Mobil
Travel Guide®

Northwest
2001

ExxonMobil Travel Publications

917.9504 MOBIL 2001

Mobil travel guide

ACKNOWLEDGMENTS

We gratefully acknowledge the help of our representatives for their efficient and perceptive inspection of the lodging and dining establishments listed; the establishments' proprietors for their cooperation in showing their facilities and providing information about them; the many users of previous editions of the Mobil Travel Guide who have taken the time to share their experiences; and for their time and information, the thousands of chambers of commerce, convention and visitors bureaus, city, state, and provincial tourism offices, and government agencies who assisted in our research.

PHOTO CREDITS

Alan Bisson/Spokane Area Convention and Visitors Bureau: 330; **FPG International:** Walter Bibikow: 155, 220, 306, 449, 482; Gary Buss: 74, 319; Wenzel Fischer: 420; R. Gage: 53; Dave Gleiter: 109; Jeri Gleiter: 167; H. Richard Johnston: 184; Alan Kearney: 442; Harvey Lloyd: 148, 375; Buddy Mays: 12, 32; E. Nagele: 400; Stan Osolinski: 385; Gary Randall: 180, 269; Ken Ross: 366; Gail Shumway: 85; Stephen Simpson: 71; John Taylor: 19; Travelpix: 409; VCG: 403, 458; Steve Wanke: 202; **Robert Holmes Photography:** 297, 434; **Markham Johnson/Backroads:** 117, 141, 350; **SuperStock:** 1, 43, 100, 125, 225, 235, 253, 262, 273, 283, 348, 363, 368, 437, 441, 467, 475, 491, 498.

Maps © MapQuest 2000, www.mapquest.com

Published by Publications International, Ltd.
7373 North Cicero Avenue
Lincolnwood, IL 60712

info@exxonmobiltravel.com

COVER PHOTO
Richard Price/FPG International

ISBN 0-7853-4638-4

Manufactured in China.
10 9 8 7 6 5 4 3 2 1

CONTENTS

Welcome xxxi
A Word to Our Readers xxxii
How to Use This Book xxxv
Making the Most of Your Trip xliii
Important Toll-Free Numbers and On-Line Information xlviii
Four- and Five-Star Establishments
  in the Northwest l

Northwest

US Mileage Chart vi
Idaho 1
Montana 53
Oregon 117
Washington 225
Wyoming 350
Canada 402

Alberta 404
British Columbia 442
Manitoba 491
Appendix A: Attraction List .501
Appendix B: Lodging List . .527
Appendix C: Restaurant List 545
City Index 552

Maps

Map Legend xxviii
Interstate Highway Map
  of the United States iv
Northwest Region viii
Distance and Driving Time . . .x
Idaho xii
Montana xiv
Oregon xvi
Washington xviii
Wyoming xx
Alberta xxii
British Columbia xxiv
Manitoba xxvi
Boise, ID 11
Billings, MT 66
Helena, MT 95
Missoula, MT 105

Eugene, OR 151
Portland, OR 191
Mount Rainier
  National Park, WA 270
Seattle, WA 301
Spokane, WA 328
Tacoma, WA 335
Casper, WY 360
Cheyenne, WY 362
Grand Teton
  National Park, WY 373
Yellowstone
  National Park, WY 398
Calgary, AB 415
Edmunton, AB 424
Vancouver, BC 455
Victoria, BC 477
Winnepeg, MB 496

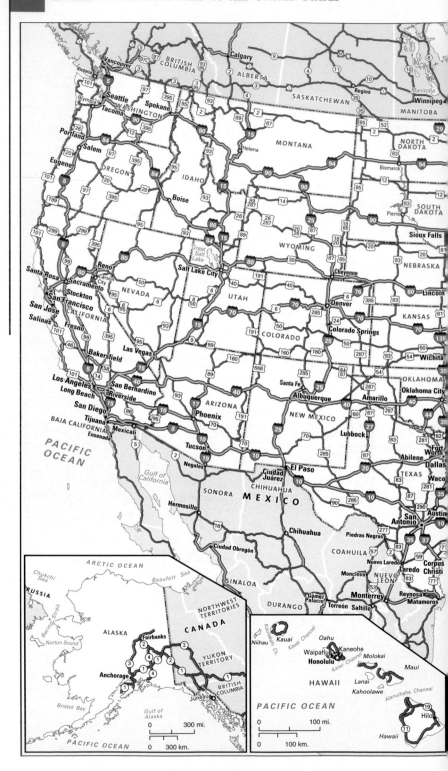

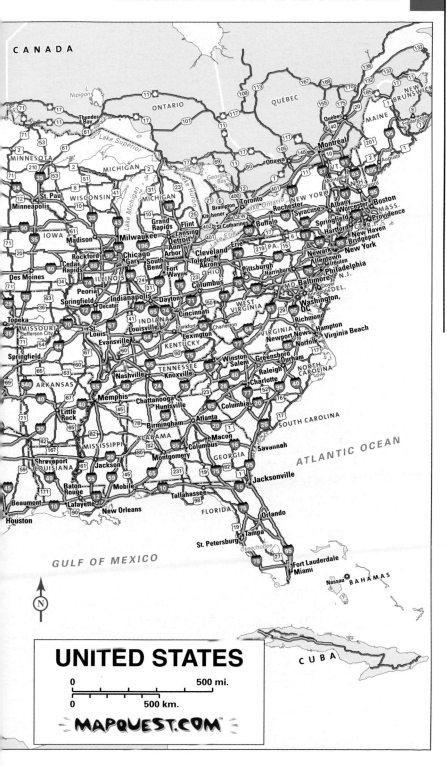

US Mileage Chart

Distances in chart are in miles. To convert miles to kilometers, multiply the distance in miles by 1.609

Example:
New York, NY to Boston, MA = 215 miles or 346 kilometers (215 x 1.609)

	ALBUQUERQUE, NM	ATLANTA, GA	BALTIMORE, MD	BILLINGS, MT	BIRMINGHAM, AL	BISMARCK, ND	BOISE, ID	BOSTON, MA	BUFFALO, NY	BURLINGTON, VT	CHARLESTON, SC	CHARLESTON, WV	CHARLOTTE, NC	CHEYENNE, WY	CHICAGO, IL	CINCINNATI, OH	CLEVELAND, OH	DALLAS, TX	DENVER, CO	DES MOINES, IA	DETROIT, MI	EL PASO, TX	HOUSTON, TX	INDIANAPOLIS, IN	JACKSON, MS	KANSAS CITY, MO	LAS VEGAS, NV
ALBUQUERQUE, NM		1490	1902	991	1274	1333	966	2240	1808	2178	1793	1568	1649	538	1352	1409	1619	754	438	1091	1608	263	994	1298	1157	894	578
ATLANTA, GA	1490		679	1889	150	1559	2218	1100	910	1158	317	503	238	1482	717	476	726	792	1403	967	735	1437	800	531	386	801	2067
BALTIMORE, MD	1902	679		1959	795	1551	2401	422	370	481	583	352	441	1665	708	521	377	1399	1690	1031	532	2045	1470	600	1032	1087	2445
BILLINGS, MT	991	1889	1959		1839	413	626	2254	1796	2181	2157	1755	2012	455	1246	1552	1597	1433	554	1007	1534	1255	1673	1432	1836	1088	965
BIRMINGHAM, AL	1274	150	795	1839		1509	2170	1215	909	1241	466	578	389	1434	667	475	725	647	1356	919	734	1292	678	481	241	753	1852
BISMARCK, ND	1333	1559	1551	413	1509		1039	1846	1388	1773	1749	1347	1604	594	838	1144	1189	1342	693	675	1126	1597	1582	1024	1548	801	1378
BOISE, ID	966	2218	2401	626	2170	1039		2697	2239	2624	2520	2182	2375	737	1708	1969	2040	1711	833	1369	1977	1206	1952	1852	2115	1376	760
BOSTON, MA	2240	1100	422	2254	1215	1846	2697		462	214	1003	741	861	1961	1003	862	654	1819	2004	1326	741	2465	1890	940	1453	1427	2757
BUFFALO, NY	1808	910	370	1796	909	1388	2239	462		375	899	431	695	1502	545	442	197	1393	1546	868	277	2039	1513	508	1134	995	2299
BURLINGTON, VT	2178	1158	481	2181	1241	1773	2624	214	375		1061	782	919	1887	930	817	567	1763	1931	1253	652	2409	1916	878	1479	1366	2684
CHARLESTON, SC	1793	317	583	2157	466	1749	2520	1003	899	1061		468	204	1783	907	622	724	1109	1705	1204	879	1754	1110	721	703	1102	2371
CHARLESTON, WV	1568	503	352	1755	578	1347	2182	741	431	782	468		265	1445	506	209	255	1072	1367	802	410	1718	1192	320	816	764	2122
CHARLOTTE, NC	1649	238	441	2012	389	1604	2375	861	695	919	204	265		1637	761	476	520	1031	1559	1057	675	1677	1041	575	625	956	2225
CHEYENNE, WY	538	1482	1665	455	1434	594	737	1961	1502	1887	1783	1445	1637		972	1233	1304	979	100	633	1241	801	1220	1115	1382	640	843
CHICAGO, IL	1352	717	708	1246	667	838	1708	1003	545	930	907	506	761	972		302	346	936	1015	337	283	1543	1108	184	750	532	1768
CINCINNATI, OH	1409	476	521	1552	475	1144	1969	862	442	817	622	209	476	1233	302		253	958	1200	599	261	1605	1079	116	700	597	1955
CLEVELAND, OH	1619	726	377	1597	725	1189	2040	654	197	567	724	255	520	1304	346	253		1208	1347	669	171	1854	1328	319	950	806	2100
DALLAS, TX	754	792	1399	1433	647	1342	1711	1819	1393	1763	1109	1072	1031	979	936	958	1208		887	752	1218	647	241	913	406	554	1331
DENVER, CO	438	1403	1690	554	1356	693	833	2004	1546	1931	1705	1367	1559	100	1015	1200	1347	887		676	1284	701	1127	1088	1290	603	756
DES MOINES, IA	1091	967	1031	1007	919	675	1369	1326	868	1253	1204	802	1057	633	337	599	669	752	676		606	1283	992	481	931	194	1429
DETROIT, MI	1608	735	532	1534	734	1126	1977	741	277	652	879	410	675	1241	283	261	171	1218	1284	606		1799	1338	318	960	795	2037
EL PASO, TX	263	1437	2045	1255	1292	1597	1206	2465	2039	2409	1754	1718	1677	801	1543	1605	1854	647	701	1283	1799		758	1489	1051	1085	717
HOUSTON, TX	994	800	1470	1673	678	1582	1952	1890	1513	1916	1110	1192	1041	1220	1108	1079	1328	241	1127	992	1338	758		1033	445	795	1474
INDIANAPOLIS, IN	1298	531	600	1432	481	1024	1852	940	508	878	721	320	575	1115	184	116	319	913	1088	481	318	1489	1033		675	485	1843
JACKSON, MS	1157	386	1032	1836	241	1548	2115	1453	1134	1479	703	816	625	1382	750	700	950	406	1290	931	960	1051	445	675		747	1735
KANSAS CITY, MO	894	801	1087	1088	753	801	1376	1427	995	1366	1102	764	956	640	532	597	806	554	603	194	795	1085	795	485	747		1358
LAS VEGAS, NV	578	2067	2445	965	1852	1378	760	2757	2299	2684	2371	2122	2225	843	1768	1955	2100	1331	756	1429	2037	717	1474	1843	1735	1358	
LITTLE ROCK, AR	900	528	1072	1530	381	1183	1808	1493	1066	1437	900	745	754	1076	662	632	882	327	984	567	891	974	447	587	269	382	1478
LOS ANGELES, CA	806	2237	2705	1239	2092	1702	1033	3046	2572	2957	2554	2374	2453	1116	2042	2215	2374	1446	1029	1703	2310	801	1558	2104	1851	1632	274
LOUISVILLE, KY	1320	419	602	1547	369	1139	1933	964	545	915	610	251	464	1197	299	106	356	852	1118	595	366	1499	972	112	594	516	1874
MEMPHIS, TN	1033	389	933	1625	241	1337	1954	1353	927	1297	760	606	614	1217	539	493	742	466	1116	720	752	1112	586	464	211	536	1611
MIAMI, FL	2155	661	1109	2554	812	2224	2883	1529	1425	1587	583	994	730	2147	1382	1141	1250	1367	2069	1632	1401	1959	1201	1196	915	1466	2733
MILWAUKEE, WI	1426	813	805	1175	763	767	1748	1100	642	1027	1003	601	857	1012	89	398	443	1010	1055	378	380	1617	1193	279	835	573	1808
MINNEAPOLIS, MN	1339	1129	1121	839	1079	431	1465	1417	958	1343	1319	918	1173	881	409	714	760	999	924	246	697	1530	1240	596	1151	441	1677
MONTRÉAL, QC	2172	1241	564	2093	1289	1685	2535	313	397	92	1145	822	1003	1799	841	815	588	1772	1843	1165	564	2363	1892	872	1514	1359	2596
NASHVILLE, TN	1248	242	716	1648	194	1315	1976	1136	716	1086	543	395	397	1240	474	281	531	681	1162	725	541	1328	801	287	423	559	1826
NEW ORLEANS, LA	1276	473	1142	1955	351	1734	2234	1563	1254	1588	783	926	713	1502	935	820	1070	525	1409	1117	1079	1118	360	826	185	932	1854
NEW YORK, NY	2015	869	192	2049	985	1641	2491	215	400	299	773	515	631	1755	797	636	466	1589	1799	1121	622	2235	1660	715	1223	1202	2552
OKLAHOMA CITY, OK	546	944	1354	1227	729	1136	1506	1694	1262	1632	1248	1022	1102	773	807	863	1073	209	681	546	1062	737	449	752	612	348	1124
OMAHA, NE	973	989	1168	904	941	616	1234	1463	1005	1390	1290	952	1144	497	474	736	806	669	541	136	743	1236	910	618	935	188	1294
ORLANDO, FL	1934	440	904	2333	591	2003	2662	1324	1221	1383	379	790	525	1926	1161	920	1045	1146	1847	1411	1180	1738	980	975	694	1245	2512
PHILADELPHIA, PA	1954	782	104	2019	897	1611	2462	321	414	371	685	454	543	1725	768	576	437	1501	1744	1091	592	2147	1572	655	1135	1141	2500
PHOENIX, AZ	466	1868	2366	1199	1723	1662	993	2706	2274	2644	2184	2035	2107	1004	1819	1876	2085	1077	904	1558	2074	432	1188	1764	1482	1360	285
PITTSBURGH, PA	1670	676	246	1719	763	1311	2161	592	217	587	642	217	438	1425	467	292	136	1246	1460	791	292	1893	1366	370	988	857	2215
PORTLAND, ME	2338	1197	520	2352	1313	1944	2795	107	560	233	1101	839	959	2059	1101	960	751	1917	2102	1424	838	2563	1988	1038	1550	1525	2855
PORTLAND, OR	1395	2647	2830	889	2599	1301	432	3126	2667	3052	2948	2610	2802	1166	2137	2398	2469	2140	1261	1798	2405	1767	2381	2280	2544	1805	1188
RAPID CITY, SD	841	1511	1626	379	1463	320	930	1921	1463	1848	1824	1422	1678	305	913	1219	1264	1077	404	629	1201	1105	1318	1101	1458	710	1035
RENO, NV	1020	2440	2623	960	2392	1372	430	2919	2460	2845	2741	2403	2595	959	1930	2191	2262	1933	1054	1591	2198	1315	2072	2073	2337	1598	442
RICHMOND, VA	1876	527	152	2053	678	1645	2496	572	485	630	428	322	289	1760	802	530	471	1309	1688	1126	627	1955	1330	641	914	1085	2444
ST. LOUIS, MO	1051	549	841	1341	501	1053	1628	1181	749	1119	850	512	704	892	294	350	560	635	855	436	549	1242	863	239	505	252	1610
SALT LAKE CITY, UT	624	1916	2100	548	1868	960	342	2395	1936	2322	2218	1880	2072	436	1406	1667	1738	1410	531	1067	1675	864	1650	1549	1813	1074	417
SAN ANTONIO, TX	818	1000	1671	1500	878	1599	1761	2092	1665	2036	1310	1344	1241	1046	1270	1231	1481	271	946	1009	1490	556	200	1186	644	812	1272
SAN DIEGO, CA	825	2166	2724	1302	2021	1765	1096	3065	2632	3020	2483	2393	2405	1179	2105	2234	2437	1375	1092	1766	2373	730	1487	2122	1780	1695	337
SAN FRANCISCO, CA	1111	2618	2840	1176	2472	1749	646	3135	2677	3062	2934	2620	2759	1176	2146	2407	2478	1827	1271	1807	2415	1181	1938	2290	2232	1814	575
SEATTLE, WA	1463	2705	2775	816	2657	1229	500	3070	2612	2997	2973	2571	2827	1234	2062	2368	2413	2208	1329	1822	2350	1944	2449	2249	2612	1872	1256
TAMPA, FL	1949	455	960	2348	606	2018	2677	1380	1276	1438	434	845	581	1941	1176	935	1101	1161	1862	1426	1194	1753	995	990	709	1259	2526
TORONTO, ON	1841	958	565	1762	958	1354	2204	570	106	419	1006	537	802	1468	510	484	303	1441	1512	834	233	2032	1561	541	1183	1028	2265
VANCOUVER, BC	1597	2838	2908	949	2791	1362	633	3204	2745	3130	3106	2705	2960	1368	2196	2501	2547	2342	1463	1956	2483	2087	2583	2383	2746	2007	1390
WASHINGTON, DC	1896	636	38	1953	758	1545	2395	458	384	517	539	346	397	1659	701	517	370	1362	1686	1025	526	2008	1433	596	996	1083	2441
WICHITA, KS	707	989	1276	1067	838	934	1346	1616	1184	1554	1291	953	1145	613	728	785	995	367	521	390	984	898	608	674	771	192	1276

LITTLE ROCK, AR	LOS ANGELES, CA	LOUISVILLE, KY	MEMPHIS, TN	MIAMI, FL	MILWAUKEE, WI	MINNEAPOLIS, MN	MONTRÉAL, QC	NASHVILLE, TN	NEW ORLEANS, LA	NEW YORK, NY	OKLAHOMA CITY, OK	OMAHA, NE	ORLANDO, FL	PHILADELPHIA, PA	PHOENIX, AZ	PITTSBURGH, PA	PORTLAND, ME	PORTLAND, OR	RAPID CITY, SD	RENO, NV	RICHMOND, VA	SALT LAKE CITY, UT	SAN ANTONIO, TX	SAN DIEGO, CA	SAN FRANCISCO, CA	SEATTLE, WA	ST. LOUIS, MO	TAMPA, FL	TORONTO, ON	VANCOUVER, BC	WASHINGTON, DC	WICHITA, KS
900	806	1320	1033	2155	1426	1339	2172	1248	1276	2015	546	973	1934	1954	466	1670	2338	1395	841	1020	1876	1051	624	818	825	1111	1463	1949	1841	1597	1896	707
528	2237	419	389	661	813	1129	1241	242	473	869	944	989	440	782	1868	676	1197	2647	1511	2440	527	549	1916	1000	2166	2618	2705	455	958	2838	636	989
1072	2705	602	993	1109	805	1121	564	716	1142	192	1354	1168	904	104	2366	246	520	2830	1626	2623	532	841	2100	1671	2724	2840	2775	960	565	2908	38	1276
1530	1239	1547	1625	2554	1175	839	2093	1648	1955	2049	1227	904	2333	2019	1199	1779	2352	889	379	960	2053	1341	1548	1500	1302	1176	816	2348	1762	949	1953	1067
381	2092	369	241	812	763	1079	1289	194	351	985	729	941	591	897	1723	763	1313	2599	1463	2392	678	501	1868	878	2021	2472	2657	606	958	2791	758	838
1183	1702	1139	1337	2224	767	431	1685	1315	1734	1641	1136	616	2003	1611	1662	1311	1944	1301	320	1372	1645	1053	960	1599	1765	1749	1229	2018	1354	1362	1543	934
1808	1033	1933	1954	2883	1748	1465	2535	1976	2234	2491	1506	1234	2662	2462	993	2161	2795	432	930	430	2496	1628	342	1761	1096	646	500	2677	2204	633	2395	1346
1493	3046	964	1353	1529	1100	1417	313	1136	1563	215	1694	1463	1324	321	2706	592	107	3126	1921	2919	572	1181	2395	2092	3065	3135	3070	1380	570	3204	458	1616
1066	2572	545	927	1425	642	958	397	716	1254	400	1262	1005	1221	414	2274	217	560	2667	1463	2460	485	749	1936	1665	2632	2677	2612	1276	106	2745	384	1184
1437	2957	915	1297	1587	1027	1343	92	1086	1588	299	1632	1390	1383	371	2644	587	233	3052	1848	2845	630	1119	2322	2036	3020	3062	2997	1438	419	3130	517	1554
900	2554	610	760	583	1003	1319	1145	543	783	773	1248	1290	379	685	2184	642	1101	2948	1824	2741	428	850	2218	1310	2483	2934	2973	434	1006	3106	539	1291
745	2374	251	606	994	601	818	822	395	926	515	1022	952	790	454	2035	217	839	2610	1422	2403	322	512	1880	1344	2503	2907	2827	581	802	2960	397	1145
754	2453	464	614	730	857	1173	1003	397	713	631	1102	1144	525	543	2107	439	980	2802	1678	2595	289	704	2072	1241	2405	2759	2827	581	802	2960	397	1145
1076	1116	1197	1217	2147	1012	881	1799	1240	1502	1755	773	497	1926	1725	1004	1425	2059	1166	305	959	1760	892	436	1046	1179	1176	1234	1941	1468	1368	1669	613
662	2042	299	539	1382	89	409	841	474	935	797	807	474	1161	768	1819	467	1101	2137	913	1930	802	294	1406	1270	2105	2146	2062	1176	510	2196	701	728
632	2215	106	493	1141	398	714	815	281	820	636	863	736	920	576	1876	292	960	2398	1219	2191	530	350	1667	1231	2234	2407	2368	935	484	2501	517	785
882	2374	356	742	1250	443	760	588	531	1070	466	1073	806	1045	437	2085	136	751	2469	1264	2262	471	560	1738	1481	2437	2470	2413	1101	303	2547	370	995
327	1446	852	466	1367	1010	999	1772	681	525	1589	209	669	1146	1501	1077	1246	1917	2140	1077	1933	1309	635	1410	271	1375	1827	2208	1161	1441	2342	1362	367
984	1029	1118	1116	2069	1055	924	1843	1162	1409	1799	681	541	1847	1744	904	1462	2102	1261	404	1054	1844	855	331	946	1092	1271	1329	1862	1512	1463	1686	521
567	1703	595	720	1632	378	246	1165	725	1117	1121	546	136	1411	1091	1558	791	1424	1798	629	1591	1126	436	1067	1009	1766	1807	1822	1426	834	1956	1025	390
891	2310	366	752	1401	380	697	564	541	1079	622	1062	743	1180	592	2074	292	838	2405	1201	2198	627	549	1675	1490	2373	2415	2350	1194	233	2483	526	984
974	801	1499	1112	1959	1617	1530	2363	1328	1118	2235	737	1236	1738	2147	432	1893	2663	1767	1105	1315	1955	1242	864	556	730	1181	1464	2102	2087	2008	898	952
447	1558	972	586	1201	1193	1240	1892	801	360	1660	449	910	1460	1572	1186	1366	1988	2381	1318	2072	1330	863	1650	200	1487	1938	2449	995	1561	2433	608	608
587	2104	12	464	1196	279	596	872	287	826	715	752	618	975	655	1764	370	1038	2280	1101	2073	641	239	1549	1186	2122	2290	2249	990	541	2383	596	674

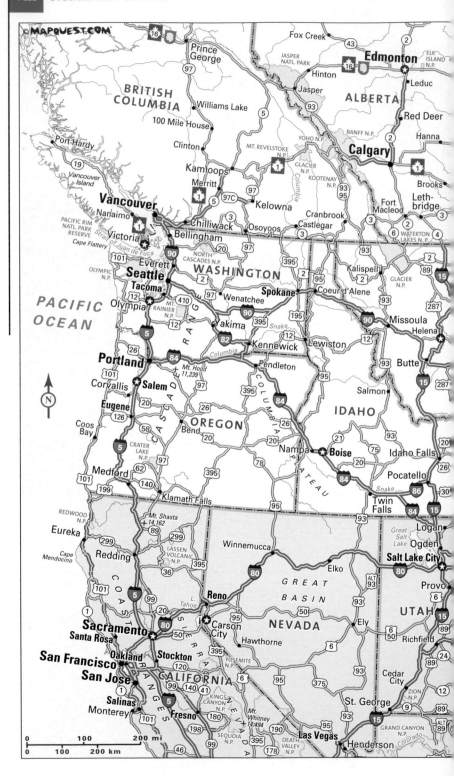

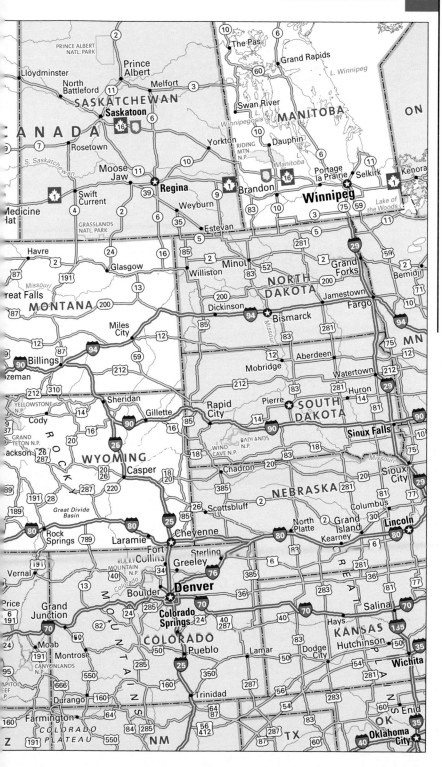

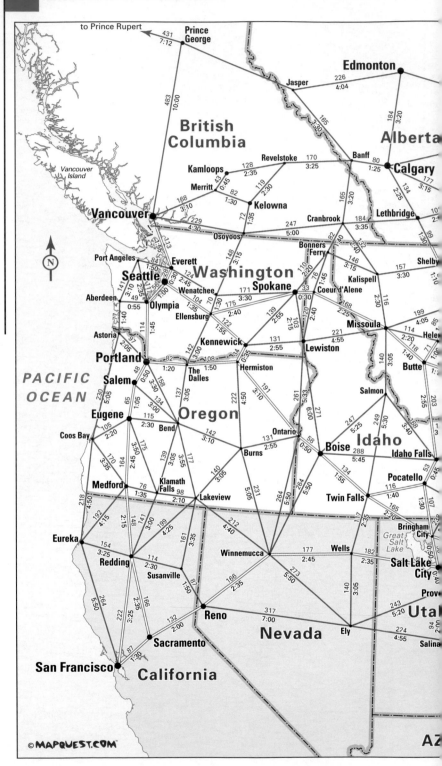

to Flin Flon

Lake Winnipeg

ON

CANADA

Prince Albert

236
5:15

327
5:42

90
2:00

243
4:50

Manitoba

470
9:25

Saskatoon

381
7:35

206
4:05

162
2:55

166
3:20

232
4:15

Yorkton

Lake Manitoba

Winnipeg

Saskatchewan

121
2:15

275
5:20

Medicine Hat

135
2:40

150
2:45

Regina

Swift Current

234
4:25

134
2:25

Brandon

Emerson

152
3:00

189
3:45

242
4:50

165
3:20

145
2:40

Havre

89
2:00

Malta

215
4:45

Minot

128
2:50

212
4:42

Grand Forks

Williston

116
2:30

79
1:15

reat Falls

133
2:55

North Dakota

202
3:05

Fargo

109
2:25

Lewistown

242
5:20

Glendive

106
2:20

197
3:00

Bismarck

MN

Montana

Miles City

74
1:05

222 125
4:50 2:45

144
2:05

112
2:25

141
2:00

Billings

288
6:20

Mobridge

zeman

131
1:50

111
2:25

Sheridan

336
7:20

107
2:25

South Dakota

99 Cody
2:10

150
3:20

248
3:35

193
3:55

Pierre

Yellowstone NP

215
4:45

149
2:10

Rapid City

Grand Teton NP

268
5:30

Casper
50
0:45

204
4:30

101
2:15

296
5:50

Chadron

Wyoming

191
4:35

225
5:40

117
2:35

Douglas

135
3:00

305
6:30

178
3:55

Nebraska

Rawlins

110
1:35

151
2:10

127
1:50

298
5:55

53
0:45

North Platte

97
1:25

Rock Springs

171
2:25

Ogallala

anston

117
2:30

Cheyenne

170
3:45

111
1:25

123
2:45

Craig

100
1:25

214
3:05

Vernal

203
4:20

175
3:50

250
3:35

Denver

Kansas

102
1:25

Green River

Grand Junction

Colorado

NM

Interstate Routes

Other Routes

277   Distance in Miles

1:50   Approximate Driving Time

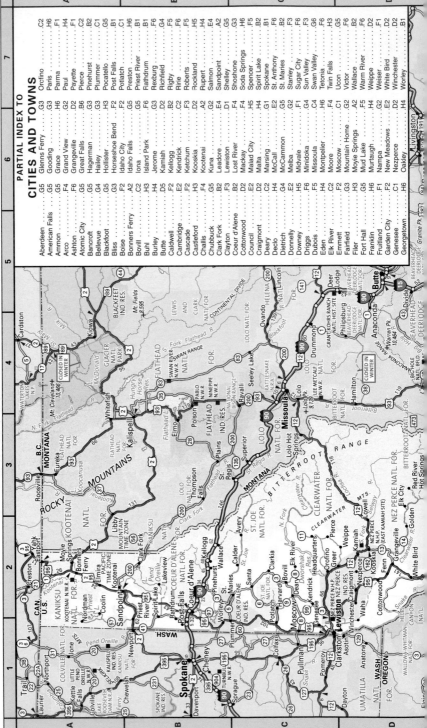

PARTIAL INDEX TO
CITIES AND TOWNS

Aberdeen	G5	Glenns Ferry	G3	Orofino	C2
American Falls	G5	Gooding	G3	Paris	H6
Ammon	G5	Grace	H6	Parma	F1
Arco	F4	Grand View	G2	Paul	H4
Ashton	F6	Grangeville	D2	Payette	F1
Atomic City	G5	Great Falls	B6	Pierce	C2
Bancroft	G5	Hagerman	G3	Pinehurst	B2
Bellevue	G4	Hailey	G4	Plummer	C1
Blackfoot	G5	Hollister	H3	Pocatello	G5
Bliss	G3	Horseshoe Bend	F2	Post Falls	B1
Boise	F2	Idaho City	F2	Potlatch	C1
Bonners Ferry	A2	Idaho Falls	G5	Preston	H6
Bovill	C2	Iona	G5	Priest River	B1
Buhl	H3	Island Park	F6	Rathdrum	B1
Burley	H4	Jerome	G3	Rexburg	F6
Butte	D5	Kamiah	D2	Richfield	G4
Caldwell	F2	Kellogg	B2	Rigby	F5
Cambridge	E2	Kendrick	C2	Ririe	F6
Cascade	F2	Ketchum	F3	Roberts	F5
Castleford	H3	Kooskia	D2	Rockland	H5
Challis	F4	Kootenai	A2	Rupert	H4
Chubbuck	G5	Kuna	G2	Salmon	E4
Clark Fork	B2	Leadore	E4	Sandpoint	A2
Clayton	F3	Lewiston	D1	Shelley	G5
Coeur d'Alene	B1	Lost River	F4	Shoshone	G3
Cottonwood	D2	Mackay	F4	Soda Springs	H6
Council	E2	Malad City	H5	Spencer	F5
Craigmont	D2	Malta	H4	Spirit Lake	B2
Deary	C2	Marsing	G1	Spokane	B1
Declo	H4	McCall	E2	St. Anthony	F6
Dietrich	G4	McCammon	G5	St. Maries	B2
Donnelly	E2	Melba	G2	Stanley	F3
Downey	H5	Midvale	F1	Sugar City	F6
Driggs	F6	Minidoka	G4	Sun Valley	G6
Dubois	F5	Missoula	C4	Swan Valley	F6
Eden	H4	Montpelier	H6	Tetonia	H3
Elk River	C2	Moore	F4	Twin Falls	H3
Emmett	F2	Moscow	C1	Ucon	G5
Fairfield	G3	Mountain Home	G2	Victor	F6
Filer	H3	Moyie Springs	A2	Wallace	B2
Fort Hall	G5	Mud Lake	F5	Warm River	F6
Franklin	H6	Murtaugh	H4	Weippe	D2
Fruitland	F1	Nampa	G2	Weiser	F1
Garden City	F2	New Meadows	E2	White Bird	D2
Genesee	C1	Nezperce	D2	Winchester	D2
Georgetown	H6	Oakley	H4	Worley	B1

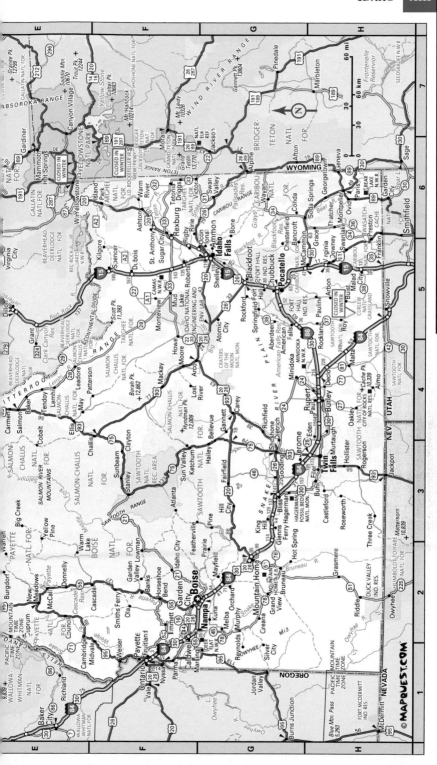

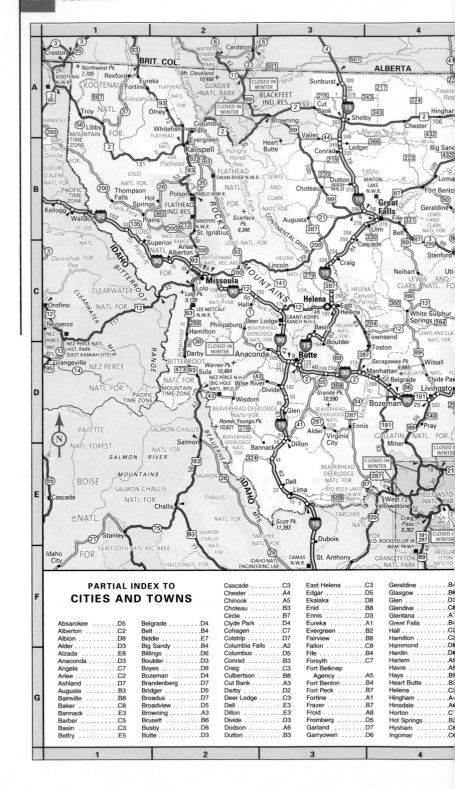

PARTIAL INDEX TO CITIES AND TOWNS

Absarokee D5	Belgrade D4	Cascade C3	East Helena C3	Geraldine .....B
Alberton C2	Belt B4	Chester A4	Edgar D5	Glasgow .....B
Albion D8	Biddle E7	Chinook A5	Ekalaka D8	Glen .....D
Alder D3	Big Sandy B4	Choteau B3	Enid B8	Glendive C
Alzada E8	Billings D6	Circle B7	Ennis D3	Glentana .....A
Anaconda D3	Boulder D3	Clyde Park D4	Eureka A1	Great Falls .....B
Angela C7	Boyes D8	Cohagen C7	Evergreen B2	Hall C
Arlee C2	Bozeman D4	Colstrip D7	Fairview B8	Hamilton C
Ashland D7	Brandenberg D7	Columbia Falls A2	Fallon C8	Hammond .....D
Augusta B3	Bridger D5	Columbus D5	Fife B4	Hardin .....D
Bainville B8	Broadus D7	Conrad B3	Forsyth C7	Harlem .....A
Baker C8	Broadview D5	Craig C3	Fort Belknap	Havre .....A
Bannack E3	Browning A3	Culbertson B8	Agency A5	Hays .....A
Barber C5	Brusett B6	Cut Bank A3	Fort Benton B4	Heart Butte .....B
Basin C3	Busby D6	Darby D2	Fort Peck B7	Helena C
Belfry E5	Butte D3	Deer Lodge C3	Fortine A1	Hingham .....A
		Dell E3	Frazer B7	Hinsdale .....A
		Dillon E3	Froid A8	Horton C
		Divide D3	Fromberg D5	Hot Springs .....B
		Dodson A6	Garland D7	Hysham .....D
		Dutton B3	Garryowen D6	Ingomar C

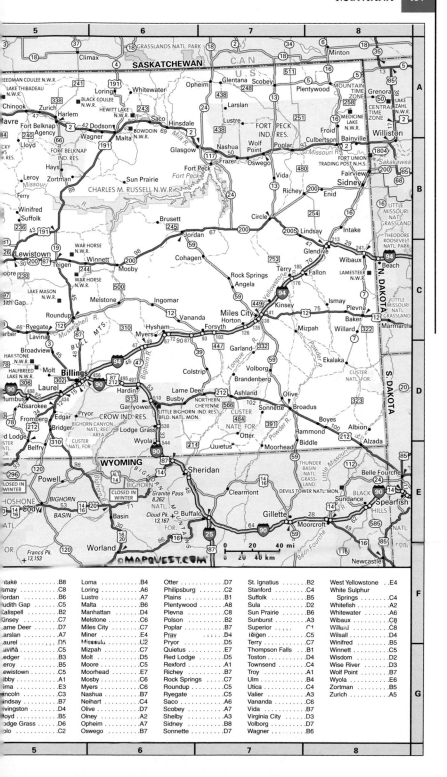

...take B8	Loma B4	Otter D7	St. Ignatius B2	West Yellowstone ..E4
...smay C8	Loring A6	Philipsburg C2	Stanford C4	White Sulphur
...ordan B6	Lustre A7	Plains B1	Suffolk B5	Springs C4
...udith Gap C5	Malta B6	Plentywood A8	Sula D2	Whitefish A2
...Kalispell B2	Manhattan D4	Plevna C8	Sun Prairie B6	Whitewater A6
...Kinsey C7	Melstone C6	Polson B2	Sunburst A3	Wibaux C8
...Lame Deer D7	Miles City C7	Poplar B7	Superior C1	Willard C8
...arslan A7	Miner E4	Pray D4	Teigen C5	Wilsall D4
...aurel D5	Missoula C2	Pryor D5	Terry C7	Winifred B5
...avina C5	Mizpah C7	Quietus E7	Thompson Falls B1	Winnett C5
...edger B3	Molt D5	Red Lodge D5	Toston D4	Wisdom D2
...eroy B5	Moore C5	Rexford A1	Townsend C4	Wise River D3
...ewistown C5	Moorhead E7	Richey B7	Troy A1	Wolf Point B7
...ibby A1	Mosby C6	Rock Springs C7	Ulm B4	Wyola E6
...ima E3	Myers C6	Roundup C5	Utica C4	Zortman B5
...incoln C3	Nashua B7	Ryegate C5	Valier A3	Zurich A5
...indsay B7	Neihart C4	Saco A6	Vananda C6	
...ivingston D4	Olive D7	Scobey A7	Vida B7	
...loyd B5	Olney A2	Shelby A3	Virginia City D3	
...odge Grass D6	Opheim A7	Sidney B8	Volborg D7	
...olo C2	Oswego B7	Sonnette D7	Wagner B6	

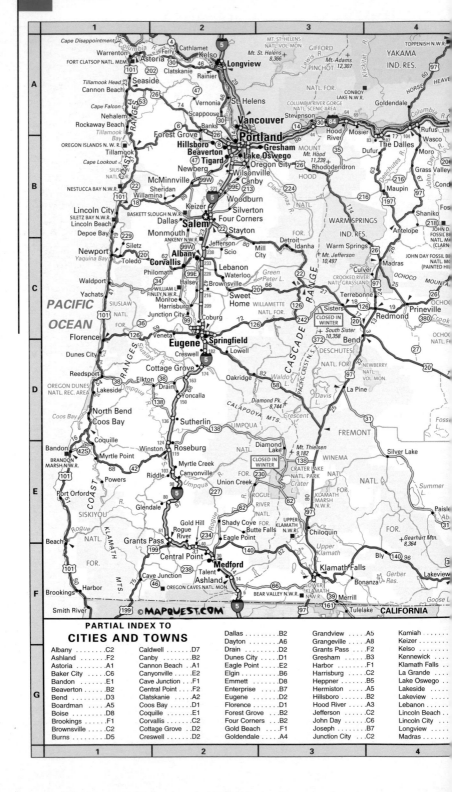

PARTIAL INDEX TO
CITIES AND TOWNS

Albany C2	Caldwell D7	Dallas B2
Ashland F2	Canby B2	Dayton A6
Astoria A1	Cannon Beach ..A1	Drain D2
Baker City C6	Canyonville E2	Dunes City D1
Bandon E1	Cave Junction ..F1	Eagle Point E2
Beaverton B2	Central Point ...F2	Elgin B6
Bend D3	Clatskanie A2	Emmett D8
Boardman A5	Coos Bay D1	Enterprise B7
Boise D8	Coquille E1	Eugene D2
Brookings F1	Corvallis C2	Florence D1
Brownsville ...C2	Cottage Grove ..D2	Forest Grove ...B2
Burns D5	Creswell D2	Four Corners ...B2
		Gold Beach F1
		Goldendale A4

Grandview A5	Kamiah ....
Grangeville ...A8	Keizer ....
Grants Pass ...F2	Kelso ....
Gresham B3	Kennewick ....
Harbor F1	Klamath Falls .
Harrisburg C2	La Grande ....
Heppner B5	Lake Oswego ..
Hermiston A5	Lakeside .....
Hillsboro B2	Lakeview .....
Hood River A3	Lebanon ......
Jefferson C2	Lincoln Beach .
John Day C6	Lincoln City ..
Joseph B7	Longview .....
Junction City ..C2	Madras ....

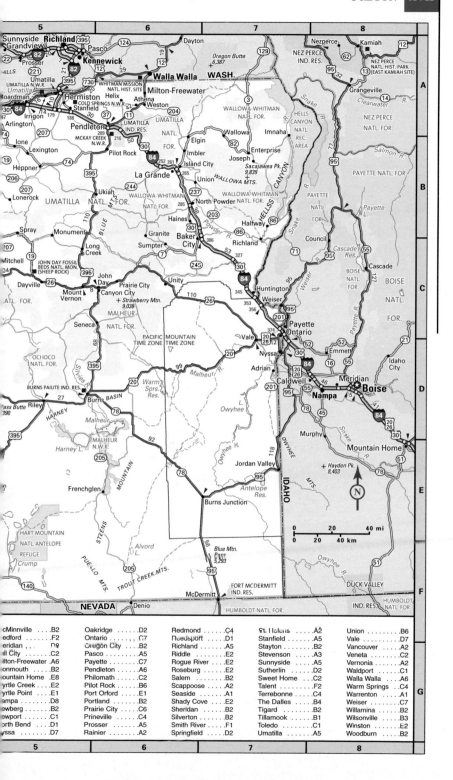

cMinnville B2	Oakridge D2	Redmond C4	St. Helens A2	Union B6
edford F2	Ontario . . . . . . , , G7	Needsport D1	Stanfield A5	Vale D7
eridian , , , ...D9	Oregon City . . .B2	Richland A5	Stayton B2	Vancouver A2
ll City C2	Pasco A5	Riddle E2	Stevenson A3	Veneta C2
ilton-Freewater .A6	Payette C7	Rogue River E2	Sunnyside A5	Vernonia A2
onmouth B2	Pendleton A6	Roseburg E2	Sutherlin D2	Waldport C1
hilomath C2	Philomath C2	Salem B2	Sweet Home . . .C2	Walla Walla A6
yrtle Creek E2	Pilot Rock B6	Scappoose A2	Talent F2	Warm Springs . .C4
yrtle Point E1	Port Orford E1	Seaside A1	Terrebonne C4	Warrenton A1
ampa D8	Portland B2	Shady Cove E2	The Dalles B4	Weiser C7
ewberg B2	Prairie City C6	Sheridan B2	Tigard B2	Willamina B2
ewport C1	Prineville C4	Silverton B2	Tillamook B1	Wilsonville B3
orth Bend D1	Prosser A5	Smith River F1	Toledo C1	Winston E2
yssa D7	Rainier A2	Springfield D2	Umatilla A5	Woodburn B2

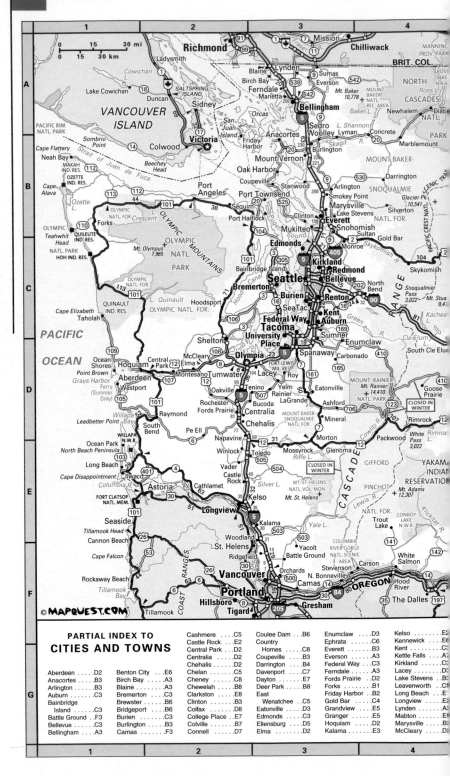

© MAPQUEST.COM

PARTIAL INDEX TO
CITIES AND TOWNS

Aberdeen D2	Benton City ...E6	Cashmere C5
Anacortes B3	Birch Bay A3	Castle Rock ...E2
Arlington B3	Blaine A3	Central Park ..D2
Auburn C3	Bremerton C3	Centralia D2
Bainbridge	Brewster B6	Chehalis D2
Island C3	Bridgeport ...B6	Chelan C5
Battle Ground ..F3	Burien C3	Cheney C8
Bellevue C3	Burlington B3	Chewelah B8
Bellingham ...A3	Camas F3	Clarkston E8
		Clinton B3
		Colfax D8
		College Place ..E7
		Colville B7
		Connell D7

Coulee Dam ...B6	Enumclaw D3	Kelso E2
Country	Ephrata C6	Kennewick E6
Homes C8	Everett B3	Kent C3
Coupeville ...B3	Everson A3	Kettle Falls ...A7
Darrington ...B4	Federal Way ..C3	Kirkland C3
Davenport C7	Ferndale A3	Lacey D3
Dayton E7	Fords Prairie ..D2	Lake Stevens ..B3
Deer Park B8	Forks B1	Leavenworth ..C5
East	Friday Harbor ..B2	Long Beach ...E1
Wenatchee ..C5	Gold Bar C4	Longview E2
Eatonville D3	Grandview E5	Lynden A3
Edmonds C3	Granger E5	Mabton E5
Ellensburg ...D5	Hoquiam D2	Marysville B3
Elma D2	Kalama E3	McCleary D2

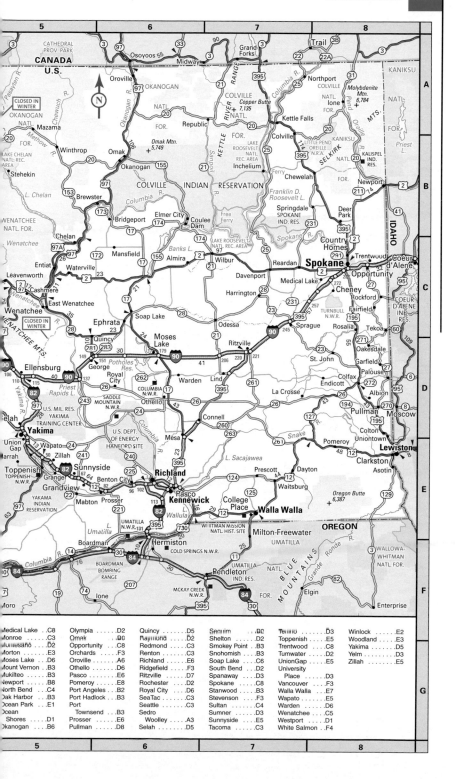

Medical Lake . . C8	Olympia D2	Quincy D5	Sequim B2	Tenino D3	Winlock E2
Monroe C3	Omak B6	Raymond D2	Shelton D2	Toppenish E5	Woodland E3
Montesano D2	Opportunity . . . C8	Redmond C3	Smokey Point . . B3	Trentwood C8	Yakima D5
Morton E3	Orchards F3	Renton C3	Snohomish B3	Tumwater D2	Yelm D3
Moses Lake . . . D6	Oroville A6	Richland E6	Soap Lake C6	UnionGap E5	Zillah E5
Mount Vernon . . B3	Othello D6	Ridgefield F3	South Bend D2	Union	
Mukilteo B3	Pasco E6	Ritzville D7	Spanaway D3	Place D3	
Newport B8	Pomeroy E8	Rochester D2	Spokane C8	Vancouver F3	
North Bend . . . C4	Port Angeles . . B2	Royal City D6	Stanwood B3	Walla Walla . . . E7	
Oak Harbor . . . B3	Port Hadlock . . B3	SeaTac C3	Stevenson F3	Wapato E5	
Ocean Park . . . E1	Port	Seattle C3	Sultan C4	Warden D6	
Ocean	Townsend . . B3	Sedro	Sumner D3	Wenatchee C5	
Shores D1	Prosser E6	Woolley A3	Sunnyside E5	Westport D1	
Okanogan B6	Pullman D8	Selah D5	Tacoma C3	White Salmon . . F4	

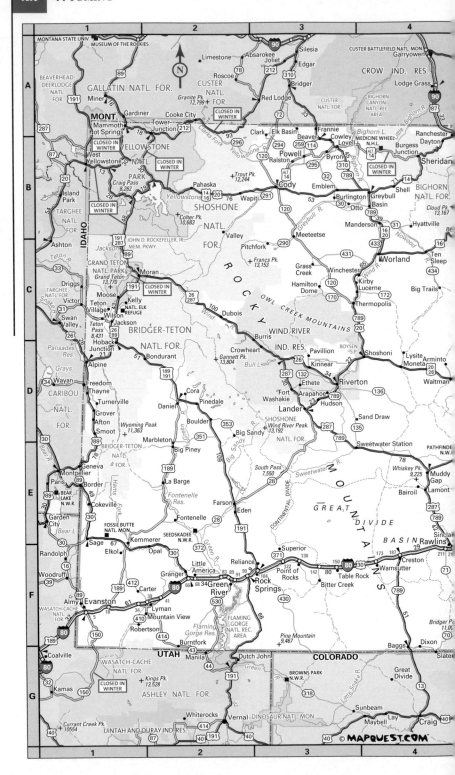

© MAPQUEST.COM

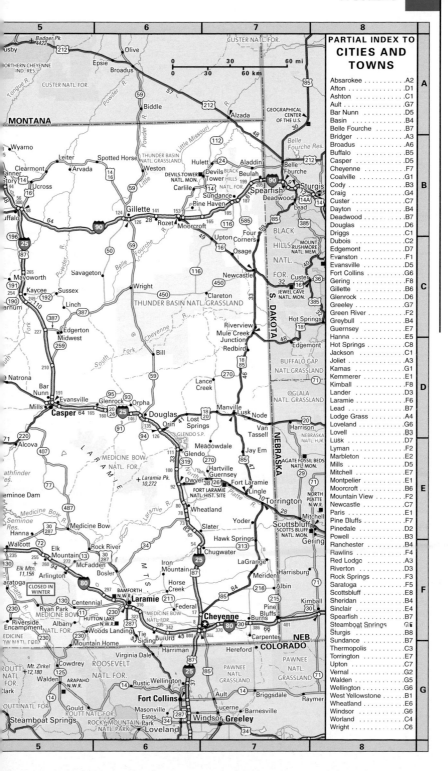

PARTIAL INDEX TO CITIES AND TOWNS

Absarokee A2
Afton D1
Ashton C1
Ault G7
Bar Nunn D5
Basin B4
Belle Fourche B7
Bridger A3
Broadus A6
Buffalo B5
Casper D5
Cheyenne F7
Coalville G1
Cody B3
Craig G4
Custer C7
Dayton B4
Deadwood B7
Douglas D6
Driggs C1
Dubois C2
Edgemont D7
Evanston F1
Evansville D5
Fort Collins G6
Gering F8
Gillette B6
Glenrock D6
Greeley G7
Green River F2
Greybull B4
Guernsey E7
Hanna E5
Hot Springs C8
Jackson C1
Joliet A3
Kamas G1
Kemmerer E1
Kimball F8
Lander D3
Laramie F6
Lead B7
Lodge Grass A4
Loveland G6
Lovell B3
Lusk D7
Lyman F2
Marbleton E2
Mills D5
Mitchell E7
Montpelier E1
Moorcroft B6
Mountain View F2
Newcastle C7
Paris E1
Pine Bluffs F7
Pinedale D2
Powell B3
Ranchester B4
Rawlins F4
Red Lodge A3
Riverton D3
Rock Springs F3
Saratoga F5
Scottsbluff E8
Sheridan B4
Sinclair E4
Spearfish B7
Steamboat Springs . . G5
Sturgis B8
Sundance B7
Thermopolis C3
Torrington E7
Upton C7
Vernal G2
Walden G5
Wellington G6
West Yellowstone . . . B1
Wheatland E6
Windsor G6
Worland C4
Wright C6

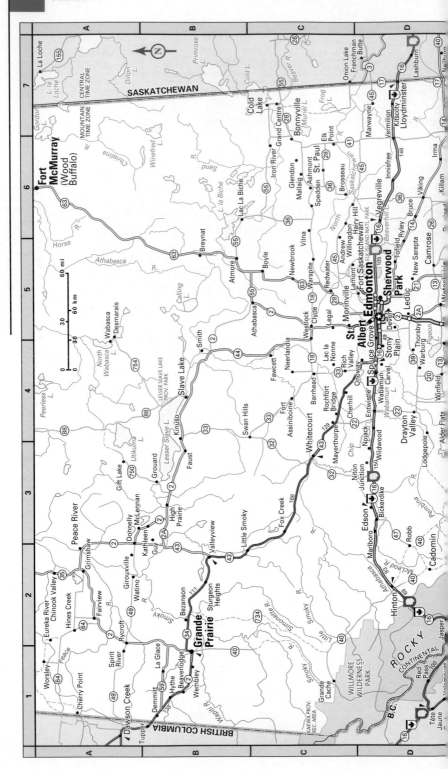

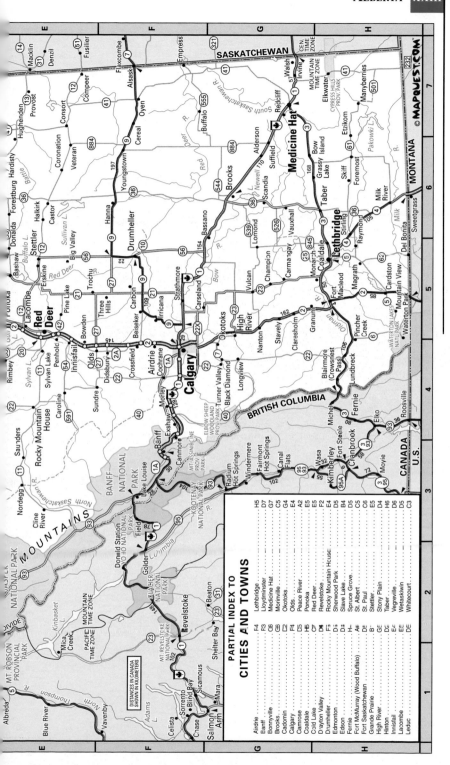

PARTIAL INDEX TO
CITIES AND TOWNS

Airdrie	F4
Banff	F3
Bonnyville	D7
Brooks	G6
Cadomin	C2
Calgary	F4
Camrose	D5
Coaldale	G6
Cold Lake	C7
Drayton Valley	D3
Drumheller	F5
Edmonton	D4
Edson	D3
Fernie	H3
Fort McMurray (Wood Buffalo)	A6
Fort Saskatchewan	D5
Grande Prairie	C1
High River	F4
Hinton	D2
Innisfail	E4
Lacombe	E4
Leduc	D4
Lethbridge	F4
Lloydminster	D7
Medicine Hat	G7
Morinville	C5
Okotoks	G4
Olds	E4
Peace River	A2
Ponoka	E5
Red Deer	E4
Revelstoke	F2
Rocky Mountain House	E4
Sherwood Park	D5
Slave Lake	B4
Spruce Grove	D5
St. Albert	C5
St. Paul	C6
Stettler	E5
Stony Plain	D4
Taber	H6
Vegreville	D6
Wetaskiwin	E4
Whitecourt	D5

DISTANCES IN CANADA SHOWN IN KILOMETERS

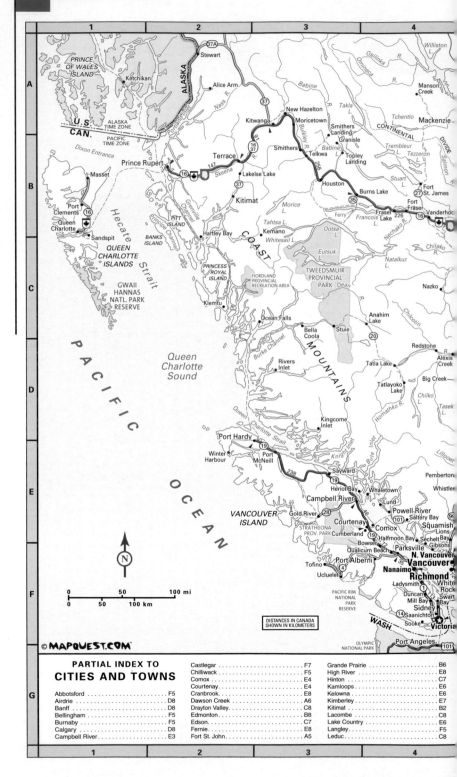

PARTIAL INDEX TO CITIES AND TOWNS

Abbotsford	F5
Airdrie	D8
Banff	D8
Bellingham	F5
Burnaby	F5
Calgary	D8
Campbell River	E3

Castlegar	F7
Chilliwack	F5
Comox	E4
Courtenay	E4
Cranbrook	E8
Dawson Creek	A6
Drayton Valley	C8
Edmonton	B8
Edson	C7
Fernie	E8
Fort St. John	A5

Grande Prairie	B6
High River	E8
Hinton	C7
Kamloops	E6
Kelowna	E6
Kimberley	E7
Kitimat	B2
Lacombe	C8
Lake Country	E6
Langley	F5
Leduc	C8

© MAPQUEST.COM

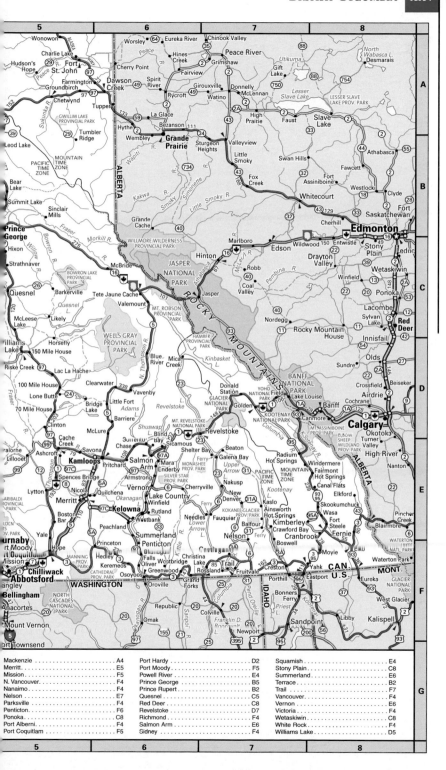

Mackenzie	A4	Port Hardy	D2	Squamish	E4
Merritt	E5	Port Moody	F5	Stony Plain	C8
Mission	F5	Powell River	E4	Summerland	E6
N. Vancouver	F4	Prince George	B5	Terrace	B2
Nanaimo	F4	Prince Rupert	B2	Trail	F7
Nelson	E7	Quesnel	C5	Vancouver	F4
Parksville	F4	Red Deer	C8	Vernon	E6
Penticton	F6	Revelstoke	D7	Victoria	F4
Ponoka	C8	Richmond	F4	Wetaskiwin	C8
Port Alberni	F4	Salmon Arm	E6	White Rock	F4
Port Coquitlam	F5	Sidney	F4	Williams Lake	D5

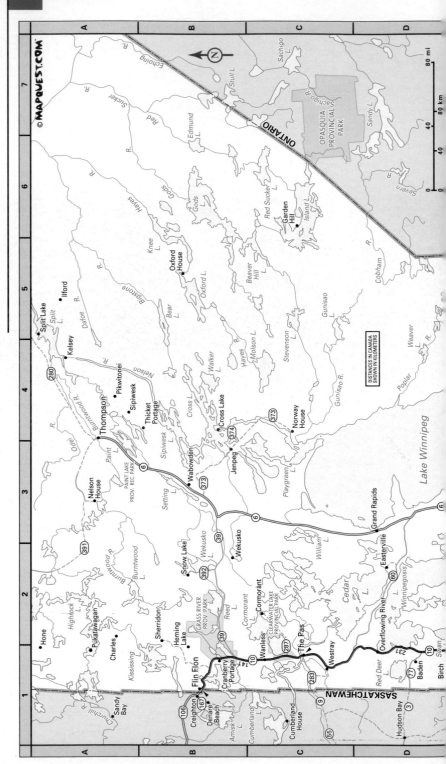

PARTIAL INDEX TO CITIES AND TOWNS

Alexander	G2	Morris	H4
Alonsa	F3	Neepawa	F3
Arborg	F4	Nelson House	A3
Arnes	F4	Newdale	F2
Ashern	F3	Ninette	H2
Baden	D1	Norway House	C4
BeauÉjour	G5	Oak Lake	G2
Benito	E1	Oak Point	F3
Binscarth	F1	Ochre River	F2
Birtle	G1	Overflowing River	D1
Bissett	F5	Petersfield	G4
Boissevain	H2	Pine Falls	F5
Brandon	G2	Pine River	E2
Camperville	E2	Plumas	G3
Cartwright	H3	Pointe du Bois	G5
Cowan	E2	Poplar Point	G3
Cranberry Portage	B1	Portage la Prairie	G3
Cross Lake	B4	Prawda	G5
Crystal City	H3	Pukatawagan	A1
Dauphin	F2	Rapid City	G2
Dauphin River	E3	Reston	H1
Deloraine	H2	Riverton	F4
Douglas	G2	Rivers	G2
Elkhorn	G1	Roblin	F1
Elm Creek	G4	Roland	H3
Elphinstone	G2	Russell	F1
Erickson	F2	Selkirk	G4
Eriksdale	F3	Sheridan	H2
Ethelbert	E2	Shoal Lake	G1
Flin Flon	B1	Sidney	G3
Gilbert Plains	F2	Skownan	E2
Gimli	F4	Snow Lake	B2
Gladstone	G3	Souris	H2
Glenboro	G3	Split Lake	A5
Grand Rapids	D3	Sprague	G5
Gretna	H4	St. Jean Baptiste	H4
Gypsumville	E3	St. Pierre-Jolys	G4
Hamiota	G2	Ste. Agathe	G4
Hartney	H2	Ste. Rose du Lac	F2
Herring Lake	B3	Steinbach	G5
Jenpeg	B4	Stonewall	G4
Kenville	E1	Sundown	G5
Killarney	H2	Swan River	E1
Lac du Bonnet	G5	The Pas	C1
Langruth	G3	Thompson	A4
Letellier	H4	Treherne	G3
Lundar	F3	Virden	G1
MacGregor	G3	Victoria Beach	F4
Manigotagan	F5	Wabowden	B2
Manitou	H3	Wanless	B1
McCreary	F2	Wasagaming	F2
Melita	H1	Wawanesa	G2
Miami	H3	Westbourne	G3
Middlebro	H5	Westray	C1
Miniota	G1	Whitemouth	G5
Minitonas	E1	Winkler	H3
Minnedosa	G2	Winnipeg	G4
Minto	H2	Winnipegosis	E2
Morden	H3		

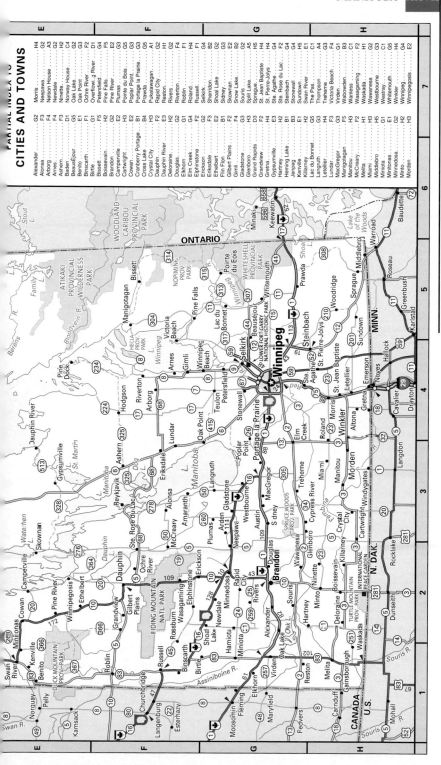

Map Legend

TRANSPORTATION

CONTROLLED ACCESS HIGHWAYS

Free

Toll; Toll Booth

Under Construction

Interchange and Exit Number

Ramp
Downtown maps only

OTHER HIGHWAYS

Primary Highway

Secondary Highway

Multilane Divided Highway
Primary and secondary highways only

Other Paved Road

Unpaved Road
Check conditions locally

HIGHWAY MARKERS

Interstate Route

U.S. Route

State or Provincial Route

County or Other Route

Business Route

Trans-Canada Highway

Canadian Provincial Autoroute

Mexican Federal Route

OTHER SYMBOLS

Distances along Major Highways
Miles in U.S.; kilometers in Canada and Mexico

Tunnel; Pass

One-way Street

Airport

Railroad
Downtown maps only

Auto Ferry; Passenger Ferry

RECREATION AND FEATURES OF INTEREST

National Park

National Forest; National Grassland

Other Large Park or Recreation Area

Military Lands

Indian Reservation

Small State Park with and without Camping

Public Campsite

Trail

Point of Interest

Golf Course
Professional tournament location

Hospital
City maps only

Ski Area

CITIES AND TOWNS

National Capital; State or Provincial Capital

County Seat
State maps only

Cities, Towns, and Populated Places
Type size indicates relative importance

Urban Area
State and province maps only

Large Incorporated Cities

OTHER MAP FEATURES

County Boundary and Name

Time Zone Boundary

Mountain Peak; Elevation
Feet in U.S.; meters in Canada and Mexico

Perennial; Intermittent River

Perennial; Intermittent or Dry Water Body

Dam

Swamp

JEFFERSON

Mt. Olympus
7,985

Whoever said the world's getting smaller never had to fuel it.

Each year millions of people become drivers. Meeting this growing demand for energy is complicated, but as ExxonMobil we try to make it look simple. So not only are the familiar faces of Exxon and

Mobil still there to help you, they now accept each other's credit cards. We figure you have enough stuff in your wallet already, so now one card works like two.

Ex̌onMobil

WHETHER YOU'RE IN A...

...TRACK RACE

...TRUCK RACE

...DRAG RACE

...OR THE RAT RACE,

...SUPERFLO® GIVES PROTECTION THAT'S FAST, PROTECTION THAT LASTS.

High-speed straightaways of the Busch Series. Treacherous mud pits of CORR (Championship Off Road Racing). Earth-shaking quarter miles of NHRA. They're all brutal on a car and its engine. Yet the drivers of these Exxon Superflo® racing vehicles can tell you firsthand, Exxon Superflo motor oil goes the distance. And if it can protect their engines, imagine what it can do for yours.

Superflo races its protection to your engine's vital parts at the start and keeps protecting mile after mile after mile. So protect your car's engine with Exxon Superflo motor oil. Protection That's Fast, Protection That Lasts!™

WELCOME

For over 40 years, the *Mobil Travel Guide* has provided North American travelers with trusted advice on finding good value, quality service, and the distinctive attractions that give a destination its unique character. Today, the *Travel Guide* is presented by ExxonMobil and is a valued member of the ExxonMobil family of travel publications.

Although you'll notice changes in the *2001 Travel Guide* format—including introduction of the ExxonMobil name—what hasn't changed is our commitment to bring reliable lodging, dining, and sightseeing information to a broad range of travelers. Our nationwide network of professional evaluators offer you their expertise on over 22,000 properties using our 5-Star rating system that has become an industry standard. Whether you're seeking a convenient business meeting locale, an elegant 5-Star celebration, or a leisurely driving trip, it is our hope that you'll rely on the *Travel Guide* as your companion.

As we continue to enhance our products to better meet the needs of the modern traveler, we hope to hear from our most important audience—you, the traveler. Please take the time to complete the customer feedback form at the back of this book or contact us on the Internet at www.exxonmobiltravel.com. We appreciate your input and wish you safe and memorable travels.

Lee R Raymond

Lee R. Raymond
Chairman
Exxon Mobil Corporation

A WORD TO OUR READERS

The exciting and complex development of the US interstate high-way system was formally—and finally—established in 1956, allowing Americans to take to the roads in enormous numbers. They are going on day trips, long weekends, extended family vacations, and business. Traveling across the country, stopping at National Parks, major cities, small towns, monuments, and landmarks remains a fantasy trip for many.

Airline travel, too, is on the increase. Whether for business or pleasure, we can take flights between relatively close cities and from coast to coast.

You, the traveler, deserve the best food and accommodations available in every city, town, or village you visit. But finding suitable accommodations can be problematic. You could try to meet and ask local residents about appropriate places to stay and eat, but that time-consuming option comes with no guarantee of getting the best advice.

That's where the *Mobil Travel Guide* comes in. This trusted, well-established tool can direct you to satisfying places to eat and stay, and to interesting events and attractions in thousands of locations across North America. Prior to the merger with Exxon Corporation, Mobil Corporation had sponsored the Mobil Travel Guide since 1958. Now ExxonMobil presents the latest edition of our annual Travel Guide series in partnership with Consumer Guide publications.

This edition has several new features. We've added driving tours, suggesting "off the beaten path" day trips (or overnight if you choose) to points of interest near a well-established destination. MapQuest has provided our maps this year, including the more-details maps for driving tours. We've also added walking tours. These allow you to stretch your legs and see the sites in and about your destination. Again, you will find maps to help you find your way to monuments, points of historic interest, and maybe even a snack.

Our three-star entries now contain more details. Clearly travelers are looking for good value, and the more information we can offer about restaurants and lodgings, the easier it will be to evaluate your many choices.

Perhaps the biggest difference this year is the addition of color to the travel guides. Pictures of places to stay, things to do, and colorful surroundings along the way might encourage you to make a stop to take your own pictures. Once a seven-volume series, The *Mobil Travel Guides* are now published as a ten book set. This allows us to add more hotel, restaurant, and attraction information, as well as several more maps in each book.

Finally, we've changed the size of the books. With more travelers carrying travel guides in their glove compartment, purse, breast pocket, or briefcase, the new size was chosen to accommodate a better fit.

The hi-tech information database that is the foundation of every title in the *Mobil Travel Guide* series is an astonishing resource: It is enormous, detailed, and continually updated, making it as accurate and useful as it can be. Highly trained field representatives, spread out across the country, generate exhaustive, computerized inspection reports. Senior staff members then evaluate these reports, along with the comments of more than 100,000 readers. All of this information is used to arrive at fair, accurate, and useful assessments of hotels, motels, and restaurants. Mobil's respected and world-famous one- to five-star rating system highlights valuable capsulized descriptions of each site. All of this dependable information, plus details about thousands of attractions and things to do, is in the dynamic Mobil database!

Space limitations make it impossible for us to include every hotel, motel, and restaurant in America. Instead, our database consists of a generous, representative sampling, with information about places that are above-average in their type. In essence, you can confidently patronize any of the restaurants, places of lodging, and attractions contained in the *Mobil Travel Guide* series.

What do we mean by "representative sampling"? You'll find that the *Mobil Travel Guide* books include information about a great variety of establishments. Perhaps you favor rustic lodgings and restaurants, or perhaps you're most comfortable with elegance and high style. Money may be no object or, like most of us, you may be on a budget. Some travelers place a high premium on 24-hour room service or special menu items. Others look for quiet seclusion. Whatever your travel needs and desires, they will be reflected in the *Mobil Travel Guide* listings.

Allow us to emphasize that we have charged no establishment for inclusion in our guides. We have no relationship with any of the businesses and attractions we list, and act only as a consumer advocate. In essence, we do the investigative legwork so you won't have to.

Look over the "How to Use This Book" section that follows. You'll discover just how simple it is to quickly and easily gather all the information you need—before your trip or while on the road. For terrific tips on saving money, travel safety, and other ways to enjoy your travels to the maximum, be sure to read our special section, "Making the Most of Your Trip."

Keep in mind that the hospitality business is ever-changing. Restaurants and places of lodging—particularly small chains or stand-alone establishments—can change management or even go out of business with surprising quickness. Although we have made every effort to double-check information during our annual updates, we nevertheless recommend that you call ahead to be sure a place you have selected is open and still offers all the features you want. Phone numbers are provided, and, when available, we also list fax and Web site information.

We hope that all your travel experiences are easy and relaxing. If any aspects of your accommodations or dining motivate you to comment, please drop us a line. We depend a great deal on our readers' remarks, so you can be assured that we will read and assimilate your comments into our research. General comments about our books are also welcome. You can write us at Mobil Travel Guide, 7373 N Cicero Ave, Lincolnwood, IL 60712, or send e-mail to info@exxonmobiltravel.com.

Take your *Mobil Travel Guide* books along on every trip. You'll be pleased by their convenience, ease of use, and breadth of dependable coverage.

Happy travels in the new millennium!

EDITORIAL CONTRIBUTORS AND CONSULTANTS FOR DRIVING TOURS, WALKING TOURS, ATTRACTIONS, EVENTS, AND PHOTOGRAPHY:

Bill McRae is a native of eastern Montana and now resides in Oregon. He is the author of eight guidebooks to the western United States and Canada including *Pacific Northwest USA: A Travel Survival Kit, Montana Handbook,* and *Utah Handbook.* His other travel writing accomplishments and credits include *The American Road Atlas* and *Travel Planner and Atlas of US National Parks.*

Julie Fanselow is a freelance writer specializing in travel. A former newspaper reporter and editor, she has authored and contributed to several travel guidebooks including *Idaho Off the Beaten Path, Traveling the Lewis & Clark Trail,* and regional guides on Texas, the Great Plains, and the Northwest. The Idaho resident's articles have appeared in many publications including *Sunset, Hemispheres,* and *Travel Choices Northwest.*

HOW TO USE THIS BOOK

The *Mobil Travel Guide* is designed for ease of use. Each state has its own chapter. The chapter begins with a general introduction, which provides both a general geographical and historical orientation to the state; it also covers basic statewide tourist information, from state recreation areas to seatbelt laws. The remainder of each chapter is devoted to the travel destinations within the state—cities and towns, state and national parks, and tourist areas—which, like the states, are arranged alphabetically.

The following is an explanation of the wealth of information you'll find regarding those travel destinations—information on the area, on things to see and do there, and on where to stay and eat.

Maps and Map Coordinates

Next to each destination is a set of map coordinates. These are referenced to the appropriate state map in the front of this book. In addition, we have provided maps of selected larger cities and of key neighborhoods within the city sections.

Destination Information

Because many travel destinations are close to other cities and towns where visitors might find additional attractions, accommodations, and restaurants, cross-references to those places are included whenever possible. Also listed are addresses and phone numbers for travel-information resources—usually the local chamber of commerce or office of tourism—as well as pertinent vital statistics and a brief introduction to the area.

What to See and Do

Almost 20,000 museums, art galleries, amusement parks, universities, historic sites and houses, plantations, churches, state parks, ski areas, and other attractions are described in the *Mobil Travel Guides*. A white star on a black background ★ signals that the attraction is one of the best in the state. Since municipal parks, public tennis courts, swimming pools, and small educational institutions are common to most towns, they are generally not represented with the white star on the black background.

Following the attraction's description, you'll find the months and days it's open, address/location and phone number, and admission costs (see the inside front cover for an explanation of the cost symbols). Note that directions are given from the center of the town under which the attraction is listed, which may not necessarily be the town in which the attraction is located. Zip codes are listed only if they differ from those given for the town.

Driving and Walking Tours

New to the *Mobil Travel Guides* are the driving and walking tours. The driving tours are usually day trips—though they can be longer—that make for interesting side trips. This is a way to get off the beaten track and visit an area often overlooked. These trips frequently cover areas of natural beauty or historical significance, and a map of the tour is included with the description. The walking tours focus on a particularly interesting area of a city or town. Again, these can be a break from more everyday tourist attractions. The tours often include places to stop for a meal or snack.

Events

Events—categorized as annual, seasonal, or special—are highlighted. An annual event is one that's held every year for a period of usually no longer than a week to ten days; festivals and fairs are typical entries. A seasonal event is one that may or may not be annual and that is held for a number of weeks or months in the year, such as horse racing, summer theater, concert or opera festivals, and professional sports. Special event listings occur infrequently and mark a certain date or event, such as a centennial or other commemorative celebration.

Major Cities

Additional information on airports and ground transportation, suburbs, and neighborhoods may be included for large cities.

Lodging and Restaurant Listings

ORGANIZATION

For both lodgings and restaurants, when a property is in a town that does not have its own heading, the listing appears under the town nearest its location with the address and town in parentheses immediately after the establishment name. In large cities, lodgings located within 5 miles of major commercial airports are listed under a separate "Airport" heading, following the city listings.

LODGING CLASSIFICATIONS

Each property is classified by type according to the characteristics below. Because the following features and services are found at most motels, lodges, motor hotels, and hotels, they are not shown in those listings:

- Year-round operation with a single rate structure unless otherwise quoted
- European plan (meals not included in room rate)
- Bathroom with tub and/or shower in each room
- Air-conditioned/heated, often with individual room control
- Cots
- Daily maid service
- In-room phones
- Elevators

Motels/Motor Lodges. Accommodations are in low-rise structures with rooms easily accessible to parking (which is usually free). Properties have outdoor room entry and small, functional lobbies. Service is often limited, and dining may not be offered in lower-rated motels and lodges. Shops and businesses are found only in higher-rated properties, as are bellhops, room service, and restaurants serving three meals daily.

Lodges. These differ from motels primarily in their emphasis on outdoor recreational activities and in location. They are often found in resort and rural areas rather than in major cities or along highways.

Hotels. To be categorized as a hotel, an establishment must have most of the following facilities and services: multiple floors, a restaurant and/or coffee shop, elevators, room service, bellhops, a spacious lobby, and recreational facilities. In addition, the following features and services not shown in listings are also found:

- Valet service (one-day laundry/cleaning service)
- Room service during hours restaurant is open
- Bellhops
- Some oversize beds

Resorts. These specialize in stays of three days or more and usually offer American plan and/or housekeeping accommodations. Their emphasis is on recreational facilities, and a social director is often available. Food services are of primary importance, and guests must be able to eat three meals a day on the premises, either in restaurants or by having access to an on-site grocery store and preparing their own meals.

All Suites. All Suites' guestrooms consist of two rooms, one bedroom and one living room. Higher rated properties offer facilities and services comparable to regular hotels.

B&Bs/Small Inns. Frequently thought of as a small hotel, a Bed and Breakfast or an inn is a place of homelike comfort and warm hospitality. It is often a structure of historic significance, with an equally interesting setting. Meals are a special occasion, and refreshments are frequently served in late afternoon. Rooms are usually individually decorated, often with antiques or furnishings representative of the locale. Phones, bathrooms, or TVs may not be available in every room.

Guest Ranches. Like resorts, guest ranches specialize in stays of three days or more. Guest ranches also offer meal plans and extensive outdoor activities. Horseback riding is usually a feature; there are stables and trails on the ranch property, and trail rides and daily instruction are part of the program. Many guest ranches are working ranches, ranging from casual to rustic, and guests are encouraged to participate in ranch life. Eating is often family style and may also include cookouts. Western saddles are assumed; phone ahead to inquire about English saddle availability.

Extended Stay. These hotels specialize in stays of three days or more and usually offer weekly room rates. Service is often limited and dining might not be offered at lower-rated extended-stay hotels.

Villas/Condos. Similar to Cottage Colonies, these establishments are usually found in recreational areas. They are often separate houses, often luxuriously furnished, and rarely offer restaurants and only a small variety of services on the premises.

Conference Centers. Conference Center Hotels are hotels with extended meeting space facilities designed to house multi-day conferences and seminars. Amenities are often geared toward groups staying for longer than one night and often include restaurants and fitness facilities. Larger Conference Center Hotels are often referred to as Convention Center Hotels.

Casinos. Casino Hotels incorporate areas that offer games of chance like Blackjack, Poker, Slot machines, etc. and are only found in states that legalize gambling. Casino Hotels offer a wide range of services and amenities, comparable to regular hotels.

Cottage Colonies. These are housekeeping cottages and cabins that are usually found in recreational areas. Any dining or recreational facilities are noted in our listing.

DINING CLASSIFICATIONS

Restaurants. Most dining establishments fall into this category. All have a full kitchen and offer table service and a complete menu. Parking on or near the premises, in a lot or garage, is assumed. When a property offers valet or other special parking features, or when only street parking is available, it is noted in the listing.

Unrated Dining Spots. These places, listed after Restaurants in many cities, are chosen for their unique atmosphere, specialized menu, or local flavor. They include delis, ice-cream parlors, cafeterias, tearooms, and pizzerias. Because they may not have a full kitchen or table service, they are not given an Mobil Travel Guide rating. Often they offer extraordinary value and quick service.

QUALITY RATINGS

The *Mobil Travel Guide* has been rating lodgings and restaurants on a national basis since the first edition was published in 1958. For years the guide was the only source of such ratings, and it remains among the few guidebooks to rate restaurants across the country.

All listed establishments were inspected by experienced field representatives or evaluated by a senior staff member. Ratings are based upon their detailed inspection reports of the individual properties, on written evaluations of staff members who stay and dine anonymously, and on an extensive review of comments from our readers.

You'll find a key to the rating categories, ★ through ★★★★★, on the inside front cover, All establishments in the book are recommended. Even a ★ place is above average, usually providing a basic, informal experience. Rating categories reflect both the features the property offers and its quality in relation to similar establishments.

For example, lodging ratings take into account the number and quality of facilities and services, the luxury of appointments, and the attitude and professionalism of staff and management. A ★ establishment provides a comfortable night's lodging. A ★★ property offers more than a facility that rates one star, and the decor is well planned and integrated. Establishments that rate ★★★ are professionally managed and staffed and often beautifully appointed; the lodging experience is truly excellent and the range of facilities is extensive. Properties that have been given ★★★★ not only offer many services but also have their own style and personality; they are luxurious, creatively decorated, and superbly maintained. The ★★★★★ properties are among the best in North America, superb in every respect and entirely memorable, year in and year out.

Restaurant evaluations reflect the quality of the food and the ingredients, preparation, presentation, service levels, as well as the property's decor and ambience. A restaurant that has fairly simple goals for menu and decor but that achieves those goals superbly might receive the same number of stars as a restaurant with somewhat loftier ambitions, but the execution of which falls short of the mark. In general, ★ indicates a restaurant that's a good choice in its area, usually fairly simple and perhaps catering to a clientele of locals and families; ★★ denotes restaurants that are more highly recommended in their area; ★★★ restaurants are of national caliber, with professional and attentive service and a skilled chef in the kitchen; ★★★★ reflect superb dining choices, where remarkable food is served in equally remarkable surroundings; and ★★★★★ represent that rare group of the best restaurants in the country, where in addition to near perfection in every detail, there's that special something extra that makes for an unforgettable dining experience.

A list of the four-star and five-star establishments in each region is located just before the state listings.

Each rating is reviewed annually and each establishment must work to maintain its rating (or improve it). Every effort is made to assure that ratings are fair and accurate; the designated ratings are published purely as an aid to travelers. In general, properties that are very new or have recently undergone major management changes are considered difficult to assess fairly and are often listed without ratings.

LODGINGS

Each listing gives the name, address, directions (when there is no street address), neighborhood and/or directions from downtown (in major cities), phone number (local and 800), fax number, number and type of rooms available, room rates, and seasons open (if not year-round). Also included are details on recreational and dining facilities on the property or nearby, the presence of a luxury level, and credit card information. A key to the symbols at the end of each listing is on the inside front cover. (Note that Exxon or Mobil Corporation credit cards cannot be used for payment of meals and room charges.)

All prices quoted in the Mobil Travel Guide publications are expected to be in effect at the time of publication and during the entire year; however, prices cannot be guaranteed. In some localities there may be short-term price variations because of special events or holidays. Whenever possible, these price charges are noted. Certain resorts have complicated rate structures that vary with the time of year; always confirm listed rates when you make your plans.

RESTAURANTS

Each listing gives the name, address, directions (when there is no street address), neighborhood and/or directions from downtown (in major cities), phone number, hours and days of operation (if not open daily year-round), reservation policy, cuisine (if other than American), price range for each meal served, children's meals (if offered), specialties, and credit card information. Additionally, special features such as chef ownership, ambience, and entertainment are noted. By carefully reading the detailed restaurant information and comparing prices, you can easily determine whether the restaurant is formal and elegant or informal and comfortable for families.

TERMS AND ABBREVIATIONS IN LISTINGS

The following terms and abbreviations are used throughout the listings:

A la carte entrees With a price, refers to the cost of entrees/main dishes that are not accompanied by side dishes.

AP American plan (lodging plus all meals).

Bar Liquor, wine, and beer are served in a bar or cocktail lounge and usually with meals unless otherwise indicated (e.g., "wine, beer").

Business center The property has a designated area accessible to all guests with business services.

Business servs avail The property can perform/arrange at least two of the following services for a guest: audiovisual equipment rental, binding, computer rental, faxing, messenger services, modem availability, notary service, obtaining office supplies, photocopying, shipping, and typing.

Cable Standard cable service; "premium" indicates that HBO, Disney, Showtime, or similar cable services are available.

Ck-in, ck-out Check-in time, check-out time.

Coin lndry Self-service laundry.

Complete meal Soup and/or salad, entree, and dessert, plus nonalcoholic beverage.

Continental bkfst Usually coffee and a roll or doughnut.

Cr cds: A, American Express; C, Carte Blanche; D, Diners Club; DS, Discover; ER, enRoute; JCB, Japanese Credit Bureau; MC, MasterCard; V, Visa.

D Followed by a price, indicates room rate for a "double"—two people in one room in one or two beds (the charge may be higher for two double beds).

Downhill/X-country ski Downhill and/or cross-country skiing within 20 miles of property.

Each addl Extra charge for each additional person beyond the stated number of persons at a reduced price.

Early-bird dinner A meal served at specified hours, typically around 4:30-6:30 pm.

Exc Except.

Exercise equipt Two or more pieces of exercise equipment on the premises.

Exercise rm Both exercise equipment and room, with an instructor on the premises.

Fax Facsimile machines available to all guests.

Golf privileges Privileges at a course within 10 miles.

Hols Holidays.

In-rm modem link Every guest room has a connection for a modem that's separate from the phone line.

Kit. or **Kits.** A kitchen or kitchenette that contains stove or microwave, sink, and refrigerator and that is either part of the room or a separate room. If the kitchen is not fully equipped, the listing will indicate "no equipt" or "some equipt."

Luxury level A special section of a lodging, covering at least an entire floor, that offers increased luxury accommodations. Management must provide no less than three of these four services: separate check-in and check-out, concierge, private lounge, and private elevator service (key access). Complimentary breakfast and snacks are commonly offered.

MAP Modified American plan (lodging plus two meals).

Movies Prerecorded videos are available for rental.

No cr cds accepted No credit cards are accepted.

No elvtr In hotels with more than two stories, it's assumed there are elevators; only their absence is noted.

No phones Phones, too, are assumed; only their absence is noted.

Parking There is a parking lot on the premises.

Private club A cocktail lounge or bar available to members and their guests. In motels and hotels where these clubs exist, registered guests can usually use the club as guests of the management; the same is frequently true of restaurants.

Prix fixe A full meal for a stated price; usually one price is quoted.

Res Reservations.

S Followed by a price, indicates room rate for a "single," i.e., one person.

Serv bar A service bar, where drinks are prepared for dining patrons only.

Serv charge Service charge is the amount added to the restaurant check in lieu of a tip.

Table d'hôte A full meal for a stated price, dependent upon entree selection; no a la carte options are available.

Tennis privileges Privileges at tennis courts within 5 miles.

TV Indicates color television.

Under certain age free Children under that age are not charged if staying in room with a parent.

Valet parking An attendant is available to park and retrieve a car.

VCR VCRs in all guest rooms.

VCR avail VCRs are available for hookup in guest rooms.

Special Information for Travelers with Disabilities

The *Mobil Travel Guide* Ⓓ symbol shown in accommodation and restaurant listings indicates establishments that are at least partially accessible to people with mobility problems.

The *Mobil Travel Guide* criteria for accessibility are unique to our publication. Please do not confuse them with the universal symbol for wheelchair accessibility. When the Ⓓ symbol appears following a listing, the establishment is equipped with facilities to accommodate people using wheelchairs or crutches or otherwise needing easy access to doorways and rest rooms. Travelers with severe mobility problems or with hearing or visual impairments may or may not find facilities they need. Always phone ahead to make sure that an establishment can meet your needs.

All lodgings bearing our Ⓓ symbol have the following facilities:

- ISA designated parking near access ramps
- Level or ramped entryways to building
- Swinging building entryway doors minimum 3900
- Public rest rooms on main level with space to operate a wheelchair; handrails at commode areas
- Elevators equipped with grab bars and lowered control buttons

- Restaurants with accessible doorways; rest rooms with space to operate wheelchair; handrails at commode areas
- Minimum 3900 width entryway to guest rooms
- Low-pile carpet in rooms
- Telephone at bedside and in bathroom
- Bed placed at wheelchair height
- Minimum 3900 width doorway to bathroom
- Bath with open sink—no cabinet; room to operate wheelchair
- Handrails at commode areas; tub handrails
- Wheelchair accessible peephole in room entry door
- Wheelchair accessible closet rods and shelves

All restaurants bearing our Ⓓ symbol offer the following facilities:

- ISA-designated parking beside access ramps
- Level or ramped front entryways to building
- Tables to accommodate wheelchairs
- Main-floor rest rooms; minimum 3900 width entryway
- Rest rooms with space to operate wheelchair; handrails at commode areas

In general, the newest properties are apt to impose the fewest barriers.

To get the kind of service you need and have a right to expect, do not hesitate when making a reservation to question the management in detail about the availability of accessible rooms, parking, entrances, restaurants, lounges, or any other facilities that are important to you, and confirm what is meant by "accessible." Some guests with mobility impairments report that lodging establishments' housekeeping and maintenance departments are most helpful in describing barriers. Also inquire about any special equipment, transportation, or services you may need.

Making the Most of Your Trip

A few hardy souls might look with fondness upon the trip where the car broke down and they were stranded for a week. Or maybe even the vacation that cost twice what it was supposed to. For most travelers, though, the best trips are those that are safe, smooth, and within their budget. To help you make your trip the best it can be, we've assembled a few tips and resources.

Saving Money

ON LODGING

After you've seen the published rates, it's time to look for discounts. Many hotels and motels offer them—for senior citizens, business travelers, families, you name it. It never hurts to ask—politely, that is. Sometimes, especially in late afternoon, desk clerks are instructed to fill beds, and you might be offered a lower rate, or a nicer room, to entice you to stay. Look for bargains on stays over multiple nights, in the off-season, and on weekdays or weekends (depending on location). Many hotels in major metropolitan areas, for example, have special weekend package plans that offer considerable savings on rooms; they may include breakfast, cocktails, and meal discounts. Prices can change frequently throughout the year, so phone ahead.

Another way to save money is to choose accommodations that give you more than just a standard room. Rooms with kitchen facilities enable you to cook some meals for yourself, reducing restaurant costs. A suite might save money for two couples traveling together. Even hotel luxury levels can provide good value, as many include breakfast or cocktails in the price of the room.

State and city sales taxes, as well as special room taxes, can increase your room rates as much as 25 percent per day. We are unable to include this specific information in the listings, but we strongly urge that you ask about these taxes when placing reservations in order to understand the total cost of your lodgings.

Watch out for telephone-usage charges that hotels frequently impose on long-distance calls, credit-card calls, and other phone calls—even those that go unanswered. Before phoning from your room, read the information given to you at check-in, and then be sure to read your bill carefully before checking out. You won't be expected to pay for charges that they did not spell out. (On the other hand, it's not unusual for a hotel to bill you for your calls after you return home.) Consider using your cell phone; or, if public telephones are available in the hotel lobby, your cost savings may outweigh the inconvenience.

ON DINING

There are several ways to get a less-expensive meal at a more-expensive restaurant. Early-bird dinners are popular in many parts of the country and offer considerable savings. If you're interested in sampling a 4- or 5-star establishment, consider going at lunchtime. While the prices then are probably relatively high, they may be half of those at dinner and come with the same ambience, service, and cuisine.

ON PARK PASSES

While many national parks, monuments, seashores, historic sites, and recreation areas may be used free of charge, others charge an entrance fee (ranging from $1 to $6 per person to $5 to $15 per carload) and/or a "use fee" for special services and facilities. If you plan to make several visits to federal recreation areas, consider one of the following National Park Service money-saving programs:

Park Pass. This is an annual entrance permit to a specific unit in the National Park Service system that normally charges an entrance fee. The pass admits the permit holder and any accompanying passengers in a private noncommercial vehicle or, in the case of walk-in facilities, the holder's spouse, children, and parents. It is valid for entrance fees only. A Park Pass may be purchased in person or by mail from the National Park Service unit at which the pass will be honored. The cost is $15 to $20, depending upon the area.

Golden Eagle Passport. This pass, available to people who are between 17 and 61, entitles the purchaser and accompanying passengers in a private noncommercial vehicle to enter any outdoor National Park Service unit that charges an entrance fee and admits the purchaser and family to most walk-in fee-charging areas. Like the Park Pass, it is good for one year and does not cover use fees. It may be purchased from the National Park Service, Office of Public Inquiries, Room 1013, US Department of the Interior, 18th and C Sts NW, Washington, DC 20240, phone 202/208-4747; at any of the 10 regional offices throughout the country; and at any National Park Service area that charges a fee. The cost is $50.

Golden Age Passport. Available to citizens and permanent residents of the United States 62 years or older, this is a lifetime entrance permit to fee-charging recreation areas. The fee exemption extends to those accompanying the permit holder in a private noncommercial vehicle or, in the case of walk-in facilities, to the holder's spouse and children. The passport also entitles the holder to a 50 percent discount on use fees charged in park areas but not to fees charged by concessionaires. Golden Age Passports must be obtained in person. The applicant must show proof of age, i.e., a driver's license, birth certificate, or signed affidavit attesting to age (Medicare cards are not acceptable proof). These passports are available at most park service units where they're used, at National Park Service headquarters (see above), at park system regional offices, at National Forest Supervisors' offices, and at most Ranger Station offices. The cost is $10.

Golden Access Passport. Issued to citizens and permanent residents of the United States who are physically disabled or visually impaired, this passport is a free lifetime entrance permit to fee-charging recreation areas. The fee exemption extends to those accompanying the permit holder in a private noncommercial vehicle or, in the case of walk-in facilities, to the holder's spouse and children. The passport also entitles the holder to a 50 percent discount on use fees charged in park areas but not to fees charged by concessionaires. Golden Access Passports must be obtained in person. Proof of eligibility to receive federal benefits is required (under programs such as Disability Retirement, Compensation for Military Service-Connected Disability, Coal Mine

Safety and Health Act, etc.), or an affidavit must be signed attesting to eligibility. These passports are available at the same outlets as Golden Age Passports.

FOR SENIOR CITIZENS

Look for the senior-citizen discount symbol in the lodging and restaurant listings. Always call ahead to confirm that the discount is being offered, and be sure to carry proof of age. At places not listed in the book, it never hurts to ask if a senior-citizen discount is offered. Additional information for mature travelers is available from the American Association of Retired Persons (AARP), 601 E St NW, Washington, DC 20049, phone 202/434-2277.

Tipping

Tipping is an expression of appreciation for good service, and often service workers rely on tips as a significant part of their income. However, you never need to tip if service is poor.

IN HOTELS

Door attendants in major city hotels are usually given $1 for getting you a cab. Bellhops expect $1 per bag, usually $2 if you have only one bag. Concierges are tipped according to the service they perform. It's not mandatory to tip when you've asked for suggestions on sightseeing or restaurants or help in making reservations for dining. However, when a concierge books you a table at a restaurant known to be difficult to get into, a gratuity of $5 is appropriate. For obtaining theater or sporting event tickets, $5-$10 is expected. Maids, often overlooked by guests, may be tipped $1-$2 per days of stay.

AT RESTAURANTS

Coffee shop and counter service wait staff are usually given 8 percent–10 percent of the bill. In full-service restaurants, tip 15 percent of the bill, before sales tax. In fine restaurants, where the staff is large and shares the gratuity, 18 percent–20 percent for the waiter is appropriate. In most cases, tip the maitre d' only if service has been extraordinary and only on the way out; $20 is the minimum in upscale properties in major metropolitan areas. If there is a wine steward, tip him or her at least $6 a bottle, more if the wine was decanted or if the bottle was very expensive. If your bus person has been unusually attentive, $2 pressed into his hand on departure is a nice gesture. An increasing number of restaurants automatically add a service charge to the bill instead of a gratuity. Before tipping, carefully review your check. If you are in doubt, ask your server.

AT AIRPORTS

Curbside luggage handlers expect $1 per bag. Car-rental shuttle drivers who help with your luggage appreciate a $1 or $2 tip

Staying Safe

The best way to deal with emergencies is to be prepared enough to avoid them. However, unforeseen situations do happen, and you can prepare for them.

IN YOUR CAR

Before your trip, make sure your car has been serviced and is in good working order. Change the oil, check the battery and belts, and make sure tires are inflated properly (this can also improve gas mileage). Other inspections recommended by the car's manufacturer should be made, too.

Next, be sure you have the tools and equipment to deal with a routine breakdown: jack, spare tire, lug wrench, repair kit, emergency tools, jumper cables, spare fan belt, auto fuses, flares and/or reflectors, flashlights, first-aid kit, and, in winter, windshield wiper fluid, a windshield scraper, and snow shovel.

Bring all appropriate and up-to-date documentation—licenses, registration, and insurance cards—and know what's covered by your insurance. Also bring an extra set of keys, just in case.

En route, always buckle up! In most states it is required by law.

If your car does break down, get out of traffic as soon as possible—pull well off the road. Raise the hood and turn on your emergency flashers or tie a white cloth to the roadside door handle or antenna. Stay near your car. Use flares or reflectors to keep your car from being hit.

IN YOUR LODGING

Chances are slim that you will encounter a hotel or motel fire. The 🅰 in a listing indicates that there were smoke detectors and/or sprinkler systems in the rooms we inspected. Once you've checked in, make sure that any smoke detector in your room is working properly. Ascertain the locations of fire extinguishers and at least two fire exits. Never use an elevator in a fire.

For personal security, use the peephole in your room's door.

PROTECTING AGAINST THEFT

To guard against theft wherever you go, don't bring anything of more value than you need. If you do bring valuables, leave them at your hotel rather than in your car, and if you have something very expensive, lock it in a safe. Many hotels have one in each room; others will store your valuables in the hotel's safe. And of course, don't carry more money than you need; use traveler's checks and credit cards, or visit cash machines.

For Travelers with Disabilities

A number of publications can provide assistance. The most complete listing of published material for travelers with disabilities is available from The Disability Bookshop, Twin Peaks Press, Box 129, Vancouver, WA 98666, phone 360/694-2462. A comprehensive guidebook to the national parks is *Easy Access to National Parks: The Sierra Club Guide for People with Disabilities* ($16), distributed by Random House.

The Reference Section of the National Library Service for the Blind and Physically Handicapped (Library of Congress, Washington, DC 20542, phone 202/707-9276 or 202/707-5100) provides information and resources for persons with mobility problems and hearing and vision impairments, as well as information about the NILS talking program (or visit your local library).

Traveling to Canada

Citizens of the United States do not need visas to enter Canada, but proof of citizenship—passport, birth certificate, or voter registration card—is required. A driver's license is not acceptable. Naturalized citizens will need their naturalization certificates or their US passport to reenter the United States. Children under 18 who are traveling on their own should carry a letter from a parent or guardian giving them permission to travel in Canada.

Travelers entering Canada in automobiles licensed in the United States may tour the provinces for up to three months without fee. Drivers are advised to carry their motor vehicle registration card and, if the car is not registered in the driver's name, a letter from the registered owner authorizing use of the vehicle. If the car is rented, carry a copy of the rental contract stipulating use in Canada. For your protection, ask your car insurer for a Canadian Non-resident Interprovince Motor Vehicle Liability Insurance Card. This card ensures that your insurance company will meet minimum insurance requirements in Canada.

The use of seat belts by drivers and passengers is compulsory in all provinces. A permit is required for the use of citizens band radios. Rabies vaccination certificates are required for dogs or cats.

No handguns may be brought into Canada. If you plan to hunt, sporting rifles and shotguns plus 200 rounds of ammunition per person will be admitted duty-free. Hunting and fishing licenses must be obtained from the appropriate province. Each province has its own regulations concerning the transportation of firearms.

The Canadian dollar's rate of exchange with the US dollar varies; contact your local bank for the latest figures. Since customs regulations can change, it's recommended that you contact the Canadian consulate or embassy in your area. Offices are located in Atlanta, Boston, Buffalo, Chicago, Dallas, Detroit, Los Angeles, Miami, Minneapolis, New York City, Seattle, and Washington, DC. For the most current and detailed listing of regulations and sources, ask for the annually revised brochure "Canada: Travel Information," which is available upon request.

IMPORTANT TOLL-FREE NUMBERS AND ON-LINE INFORMATION

Hotels and Motels

Adam's Mark 800/444–2326
www.adamsmark.com

Baymont Inns and Suites
800/428–3438
www.budgetel.com

Best Western 800/780–7234,
TDD 800/528–2222
www.bestwestern.com

Budget Host 800/283–4678
www.budgethost.com

Clarion 800/252–7466

Comfort Inn 800/228–5150
www.choicehotels.com

Courtyard by Marriott 800/321–2211
www.courtyard.com

Days Inn 800/325–2525
www.daysinn.com

Doubletree 800/222–8733
www.doubletreehotels.com

Drury Inns 800/325–8300
www.drury-inn.com

Econo Lodge 800/446–6900
www.econolodge.com

Embassy Suites 800/362–2779
www.embassy-suites.com

Exel Inns of America 800/356–8013
www.exelinns.com

Fairfield Inn
by Marriott 800/228–2800
www.fairfieldinn.com

Fairmont Hotels 800/527–4727
www.fairmont.com

Forte 800/225–5843
www.forte-hotels.com

Four Seasons 800/819–5053
www.fourseasons.com

Friendship Inns 800/453–4511
www.hotelchoice.com

Hampton Inn 800/426–7866
www.hampton-inn.com

Hilton 800/445–8667,
TDD 800/368–1133
www.hilton.com

Holiday Inn 800/465–4329,
TDD 800/238–5544
www.holiday-inn.com

Howard Johnson 800/446–4656,
TDD 800/654–8442
www.hojo.com

Hyatt & Resorts 800/233–1234
www.hyatt.com

Inns of America 800/826–0778
www.innsamerica.com

Inter-Continental 800/327–0200
www.interconti.com

La Quinta 800/531–5900,
TDD 800/426–3101
www.laquinta.com

Loews 800/235–6397
www.loewshotels.com

Marriott 800/228–9290
www.marriott.com

Master Hosts Inns 800/251–1962
www.reservahost.com

Meridien 800/225–5843
www.forte-hotels.com

Motel 6 800/466–8356
www.motel6.com

Nikko Hotels
International 800/645–5687
www.nikkohotels.com

Omni 800/843–6664
www.omnihotels.com

Quality Inn 800/228–5151
www.qualityinn.com

Radisson 800/333–3333
www.radisson.com

Ramada 800/228–2828,
TDD 800/228–3232
www.ramada.com

Red Carpet Inns 800/251–1962
www.reservahost.com

Red Lion 800/733–5466
www.redlion.com

Red Roof Inn 800/843–7663
www.redroof.com

Renaissance 800/468–3571
www.renaissancehotels.com

Residence Inn
by Marriott 800/331–3131
www.marriott.com

Ritz-Carlton 800/241–3333
www.ritzcarlton.com

Rodeway 800/228–2000
www.rodeway.com

Sheraton 800/325–3535
www.sheraton.com

Shilo Inn 800/222–2244
www.shiloinns.com

Signature Inns 800/822–5252
www.signature-inns.com

Sleep Inn 800/753–3746
www.sleepinn.com

Super 8 800/800–8000
www.super8motels.com

Susse Chalet 800/524–2538
www.sussechalet.com

Travelodge 800/578–7878
www.travelodge.com

Vagabond Inns 800/522–1555
www.vagabondinns.com

Westin Hotels
& Resorts 800/937–8461
www.westin.com

Wyndham Hotels
& Resorts 800/996–3426
www.travelweb.com

Airlines

Air Canada 800/776–3000
www.aircanada.ca

Alaska 800/252–7522
www.alaska-air.com

American 800/433–7300
www.aa.com

America West 800/235–9292
www.americawest.com

British Airways 800/247–9297
www.british-airways.com

Canadian 800/426–7000
www.cdnair.ca

Continental 800/523–3273
www.flycontinental.com

Delta 800/221–1212
www.delta-air.com

IslandAir 800/323–3345

Mesa 800/637–2247
www.mesa-air.com

Northwest 800/225–2525
www.nwa.com

SkyWest 800/453–9417
www.skywest.com

Southwest 800/435–9792
www.iflyswa.com

TWA 800/221–2000
www.twa.com

United 800/241–6522
www.ual.com

USAir 800/428–4322
www.usair.com

Trains

Amtrak 800/872–7245
www.amtrak.com

Buses

Greyhound 800/231–2222
www.greyhound.com

Car Rentals

Advantage 800/777–5500
www.arac.com

Alamo 800/327–9633
www.goalamo.com

Allstate 800/634–6186
www.bnm.com/as.htm

Avis 800/831–2847
www.avis.com

Budget 800/527–0700
www.budgetrentacar.com

Dollar 800/800–3665
www.dollarcar.com

Enterprise 800/325–8007
www.pickenterprise.com

Hertz 800/654–3131
www.hertz.com

National 800/227–7368
www.nationalcar.com

Payless 800/729–5377
www.800-payless.com

Rent-A-Wreck 800/944–7501
www.rent-a-wreck.com

Sears 800/527–0770
www.budget.com

Thrifty 800/847–4369
www.thrifty.com

FOUR-STAR AND FIVE-STAR ESTABLISHMENTS IN THE NORTHWEST

Montana

★★★★ Lodging
Averill's Flathead Lake Lodge, *Bigfork*

Oregon

★★★★ Lodgings
The Westin Portland, *Portland*

★★★★ Restaurants
Couvron, *Portland*
Genoa, *Portland*

Washington

★★★★ Lodgings
Bellevue Club Hotel, *Bellevue*
Four Seasons Hotel Seattle, *Seattle*
W Seattle, *Seattle*
Woodmark Hotel on Lake Washington, *Bellevue*

★★★★ Restaurants
Brasa, *Seattle*
Georgian Room, *Seattle*
Rover's, *Seattle*

Wyoming

★★★★ Lodgings
Jenny Lake Lodge, *Grand Teton National Park*
Lost Creek Ranch, *Grand Teton National Park*
Rusty Parrot Lodge, *Jackson*

★★★★ Restaurant
The Alpenhof Dining Room, *Jackson*

Alberta

★★★★ Lodgings
Hotel Macdonald, *Edmonton*
Post Hotel, *Lake Louise*

★★★★ Restaurants
Post Hotel Dinning Room, *Lake Louise*

British Columbia

★★★★ Lodgings
The Aerie Resort, *Victoria*
The Fairmont Vancouver Airport, *Vancouver*
Four Seasons Hotel Vancouver, *Vancouver*
Hastings House, *Victoria*
The Metropolitan Hotel, *Vancouver*
The Pan Pacific Vancouver, *Vancouver*
Renaissance Vancouver Hotel Harbourside, *Vancouver*
Sheraton Suites Le Soleil, *Vancouver*
The Sutton Place Hotel, *Vancouver*
The Westin Grand Vancouver, *Vancouver*
The Westin Resort and Spa, *Whistler*
The Wickaninnish Inn, *Vancouver*

★★★★ Restaurants
The Aerie Dining Room, *Victoria*
Bear Foot Bistro, *Whistler*
Bishop's, *Vancouver*
La Belle Auberge, *Vancouver*
Lumiere, *Vancouver*
Restaurant Matisse, *Victoria*

IDAHO

When Idaho Territory was created (it included much of Montana and Wyoming as well as the present state), President Abraham Lincoln had difficulty finding a governor who was willing to come to this wild and rugged land. Some appointees, including Gilman Marston and Alexander H. Conner, never appeared.

They had good reason to be timorous—the area was formidable and still is. For there is not just one Idaho; there are at least a half dozen: a land of virgin rain forests (more than one-third of the state is wooded); a high desert covering an area bigger than Rhode Island and Delaware combined; gently sloping farmland, where soft Pacific winds carry the pungency of growing alfalfa; an alpine region of icy, isolated peaks and densely forested valleys hiding more lakes and streams than have been named, counted, or even discovered; an atomic energy testing station as modern as tomorrow, only a few miles from the Craters of the Moon, where lava once poured forth and congealed in fantastic formations; and the roadless, nearly uninhabited, 2.3-million-acre Frank Church—River of No Return Wilderness, where grizzly bear, moose, and bighorn sheep still run wild.

Stretching southward from Canada for nearly 500 miles and varying dramatically in terrain, altitude, and climate, Idaho has the deepest canyon in North America (Hell's Canyon, 7,913 feet), the largest stand of white pine in the world (in Idaho Panhandle National Forests), the finest big game in the country (Chamberlain Basin and Selway), the largest wilderness area in the United States (the Frank Church—River of No Return Wilderness), and the largest contiguous irrigated area in the United States (created by American Falls and several lesser dams). Idaho's largest county, named after the state itself, would hold the entire state of Massachusetts; its second-largest county, Owyhee, would hold New Jersey.

In addition to superlative scenery, fishing, and hunting, the visitor will find such diversions as buried bandit treasure, lost gold mines, hair-raising boat trips down the turbulent Salmon River (the "River of No

Population: 1,251,700
Area: 82,413 square miles
Elevation: 710-12,662 feet
Peak: Borah Peak (Custer County)
Entered Union: July 3, 1890 (43rd state)
Capital: Boise
Motto: It is forever
Nickname: The Gem State
Flower: Syringa
Bird: Mountain Bluebird
Tree: White Pine
Fair: Eastern, September 1-8, 2001, in Blackfoot; Western, August 17-25, 2001, in Boise
Time Zone: Mountain and Pacific
Website: www.visitid.org

The Sawtooths, Stanley

Return"), and ghost mining towns. For those who prefer something less strenuous, Sun Valley and Coeur d'Alene have luxurious accommodations.

Millions of years ago herds of mammoth, mastodon, camels, and a species of enormous musk ox roamed the Idaho area. When Lewis and Clark entered the region in 1805, they found fur-bearing animals in such great numbers that they got in each other's way. The promise of riches in furs brought trappers, who fought the animals, the Native Americans, the country, and each other with equal gusto. They were aided and abetted by the great fur companies, including the legendary Hudson's Bay Company. The first gold strike in the Clearwater country in 1860, followed by rich strikes in the Salmon River and Florence areas, the Boise Basin, and Coeur d'Alene (still an important mining area in the state) brought hordes of miners who were perfectly willing to continue the no-holds-barred way of life initiated by fur trappers. Soon afterward the shots of warring sheepmen and cattlemen mingled with those of miners.

Mining, once Idaho's most productive and most colorful industry, has yielded its economic reign, but the state still produces large amounts of silver, zinc, pumice, antimony, and lead. It holds great reserves (268,000 acres) of phosphate rock. Copper, thorium, limestone, asbestos, graphite, talc, tungsten, cobalt, nickel, cinnabar, bentonite, and a wealth of other important minerals are found here. Gems, some of the finest quality, include agate, jasper, garnets, opals, onyx, sapphires, and rubies.

Today, Idaho's single largest industry is farming. On more than 3.5 million irrigated acres, the state produces an abundance of potatoes, beets, hay, vegetables, fruit, and livestock. The upper reaches of the Snake River Valley, once a wasteland of sagebrush and greasewood, are now among the West's most fertile farmlands. Manufacturing and processing of farm products, timber, and minerals is an important part of the state's economic base. Tourism is also important to the economy.

When to Go/Climate

Summer and fall are usually pleasant times to visit Idaho, although it can snow at almost any time of year here. The state's varied topography makes for a wide range of weather conditions. Winter temperatures are cold but not so cold as to make outdoor acitivities uncomfortable.

AVERAGE HIGH/LOW TEMPERATURES (°F)

BOISE

Jan 36/22	**May** 71/44	**Sep** 77/48
Feb 44/28	**June** 81/58	**Oct** 65/39
Mar 53/32	**July** 90/58	**Nov** 49/31
Apr 61/37	**Aug** 88/57	**Dec** 38/23

POCATELLO

Jan 32/14	**May** 68/40	**Sep** 75/43
Feb 38/20	**June** 78/53	**Oct** 63/34
Mar 47/26	**July** 88/53	**Nov** 45/26
Apr 58/32	**Aug** 86/51	**Dec** 34/16

Parks and Recreation Finder

Directions to and information about the parks and recreation areas below are given under their respective town/city sections. Please refer to those sections for details.

NATIONAL PARK AND RECREATION AREAS

Key to abbreviations. I.H.S. = International Historic Site; I.P.M. = International Peace Memorial; N.B. = National Battlefield; N.B.P. = National Battlefield Park; N.B.C. = National Battlefield and Cemetery; N.C.A. = National Conservation Area; N.E.M. = National Expansion Memorial; N.F. = National Forest;

N.G. = National Grassland; N.H.P. = National Historical Park; N.H.C. = National Heritage Corridor; N.H.S. = National Historic Site; N.L. = National Lakeshore; N.M. = National Monument; N.M.P. = National Military Park; N.Mem. = National Memorial; N.P. = National Park; N.Pres. = National Preserve; N.R.A. = National Recreational Area; N.R.R. = National Recreational River; N.Riv. = National River; N.S. = National Seashore; N.S.R. = National Scenic Riverway; N.S.T. = National Scenic Trail; N.Sc. = National Scientific Reserve; N.V.M. = National Volcanic Monument.

Place Name	Listed Under
Boise N.F.	BOISE
Caribou N.F.	MONTPELIER , POCATELLO
Challis N.F.	CHALLIS
City of Rocks N.Res.	BURLEY
Clearwater N.F.	LEWISTON
Craters of the Moon N.M.	same
Idaho Panhandle N.F.	COEUR D'ALENE, PRIEST LAKE AREA, ST. MARIE'S
Nez Perce N.F.	GRANGEVILLE
Nez Perce N.H.P.	LEWISTON
Payctte N.F.	McCALL
Salmon N.F.	SALMON
Sawtooth N.F.	BELLEVUE, BURLEY, STANLEY
Targhee N.F.	ASHTON

STATE PARK AND RECREATION AREAS

Key to abbreviations. I.P. = Interstate Park; S.A.P. = State Archaeological Park; S.B. = State Beach; S.C.A. = State Conservation Area; S.C.P. = State Conservation Park; S.Cp. = State Campground; S.F. = State Forest; S.G. = State Garden; S.H.A. = State Historic Area; S.H.P. = State Historic Park; S.H.S. = State Historic Site; S.M.P. = State Marine Park; S.N.A. = State Natural Area; S.P. = State Park; S.P.C. = State Public Campground; S.R. = State Reserve; S.R.A. = State Recreation Area; S.Res. = State Reservoir; S.Res.P. = State Resort Park; S.R.P. = State Rustic Park.

Place Name	Listed Under
Bear Lake S.P.	MONTPELIER
Bruneau Dunes S.P.	MOUNTAIN HOME
Eagle Island S.P.	BOISE
Farragut S.P.	COEUR D'ALENE
Harriman S.P.	ASHTON
Hell's Gate S.P.	LEWISTON
Henrys Lake S.P.	ASHTON
Heyburn S.P.	ST. MARIE'S
Lucky Peak S.P.	BOISE
Malad Gorge S.P.	JEROME
Massacre Rocks S.P.	AMERICAN FALLS
Old Mission S.P.	KELLOGG
Ponderosa S.P.	McCALL
Priest Lake S.P. (Dickensheet, Indian Creek, and Lionhead units)	PRIEST LAKE AREA
Round Lake S.P.	SANDPOINT

Water-related activities, hiking, riding, various other sports, picnicking, visitor centers, and camping are available in most of these areas. Camping: $14/site/night with all hookups; $10/site/night with water; $7/site/night for primitive site. Extra vehicle $5/night. 15-day maximum stay at most parks. Reservations available only at Bear Lake, Farragut, Hell's Gate, Ponderosa and Priest Lake parks ($6 fee). Motorized vehicle entrance fee (included in camping fee), $2/day or $30 annual pass; no entrance fee for persons walking, riding a bicycle, or horseback riding. All camping parks in the Idaho system feature at least one site designed for use by the disabled. Most visitor centers and restrooms also accommodate the disabled. For further information contact the Idaho Dept of Parks & Recreation, PO Box 83720, Boise 83720-0065; 208/334-4199 or 800/VISIT-ID.

SKI AREAS

Place Name	Listed Under
Bogus Basin Ski Resort	BOISE
Brundage Mt Ski Area	McCALL

CALENDAR HIGHLIGHTS

FEBRUARY

Pacific Northwest Sled Dog Championship Races (Priest Lake Area). At Priest Lake Airport. Approx 100 teams from the US and Canada compete in various races from ½ mi to 35 mi. Phone Chamber of Commerce, 208/443-3191.

Lionel Hampton/Chevron Jazz Festival (Moscow). University of Idaho. Four-day festival hosted by Lionel Hampton featuring all-star headliners and student performers. Phone 208/885-6765.

APRIL

Cowboy Poet Festival (St. Anthony). Entertainment, clogging demonstrations. Phone South Fremont Chamber of Commerce, 208/624-4870.

JUNE

Western Days (Twin Falls). Three-day event featuring shoot-out, barbecue contests, dances, parade. Phone 800/255-8946.

National Oldtime Fiddlers' Contest (Weiser). One of the oldest such contests in the country, attracting some of the nation's finest fiddlers. Also parade, barbecue, arts and crafts. Phone 800/437-1280.

Boise River Festival (Boise). Night-time parade, contests, entertainment, fireworks. Phone 208/338-8887.

JULY

smART Festival (St. Marie's). St. Marie's City Park. Paintings and crafts by local and regional artists. Food; entertainment; swimming. Phone 208/245-3417.

Snake River Stampede (Nampa). Among nation's top professional rodeos. All seats reserved. Phone 208/466-8497.

AUGUST

Shoshone-Bannock Indian Festival (Blackfoot). Fort Hall Indian Reservation. Tribes from many western states and Canada gather for this festival. Dancing, parades, rodeo, Native American queen contest, buffalo feast, and other events. Phone 208/785-2080.

Western Idaho Fair (Boise). Largest fair in state. Four entertainment stages, grandstand for nationally known musicians. Livestock, rodeo, agricultural pavilion, antique tractors, indoor and outdoor commercial exhibits, midway rides. Phone 208/376-3247.

SEPTEMBER

Eastern Idaho State Fair (Blackfoot). Seventy-acre fairground. Livestock, machinery exhibits, 4-, 6-, and 8-horse hitch competition, racing (pari-mutuel betting), rodeo, tractor pull, demolition derby, parade, nightly outdoor musical shows. Phone 208/785-2480.

Grand Targhee Ski and Summer Resort	DRIGGS
Lookout Pass Ski Area	WALLACE
Pebble Creek Ski Area	POCATELLO
Pomerelle Ski Area	BURLEY
Schweitzer Mt Resort	SANDPOINT
Silver Mt Ski Area	KELLOGG
Snowhaven Ski Area	GRANGEVILLE
Soldier Mt Ski Area	MOUNTAIN HOME
Sun Valley Resort	SUN VALLEY AREA

FISHING AND HUNTING

Nowhere in Idaho is the outdoor enthusiast more than an hr's drive from a clear-water fly fishing stream. From 2,000 lakes, 90 reservoirs, and 16,000 mi of rivers and streams, anglers take several million fish each year. Kokanee, trout (steelhead, rainbow, Kamloops, cutthroat, brown, brook, Dolly Varden, and Mackinaw), bass, perch, channel catfish, and sunfish are the most common varieties, with trout the most widespread and certainly among the scrappiest. Big game incl whitetail and mule deer, elk, antelope, bighorn sheep, mountain goat, and black bear. There are 12 kinds of upland game birds; ducks, Canada geese, and doves in season.

Nonresident fishing license: season $51.50; 1-day $7.50; each addl day $3/day; 3-day salmon/steelhead $31.50. Nonresident hunting license: game $101.50; turkey tag $36.50; deer tag $232.50; elk tag $332.50; other tag fees required for some game. There are nonresident quotas for deer and elk; apply mid-Dec. State permit validation is required for hunting waterfowl and some upland bird species, $6.50; archery and muzzleloader permits, $9. Prices may vary; for full information contact the Idaho Dept of Fish and Game, 600 S Walnut St, Box 25, Boise 83707; 208/334-3700 or 800/635-7820.

RIVER EXPEDITIONS

See Grangeville, Lewiston, Pocatello, Salmon, Stanley, Sun Valley Area, and Weiser. Contact Idaho Outfitters and Guides Assn, PO Box 95, Boise 83701; 800/71-IDAHO.

Driving Information

Safety belts are mandatory for all persons in front seat of vehicle. Children under 4 yrs must be in an approved safety seat anywhere in vehicle. For further information phone 208/334-8100.

INTERSTATE HIGHWAY SYSTEM

The following alphabetical listing of Idaho towns in *Mobil Travel Guide* shows that these cities are within 10 miles of the indicated Interstate highways. A highway map, however, should be checked for the nearest exit.

Highway Number	Cities/Towns within 10 miles
Interstate 15	Blackfoot, Idaho Falls, Lava Hot Springs, Pocatello.
Interstate 84	Boise, Burley, Caldwell, Jerome, Mountain Home, Nampa, Twin Falls.
Interstate 86	American Falls, Pocatello.
Interstate 90	Coeur d'Alene, Kellogg, Wallace.

Additional Visitor Information

Idaho Travel Council, PO Box 83720, 700 W State St, Boise 83720-0093, publishes a number of attractive and helpful pamphlets, among them an Idaho Travel Guide. Phone 208/334-2470 or 800/71-IDAHO.

Visitor centers in Idaho are located in or near the Oregon/Idaho, Washington/Idaho, and Utah/Idaho borders, as well as throughout the state. Visitors who stop by will find information and brochures helpful in planning stops at points of interest.

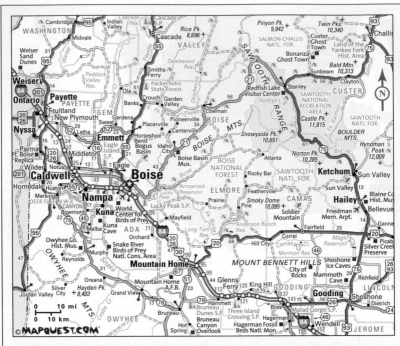

This route, which begins and ends on the arid Snake River plateau, climbs through Idaho's most extravagant mountain scenery. Highlights include stops at Idaho City, one of the state's oldest cities and the site of early gold mining history and frontier architecture, and several Wild West ghost town attractions, such as old saloons, summer melodrama theaters, and gold panning. Climbing high into the Rockies, the route tops a 6,110-foot pass and drops down to the Sawtooth National Recreation Area, where the serrated peaks of the Sawtooth Mountains loom on the western horizon. There are several lake basins along the face of the Sawtooths that feature easy hikes and picnicking. The route continues up to crest Galena Summit at 8,700 feet, then drops down to Ketchum and Sun Valley, towns famous for their ski resorts, fine restaurants, galleries, and celebrity spotting opportunities. Make a pilgrimage to Hemingway's memorial, or drive down the road to Hailey to catch a glimpse of Ezra Pound's humble birthplace. After descending from the Rockies to the parched plains along the Snake River, stop at the Shoshone Indian Ice Caves (natural caverns filled with ice formations) for welcome relief from fierce summer heat. **(Approx 267 mi)**

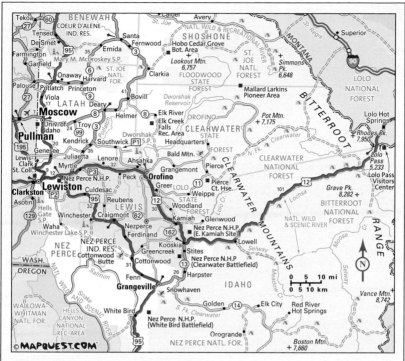

This route begins in the Snake River canyon and follows a series of dramatic river valleys into the very heart of the Rockies, finally climbing up to crest the Continental Divide. Lewiston, where jet boat trips to popular Hells Canyon of the Snake River begin, sits at the junction of the Snake and Clearwater rivers, which meet beneath 1,000-foot desert cliffs. Highway 30 follows the Clearwater River east, where the valley quickly turns forested and green. This portion of the route passes through the Nez Perce National Historic Park, and several sites of mythic and historic interest to the Nez Perce people are highlighted and interpreted. As the route continues east, the valley becomes more narrow and dramatic, with small, venerable fishing resorts clinging to the rocky river bank. East from Kooskia, Highway 12 wedges into the canyon of the Lochsa River, a mountain terrain so formidable (and scenically dramatic) that completion of this section of the highway was not possible until 1962, with the availability of modern engineering and construction processes. This near wilderness area is popular with experienced whitewater rafters, who are often seen on the coursing river. Near the pass into Montana, easy hiking trails lead to undeveloped, natural hot springs. **(Approx 172 mi)**

American Falls

(G-5) *See also Pocatello*

Pop 3,757 **Elev** 4,404 ft
Area code 208 **Zip** 83211
Information Chamber of Commerce, 239 Idaho St, PO Box 207; 208/226-7214

After a party of American Fur Company trappers was caught in the current of the Snake River and swept over the falls here, the fur company gave its name to both the community and the falls. American Falls boasts an important hydroelectric plant and is the capital of a vast dry-farming wheat belt; agricultural reclamation projects stretch westward for 170 miles.

What to See and Do

American Falls Dam. Impounds 25 mi-long lake; Willow Bay Recreation Area has swimming (beaches), fishing, boating (ramp; fee); picnicking, camping (hookups; fee). I-86 exit 40, follow signs on ID 39 Bypass. Phone 208/226-7214.

Indian Springs. Hot mineralized springs, pools, and baths; camping. (May-Labor Day, daily) 4 mi S on ID 37. Phone 208/226-2174. ¢¢

Massacre Rocks State Park. Nine hundred ninety-five acres. Along the Old Oregon Trail, emigrants carved their names on Register Rock. Nearby, at Massacre Rocks, is the spot where a wagon train was ambushed in 1862. River, juniper-sagebrush area; extensive bird life. Waterskiing, fishing, boating (ramps); hiking, bird-watching, picnicking. Fifty-two tent and trailer sites (dump station). Interpretive programs, info center. Standard fees. (Daily) 12 mi SW on I-86 at exit 28. Phone 208/548-2672. ¢

Trenner Memorial Park. Honors engineer who played key role in development of area; miniature power station, fountain, lava terrace. Near Idaho Power Co plant, SW of dam. **FREE**

Annual Event

Portneuf Muzzleloader Blackpowder Rendezvous. Massacre Rocks State Park. First wkend June.

Arco (F-4)

Settled 1879 **Pop** 1,016 **Elev** 5,318 ft
Area code 208 **Zip** 83213

Arco, seat of Butte County, was the first town to be lighted by power derived from atomic energy. Wildcat Peak casts its shadow on this pleasant little community located in a bend of the Big Lost River. Visitors pause here while exploring the Craters of the Moon National Monument (see), 20 miles southwest.

What to See and Do

Craters of the Moon National Monument. (see) 20 mi SW on US 20/26/93.

Experimental Breeder Reactor Number I (EBR-1). The first nuclear reactor developed to generate electricity (Dec 20, 1951). Visitor center exhibits incl the original reactor and 3 other nuclear reactors, equipment, and control rm, as well as displays on the production of electricity. Self-guided or 1-hr tours (Memorial Day wkend-Labor Day, daily; rest of yr, by appt). Contact INEL Tours, PO Box 1625, Idaho Falls 83415-3695. 18 mi SE via US 20/26. Phone 208/526-0050. **FREE**

Ashton

(F-6) *See also Driggs, Rexburg, St. Anthony*

Pop 1,114 **Elev** 5,260 ft
Area code 208 **Zip** 83420
Information Chamber of Commerce, City Hall, 64 N 10th St, PO Box 689; 208/652-3987

Ashton's economy is centered on the flow of products from the rich agricultural area that extends to Blackfoot. Equally important to the town, which has a view of the Twin Teton Peaks in Wyoming, is the influx of vacationers bound for the Targhee National Forest, Warm River recreation areas, and Bear Gulch winter sports area. A Ranger District office of the forest is located here.

What to See and Do

Harriman State Park. Located in the heart of a 16,000-acre wildlife refuge; home of the rare trumpeter swan. Nature is the main attraction here with Golden and Silver lakes, wildflowers, lodgepole pines, and thriving wildlife. The world-famous fly-fishing stream, Henry's Fork of the Snake River, winds through the park. Historic Railroad Ranch. Hiking, horseback riding, cross-country skiing. (Daily) Standard fees. HC 65, Box 500, Island Park. Phone 208/558-7368. Per vehicle ¢

Henry's Lake State Park. This 586-acre park offers waterskiing, boating (ramp); hiking, picnicking, 50 campsites (26 with hookups, 24 without hookups; dump station). (Mid-May-Oct, daily) Standard fees. 37 mi N on US 20, then 1 mi W; N of Island Park, on the S shore of famous fishing area, Henry's Lake. Phone 208/558-7368. Per vehicle ¢

⭐ **Targhee National Forest.** Approx 1.8 million acres incl two wilderness areas: Jedediah Smith (W slope of the Tetons, adj Grand Teton National Park) and Winegar Hole (grizzly bear habitat, bordering Yellowstone National Park); no motorized vehicles allowed in wilderness areas. Fishing (incl trout fishing on Henry's Fork of the Snake River and Henry's Lake Reservoir); big game hunting, camping (fee), picnicking, winter sports, Grand Targhee Resort (see DRIGGS) ski area. Float trips on the Snake River; boating, sailing, waterskiing, and canoeing on the Palisades Reservoir; outfitters and guides for the Jedediah Smith Wilderness. Closed Sat and Sun. Contact the Supervisor, 420 N Bridge St, PO Box 208, St. Anthony 83445. N on US 20/191. Phone 208/624-3151. In the forest are

Big Springs. Source of North Fork of Snake River which gushes from subterranean cavern at constant 52°F; it quickly becomes 150 ft wide. Schools of salmon and rainbow trout can be seen from bridge. The stream was designated the 1st National Recreation Water Trail. Moose, deer, sandhill cranes, trumpeter swans, and bald eagles can be seen along the banks. 33 mi N on

US 20/191 to Mack's Inn, then 5 mi E on paved road.

Lower Mesa Falls. North Fork drops another 65 ft here; scenic overlook, camping. 14 mi NE on ID 47.

Upper Mesa Falls. North Fork of Snake River takes a 114-ft plunge here; scenic overlook. 18 mi NE on ID 47 on Forest Service land.

Bellevue

(G-4) *See also Shoshone, Sun Valley Area*

Pop 1,275 **Elev** 5,190 ft
Area code 208 **Zip** 83313

What to See and Do

Sawtooth National Forest. Elevations from 4,500-12,100 ft. Swimming, water sports, fishing, boating; nature trails, downhill and cross-country skiing, snowmobiling. picnicking, saddle and pack trips, hunting, camping. Fee at certain designated campgrounds. N & W. Contact Forest Supervisor, 2647 Kimberly Rd E, Twin Falls 83301-7976. Phone 208/737-3200. **FREE**

Blackfoot

(G-5) *See also Idaho Falls, Pocatello*

Founded 1878 **Pop** 9,646
Elev 4,504 ft **Area code** 208
Zip 83221
Information Chamber of Commerce, Riverside Plaza, #1, PO Box 801; 208/785-0510

Blackfoot's economy has been stimulated by the establishment of an atomic reactor center, about 45 miles west (see ARCO), and deep-well drilling techniques that have increased agricultural productivity. The town, once called Grove City, was established in anticipation of the Utah Northern Railroad's arrival on Christmas Day. Its present name is linked to a legend about Native Americans who crossed a fire-blackened range. To the south is the

528,000-acre Fort Hall Indian Reservation. Excellent Shoshone and Bannock handicraft work is available at local stores and at the tribal office in Fort Hall agency on US 91.

What to See and Do

Bingham County Historical Museum. Restored 1905 homestead containing gun collection, Native American artifacts, early 20th-century furnishings and kitchen utensils. (Mar-Nov, Wed-Fri; closed hols) 190 N Shilling Ave. Phone 208/785-8065. **Donation**

Parks. Airport. Rodeo grounds, racetrack, picnicking, playground, golf. **Jensen Grove.** Boating, waterskiing, paddleboat rentals, varied water activities. Airport Rd, on Snake River. Parkway Dr, ½ mi N via I-15 exit 93.

Annual Events

Blackfoot Pride Days. Mid-Late June.

Shoshone-Bannock Indian Festival. Fort Hall Indian Reservation, S on I-15, Simplot Rd exit 80, then 2 mi W. Tribes from many western states and Canada gather for this festival. Dancing, parades, rodeo, Native American queen contest, buffalo feast, and other events. Phone 208/785-2080. Early Aug.

Eastern Idaho State Fair. Seventy-acre fairground, N of town. Livestock, machinery exhibits, 4-, 6-, and 8-horse hitch competition, racing (pari-mutuel betting), rodeo, tractor pull, demolition derby, parade, nightly outdoor musical shows. Phone 208/785-2480. Sep 1-8, 2001.

Boise

(F-2) *See also Nampa*

Settled 1862 **Pop** 125,738
Elev 2,726 ft **Area code** 208
Web www.boise.org

Information Convention and Visitors Bureau, 168 N 9th St, Suite 200, PO Box 2106, 83701; 208/344-7777 or 800/635-5240

Capital and largest city in Idaho, Boise (BOY-see) is also the business, financial, professional, and transportation center of the state. It is home to Boise State University (1932) and the National Interagency Fire Center, the nation's logistical support center for wildland fire suppression. Early French trappers labeled this still tree-rich area as *les bois* (the woods). Established during gold rush days, Boise was overshadowed by nearby Idaho City until designated the territorial capital in 1864. Abundant hydroelectric power stimulated manufacturing, with electronics, steel fabrication, and mobile homes the leading industries. Several major companies have their headquarters here. Lumber, fruit, sugar beets, and livestock are other mainstays of the economy; the state's main dairy region lies to the west of Boise. Natural hot water from the underground springs (with temperatures up to 170°F) heats some of the homes in the eastern portion of the city. A Ranger District office and the headquarters of the Boise National Forest are located here.

Extending alongside the Boise River is the Greenbelt, a trail used for jogging, skating, biking, and walking. When complete, the 22-mile trail will connect Eagle Island State Park on the west side of the city with Lucky Peak State Park on the east side of the city.

What to See and Do

Basque Museum and Cultural Center. (1864) The only museum in North America dedicated solely to Basque heritage; historical displays, paintings by Basque artists, changing exhibits, restored boarding house used by Basque immigrants in 1900s. (Tues-Sat, limited hrs) Phone 208/343-2671. ¢

Bogus Basin Ski Resort. Six double chairlifts, high-speed quad, paddle tow; patrol, school, rentals; two lodges, restaurants, bar, day care. Longest run 1½ mi; vertical drop 1,800 ft. Night skiing. (Dec-mid-Apr, daily) Cross-country trails. 16 mi N on Bogus Basin Rd. Phone 208/342-2100 (snow conditions) or 800/367-4397 (exc ID). ¢¢¢¢

Boise National Forest. This 2,646,341-acre forest incl the headwaters of the Boise and Payette rivers, 2 scenic byways, abandoned mines and ghost towns, and access

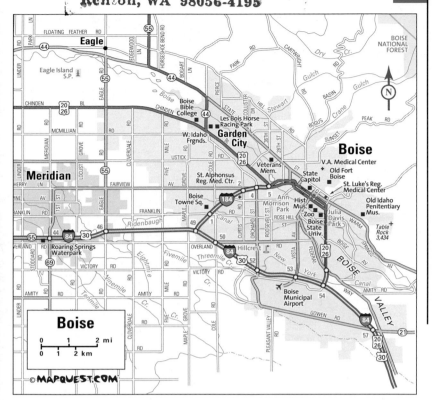

Boise

0   1   2 mi
0 1 2 km

©MAPQUEST.COM

to the Sawtooth Wilderness and the Frank Church—River of No Return Wilderness. Trout fishing, swimming, rafting; hunting, skiing, snowmobiling, mountain biking, motorized trail biking, hiking, picnicking, camping. (Mon-Fri) Contact the Supervisor, 1750 Front St, 83702. 1387 S Vinnell. Phone 208/373-4007.

Discovery Center of Idaho. Hands-on exhibits explore various principles of science; large bubblemaker, catenary arch, magnetic sand. (Tues-Sun; closed hols) 131 Myrtle St. Phone 208/343-9895. ¢¢

Eagle Island State Park. This 546-acre park was once a prison farm. Situated between the north and south channels of the Boise River, the park has cottonwoods, willows, and a variety of native flowers, as well as an abundance of wildlife incl the great blue heron, eagle, hawk, beaver, muskrat, fox, and weasel. Facilities incl 15-acre man-made lake (no fishing), swimming beach, water slide (fee); picnicking, concession. No pets. No glass beverage bottles. (Memorial Day-Labor Day, daily) 8 mi W via ID 20/26 to Linder Rd. Phone 208/939-0696. ¢

Idaho Botanical Gardens. Eleven theme and display gardens including meditation, cactus, rose, water, and butterfly/hummingbird gardens; ¾-mi nature trail, plaza. (Daily) 2355 N Penitentiary Rd. Phone 208/343-8649. ¢¢

Julia Davis Park. Rose garden, tennis courts, picnicking, (shelters); playground. Boat rentals, bandshell. 1104 Royal Blvd, off 9th St. Phone 208/384-4240. On grounds are

  Zoo Boise. Home to 285 animals; large birds of prey area; otter exhibit, primates, variety of cats, petting zoo. Education center; gift shop. (Daily; closed Jan 1, Thanksgiving, Dec 25) 355 N Julia Davis Dr. Phone 208/384-4045. ¢¢

Idaho State Historical Museum. History of Idaho and Pacific Northwest. Ten historical interiors;

Native American exhibits; fur trade, mining, ranching, forestry displays. (Daily) 610 N Julia Davis Dr. Phone 208/334-2120. **Donation**

Boise Art Museum. Northwest, Asian, and American art featured in changing and permanent exhibits. (Tues-Sun; closed hols) 670 S Julia Davis Dr. Phone 208/345-8330. ¢¢

Boise Tour Train. Narrated, 1-hr tour of the city and historical areas aboard motorized 1890s-style tour train. Departure point in Julia Davis Park. (Memorial Day-Labor Day, daily; early May-Memorial Day and after Labor Day-Oct, wkends) Phone 208/342-4796. ¢¢¢

Lucky Peak State Park. A 237-acre park comprised of 3 units: Spring Shores Marina (boating, day use), Sandy Point (swimming beach below dam), and Discovery unit (picnicking, 3 group shelters, river). Standard fees. 10 mi SE on ID 21. Phone 208/334-2679. Per vehicle ¢

M-K Nature Center. River observatory allows visitors to view activities of fish life; aquatic and riparian ecology displays; also visitor center with hands-on computerized exhibits; nature trails. (Daily) 600 S Walnut St. Phone 208/368-6060. Grounds **FREE**; Visitor center ¢¢

Old Idaho Penitentiary. (1870) Self-guided tour through the cells, compounds, and other areas of the

Boise skyline

prison. Guided tours by appt (Memorial Day-Labor Day). Displays about famous inmates, lawmen, and penal methods. Slide show on history. (Daily; closed hols) Under 13 only with adult. 2½ mi E via Warm Springs Ave (ID 21) to 2445 Old Penitentiary Rd. Phone 208/368-6080. ¢¢

St. Michael's Episcopal Cathedral. (1900) Tiffany window in south transept is fine example of this type of stained glass. (Mon-Fri, call for schedule) 518 N 8th St. Phone 208/342-5601.

State Capitol. (1905-22) Neo-classical design, faced with Boise sandstone; mounted statue of George Washington in lobby on second floor. Murals on 4th floor symbollically tell state's past, present, and future. Changing exhibits. Self-guided tours (Mon-Sat). Guided tours (Mon-Fri, by appt). 8th & Jefferson Sts. Phone 208/334-5174. **FREE**

Table Rock. Provides panoramic view of entire valley, 1,100 ft below. Road may be closed in winter. 4 mi E at end of Shaw Mt Rd.

World Center for Birds of Prey. Originally created to prevent extinction of peregrine falcon; scope has been expanded to include national and international conservation of birds of prey and their environments. Visitors can see breeding chamber of California condors and other raptors at interpretive center; gift shop. (Tues-Sun; closed Jan 1, Thanksgiving, Dec 25) 5666 W Flying Hawk Lane, I-84, exit 50 to S Cole Rd, then 6 mi S. Phone 208/362-TOUR. ¢¢

Annual Events

Boise River Festival. Night parade, contests, entertainment, fireworks. Phone 208/338-8887. Last full wkend June.

Western Idaho Fair. Largest fair in state. Phone 208/376-3247. Aug 17-25, 2001.

Seasonal Events

Jazz Festival. Boise State University. 1910 University Dr. Phone 208/385-1203. Apr.

Thoroughbred racing. Les Bois Park. 5610 Glenwood Rd. Wed and Sat evenings, matinees Sun. Simulcast racing yr-round (daily). Phone 208/376-RACE (7223). May-mid-Aug.

Idaho Shakespeare Festival. Amphitheater. Repertory theater. Phone 208/323-9700. June-Sep.

Motels/Motor Lodges

★★ **BEST REST INN.** *8002 Overland Rd (83709).* 208/322-4404; fax 208/322-7487; res 800/733-1481. 87 rms, 2 story. June-mid-Sep: S $50; D $56; under 18 free; ski plans; lower rates rest of yr. Crib free. Pet accepted. TV; cable (premium), VCR (movies). Pool; whirlpool. Ck-out noon. Business servs avail. Sundries. Gift shop. Cr cds: A, D, DS, MC, V.
D ⊷ ⇔ ⊠ 🔥

★★ **BEST WESTERN AIRPORT MOTOR INN.** *2660 Airport Way (83715), near Air Terminal Airport.* 208/384-5000; fax 208/384-5566; res 800/528-1234; toll-free 800/727-5004. Email bradley@innamerica.com; www.bestwestern.com. 50 rms, 2 story. May-Sep: S $65; D $72; each addl $4; under 18 free; lower rates rest of yr. Crib avail. Parking lot. Pool. TV; cable (premium). Complimentary continental bkfst, coffee in rms, newspaper, toll-free calls. Restaurant. Fax servs avail. Dry cleaning, coin lndry. Exercise privileges. Cr cds: A, D, DS, MC, V.
⇔ 🏃 ✈ ⊠ 🔥

★★ **BEST WESTERN SAFARI INN.** *1070 Grove St (83702).* 208/344-6556; fax 208/344-7240; res 800/WESTERN; toll-free 800/541-6556. Email safari1@bigplanet.com; www.bwsafari.com. 100 rms, 3 story, 3 suites. S $59; D $75; each addl $6; suites $79; under 18 free. Pet accepted, some restrictions. Parking garage. Pool, whirlpool. TV; cable (premium). Complimentary continental bkfst, coffee in rms, toll-free calls. Restaurant nearby. Ck out 1 pm, ck-in 3 pm. Meeting rm. Business servs avail. Dry cleaning. Free airport transportation. Exercise equipt, sauna. Golf. Downhill skiing. Cr cds: A, C, D, DS, MC, V.
D ⊷ ⇔ 🏋 ⇔ ⊠ 🔥

★★ **BOISE RIVER INN.** *1140 Colorado Ln (83706).* 208/344-9988; fax

208/336-9471. 88 kit. suites, 2 story. S, D $53-$58; under 16 free; each addl $5; wkly rates. Crib free. TV; cable. Heated pool. Complimentary continental bkfst. Restaurant nearby. Ck-out noon. Coin lndry. Balconies. Picnic tables, grills. On river. Cr cds: A, D, DS, MC, V.
D ⇔ ⊠ 🔥

★★ **CAVANAUGH'S PARKCENTER SUITES.** *424 E Parkcenter Blvd (83706).* 208/342-1044; fax 208/342-2763; toll-free 800/342-1044. 238 kit. units, 3 story. S, D $120-$130; under 12 free; wkend, wkly rates; higher rates Boise River Festival. Crib free. Pet accepted; $100. TV; cable (premium). Pool; whirlpool. Complimentary continental bkfst, coffee in rms. Restaurant nearby. Bar 5-10 pm. Ck-out noon. Coin lndry. Meeting rms. Business center. In-rm modem link. Valet serv. Free airport, railroad station, bus depot transportation. Exercise equipt. Minibars. Cr cds: A, D, DS, MC, V.
D ⊷ ⇔ 🏃 ⊠ 🔥 SC 🏃

★★ **COMFORT INN.** *2526 Airport Way (83705), near Air Terminal Airport.* 208/336-0077; fax 208/342-6592; res 800/228-5150. 62 rms, 2 story. Apr-Oct: S $49; D $62; each addl $6; suites $62-$76; under 18 free; lower rates rest of yr. Crib $2. TV; cable (premium), VCR avail. Indoor pool; whirlpool. Complimentary continental bkfst. Restaurant adj open 24 hrs. Ck-out 11:30 am. In-rm modem link. Free airport transportation. Downhill ski 20 mi. Refrigerator in suites. Cr cds: A, DS, MC, V.
🏃 ⇔ ➤ 🔥

★ **ECONO LODGE.** *4060 Fairview Ave (83706).* 208/344-4030; fax 208/542-1635; res 800/553-2666. 52 rms, 3 story. S $40-$45; D $45-$50; each addl $6; under 18 free. Crib free. Pet accepted, some restrictions. TV; cable (premium), VCR avail. Complimentary continental bkfst. Restaurants nearby. Ck-out 11 am. Cr cds: A, DS, MC, V.
➤ 🔥

★★ **INN AMERICA.** *2275 Airport Way (83705), I-84, Exit 53, near Air Terminal Airport.* 208/389-9800; fax 208/338-1303; toll-free 800/469-4667. Email bradley@innamerica.com; www.

innamerica.com. 73 rms, 3 story. May-Sep: S $49; D $56; each addl $4; under 17 free; lower rates rest of yr. Crib avail. Parking lot. Pool. TV; cable (premium). Complimentary toll-free calls. Restaurant. Fax servs avail. Dry cleaning, coin lndry. Golf. Cr cds: A, D, DS, MC, V.

★★ **QUALITY INN AIRPORT SUITES.** *2717 Vista Ave (83705). 208/343-7505; fax 208/342-4319; res 800/228-5151.* 79 suites, 2 story, 50 kit. units. May-Oct: suites, kit. units $57-$64; under 18 free; wkly rates; lower rates rest of yr. Crib $2. Pet accepted, some restrictions; $10. TV; cable (premium), VCR avail. Pool. Complimentary continental bkfst. Restaurant nearby. Ck-out noon. Coin lndry. Free airport transportation. Refrigerators. Cr cds: A, C, D, DS, ER, JCB, MC, V.

★★ **RODEWAY INN.** *1115 N Curtis Rd (83706). 208/376-2700; fax 208/ 377-0324; res 800/228-2000; toll-free 800/727-5002. Email rodewayboise@ prodigy.net; www.rodeway.com.* 88 rms, 2 story, 10 suites. May-Aug: S $70; D $80; each addl $10; suites $100; under 17 free; lower rates rest of yr. Crib avail. Pet accepted, some restrictions, fee. Parking lot. Pool, whirlpool. TV; cable (premium), VCR avail. Complimentary full bkfst, coffee in rms, newspaper, toll-free calls. Restaurant 6:30 am-9:30 pm. Bar. Ck-out noon, ck-in 2 pm. Meeting rms. Business center. Dry cleaning. Free airport transportation. Golf, 18 holes. Tennis, 2 courts. Downhill skiing. Picnic facilities. Cr cds: A, C, D, DS, MC, V.

★★ **SHILO INN AIRPORT.** *4111 Broadway Ave (83705), near Air Terminal Airport. 208/343-7662; fax 208/344-0318; res 800/222-2244. www.shiloinns.com.* 125 rms, 4 story, 87 suites. S, D $75-$79; each addl $10; suites $85-$89; under 13 free. Pet accepted; $7. TV; cable (premium), VCR. Pool; whirlpool. Complimentary continental bkfst, coffee in rms. Restaurant adj open 24 hrs. Ck-out noon. Coin lndry. Meeting rms. Business servs avail. Valet serv. Free airport, bus depot transportation. Exercise equipt; sauna. Refrig-

erators, microwaves, bathrm phones; some wet bars. Cr cds: A, D, DS, MC, V.

★ **SLEEP INN.** *2799 Airport Way (83705), near Air Terminal Airport. 208/336-7377; fax 208/336-2035; toll-free 800/321-4661.* 69 rms, shower only, 2 story. S $60; D $67; each addl $5; under 18 free. Crib free. TV; cable (premium), VCR (movies). Complimentary continental bkfst, coffee in rms. Restaurant nearby. Ck-out 1 pm. Business servs avail. In-rm modem link. Free airport, bus depot transportation. Some refrigerators. Cr cds: A, C, D, DS, ER, JCB, MC, V.

★ **SUPER 8.** *2773 Elder St (83705), near Air Terminal Airport. 208/344-8871; fax 208/344-8871; res 800/800-8000. www.super8.com.* 108 rms, 3 story. June-Sep: S $55; D $65; each addl $5; under 12 free; lower rates rest of yr. Crib avail. Parking lot. Indoor pool. TV; cable (premium), VCR avail. Complimentary continental bkfst, toll-free calls. Ck-out 11 am, ck-in 3 pm. Business servs avail. Coin lndry. Golf, 18 holes. Cr cds: A, C, D, DS, MC, V.

★ **TRAVELODGE.** *1314 Grove St (83702). 208/342-9351; fax 208/336-5828; res 800/578-7878. www.trave lodge.com.* 48 rms, 41 with shower only, 2 story. May-mid-Sep: S $45-53; D $50-$60; each addl $5; under 18 free; lower rates rest of yr. Crib free. Pet accepted. TV; cable (premium). Pool. Complimentary continental bkfst, coffee in rms. Restaurant nearby. Ck-out noon. Free airport transportation. Cr cds: A, C, D, DS, ER, JCB, MC, V.

★★ **UNIVERSITY INN.** *2360 University Dr (83706), adj to Boise State Univ. 208/345-7170; fax 208/345-5118; toll-free 800/345-7170.* 82 rms, 2 story. S $46.50-$65.50; D $55.50-$65; each addl $6; suites $80-$100; under 18 free. Crib free. TV; cable (premium). Heated pool; whirlpool, poolside serv. Restaurant 6 am-2 pm; Sun 7 am-3 pm. Bar. Ck-out noon. Business servs avail. Valet serv. Free airport transportation. Downhill ski 20 mi. Cr cds: A, C, D, DS, MC, V.

Hotels

★★ BEST WESTERN VISTA INN.
2645 Airport Way (83705), near Air Terminal Airport. 208/336-8100; fax 208/342-3060; res 800/528-1234. Email bradley@innamerica.com; www.bestwestern.com. 87 rms, 2 story. May-Sep: S $75; D $85; each addl $4; under 17 free; lower rates rest of yr. Crib avail. Parking lot. Indoor pool. TV; cable (premium). Complimentary continental bkfst, coffee in rms, newspaper, toll-free calls. Restaurant. Ck-out 1 pm, ck-in 3 pm. Meeting rms. Business servs avail. Dry cleaning, coin lndry. Sauna. Golf. Cr cds: A, C, D, DS, MC, V.

★★★ DOUBLETREE. *1800 Fairview Ave (83702).* 208/344-7691; fax 208/336-3652; res 800/222-8733; toll-free 800/547-8010. 180 rms, 7 story, 2 suites. May-Sep: S $109; D $119; each addl $10; suites $195; under 12 free; lower rates rest of yr. Crib avail. Pet accepted, fee. Parking lot. Pool, whirlpool. TV; cable (DSS), VCR avail. Complimentary coffee in rms, newspaper. Restaurant 6 am-10 pm. Bar. Ck-out noon, ck-in 3 pm. Meeting rms. Business servs avail. Bellhops. Dry cleaning. Gift shop. Free airport transportation. Exercise privileges. Golf. Tennis. Bike rentals. Cr cds: A, C, D, DS, ER, JCB, MC, V.

★★★ DOUBLETREE CLUB HOTEL - BOISE. *475 Parkcenter Blvd (83706).* 208/345-2002; fax 208/345-7823; res 800/-222-TREE. Email boipc@micron.net; www.doubletree.com. 156 rms, 6 story, 2 suites. S $79; D $89; each addl $10; suites $175; under 18 free. Crib avail, fee. Parking lot. Pool, whirlpool. TV; cable (premium). Complimentary coffee in rms, newspaper, toll-free calls. Restaurant 6 am-11 pm. Bar. Ck-out 1 pm, ck-in 3 pm. Meeting rms. Business center. Bellhops. Dry cleaning. Exercise privileges. Golf, 18 holes. Downhill skiing. Bike rentals. Video games. Cr cds: A, C, D, DS, ER, JCB, MC, V.

★★★ DOUBLETREE HOTEL RIVERSIDE. *2900 Chinden Blvd (83714).* 208/343-1871; fax 208/344-1079; res 800/222-8733. Email dtsales@micron.net; www.doubletree.com. 304 rms, 2 story, 35 suites. Crib avail, fee. Pet accepted. Parking lot. Pool, children's pool, whirlpool. TV; cable (premium). Complimentary coffee in rms, newspaper, toll-free calls. Restaurant. Bar. Ck-out noon, ck-in 4 pm. Conference center, meeting rms. Business center. Bellhops. Dry cleaning, coin lndry. Gift shop. Free airport transportation. Exercise equipt, sauna, steam rm. Golf. Tennis. Downhill skiing. Hiking trail. Picnic facilities. Cr cds: A, C, D, DS, ER, JCB, MC, V.

★★ HOLIDAY INN. *3300 Vista Ave (83705), near Air Terminal Airport.* 208/344-8365; fax 208/343-9635; toll-free 800/465-4329. Email gmboi@lodgian.com; www.holiday-inn.com/boise-airport. 265 rms, 2 story, 3 suites. Mar, June-Aug: S, D $89; suites $199; under 18 free; lower rates rest of yr. Crib avail. Pet accepted. Parking lot. Indoor pool, lap pool, children's pool, lifeguard, whirlpool. TV; cable (premium). Complimentary coffee in rms, newspaper, toll-free calls. Restaurant 5 am-11 pm. Bar. Ck-out noon, ck-in 3 pm. Conference center, meeting rms. Business center. Bellhops. Dry cleaning, coin lndry. Free airport transportation. Exercise equipt. Golf. Tennis, 9 courts. Downhill skiing. Supervised children's activities. Hiking trail. Picnic facilities. Cr cds: A, C, D, DS, ER, JCB, MC, V.

★★★ OWYHEE PLAZA HOTEL.
1109 Main St (83702). 208/343-4611; fax 208/381-0695; toll-free 800/233-4611. Email info@owyheeplaza.com; www.owyheeplaza.com. 98 rms, 3 story, 2 suites. S $79; D $89; each addl $10; suites $235; under 18 free. Crib avail. Pet accepted, some restrictions, fee. Parking lot. Pool. TV; cable, VCR avail. Complimentary coffee in rms, newspaper. Restaurant 6 am-10 pm. Bar. Ck-out noon, ck-in 3 pm. Meeting rms. Business servs avail. Bellhops. Dry cleaning. Salon/barber. Free airport transportation. Exercise privileges. Golf. Tennis. Cr cds: A, MC, V.

★★ **PLAZA SUITE HOTEL.** *409 S Cole Rd (83709). 208/375-7666; fax 208/376-3608; toll-free 800/376-3608.* 36 rms, 4 story, 2 suites. S, D $88; each addl $9; suites $125; under 5 free. Crib avail. Parking lot. Indoor pool. TV; cable (premium), VCR avail. Complimentary continental bkfst, coffee in rms, newspaper, toll-free calls. Restaurant nearby. Ck-out 1 pm, ck-in 3 pm. Meeting rms. Business center. Dry cleaning. Exercise privileges. Golf. Tennis. Downhill skiing. Cr cds: A, C, D, DS, ER, JCB, MC, V.

★★ **SHILO INN RIVERSIDE.** *3031 Main St (83702). 208/344-3521; fax 208/384-1217; toll-free 800/222-2244. Email boiseriverside@shiloinns.com; www.shiloinns.com.* 112 rms, 3 story. June-Aug: S, D $85; each addl $10; under 12 free; lower rates rest of yr. Crib avail. Pet accepted, some restrictions, fee. Parking lot. Indoor pool, whirlpool. TV; cable (premium). Complimentary continental bkfst, coffee in rms, newspaper, toll-free calls. Restaurant nearby. Ck-out noon, ck-in 2 pm. Meeting rm. Business servs avail. Dry cleaning, coin lndry. Free airport transportation. Exercise equipt, sauna, steam rm. Golf. Downhill skiing. Hiking trail. Picnic facilities. Video games. Cr cds: A, C, D, DS, ER, JCB, MC, V.

★★ **STATEHOUSE INN.** *981 Grove St (83702). 208/342-4622; fax 208/344-5751; res 800/243-4622.* 88 rms, 6 story. S $90-$95; D $100-$110; each addl $10; suites $175; under 18 free. Crib free. TV; cable (premium), VCR. Complimentary full bkfst. Restaurant 6 am-10 pm. Bar 4 pm-midnight. Ck-out 1 pm. Meeting rms. Business servs avail. Free garage parking. Free airport, railroad station, bus depot transportation. Exercise equipt; sauna. Some refrigerators. Cr cds: A, DS, MC, V.

B&B/Small Inn

★★ **IDAHO HERITAGE INN.** *109 W Idaho St (83702). 208/342-8066; fax 208/343-2325. Email info@id heritageinn.com; www.idheritageinn. com.* 6 rms, 3 story, 2 suites. S $65; D $70; each addl $10; suites $95. Parking lot. TV; cable, VCR avail. Complimentary full bkfst, coffee in rms, newspaper, toll-free calls. Restaurant nearby. Ck-out 11 am, ck-in 3 pm. Business servs avail. Exercise privileges. Golf. Tennis. Downhill skiing. Bike rentals. Cr cds: A, DS, MC, V.

All Suite

★★ **RESIDENCE INN BY MARRIOTT.** *1401 Lusk Ave (83706), Yale at Capitol Blvd. 208/344-1200; fax 208/384-5354; res 208/344-1200; toll-free 800/331-3131. Email resinboise@ aol.com.* 104 rms, 2 story. S $100-$110; D $115-$140. Crib free. Pet accepted, some restrictions; $10/day. TV; cable (premium). Pool; whirlpool. Complimentary coffee. Restaurant nearby. Ck-out noon. Coin lndry. Meeting rms. Business servs avail. Free airport, railroad station, bus depot transportation. Downhill/x-country ski 20 mi. Lawn games. Refrigerators. Private patios, balconies. Picnic tables, grills. Cr cds: A, DS, MC, V.

Restaurants

★★ **MILFORD'S FISH HOUSE.** *405 S 8th St #100 (83702). 208/342-8382.* Specializes in fresh Northwest seafood. Hrs: 11:30 am-10 pm; Sat, Sun from 5 pm. Closed hols. Res accepted. Bar. Lunch $9-$14; dinner $14-$30. Former railroad freight warehouse. Cr cds: A, DS, MC, V.

★ **ONATI-THE BASQUE RESTAURANT.** *3544 Chinden Blvd (83714), 2 mi NW on Chinden Blvd. 208/343-6464.* Specializes in lamb, seafood. Hrs: 5-9:30 pm; Fri from 11 am. Closed Jan 1, July 4, Dec 24. Res accepted. Bar. Lunch complete meals: $4.25-$7.95; dinner complete meals: $9.95-$17. Entertainment: basque-style dancing. Basque artwork on display. Cr cds: A, D, DS, MC, V.

★ **RICK'S CAFE AMERICAN AT THE FLICKS.** *646 Fulton St (83702), in theater complex. 208/342-4288. Email the-flicks@rmci.net; www.the flicksboise.com.* Specializes in grilled

Italian sandwiches. Hrs: 4-9:30 pm; Fri-Sun from noon. Wine, beer. Lunch, dinner $5-$15. Designed after Humphrey Bogart's famous cafe in Casablanca; movie memorabilia, directors chairs, hologram image. Cr cds: A, DS, MC, V.

D

Bonner's Ferry

(A-2) *See also Sandpoint*

Settled 1864 **Pop** 2,193 **Elev** 1,777 ft
Area code 208 **Zip** 83805
Information Visitors Center, PO Box X; 208/267-5922

E.L. Bonner offered ferry service from this point on the Kootenai River, near the northern tip of the state, and gave this community its name. Today Bonner's Ferry services the agricultural and lumbering districts of Boundary County, of which it is the county seat. From here the broad, flat, and fertile Kootenai Valley stretches north to British Columbia. This is a scenic area featuring many lakes and streams; fishing, hunting, and hiking are popular pastimes. A Ranger District office of the Idaho Panhandle National Forest-Kaniksu (see PRIEST LAKE AREA) is located here.

What to See and Do

Kootenai National Wildlife Refuge. This 2,774-acre refuge was created as a resting area for waterfowl during migration. Its wide variety of habitat supports many species of birds and mammals, incl bald eagles. Auto tour (4½ mi). Hunting, fishing. For further info contact Refuge Mgr, HCR 60, Box 283. 5 mi W on Riverside Rd. Phone 208/267-3888. **FREE**

Moyie Falls. Park and look down into 400-ft canyon at spectacular series of plunges. Greater flow during the spring runoff. 9 mi E on US 2, then N at Moyie Springs on small road; watch for sign for overlook just E of first bridge over Moyie River.

Annual Event

Kootenai River Days. Three wks June.

Motels/Motor Lodges

★ **KOOTENAI VALLEY MOTEL.** *Hwy 95 (83805), S on US 95. 208/267-7567; fax 208/267-2600.* 22 rms, 2 kit. units, some with showers only. June-Sep: S $55; D $65-$125; each addl $5; kit. units $75-$90; higher rates special events; lower rates rest of yr. Crib free. TV; cable (premium). Whirlpool. Playground. Restaurant adj 4:30 am-8 pm. Ck-out 11 am. Business servs avail. Picnic tables. Cr cds: MC, V.
⊠ 🔥

★ **SUNSET MOTEL.** *2705 Canyon St (Hwy 3E), 33 mi N via US 2/95 to ID 1, then 7 mi N. 250/428-2229; fax 250/428-2251; toll-free 800/663-7082. Email sunset@kootenay.com; www. kootenay.com/~sunset/iframe/index.htm.* 16 rms, 2 story, 8 suites. May-Oct: S $58; D $64; suites $71; lower rates rest of yr. Pet accepted, some restrictions, fee. Parking lot. Pool. TV; cable (premium), VCR avail. Complimentary coffee in rms, newspaper, toll-free calls. Restaurant nearby. Meeting rm. Business servs avail. Golf, 18 holes. Picnic facilities. Cr cds: A, C, D, DS, ER, MC, V.
🐟 🎿 ⊨ ⊠ 🔥

★ **TOWN & COUNTRY MOTEL.** *US 95 S (83805), at Rte 4. 208/267-7915; fax 208/267-7915.* 12 rms, 2 story. July-Aug: S $60; D $65; each addl $5; under 2 free; lower rates rest of yr. Pet accepted, some restrictions, fee. Parking lot. TV; cable (DSS). Complimentary coffee in rms, toll-free calls. Restaurant nearby. Ck-out 11 am, ck-in 2 pm. Business servs avail. Gift shop. Golf. Downhill skiing. Cr cds: A, C, D, DS, MC, V.
D 🐟 🎿 🦌 ⊠ 🔥

Restaurant

★ **PANHANDLE RESTAURANT.** *230 Main St (83805). 208/267-2623.* Specializes in chicken-fried steak, fish and chips. Own soups. Hrs: 6 am-8 pm; Sat, Sun from 7 am. Closed hols. Bkfst $2-$6.95; lunch $2.50-$5.25; dinner $6-$12. Cr cds: DS, MC, V.
D 🍴

Buhl

(H-3) *See also Twin Falls*

Pop 3,516 **Elev** 3,793 ft
Area code 208 **Zip** 83316
Information Chamber of Commerce, 716 US 30 E; 208/543-6682

Named for Frank Buhl, an early empire builder, this community processes the outpouring of farm goods produced in the farmlands of "Magic Valley." A Ranger District office of Nevada's Humboldt National Forest is located here.

What to See and Do

Balanced Rock. This 40-ft rock tower, resembling the mushroom cloud of an atomic bomb, rests on an 18-by-36-inch base; picnic area nearby. 12 mi SW on local roads.

Annual Events

Farmers Market. Last wk June-Sep.
Sagebrush Days. Sidewalk sales, arts in the park, fireworks, parade. Early July.
Twin Falls County Fair and Rodeo. 6 mi E in Filer. Carnival, 4-H exhibits, flower, art and antique shows; RCA rodeo. Four days beginning Wed after Labor Day.

Burley

(H-4) *See also Twin Falls*

Pop 8,702 **Elev** 4,165 ft
Area code 208 **Zip** 83318
Web http:www.cyberhighway.net/~mcidcham/
Information Mini-Cassia Chamber of Commerce, 324 Scott Ave, Rupert, 83350; 208/678-7230 or 800/333-3408

Created by a 210,000-acre irrigation project that turned a near desert area into a thriving agricultural center ideal for alfalfa, grain, sugar beet, and potatoes. Burley is a center for potato processing and has one of the largest sugar beet processing plants in the world. A Ranger District office of the Sawtooth National Forest is located here.

What to See and Do

Boating. 30 mi of the Snake River, with constant water levels, provide great boating opportunities throughout the summer.
Cassia County Historical Museum. Railroad cars, pioneer cabins, wagon collection, other pioneer relics. (Apr-mid-Nov, Tues-Sat; closed July 4) E Main & Hiland Ave. Phone 208/678-7172. **Donation**
City of Rocks National Reserve. A pioneer stopping place, this 25-sq-mi area of granite spires and sculptured rock formations resembles a city carved from stone; granite walls are inscribed with messages and names of westward-bound settlers, and remnants of the California Trail are still visible. Well-known for technical rock climbing. Hiking, picnicking, primitive camping. 22 mi S on ID 27 to Oakley, then 16 mi S and follow signs; or 32 mi S on ID 77 to Almo, then 2 mi W and follow signs. Phone 208/824-5519.
Sawtooth National Forest. Fishing; camping, hiking, horseback riding, snowmobiling, cross-country and downhill skiing, scenic views. Incl Howell Canyon, Lake Cleveland, and 4 other glacial lakes. Fee for certain designated campgrounds. Contact the Supervisor, 2647 Kimberly Rd E, Twin Falls 83301-7976. 9 mi E on US 30 to Declo, then 15 mi S on ID 77; other areas E & W. Phone 208/737-3200. In forest is
   Pomerelle Ski Area. Double, triple chairlifts, rope tow; patrol, school, rentals; cafeteria. Longest run 2.2 mi; vertical drop 1,000 ft. (Mid-Nov-Mar, daily; Apr, wkends) Night skiing (Jan-mid-Mar, Tues-Sat). 25 mi SE on ID 77, off I-84 exit 216. Phone 208/638-5599 (office) or 208/638-5555 (recorded snow report). ¢¢¢¢

Annual Events

Idaho Powerboat Regatta. Burley Marina. Boat racers from throughout the western US compete in this American Power Boat Association's national championship series event. Last wkend June.

Caldwell

(F-2) *See also Boise, Nampa*

Founded 1883 **Pop** 18,400
Elev 2,369 ft **Area code** 208
Zip 83605 **Web** www.caldwellid.org
Information Chamber of Commerce,
300 Frontage Rd, PO Box 819, 83606;
208/459-7493

Caldwell, seat of Canyon County, is situated in the triangle formed by the confluence of the Snake and Boise rivers. Founded by the Idaho and Oregon Land Improvement Company, the town was named for the company's president, C.A.Caldwell. Livestock, diversified agriculture, and vegetable processing plants are mainstays of the economy.

Needle Rock, City of Rocks

Cassia County Fair & Rodeo. County Fairgrounds, E end of E 10th & E 12th Sts. Racing, pari-mutuel betting. Third wk Aug.

Conference Center

★★ **BEST WESTERN BURLEY INN & CONVENTION CENTER.** *800 N Overland Ave (83318), I-84 Exit 208. 208/678-3501; fax 208/678-9532; res 800/528-1234; toll-free 800/599-1849. Email staycee@cyberhighway.net; www. bestwestern.com.* 121 rms, 2 story, 5 suites. May-Aug: S $69; D $79; each addl $6; suites $100; under 17 free; lower rates rest of yr. Crib avail. Pet accepted, some restrictions. Parking lot. Pool, children's pool, whirlpool. TV; cable (premium), VCR avail. Complimentary coffee in rms, newspaper, toll-free calls. Restaurant. Bar. Meeting rms. Business center. Dry cleaning, coin lndry. Free airport transportation. Exercise privileges. Golf, 18 holes. Tennis, 2 courts. Downhill skiing. Bike rentals, Supervised children's activities. Hiking trail. Picnic facilities. Cr cds: A, C, D, DS, ER, JCB, MC, V.

What to See and Do

Albertson College of Idaho. (1891) 800 students. Oldest 4-yr college in state. Private liberal arts college. Evans Mineral Collection, the Orma J. Smith Natural Science Museum, and a planetarium are in Boone Science Hall; Blatchley Hall houses the Rosenthal Gallery of Art (Sep-May, inquire for hrs). On Cleveland Blvd at 20th St. Phone 208/459-5500.

Ste. Chapelle Winery & Vineyards. Vineyards spread over slopes of the beautiful Snake River Valley. Reception area, tasting room, 24-ft cathedral windows offer spectacular view of valley and distant Owyhee Mts. Half-hr tours. (Daily) 12 mi S via ID 55. Phone 208/459-7222. **FREE**

Succor Creek Canyon. Two-mile stretch of spectacular canyon scenery and interesting earth formations. An abundance of prehistoric fossils has been found here. 33 mi W on ID 19, just across Oregon line.

Warhawk Air Museum. Displays WWII aviation artifacts. (Daily; call for schedule) 4917 Aviation Way, Caldwell Industrial Airport. Phone 208/454-2854. ¢

Annual Events

Caldwell Exchange Youth Rodeo. Second wk July.

Canyon County Fair. Late July.
Night Rodeo. Second or 3rd wk Aug.

Motels/Motor Lodges

★★ **BEST INN AND SUITES.** *901 Specht Ave (83605). 208/454-2222; fax 208/454-9334; res 800/237-8466. Email bestinn@cyberhighway.net; www. hotels-west.com.* 59 rms, 3 story, 6 suites. May-Sep: S $69; D $74; suites $110; lower rates rest of yr. Crib avail. Pet accepted. Parking lot. Indoor pool, children's pool, whirlpool. TV; cable, VCR avail. Complimentary continental bkfst, coffee in rms, newspaper, toll-free calls. Restaurant 6 am-11 pm. Ck-out 1 pm, ck-in 2 pm. Meeting rms. Business center. Dry cleaning, coin lndry. Gift shop. Exercise equipt. Golf. Downhill skiing. Picnic facilities. Cr cds: A, D, DS, JCB, MC, V.
🅳 🔧 ⚓ 🎿 🏃 🏊 🐾 🆂🅲 🏹

★ **SUNDOWNER MOTEL.** *1002 Arthur (83605). 208/459-1585; fax 208/459-6471; res 800/454-9487.* 65 rms, 2 story. S $40; D $43. Pet accepted, some restrictions, fee. Parking lot. TV; cable. Complimentary continental bkfst, toll-free calls. Restaurant nearby. Ck-out 11 am. Fax servs avail. Golf. Cr cds: A, D, DS, MC, V.
🐾 🎿 🏊 🐾

Challis (F-4)

Founded 1876 **Pop** 1,073
Elev 5,288 ft **Area code** 208
Zip 83226

Cloud-capped mountains, rocky gorges, and the Salmon River make this village one of the most picturesque in the Salmon River "Grand Canyon" area. This is the seat of Custer County and the headquarters for Challis National Forest. Two Ranger District offices of the forest are also located here.

What to See and Do

Challis National Forest. More than 2½ million acres of forest land surrounds Challis on all sides, crossed by US 93 & ID 75. Hot springs, ghost towns, nature viewing via trails; por-

tion of the Frank Church—River of No Return Wilderness; trout fishing; camping, picnicking, hunting. Guides, outfitters avail in Challis and vicinity. Idaho's highest point is here—Mt Borah (12,665 ft). Contact the Recreation Staff Officer, Forest Supervisor Bldg, HC 63, Box 1671. Phone 208/879-2285. Flowing through the forest is the

Middle Fork of the Salmon Wild and Scenic River. One of the premier whitewater rafting rivers in the US. Permits are required to float this river (apply Oct-Jan, permits issued June-Sep by lottery; fee). For permit info contact Middle Fork Ranger, PO Box 750. Phone 208/879-4101.

Grand Canyon in miniature. Walls cut 2,000 ft down on either side. Best seen at dusk. 10-13 mi S & SE on US 93.

Motels/Motor Lodges

★ **NORTHGATE INN.** *Hwy 93 (83226), ¼ mi N. 208/879-2490; fax 208/879-5767.* 56 rms, 3 story. S $35-$40; D $40-$50; each addl $4; under 12 free. Crib free. Pet accepted; $4. TV; cable. Complimentary continental bkfst. Ck-out 10 am. Meeting rm. Cr cds: A, D, DS, MC, V.
🅳 🔧 🏊 🐾 🆂🅲

★ **VILLAGE INN.** *US 93 (83226). 208/879-2239; fax 208/879-2813.* 54 rms, 6 kits. S $30-$42; D $42-$52; each addl $2; kit. units $2 addl; under 3 free. Pet accepted; $3. TV; cable (premium). Whirlpool. Restaurant 6 am-10 pm. Ck-out 11 am. Meeting rm. Downhill ski 7 mi; x-country ski 10 mi. Some refrigerators. Cr cds: A, D, DS, MC, V.
🅳 🔧 🎿 🏊 🐾

Coeur d'Alene

(B-2) *See also Kellogg; also see Spokane, WA*

Settled 1878 **Pop** 24,563 **Elev** 2,152 ft
Area code 208 **Zip** 83814
Web www.coeurdalene.com

Information Coeur d'Alene Area Chamber of Commerce, PO Box 850, 83816; 208/664-3194

Nestled amid lakes and rivers, Coeur d'Alene (cor-da-LANE) is a tourist and lumbering community, but particularly a gateway to a lush vacation area in the Idaho Panhandle. Irrigation has opened vast sections of nearby countryside for agricultural development; grass seed production is of major importance. This is the headquarters for the three Idaho Panhandle National Forests, and there are three Ranger District offices here.

What to See and Do

Coeur d'Alene Greyhound Park. Parimutuel betting; clubhouse, restaurant, concessions. (Tues-Sun nights; matinees Sat and Sun) 11 mi W via I-90, at Idaho/Washington state line. Phone 208/773-0545. ¢

Farragut State Park. Four thousand acres on S end of Lake Pend Oreille; some open landscape, heavy woods. Swimming, bathhouse, fishing, boating (ramps); hiking and bicycle route, cross-country skiing, sledding, and snowshoeing in winter. Model airplane field. Picnicking. Tent and trailer sites (hookups Apr-mid-Oct, dump station; res recommended). Campfire programs; interpretive displays and talks; info center. (Daily) Standard fees. 20 mi N on US 95, then 4 mi E on ID 54, in Athol. Phone 208/683-2425. Per vehicle ¢

Idaho Panhandle National Forests— Coeur d'Alene. Boating, fishing; camping (fee), cabins, picnicking, hiking, cross-country skiing, snowmobiling trails. Visitors are welcome at the Coeur d'Alene Tree Nursery, 1 mi NW on Ramsey Rd. Contact the Forest Supervisor, 1201 Ironwood Dr. N on US 95 & E on I-90. Phone 208/765-7223. Other national forests that lie in the Panhandle are Kaniksu (see PRIEST LAKE AREA) and St. Joe (see ST. MARIE'S).

Lake Coeur d'Alene. Partially adj to the Idaho Panhandle National Forest. This lake, 26 mi long with a 109-mi shoreline, is considered one of the loveliest in the country. Popular for boating, fishing, swimming. Municipal beach, picnic grounds at point where lake and town meet. At S end of lake is

St. Joe River. One of the rivers that feed Lake Coeur d'Alene. Trout and lovely scenery abound. Stretch between Lake Chatcolet and Round Lake is said to be the world's highest navigable river.

Lake Coeur d'Alene Cruises, Inc. Makes 6-hr trip up Lake Coeur d'Alene into the St. Joe River (mid-June-early Sep, Wed and Sun; mid-May-Oct, Sun only). Also 90-min lake cruises (mid-May-mid-Oct, daily). Dinner cruises (June-mid-Sep, Mon). Sun brunch cruises (mid-June-Sep). 1115 S Second St. Phone 208/765-4000. ¢¢¢- ¢¢¢¢

Museum of North Idaho. Exhibits feature steamboating, timber industry, and Native American history. Also, a big game trophy collection. (Apr-Oct, Tues-Sat) 115 NW Blvd, adj to City Park, near waterfront. Phone 208/664-3448. ¢ Admission includes

Fort Sherman Museum. North Idaho College campus. Housed in old powder house of Fort Coeur d'Alene (ca 1880). Exhibits incl log cabin once used by US Forest Service firefighters. Logging, mining, and pioneer implements are among featured exhibits. (May-Sep, Tues-Sat) Phone 208/664-3448.

✖ Scenic drives. Some of the most spectacular drives are S on US 97, along E shore of Lake Coeur d'Alene; E on US 10, through 4th of July Canyon; and N, along US 95. In any direction from city.

Silverwood Theme Park. Turn-of-the-century park and village with Victorian buildings incl restaurants, saloon, general store, theater featuring old newsreels and classic movies, aircraft museum, air shows, and entertainment; adj amusement park w/rides and attractions. (Memorial Day wkend-Labor Day, daily) 15 mi N on US 95, in Athol. Phone 208/683-3400. ¢¢¢¢

Annual Events

Art on the Green. First wkend Aug.

Northern Idaho Fair. Late Aug.

Motels/Motor Lodges

★★ **BEST WESTERN CAVANAUGH'S TEMPLIN'S RESORT.** *414 E 1st Ave (83854), W via I-90, Exit 5. 208/773-1611; fax 208/773-4192; res 800/325-4000; toll-free 800/283-6754. www.westcoast hotels.com.* 167 rms, 2-3 story. May-mid-Sep: S $93-$112; D $100-$121; each addl $15; suites $119-$269; under 12 free; lower rates rest of yr. Crib $10. Pet accepted, some restrictions. TV; cable (premium). Indoor pool. Restaurant 6 am-10 pm. Bar 10 pm-1 am; entertainment. Ck-out noon. Meeting rms. Business servs avail. In-rm modem link. Airport transportation. Tennis. Exercise equipt; sauna. Lawn games. Some refrigerators. Private patios, balconies. Picnic tables. On river; marina, guest docking, boat rentals. Cr cds: A, D, DS, MC, V.

★★ **COEUR D'ALENE INN & CONFERENCE CENTER.** *414 W Appleway Ave (83814), jct US 95 and I-90. 208/765-3200; fax 208/664-1962; toll-free 800/251-7829. www.cdainn.com.* 120 rms, 2 story, 2 suites. June-Aug: S, D $139; each addl $10; suites $225; under 17 free; lower rates rest of yr. Crib avail. Pet accepted, fee. Parking lot. Indoor/outdoor pools, lap pool, whirlpool. TV; cable (premium). Complimentary coffee in rms, newspaper, toll-free calls. Restaurant 6 am-10 pm. Bar. Ck-out noon, ck-in 4 pm. Meeting rms. Business center. Dry cleaning. Gift shop. Exercise privileges. Golf, 18 holes. Tennis, 3 courts. Downhill skiing. Beach access. Bike rentals. Supervised children's activities. Hiking trail. Picnic facilities. Video games. Cr cds: A, C, D, DS, JCB, MC, V.

★ **DAYS INN.** *2200 NW Blvd (83814). 208/667-8668; fax 208/765-0933; res 800/DAYSINN.* 61 rms, 2 story. June-Aug: S $65; D $70; each addl $5; under 18 free; lower rates rest of yr. Crib free. Pet accepted. TV; VCR avail. Complimentary continental bkfst. Ck-out noon. Meeting rm. Sundries. Exercise equipt; sauna. Cr cds: A, D, DS, MC, V.

★ **FLAMINGO MOTEL.** *718 E Sherman Ave (83814). 208/664-2159; fax 208/667-8576.* 13 rms, 2 kits, 3 bungalows. May-Sep: S, D $65.50-$78; each addl $5; suites $89-$95; bungalows $125-$130; under 12 free; lower rates rest of yr. Crib free. TV; cable (premium). Pool. Coffee avail. Restaurant nearby. Ck-out 11 am. Airport transportation. Cr cds: A, C, D, DS, MC, V.

★ **HOWARD JOHNSON EXPRESS INN.** *3705 W 5th Ave (83854), 10 mi W via I-90 Exit 2, then E on 5th Ave. 208/773-4541; fax 208/773-0235; res 800/igohojo; toll-free 800/829-3124.* 100 rms, 2-4 story. June-Sep: S, D $70-$75; each addl $5; under 18 free; package plans; lower rates rest of yr. Crib $5. Pet accepted; $10. TV; cable (premium), VCR avail. Indoor pool; whirlpool. Complimentary continental bkfst. Restaurant opp open 24 hrs. Ck-out noon. Game rm. Cr cds: A, C, D, DS, MC, V.

★ **MOTEL 6.** *416 W Appleway Ave (83814). 208/664-6600; fax 208/667-9446; res 800/664-8356.* 109 rms, 2 story. S $39.99; D $45.99; each addl $3; under 18 free. Crib free. Pet accepted. TV; cable (premium). Pool. Restaurant adj 6 am-10 pm. Ck-out noon. Cr cds: A, C, D, DS, MC, V.

★★ **RIVERBEND INN.** *4105 W Riverbend Ave (83854), 10 mi W via I-90 Exit 2 to Riverbend Ave. 208/773-3583; fax 208/773-1306; toll-free 800/243-7666.* 71 rms, 2 story. S $55-$65; D $70-$75; each addl $5; under 12 free. Crib free. TV; cable (premium). Heated pool; whirlpool. Complimentary continental bkfst. Ck-out noon. Coin lndry. Cr cds: A, DS, MC, V.

★ **SUPER 8 MOTEL.** *505 W Appleway Ave (83814). 208/765-8880; fax 208/765-8880; res 800/800-8000.* 95 units, 3 story. June-Sep: S $60-$70; D $75-$85; each addl $5; suites $80.88-$90.88; under 12 free; wkly rates winter; lower rates rest of yr. Crib free. Pet accepted. TV; cable (premium), VCR avail. Complimentary coffee. Ck-out 11 am. Cr cds: A, C, D, DS, JCB, MC, V.

Hotels

★★ **BEST INN & SUITES.** *280 W Appleway (83814). 208/765-5500; fax 208/664-0433; toll-free 800/237-8466.* 44 rms, 3 story, 7 suites. June-Sep: S $89; D $109; suites $199; lower rates rest of yr. Crib avail. Pet accepted. Parking lot. Indoor pool, whirlpool. TV; cable (premium), VCR avail. Complimentary continental bkfst, coffee in rms, newspaper, toll-free calls. Restaurant. Ck-out noon, ck-in 2 pm. Meeting rm. Fax servs avail. Dry cleaning, coin lndry. Gift shop. Exercise privileges, sauna. Golf. Tennis. Picnic facilities. Cr cds: A, C, D, DS, ER, JCB, MC, V.

★★ **SHILO INN.** *702 W Appleway Ave (83814). 208/664-2300; fax 208/667-2863; toll-free 800/222-2244. Email coeurdalene@shiloinns.com; www.shiloinns.com.* 138 rms, 4 story. June-Aug: S, D $129; each addl $12; suites $159; under 12 free; lower rates rest of yr. Crib avail. Pet accepted, fee. Street parking. Indoor pool. TV; cable (premium). Complimentary continental bkfst, coffee in rms, newspaper, toll-free calls. Restaurant nearby. Ck-out noon, ck-in 4 pm. Meeting rm. Business center. Dry cleaning, coin lndry. Exercise equipt, sauna, steam rm. Golf. Tennis. Supervised children's activities. Hiking trail. Picnic facilities. Video games. Cr cds: A, C, D, DS, ER, JCB, MC, V.

Resort

★★★ **THE COEUR D'ALENE - A RESORT ON THE LAKE.** *115 S 2nd St (83814). 208/765-4000; fax 208/664-7276; res 800/688-5253. Email cdabus@cdaresort.com.* 336 rms, 18 story. Mid-June-Sep: S, D $150-$390; each addl $10; suites $350-$2,750; under 18 free; lower rates rest of yr. Crib free. TV; cable (premium), 2 heated pools, 1 indoor; wading pool, whirlpool, poolside serv. Playground adj. Supervised children's activities. Restaurants (see BEVERLY'S). Bars; entertainment. Ck-out noon, ck-in after 4 pm. Convention facilities. Business center. Valet serv. Shopping arcade. Airport, bus depot transportation. Tennis. 18-hole golf. Marina. Boat rentals. Tour boats. Seaplane rides. Cross country ski on site. Bowling. Exercise rm; sauna, steam rm. Massage. Spa. Refrigerators. Balconies. Atrium areas. Cr cds: A, D, DS, MC, V.

B&Bs/Small Inns

★★ **BLACKWELL HOUSE.** *820 E Sherman Ave (83814). 208/664-0656; fax 208/664-0656; res 800/899-0656.* 8 rms, 2 share bath, 4 A/C, 3 story, 3 suites. No elvtr. No rm phones. S $70-$135; D $75-$140; each addl $10; suites $110-$140; wkly rates. Children over 12 yrs only. TV in lobby; cable. Complimentary full bkfst; afternoon refreshments. Ck-out noon, ck-in 2 pm. Some street parking. Restored, late Victorian house (1904); music rm, sitting rm, antiques. Gazebo. Cr cds: A, DS, MC, V.

★★ **THE ROOSEVELT.** *105 E Wallace Ave (83814). 208/765-5200; fax 208/664-4142; res 800/290-3358. Email info@therooseveltinn.com.* 16 rms, 4 story, 4 suites. May-Oct: S $60-$80; D $69.50-$122.50; each addl $20; suites $140; under 8 free; package plans; lower rates rest of yr. Children over 8 yrs only in summer. TV in common rm; VCR avail. Complimentary full bkfst; afternoon refreshments. Ck-out noon, ck-in 2 pm. Street parking. Downhill ski 20 mi; x-country ski 1 mi. Built in 1905; was an old elementary school named after Theodore Roosevelt. Totally nonsmoking. Cr cds: A, DS, MC, V.

Restaurants

★★★ **BEVERLY'S.** *115 S 2nd St. 208/765-4000.* Specializes in broiled salmon with shiitake mushrooms, rack of lamb, tenderloin of beef. Hrs: 11 am-10 pm; Sun from 5 pm. Res accepted. Bar. Wine cellar. Lunch a la carte entrees: $7.95-$13.95; dinner a la carte entrees: $19.95-$29.95.

Child's menu. Northwestern cuisine.
Cr cds: A, D, DS, MC, V.
D

★ **IRON HORSE.** *407 Sherman Ave
(83814). 208/667-7314.* Specializes in
prime rib, burgers. Hrs: 7 am-10 pm;
Sat from 8 am; Sun from 9 am.
Closed Jan 1, Dec 25. Bar. Bkfst
$2.65-$6.95; lunch $4.75-$10.95;
dinner $4.75-$15.95. Child's menu.
RR train decor. Cr cds: MC, V.
SC ◻

★★ **JIMMY D'S CAFE.** *320 Sherman
Ave (83814). 208/664-9774. www.
jimmyds.com.* Specializes in fresh
seafood, steaks. Hrs: 11 am-9 pm.
Closed Jan 1, Thanksgiving, Dec 25.
Bar. Lunch $4.75-$8.95; dinner
$9.95-$19.95. Sidewalk cafe atmosphere. Cr cds: A, DS, MC, V.
D

Craters of the Moon National Monument

(18 mi SW of Arco on US 20/26/93)

So named because it resembles the
surface of the moon as seen through
a telescope, this 83-square-mile
monument has spectacular lava
flows, cinder cones, and other
volcanic creations. Geologists believe
a weak spot in the earth's crust
permitted outbursts of lava at least
eight times during the last 15,000
years. These eruptions produced the
lava flows, the 25 cinder cones,
spatter cones, lava tubes, natural
bridges, and tree molds within the
monument. Geological and historical
exhibits are on display at the visitor
center (daily; closed winter hols).
Autos may follow the seven-mile
loop drive; closed by snow in
winter. Interpretive programs of
nature walks, campfire talks (mid-
June-Labor Day). Campground (no
hookups) near entrance (mid-May-
Oct; fee). Golden Eagle, Golden Age,
Golden Access passports accepted
(see MAKING THE MOST OF YOUR
TRIP). For further info contact PO
Box 29, Arco 83213; 208/527-3257.
Per vehicle ¢¢

Driggs

*(F-6) See also Ashton, Rexburg, St.
Anthony*

Pop 846 **Elev** 6,116 ft **Area code** 208
Zip 83422

A Ranger District office of the
Targhee National Forest (see ASH-
TON) is located here.

What to See and Do

**Grand Targhee Ski and Summer
Resort.** Three chairlifts, surface lift;
patrol, school, rentals; 3 lodges, 3
restaurants, cafeteria, bar, nursery;
hot tubs, heated outdoor pool.
Longest run 2.7 mi; vertical drop
2,200 ft. (Mid-Nov-early Apr, daily)
Second mountain for powder skiing
only. Cross-country trails; snowboard
half-pipe. Summer activities incl fishing, rafting; horseback riding, biking,
hiking, golf, tennis, music festivals
(July-Aug), chairlift rides (June-Aug,
daily). Half-day rates. 12 mi E on
county road, in Alta, WY. Phone
307/353-2300 or 800/TARGHEE.
¢¢¢¢

Motels/Motor Lodges

★ **INTERMOUNTAIN LODGE.** *34
Ski Hill Rd (98403). 208/354-8153.* 14
rms. Dec-Jan, July-Sep: S, D $69; each
addl $5; children $5; lower rates rest
of yr. Crib avail. TV; cable (DSS), VCR
avail. Restaurant nearby. Ck-out 11
am, ck-in 3 pm. Gift shop. Golf.
Downhill skiing. Hiking trail. Cr cds:
A, DS, MC, V.
🐾 ⛷ 🏊 🧍 🖾 🏌

★ **SUPER 8 TETON WEST.** *133 State
Hwy 33 (83422). 208/354-8888; fax
208/354-2962; res 800/800-8000.* 43
rms, 2 story, 3 suites. June-Sep: S, D
$80; suites $125; lower rates rest of
yr. Crib avail. Parking lot. Indoor
pool, children's pool, whirlpool. TV;
cable (DSS), VCR avail. Compli-men-
tary continental bkfst, toll-free calls.
Ck-out noon, ck-in 3 pm. Meeting
rm. Coin lndry. Free airport transportation. Sauna. Golf, 18 holes.
Downhill skiing. Cr cds: ER, JCB,
MC, V.
D 🏊 🧍 🖾

★ **TETON MOUNTAIN VIEW LODGE.** *510 Egbert Ave (83452), 7 mi N. 208/456-2741; fax 208/456-2232; toll-free 800/625-2232. Email tmvl@ axxess.net.* 24 rms, 10 with shower only, 2 story. July-Sep: S $79.95; D $89.95; each addl $5; suite $109.95; under 16 free; wkly rates; lower rates rest of yr. Crib free. Pet accepted, some restrictions. TV; cable. Complimentary coffee in lobby. Restaurant nearby. Ck-out noon. Whirlpool. Cr cds: A, DS,MC, V.

Hotel

★★ **BEST WESTERN TETON WEST.** *476 N Main St (83422). 208/354-2363; fax 208/354-2962; res 800/528-1234.* 40 rms, 2 story. July-Sep: S $79; D $89; each addl $8; lower rates rest of yr. Crib avail. Parking lot. Indoor pool, whirlpool. TV; cable. Complimentary continental bkfst, coffee in rms, toll-free calls. Restaurant nearby. Ck-out noon, ck-in 3 pm. Meeting rm. Coin lndry. Free airport transportation. Golf, 9 holes. Tennis, 2 courts. Downhill skiing. Cr cds: A, C, D, DS, MC, V.

Resorts

★★★ **GRAND TARGHEE.** *PO Box SKI (83342), 12 mi E on Ski-Hill Rd (Lodge is accessible only from ID). 307/353-2300; fax 307/353-8148; toll-free 800/827-4433. Email info@grand targhee.com; www.grandtarghee.com.* 97 rms, 3 story, 32 suites. Dec-Mar: S, D $200; suites $269; under 5 free; lower rates rest of yr. Crib avail. Parking lot. Pool, whirlpool. TV; cable (DSS), VCR avail. Complimentary coffee in rms, newspaper. Restaurant. Bar. Meeting rms. Business center. Coin lndry. Gift shop. Exercise privileges, sauna. Golf, 9 holes. Tennis, 2 courts. Downhill skiing. Bike rentals. Supervised children's activities. Hiking trail. Picnic facilities. Cr cds: A, DS, MC, V.

★★★ **TETON RIDGE RANCH.** *200 Valley View Rd (83452), N on ID 33, then 1.7 mi E on unnumbered road toward Leigh Creeks, then turn at first left going N to Dry Ridge, follow signs to Ranch. 208/456-2650; fax 208/456-2218. Email info@tetonridge.com.* 7 units. July-Aug, AP: S $350; D $475; each addl $100; lower rates rest of yr. Closed Nov-mid-Dec, Apr-May. Children over 12 yrs only. Pet accepted, some restrictions. TV in public rms; cable (premium). Box lunches. Setups. Ck-out, ck-in noon. Grocery. Guest lndry. Package store 9 mi. Meeting rms. Airport transportation. Downhill ski 20 mi; x-country ski on site. Sleighing. Horse stables. Hiking. Mountain bikes (rentals). Rec rm. Fishing/hunting guides, clean and store. Balconies. Secluded mountain valley ranch situated on west side of Grand Tetons. Cr Cds: MC, V.

Fort Hall

(see Blackfoot)

Grangeville (D-2)

Founded 1876 **Pop** 3,226
Elev 3,390 ft **Area code** 208
Zip 83530
Information Chamber of Commerce, US 95 & Pine St, PO Box 212; 208/983-0460

Grangeville is a light industry and agricultural community. It was a focal point in the Nez Perce Indian War and a gold rush town in the 1890s when rich ore was found in the Florence Basin and the Elk City areas. The seat of Idaho County, it is also the gateway to several wilderness areas. The headquarters and two Ranger District offices of the Nez Perce National Forest are located here.

What to See and Do

Hell's Canyon National Recreation Area. Created by the Snake River, at the Idaho/Oregon border, Hell's

Canyon is the deepest gorge in North America—1½ mi from He Devil Mt (elevation 9,393 ft) to the Snake River at Granite Creek (elevation 1,408 ft). Overlooks at Heaven's Gate, W of Riggins, and in Oregon (see JOSEPH, OR). The recreation area incl parts of the Nez Perce and Payette National Forest in Idaho and the Wallowa-Whitman National Forest in Oregon. Activities incl float trips, jet boat tours; auto tours, backpacking, and horseback riding; boat trips into canyon from Lewiston, Grangeville, and Riggins, also via Pittsburg Landing or the Hell's Canyon Dam (see WEISER). Developed campgrounds in Oregon and Idaho; much of the area is undeveloped, some is designated wilderness. Be sure to inquire about road conditions before planning a trip; some roads are rough and open for a limited season. For further information contact Hell's Canyon National Recreation Area, 88401 Hwy 82, Enterprise, OR 97828. Access approx 16 mi S on US 95 to White Bird, then W on County 493 to Pittsburg Landing; access also from Riggins, from US 95 take Rd 241 (Race Creek) N of Riggins; paved access via ID 71 from Cambridge (see WEISER). Phone 541/426-4978; or 2535 Riverside Dr, Box 699, Clarkston, WA 99403, phone 509/758-0616. For river info and float res, phone 509/758-1957.

✪ **Nez Perce National Forest.** More than 2.2 million acres with excellent fishing; camping, cabins (fee at some campgrounds), picnicking, crosscountry skiing, and snowmobiling. The Salmon (the River of No Return), Selway, South Fork Clearwater, and Snake rivers, all classified as wild and scenic, flow through or are adj to the forest. Pack and float trips are avail; contact the Idaho Outfitters and Guides Assn, PO Box 95, Boise 83701; 208/342-1438. High elevations are open only in summer and fall; low elevations are open Mar-Nov. For further info contact Office of Info, Rte 2, Box 475. S on US 95. Phone 208/983-1950.

Skiing. Snowhaven. T-bar, rope tow; patrol, school, rentals; cafeteria. Vertical drop 400 ft. (Dec-early Mar, Fri-Sun) Night skiing; half-day rates. 7 mi SE via Fish Creek Rd. Phone 208/983-2299. ¢¢- ¢¢¢

White Bird Hill. Site of the famous Whitebird Battle of the Nez Perce Indian Wars. View of Camas Prairie, canyons, mountains, and Seven Devils Peaks. Self-guided tour brochures avail from Chamber of Commerce. 5 mi S on US 95.

Annual Events

Border Days. Three-day rodeo and parades, dances. Art-in-the-park; food. Phone 208/983-0460. July 4 wkend.

Oktubberfest. Three-day event features tub races on Main St, arts and crafts, street dance, entertainment. Last wkend Sep.

Idaho City

(F-2) *See also Boise*

Settled 1862 **Pop** 322 **Elev** 3,906 ft **Area code** 208 **Zip** 83631
Information Chamber of Commerce, PO Box 70; 208/392-4148

Flecks of gold persist in the gravel beneath most of Idaho City, and the community is steeped in gold rush lore. From the 18-square-mile Boise Basin, said to have produced more gold than all of Alaska, Idaho City's fame once spread far and wide. Idaho City also is home to the state's first Pioneer Lodge (established 1864) and the birthplace of the Grand Lodge of Idaho (established 1867).

What to See and Do

Boise Basin Museum. (1867) Restored building houses artifacts of gold rush era. Walking tours of Idaho City avail (fee). (Memorial Day-Labor Day, daily; May and Sep, wkends only; rest of yr, by appt) Montgomery & Wall Sts. Phone 208/392-4550. ¢

Boise National Forest. Surrounding area. Fishing, swimming; hunting, camping, skiing, and snowmobiling. A Ranger District office of the forest is located here. Contact the Supervisor, 1750 Front St, Boise 83702.

Boot Hill. Restored 40-acre cemetery, last resting place of many gunfight victims.

Gold Hill. Rich Boise Basin placer ground. 1 mi N on Main St.

Idaho Falls

(G-5) *See also Blackfoot, Pocatello, Rexburg*

Pop 43,929 **Elev** 4,710 ft
Area code 208
Information Chamber of Commerce, 505 Lindsay Blvd, PO Box 50498, 83405; 208/523-1010 or 800/634-3246

An industrial, transportation, and trading center in the upper Snake River Valley, Idaho Falls is a center of potato production and headquarters for the Idaho Operations Office of the Department of Energy. The Idaho National Engineering Laboratory is located on the Lost River Plains, 30 miles west on US 20. Potato processing is important; stockyards here are the state's largest; and one of the nation's leading safety research centers for nuclear reactors is located here. A Ranger District office of Targhee National Forest (see ASHTON) is also in Idaho Falls.

What to See and Do

Bonneville Museum. Displays of early county, state, and city history; natural history; Native American artifacts; early settler and mountain-man relics; replica of early (ca 1890) Idaho Falls (Eagle Rock); 30-min video on county history and other subjects of local interest. Art exhibits featuring works of area artists; special and traveling exhibits. (Mon-Fri; also Sat afternoons; closed Jan 1, Thanksgiving, Dec 25) 200 N Eastern Ave. Phone 208/522-1400. ¢

Heise Hot Springs. Mineral water pool, freshwater pools, water slide, fishing; golf, camping. (Mid-May-Sep) Fee for activities. 23 mi E on US 26, in Ririe. Phone 208/538-7312.

Idaho Falls. Falls run for 1,500 ft along Snake River. Picnic tables nearby.

The Lavas. Lava-created caves, fissures, and rock flows, fringed by dwarf trees. Native American relics are also plentiful. 10 mi S via US 91 to Shelley, then 4 mi W on local road.

Tautphaus Park. Zoo (fee); amusement rides (Memorial Day wkend-Labor Day wkend; fee); picnic and barbecue areas; lighted tennis courts and softball diamonds; horseshoe pits; ice-skating, hockey (seasonal). Park (daily; closed Jan 1, Thanksgiving, Dec 25). Rollandet Ave or South Blvd. **FREE**

Annual Event

War Bonnet Roundup. Sandy Downs Park Rodeo Grounds. Rodeo. Four nights early Aug.

Motels/Motor Lodges

★★ **AMERITEL INN.** *645 Lindsay Blvd (83402). 208/523-1400; fax 208/523-0004; res 800/600-6001.* 126 rms, 4 story, 26 suites. June-Sep: S, D $99.75; each addl $8; suites $119-$229; under 12 free; lower rates rest of yr. Crib free. TV; cable (premium). Complimentary full bkfst, coffee in rms. Restaurant nearby. Ck-out noon. Meeting rms. Business servs avail. In-rm modem link. Sundries. Free airport transportation. Exercise equipt. Indoor pool; whirlpool. Bathrm phones; some refrigerators, microwaves. Cr cds: A, C, D, DS, JCB, MC, V.
D ☒ ✕ ☒ ☒

★★ **BEST WESTERN COTTON TREE INN.** *900 Lindsay Blvd (83402), near Fanning Field Airport. 208/523-6000; fax 208/523-0000; res 800/528-1234, toll-free 800/662-6886.* 94 rms, 3 story, 9 suites, 6 kit. units. S, D $65-$75; each addl $5; suites $90-$110; kit. units $90-$110; under 18 free. Crib $8. TV; cable (premium). Indoor pool; whirlpool. Complimentary continental bkfst. Restaurant nearby. Ck-out noon. Coin lndry. Meeting rms. Business servs avail. Valet serv. Free airport transportation. Exercise equipt. Microwaves avail. Near river. Cr cds: A, D, DS, MC, V.
D ☒ ✕ ☒ ☒

★★ **COMFORT INN.** *195 S Colorado Ave (83402), I-15, Exlt 118, near Fanning Field Airport. 208/528-2804; fax 208/522-3083; res 800/228-5150.* 56 rms, 2 story, 14 suites. June-Sep: S $59.99; D $69.99; each addl $7; suites $74.99-$120; under 12 free; lower rates rest of yr. Crib free. Pet accepted, some restrictions. TV; cable. Indoor pool; whirlpool. Complimentary continental bkfst. Restaurant

nearby. Ck-out 11 am. Refrigerators.
Cr cds: A, D, DS, MC, V.

[D] [icons]

★★ **HAMPTON INN.** *2500 Channing Way (83404). 208/529-9800; fax 208/529-9455; res 800/HAMPTON.* 63 rms, 3 story, 7 suites. Late May-Aug: S $64; D $69; suites $74-$99; under 18 free; lower rates rest of yr. Crib free. TV; cable (premium). Complimentary continental bkfst. Restaurant nearby. Ck-out noon. Meeting rm. Business servs avail. Bellhops. Exercise equipt. Indoor pool; whirlpool. Refrigerator, microwave in suites. Cr cds: A, C, D, DS, MC, V.

[D] [icons]

Hotel

★★ **SHILO INN.** *780 Lindsay Blvd (83402). 208/523-0088; fax 208/522-7420; toll-free 800/222-2244. Email idahofalls@shiloinns.com; www.shilo inns.com.* 116 rms, 4 story. June-Aug: S, D $119; each addl $15; suites $149; under 12 free; lower rates rest of yr. Crib avail. Pet accepted, some restrictions, fee. Parking lot. Indoor pool, whirlpool. TV; cable (premium). Complimentary continental bkfst, coffee in rms, newspaper, toll-free calls. Restaurant. Bar. Ck-out noon, ck-in 2 pm. Meeting rms. Fax servs avail. Coin lndry. Exercise equipt, sauna, steam rm. Golf. Picnic facilities. Video games. Cr cds: A, C, D, DS, ER, JCB, MC, V.

[D] [icons] SC

Restaurant

★ **JAKERS.** *851 Lindsay Blvd (83402). 208/524-5240.* Specializes in pan-fried shrimp, prime rib, steaks and ribs. Hrs: 11 am-9 pm; Fri to 10 pm; Sat 4-10 pm; Sun 4-9 pm. Closed Jan 1, Thanksgiving, Dec 25. Res accepted. Bar. Lunch $2.25-$7.95; dinner $8.95- $22.95. Child's menu. Contemporary rustic decor. Cr cds: A, D, DS, MC, V.

[D]

Jerome

(G-3) *See also Shoshone, Twin Falls*

Pop 6,529 **Elev** 3,781 ft
Area code 208 **Zip** 83338
Information Chamber of Commerce, 101 W Main St, Suite 6; 208/324-2711

What to See and Do

Jerome County Historical Museum. Located in historic Pioneer Hall building. Changing displays. Guided tours. (May-Sep, Mon-Sat; rest of yr, Tues-Sat) 220 N Lincoln. Phone 208/324-5641. **FREE**

Malad Gorge State Park. More than 650 acres with the 2½-mi-long, 250-ft-deep Malad Gorge. Footbridge spans waterfall at Devil's Washbowl. Interpretive trails, picnicking. (Schedule varies) Phone 208/837-4505.

Annual Events

Horse Racing. Jerome County Fairgrounds. Pari-mutuel racing. Phone 208/324-7209. Two wkends mid-June.

Jerome County Fair. Concert, rodeo, carnival, parade. Phone 208/324-7209. First wk Aug.

Seasonal Event

Chariot Races. Jerome County Fairgrounds. Phone 208/324-7209. Wkends, Dec-Feb.

Motel/Motor Lodge

★ **SLEEP INN.** *1200 S Centennial Spur (83338). 208/324-6400; toll-free 800/753-3746.* 73 rms, 3 story. May-Sep: S $45-$55; D $49-$59; each addl $5; under 19 free; lower rates rest of yr. Crib free. TV; cable (premium), VCR (movies). Restaurant adj open 24 hrs. Ck-out noon. Meeting rm. Business servs avail. In-rm modem link. Sundries. Coin lndry. Whirlpool. Cr cds: A, C, D, DS, JCB, MC, V.

[D] [icons] SC

Hotel

★★ **SAWTOOTH INN BEST WESTERN.** *2653 S Lincoln Ave (83338). 208/324-9200; fax 208/324-*

*9292; toll-free 800/528-1234. www.
bestwestern.com/sawtoothinnsuites.* 47
rms, 2 story, 10 suites. May-Oct: S
$69; D $89; each addl $10; suites $99;
under 18 free; lower rates rest of yr.
Crib avail, fee. Pet accepted, some
restrictions. Parking lot. Indoor pool,
whirlpool. TV; cable (premium). Complimentary continental bkfst, coffee
in rms, newspaper, toll-free calls.
Restaurant. Ck-out noon, ck-in 4 pm.
Meeting rms. Business servs avail.
Bellhops. Dry cleaning, coin lndry.
Exercise privileges. Golf, 18 holes.
Tennis, 2 courts. Picnic facilities. Cr
cds: A, C, D, DS, ER, JCB, MC, V.

[symbols]

Kellogg

(B-2) *See also Coeur d'Alene, Wallace*

Pop 2,591 **Elev** 2,308 ft
Area code 208 **Zip** 83837
Web www.nidlink.com/~kellogg
Information Greater Kellogg Area
Chamber of Commerce, 608 Bunker
Ave; 208/784-0821

In this rich mining region are the
country's largest silver and lead
mines. One of the state's most violent miners' strikes took place here
in 1899. Today, the former mining
town is being transformed into a ski
resort.

What to See and Do

Old Mission State Park. (1850) A
100-acre park. Tours of the Coeur
d'Alene Mission of the Sacred Heart,
a restored Native American mission;
oldest existing building in state. Picnicking; info center; interpretive programs; history trail. Standard fees.
(Daily) 10 mi W off I-90 exit 39, in
Cataldo. Phone 208/682-3814.

Silver Mountain Ski Area. Double,
quad, triple chairlifts, surface lift;
patrol, school, rentals; lodges, restaurants, cafeteria, bar, nursery. Fifty
trails, longest run 2.5 mi; vertical
drop 2,200 ft. (Mid-Nov-Apr, daily)
Summer activities include amphitheater performances, hiking, mountain
biking; 3-mi gondola rides. ½ mi
SW, off I-90 exit 49. Phone 208/783-
1111. ¢¢¢

Sunshine Mine Disaster Memorial.
Double-life-size statue constructed of
steel is memorial to all miners; created by Kenn Lonn, a native of Kellogg. The helmet's light burns
perpetually and the miner holds a
typical jackleg drill. 3 mi E on I-90,
exit 54, Big Creek.

Annual Event

Christmas Dickens Festival. Entire
town dressed in period costume.
Plays, skits, puppet shows, parade.
608 Bunker Ave. Second wkend Dec.

Motels/Motor Lodges

★ **SILVERHORN MOTOR INN &
RESTAURANT.** *699 W Cameron Ave
(83837).* 208/783-1151; fax 208/784-
5081; toll-free 800/437-6437. Email
sminn@nidlink.com. 40 rms, 2 story.
June-Sep: S $53; D $58; each addl $5;
under 13 free; lower rates rest of yr.
Crib avail, fee. Pet accepted. Parking
lot. TV; cable, VCR avail, CD avail.
Restaurant 6 am-9 pm. Ck-out noon,
ck-in noon. Meeting rm. Business
servs avail. Dry cleaning, coin lndry.
Gift shop. Whirlpool. Golf. Tennis, 2
courts. Downhill skiing. Bike rentals.
Hiking trail. Picnic facilities. Cr cds:
A, C, D, DS, MC, V.

[symbols]

★ **SUPER 8 MOTEL.** *601 Bucker Ave
(83837).* 208/783-1234; fax 208/784-
0461; res 800/800-8000; toll-free 800/
785-5443. Email supr8klg@nidlink.
com. 61 rms, 2 story. Mid-June-mid-
Sep: S $53-$58; D $58-$63; each addl
$5; suites $75-$100; under 13 free;
ski plans; lower rates rest of yr. Crib
free. Pet accepted. TV; cable (premium), VCR avail. Complimentary
continental bkfst. Restaurant opp 11
am-10 pm. Ck-out 11 am. Meeting
rms. Business servs avail. Downhill
ski on site. Indoor pool; whirlpool.
Some refrigerators, microwaves. Picnic tables. Cr cds: A, DS, MC, V.

[symbols]

Ketchum

(see Sun Valley Area)

Lava Hot Springs

See also Pocatello

Pop 420 **Elev** 5,060 ft **Area code** 208 **Zip** 83246

Hot water pouring out of the mountains and bubbling up in springs, believed to be the most highly-mineralized water in the world, makes Lava Hot Springs a busy year-round resort. Fishing, swimming; hunting, camping, and golf are available in the surrounding area.

What to See and Do

Lava Hot Springs. Outdoor mineral pools, fed by 30 different springs, range from 104-112°F. Olympic-size swimming pool with diving tower (Memorial Day-Labor Day). (Daily; closed Thanksgiving, Dec 25) ½ mi E on US 30N. Phone 208/776-5221. ¢¢

South Bannock County Historical Center. Museum artifacts, photographs, transcripts, and memorabilia trace history of town from the era of Native American and fur trappers to its development as a resort area. Slide show and guided walking tour (by appt). (Daily) 110 Main St. Phone 208/776-5254. **Donation**

Lewiston

(D-1) *See also Moscow; also see Clarkston, WA*

Founded 1861 **Pop** 28,082 **Elev** 739 ft
Area code 208 **Zip** 83501
Web www.lewistonchamber.org
Information Chamber of Commerce, 111 Main St, Suite 120; 208/743-3531 or 800/473-3543

The Clearwater River, starting in the Bitterroot Mountains and plunging through the vast Clearwater National Forest, joins the Snake River at Lewiston. The two rivers and the mountains that surround the town give it one of the most picturesque settings in the state. A thriving tourist trade supplements Lewiston's grain, lumber, and livestock industries.

What to See and Do

⭐ **Auto tours.** The Lewis and Clark Hwy (US 12) parallels the famous Lewis and Clark Trail E to Montana. Interpretive signs along the way explain the human and natural history of the canyon. A Forest Service Information Station is at Lolo Pass on the Idaho/Montana border. The Chamber of Commerce has maps for other tours.

Castle Museum. Three-story, handmade cement block house built in 1906 and patterned after Scottish castle; embossed metal ceilings, antiques. (Apr-Oct, daily; rest of yr, by appt) 23 mi N on ID 3 in Juliaetta; 1 blk off main hwy. Phone 208/276-3081. **Donation**

Clearwater National Forest. About 1,850,000 acres with trout fishing; hunting, skiing and snowmobiling trails, camping (fee for some developed campsites), cabins, picnicking. Pack trips. Higher elevations accessible July-Sep; lower elevations accessible Mar-Oct or Nov. Lolo Pass Visitor Center and Lochsa Historical Ranger Station on US 12 (mid-May-mid-Sep; daily). For further info contact the Supervisor, 12730 US Hwy 12, Orofino 83544. US 12 in Orofino. Phone 208/476-4541.

Hell's Canyon Excursions. Jet boat trips and fishing charters into Hell's Canyon National Recreation Area (see GRANGEVILLE). For info contact the Chamber of Commerce.

Hell's Gate State Park. Nine hundred sixty acres on Snake River, 40 mi N of Hell's Canyon National Recreation Area (see GRANGEVILLE). Swimming, fishing, boating (marina, concession, ramp); hiking and paved bicycle trails, horseback riding area, picnicking, playground, tent and trailer campsites (hookups, dump station; 15-day max). Info center, interpretive programs, exhibits; excursion boats. Park (Mar-Nov). Standard fees. 4 mi S on Snake River Ave. Phone 208/799-5015.

Luna House Museum. On site of first hotel in town (1861). Exhibits on Nez Perce and pioneers; displays on town and county history. (Tues-Sat;

closed hols) 3rd & C Sts. Phone 208/743-2535. **FREE**

Nez Perce National Historical Park. The park is composed of 38 separate sites scattered throughout Washington, Oregon, Montana, and Idaho. All of the sites relate to the culture and history of the Nez Perce; some relate to the westward expansion of the nation into homelands. Visitor center and museum (daily; closed Jan 1, Thanksgiving, Dec 25). Headquarters, 11 mi E on US 95 in Spalding. Phone 208/843-2261. **FREE**

Annual Events

Lewiston Round-Up. Lewiston Round-Up grounds, 7000 Tammany Creek Rd. Wkend after Labor Day.

Nez Perce County Fair. Four days late Sep.

Motels/Motor Lodges

★ **HOWARD JOHNSON.** *1716 Main St (83501). 208/743-9526; fax 208/746-6216. Email 10237@hotel.cendant.com.* 66 rms, 1-2 story, 4 kit. units. S $62-$67; D $62-$82; under 18 free. Pet accepted. TV; cable (premium). Complimentary continental bkfst. Coffee in rms. Heated pool. Ck-out noon. Free lndry facilities. In-rm modem link. Refrigerators. Cr cds: A, DS, MC, V.

🅳 ⌇ ⬛ 🐾

★★ **INN AMERICA - A BUDGET MOTEL.** *702 21st St (83501). 208/746-4600; fax 208/746-7756; toll-free 800/469-4667. Email daved@inn america.com; www.lewiston.innamerica.com.* 57 rms, 3 story, 4 suites. May-Sep: S $52; D $62; each addl $5; suites $90; under 17 free; lower rates rest of yr. Crib avail. Parking lot. Pool. TV; cable. Complimentary continental bkfst, toll-free calls. Restaurant nearby. Ck-out 1 pm, ck-in 2 pm. Business servs avail. Coin lndry. Free airport transportation. Exercise privileges. Golf. Tennis, 10 courts. Cr cds: A, C, D, DS, ER, JCB, MC, V.

🅳 🏋 ⌇ ⬛ 🐾 ⬛

★ **RED LION HOTEL.** *621 21st St (83501). 208/799-1000; fax 208/799-1000; res 800/232-6730. Email lion hotel@aol.com; www.redlionlewiston.com.* 134 rms, 4 story. S $66; D $76; each addl $10; suites $89-$400;

under 18 free; wkly rates; golf plans. Crib free. Pet accepted. TV; cable (premium). 2 pools, 1 indoor; whirlpool, poolside serv. Coffee in rms. Restaurant 6 am-10 pm. Bar 4 pm-1:30 am. Ck-out noon. Coin lndry. Meeting rms. Valet serv. Concierge. Sundries. Free airport, railroad station, bus depot transportation. Some bathrm phones. Cr cds: A, C, D, DS, ER, JCB, MC, V.

🅳 🐾 ⬛ 🐾 🐾 SC

★★ **RIVERVIEW INN.** *1325 Main St (83501). 208/746-3311; fax 208/746-7955; toll-free 800/806-7666.* 75 rms, 4 story. S $34; D $47; each addl $6; under 12 free. Crib avail. Pet accepted. Parking lot. TV; cable. Complimentary continental bkfst, coffee in rms, toll-free calls. Restaurant. Bar. Ck-out noon, ck-in 1 pm. Meeting rm. Fax servs avail. Exercise privileges. Golf. Downhill skiing. Hiking trail. Cr cds: A, D, DS, MC, V.

🅳 🐾 🎿 🏋 🏋 🐾 ⬛ 🐾

★★ **SACAJAWEA SELECT INN.** *1824 Main St (83501), near Nez Perce County Regional Airport. 208/746-1393; fax 208/743-3620; toll-free 800/333-1393.* 78 rms, 2 story, 12 suites. S $51; D $58; each addl $3; suites $58; under 13 free. Crib avail, fee. Pet accepted, fee. Parking lot. Pool, whirlpool. TV; cable (premium), VCR avail. Complimentary continental bkfst. Restaurant 6 am-10 pm. Bar. Ck-out noon, ck-in noon. Meeting rms. Business center. Dry cleaning, coin lndry. Free airport transportation. Exercise equipt. Golf. Tennis, 10 courts. Hiking trail. Cr cds: A, C, D, DS, MC, V.

🅳 🐾 🎿 🏋 🏋 ⬛ 🏋 🐾 ⬛ 🐾 🐾

★ **SUPER 8 MOTEL.** *3120 N & S Hwy (83501). 208/743-8808; fax 208/743-8808; res 800/800-8000.* 62 rms, 2 story. Apr-Sep: S $46.99; D $53.99-$58.99; each addl $5; under 12 free; higher rates special events; lower rates rest of yr. Crib free. TV; cable (premium), VCR. Complimentary coffee. Ck-out 11 am. Refrigerators, microwaves avail. On river. Cr cds: A, C, D, DS, ER, JCB, MC, V.

🅳 ⬛ 🐾 SC

McCall (E-2)

Pop 2,005 **Elev** 5,030 ft
Area code 208 **Zip** 83638
Information Chamber of Commerce,
PO Box D; 208/634-7631 or
800/260-5130

At the southern tip of Payette Lake,
McCall is a resort center for one of
the state's chief recreational areas.
Fishing, swimming, boating, and
waterskiing are available on Payette
Lake. McCall is also the headquarters
for Payette National Forest, and three
Ranger District offices of the forest
are located here.

River of No Return

What to See and Do

Brundage Mountain Ski Area. Triple,
2 double chairlifts, Quadlift, Pomalift, rope tow; patrol, school, rentals;
bar, cafeteria, nursery. (Mid-Nov-mid-
Apr, daily) 3890 Gooselake Rd.
Phone 208/634-4151 or 208/634-
5650 (snow conditions). ¢¢¢¢¢

Cascade Dam Reservoir. Fishing, boating. 25 mi S on ID 55, in Cascade.

Pack trips into Idaho primitive areas.
Check with Chamber of Commerce
for list of outfitters.

Payette National Forest. More than
2.3 million acres surrounded by the
Snake and Salmon rivers, the River of
No Return Wilderness, Hell's Canyon
National Recreation Area, and the
Boise National Forest. Trout and
salmon fishing in 300 lakes and
3,000 mi of streams, boating; 2,100

mi of hiking trails, hunting, camping, and picnic areas, winter sports.
For further info contact the Supervisor, PO Box 1026. 800 W Lakeside,
PO Box 1026. Phone 208/634-0700.

Ponderosa State Park. Approx 1,280
acres. Large stand of ponderosa
pines. Swimming, waterskiing, fishing, boating (ramps); hiking, cross-
country skiing, picnicking, camping
(exc winter; res accepted Memorial
Day-Labor Day), tent and trailer sites
(hookups; 15-day max; dump station). Park (daily). Standard fees.
Contact Park Manager, PO Box A. 2
mi NE, on Payette Lake. Phone
208/634-2164.

**River rafting. Salmon River Outfit-
ters.** Offers 5- and
6-day guided raft
trips along the
Salmon River. For
info and res, con-
tact PO Box 307,
Columbia, CA
95310. Phone
800/346-6204.
¢¢¢¢¢

Annual Events

Winter Carnival.
Parades, fireworks;
ice sculptures,
snowmobile and
ski races, snow-
man-building con-
test, carriage and
sleigh rides, ball.
Ten days early Feb.

Music Festival. Fiddle music; Western,
swing, Irish, folk, blues, and jazz;
square dancing. Third wkend July.

Motels/Motor Lodges

★★ **BEST WESTERN MCCALL.**
*415 N 3rd St (83638). 208/634-6300;
fax 208/634-2967; toll-free 800/528-
1234.* 79 rms, 2 story. Mid-June-mid-
Sep: S $70-$120; D $75-$125; under
18 free; lower rates rest of yr. Crib
free. Pet accepted, some restrictions.
TV; cable (premium), VCR avail.
Indoor pool; whirlpool. Complimentary coffee in lobby. Ck-out 11 am.
Coin lndry. Meeting rms. Business
servs avail. In-rm modem link. Exercise equipt. Downhill/x-country ski
10 mi. Refrigerators, microwaves. Cr
cds: A, C, D, DS, ER, JCB, MC, V.

◻ ◻ ◻ ◻ ◻ ◻ ◻ **SC**

★ **WOODSMAN MOTEL AND CAFE.** *402 N 3rd St (83638), ½ mi S on ID 55. 208/634-7671; fax 208/634-3191.* 60 rms, 1-2 story. No A/C. S $42-$46; D $52-$56. TV, some B/W; cable. Restaurant 7 am-9:30 pm. Ck-out 11 am. Airport, bus depot transportation. Downhill ski 10 mi; x-country ski on site. Cr cds: A, DS, MC, V.

🏊 🗙 🔥

Hotel

★★ **HOTEL MCCALL.** *1101 N 3rd St (83638). 208/634-8105; fax 208/ 634-8755.* 22 rms, 3 story, 2 suites. Dec-Feb, June-Oct: S, D $50-$195; each addl $10; under 11 free; ski plan. Crib avail. Parking lot. TV; cable, VCR avail. Complimentary continental bkfst, newspaper, toll-free calls. Restaurant 10 am-8 pm. Ck-out 11 am, ck-in 2 pm. Meeting rm. Business servs avail. Gift shop. Free airport transportation. Golf. Tennis. Downhill skiing. Beach access. Hiking trail. Picnic facilities. Cr cds: A, DS, MC, V.

🆔 🏌 🎿 🏊 🧗 🏃 🎣 🛩 🔥

Resort

★★★ **SHORE LODGE.** *501 W Lake St (83638). 208/634-2244; fax 208/634-7504; toll-free 800/657-6464. Email shlodge@cyberhighway.net; www. shorelodge.com.* 3 story, 81 suites. June-Sep: S $175; D $225; each addl $25; suites $375; under 12 free; lower rates rest of yr. Crib avail, fee. Valet parking avail. Pool, lap pool, lifeguard. TV; cable (DSS), VCR avail. Complimentary toll-free calls. Restaurant 5-10 pm. Bar. Ck-out 11 am, ck-in 1 pm. Meeting rms. Business servs avail. Bellhops. Concierge. Gift shop. Free airport transportation. Exercise equipt, sauna, steam rm. Golf, 18 holes. Tennis, 2 courts. Downhill skiing. Beach access. Bike rentals. Supervised children's activities. Hiking trail. Video games. Cr cds: A, C, D, DS, MC, V.

🆔 🏌 🎿 🏊 🧗 🏃 🎣 🛩 🔥

Restaurant

★★ **MILL STEAKS & SPIRITS.** *324 N 3rd St (83638). 208/634-7683. www.*

themillmccallidaho.com. Specializes in steak, prime rib, seafood. Hrs: 5:30-10 pm; Fri, Sat to 11 pm. Closed Thanksgiving, Dec 25. Bar. Dinner $8.45-$25.95. Child's menu. Entertainment: wkends. Photo collection of history of the Northwest. Family-owned. Cr cds: A, D, DS, MC, V.

🍽

Montpelier (H-6)

Founded 1864 **Pop** 2,656
Elev 5,964 ft **Area code** 208
Zip 83254
Information Bear Lake Convention & Visitors Bureau, PO Box 26, Fish Haven 83287; 208/945-2072 or 800/448-2327

Located in the highlands of Bear Lake Valley, Montpelier is surrounded by lakes, rivers, creeks, and grazing ranges. The average yearly temperature is 46°F. First called Clover Creek, then Belmont, it was finally designated by the Mormon leader Brigham Young as Montpelier, after the capital of Vermont. There are Mormon tabernacles throughout this area. Phosphate is mined extensively nearby. A Ranger District office of the Caribou National Forest is located here.

What to See and Do

Bear Lake. Covering 71,000 acres, this 20-mi-long, 200-ft-deep body of water lies across the Idaho/Utah border. Fishing for Mackinaw, cutthroat, whitefish, and the rare Bonneville cisco. 20 mi S on US 89. On N shore is

Bear Lake State Park. Provides swimming beach, waterskiing, fishing, boating (ramp); picnicking, park (mid-May-mid-Sep), camping on E shore (dump station, hookups). Standard fees. Phone 208/945-2790.

Bloomington Lake. Spring-fed lake of unknown depth. Camping; fishing. 12 mi S on US 89, then W on local road, W of Bloomington.

Caribou National Forest. Fishing; camping (fee at certain designated campsites), hunting, picnicking, winter sports. For further info contact Ranger District, 431 Clay St. W, N & S of US 89; N & S of US 30. Phone 208/945-2407. Within the forest is **Minnetonka Cave.** Cave is ½ mi long and has 9 rms; 40°F. Guided tours (mid-June-Labor Day, daily). 10 mi W of St Charles off US 89. Phone 208/847-0375. ¢¢

Annual Events

Oregon Trail Rendezvous Pageant. Fri closest to July 24.

Bear Lake County Fair and Rodeo. Third wkend Aug.

Motels/Motor Lodges

★★ **BEST WESTERN CLOVER CREEK INN.** *243 N 4th St (83254). 208/847-1782; fax 208/847-3519; res 800/528-1234.* 65 rms, 2 story. May-Oct: S $60; D $66; each addl $6; suites $89; under 12 free; lower rates rest of yr. Crib $6. Pet accepted, some restrictions. TV; cable (premium), VCR avail (movies). Complimentary continental bkfst, coffee in rms. Restaurant opp 6 am-10 pm. Ck-out 11 am. Meeting rm. Business servs avail. Exercise equipt. Whirlpool. Some refrigerators, microwaves. Cr cds: A, C, D, DS, MC, V.

★ **SUPER 8.** *276 N 4th St (83254). 208/847-8888; fax 208/847-3888; res 800/800-8000.* 50 rms, 2 story, 5 suites. June-Sep: S $47.88; D $50.88-$54.88; each addl $4; suites $61.88; under 12 free; golf plans; lower rates rest of yr. Crib free. TV; cable. Complimentary continental bkfst. Restaurant nearby. Ck-out 11 am. Meeting rms. Business servs avail. Gift shop. Exercise equipt. Some refrigerators, microwaves. Cr cds: A, D, DS, MC, V.

Moscow (C-1)

Pop 18,519 **Elev** 2,583 ft
Area code 208 **Zip** 83843
Web www.moscow.com/chamber

Information Chamber of Commerce, PO Box 8936; 208/882-1800 or 800/380-1801

Moscow is the seat of Latah County in the heart of the Palouse Hills country and beautiful Paradise Valley. It is known as the "Dry Pea and Lentil Capital of the Nation."

What to See and Do

Appaloosa Museum & Heritage Center. Exhibit of paintings and artifacts relating to the appaloosa horse; early cowboy equipment, saddle collection, Nez Perce clothing, tools. (June-Aug, Mon-Sat; rest of yr, Mon-Fri; closed hols) Also houses national headquarters of the Appaloosa Horse Club, Inc. Moscow-Pullman Hwy. Phone 208/882-5578. **FREE**

Latah County Historical Society. Period furnishings, exhibits, and artifacts depicting local history. Local history and genealogy library. Museum (Tues-Sat, limited hrs; closed hols); library, 327 E 2nd St (Tues-Fri). McConnell Mansion (1886), 110 S Adams St. Phone 208/882-1004. **Donation**

University of Idaho. (1889) 11,000 students. Graduate and undergraduate programs. On campus is a major collection of big game specimens from the estate of well-known hunter Jack O'Connor; art gallery and performing arts center; mining, forestry, and wildlife exhibits in the mining and forestry buildings; 18,000-seat, covered Kibbie-ASUI Activities Center with award-winning barrel-arch dome. Tours (daily). W off US 95. Phone 208/885-6424.

Annual Events

Lionel Hampton/Chevron Jazz Festival. University of Idaho. Four-day festival hosted by Lionel Hampton featuring all-star headliners and student performers. Phone 208/885-6765. Late Feb.

Rendezvous in the Park. In East City Park. Arts and crafts festival, juried art shows, silent movies, concerts under the stars. Phone 208/882-1178. Two wkends July.

Latah County Fair. Fairgrounds, E of town. Phone 208/883-0694. Second wk Sep, after Labor Day.

Seasonal Event

Idaho Repertory Theater. E.W. Hartung Theater, University of Idaho. Shakespeare, musicals, dramas, comedies. Phone 208/885-7212 or 800/345-7402. July-early Aug.

Motels/Motor Lodges

★ **HILLCREST MOTEL.** *706 N Main St (83843). 208/882-7579; fax 208/882-0310; toll-free 800/368-6564. Email hillcrest@moscow.com.* 49 rms, 1 story, 3 suites. S $32; D $36; each addl $2; suites $45; under 6 free. Crib avail. Pet accepted, some restrictions, fee. Parking lot. TV; cable. Complimentary toll-free calls. Restaurant. Ck-out 11 am, ck-in 2 pm. Business servs avail. Coin lndry. Free airport transportation. Golf. Cr cds: A, MC, V.

★★ **MARK IV MOTOR INN.** *414 N Main St (83843). 208/882-7557; fax 208/883-0684; res 800/833-4240.* 86 units, 2 story. S $32-$41; D $40-$51; each addl $5; suites $50-$87; under 12 free; higher rates special events. Crib avail. Pet accepted; $5. TV; cable (premium). Indoor pool; whirlpool. Restaurant 6 am-9 pm. Bar 3:30 pm-midnight. Ck-out noon. Meeting rm. Business servs avail. In-rm modem link. Free airport, bus depot transportation. Cr cds: A, C, D, DS, ER, MC, V.

★ **SUPER 8.** *175 Peterson Dr (83843). 208/883-1503; fax 208/883-4769; res 800/800-8000.* 60 rms, 3 story. No elvtr. S $39.88; D $47.88-$70.88; each addl $3; under 12 free; higher rates special events. Crib free. TV; cable (premium). Ck-out 11 am. Meeting rms. Cr cds: A, C, D, DS, ER, MC, V.

Hotel

★★ **BEST WESTERN UNIVERSITY INN.** *1516 Pullman Rd (83843). 208/882-0550; fax 208/883-3056; res 800/528-1234; toll-free 800/325-8765. Email uibw@moscow.com; www.uinn moscow.com.* 168 rms, 2 story, 5 suites. S $74; D $84; each addl $5; suites $175; under 17 free. Crib avail.

Pet accepted, some restrictions, fee. Parking lot. Indoor pool, children's pool, whirlpool. TV; cable (premium). Complimentary continental bkfst, coffee in rms, newspaper, toll-free calls. Restaurant 6 am-2 pm. Bar. Ck-out noon, ck-in 4 pm. Meeting rms. Business center. Dry cleaning. Gift shop. Free airport transportation. Exercise equipt, sauna. Golf, 18 holes. Tennis, 10 courts. Hiking trail. Picnic facilities. Video games. Cr cds: A, D, DS, MC, V.

Mountain Home

(G-2) *See also Boise*

Pop 7,913 **Elev** 3,143 ft
Area code 208 **Zip** 83647
Web mhchamber@mhiconn.net
Information Desert Mountain Visitor Center, 2900 American Legion Blvd, PO Box 3; 208/587-4464

A transportation center in the Boise-Owyhee Valley of southwest Idaho, Mountain Home affords a fine starting point for side trips. Within a few hours' drive are forested ranges of the Boise National Forest, sand dunes, ghost towns, reservoirs, and canyons; a Ranger District office of the forest (see BOISE) is located here.

What to See and Do

Bruneau Canyon. A 61-mi gorge, 2,000 ft deep but narrow enough in places to toss a rock across. **Bruneau Dunes State Park** (4,800 acres) has small lakes, sand dunes, and the highest single structured dune in North America (470 ft). Fishing for bass and bluegill, boating (ramps; no motors); nature trails, picnicking, tent and trailer sites (15-day max; hookups, dump station). Info center, public observatory, interpretive programs (by appt). Standard hrs, fees. 20 mi S on ID 51 to Bruneau, then SE on local road, near Bruneau. Phone 208/366-7919.

Elmore County Historical Foundation Museum. Contains historical info about Mountain Home and Elmore County. (Mar-Dec, Fri and Sat afternoons) 180 S 3rd St E. Phone 208/587-2104. ¢

Fishing, swimming, boating, camping. Strike Reservoir, 23 mi S on ID 51; or Anderson Ranch Reservoir, 22 mi NE on ID 20.

Soldier Mountain Ski Area. Two double chairlifts, rope tow; patrol, school, rentals, snowmaking; cafeteria, concession. Longest run 2 mi; vertical drop 1,400 ft. Half-day rates. (Mid-Nov-Apr, Thurs-Sun and hols; Christmas and Easter wks, daily) NE on US 20 to Fairfield, then 10 mi N on Soldier Creek Rd. Phone 208/764-2300. ¢¢¢¢¢

Motels/Motor Lodges

★★ **BEST WESTERN FOOTHILLS MOTOR INN.** *1080 Hwy 20 (83647), I-84 Exit 95. 208/587-8477; fax 208/ 587-5774; res 800/528-1324; toll-free 800/528-1234. www.bestwestern. com/foothillsmotorinn.* 76 rms, 2 story. May-Sep: S $60; D $70; each addl $5; under 12 free; lower rates rest of yr. Crib avail. Pet accepted, some restrictions. Parking lot. Pool, whirlpool. TV; cable. Complimentary continental bkfst, coffee in rms, newspaper, toll-free calls. Restaurant. Meeting rm. Business servs avail. Coin lndry. Gift shop. Exercise equipt. Golf, 18 holes. Cr cds: A, C, D, DS, ER, JCB, MC, V.

🄳 🐾 🛏 ⇋ 🏋 📳 🔥

★ **HILANDER MOTEL & STEAK HOUSE.** *615 S 3rd W (83647). 208/587-3311; fax 208/580-2152.* 33 rms, 2 story. June-Aug: S $35; D $40; each addl $4; lower rates rest of yr. Crib avail. Pet accepted, some restrictions, fee. Parking lot. Pool. TV; cable. Complimentary coffee in rms, toll-free calls. Restaurant 4-10 pm, closed Sun. Bar. Ck-out 11 am, ck-in 11 pm. Fax servs avail. Cr cds: A, D, DS, MC, V.

🐾 ⇋ 🏋 📳 🔥

★ **SLEEP INN.** *1180 US 20 (83647). 208/587-9743; fax 208/587-7382; toll-free 800/300-0039.* 60 rms. May-July, Sep: S $55; D $60; each addl $5; under 12 free; lower rates rest of yr. Crib avail. Pet accepted, some restrictions. Parking lot. TV; cable, VCR avail. Complimentary continental

bkfst, coffee in rms, newspaper, toll-free calls. Restaurant. Meeting rm. Golf, 18 holes. Cr cds: A, C, DS, MC, V.

🄳 🐾 🛏 📳 🔥

Nampa

(G-2) *See also Boise*

Founded 1885 **Pop** 28,365
Elev 2,490 ft **Area code** 208
Web www.nampa.com

Information Chamber of Commerce, 1305 3rd St S, PO Box A, 83653; 208/466-4641

Nampa, the largest city in Canyon County, is located in the heart of the agriculturally rich Treasure Valley of southwestern Idaho.

What to See and Do

Canyon County Historical Society Museum. Historical artifacts and memorabilia inside a 1903 train depot once used as offices of the Union Pacific Railroad. (Tues-Sat, limited hrs) 1200 Front St. Phone 208/467-7611. **Donation**

Deer Flat National Wildlife Refuge. Thousands of migratory waterfowl pause at this 10,500-acre refuge while on their journey (Oct-Dec). Wildlife observation. Fishing; hunting in season. Visitor center (Mon-Fri; closed hols). 5 mi SW off I-84. Phone 208/467-9278. **FREE** Within the refuge is

Lake Lowell. Approx 8,800 acres. Waterskiing, boating, sailing; picnicking; (mid-Apr-Sep, daily).

Lakeview Park. A 90-acre park with gardens, sports facilities, tennis, archery range, picnic areas. Pool (June-Labor Day; fee). Antique fire engine, locomotive, steam roller, jet fighter plane on display. Amphitheater. Park (daily). Garrity Blvd & 16th Ave N. Phone 208/465-2215. **FREE**

Annual Event

Snake River Stampede. Among nation's top professional rodeos. All seats reserved. For tickets contact PO

Box 231, 83653; 208/466-8497. Tues-
Sat, 3rd wk July.

Motels/Motor Lodges

★ **DESERT INN.** *115 9th Ave S
(83606). 208/467-1161; fax 208/467-
5268; toll-free 800/588-5268.* 40 rms,
2 story. S $35; D $43; each addl $3;
under 12 free. TV; cable (premium).
Pet accepted; $12.50/day. Pool. Com-
plimentary continental bkfst. Restaurant adj 6 am-10 pm. Ck-out 11 am.
Some refrigerators, microwaves. Cr
cds: DS, MC, V.

★★ **INN AMERICA.** *130 Shannon Dr
(83687). 208/442-0800; fax 208/442-
0229; toll-free 800/469-4667. Email
rpreston@innamerica.com; www.
innamerica.com.* 61 rms, 3 story, 6
suites. Apr-July: S $50; D $62; each
addl $5; suites $52; lower rates rest of
yr. Crib avail. Parking lot. Pool. TV;
cable (premium). Complimentary
continental bkfst, toll-free calls.
Restaurant. Business servs avail. Dry
cleaning, coin lndry. Free airport
transportation. Golf. Cr cds: A, D,
DS, MC, V.

★★ **SHILO INN.** *1401 Shilo Dr
(83687). 208/465-3250; fax 208/465-
5929; res 800/334-1049; toll-free
800/222-2244.* 83 suites, 4 story, 8
kits. S $55; D$65-$85; each addl $10;
kit. suites $79-$89; under 13 free.
Crib free. Pet accepted; $7. TV; cable
(premium). Indoor pool; whirlpool.
Coffee in rms. Restaurant adj 6 am-
10 pm. Ck-out noon. Coin lndry.
Meeting rms. Sundries. Free airport,
railroad station, bus depot transportation. Exercise equipt; sauna.
Bathrm phones, refrigerators, microwaves; many wet bars. Cr cds: A, C,
JCB, MC, V.

★★ **SHILO INN.** *617 Nampa Blvd
(83687). 208/466-8993; fax 208/465-
3239; res 800/222-2244.* 61 rms, 3
story. No elvtr. S, D $53-$75; each
addl $8; under 13 free. Crib free. Pet
accepted; $7. TV; cable (premium).
Heated pool; whirlpool. Complimentary continental bkfst, coffee in rms.
Ck-out noon. Coin lndry. Valet serv.
Sauna, steam rm. Refrigerators,

microwaves. Cr cds: A, D, DS, JCB,
MC, V.

Pocatello

(G-5) *See also Blackfoot, Idaho Falls*

Founded 1882 **Pop** 46,080
Elev 4,464 ft **Area code** 208
Information Greater Pocatello Cham-
ber of Commerce, 343 W Center St,
PO Box 626, 83204; 208/233-1525

At the heart of the intermontane
transportation system is Pocatello.
Once the site of a reservation, the
city was named for the Native American leader who granted the railroad
rights of way and building privileges.
A Ranger District office and the
headquarters of the Caribou National
Forest are located here.

What to See and Do

Caribou National Forest. Fishing;
hunting, scenic drives, pack trips,
camping (fee in some designated
developed campgrounds), picnic
grounds, downhill and cross-country
skiing, snowmobiling. For further
info contact the Forest Supervisor,
250 S 4th Ave, Suite 187, 83201. S,
W & E of city. Phone 208/236-7500.
In forest is

Pebble Creek Ski Area. Triple, two
double chairlifts; beginner-to-
expert trails; patrol, school, rentals;
restaurant, bar, day care. Longest
run 1¼ mi; vertical drop 2,000 ft.
Night skiing. Half-day rates. (2nd
wk Dec-early Apr, Tues-Sun) 10 mi
SE on I-15 to Inkom, then 5 mi E
on Green Canyon Rd. Phone
208/775-4452. ¢¢¢¢

Idaho State University. (1901) 11,155
students. Undergraduate and graduate programs. Art gallery in Fine Arts
Bldg has changing exhibits (academic yr, daily; summer by appt,
phone 208/236-3532); art gallery in
Student Union Bldg (daily); both galleries free. On campus is 12,000-seat
Holt Arena, indoor football stadium
and sports arena. Tours. 741 S 7th
Ave. For info, schedules phone
208/236-3620. Also here is

Idaho Museum of Natural History. Exhibits on Idaho fossils, especially large mammals of the Ice Age; Native American basketry and beadwork; "Discovery Room" for educational activities; prearranged tours; museum shop. (Mon-Fri; closed hols) Phone 208/236-3168 or 208/236-2262. **FREE**

Rocky Mountain River Tours. Six-day wilderness rafting tours; equipment provided. Middlefork Salmon River Canyon. Phone 208/345-2400.

Ross Park. Zoo; swimming pool (June-Aug), water slide; playground, picnic area with shelter, band shell. Park (daily). Fee for some activities. S 2nd Ave. Phone 208/234-6232. On upper level are

> **Old Fort Hall Replica.** Reproduction of 1834 Hudson's Bay Trading Post; period displays. (June-mid-Sep, daily; Apr-May, Tues-Sat) ¢
>
> **Bannock County Historical Museum.** Relics of the early days of Pocatello and Bannock County; Bannock and Shoshone display. (Memorial Day-Labor Day, daily; rest of yr, Tues-Sat, limited hrs; closed hols, also mid-Dec-mid-Jan) Phone 208/233-0434. ¢

Standrod House. Restored Victorian mansion lavishly decorated with woodwork and marble; furnished with antiques. (Tues-Fri) 648 N Garfield Ave. Phone 208/233-4198. ¢

Annual Events

Shoshone-Bannock Indian Festival. Begins 2nd Wed Aug.

Bannock County Fair and Rodeo. North: Bannock County Fairgrounds. South: Downey Fairgrounds. Carnival, rodeo, exhibits, food booths, livestock and horse shows. Mid-Aug.

Seasonal Event

Summer Band Concert Series. Guy Gates Memorial Band Shell, in lower level of Ross Park. Sun, July-Aug.

Motels/Motor Lodges

★★ **AMERITEL INN.** *1440 Bench Rd (83201), I-15 Exit 71. 208/234-7500; fax 208/234-0000; res 800/600-6001.* 148 rms, 3 story, 14 kit. units. June-Aug: S, D $79; each addl $8; suites, kit. units $109-$189; under 13 free; lower rates rest of yr. Crib free. TV; cable (premium). Indoor pool; whirlpool. Complimentary continental bkfst. Restaurant nearby. Ck-out noon. Coin lndry. Meeting rms. In-rm modem link. Valet serv. Free airport transportation. Exercise equipt. Some refrigerators; microwaves avail. Cr cds: A, D, DS, MC, V.
🅳 ➤ 🏋 ⬛ 🔥

★★ **COMFORT INN.** *1333 Bench Rd (83201). 208/237-8155; fax 208/237-5695; res 800/228-5150.* 52 rms, 2 story, 14 suites. June-Sep: S $59; D $69; suites $74; under 18 free; lower rates rest of yr. Crib free. Pet accepted. TV; cable (premium). Indoor pool; whirlpool. Complimentary continental bkfst. Restaurant nearby. Ck-out 11 am. Microwaves avail. Cr cds: A, DS, MC, V.
➤ ➤ 🔥

★★ **HOLIDAY INN.** *1399 Bench Rd (83201). 208/237-1400; fax 208/238-0225; toll-free 800/446-4656.* 202 rms, 2 story. S, D $69; each addl $6; suites $139; under 18 free; wkly, wkend, hol rates. Crib free. Pet accepted, some restrictions; $25 deposit. TV; cable (premium), VCR avail. Complimentary continental bkfst, coffee in rms. Restaurant 6 am-2 pm, 5-10 pm. Rm serv 6 am-10 pm. Bar 5 pm-1 am. Ck-out noon. Meeting rms. Business servs avail. Bellhops. Sundries. Coin lndry. Free airport transportation. Indoor putting green. Exercise equipt; sauna. Indoor pool; whirlpool. Game rm. Cr cds: A, C, D, DS, JCB, MC, V.
➤ ➤ 🏋 ⬛ 🔥 SC

★ **POCATELLO SUPER 8.** *1330 Bench Rd (83201). 208/234-0888; fax 208/232-0347; res 280/800-8000.* 80 rms, 3 story. June-Aug: S $58; D $62; each addl $4; under 12 free; lower rates rest of yr. Crib avail. Pet accepted, some restrictions, fee. Parking lot. TV; cable, VCR avail. Complimentary continental bkfst, toll-free calls. Restaurant 6 am-11 pm. Ck-out 11 am, ck-in 2 pm. Business servs avail. Coin lndry. Golf, 18 holes. Downhill skiing. Cr cds: A, C, D, DS, MC, V.
🅳 ➤ 🎿 🏋 ⬛ 🔥 SC

Hotels

★★ **BEST WESTERN COTTON TREE INN.** *1415 Bench Rd (83201). 208/237-7650; fax 208/238-1355; res*

800/528-1234; toll-free 800/662-6886. Email mike@cottontree.net; www.cotton tree.net. 102 rms, 3 story, 47 suites. S, D $66; suites $81. Crib avail. Pet accepted. Parking lot. Indoor pool, whirlpool. TV; cable. Complimentary continental bkfst, coffee in rms, newspaper, toll-free calls. Restaurant nearby. Bar. Meeting rms. Business center. Bellhops. Dry cleaning, coin lndry. Free airport transportation. Exercise privileges. Golf. Tennis, 2 courts. Downhill skiing. Supervised children's activities. Video games. Cr cds: A, C, D, DS, ER, JCB, MC, V.

★★ WESTCOAST POCATELLO HOTEL. 1555 Pocatello Creek Rd (83201), jct I-15 and I-86. 208/233-2200; fax 208/234-4524; res 800/325-4000; toll-free 800/527-5202. www. westcoasthotels.com. 144 rms, 2 story, 6 suites. S, D $79; each addl $10; suites $145; under 17 free. Crib avail. Pet accepted. Parking lot. Indoor pool, children's pool, whirlpool. TV; cable. Complimentary coffee in rms, toll-free calls. Restaurant 5:30 am-10 pm. Bar. Ck-out noon, ck-in 3 pm. Meeting rms. Business center. Dry cleaning, coin lndry. Free airport transportation. Sauna. Golf. Down-hill skiing. Video games. Cr cds: A, C, D, DS, MC, V.

Priest Lake Area

See also Sandpoint

(25 mi N of Priest River via ID 57)

Area code 208

Information Chamber of Commerce, PO Box 174, Coolin 83821; 208/443-3191

Among the few remaining unspoiled playgrounds of the Pacific Northwest are lovely and spectacular Priest Lake and the Idaho Panhandle National Forest. North of the confluence of the Pend Oreille and Priest rivers, giant lake trout, big game, towering mountains, waterfalls, lakes, and tall trees make this area one of the most

attractive in the country. Mountain ranges and Pacific breezes keep the climate moderate.

This entire water and forest domain was explored by a Jesuit priest, Father Peter John DeSmet, also known as "great black robe" and the "first apostle of the Northwest." Priest Lake and Priest River were both named in his honor. A Ranger District office of the Idaho Panhandle National Forests-Kaniksu is located at Priest Lake.

What to See and Do

Idaho Panhandle National Forests—Kaniksu. Surrounds Priest Lake and Lake Pend Oreille; other areas NE. Rich with huge trees, wildflowers, fishing streams. Boating, swimming, fishing in Pend Oreille and Priest lakes; big game hunting, cross-country skiing, snowmobiling trails, picnicking, 12 forest-run camp-grounds on the west side of Priest Lake (may be fee); other state-run campgrounds in the area. Contact the Priest Lake Ranger District, HCR 5, Box 207, Priest River 83856. Phone 208/443-2512.

Priest Lake. Lower Priest, the main lake, is 18½ mi long, about 4 mi wide, and has a 63-mi shoreline. Upper Priest (inaccessible by road; best reached by boat) is 3¼ mi long, 1 mi wide, and has an 8-mi shoreline. The area is very popular for picnics, overnight cruises, and campouts. There are 3 state-run campgrounds on the E side: Dickensheet, Indian Creek, and Lionhead; the US Forest Service operates other campgrounds in the area, on the W side. Nearby is the Roosevelt Grove of ancient cedars with 800-year-old trees standing as tall as 150 ft. Granite Falls is within the grove. Priest Lake is famous for its giant-size lake trout (Mackinaw trout) and cutthroat trout. The main lake contains 6 islands ideal for picnicking and camping (10-day max). Recreation around the lake incl swimming, boating (ramp), ice fishing; cross-country skiing, snowmobiling, ice-skating, sledding. 22 mi N of town of Priest River via ID 57, then approx 6 mi E on East Shore Rd; or approx 6 mi farther on ID 57, then 1 mi E on Out-let Bay Rd. On the E side of the lake is

Priest Lake State Park. This park comprises 3 state-run campgrounds: **Dickensheet** unit is 1 mi off ID 57, on the Coolin Rd (46 acres; 11 campsites); **Indian Creek** unit is 11 mi N of Coolin, on the Eastshore Rd (park headquarters; 295 acres; 93 campsites, store, boating facilities, RV hookups, trails); and **Lionhead** unit is 23 mi N of Coolin, on the Eastshore Rd (415 acres; 47 tent sites, group camp, boating facilities, trails). Res are available for Indian Creek campsites; res are required for the group camp at Lionhead. Phone 208/443-2200.

Priest River. Old logging roads parallel much of it. Only at north and south stretches is it easily reached from ID 57. Long whitewater stretches provide adventure for canoe experts; riffles, big holes, smooth-flowing sections make it a tantalizing trout stream (fishing: June-Oct). Winds for 44 mi S of lake through wild, forested country.

Annual Events

Pacific Northwest Sled Dog Championship Races. On ID 57 at Priest Lake Airport, W shore. Last wkend Jan.

Spring Festival. Auction, parade. Memorial Day wknd.

Resorts

★★ **ELKINS ON PRIEST LAKE.** *404 Elkins Rd (83848), W shore of Priest Lake. 208/443-2432; fax 208/443-2527. Email info@elkinsresort.com; www.elkinsresort.com.* 30 air-cooled kit. cottages. July-Aug (1-wk min), Sep-June (2-day min): S, D $75-$280; wkly rates; higher rates hol wknds; lower rates rest of yr. Crib free. Pet accepted; $5. Restaurant 8 am-9 pm; closed Mar and Apr. Box lunches, picnics. Bar. Ck-out 11 am, ck-in 4 pm. Gift shop. Grocery. Coin lndry 2 mi. Meeting rms. Game rm. Private beach. Boats. X-country ski on site. Picnic tables. Cr cds: DS, MC, V.

⬛ 🐾 🚶 ⛄ 🔥

★★ **GRANDVIEW RESORT.** *3492 Reeder Bay Rd (83848), W shore of Priest Lake, via ID 57 to Reeder Bay Rd. 208/443-2433; fax 208/443-3033; toll-free 888/806-3033. Email grandview@nidlink.com; www.gvr.com.* 8 rms, 2 story, 10 suites. June-Aug: S, D $165;

suites $165; lower rates rest of yr. Parking lot. Pool, children's pool. TV; cable. Complimentary coffee in rms, newspaper. Restaurant. Bar. Meeting rm. Business servs avail. Coin lndry. Gift shop. Golf. Beach access. Hiking trail. Picnic facilities. Cr cds: MC, V.

🔌 🐾 🚶 ⛄ 🔥 🎿

★★ **HILLS RESORT.** *4777 W Lakeshore Rd (83856), W shore of Priest Lake via ID 57 to Luby Bay Rd. 208/443-2551; fax 208/443-2363.* 50 kit. chalets, cabins, 1-2 story. No A/C. Last wk June-Labor Day: $800-$1,850/wk; lower rates rest of yr. Crib $5. Pet accepted; $10. Dining rm 8 am-9:30 pm. Box lunches. Bar 1 pm-1 am. Ck-out 11 am. Grocery. Coin lndry. Meeting rms. Business servs avail. Tennis. Beach, boats, rowboats, canoes, waterskiing. X-country ski on site. Sleighing, tobogganing, snowmobiles. Bicycles (rentals). Lawn games. Entertainment, dancing, movies. Game rm. Housekeeping units. Fireplaces. Balconies. Picnic tables, grills. Cr cds: DS, MC, V.

⬛ 🐾 🚶 🔥

Rexburg

(F-6) See also Ashton, Idaho Falls, St. Anthony

Founded 1883 **Pop** 14,302
Elev 4,865 ft **Area code** 208
Zip 83440 **Web** www.rexcc.com

Information Chamber of Commerce Tourist & Information Center, 420 W 4th S; 208/356-5700

Rexburg enjoys its position as a farm and trading center. Founded on instructions of the Mormon Church, the community was named for Thomas Ricks; usage changed it to Rexburg.

What to See and Do

Idaho Centennial Carousel. Restored Spillman Engineering carousel. (June-Labor Day, daily) Porter Park. Phone 208/359-3020. ¢

Parks.

Beaver Dick. A 12-acre preserve on W bank of the North Fork of Snake

River. Fishing, boating, ramp; picnic facilities, primitive camping. (Mar-Dec) 7 mi W on ID 33.

Twin Bridges. A 30-acre preserve on N bank of the South Fork of Snake River. Fishing, boating, ramp; picnic facilities, camping. (Apr-Nov) 13 mi SE on Archer-Lyman Rd.

Teton Flood Museum. Artifacts, photographs, and films document the 1976 flood caused by the collapse of the Teton Dam, which left 11 persons dead and $1 billion in damage. Also various historical displays. (May-Aug, Mon-Sat; rest of yr, Mon-Fri, limited hrs; closed hols exc July 4) 51 N Center. Phone 208/356-9101. **FREE**

Annual Event

International Street Festival. Dance teams from around the world, events. Last wk July-1st wkend Aug.

Motels/Motor Lodges

★★ **BEST WESTERN COTTON TREE INN.** *450 W 4th St S (83440). 208/356-4646; fax 208/356-7461; res 800/528-1234; toll-free 800/662-6886.* 101 rms, 2 story. S $64; D $69-$74; each addl $5; suite $195; under 18 free. Crib free. Pet accepted. TV; cable. Indoor pool; whirlpool. Restaurant adj 7 am-10 pm. Ck-out noon. Coin lndry. Meeting rms. Business servs avail. Health club privileges. Some refrigerators, microwaves. Balconies. Cr cds: A, D, DS, MC, V.
D ⬛ 🛏 🏃 ⛷ 🔥 ☀

★★ **COMFORT INN.** *1565 W Main St (83440). 208/359-1311; fax 208/359-1387.* 48 rms, 2 story, 4 suites. June-Aug: S, D $69; suites $84; under 18 free; lower rates rest of yr. Crib avail, fee. Pet accepted, some restrictions. Parking lot. Indoor pool; whirlpool. TV; cable. Complimentary continental bkfst, coffee in rms, newspaper, toll-free calls. Restaurant nearby. Ck-out 11 am, ck-in 3 pm. Meeting rm. Business center. Exercise equipt. Golf. Tennis. Downhill skiing. Cr cds: A, C, D, DS, JCB, MC, V.
D ⬛ 🛏 🏃 ⛷ 🏃 🔥 ⛷

★ **SUPER 8.** *215 W Main St (83440). 208/356-8888; fax 208/356-8896; res* 800/800-8000. 42 rms, 2 story. June-Sep: S $42.88; D $46.88-$50.88; each addl $4; under 12 free; lower rates rest of yr. Crib free. TV; cable. Complimentary continental bkfst. Restaurant nearby. Ck-out 11 am. Business servs avail. Cr cds: A, D, DS, MC, V.
D 🛏 🔥 ☀

Restaurant

★ **FRONTIER PIES RESTAURANT.** *460 W 4th St (83440). 208/356-3600.* Specializes in Navajo taco, broiled chicken Hawaiian. Own soups, pies. Hrs: 7 am-10 pm; Fri, Sat to 11 pm; Sun to 9 pm. Closed Dec 25. Bkfst $2.95-$5.59; lunch $4.59-$7.29; dinner $4.99-$10.99. Child's menu. Rustic decor; Old West antiques. Cr cds: A, DS, MC, V.
D SC

Salmon (E-4)

Settled 1866 **Pop** 2,941 **Elev** 4,004 ft
Area code 208 **Zip** 83467
Information Salmon Valley Chamber of Commerce, 200 Main St, Suite 1; 208/756-2100 or 208/756-4935

This town, at the junction of the Salmon and Lemhi rivers, serves as a doorway to the Salmon River country. It has towering mountains, lush farmland, timberland, and rich mines. The Salmon River runs through the town on its way to the Columbia River and the Pacific Ocean. Fishing and boating are available along the Salmon and Lemhi rivers and in more than 250 lakes. The headquarters and two Ranger District offices of the Salmon National Forest are located here.

What to See and Do

Lemhi Ghost Town. The village, like the forest, county, mountain range, valley, and river, is named for Lemhi, a character in *The Book of Mormon.* Mormons attempted to colonize here in 1855 and built a fort, but by 1858, Native Americans had driven them out. The walls of old Fort Lemhi still stand. For info on other ghost towns in the area contact the Salmon Valley Chamber of Commerce. 29 mi SE on ID 28.

River rafting, backpack, fishing, and pack trips. along the Lemhi, Salmon, Middle Fork, and other rivers can be arranged. Contact the Chamber of Commerce for a list of outfitters in the area.

Salmon National Forest. Approx 1.8 million acres. Boat trips, fishing; hunting, picnicking, camping. Includes portion of the Frank Church—River of No Return Wilderness. For further info contact the Supervisor, PO Box 729. N, E, and W of town along US 93. Phone 208/756-2215.

Annual Events

High School Rodeo. First wkend June.

Salmon River Days. July 4.

The Great Salmon BalloonFest. Hot-air balloon festival. Aug.

Lemhi County Fair & Rodeo. Third wk Aug.

Motel/Motor Lodge

★★ **STAGECOACH INN MOTEL.** *201 Hwy 93 N (83467). 208/756-4251.* 100 rms, 3 story. S $47; D $55; each addl $6; children $6; under 12 free. Crib avail, fee. Parking lot. Pool. TV; cable. Complimentary continental bkfst. Restaurant 5-10 pm. Ck-out 11 am, ck-in 3 pm. Meeting rms. Coin lndry. Free airport transportation. Exercise privileges. Golf, 9 holes. Tennis. Downhill skiing. Beach access. Picnic facilities. Cr cds: A, C, D, MC, V.

🄳 🐾 ⚡ 🍴 ⛷ 🏊 🏃 🔌 🔥

Restaurant

★ **SALMON RIVER COFFEE SHOP.** *606 Main St (83467). 208/756-3521.* Specializes in steak, seafood. Salad bar. Hrs: 5 am-10 pm; Fri, Sat to 11 pm. Closed Jan 1, Thanksgiving, Dec 25. Bar. Bkfst $3-$6.95; lunch $3.75-$6.25; dinner $6.25-$20. Child's menu. Entertainment: Mon-Sat. Cr cds: A, C, D, MC, V.

🄳 ⬛

Sandpoint

(A-2) *See also Priest Lake Area*

Pop 5,203 **Elev** 2,085 ft
Area code 208 **Zip** 83864
Web www.keokee.com/chamber/index.html
Information Chamber of Commerce, 900 N 5th, PO Box 928; 208/263-2161 or 800/800-2106

At the point where the Pend Oreille River empties into Lake Pend Oreille (pon-da-RAY, from a Native American tribe given to wearing pendant ear ornaments), Sandpoint straddles two major railroads and three US highways. All of these bring a stream of tourists into town. In the surrounding area are dozens of smaller lakes and streams. A Ranger District office of the Idaho Panhandle National Forests-Coeur d'Alene (see COEUR D'ALENE) is located here.

What to See and Do

Bonner County Historical Society Museum. Exhibits depict history of Bonner County. Research library with newspaper collection dating from 1899. (Apr-Oct, Tues-Sat; rest of yr, Thurs; closed hols) In Lakeview Park, 611 S Ella. Phone 208/263-2344. ¢

Coldwater Creek on the Cedar St Bridge. Shopping mall built on a bridge over Sand Creek. Inspired by the Ponte Vecchio in Florence, Italy, the Coldwater Creek shops provide panoramic views of Lake Pend Oreille and nearby mountains. (Daily)

Lake Pend Oreille. Largest in Idaho, one of the largest natural lakes wholly within US; more than 43 mi long, 6 mi wide, with more than 111 mi of shoreline. Approx 14 varieties of game fish incl famous Kamloops, largest rainbow trout in world (avg 16-26 lbs). Boating, swimming, waterskiing; camping, picnicking.

Round Lake State Park. Approx 140 acres of coniferous woods. Swimming, skin diving, fishing, ice fishing, ice skating, boating (ramp, no motors); hiking, cross-country skiing, sledding, tobogganing, snowshoeing in winter, picnicking. Camping (15-day max; no hookups), dump station. Campfire programs. Park (daily). Standard fees. 10 mi S on US

95, then 2 mi W, near Sagle. Phone 208/263-3489.

Sandpoint Public Beach. Nearly 20 acres. Bathhouse, swimming, water-skiing, boat docks, ramps; picnic tables, fireplaces, volleyball and tennis courts; concession (seasonal). Park (daily). Foot of Bridge St, E edge of town. **FREE**

Skiing. Schweitzer Mountain Resort. Five chairlifts, high-speed quad; school, rentals; lodging, restaurants, bars, cafeteria, nursery. Longest run 2.7 mi; vertical drop 2,400 ft. (Nov-Apr, daily) Summer chairlift rides (fee). 11 mi NW off US 2 & US 95, in Selkirk Mts of Idaho Panhandle National Forests. Phone 800/831-8810.

Annual Event

Winter Carnival. Two wkends of festivities incl snow sculpture, snow-shoe softball, and other games, races, torchlight parade. Mid-Jan.

Motels/Motor Lodges

★ ★ **EDGEWATER RESORT.** *56 Bridge St (83864), E of US 95. 208/ 263-3194; fax 208/263-3194; toll-free 800/635-2534. Email edgewater@netw. com; www.keokee.com@sandida/home. html.* 55 rms, 3 story. No elvtr. S $106-$115; D $110-$119; each addl $10; suites $120-$150; under 16 free; package plans. Crib $5. Pet accepted; $5. TV; cable, VCR avail. Restaurant 11 am-10 pm; Sun to 9 pm. Bar. Ck-out noon. Meeting rms. Business servs avail. Whirlpool. Sauna. Private patios, balconies. On Lake Pend Oreille; swimming beach. Cr cds: A, C, D, DS, ER, JCB, MC, V.

★ ★ **SANDPOINT QUALITY INN.** *807 N 5th Ave (83864). 208/263-2111; fax 208/263-3289; res 800/635-2534.* 62 rms, 2 story. S $59-$88; D $65-$95; each addl $6; under 18 free; ski plan. Crib free. Pet accepted; $5. TV; cable, VCR avail. Indoor pool; whirlpool. Coffee in rms. Restaurant 5:30 am-10 pm. Bar

11-2 am. Ck-out noon. Business servs avail. Coin lndry. Sundries. Downhill/x-country ski 11 mi. Cr cds: A, C, D, DS, JCB, MC, V.

★ **SUPER 8 MOTEL.** *476841 Hwy 95 N (83864). 208/263-2210; fax 208/ 263-2210; res 800/800-8000.* 61 rms, 2 story. Mid-June-mid Aug: S $45-$65; D $45-$85; each addl $5; under 13 free; family rates; package plans; higher rates special events; lower rates rest of yr. Crib free. Pet accepted. TV; cable (premium). Complimentary coffee in lobby. Restaurant adj 8 am-9 pm. Ck-out 11 am. Business servs avail. In-rm modem link. Downhill ski 9 mi; x-country ski 1 mi. Microwaves avail. Cr cds: A, C, D, DS, ER, JCB, MC, V.

Hotels

★ ★ ★ **CONNIE'S HAWTHORN INN & SUITES.** *415 Cedar St (83864), downtown. 208/263-9581; fax 208/ 263-3395; res 800/527-1133; toll-free 800/282-0660. Email connies2@bossig. com; www.hotels-west.com.* 53 rms, 3 story. July-Aug: S $69-$79; D $79-$89; each addl $8; suites $129-$179; under 17 free; golf, ski plans; lower rates rest of yr. Crib $8. TV; cable (premium), VCR avail. Heated pool; whirlpool. Restaurant 6 am-10 pm; Fri, Sat to midnight. Rm serv 7 am-10 pm. Bar 11-1 am. Ck-out 1 pm. Meeting rm. Business servs avail. In-rm modem link. Valet serv. Downhill/x-country ski 9 mi. Health club privileges. Some bathrm phones,

Lake Pend Oreille

refrigerators. Balconies. Cr cds: A, DS, MC, V.

★ **LAKESIDE INN.** *106 Bridge St (83864). 208/263-3717; fax 208/265-4781; toll-free 800/543-8126. Email lakeside@televar.com; www.keokee. com/lakeside.* 54 rms, 4 suites. Dec-Feb, June-Aug: S $74; D $79; each addl $5; under 12 free; lower rates rest of yr. Crib avail, fee. Pet accepted, some restrictions, fee. Parking lot. TV; cable (DSS), VCR avail. Complimentary continental bkfst, coffee in rms, newspaper, toll-free calls. Restaurant. Ck-out 11 am, ck-in 2 pm. Business center. Coin lndry. Free airport transportation. Exercise privileges, sauna, whirlpool. Golf, 18 holes. Tennis, 6 courts. Downhill skiing. Beach access. Bike rentals. Picnic facilities. Cr cds: A, D, DS, MC, V.

Restaurants

★★ **BANGKOK CUISINE.** *202 N 2nd Ave (83864). 208/265-4149.* Specializes in vegetarian dishes, curries. Hrs: 11:30 am-9 pm. Closed Sun; Labor Day, Thanksgiving, Dec 25. Res accepted. Lunch a la carte entrees: $4.75-$5.50; dinner a la carte entrees: $6.95-$12.95. Street parking. Thai decor; fish tank. Cr cds: A, D, DS, MC, V.

★★ **FLOATING RESTAURANT.** *ID 200E (83836), 17 mi E on ID 200, adj to Hope Marina. 208/264-5311.* Specializes in fish, pasta. Own baking. Hrs: 11 am-9 pm. Closed Oct-Apr. Res accepted. Bar. Lunch a la carte entrees: $4.25-$9; dinner a la carte entrees: $4.95-$8.95. Sun brunch $8.95. Child's menu. Parking. On lake. Cr cds: A, DS, MC, V.

★ **HYDRA.** *115 Lake St (83864). 208/263-7123.* Specializes in beef, seafood, pasta. Salad bar. Hrs: 11:30 am-10 pm; Fri, Sat to 10:30 pm; Sat, Mon from 5 pm; Sun 10 am-9 pm; Sun brunch to 2 pm. Closed Thanksgiving, Dec 25. Bar. Lunch buffet: $5.89; dinner $5.25-$16.95. Sun brunch $7.25. Eclectic decor; cutglass by local artist. Cr cds: A, D, DS, MC, V.

★★ **IVANO'S RISTORANTE.** *124 S 2nd Ave (83864). 208/263-0211.* Specializes in pasta, seafood. Hrs: 5-9 pm; Sun 4:30-8:30 pm. Closed Easter, Thanksgiving, Dec 25. Res accepted. Bar. Dinner $7.95-$19.95. Child's menu. Cathedral ceiling in main dining rm. Cr cds: A, D, DS, MC, V.

★ **JALAPENO'S.** *314 N 2nd Ave (83864). 208/263-2995. www.jalapenosrestaurant.com.* Specializes in garlic shrimp, pork carnitas, carne asada. Hrs: 11 am-9 pm. Closed hols. Lunch $5-$9; dinner $5-$11. Child's menu. Street parking. Wall murals. Cr cds: A, DS, MC, V.

Shoshone
(G-3) *See also Jerome, Twin Falls*

Founded 1882 **Pop** 1,249
Elev 3,970 ft **Area code** 208
Zip 83352
Information City Hall, 207 S Rail St W, Box 208; 208/886-2030

Shoshone (sho-SHOWN or sho-SHO-nee) is the seat of Lincoln County and the marketplace for a farming and livestock area fed by irrigation.

What to See and Do

Mary L. Gooding Memorial Park. Playground, pool (May-Aug, daily), picnic area along Little Wood River. (Daily) 300 N Rail St. Phone 208/886-2030.

Shoshone Indian Ice Caves. Natural refrigerator, with temperatures ranging from 18-33° F. Cave is 3 blks long, 30 ft wide, and 40 ft high. On grounds are statue of Shoshone Chief Washakie and a museum of Native American artifacts; minerals, gems (free). 40-min guided tours (May-Sep, daily). 17 mi N on ID 75. Phone 208/886-2058. ¢¢

Annual Events

Arts in the Park. Arts and crafts fair. Second wkend July.

Manty Shaw Fiddlers' Jamboree. Second wkend July.

Lincoln County Fair. Third wk July.

St. Anthony

(F-6) *See also Ashton, Idaho Falls, Rexburg*

Pop 3,010 **Elev** 4,972 ft
Area code 208 **Zip** 83445
Information Chamber of Commerce, City Hall, 114 N Bridge St; 208/624-3494

Seat of Fremont County, headquarters for the Targhee National Forest and a center of the seed potato industry, St. Anthony is named for Anthony Falls, Minnesota. Tourists make it a base for exploring Idaho's tiny (30 miles long, 1 mile wide) "sahara desert," the St. Anthony Sand Dunes.

What to See and Do

Fort Henry Trading Post Site. (1810) First fort on what early voyageurs called the "accursed mad river." 7 mi W along Henry's Fork of Snake River.
St. Anthony Sand Dunes. 12 mi W. Phone 208/624-3494.

Annual Events

Cowboy Poet Festival. Entertainment, clogging demonstrations. Apr.
Fremont County Pioneer Days. Rodeo, parade, carnival. Late July.
Fremont County Fair. Fairgrounds. Features demolition derby. Aug.
Summerfest. Main St Booth fair. Aug.

St. Marie's

(B-2) *See also Coeur d'Alene*

Pop 2,442 **Elev** 2,216 ft
Area code 208 **Zip** 83861
Information Chamber of Commerce, 906 Main, PO Box 162; 208/245-3563

St. Marie's (St. Mary's) is a center for lumbering and the production of plywood, a crossroads for lake, rail, and road transportation, and the jumping-off place for exploring the shadowy St. Joe River country. A Ranger District office of the Idaho Panhandle National Forests-St. Joe is located in St. Marie's.

What to See and Do

Benewah, Round, and Chatcolet lakes. Famous as one of state's best bass fishing and duck hunting areas. The 3 lakes became 1 lake with the construction of Post Falls Dam. Along St. Joe River. Also here is

Heyburn State Park. More than 7,800 acres. Swimming beach, fishing, boating (ramps), ice skating, ice fishing; hiking and bridle trails, self-guided nature walks, picnicking, concession, tent and trailer campsites (15-day max; hookups), dump station. Campfire and interpretive programs. Park (daily). Standard fees. 7 mi W on ID 5. Phone 208/686-1308.

Idaho Panhandle National Forests—St. Joe. Fishing; hunting, hiking, camping, cabins, picnicking, summer and winter sports areas, cross-country skiing, snowmobiling trails; digging for garnets; scenic drives. Contact the St. Marie's Ranger District, PO Box 407. Access from US 95 & I-90; other areas E on local roads. Phone 208/245-2531; or the Avery Ranger District, HC Box 1, Avery 83802, phone 208/245-4517; or the Supervisor, 1201 Ironwood Dr, Coeur d'Alene 83814, phone 208/765-7223. Other forests in the Panhandle are Coeur d'Alene (see COEUR D'ALENE) and Kankisu (see PRIEST LAKE AREA).

St. Joe Baldy Mountain. Lookout at top has view of Washington and Montana. 8 mi E on St. Joe River Rd (Forest Hwy 50).

St. Joe River. Called "the river through the lakes," one of the world's highest navigable rivers. Connects St. Marie's with Lake Coeur d'Alene. Just E on ID 5.

Annual Events

smART Festival. St. Marie's City Park. Paintings and crafts by local and regional artists. Food, entertainment, swimming. Phone 208/245-3417. Third wkend July.

Paul Bunyan Days. Incl parade, fireworks, logging events, water show, carnival. Labor Day wkend.

Stanley (F-3)

Pop 71 **Elev** 6,260 ft **Area code** 208
Zip 83278 **Web** www.stanleycc.org
Information Chamber of Commerce,
PO Box 8; 208/774-3411

Situated on the Salmon River (the
famous "river of no return"), Stanley
is located at the center of the Sawtooth Wilderness, Sawtooth Valley,
and scenic Stanley Basin. A Ranger
District office of the Sawtooth
National Forest (see BELLEVUE, BUR-
LEY) is located here.

What to See and Do

Salmon River. Rafting, kayaking, fishing; camping.

　River Expeditions. Many outfitters
　offer wilderness float trips on the
　Middle Fork of the Salmon River.
　Along the river are Native Ameri-
　can pictographs, caves, abandoned
　gold mines, and abundant wildlife.
　Activities incl boating, fishing, nat-
　ural hot water springs; hunting
　and photography. For a list of out-
　fitters contact the Chamber of
　Commerce or the Idaho Company
　Outfitters and Guides Assn. Phone
　208/774-3411.

Sawtooth National Recreation Area.
Fishing, boating, waterskiing; hiking,
biking, camping (fee). Many lakes are
here, including Stanley, Redfish, and
Alturas. Contact Area Ranger, Star
Rte, Ketchum 83340. (Also see SUN
VALLEY AREA) In Sawtooth National
Forest. Phone 208/727-5000. In
recreation area are

　Redfish Lake Visitor Center. Histor-
　ical, geological, naturalist displays
　and dioramas. Self-guiding trails.
　Campfire programs, guided tours.
　(Memorial Day-Labor Day, daily) 5
　mi S on ID 75, then 2 mi SW.
　FREE

　Sawtooth Wilderness. Many lakes;
　wilderness hiking, backpacking,
　and mountain climbing. 8 mi N,
　in Ketchum. Phone 208/726-7672.

Sawtooth Valley & Stanley Basin.
Fishing; cross-country skiing, snowmobiling, mountain biking, backpacking, hunting. Dude ranches
featuring pack trips; big game guides.
Contact Chamber of Commerce.

Annual Events

**Sawtooth Mountain Mamas Arts &
Crafts Fair.** Third wkend July.
Sawtooth Quilt Festival. Community
Bldg. Third wkend Sep.

Resort

★★ **MOUNTAIN VILLAGE LODGE.**
*Corner of Hwy 75 & 21 PO Box 150
(83278). 208/774-3661; fax 208/774-
3761; res 800/843-5475. Email
info@mountainvillage.com; www.
mountainvillage.com.* 58 rms, 2 story,
3 suites. June-Sep: S, D $74; each
addl $5; suites $109; under 10 free;
lower rates rest of yr. Crib avail. Pet
accepted, some restrictions, fee. Parking lot. TV; cable (premium), VCR
avail. Complimentary coffee in rms.
Restaurant 7 am-9 pm. Bar. Ck-out
11 am, ck-in 3 pm. Meeting rm. Business center. Coin lndry. Free airport
transportation. Hiking trail. Picnic
facilities. Cr cds: A, DS, MC, V.
🅳 ➥ 🐾 ⚡ 🎿 ✈ 🛏 🎱 🚶

Guest Ranch

★★ **IDAHO ROCKY MOUNTAIN
RANCH.** *HC 64 Box 9934 (83278),
approx 9 mi S. 208/774-3544; fax
208/774-3477. Email idrocky@ruralnet
work.net; www.idahorocky.com.* 4 rms.
S $162. Parking lot. Pool. TV; cable
(premium), VCR avail. Complimentary full bkfst. Ck-out 11 am, ck-in 3
pm. Business servs avail. Coin lndry.
Downhill skiing. Bike rentals. Hiking
trail. Cr cds: DS MC, V.
🐾 ⚡ 🎿 ♒ ✈

Sun Valley Area

(F-3)

Elev 5,920 ft **Area code** 208
Web www.visitsunvalley.com
Information Sun Valley/Ketchum
Chamber of Commerce, PO Box
2420, Sun Valley 83353; 208/726-
3423 or 800/634-3347

In a sun-drenched, bowl-shaped valley, this is one of the most famous
resorts in the world. Developed by
the Union Pacific Railroad, this area
was established after an extensive

survey of the West. Sheltered by surrounding ranges, it attracts both winter and summer visitors and offers nearly every imaginable recreational opportunity. Powder snow lasts until late spring, allowing long skiing seasons, and there is hunting, mountain biking, and superb fly fishing. Two Ranger District offices of the Sawtooth National Forest (see BELLE-VUE, BURLEY) are located in Ketchum.

What to See and Do

Sawtooth National Recreation Area. Fishing, boating, waterskiing; hiking, camping (fee). Many lakes are here, incl Stanley, Redfish, and Alturas. Contact Area Ranger, Star Rte, Ketchum 83340. (See also STANLEY) NW via ID 75, in Sawtooth National Forest. Phone 208/726-7672. In recreation area on ID 75 is

Headquarters Visitor Information Center. Orientation exhibits, maps, brochures, interpretive material. Evening programs (summer). Center (daily; schedule may vary). Phone 208/727-5013. **FREE**

Sun Valley Resort. Year-round activities. Sports director, supervised recreation for children; 3 outdoor pools, 2 glass-enclosed, lifeguard, sauna; massage, bowling, indoor and outdoor ice skating, movies, dancing; Sun Valley Center for the Arts and Humanities. Special activities. Contact Sun Valley Resort. 1 Sunvally Rd. Phone 208/622-4111 or 208/622-2231 (sports center).

Winter. Seventeen ski lifts to slopes for every level of skier; ski school, rentals. Longest run 3 mi; vertical drop 3,400 ft. Ice skating, sleigh rides, and groomed cross-country trails. (Thanksgiving-Apr, daily)

Summer. Three outdoor pools, fishing, boating, whitewater river raft trips; tennis (school), 18-hole Robert Trent Jones golf course (pro), Olympic ice show, skeet, and trap shooting, lawn games, horseback riding (school), mountain biking, hiking, pack trips, hay rides. Auto trips may be arranged to Redfish Lake near Stanley.

Annual Event

Wagon Days. Celebration of the area's mining history; large, non-motorized parade, band concerts, entertainment, arts and crafts fair, dramas. Labor Day wkend.

Motels/Motor Lodges

★ **AIRPORT INN.** *820 4th Ave S (83333), 8 blks S on ID 75, near Hailey Airport. 208/788-2477; fax 208/788-3195. Email bookings@miczon.net; www.taylorhotelgroup.com.* 30 rms, 1-2 story, 4 kits. S $58; D $66; each addl $8; suites $75; under 12 free. Crib free. TV; cable, VCR avail. Restaurant nearby. Ck-out 11 am. Coin lndry. Downhill ski 12 mi; x-country ski adj. Whirlpool. Some refrigerators, microwaves. Cr cds: A, C, D, DS, MC, V.

🐾 ➷ 🐾 SC

★★ **BEST WESTERN KENTWOOD LODGE.** *180 S Main St (83340). 208/726-4114; fax 208/726-2417; res 800/528-1234; toll-free 800/805-1001.* 57 rms, 3 story. Feb-mid-Apr, mid-June-mid-Sep, mid-Dec-early Jan: S, D $145; each addl $10; suites, kit. units $145; under 12 free; 2-day min some wkends, 3-day min some hols; lower rates rest of yr. Crib $5. TV; cable. Indoor pool; whirlpool. Restaurant adj 8 am-3 pm. Ck-out 11 am. Coin lndry. Meeting rm. Business servs avail. Valet serv. Exercise equipt. Refrigerators; microwaves avail. Some balconies. Totally non-smoking. Cr cds: A, DS, MC, V.

🏊 ✕ ➷ 🐾

★★ **BEST WESTERN TYROLEAN LODGE.** *260 Cottonwood Ave (83340), 1 mi N on ID 75, then W on River Run Rd; near base of Mt Baldy and River Run Ski Lift. 208/726-5336; fax 208/726-2081; toll-free 800/333-7912.* 56 rms, 3 story, 7 suites. No A/C. Mid-Dec-early Jan: S $85; D $90-$100; each addl $8; suites $125-$155; under 12 free; ski plan; lower rates rest of yr. Crib free. Pet accepted, some restrictions; fee. TV; cable. Pool; whirlpool. Complimentary continental bkfst. Restaurant nearby. Ck-out 11 am. Coin lndry. Meeting rms. Business servs avail. Downhill/x-country ski adj. Exercise equipt; sauna. Game rm. Microwaves avail. Cr cds: A, DS, MC, V.

★★ **HEIDELBERG INN.** *1908 Warm Springs Rd (83340), N on ID 75, then W on Warm Springs Rd.* 208/726-5361; fax 208/726-2084; toll-free 800/284-4863. 30 rms, 2 story, 14 kits. S $60-$85; D $65-$100; kit. units $60-$100; each addl $8. Crib free. Pet accepted; $5. TV; cable, VCR (movies $2). Heated pool; whirlpool. Complimentary continental bkfst, coffee in rms. Restaurant nearby. Ck-out 11 am. Coin lndry. Downhill ski 1 mi; x-country ski adj. Sauna. Refrigerators, microwaves; some fireplaces. Picnic tables, grills. Cr cds: A, C, D, DS, MC, V.

★ **TAMARACK LODGE.** *Sun Valley Rd and Walnut Ave (83353), 3 blks E of ID 75.* 208/726-3344; fax 208/726-3347; toll-free 800/521-5379. Email reservations@tamaracksunvalley.com; www.tamaracksunvalley.com. 21 rms, 3 story, 5 suites. Feb-Mar, June-Oct: S, D $96; each addl $10; suites $149; under 16 free; lower rates rest of yr. Crib avail. Pet accepted, some restrictions, fee. Parking lot. Indoor pool, whirlpool. TV; cable (premium). Complimentary coffee in rms, toll-free calls. Restaurant nearby. Business center. Dry cleaning. Exercise privileges. Golf. Tennis, 4 courts. Downhill skiing. Bike rentals. Hiking trail. Picnic facilities. Cr cds: A, C, D, DS, JCB, MC, V.

Resorts

★★★ **ELKHORN RESORT.** *1 Elkhorn Rd (83354).* 208/622-4511; fax 208/622-3261; toll-free 800/355-4676. Email elkhorn1@micron.net; www.elkhornresort.com. 125 rms, 4 story, 7 suites. Feb-Mar, June-Sep: S, D $128; each addl $10; suites $299; under 18 free; lower rates rest of yr. Crib avail, fee. Pet accepted, some restrictions, fee. Parking lot. Pool, children's pool, lifeguard, whirlpool. TV; cable, VCR avail. Complimentary coffee in rms, newspaper. Bar. Meeting rms. Business servs avail. Bellhops. Concierge. Dry cleaning. Gift shop. Free airport transportation.

Exercise rm, sauna. Golf, 18 holes. Tennis, 17 courts. Downhill skiing. Bike rentals. Supervised children's activities. Hiking trail. Picnic facilities. Cr cds: A, C, D, DS, MC, V.

★★★ **SUN VALLEY RESORT.** *1 Sun Valley Rd (83353).* 208/622-4111; fax 208/622-2030; res 800/786-8259. Email ski@sunvalley.com; www.sun valley.com. 520 rms, 4 story, 8 suites. Dec-Mar, June-Sep: S $159; D $229; each addl $15; suites $399; under 12 free; lower rates rest of yr. Crib avail. Valet parking avail. Pool, lap pool, children's pool, lifeguard, whirlpool. TV; cable (premium). Complimentary newspaper. Restaurant 7 am-11 pm (see GRETCHEN's). Bar. Ck-out 11 am, ck-in 4 pm. Conference center, meeting rms. Business center. Bellhops. Concierge. Dry cleaning, coin lndry. Gift shop. Salon/barber. Free airport transportation. Exercise equipt, sauna. Golf, 18 holes. Tennis, 18 courts. Downhill skiing. Bike rentals. Supervised children's activities. Hiking trail. Picnic facilities. Cr cds: A, D, DS, MC, V.

B&Bs/Small Inns

★★★ **IDAHO COUNTRY INN.** *134 Latigo Ln (83353), ½ mi N on ID 75 right on Saddle Rd, turn left on Valley-wood to Latigo Ln.* 208/727-4000; fax 208/726-5718; toll-free 800/635-4444. 11 rms, 6 A/C, 2 story. Jan-Mar and June-Sep: S, D $125-$185; higher rates wk of Dec 25; lower rates rest of yr. TV; cable. Complimentary full bkfst; afternoon refreshments. Restaurant nearby. Ck-out 11 am, ck-in 3 pm. Downhill/x-country ski ½ mi. Whirlpool. Refrigerators. Balconies. Library, warming rm; individually decorated rms. Stone fireplace. View of Bald Mountain. Totally nonsmoking. Cr cds: A, MC, V.

★★★ **THE RIVER STREET INN.** *100 River St W (83340).* 208/726-3611; fax 208/726-2439; res 208/726-3611; toll-free 888/746-3611. Email innkeeper@theriverstreetinn.com; www. theriverstreetinn.com. 8 rms, 2 story. Jan-Apr, June-July, Sep: S $165; D $175; each addl $25; lower rates rest of yr. Street parking. TV; cable, VCR avail. Complimentary full bkfst, coffee in rms, newspaper. Restaurant nearby. Ck-out 11 am, ck-in 2 pm. Meeting rm. Business servs avail. Concierge. Gift shop. Exercise privileges, whirlpool. Golf. Tennis, 10 courts. Downhill skiing. Bike rentals. Hiking trail. Picnic facilities. Cr cds: A, MC, V.

🄳 🗲 🐾 🎿 🛝 🚶 🎿 🛝 🛶

Restaurants

★★ **CHANDLER'S RESTAURANT.** *200 S Main St (83340). 208/726-1776. Email chandlers@sunvalley.com.* Specializes in fresh Hawaiian ahi, elk loin, Yankee pot roast. Hrs: 6-10 pm. Closed Dec 25. Res accepted. Wine, beer. Dinner $14-$29. Prix fixe: $16.95. Child's menu. 1940s home has antique furnishings, open beamed ceilings. Cr cds: A, DS, MC, V.

★★★ **EVERGREEN BISTRO.** *171 First Ave (83340). 208/726-3888.* Specializes in venison, rack of lamb, fresh fish. Hrs: 6:30-10 pm. Closed May, Nov. Res accepted. Wine cellar. Dinner $16.95-$30. In converted house; view of Mt Baldy. Cr cds: A, MC, V.
🄳

★★★ **GRETCHEN'S.** *1 Sun Valley Rd. 208/622-2144. Email svmktpr@sun valley.com; www.sunvalley.com.* Specializes in hazelnut-crusted elk loin, spicy farfalle pasta with roasted roma tomatoes, raspberry chocolate mousse. Own baking. Hrs: 7 am-9 pm. Res accepted. Bar. Bkfst $5-$8; lunch $6.25-$9.75; dinner $14.50-$22. Child's menu. Cozy, country-French atmosphere. Cr cds: A, D, DS, MC, V.
🄽

★★ **WARM SPRINGS RANCH RESTAURANT.** *1801 Warm Springs Rd (83340). 208/726-2609.* Specializes in scones, seafood, barbecued ribs. Hrs: 6-9 pm. Res accepted. Bar. Dinner $10.95-$20.95. Child's menu. Parking. Overlooks mountains and stocked, spring-fed ponds. Family-owned. Cr cds: A, MC, V.

Twin Falls

(H-3) *See also Buhl, Burley, Jerome, Shoshone*

Founded 1904 **Pop** 27,591
Elev 3,745 ft **Area code** 208
Zip 83301 **Web** www.cyberhighway. net/~tfidcham/

Information Chamber of Commerce, 858 Blue Lakes Blvd N; 208/733-3974 or 800/255-8946

After rising "like magic" on the tide of irrigation that reached this valley early in the century, Twin Falls has become the major city of south central Idaho's "Magic Valley" region. Seat of agriculturally rich Twin Falls County, it is also a tourist center, boasting that visitors in the area can enjoy almost every known sport. The headquarters and a Ranger District office of the Sawtooth National Forest (see BELLEVUE, BURLEY, STANLEY) are located here.

What to See and Do

Fishing. In Snake River and numerous other rivers and lakes. Sturgeon of up to 100 pounds may be caught, but by law cannot be removed from the water. Twin Falls Chamber of Commerce can provide detailed info.

Herrett Center. Exhibits on archaeology of North, Central, and South America; gallery of contemporary art; Faulkner Planetarium. (Tues-Sat; closed hols) 315 Falls Ave, on College of Southern Idaho campus. Phone 208/733-9554, ext 2655.

Perrine Memorial Bridge. Bridge, 486 ft high and 1,500 ft long, crosses the Snake River canyon. 1½ mi N on US 93.

Sawtooth Twin Falls Ranger District. Fishing; camping (fee at some designated campgrounds), picnicking, hiking trails, snowmobile trails, downhill and cross-country skiing. 9 mi E on US 30 to Hansen, then 28 mi S on local roads, in Sawtooth National Forest. Phone 208/737-3200.

✠ **Shoshone Falls.** "Niagara of the West" drops 212 ft (52 ft more than Niagara Falls). During irrigation season, the flow is limited; it is best during spring and fall. 5 mi NE, on

Snake River. Access to the falls is avail through

Shoshone Falls Park. Picnic tables, stoves, fireplace, trails, waterskiing. (Mar-Nov, daily) S bank of river. Phone 208/736-2265 or 208/736-2266. Per vehicle (mid-May-Aug) ¢

Twin Falls. 5½ mi NE. These 132-ft falls are accessible via

Twin Falls Park. Picnic area w/electric outlets, hot plates (free); boating (dock, ramp), fishing, waterskiing. (Daily) 3593 Twin Falls Grade. Phone 208/423-4223.

Annual Events

Western Days. Three-day event featuring shoot-out, barbecue contests, dances, parade. Dates may vary, phone 800/255-8946 for schedule; usually wkend following Memorial Day.

Twin Falls County Fair & Rodeo. County Fairgrounds, 6 mi W via US 30 in Filer. One wk starting Wed before Labor Day.

Motels/Motor Lodges

★★ **AMERITEL INN-TWIN FALLS.** *1377 Blue Lakes Blvd N (83301). 208/736-8000; fax 208/734-7777; res 800/600-6001. www.ameritelinns.com.* 118 rms, 3 story, 14 suites. S, D $100; each addl $8; suites $110; under 18 free. Crib avail. Parking lot. Indoor pool, whirlpool. TV; cable, VCR avail. Complimentary continental bkfst, coffee in rms, newspaper. Restaurant nearby. Ck-out noon, ck-in 3 pm. Meeting rm. Business center. Free airport transportation. Exercise equipt. Golf. Cr cds: A, D, DS, MC, V.

★★ **BEST WESTERN CANYON SPRINGS PARK HOTEL.** *1357 Blue Lakes Blvd N (83301). 208/734-5000; fax 208/734-5000; toll-free 800/528-1234.* 112 rms, 2 story. S $69.75; D $75.75; each addl $6; under 12 free. Crib free. TV; cable (premium). Heated pool. Restaurant 6 am-10 pm; Fri, Sat to 11 pm. Bar 4 pm-1 am. Ck-out 1 pm. Meeting rms. Bellhops. Valet serv. Free airport transportation. Exercise equipt. Balconies. Cr cds: A, C, D, DS, MC, V.

★★ **TWIN FALLS COMFORT INN.** *1893 Canyon Springs Rd (83301). 208/734-7494; fax 208/735-9428; res 800/228-5150.* 52 rms, 2 story, 15 suites. S $52.99; D $59.99; each addl $7; suites $67.99; under 18 free. Crib free. Pet accepted. TV; cable (premium). Indoor pool; whirlpool. Complimentary continental bkfst. Ck-out 11 am. Health club privileges. Cr cds: A, D, DS, MC, V.

Hotel

★★ **SHILO INN.** *1586 Blue Lakes Blvd N (83301). 208/733-7545; fax 208/736-2019; toll-free 800/222-2244. Email twinfalls@shiloinns.com; www.shiloinns.com.* 128 rms, 4 story. June-Aug: S, D $109; each addl $10; suites $139; under 12 free; lower rates rest of yr. Crib avail. Pet accepted, some restrictions, fee. Parking lot. Indoor pool, whirlpool. TV; cable (premium). Complimentary continental bkfst, coffee in rms, newspaper, toll-free calls. Restaurant nearby. Ck-out noon, ck-in 2 pm. Meeting rms. Fax servs avail. Coin lndry. Free airport transportation. Exercise equipt, sauna, steam rm. Golf. Hiking trail. Picnic facilities. Video games. Cr cds: A, C, D, DS, ER, JCB, MC, V.

Restaurant

★★ **JAKER'S.** *1598 Blue Lakes Blvd (83301). 208/733-8400.* Specializes in prime rib, pasta, seafood. Hrs: 11 am-10 pm; Fri, Sat to 11 pm; Sun to 9 pm. Closed hols. Res accepted. Bar. Lunch $2.95-$9.95; dinner $6.95-$29.95. Child's menu. Cr cds: A, D, DS, MC, V.

Wallace

(B-2) *See also Coeur d'Alene, Kellogg*

Founded 1884 **Pop** 1,010
Elev 2,744 ft **Area code** 208
Zip 83873

Information Chamber of Commerce, 10 River St, PO Box 1167; 208/753-7151

Gold was discovered in streams near here in 1882; lead, zinc, silver, and copper deposits were found in 1884. A Ranger District office of the Idaho Panhandle National Forests-Coeur d'Alene (see COEUR D'ALENE) is located in nearby Silverton.

What to See and Do

Auto tour. Fifteen-mi drive through spectacular scenery in Idaho Panhandle National Forests—Coeur d'Alene and St. Joe. Local roads follow Nine Mile Creek, Dobson Pass, and Two Mile Creek to Osburn. This trip may be extended by traveling N and E out of Dobson Pass along Beaver and Trail creeks to Murray, then W to Prichard; then follow Coeur d'Alene River W & S to Kingston; return to Wallace on US 10, I-90.

Lookout Pass Ski Area. Chairlift, rope tow; patrol, school, rentals; cafeteria, bar. Longest run 1 mi; vertical drop 850 ft. Half-day rate. (Mid-Nov-mid-Apr, Thurs-Sun) Cross-country skiing is also avail. Snowmobiling. 12 mi E on I-90, in Idaho Panhandle National Forests. Phone 208/744-1392. ¢¢¢¢

Northern Pacific Depot Railroad Museum. (1901) Houses artifacts, photographs, and memorabilia that portray railroad history of the Coeur d'Alene Mining District; display of railroad depot (ca 1910). (May-Oct, daily) 219 6th St. Phone 208/752-0111. ¢

Oasis Bordello Museum. Former bordello (ca 1895); moonshine still. (May-Oct, daily; closed hols) 605 Cedar St. Phone 208/753-0801. ¢¢¢

Sierra Silver Mine Tour. Offers 1¼-hr guided tour through depleted silver mine. Demonstrations of mining methods, techniques, and operation of modern-day equipment. Departs every 30 min. (May-mid-Sep, daily) 420 5th St. Phone 208/752-5151. ¢¢¢

Wallace District Mining Museum. Material on the history of mining, 20-min video, old mining machinery. Info on mine tours and old mining towns in the area. (May-Sep, daily; rest of yr, Mon-Sat) 509 Bank St. Phone 208/556-1592. ¢

Motel/Motor Lodge

★ **STARDUST MOTEL.** *410 Pine St (83873). 208/752-1213; fax 208/753-0981; toll-free 800/643-2386. Email rshaffer@midlink.com.* 42 rms, 22 A/C, 2 story. S $44.50; D $52.50; each addl $8; under 12 free. Crib $6. Pet accepted; $25 deposit. TV; cable (premium). Pool privileges. Restaurant nearby. Ck-out noon. Meeting rms. Airport transportation. Downhill ski 10 mi; x-country ski 11 mi. Cr cds: A, DS, MC, V.

⬛ 🔧🍴 🛒 ⛷ 🚶

Hotel

★★ **BEST WESTERN WALLACE INN.** *100 Front St (83873), I-90 Exit 61. 208/752-1252; fax 208/753-0981; res 800/523-1234; toll-free 800/643-2386. Email rshaffer@nidlink.com.* 63 rms, 2 story. S $70-$75; D $80-$85; each addl $8; suites $225-$250; under 12 free. Crib $8. TV; cable (premium), VCR avail. Indoor pool; whirlpool, poolside serv. Restaurant 7 am-9 pm. Bar. Ck-out noon. Meeting rms. Business servs avail. Gift shop. Bus depot transportation. Exercise equipt sauna. Refrigerator, minibar in suites. Cr cds: A, DS, MC, V.

⬛ 🔧🍴 🛒 🚶 🏃

Restaurant

★★ **JAMESON.** *304 6th St (83873). 208/556-1554.* Specializes in steak, pasta. Hrs: 11 am-9 pm; winter hrs vary. Closed Tues. Res accepted. Bar. Lunch, dinner $6-$18.95. Street parking. Old West atmosphere; saloon decor. In Jameson hotel. Cr cds: A, D, MC, V.

⬛ 🆂🅲

Weiser

(F-1) *See also Ontario, OR*

Founded 1888 **Pop** 4,571
Elev 2,117 ft **Area code** 208
Zip 83672

Information Chamber of Commerce, 8 E Idaho St; 208/549-0452 or 800/437-1280

Located at the confluence of the Weiser and Snake rivers, the town of Weiser (WEE-zer) is both a center for tourism for Hell's Canyon National Recreation Area to the north and a center for trade and transportation for the vast orchards, onion, wheat, and sugar beet fields of the fertile Weiser Valley to the east. Lumbering, mining, the manufacture of mobile homes, and the raising of cattle also contribute to the town's economy. A Ranger District office of the Payette National Forest (see McCALL) is located in Weiser.

What to See and Do

Fiddlers' Hall of Fame. Mementos of past fiddle contests, pictures of champion fiddlers, state winners; collection of old-time fiddles; state scrapbook on view. (Mon-Fri; also wkend during Fiddlers' Contest; closed hols) 10 E Idaho St. Phone 208/549-0452. **FREE**

Hell's Canyon National Recreation Area. Spanning the Idaho/Oregon border, this canyon, the deepest in North America, was created by the Snake River, which rushes nearly 8,000 feet below Seven Devils rim on the Idaho side. Three dams built by the Idaho Power Company have opened up areas that were once inaccessible and created man-made lakes that provide boating, fishing, and waterskiing. Whitewater rafting and jet boat tours are available below the dams, on the Snake River. Stretching north for 100 miles; access approx 55 mi NW via US 95 to Cambridge, then via ID 71. Also here are

   Brownlee Dam. The southernmost dam of the 3, at end of ID 71. This 395-ft rockfill dam creates Brownlee Lake, 57½ mi long, reaching to 10 mi N of Weiser. Woodhead Park, a short distance S, and McCormick Park, a short distance N, provide picnicking, boat ramps; tent and trailer sites, showers. ¢¢¢

   Oxbow Dam. This 205-ft-high barrier makes a 12½-mi-long reservoir. Copperfield Park, just below the dam on the Oregon side, has tent and trailer sites, showers, and day-use picnicking; 9 mi N of dam on

the Idaho side is Hell's Canyon Park, offering boat ramp; tent and trailer sites, showers, picnicking. 12½ mi N of Brownlee Dam. ¢¢¢

Hells Canyon Dam. This structure (330 ft high) creates another water recreation area. The improved Deep Creek trail, Idaho side, provides fishing and other recreational access to the Snake River below Hell's Canyon Dam. 23 mi N of Oxbow Dam.

Snake River Heritage Center. Artifacts and memorabilia portray the history of Snake River Valley. (By appt only) 2295 Paddock Ave, in Hooker Hall. Phone 208/549-0205. ¢

Trips into Hell's Canyon. Several companies offer river rafting, jet boat, and pack trips into and around Hell's Canyon National Recreation Area. For info on additional outfitters, contact the Chamber of Commerce.

   Hell's Canyon Adventures. Jet boat tours, rafting. Contact PO Box 159, Oxbow, OR 97840. Phone 503/785-3352 or 800/422-3568.

   Hughes River Expeditions. Outfitters for whitewater and fishing trips on backcountry rivers of Idaho and eastern Oregon, incl 3-, 4-, and 5-day trips on the Snake River through Hell's Canyon. (May-Oct, several dates) Advance res required. 26 mi N on US 95, at 95 First St in Cambridge. Phone 208/257-3477. ¢¢¢¢

Annual Event

National Oldtime Fiddlers' Contest. One of the oldest such contests in the country, attracting some of the nation's finest fiddlers. Also parade, barbecue, arts and crafts. Phone 800/437-1280. Mon-Sat, 3rd full wk June.

MONTANA

This magnificent state took its name from the Spanish *montaña* —meaning mountainous. The altitude of about half the state is more than 5,000 feet, and the sprawling ranges of the Continental Divide rise more than two miles into air so clear that photographers must use filters to avoid overexposure. The names of many towns, though, indicate that Montana has more than mountains. Grassrange, Roundup, and Buffalo tell of vast prairie regions, where tawny oceans of wheat stretch to the horizon and a cattle ranch may be 30 miles from front gate to front porch. Big Timber and Highwood suggest Montana's 22 million acres of forests; Goldcreek and Silver Gate speak of the roaring mining days (the roaring is mostly over, but you can still pan for gold in almost any stream); and Jim Bridger reminds us of the greatest mountain man of them all. Of special interest to the vacationing visitor are Antelope, Lame Deer, and Trout creeks, which indicate hunting and fishing *par excellence*.

Population: 799,065
Area: 145,392 square miles
Elevation: 1,800-12,799 feet
Peak: Granite Peak (Park County)
Entered Union: November 8, 1889 (41st state)
Capital: Helena
Motto: Oro y Plata ("Gold and Silver" in Spanish)
Nickname: The Treasure State, Big Sky Country
Flower: Bitterroot
Bird: Western Meadowlark
Tree: Ponderosa Pine
Fair: July 28-August 4, 2001, in Great Falls
Time Zone: Mountain
Website: www.visitmt.com or www.travel.state.mt.us

First glimpsed by French traders Louis and François Verendrye in 1743, Montana remained unexplored and largely unknown until Lewis and Clark crossed the region in 1805. Two years later, Manuel Lisa's trading post at the mouth of the Big Horn ushered in a half century of hunting and trapping.

The Treasure State's natural resources are enormous. Its hydroelectric potential is the greatest in the world—annual flow of the four major rivers is enough to cover the whole state with six inches of water. The 25 major dams include

Montana cowboy herds cattle

Fort Peck, one of the world's largest hydraulic earthfill dams. Near Great Falls, one of the world's largest freshwater springs pours out nearly 400 million gallons of water every day. In more than 1,500 lakes and 16,000 miles of fishing streams the water is so clear you may wonder if it's there at all.

For a hundred years the state has produced gold and silver, with Virginia City (complete with Robbers' Roost situated within convenient raiding distance) probably the most famous mining town. Montana produces about $1 billion worth of minerals a year. Leading resources are coal, copper, natural gas, silver, platinum, and palladium. Montana also produces more gem sapphires than any other state. Farms and ranches totaling 67 million acres add $2 billion a year to the state's economy.

Along with the bounty of its resources, Montana's history has given us Custer's Last Stand (June 25, 1876), the last spike in the Northern Pacific Railroad (September 8, 1883), the country's first Congresswoman (Jeannette Rankin of Missoula, in 1916), the Dempsey-Gibbons fight (July 4, 1923), and a state constitution originally prefaced by the Magna Carta, the Declaration of Independence, the Articles of Confederation, and the US Constitution.

If you come in winter, bring your mittens. Temperatures can drop below zero, but the climate is milder than perceived because of the state's location in the interior of the continent. Snowmobiling and downhill and cross-country skiing are popular sports here. Summer days are warm, dry, and sunny.

When to Go/Climate

Montana's weather is changeable and temperatures are cold for much longer than they are warm. To the east of the divide, weather is more extreme than in the west, due to winds blowing unhindered across the plains. There is heavy snowfall in the mountains and summer doesn't really begin until July. Summer is tourist season; early fall is less crowded and temperatures are still good for outdoor adventures.

AVERAGE HIGH/LOW TEMPERATURES (°F)

BILLINGS

Jan 32/14	May 67/43	Sep 72/47
Feb 39/19	June 78/58	Oct 61/38
Mar 46/25	July 87/58	Nov 45/26
Apr 57/34	Aug 85/57	Dec 34/17

MISSOULA

Jan 30/15	May 66/38	Sep 71/40
Feb 37/21	June 74/50	Oct 57/31
Mar 47/25	July 83/50	Nov 41/24
Apr 58/31	Aug 82/50	Dec 30/16

Parks and Recreation Finder

Directions to and information about the parks and recreation areas below are given under their respective town/city sections. Please refer to those sections for details.

NATIONAL PARK AND RECREATION AREAS

Key to abbreviations. I.H.S. = International Historic Site; I.P.M. = International Peace Memorial; N.B. = National Battlefield; N.B.P. = National Battlefield Park; N.B.C. = National Battlefield and Cemetery; N.C.A. = National Conservation Area; N.E.M. = National Expansion Memorial; N.F. = National Forest; N.G. = National Grassland; N.H.P. = National Historical Park; N.H.C. = National Heritage Corridor; N.H.S. = National Historic Site; N.L. = National Lakeshore; N.M. = National Monument; N.M.P. = National Military Park; N.Mem. = National Memorial; N.P. = National Park; N.Pres. = National Preserve;

CALENDAR HIGHLIGHTS

JANUARY

Montana Pro Rodeo Circuit Finals (Great Falls). Four Seasons Arena. Best riders in the state compete for a chance to reach the nationals. Phone 406/727-8115.

FEBRUARY

Chocolate Festival (Anaconda). Chocolate baking contest with winners sold at charity bake sale. Free chocolates at local merchants. Various "sweetheart" activities throughout town. Phone 406/563-2422.

JULY

Wild Horse Stampede (Wolf Point). One of Montana's best and oldest rodeos. Phone Chamber of Commerce & Agriculture, 406/653-2012.

State Fair (Great Falls). Fairgrounds. Rodeo, livestock exhibits, horse racing, petting zoo, commercial exhibits, entertainment, carnival. Phone 406/727-8900.

AUGUST

Western Montana Fair and Rodeo (Missoula). Fairgrounds. Live horse racing, 3-night rodeo, nightly fireworks. Carnival, livestock, commercial exhibits. Musical performance, demolition derby, blacksmith competition. Phone 406/721-FAIR.

Montana Cowboy Poetry Gathering (Lewistown). Modern-day cowboys and admirers of Western folklore relate life "down on the range" through original poetry. Phone 406/538-5436.

OCTOBER

Bridger Raptor Festival (Bozeman). Bridger Bowl ridge area. View birds of prey, incl the largest concentration of migrating Golden Eagles in the contiguous 48 states, on their trip south. Phone 406/585-1211.

N.R.A. = National Recreational Area; N.R.R. = National Recreational River; N.Riv. = National River; N.S. = National Seashore; N.S.R. = National Scenic Riverway; N.S.T. = National Scenic Trail; N.Sc. = National Scientific Reserve; N.V.M. = National Volcanic Monument.

Place Name	Listed Under
Bear's Paw Battleground	CHINOOK
Beaverhead N.F.	DILLON
Big Hole N.B.	same
Bitterroot N.F.	HAMILTON
Custer N.F.	HARDIN
Deerlodge N.F.	BUTTE
Flathead N.F.	KALISPELL
Fort Union Trading Post N.H.S.	SIDNEY
Gallatin N.F.	BOZEMAN
Glacier N.P.	same
Grant-Kohrs Ranch N.H.S.	DEER LODGE
Helena N.F.	HELENA
Kootenai N.F.	LIBBY
Lewis and Clark N.F.	GREAT FALLS
Little Bighorn Battlefield N.M.	same
Lolo N.F.	MISSOULA

The national forests of Montana are part of the more than 25,000,000 acres that make up the Northern Region of the Forest Service. The terrain runs from rugged mountains to rolling hills, from lodgepole pine and Douglas fir to grass. The highest point in the region is Granite Peak in the Beartooth Mountains, 12,799 feet. Recreation opportunities abound: hiking, rock hounding, fishing, boating, mountain camping, hunting, and horseback riding. For further information contact the Forest Service, Northern Region, Federal Bldg, PO Box 7669, Missoula 59807; 406/329-3511. For reporting forest fires, phone 406/329-3857.

STATE PARK AND RECREATION AREAS

Key to abbreviations. I.P. = Interstate Park; S.A.P. = State Archaeological Park; S.B. = State Beach; S.C.A. = State Conservation Area; S.C.P. = State Conservation Park; S.Cp. = State Campground; S.F. = State Forest; S.G. = State Garden; S.H.A. = State Historic Area; S.H.P. = State Historic Park; S.H.S. = State Historic Site; S.M.P. = State Marine Park; S.N.A. = State Natural Area; S.P. = State Park; S.P.C. = State Public Campground; S.R. = State Reserve; S.R.A. = State Recreation Area; S.Res. = State Reservoir; S.Res.P. = State Resort Park; S.R.P. = State Rustic Park.

Place Name	Listed Under
Bannack S.P.	DILLON
Canyon Ferry S.P.	HELENA
Deadman's Basin Fishing Access Site	HARLOWTON
Flathead Lake S.P. (Big Arm, Elmo, and Finley Point units)	POLSON
Flathead Lake S.P. (Wayfarers and Yellow Bay units)	BIGFORK
Fort Owen S.P.	HAMILTON
Giant Springs S.P.	GREAT FALLS
Hell Creek S.P.	GLASGOW
Lewis and Clark Caverns S.P.	THREE FORKS
Lost Creek S.P.	ANACONDA
Makoshika S.P.	GLENDIVE
Missouri River Headwaters S.P.	THREE FORKS
Painted Rocks S.P.	HAMILTON
Pictograph Cave S.P.	BILLINGS
Whitefish S.P.	WHITEFISH

Water-related activities, hiking, riding, various other sports, picnicking, and visitor centers, as well as camping, are available in many of these areas. Parks are open approx May-Sep. Day-use fee, $4 per vehicle, $1 per walk-in visitor. Camping (limited to 14 days), $7-$9/site/night. Additional fees may be charged at some areas for other activities. Pets on leash only. For information on state parks write Parks Division, Montana Dept of Fish, Wildlife, and Parks, 1420 E Sixth Ave, Helena 59620; 406/444-3750.

SKI AREAS

Place Name	Listed Under
Big Mt Ski and Summer Resort	WHITEFISH
Big Sky Ski and Summer Resort	BIG SKY
Bridger Bowl Ski Area	BOZEMAN
Discovery Basin Ski Area	ANACONDA
Lost Trail Powder Mt Ski Area	HAMILTON
Marshall Mt Ski Area	MISSOULA
Maverick Mt Ski Area	DILLON
Montana Snowbowl Ski Area	MISSOULA
Red Lodge Mountain Ski Area	RED LODGE
Showdown Ski Area	WHITE SULPHUR SPRINGS
Turner Mt Ski Area	LIBBY

FISHING AND HUNTING

Game fish incl all species of trout as well as salmon, whitefish, grayling, sauger, walleye, paddlefish, sturgeon, pike, burbot, channel catfish, and bass. Nonresident fishing license: annual, $45; 2-day consecutive license, $10; nonfee permit needed in Glacier or Yellowstone national parks.

Big game incl moose, elk, deer, antelope, bighorn sheep, mountain goat, mountain lion, and black bear; game birds incl both mountain and prairie species. Nonresident hunting license: game birds, $110; various types of elk and deer combination licenses are available. Licenses for moose, sheep, goat, antelope are awarded through special drawings. License for mountain lion must be purchased by August 31.

A $5 conservation license is a prerequisite to hunting or fishing license. For detailed info write Montana Fish, Wildlife, and Parks, 1420 E Sixth Ave, PO Box 200701, Helena 59620-0701; 406/444-2535 (general info) or 406/444-2950 (special licensing).

Driving Information

Safety belts are mandatory for all persons anywhere in vehicle. Children under 4 yrs or under 40 pounds in weight must be in an approved safety seat anywhere in vehicle. For information phone 406/444-3412.

INTERSTATE HIGHWAY SYSTEM

The following alphabetical listing of Montana towns in *Mobil Travel Guide* shows that these cities are within 10 miles of the indicated Interstate highways. A highway map, however, should be checked for the nearest exit.

Highway Number	Cities/Towns within 10 miles
Interstate 15	Butte, Dillon, Great Falls, Helena.
Interstate 90	Anaconda, Big Timber, Billings, Bozeman, Butte, Deer Lodge, Hardin, Livingston, Missoula, Three Forks.
Interstate 94	Billings, Glendive, Miles City.

Additional Visitor Information

Several pamphlets and brochures, which comprise a "Vacation Planning Guide," list points of interest, motels, campgrounds, museums, events, and attractions. They may be obtained from Travel Montana, 1424 9th Avenue, PO Box 200533, Helena, 59620-0533; 800/VISIT-MT.

Three periodicals are recommended to the Montana visitor. They are: *Montana: Magazine of Western History,* quarterly, Montana Historical Society, 225 N Roberts St, Helena 59601; *Montana Magazine Inc,* bimonthly, 3020 Bozeman, Helena 59624; and *Montana Outdoors,* bimonthly, Dept of Fish, Wildlife, and Parks, 1420 E Sixth Ave, PO Box 200701, Helena 59620-0701.

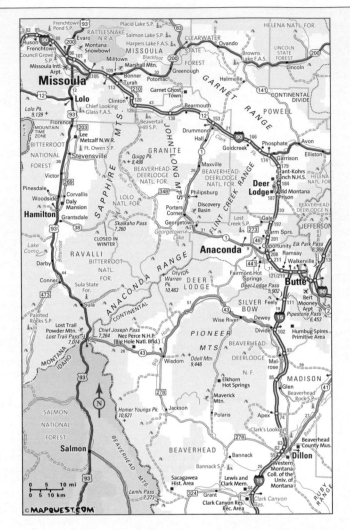

This route is a highly scenic alternative to freeway driving along I-15 and I-90. From Missoula, follow Highway 93 south along the Bitterroot River. At first, the valley is wide and filled with farms, then the mountains close in: the jagged Bitterroot Range rears to the west and the gentle Sapphire Range rises to the east. This is one of Montana's most scenic valleys, with some of its best fishing. Near Florence, visit the Daly Mansion, which was home to one of the super-rich Copper Kings in the 1880s. Just below the Continental Divide, stop at the Lost Trail Hot Springs. After climbing up to Lost Trail Pass, turn back toward Montana on Highway 43 and drop into the Big Hole National Battlefield where the Battle of the Big Hole, one of the West's most dramatic Army/Indian battles, was fought. Paths lead to the battle site where Chief Joseph and the Nez Perce defeated the US Army; there's also a good interpretive center. The little ranch town of Wisdom, with its excellent fine-art gallery, is the fishing capital of the Big Hole (the Big Hole River is a "blue ribbon" fishing river), a very broad prairielike valley filled with historic cattle ranches flanked by towering mountain ranges. Continue along Highway 278 through lovely high prairies, stopping by Bannack, the territorial capital of Montana and one of the best preserved ghost towns in the West (also a state park). Join I-15 at Dillon, a handsome Victorian town that is home to Montana's oldest college and much historic architecture. **(Approx 207 mi)**

Stanford is in the center of the Judith Basin, an area of high prairie ringed by low-slung mountain ranges. This was one of the centers of the old open-range cattle ranges, and cowboy artist Charlie Russell painted many of the unique, monumental buttes and mountains in the area. From the farm and ranch lands around Stanford, leave Highway 200 and cut north on Highway 80. The horizon is filled with odd blocklike buttes rising directly out of the plains. The largest is Square Butte, which from a distance looks like a completely square block of rock towering thousands of feet above the range. These odd formations are lava batholiths, which formed as subterranean lakes of molten rock that cooled and were later exposed by erosion. Square Butte is protected by the Bureau of Land Management, but anyone with a high clearance vehicle can climb up the side to a plateau 1,000 feet above the prairie for views that stretch hundreds of miles. The prairie ecosystem on the butte is considered pristine, an example of the flora that once greeted Lewis and Clark. Past Square Butte, the road dips into a vast abandoned river channel that once carried the Ice-Age Missouri River. As the route approaches the present-day river you can see glimpses of the famed White Cliffs of the Missouri, which so impressed Lewis and Clark. (This section of the Missouri is protected as a Wild and Scenic River and is otherwise essentially roadless.) The route drops onto the Missouri at Fort Benton, the upper terminus of the Missouri riverboat trade in the 1850s. Fort Benton is one of the oldest towns in the state and has several good museums and historic buildings. Here the route joins Highway 87. (Approx 48 mi)

Anaconda

(D-3) *See also Butte, Deer Lodge*

Founded 1883 **Pop** 10,278
Elev 5,265 ft **Area code** 406
Zip 59711
Information Chamber of Commerce,
306 E Park St; 406/563-2400

Chosen by Marcus Daly, a copper
king, as the site for a copper
smelter, the city was first dubbed
with the tongue-twisting name of
Copperopolis, but was later
renamed. In 1894, the "war of the
copper kings" was waged between
Daly and W. A. Clark over the location of the state capital. Clark's
Helena won by a small margin.
After his rival's death, the world's
largest copper smelter was built,
standing 585 feet 1½ inches.

What to See and Do

Anaconda's Old Works. Eighteen-
hole Jack Nicklaus signature golf
course located on developed grounds
of former copper smelters. Also features fully accessible trail that skirts
the foundations of the old works and
allows interpretation of town's smelting heritage (free). Clubhouse, dining
rm, pro shop. (Late May-Oct, daily,
weather permitting) 1205 Pizzini
Way. Phone 406/563-5989. ¢¢¢¢

Big Hole Basin. Fishing, raft races;
hunting, lodge, skiing. 25 mi SW on
MT 274.

Big Hole National Battlefield. (see)
22 mi SW on MT 274, then 40 mi
SW on MT 43.

**Copper Village Museum and Arts
Center.** Local and traveling art exhibitions; theater, music, films;
museum of local pioneer and industrial history. (Summer, daily; rest of
yr, Tues-Sat; closed hols) 401 E Commercial St. Phone 406/563-2422.
FREE

Georgetown Lake. Waterskiing, boating, fishing, swimming; camping,
picnicking, wilderness area, skiing,
snowmobiling. 15 mi W on Pintler
Scenic Route (MT 1).

Ghost towns & Sapphire mines. Near
Georgetown Lake on Pintler Scenic

Route (MT 1). Inquire at local chambers or visitor centers.

Lost Creek State Park. Lost Creek
Falls is the feature of a deep canyon
carved through mountains of limestone. Hiking, picnicking, grills, camping. Interpretive display. Standard fees.
1½ mi E on MT 1, then 2 mi N on MT
273, then 6 mi W on unnumbered
road. Phone 406/542-5500.

Skiing. Discovery Basin. Three double
chairlifts, 2 beginner lifts; patrol,
school, rentals, snowmaking; restaurant, bar. Longest run 2 mi; vertical
drop 1,480 ft. (Thanksgiving-Easter,
daily) Cross-country trail. 18 mi NW
on MT 1. Phone 406/563-2184. ¢¢¢¢

⚡ Visitor Center. Display of smelter
works photographs; outdoor railroad
exhibit; self-guided walking tours;
historic bus tours (Memorial Day-
Labor Day, daily); video presentation
(20 min) showing area attractions;
tourist info for both city and state.
(Summer, daily; rest of yr, Mon-Fri)
306 E Park St. Bus tours ¢¢

Annual Event

Wayne Estes Memorial Tournament.
One of the largest basketball tournaments in the NW. Slamdunk, 3-point
contest. Last wkend Mar.

Resort

★★ **FAIRMONT HOT SPRINGS
RESORT.** *1500 Fairmont Rd (59711),
4 mi S of I-90 Exit 211. 406/797-3241;
fax 406/797-3337; toll-free 800/332-
3272. Email fairmontmt@aol.com;
www.fairmontmontana.com.* 152 rms,
3 story. June-Sep: S, D $99-$109;
each addl $10; suites, kit. units $119-
$299; under 12 free; ski plan; lower
rates rest of yr. Crib free. TV; cable,
VCR avail (movies). 4 pools, 2
indoor; lifeguard. Restaurants 6:30
am-10 pm. Bar to 1:30 am; entertainment Tues-Sat. Ck-out 11 am. Ck-in
3 pm. Meeting rms. Business servs
avail. Gift shop. Airport transportation. Tennis. 18-hole golf, greens fee
$30, driving range. Bicycle rentals.
Exercise equipt. Massage. Game rm.
Lawn games. Hayrides. Private patios,
balconies. Cr cds: A, C, D, DS, MC, V.
🏊 🎿 🛎 ⛵ 🏃 🎣 ⛷ 🔥

Restaurant

★ ★ **BARCLAY II.** *1300 E Commercial (59711), 1 mi E on US 10A. 406/563-5541.* Specializes in tenderloin steak, halibut, breaded veal. Hrs: 5-10 pm; Sun 4-9:30 pm. Closed Mon; hols. Bar. Dinner complete meals: $9-$25. Cr cds: A, DS, MC, V. D

Bigfork

See also Kalispell, Polson

Pop 1,080 (est) **Elev** 2,968 ft
Area code 406 **Zip** 59911
Information Chamber of Commerce, PO Box 237; 406/837-5888

Surrounded by lakes, a river, and a dam, Bigfork's businesses are electric power and catering to tourists who visit the east shore of Flathead Lake (see POLSON). A Ranger District office of the Flathead National Forest (see KALISPELL) is located here.

What to See and Do

Bigfork Art & Cultural Center. Exhibits of artists and crafters of NW Montana; gift shop. (spring and fall, Wed-Sat; summer, Tues-Sat) 525 Electric Ave. Phone 406/837-6927. **FREE**

Flathead Lake Biological Station, University of Montana. Laboratories for teaching and research in natural sciences; museum; self-guided nature trips. (Mon-Fri; closed hols) MT 35, milepost 17½, midway between Bigfork and Polson. Phone 406/982-3301. **FREE**

Flathead Lake State Park. On Flathead Lake (see POLSON). At all units: swimming, fishing, boating (ramp); picnicking, camping (no hookups). Standard fees.

Wayfarers Unit. Hiking trails. Camping (dump station, patrons only). Off MT 35. Phone 406/837-4196 (summer) or 406/752-5501.

Yellow Bay Unit. Joint state/tribal fishing license required. No RVs or trailers permitted. 10 mi S on MT 35. Phone 406/752-5501.

Swan Lake. About 10 mi long. Swimming, waterskiing, fishing, boating. 14 mi SE on MT 83.

Annual Event

Wild West Day. Sep.

Seasonal Event

Bigfork Summer Playhouse. 526 Electric Ave. Broadway musicals. Mon-Sat nights. Phone 406/837-4886. May-late Aug.

Motels/Motor Lodges

★ **SWAN VALLEY SUPER 8 LODGE.** *Hwy 83, (59826), at mile marker 46.5. 406/754-2688; fax 406/754-2688; res 800/800-8000.* 22 rms, 2 story. No A/C. June-Sep: S $55.88; D $59.88-$65.88; each addl $2; under 18 free; lower rates rest of yr. Crib free. TV; cable. Complimentary coffee in lobby. Ck-out 11 am. Business servs avail. Some refrigerators. Cr cds: A, DS, MC, V.
D 🐕 ❄ 🐾 🔌 🏊

★ **TIMBERS.** *8540 Hwy 35 (59911), at jct MT 35 and 209. 406/837-6200; fax 406/837-6203; toll-free 800/821-4546. Email timbers@digisys.net; www.timbersmotel.com.* 40 rms, 2 story. June-Aug: S $68; D $78; lower rates rest of yr. Crib avail, fee. Pet accepted, fee. Parking lot. Pool, whirlpool. TV; cable (premium). Complimentary continental bkfst, coffee in rms. Restaurant. Business servs avail. Coin lndry. Exercise privileges, sauna. Golf. Tennis, 2 courts. Downhill skiing. Supervised children's activities. Picnic facilities. Cr cds: A, DS, MC, V.
D 🐕 🐾 🔌 ⛳ 🏊

Resort

★ ★ **MARINA CAY RESORT & CONFERENCE CENTER.** *180 Vista Ln (59911). 406/837-5861; fax 406/837-1118; res 800/433-6516. Email mcr@marinacay.com; www. marinacay.com.* 70 rms, 3 story, 30 suites. June-Sep: S, D $120; suites $180; under 10 free; lower rates rest of yr. Crib avail, fee. Parking lot. Pool, whirlpool. TV; cable, VCR avail. Complimentary coffee in rms, toll-free calls. Restaurant 11 am-2 pm.

Bar. Ck-out 11 am, ck-in 3 pm. Meeting rms. Business servs avail. Bellhops. Dry cleaning, coin lndry. Gift shop. Exercise privileges. Golf, 18 holes. Tennis, 4 courts. Downhill skiing. Hiking trail. Picnic facilities. Cr cds: A, D, DS, MC, V.

🄳 🛌 🐾 🎿 🚶 ⛵ ⛷ 🔥

B&Bs/Small Inns

★ **COYOTE ROADHOUSE INN.**
600 & 602 Three Eagle Ln (54521), 4 mi E on MT 209. 406/837-4250. Email coyote@cyberport.net; www.glacier country.com/coyote. 8 rms, 2 with shower only, 2 story. No A/C. No rm phones. June-Sep: S $75; D $75-$150; lower rates Apr-May, Oct. Closed rest of yr. Complimentary full bkfst. Ck-out 11 am, ck-in 3 pm. Many in-rm whirlpools. On Swan River. Many antiques. Totally nonsmoking. Cr cds: MC, V.

🄳 🛌 ⛵ 🔥

★★ **O'DUACHAIN COUNTRY INN.**
675 N Ferndale Dr (59911), 3½ mi E off MT 209. 406/837-6851; fax 413/451-0981; toll-free 800/837-7460. www.montanainn.com. 5 rms, 2 story, 1 suite. Apr-Oct: S, D $120; each addl $20; suites $195; lower rates rest of yr. Crib avail. Pet accepted, some restrictions, fee. Parking lot. TV; cable, VCR avail. Complimentary full bkfst. Restaurant nearby. Bar. Ck-out 11 am, ck-in 3 pm. Meeting rms. Fax servs avail. Sauna, whirlpool. Golf. Tennis, 6 courts. Downhill skiing. Hiking trail. Picnic facilities. Cr cds: A, DS, MC, V.

🄳 🐾 ⛵ 🎿 ⛷ 🚶 🔥

Guest Ranch

★★★★ **AVERILL'S FLATHEAD LAKE LODGE.** *150 Flathead Lake Lodge Rd (59911), ½ mi SW of MT 35. 406/837-4391; fax 406/837-6977. Email fll@digisys.net; www.averills.com.* This 2,000-acre Rocky Mountain ranch just south of Glacier National Park is family operated and provides a casual, down-to-earth vacation for guests of all ages. Rates include meals and various recreations, such as horseback riding, lake cruising, and trail hiking. Visitors can even learn the inner workings of an authentic dude ranch through roping cattle

and helping out around the corral. 19 rms in 2-story lodge, 22 cottages. No A/C. AP, mid-June-Sep, wkly: S, D $1,850; 13-19 yrs $1,380; 6-12 yrs $1,150; 3-5 yrs $840; under 3 yrs $96. Closed rest of yr. Crib free. Heated pool. Free supervised children's activities (June-Sep); ages 6-teens. Dining rm 8 am-6:30 pm. Patio barbecues. Ck-out 11 am, ck-in 1 pm. Grocery, package store 1 mi. Coin lndry. Business servs avail. Valet serv. Gift shop. Airport, railroad station transportation. Tennis. Private beach; boats, motors, canoes, sailboats, raft trips, waterskiing, instruction. Lake cruises. Fly-fishing instruction. Hiking. Whitewater rafting. Mountain bike rental. Soc dir. Indoor, outdoor games. Rec rm. Health club privileges. Many private patios, balconies. Picnic tables, grills. Cr cds: A, MC, V.

🄳 🛌 🏊 🎿 ⛵ ⛷ 🚶 🔥

Restaurants

★★ **BIGFORK INN.** *604 Electric Ave (59911), on grounds of Bigfork Inn Hotel. 406/837-6680.* Specializes in fresh seafood, chicken. Hrs: 5-10 pm. Closed Thanksgiving, Dec 25. Res accepted. Bar. Dinner $12-$18. Child's menu. Entertainment: Fri, Sat. Swiss chalet country inn. Cr cds: A, DS, MC, V.

🍽

★★★ **COYOTE RIVERHOUSE.** *600 Three Eagle Ln (59911), E on MT 209. 406/837-1233.* Specializes in Cajun stuffed breast of chicken, sauteed Provimi veal. Own desserts. Hrs: 5:30-8:30 pm. Closed Mon, Tues. Res accepted. Bar. Dinner $17-$20. Child's menu. Secluded country dining with view of Swan River; flower gardens. Cr cds: MC, V.

🄳

★★ **SHOWTHYME.** *548 Electric Ave (59911). 406/837-0707. www. showthyme.com.* Specializes in fresh seafood, duck, lamb. Hrs: 5-9:30 pm. Closed Dec 25. Dinner a la carte entrees: $12-$20. Child's menu. In old bank bldg (1910). Cr cds: A, DS, MC, V.

Big Hole National Battlefield

(10 mi W of Wisdom on MT 43 or 16 mi E of Lost Trail Pass on MT 43, off MT 93, near Idaho border.)

Fleeing the US Army from what is now Idaho and Oregon, five "nontreaty" bands of Nez Perce were attacked here before dawn by US troops and citizen volunteers on August 9, 1877. More than 655 acres of the battlefield are preserved today. The Nez Perce escaped, but were pursued by the army to what is now called Bear Paw Battleground (see CHINOOK), where Chief Joseph and the surviving Nez Perce surrendered after a six-day battle. Ironically, the tribe had previously been on good terms with the settlers until a treaty, forced on them in 1863, diminished the land originally granted to them in 1855. Those left out refused to recognize the 1863 treaty.

Three self-guided trails lead through the Siege Area, the Nez Perce Camp, and the Howitzer Capture Site. Wildlife roam the area; fishing is permitted with a license. Visitor Center Museum exhibits firearms and relics of the period (summer, daily; winter, Mon-Sat; closed Jan 1, Thanksgiving, Dec 25). Interpretive walks presented daily in summer. Some access roads are closed in winter. For further info contact PO Box 237, Wisdom 59761; 406/689-3155. Per vehicle (Memorial Day-Labor Day) ¢¢

Big Sky (Gallatin County)

See also Bozeman

Pop 450 (est) **Elev** 5,934 ft
Area code 406 **Zip** 59716
Web www.bigskyresort.com

Information Sky of Montana Resort, PO Box 160001; 406/995-5000 or 800/548-4486

Located 45 miles southwest of Bozeman in Gallatin National Forest, Big Sky is a resort community developed by the late newscaster and commentator, Chet Huntley. Golf, tennis, skiing, fishing, whitewater rafting, and horseback riding are among the many activities available in the area.

What to See and Do

Big Sky Ski and Summer Resort. Quad, 3 high-speed quads, 3 triple, 3 double chairlifts, 3 surface tows; patrol, school, rentals; bar, concession area, cafeteria, nursery. Longest run 3 mi; vertical drop 4,180 ft. (Mid-Nov-mid-Apr, daily) Fifty mi of cross-country trails. Gondola. Tram. Also summer activities. Phone 406/995-5000 or 800/548-4486. ¢¢¢¢

River trips. Yellowstone Raft Company. Half- and full-day whitewater raft trips on Gallatin and Madison rivers. No experience necessary. Paddle or oar powered rafts. Contact PO Box 160262. Phone 406/995-4613 or 800/348-4376. ¢¢¢¢

Motels/Motor Lodges

★★ **BEST WESTERN BUCKS T-4 LODGE.** *Hwy 191, 46625 Gallatin Rd (59716), 1½ mi S of US 191 Big Sky Exit. 406/995-4111; fax 406/995-2191; res 800/528-1234; toll-free 800/822-4484. Email buckst4@mcn.net; www.buckst4.com.* 72 rms, 3 story, 2 suites. Feb-Mar, July-Sep, Dec: S $139; D $154; each addl $10; suites $269; under 12 free; lower rates rest of yr. Crib avail, fee. Pet accepted, some restrictions, fee. Parking lot. TV; cable (premium), VCR avail. Complimentary continental bkfst, coffee in rms, newspaper, toll-free calls. Restaurant 5-9:30 pm. Bar. Ck-out 11 am, ck-in 4 pm. Meeting rms. Business center. Concierge. Coin lndry. Gift shop. Whirlpool. Golf, 18 holes. Tennis, 4 courts. Downhill skiing. Hiking trail. Cr cds: A, C, D, DS, ER, JCB, MC, V.

D ⊷ ⊠ ☾ ⛷ ⤢ ⊠ ⚒

★★ **COMFORT INN.** *47214 Gallatin Rd (59716). 406/995-2333; fax 406/995-2277; res 877/466-7222.* 61 rms,

3 story, 14 suites. No elvtr. June-mid-Sep: S, D $89-$150; each addl $10; suites $130-$240; under 18 free; ski plans; higher rates special events; lower rates rest of yr. Crib free. Pet accepted; $50 deposit. TV; cable (premium), VCR avail. Complimentary continental bkfst, coffee in rms. Restaurant nearby. Ck-out 11 am. Meeting rms. Business servs avail. Gift shop. Coin lndry. Downhill ski 10 mi; x-country ski 2 mi. Exercise equipt. Indoor pool; whirlpool, waterslide. Some refrigerators, microwaves. Cr cds: A, C, D, DS, JCB, MC, V.

★★ **RIVER ROCK LODGE.** *3080 Pine Dr (59716). 406/995-2295; fax 406/995-2727; toll-free 800/995-9966. www.montana.avicom.net/bigsky.* 29 rms, 2 story. Mid-Nov-mid-Apr: S $115; D $130; each addl $15; suite $230; under 12 free; lower rates rest of yr. Crib $15. TV; cable, VCR (movies). Restaurant nearby. Ck-out 10:30 am. Meeting rms. Business servs avail. Concierge. Sundries. Downhill/x-country ski 6 mi. Refrigerator. Totally nonsmoking. Cr cds: A, C, D, DS, MC, V.

Resort

★★★ **BIG SKY RESORT.** *1 Lone Mountain Trl (59716), 9 mi W of US 191. 406/995-5000; fax 406/995-5001; toll-free 800/548-4486. Email info@bigskyresort.com; www.bigsky resort.com.* 315 rms, 10 story, 95 suites. Feb-Mar, July-Aug: S, D $137-$186; each addl $22; ski plan; under 10 free; lower rates rest of yr. Crib avail. Valet parking avail. Pool, lap pool, whirlpool. TV; cable (premium), VCR avail. Complimentary full bkfst, coffee in rms, newspaper. Restaurant. Bar. Ck-out 10 am, ck-in 5 pm. Conference center, meeting rms. Business center. Bellhops. Concierge. Dry cleaning, coin lndry. Gift shop. Exercise rm, sauna. Golf, 18 holes. Tennis, 4 courts. Downhill skiing. Bike rentals. Supervised children's activities. Hiking trail. Picnic facilities. Cr cds: A, D, DS, MC, V.

B&B/Small Inn

★★ **RAINBOW RANCH.** *42950 Gallatin Rd (59716). 406/995-4132; fax 406/995-2861; res 800/937-4132. Email info@rainbowranch.com; www. rainbowranch.com.* 16 rms, 1 story. Jan, Mar, July-Sep: S, D $250; each addl $50; under 5 free; lower rates rest of yr. Crib avail. Pet accepted, some restrictions, fee. Parking lot. TV; cable (DSS), VCR avail. Complimentary continental bkfst, coffee in rms, newspaper, toll-free calls. Restaurant 6-10:30 pm. Bar. Ck-out 11 am, ck-in 3 pm. Meeting rm. Business servs avail. Concierge. Gift shop. Whirlpool. Golf, 18 holes. Tennis, 4 courts. Downhill skiing. Hiking trail. Cr cds: A, DS, MC, V.

Guest Ranches

★★★ **LONE MOUNTAIN.** *Lone Mountain Acess Rd (59716), 4½ mi W on US 191, then 1 mi N. 406/995-4644; fax 406/995-4670; toll-free 800/514-4644. Email lmr@lmranch.com; www.lmranch.com.* 30 cabins. No A/C. AP, Dec-Apr, June-Oct: S $2,200-$3,475/wk; D $3,200/wk; each addl $1,650/wk. Children age 2-3 addl $425/wk, age 4-5 addl $1150/wk. Closed rest of yr. Crib free. Whirlpool. Playground. Supervised children's activities (June-Labor Day). Restaurant (see LONE MOUNTAIN RANCH DINING ROOM). Bar 3:30 pm-midnight. Ck-out 11 am, ck-in 3 pm. Coin lndry. Meeting rms. Sundries. Gift shop. Free airport transportation. Downhill ski 6 mi; x-country ski on site. Ski rentals, lessons. Sleigh ride dinners. Massage. Soc dir; entertainment. Game rm. Fishing guides. Fireplaces. Private porches. Picnic tables, boxed lunches avail. Rustic setting. Totally nonsmoking. Cr cds: DS, MC, V.

★★ **NINE QUARTER CIRCLE RANCH INC.** *5000 Taylor Fork Rd (59730), 14 mi S to Taylor Fork, then 5 mi W. 406/995-4276. Email nineqtr circle@mcn.net; www.ninequartercircle. com.* 15 cabins (1-bedrm), 8 cabins (2-bedrm). No A/C. AP, mid-June-mid-Sep: S $1,162/wk; D $2,184/wk; family rates. Closed rest of yr. Crib free. Pool. Playground. Free supervised children's activities (mid-June-mid-Sep). Dining rm sittings: 7 am, noon, 6:30 pm. Ck-out varies, ck-in noon. Coin lndry. Meeting rms. Airport transportation. Lawn games.

Some fireplaces. 4,000-ft landing strip. Cr cds: A, DS, MC, V.

Restaurants

★ **CAFE EDELWEISS.** *Big Sky Spur Rd (59716). 406/995-4665. www. edelweiss@avicom.net.* Specializes in Wienerschnitzel, rack of lamb, chicken lienz. Hrs: 11 am-3 pm, 6-9:30 pm; winter hrs vary. Res accepted. Bar. Lunch $4.50-$8; dinner $14-$22. Child's menu. Original Austrian wood carvings. World Cup ski trophies on display. Cr cds: A, MC, V.

★★ **FIRST PLACE.** *Little Coyote Rd (59716), 1¾ mi W of US 191 Big Sky Exit. 406/995-4244.* Specializes in fresh fish, wild game. Hrs: 5-10 pm. Closed mid-Apr-May. Res accepted. Bar. Dinner $12.50-$22.75. Child's menu. Scenic mountain view. Cr cds: A, C, D, DS, ER, MC, V.

★★★ **LONE MOUNTAIN RANCH DINING ROOM.** *Lone Mountain Access Rd. 406/995-2782. Email lmr@ lmranch.com; www.lmranch.com.* Specializes in symphony of lamb, beef tenderloin tournedos. Hrs: 7-9 am, noon-2 pm, 6-8:30 pm. Closed Apr-mid-June, mid-Sep-Nov. Res accepted; required dinner. Bar. Bkfst buffet: $7.95; lunch buffet: $9.95; dinner prix fixe: $32. Western ranch atmosphere. Cr cds: DS, MC, V.

Big Timber

See also Bozeman, Livingston

Pop 1,557 **Elev** 4,081 ft
Area code 406 **Zip** 59011

Some of the tall cottonwoods that gave this settlement its name and the grasses that endowed the county with the name Sweet Grass remain. Livestock ranches make Big Timber their selling and shopping center. This is also a popular dude ranch area, with good hunting and fishing facilities. The Yellowstone and Boulder rivers provide good

trout fishing. The first dude ranch in the state was started here around 1911. Natural bridge and falls area is located approximately 25 miles south of town.

A Ranger District office of the Gallatin National Forest (see BOZEMAN) is located here.

Annual Event

NRA/MRA Rodeo. Phone 406/252-1122. Mid-May-mid-Sep.

Motel/Motor Lodge

★ **SUPER 8 MOTEL.** *Box 1441 (59011), I-90 Exit 367. 406/932-8888; fax 406/932-4103; res 800/800-8000.* June-Sep: S $70; D $75; each addl $5; suites $80; under 12 free; lower rates rest of yr. Crib avail. Parking lot. TV; cable. Complimentary continental bkfst, newspaper. Restaurant 6 am-9 pm. Ck-out 11 am, ck-in 2 pm. Business servs avail. Coin lndry. Gift shop. Golf, 9 holes. Cr cds: A, D, DS, MC, V.

Restaurant

★★ **THE GRAND.** *139 McLeod St (59011). 406/932-4459. www.the grand-hotel.com.* Specializes in pan-roasted salmon, rack of lamb, tenderloin. Hrs: 11 am-2 pm, 5-9 pm; Sun brunch 11 am-2 pm. Res accepted. Bar. Lunch $6-$9; dinner $9.90-$24. Sun brunch $8.95. Child's menu. 1890 hotel dining rm. Cr cds: DS, MC, V.

Billings

(D-6) *See also Hardin*

Founded 1882 **Pop** 81,151
Elev 3,124 ft **Area code** 406
Web www.travel.state.mt.us/ billingscvb

Information Billings Area Chamber of Commerce, 815 S 27th St, PO Box 31177, 59107; 406/252-4016 or 800/735-2635

On the west bank of the Yellowstone River, Billings, seat of Yellowstone County, was built by the Northern Pacific Railway and took the name of railroad President Frederick K. Billings. Today, it is the center of a vast trade region. Billings is a major distribution point for Montana's and Wyoming's vast strip-mining operations. Industries include agriculture, tourism, and oil trade. Billings offers excellent medical facilities and is a regional convention center. It is also the headquarters of the Custer National Forest (see HARDIN).

What to See and Do

Boothill Cemetery. Final resting place of Billings' gunmen and lawmen who died with their boots on. E end of Chief Black Otter Trail.

Chief Black Otter Trail. Drive above city, past Boothill Cemetery, up Kelly Mt, and down along edge of sheer cliff. Excellent view of Billings. Starts at E end of city.

Geyser Park. Eighteen-hole mini golf course; water bumper boats, Lazer-Tag, Go-Karts, and track; concessions. (May-Oct, daily; closed hols) 4910 Southgate Dr. Phone 406/254-2510. ¢¢¢

Moss Mansion. In 1901 architect H.J. Hardenbergh created the 3-story estate. Authentically furnished. (Daily) 914 Division St. Phone 406/256-5100. ¢¢¢

Peter Yegen, Jr—Yellowstone County Museum. Native American artifacts, antique steam locomotive, horse-drawn vehicles; dioramas depict homesteading days and Native American sacrificial ceremony; vast display of valuable guns, saddles, precious stones. Breathtaking view of Yellowstone Valley and the mountains. (Sun-Fri; closed hols) At Logan Field Airport, on MT 3. Phone 406/256-6811. **Donation**

Pictograph Cave State Park. Inhabited 4,500 yrs ago; pictographs on walls. Picnicking. (Mid-Apr-mid-Oct) I-90 at Lockwood Exit, 6 mi S on

county road. Phone 406/245-0227. Per vehicle ¢¢

Range Rider of the Yellowstone. Life-size bronze statue of cowboy and his mount; posed for by William S. Hart, an early silent film cowboy star. Near airport, off Chief Black Otter Trail.

Rocky Mountain College. (1878) 850 students. First college in Montana. Sandstone buildings are some of Billings's oldest permanent structures. 1511 Poly Dr. Phone 406/657-1000.

Western Heritage Center. Featuring rotating exhibits relating to the history of the Yellowstone Valley from prehistoric to modern times. (Tues-Sun; closed hols) 2822 Montana Ave. Phone 406/256-6809. **Donation**

Yellowstone Art Museum. Contemporary and historic art exhibitions, lectures, chamber concerts, films. (Tues-Sun; closed Jan) 401 N 27th St. Phone 406/256-6804. ¢¢

ZooMontana. The state's only wildlife park features homestead petting zoo. (Mid-Apr-mid-Oct, daily; rest of yr, wkends, weather permitting) 2100 S Shiloh Rd. Phone 406/652-8100. ¢¢

Annual Events

Peaks to Prairies Triathlon. Apr.

Montana Fair. MetraPark. Phone 406/256-2400. Mid-Aug.

Northern International Livestock Exposition. Oct.

Motels/Motor Lodges

★★ **BEST WESTERN BILLINGS.** *5610 S Frontage Rd (59101), I-90 Exit 446. 406/248-9800; fax 406/248-2500; res 800/WESTERN.* 80 rms, 3 story, 12 suites. June-Aug: S $54-$58; D $66-$76; each addl $5; suites $78-$110; under 18 free; lower rates rest of yr. Crib free. Pet accepted, some restrictions. TV; cable (premium). Indoor pool; whirlpool. Complimentary continental bkfst. Coffee in rms. Restaurant adj open 24 hrs. Ck-out noon. Coin lndry. Meeting rms. Business servs avail. Valet serv. Sauna. Some refrigerators; microwave avail in suites. Cr cds: A, C, D, DS, MC, V.

D ⊛ ⤢ ⤢ ⤢ ⤢ ⤢

★★ **BEST WESTERN PONDEROSA INN.** *2511 1st Ave N (59101), I-90*

Exit 27th St S, near Logan Field Airport. 406/259-5511; fax 406/245-8004; toll-free 800/528-1234. 130 rms, 2 story. S $50-$60; D $60-$70; each addl $5. Crib free. Pet accepted, some restrictions. TV; cable (premium). Pool. Complimentary coffee in rms. Restaurant open 24 hrs. Bar 3 pm-2 am; closed Sun. Ck-out 11 am. Coin lndry. Meeting rm. Business servs avail. Valet serv. Free airport transportation. Exercise equipt; sauna. Cr cds: A, C, D, DS, ER, JCB, MC, V.

⊛ ⤢ 🍴 ✈ ⤢ SC

★★ **THE BILLINGS INN.** *880 N 29th St (59101), I-90 Exit 27th St, then 2 mi N, near Logan Field Airport. 406/252-6800; fax 406/252-6800; res 800/231-7782. Email tbi@wtp.net.* 60 rms, 4 story. S $49; D $53; each addl $5; under 12 free. Crib $5. Pet accepted, some restrictions; $5. TV; cable. Complimentary continental bkfst. Ck-out 11 am. Coin lndry. Valet serv. Sundries. Airport transportation. Some refrigerators, microwaves. Cr cds: A, DS, MC, V.

⊛ ✈ ⤢

★★ **C'MON INN.** *2020 Overland Ave (59102). 406/655-1100; fax 406/652-7672; toll-free 800/655-1170.* 80 rms, 2 story, 8 suites. May-Aug: S $62.95; D $70.95-$79.95; each addl $6; suites $113; under 13 free; lower rates rest of yr. Crib free. TV; cable (premium). Indoor pool; wading pool, whirlpool. Complimentary continental bkfst. Restaurant nearby. Ck-out noon. Meeting rms. Business servs avail. Exercise equipt. Valet serv. Game rm. Minibars; refrigerator, microwave in suites. Cr cds: A, DS, MC, V.

D ⤢ 🍴 ⤢ ⤢ SC

★★ **COMFORT INN.** *2030 Overland Ave (59102). 406/652-5200; fax 406/652-5200; toll-free 800/228-5150.* 60 rms, 2 story. June-mid-Sep: S $69.95; D $79.95; each addl $5; suites $84-$90; under 18 free; lower rates rest of yr. Crib free. Pet accepted, some restrictions. TV; cable (premium). Indoor pool; whirlpool. Complimentary continental bkfst. Ck-out 11 am. Business servs avail. Game rm. Some refrigerators. Cr cds: A, C, D, DS, ER, JCB, MC, V.

D ⊛ ⤢ ⤢ ⤢ SC

★ **DAYS INN.** *843 Parkway Ln (59101). 406/252-4007; fax 406/896-1147; res 800/DAYSINN. www.daysinn. com.* 63 rms. S $65; D $55-$80; each addl $5; under 12 free. Crib free. Pet accepted, some restrictions. TV; cable, VCR avail (movies). Complimentary continental bkfst. Restaurant nearby. Ck-out noon. Coin lndry. Sundries. Whirlpool. Cr cds: A, C, D, DS, MC, V.

★★ **FAIRFIELD INN BY MAR-RIOTT.** *2026 Overland Ave (59102). 406/652-5330; fax 406/652-5330; res 800/228-2800.* 63 rms, 3 story. June-mid-Sep: S $62.95; D $72.95; each addl $5; under 18 free; lower rates rest of yr. Crib free. TV; cable (premium). Indoor pool; whirlpool. Complimentary continental bkfst. Restaurant nearby. Ck-out noon. Meeting rms. Business servs avail. Game rm. Some refrigerators. Cr cds: A, D, DS, MC, V.

★★ **HILLTOP INN.** *1116 N 28th St (59101). 406/245-5000; fax 406/245-7851; toll-free 800/878-9282. Email hilltop@wtp.net.* 47 rms, 4 story, 10 suites. S $55; D $59; each addl $5; suites $64. Crib avail, fee. TV; cable (premium). Restaurant nearby. Ck-out 11 am, ck-in 2 pm. Golf, 18 holes. Tennis, 8 courts. Cr cds: A, D, DS, MC, V.

★ **HOWARD JOHNSON EXPRESS INN.** *1001 S 27th St (59101). 406/248-4656; fax 406/248-7268; res 800/446-4656.* 173 rms, 3 story. June-Sep: S $68; D $72; each addl $4; under 18 free. Crib free. Pet accepted, some restrictions; deposit. TV; cable. Complimentary continental bkfst. Coffee in rms. Ck-out noon. Coin lndry. Meeting rms. Business servs avail. In-rm modem link. Free airport transportation. Cr cds: A, C, D, DS, MC, V.

★★ **RAMADA INN.** *1345 Mullowney Ln (59101), at jct I-90 and King Ave Exit. 406/252-2584; fax 406/252-2584; res 800/272-6232. www.ramada. com.* 115 rms, 2 story, 1 suite. June-Aug: S $65; D $75; each addl $5; suites $175; under 17 free; lower rates rest of yr. Crib avail. Pet

accepted, fee. Parking lot. Pool. TV; cable (premium). Complimentary continental bkfst, newspaper, toll-free calls. Fax servs avail. Dry cleaning, coin lndry. Exercise equipt. Golf. Downhill skiing. Cr cds: A, C, D, DS, ER, JCB, MC, V.

★ **SLEEP INN.** *4904 Southgate Dr (59101), at I-90 Exit 447. 406/254-0013; fax 406/254-9878; res 800/753-3746.* 75 rms, shower only, 2 story. S $51; D $58-$63; each addl $6; under 18 free. Crib free. TV; cable (premium). Complimentary continental bkfst. Restaurant nearby. Ck-out 11 am. Cr cds: A, DS, MC, V.

★ **SUPER 8 MOTEL.** *5400 Southgate Dr (59102), at I-90 Exit 446. 406/248-8842; fax 406/248-8842; toll-free 800/800-8000.* 114 rms, 2 story. S $54.88; D $62.88-$64.99; each addl $5; suites $72.11; under 12 free. Crib free. Pet accepted, some restrictions; $20. TV; cable (premium), VCR avail (movies). Restaurant nearby. Ck-out 11 am. Cr cds: A, C, D, DS, ER, JCB, MC, V.

Hotels

★★ **QUALITY INN.** *2036 Overland Ave (59102). 406/652-1320; fax 406/652-1320; toll-free 800/228-5151. Email brutger@aol.com; www.qualityinn.com/ hotel/mt015.* 119 rms, 2 story, 60 suites. May-Aug: S $62; D $89; each addl $5; suites $99; under 18 free; lower rates rest of yr. Crib avail. Pet accepted, some restrictions. Parking lot. Indoor pool. TV; cable (premium), VCR avail. Complimentary full bkfst, coffee in rms, newspaper, toll-free calls. Restaurant 6 am-9 pm. Ck-out noon, ck-in 3 pm. Meeting rms. Bellhops. Dry cleaning. Gift shop. Free airport transportation. Exercise privileges, sauna. Golf. Tennis, 24 courts. Downhill skiing. Picnic facilities. Cr cds: A, C, D, DS, ER, JCB, MC, V.

★★★ **RADISSON NORTHERN HOTEL.** *19 N 28th St (59101), Downtown. 406/245-5121; fax 406/259-9862; res 800/333-3333; toll-free 800/542-5121. Email radsales@wtp.net.* 160 rms, 10 story. S, D $79-$119; each addl $10; under 18 free. Crib free. Pet accepted, some restrictions. TV; cable (premium). Restaurant 6:30 am-10 pm. Bar 11-1 am. Ck-out noon, ck-in 3 pm. Meeting rms. Business servs avail. Gift shop. Free covered parking. Airport transportation. Exercise equipt. Some refrigerators. Cr cds: A, DS, MC, V.

[icons]

★★★ **SHERATON.** *27th St N 27 (59101), near Logan Field Airport. 406/252-7400; fax 406/252-2401; res 800/325-3535; toll-free 800/588-7666. Email sheraton2@mcn.net; www. sheraton.com\billings.* 272 rms, 23 story, 10 suites. S, D $99; each addl $10; suites $155; under 17 free. Crib avail. Pet accepted. Parking garage. Indoor pool, children's pool, whirlpool. TV; cable (DSS), CD avail. Complimentary coffee in rms, toll-free calls. Restaurant 6 am-10:30 pm. Bar. Ck-out noon, ck-in 3 pm. Conference center, meeting rms. Business center. Bellhops. Concierge. Dry cleaning. Gift shop. Salon/barber. Free airport transportation. Exercise privileges, sauna, steam rm. Golf, 18 holes. Tennis, 3 courts. Cr cds: A, C, D, DS, ER, JCB, MC, V.

[icons]

Conference Center

★★ **HOLIDAY INN GRAND MONTANA.** *5500 Midland Rd (59101). 406/248-7701; fax 406/248-8954; res 800/465-4983; toll-free 877/554-7263. Email hi429sales@sagehotel.com; www. holiday-inn.com/billings-west.* 289 rms, 7 story, 28 suites. June-Aug: S, D $99; each addl $10; suites $129; under 18 free; lower rates rest of yr. Crib avail, fee. Pet accepted, some restrictions, fee. Parking lot. Indoor pool, whirlpool. TV; cable (premium), VCR avail. Complimentary coffee in rms. Restaurant 6 am-9 pm. Bar. Ck-out noon, ck-in 4 pm. Conference center, meeting rms. Business center. Bellhops. Concierge. Dry cleaning. Gift shop. Free airport transportation. Exercise equipt, sauna, steam rm. Golf. Cr cds: A, C, D, DS, JCB, MC, V.

[icons]

Restaurants

★ **BRUNO'S ITALIAN SPECIALTIES.** *1002 N 1st Ave (59101). 406/248-4146.* Specializes in fresh pasta, pizza. Hrs: 11 am-10 pm; Sat from 5 pm. Closed Sun; hols. Res accepted. Bar. Lunch $4.95-$6.25; dinner $6.95-$12. Child's menu. Parking. Cozy atmosphere; many antiques. Cr cds: DS, MC, V.

[icon]

★★ **GEORGE HENRY'S.** *404 N 30th St (59101). 406/245-4570.* Specializes in chicken, steaks, seafood. Own soups, desserts. Hrs: 11 am-2 pm, 5:30-9 pm; Sat from 5:30 pm. Closed Sun; hols. Res accepted. Wine, beer. Lunch $5.75-$7.75; dinner $8.95-$18.95. Child's menu. Parking. Built 1882; former boardinghouse and tea rm; some original fixtures. Cr cds: A, DS, MC, V.

★★ **GREAT WALL.** *1309 Grand Ave (59102). 406/245-8601.* Specializes in marinated crisp duck, Taiwanese seafood in bird's nest, hot amazing chicken. Hrs: 11 am-9 pm; Fri, Sat to 10 pm. Closed Thanksgiving, Dec 25. Res accepted. Wine, beer. Lunch $5.25-$8.25. Buffet $6.25; dinner $5.75-$16.95. Child's menu. Parking. Cr cds: A, DS, MC, V.

[icon]

★★★ **JULIANO'S.** *2912 N 7th Ave (59101). 406/248-6400. Email shunzo@aol.com.* Specializes in peppered Montana ostrich, seared sesame-crusted (rare) tuna. Own baking. Hrs: 11:30 am-2 pm, 5:30-9 pm; Wed-Sat from 5:30 pm. Closed Sun; Thanksgiving, Dec 25. Res accepted. Bar. Wine list. Lunch $6.95-$7.95; dinner $13.95-$21.95. Parking. Converted Victorian home (1902); turn-of-the-century decor. Cr cds: A, C, D, DS, MC, V.

[icon]

★★ **MATTHEW'S TASTE OF ITALY.** *1233 N 27th (59101). 406/254-8530.* Specializes in scallopini di pollo, pasta con pollo al sugo bianco. Hrs: 11 am-10 pm; Sat from 4 pm; Sun 4-9 pm. Closed Thanksgiving, Dec 25. Res accepted. Bar. Lunch $5.95-$9.95; dinner $7.95-$16.95. Child's menu. Italian bistro decor. Cr cds: A, MC, V.

[icon]

★★ **REX.** *2401 Montana Ave (59101). 406/245-7477. Email chef@imt.net.* Specializes in hand-cut steak, prime rib, fresh seafood. Hrs: 11:30 am-10:30 pm. Closed Thanksgiving, Dec 25. Res accepted. Bar.

Lunch $8.95-$12.95; dinner $12.95-$27.95. In National Historic District. Cr cds: A, D, DS, MC, V.

★★★ **WALKER'S GRILL.** *301 N 27th St (59101). 406/245-9291. www.walkersgrill.com.* Specializes in dry-aged beef, fresh fish, pasta. Hrs: 11 am-1:30 pm, 5:30-10 pm; Sat from 5:30 pm. Closed Sun; hols. Res accepted. Bar. Lunch $7.95-$12.95; dinner $12.95-$19.95. Child's menu. Entertainment. Parking. Bistro atmosphere. Cr cds: A, DS, MC, V.

Bozeman

(D-4) *See also Livingston, Three Forks, White Sulphur Springs*

Settled 1864 **Pop** 22,660 **Elev** 4,810 ft
Area code 406
Web www.bozemanchamber.com
Information Chamber of Commerce, 2000 Commerce Way, 59718; 406/586-5421 or 800/228-4224

Blazing a trail from Wyoming, John M. Bozeman led a train of immigrants who settled here and named the town for their leader. The first settlements in the Gallatin Valley were agricultural, but were economically surpassed by the mines nearby. Today, small grain farming, livestock, dairying, tourism, and the state university are important sources of income. The city is the marketplace for the cattle-producing Gallatin Valley.

What to See and Do

Bridger Bowl Ski Area. Quad, 5 double chairlifts; ski school, patrol, rentals; lodge, cafeteria, bar. Longest run 2½ mi; vertical drop 2,000 ft. (Mid-Dec-Apr, daily) 16 mi NE via MT 86, in Gallatin National Forest. Phone 406/587-2111 or 800/223-9609. ¢¢¢¢

Gallatin National Forest. Has 1,735,412 acres. Mountain peaks, pine and fir forest, winter sports, pack trips, picnicking, camping, fishing, hunting; 574,788-acre Absaroka-Beartooth Wilderness S of

Livingston, 253,000-acre Lee Metcalf Wilderness, Gallatin Gateway to Yellowstone. Forest rangers provide interpretive programs in summer at the Madison River Canyon Earthquake Area (see WEST YELLOWSTONE); exhibits. For info contact Supervisor, 10 E Babcock St, PO Box 130, 59771. N & S of town. Phone 406/587-6701. A Ranger District office is located here.

Montana State University. (1893) 11,000 students. 11th Ave, College St, 7th Ave, and Lincoln St, at S edge of town. On campus is

Museum of the Rockies. Pioneer, Native American exhibits; dinosaurs; art and science displays. Taylor Planetarium. (Daily; closed hols) 600 W Kagy Blvd. Phone 406/994-2251. ¢¢

Annual Events

Montana Winter Fair. Second wk Feb.

Gallatin County Fair. Third wkend July.

Sweet Pea Festival. First full wkend Aug.

Bridger Raptor Festival. Bridger Bowl ridge area. View birds of prey, incl the largest concentration of migrating Golden Eagles in the contiguous 48 states, on their trip S. Usually first 2 wks Oct.

Motels/Motor Lodges

★★ **COMFORT INN.** *1370 N 7th Ave (59715), I-90 Exit 306. 406/587-2322; fax 406/587-2423; res 800/228-5150; toll-free 800/587-3833. Email info@comfortinnbozeman.com; www.comfortinnbozeman.com.* 87 rms, 3 story. June-Sep: S $69; D $73-$83; each addl $4; suites $79-$100; under 18 free; lower rates rest of yr. Crib $4. Pet accepted, some restrictions. TV; cable. Indoor pool; whirlpool. Complimentary continental bkfst. Coffee in rms. Restaurant opp 6:30 am-11 pm. Ck-out 11 am. Coin lndry. Meeting rm. Business center. Exercise equipt; sauna. Cr cds: A, DS, MC, V.

★★ **FAIRFIELD INN.** *826 Wheat Dr (59715), I-90 7th Ave Exit. 406/587-2222; fax 406/587-2222; toll-free 800/228-2800.* 57 rms, 3 story. June-Aug: S $79; D $84-$89; each addl $5;

suites $94-$99; under 18 free; lower rates rest of yr. Crib free. TV; cable (premium). Indoor pool; whirlpool. Complimentary continental bkfst. Restaurant opp open 24 hrs. Ck-out noon. Business servs avail. Valet serv. Sundries. Downhill/x-country ski 16 mi. Game rm. Refrigerator, microwave in suites. Cr cds: A, C, D, DS, MC, V.

★★ **HAMPTON INN.** *75 Baxter Ln (59718). 406/522-8000; fax 406/522-7446.* 70 rms, 2 story. June-mid-Sep: S, D $81; under 18 free; lower rates rest of yr. Crib free. TV; cable (premium). Complimentary continental bkfst, coffee in rms. Restaurant adj 6:30 am-10 pm. Ck-out 11 am. Meet-

Where the deer and the antelope play

ing rms. Business servs avail. Bellhops. Coin lndry. Free airport transportation. Downhill/x-country ski 16 mi. Exercise equipt. Indoor pool; whirlpool. Cr cds: A, D, DS, MC, V.

★★ **HOLIDAY INN EXPRESS.** *6261 Jackrabbit Ln (59714), 8 mi W. 406/388-0800; fax 406/388-0804; res 800/HOLIDAY; toll-free 800/542-6791.* 67 rms, 3 story. June-Aug: S, D $59.95-$69.95; under 12 free; lower rates rest of yr. Crib free. Pet accepted. TV; cable (premium). Complimentary coffee in lobby. Restaurant adj open 24 hrs. Ck-out 11 am.

Exercise equipt. Cr cds: A, C, D, DS, JCB, MC, V.

★★ **RAMADA INN.** *2020 Wheat Dr (59715). 406/585-2626; fax 406/585-2727.* 50 rms, shower only, 2 story. June-Aug: S $79; D $99-$109; suites $119-$139; lower rates rest of yr. Crib free. Pet accepted. TV; cable (premium). Indoor pool; whirlpool, waterslide. Complimentary continental bkfst. Restaurant nearby. Ck-out noon. Valet serv. Downhill/x-country ski 16 mi. Cr cds: A, D, DS, MC, V.

★ **ROYAL 7.** *310 N 7th Ave (59715), on Business Loop from I-90, Exit 306W. 406/587-3103; toll-free 800/587-3103. Email royal7inn@cs.com; www.av-com.net/royal7.* 47 rms, 1 story. May-Sep: S $42; D $49; lower rates rest of yr. Crib avail, fee. Pet accepted, some restrictions. Parking lot. TV; cable. Restaurant 7 am-10 pm. Ck-out noon, ck-in 2 pm. Downhill skiing. Picnic facilities. Cr cds: A, D, DS, MC, V.

★ **SLEEP INN.** *817 Wheat Dr (59715). 406/585-7888; fax 406/585-8842; res 800/221-2222; toll-free 800/377-8240. Email bozemansleepinn@aol.com; www.sleepinn.com\hotel\mt410.* 50 rms, 2 story, 6 suites. June-Aug: S $79; D $89; suites $99; lower rates rest of yr. Crib avail. Pet accepted. Parking lot. Indoor pool, whirlpool. TV; cable (premium), VCR avail. Complimentary continental bkfst, coffee in rms, newspaper, toll free calls. Restaurant. Ck-out 11 am, ck-in 3 pm. Business servs avail. Dry cleaning, coin lndry. Exercise privileges, sauna. Golf. Tennis, 10 courts. Downhill skiing. Hiking trail. Cr cds: A, C, D, DS, ER, JCB, MC, V.

★ **TLC INN.** *805 Wheat Dr (59715), I-90 7th Ave Exit. 406/587-2100; fax 406/587-4941; toll-free 877/466-7852. Email info@tlc-inn.com; www.tlc-inn. com.* 40 rms, 3 story, 2 suites. June-Sep: S $58; D $66; each addl $5; suites $70; under 18 free; lower rates rest of yr. Crib avail. Pet accepted, fee. Parking lot. TV; cable. Complimentary continental bkfst, coffee in rms, toll-free calls. Restaurant 6 am-midnight. Ck-out 11 am, ck-in 3 pm. Fax servs avail. Sauna, whirlpool. Golf. Downhill skiing. Cr cds: A, C, D, DS, JCB, MC, V.

ᗪ ➔ 🏋 🧍 ⛷ 🔥

Hotels

★★ **BEST WESTERN GRANTREE INN.** *1325 N 7th Ave (59715). 406/587-5261; fax 406/587-9437; res 800/528-1234; toll-free 800/624-5865. Email grantree@grantreeinn.com; www. bestwestern.com/grantreeinn.* 97 rms, 2 story, 6 suites. May-Sep: S, D $105; each addl $4; suites $115; under 17 free; lower rates rest of yr. Crib avail. Pet accepted, some restrictions. Parking lot. Indoor pool, whirlpool. TV; cable (premium). Complimentary coffee in rms, toll-free calls. Restaurant 6 am-9 pm. Bar. Ck-out 11 am, ck-in 3 pm. Meeting rms. Business center. Bellhops. Concierge. Dry cleaning, coin lndry. Gift shop. Free airport transportation. Exercise privileges. Golf, 18 holes. Tennis, 10 courts. Downhill skiing. Hiking trail. Video games. Cr cds: A, C, D, DS, ER, JCB, MC, V.

ᗪ ➔ 🏌 🏋 🛏 ⛷ 🔥 SC

★★ **BOZEMAN'S WESTERN HERITAGE INN.** *1200 E Main St (59715). 406/586-8534; fax 406/587-8729; toll-free 800/877-1094. Email western@ avicom.net; www.avicom.net/western heritage.* 35 rms, 3 story, 3 suites. June-Aug: S $63; D $73; each addl $5; suites $125; under 16 free; lower rates rest of yr. Crib avail, fee. Pet accepted, some restrictions, fee. Parking lot. TV; cable (premium), VCR avail. Complimentary continental bkfst. Restaurant. Ck-out 11 am, ck-in 2 pm. Meeting rm. Business center. Coin lndry. Gift shop. Exercise equipt, steam rm, whirlpool. Golf, 18 holes. Tennis, 12 courts. Downhill

skiing. Picnic facilities. Cr cds: A, C, D, DS, MC, V.

🏊 ➔ 🏋 🏌 🧍 ⛷ 🔥 SC 🏌

★ **DAYS INN.** *1321 N 7th Ave (59715). 406/587-5251; fax 406/587-5351; res 800/329-7466. Email 6765@ hotel.cendant.com; www.the.daysinn. com/bozeman06765.* 79 rms, 2 story. S $60-$88; D $80-$95; suites $90-$100; each addl $5; under 12 free. Crib free. Pet accepted; $25 deposit. TV; cable (premium), VCR avail (movies). Complimentary full bkfst. Restaurant adj 6 am-10 pm. Ck-out noon. Business servs avail. Downhill/x-country ski 17 mi. Whirlpool, sauna. Cr cds: A, DS, MC, V.

ᗪ ➔ 🏊 🔥

★★ **HOLIDAY INN.** *5 Baxter Ln (59715), 1½ mi NW on N 7th St, S of I-90, N 7th Ave Exit. 406/587-4561; fax 406/587-4413; toll-free 800/366-5101. www.bznholinn.com.* 179 rms, 2 story, 1 suite. June-Sep: S, D $109; each addl $10; suites $179; lower rates rest of yr. Crib avail. Pet accepted, fee. Parking lot. Indoor pool, whirlpool. TV; cable (premium). Complimentary coffee in rms, toll-free calls. Restaurant 5:30 am-10 pm. Bar. Ck-out 11 am, ck-in 4 pm. Meeting rms. Business servs avail. Bellhops. Dry cleaning, coin lndry. Free airport transportation. Exercise equipt. Golf, 18 holes. Tennis, 2 courts. Downhill skiing. Video games. Cr cds: A, DS, MC, V.

ᗪ ➔ 🐾 🏌 ⛷ 🏋 🧍 ⛷ 🛏 🔥 SC

B&Bs/Small Inns

★★★ **FOX HOLLOW BED & BREAKFAST.** *545 Mary Rd (59718). 406/582-8440; fax 406/582-9752; toll-free 800/431-5010. Email foxhollow@ bozeman-mt.com; www.bozeman-mt. com.* 3 rms, 2 story, 2 suites. S, D $95; each addl $15; suites $128; under 12 free. Parking lot. TV; cable, VCR avail. Complimentary full bkfst, coffee in rms, newspaper. Ck-out 11 am, ck-in 4 pm. Meeting rm. Business servs avail. Concierge. Whirlpool. Golf. Tennis. Downhill skiing. Picnic facilities. Cr cds: A, D, DS, MC, V.

➔ 🏌 🧍 🔥

★★★ **GALLATIN GATEWAY.** *76405 Gallatin Rd (US 191) (59715). 406/763-4672; fax 406/763-4672; toll-*

free 800/676-3522. Email gatewayinn@ gallatingatewayinn.com; www.gallatin gatewayinn.com. 30 rms, 2 story, 4 suites. July-Sep: S $105; D $120; each addl $15; suites $160; under 17 free; lower rates rest of yr. Crib avail, fee. Parking lot. Pool, whirlpool. TV; cable, VCR avail. Complimentary continental bkfst, coffee in rms. Restaurant. Bar. Ck-out 11 am, ck-in 4 pm. Meeting rms. Business center. Dry cleaning, coin lndry. Golf, 18 holes. Tennis, 3 courts. Downhill skiing. Bike rentals. Picnic facilities. Cr cds: A, DS, MC, V.

★★ **SILVER FOREST.** *15325 Bridger Canyon Rd (59715). 406/586-1882; fax 406/582-0492; toll-free 888/835-5970. www.silverforestinn.com.* 6 rms, some share bath, 5 with shower only. No A/C. No rm phones. S, D $90-$125; each addl $10; under 12 free; package plans. Crib free. TV; cable (premium), VCR avail (movies). Ck-out noon, ck-in 4-6 pm. Luggage handling. Guest lndry. Downhill/x-country ski ¼ mi. Built in 1931; rustic decor. Totally nonsmoking. Cr cds: A, MC, V.

★★ **TORCH & TOES BED & BREAKFAST.** *309 S 3rd Ave (59715). 406/586-7285; fax 406/585-2749; toll-free 800/446-2138.* 4 rms in 2 bldgs, 2 story. No A/C. No rm phones. S, D $70-$90; each addl $10; under 5 free; wkly rates. Crib free. TV in sitting rm. Complimentary full bkfst. Restaurant nearby. Ck-out 11 am, ck-in 4-6 pm. Colonial Revival-style house (1906); large front porch with swing; antiques, library. Totally nonsmoking. Cr cds: MC, V.

★★ **VOSS INN.** *319 S Willson Ave (59715). 406/587-0982; fax 406/585-2964. Email vossinn@imt.net.* 6 rms, 2 A/C, 2 story. S $75-$85; D $85-$95; each addl $10. TV in sitting rm. Complimentary full bkfst; afternoon refreshments. Ck-out noon, ck-in 2 pm. Downhill/x-country ski 16 mi. Built 1883; Victorian decor, antiques; brass and iron beds. Totally nonsmoking. Cr cds: A, DS, MC, V.

Restaurants

★★ **BOODLES.** *215 E Main St (59715). 406/587-2901.* Specializes in fish, steaks. Hrs: 11:30 am-2 pm, 5:30-9:30 pm; Sun from 5:30 pm. Closed Thanksgiving, Dec 25. Res accepted. Bar. Lunch $6-$9; dinner $13-$27. Entertainment: jazz Fri, Sat. Street parking. In 1880s saloon bldg; old English club decor. Cr cds: A, DS, MC, V.

★★★ **GALLATIN GATEWAY INN.** *76405 Gallatin Rd. 406/763-4672. Email gatewayinn@gallatingatewayinn. com; www.gallatingatewayinn.com.* Specializes in pasta, fresh seafood, wild game. Hrs: 6-9:30 pm. Res accepted. Bar. Wine list. Dinner $13.50-$25. Child's menu. Spanish decor. Cr cds: A, DS, MC, V.

★★ **JOHN BOZEMAN BISTRO.** *125 W Main St (59715). 406/587-4100.* Specializes in fresh seafood, Montana steaks, fresh sushi. Hrs: 11:30 am-2:30 pm, 5-10 pm. Closed Sun, Mon. Res accepted. Wine, beer. Lunch $4.95-$8.95; dinner $13.95-$24.95. Child's menu. Parking. Eclectic decor; original art. Cr cds: A, D, DS, MC, V.

★★ **SPANISH PEAKS BREWERY.** *120 N 19th St (59715). 406/585-2296. Email chug@spanishpeaks.com; www.spanishpeaks.com.* Specializes in homemade pasta, wood-fired pizza. Hrs: 11:30 am-10:30 pm; Sun noon-10 pm. Res accepted. Bar. Lunch $5.95-$8.95; dinner $7.95-$18.95. Parking. Contemporary decor. Beer brewed on site. Cr cds: MC, V.

Unrated Dining Spots

LEAF & BEAN COFFEE HOUSE. *35 W Main St (59715). 406/587-1580.* Specializes in selection of specialty coffees, teas, and desserts. Hrs: 6:30-10 pm; Fri, Sat to 11 pm. Closed Thanksgiving, Dec 25. Entertainment: Fri, Sat. Cr cds: MC, V.

MACKENZIE RIVER PIZZA. *232 E Main St (59715). 406/587-0055.* Spe-

cialies in gourmet pizza. Hrs: 11:30 am-10 pm; Sun from 5 pm. Closed hols. Lunch $4.95-$16.75; dinner $4.95-$16.75. Cr cds: A, DS, MC, V.
⟦D⟧

Browning

(A-3) *See also East Glacier Area under Glacier National Park*

Pop 1,170 **Elev** 4,362 ft
Area code 406 **Zip** 59417

Eastern gateway to Glacier National Park (see), Browning is the capital of the Blackfeet Nation. The town was named for a US Commissioner of Indian Affairs. The reservation itself covers 2,348,000 acres.

What to See and Do

Museum of Montana Wildlife and Hall of Bronze. Miniature dioramas, mounted specimens; paintings, sculpture. (May-Sep, daily) Just E of Museum of the Plains Indian on US 2, 89. Phone 406/338-5425. ¢

Museum of the Plains Indian. Collection of Blackfeet and Northern Plains Native American tribal artifacts plus history of tribes of the northern Great Plains. Administered by Dept of Interior, Indian Arts and Crafts Board. (June-Sep, daily; rest of yr, Mon-Fri; closed Jan 1, Thanksgiving, Dec 25) W at jct US 2, 89; 13 mi from Glacier National Park. Phone 406/338-2230. June-Sep ¢¢ Rest of yr **FREE**

Annual Event

North American Native American Days Powwow. Blackfeet Reservation. Phone 406/338-7276. Mid-July.

Butte

(D-3) *See also Anaconda, Three Forks*

Settled 1864 **Pop** 33,336 **Elev** 5,549 ft
Area code 406 **Zip** 59701
Web www.butteinfo.org
Information Butte-Silver Bow Chamber of Commerce, 1000 George St; 800/735-6814

Settled more than 100 years ago, Butte, atop the "richest hill on earth," harvests treasures of copper along with by-product gold, silver, and other metals from 1,000 acres of mines. Although mined for more than a century, this treasure chest seems to be inexhaustible. Butte's famous old properties continue to produce high-grade ores. Modern mining techniques have exposed vast new low-grade mineral resources.

Butte was born as a bonanza silver camp. When the silver ores became lower grade at comparatively shallow depths, copper ores were discovered. Although development of the copper mines was a slow process, culminating in the "war of the copper kings," fortunes

The one that got away

were made and lost and battles were fought in court for control of ore on surface and underground.

The brawny, colorful mining-camp days of Butte are over. Although copper mining still plays an important role in the Butte economy, it is also a retailing, distribution, and diversified industrial center. A Ranger District office of the Deerlodge National Forest is located here.

What to See and Do

Arts Chateau. (1898) Originally home of Charles Clark, now a heritage museum and arts center. Stairway leads from 1st floor galleries to 4th floor ballroom. Stained-glass windows, intricate moldings. (Tues-Sat) 321 W Broadway. Phone 406/723-7600. ¢¢

Berkeley Pit. Located just outside of downtown Butte, the former open-pit copper mine is over 1,800 ft deep and more than 1 mi across. When filled, it is Montana's deepest, and most toxic, body of water. Can be seen from viewing stand (March-Nov). 200 Shields St. Phone 406/723-3177.

Copper King Mansion. (ca 1888) Restored 32-rm home of Senator W.A. Clark, prominent political figure of Montana's early mining days; of particular interest are frescoed ceilings and walls, stained-glass windows, 9 hand-carved fireplaces, antique pipe organ; silver and crystal collections. (May-Sep, daily) 219 W Granite St. Phone 406/782-7580. ¢¢

Deerlodge National Forest. A 1,176,452-acre forest that incl 158,516-acre Anaconda-Pintler Wilderness, alpine lakes, ghost towns. Fishing, hunting; bridle trails, winter sports, picknicking, camping. Contact Forest Supervisor, 400 N Main St, PO Box 400. Sections surround town, reached by I-90, I-15, MT 2, MT 1 (Pintler scenic route). Phone 406/496-3400.

Dumas Brothel Museum. Listed on the National Register of Historic Places, museum is one of the few remaining bldgs in the West purposely built as a brothel. Various brothel-related exhibits. Gift shop. Not recommended for children. Tours (Memorial Day-Labor Day,

daily; rest of yr by appt) 45 E Mercury St. Phone 406/723-6128. ¢¢

Montana Tech of the University of Montana. (1893) 1,900 students. Mineral energy-oriented college near mining operations. On W Park St. Phone 406/496-4266. On campus is

> **Mineral Museum.** Mineral display; some fossils; specimens from collection of 15,100 rotate periodically; special fluorescent and Montana minerals. Guided tours. (Mon-Fri; also by appt; closed hols) Phone 406/496-4414. **FREE**

Old No. 1. Tour of city aboard replica of early-day streetcar departs from Chamber of Commerce office. (June-Labor Day, Mon-Fri; closed July 4) Phone 800/735-6814. ¢¢

Our Lady of the Rockies. Ninety-ft likeness of Mary, Mother of Jesus, sits atop Continental Divide overlooking town. Trips to mountaintop avail in summer. Phone 406/494-2656 for res (fee) or 406/782-1221 (info).

World Museum of Mining and 1899 Mining Camp. Outdoor and indoor displays of mining mementos; turn-of-the-century mining camp, Hell Roarin' Gulch. Picnic area. (Memorial Day-Labor Day, daily; rest of yr, limited hours) W Park St. Phone 406/723-7211. ¢

Annual Event

Vigilante Rodeo. July.

Motels/Motor Lodges

★★ **HOLIDAY INN EXPRESS-PARKSIDE.** *1 Holiday Park (59701). 406/494-6999; fax 406/494-1300; res 800/465-4329. Email BTMEX@MON-TANA.COM.* 83 rms, 5 story, 17 suites. June-Sep: S, D $72; suites $85-$99; under 18 free; lower rates rest of yr. Crib free. TV; cable (premium). Complimentary continental bkfst. Restaurant adj open 24 hrs. Ck-out noon. Meeting rms. Business center. Coin lndry. Free airport transportation. Exercise equipt. Bathrm phones; refrigerator in suites. Cr cds: A, DS, MC, V.

★★ **RAMADA INN.** *4655 Harrison Ave (59701), S of I-90, Harrison Ave Exit, near Bert Mooney Airport. 406/494-6666; fax 406/494-3274; res*

800/2RAMADA; toll-free 800/332-8600. 146 rms, 2 story. S, D $88-$98; each addl $10; suites $165; under 18 free. Crib free. Pet accepted. TV; cable. Indoor pool. Coffee in rms. Restaurants 6 am-9 pm. Bar 11-2 am; entertainment Fri, Sat. Ck-out noon. Coin lndry. Meeting rms. Business servs avail. Bellhops. Free airport transportation. Indoor tennis. Exercise equipt; sauna. Private patios. Cr cds: A, C, D, DS, MC, V.

★ **SUPER 8 MOTEL.** 2929 Harrison Ave (59701). 406/494-6000; fax 406/494-6000; toll-free 800/800-8000. 104 rms, 3 story. No elvtr. Mid-May-mid-Sep: S $52.88; D $56.88-$60.88; each addl $4; suites $70.88; under 12 free; lower rates rest of yr. Crib free. TV; cable, VCR avail (movies). Complimentary continental bkfst. Restaurant opp 6 am-11 pm. Ck-out 11 am. Cr cds: A, C, D, DS, MC, V.

Hotels

★★ **COMFORT INN OF BUTTE.** 2777 Harrison Ave (59701), near Bert Mooney Airport. 406/494-8850; fax 406/494-2801; res 800/442-4667. www.townpump.com. 137 rms, 3 story, 9 suites. May-Sep: S $75; D $80; each addl $5; suites $140; under 18 free; lower rates rest of yr. Crib avail. Pet accepted, some restrictions, fee. Parking lot. Indoor pool, whirlpool. TV; cable (premium), VCR avail. Complimentary continental bkfst. Restaurant nearby. Ck-out 11 am, ck-in 4 pm. Meeting rms. Business servs avail. Bellhops. Dry cleaning, coin lndry. Gift shop. Free airport transportation. Exercise equipt, sauna. Golf, 18 holes. Downhill skiing. Cr cds: A, C, D, DS, ER, JCB, MC.

★ **DAYS INN.** 2700 Harrison Ave (59701). 406/494-7000; fax 406/494-7000; toll-free 800/329-7466. 74 rms, 3 story, 2 suites. May-Sep: S $72; D $89; each addl $8; suites $200; under 11 free; lower rates rest of yr. Crib avail. Pet accepted, some restrictions. Parking lot. Indoor pool, lap pool, whirlpool. TV; cable, VCR avail. Complimentary continental bkfst, coffee in rms, toll-free calls. Restaurant. 24-hr rm serv. Ck-out 11 am, ck-in 3 pm. Meeting rms. Business

servs avail. Dry cleaning, coin lndry. Gift shop. Free airport transportation. Exercise equipt. Golf, 18 holes. Tennis, 6 courts. Downhill skiing. Hiking trail. Picnic facilities. Cr cds: A, C, D, DS, ER, JCB, MC, V.

Restaurants

★★★ **LYDIA'S.** 4915 Harrison Ave (59701), 3 blks S of airport turnoff. 406/494-2000. Specializes in tenderloin steaks, homemade ravioli, seafood. Hrs: 5:30-11 pm. Closed Sat, Sun; hols. Dinner complete meals: $9.25-$18.50. Child's menu. Victorian decor; stained-glass windows. Family-owned. Cr cds: A, D, DS, MC, V.

★★ **SPAGHETTINI'S.** 804 Utah Ave (59701). 406/782-8855. Specializes in seafood, chicken, fresh pasta. Hrs: 11 am-2:30 pm, 5:30-9:30 pm. Closed hols. Res accepted. Wine, beer. Lunch $4-$5; dinner $7-$16. Former 1890s warehouse with Italian decor. Cr cds: A, C, D, DS, MC, V.

★★★ **UPTOWN CAFE.** 47 E Broadway (59701). 406/723-4735. Email uptown@montana.com; www.montana.com/uptown. Specializes in beef, fresh seafood. Own desserts. Hrs: 11 am-2 pm, 5-10 pm; early-bird dinner 5-6:30 pm. Closed hols. Res accepted. Lunch buffet: $5; dinner complete meals: $8.95-$29. Monthly art display. Cr cds: A, DS, MC, V.

Chinook

(A-5) See also Havre

Pop 1,512 **Elev** 2,438 ft
Area code 406 **Zip** 59523
Information Chamber of Commerce, PO Box 744; 406/357-2100

Gas wells, farming, and grazing are the main concerns of this town, which takes its name from the much-desired January and February winds that melt the snow, exposing grass for cattle.

What to See and Do

Bear's Paw Battleground. Scene of final battle and surrender of Chief Joseph of the Nez Perce following trek N from the Big Hole River, ending Montana's Native American wars in 1877. It was here that Chief Joseph spoke the eloquent words "From where the sun now stands, I will fight no more forever." This is the newest addition to the Nez Perce National Historic Park system. Picnicking. (See BIG HOLE NATIONAL BATTLEFIELD) 16 mi S on MT Sec 240.

Blaine County Museum. Local historical exhibits. (June-Aug, Tues-Sat, Sun afternoons; rest of yr, Mon-Fri) 501 Indiana. Phone 406/357-2590. **FREE**

Annual Event

Blaine County Fair. July.

Motel/Motor Lodge

★ **BEAR PAW COURT.** *114 Montana St (59523). 406/357-2221; toll-free 888/357-2224.* 16 rms, 1 story. S $41; D $47. TV; cable. Complimentary coffee in rms, toll-free calls. Restaurant nearby. Cr cds: A, DS, MC, V.
✈ ⊷ 🐾

Columbia Falls

(A-2) *See also Kalispell, Whitefish*

Pop 2,942 **Elev** 3,087 ft
Area code 406 **Zip** 59912
Web www.fcvb.org
Information Flathead Convention & Visitor Bureau, 15 Depot Park, Kalispell, 55901; 406/756-9091 or 800/543-3105

A gateway to Glacier National Park (see), and the north fork of the Flathead River, this is an area of superb hunting and fishing. Here also is the *Hungry Horse News*, Montana's only Pulitzer Prize-winning newspaper.

What to See and Do

Big Sky Water Slide. Nine water slides, inner tube river run, hot tubs. Picnicking, concessions. (Memorial Day-Labor Day, daily) Jct US 2, MT 206; 1 mi SE via US 2. Phone 406/892-5025. ¢¢¢

Glacier Maze. A 2-level, 3-dimensional maze with passages more than 1 mi long; also 18-hole miniature golf course. Picknicking, concessions. (May-Labor Day, daily) 10 mi NE on US 2E. Phone 406/387-5902. ¢¢

Hungry Horse Dam and Power Plant. One of world's largest concrete dams (564 ft), set in a wooded canyon near Glacier National Park. The 2,115-ft-long crest is crossed by a 30-ft-wide roadway. The reservoir is approximately 34 mi long and 3½ mi at its widest point. Self-guided tours, pictorial and interactive displays; video (mid-May-late Sep, daily). Several recreation and camping sites of the Flathead National Forest (see KALISPELL) are on the reservoir. US 2 E 6 mi. **FREE**

Annual Event

Heritage Days. July.

Resort

★★★ **MEADOW LAKE.** *100 St. Andrews Dr (59912). 406/892-8700; fax 406/892-0330; toll-free 800/321-4653. Email vacation@meadowlake.com; www.meadowlake.com.* 24 rms, 3 story, 16 suites. July-Aug: D $139; each addl $15; suites $175; under 16 free; lower rates rest of yr. Crib avail. Pet accepted, some restrictions, fee. Parking garage. Indoor/outdoor pools, children's pool, whirlpool. TV; cable (premium), VCR avail, CD avail. Complimentary coffee in rms, toll-free calls. Restaurant 7 am-10 pm. Bar. Ck-out 10 am, ck-in 4 pm. Meeting rm. Business servs avail. Concierge. Dry cleaning, coin lndry. Gift shop. Free airport transportation. Exercise equipt, sauna. Golf, 18 holes. Tennis. Downhill skiing. Bike rentals. Supervised children's activities. Hiking trail. Picnic facilities. Cr cds: A, D, DS, MC, V.
🄳 🦮 🍸 ⛷ 📶 🎿 🏌 ⛺ 🚶 🎿 🚵 🐾

B&Bs/Small Inns

★★★ **BAD ROCK COUNTRY BED & BREAKFAST.** *480 Bad Rock Dr (59912), 2½ mi S of MT 206. 406/892-2829; fax 406/892-2930; toll-free 888/892-2829. Email stay@badrock.com; www.badrock.com.* 7 rms, 2 story. June-Sep: D $169; lower rates rest of yr. Street parking. TV; cable (premium), VCR avail, CD avail. Complimentary full bkfst, newspaper. Restaurant nearby. Bar. Ck-out 11 am, ck-in 3 pm. Business center. Concierge. Free airport transportation. Golf. Downhill skiing. Hiking trail. Cr cds: A, C, D, DS, MC, V.

★★ **MOUNTAIN TIMBERS LODGE.** *5385 Rabe Rd (59936), 10 mi N on MT 486 to Blankenship Rd, turn E and continue for 2 mi to "Y" intersection, then S 1 mi. 406/387-5830; fax 406/387-5835; toll-free 800/841-3835. Email mtntmbrs@digisys.net.* 6 rms, 3 story. June-Sep: S $55; D $85; suites $125; lower rates rest of yr. Parking lot. TV; cable (premium), VCR avail, CD avail, VCR avail. Complimentary full bkfst. Ck-out 11 am, ck-in 4 pm. Meeting rm. Business center. Whirlpool. Golf, 18 holes. Downhill skiing. Hiking trail. Picnic facilities. Cr cds: A, MC, V.

★★ **PLUM CREEK HOUSE.** *985 Vans Ave (59912). 406/892-1816; fax 406/892-1876; toll-free 800/682-1429. Email plumcreek@in-tch.com, www.wtp.net/go/plumcreek.* 6 rms, 2 with shower only. No A/C. June-mid-Sep: S $95-$105; D $105-$115; each addl $15; under 12 free; wkly rates; lower rates rest of yr. Children over 8 yrs only. TV; cable, VCR (free movies). Pool; whirlpool. Complimentary full bkfst, coffee in rms. Ck-out 11 am, ck-in 3 pm. On bluff overlooking Flathead River. Built 1957 as home for timber mill owner; many antiques. Totally nonsmoking. Cr cds: A, C, D, DS, MC, V.

Cooke City

See also Red Lodge; Cody, WY

Settled 1873 **Pop** 100 (est)
Elev 7,651 ft **Area code** 406
Zip 59020
Information Chamber of Commerce, PO Box 1071; 406/838-2272

Once the center of a gold rush area in which $1 million was panned from the rushing streams, Cooke City today is busy serving tourists on their way to Yellowstone National Park (see WYOMING). Available locally are jeep, horse, and snowmobile trips.

What to See and Do

Grasshopper Glacier. One of the largest icefields in US; so named because of the millions of grasshoppers frozen in its 80-ft ice cliff. Accessible only by trail, the last 2 mi reached only by foot; be prepared for adverse weather. Grasshoppers are visible only during brief time periods; glacial ice must be exposed by snow melt, which generally does not occur until mid-Aug, while new snow begins to accumulate late Aug. 14 mi NE on mountain trail in the Absaroka-Beartooth Wilderness, Custer National Forest (see HARDIN).

Motels/Motor Lodges

★ **HIGH COUNTRY MOTEL.** *113 Main (59020). 406/838-2272.* 15 rms, 1-2 story, 4 kits. No A/C. S $40; D $40-$58; each addl $5; kit. units $52-$65. Crib $2. Pet accepted. TV. Restaurant nearby. Ck-out 10 am. X-country ski 1 mi. Some refrigerators. Cabins avail. Cr cds: A, D, DS, MC, V.

★ **HOOSIER'S MOTEL & BAR.** *Corner Hwy 212 & Huston N (59020). 406/838-2241.* 12 rms, 2 story. June-Oct: S, D $60; each addl $5; lower rates rest of yr. Parking lot. TV; cable (DSS). Restaurant nearby. Bar. Ck-out 10 am, ck-in 2 pm. Hiking trail. Cr cds: DS, MC, V.

Restaurant

★ **LOG CABIN CAFE.** *US 212 (59081), 3 mi W on US 212. 406/838-2367. Email kayking@juno.com.* Specializes in rainbow trout, steak, hickory-smoked barbeque. Own desserts. Hrs: 7 am-10 pm. Closed Sep-May. Bkfst $1.75-$7.45; lunch $1.75-$7.95; dinner $8.95-$22.95. Rustic Western log cabin (1938). View of mountains. Cr cds: MC, V.

Deer Lodge

(C-3) See also Anaconda, Helena

Settled 1862 **Pop** 3,378 **Elev** 4,521 ft **Area code** 406 **Zip** 59722
Information Powell County Chamber of Commerce, 1171 S Main St; 406/846-2094

Near Montana's first important gold discovery at Gold Creek, this town was first a trapping and trading center, later an important stage and travel station between the early gold camps. Remnants of old mining camps are a few miles from town.

What to See and Do

Deerlodge National Forest. (See BUTTE) A Ranger District office is located here. Self-guided auto tour (inquire locally). W & E of town.

Frontier Montana. Museum houses western memorabilia incl weapons, clothing, bar. (Memorial Day-Labor Day) 1106 Main St. Phone 406/846-3111 or 406/846-3114. ¢¢ Incl in fee is

Montana Territorial Prison. Montana prison from 1871-1979. A sandstone wall, built in 1893, surrounds the 5-acre complex. The 1912 castlelike cell block remains intact and offers the visiting public a rare view of early prison life. Montana Law Enforcement Museum on grounds. (Daily) 1106 Main St. Phone 406/846-3111.

Powell County Museum. Displays reflecting the history of Powell County and SW Montana. (June-Labor Day, daily) 1193 Main St. Phone 406/846-3111.

Towe Ford Museum. Collection of antique Ford cars. One hundred on display, dating from 1903. Picnic area. (Daily) 1106 Main St. Phone 406/846-3111.

Yesterday's Playthings. Extensive doll collection from different time periods and cultures. Antique toys. (Mid-May-mid-Sep, daily) 1017 Main St. Phone 406/846-1480.

Grant-Kohrs Ranch National Historic Site. Preserved in its pioneer state, this was once headquarters for over a million acres of ranchland. The house was called the "finest home in Montana Territory." Original furniture, horse-drawn vehicles, and buildings provide an authentic look into history. Visitors may tour the house, barns, and bunkhouse. In season, see blacksmith and ranch hands at work, 19th-century style. (Daily; closed Jan 1, Thanksgiving, Dec 25) N edge of town. Phone 406/846-2070. Per person ¢; per vehicle ¢¢

Annual Events

Territorial Days. Third wkend June.

Tri-County Fair and Rodeo. Third wkend Aug.

Motel/Motor Lodge

★ **SUPER 8 MOTEL.** *1150 N Main (59722). 406/846-2370; fax 406/846-2373; res 800/800-8000.* 54 rms, 2 story. June-Aug: S $52.68; D $57.88-$62.88; each addl $5; suites $70.88; under 6 free; lower rates rest of yr. Crib free. Pet accepted; $5. TV; cable. Complimentary coffee in lobby. Restaurant adj open 24 hrs. Ck-out 11 am. Meeting rms. Cr cds: A, DS, MC, V.

Dillon *(E-3)*

Founded 1880 **Pop** 3,991
Elev 5,096 ft **Area code** 406
Zip 59725

Information Tourist Information Center & Chamber of Commerce, 125 S Montana, PO Box 425; 406/683-5511

Named after a president of the Union Pacific Railroad, Dillon is in a ranching community. Its farms and ranches produce more than 200,000 tons of hay each year. Livestock raising is also important.

What to See and Do

Bannack State Park. First territorial capital, now ghost town. Created by big gold strike on Grasshopper Creek (1862). Fishing; picnicking, camping (no hookups). Standard fees. 5 mi S on I-15, then 21 mi W on MT 278, then 4 mi S on county road. Phone 406/834-3413. Per car ¢¢

Beaverhead County Museum. Geological displays, mining, livestock and commercial artifacts, pioneer housewares, outdoor interpretive area. (Apr-early Nov, daily; closed hols) 15 S Montana St. Phone 406/683-5027. **FREE**

Beaverhead National Forest. More than 2 million acres. Rugged mountains, alpine lakes, hot springs. Fishing; hunting, skiing, snowmobiling, picknicking, camping (standard fees). A Ranger District office also is located here. E & W off US 91, I-15. For info contact Supervisor, 420 Barrett St. Phone 406/683-3900.

Maverick Mountain Ski Area. Double chairlift, pony lift; school, rentals, patrol; cafeteria and bar. Longest run 2¼ mi; vertical drop 2,100 ft. (Thanksgiving-Easter, Thurs-Sun; closed Dec 25) Cross-country trails. 40 mi NW on MT 278. Phone 406/834-3454. ¢¢¢¢

Annual Events

Bannack Days. Bannack State Park. Reliving of Gold Rush days in Bannack. Gold panning, demonstrations. Third wkend July.

Beaverhead County Fair. Five days before Labor Day.

Motels/Motor Lodges

★★ **BEST WESTERN PARADISE INN.** *650 N Montana St (59725). 406/683-4214; fax 406/683-4216; res 800/528-1234.* 62 rms, 2 story, 3 suites. May-Oct: S $51; D $57; each addl $3; suites $83; lower rates rest of yr. Crib avail, fee. Pet accepted. Parking lot. Indoor pool, whirlpool. TV; cable. Complimentary newspaper, toll-free calls. Restaurant 6 am-10

pm. Bar. Ck-out 11 am, ck-in 2 pm. Business servs avail. Gift shop. Exercise equipt. Golf, 9 holes. Cr cds: A, C, D, DS, ER, MC, V.

★ **SUPER 8 MOTEL.** *550 N Montana St (59725). 406/683-4288; fax 406/683-4288; toll-free 800/800-8000.* 48 rms, 3 story. No elvtr. May-Aug: S $50; D $60; each addl $5; under 12 free; lower rates rest of yr. Crib free. Pet accepted; $25. TV; cable (premium). Restaurant opp open 24 hrs. Ck-out 11 am. Cr cds: A, C, D, DS, MC, V.

Hotel

★★ **COMFORT INN OF DILLON.** *450 N Interchange (59725), 450 N Interchange, ½ blk from I-15 Exit 63. 406/683-6831; fax 406/683-2021; res 800/442-4667. www.townpump.com.* 46 rms, 2 story, 2 suites. May-Sep: S $56; D $66; each addl $5; suites $71; under 18 free; lower rates rest of yr. Crib avail. Pet accepted, some restrictions, fee. Parking lot. Indoor pool. TV; cable (premium), VCR avail. Complimentary continental bkfst, toll-free calls. Restaurant nearby. Bar. Ck-out 11 am, ck-in 4 pm. Meeting rm. Business servs avail. Bellhops. Dry cleaning, coin lndry. Gift shop. Golf, 18 holes. Downhill skiing. Cr cds: A, C, D, DS, ER, JCB, MC, V.

B&B/Small Inn

★ **THE CENTENNIAL INN.** *122 South Washington St (59725). 406/683-4454. Email centenn@bmt.net; www.bmt.net/~centenn.* 4 rms, 2 story. July-Aug: D $79; each addl $5; lower rates rest of yr. Crib avail. Pet accepted, some restrictions. Parking lot. TV; cable, VCR avail. Complimentary full bkfst. Restaurant. Ck-out 11 am. Meeting rms. Business center. Coin lndry. Gift shop. Free airport transportation. Golf, 18 holes. Downhill skiing. Bike rentals. Hiking trail. Picnic facilities. Cr cds: A, DS, MC, V.

Restaurant

★★ **THE OLD HOTEL.** *101 E 5th Ave (59754), 30 mi N on MT 43. 406/684-5959. www.theoldhotel.com.*

Specializes in Scottish potted eggs, parmesan-encrusted halibut, chili honey-glazed pork. Hrs: 11 am-2 pm, 5:30-9:30 pm; Sun brunch 7:30 am-2 pm. Closed Mon; hols. Res required. Wine, beer. Bkfst $2-$8; lunch $3-$12; dinner $15-$30. Sun brunch $2-$15. Entertainment. Parking. In 1890 hotel bldg; unique Scottish atmosphere. Cr cds: DS, MC, V.
D

Ennis

(D-3) *See also Three Forks, Virginia City*

Settled 1864 **Pop** 773 **Elev** 4,939 ft **Area code** 406 **Zip** 59729

Surrounded by three Rocky Mountain ranges in the Madison River valley and encircled by cattle ranches, Ennis has good trout fishing and big-game hunting. Beartrap Canyon offers whitewater floats. Swimming, boating, snowmobiling, and Nordic skiing are popular. A Ranger District office of the Beaverhead National Forest (see DILLON) is located here.

What to See and Do

National Fish Hatchery. Raises rainbow trout. (Daily) 12 mi S off US 287. Phone 406/682-4847. **FREE**

Motels/Motor Lodges

★ **FAN MOUNTAIN INN.** *204 N Main St (59729). 406/682-5200; fax 406/682-5266; toll-free 877/682-5200. Email fanmtnin@3rivers.net.* 28 rms, 2 story. S $39.50; D $48-$56; each addl $5; suite $75. Pet accepted; $5. TV; cable (premium), VCR avail (movies). Complimentary coffee in lobby. Restaurant nearby. Ck-out 11 am. Meeting rm. Cr cds: A, C, D, DS, MC, V.
D 🐾 🏋 ⚡ 🎿 📐 🐾

★ **IMA RAINBOW VALLEY MOTEL.** *S US Hwy 287 (59729), ½ mi S on US 287. 406/682-4264; fax 406/682-5012. Email rnbwvlly@3rivers.net; www. rainbowvalley.com.* 24 rms, 6 kits. June-Nov: S $55; D $70; each addl

$5-$15; kit. units $55-$100; lower rates rest of yr. TV; cable (premium). Heated pool. Restaurant nearby. Ck-out noon. Coin lndry. River float trips. Refrigerators avail. Picnic tables. Grills. Cr cds: A, C, D, DS, MC, V.
D ⚡ 🎿 🐾

Extended Stay

★★ **EL WESTERN RESORT.** *US 287 S (59729), ½ mi S on US 287. 406/682-4217; fax 406/682-5207; toll-free 800/831-2773. Email elwestrn@3rivers.net; www.elwestern.com.*, 1 story, 23 suites. June-Sep: S, D $65; suites $125; under 10 free; lower rates rest of yr. Crib avail, fee. Pet accepted, some restrictions, fee. Street parking. TV; cable, VCR avail. Complimentary toll-free calls. Restaurant nearby. Ck-out 11 am, ck-in 3 pm. Meeting rm. Business center. Concierge. Golf, 9 holes. Tennis, 4 courts. Bike rentals. Hiking trail. Cr cds: A, DS, MC, V.
🐾 🏋 🎿 🍴 📐 🐾 🚶

Fort Benton

(B-4) *See also Great Falls*

Founded 1846 **Pop** 1,660 **Elev** 2,632 ft **Area code** 406 **Zip** 59442
Information City Clerk, PO Box 8; 406/622-5494

Established as a fur-trading post and named in honor of Senator Thomas Hart Benton of Missouri, this famous frontier outpost at the head of navigation on the Missouri River became a strategic commercial stronghold. Supplies were received here and shipped overland to trappers and miners throughout Montana. The seat of Chouteau County and one of the oldest communities in the state, it continues as a trading center. The Lewis and Clark State Memorial in Fort Benton Park honors the surveyors who opened the area for trade and commerce.

What to See and Do

Museum of the Northern Great Plains. Agricultural and homestead history displays. (Memorial Day-Labor Day, daily) 20th & Washington. Phone 406/622-5494. ¢¢

Museum of the Upper Missouri River. Displays of steamboats, freighting, stagecoaches, fur, and Canadian trade. (Mid-May-mid-Sep, daily) 18th & Front Sts. Phone 406/622-5494. ¢¢

Ruins of Old Fort Benton. (1847) One building and parts of another remain of old trading post and blockhouse. On riverfront, near Main St.

Annual Events

Summer Celebration. Last wkend June.

Chouteau County Fair. Late Aug.

Gardiner

Founded 1883 **Pop** 600 (est)
Elev 5,314 ft **Area code** 406
Zip 59030

Gardiner was established as the original entrance to Yellowstone Park. Named for a trapper who worked this area, Gardiner is the only gateway open throughout the year to Yellowstone National Park (see WYOMING). A Ranger District office of the Gallatin National Forest (see BOZEMAN) is located here.

What to See and Do

Rafting. Yellowstone Raft Company. Half- and full-day whitewater raft trips on the Yellowstone, Gallatin, and Madison rivers. Departures from Gardiner and Big Sky (see). Res recommended. Phone 406/848-7777 or 800/858-7781. ¢¢¢¢¢

Annual Event

Gardiner Rodeo. NRA sanctioned rodeo. Phone 406/848-7971. June.

Motels/Motor Lodges

★ **ABSAROKA LODGE.** *US 89 and Yellowstone River Bridge (59030). 406/848-7414; fax 406/848-7560; toll-free 800/755-7414. Email ablodge@aol.com; www.yellowstonemotel.com.* 33 rms, 3 story, 8 suites. June-Sep: S, D $90;

each addl $5; suites $100; under 11 free; lower rates rest of yr. Pet accepted, some restrictions, fee. Parking lot. TV; cable. Complimentary toll-free calls. Restaurant nearby. Ck-out 11 am, ck-in 2 pm. Business servs avail. Concierge. Gift shop. Exercise privileges. Beach access. Hiking trail. Cr cds: A, C, D, DS, MC, V.

★ **MOTEL 6 GARDINER.** *109 Hell Roaring (59030). 406/848-7520; fax 406/848-7555; toll-free 877/266-8356.* 40 rms, 4 story. June-Aug: S $75; D $81; each addl $6; under 17 free; lower rates rest of yr. Crib avail. Pet accepted. Parking lot. TV; cable. Ck-out 11 am, ck-in 3 pm. Fax servs avail. Coin lndry. Hiking trail. Picnic facilities. Cr cds: A, C, D, DS, MC, V.

★ **YELLOWSTONE SUPER 8.** *US 89 S (59030), ¼ mi N on US 89. 406/848-7401; fax 406/848-9410; res 800/800-8000. Email super8@gomontan.com; www.yellowstonesuper8.com.* 66 rms, 3 story, 1 suite. May-Sep: S, D $99; each addl $5; suites $134; under 11 free; lower rates rest of yr. Crib avail. Pet accepted, some restrictions, fee. Parking lot. Indoor pool. TV; cable (premium). Complimentary newspaper, toll-free calls. Restaurant nearby. Fax servs avail. Concierge. Hiking trail. Cr cds: A, C, D, DS, MC, V.

Hotels

★ **RODEWAY INN & SUITES.** *107 Hell Roaring St (59030), on US 89. 406/848-7536; fax 406/848-7062; res 800/228-2000. Email rdwayinnyellow stone@yahoo.com; www.rodeway innyellowstone.com.* 78 rms, 3 story, 2 suites. June-Sep: S $99; D $139; each addl $8; suites $139; lower rates rest of yr. Crib avail, fee. Parking lot. TV; cable, VCR avail. Complimentary continental bkfst, coffee in rms, newspaper, toll-free calls. Restaurant nearby. Ck-out 10 am, ck-in 4 pm. Meeting rm. Coin lndry. Whirlpool. Downhill skiing. Hiking trail. Cr cds: A, C, D, DS, MC, V.

★★ **YELLOWSTONE VILLAGE INN.** *Yellowstone Park N entrance, Gardiner (82190). 406/848-7417; fax 406/848-7418; toll-free 800/228-8158. Email*

elk@yellowstoneinn.com; www.yellow-
stoneinn.com. 40 rms, 2 story, 4
suites. June-Sep: S, D $69; each addl
$5; suites $50; under 12 free; lower
rates rest of yr. Crib avail. Parking lot.
Indoor pool. TV; cable (premium),
VCR avail. Complimentary continental bkfst, coffee in rms, toll-free calls.
Restaurant. Business servs avail.
Concierge. Coin lndry. Sauna. Tennis,
4 courts. Bike rentals. Supervised children's activities. Hiking trail. Picnic
facilities. Cr cds: A, DS, MC, V.

Resort

★★ **BEST WESTERN BY MAM-
MOTH HOT SPRINGS.** *S Hwy 89,
PO Box 646 (59030), ½ mi N, at N
entrance to Yellowstone Park. 406/848-
7311; fax 406/848-7120; res 800/528-
1234; toll-free 800/828-9080. www.
bestwestern.com/mammoth.* 81 rms, 2
story, 4 suites. June-Sep: S, D $87;
each addl $5; suites $185; under 12
free; lower rates rest of yr. Crib avail,
fee. Pet accepted, some restrictions,
fee. Parking lot. Indoor pool, whirlpool. TV; cable, VCR avail. Restaurant 5-9:30 pm. Bar. Ck-out 11 am,
ck-in 4 pm. Meeting rm. Business
center. Coin lndry. Gift shop. Sauna,
steam rm. Beach access. Hiking trail.
Cr cds: A, C, D, DS, ER, JCB, MC, V.

Restaurant

★★ **YELLOWSTONE MINE.** *US 89
(59030), ½ mi N, near N entrance to
park. 406/848-7336.* Specializes in
prime rib, seafood, stuffed chicken.
Hrs: 6-11 am, 5-10 pm; Sat to 11 pm;
Sun to noon. Bar. Bkfst buffet: $6.50;
dinner $6.95-$19.95. Child's menu.
Old West mining decor. Cr cds: A,
DS, MC, V.

Glacier
National Park

Big, rugged, and primitive, Glacier
National Park is nature's unspoiled
domain. Human civilization is
reduced to insignificance by the wild

grandeur of these million acres. It's
the place for a snowball fight in midsummer, for glacial solitude, for
fishing, for alpine flowers, lonely and
remote campgrounds along fir-
fringed lakes. The park is also a living
textbook in geology.

Declared a national park on May
11, 1910, these 1,013,595 acres of
spectacular scenery are preserved
year after year much as they were
when Meriwether Lewis saw them in
the distance in 1806. The United
States and Canada share these treasures of nature; the 204 square miles
of Canada that are linked to Glacier
are known as the Waterton-Glacier
International Peace Park. Glacier
National Park contains 50 glaciers,
among the few in the United States,
some of which are comparatively
accessible. There are more than 200
lakes and 1,400 varieties of plants, 63
species of animals—from mice to
moose—and 272 varieties of birds.

Visitors here can choose a variety
of activities during their stay; they
can enjoy the scenery from the
shadow of a hotel or chalet, share
the camaraderie of a community
campground, or seek solitude in the
wilderness. The delights of Glacier,
however, should be savored cau-
tiously. Rangers recommend that visitors stay on the trails and never hike
alone. The behavior of wild animals
can be unpredictable.

This is a land where winter does
not beat a full retreat until mid-
June, and sometimes returns in
mid-September. The summer season
extends between those periods, but
until July, high snowbanks line the
roads and the mountains are capped
with snow. Late June is a time of
cascading waterfalls and profuse
wildflowers. In the fall, the dense
forests are a blaze of colors set
against a background of snow-cov-
ered peaks. Winter brings deep-
snow peace, which only the most
hardy invade for cross-country skiing or photography.

Spectacular views of the park may
be seen from your car, particularly
when crossing the Continental
Divide on the Going-to-the-Sun
Road; it is 50 miles long and one of
the most magnificent drives in the
world (approximately mid-June-mid-

October). As of January, 1994, vehicles in excess of 21 ft in length (including combinations of units) and 8 feet in width (including mirrors) are prohibited on the Going-to-the-Sun Road between Avalanche and Sun Point. Vehicles exceeding these restrictions may use US 2 or can be parked at Avalanche or Sun Point parking areas. The road continuously winds up and down in tight curves and requires caution. This unforgettable ride links the east and west sides of the park, passing over Logan Pass (a visitor center with exhibits is here; June-September, daily; closed rest of yr) for a 100-mile view from an elevation of 6,646 ft. It connects with US 89 at St. Mary (here is a visitor center with exhibits, programs; May-September, daily) and with US 2 at West Glacier. US 89 on the east side of the park is the Blackfeet Highway, extending from Browning to Canada. The road to Many Glacier Valley branches from US 89, 9 miles north of St. Mary. The road to Two Medicine Lake leaves MT 49, 4 miles north of East Glacier Park. Chief Mountain International Highway (MT 17) leads to Waterton Lakes National Park in Canada (see).

Most of the park, however, including the glaciers, is accessible only by trail. There are 732 maintained miles of trails penetrating to remote wilderness areas. By foot or on horseback, magnificent and isolated parts of Glacier await discovery.

There are eight major and five semiprimitive campgrounds. The camping limit is seven days. Most campgrounds are available on a first come, first served basis. Fish Creek and St. Mary campgrounds may be reserved ahead of time through the National Park Reservation System by calling 800/365-2267. A fee is charged for camping. Visitors planning to camp overnight in Glacier's backcountry must obtain a Backcountry User Permit and camp in designated sites; 406/888-7800.

Place-name signs and roadside exhibits mark the major roads from late May-September 15. Also, ranger-naturalists conduct daily walks and campfire programs that are both rewarding and scenic. Park-wide guided hikes for day and overnight trips available through Glacier Wilderness Guides, PO Box 535, West Glacier 59936. Guided bus tours available through Glacier Park, Inc, Dial Tower, Dial Corporate Center, Phoenix, AZ 85077 (October-mid-May); or East Glacier Park 59434 (rest of year). Saddle horses available through Mule Shoe Outfitters, LLC, PO Box 322, Kila 59920; also at Many Glacier, Lake McDonald Lodge, and Apgar Village Lodge. Launch service operates on Two Medicine, Swiftcurrent, Josephine, St. Mary, and McDonald lakes through Glacier Park Boat Co, PO Box 5262, Kalispell 59903; and between the townsite in Waterton Lakes National Park, Canada, and the head of Waterton Lake in Glacier National Park through Waterton Shoreline Cruises, PO Box 126, Waterton, Alberta, Canada TOK 2MO (June-August).

Contact the Superintendent, Glacier National Park, West Glacier 59936; 406/888-9800, for detailed info. Golden Eagle Passport accepted (see MAKING THE MOST OF YOUR TRIP). Seven-day pass: per vehicle ¢¢¢; Per person ¢¢

What to See and Do

Avalanche Creek. Flows through deep gorge filled with spray. Two-mi hike to Avalanche Lake Basin with waterfalls, 2,000-ft-high cliffs. Camping, picnicking.

Belly River Country. Trails, lake fishing, backcountry camping, glacial valleys.

Cut Bank. A primitive, densely wooded valley. At head of valley is 8,011-ft Triple Divide Peak. Hiking, camping.

Flattop Mountain. Between the Lewis Range and the Livingston Range; meadows and groves of trees contrast with dense forest growth elsewhere.

Granite Park. Much of this area is a mass of lava; trails, glacial valleys, alpine flowers. Accessible only by foot or horseback.

✪ Lake McDonald. Largest in park: 10 mi long, 1 mi wide; heavily forested shores with peaks rising 6,000 ft above lake. Trail to Sperry Glacier. One-hr boat tours, horseback riding trips leave from Lake McDonald Lodge (mid-June-mid-Sep, daily).

Many Glacier Area. Fishing, boating (trips); camping, hiking, riding, trails to Morning Eagle Falls, Cracker Lake, Grinnell Glacier and Lake, Iceberg

Lake. Footpaths go around Swiftcurrent and Josephine lakes and to Appekunny Falls and Cirque. Self-guided trail from hotel.

Red Eagle Lake. Located in a glacially carved basin with dramatic falls and gorge. Backcountry camping.

River Rafting. Four companies offer several ½- to 6-day trips on the Middle and N forks of the Flathead River. Guided fishing trips, combination trips.

Glacier Raft Company. Phone 406/888-5454 or 800/332-9995. ¢¢¢¢

Great Northern Whitewater. Phone 406/387-5340 or 800/735-7897 (res). ¢¢¢¢

Wild River Adventures. Phone 406/387-9453 or 800/826-2724. ¢¢¢¢

Montana Raft Company & Glacier Wilderness Guides. Phone 406/387-5555 or 800/521-RAFT. ¢¢¢¢

Sperry and Grinnell Glaciers. Largest in the park. Inquire about trips to Grinnell.

St. Mary Lake. Emerald green, with peaks on 3 sides. Fishing, boating, hiking. One-and-a-half-hr boat tours leave from Rising Sun Boat Landing (mid-June-mid-Sep, daily). Self-guided trail from Sun Point.

Two Medicine Valley. Deep valleys, towering peaks surround mountain lake. Brook, rainbow trout, boating; hiking trails, camping.

East Glacier Area

Area code 406 Zip 59434

Motels/Motor Lodges

★★ **MOUNTAIN PINE.** *MT 49 (59434), ½ mi N of US 2.* 406/226-4403; fax 406/226-9290. 26 rms. No A/C. Mid-June-mid-Sep: S $51; D $56; each addl $3; family units $98-$110; log house $175; lower rates May-mid-June, late Sep. Closed rest of yr. Crib free. TV; cable. Restaurant nearby. Ck-out 11 am. Free railroad station transportation. Picnic tables. Cr cds: A, D, DS, MC, V.

Sunrise against the beautiful backdrop of Glacier National Park

★★ **THE RESORT AT GLACIER.** *Jct Hwy 89 & Going to Sun Rd (59417), at Going to the Sun Rd.* 406/732-4431; fax 406/732-7265; res 800/368-3689. Email stmary@gfcpark.com; www.gfcpark.com. 106 rms, 3 story, 18 suites. July-Aug: S $89; D $109; each addl $10; under 12 free; lower rates rest of yr. Crib avail, fee. TV; cable (DSS). Restaurant 7 am-10 pm. Bar. Ck-out 11 am, ck-in 4 pm. Meeting rms. Cr cds: A, DS, MC, V.

★ **SWIFTCURRENT INN.** *12 mil W of Babb Mt (59434), ¾ mi SW of Swiftcurrent Lake.* 406/732-5531, fax 406/732-5594. 88 units, 26 cottages. No A/C. Mid-June-mid-Sep: S $29-$75; D $35-$81; each addl $10. Closed rest of yr. Restaurant 7 am-9:30 pm. Ck-out 11 am. Coin lndry. Sundries. Trail center for hikers. Cr cds: A, DS, MC, V.

★ **VILLAGE INN.** *Apgar Village - West Glacier (59434), 12 mi W of Babb off US 89. 406/756-2444; fax 406/257-0384; res 406/756-2444. www.glacierparkinc.com.* 210 rms, 5 story. No A/C. No elvtr. Early June-mid-Sep: S $91-$174; D $97-$174; each addl $10; suites $163-$174; under 12 free. Closed rest of yr. Crib free. Restaurant 6:30 am-9:30 pm. Bar 11:30 am-midnight; entertainment. Ck-out 11 am. Gift shop. Hiking. Overlooks Swiftcurrent Lake. A Glacier Park, Inc, hotel. Cr cds: A, D, DS, MC, V.

Cottage Colony

★ **JACOBSON'S COTTAGES.** *1204 MT 49 PO Box 454 (59534), ½ mi N. 406/226-4422; toll-free 888/226-4422.* 12 cottages, 1 kit. No A/C. No rm phones. Mid-May-Oct: S $48; D $52-$58; each addl $3; kit. cottage $65; under 6 free. Closed rest of yr. Crib free. TV; cable. Restaurant adj 6:30 am-10:30 pm. Ck-out 11 am. Picnic table. Cr cds: A, DS, MC, V.

Restaurants

★★ **GLACIER VILLAGE.** *304-308 Hwy 2E (59434), Town Center. 406/226-4464.* Specializes in broiler items, seafood, roast turkey. Own bread, desserts. Hrs: 6:30 am-10 pm; winter hrs vary. Closed late Sep-early May. Res accepted. Wine, beer. Bkfst $2.25-$6.95; lunch $4.50-$6.95; dinner $5.95-$13.95. Family-owned since 1954. Cr cds: DS, MC, V.

★★ **SNOW GOOSE GRILLE.** *St. Mary (East Glacier Area), jct US 89 and Going to the Sun Rd, at E entrance to park. 406/732-4431. www.glcpark.com.* Specializes in sourdough scones, range-fed buffalo, locally caught whitefish. Hrs: 7:30-10:30 am, 11:30 am-2 pm, 5:30-10 pm. Closed Oct-mid-May. Bar. Bkfst $3.75-$7.50; lunch $4.95-$8.95; dinner $9.95-$18.95. Child's menu. Family-owned. Cr cds: A, D, DS, MC, V.

West Glacier Area

Area code 406 **Zip** 59936

Hotel

★ **LAKE MCDONALD LODGE.** *Going to the Sun Rd (59434), 12 mi NE on Lake McDonald. 406/888-5431; fax 406/888-5681.* 32 rms in lodge, 38 cabins, 30 motel rms, 1-2 story. No A/C. Early June-late Sep: lodge: S $115; D $121; each addl $10; under 12 free; cabins: S $65-$113; D $71-$119; each addl $10; motel: S $78; D $83; each addl $10. Closed rest of yr. Crib free. Restaurant. Bar 11 am-midnight. Ck-out 11 am. Gift shop. Boating; launch cruises. Hiking. Camp store. Rustic hunting lodge amid giant cedars. Lodge totally non-smoking. Cr cds: DS, MC, V.

B&B/Small Inn

★★ **IZAAK WALTON INN.** *123 Izaak Walton Inn Rd (59916), Essex Exit off US 2, halfway between East and West Glacier. 406/888-5700; fax 406/888-5200. Email izaakw@digisys.net.* 33 rms, 3 story. No A/C. No rm phones. S, D $98; each addl $5; suites $150; caboose kit. cottages (3-day min) $475; wkly rates; package plans. Crib free. Dining rm 7 am-8 pm. Bar. Ck-out 11 am, ck-in 3 pm. Coin lndry. Meeting rm. Business servs avail. X-country ski on site; rentals. Sauna. Game rm. Rec rm (movies). Lawn games. Bicycle rentals. Picnic tables. Old railroad hotel (1939); restored sleeper cars avail for rental (3-day min). Adj to Glacier National Park. Totally non-smoking. Cr cds: A, DS, MC, V.

Glasgow (B-6)

Founded 1887 **Pop** 3,572
Elev 2,090 ft **Area code** 406
Zip 59230

Information Glasgow Area Chamber of Commerce & Agriculture, 740 US 2E, PO Box 832; 406/228-2222

Glasgow has had four booms in its history. The first was opening of land to white settlement in 1888, the second when another 18,000,000 acres were opened around 1910. In the 1930s, Glasgow was headquarters for the 10,000 construction workers on Fort Peck Dam. Glasgow AFB made its home 18 miles northeast of town from 1954-68; the flight facilities are now owned by Boeing and the residential area is being developed into a military retirement community. Wheat and livestock are raised in Valley County.

What to See and Do

Fort Peck Dam and Lake. Built by Army Corps of Engineers. Largest hydraulic earthfill dam in the world, forming huge reservoir with 1,600-mi lakeshore. Dam rises 280½ ft above Missouri River; total length 21,026 ft; road follows crest of the dam, leading to mi-long concrete spillway. Information center; museum. Guided tours of power plant (Memorial Day-Labor Day, daily; rest of yr, by appt). Self-guided nature trail. There are several recreation areas with fishing, boating (ramps); camping (fee), trailer sites, concession. 20 mi SE on MT 24. **FREE**

Hell Creek State Park. Swimming, fishing, boating (ramp, rentals); picnicking, camping (no hookups). Standard fees. 50 mi S on MT 24, then 6 mi W on county road. Phone 406/232-4365.

Pioneer Museum. Displays of Native American artifacts; photos of pioneers and events of their time; pioneer farm machinery. Also fossils and aviation display. (Memorial Day-Labor Day, daily) ½ mi W on US 2. Phone 406/228-8692. **FREE**

Annual Events

Longest Dam Run. Kiwanis Park, foot of Fort Peck Dam. 5K and 10K run/walk crosses 1.8 mi of Dam. Refreshments, prizes. Phone 406/228-2222. Third wk June.

Montana Governor's Cup Walleye Tournament. Fort Peck Lake. Phone 406/228-2222. Early July.

Northeast Montana Fair & Rodeo. Fairgrounds at W edge of city. Exhibits, midway, rodeo, nightly shows. Three days Late July or early Aug.

Seasonal Events

Fort Peck Summer Theater. 17 mi SE on MT 24 in Fort Peck. Professional cast performs musicals, comedies. Fri-Sun. Historical landmark. Phone 406/228-9219. Late June-Labor Day.

Hiline Festival games. Scottish games and music. Mid-Sep.

Conference Center

★ **COTTONWOOD INN.** *Hwy Two E (59230), 1 mi E on US 2, near City-County Airport. 406/228-8213; fax 406/228-8248; toll-free 800/321-8213. Email cwinn@nemontel.net.* 92 rms, 2 story. June-Aug: S $50; D $60; each addl $5; under 12 free; lower rates rest of yr. Crib avail. Pet accepted, some restrictions. Parking lot. Indoor pool, whirlpool. TV; cable (premium), VCR avail. Complimentary toll-free calls. Restaurant 6 am-10 pm. Bar. Ck-out 11 am, ck-in 1 pm. Meeting rms. Business servs avail. Dry cleaning, coin lndry. Gift shop. Free airport transportation. Sauna. Golf, 9 holes. Tennis, 2 courts. Cr cds: A, C, D, DS, MC, V.

Restaurant

★★ **SAM'S SUPPER CLUB.** *307 Klein (US 2) (59230). 406/228-4614.* Specializes in char-broiled steak, walleye pike, fresh pasta. Hrs: 11 am-2 pm, 5-10 pm; Sat from 4 pm. Closed Sun, Mon; July 4, Thanksgiving, Dec 25. Res accepted. Bar. Lunch $2-$6.75; dinner $6-$19.50. Child's menu. Cr cds: A, MC, V

Glendive (C-8)

Settled 1864 **Pop** 4,802 **Elev** 2,078 ft
Area code 406 **Zip** 59330
Web www.midrivers.com/chamber
Information Chamber of Commerce
& Agriculture, 313 S Merrill Ave;
406/365-5601

Glendive is the shipping center for the crops of Dawson County. It also serves the oil wells, railroad yards, and natural gas fields that ring the city.

What to See and Do

Fishing. The unusual spatula-nosed paddlefish (*Polyodon spathula*) is found here in the Yellowstone River. Fishing for this rare, prehistoric species is permitted mid-May-June only.

Frontier Gateway Museum. Collection depicts Glendive and early Dawson County; "Main Street 1881" exhibit in basement; 1-rm schoolhouse, blacksmith shop, display of early farm machinery on grounds, and 5 other buildings in complex. (June-Aug, daily) Belle Prairie Frontage Rd, 1 mi E off I-94, Exit 215. Phone 406/365-8168. **FREE**

Hunt moss agates. Along Yellowstone River.

Makoshika (Ma-KO-she-ka) **State Park.** Spectacular badlands scenery; fossils. The eroded sandstone cliffs are particularly striking at sunrise and sunset. Visitor Center. Hiking, picnicking, camping (no hookups). Standard fees. ¼ mi SE on Snyder Ave. Phone 406/365-8596.

Annual Events

Buzzard Day. Makoshika State Park. Day-long activities; softball tournaments, concerts, BBQ. Early June.

Dawson County Fair & Rodeo. Four days mid-Aug.

Motel/Motor Lodge

★ **DAYS INN.** *2000 N Merrill Ave (59330), I-94 Exit 215.* 406/365-6011; *fax* 406/365-2876; *res* 800/389-7466. 59 rms, 2 story. May-Sep: S $50; D $65; each addl $4; children $3; under 12 free; lower rates rest of yr. Crib avail. Pet accepted, some restrictions. Parking lot. TV; cable (premium). Complimentary continental bkfst, newspaper, toll-free calls. Restaurant nearby. Ck-out 11 am, ck-in 2 pm. Fax servs avail. Dry cleaning. Exercise privileges. Golf. Downhill skiing. Picnic facilities. Cr cds: A, C, D, DS, MC, V.

Great Falls

(B-4) *See also Fort Benton*

Founded 1884 **Pop** 55,097
Elev 3,333 ft **Area code** 406
Web www.greatfallschamber.org
Information Chamber of Commerce, 710 1st Ave N, PO Box 2127, 59403; 406/761-4434

Great Falls's growth has been powered by thriving diversified industry, agriculture and livestock, construction and activity at nearby Malmstrom AFB. The city takes its name from the falls of the Missouri River, a source of electric power.

What to See and Do

✪ **C. M. Russell Museum Complex & Original Log Cabin Studio.** Charles Russell paintings, bronzes, original models, and illustrated letters; exhibits of Russell's contemporaries. Browning Firearms Collection. (Daily; winter, Tues-Sun) 400 13th St N. Phone 406/727-8787. ¢¢

Giant Springs State Park and State Trout Hatchery. One of the largest freshwater springs in the world produces nearly 390 million gallons of water every 24 hrs. The hatchery next to the springs raises trout. Picnic grounds. (Daily) 4 mi NE on River Dr. Phone 406/454-5840. ¢

Lewis and Clark National Forest. More than 1.8 million acres of canyons, mountains, meadows, and wilderness. Parts of the Scapegoat Wilderness and the Bob Marshall Wilderness (384,407 acres), with the 15-mi-long, 1,000-ft-high Chinese Wall, are here. Activities incl stream and lake fishing; scenic drives, big-game hunting, hiking, camping (fee), picnicking, winter sports. For info contact Supervisor, 1101 15th St N, PO Box 869, 59403. E on US 87, 89, MT 200. Phone 406/791-7700.

Lewis and Clark National Historical Trail Interpretive Center. Exhibits follow the historical expedition's journey, incl canoe-pulling simulation, Mandan Indian earth lodge, Shoshone tepee, and replicas of the boats used in the expedition. Twenty-min film on the expedition in 158-seat theater. (Daily) 3 mi NW on Giant Springs Rd. Phone 406/791-7717. ¢¢

Malmstrom AFB. Home of the 43rd Air Refueling Wing and center of one of the largest intercontinental ballistic missile complexes in the world. Museum featuring historical military displays (Memorial Day-Labor Day, Fri mornings; rest of yr, by appt). 1 mi E of 2nd Ave N and Bypass Rd. Phone 406/731-4046. **FREE**

Paris Gibson Square Museum of Art. Historical school bldg contains a gallery with changing displays of contemporary regional art, plus the Cascade County Historical Museum. Two gift shops; lunchtime cafe. 1400 1st Ave N. Phone 406/727-8255. **FREE**

University of Great Falls. (1932) 1,200 students. A 40-acre campus. Chapel sculpture and stained-glass windows designed and produced at college. The pool in McLaughlin Memorial Center is open to public (inquire for days, hrs, fees). 1301 20th St S. Phone 406/761-8210.

Annual Events

Montana Pro Rodeo Circuit Finals. Four Seasons Arena. Phone 406/727-8900. Mid-Jan.

State Fair. Fairgrounds. Rodeo, livestock exhibits, horse racing, petting zoo, commercial exhibits, entertainment, carnival. Phone 406/727-8900. Late July-early Aug.

Motels/Motor Lodges

★ **BUDGET INN.** *2 Treasure State Dr (59404), W of I-15 10th Ave Exit S, near Intl Airport. 406/453-1602; fax 406/453-1602; toll-free 800/362-4842. Email bwheritage@montana.com.* 60 rms, 2 story. June-Aug: S, D $55; lower rates rest of yr. Crib avail. Pet

accepted, some restrictions. Parking lot. Indoor pool, whirlpool. TV; cable (premium). Complimentary continental bkfst, coffee in rms, toll-free calls. Restaurant nearby. Ck-out noon, ck-in 2 pm. Business servs avail. Bellhops. Dry cleaning, coin lndry. Gift shop. Free airport transportation. Exercise privileges, sauna. Golf. Tennis, 2 courts. Downhill skiing. Hiking trail. Picnic facilities. Cr cds: A, C, D, DS, MC, V.

[D] [symbols] [SC]

★★ **COMFORT INN.** *1120 S 9th St (59405). 406/454-2727; fax 406/454-2727; res 800/228-5150.* 64 rms, 3 story. S, D $69.95; each addl $5; suites $79.95; under 18 free. Crib free. Pet accepted; $5. TV; cable (premium). Indoor pool; whirlpool. Complimentary continental bkfst. Restaurant nearby. Ck-out 11 am. Business servs avail. Health club privileges. Cr cds: A, D, DS, MC, V.

[D] [symbols]

★ **DAYS INN OF GREAT FALLS.** *101 NW 14th Ave (59404). 406/727-6565; fax 406/727-6308; res 800/329-7466. www.daysinn.com.* 62 rms, 2 story. June-Sep: S $59; D $65; each addl $6; under 13 free. Crib free. Pet accepted. TV; cable. Complimentary continental bkfst. Ck-out 11 am. Coin lndry. Cr cds: A, DS, MC, V.

[D] [symbols]

★★ **FAIRFIELD INN.** *1000 9th Ave S (59405), opp Holiday Village Shopping Center. 406/454-3000; fax 406/454-3000; toll-free 800/228-2800.* 63 rms, 3 story, 16 suites. S $69.95; D $74.95; each addl $5; suites $79.95; under 18 free. Crib free. TV; cable. Indoor pool; whirlpool. Complimentary continental bkfst. Restaurant opp open 24 hrs. Ck-out 11 am. Valet serv. Game rm. Refrigerator, microwave in suites. Cr cds: A, D, DS, MC, V.

[D] [symbols] [SC]

Hotels

★★ **BEST WESTERN HERITAGE INN.** *1700 Fox Farm Rd (59404), I-15 Exit 10th Ave S. 406/761-1900; fax 406/761-0136; toll-free 800/548-8256. Email bwheritage@montana.com; www. bestwestern.com/heritageinngreatfalls.* 231 rms, 2 story, 9 suites. June-Aug:

S, D $99; suites $129; lower rates rest of yr. Crib avail. Pet accepted, some restrictions. Parking lot. Indoor pool, whirlpool. TV; cable. Complimentary coffee in rms, toll-free calls. Restaurant 6 am-10 pm. Bar. Ck-out noon, ck-in 2 pm. Meeting rms. Business servs avail. Bellhops. Dry cleaning, coin lndry. Gift shop. Free airport transportation. Exercise privileges, sauna. Golf. Tennis, 2 courts. Downhill skiing. Hiking trail. Picnic facilities. Video games. Cr cds: A, C, D, DS, MC, V.

★★ **HOLIDAY INN.** *400 10th Ave S (59405). 406/727-7200; fax 406/727-7200; res 800/257-1998; toll-free 800 /626-8009. Email hlidayinn@initco.net.* 169 rms, 7 story. S, D $75; suites $145. Crib free. Pet accepted, some restrictions. TV; cable (premium). Indoor pool; whirlpool. Coffee in rms. Restaurant 6 am-10 pm. Bar noon-2 am. Ck-out noon. Meeting rms. Business servs avail. Free airport, bus depot transportation. Sauna. Health club privileges. Cr cds: A, C, D, DS, ER, JCB, MC, V.

★ **TOWN HOUSE INN OF GREAT FALLS.** *1411 S 10th Ave (59405). 406/761-4600; fax 406/761-7603; res 800/442-4667. www.townpump.com.* 107 rms, 2 story, 2 suites. May-Sep: S $70; D $76; each addl $5; suites $135; under 18 free; lower rates rest of yr. Crib avail. Pet accepted, some restrictions, fee. Parking lot. Indoor pool, whirlpool. TV; cable (premium), VCR avail. Complimentary toll-free calls. Restaurant 7 am-10 pm. Bar. ck-out 11 am, ck-in 4 pm. Meeting rms. Business servs avail. Bellhops. Dry cleaning, coin lndry. Gift shop. Free airport transportation. Sauna. Golf, 18 holes. Downhill skiing. Cr cds: A, C, D, DS, ER, JCB, MC.

Restaurants

★ **EDDIE'S SUPPER CLUB.** *38th and N 2nd Ave (59401). 406/453-1616.* Specializes in steak, hamburgers. Hrs: 9:30 am-11 pm; Fri, Sat to midnight. Bar. Lunch $3-$7; dinner $9.95-$20.95. Entertainment: Fri, Sat. Cr cds: DS, MC, V.

★★ **JAKER'S STEAK, RIBS & FISH HOUSE.** *1500 S 10th Ave (59405). 406/727-1033. www.puimcgf@in/tch. com.* Specializes in prime rib, babyback ribs, seafood. Hrs: 11 am-10 pm. Closed Dec 25. Res accepted. Lunch $4.95-$7.95; dinner $6.45-$19.95. Child's menu. Cr cds: A, D, DS, MC, V.

Hamilton

(C-2) *See also Missoula*

Pop 2,737 **Elev** 3,572 ft
Area code 406 **Zip** 59840
Web www.bvchamber.com
Information Bitterroot Valley Chamber of Commerce, 105 E Main; 406/363-2400

Hamilton is the county seat and main shopping center for Ravalli County and headquarters for the Bitterroot National Forest.

What to See and Do

Big Hole National Battlefield. (see) S on US 93.

Bitterroot National Forest. (1,579,533 acres) Lake and stream fishing, big-game hunting; Anaconda-Pintler Wilderness, Selway-Bitterroot Wilderness, and River of No Return Wilderness. Mountain lakes, hot springs. Scenic drives in Bitterroot Valley; Skalkaho Falls. Hiking and riding trails, winter sports, camp and picnic sites. Inquire locally for wilderness pack trips. Fees may be charged at recreation sites. Contact Supervisor, 1801 N 1st St. Surrounding Hamilton with access by US 93, MT 38. Phone 406/363-7161.

Daly Mansion. (ca 1890) This 42-rm mansion was the home of Marcus Daly, an Irish immigrant who became one of Montana's "copper kings" through the copper mines near Butte. Seven Italian marble fireplaces, original furniture, transplanted exotic trees, "dollhouse" built for Daly children. Tours (May-Sep, daily; rest of yr, by appt). 2 mi NE on County 269. Phone 406/363-6004. ¢¢

Fort Owen State Park. Restoration of Montana's first white settlement, more a trading post than a fort. Day use only. 20 mi N, off US 93 to Stevensville, then 5 mi E on MT 269. **FREE**

Painted Rocks State Park. Swimming, fishing, boating (ramp); picnicking, camping (no hookups). Standard fees. 20 mi S on US 93, then 23 mi SW on MT 473, in the Bitterroot Mts. Phone 406/542-5500.

Skiing. Lost Trail Powder Mountain. Two chairlifts, 2 rope tows; patrol, ski school, rentals; concession area. Vertical drop 1,100 ft. (Dec-Apr, Thurs-Sun, hols) Cross-country trails. 50 mi S on US 93. Phone 406/821-3211. ¢¢¢¢

St. Mary's Mission. (1841) Picturesque log church and residence; one of the oldest churches in Northwest (present structure built in 1866); also old pharmacy (1868). Restored and furnished to period. Pioneer relics, Chief Victor's house and cemetery. Site is 1st in religion, education, agriculture, music in Montana. Gift shop. Guided tours. Park, picnicking. (Mid-Apr-mid-Oct, daily) 20 mi N off US 93; W end of 4th St in Stevensville. Phone 406/777-5734. ¢

Annual Events

Chief Victor Days. June.

Good Nations Powwow. July.

Ravalli County Fair, Rodeo, and Horse Races. Late Aug.

McIntosh Apple Days. Oct.

Motel/Motor Lodge

★★ BEST WESTERN HAMILTON INN. 409 S 1st St (59810). 406/363-2142; fax 406/363-2142; res 800/528-1234; toll-free 800/426-4586. 36 rms, 2 story, 2 suites. June-Aug: S $63; D $66; each addl $50; suites $69; under 12 free; lower rates rest of yr. Crib avail. Parking lot. TV; cable (premium), VCR avail. Complimentary continental bkfst, coffee in rms. Restaurant nearby. Ck-out 11 am, ck-in 3 pm. Meeting rm. Business center. Exercise privileges, whirlpool. Golf, 18 holes. Downhill skiing. Hiking trail. Cr cds: A, C, D, DS, MC, V.
🄳 🐾 🕆 🏊 🎿 🏇 🔥 SC 🎿

Hotel

★★ COMFORT INN OF HAMILTON. 1113 N 1st St (59840), 1 mi N on US 93. 406/363-6600; fax 406/363-5644; res 800/442-4667. www.townpump. com. 63 rms, 2 story, 2 suites. May-Sep: S $57; D $64; each addl $5; suites $72; under 18 free; lower rates rest of yr. Crib avail. Pet accepted, some restrictions, fee. Parking lot. TV; cable (premium), VCR avail. Complimentary continental bkfst, toll-free calls. Restaurant 7 am-9 pm. Bar. Ck-out 11 am, ck-in 4 pm. Meeting rm. Business servs avail. Bellhops. Dry cleaning, coin lndry. Gift shop. Sauna, whirlpool. Golf, 18 holes. Tennis, 10 courts. Downhill skiing. Cr cds: A, C, D, DS, ER, JCB, MC, V.
🄳 🐾 🏊 🕆 🏇 🎿 🔥 SC

B&B/Small Inn

★ DEER CROSSING BED & BREAKFAST. 396 Hayes Creek Rd (59840). 406/363-2232; toll-free 800/763-2232. Email deercros@bitterroot.net; www.wtp. net/go/deercrossing. 2 rms, 3 story, 2 suites. Apr-Sep: S $80; each addl $15; suites $125; lower rates rest of yr. Pet accepted, some restrictions, fee. TV; cable (DSS), VCR avail. Complimentary full bkfst, coffee in rms. Restaurant. Ck-out 11 am, ck-in 3 pm. Business center. Gift shop. Golf. Downhill skiing. Hiking trail. Cr cds: A, MC, V.
🐾 🐴 🕆 🏊 🏇 🔥 🎿 🚶

Guest Ranch

★★★ TRIPLE CREEK RANCH. 5551 W Fork Rd (59829), approx 23 mi S on US 93, W on County Rd 473 for approx 5 mi. 406/821-4600; fax 406/821-4666; res 406/821-4600; toll-free 800/654-2943. Email ter@bitter root.net. 8 cabins, showers only, 2 kit. cabins. AP: S $460-$945; D, kit. cabins $510-$995; each addl $200. Children over 16 yrs only. TV; cable (premium), VCR (movies). Pool; poolside serv. Complimentary coffee in lobby. Restaurant 8-2 pm, 6-8:30 pm. Box lunches, picnics. Bar 6-11 pm; entertainment Wed, Sat, Sun. Ck-out noon, ck-in 3 pm. Gift shop. Meeting rms. Business servs avail. In-rm modem link. Airport transportation. Sports dir. Tennis. Putting green. X-country ski on site. Horse stables. Snowmobiles. Hiking. Lawn games. Soc dir. Exercise equipt. Massage. Refrigerators, wetbars, fireplaces; some in-rm whirlpools. Picnic tables. Cr cds: A, DS, MC, V.

Hardin

(D-6) *See also Billings*

Pop 2,940 **Elev** 2,902 ft
Area code 406 **Zip** 59034
Web www.mcn.net/~custerfight/
Information Chamber of Commerce, 21 E 4th St; 406/665-1672

Hardin became the seat of Big Horn County after the area was opened to white settlers in 1906. It is the trading center for ranchers, farmers, and Native Americans from the Crow Reservation.

What to See and Do

Bighorn Canyon National Recreation Area. (See LOVELL, WY) 43 mi S on MT 313.

Custer National Forest. Approx 1.2 million acres in Montana and South Dakota; Little Missouri Grasslands, an additional 1.2 million acres in North Dakota, is also included. Rolling pine hills and grasslands; picnicking, saddle and pack trips, big-game hunting, camping. E via US 212; incl Beartooth Hwy, a National Forest Scenic Byway (see RED LODGE). Headquarters: 2602 1st Ave N, Billings 59103. Phone 406/657-6361.

Little Bighorn Battlefield National Monument. (see) 13 mi SE off I-90.

Annual Events

Little Big Horn Days. Custer's last stand reenactment. Military Ball, rodeo, street dance, bed races, children's games. Third wkend June.

Crow Fair. Crow Reservation, S on MT 313. Features largest all Native American rodeo in the country. Aug.

Motels/Motor Lodges

★ **AMERICAN INN.** *1324 N Crawford Ave (59034), at I-90 City Center Exit. 406/665-1870; fax 406/665-1615; toll-free 800/582-8094.* 42 rms, 2 story. May-Oct: S $45; D $56-$63; each addl $5; lower rates rest of yr. Crib $2. TV; cable. Pool; whirlpool, waterslide. Playground. Restaurant adj 7 am-10 pm. Ck-out 11 am. Coin lndry. Exercise equipt. Game rm. Cr cds: A, C, D, DS, MC, V.

★ **SUPER 8 MOTEL.** *201 W 14th St (57785). 406/665-1700; fax 406/665-2746; toll-free 800/800-8000.* 53 rms, 2 story. May-Sep: S $47.88; D $49.88-$53.88; each addl $4; under 12 free; higher rates special events; lower rates rest of yr. Crib $2. Pet accepted. TV; cable. Complimentary continental bkfst. Ck-out 11 am. Coin lndry. Meeting rms. Cr cds: A, C, D, DS, MC, V.

Harlowton

Pop 1,049 **Elev** 4,167 ft
Area code 406 **Zip** 59036
Information Chamber of Commerce, PO Box 694; 406/632-4694

A Ranger District office of the Lewis and Clark National Forest (see GREAT FALLS) is located here.

What to See and Do

Deadman's Basin Fishing Access Site. Swimming, fishing, boating; picnicking. Standard fees. 23 mi E on US 12 to milepost 120, then 1 mi N on county road.

Fishing, camping. Martinsdale, Harris, and North Fork lakes. W on US 12. **Lebo Lake.** 9 mi W on US 12 to Twodot, then 7 mi S on County 296.

Annual Event

Rodeo. Chief Joseph Park. NRA approved; parade, concessions, campgrounds. Early July.

Havre

(A-5) *See also Chinook*

Founded 1887 **Pop** 10,201
Elev 2,494 ft **Area code** 406
Zip 59501
Web www.nmclites.edu/havre
Information Chamber of Commerce,
518 1st St, PO Box 308; 406/265-4383

Center of a cattle and wheat-producing area, Havre (HAVE-er) is an important retail and wholesale distribution point for northern Montana. It is one of the oldest and largest division points on the Burlington Northern Santa Fe (formerly Great Northern) Railway.

What to See and Do

Beaver Creek Park. Ten thousand acres. Swimming, fishing, boating; skiing, cross-country skiing, snowmobiling, camping (fee). **Fresno Lake.** Waterskiing, boating; camping. 15 mi NW. About 10 mi S, in Bear Paw Mts. Phone 406/395-4565. **FREE**

Fort Assinniboine. Built in 1879-83 and used as a military fort until 1911. In 1913 it became an agricultural experiment station. Some original buildings still stand. Tours (May-Sep). 6 mi SW on US 87. Phone 406/265-4383. ¢¢

Havre Beneath the Streets. Tour an "underground mall" where many of the 1st businesses in the town were established. Incl turn-of-the-century Sporting Eagle Saloon, Holland and Son Mercantile, Wah Sing Laundry, even an opium den. Tours take approx 1 hr. Res required. (Daily) 100 3rd Ave. Phone 406/265-8888. ¢¢

H. Earl Clack Memorial Museum. Regional history. (Memorial Day-Labor Day, daily, rest of yr, by appt) 306 3rd Ave, in Havre Heritage Center. Phone 406/265-4000. **FREE** Museum manages

> **Wahkpa Chu'gn.** Archealogical excavation of prehistoric bison jump site. Also campground (fee). Tours (Memorial Day-Labor Day, Tues-Sun). ½ mi W on US 2. Phone 406/265-6417 or 406/265-7550. ¢¢

Annual Events

Rocky Boy Powwow. First wkend Aug.
Great Northern Fair. Phone 406/265-7121. Second wk Aug.
Havre Festival Days. Third wkend Sep.

Motel/Motor Lodge

★ **TOWNHOUSE INN.** *601 W 1st St (59501). 406/265-6711; fax 406/265-6213; toll-free 800/442-4667. www.townpump.com.* 104 rms, 1-2 story. S $58; D $62-$66; each addl $4; suites $88-$170. Crib free. Pet accepted, some restrictions; $4. TV; cable (premium). Indoor pool; whirlpool. Restaurant opp open 24 hrs. Bar 8-2 am. Ck-out noon. Coin lndry. Meeting rm. Free airport, railroad station, bus depot transportation. Cr cds: A, C, D, DS, MC, V.

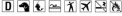

Helena

(C-3) *See also Deer Lodge, White Sulphur Springs*

Settled 1864 **Pop** 24,569 **Elev** 4,157 ft
Area code 406 **Zip** 59601
Web www.helenachamber.com
Information Helena Area Chamber of Commerce, 225 Cruse Ave, Suite A; 406/442-4120 or 800/7-HELENA (outside MT)

Montana's state capital and fourth largest city, Helena was the site of one of the state's largest gold rushes. In 1864, a party of discouraged prospectors decided to explore a gulch—now Helena's Main Street—as their "last chance." This gulch and the area surrounding it produced more than $20 million in gold. A hundred cabins soon appeared. The mining camp, known as "Last Chance," was renamed Helena, after a town in Minnesota. Besides being the governmental center for Montana, today's Helena hosts agricultural and industrial business, including an important smelting and ore refining plant in East Helena.

What to See and Do

The Archie Bray Foundation.
World-famous ceramic artists' studio workshop, gallery, and classroom. 2915 Country Club Ave. Phone 406/443-3502.

Canyon Ferry State Park. (Chinamans Unit) There are numerous recreation sites around this reservoir, which was created in 1954 by the construction of the Canyon Ferry Dam. Swimming, waterskiing, fishing, boating; picnicking, camping (no hookups). Standard fees. 10 mi E on US 12/287, then 6 mi N on MT 284.

Cathedral of St. Helena. Gothic cathedral with 230-ft spires and 68 stained-glass windows made in Germany. Modeled after cathedral in Cologne. (Daily) Lawrence & Warren Aves.

Frontier Town. Rustic pioneer village shaped with solid rock and built with giant logs. Seventy-five-mi view of the Continental Divide. Restaurant, bar. (Mother's Day-early Oct, daily) 15 mi W on US 12, atop Mac-Donald Pass. Phone 406/442-4560. **FREE**

Gates of the Mountains. Twelve-mi, 2-hr Missouri River cruise explores deep gorge in Helena National Forest, discovered and named by Lewis and Clark. Views of cliffs, canyons, wildlife, and wilderness. (Memorial Day wkend-mid-Sep, daily) Launching facilities (Apr-Nov). 16 mi N, off I-15. Phone 406/458-5241. ¢¢

Gold Collection. Collection incl nuggets, wire and leaf gold, gold dust, and coins. (Mon-Fri; closed hols) Norwest Bank Helena, 350 N Last Chance Gulch. Phone 406/447-2000. **FREE**

Helena National Forest. Approx 975,000 acres incl part of the Scapegoat Wilderness and the Gates of the Mountains Wilderness, camp and picnic sites. Scenic drives, fishing, hunting for deer and elk. For info contact Forest Supervisor, 2880 Skyway Dr, 59626. Adj to Helena, accessible from US 12, 91, 287, I-15, MT 200. Phone 406/449-5201.

Holter Museum of Art. Changing exhibits featuring paintings, sculpture, photography, ceramics, weaving. (June-Sep, daily; Oct-May, Tues-Sun; closed hols) 12 E Lawrence. Phone 406/442-6400. **Donation**

★ **Last Chance Tour Train.** Departs from historical museum. Covered trains tour the city's major points of interest, incl Last Chance Gulch. (Mid-May-Sep, daily) Phone 406/442-1023. ¢¢

Marysville Ghost Town. A ghost town, with abandoned saloons, churches, etc., complete with a fully functioning restaurant—**Marysville House**—amidst the ruins. (Restaurant Wed-Sat; summer, Tues-Sat). No phone number avail for restaurant. 7 mi N, off Hwy 279.

★ **Montana Historical Society Museum.** History of Montana in Montana Homeland exhibit; notable collection of Charles M. Russell's art, Haynes Gallery of early Yellowstone Park Photography; military history rm; changing exhibits. Montana Historical Library is on 2nd floor. (Memorial Day-Labor Day, daily; rest of yr, Mon-Sat; closed Jan 1, Thanksgiving, Dec 25) 225 N Roberts St. Phone 406/444-2694. **FREE**

Old Governor's Mansion. (1888) Restored 22-rm brick house used as governor's residence 1913-59. Tours (Mar-Dec, daily). 304 N Ewing St. Phone 406/444-4789. **FREE**

Pioneer Cabin. (1864) Depicts frontier life (1863-83); many authentic furnishings. (Memorial Day-Labor Day, Mon-Fri; rest of yr, by appt) 212 S Park Ave. Phone 406/443-7641. **Donation**

Reeder's Alley. This area previously housed miners, muleskinners, and Chinese laundry workers; now houses specialty shops and a restaurant. Near S end of Last Chance Gulch.

State Capitol. (Closed until July 2001) Neoclassic structure faced with Montana granite and sandstone, topped with a copper dome. Murals by Charles M. Russell, E.S. Paxson, and other artists on display inside. (Daily; guided tours mid-June-Labor Day) Bounded by Lockey & Roberts Sts, 6th & Montana Aves. Phone 406/444-2694. **FREE**

Annual Events

"Race to the Sky" Dog Sled Races. Feb.

Governor's Cup Marathon. Early June.

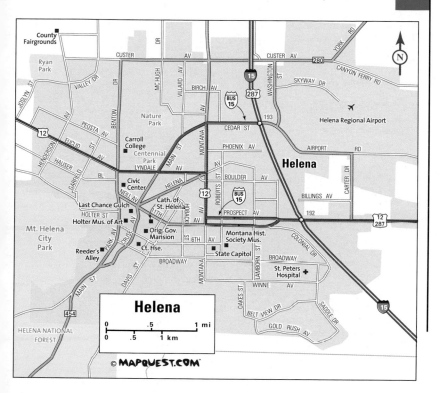

Helena

© MAPQUEST.COM

Montana Traditional Jazz Festival. Mid-June.

Last Chance Stampede & Fair. Lewis and Clark County Fairgrounds. Rodeo. July.

Western Rendezvous of Art. Early Aug.

Seasonal Event

Eagle Watch. Bald eagles migrate to nearby Missouri River to feed on salmon. Mid-Nov-mid-Dec.

Motels/Motor Lodges

★★ **CAVANAUGH'S COLONIAL HOTEL.** *2301 Colonial Dr (59601). 406/443-2100; fax 406/442-0301; toll-free 800/422 1003.* 149 rms, 2 story. S $72-90; D $79-$102; under 18 free. Crib free. TV; cable (premium). 2 heated pools, 1 indoor; poolside serv. Coffee in rms. Restaurant 6 am-9 pm. Bar 5 pm-1:30 am. Ck-out 1 pm. Coin lndry. Meeting rms. Business servs avail. Bellhops. Valet serv. Gift shop. Barber, beauty shop. Free airport transportation. Exercise equipt.

Some bathrm phones, in-rm whirlpools, refrigerators; microwaves avail. Cr cds: A, C, D, DS, MC, V.
D ☒ ⚲ ☒ ☒ SC

★★ **COMFORT INN.** *750 Fee St (59601). 406/443-1000; fax 406/443-1000; toll-free 800/228-5150.* 56 rms, 2 story, 14 suites. June-Aug: S $70; D $75; each addl $5; suites $80-$85; under 18 free; lower rates rest of yr. Crib free. Pet accepted. TV; cable (premium). Indoor pool; whirlpool. Complimentary continental bkfst, coffee in lobby. Restaurant opp open 24 hrs. Ck-out 11 am. Ck-in 2 pm. Business servs avail. Cr cds: A, C, D, DS, ER, JCB, MC, V.
D ☒ ☒ ☒ ☒ SC

★★ **FAIRFIELD INN.** *2150 11th Ave (59601). 406/449-9944; fax 406/449-9949; res 800/228-2800. Email mkeelr@aol.com.* 60 rms, 3 story. June-Aug: S $64; D $69-$79; each addl $5; under 18 free; lower rates rest of yr. Crib free. TV; cable (premium). Complimentary continental bkfst. Restaurant nearby. Ck-out noon. Business servs avail. Coin lndry. Exercise equipt. Indoor pool. Many refrigerators, microwaves. Cr cds: A, C, D, DS, MC, V.

★★ **HOLIDAY INN EXPRESS.** *701 Washington Ave (05701). 406/449-4000; fax 406/449-4522; res 800/465-4329. Email hlnexpress@aol.com.* 68 rms, 3 story, 7 suites. June-Sep: S, D $85; suites $109; lower rates rest of yr. Crib avail. Parking lot. TV; cable (premium). Complimentary continental bkfst, coffee in rms, newspaper, toll-free calls. Restaurant nearby. Ck-out noon, ck-in 3 pm. Meeting rm. Business center. Dry cleaning, coin lndry. Free airport transportation. Exercise equipt. Golf. Tennis. Downhill skiing. Hiking trail. Picnic facilities. Cr cds: A, C, D, DS, JCB, MC, V.

★★ **JORGENSON'S INN AND SUITES.** *1714 11th Ave (59601), 3 blks W of I-15 Capitol Exit. 406/442-1770; fax 406/449-0155; toll-free 800/272-2770.* 117 rms, 3 story. June-Sep: S $46-$62; D $51-$82; each addl $5; suites $92-$99; under 12 free; lower rates rest of yr. Crib $3. TV; cable (premium). Indoor pool. Complimentary coffee in lobby. Restaurant 6:30 am-10 pm. Bar 11:30 am-11 pm. Ck-out noon. Meeting rms. Business servs avail. Free airport transportation. Exercise equipt. Health club privileges. Many bathrm phones; refrigerator in suites. Cr cds: A, D, DS, MC, V.

★★ **SHILO INN.** *2020 Prospect Ave (59601), W of I-15 on US 12, Capitol Exit. 406/442-0320; fax 406/449-4426. Email helena@shiloinns.com.* 47 rms, 3 story, 3 kits. No elvtr. S, D $75; each addl $10; kit. units $85. Crib free. Pet accepted; $7. TV; cable (premium); VCR (movies $5). Indoor pool; whirlpool. Sauna, steam rm. Complimentary continental bkfst. Coffee in rms. Restaurant adj open 24 hrs. Ck-out noon. Coin lndry. Meeting rm. Valet serv. Free airport, bus depot transportation. Bathrm phones, refrigerators. Cr cds: A, C, D, DS, ER, JCB, MC, V.

★ **SUPER 8 MOTEL.** *2200 11th Ave (59601). 406/443-2450; fax 406/443-*2450; toll-free 800/800-8000. 102 rms, 3 story. No elvtr. S $49.88-$62.99; D $58.99-$62.88; each addl $5. Crib free. TV; cable (premium). Restaurant adj 11 am-10 pm. Ck-out 11 am. Coin lndry. Meeting rm. Exercise equipt. Cr cds: A, C, D, DS, MC, V.

B&Bs/Small Inns

★★ **APPLETON INN BED & BREAKFAST.** *1999 Euclid Ave (59601). 406/449-7492; toll-free 800/956-1999. Email appleton@ixi.net; www.appleton inn.com.* 5 rms, 3 story, 1 suite. May-Oct: S $98; D $125; each addl $15; suites $175; lower rates rest of yr. Pet accepted, some restrictions. Parking lot. TV; cable, VCR avail, CD avail. Complimentary full bkfst, newspaper, toll-free calls. Restaurant nearby. Business center. Gift shop. Free airport transportation. Exercise privileges. Golf, 18 holes. Tennis, 5 courts. Downhill skiing. Bike rentals. Hiking trail. Cr cds: A, D, DS, MC, V.

★★ **BARRISTER BED & BREAKFAST.** *416 N Ewing St (59601). 406/443-7330; fax 406/442-7964; toll-free 800/823-1148. Email barister@rcisys. net; www.wtp.net/go/montana/sites/ barrister.html.* 5 rms, 3 story, 1 suite. S, D $90; each addl $15; suites $125. Parking lot. TV; cable. Complimentary full bkfst, coffee in rms, newspaper, toll-free calls. Restaurant nearby. Ck-out 11 am, ck-in 4 pm. Meeting rms. Business center. Free airport transportation. Golf. Tennis. Downhill skiing. Bike rentals. Hiking trail. Picnic facilities. Cr cds: A, D, DS, MC, V.

★★★ **THE SANDERS - HELENA'S BED & BREAKFAST.** *328 N Ewing (59601). 406/442-3309; fax 406/443-2361. Email thefolks@sandersbb.com; www.sandersbb.com.* 7 rms, 2 story. Apr-Oct: S $80; D $105; each addl $20; lower rates rest of yr. Street parking. TV; cable, VCR avail, CD avail. Complimentary full bkfst, coffee in rms, newspaper, toll-free calls. Restaurant nearby. Ck-out 11 am, ck-in 4 pm. Meeting rm. Business center. Exercise privileges. Golf. Tennis, 18 courts. Downhill skiing. Cr cds: A, D, DS, V.

Restaurants

★ **JADE GARDEN.** *3128 N Montana Ave (59602). 406/443-8899.* Specializes in broccoli beef, imperial shrimp, Mandarin pork. Hrs: 11 am-9:30 pm; Fri, Sat to 10 pm. Closed Sun. Wine, beer. Lunch $5.50-$8.75; dinner $4.50-$17.95. Child's menu. Parking. Contemporary Chinese decor. Cr cds: A, DS, MC, V.
D

★★ **ON BROADWAY.** *106 Broadway (59601). 406/443-1929.* Specializes in oven-roasted fresh salmon, pan-blackened tuna, fresh East Coast mussels. Hrs: 5:30-9:30 pm; Fri, Sat to 10 pm. Closed Sun; hols. Bar. Dinner $9.75-$17.75. In 1889 grocery store. Cr cds: A, DS, MC, V.

★★ **STONEHOUSE.** *120 Reeder's Alley (59601). 406/449-2552.* Specializes in wild game, sauteed salmon, bread pudding with rum sauce. Hrs: 5:30-9 pm; Fri, Sat to 9:30 pm. Closed Sun; hols. Res accepted. Wine, beer. Dinner $11.95-$19.95. Child's menu. Turn-of-the-century house. Cr cds: A, DS, MC, V.
D SC

★ **WINDBAG SALOON.** *19 S Last Chance Gulch (59601). 406/443-9669.* Specializes in Northwestern seafood, prime rib, fresh cobb salads. Hrs: 11 am-2:30 pm, 5-9:30 pm; Sat from 5 pm. Closed Sun; hols. Bar. Lunch $5-$7.75; dinner $6.25-$18.95. In former bordello; antique bar. Cr cds: A, DS, MC, V.
D

Kalispell

(B-2) *See also Bigfork, Columbia Falls, Whitefish*

Founded 1891 **Pop** 11,917
Elev 2,955 ft **Area code** 406
Zip 59901 **Web** www.fcvb.org
Information Flathead Convention & Visitor Bureau, 15 Depot Park; 406/756-9091 or 800/543-3105

Center of a mountain vacationland, Kalispell is the convention center of the Flathead Valley. Seed potatoes and sweet cherries are grown and processed in great quantities. Recreational activities abound in the area.

What to See and Do

Conrad Mansion. (1895) A 23-rm Norman-style mansion, authentically furnished and restored. Tours (mid-May-mid-Oct, daily). 6 blks E of Main St on 4th St E. Phone 406/755-2166. ¢¢

Flathead Lake. (See POLSON) 9 mi S on US 93.

Flathead National Forest. A 2.3 million-acre forest; incl part of 1,009,356-acre Bob Marshall Wilderness; 286,700-acre Great Bear Wilderness and the 73,573-acre Mission Mts Wilderness; 15,368-acre Jewel Basin hiking area and the 219-mi Flathead National Wild & Scenic river system. Spectacular geological formations; glaciers, wild areas. Swimming, fishing, boating, canoeing; riding, picnicking, camping (June-Sep; fee), hunting, outfitters and guides, winter sports, recreation resorts, scenic drives. Contact Supervisor, 1935 3rd Ave E. Near US 2, 93, adj to W & S sides of Glacier Natl Park. Phone 406/755-5401.

Glacier National Park. (see)

Hockaday Center for the Arts. Changing exhibits; sales gallery. (Tues-Sat; closed hols) 3rd St & 2nd Ave E. Phone 406/755-5268. ¢

Lawrence Park. Preserved in natural state. Picnic, playground facilities. E off N Main St. **FREE**

Woodland Park. Thirty-seven acres. Flower and rock gardens, bird exhibit, mi-long lagoon, skating rink (winter), picnicking, kitchen, playground, pool, wading pool (fees). (Daily) 8 blks E of Main St on 2nd St E. **FREE**

Annual Events

Agriculture-Farm Show. Two days mid Feb.

Youth Horse Show. May.

Flathead Music Festival. July.

Quarter Horse Show. July.

Northwest Montana Fair & Rodeo. Flathead County Fairgrounds. Mid-Aug.

Glacier Jazz Stampede. Oct.

Motels/Motor Lodges

★★ **BEST WESTERN OUTLAW HOTEL.** *1701 Hwy 93 S (59901). 406/755-6100; fax 406/756-8994. Email rhonda.dominick@westcoast hotels.com.* 220 rms, 3 story. S $82-$135; D $92-$175; each addl $10; under 12 free; package plans. Crib $7. Pet accepted; $10. TV; cable (premium). 2 indoor pools; wading pool, whirlpool. Playground. Coffee in rms. Restaurant 6 am-10 pm. Bar 11-2 am. Ck-out 11 am. Coin lndry. Meeting rms. Business servs avail. Bellhops. Valet serv. Sundries. Gift shop. Barber, beauty shop. Tennis. Exercise equipt; sauna. Game rm. Microwaves avail. Some balconies. Casino. Western art gallery. Cr cds: A, DS, MC, V.

[D] [icons] SC

★ **DAYS INN.** *1550 Hwy 93 N (59901). 406/756-3222; fax 406/756-3277; toll-free 800/329-7466.* 53 rms, 2 story. Mid-May-Sep: S $59-$69; D $74-$79; each addl $5; suites $75-$85; under 12 free; lower rates rest of yr. Crib free. TV; cable (premium). Complimentary continental bkfst. Restaurant nearby. Ck-out 11 am. Meeting rm. Cr cds: A, C, D, DS, JCB, MC, V.

[D] [icons] SC

★★ **HAMPTON INN.** *1140 W US 2 (59901). 406/755-7900; fax 406/755-5056; res 800/HAMPTON. www.north westinns.com.* 120 rms, 3 story. June-Sep: S $83; D $93; suites $155-$205; under 19 free; lower rates rest of yr. Crib free. Pet accepted. TV; cable (premium), VCR. Complimentary continental bkfst, coffee in rms. Restaurant adj 7 am-10 pm. Ck-out noon. Meeting rms. Business center. Bellhops. Valet serv. Sundries. Gift shop. Coin lndry. Free airport transportation. Downhill/x-country ski 16 mi. Exercise equipt. Indoor pool; whirlpool. Rec rm. Refrigerators; in-rm whirlpool, microwave, wet bar, fireplace in suites. Cr cds: A, C, D, DS, JCB, MC, V.

[D] [icons]

★★★ **WEST COAST KALISPELL CENTER.** *20 N Main St (59901). 406/752-6660; fax 406/751-5051; res 800/325-4000.* 132 rms, 3 story, 14 suites. Mid-May-Sep: S $98; D $105; each addl $12; suites $120-$190; kit. units $150, under 18 free; ski, golf plans; lower rates rest of yr. Crib free. Pet accepted, some restrictions. TV; cable. Indoor pool; whirlpools. Coffee in rms. Restaurant 6:30 am-10 pm. Bar 4 pm-2 am; entertainment Fri, Sat. Ck-out noon. Meeting rms. Business servs avail. Bellhops. Shopping arcade. Barber, beauty shop. Downhill ski 20 mi; x-country ski 15 mi. Exercise equipt; sauna. Casino. Adj to 50-store indoor shopping mall. Cr cds: A, D, DS, MC, V.

[D] [icons]

Hotel

★ **KALISPELL GRAND HOTEL.** *100 Main St (59901). 406/755-8100; fax 406/752-8012; toll-free 800/858-7422. Email grand@kalispellgrand.com; www. kalispellgrand.com.* 38 rms, 3 story, 2 suites. June-Sep: S $74; D $81; each addl $7; under 12 free; lower rates rest of yr. Crib avail. Pet accepted. Parking lot. TV; cable (premium). Complimentary continental bkfst, toll-free calls. Restaurant 11:30 am-5:30 pm, closed Sun. Bar. Ck-out 11 am, ck-in 3 pm. Meeting rm. Business servs avail. Dry cleaning. Salon/barber. Exercise privileges. Golf. Tennis, 2 courts. Downhill skiing. Cr cds: A, D, DS, MC, V.

[icons]

Villa/Condo

★★★ **ANGEL POINT GUEST SUITES.** *829 Angel Point Rd (59922), 14 mi S on US 93. 406/844-2204; toll-free 800/214-2204. Email anglpt@ in-tch.com; www.mtcondos.com.* 2 suites. Each addl $35; suites $115; children $35; lower rates rest of yr. Parking lot. TV; cable (premium). Restaurant. Ck-out 11 am, ck-in 3 pm. Golf. Downhill skiing. Beach access. Hiking trail. Picnic facilities. No cr cds accepted.

[icons]

Restaurant

★★ **FIRST AVENUE WEST.** *139 W 1st Ave (59901). 406/755-4441.* Italian menu. Specializes in grilled fresh seafood, pasta. Hrs: 5-9:30 pm; Fri, Sat to 10 pm. Closed Thanksgiving, Dec 25. Res accepted. Bar. Dinner $4.95-$16.95. Child's menu. Casual, bistro atmosphere. Cr cds: MC, V.

[D] [icons]

Lewistown (C-5)

Founded 1881 **Pop** 6,051
Elev 3,963 ft **Area code** 406
Zip 59457
Web www.lewistown.net/~lewchamb
Information Chamber of Commerce,
PO Box 818; 406/538-5436

At the geographic center of the state,
amid some of Montana's finest farming and ranching country, Lewistown
is a farm trade community. The area
is famous for hard, premium wheat
and high-grade registered cattle.
Originally a small trading post on
the Carroll Trail, it was first called
"Reed's Fort," and later renamed to
honor a Major Lewis who established
a fort two miles south in 1876.

What to See and Do

Big Spring Creek. One of the top
rainbow trout streams in the country.
Picnic grounds. Running N and S.

**Charles M. Russell National Wildlife
Refuge.** Missouri River "Breaks" and
prairie lands; wildlife incl pronghorn, elk, mule, and whitetail deer;
bighorn sheep, sage, and sharptail
grouse. Refuge (daily, 24 hrs). Lewistown headquarters (Mon-Fri; closed
hols). 70 mi NE via US 191 or MT
200. Phone 406/538-8706. **FREE**

Fort Maginnis. Ruins of 1880 frontier
post. 15 mi E on US 87, then 10 mi N.

**Historical points of 19th-century gold
mining. Maiden.** 10 mi N on US 191,
then 6 mi E. **Kendall.** 16 mi N on US
191, then 6 mi W on gravel road.
Giltedge. 14 mi E on US 87, then 6
mi NW.

Annual Events

**Central Montana Horse Show, Fair,
Rodeo.** Fergus County Fairgrounds.
Last full wk in July.

Montana Cowboy Poetry Gathering.
Modern-day cowboys and admirers
of Western folklore relate life "down
on the range" through original
poetry. Third wkend Aug.

Seasonal Events

Drag Races. Quarter-mile races.
NHRA sanctioned. Late May-Sep.

Charlie Russell Chew-Choo. Three-
and-a-half-hr dinner train runs
through rugged beauty of Central
Montana. Sat. June-Sep.

Motel/Motor Lodge

★ **LEWISTOWN SUPER 8 MOTEL.**
102 Wendell Ave (59457). 406/538-
2581; fax 406/538-2702; res 800/800-
8000. 44 rms, 2 story. June-Sep: S
$42.88; D $45.88-$48.88; each addl
$4; under 12 free; lower rates rest of
yr. Crib free. TV; cable (premium).
Complimentary coffee in lobby.
Restaurant opp 7 am-10 pm. Ck-out
11 am. Coin lndry. Cr cds: A, DS,
MC, V.

Restaurant

★ **WHOLE FAMDAMILY.** *206 W
Main St (59457), on US 87.* 406/538-
5161. Own desserts. Hrs: 11 am-8
pm; Sat to 5 pm. Closed Sun; hols.
Res accepted. Wine, beer. Lunch $4-
$7; dinner $5.95-$6.50. Child's
menu. Decorated with family portraits. Cr cds: A, DS, MC, V.
D

Libby

*(A-1) See also Kalispell; also see Bonners
Ferry, ID; Sandpoint, ID*

Settled 1863 **Pop** 2,532 **Elev** 2,086 ft
Area code 406 **Zip** 59923
Web www.libby.org

Information Chamber of Commerce,
905 W 9th St, PO Box 704; 406/293-
4167

Nestled in the Cabinet Mountains,
Libby, formerly a gold town, is now
busy processing logs. It is headquarters for Kootenai National Forest,
which has three Ranger District
offices.

What to See and Do

Camping. Libby Ranger District;.
406/293-7773 incl 3 campgrounds.
Howard Lake Campground; 26 mi S
on Hwy 2, 5 mi on W Fisher Rd.
McGillvray Campground; 13 mi
NE, near Lake Koocanusa. **McGregor
Lake;** 53 mi SE on Hwy 2.

Heritage Museum. Located in 12-
sided log bldg and featuring various
exhibits on area pioneers; animal
exhibits; art gallery; exhibits by the
Forest Service, mining interests, the
lumber industry. (June-Aug, Mon-Sat,
also Sun afternoons) 1¼ mi S via US
2. Phone 406/293-7521. **Donation**

Kootenai National Forest. More than
2.2 million acres. Incl 94,360-acre
Cabinet Mts Wilderness. Scenic drives along Yaak River, Lake Koocanusa
Reservoir, Fisher River, Bull River;
Giant Cedars Nature Trail. Ross Creek
Cedars. Fishing, boating, canoeing;
hiking trails, cross-country skiing,
picknicking, camping. For info contact Supervisor's Office, 1101 W Hwy
2. Surrounds Libby, accessible on US
2, MT 37 and Hwy 56. Phone
406/293-6211. In the forest is

> **Turner Mountain Ski Area.** T-bar,
> rope tow; patrol; school; snack bar.
> (Late Dec-early Jan, daily; rest of
> Dec, early Jan-Mar, Sat-Sun) 23 mi
> NW on Pipe Creek Rd. ¢¢¢¢

Libby Dam. Lake Koocanusa extends
90 mi upstream. A US Army Corps of
Engineers project. Fishing, boating
(dock); picnicking. (Daily) Visitor
center and gift shop; tours of dam
and powerhouse
(hrly); viewpoints
(Memorial Day-
Labor Day, daily).
17 mi NE on MT
37. Phone
406/293-5577.
FREE

Annual Events

Logger Days. Adult
and child logging
contests. Carnival,
parade, karaoke
contest. Vendors,
food. Early July.

Nordicfest. Scandi-
navian festival,
parade, dances,
food, melodrama.
Third wkend Sep.

Little Bighorn Battlefield National Monument

See also Billings, Hardin

*(2 mi SE of Crow Agency. Entrance 1 mi
E of I-90 on US 212)*

Scene of Custer's "last stand," this
monument memorializes one of the
last armed clashes between Northern
Plains tribes, fighting to preserve their
traditional way of life, and the forces
of the United States, charged with
safeguarding westward expansion.
Here, on June 25, 1876, Lieutenant
Colonel George A. Custer and
approximately 263 men of the US
Army 7th Cavalry and attached
personnel were killed in a battle
against an overwhelming force of
Lakota and Cheyenne warriors. Also
here are a national cemetery,
established in 1879; and the Reno-
Benteen Battlefield, five miles
southeast, where the remainder of the
7th Cavalry withstood until late on
June 26. Headstones show where the
soldiers fell and a large obelisk marks
the mass grave of the 7th Cavalry. A
visitor center contains a bookstore and
museum with dioramas and exhibits
(daily; closed Jan 1, Thanksgiving, Dec
25). National Park Service personnel

Custer National Cemetery

provide interpretive programs (Memorial Day-Labor Day), guided tours of Custer National Cemetery. For further info contact PO Box 39, Crow Agency 59022; 406/638-2621. ¢¢-¢¢¢

Livingston

(D-4) *See also Big Timber, Bozeman*

Settled 1882 **Pop** 6,701 **Elev** 4,503 ft
Area code 406 **Zip** 59047
Web www.livingston.avicom.net
Information Chamber of Commerce, 208 W Park; 406/222-0850

Railroading has been a key to the town's history and economy since railroad surveyors first named it Clark City; later the present name was adopted to honor a director of the Northern Pacific Railway. Today agriculture, ranching, and tourism are the chief industries. Farm products from Paradise and Shields valleys also pass through the town. Trout fishing is excellent in the Yellowstone River. A Ranger District office of the Gallatin National Forest (see BOZEMAN) is located here.

What to See and Do

Depot Center. Changing exhibits and cultural art shows. Gift shop. (Mid-May-mid-Oct, Mon-Sat, also Sun afternoons) Park & 2nd Sts. Phone 406/222-2300. ¢

Emigrant Gulch. Gold was discovered here in 1862. Chico and Yellowstone City boomed busily but briefly—the gold supply was limited and the Crow were aggressive. Both are ghost towns now. 37 mi S, off US 89.

Park County Museum. "House of Memories"; pioneer tools, library, old newspapers, sheep wagon, stagecoach, Native American and archaeological exhibits. Northern Pacific Railroad Rm. (June-Labor Day, afternoons; rest of yr, by appt) 118 W Chinook. Phone 406/222-4184. ¢- ¢¢

Annual Event

Round-up Rodeo. Fairgrounds. Early July.

Motels/Motor Lodges

★★ **BEST WESTERN/YELLOWSTONE MOTOR INN.** *1515 W Park St (59047). 406/222-6110; fax 406/222-3976; res 800/826-1214.* 99 rms, 3 story. Mid-May-mid-Sep: S, D $72-$99; each addl $7; kit. unit $144; under 13 free; wkly rates; lower rates rest of yr. Crib free. Pet accepted; $8. TV; cable. Complimentary coffee in lobby. Restaurant 6 am-10 pm. Bar noon-2 am. Ck-out noon. Meeting rms. Business servs avail. Bellhops. Sundries. Barber, beauty shop. Indoor pool. Cr cds: A, C, D, DS, MC, V.
🄳 🐾 ⛱ 🛜 🔥 SC

★★ **COMFORT INN.** *114 Love Ln (59047), I-90 Exit 333. 406/222-4400; fax 406/222-7658.* 49 rms, 2 story. July-Aug: S $74.95; D $79.95-$84.95; each addl $5; suites $96.95-$106.95; under 18 free; lower rates rest of yr. Crib free. TV; cable (premium). Complimentary continental bkfst. Restaurant nearby. Ck-out 11 am. Meeting rm. Bellhops. Sundries. Coin lndry. Indoor pool; whirlpool. Game rm. Refrigerator, wet bar in suites. Cr cds: A, C, D, DS, MC, V.
🄳 ⛱ 🛜 🔥 SC

★ **LIVINGSTON SUPER 8.** *105 Centennial Dr (59047), I-90 Exit 333. 406/222-7711; fax 406/222-8654; res 800/800-8000.* 36 rms, 2 story. June-Aug: S $57; D $65; each addl $4; suites $71; under 13 free; lower rates rest of yr. Crib avail. Parking lot. TV; cable (premium). Complimentary continental bkfst, toll-free calls. Restaurant nearby. Ck-out 11 am, ck-in 2 pm. Fax servs avail. Coin lndry. Golf, 9 holes. Downhill skiing. Cr cds: A, D, DS, JCB, MC, V.
🄳 🏌 🐾 🎿 ⛱ 🔥

★ **PARADISE INN.** *Park Rd and Rogers Ln (59047), Exit 333. 406/222-6320; fax 406/222-2481; toll-free 800/437-6291.* 43 rms. Mid-May-Sep: S, D $79-$89; each addl $5; suites $99-$129; lower rates rest of yr. Crib $5. Pet accepted; $5. TV; cable (premium). Indoor pool. Restaurant 6 am-10:30 pm. Bar 3 pm-2 am. Ck-out 11 am. Cr cds: A, MC, V.
🄳 🐾 🏌 🎿 ⛱ 🎿 🛜 🐾

Resort

★★ CHICO HOT SPRINGS RESORT. *Old Chico Rd (59065), approx 25 mi S on US 89 to Emigrant, then E on MT 540.* 406/333-4933; fax 406/333-4694; toll-free 800/468-9232. Email chico@chicohotsprings.com; www.chicohotsprings.com. 102 rms, 2 story, 7 suites. Dec-Jan, June-Sep: S, D $85; each addl $5; suites $189; under 6 free; lower rates rest of yr. Crib avail, fee. Pet accepted, fee. Street parking. Pool, lap pool, children's pool. TV; cable (premium). Complimentary coffee in rms. Restaurant 5-midnight. Bar. Ck-out 11 am, ck-in 3 pm. Meeting rms. Business servs avail. Concierge. Gift shop. Golf, 9 holes. Downhill skiing. Bike rentals. Supervised children's activities. Hiking trail. Cr cds: A, DS, MC, V.

Guest Ranch

★★★ MOUNTAIN SKY GUEST RANCH. *Big Creek Rd (59027), 35 mi S of Livingston; off US 89, turn at Big Creek Rd.* 406/333-4911; fax 406/587-3397; toll-free 800/548-3392. Email mountainsky@mcn.net; www.mtnsky.com. 27 cabins, 1-3 bedrm. No rm phones. AP, June-Sep: S, D $2,030-$2,450/wk; family rates; 50% deposit required to confirm res. Closed rest of yr. Heated pool; whirlpool. Playground. Free supervised children's activities (mid-June-Aug). Coffee in rms. Ck-out 10 am, ck-in 3 pm. Guest lndry. Meeting rms. Business servs avail. Airport transportation. Tennis, pro. Sauna. Float trips. Lawn games. Hiking. Soc dir; entertainment. Rec rm. Refrigerators. 30 mi N of Yellowstone National Park. Cr cds: MC, V.

Restaurants

★★★ LIVINGSTON. *130 N Main St (59047).* 406/222-7909. Specializes in baked poussin, fresh grouper, New York strip steak. Own baking. Hrs: 5-10 pm. Closed Thanksgiving, Dec 25. Res accepted. Bar. Wine list. Dinner $18-$20. Child's menu. Street parking. Turn-of-the-century bldg has 100-yr-old mahogany bar; overlooks downtown. Cr cds: A, DS, MC, V.

★★ UNCLE LOOIE'S. *119 W Park St (59047).* 406/222-7177. Specializes in pasta, beef, seafood. Hrs: 11:30 am-2:30 pm, 5:30-10 pm; Sat, Sun from 5:30 pm. Closed Thanksgiving, Dec 25. Res accepted. Bar. Lunch $5.95-$10.95. Buffet: $5.95; dinner $7.95-$21.95. Child's menu. Italian, Mediterranean theme. Cr cds: DS, MC, V.

Malta (B-6)

Pop 2,340 **Elev** 2,255 ft
Area code 406 **Zip** 59538
Information Malta Area Chamber of Commerce, PO Box 1420; 406/654-1776 or 800/704-1776

What to See and Do

Bowdoin National Wildlife Refuge. Approx 15,500 acres provide excellent nesting, resting, and feeding grounds for migratory waterfowl. The refuge also supports whitetailed deer and pronghorns. Use of the self-guided drive-through trail is recommended. (Daily; weather permitting) 7 mi E via Old US 2. Phone 406/654-2863. **FREE**

Phillips County Museum. Features Native American, homestead, and dinosaur exhibits. (Mid-May-Labor Day, Tues-Sat) US 2 E. Phone 406/654-1037. ¢¢

Motel/Motor Lodge

★ MALTANA. *138 S 1st Ave W (59538).* 406/654-2610; fax 406/654-1663; toll-free 800/735-9278. Email elmendel@ttc-cmc.net. 18 rms, 1 story, 1 suite. S $37; D $44; each addl $4. Crib avail, fee. Parking lot. TV; cable. Complimentary coffee in rms, toll-free calls. Restaurant nearby. Fax servs avail. Free airport transportation. Golf. Cr cds: A, C, D, DS, MC, V.

Miles City (C-7)

Pop 8,461 **Elev** 2,358 ft
Area code 406 **Zip** 59301
Web www.midrivers.com/
~mcchamber
Information Chamber of Commerce,
901 Main St; 406/232-2890

This trade, industrial, and energy-concerned city is also a livestock and agricultural center. Seat of Custer County, the city is named for a US infantry general. Here are the Livestock Auction Saleyards where about 25 percent of Montana's livestock is processed.

What to See and Do

Custer County Art Center. Housed in former holding tanks of old Miles City Water Works, overlooking the Yellowstone River. Contemporary art exhibits. Gift shop. (Tues-Sun afternoons; closed hols) Water Plant Rd, W via US 10, 12. Phone 406/232-0635. **FREE**

Range Riders Museum and Pioneer Memorial Hall. Exhibits and memorabilia of the days of the open range. Bert Clark gun collection, one of the largest in the Northwest. (Apr-Oct) W end of Main St. Phone 406/232-6146. ¢¢

Annual Events

Bucking Horse Sale. Fairgrounds. Exit 135 off I-94. Born in 1951, it grew out of the Miles City Roundup. Features Wild Horse Stampede, bronc and bull riding, and the sale of both bucking horses and bulls. Third wkend May.

Ballon Roundup. Fourth wkend June.

Eastern Montana Fair. Fairgrounds. Exit 135 off I-94. Four days late Aug.

Motels/Motor Lodges

★★ **BEST WESTERN INN.** *1015 S Haynes Ave (59301), off I-90 Exit 138. 406/232-4560; fax 406/232-0363; toll-free 800/528-1234.* 54 rms, 2 story. May-Sep: S $66; D $71; each addl $6; suites $100; under 18 free; higher rates Bucking Horse Sale; lower rates rest of yr. Crib $6. Pet accepted. TV; cable (premium). Indoor pool; whirl-pool. Complimentary continental bkfst. Ck-out noon. Meeting rms. Cr cds: A, C, D, DS, JCB, MC, V.

★★ **COMFORT INN.** *1615 S Haynes Ave (59301). 406/232-3141; fax 406/232-2924; toll-free 800/228-5150. Email rbls@midrivers.com.* 49 rms, 2 story. May-Aug: S $52.95; D $57.95-$62.95; each addl $5; under 18 free; higher rates Bucking Horse Sale; lower rates rest of yr. Crib free. TV; cable (premium). Indoor pool; whirl-pool. Complimentary continental bkfst. Ck-out 11 am. Coin lndry. Meeting rms. Business servs avail. Cr cds: A, D, DS, MC, V.

Hotel

★★ **HOLIDAY INN EXPRESS.** *1720 S Haynes (59301). 406/232-1000; fax 406/232-1365; res 800/465-4389; toll-free 800/700-0402. Email hiexpmc@ mcn.net; www.hiexpress.com.* 46 rms, 2 story, 6 suites. June-Aug: S, D $85; suites $115; lower rates rest of yr. Crib avail. Parking lot. Indoor pool, whirlpool. TV; cable (premium), VCR avail. Complimentary continental bkfst, coffee in rms, toll-free calls. Restaurant. Ck-out 11 am, ck-in 3 pm. Meeting rm. Business servs avail. Dry cleaning, coin lndry. Exercise privileges. Golf, 9 holes. Tennis, 8 courts. Cr cds: A, C, D, DS, JCB, MC, V.

Missoula

(C-2) *See also Hamilton*

Settled 1860 **Pop** 42,918 **Elev** 3,200 ft
Area code 406
Information Chamber of Commerce, 825 E Front, PO Box 7577, 59807; 406/543-6623

Since the days of the Lewis and Clark Expedition, Missoula has been a trading and transportation crossroads. It is a lumber and paper manufacturing center, the hub of large reserves of timber, and the regional headquarters of the United States Forest Service and Montana State Forest Service.

What to See and Do

⭐ **Aerial Fire Depot.** Forest Service headquarters for aerial attack on forest fires in western US. Smokejumpers trained and based here during summer. 7 mi W on US 10, I-90, ½ mi W of Johnson Bell Airport. Phone 406/329-4900.

Northern Forest Fire Laboratory. Conducts research in fire prevention and control and the beneficial uses of fire in forest management. Tours by appt. Phone 406/329-4934.

Smokejumper Center. Training and dispatching center for airborne fire crews; parachute and fire training. **FREE**

Visitor Center. Fire management exhibits, guided tour of parachute loft and training facilities; films, information on recreational facilities in 13 national forests in region. (Memorial Day-Labor Day, daily; rest of yr, by appt) Phone 406/329-4934. **Donation**

Historical Museum at Fort Missoula. Established to interpret the history of Missoula County and forest management and timber production in western Montana. The museum features indoor galleries with permanent and changing exhibits; outdoor area incl 10 historic structures, 4 restored. Located in the core of what was originally Fort Missoula (1877-1947). Several original bldgs remain. Other areas incl railroad and military history. (Tues-Sun; closed hols) 5 mi S from I-90 via Reserve St to South Ave, then 1 mi W. Phone 406/728-3476. ¢¢

Lolo National Forest. Foot trails to 100 lakes and peaks, camping (mid-May-Sep, full service campgrounds, some free); fishing; picnicking, hunting, winter sports, scenic drives through 2,062,545 acres. Incl Welcome Creek Wilderness and Rattlesnake National Recreation Area and Wilderness, part of Scapegoat Wilderness, and Selway-Bitterroot Wilderness. The Pattee Canyon Recreation Area is 5 mi from town. Historic Lolo Trail and Lewis & Clark Hwy (US 12) over Bitterroot Mts take visitors along route of famed exploration. Contact Supervisor, Fort Missoula, Bldg 24, 59801. Surrounds Missoula, accessible on US 10, 12, 93, MT 200, 83, I-90. Phone 406/329-3750. A Ranger District office is also located here.

Missoula Carousel. Carousel features hand-carved horses—the first such carousel in the US to do so in over 60 yrs. Gift shop. (Daily) In Caras Park, just W of the Higgins Bridge. Phone 406/728-0447.

Missoula Museum of the Arts. Art of the western states. Changing exhibits. Educational programs. Museum shop. (Mon-Sat afternoons) 335 N Pattee. Phone 406/728-0447. **FREE**

Missoula Public Library. Outstanding collection of historical works on Montana and the Northwest and genealogical materials. 301 E Main St. Phone 406/721-2665.

Paxson Paintings. Eight murals depicting Montana's history by one of the West's outstanding artists. (Mon-Fri; closed hols) County Courthouse, 200 W Broadway between Orange and Higgins Sts. Phone 406/721-5700, ext 3200. **FREE**

St. Francis Xavier Church. (1889) Steeple highlights this structure built the same year Montana became a state. (Daily) 420 W Pine St. Phone 406/542-0321.

Skiing.

Marshall Mountain Ski Area. Triple chairlift, T-bar, rope tow; school, patrol, rentals, snowmaking; half-day rates; cafeteria, snack bar. Longest run 2 mi; vertical drop 1,500 ft. (Dec-Mar, Wed-Sun) 7 mi NE via I-90, E Missoula exit. Phone 406/258-6000. ¢¢¢¢

Montana Snowbowl. 2 double chairlifts, T-bar, rope tow; patrol, school, rentals; cafeteria, bar. Longest run 3 mi; vertical drop 2,600 ft. (Late Nov-Apr, daily) Lifts fee; tow free. Summer chairlift. Hiking trails; mountain biking; 9-hole disc golf course. (Last wkend June-mid-Sep, Fri-Sun) 3 mi NW on I-90 (Reserve St Exit), then 9 mi N on Giant Creek Rd to Snow Bowl Rd. Phone 406/549-9777. Summer ¢¢¢; Winter ¢¢¢¢

University of Montana. (1893) 10,000 students. At the foot of Mt Sentinel. University Center Gallery and

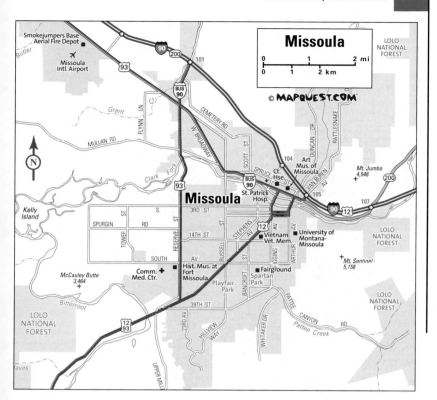

Gallery of Visual Arts. Campus tours. University & Arthur Aves. Phone 406/243-2522.

Annual Events

International Wildlife Film Festival. Downtown. Phone 406/728-9380. Early Apr.

Western Montana Quarter Horse Show. Fairgrounds. Early July.

Western Montana Fair. Fairgrounds. Mid-Aug.

Motels/Motor Lodges

★ **BEST INN AND CONFERENCE CENTER.** *3803 Brooks St (59804). 406/251-2665; fax 406/251-5733; res 800/237-8466; toll-free 800/272-9500. Email mtgs-4-u@bigsky.net; www. bestinn.com.* 81 rms, 3 story, 4 suites. Apr-Sep: S, D $69; suites $120; lower rates rest of yr. Crib avail, fee. Pet accepted, fee. Parking lot. TV; cable. Complimentary continental bkfst, newspaper. Restaurant. Ck-out noon, ck-in 2 pm. Meeting rms. Business servs avail. Dry cleaning, coin lndry. Free airport transportation. Golf, 18 holes. Tennis, 4 courts. Downhill skiing. Cr cds: A, DS, MC, V.

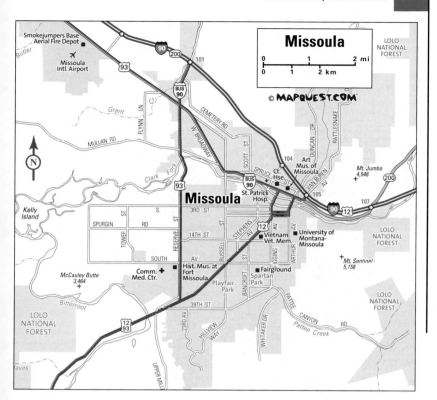

★ **BEST INN NORTH.** *4953 N Reserve St (59808), I-90 Exit 101. 406/542-7550; fax 406/721-5931; res 800/237-8466; toll-free 800/272-9500. www.bestinn.com.* 67 rms, 3 story. May-Sep: S, D $69; under 18 free; lower rates rest of yr. Crib avail. Pet accepted, fee. Parking lot. TV; cable (premium). Complimentary continental bkfst, coffee in rms, toll-free calls. Restaurant noon-midnight. Ck-out noon, ck-in 2 pm. Business servs avail. Dry cleaning, coin lndry. Free airport transportation. Whirlpool. Golf. Tennis, 4 courts. Downhill skiing. Cr cds: A, C, D, DS, MC, V.

★★ **HAMPTON INN.** *4805 N Reserve St (59802). 406/549-1800; fax 406/549-1737; toll-free 800/426-7866.* 60 rms, 4 story. S $69-$79; D $79-

$89; under 18 free. Crib free. Pet accepted; $5. TV; cable (premium). Indoor pool; whirlpool. Complimentary continental bkfst. Restaurant nearby. Ck-out noon. Meeting rms. Business servs avail. Bellhops. Valet serv. Free airport transportation. Exercise equipt. Cr cds: A, C, D, DS, MC, V.

D ⬛ ⬛ ⬛ ⬛ ⬛ SC

★★ **HOLIDAY INN PARKSIDE.** *200 S Pattee St (59802). 406/721-8550; toll-free 800/379-0408. Email info@ park-side.com.* 200 rms, 4 story. S, D $88-$99; suites $125-$150; under 18 free. Pet accepted. TV; cable. Indoor pool; whirlpool. Restaurant 6:30 am-2 pm, 5:30-10:30 pm. Bar 2 pm-2 am; entertainment Fri, Sat. Ck-out noon. Meeting rms. Business servs avail. Bellhops. Gift shop. Free airport transportation. Downhill ski 12 mi; x-country ski 5 mi. Exercise equipt; sauna. Balconies. Open atrium, outside patio dining. On Clark Fork River and park. Cr cds: A, DS, MC, V.

D ⬛ ⬛ ⬛ ⬛ ⬛ ⬛ ⬛ SC

★ **ORANGE STREET BUDGET MOTOR INN MISSOULA.** *801 N Orange St (59806). 406/721-3610; fax 406/721-8875; toll-free 800/328-0801. Email krisd@bigsky.net.* 81 rms, 3 story. May-Sep: S $46; D $50; lower rates rest of yr. Crib avail, fee. Pet accepted, some restrictions, fee. Parking lot. TV; cable (premium), VCR avail. Complimentary continental bkfst. Restaurant nearby. Ck-out 11 am, ck-in noon. Meeting rm. Business center. Dry cleaning. Free airport transportation. Exercise equipt. Golf, 18 holes. Tennis, 2 courts. Downhill skiing. Picnic facilities. Cr cds: A, C, D, DS, MC, V.

D ⬛ ⬛ ⬛ ⬛ ⬛ ⬛ ⬛

★ **RED LION INN.** *700 W Broadway (59802), ½ mi S of I-90 Orange St Exit. 406/728-3300; fax 406/728-4441; res 800/733-5466. Email rlmi@hotmail. com; www.redlion.com.* 76 rms, 2 story. May-Sep: S, D $99; each addl $10; under 18 free; lower rates rest of yr. Crib avail. Pet accepted, some restrictions, fee. Parking lot. Pool, whirlpool. TV; cable (premium), VCR avail. Complimentary continental bkfst, coffee in rms, newspaper, toll-free calls. Restaurant 11 am-10 pm. Ck-out noon, ck-in 3 pm. Meeting

rm. Business center. Dry cleaning, coin lndry. Gift shop. Free airport transportation. Exercise equipt. Golf. Tennis. Downhill skiing. Hiking trail. Cr cds: A, C, D, DS, MC, V.

D ⬛ ⬛ ⬛ ⬛ ⬛ ⬛ ⬛ ⬛ ⬛ SC ⬛

★ **SLEEP INN.** *3425 Dore Ln (59801). 406/543-5883; fax 406/543-5883; toll-free 800/228-5050.* 59 rms, 3 story, 10 suites. Mid-May-Aug: S $59.95; D $64.95-$69.95; each addl $5; suites $74.95-$79.95; under 18 free; higher rates Univ of Montana graduation; lower rates rest of yr. Crib free. Pet accepted, some restrictions. TV; cable (premium). Complimentary continental bkfst. Restaurant opp 6:30 am-10 pm. Ck-out 11 am. Business servs avail. Bellhops. Indoor pool; whirlpool. Cr cds: A, D, DS, JCB, MC, V.

D ⬛ ⬛ ⬛ ⬛ SC

★ **SUPER 8.** *4703 N Reserve St (59804). 406/549-1199; fax 406/549-0677; res 800/800-8000; toll-free 888/900-9010. Email gm@super8mt.com; www.super8mt.com.* 57 rms, 3 story, 1 suite. Apr-Sep: S $60; D $65; each addl $5; suites $117; under 12 free; lower rates rest of yr. Crib avail. Parking lot. TV; cable (premium). Complimentary continental bkfst. Restaurant. Business servs avail. Free airport transportation. Whirlpool. Golf. Downhill skiing. Picnic facilities. Cr cds: A, C, D, DS, MC, V.

D ⬛ ⬛ ⬛ ⬛ ⬛ ⬛ ⬛

★ **SUPER 8.** *3901 S Brooks St (59801). 406/251-2255; fax 406/251-2989; res 800/800-8000; toll-free 888/900-9010. Email gm@super8mt.com; www.super8mt.com.* 104 rms, 3 story. No elvtr. S $44.88; D $49.88-$54.88; each addl $3; ski plan. Crib free. TV; cable (premium). Restaurant nearby. Ck-out 11 am. Downhill/x-country ski 20 mi. Cr cds: A, DS, MC, V.

D ⬛ ⬛ ⬛ ⬛ ⬛

★ **TRAVELODGE.** *420 W Broadway St (59802), ½ mi S of I-90 Orange St Exit. 406/728-4500; fax 406/543-8118; toll-free 800/578-7878.* 60 rms, 3 story, no ground floor rms. Mid-May-mid-Sep: S $49-$55; D $55-$62; each addl $2; suites $68-$82; under 18 free; lower rates rest of yr. Crib free. TV; cable (premium). Ck-out noon. Sundries. Downhill/x-country ski 10 mi. Balconies. Cr cds: A, C, D, DS, MC, V.

★ **VAL-U-INN.** *3001 SW Brooks St (59801). 406/721-9600; fax 406/721-7208; res 800/443-7777.* 82 rms, 3 story, 2 suites. June-Aug: S $55; D $70; each addl $6; suites $85; under 12 free; lower rates rest of yr. Crib avail, fee. TV; cable (premium), VCR avail. Restaurant nearby. Ck-out noon. Meeting rms. Golf. Cr cds: A, C, D, DS, MC, V.

Hotels

★★ **BEST WESTERN GRANT CREEK INN.** *5280 Grant Creek Rd (59802). 406/543-0700; fax 406/543-0777; res 800/528-1234; toll-free 888/543-0700. www.bestwestern.com/grant creekinn.* 116 rms, 4 story, 10 suites. June-Sep: S, D $99; each addl $10; suites $169; under 12 free; lower rates rest of yr. Crib avail, fee. Pet accepted, some restrictions, fee. Parking lot. Indoor pool, whirlpool. TV; cable (DSS). Complimentary continental bkfst, coffee in rms, toll-free calls. Restaurant 1 am-midnight. Ck-out noon, ck-in 2 pm. Meeting rms. Business servs avail. Dry cleaning, coin lndry. Gift shop. Free airport transportation. Exercise equipt, sauna, steam rm. Golf. Downhill skiing. Hiking trail. Video games. Cr cds: A, C, D, DS, MC, V.

★★ **HOLIDAY INN EXPRESS.** *1021 E Broadway St (59802). 406/549-7600; fax 406/543-2223. Email holiday@ bigsky.net.* 95 rms, 5 with shower only, 4 story, 14 suites. May-Aug: S, D $77; suites $99; under 18 free; higher rates special events; lower rates rest of yr. Crib free. TV; cable (premium). Complimentary continental bkfst. Restaurant nearby. Ck-out noon. Meeting rms. Business center. In-rm modem link. Bellhops. Coin lndry. Free airport transportation. Downhill/x-country ski 5 mi. Exercise equipt. Pool privileges. Bathrm phones. Refrigerator, microwave, wet bar in suites. Some balconies. On river. Cr cds: A, DS, MC, V.

B&Bs/Small Inns

★★★ **THE EMILY A. BED & BREAKFAST.** *Mile Marker 20 Hwy 83N (59868), 5 mi N of Seeley Lake. 406/677-3474; fax 406/677-3474; toll-free 800/977-4639. Email slk3340@ blckfoot.net; www.theemilya.com.* 6 rms, 3 share bath, 2 story, 1 suite, 1 guest house. No A/C. No rm phones. S, D $115; each addl $15; suite $150; guest house $150. Crib free. Pet accepted, some restrictions. Premium cable TV in common rm; VCR avail (movies). Complimentary full bkfst. Ck-out 11 am, ck-in 2-7 pm. Business servs avail. Coin lndry. Airport transportation. X-country ski on site. Rec rm. Some balconies. Picnic tables, grills. Log interior and exterior; Western art works. Totally nonsmoking. Cr cds: A, DS, MC, V.

★★ **GOLDSMITH'S BED & BREAK-FAST INN.** *809 E Front St (59802), I-90 Van Buren St Exit. 406/721-6732; fax 406/543-0045; res 406/728-1585. Email dickgsmith@aol.com; www. goldsmithsinn.com.* 7 rms, 2 story, 4 suites. May-Sep: S $89; D $99; each addl $15; suites $119; lower rates rest of yr. Crib avail. Parking lot. TV; cable. Complimentary full bkfst, toll-free calls. Restaurant 5-10 pm. Bar. Ck-out 11 am, ck-in 2 pm. Exercise privileges. Golf. Downhill skiing. Hiking trail. Cr cds: DS, MC, V.

Restaurants

★★ **DEPOT.** *201 W Railroad St (59801), S of I-90 Orange St Exit. 406/728-7007.* Specializes in fresh seafood, prime rib, hand-cut steak. Salad bar. Hrs: 5:30-10:30 pm. Closed Thanksgiving, Dec 25. Res accepted. Bar. Dinner $10.95-$22.95. Parking. Cr cds: A, D, DS, MC, V.

★★ **ZIMORINO RED PIES OVER MONTANA.** *424 N Higgins Ave (59802). 406/721-7757. www. zimorinos.com.* Specializes in pizza, chicken, manicotti. Hrs: 5-9 pm; Fri, Sat to 10 pm. Closed hols. Bar. Dinner $8-$15. Child's menu. Italian bistro decor. Cr cds: A, DS, MC, V.

Polson

(B-2) *See also Bigfork*

Pop 3,283 **Elev** 2,931 ft
Area code 406 **Zip** 59860
Web www.polsonchamber.com
Information Chamber of Commerce, 7 Third Ave W, PO Box 667; 406/883-5969

At the south edge of Flathead Lake, Polson is the trade center for a productive farming area and a provisioning point for mountain trips. According to legend, Paul Bunyan dug the channel from Flathead Lake to Flathead River.

What to See and Do

Flathead Lake Cruise. *Port Polson Princess* departs from Kwataqnuk Resort for sightseeing around Flathead Lake. View the Narrows, Bird Island, and Wildhorse Island. (June-Sep, daily) Res recommended. Phone 406/883-3636. ¢¢¢¢-¢¢¢¢¢

Flathead Lake State Park. Twenty-eight mi long, 15 mi wide, average depth 220 ft; formed by glacial action. Fishing best in early spring, late fall; swimming, boating, water-skiing. There are 6 state park units surrounding the lake (also see BIG-FORK).

Big Arm Unit. Also fishing (joint state/tribal license required). Camping (no hookups, dump station). 13 mi N, along W shore on US 93.

Elmo Unit. 16 mi N on US 93.

Finley Point Unit. 12 mi N off MT 35.

National Bison Range. Visitor center, exhibits, nature trails; picnic grounds near headquarters. Bison, antelope, bighorn sheep, deer, elk, and other big game species roam over 18,500 acres of fenced-in range. A 19-mi self-guided tour route rises 2,000 ft over Mission Valley (mid-May-mid-Oct, daily). Motorcycles and bicycles are not permitted on the drives. 32 mi S on US 93, then 13 mi SW on US 212 to main entrance in Moiese. **FREE**

Ninepipe and Pablo National Wildlife Refuges. More than 180 species of birds have been observed on these waterfowl refuges, incl ducks, geese, grebes, great blue herons, and cormorants. Fishing permitted at certain times and areas in accordance with tribal and state regulations. Joint state/tribal recreation permit and fishing stamp required. Portions of (or all) refuges may be closed during waterfowl season and nesting period. Visitors may obtain more information, incl regulations, from Refuge Manager at National Bison Range, 132 Bison Range Rd, Moiese 59824. Pablo is 7 mi S on US 93; Ninepipe is 18 mi S on US 93. Phone 406/644-2211.

Polson-Flathead Historical Museum. Native American artifacts, farm and household items from the opening of the Flathead Reservation in 1910; home of Rudolph, a Scotch-Highland steer, who appeared in over 136 parades in 5 states and Canada; wildlife display and old stagecoach. (Summer, daily) 8th Ave & Main St. Phone 406/883-3049. **Donation**

River Rafting. Flathead Raft Company. Offers half-day whitewater trips on Lower Flathead River, leaving from Port Polson, S end of Flathead Lake. Phone 406/883-5838 (Polson office in-season) or 800/654-4359 (West Glacier office off-season). ¢¢¢¢¢

Resort

★★ **BEST WESTERN KWATAQNUK RESORT.** *303 US Hwy 93 E (59860).* 406/883-3636; fax 406/883-5392; res 800/882-6363. Email bwktn@ptinet.net; www.kwataqnuk.com. 112 rms, 3 story. Mid-June-mid-Sep: S $92-$113; D $102-$123; each addl $10; suites $179; under 12 free; lower rates rest of yr. Crib free. TV; cable (premium), VCR avail. 2 pools, 1 indoor; whirlpool. Coffee in rms. Restaurant 6 am-11 pm. Ck-out 11 am. Meeting rms. Business servs avail. Bellhops. Sundries. Gift shop. Game rm. Many balconies. On Flathead Lake; swimming, boat cruises (fee). Cr cds: A, C, D, DS, MC, V.
⊡ 🐾 ⤫ ⤬ 🐾 SC

Red Lodge

(D-5) *See also Cooke City; also see Cody, WY*

Pop 1,958 **Elev** 5,553 ft
Area code 406 **Zip** 59068
Web www.wtp.net/redlodge
Information Chamber of Commerce, PO Box 988; 406/446-1718

The seat of Carbon County and a busy resort town, Red Lodge was, according to legend, named for a Native American band whose tepees were painted red. It is a most magnificent approach to Yellowstone National Park (see WYOMING) and gateway to the half-million-acre Beartooth-Absaroka Wilderness Area. A Ranger District office of the Custer National Forest (see HARDIN) is located here.

What to See and Do

Beartooth Highway (National Forest Scenic Byway). US 212 travels 64 mi over an 11,000-ft pass in the Beartooth Mts to the NE entrance of Yellowstone National Park. Incl Rock Creek Vista Point; Granite Peak, highest point in Montana (12,799 ft); a 345,000-acre portion of the Absaroka-Beartooth Wilderness; Grasshoper Glacier (see COOKE CITY). The area is characterized by alpine plateaus, rugged peaks, and hundreds of lakes. Offers winter sports and trout fishing. Views of glaciers, lakes, fields of alpine flowers, peaks, and canyons. There are no service areas or gas stations on the 64-mi (2½-hr) stretch between Red Lodge and Cooke City. Beartooth Hwy is closed each winter between Red Lodge and Cooke City (closing dates depend on snow conditions) and is open approx June-Sep.

Red Lodge Mountain Ski Area. Triple, 2 high-speed detachable quads, 4 double chairlifts, mitey-mite; patrol, school, rentals, snowmaking; restaurant, cafeteria, bar. Longest run 2½ mi; vertical drop 2,016 ft. (Thanks-giving-Easter, daily) 6 mi W off US 212, in Custer National Forest. Phone 406/446-2610. ¢¢¢¢

Annual Events

Winter Carnival. Ski races, snow sculpting, entertainment. Mar.

Music Festival. Features performances by faculty members from schools throughout the country. June.

Festival of Nations. Exhibits, nightly entertainment reflecting several European cultures. Art demonstrations and displays. Early-mid-Aug.

Scenic Beartooth Highway

Motels/Motor Lodges

★★ **BEST WESTERN LUPINE INN.** *702 S Hauser Ave (59068). 406/446-1321; fax 406/446-1465; toll-free 888/567-1321. Email bwlupine@bestwestern lupine.com; www.bestwesternlupine. com.* 46 rms, 2 story, 1 suite. June-Sep, Dec: S, D $89; lower rates rest of yr. Crib avail. Pet accepted, some restrictions. Parking lot. Indoor pool, whirlpool. TV; cable (DSS), VCR avail. Complimentary continental bkfst, coffee in rms, toll-free calls. Ck-out noon, ck-in 3 pm. Meeting rm. Business servs avail. Coin lndry. Exercise equipt, sauna. Golf, 18 holes. Tennis, 2 courts. Downhill skiing. Cr cds: A, C, D, DS, MC, V.

★★ **COMFORT INN.** *612 N Broadway (59068). 406/446-4469; fax 406/446-4669; toll-free 888/733-4661. Email 1stpic@wtp.net; www.wtp.net/ comfortinn.* 53 rms, 2 story. Dec-Mar, June-Sep: S, D $90; each addl $10; under 18 free; lower rates rest of yr. Crib avail. Pet accepted, some restrictions, fee. Parking lot. Indoor pool, whirlpool. TV; cable, VCR avail. Complimentary continental bkfst, coffee in rms, newspaper, toll-free calls. Restaurant nearby. Ck-out 11 am, ck-in 2 pm. Meeting rm. Business center. Coin lndry. Exercise privileges. Golf, 18 holes. Tennis, 2 courts. Downhill skiing. Supervised children's activities. Hiking trail. Picnic facilities. Cr cds: A, C, D, DS, JCB, MC, V.

★ **SUPER 8.** *1223 S Broadway Ave (59068). 406/446-2288; fax 406/446-3162; res 800/800-8000; toll-free 800/813-8335.* 50 rms, 2 story. S $59; D $59-$89. Crib free. Pet accepted, some restrictions. TV; cable (premium). Indoor pool; whirlpool. Complimentary continental bkfst. Ck-out 11 am. Coin lndry. Meeting rm. Downhill/x-country ski 5 mi. Some refrigerators, in-rm whirlpools; microwaves avail. Some rms with view of mountains. Cr cds: A, D, DS, MC, V.

Hotel

★★ **POLLARD HOTEL.** *2 N Broadway (59068). 406/446-0001; fax 406/446-0002; res 800/765-5273. Email pollard@pollardhotel.com.* 36 rms, 5 with shower only, 3 story, 4 suites. Mid-June-mid-Sep, mid-Dec-mid-Apr: S, D $85-$110; each addl $20; suites $170-$185; ski plan; lower rates rest of yr. Crib free. TV; cable. Complimentary full bkfst. Restaurant (see GREENLEE'S). No rm serv. Ck-out noon. Meeting rms. Business servs avail. Concierge. Gift shop. Downhill/x-country ski 6 mi. Exercise rm; sauna. Whirlpool. Racquetball courts. Some in-rm whirlpools. Restored hotel built 1893. Totally nonsmoking. Cr cds: A, DS, MC, V.

Resort

★★★ **ROCK CREEK RESORT.** *(59068), 5 mi S on US 212. 406/446-1111; fax 406/446-3688; res 800/667-1119. Email rcresort@wtp.net; www.rcresort.com.* 90 rms, 2-3 story, 39 kits. No A/C. S $88; D $88-$93; kit. units $99-$285. Crib free. TV; cable (premium), VCR avail. Indoor pool; whirlpool. Playground. Dining rm 7 am-2 pm. Ck-out 11 am, ck-in 3 pm. Coin lndry. Meeting rms. Business servs avail. Gift shop. Tennis. Downhill ski 11 mi. Exercise equipt. Lawn games. Some in-rm whirlpools; microwaves avail. Balconies. Cr cds: A, D, DS, MC, V.

Restaurants

★★★ **GREENLEE'S.** *2 N Broadway. 406/446-0001. Email pollard@pollard hotel.com; www.pollardhotel.com.* Continental menu. Specializes in pistachio salmon, Montana ostrich, steaks. Own desserts. Hrs: 7 am-9 pm. Res accepted. Bar. Wine cellar. Bkfst $3.50-$5.75; lunch $5.50-$7.50; dinner $14.25-$27. Child's menu. Victorian hotel dining rm; original art. Cr cds: A, DS, MC, V.

★★ **OLD PINEY DELL.** *US 212. 406/446-1196.* Specializes in steak, seafood, chicken. Hrs: 5:30-9 pm. Res accepted. Bar. Dinner $13.50-$22. Child's menu. Entertainment. View of Beartooth Mts. Family-owned. Cr cds: A, D, MC, V.

Sidney (B-8)

Pop 5,217 **Elev** 1,931 ft
Area code 406 **Zip** 59270
Web www.mtsid.mt1ib.org

Information Chamber of Commerce, 909 S Central; 406/482-1916

Irrigation in Richland County produces bountiful crops of sugar beets and wheat, which are marketed at Sidney, the county seat. Oil fields, open-pit coal mining, and livestock feeding contribute to the town's economy.

What to See and Do

Blue Rock Products Company-Pepsi Cola Bottling Plant. Guided tours of the mixing and bottling process of the Pepsi Cola soft drink. (Mon-Fri) 501 9th Ave NE. Phone 406/482-3403. **FREE**

Fort Union Trading Post National Historic Site. (See WILLISTON, ND) 22 mi N via MT 200 to Fairview, N 18 mi on Williams County 58.

MonDak Heritage Center. Seventeen-unit street scene displaying historical artifacts of the area; changing art exhibits; historical and art library, gift shop. (Tues-Sun afternoons; daily in summer; closed hols) 120 3rd Ave SE. Phone 406/482-3500. ¢¢

Annual Events

Peter Paddlefish Day. The sighting of Peter on his spawning run up the Yellowstone River indicates a normal run-off on the Yellowstone and a normal season. Phone 406/482-1916. Last Sat Apr.

Sunrise Festival of the Arts. Central Park. Second Sat July.

Richland County Fair and Rodeo. Exhibits, livestock shows, petting zoo, carnival, PRCA rodeos, country-western show. Phone 406/482-2801. Early Aug.

Three Forks

See also Bozeman, Butte, Ennis

Pop 1,203 **Elev** 4,080 ft
Area code 406 **Zip** 59752

In 1805, Lewis and Clark discovered the source of the Missouri River, beginning of the world's largest river chain, at the confluence of the Jefferson, Madison, and Gallatin rivers here. Native Americans resisted settlement of the valley, a favorite bison hunting ground, but before long it became a trading post headquarters for hunters and trappers.

What to See and Do

Lewis and Clark Caverns State Park. Underground wonderland of colorful rock formations; ¾-mi lighted path; 50°F. Two-hr (2-mi) guided tour (May-Sep, daily) Picnicking, camping (no hookups, dump station), visitor center. Standard fees. 19 mi W on MT 2, milepost 271. Phone 406/287-3541. Tour ¢¢

Madison Buffalo Jump State Monument. Native American hunting technique of herding charging buffalo over cliffs is illustrated. Hiking, picnicking. Day use only. E on I-90, then 7 mi S on Buffalo Jump Rd. ¢

Missouri River Headwaters State Park. Where Lewis and Clark discovered the source of the Missouri. Fishing, boating (ramp); picnicking, camping (no hookups, dump station). Standard fees. 3 mi E on I-90, then E on MT Secondary 205, then 3 mi N on MT Secondary 286. Phone 406/994-4042.

Motel/Motor Lodge

★ **FORT THREE FORKS.** *10776 US 287 (59752), I-90 Exit 274. 406/285-3233; fax 406/285-4362; res 406/285-3233; toll-free 800/477-5690. Email fort3forks@aol.com; www.fortthreeforks. com.* 24 rms, 2 story, 2 suites. June-Sep: S $42; D $50; each addl $4; suites $79; under 11 free; lower rates rest of yr. Crib avail, fee. Pet accepted, some restrictions, fee. Parking lot. TV; cable (DSS), VCR avail. Complimentary continental bkfst, newspaper, toll-free calls. Restaurant nearby. Business center. Bellhops. Coin lndry. Gift shop. Exercise privileges, whirlpool. Golf, 9 holes. Tennis, 2 courts. Downhill skiing. Supervised children's activities. Hiking trail. Picnic facilities. Cr cds: A, D, DS, MC, V.

🄳 ➤ 🐾 ♿ 🏊 🏃 ⛷ 🎿 🏃 ⛷ 🔥 🏃

Virginia City

(D-3) *See also Ennis*

Settled 1863 **Pop** 142 **Elev** 5,822 ft
Area code 406 **Zip** 59755

Information Bovey Restoration, PO Box 338; 406/843-5377 or 800/648-7588. Chamber of Commerce; 800/829-2969

On May 26, 1863, gold was found in Alder Gulch. The old days of the rough 'n' tough West are rekindled in this restored gold boomtown, once the capital of the territory. Alder Gulch (Virginia and Nevada cities) sprouted when six men who had escaped from Native Americans discovered history's richest placer deposit. Ten thousand gold miners arrived within a month, followed by bands of desperadoes; 190 murders were committed in seven months. Vigilantes hunted down 21 road agents and discovered that the sheriff was the leader of the criminals. Nearly $300 million in gold was washed from Alder Gulch, but the area faded as the diggings became less productive and Nevada City became a ghost town. In 1946 a restoration program began, which has brought back much of the early mining-town atmosphere.

What to See and Do

Boot Hill. Graves of 5 criminals hanged by the vigilantes.

Restored buildings. incl the offices of the Montana *Post,* first newspaper in the state; the Gilbert Brewery, dressmaker's shop, Wells Fargo Express office, livery stable, barbershop, blacksmith shop, general store, many others. Phone 406/843-5377 or 800/648-7588. Includes

  Gilbert's Brewery. Virginia City's 1st brewery was built in 1864. The main bldg has been restored and original brewery is still inside. Musical variety shows (mid-June-mid-Sep, Wed-Mon nights). E Cover St. Phone 406/843-5377. ¢¢¢

  Nevada City. Authentic buildings incl early mining camp stores, homes, school, offices. Music Hall has large collection of mechanical musical machines. (Memorial Day-mid-Sep, daily) 1½ mi W on MT 287. **FREE**

  Nevada City Depot. Houses steam railroad museum (fee) of early-day engines and cars. Train ride to Virginia City. (Early June-Labor Day, daily; fee)

Robbers' Roost. Old-time stage station often used by outlaws. 15 mi W on MT 287.

St. Paul's Episcopal Church. Elling Memorial (1902) Built on site of 1867 building; oldest Protestant congregation in state. Tiffany windows. Idaho St.

Thompson-Hickman Memorial Museum. Relics of the gold camps. (May-Sep, daily) Wallace St. **Donation**

Virginia City-Madison County Historical Museum. Traces western Montana history. (Early June-Labor Day, daily) Wallace St. ¢¢

Seasonal Event

Classic melodramas. In Old Opera House, foot of Wallace St. Virginia City Players present 19th-century entertainment. Tues-Sun. Res required. Phone 406/843-5377. Early June-Labor Day.

West Yellowstone (E-4)

Pop 913 **Elev** 6,666 ft **Area code** 406 **Zip** 59758
Information Chamber of Commerce, 30 Yellowstone Ave, PO Box 458; 406/646-7701

At the west entrance to Yellowstone National Park (see WYOMING), this town serves as a hub for incoming tourists. Not too long ago, West Yellowstone was abandoned and snowbound in the winter; today winter sports and attractions allow the town to serve visitors all year. A Ranger District office of the Gallatin National Forest (see BOZEMAN) is located here.

What to See and Do

Grizzly Discovery Center. Bear and wolf preserve and educational facility. Interactive exhibits, films, presentations. Wildlife-themed gift shop. (Daily; closed hols) 201 S Canyon St. Phone 406/646-7001. ¢¢¢

Interagency Aerial Fire Control Center. A US Forest Service facility. Guided tour by smokejumpers who explain firefighting techniques. (Late

June-Labor Day, daily) 2 mi N on US 191. Phone 406/646-7691. **FREE**

Madison River Canyon Earthquake Area. Incl Quake Lake, formed by earthquake of Aug 17, 1959. This area, with its slides and faults, is a graphic demonstration of earthquake damage. Camping (mid-June-mid-Sep; Beaver Creek Campground, fee/night). Visitor Center (on US 287, 22 mi W of US 191) with talks, exhibits; list of self-guided tours (Memorial Day-Labor Day, daily). Road through area (all yr). For details inquire at the Chamber of Commerce or at the US Forest Service Office on US 191/287 N of town; or contact PO Box 520. 8 mi N on US 191, then 3 mi W on US 287, in Gallatin National Forest (see BOZEMAN). Phone 406/646-7369. **FREE**

National Geographic Theatre. Six-story-high screen shows "Yellowstone," a film interpreting the history, wildlife, geothermal activity, and grandeur of America's first national park. Exhibits incl wildlife photography, props used in film, and "Effects of the Yellowstone Hot Spot." (Daily, shows hourly) 101 S Canyon St. Phone 406/646-4100. *¢¢¢*

Sightseeing tours.

Buffalo Bus Lines. Phone 406/646-9564 or 800/426-7669.

Gray Line bus tours. Phone 800/523-3102.

Amfac Parks & Resorts, Inc. Offers guided snowcoach tours and cross-country ski trips through Yellowstone National Park (see WYOMING) departing from West Yellowstone and other locations surrounding the park (mid-Dec-early Mar). Summer season offers full-day bus tours, boat tours, and horseback rides in the park (June-Aug). Res recommended. Phone 307/344-7311.

Annual Events

Great American Ski Chase. Mar.

World Snowmobile Expo. Third wkend Mar.

Seasonal Event

Playmill Theater. 29 Madison Ave. Musical comedies and melodramas.

Mon-Sat. Phone 406/646-7757. Memorial Day-Labor Day.

Motels/Motor Lodges

★ **DAYS INN.** *301 Madison (59758). 406/646-7656; fax 406/646-7965; res 800/DAYSINN; toll-free 800/548-9551. www.wyellowstone.com/loomis.* 45 rms, 2 story. June-Oct, Dec-mid-Mar: S, D $89; each addl $5; suites $152; kit. unit $152; under 13 free; lower rates rest of yr. Crib free. TV; cable (premium). Indoor pool; whirlpool. Complimentary continental bkfst. Restaurant adj 7 am-10 pm. Ck-out 11 am. Business servs avail. Sauna. Some refrigerators. Cr cds: A, D, DS, MC, V.

⬛ 🛆 🛠 🛬 🛋 🖎 🐾

★★ **FAIRFIELD INN.** *105 S Electric St (59758). 406/646-4892; fax 406/646-4893; res 800/228-2800; toll-free 800/565-6803. Email fairfieldinn@wyellowstone.com; www.fairfieldinn.com.* 77 rms, 3 story. Mid-June-mid-Sep: S, D $120-$130; each addl $8; suites $150-$160; under 18 free; lower rates rest of yr. Crib free. TV; cable (premium). Complimentary continental bkfst. Restaurant nearby. Ck-out noon. Business servs avail. In-rm modem link. Coin lndry. X-country ½ blk. Indoor pool; whirlpool. Cr cds: A, DS, MC, V.

⬛ 🛆 🛠 🛬 🐾 🛋

★★ **HOLIDAY INN SUNSPREE RESORT.** *315 Yellowstone Ave (59758), 3 blks W of park entrance. 406/646-7365; fax 406/646-4433; res 800/HOLIDAY. Email resc@yellowstone-cons-hotel.com; www.yellowstone-cons-hotels.com.* 123 rms, 3 story. Mid-June-Sep: S, D $129-$200; each addl $8; under 12 free; lower rates rest of yr. Crib free. TV; cable. Indoor pool; whirlpool. Complimentary coffee in rms. Restaurant 6:30 am-10 pm. Bar 11-2 am. Ck-out 11 am. Coin lndry. Meeting rms. Business servs avail. Bellhops. Valet serv. Gift shop. Exercise equipt; sauna. Refrigerators, microwaves; some in-rm whirlpools. Cr cds: A, DS, MC, V.

⬛ 🛆 🛠 🛬 🏃 🛋 ✖ 🖎 🐾

★★ **KELLY INN.** *104 S Canyon (59758). 406/646-4544; fax 406/646-9838; res 800/635-3559; toll-free 800/259-4672. www.wyellowstone.com/kellyinn.* 78 rms, 3 story. June-Sep: S, D

$120-$130; each addl $8; under 12 free; lower rates rest of yr. Crib free. Pet accepted. TV; cable. Complimentary continental bkfst. Restaurant nearby. Ck-out 11 am. Business servs avail. Coin lndry. X-country ski 3 blks. Indoor pool; whirlpool. Sauna. Many refrigerators, microwaves. Cr cds: A, C, D, DS, MC, V.

★★ **STAGECOACH INN.** *209 Madison Ave (59758), at Dunraven Ave. 406/646-7381; fax 406/646-9575; toll-free 800/842-2882. Email sci@yellow stoneinn.com; www.yellowstoneinn.com.* 80 rms, 1-2 story. Early June-mid-Sep: S $79-$125; D $79-$131; each addl $6; under 12 free; lower rates rest of yr. Crib free. TV; cable. Restaurant 6:30 am-10 pm. Bar noon-1 am; entertainment Tues-Sat (in season). Ck-out 11 am. Coin lndry. Meeting rms. Gift shop. X-country ski ¼ mi. Sauna. Whirlpools. Snowmobiling. Cr cds: A, C, D, DS, MC, V.

★ **SUPER 8 LIONSHEAD RESORT.** *1545 Targhee Pass Hwy (59758), approx 7 mi S on US 20. 406/646-9584; fax 406/646-7404; res 800/800-8000.* 44 rms, 2 story. Memorial Day-Labor Day: S $79.88; D $79.88-$82.88; each addl $5; under 13 free; lower rates rest of yr. Crib $5. TV; cable (premium). Playground. Restaurant 7-11 am, 5-9:30 pm. Ck-out 11 am. Coin lndry. Sauna. Whirlpool. Cr cds: A, C, D, DS, MC, V.

Hotels

★★ **COMFORT INN.** *638 Madison Ave (59758). 406/646-4212; fax 406 /646-4212; res 800/228-5150; toll-free 888/264-2466.* 68 rms, 3 story, 10 suites. Jan-Mar, June-Sep: S, D $129; each addl $8; suites $189; under 18 free; lower rates rest of yr. Crib avail. Parking lot. Indoor pool, whirlpool. TV; cable (DSS). Complimentary continental bkfst, newspaper, toll-free calls. Ck-out 10 am, ck-in 3 pm. Meeting rm. Coin lndry. Exercise privileges. Downhill skiing. Cr cds: A, C, D, DS, JCB, MC, V.

★★ **GRAY WOLF INN & SUITES.** *250 S Canyon St (59758). 406/646-0000; fax 406/646-4232; res 800/561-*

0815; toll-free 800/852-8602. Email graywolf@graywolf-inn.com; www.gray wolf-inn.com. 85 rms, 3 story, 18 suites. Feb, July-Aug: S, D, $129; each addl $10; suites $190; under 18 free; higher rates rest of yr. Crib avail. Pet accepted, fee. Parking garage. Indoor pool, whirlpool. TV; cable, VCR avail. Complimentary continental bkfst, coffee in rms. Ck-out 11 am, ck-in 2 pm. Dry cleaning, coin lndry. Free airport transportation. Video games. Cr cds: A, C, D, DS, JCB, MC, V.

Restaurant

★★ **THREE BEAR.** *205 Yellowstone Ave (59758). 406/646-7811.* Specializes in seafood, hand-cut steaks, pasta. Hrs: 7-11 am, 5-10 pm. Closed Dec 25; mid-Mar-early-May, mid-Oct-mid-Dec. Bar. Bkfst $3.25-$8.75; dinner $10.95-$20.95. Child's menu. Family-owned. Cr cds: MC, V.

Whitefish

(A-2) *See also Columbia Falls, Kalispell*

Pop 4,368 **Elev** 3,036 ft
Area code 406 **Zip** 59937
Web www.fcvb.org

Information Flathead Convention & Visitor Bureau, 15 Depot Park, Kalispell, 59901; 406/756-9091 or 800/543-3105

On the shore of Whitefish Lake, this community prospers from tourism and railroading. The town is headquarters for a four-state summer vacation area and is a winter ski center. A growing forest products industry and the railroad constitute the other side of Whitefish's economy. A Ranger District office of the Flathead National Forest (see KALISPELL) is located here.

What to See and Do

Big Mountain Ski and Summer Resort. Double, 4 triple, 2 quad chairlifts, T-bar, platter lift; patrol, school, rentals; hotels, restaurants, bars, nursery, cafeteria, concession area; sleigh rides. Longest run 2½ mi;

vertical drop 2,100 ft. (Thanksgiving-mid-Apr, daily) Cross-country trails. Gondola (also operates in summer) provides views of Rockies, Flathead Valley; travels 6,800 ft to summit of Big Mt. Summer activites (mid-May-early Oct): gondola rides overlooking Glacier National Park (see), horseback riding, hiking, mountain biking, tennis; outdoor theater, events. 8 mi N on County 487 in Flathead National Forest (see KALISPELL); shuttle bus trips daily in winter. Phone 800/858-5439. Winter ¢¢¢¢; Summer ¢¢¢

Glacier National Park. (see)

🌟 **Whitefish Lake.** Seven mi long, 2 mi wide. Studded with resorts, particularly on E shore; swimming, water-skiing, fishing, sailing; picnicking. On lake is

> **Whitefish State Park.** Swimming, fishing, boating (ramp); picnicking, camping (no hookups). Standard fees. ½ mi W on US 93, milepost 129, then 1 mi N. Phone 406/862-3991 (summer) or 406/752-5501.

Annual Event

Winter Carnival. First wkend Feb.

Motel/Motor Lodge

★ **SUPER 8 MOTEL.** *800 Spokane Ave (59937). 406/862-8255; fax 406/862-8255; res 800/800-8000.* 40 rms, 3 story. July-Aug: S $77; D $83; each addl $5; under 12 free; lower rates rest of yr. Crib avail. Pet accepted, some restrictions, fee. Parking lot. TV; cable. Complimentary continental bkfst, toll-free calls. Restaurant nearby. Ck-out 11 am, ck-in 3 pm. Fax servs avail. Coin lndry. Golf. Downhill skiing. Picnic facilities. Cr cds: A, C, D, DS, MC, V.

🄳 🐾 ⚓ 🏊 🍴 🔄 🛶 🔥 SC

Hotels

★★ **KANDAHAR LODGE.** *3824 Big Mt Rd (59937), 8 mi N on Big Mt Rd, at Big Mt Village. 406/862-6098; fax 406/862-6095; toll-free 800/862-6094. Email kandahar@digisys.net; www.kandaharlodge.com.* 48 rms, 4 story, 10 suites. Feb-Mar, July-Aug: S $139; D $151-165; each addl $10; suite $275; kit. $175; under 12 free; higher rates week of Dec 25, last 2 wks of Feb; lower rest of yr. Crib avail. Park-ing lot. TV; cable, VCR avail. Complimentary coffee in rms. Restaurant. Bar. Ck-out 11 am, ck-in 4 pm. Meeting rms. Business servs avail. Bellhops. Concierge. Coin lndry. Sauna, steam rm, whirlpool. Golf. Downhill skiing. Hiking trail. Picnic facilities. Cr cds: A, DS, MC, V.

⚓ 🏊 🍴 🔄 🛶 🔥

★★ **PINE LODGE.** *920 Spokane Ave (59937). 406/862-7600; fax 406/862-7616; toll-free 800/305-7463. Email info@thepinelodge.com; www.thepinelodge.com.* 66 rms, 4 story, 10 suites. June-Sep: S $120; D $130; suites $160; under 17 free; lower rates rest of yr. Crib avail, fee. Pet accepted. Indoor/outdoor pools, lap pool, children's pool, whirlpool. TV; cable (premium), VCR avail. Complimentary continental bkfst, coffee in rms, toll-free calls. Restaurant. Ck-out 11 am, ck-in 4 pm. Meeting rm. Business servs avail. Dry cleaning, coin lndry. Gift shop. Free airport transportation. Exercise equipt. Golf. Tennis, 3 courts. Downhill skiing. Beach access. Hiking trail. Picnic facilities. Cr cds: A, C, D, DS, ER, MC, V.

🄳 🐾 ⚓ 🏊 🍴 🔄 🛶 🗿 🔥 SC

★★ **ROCKY MOUNTAIN LODGE.** *6510 US 93 S (59068). 406/862-2569; fax 406/862-1154; toll-free 800/862-2569. Email info@rockymtnlodge.com; www.rockymtnlodge.com.* 72 rms, 3 story, 5 suites. July-Aug: S $129; D $139; each addl $10; suites $179; under 17 free; lower rates rest of yr. Crib avail, fee. Pet accepted, some restrictions. Parking lot. Pool, whirlpool. TV; cable (premium), VCR avail. Complimentary continental bkfst, coffee in rms, newspaper, toll-free calls. Restaurant. Meeting rms. Business center. Bellhops. Concierge. Dry cleaning, coin lndry. Free airport transportation. Exercise privileges. Golf. Tennis. Downhill skiing. Picnic facilities. Cr cds: A, C, D, DS, MC, V.

🄳 🐾 🏊 🍴 🔄 🛶 🗿 🔥 SC 🎿

Resort

★★ **GROUSE MOUNTAIN LODGE.** *2 Fairway Dr (59937), on Whitefish Lake Golf Course. 406/862-3000; fax 406/862-0326; res 877/862-1505; toll-free 800/321-8822. Email info@ montanasfinest.com; www.montanas*

finest.com. 133 rms, 3 story, 12 suites. July-Aug, Dec: D $179; each addl $10; suites $219; under 12 free; lower rates rest of yr. Crib avail. Parking lot. Indoor pool, whirlpool. TV; cable, VCR avail. Complimentary coffee in rms, newspaper. Restaurant. Bar. Ck-out 11 am, ck-in 4 pm. Meeting rms. Business center. Concierge. Dry cleaning, coin lndry. Gift shop. Free airport transportation. Exercise equipt, sauna. Golf. Tennis, 3 courts. Downhill skiing. Bike rentals. Hiking trail. Picnic facilities. Cr cds: A, C, D, DS, ER, MC, V.

D ⬚ ⬚ ⬚ ⬚ ⬚ ⬚ ⬚ ⬚ ⬚ ⬚ ⬚

B&B/Small Inn

★★ **GOOD MEDICINE LODGE.** *537 Wisconsin Ave (59937). 406/862-5488; fax 406/862-5489; toll-free 800/ 860-5488. Email goodrx@digisys.net; www.wtp.net/go/goodrx.* 9 rms, 2 story, 2 suites. June-Sep, Dec: S $95; D $105; each addl $20; suites $145; under 10 free; lower rates rest of yr. Crib avail, fee. Parking lot. TV; cable, VCR avail. Complimentary full bkfst. Restaurant nearby. Ck-out 11 am, ck-in 3 pm. Meeting rms. Business servs avail. Concierge. Coin lndry. Gift shop. Whirlpool. Golf. Tennis. Downhill skiing. Picnic facilities. Cr cds: A, DS, MC, V.

D ⬚ ⬚ ⬚ ⬚ ⬚ ⬚

Restaurant

★★ **FENDERS.** *US 93 N (59937), 7 mi S. 406/752-3000.* Specializes in prime rib, seafood. Hrs: 4-10 pm; Sun 11 am-midnight. Res accepted. Bar. Lunch $4.95-$7.95; dinner $9.95-$19.95. Child's menu. Entertainment. Many collectibles, old cars. Cr cds: A, MC, V.

D

White Sulphur Springs

(C-4) *See also Bozeman, Helena*

Pop 963 **Elev** 5,100 ft **Area code** 406 **Zip** 59645

Mineral springs, as well as fine hunting and fishing, make this a popular summer and fall resort town. It lies in a mile-high valley ringed by mountains—the Castles, Crazies, and Big and Little Belts. Agates may still be found in the area. A Ranger District office of the Lewis and Clark National Forest (see GREAT FALLS) is located here.

What to See and Do

Showdown Ski Area. Two chairlifts, Pomalift, free beginners tow; patrol, school, rentals; cafeteria, bar, day care. Longest run 2 mi; vertical drop 1,400 ft. (Late Nov-mid-Apr, Wed-Sun) 29 mi N on US 89, in Lewis and Clark National Forest. Phone 406/236-5522. ¢¢¢¢

Wolf Point (B-7)

Pop 2,880 **Elev** 1,997 ft
Area code 406 **Zip** 59201
Information Chamber of Commerce & Agriculture, 218 3rd Ave S, Suite B; 406/653-2012

During the winters of the 1870s, trappers poisoned wolves and hauled the frozen carcasses to this point on the Missouri River for spring shipment to St. Louis. Wolf Point is the seat of Roosevelt County and a trading point for oil, wheat, and cattle. Hunting for antelope, deer, and sharp-tailed and sage grouse is popular here.

Annual Events

Wild Horse Stampede. One of Montana's best and oldest rodeos. Contact Chamber of Commerce & Agriculture for info. Second wkend July.

Wadopana Powwow. Phone 406/653-3476. First wkend Aug.

OREGON

This is the end of the famous Oregon Trail, over which came scores of pioneers in covered wagons. The state abounds in the romance of the country's westward expansion. Meriwether Lewis and William Clark, sent by President Thomas Jefferson to explore the vast area bought in the Louisiana Purchase, ended their explorations here. This was also the scene of John Jacob Astor's fortune-making fur trade and that of Hudson's Bay Company, which hoped to keep the area for England, as well as gold rushes and the traffic of stately clippers of the China trade.

English Captain James Cook saw the coast in 1778. Others had seen it before him and others after him, but it remained for Lewis and Clark to discover what a prize Oregon was. On their return to St. Louis in 1806 they spread the word. In 1811, Astor's Pacific Fur Company built its post at Astoria, only to be frightened into selling to the British North West Company during the War of 1812. (In 1818 it again became US territory.) Other fur traders, missionaries, salmon anglers, and travelers followed them, but the Oregon territory was far away and hard to reach. The first true settlers did not make their way there until 1839, four years before a great wagon train blazed the Oregon Trail.

Cattle and sheep were driven up from California and land was cleared for farms. Oregon was settled not by people hungry for gold, but by pioneers looking for good land that could support them. The Native Americans resented the

Population: 2,842,321
Area: 97,060 square miles
Elevation: 0-11,239 feet
Peak: Mount Hood (Between Clackamas, Hood River Counties)
Entered Union: February 14, 1859 (33rd state)
Capital: Salem
Motto: The Union
Nickname: Beaver State
Flower: Oregon Grape
Bird: Western Meadowlark
Tree: Douglas Fir
Fair: Late August-early September, 2001, in Salem
Time Zone: Mountain and Pacific
Website: www.traveloregon.com

An afternoon of cycling along the coast of Oregon

early settlers and fought them until 1880. The Oregon Territory, established in 1848, received a flood of immigrants; they continued to arrive after statehood was proclaimed, under President James Buchanan, 11 years later.

The rich forests grew rapidly in the moist climate west of the mountains called the Cascades, and lumber was an early product of this frontier. The streams were full of fish, the woods offered nuts and berries, and the lush, green scenery lifted hearts and hopes at the end of the weary journey. The rivers—Columbia, Willamette, Rogue, and many others—offered transportation to the sea. Steamboats plied the Willamette and Columbia as early as 1850. The first full ship's cargo of wheat went from Portland to Liverpool in 1868, and when the railroad reached Portland in 1883, the world began receiving the fish, grain, lumber, and livestock that Oregon was ready to deliver.

Vast rivers provide more than transportation. Dammed, they are the source of abundant electric power and of water used to irrigate farms east of the Cascades. Timber is still important; a quarter of Oregon is national forest land. Sustained yield practices by the big lumber companies ensure a continuing supply.

One of the most beautiful drives in Oregon extends from Portland (see) to The Dalles (see) along the Columbia River. Here is the spectacular Columbia Gorge, designated a National Scenic Area, where waterfalls, streams, and mountains abound. The area offers many recreational activities such as camping—the Cascade Locks Marina Park lies four miles east of the Bonneville Dam (see HOOD RIVER), skiing (see MOUNT HOOD NATIONAL FOREST), snowmobiling, windsurfing, and hiking.

Whether one's taste is for an ocean beach, a ski slope, a mountain lake, or ranch life with riding and rodeos, the visitor who loves the outdoors or the American West loves Oregon. Each year, millions of tourists enjoy the state's magnificent coastline, blue lakes, mountains, and forests.

When to Go/Climate

Temperatures along the Pacific coast are mild, while Portland and the Willamette Valley experience more extreme weather conditions. Heavy snow falls in the Cascades; and to the east there's a high desert area that experiences typical desert heat and dry conditions.

AVERAGE HIGH/LOW TEMPERATURES (°F)

BURNS

Jan 34/13	**May** 66/36	**Sep** 74/36
Feb 40/19	**June** 74/42	**Oct** 62/28
Mar 48/25	**July** 85/47	**Nov** 45/22
Apr 57/29	**Aug** 83/45	**Dec** 35/15

PORTLAND

Jan 45/34	**May** 67/47	**Sep** 75/52
Feb 51/36	**June** 74/53	**Oct** 64/45
Mar 56/39	**July** 80/57	**Nov** 53/40
Apr 61/41	**Aug** 80/57	**Dec** 46/35

Parks and Recreation Finder

Directions to and information about the parks and recreation areas below are given under their respective town/city sections. Please refer to those sections for details.

NATIONAL PARK AND RECREATION AREAS

Key to abbreviations. I.H.S. = International Historic Site; I.P.M. = International Peace Memorial; N.B. = National Battlefield; N.B.P. = National Battlefield Park; N.B.C. = National Battlefield and Cemetery; N.C.A. = National Conservation

Area; N.E.M. = National Expansion Memorial; N.F. = National Forest; N.G. = National Grassland; N.H.P. = National Historical Park; N.H.C. = National Heritage Corridor; N.H.S. = National Historic Site; N.L. = National Lakeshore; N.M. = National Monument; N.M.P. = National Military Park; N.Mem. = National Memorial; N.P. = National Park; N.Pres. = National Preserve; N.R.A. = National Recreational Area; N.R.R. = National Recreational River; N.Riv. = National River; N.S. = National Seashore; N.S.R. = National Scenic Riverway; N.S.T. = National Scenic Trail; N.Sc. = National Scientific Reserve; N.V.M. = National Volcanic Monument.

Place Name	Listed Under
Crater Lake N.P.	same
Deschutes N.F.	BEND
Fort Clatsop N.Mem.	same
Fremont N.F.	LAKEVIEW
Hells Canyon N.R.	JOSEPH
John Day Fossil Beds N.M.	JOHN DAY
Malheur N.F.	JOHN DAY
Mount Hood N.F.	same
Newberry N.V.M.	BEND
Ochoco N.F.	PRINEVILLE
Oregon Caves N.M.	same
Oregon Dunes N.R.	REEDSPORT
Rogue River N.F.	MEDFORD
Siskiyou N.F.	GRANTS PASS
Siuslaw N.F.	CORVALLIS
Umatilla N.F.	PENDLETON
Umpqua N.F.	ROSEBURG
Wallowa-Whitman N.F.	BAKER CITY
Willamette N.F.	EUGENE
Winema N.F.	KLAMATH FALLS

STATE PARK AND RECREATION AREAS

Key to abbreviations. I.P. = Interstate Park; S.A.P. = State Archaeological Park; S.B. = State Beach; S.C.A. = State Conservation Area; S.C.P. = State Conservation Park; S.Cp. = State Campground; S.F. = State Forest; S.G. = State Garden; S.H.A. = State Historic Area; S.H.P. = State Historic Park; S.H.S. = State Historic Site; S.M.P. = State Marine Park; S.N.A. = State Natural Area; S.P. = State Park; S.P.C. = State Public Campground; S.R. = State Reserve; S.R.A. = State Recreation Area; S.Res. = State Reservoir; S.Res.P. = State Resort Park; S.R.P. = State Rustic Park.

Place Name	Listed Under
Benson S.R.A.	PORTLAND
Beverly Beach S.P.	NEWPORT
Bullards Beach S.P.	BANDON
Cape Arago S.P.	COOS BAY
Cape Blanco S.P.	PORT ORFORD
Cape Lookout S.P.	TILLAMOOK
Cape Sebastian S.P.	GOLD BEACH
Carl G. Washburne Memorial S.P.	FLORENCE
Catherine Creek S.P.	LA GRANDE
Champoeg S.H.A.	NEWBERG
Cline Falls S.P.	REDMOND
Collier Memorial S.P.	KLAMATH FALLS

Crown Point S.P.	PORTLAND
Dabney S.P.	PORTLAND
Darlingtonia S.P.	FLORENCE
Devil's Elbow S.P.	FLORENCE
Devil's Lake S.P.	LINCOLN CITY
Devil's Punch Bowl S.P.	NEWPORT
Ecola S.P.	CANNON BEACH
Emigrant Springs S.P.	PENDLETON
Face Rock S.P.	BANDON
Farewell Bend S.P.	ONTARIO
Fogarty Creek S.P.	DEPOE BAY
Fort Stevens S.P.	ASTORIA
Guy W. Talbot S.P.	PORTLAND
Harris Beach S.P.	BROOKINGS
Hat Rock S.P.	UMATILLA
Hilgard Junction S.R.A.	LA GRANDE
Humbug Mountain S.P.	PORT ORFORD
Jackson F. Kimball S.P.	KLAMATH FALLS
Jessie M. Honeyman Memorial S.P.	FLORENCE
Joseph P. Stewart S.P.	MEDFORD
Lake Owyhee S.P.	ONTARIO
LaPine S.P.	BEND
Lewis and Clark S.P.	PORTLAND
Loeb S.P.	BROOKINGS
Mayer S.P.	THE DALLES
Milo McIver S.P.	OREGON CITY
Neptune S.P.	YACHATS
Ona Beach S.P.	NEWPORT
Ontario S.P.	ONTARIO
Oswald West S.P.	CANNON BEACH
Peter Skene Ogden Wayside S.P.	REDMOND
Pilot Butte S.P.	BEND
Rooster Rock S.P.	PORTLAND
Saddle Mountain S.P.	SEASIDE
Samuel H. Boardman S.P.	BROOKINGS
Shore Acres S.P.	COOS BAY
Silver Falls S.P.	SILVERTON
Smith Rock S.P.	REDMOND
South Beach S.P.	NEWPORT
Sunset Bay S.P.	COOS BAY
The Cove Palisades S.P.	MADRAS
Tou Velle S.P.	MEDFORD
Tumalo S.P.	BEND
Ukiah-Dale Forest S.P.	PENDLETON
Umpqua Lighthouse S.P.	REEDSPORT
Unity Lake S.P.	BAKER CITY
Valley of the Rogue S.P.	GRANTS PASS
Wallowa Lake S.P.	JOSEPH
Willamette Stone S.P.	PORTLAND
William M. Tugman S.P.	REEDSPORT
Yachats S.R.A.	YACHATS
Yaquina Bay S.P.	NEWPORT

CALENDAR HIGHLIGHTS

MAY

Boatnik Festival (Grants Pass). Riverside Park. Parade, concessions, carnival rides, boat races; entertainment. A 25-mile whitewater hydroboat race from Riverside Park to Hellgate Canyon and back. Square dance festival at Josephine County Fairgrounds. Phone 800/547-5927.

JUNE

Return of the Sternwheeler Days (Hood River). Celebration of the sternwheeler Columbia Gorge's return to home port for the summer. Wine and cheese tasting, crafts, food. Phone 541/374-8619.

Sandcastle Contest (Cannon Beach). Nationally known event features sand sculptures on beach. Phone 503/436-2623.

Portland Rose Festival (Portland). Held for more than 80 years, this festival incl the Grand Floral Parade (reservations required for indoor parade seats) and 2 other parades; band competition; rose show; championship auto racing; hot-air balloons; air show; carnival; Navy ships. Phone 503/227-2681. Web www.rosefestival.org

Scandinavian Midsummer Festival (Astoria). Parade, folk dancing, display booths, arts and crafts demonstrations, Scandinavian food. Phone Astoria Warrenton Chamber of Commerce, 503/325-6311.

Bach Festival (Eugene). Numerous concerts by regional and international artists; master classes; family activities. Phone 800/457-1486.

JULY

Oregon Coast Music Festival (Coos Bay). Variety of musical presentations ranging from jazz and dance to chamber and symphonic music. Phone 877/897-9350.

Da Vinci Days (Corvallis). Festival celebrating the relationship between art, science, and technology. Phone 541/757-6363.

Salem Art Fair & Festival (Salem). Bush's Pasture Park. Arts and crafts booths and demonstrations, children's art activities and parade, ethnic folk arts, performing arts, street painting, 5K run, food; tours of historic Bush House. Phone 503/581-2228.

AUGUST

Oregon State Fair (Salem). Fairgrounds. Horse racing, wine competition and tastings, agricultural exhibits, horse show, livestock, food, carnival, entertainment. Phone 503/378-FAIR.

SEPTEMBER

Pendleton Round-Up (Pendleton). Stadium. Rodeo and pageantry of Old West, annually since 1910. Gathering of Native Americans, PRCA working cowboys, and thousands of visitors. Phone 800/457-6336.

Water-related activities, hiking, riding, various other sports, picnicking and visitor centers, as well as camping, are available in many of these areas. Many camping facilities in state parks stay open yr-round, while others remain open as long as weather permits, usually Mar-Oct. All campgrounds are open mid-Apr-late Oct. Campers are limited to 10 days in any 14-day period from May 15-Sept 14; and 14 days out of 18 the rest of the yr. Discount rates are available at most campgrounds Oct-Apr. Summer fees per night: primitive campsite $8-$13; tent sites $14-$16; electrical sites $13-$19; full hookup sites $17-$20; extra vehicle $7; firewood is available (fee varies). Campsites may be reserved at 25 state parks throughout the year with a $6 fee plus first night's camping rate. A day-use fee of $3 is charged for each motor vehicle entering 24 state parks. For more information, contact Oregon Parks & Recreation Department, 1115 Commercial St NE, Salem 97301. For campsite res phone 800/452-5687; for information phone 503/378-6305 or 800/551-6949.

SKI AREAS

Place Name	Listed Under
Anthony Lakes Ski Area	BAKER CITY
Mt Ashland Ski Area	ASHLAND
Mt Bachelor Ski Area	BEND
Mt Hood Meadows Ski Area	MOUNT HOOD NATIONAL FOREST
Spout Springs Ski Area	LA GRANDE
Timberline Lodge	MOUNT HOOD NATIONAL FOREST
Williamette Pass Ski Area	EUGENE

FISHING AND HUNTING

Nonresident fishing license, annual $48.50; 7-day license $34.75; combined angling harvest card, $16.50; 1-day license, $8. Nonresident hunting license, annual $58.50. Special tags required in addition to license for big game. All licenses include agent-writing fee.

Oregon has 15,000 mi of streams, hundreds of lakes, and surf and deep-sea fishing. Fishing is good for Chinook and coho salmon, steelhead, rainbow and cutthroat trout, striped bass, perch, crappies, bluegill, catfish, and many other varieties. The hunter will find mule and blacktail deer, elk, ring-necked pheasant, Hungarian and chukar partridge, quail, blue and ruffed grouse, band-tailed pigeons, mourning doves, waterfowl, jackrabbits, coyote, fox, and bear.

For synopses of the latest angling and big-game regulations, contact Oregon Dept of Fish and Wildlife, PO Box 59, Portland 97207; 503/872-5268.

Driving Information

Safety belts are mandatory for all persons anywhere in vehicle. Under age 4 (or 40 lbs) must use an approved safety seat. For further information phone 503/986-4190 or 800/922-2022 (OR).

INTERSTATE HIGHWAY SYSTEM

The following alphabetical listing of Oregon towns in *Mobil Travel Guide* shows that these cities are within 10 miles of the indicated Interstate highways. A highway map, however, should be checked for the nearest exit.

Highway Number	Cities/Towns within 10 miles
Interstate 5	Albany, Ashland, Beaverton, Corvallis, Cottage Grove, Eugene, Grants Pass, Jacksonville, Medford, Oregon City, Portland, Roseburg, Salem.
Interstate 84	Baker City, Beaverton, Biggs, Hermiston, Hood River, La Grande, Ontario, Oregon City, Pendleton, Portland, The Dalles, Umatilla.

Additional Visitor Information

The Oregon Tourism Commission, 775 Summer St NE, Salem 97310; 800/547-7842, will provide visitors with an Oregon travel guide and other informative brochures on request.

There are 9 staffed state welcome centers in Oregon (Apr-Oct). They are: Astoria (downtown); Brookings (OR-CA border, S on US 101); Lakeview (downtown); Siskiyou (OR-CA border, S on I-5); Ontario (OR-ID border, E on I-84); Seaside (at Chamber of Commerce on US 101); Umatilla (on Brownell Blvd); Jantzen Beach-Portland (I-5 exit 308); Klamath Falls (OR-CA border, S on US 97).

This day trip or overnight from Portland affords a good look at the Oregon coast, with plenty of history, too. Take US Highway 30 northwest along the Columbia River to Astoria. Attractions include the Columbia River Maritime Museum and the Astoria Column. Next visit Fort Clatsop National Memorial, where Lewis and Clark—having finally reached the Pacific—spent the winter of 1805–06 before returning back east. Drive south on US Highway 101 to the classic beach town of Seaside, with its boardwalks and arcades. Continue south to Cannon Beach to see Haystack Rock, possibly the most famous landmark on the Oregon coast. Backtrack a few miles north to US Highway 26, which will take you back east to Portland. **(Approx 210 mi)**

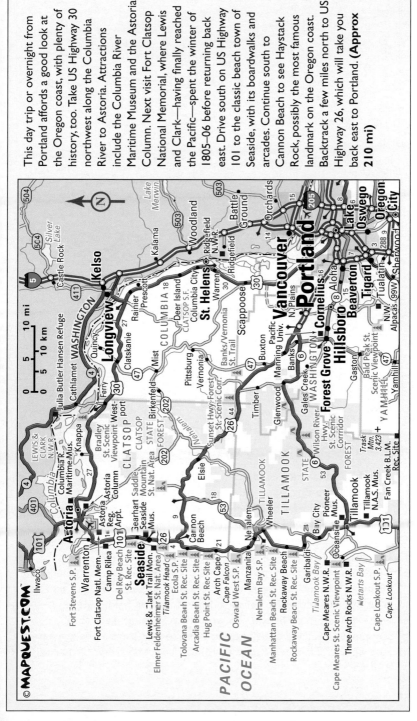

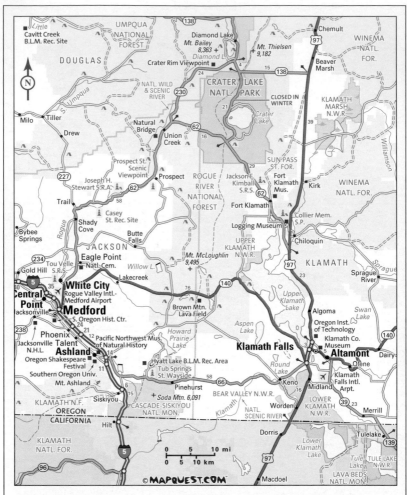

The deepest lake in the United States is the centerpiece of this beautiful drive through southwest Oregon. Begin in Medford and drive northeast on State Highways 62, 230, and 138 to the north entrance of Crater Lake National Park (this entrance is open only in summer). Explore the park on the Rim Drive, then hike down the Cleetwood Trail for a boat trip to the lake's landmarks. From the park's south entrance (open all year), take State Highway 62 and US Highway 97 south along Annie Creek and Upper Klamath Lake—a great spot to see white pelicans in summer and bald eagles in winter. Take State Highway 66 west from Klamath Falls to I-5, stopping in Ashland for dinner and maybe an Oregon Shakespeare Festival performance. Return north to Medford via I-5. **(Approx 250 mi)**

Albany

(C-2) *See also Corvallis, Salem, Sweet Home*

Founded 1848 **Pop** 29,462 **Elev** 212 ft
Area code 541 **Zip** 97321
Web www.albanyvisitors.com
Information Visitors Convention & Association, 300 SW 2nd Ave, PO Box 965; 541/928-0911 or 800/526-2256

Gateway to Oregon's covered bridge country, Albany was founded by Walter and Thomas Monteith and named for their former home, Albany, New York. The city boasts the largest collection of Victorian homes in the state. Albany is nestled in the heart of the Willamette Valley along the I-5 corridor of the Cascades. The Calapooia River joins the Willamette here. The seat of Linn County, Albany has diversified industry ranging from agriculture, timber, and wood products to rare metals.

What to See and Do

Flinn's Heritage Tours. Twenty different narrated tours take visitors through historic areas in the mid-Williamette Valley. Tours range from 45 min-6 hrs; feature covered bridges of Linn County, Albany's 3 historic districts, ghost towns, 100-yr-old apple orchard, or historic homes. (Daily; closed Dec 25) 222 Flist Ave W. Phone 541/928-5008 or 800/636-5008. ¢¢¢-¢¢¢¢¢

Annual Events

World Championship Timber Carnival. Timber Linn Park, E edge of town. Phone 541/928-2391. July 4 wkend.

Historic Interior Homes Tours. Phone 541/928-0911 or 800/526-2256. Summer and late Dec.

Great Balloon Escape. Last wkend July.

Veteran's Day Parade. One of the nation's largest. Phone 541/451-5799. Nov 11.

Motels/Motor Lodges

★★ **HAWTHORN INN AND SUITES.** *251 Airport Rd SE (97321). 541/928-0921; fax 541/928-8055; res 800/527-1133. Email hawthorn@ proaxis.com.* 50 rms, 3 story. Apr-Aug: S $60-$75; D $67-$82; each addl $7; suites $150; kit. units $70-$107; under 18 free; package plans; higher rates special events; lower rates rest of yr. Crib free. Pet accepted. TV; cable. Indoor pool; whirlpool. Complimentary continental bkfst. Restaurant opp 5 am-11 pm. Ck-out noon. Coin lndry. Meeting rms. Business servs avail. Gift shop. Exercise equipt; sauna. Refrigerators avail. Cr cds: A, DS, MC, V.

Covered bridge over Crabtree Creek, Linn County

★ **MOTEL ORLEANS.** *1212 SE Price Rd (97321), off I-5 Exit 233. 541/926-0170; fax 541/967-3283; toll-free 800/626-1900.* 72 rms, 2 story, 4 suites. May-Sep: S $50; D $56; each addl $6; suites $80; under 16 free; lower rates rest of yr. Crib avail, fee. Pet accepted, some restrictions. Parking lot. Pool. TV; cable (premium). Restaurant. Bar. Ck-out 11 am, ck-in

2 pm. Meeting rm. Business servs avail. Coin lndry. Golf. Cr cds: A, C, D, DS, MC, V.

Hotel

★★ **BEST WESTERN PONY SOLDIER INN.** *315 Airport Rd SE (97321), off I-5 Exits 234A(N), 234(S). 541/928-6322; fax 541/928-8124; toll-free 800/634-7669. Email ponyalb@aol.com; www.ponysoldierinns.com.* 73 rms, 2 story, S, D $70-$87; each addl $5; under 18 free. Crib avail. Parking lot. Pool, whirlpool. TV; cable (premium). Complimentary continental bkfst, coffee in rms, newspaper, toll-free calls. Restaurant 6 am-11 pm. Ck-out noon, ck-in 3 pm. Meeting rm. Dry cleaning, coin lndry. Exercise equipt, sauna, steam rm. Golf. Picnic facilities. Video games. Cr cds: A, C, D, DS, JCB, MC, V.

Ashland

(F-2) See also Jacksonville, Medford

Founded 1852 **Pop** 16,234
Elev 1,951 ft **Area code** 541
Zip 97520
Web www.ashlandchamber.com
Information Chamber of Commerce, 110 E Main St, PO Box 1360; 541/482-3486

When the pioneers climbed over the Siskiyou Mountains and saw the green expanse of the Rogue River Valley ahead of them, many decided to go no further. Later, when mineral springs were found, their Lithia water was piped in and now gushes from fountains on this city's plaza. Tourism, education, and small industry support the town. Southern Oregon University College (1926) makes this a regional education center. Rogue River National Forest (see MEDFORD) is on three sides; a Ranger District office is located here.

What to See and Do

Lithia Park. Has 100 acres of woodlands and ponds. Nature trails, tennis, picnicking, sand volleyball. Rose and Japanese gardens. Concerts. (Daily) Adj to City Plaza. Phone 541/488-5340. **FREE**

Mount Ashland Ski Area. Area has 2 triple, 2 double chairlifts; patrol, school, rentals; cafeteria, bar. Longest run 1 mi; vertical drop 1,150 ft. (Thanksgiving-Apr) 9 mi S on I-5, then 9 mi W on access road. Phone 541/482-2897; or 541/482-2754 (snow conditions). ¢¢¢¢

Seasonal Events

Oregon Cabaret Theatre. 1st & Hargadine Sts. Musicals, reviews, and comedies in dinner club setting. Schedule varies. Phone 541/488-2902. Feb-Dec.

Oregon Shakespeare Festival. Elizabethan Theater (outdoor); Angus Bowmer Theater (indoor); Black Swan Theater (indoor). Series of 12 classic and contemporary plays. Tues-Sun. Wheelchair seating by advance arrangement. Phone 541/482-4331. Mid-Feb-Oct.

Motels/Motor Lodges

★★ **BEST WESTERN.** *132 N Main St (97520). 541/482-0049; fax 541/488-3259; res 800/937-8376; toll-free 800/533-9627. Email barbsinn@symbolmindsprings.com.* 92 rms, 2-3 story. June-Oct: S $92-$115; D $106-$128; each addl $10; lower rates rest of yr. Crib $10. Pet accepted; $10. TV; cable (premium). Pool; whirlpool. Ck-out 11 am. Business servs avail. Airport transportation. Downhill/x-country ski 15 mi. Refrigerators. Near Shakespeare Festival theater. Cr cds: A, D, DS, MC, V.

★★ **BEST WESTERN WINDSOR INN.** *2520 Ashland St (97520). 541/488-2330; fax 541/482-1068; res 800/528-1234; toll-free 800/334-2330. www.windsorinn.com.* 60 rms, 2 story, 5 kit. units. Mid-May-Sep: S $60.75-$93.75; D $65.75-$93.75; each addl $6; kit. units $93.75-$103.75; lower rates rest of yr. Crib $6. Pet accepted, some restrictions; $6. TV; cable, VCR (movies). Heated pool. Complimentary continental bkfst. Restaurant adj open 24 hrs. Ck-out 1 pm. Business servs avail. Airport transportation. Downhill/x-country ski 13 mi. Microwave in suites. Cr cds: A, C, D, DS, ER, JCB, MC, V.

D 🐾 🏊 🛏 🖥 🔥

★ **CEDARWOOD INN MOTEL ASHLAND.** *1801 Siskiyou Blvd (97520). 541/488-2000; fax 541/482-2000; res 800/547-4141.* 59 rms, 14 with shower only, 2-3 story, 24 kit. units. Mid-May-mid-Oct: S $68; D $72; each addl $6; kit. units $78-$125; under 2 free; ski plans; lower rates rest of yr. Crib $6. Pet accepted, some restrictions. TV; cable, VCR avail (movies). Complimentary coffee in rms. Restaurant nearby. Bar. Ck-out 11 am. Business servs avail. Downhill/x-country ski 15 mi. 2 pools, 1 indoor; whirlpool. Microwaves avail. Picnic tables, grills. Cr cds: A, D, DS, MC, V.

D 🐾 🏊 🛏 🔥 SC

★ **KNIGHTS INN.** *2359 Hwy 66 (97520), at I-5 Exit 14. 541/482-5111; fax 541/488-1589; res 800/843-5644; toll-free 800/547-4566.* 40 rms, 1-2 story. June-Sep: S $38-$51; D $42-$62; each addl $6; ski plans; lower rates rest of yr. Crib $6. Pet accepted, some restrictions; $6. TV; cable. Heated pool; whirlpool. Complimentary coffee in lobby. Restaurant 7 am-10 pm. Bar 11 am-midnight. Ck-out 11 am. Downhill ski 15 mi. Cr cds: A, D, DS, MC, V.

🐾 🛗 🏊 🛏 🖥 🔥

★ **RODEWAY INN.** *1193 Siskiyou Blvd (97520). 541/482-2641; fax 541/482-0139; toll-free 800/547-6414.* 64 rms, 1-3 story. S $72-$80; D $72-$82; each addl $6. Crib $6. Pet accepted, some restrictions; $6. TV; cable (premium). Heated pool. Coffee in rms. Restaurant adj. Ck-out 11 am. Business servs avail. Downhill/x-country ski 18 mi. Microwaves avail. College opp. Cr cds: A, C, D, DS, MC, V.

D 🐾 🏊 🛏 🖥 🔥

★★ **STRATFORD INN.** *555 Siskiyou Blvd (97520). 541/488-2151; fax 541/482-0479; toll-free 800/547-4741.* 55 rms, 3 story, 6 kits. June-Sep: S $94; D $995; each addl $5; kit. units $105-$135; lower rates rest of yr. Crib

free. TV; cable (premium). Indoor pool; whirlpool. Complimentary continental bkfst. Restaurant nearby. Ck-out 11 am. Downhill/x-country ski 18 mi. Refrigerators; some microwaves. Locker rm for skis and bicycles. Cr cds: A, D, DS, MC, V.

D 🛗 ⚡ 🏊 🛏 🔥 🖥 🔥

Hotel

★★★ **WINDMILL INN.** *2525 Ashland St (97520), E of I-5 Exit 14. 541/482-8310; fax 541/488-1783; toll-free 800/547-4747. Email marief@jeld-wen. com; www.windmillinns.com.* 230 rms, 3 story, 86 suites. May-Sep: S, D $89; each addl $6; suites $109; under 17 free; lower rates rest of yr. Crib avail, fee. Pet accepted. Parking lot. Pool, lap pool, whirlpool. TV; cable (premium), VCR avail. Complimentary continental bkfst, newspaper, toll-free calls. Restaurant nearby. Ck-out 11 am, ck-in 4 pm. Meeting rms. Fax servs avail. Bellhops. Dry cleaning, coin lndry. Salon/barber. Free airport transportation. Exercise equipt. Golf. Tennis, 2 courts. Downhill skiing. Bike rentals. Picnic facilities. Cr cds: A, D, DS, MC, V.

D 🐾 🏊 🛗 🖥 🏊 🚶 🖥 🔥

B&Bs/Small Inns

★★★ **CHANTICLEER INN.** *120 Gresham St (97520). 541/482-1919; fax 541/488-4810; res 800/898-1950.* 6 rms, 3 story. June-Oct: S, D $125-$160; each addl $25; lower rates rest of yr. Complimentary full bkfst; afternoon refreshments. Restaurant nearby. Ck-out 11 am, ck-in 3-6 pm. Free local airport, bus depot transportation. Downhill/x-country ski 14 mi. Lawn games. Antiques, comforters. Country French inn; river rock fireplace. Patio. Cr cds: A, DS, MC, V.

🏊 🖥 🔥 🖥

★★★ **COUNTRY WILLOWS BED & BREAKFAST INN.** *1313 Clay St (97520). 541/488-1590; fax 541/488-1611; toll-free 800/945-5697. Email willows@willowsinn.com; www.willows inn.com.* 9 rms, 2 story, 3 suites. Apr-Oct: S $120; D $125; each addl $30; suites $190; lower rates rest of yr. Parking lot. Pool, lap pool, whirlpool. TV; cable, VCR avail, CD avail.

Complimentary full bkfst, coffee in rms, newspaper, toll-free calls. Restaurant. Ck-out 11 am, ck-in 3 pm. Meeting rm. Business center. Concierge. Gift shop. Exercise privileges. Golf. Tennis. Downhill skiing. Bike rentals. Hiking trail. Picnic facilities. Cr cds: A, DS, MC, V.

★★ **MCCALL HOUSE.** *153 Oak St (97520). 541/482-9296; fax 541/482-2125; res 800/808-9749. Email mccall@mccallhouse.com; www.mccall house.com.* 9 rms, 2 story. Rm phones avail. June-Oct: S, D $115-$170; each addl $30; varied lower rates rest of yr. Children over 12 yrs only. Complimentary full bkfst. Restaurant nearby. Ck-out 11 am, ck-in 3-6 pm. Former residence (1883) of Civil War veteran and mayor of Ashland. Totally nonsmoking. Cr cds: MC, V.

★★★ **MT ASHLAND INN.** *550 Mt Ashland Ski Rd (97520), W of I-5 Exit 6. 541/482-8707; toll-free 800/830-8707. www.mtashlandinn.com.* 4 story, 5 suites. S $130; D $135; each addl $30; suites $200. Parking lot. TV; cable, VCR avail, CD avail. Complimentary full bkfst, newspaper, toll-free calls. Ck-out 11 am, ck-in 3 pm. Gift shop. Sauna, whirlpool. Downhill skiing. Bike rentals. Hiking trail. Picnic facilities. Cr cds: DS, MC, V.

★★ **OAK HILL BED & BREAKFAST.** *2190 Siskiyou Blvd (97520). 541/482-1554; fax 541/482-1378; toll-free 800/888-7434. Email oakhill@mind.net; www.oakhillbb.com.* 6 rms, 2 story. Apr-Oct: D $115; each addl $25; lower rates rest of yr. Parking lot. TV; cable, VCR avail, CD avail. Complimentary full bkfst, coffee in rms, newspaper, toll-free calls. Restaurant nearby. Ck-out 11 am, ck-in 3 pm. Business servs avail. Gift shop. Exercise privileges. Golf. Tennis. Downhill skiing. Hiking trail. Picnic facilities. Cr cds: A, DS, MC, V.

★★ **PEDIGRIFT HOUSE B&B.** *407 Scenic Dr (97520). 541/482-1888; fax 541/482-8867; toll-free 800/262-4073. www.opendoor.com/pedigrift.* 4 rms, 2 story. S $115; D $130; each addl $25; under 12 free. Parking lot. TV; cable, VCR avail, CD avail. Complimentary

full bkfst, newspaper. Ck-out 11 am, ck-in 3 pm. Exercise privileges. Downhill skiing. Bike rentals. Supervised children's activities. Hiking trail. Cr cds: MC, V.

★★★ **ROMEO INN.** *295 Idaho St (97520). 541/488-0884; fax 541/488-0817; toll-free 800/915-8899. Email romeo@mind.net; www.romeoinn.com.* 4 rms, 2 story, 2 suites. May-Oct: D $160; each addl $30; suites $185; lower rates rest of yr. Parking lot. Pool, whirlpool. TV; cable, VCR avail, CD avail. Complimentary full bkfst, coffee in rms, newspaper. Restaurant nearby. Ck-out 11 am, ck-in 3 pm. Fax servs avail. Gift shop. Golf. Downhill skiing. Cr cds: DS, MC, V.

★★★ **WINCHESTER COUNTRY INN.** *35 S 2nd St (97520). 541/488-1113; fax 541/488-4604; toll-free 800 /972-4991. Email ashlandinn@aol.com; www.mind.net/winchesterinn.* 18 rms, 3 story. June-Oct: S $105-$135; D $110-$140; suites $135-$200; each addl $30; under 6 free; some wkend rates off-season; lower rates rest of yr. Complimentary full bkfst; afternoon refreshments. Restaurant (see WINCHESTER COUNTRY INN). Ck-out 11 am, ck-in 3 pm. Downhill/x-country ski 15 mi. Some whirlpools, fireplaces in suites. Some balconies. Patio tables. Restored Victorian house (1886) once served as the area's first hospital. Individually decorated rms; period furnishings. Gazebo, flower gardens. Cr cds: A, DS, MC, V.

★★ **WOODS HOUSE BED & BREAKFAST.** *333 N Main St (97520). 541/488-1598; fax 541/482-8027; toll-free 800/435-8260. Email woodsinfo@ woodshouse.com; www.woodshouse. com.* 6 rms, 2 story. June-Oct: S $115; D $125; each addl $35; under 11 free; lower rates rest of yr. Parking lot. TV; cable, VCR avail, CD avail. Complimentary full bkfst, coffee in rms, newspaper, toll-free calls. Restaurant nearby. Ck-out 11 am, ck-in 2 pm. Business servs avail. Gift shop. Exercise privileges. Golf, 9 holes. Tennis, 3 courts. Downhill skiing. Cr cds: DS, MC, V.

Restaurants

★ **ASHLAND BAKERY & CAFE.** *38 E Main St (97520).* 541/482-2117. *Email ashbkry38@aol.com.* Specializes in baked goods, vegetarian dishes. Hrs: 8 am-8 pm; Mon, Tues to 3 pm. Closed Thanksgiving, Dec 25. Wine, beer. Bkfst $3.25-$9.75; lunch $2.75-$9.75; dinner $2.75-$10.75. Cr cds: MC, V.

★★ **CHATEAULIN.** *50-52 E Main St (97520).* 541/482-2264. *Email chateau@jeffnet.org; www.chataulin. com.* Specializes in fresh seafood, lamb, roast duckling. Hrs: 5-9 pm. Closed Thanksgiving, Dec 24, 25; Mon in winter. Res accepted. Bar. Dinner $9-$27. Child's menu. Cr cds: A, D, MC, V.

★ **MACARONI'S.** *58 E Main St (97520).* 541/488-3359. Specializes in pizza, pasta, salad. Hrs: 11:30 am-10 pm; Fri, Sat to midnight; winter hrs vary. Closed Jan 1, Thanksgiving, Dec 25. Bar. Lunch $6-$15.95; dinner $9.50-$15.95. Cr cds: A, D, DS, MC, V.

★★ **WINCHESTER COUNTRY INN.** *35 S Second St.* 541/488-1115. *Email ashlandinn@aol.com; www. mind.net/winchesterinn.* Specializes in fresh salmon, beef, lamb. Hrs: 5-8 pm; Fri, Sat 5:30-8:30 pm. Dinner $14.95-$22.95. Built 1886. Cr cds: A, DS, MC, V.

Astoria

(A-1) *See also Cannon Beach, Seaside*

Settled 1811 **Pop** 10,069 **Elev** 18 ft
Area code 503 **Zip** 97103
Web www.el.com/to/astoria

Information Astoria-Warrenton Chamber of Commerce, 111 W Marine Dr, PO Box 176; 503/325-6311 or 800/875-6807

John Jacob Astor's partners sailed around Cape Horn and picked this point of land ten miles from the Pacific, overlooking the mouth of the Columbia River, for a fur trading post. The post eventually lost its importance, but the location and the natural resources attracted immigrants, and the town continued to grow. A four-mile-long bridge crosses the mouth of the Columbia.

What to See and Do

Astoria Column. (1926) A 125-ft tower commemorates first settlement; observation deck at top. (Daily) Info booth (Memorial Day-Labor Day, daily). Follow scenic drive signs to Coxcomb Hill. **FREE**

Columbia River Maritime Museum. Rare maritime artifacts and memorabilia of Columbia River, its tributaries, and the NW coast. *Columbia,* Lightship 604 at moorage in Maritime Park. Fishing industry, discovery and exploration, steamship, shipwreck, navigation and steamboat exhibits. Coast Guard and Navy exhibits. (Daily; closed Thanksgiving, Dec 25) 17th & Marine Dr. Phone 503/325-2323. ¢¢

Flavel House. (1883-87) Built by Captain George Flavel, pilot and shipping man; outstanding example of Queen Anne architecture. Restored Victorian home houses antique furnishings and fine art; collection of 19th- and 20th-century toys. (Daily; closed hols) Admission incl Heritage Museum at 16th & Duane and/or the Uppertown Firefighters' Mueseum at 30th & Marine Dr. 441 8th St. Phone 503/325-2203. ¢¢

✪ **Fort Clatsop National Memorial.** (see) 6 mi SW on US 101A.

Fort Stevens State Park. A 3,763-acre park adj old Civil War fort. Wreck of the *Peter Iredale* (1906) is on the ocean shore. Fort Stevens is the only military post in the lower 48 states to be fired upon by foreign forces since 1812. On June 21, 1942, a Japanese submarine fired several shells from its 5-inch gun; only 1 hit land while the others fell short. Visitor center and self-guided tour at the Old Fort Stevens Military Complex. Ocean beach, lake swimming, fishing, clamming on beach, boating (dock, ramp); bicycling, picnicking at Coffenbury Lake, improved tent and trailer sites (daily; standard fees, dump station). 5 mi W on US 101, then 5 mi N on Ridge Rd. Phone 503/861-1671.

Annual Events

Astoria-Warrenton Crab & Seafood Festival. Hammond Mooring Basin on Columbia River. Crab feast, Oregon wines, food and craft booths. Carnival, water taxi, crabbing and fishing boats. Last wkend Apr.

Maritime Week. Wk-long celebration of Astoria's maritime heritage includes Coast Guard demonstrations, ship model competition, Lower Columbia "row in." Phone 503/325-2323. Mid-May.

Scandinavian Midsummer Festival. Parade, folk dancing, display booths, arts and crafts demonstrations, Scandinavian food. Phone 503/325-1630. Mid-June.

Astoria Regatta. Parade, arts festival, public dinner, barbecue, boating competition. Mid-Aug.

Great Columbia Crossing Bridge Run. One of the most unusual and scenic runs; 8-mi course begins at Chinook, WA and ends at Astoria port docks. Mid-Oct.

Motels/Motor Lodges

★ **ASTORIA DUNES MOTEL.** *288 W Marine Dr (97103), foot of Astoria Megler Bridge. 503/325-7111; fax 503/ 325-0814; res 800/441-5519; toll-free 800/441-3319.* 58 rms, 18 A/C, 2-3 story. No elvtr. June-Sep: S, D $60-$95; each addl $7; lower rates rest of yr. TV; cable (premium). Indoor pool; whirlpool. Complimentary coffee. Restaurant nearby. Ck-out 11 am. Coin lndry. Business servs avail. Some refrigerators. Opp river. Cr cds: A, DS, MC, V.

⊷ ⊠ 🐾

★ **BAYSHORE MOTOR INN.** *555 Hamburg Ave (97103). 503/325-2205; fax 503/325-5550; toll-free 800/621-0641.* 71 rms, 4 story, 3 suites. July-Aug: S $69; D $79; each addl $6; suites $89; under 18 free; lower rates rest of yr. Crib avail. Pet accepted, some restrictions, fee. Parking lot. Indoor pool, whirlpool. TV; cable, VCR avail. Complimentary continental bkfst, toll-free calls. Restaurant nearby. Ck-out 11 am, ck-in 2 pm.

Meeting rm. Business servs avail. Coin lndry. Exercise privileges, sauna. Golf. Tennis. Cr cds: A, D, DS, JCB, MC, V.

🄳 ⊷ ⊷ 🌠 🎿 ⊷ 🏃 ✈ ⊠ 🐾 🆂🅲

★★ **CREST MOTEL.** *5366 Lief Erickson Dr (97103). 503/325-3141; fax 503/325-3141; toll-free 800/421-3141. Email thecrest@pacifier.com; www.crestmotel.com.* 40 rms, 2 story, 10 suites. June-Sep: S $55; D $73; each addl $7; suites $96; under 12 free; lower rates rest of yr. Crib avail. Pet accepted. Parking lot. TV; cable (premium). Complimentary continental bkfst, coffee in rms. Restaurant nearby. Ck-out noon, ck-in 2 pm. Fax servs avail. Coin lndry. Whirlpool. Golf. Beach access. Hiking trail. Picnic facilities. Cr cds: A, C, D, DS, MC, V.

🄳 ⊷ ⊷ 🌠 ⊠ 🔥

Hotel

★★ **SHILO INN.** *1609 E Harbor Dr (97146), 2 mi S on US 101, near airport. 503/861-2181; fax 503/861-2980; res 800/222-2244. Email warrenton@ shiloinns.com; www.shiloinns.com.* 4 story, 63 suites. June-Aug: S, D $149; each addl $15; suites $249; under 12 free; lower rates rest of yr. Crib avail. Pet accepted, fee. Parking lot. Indoor pool. TV; cable (DSS). Complimentary full bkfst, coffee in rms, newspaper, toll-free calls. Restaurant 6 am-9 pm. Bar. Ck-out noon, ck-in 4 pm. Meeting rms. Business servs avail. Dry cleaning, coin lndry. Free airport transportation. Exercise equipt, sauna, steam rm. Golf, 18 holes. Video games. Cr cds: A, D, DS, ER, JCB, MC, V.

🄳 ⊷ ⊷ 🌠 🌠 ⊷ 🏃 ✈ ⊠ 🐾

Resort

★ **RED LION INN.** *400 Industry St (97103), W of bridge, on US 101. 503/325-7373; fax 503/325-5786; toll-free 800/733-5446. Email redliona@pacifier.com; www.redlion oregon.com.* 124 rms, 2 story, 3 suites. July-Aug: S, D $109; each addl $10; suites $150; under 17 free; lower rates rest of yr. Crib avail. Pet accepted, fee. Parking lot. TV; cable, VCR avail. Complimentary continental bkfst, coffee in rms, newspaper, toll-free calls. Restaurant 6 am-10 pm. Bar. Ck-out 3 pm, ck-in noon. Meeting rms. Dry cleaning. Supervised children's activities. Hiking trail. Picnic facilities. Cr cds: A, C, D, DS, MC, V.

🅳 ▣ 🖻 ▨ ▨ 🆂🅲

B&Bs/Small Inns

★ **COLUMBIA RIVER INN.** *1681 Franklin Ave (97103). 503/325-5044; toll-free 800/953-5044. www.moriah. com/columbia.* 2 rms, 2 story. June-Aug: S, D $75-$125; each addl $10; children $12; lower rates rest of yr. Parking garage. Indoor/outdoor pools, children's pool. TV; cable, VCR avail. Complimentary full bkfst, coffee in rms. Restaurant. Bar. Ck-out 3 pm, ck-in 11 pm. Meeting rms. Gift shop. Cr cds: A, DS, MC, V.

▨ ▣ ▨

★ **FRANKLIN STREET STATION BED & BREAKFAST.** *1140 Franklin Ave (97103). 503/325-4314; fax 801/ 681-5641; res 800/448-1098. Email franklinststationbb@yahoo.com; www. franklin-st-station-bb.com.* 5 rms, 4 story, 3 suites. Apr-Sep: S $65; D $80; each addl $15; suites $110; children $15; lower rates rest of yr. Street parking. TV; cable (premium), VCR avail, CD avail. Complimentary full bkfst, coffee in rms, newspaper, toll-free calls. Restaurant. Ck-out 11 am. Meeting rm. Internet dock/port avail. Exercise privileges. Golf, 18 holes. Tennis, 4 courts. Cr cds: A, DS, MC, V.

▨ ▣ ▨ ▣ ▨ ▨ 🆂🅲

★★ **ROSE BRIAR HOTEL.** *636 14th St (97103). 503/325-7427; fax 503/ 325-6937; toll-free 800/487-0224. Email Rosebriar@oregoncoastlodgings. com, www.rosebriarhotel.com.* 10 rms, 2 story. No A/C. S, D $65-$139; each addl $10. Complimentary bkfst. Restaurant nearby. Ck-out 11 am, ck-in 3 pm. Business servs avail. Some fireplaces. Built in 1902 as a residence; was also used as a convent. Many antiques. Overlooks town and river. Totally nonsmoking. Cr cds: A, D, DS, MC, V.

🅳 🖻 ▣ ▣ ▨ ▨

Restaurants

★★ **PIER 11 FEED STORE.** *77 11th St (97103). 503/325-0279.* Specializes in seafood, steak. Salad bar. Hrs: 8:30 am-9 pm; Fri, Sat to 10 pm. Closed Thanksgiving, Dec 25. Res accepted. Bar. Bkfst $2.95-$8.50; lunch $5.50-$9; dinner $8-$24.50. Old feed store on pier (late 1800s); natural beamed ceilings. View of Columbia River. Cr cds: A, D, MC, V.

🅳 ▣

★★ **SHIP INN.** *1 2nd St (97103). 503/325-0033.* Specializes in Cornish and chicken pasties, seafood. Salad bar. Hrs: 11:30 am-9:30 pm. Closed hols. Bar. Lunch, dinner $5-$12. Complete meals: $8.50-$16.50. View of Columbia River. Cr cds: C, MC, V.

🅳

Baker City

(C-6) *See also La Grande*

Pop 9,140 **Elev** 3,443 ft
Area code 541 **Zip** 97814
Web www.neoregon.com/visitBaker.html

Information Baker County Visitor & Convention Bureau, 490 Campbell St; 541/523-3356 or 800/523-1235

The Baker City Historic District includes more than 100 commercial and residential buildings, many built from stone quarried in town at the same place where gold was found. A 15-block area, from the Powder River to 4th St and from Estes to Campbell Sts, has many structures built between 1890-1910 that are being restored. Baker City, on the "old Oregon trail," is also the home of the Armstrong Gold Nugget found June 19, 1913, by George Armstrong. It weighs more than 80 ounces. A Ranger District office and the office of the supervisor of the Wallowa-Whitman National Forest is located here.

What to See and Do

Eastern Oregon Museum. Large collection of relics and implements used in the development of the West; turn-of-the-century logging and mining tools; period rms; doll collection; children's antique furniture. On grounds is 1884 railroad depot. (Mid-Apr-mid-Oct, daily) 9 mi NW on old US 30. Phone 541/856-3233. **Donation**

Hells Canyon Tours. One- to 6-day float trips; horseback and rafting combinations. Guides, oar powered or paddle rafts, camping equipment, meals provided. (May-Sep) Also 2-hr, 3-hr, and all day (includes lunch) canyon tours by jet boat. E on OR 86 to Oxbow then N to Hells Canyon Dam. Phone 541/785-3352 or 800/422-3568. ¢¢¢¢¢

Horse-Drawn Trolley Tours. Narrated tours covering pioneer, gold rush, and Oregon Trail histories. (June-Sep, Fri and Sat) Phone 800/523-1235. ¢¢¢

National Historic Oregon Trail Interpretive Center. Exhibits, living history presentations, multi-media displays. (Daily; closed Jan 1, Dec 25) 5 mi E on OR 86, at summit of Flagstaff Hill. Phone 800/523-1235. ¢¢¢

Oregon Trail Regional Museum. Houses one of the most outstanding collections of rocks, minerals, and semiprecious stones in the West. Also, an elaborate sea-life display; wildlife display; period clothing and artifacts of early Baker County. (Late Mar-Oct, daily) 2490 Grove St. Phone 800/523-1235. ¢

Sumpter Valley Railroad. Restored gear-driven Heisler steam locomotive and 2 observation cars travel 7 mi on narrow-gauge track through a wildlife game habitat area where beaver, muskrat, geese, waterfowl, herons, and other animals may be seen. Also passes through the Sumpter mining district, location of the Sumpter Dredge which brought up more than $10 million in gold between 1913-54 from as far down as 20 ft. (May-Sep, Sat, Sun, hols) 30 mi SW on OR 7. Phone 800/523-1235. ¢¢¢

Unity Lake State Park. A 39-acre park with swimming, fishing, boat ramp on Unity Lake; picnicking, tent and improved-site camping. Standard fees. 45 mi SW on OR 245, near jct US 26. Phone 541/575-2773.

Wallowa-Whitman National Forest. Reached via OR 7, 26, 86, 203, 82, I-84. More than 2 million acres with 14,000-acre North Fork John Day Wilderness; 7,000-acre Monument Rock Wilderness; 358,461-acre Eagle Cap Wilderness; 215,500-acre Hells Canyon Wilderness. Snowcapped

peaks, Minam River; alpine meadows, rare wild flowers; national scenic byway, scenic drive Hells Canyon Overlook, which overlooks deepest canyon in North America— Hells Canyon National Recreation Area (see JOSEPH); Buckhorn Lookout; Anthony Lake, and Phillips Lake. Stream and lake trout fishing, float and jet boat trips; elk, deer, and bear hunting, saddle and pack trips. Picnic area. Camping. For further info contact Supervisor, PO Box 907. Sections W, NE & S. Phone 541/523-6391. In forest is

Anthony Lakes Ski Area. Double chairlift, pomalift; patrol, school, rentals; nursery; day lodge, cafeteria, concession area, bar. Longest run more than 1 mi; vertical drop 860 ft. (Mid-Nov-mid-Apr, Thurs-Sun) Cross-country trails. Fishing, hiking, cabin rentals, store (summer). 35 mi NW, off I-84 at North Powder. Phone 800/523-1235. ¢¢¢¢

Annual Event

Miner's Jubilee. Third wkend July.

Motels/Motor Lodges

★★ **BEST WESTERN.** *1 Sunridge Ln (97814).* 541/523-6444; fax 541/523-6446; toll-free 800/233-2368. 155 rms, 2 story. S $54-$64; D $58-$68; each addl $4; suites $150-$175. Crib $5. TV; cable (premium), VCR avail. Heated pool; whirlpool. Coffee in rms. Restaurant 5:30 am-10 pm. Ck-out noon. Meeting rms. Business servs avail. In-rm modem link. Sundries. Free airport transportation. Private patios, balconies. Cr cds: A, C, D, DS, ER, MC, V.

D ⛱ 📶 👍 SC

★★ **ELDORADO INN.** *695 Campbell St (97814), at I-84 N City Center Exit.* 541/523-6494; fax 541/523-6494; toll-free 800/537-5756. 56 rms, 2 story. S, D $43-$55; family rates. Crib $3. Pet accepted; $2/day. TV; cable, VCR avail. Indoor pool. Complimentary coffee. Restaurant open 24 hrs. Ck-out noon. Business servs avail. Refrigerators avail. Cr cds: A, C, D, DS, MC, V.

🐾 ⛱ 📶 👍 SC

★★ **QUALITY INN.** *810 Campbell St (97814).* 541/523-2242; fax 541/523-

2242; res 800/228-5151. 54 rms, 2 story. Mid-May-mid-Sep: S $50-$54; D $57-$61; each addl $5; under 19 free; lower rates rest of yr. Crib $3. Pet accepted; $2/day. TV; cable. Pool privileges. Complimentary continental bkfst. Restaurant nearby. Ck-out noon. Meeting rms. Some refrigerators. Cr cds: A, DS, MC, V.

★ **SUPER 8 MOTEL.** *250 Campbell St (97814). 541/523-8282; fax 541/ 523-9137; res 888/726-2466; toll-free 800/800-8000.* 72 rms, 2 story, 2 kit. units. Apr-Sep: S $43.88; D $49.88; each addl $4; kit. units $71.88; under 13 free; lower rates rest of yr. Crib $4. TV; cable (premium), VCR avail (movies). Indoor pool; whirlpool. Complimentary continental bkfst. Restaurant nearby. Ck-out 11 am. Coin lndry. Business servs avail. Refrigerators. Cr cds: A, C, D, DS, JCB, MC, V.

Bandon

(E-1) *See also Coos Bay, North Bend, Port Orford*

Pop 2,215 **Elev** 67 ft **Area code** 541 **Zip** 97411
Information Chamber of Commerce, PO Box 1515; 541/347-9616

A fine beach, known for its picturesque beauty, legendary rocks, and a harbor at the mouth of the Coquille River attracts many tourists to Bandon. From November through March, the town is known for its short-lived storms followed by sunshine, and even has a group called the Storm Watchers. Popular seashore activities include beachcombing, hiking, fishing from the south jetty, and crabbing from the docks. Summer and early autumn bring the salmon run in the Coquille River. Rockhounds search for agate, jasper, and petrified wood.

What to See and Do

Bandon Museum. Exhibits on maritime activities of early Bandon and Coquille River; coastal shipwrecks, Coast Guard operations; extensive collection of Native American artifacts; old photos. (Schedule varies) US 101 & Filmore Ave. Phone 541-347-2164. ¢

Bullards Beach State Park. A 1,266-acre park with 4 mi of ocean beach. Fishing, boating (dock, ramp with access to Coquille River); picnicking, improved trailer campsites (dump station). Coquille Lighthouse (1896); interpretive plaques (daily). Standard fees. 2 mi N on US 101. Phone 541/347-3501.

Face Rock State Park. An 879-acre park on coastal dune area with access to beach, fishing; picnicking. 4 mi S on US 101, then 1 mi W on Bradley Lake Rd. Phone 541/347-3501.

West Coast Game Park. A 21-acre park with more than 450 exotic animals and birds. Visitors meet and walk with free-roaming wildlife. Animal keepers demonstrate the personalities of many large predators residing at the park. (Mar-Nov, daily; rest of yr, wkends and hols) 7 mi S on US 101. Phone 541/347-3106. ¢¢¢

Annual Events

Seafood and Wine Festival. Memorial Day wkend.

Cranberry Festival. Parade, barbecue, square dances, harvest ball, sports events. Late Sep.

Motels/Motor Lodges

★ **HARBOR VIEW MOTEL.** *355 OR 101 PO Box 1409 (97411). 541/347-4417; fax 541/347-3616; toll-free 800/526-0209. Email hvmbandon@ harborside.com; www.harborview motelbandon.com.* 58 rms, 3 story, 1 suite. May-Sep: S $79; D $84; each addl $5; suites $125; under 6 free; lower rates rest of yr. Crib avail, fee. Parking lot. TV; cable (premium). Complimentary coffee in rms. Restaurant nearby. Ck-out 11 am. Fax servs avail. Whirlpool. Golf. Cr cds: A, C, D, DS, MC, V.

★ **SUNSET OCEANFRONT ACCOMMODAT.** *1865 Beach Loop Dr SW (97411), ½ mi W of US 101. 541/ 347-2453; fax 541/347-3636; toll-free 800/842-2407. Email sunset@harbor side.com.* 58 rms, 1-3 story, 8 kits. S, D $45-$105; suites $110-$215; kit. units $66-$120; cottages with kits $125-$215. Crib free. Pet accepted, some restrictions; $5/day. TV; cable. Restaurant 11 am-3 pm, 5-9 pm. Ck-out 11 am. Coin lndry. Business servs avail. Free airport transportation. Whirlpool. Ocean view; beach access. Cr cds: A, DS, MC, V.

🖐 🖼

Restaurants

★★ **BANDON BOATWORKS.** *275 Lincoln Ave SW (97411), near South Jetty Rd. 541/347-2111. www. destinationbandon.com.* Specializes in seafood, steak, chicken. Salad bar. Hrs: 11:30 am-9 pm; Sun 11 am-8:30 pm. Closed Dec 25. Res accepted. Wine, beer. Lunch $5-$8; dinner $9-$21.95. Child's menu. View of jetty, lighthouse. Cr cds: A, D, MC, V.

D SC

★★★ **LORD BENNETT'S.** *1695 Beach Loop Dr (97411). 541/347-3663.* Specializes in fresh seafood. Hrs: 11 am-3 pm, 5-10 pm; Sun brunch to 3 pm; winter to 9 pm. Closed Dec 25. Res accepted. Lunch $4.50-$8.25; dinner $10-$18. Sun brunch $4.50-$8.75. Child's menu. Entertainment. Overlooks ocean. Cr cds: A, D, MC, V.

D ⟶

★★ **WHEELHOUSE.** *125 Chicago Ave (97411), at Old Town Mall. 541/347-9331.* Specializes in seafood, local lamb. Hrs: 11:30 am-10 pm; winter to 9 pm. Bar. Lunch $5-$10; dinner $8-$20. In restored fish ware-house. View of boat harbor and fish-ing boats. Cr cds: A, MC, V.

D ⟶

Beaverton

(B-2) *See also Forest Grove, Hillsboro, Oregon City, Portland*

Pop 53,310 **Elev** 189 ft **Area code** 503
Zip 97005 **Web** www.beaverton.org

Information Beaverton Area Chamber of Commerce, 4800 SW Griffith Dr, Suite 100; 503/644-0123

Motels/Motor Lodges

★★★ **GREENWOOD INN.** *10700 SW Allen Blvd (97005). 503/643-7444; fax 503/626-4545; toll-free 800/289-1300. Email info@greenwoodinn.com.* 250 rms, 2 story, 24 kits. S $99-$133; D $114-$148; each addl $10; kit. suites $180-$400; under 12 free; wknd rates. Crib free. Pet accepted; $10. TV; cable (premium). Pools; whirlpool. Complimentary coffee in rms. Restaurant (see PAVILLION). Bar 4 pm-1:30 am; entertainment exc Sun. Ck-out 1 pm. Meeting rms. Business center. In-rm modem link. Sundries. Gift shop. Exercise equipt; sauna. Some refrigerators. Cr cds: A, DS, MC, V.

🖐 ⊷ 🧍 🏃 🖼

★★ **PEPPERTREE INN.** *10720 SW Allen Blvd (97005). 503/641-7477; fax 503/641-7477; toll-free 800/453-6219. Email sales@peppertreeinn.com; www.peppertreeinn.com.* 73 rms, 2 story. S $65; D $70. Crib avail, fee. Parking lot. Indoor pool, whirlpool. TV; cable (premium), VCR avail. Complimentary continental bkfst, coffee in rms, newspaper, toll-free calls. Ck-out 11 am, ck-in 2 pm. Business servs avail. Dry cleaning, coin lndry. Exercise privileges. Golf, 18 holes. Cr cds: A, D, DS, JCB, MC, V.

D 🧍 🧍 ⟶ 🖼

★★ **PHOENIX INN TIGARD.** *9575 SW Locust (97223), 2 blks N on OR 217 Exit Greenburg Rd, near Washing-ton Square Shopping Mall. 503/624-9000; fax 503/968-8184; toll-free 800/624-6884.* 56 rms, 3 story. S $72-$77; D $79-$89; each addl $10; under 18 free; wknd rates. Crib free. TV; cable (premium). Compli-mentary continental bkfst, compli-mentary coffee in rms. Restaurant nearby. Ck-out noon. Meeting rms. Business servs avail. Valet serv. Sun-dries. Coin lndry. Exercise equipt. Indoor pool; whirlpool. Refrigera-tors, microwaves; some wet bars. Cr cds: A, DS, MC, V.

⊷ 🧍 🖼

★★ **RAMADA INN.** *13455 SW Canyon Rd (97005). 503/643-9100; fax 503/643-0514; res 888/298-2054.*

142 rms, 3 story, 18 kits. S, D $115-$144; each addl $10; kit. units $120-$150; under 18 free. Crib free. TV, cable (premium). Heated pool. Complimentary continental bkfst, coffee in rms. Restaurant adj open 24 hrs. Ck-out noon. Business servs avail. Exercise equipt. Cr cds: A, D, DS, MC, V.

Hotels

★★ **BEAVERTON FAIRFIELD INN.** *15583 NW Gateway Ct (97006). 503/972-0048; fax 503/972-0049; res 800/228-2800. www.fairfieldinn.com/pdxfh.* 106 rms, 4 story. May-Aug: S, D $77; lower rates rest of yr. Crib avail. Pet accepted, some restrictions. Parking lot. Indoor pool, whirlpool. TV; cable (DSS). Complimentary continental bkfst, coffee in rms, newspaper, toll-free calls. Restaurant nearby. Ck-out noon, ck-in 3 pm. Business center. Dry cleaning, coin lndry. Exercise privileges. Golf. Tennis, 16 courts. Downhill skiing. Hiking trail. Picnic facilities. Video games. Cr cds: A, D, DS, MC, V.

★★ **COURTYARD BY MARRIOTT.** *8500 SW Nimbus Ave (97008). 503/641-3200; fax 503/641-1287; toll-free 800/831-0224.* 137 rms, 3 story, 12 suites. S, D $79; suites $119. Crib avail. Parking lot. Indoor pool, whirlpool. TV; cable (premium). Complimentary coffee in rms, newspaper. Restaurant. Bar. Ck-out noon, ck-in 3 pm. Meeting rms. Business servs avail. Dry cleaning, coin lndry. Exercise equipt. Golf, 18 holes. Tennis, 2 courts. Cr cds: A, D, DS, MC, V.

Restaurants

★★ **KOJI OSAKAYA.** *11995 SW Beaverson (Hillsdale Hwy) (97005). 503/646-5697.* Specializes in sushi, Japanese-style noodles. Hrs: 11:30 am-2:30 pm; 5-11 pm; Sat 11:30 am-11 pm; Sun 11:30 am-10 pm. Closed hols. Bar. Lunch $6-$12; dinner $6-$18.95. Japanese decor. Cr cds: A, MC, V.

★★★ **PAVILION.** *10700 SW Allen Blvd. 503/626-4550. www.pavilion trattoria.citysearch.com.* Specializes in salmon, prime rib. Hrs: 6:30 am-10 pm; Sat, Sun from 7 am; early-bird dinner Sun-Thurs 4-6 pm; Sun brunch 9 am-2 pm. Res accepted. Bar. Bkfst $4-$9.25; lunch $5.95-$9.50; dinner $8-$19. Sun brunch $19.95. Child's menu. Entertainment: Thurs-Sat. Casual decor. Cr cds: A, D, DS, MC, V.

★★ **SAYLER'S OLD COUNTRY KITCHEN.** *4655 SW Griffith Dr (97005). 503/644-1492.* Specializes in steak, prime rib, chicken. Hrs: 11:30 am-10 pm; Fri to 11 pm; Sat 3-11 pm; Sun noon-11 pm. Closed July 4, Thanksgiving, Dec 24, 25. Bar. Lunch $8.95-$16.95; dinner $8.95-$21.95. Child's menu. Family-owned. Cr cds: A, MC, V.

Bend

(D-3) *See also Prineville, Redmond*

Settled 1900 **Pop** 20,469 **Elev** 3,628 ft **Area code** 541
Web www.bendchamber.org
Information Chamber of Commerce, 63085 N US 97, 97701; 541/382-3221 or 800/905-2363

The early town was named Farewell Bend after a beautiful wooded area on a sweeping curve of the Deschutes River, where pioneer travelers had their last view of the river. The Post Office Department shortened it, but there was good reason for this nostalgic name. As westward-bound settlers approached, they found the first lush, green forests and good water they had seen in Oregon.

Tourists are attracted year-round to the region by its streams and lakes, mountains, great pine forests, ski slopes, and golf courses. There is also much of interest to the geologist and rockhound in this area. Movie and television producers take advantage of the wild western scenery.

Two Ranger District offices of the Deschutes National Forest are located here.

What to See and Do

✪ Driving Tour In Deschutes National Forest. An 89-mi paved loop (Century Drive, Cascade Lakes Hwy) provides a clear view of Three Sisters peaks, and passes many mountain lakes and streams. Go W on Franklin Ave past Drake Park, follow the signs. Continue S past Mt Bachelor, Elk Lake, Lava Lakes, and Cultus Lake. After passing Crane Prairie Reservoir, turn left (E) on Forest Rd 42 to US 97, then left (N) for return to Bend. Also in the forest are Newberry National Volcanic Monument, the Lava Cast Forest and Lava Butte Geological Area, Mt Bachelor Ski Area, Crane Prairie Osprey Management Area, as well as Mt Jefferson, Diamond Peak, Three Sisters, and Mt Washington wildernesses. Fishing, hiking, camping, picnicking, and rafting are popular. The forest includes 1.6 million acres with headquarters in Bend. 10 mi S of Bend, at the base of Lava Butte, is Lava Lands Visitor Center, operated by the US Forest Service, with dioramas and exhibits on history and geology of volcanic area. For further information contact Supervisor, 1645 US 20E, 97701. Phone 541/388-2715.

The High Desert Museum. Regional museum with indoor/outdoor exhibits featuring live animals and cultural history of Intermountain Northwest aridlands; hands-on activities; on-going presentations. Galleries house wildlife, Western art, and Native American artifacts; landscape photography; walk-through dioramas depicting opening of American West. Desertarium showcases seldom-seen bats, burrowing owls, amphibians, and reptiles. Visitor center. (Daily; closed Jan 1, Thanksgiving, Dec 25) 6 mi S on US 97. Phone 541/382-4754. ¢¢¢

Lava Butte and Lava River Cave. Lava Butte is an extinct volcanic cone. Paved road to top provides view of Cascades; interpretive trails through pine forest and lava flow. One mi S, Lava River Cave offers a lava tube 1.2 mi long; ramps and stairs ease walking. Visitor center has audiovisual shows (May-Sep, daily). 11 mi S on US 97. Phone 541/593-2421. ¢

Mount Bachelor Ski Area. Panoramic, scenic view of forests, lakes, and Cascade Range. Facilities at base of 6,000 ft; 6,000 acres. Ten chairlifts; patrol, school, rentals; cafeterias, concession areas, bars, lodges; day care. Longest run 2 mi; vertical drop 3,100 ft. (Mid-Nov-early July, daily) 56 mi of cross-country trails. Half-day rates. 22 mi SW on Century Dr. Phone 541/382-2442 or 541/382-2607, or 800/829-2442 for res. ¢¢¢¢

Newberry National Volcanic Monument. Wide range of volcanic features and deposits similar to Mt Etna; obsidian flow, pumice deposits. On same road are East and Paulina lakes. There is a view of entire area from Paulina Peak. Both lakes have excellent fishing, boat landings; hiking, picnicking (stoves, fireplaces), resorts, tent and trailer sites. 24 mi S on US 97, then 14 mi E on Forest Road 21, in Deschutes National Forest. Phone 541/388-2715. Camping ¢¢¢

Pine Mountain Observatory. University of Oregon astronomical research facility. Visitors may view stars, planets, and galaxies through telescopes. (May-Oct, Fri and Sat) 26 mi SE near Millican, via US 20, then 9 mi S on marked rd. Phone 541/382-8331 for appt. **Donation**

State parks and recreation areas.

LaPine. A 2,333-acre park on Deschutes River in Ponderosa pine forest. Scenic views. Swimming, bathhouse, fishing, boating; picnicking, improved trailer campsites (dump station). Standard fees. 22 mi S on US 97, then 4 mi W. Phone 541/388-6055.

Pilot Butte. A 101-acre park noted for a lone cinder cone rising 511 feet above the city. Summit affords an excellent view of the Cascade Range. No water, no camping. 1 mi E on US 20. Phone 541/388-6055.

Tumalo. A 320-acre park situated along the banks of the Deschutes River; swimming nearby, fishing; hiking, picnicking, tent and trailer campsites, solar-heated showers. Standard fees. 5½ mi NW off US 20. Phone 541/382-3586 or 541/388-6055.

Tumalo Falls. A 97-ft waterfall deep in pine forest devastated by 1979 fire. W via Franklin Ave & Galveston Ave, 12 mi beyond city limits, then 2 mi via unsurfaced forest road.

Whitewater Rafting. Sun Country Tours. Choose from 2-hr or all-day trips. Also canoeing and special programs. (May-Sep) Phone 541/382-6277 for more information. ¢¢¢¢

Motels/Motor Lodges

★★ **BEST WESTERN ENTRADA LODGE.** *19221 Century Dr (97702). 541/382-4080; fax 541/382-4080; res 800/528-1234. www.bestwestern.com/ entradalodge.* 78 rms, 1 story, 1 suite. June-Sep, Dec: S, D $89; each addl $5; suites $129; lower rates rest of yr. Crib avail. Pet accepted, some restrictions, fee. Parking lot. Pool, whirlpool. TV; cable. Complimentary continental bkfst, coffee in rms, toll-free calls. Restaurant nearby. Ck-out noon, ck-in 3 pm. Business servs avail. Coin lndry. Golf, 18 holes. Tennis, 10 courts. Downhill skiing. Hiking trail. Cr cds: A, C, D, DS, MC, V.

★ **CIMARRON MOTEL SOUTH.** *201 NE 3rd St (97701). 541/382-8282; fax 541/388-6833.* 58 rms, 2 story, 2 suites. May-Oct: S $59; D $69; each addl $5; suites $89; lower rates rest of yr. Crib avail. Pet accepted, fee. Pool. TV; cable (premium). Complimentary continental bkfst, toll-free calls. Ck-out 11 am, ck-in 2 pm. Fax servs avail. Golf. Cr cds: A, D, DS, MC, V.

★★ **MOUNT BACHELOR VILLAGE RESORT.** *19717 Mount Bachelor Dr (97702). 541/389-5900; fax 541/388-7820; toll-free 800/452-9846. www. mountbachelorvillage.com.* 130 condominiums, some A/C, 2 story. Condos $97-$329; ski, golf plans. Crib $5. TV; cable. Heated pool; whirlpools. Complimentary coffee in lobby. Restaurant 11:30 am-10 pm. Ck-out noon. Coin lndry. Meeting rm. Business center. Downhill ski 18 mi; x-country ski 14 mi. Health club privileges. Refrigerators, fireplaces; some microwaves. Private patios, balconies. Picnic tables. Woodland setting along Deschutes River. Cr cds: A, DS, MC, V.

★ **RED LION INN NORTH.** *1415 NE 3rd St (97701). 541/382-7011; fax 541/382-7934; res 800/222-8733.* 75 rms, 2 story. S, D $79; each addl $10; under 18 free. Crib free. Pet accepted. TV; cable (premium). Heated pool; whirlpool. Restaurant 6 am-10 pm. Ck-out noon. Meeting rms. Business servs avail. In-rm modem link. Sundries. Saunas. Cr cds: A, D, DS, MC, V.

Guest Ranch

★★ **ROCK SPRINGS GUEST RANCH.** *64201 Tyler Rd (97701), 9 mi NW of Bend off US 20. 541/382-1957; fax 541/382-7774; toll-free 800/ 225-3833. Email info@rocksprings.com; www.rocksprings.com.* 26 cottages. S $1,430/wk; family rates; AP late June-Aug; MAP Thanksgiving. TV in sitting rm. Heated pool; whirlpool. Free supervised children's activities (late June-Aug); ages 3-16. Dining rm (sittings) 8-9 am, noon-1 pm, 6:30-7:30 pm. Box lunches. Picnics. Ck-out 11 am, ck-in 4:30 pm. Grocery 3 mi. Guest lndry. Meeting rm. Business servs avail. Free airport transportation. Lighted tennis, pro. Downhill/X-country ski 20 mi. Exercise equipt. Massage. Lawn games. Western trail rides. Game rm. Fish pond. Refrigerators, fireplaces. Picnic tables. Cr cds: A, C, D, DS, MC, V.

Hotels

★★ **HAMPTON INN.** *15 NE Butler Market Rd (97701). 541/388-4114; fax 541/389-3261; res 800/426-7866. Email benor01@hi-hotel.com.* 99 rms, 2 story. May-Sep: S $84; D $89; under 16 free; lower rates rest of yr. Crib avail. Pet accepted, some restrictions. Parking lot. Pool, whirlpool. TV; cable (premium). Complimentary continental bkfst, coffee in rms, newspaper, toll-free calls. Restaurant nearby. Ck-out noon, ck-in 4 pm. Meeting rm. Business servs avail. Dry cleaning. Exercise privileges. Golf.

Downhill skiing. Cr cds: A, C, D, DS, MC, V.

★★ **SHILO INN.** *3105 NE O.B. Riley Rd (97701), opp Bend River Mall. 541/389-9600; fax 541/382-4310; toll-free 800/222-2244. Email bend@shiloinns.com; www.shiloinns.com.* 151 rms, 3 story. June-Aug: S, D $169; each addl $10; suites $185; under 12 free; lower rates rest of yr. Crib avail. Pet accepted, some restrictions, fee. Parking lot. Indoor/outdoor pools, whirlpool. TV; cable (premium). Complimentary continental bkfst, coffee in rms, newspaper, toll-free calls. Restaurant 7 am-9 pm. Bar. Ck-out noon, ck-in 4 pm. Meeting rms. Business servs avail. Dry cleaning, coin lndry. Free airport transportation. Exercise equipt, sauna, steam rm. Golf. Tennis. Downhill skiing. Bike rentals. Supervised children's activities. Hiking trail. Picnic facilities. Video games. Cr cds: A, C, D, DS, ER, JCB, MC, V.

Resorts

★★ **BLACK BUTTE RANCH.**
13653 Hawks Beard Rd (97759), 30 mi NW via US 20. 541/595-6211; fax 541/595-2077; toll-free 800/452-7455. www.blackbutteranch.com. 132 condo and house units (1-4 bedrm), 69 with kit. Condo units $85-$178; houses $130-$280; golf, ski plans. Crib $5. TV; VCR (movies $3-$5). 4 heated pools; wading pool, lifeguard. Playground. Supervised children's activities (June-Labor Day). Dining rm 8 am-3 pm, 5-9 pm. Snack bar. Bar 11 am-10 pm. Ck-out 11 am, ck-in 4 pm. Meeting rms. Business servs avail. Grocery. Sports dir. Lighted tennis, pro. Two 18-hole golf courses, pro, greens fee $55, putting green, driving range. Downhill/x-country ski 15 mi; x-country rental equipt. Exercise equipt. Massage. Game rm. Bicycles. Many microwaves, fireplaces. Private patios. On 1,830 wooded acres. Cr cds: A, D, DS, MC, V.

★★★ **THE INN OF THE SEVENTH MOUNTAIN.** *18575 SW Century Dr (97702), 7 mi W. 541/382-8711; fax 541/382-3517; res 541/382-8711; toll-free 541/452-6810. Email reservations@7thmtn.com; www.7thmtn.com.* 320 rooms. June-Sep: S $74; D $104; each addl $20; suites $104; under 12 free; lower rates rest of yr. Crib avail, fee. Parking lot. Indoor/outdoor pools, children's pool, lifeguard, whirlpool. TV; cable, VCR avail. Restaurant 7 am-10 pm. Bar. Ck-out noon, ck-in 5 pm. Meeting rms. Business center. Dry cleaning, coin lndry. Gift shop. Exercise privileges. Golf. Tennis, 4 courts. Downhill skiing. Bike rentals. Supervised children's activities. Hiking trail. Picnic facilities. Cr cds: A, D, DS, MC, V.

★★★ **RIVERHOUSE RESORT.** *3075 N Hwy 97 (97701). 541/389-3111; fax 541/389-0870; toll-free 800/547-3928. Email admin@riverhouse.com; www. riverhouse.com.* 200 rms, 2 story, 20 suites. May-Sep: S $77; D $89; each addl $6; suites $99; under 6 free; lower rates rest of yr. Crib avail, fee. Pet accepted, some restrictions. Parking lot. Indoor/outdoor pools, lap pool, whirlpool. TV; cable (premium), VCR avail. Complimentary continental bkfst, coffee in rms. Restaurant. Bar. Meeting rms. Business center. Bellhops. Dry cleaning, coin lndry. Exercise equipt. Downhill skiing. Hiking trail. Picnic facilities. Cr cds: A, D, DS, MC, V.

★★★ **SUNRIVER RESORT.** *1 Center Dr (97707), 15 mi S of Bend, 2 mi W of US 97. 541/593-1000; fax 541/593-1000; res 541/593-2300; toll-free 800/547-3922.* 211 units (1-3 bedrm) in 2 story lodge units, 77 kits., 230 houses (1-4 bedrm). Mid-June-Sep: S, D $130-$139; kit. suites $190; houses (up to 8 persons) $165-$325; higher rates hols; lower rates rest of yr. TV; cable (premium), VCR avail (movies $3). 3 pools; 3 wading pools, outdoor whirlpools, lifeguard. Playground. Supervised children's activities (June-Sep); ages 3-14. Dining rms 7 am-10 pm (see MEADOWS). Ck-out 11 am, ck-in 4 pm. Coin lndry. Meeting rms. Business center. Gift shop. Grocery. Barber, beauty shop. Airport transportation. Ski bus. Sports dir. 28 tennis courts. Three 18-hole golf courses, 6 pros, putting greens, driving ranges, pro shops. Canoes; whitewater rafting. Downhill ski 18 mi; x-country ski on site. Skating rink, equipt (fee). Racquetball. Bicycles; 30 mi of bike trails. Nature center. Stables. Indoor, outdoor games. Game rm (fee). Entertainment. Massage. Health club privileges. Fishing guide service. 5,500-ft airstrip. Marina. Houses with full amenities and private patios. Some microwaves. Balconies. Picnic tables. 3,300 acres on Deschutes River. Cr cds: A, DS, MC, V.

Restaurants

★★★ **ERNESTO'S ITALIAN RESTAURANT.** *1203 NE 3rd St (97701), on US 97.* 541/389-7274. Specializes in pizza, calzone. Hrs: 11:30 am-2:30 pm, 4:30-9 pm; Fri to 10 pm; Sat 4:30-10 pm; Sun 4:30-9 pm. Bar. Dinner $7.95-$15.50. Child's menu. Parking. Housed in former church. Cr cds: A, D, DS, MC, V.
SC

★★ **MEADOWS.** *1 Center Dr.* 541/593-1000. www.sunriverresort.com. Own pastries, desserts. Hrs: 6:30 am-9 pm. Res accepted. Extensive wine list. Lunch, dinner a la carte entrees: $11-$25. Cr cds: A, C, D, DS, MC, V.
D

★★ **PINE TAVERN.** *967 NW Brooks (97701), on Mirror Pond, downtown.* 541/382-5581. www.pinetav.com. Specializes in fresh trout, prime rib, seafood. Salad bar (lunch). Hrs: 11:30 am-9:30 pm; Sun from 5:30 pm. Res accepted. Bar. Lunch $5.95-$8.95; dinner $10.50-$17.50. Child's menu. 100-ft pine tree in dining rm. Overlooks Deschutes River, garden. Cr cds: A, D, MC, V.
D

★ **ROSZAK'S FISH HOUSE.** *1230 NE 3rd St (97701).* 541/382-3173. Specializes in prime rib, seafood. Hrs: 11:30 am-9:30 pm. Closed Sun; Memorial Day, Labor Day. Res accepted. Bar. Lunch $6.25-$8.95; dinner $10.95-$22.95. Child's menu. Parking. Cr cds: A, D, DS, MC, V.
D

★ **TONY'S.** *415 NE 3rd St (97701).* 541/389-5858. Specializes in pizza. Hrs: 6:30 am-2 pm, 5-9 pm; Sun 7 am-2 pm. Closed Dec 25. Res

accepted. Bar. Bkfst $2.75-$6.95; lunch $2.95-$5.95; dinner $6.95-$12.95. Child's menu. Parking. Early American bldg; original paintings, fireplace. Family-owned. Cr cds: D, DS, MC, V.
D **SC**

Unrated Dining Spot

WESTSIDE BAKERY & CAFE. *1005 NW Galveston Ave (97701).* 541/382-3426. Specializes in baked goods, omelettes. Hrs: 6:30 am-2:30 pm. Closed Thanksgiving, Dec 25. Bkfst $5-$8; lunch $5-$8. Child's menu. Parking. 3 dining rms; many antiques and toys. Cr cds: DS, MC, V.
D

Biggs
See also The Dalles

Pop 30 (est) **Elev** 173 ft
Area code 541 **Zip** 97065

What to See and Do

John Day Locks and Dam. A $487-million unit in the US Army Corps of Engineers Columbia River Basin project. Visitors may view turbine generators from powerhouse observation rm; fish-viewing stations. Self-guided tours (daily; guided tours by appt; closed hols). 5 mi E off I-84N. **FREE** The dam creates

Lake Umatilla. A 100-mi reservoir. The eastern part of lake is a national wildlife management area for the preservation of game waterfowl and fish.

Motel/Motor Lodge

★★ **RIVIERA.** *91484 Biggs (97065), 1 blk W of US 97, 1 blk S of I-84N, Exit 104.* 541/739-2501; fax 541/739-2091; toll-free 800/538-1234. 40 rms, 1-2 story. S $53; D $62; each addl $5; suites $69-$93. Crib $5. Pet accepted; $7. TV. Pool. Complimentary continental bkfst. Restaurant adj 6 am-10 pm. Ck-out noon. Business servs avail. Cr cds: A, C, D, DS, MC, V.

Brookings

(F-1) *See also Coos Bay, Gold Beach*

Pop 4,400 **Elev** 130 ft **Area code** 541
Zip 97415
Information Brookings-Harbor
Chamber of Commerce and Information Center, 16330 Lower Harbor Rd,
PO Box 940; 800/535-9469

Beachcombers, whale watchers, and
anglers find this coastal city a haven
for their activities. A commercial and
sportfishing center, Brookings lies in
an area that produces a high percentage of the nation's Easter lily bulbs.
A Ranger District office of the
Siskiyou National Forest (see
GRANTS PASS) is located here.

What to See and Do

Azalea Park. A 36-acre city park with
5 varieties of large native azaleas,
some blooming twice a yr (see
ANNUAL EVENT). Observation
point. Hiking. Picnicking. Just E off
US 101.

State parks.

Harris Beach. A 171-acre park
with scenic rock cliffs along
ocean. Ocean beach, fishing; hiking trails, observation point, picnicking, improved tent and trailer
campsites (dump station). Standard fees. 2 mi N on US 101.
Phone 541/469-2021.

Loeb. A 320-acre park on the
Chetco River with an area of beautiful old myrtle trees; also redwoods. Swimming, fishing;
picnicking, improved camping.
Standard fees. 10 mi NE off US
101. Phone 541/469-2021.

Samuel H. Boardman. A 1,473-acre
park with observation points along
11 mi of spectacular coastline.
Fishing, clamming; hiking, picnicking. 4 mi N on US 101. Phone
541/469-2021.

Annual Event

Azalea Festival. Azalea Park. Parade,
seafood, art exhibits, street fair, crafts
fair, music. Memorial Day wkend.

Motel/Motor Lodge

★ **SPRINDRIFT MOTOR INN.** *1215
Chetco Ave, PO Box 6026 (97415).
541/469-5345; fax 541/469-5213; toll-free 800/292-1171.* 35 rms, 2 story.
May-Sep: S $52; D $69; each addl $6;
children $6; under 12 free; lower
rates rest of yr. Crib avail, fee. Parking lot. TV; cable (premium). Complimentary toll-free calls. Restaurant.
Ck-out 11 am, ck-in 11 pm. Fax servs
avail. Free airport transportation.
Exercise privileges. Golf, 18 holes.
Beach access. Picnic facilities. Cr cds:
A, C, D, DS, MC, V.

Burns (D-5)

Pop 2,913 **Elev** 4,170 ft
Area code 541 **Zip** 97720
Web www.oregon1.org/harney/
Information Harney County Chamber of Commerce, 18 West D Street;
541/573-2636

This remote trading center and
county seat serves a livestock-raising
and forage production area bigger
than many eastern states. Ranger
District offices of the Malheur
National Forest (see JOHN DAY) and
Ochoco National Forest (see
PRINEVILLE) are located here.

What to See and Do

Harney County Historical Museum.
Displays incl arrowheads, quilts,
wildlife, artifacts, furniture, clothing,
cut glass, old-fashioned kitchen, Pete
French's safe, and spurs. The Hayes
Rm contains a bedrm and dining rm
furnished in antiques. Also old wagons, tools, and machinery. (Apr-Oct,
Tues-Sat, daily; closed July 4) 18 West
D Street. Phone 541/573-2636. ¢¢
Malheur National Wildlife Refuge.
Established in 1908 by Theodore
Roosevelt, the 185,000-acre refuge
was set aside primarily as a nesting
area for migratory birds. It is also an
important fall and spring gathering
point for waterfowl migrating
between the northern breeding
grounds and the California wintering
grounds. More than 320 species of
birds and 58 species of mammals

have been recorded on the refuge. Headquarters has museum. (Daily) 32 mi S on OR 205. Refuge Manager, phone 541/493-2612. **FREE**

Annual Events

John Scharff Migratory Bird Festival. Incl bird-watching and historical tours, films, arts and crafts. First wkend Apr.

Steens Mountain Rim Run. In Frenchglen, approx 48 mi S on OR 205. Six-mi run at high elevation, pit barbecue, all-night street dance, team-roping, horse cutting. First wkend Aug.

Harney County Fair, Rodeo & Race Meet. Incl rodeo and pari-mutuel racing. Wed-Sun after Labor Day.

Motels/Motor Lodges

★ **PONDEROSA.** *577 W Monroe St (97720). 541/573-2047; fax 541/573-3828; res 800/303-2047.* 52 rms, 2 story. S $48-$53; D $53-$63; each addl $5. Pet accepted; $10. TV; cable (premium). Pool. Complimentary continental bkfst. Restaurant nearby. Ck-out 11 am. Business servs avail. Cr cds: A, C, D, DS, MC, V.
D 🐾 ⚂ ⚄ 🔥 **SC**

★ **SILVER SPUR MOTEL.** *789 N Broadway Ave (97720). 541/573-2077; fax 541/573-3921; toll-free 800/400-2077.* 26 rms, 2 story. S $35-$40; D $45-$55; each addl $5. Crib $5. TV; cable (premium). Pet accepted; $5. Complimentary continental bkfst, coffee in rms. Ck-out 11:30 am. Free airport transportation. Health club privileges. Refrigerators, microwaves. Cr cds: A, DS, MC, V.
D 🐾 ⚗ ✈

Restaurant

★ ★ **PINE ROOM CAFE.** *543 W Monroe (97720). 541/573-6631.* Specializes in brochette of tenderloin, stuffed prawns Mornay. Hrs: 11 am-10 pm; winter to 9 pm. Closed Sun, Mon; hols. Res. Pictures of Harney County by local artist. Bar. Lunch, dinner $7.25-$17.25. Family-owned. Cr cds: A, DS, MC, V.
D ⚃

Cannon Beach

(A-1) *See also Astoria, Seaside*

Pop 1,221 **Elev** 25 ft **Area code** 503 **Zip** 97110
Information Visitor Information Center, 207 N Spruce, PO Box 64; 503/436-2623

The cannon and capstan from the schooner USS *Shark,* which was washed ashore near here in 1846, are now on a small monument four miles south of this resort town. Swimming (lifeguard on duty in summer), surfing, and surf fishing can be enjoyed here and the seven-mile stretch of wide beach is wonderful for walking. Among the large rocks offshore is the 235-foot Haystack Rock, third-largest monolith in the world.

What to See and Do

Ecola State Park. End of the trail for Lewis and Clark expedition. A 1,303-acre park with 6 mi of ocean frontage; sea lion and bird rookeries on rocks and offshore islands; Tillamook Lighthouse. Beaches, fishing; hiking (on the Oregon Coast Trail), picnicking at Ecola Point,

Oswald West State Park

whale watching at observation point. 2 mi N off US 101.

Fort Clatsop National Memorial. (see) Approx 15 mi N off US 101A.

Oswald West State Park. A 2,474-acre park with outstanding coastal headland; towering cliffs; low dunes; rain forest with massive spruce and cedar trees; road winds 700 ft above sea level and 1,000 ft below peak of Neahkahnie Mt. Surfing (at nearby Short Sands Beach), fishing; hiking trails (on the Oregon Coast Trail), picnicking, primitive campgrounds accessible only by ¼-mi foot trail. 10 mi S on US 101, walk last ¼ mi.

Annual Event

Sandcastle Contest. Nationally known event features sand sculptures on beach. Early June.

Motel/Motor Lodge

★★★ **HALLMARK RESORT.** *1400 S Hemlock St (97110). 503/436-1566; fax 503/436-0324; toll-free 800/345-5676.* 132 rms, 3 story, 63 kits., 5 cottages. July-Sep: S, D $109-$189; suites $125-$229; kit. units $125-$229; cottages $265-$425; lower rates rest of yr. Crib free. Pet accepted; $8/day. TV; cable (premium), VCR avail (movies). Indoor pool; wading pool, whirlpool. Complimentary coffee. Restaurant adj 8 am-9 pm. Ck-out noon, ck-in 4 pm. Coin lndry. Meeting rms. Business servs avail. Gift shop. Exercise equipt; sauna. Health club privileges. Refrigerators; some in-rm whirlpools, fireplaces. Balconies. On beach. Cr cds: A, DS, MC, V.

[D] 🦭 ≈ 🏃 ≥ 🔥 SC ✈

Resorts

★★ **SCHOONERS COVE OCEAN FRONT MOTEL.** *188 N Larch (97110). 503/436-2300; fax 503/436-2156; toll-free 800/843-0128. Email stay@schoonerscove.com; www.schoonerscove.com.* 30 rms, 2 story, 26 suites. June-Oct: S, D $149; each addl $10; children $10; lower rates rest of yr. Crib avail, fee. Parking lot. TV; cable (premium), VCR avail. Complimentary coffee in rms, toll-free calls. Restaurant nearby. Meeting rm. Coin lndry. Whirlpool.

Golf. Beach access. Picnic facilities. Cr cds: A, C, D, DS, MC, V.

[D] 🏃 ≥ 🔥 SC

★★★ **SURFSAND RESORT HOTEL.** *Oceanfront (97110), S on Hemlock St, at Gower St. 503/436-2274; fax 503/436-9116; toll-free 800/547-6100. Email info@surfsand.com; www.surfsand.com.* 54 rms, 4 story, 28 suites. June-Sep: S, D $249; suites $319; lower rates rest of yr. Crib avail. Pet accepted, fee. Parking lot. Indoor pool, whirlpool. TV; cable (DSS), VCR avail. Complimentary coffee in rms, newspaper, toll-free calls. Restaurant 8 am-11 pm. Bar. Ck-out noon, ck-in 4 pm. Meeting rms. Business servs avail. Bellhops. Concierge. Gift shop. Exercise privileges. Golf, 18 holes. Tennis. Beach access. Supervised children's activities. Video games. Cr cds: A, DS, MC, V.

[D] 🦭 🏃 🚶 ≈ 🏃 ≥ 🔥

★★ **TOLOVANA INN.** *3400 S Hemlock (97145), 1½ mi S; ¼ mi W of US 101. 503/436-2211; fax 503/436-0134; toll-free 800/333-8890. www.tolovanainn.com.* 80 rms, 3 story, 95 suites. June-Sep: S, D $71; suites $139; lower rates rest of yr. Crib avail. Pet accepted, some restrictions, fee. Parking lot. Indoor pool, whirlpool. TV; cable, VCR avail. Complimentary coffee in rms, newspaper, toll-free calls. Restaurant 11 am-9 pm. Bar. Ck-out noon, ck-in 4 pm. Meeting rm. Business servs avail. Bellhops. Coin lndry. Gift shop. Exercise privileges, sauna. Golf, 18 holes. Tennis. Beach access. Hiking trail. Picnic facilities. Cr cds: A, D, DS, MC, V.

[D] 🦭 🛢 🚶 🏃 🚶 ≈ 🏃 ≥ 🔥

B&Bs/Small Inns

★ **GREY WHALE INN.** *164 Kenai St (97110). 503/436-2848.* 5 rms, shower only, 3 kit. units. No A/C. June-Sep: S, D $74-$94; each addl $10; lower rates rest of yr. TV; cable, VCR. Complimentary coffee in rms. Ck-out 11 am, ck-in 3 pm. Totally nonsmoking. Cr cds: MC, V.

≥ 🔥

★★★ **HEARTHSTONE INN.** *107 Jackson St E (97110). 503/436-1392; fax 503/436-1396; toll-free 800/238-4107. www.oregoncoastlodgings.com/cannonbeach/cbhl/hearthstone.* 3 rms, 1 story, 1 suite. June-Sep: S, D $125; each addl $10; children $10; lower rates rest of yr. Crib avail. Parking lot. TV; cable, VCR avail. Complimentary coffee in rms, toll-free calls. Restaurant nearby. Ck-out 11 am, ck-in 3 pm. Fax servs avail. Golf. Tennis. Beach access. Picnic facilities. Cr cds: A, C, D, DS, MC, V.

⛵ ✈ 🛎 ✈ ✈ ✈ ➷ 🔥

Restaurant

★★ **DOOGER'S.** *1371 S Hemlock (97110). 503/436-2225.* Specializes in steak, seafood. Hrs: 8 am-9:30 pm. Closed Thanksgiving, Dec 25; also 2 wks Jan. Bar. Bkfst $2.75-$8.95; lunch $3-$9.50; dinner $7.95-$34.95. Child's menu. Cr cds: A, D, DS, MC, V.

🅳

Cave Junction

(F-1) *See also Grants Pass*

Pop 1,126 **Elev** 1,295 ft
Area code 541 **Zip** 97523
Information Illinois Valley Chamber of Commerce, 201 Caves Hwy, PO Box 312; 541/592-3326

A Ranger District office of the Siskiyou National Forest (see GRANTS PASS) is located here.

What to See and Do

Kerbyville Museum. Home (ca 1870) furnished in the period; outdoor display of farm, logging, and mining tools; Native American artifacts; rock display; log schoolhouse, blacksmith shop, general store. Picnic tables. (May-Sep, daily) 2 mi N on US 199 in Kerby. Phone 541/592-2076 or 541/592-4478. ¢

Oregon Caves National Monument. (see) 20 mi E on OR 46.

Annual Events

Annual Moon Tree Country Run. Siskiyou Smoke Jump Base. Phone 541/596-2621. Mid-June.

Wild Blackberry Festival. Blackberry foods, cooking, games, crafts, and music. Mid-Aug.

Lion's Club Parade & Labor Day Festival. Labor Day wkend.

Motel/Motor Lodge

★★ **OREGON CAVES LODGE.** *20000 Cave Hwy (97523). 541/592-3400; fax 541/592-6654. Email info@ crater-lake.com.* 22 rms, 3 story, 3 suites. No A/C. No elvtr. No rm phones. S, D $89; each addl $10; suites $119; under 6 free. Closed Nov-Apr. Crib $10. Restaurants from 7 am. Ck-out 11 am. Meeting rms. Business center. Sundries. Gift shop. X-country ski on-site. Picnic tables, grills. Totally nonsmoking. Cr cds: A, DS, MC, V.

🎣 ⛷ ➷ 🔥

Coos Bay

(D-1) *See also Bandon, Brookings, North Bend, Reedsport*

Founded 1854 **Pop** 15,076 **Elev** 11 ft
Area code 541 **Zip** 97420
Web www.ucinet.com/~bacc
Information Bay Area Chamber of Commerce, 50 E Central, PO Box 210; 541/269-0215 or 800/824-8486

Coos Bay, one of the world's largest shipping ports for forest products, is also a deep-sea fishing haven. Dairy herds graze in the surrounding area, providing milk for the production of butter and cheddar cheese. Local cranberry bogs supply fruit for processing.

What to See and Do

Charleston Marina Complex. Charter boats, launching and moorage facilities (fee), car and boat trailer parking (free), dry boat storage, marine fuel dock; travel park, motel, tackle shops, restaurants. Office (Mon-Fri). 9 mi SW in Charleston. Phone 541/888-2548.

The Oregon Connection/House of Myrtlewood. Manufacturing of myrtlewood gift items. Tours. (Daily; closed Jan 1, Thanksgiving, Dec 25)

1125 S 1st St, just off US 101 in S Coos Bay. Phone 541/267-7804. **FREE**

South Slough National Estuarine Research Reserve. A 4,400-acre area reserved for the study of estuarine ecosystems and life. Previous studies here incl oyster culture techniques and water pollution. Special programs, lectures, and exhibits at Interpretive Center. Trails and waterways (daily); guided trail walks and canoe tours (June-Aug; fee). Interpretive Center (June-Aug, daily; rest of yr, Mon-Fri). 4 mi S on Seven Devils Rd, in Charleston. Phone 541/888-5558.

State parks.

Cape Arago. This 134-acre promontory juts ½ mi into ocean. Two beaches, fishing; hiking (on Oregon Coast Trail), picnicking. Observation point (whale and seal watching). 14 mi SW off US 101 on Cape Arago Hwy. Phone 541/888-8867.

Shore Acres. Former grand estate of Coos Bay lumberman, noted for its unusual botanical and Japanese gardens and spectacular ocean views (743 acres). Ocean beach; hiking (on the Oregon Coast Trail), picnicking. Standard fees. 13 mi SW off US 101 on Cape Arago Hwy. Phone 541/888-3732 or 541/888-8867.

Sunset Bay. A 395-acre park with swimming beach on sheltered bay, fishing; hiking, picnicking, tent and trailer sites. Observation point. Standard fees. 12 mi SW off US 101 on Cape Arago Hwy. Phone 541/888-4902.

Annual Events

Oregon Coast Music Festival. Variety of musical presentations ranging from jazz and dance to chamber and symphonic music. Also free outdoor picnic concerts. Phone 800/676-7563. Last 2 full wks July.

Blackberry Arts Festival. Fourth Sat Aug.

Bay Area Fun Festival. Third wkend Sep.

Motel/Motor Lodge

★★ **BEST WESTERN HOLIDAY MOTEL.** *411 N Bayshore Dr (97420),* *on US 101. 541/269-5111; fax 541/269-5111; res 800/528-1234. www.best western.com.* 77 rms, 2 story. July-Aug: S, D $71-$91; each addl $5; suites $100-$140; kits. units $69-$99; lower rates rest of yr. Crib avail. TV; cable (premium). Indoor pool; whirlpool. Complimentary coffee in lobby. Restaurant adj open 24 hrs. Guest lndry. Ck-out noon. Exercise equipt. Microwaves avail. Whirlpools in suites. Cr cds: A, C, D, DS, MC, V.

D 🛖 🏋 🖥 🔥

Hotel

★ **RED LION HOTEL.** *1313 N Bayshore Dr (97420), on US 101. 541/267-4141; fax 541/267-2884; res 800/733-5466. Email coosbay@harbor side.com; www.redlion.com.* 137 rms, 2 story, 6 suites. S $79; D $84; each addl $10; suites $109; under 18 free. Crib avail. Pet accepted, some restrictions. Parking lot. Pool, whirlpool. TV; cable (DSS). Complimentary coffee in rms, newspaper, toll-free calls. Restaurant 6:30 am-10 pm. Bar. Ck-out noon, ck-in 3 pm. Meeting rms. Business center. Dry cleaning, coin lndry. Free airport transportation. Exercise equipt. Golf. Video games. Cr cds: A, C, D, DS, MC, V.

D 🐾 🍴 🛖 🏋 🖥 🐾 SC 🏋

Restaurant

★★ **PORTSIDE.** *8001 Kingfisher Rd (97420), 9 mi SW on US 101, at the Charleston Boat Basin. 541/888-5544. Email dine@portsidebythebay.com; www.portsidebythebay.com.* Specializes in bouillabaisse, live lobster, fresh salmon. Own desserts. Hrs: 11:30 am-11 pm. Res accepted. Bar. Lunch $4.95-$22.95; dinner $10.95-$24.95. Child's menu. Entertainment: Fri-Sun. Cr cds: A, DS, MC, V.

D

Corvallis

(C-2) *See also Albany, Eugene, Salem*

Settled 1845 **Pop** 44,757 **Elev** 225 ft
Area code 541
Web www.visitcorvallis.com

Information Convention & Visitors Bureau, 420 NW 2nd, 97330; 541/757-1544 or 800/334-8118

Located in the heart of Oregon's fertile Willamette Valley and built on the banks of the Willamette River, Corvallis is a center for education, culture, and commerce. It is the home of Oregon State University, the state's oldest institution of higher education. A prosperous business environment is supported by several international firms located here. Siuslaw National Forest headquarters is here.

What to See and Do

Avery Park. A 75-acre park on the Marys River. Bicycle, cross-country, and jogging trails; picnicking; ballfield. Rose and rhododendron gardens, community gardens, 1922 Mikado locomotive. Playground (accessible to the disabled). (Daily) S 15th St and US 20. Phone 541/757-6918. **FREE**

Benton County Historical Museum. Located in the former Philomath College bldg. Features displays on history of the county; art gallery. Reference library (by appt). (Tues-Sat) 6 mi W at 1101 Main St in Philomath. Phone 541/929-6230. **FREE**

Oregon State University. (1868) 14,500 students. On its 400-acre campus are Memorial Union Con course Gallery (daily; phone 541/737-2416); Fairbanks Gallery (daily; phone 541/737-5009); Guistina Gallery at La Sells Stewart Center (Mon-Fri; phone 541/737-2402). Campus tours. Bounded by 11th and 53rd Sts, Monroe Ave & US 20. Phone 541/737-0123 or 541/737-1000. **FREE**

Siuslaw National Forest. Incl 50 mi of ocean frontage with more than 30 campgrounds; public beaches, sand dunes and overlooks; visitor center and nature trails in the Cape Perpetua Scenic Area. Marys Peak, highest peak in the Coast Range, has a road to picnic grounds and campground near the summit. Swimming; ocean, lake, and stream fishing; clam digging; boating; hunting for deer, bear, elk, and migratory birds; hiking; picnicking; camping (fee in most areas); dune buggies (in designated areas). Forest contains 630,000 acres incl the Oregon Dunes National Recreation Area. For further info contact Forest Supervisor, 97333. W via OR 34. Phone 541/750-7000.

Tyee Wine Cellars. Located on 460-acre Century farm. Offers tastings, tours, interpretive hikes, picnicking. (July-Sep, Fri-Mon; May-June and Oct-Dec, wkends; also by appt) 7 mi S via US 99W, 3 mi W on Greenberry Rd. Phone 541/753-8754. **FREE**

Annual Events

Oregon Folklife Festival. Traditional and contemporary folk music; crafts. Phone 541/758-3243. Late June.

Da Vinci Days. Festival celebrating the relationship between art, science, and technology. Phone 541/757-6363. Third wkend July.

Benton County Fair and Rodeo. Phone 541/757-1521. Late July-early Aug.

Fall Festival. Phone 541/752-9655. Last wkend Sep.

Motels/Motor Lodges

★ **BEST INNS & SUITES.** *935 NW Garfield Ave (97330). 541/758-9125; fax 541/758-0544; res 800/237-8466; toll-free 800/626-1900.* 61 rms, 3 story. No elvtr. S $45-$50; D $51-$54; each addl $4; suites $56-$64; under 12 free. Crib $5. Pet accepted, some restrictions. TV; cable. Pool privileges. Complimentary coffee in lobby. Restaurant nearby. Ck-out 11 am. Coin lndry. Whirlpool. Microwaves avail. Cr cds: A, C, D, DS, MC, V.

🄳 🍴 🐾 🔧 🖼 🔥

★ ★ **BEST WESTERN GRAND MANOR INN.** *925 NW Garfield Ave (97330). 541/758-8571; fax 541/758-0834; res 800/528-1234; toll-free 800/626-1900.* 55 rms, 3 story. S $71-$160; D $78-$160; each addl $6; suites $98 $160, under 12 free. Crib $6. TV; cable (premium). Heated pool. Complimentary continental bkfst. Restaurant nearby. Ck-out 11 am. Business servs avail. In-rm modem link. Exercise equipt. Refrig-

erators; some microwaves. Cr cds: A,
D, DS, MC, V.

★★ **SHANICO INN.** *1113 NW 9th
St (97330). 541/754-7474; fax
541/754-2437; toll-free 800/432-1233.
Email shanicoinn@aol.com.* 76 rms, 3
story. S $49; D $57-$67; each addl
$5; suites $67; under 12 free. Crib
free. Pet accepted, some restrictions.
TV. Heated pool. Complimentary
continental bkfst. Restaurant adj
open 24 hrs. Ck-out noon. Meeting
rm. Cr cds: A, C, D, DS, MC, V.

B&Bs/Small Inns

★★★ **BED & BREAKFAST ON THE
GREEN.** *2515 SW 45th St (97333).
541/757-7321; fax 541/753-4332; toll-
free 888/757-7321. Email neoma@
banbonthegreen.com; www.banbon
thegreen.com.* 4 rms, 2 story. S $85; D
$95. Parking lot. TV; cable (DSS),
VCR avail. Complimentary full bkfst,
toll-free calls. Ck-out 11 am, ck-in 4
pm. Business center. Concierge. Golf.
Cr cds: A, D, DS, MC, V.

★★★ **HARRISON HOUSE BED &
BREAKFAST.** *2310 NW Harrison Blvd
(97330). 541/752-6248; fax 541/754-
1353; toll-free 800/233-6248. Email
stay@corvallis-lodging.com; www.
corvallis-lodging.com.* 4 rms, 2 story. S,
D $100; each addl $20; under 5 free.
Parking lot. TV; cable. Complimentary full bkfst, newspaper. Restaurant.
Bar. Ck-out 11 am, ck-in 4 pm. Business servs avail. Exercise privileges.
Golf. Cr cds: A, C, D, DS, JCB, MC, V.

Restaurants

★★ **GABLES.** *1121 NW 9th St
(97330). 541/752-3364. www.b-sphere.
com/gables.html.* Specializes in fresh
seafood, steak, prime rib. Own
desserts. Hrs: 5-9 pm; Sun to 8 pm.
Res accepted. Bar. Dinner $10.95-
$25.95. Child's menu. Wine cellar
dining area. Family-owned. Cr cds:
A, D, DS, MC, V.

★★ **MICHAEL'S LANDING.** *603
NW Second St (97330). 541/754-
6141. www.michaelslanding.com.* Specializes in prime rib, pasta, seafood.

Hrs: 11:30 am-9 pm; Sun from 10
am. Closed Dec 25. Res accepted.
Bar. Lunch $5.25-$10.25; dinner
$10.95-$18.95. Child's menu. Old
railroad depot overlooking river;
built in 1909. Cr cds: A, C, D, DS,
MC, V.

Cottage Grove

(D-2) *See also Eugene*

Pop 7,402 **Elev** 641 ft **Area code** 541
Zip 97424
Information Cottage Grove Area
Chamber of Commerce, 330 Hwy 99
S, PO Box 587; 541/942-2411

Cottage Grove is the lumber, retail,
and distribution center for south
Lane County. A Ranger District office
of the Umpqua National Forest (see
ROSEBURG) is located here.

What to See and Do

Chateau Lorane Winery. Thirty-acre
vineyard located on 200-acre wooded
estate features lakeside tasting rm in
which to enjoy great variety of traditional, rare, and handmade wines.
(June-Aug, Tues-Sun; Mar-May and
Sep-Dec, wkends and hols; also by
appt) 12 mi W on Cottage Grove-
Lorane Rd to Siuslaw River Rd. Phone
541/942-8028. **FREE**

Cottage Grove Lake. Three-mi-long
lake. Lakeside (W shore) and Wilson
Creek (E shore) parks have swimming, boat launch; picnicking. Short-
ridge Park (E shore) has swimming,
waterskiing, fishing; picnicking.
Primitive and improved camping
(showers, dump station) at Pine
Meadows on E shore (Mid-May-mid-
Sep, 14-day limit; no res; fee). S via I-
5, Cottage Grove Lake Exit 170, turn
left, then 5 mi S on London Rd.
Phone 541/942-8657 or 541/942-
5631. Per vehicle ¢¢¢

Cottage Grove Museum. Displays of
pioneer homelife and Native American artifacts housed in a former
Roman Catholic Church (1897),
octagonal, with stained-glass
windows made in Italy. Adj annex
houses model of ore stamp mill
showing how gold was extracted

from the ore; working model of a green chain; antique tools. (Mid-June-Labor Day, Wed-Sun afternoons; rest of yr, wkends) Birch Ave & H Street. Phone 541/942-3963. **FREE**

Covered Bridges. Five old-time covered bridges within 10-mi radius of town. Inquire at Chamber of Commerce.

Dorena Lake. Five-mi-long lake. Schwarz Park (camping fee), on Row River below dam, has fishing; picnicking and camping (dump station). Lane County maintains Baker Bay Park, on S shore, and offers swimming, waterskiing, fishing, boating (launch, marina, rentals); picnicking, concession, and camping (fee); and Harms Park, on N shore, offers boat launching; picnicking. For further info inquire at Cottage Grove project office. 5 mi E on Row River Rd. Phone 541/942-1418. Schwarz Park per vehicle ¢¢¢

Annual Events

Bohemia Mining Days Celebration. Commemorates area's gold-mining days; parades; flower, art shows; rodeo, entertainment. Third wk July.

Covered Bridge Celebration. Guided tours, food, art show, children's activities. First Sat Aug.

Motel/Motor Lodge

★★ **BEST WESTERN VILLAGE GREEN.** *725 Row River Rd (97424), off I-5 Exit 174. 541/942-2491; fax 541/942-2386; res 800/937-8376; toll-free 800/343-7666. www.bestwestern. com.* 96 rms. June-Oct: S $69-$99; D $79-$110; each addl $5; suites $99-$165; under 12 free; lower rates rest of yr. Crib free. Pet accepted. TV; cable (premium). Heated pool; whirlpool. Playground. Restaurant 6:30 am-9 pm. Bar 4 pm-midnight. Ck-out 11 am. Coin lndry. Meeting rms. Business servs avail. Sundries. Covered parking. Tennis. Some refrigerators. Private patios. 18-hole golf course adj. Cr cds: A, D, DS, MC, V.

Restaurant

★ **COTTAGE.** *2915 Row River Rd (97424). 541/942-3091.* Specializes in fresh seafood, steak, chicken. Salad bar. Own desserts. Hrs: 11 am-9 pm. Closed Sun; wk of Thanksgiving. Bar. Lunch, dinner $2.75-$19. Child's menu. Bldg solar heated. Cr cds: A, MC, V.

Crater Lake National Park

(57 mi N of Klamath Falls on US 97, OR 62)

One of Crater Lake's former names, Lake Majesty, probably comes closest to describing the feeling visitors get from these deep blue waters in the caldera of dormant Mount Mazama. More than 7,700 years ago, following climactic eruptions, this volcano collapsed and formed a deep basin. Rain and snow accumulated in the empty caldera, forming the deepest lake in the United States (1,932 ft). Surrounded by 25 miles of jagged rim rock, the 21-square-mile lake is broken only by Wizard and Phantom Ship Islands. Entrance by road from any direction brings you to the 33-mile Rim Drive (July-mid-October or first snow), leading to all observation points, park headquarters, and a visitor center at Rim Village (June-September, daily). The Sinnott Memorial Overlook with broad terrace permits a beautiful view of the area. On summer evenings, rangers give campfire talks at Mazama Campground (late June-September, phone 541/594-2211). The Steel Center located at Park Headquarters (daily) has exhibits about the natural history of the park and a movie is shown daily.

The park can be explored on foot or by car, by following spurs and trails extending from Rim Drive. Going clockwise from Rim Village, to the west, The Watchman Peak is reached by a trail almost one mile long that takes the hiker 1,800 feet above the lake with a full view in all directions; Mount Shasta in California, 105 miles away, is visible on a clear day. The road to the north entrance passes through the Pumice

Crater Lake as seen from above

Desert, once a flood of frothy debris from the erupting volcano.

On the northeast side, Cleetwood Trail descends one mile to the shore and a boat landing where two-hour launch trips depart hourly each day in summer (fee). From the boats, Wizard Island, a small volcano, and Phantom Ship, a craggy mass of lava, can be seen up close.

Six miles farther on Rim Drive, going clockwise, is the start of a two and a half mile hiking trail, 1,230 feet to Mount Scott, soaring 8,926 feet, the highest point in the park. Just to the west of the beginning of this trail is a one mile drive to the top of Cloudcap, 8,070 feet high and 1,600 feet above the lake. Four miles beyond this point, a road leads seven miles from Rim Drive to The Pinnacles, pumice spires rising like stone needles from the canyon of Wheeler Creek.

Back at Rim Village, two trails lead in opposite directions. Counterclockwise, a one and a half mile trek mounts the top of Garfield Peak. The other trail goes to Discovery Point, where in 1853 a young prospector, John Hillman, became the first settler to see the lake.

In winter, the south and west entrance roads are kept clear in spite of the annual 45-foot snowfall; the north entrance road and Rim Drive are closed from mid-October-June, depending on snow conditions. A cafeteria is open daily at Rim Village for refreshments and souvenirs.

Depending on snow, the campground (fee) is open from late-June-mid-October. Mazama, at the junction of the S and W entrance drives, has a camper store, fireplaces, showers, laundry facilities, toilets, water, and tables; no reservations. There are six picnic areas on Rim Drive. The wildlife includes black bears—keep your distance and never feed them. There are also deer, golden-mantled ground squirrels, marmots, and coyotes. Do not feed any wildlife in park.

The park was established in 1902 and covers 286 square miles. For park information contact Superintendent, Crater Lake National Park, PO Box 7, Crater Lake 97604; 541/594-2211 ext 402. Golden Eagle Passport (see MAKING THE MOST OF YOUR TRIP). Per vehicle ¢¢¢

Note: Conservation measures may dictate the closing of certain roads and recreational facilities. In winter, inquire locally before attempting to enter the park.

Motel/Motor Lodge

★★★ **CRATER LAKE LODGE.** *565 Rim Village Dr (97604). 541/594-2255; fax 541/594-2342; res 571/830-8700. Email mike@crater-lake.com.* 71 rms, 4 story. No A/C. No rm phones. S, D $99-$120; under 12 free. Closed mid-Oct-mid-May. Complimentary coffee in lobby. Restaurant 7-10:30 am, 11:30 am-2:30 pm, 5-10 pm. Ck-out 11 am. Bellhops. Picnic tables, grills. On lake. Totally nonsmoking. Cr cds: MC, V.

🄳 ⏃ 🄵 ⊠ 🔥

Dalles

(see The Dalles)

Depoe Bay

(B-I) *See also Lincoln City, Newport*

Pop 870 **Elev** 58 ft **Area code** 541
Zip 97341
Information Chamber of Commerce,
PO Box 21; 541/765-2889

The world's smallest natural, navigable harbor, with six acres, Depoe Bay
is a base for the United States Coast
Guard and a good spot for deep-sea
fishing. The shoreline is rugged at
this point. Seals and sea lions inhabit
the area, and whales are so often
seen that Depoe Bay claims to be the
"whale watching capital of the Oregon coast." In the center of town are
the "spouting horns," natural rock
formations throwing geyserlike
sprays high in the air. There are nine
state parks within a few miles of this
resort community.

What to See and Do

Depoe Bay Park. Covers 3 acres.
Ocean observation bldg with view of
bay, spouting horn, and fishing fleets.
Small picnic area. N on US 101.

Fogarty Creek State Park. A 142-acre
park with beach area and creek, swimming (dressing rms), fishing; hiking,
picnicking. Standard fees. 2 mi N on
US 101. Phone 541/265-9278.

Thundering Seas. (Oregon State University School for the Crafts) Professional school for goldsmiths and
silversmiths lies 60 ft above the Pacific
Ocean; unusual museum. Tours
(daily). Phone 541/765-2604. **FREE**

Annual Events

**Classic Wooden Boat Show & Crab
Feed.** Last wkend Apr.

Fleet of Flowers Ceremony. After services on shore, flowers are cast on
the water to honor those who lost
their lives at sea. Memorial Day.

Salmon Bake. Depoe Bay Park.
Salmon prepared in the Native American manner. Third Sat Sep.

Motels/Motor Lodges

★★ **INN AT OTTER CREST.** *301
Otter Crest Loop Rd (97369), 5 mi S, W
of US 101 Exit Otter Rock. 541/765-*

*2060; fax 541/765-2047; toll-free
800/452-2101. www.ottercrest.com.*
120 units. S, D $99-$299. Crib free.
TV; cable (premium), VCR avail.
Heated pool; whirlpool. Restaurant 8
am-10 pm; mid-Oct-mid-June to 8
pm. Bar. Ck-out noon. Coin lndry.
Meeting rms. Business servs avail.
Bellhops. Sundries. Gift shop. Outdoor tennis. Exercise equipt; sauna.
Lawn games. Sun deck. Refrigerators;
some microwaves. Private balconies.
On 35 acres; duck pond. Ocean view;
beach access. Cr cds: A, DS, MC, V.

[D] [symbols]

★★ **SURFRIDER RESORT.** *3115
NW Hwy 101 (97341), 2 mi N at Fogarty Creek State Park. 541/764-2311; fax
541/764-2634; toll-free 800/662-2378.*
52 rms, 2 story, 20 kits. No A/C.
June-Sep, wkends, hols: S, D $75-$95;
each addl $10; studio rms, suites, kit.
units $105-$125; under 12 free;
lower rates rest of yr. Crib $5. TV;
cable (premium). Indoor pool; whirlpool. Restaurant 7 am-10 pm. Bar 11-
1 am. Ck-out 11 am. Gift shop. Free
airport transportation. Sauna. Many
fireplaces; some in-rm whirlpools.
Many private patios, balconies. All
rms with ocean view. Cr cds: A, C, D,
DS, MC, V.

[D] [symbols]

B&B/Small Inn

★★ **CHANNEL HOUSE.** *35 Elling-
son St (97341). 541/765-2140; fax
541/765-2191; toll-free 800/447-2140.
Email cfinseth@channelhouse.com;
www.channelhouse.com.* 14 rms, 3
story, 9 suites, 2 kit. units. No elvtr.
Mar-Dec: S, D $80-$150; each addl
$30; suites $175-$225; kit. units
$225; lower rates rest of yr. Children
over 12 yrs only. TV; cable (premium). Complimentary bkfst.
Restaurants nearby. Ck-out 11 am,
ck-in 4 pm. Business servs avail.
Street parking. Some balconies. Modern oceanfront bldg overlooking
Depoe Bay. Totally nonsmoking. Cr
cds: A, DS, MC, V.

[symbols]

Enterprise

(see Joseph)

Eugene

(D-2) *See also Corvallis, Cottage Grove*

Settled 1846 **Pop** 112,669 **Elev** 419 ft
Area code 541
Web www.cvalco.org/travel.html
Information Lane County Convention & Visitors Association, 115 W 8th, Suite 190, PO Box 10286, 97440; 541/484-5307 or 800/547-5445

Eugene sits on the west bank of the Willamette (Wil-AM-et) River, facing its sister city Springfield on the east bank. The Cascade Range rises to the east, mountains of the Coast Range to the west. Bicycling, hiking, and jogging are especially popular here, with a variety of trails to choose from. Forests of Douglas fir support a lumber industry that accounts for 40 percent of the city's manufacturing. Eugene-Springfield is at the head of a series of dams built for flood control of the Willamette River Basin. Willamette National Forest headquarters are located here.

What to See and Do

Armitage County Park. A 57-acre park on partially wooded area on the S bank of the McKenzie River. Fishing, boating (ramp); hiking, picnicking. Standard fees. 6 mi N off I-5 on Coburg Rd. Phone 541/682-2000.

Camp Putt Adventure Golf Park. Eighteen-hole course with challenging holes like "Pond O' Peril," "Thunder Falls," and "Earthquake." Lakeside patio with ice cream bar. (Late Mar-mid-Nov, daily) 4006 Franklin Blvd. Phone 541/741-9828. ¢¢

Fall Creek Dam and Lake. Winberry Creek Park has swimming beach, fishing, boating (ramp); picnicking (May-Sep). Some fees. N Shore Ramp has fishing, boat launching facilities; picnicking. (Daily with low-level ramp) Cascara Campground has swimming, fishing, boating (ramp),

camping (May-Sep). Some fees. 20 mi SE on OR 58 to Lowell, then follow signs to Big Fall Creek Rd. N county road. Phone 541/937-2131 for further info.

Hendricks Park Rhododendron Garden. A 20-acre, internationally known garden features more than 6,000 aromatic plants, incl rare species and hybrid rhododendrons from the local area and around the world (peak bloom mid-Apr-mid-May). Walking paths, hiking trails; picnic area. (Daily) Summit & Skyline Drs. Phone 541/682-4800. **FREE**

Hult Center. Performing arts center offering more than 300 events each year ranging from Broadway shows and concerts to ballet. 7th Ave & Willamette St; One Eugene Center. Phone 541/682-5000 for tickets or 541/682-5746 (24-hr event recording), or phone 541/682-5087 for tour info.

Lane County Historical Museum. Changing exhibits depict history of county from mid-19th century-1930s; incl artifacts of pioneer and Victorian periods; textiles; local history research library. (Wed-Fri, also Sat afternoons) 740 W 13th Ave. Phone 541/687-4239. ¢

Lookout Point and Dexter Dams and Lakes. The 14-mi-long Lookout Point Lake has Black Canyon Campground (May-Oct; fee) with trailer parking. Fishing; picnicking. Hampton Boat Ramp with launching facilities; 4 camp sites (all yr; fee) with trailer parking. Fishing; picnicking; closed to launching during low water (usually Oct-Apr). **Lowell Park** on 3-mi-long Dexter Lake has swimming, waterskiing, boating (moorage, ramp), sailboating; picnicking. **Dexter Park** has waterskiing, fishing, boating (ramp), sailboating; picnicking. The Powerhouse at Lookout Point Dam is open to the public (by appt). For further info inquire at Project Office, Lookout Point Dam. 20 mi SE on OR 58. Phone 541/937-2131.

Owen Municipal Rose Garden. A 5-acre park with more than 300 new and rare varities of roses, as well as wild species (best blooms late June-early July); a recognized test garden for experimental roses. Also here is a collection of antiques and minia-

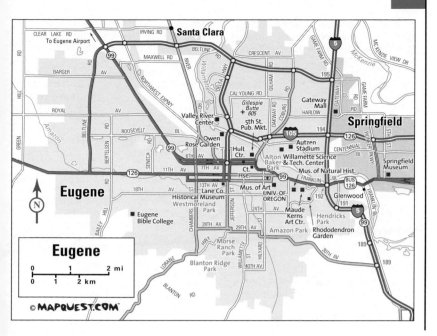

tures. Picnic area. (Daily) N end of Jefferson St, along the Willamette River. Phone 541/682-4800. **FREE**

Spencer Butte Park. Park has 305 acres of wilderness, with Spencer Butte Summit, at 2,052 ft, dominating the scene. Hiking trails. Panoramic views of Eugene, Cascade Mts. (Daily) 2 mi S of city limits on Willamette St. Phone 541/682-4800. **FREE** Starting at edge of park is

South Hills Ridgeline Trail. A 5-mi trail extending from Blanton Rd E to Dillard Rd; a spur leads to top of Butte. Trail offers magnificent views of the Cascade Mts, Coburg Hills, and Mt Baldy; wildflowers along the trail reach peak bloom late Apr. Begins at 52nd St & Willamette St.

University of Oregon. (1876) 17,000 students. The 250-acre campus incl more than 2,000 varieties of trees. Points of interest incl the Museum of Natural History, Robinson Theatre, Beall Concert Hall, Hayward Field, and the Erb Memorial Union. Campus tours depart from Information and Tour Services, Oregon Hall (Mon-Sat). Bounded by Franklin Blvd & Agate St, Alder & 18th Sts. Phone 541/346-3014. Also on campus are

Knight Library. With more than 2 million volumes, this is the largest library in Oregon. Main lobby features changing exhibits of rare books, manuscripts; Oregon Collection on 2nd floor. Fine arts pieces, wrought iron gates, and carved panels. (Daily) Phone 541/346-3054.

Museum of Art. Diverse collections incl large selection of Asian art representing cultures of China, Japan, Korea, Cambodia, and American and British works of Asian influence; official court robes of the *Ch'ing* dynasty (China, 1644-1911); Russian icon paintings from the 17th-19th centuries; Persian miniatures and ceramics; photography; works by contemporary artists and craftsmen from the Pacific Northwest, incl those of Morris Graves. Special exhibits. Gift shop. (Wed-Sun afternoons; closed hols). Phone 541/346-3027. **FREE**

Whitewater rafting. Numerous companies offer trips on the McKenzie, North Umpqua, Deschutes, and Willamette rivers. Trips range from 2 hrs-5 days. Contact Convention & Visitors Association for details.

Willamette National Forest. More than 1.5 million acres. Home to more than 300 species of wildlife; incl Cascade Mt Range summit; Pacific Crest National Scenic Trail with views of snowcapped Mt Jefferson, Mt Washington, Three Fingered Jack, Three Sisters, Diamond Peak; Koosah and Sahalie Falls on the Upper McKenzie River; Clear Lake; the lava beds at summit of McKenzie Pass; Waldo Lake near summit of Willamette Pass. Fishing; hunting, hiking, skiing, snowmobiling, camping (fee at some sites). E via US 20, OR 126. For further info contact Supervisor, 211 E 7th Ave, 97401.

Willamette Pass Ski Area. Double, 4 triple chairlifts; patrol, school, rentals (ski and snowboard). Lodge, restaurant, lounge. Longest run 2.1 mi; vertical drop 1,563 ft. Also 20 km of groomed nordic trails. (Mid-Nov-mid-Apr) Night skiing (late Dec-late Apr, Fri-Sat). S via I-5, E on OR 58. Phone 541/484-5030. ¢¢¢¢¢

Willamette Science & Technology Center. Participatory science center encourages hands-on learning; features exhibits illustrating physical, biological, and earth sciences and related technologies. Planetarium shows. Phone 541/682-7888 or 541/687-STAR (planetarium). ¢¢

Annual Events

Northwest Microbrew Expo & Willamette Winter Wine Festival. Early Feb.

Bach Festival. Numerous concerts by regional and intl artists; master classes; family activities. Phone 800/457-1486. June-July.

Lane County Fair. Mid-Aug.

Motels/Motor Lodges

★ **BEST INN AND SUITES.** *3315 Gateway St (97477), 3½ mi NE, E of I-5 Exit 195A. 541/746-1314; fax 541/746-3884; toll-free 800/626-1900.* 72 rms, 3 story. No elvtr. S $42-$46; D $46-$54; each addl $5; suites $58-$66; under 12 free. Crib $5. TV; cable. Complimentary coffee in lobby. Restaurant nearby. Ck-out 11 am. Coin lndry. Business servs avail. In-rm modem link. Health club privileges. Whirlpool. Microwaves avail. Cr cds: A, C, D, DS, MC, V.
🄳 🖼 🐾 SC

★★ **BEST WESTERN GRAND MANOR.** *971 Kruse Way (97477), N on I-5, Exit 195. 541/726-4769; fax 541/744-0745; res 800/528-1234; toll-free 800/626-1900.* 62 rms, 3 story, 3 suites. June-Oct: S $84; D $89; each addl $8; suites $107; under 12 free; lower rates rest of yr. Crib avail. TV; cable (premium), VCR avail. Restaurant. Ck-out 11 am, ck-in 2 pm. Meeting rms. Golf, 18 holes. Tennis, 2 courts. Cr cds: A, D, DS, MC, V.
🖼 🖼 🖼 🖼

★★ **BEST WESTERN NEW ORE-GON MOTEL.** *1655 Franklin Blvd (97440), opp Univ of Oregon. 541/683-3669; fax 541/484-5556; toll-free 800/528-1234. Email neworegon@aol.com; www.bestwestern.com/neworegon motel.* 128 rms, 2 story, 12 suites. May-Sep: S $68; D $74; each addl $4; suites $125; under 12 free; lower rates rest of yr. Crib avail. Pet accepted, some restrictions. Parking lot. Indoor pool, whirlpool. TV; cable (premium). Complimentary toll-free calls. Restaurant 6 am-10 pm. Ck-out noon, ck-in 4 pm. Business servs avail. Dry cleaning, coin lndry. Exercise equipt, sauna. Golf. Hiking trail. Cr cds: A, C, D, DS, ER, JCB, MC, V.
🄳 🐾 🖼 🖼 🖼 🖼 🖼

★ **CAMPUS INN.** *390 E Broadway (97401). 541/343-3376; fax 541/458-9392; res 800/888-6213; toll-free 800/888-6313. Email eugene@campus-inn.com; www.campus-inn.com.* 58 rms, 2 story. S $46; D $48-$70; each addl $8; under 18 free. Pet accepted; $20 refundable. TV; cable (premium). Complimentary continental bkfst. Restaurant nearby. Ck-out 11 am. In-rm modem link. Cr cds: A, DS, MC, V.
🐾 🖼 🐾 SC

★★ **HOLIDAY INN EXPRESS.** *3480 Hutton St (97477), off I-5 Exit 195A. 541/746-8471; fax 541/747-1541; res 800/HOLIDAY; toll-free 800/363-8471. www.hiexpress.com.* 58 rms, 3 story. June-Aug: S, D $89; each addl $6; under 18 free; lower rates rest of yr. Crib avail. Pet accepted, some restrictions, fee. Parking lot. Indoor pool. TV; cable (premium), VCR avail. Complimentary continental bkfst, coffee in rms, newspaper, toll-free calls. Restaurant. Ck-out noon, ck-in 3 pm. Meeting rm. Business center. Dry cleaning, coin lndry. Exercise privileges. Golf. Tennis. Cr cds: A, C, D, DS, JCB, MC, V.
🄳 🐾 🖼 🖼 🖼 🖼 🖼 SC 🖼

★ **PACIFIC 9 MOTOR INN.** *3550 Gateway St (97477), 3½ mi NE, E of I-5 Exit 195A.* 541/726-9266; *fax 541/744-2643; toll-free 800/722-9462. Email pacific9@pacific9.com; www. pacific9.com.* 119 rms, 3 story. Apr-Sep: S $48; D $60; each addl $6; under 17 free; lower rates rest of yr. Crib avail. Parking lot. Pool. TV; cable (DSS). Complimentary continental bkfst, toll-free calls. Restaurant nearby. Ck-out 11 am, ck-in 4 pm. Fax servs avail. Golf. Cr cds: A, C, D, DS, MC, V.

D ⛄ ⛱ ⛬ 🔥 SC

★★ **SHILO INN.** *3350 Gateway St (97477), 3½ mi NE, E of I-5 Exit 195A.* 541/747-0332; *fax 541/726-0587; toll-free 800/222-2244.* 143 rms, 2 story, 43 kits. S, D $65-$75; each addl $10; kit. units $79-$89; under 12 free; package plans. Pet accepted, some restrictions; $7/day. TV; cable (premium), VCR avail (movies). Pool. Complimentary continental bkfst. Restaurant 6 am-11 pm. Bar 11-2 am. Ck-out noon. Coin lndry. Meeting rms. Business servs avail. Free airport transportation. Some microwaves. Cr cds: A, C, D, DS, ER, JCB, MC, V.

D ⛄ ⛱ ⛬ 🔥 SC

★ **TRAVELODGE.** *1859 Franklin Blvd (97403), near Univ of Oregon.* 541/342-6383; *fax 541/342-6383; toll-free 800/144-6383.* 60 rms, 2-3 story. S $52-$61; D $70-$80; each addl $5; suites $80-$85; under 12 free. Crib free. Pet accepted, some restrictions. TV; cable. Complimentary continental bkfst. Coffee in rms. Restaurant adj 7 am-11 pm. Ck-out 11 am. Business servs avail. Sauna. Whirlpool. Microwaves avail; refrigerator in suites. Cr cds: A, C, D, DS, MC, V.

D ⛄ ⛬ 🔥 SC

Hotels

★★★ **HILTON.** *66 E 6th Ave (97401).* 541/342-2000; *fax 541/302-6660; res 800/445-8667. www.eugene. hilton.com.* 272 rms, 12 story. S $130; D $145; each addl $15; suites $290-$360; under 18 free. Pet accepted, some restrictions; $25. TV; cable (premium). Indoor pool; whirlpool. Restaurant 6:30 am-10 pm. Rm serv to 1 am. Bar; entertainment. Ck-out noon. Convention facilities. Business center. Concierge. Gift shop. Free covered parking. Free airport, railroad station, bus depot transportation. Exercise equipt. Health club privileges. Some refrigerators; microwaves avail. Balconies. Luxury level. Cr cds: A, C, D, DS, MC, V.

D ⛄ ⛬ ⛱ 🏃 ⛷ ⛬ 🔥

★★ **PHOENIX INN.** *850 Franklin Blvd (97403).* 541/344-0001; *fax 541/686-1288. www.phoenixinn.com.* 4 story, 97 suites. S $89; D $99; each addl $10; under 17 free. Crib avail, fee. Parking lot. Indoor pool, whirlpool. TV; cable, VCR avail. Complimentary continental bkfst, coffee in rms, newspaper, toll-free calls. Restaurant nearby. Ck-out noon, ck-in 4 pm. Meeting rms. Business center. Dry cleaning, coin lndry. Exercise equipt. Golf. Cr cds: A, D, DS, MC, V.

D ⛄ 🏃 ⛷ ⛬ 🔥 🏃

★ **RED LION HOTEL EUGENE.** *205 Coburg Rd (97401), I-5 Exit 194B, then I-105 1 mi to Exit 1.* 541/342-5201; *fax 541/485-2314; toll-free 800/733-5466. Email redlion541@ aol.com; www.redlion.com.* 137 rms, 2 story. May-Sep: S, D $99; under 17 free; lower rates rest of yr. Crib avail. Pet accepted. Parking lot. Pool, whirlpool. TV; cable (premium). Complimentary coffee in rms, newspaper, toll-free calls. Restaurant 6 am-10 pm. Bar. Ck-out noon, ck-in 3 pm. Meeting rms. Business center. Bellhops. Dry cleaning, coin lndry. Free airport transportation. Exercise equipt. Golf. Tennis, 15 courts. Hiking trail. Cr cds: A, C, D, DS, ER, JCB, MC, V.

D ⛄ ⛏ ⛷ ⛱ 🏃 ⛷ ⛬ 🔥 SC 🏃

★★★ **VALLEY RIVER INN.** *1000 Valley River Way (97401), off I-5 Exit 194B, follow signs to Valley River Center.* 541/687-0123; *fax 541/683-5121; toll-free 800/543-8266. Email sales@ valleyriverinn.com; www.valleyriverinn. com.* 245 rms, 3 story, 12 suites. Apr-Oct: S $180; D $200; each addl $20; suites $300; under 18 free; lower rates rest of yr. Crib avail. Pet accepted, some restrictions, fee. Valet parking avail. Pool, lap pool, children's pool, whirlpool. TV; cable (premium), VCR avail. Complimentary coffee in rms, newspaper, toll-free calls. Restaurant. Bar. Meeting rms. Business servs avail. Bellhops. Concierge. Dry cleaning. Gift shop. Free airport transportation. Exercise privileges, sauna, steam rm. Golf. Bike rentals. Supervised children's activities. Hiking trail. Picnic facilities. Video games. Cr cds: A, D, DS, MC, V.

D ⊛ 🏃 🏊 ≈ 🏃 🏄 🔥 ⊛

B&B/Small Inn

★★★ **THE CAMPBELL - A CITY INN.** *252 Pearl St (97401), in Historic Skinner Butte District. 541/343-1119; fax 541/343-2258; toll-free 800/264-2519. Email campbellhouse@campbell house.com; www.campbellhouse.com.* 17 rms, 3 story, 1 suite. Apr-Oct: S, D $149; each addl $15; suites $289; lower rates rest of yr. Crib avail, fee. Parking lot. TV; cable, VCR avail, CD avail. Complimentary full bkfst, newspaper, toll-free calls. Restaurant nearby. Ck-out noon, ck-in 4 pm. Meeting rms. Business center. Concierge. Dry cleaning. Gift shop. Exercise privileges. Golf. Tennis. Bike rentals. Hiking trail. Picnic facilities. Cr cds: A, DS, MC, V.

D ⊛ 🏃 🏄 🏃 🏃 🏄 🔥 ⊛ 🏃

Restaurants

★★ **AMBROSIA.** *174 E Broadway (97401). 541/342-4141.* Specializes in Italian dishes. Hrs: 11:30 am-10 pm; Sun from 4 pm. Closed hols. Bar. Lunch $8-$10; dinner $10-$17. Many antiques. Cr cds: MC, V.

D

★ **CAFE NAVARRO.** *454 Willamette St (97401). 541/344-0943. Email navarro@efn.org.* Hrs: 5-9 pm; Sat, Sun 9 am-2 pm, 5-9 pm. Closed Mon; July 4, Thanksgiving, Dec 25. Wine, beer. Bkfst $3.95-$6.95; lunch $3.95-$6.95; dinner $7.50-$13.95. Entertainment. Cr cds: MC, V.

D SC

★★★ **CHANTERELLE.** *207 E 5th Ave (97401), in Fifth Pearl Bldg. 541/484-4065.* Specializes in wild game, rack of lamb, seafood. Hrs: 5-10 pm. Closed Sun, Mon; hols. Res accepted. Dinner complete meals: $13.95-$23.95. Casual, intimate dining. Cr cds: A, JCB, MC, V.

D

★ **EXCELSIOR INN.** *754 E 13th (97401). 541/342-6963. Email mpaparo@excelsiorinn.com; www. excelsiorinn.com.* Specializes in fresh seafood. Hrs: 7 am-midnight, Sat from 5 pm; Sun brunch 10 am-2 pm. Res accepted. Bar. Bkfst $3-$8; lunch $6-$12.50; dinner $13.95-$21.95. Sun brunch $6.95-$13.95. Child's menu. Intimate, informal dining. Cr cds: A, C, D, DS, MC, V.

D

★★ **NORTH BANK.** *22 Club Rd (97401), W of Ferry St Bridge. 541/343-5622. www.teleport.com/~casado/northbank.* Specializes in fresh seafood, steak, prime rib. Hrs: 11-1 am; Sun noon-midnight. Closed Dec 25. Res accepted. Bar. Lunch a la carte entrees: $3.25-$8.95; dinner a la carte entrees: $9.95-$19.95. Parking. Cr cds: A, DS, MC, V.

D

★★ **OREGON ELECTRIC STATION.** *27 E Fifth St (97401). 541/485-4444.* Specializes in prime rib, seafood, chicken. Hrs: 11:30 am-2:30 pm, 5-10 pm; Fri to 10:30 pm; Sat 4:30-10:30 pm; Sun 4:30-9:30 pm. Closed July 4, Dec 25. Res accepted. Bar. Lunch $3.75-$10.95; dinner $10.95-$29.95. Child's menu. Parking. Former railroad station (1912); memorabilia. Cr cds: A, C, D, DS, MC, V.

D

★★★ **SWEETWATERS.** *1000 Valley River Way. 541/687-0123. Email reserve@valleyriverinn.com; www.valley riverinn.com.* Specializes in seafood, fowl, Pacific Northwest regional cuisine. Hrs: 6:30 am-2 pm, 5:30-9:30 pm; Sun from 7:30 am; Sun brunch 9 am-2 pm. Res accepted. Bar. Wine list. Bkfst $4-$8; lunch $7-$9; dinner $15-$22. Sun brunch $15.75. Child's menu. Parking. Fireplace. Overlooks Willamette River; view from every table. Cr cds: A, D, DS, MC, V.

D

★★ **ZENON CAFE.** *898 Pearl St (97401). 541/343-3005.* Specializes in local pork, lamb. Own desserts. Hrs: 8 am-11 pm; Fri, Sat to midnight; Sun brunch to 2 pm. Closed Thanksgiving, Dec 25. Wine, beer. Bkfst $5.25-$8; lunch $5.75-$9.50; dinner $8.75-$17.50. Sun brunch $5.75-$9.75. Cr cds: MC, V.

D

Unrated Dining Spot

GOVINDA'S VEGETARIAN BUFFET.
270 W 8th St (97401). 541/686-3531.
Specializes in vegetable, rice, and
pasta dishes. Salad bar. Hrs: 11:30
am-2:30 pm, 5-8 pm; Sat from 5 pm.
Closed Sun; Jan 1, July 4, Dec 25. Res
accepted. Lunch a la carte entrees:
$2-$4. Buffet: $5-$6; dinner a la carte
entrees: $2-$4.50. Child's menu.
Parking. Far Eastern atmosphere. Cr
cds: A, DS, MC, V.
[D] [SC]

Florence

(D-I) *See also Reedsport, Yachats*

Settled 1876 **Pop** 5,162 **Elev** 23 ft
Area code 541 **Zip** 97439
Web www.presys.com/wtc/discover
florence
Information Florence Area Chamber
of Commerce, PO Box 26000;
541/997-3128

At the northern edge of the National
Dunes Recreation Area, with some of
the highest sand dunes in the world,
Florence is within reach of 17 lakes
for fishing, swimming, and boating.
River and ocean fishing, crabbing,
and clamming are also popular.
Along the Siuslaw River is "Old
Town," an historic area with gal-
leries, restaurants, and attractions.

What to See and Do

C & M Stables. Experience spectacular scenery of Oregon coast on horseback. Beach (1½-2 hrs), dune trail
(1-1½ hrs), sunset (2 hr, with or
without meal), and coast range (½-
day or all day) rides. Must be 8 yrs or
older. (Daily; closed Thanksgiving,
Dec 25) 8 mi N on US 101. Phone
541/997-7540. ¢¢¢¢

Heceta Head Lighthouse. (1894) Picturesque beacon set high on rugged
cliff. 12 mi N on US 101.

Sand Dunes Frontier. Excursions
aboard 20-passenger dune buggies or
drive-yourself Odysseys; miniature
golf; flower garden; arcade, gift shop,

snack bar. (Daily) 3½ mi S on US
101. Phone 541/997-3544. Dune
buggy rides ¢¢¢¢

✪ **Sea Lion Caves.** Descend 208 ft
under basaltic headland into cavern
(1,500 ft long); home of wild sea
lions. These mammals (up to 12 ft
long) are generally seen on rocky
ledges outside the cave in spring and
summer and inside the cave in fall
and winter. Self-guided tours; light
jacket and comfortable shoes suggested. (Daily; closed Dec 25) 12 mi
N on US 101. Phone 541/547-3111.
¢¢¢

Siuslaw Pioneer Museum. Exhibits
preserve the history of the area;
impressive display of artifacts and
items from early settlers and Native
Americans. Library rm; extensive
genealogy records; hundreds of old
photographs. (Jan-Nov, Tues-Sun;
closed hols) 85294 US 101S, 1 mi S.
Phone 541/997-7884. **FREE**

State parks.

Carl G. Washburne Memorial.
This 1,089-acre park is a good
area for study of botany. Two-mi-
long beach, swimming, fishing,
clamming; hiking, picnicking,
tent and trailer campsites with
access to beach. Elk may be seen
in campgrounds and nearby
meadows. 14 mi N on US 101.
Phone 541/547-3416.

Darlingtonia. An 18-acre park with
short loop trail through bog area

Haceta Head Lighthouse

noted for Darlingtonia, a carnivorous, insect-eating plant also known as cobra lily. Picnicking. Viewing deck. 5 mi N on US 101. Phone 541/997-3641.

Devil's Elbow. A 545-acre park. Ocean beach, fishing; hiking, picnicking. Observation point. 13 mi N on US 101, below Heceta Head Lighthouse. Phone 541/997-3641. ¢¢

Jessie M. Honeyman Memorial. Park has 522 coastal acres with wooded lakes and sand dunes, an abundance of rhododendrons, and an excellent beach. Swimming, waterskiing; fishing, boat dock and ramps; hiking, picnicking, improved camping, tent and trailer sites (dump station). (Daily) Standard fees. 3 mi S on US 101. Phone 541/997-3641.

Westward Ho! Sternwheeler. One-hr cruises incl Classical Continental Breakfast & Birdwatch, Jazzy Lunch Adventure, Afternoon Blues Cruise. Also 2-hr Sunset Buffet Cruise (Fri-Sun eves, res required) and 30-min Bay Rides (Sun and hols). (Apr-Oct, daily) Old Town Dock. Phone 541/997-9691. ¢¢¢-¢¢¢¢¢

Annual Events

Rhododendron Festival. Third wkend May.

Fall Festival. Last wkend Sep.

Motels/Motor Lodges

★★ **BEST WESTERN PIER POINT INN.** 85625 Hwy 101 S (97439). 541/997-7191; fax 541/997-3828; res 800/528-1234. 55 rms, 3 story. Mid-May-early Sep: S $75-$99; D $95-$129; each addl $10; lower rates rest of yr. TV; cable (premium). Complimentary continental bkfst. Coffee in rms. Ck-out 11 am. Meeting rms. Sauna. Whirlpool. Balconies. Overlooks Siuslaw River. Cr cds: A, D, DS, MC, V.
⊡ ⬤ ⚡ ⊠ ▨

★★ **HOLIDAY INN EXPRESS.** 2475 Hwy 101 (97439). 541/997-7797; fax 541/997-7895; res 800/465-4329. 51 rms, 2 story. S, D $55-$99; each addl $10; under 19 free. TV; cable (premium). Complimentary continental bkfst. Restaurant adj 6 am-9 pm. Ck-out 11 am. Meeting rms. Exercise equipt. Whirlpool. Cr cds: A, C, D, DS, MC, V.
⊡ ⬤ ⚡ 🏋 ⊠ ▨

★ **MONEY SAYER MOTEL.** 170 Hwy 101 (97439), N of bridge. 541/997-7131; fax 541/997-6263; toll-free 877/997-7131. Email moneysaver@harborside.com. 40 rms, 2 story. July-Sep: S, D $59; each addl $7; under 12 free; lower rates rest of yr. Parking lot. TV; cable. Complimentary toll-free calls. Restaurant nearby. Ck-out 11 am, ck-in 2 pm. Golf. Cr cds: A, DS, MC, V.
⊡ 🐾 ✈ ⊠ ▨ SC

★ **RIVER HOUSE MOTEL.** 1202 Bay St (97439). 541/997-3933; fax 541/997-6263; toll-free 877/997-3933. Email riverhouse@harborside.com; www.riverhouseflorence.com. 40 rms, 2 story. No A/C. June-Sep: S, D $64-$120; each addl $6; higher rates hols; lower rates rest of yr. Crib $6. TV; cable. Complimentary coffee in lobby. Restaurant nearby. Ck-out 11 am. Coin lndry. On river. Cr cds: A, DS, MC, V.
✈ ▨

Restaurant

★★ **WINDWARD INN.** 3757 US 101N (97439). 541/997-8243. Specializes in steak, fresh seafood. Own baking. Hrs: 7 am-10 pm. Closed Dec 25. Res accepted. Bar. Bkfst $2.95-$8.95; lunch $3.95-$10.95; dinner $6.95-$18.95. Child's menu. Entertainment: pianist wkends. Cr cds: DS, MC, V.
⊡ SC

Forest Grove

(B-2) See also Beaverton, Hillsboro, Portland

Settled 1845 **Pop** 13,559 **Elev** 175 ft
Area code 503 **Zip** 97116
Web www.grovenet.org/forestgrove/chamber/index.html

Information Chamber of Commerce, 2417 Pacific Ave; 503/357-3006

Forest Grove traces its beginning to missionaries who brought religion to what they called the "benighted Indian." The town is believed to have been named for a forest of firs which met a grove of oaks.

What to See and Do

Pacific University. (1849) 1,600 students. Founded as Tualatin Academy, it is one of the Northwest's oldest schools. On campus is art gallery and Old College Hall (academic yr, Tues, Thurs; also by appt). Tours of campus. Main entrance on College Way. Phone 503/357-6151.

Scoggin Valley Park and Hagg Lake. Features 11 mi of shoreline. Swimming, windsurfing, fishing, boating (ramps), picnic sites. (Apr-Oct) 7 mi SW via OR 47, Scoggin Valley Rd exit.

Annual Events

Barbershop Ballad Contest. Phone 503/292-5673. First wkend Mar.

Hawaiian Luau. Pacific University. Hawaiian traditions celebrated in food, fashions, and dance. Phone 503/357-6151. Mid-Apr.

Concours d'Elegance. Pacific University. Classic and vintage auto display. Phone 503/357-2300. Third Sun June.

Founders Day Corn Roast. Phone 503/357-3006. Late Sep.

Motels/Motor Lodges

★ **FOREST GROVE INN.** *4433 Pacific Ave (97116). 503/357-9700; fax 503/357-3135; toll-free 800/240-6504.* 20 rms, 2 story, 4 kit. units. S $41-$46; D $46-$49; each addl $7; kit. units $70. Crib free. TV; cable (premium). Complimentary coffee in rms. Restaurant nearby. Ck-out 11 am. Business servs avail. Refrigerators. Cr cds: A, D, DS, MC, V.
D ⚛ ⚒ ⚑ ⚐ ⚐

★ **TRAVELODGE SUITES.** *3306 Pacific Ave (97116). 503/357-9000; fax 503/359-4134; toll-free 800/578-7878.* 41 rms, 2 story. May-Sep: S $55-$65; D $60-$70; each addl $6; under 12 free; lower rates rest of yr. Crib free. TV; cable (premium). Indoor pool; whirlpool. Complimentary continental bkfst. Coffee in rms. Restaurant adj 6-1 am. Bar 11 am-11 pm. Ck-out 11 am. Coin lndry. Meeting rms. Business servs avail. In-rm modem

link. Exercise equipt. Refrigerators. Cr cds: A, C, D, DS, ER, JCB, MC, V.
D ⚛ ⚒ ⚑ ⚐ SC

Fort Clatsop National Memorial

See also Astoria, Cannon Beach, Seaside

(6 mi SW of Astoria off US 101A)

This site marks the western extremity of the territory explored by Meriwether Lewis and William Clark in their expedition of 1804-06. The fort is a reconstruction of their 1805-06 winter quarters. The original fort was built here because of its excellent elk hunting grounds, its easy access to ocean salt, its protection from the westerly coastal storms, and the availability of fresh water.

The expedition set out on May 14, 1804, to seek "the most direct and practicable water communication across this continent" under orders from President Thomas Jefferson. The first winter was spent near Bismarck, North Dakota. In April, 1805, the party, then numbering 33, resumed the journey. On November 15, they had their first view of the ocean from a point near McGowan, Washington. The company left Fort Clatsop on March 23, 1806, on their return trip and was back at St. Louis on September 23 of the same year. The Lewis and Clark Expedition was one of the greatest explorations in the history of the United States, and its journals depict one of the most fascinating chapters in the annals of the American frontier. The visitor center has museum exhibits and provides audiovisual programs. The canoe landing has replicas of dugout canoes of that period. Ranger talks and living history demonstrations are presented mid-June-Labor Day. (Daily; closed Dec 25) For further info contact Superintendent, Rte 3, Box 604 FC, Astoria 97103; 503/861-2471. Apr-Sep ¢¢; Rest of year **FREE**

Gleneden Beach

(see Lincoln City)

Gold Beach

(F-1) *See also Brookings, Port Orford*

Pop 1,546 **Elev** 51 ft **Area code** 541
Zip 97444 **Web** www.goldbeach.org
Information Chamber of Commerce
& Visitors Center, 29279 Ellensburg
Ave #3; 541/247-7526 or 800/525-
2334

Until floods in 1861 washed the
deposits out to sea, placer mining
in the beach sands was profitable
here; hence the name. There is still
some mining farther up the Rogue
River. Gold Beach is at the mouth of
the Rogue River, on the south
shore; Wedderburn is on the north
bank. Agate hunting is popular at
the mouth of the Rogue River. The
river is also well-known for steelhead and salmon fishing. Surf fishing and clamming are possible at
many excellent beaches. The
Siskiyou National Forest (see
GRANTS PASS) is at the edge of
town and a Ranger District office of
the forest is located here.

What to See and Do

Boat trips.

⊠ **Court's White Water Trips.** A
104-mi round-trip to Blossom Bar
Rapids; stopover for lunch at Paradise Lodge with overnight
option. Also 6-hr (64-mi) trip. Res
advised. Departs from Jerry's Rogue
River Jets, S end of Rogue River
Bridge on US 101. Phone 541/247-
6022, 541/247-6504. ¢¢¢¢

Jerry's Rogue River Jet Boat Trips.
A 6-hr (64-mi) round-trip into
wilderness area; 2-hr lunch or dinner stop at Agness. Also 8-hr (104-
mi) and 6-hr (80-mi) round trip
whitewater excursions. Rogue River
Museum & Gift Shop (all yr).
(May-Oct, daily). S end of Rogue
River Bridge at port of Gold Beach

Boat Basin. Phone 541/247-4571 or
800/451-3645. ¢¢¢¢

Mail Boat Whitewater Trips. A
104-mi round trip by jet boat into
wilderness and white water of the
upper Rogue River. The narrated
7½-hr trip includes 2-hr lunch
stop at a wilderness lodge. (May-
Oct, daily) Also 80-mi round trip
to the middle Rogue River. Narrated 6¾-hr trip departs twice
daily; incl lunch or dinner stop.
(Mid-June-Sep) Res advised for all
trips. Mail Boat Dock. Phone
800/458-3511 or 541/247-7033.
¢¢¢¢¢

**Official Rogue River Mail Boat
Hydro-Jet Trips.** A 64-mi round trip
by jet boat up the wild and scenic
Rogue River; 2-hr lunch stop at
Agness. (May-Oct, daily) Res
advised. Mail Boat Dock, ¼ mi
upstream from N end of Rogue
River Bridge in Wedderburn, on N
bank of the Rogue River. Phone
800/458-3511 or 541/247-7033.
¢¢¢¢¢

Cape Sebastian State Park. Approx
1,100 acres of open and forested
land. Cape Sebastian is a precipitous
headland, rising more than 700 ft
above tide with a view of many mi
of coastline. A short roadside
through the forest area is marked by
wild azaleas, rhododendrons, and
blue ceanothus in season. Trails; no
rest rms or water. 7 mi S on US 101.
Phone 541/469-2021.

Curry County Historical Museum.
Collections and interpretive displays
of early life in Curry County. (June-
Sep, Tues-Sat afternoons; rest of yr,
Sat afternoons) Fairgrounds. Phone
541/247-6113. **Donation**

Prehistoric Gardens. Life-size sculptures of dinosaurs and other prehistoric animals that disappeared more
than 70 million yrs ago are set
among primitive plants, which have
survived. (Daily) 14 mi N on US 101,
located in Oregon's rain forest.
Phone 541/332-4463. ¢¢

Annual Events

Whale of a Wine Festival. Jan.

SUDS Festival. Food and brew festival. Mar.

Clam Chowder Festival. First wkend
May.

Curry County Fair. Last wkend July.

Festival of Quilts. Third wknd Sep.

Motels/Motor Lodges

★★ **SHORE CLIFF INN.** *29346 Ellensburg Ave (97444). 541/247-7091; fax 541/247-7170; toll-free 888/663-0608.* 38 rms, 1-2 story. S, D $59-$75; each addl $5. TV; cable (premium). Complimentary coffee in lobby. Restaurant adj 6 am-10 pm. Ck-out 11 am. Balconies. On beach. Cr cds: MC, V.
[D] [⛄] [🔥]

★★★ **TU TU' TUN LODGE.** *96550 N Bank Rogue (97444). 541/247-6664; fax 541/247-0672; toll-free 800/864-6357. Email tututun@harbor side.com.* 16 rms, 2 suites, 1 garden house. S, D $135-$325; each addl $25; suites $185-$225; garden house $235, $125 off-season. Two River Suites and Garden House avail all yr. (in season and off season rates vary). Remodeled lodge with 2 stone fireplaces. Heated pool. Complimentary hors d'oeuvres. Dining rm open May-Oct (public by res): bkfst 7:30-9:30 am, lunch sitting (registered guests only) 1 pm; dinner sitting 7 pm. Bar. Ck-out 11 am, ck-in 3 pm. Business center. In-rm modem link. Free airport transportation. Dock; guides, whitewater boat trips. 4-hole pitch and putt golf; horseshoes. Private patios, balconies. Library. Cr cds: DS, MC, V.
[D] [🐾] [⛏] [🍴] [🏊] [🎣] [🚶] [✈] [⛄] [🔥]

B&B/Small Inn

★★ **INN AT NESIKA BEACH.** *33026 Nesika Rd (97444), 6 mi N on US 101. 541/247-6434. Email leminn@ harborside.com; www.moriah.com.* 4 rms, 3 story. June-Aug: D $100; suites $130; lower rates rest of yr. Parking lot. TV; cable, VCR avail, CD avail. Complimentary full bkfst. Ck-out 11 am, ck-in 3 pm. Golf, 18 holes. Beach access. Hiking trail. No cr cds accepted.
[🐾] [🍴] [🏊] [⛄]

Restaurants

★ **CHOWDERHEAD.** *29430 Ellensburg US 101 (97444). 541/247-0588.* Specializes in seafood, steak. Salad bar. Hrs: 11 am-9 pm. Lunch $4.95-

$9.95; dinner $10.75-$33. Child's menu. Rustic decor; dining rm with ocean view. Cr cds: DS, MC, V.
[D]

★★ **NOR'WESTER SEAFOOD.** *10 Harbor Way (97444), at Port of Gold Beach. 541/247-2333.* Specializes in seafood, steak. Hrs: 5-10 pm; off-season to 9 pm. Closed Dec, Jan. Bar. Dinner $12.95-$22.95. Child's menu. Entertainment. Overlooks bay and ocean. Cr cds: A, MC, V.

Grants Pass

(F-2) See also Cave Junction, Jacksonville, Medford

Pop 17,488 **Elev** 948 ft **Area code** 541
Web www.grantspass.com

Information Visitor & Convention Bureau, PO Box 1787, 97528; 541/476-5510 or 800/547-5927; 800/460-7700 (events line)

Grants Pass was named by the rail constructors who were here when news reached them of General Grant's victorious siege of Vicksburg in 1863. On the Rogue River, Grants Pass is the seat of Josephine County. Tourism is the chief source of income; agriculture and electronics are next in importance. Fishing in the Rogue River is a popular activity. A Ranger District office and headquarters of the Siskiyou National Forest is located here.

What to See and Do

Grants Pass Museum of Art. Permanent and changing exhibits of photography, paintings, art objects. (Tues-Sat afternoons; closed hols) In Riverside Park, on the Rogue River off of 7th & Park Sts. Phone 541/479-3290. **FREE**

Oregon Caves National Monument. (see) 28 mi SW on US 199 to Cave Junction, then 20 mi E on OR 46.

Rogue River Raft Trips. One- to 5-day whitewater scenic or fishing trips through the wilderness, past abandoned gold-mining sites; overnight lodges or camping en route. Some of these are seasonal; some all yr. For details contact the Visitor & Convention Bureau. Also avail is

Hellgate Jetboat Excursions. Interpretive jet boat trips down the Rogue River: 2-hr scenic excursion (May-Sep, daily); 4-hr country dinner excursion (mid-May-Sep); 4-hr champagne brunch excursion (mid-May-Sep, wkends); 5-hr whitewater trip (May-Sep, daily). Depart from Riverside Inn. Phone 800/648-4874 or 541/479-7204.

¢¢¢¢

Siskiyou National Forest. Over 1 million acres. Famous for salmon fishing in lower Rogue River gorge and early-day gold camps. Many species of trees and plants are relics of past ages; a botanist's paradise. An 84-mi stretch of Rogue River between Applegate River and Lobster Creek Bridge is designated a National Wild and Scenic River; nearly half is in the forest. Boat, pack, and saddle trips into rugged backcountry. Picnic sites. Camping. For further information contact Visitor Information Office, PO Box 440, 200 NE Greenfield Rd. N, S & W off US 199 or W of I-5. Phone 541/471-6516.

Valley of the Rogue State Park. A 275-acre park with fishing, boat ramp to Rogue River; picnicking, improved tent and trailer sites (daily; dump station). Standard fees. 8 mi S on I-5. Phone 541/582-1118.

Annual Events

Amazing May. Eclectic mixture of events heralding the arrival of spring. May.

Boatnik Festival. Riverside Park. Parade, concessions, carnival rides, boat races; entertainment. A 25-mi whitewater hydroboat race from Riverside Park to Hellgate Canyon and back. Square dance festival at Josephine County Fairgrounds. Memorial Day wkend.

Pari-mutuel Horse Racing. Fairgrounds. Phone 541/476-3215. Late May-early July.

Josephine County Fair. Fairgrounds, Redwood Hwy and W Park St. Phone 541/476-3215. Mid-Aug.

Jedediah Smith Mountain Man Rendezvous & Buffalo Barbecue. Sportsman Park. Muzzleloader/black powder shoots, costume contests,

exhibits. Phone 541/479-8929. Labor Day wkend.

Josephine County Air Fair. Airport, Brookside Dr. Antique aircraft, contests, airplane and helicopter rides. Phone 541/474-5285 or 541/474-0665. Early Sep.

Heritage Days. Historical and ethnic related events of the pioneers that settled the southern Oregon territory. Sep-mid-Oct.

Motels/Motor Lodges

★★ **BEST WESTERN GRANTS PASS INN.** *111 NE Agness Ave (97526). 541/476-1117; fax 541/479-4315; toll-free 800/553-7666. Email bwgpi@chatlink.com.* 80 rms, 2 story, 4 suites. May-Sep: S $82; D $90; each addl $5; under 17 free; lower rates rest of yr. Crib avail. Pet accepted, fee. Parking lot. Pool, whirlpool. TV; cable (premium), VCR avail. Complimentary continental bkfst, coffee in rms, toll-free calls. Restaurant 6 am-9 pm. Ck-out 11 am, ck-in 2 pm. Business servs avail. Bellhops. Dry cleaning, coin lndry. Golf. Downhill skiing. Cr cds: A, D, DS, MC, V.

⧉ ⧉ ⧉ ⧉ ⧉ ⧉ ⧉

★★ **COMFORT INN.** *1889 NE 6th (97526). 541/479-8301; fax 541/955-9721; res 800/228-5150; toll-free 800/626-1900.* 59 rms, 2 story. S $49.99; D $59.99-$64.99; each addl $5. Crib $5. TV; cable (premium). Heated pool. Complimentary continental bkfst. Restaurant adj open 24 hrs. Ck-out 11 am. Microwaves avail. Cr cds: A, DS, MC, V.

⧉ ⧉ ⧉ ⧉ **SC**

★ **MOTEL DEL ROGUE.** *2600 Rogue River Hwy (97527). 541/479-2111.* 14 rms, 1-2 story, 13 kits. (oven in 10). S $40; D $65; each addl $5-$10; suites, kit. units $45-$65; lower rates rest of yr. TV; cable. Restaurant nearby. Ck-out 11 am. Coin lndry. Many microwaves. Porches. Picnic tables, grills. Shaded grounds; on river. Cr cds: MC, V.

⧉ ⧉ ⧉

★★ **REDWOOD MOTEL.** *815 NE 6th St (97526). 541/476-0878; fax 541/476-1032. Email redwood@chatlink.com; www.chatlink.com/~redwood.* 26 rms, 9 kits. Mid-May-Sep: S $55-$80; D $60-$82; each addl $5; kit. units $68-$95; whirlpool suites $97; lower rates rest of yr. Crib $5. Pet accepted, some restrictions; $10. TV; cable (premium). Heated pool; whirlpool. Playground. Complimentary continental bkfst. Restaurant opp 6 am-10 pm. Guest lndry. Ck-out 11 am. Many refrigerators, microwaves. Picnic tables. Cr cds: A, D, DS, MC, V.

🄳 🔌 🕭 🞫 🔥 SC

★ **ROGUE VALLEY MOTEL.** *7799 Rogue River Hwy (97527), I-5 Exit 48.* 541/582-3762. 8 rms, 6 with shower only, 1 story. June-Sep: S $45-49; D $72; each addl $5; lower rates rest of yr. Crib free. Pet accepted, some restrictions. TV; cable. Heated pool. Complimentary coffee in rms. Ck-out 11 am. Refrigerators; many microwaves. Picnic tables. On river. Cr cds: MC, V.

🄳 🔌 🕭 🞫 🞫 🔥

★ **ROYAL VIEW MOTOR HOTEL.** *110 NE Morgan Ln (97526).* 541/479-5381; fax 541/479-5381; toll-free 800/547-7555. 60 rms, 2 story. S $40-$44; D $49-$66; suites $64. Crib $4. Pet accepted. TV; cable (premium), VCR avail. Heated pool; whirlpool, poolside serv. Coffee in rms. Restaurant 6 am-10 pm. Bar 11-2 am; entertainment Thurs-Sun. Ck-out noon. Coin lndry. Sauna, steam rm. Refrigerator, minibar in suites. Balconies. Cr cds: A, C, D, DS, MC, V.

🔌 🞫 🞫 🔥 SC

★★ **SHILO INN.** *1880 NW 6th St (9/526).* 541/479-8391; fax 541/474-7344. 70 rms, 2 story. May-Sep: S, D $59-$79; each addl $10; under 12 free; lower rates rest of yr. Crib free. Pet accepted; $7. TV; cable (premium). Pool. Continental bkfst. Restaurant adj open 24 hrs. Ck-out noon. Meeting rm. Sauna, steam rm. Microwaves avail. Cr cds: A, D, DS, MC, V.

🄳 🔌 🕭 🕯 🞫 🛉 🞫 🔥

Hotels

★★ **BEST WESTERN INN AT THE ROGUE.** *8959 Rogue River Hwy (97527).* 541/582-2200; fax 541/582-1415; toll-free 800/238-0700. Email rogueinn@is-plus.net. 48 rms, 2 story, 6 suites. May-Sep: S, D $79; each addl $5; suites $149; under 12 free; lower rates rest of yr. Crib avail, fee. Pet accepted, some restrictions, fee.

Parking lot. Pool, whirlpool. TV; cable (premium), VCR avail. Complimentary continental bkfst, coffee in rms. Restaurant nearby. Bar. Ck-out 11 am, ck-in 2 pm. Meeting rms. Business center. Coin lndry. Gift shop. Exercise equipt. Golf. Bike rentals. Supervised children's activities. Hiking trail. Picnic facilities. Cr cds: A, C, D, DS, MC, V.

🄳 🔌 🕭 🕯 🞫 🛉 🞫 🔥 SC 🛉

★★ **HOLIDAY INN EXPRESS GRANTS PASS.** *105 NE Agness Ave (97526), I-5 Exit 55.* 541/471-6144; fax 541/471-9248; res 800/HOLIDAY; toll-free 800/838-7666. Email holidayexpress@terragon.com; www.rogueweb.com/holiday. 72 rms, 4 story, 8 suites. May-Sep: S $85; D $90; each addl $5; suites $132; under 18 free; lower rates rest of yr. Crib avail. Pet accepted, some restrictions, fee. Parking lot. Pool, whirlpool. TV; cable (premium). Complimentary continental bkfst. Restaurant. Meeting rm. Business center. Dry cleaning, coin lndry. Exercise privileges. Golf, 18 holes. Tennis, 2 courts. Cr cds: A, C, D, DS, JCB, MC, V.

🄳 🔌 🕯 🞫 🛉 🞫 🔥 🛉

★★★ **RIVERSIDE INN.** *971 SE 6th St (97526).* 541/476-6873; fax 541/474-9848; toll-free 800/334-4567. Email sue@riverside-inn.com; www.riverside-inn.com. 174 rms, 2 story, 15 suites. May-Aug: S $99; D $109; each addl $10; suites $175; under 12 free; lower rates rest of yr. Crib avail, fee. Pet accepted, some restrictions, fee. Parking lot. Pool. TV; cable (premium), VCR avail. Complimentary coffee in rms, toll-free calls. Restaurant 7 am-10 pm. Bar. Ck-out 11 am, ck-in 4 pm. Meeting rms. Business servs avail. Gift shop. Salon/barber. Exercise privileges. Golf, 18 holes. Tennis, 2 courts. Picnic facilities. Cr cds: A, D, DS, JCB, V.

🄳 🔌 🕭 🕯 🕯 🞫 🛉 🞫 🔥

B&Bs/Small Inns

★★ **FLERY MANOR.** *2000 Jump Off Joe Creek Rd (97526).* 541/476-3591; fax 541/471-2303. Email flery@flerymanor.com; www.flerymanor.com. 4 rms, 3 story. No elvtr. S, D $75-$125; wkly rates. Children over 10 yrs only. TV in common rm; VCR avail

(movies). Complimentary full bkfst; afternoon refreshments. Ck-out 11 am, ck-in 4-6 pm. Business servs avail. Picnic tables, grills. Country decor; fireplace, antiques. Totally nonsmoking. Cr cds: A, DS, MC, V.
🖼️ 🖼️ **SC**

★★ **HOME FARM BED AND BREAKFAST.** *157 Savage Creek Rd (97527), I-5 Exit 48, cross river, N on OR 99. 541/582-0980; fax 541/582-3480; res 800/522-7967. Email home-farm@chatlink.com.* 4 rms. No rm phones. S $60-$75, D $65-$80; each addl $10; wkly rates. TV in parlor. Complimentary full bkfst. Ck-out 11 am, ck-in 3-6 pm. Game rm. Lawn games. Picnic tables. Farm house built 1944; many antiques. On 4½ acres. Totally nonsmoking. Cr cds: A, DS, MC, V.
D 🖼️ 🖼️

★★ **MORRISON'S ROGUE RIVER LODGE.** *8500 Galice Rd (97532), NW on I-5 to Merlin, 12 mi W on Galice Rd. 541/476-3825; fax 541/476-4953; toll-free 800/826-1963. Email info@ morrisonslodge.com; www.morrisons lodge.com.* 4 rms, 2 story. Sep-Nov: S $175; D $300; each addl $70; children $50; under 13 free; lower rates rest of yr. Crib avail. Parking garage. Pool. TV; cable (premium), VCR avail, VCR avail. Complimentary full bkfst, coffee in rms, toll-free calls. Restaurant. Bar. Meeting rm. Fax servs avail. Coin lndry. Gift shop. Golf. Tennis, 2 courts. Beach access. Supervised children's activities. Cr cds: DS, MC, V.
🖼️ 🖼️ 🖼️ 🖼️ 🖼️ 🖼️ 🖼️

★★ **PINE MEADOW INN.** *1000 Crow Rd (97532), I-5 Exit Merlin. 541/471-6277; fax 541/471-6277; toll-free 800/554-0806. Email pmi@pinemeadow inn.com; www.pinemeadowinn.com.* 4 rms, 2 story. Apr-Sep: D $100; lower rates rest of yr. Parking lot. TV; cable (premium), VCR avail, VCR avail. Complimentary full bkfst. Ck-out 11 am. Golf. Hiking trail. Cr cds: A, DS, MC, V.
🖼️ 🖼️ 🖼️ 🖼️ 🖼️ 🖼️

★★★ **WEASKU INN.** *5560 Rogue River Hwy (97527), 8 mi N on Red-wood Hwy 99, I-5 Exit 48. 541/476-4190; fax 541/471-7038. www. weasku.com.* 22 rms, many with A/C, 2 story, 3 suites. S, D $85-

$250; suites $195-$295. TV; cable, VCR (movies). Complimentary continental bkfst; afternoon refreshments. Ck-out noon, ck-in 3 pm. Business servs avail. Gift shop. Health club privileges. Lawn games. Some fireplaces. Some balconies. On river. Built in 1924; antiques. Cr cds: A, DS, MC, V.
D 🖼️ 🖼️ 🖼️ 🖼️

Restaurant

★★ **YANKEE POT ROAST.** *720 NW Sixth St (97526). 541/476-0551. Email yankee@tarrogon.com; www.yankee-pot roast.com.* Specializes in Yankee pot roast, fresh halibut. Hrs: 5-9 pm; Sun from 2 pm. Closed Mon, Tues; Dec 25. Dinner $7.95-$16.95. Child's menu. Restored historic home; built 1905. Cr cds: A, MC, V.

Hermiston

(A-5) *See also Pendleton, Umatilla*

Pop 10,040 **Elev** 457 ft **Area code** 541 **Zip** 97838

Information Greater Hermiston Chamber of Commerce, 415 S US Hwy 395, PO Box 185; 541/567-6151 or 541/564-9109

Centrally located between the major cities of the Northwest, Hermiston offers an abundant array of recreational opportunities. The Columbia River, second largest river in the country, flows five miles to the north and the Umatilla River skirts the city limits; both are popular for fishing. The nearby Blue Mountains offer a variety of summer and winter activities. Agriculture, processing, and production form the economic base of this community, which has become a trading center for this area of the Columbia River Basin.

Seasonal Event

Stock Car Racing. Race City, USA, on US 395. Phone 541/567-8320. Apr-Oct.

Motel/Motor Lodge

★ **ECONOMY INN.** *835 N 1st St (97838). 541/567-5516; fax 541/567-5516; toll-free 888/567-9521.* 39 rms, 3 kit, 1-2 story. S $35; D $42; each addl $5; suites $65; wkly rates. Crib $10. Pet accepted; $5. TV; cable (premium). Pool. Restaurant adj 6 am-10 pm. Bar adj. Ck-out 11 am. Business servs avail. Refrigerators, microwaves. Cr cds: A, D, DS, MC, V.

🐾 🦾 📠 🛥 🕴 🐕 ⛷ 🔥

Hillsboro

(B-2) *See also Beaverton, Forest Grove, Oregon City, Portland*

Pop 37,520 **Elev** 165 ft **Area code** 503 **Web** www.hilchamber.org

Information Greater Hillsboro Chamber of Commerce, 334 SE 5th Ave, 97123; 503/648-1102

Motel/Motor Lodge

★ **TRAVELODGE.** *622 SE 10th St (97123). 503/640-4791; fax 503/640-8127; res 800/578-7878. www.travelodge.com.* 58 rms, 2 story. S $60; D $65; each addl $10. Crib $10. TV; cable (premium). Complimentary coffee in rms. Restaurant adj 6 am-10 pm. Ck-out 11 am. Coin lndry. Business servs avail. Refrigerators. Cr cds: A, DS, MC, V.

Ⅾ 🦾 📠 🐕 ⛷ 🔥

Hood River

(A-3) *See also The Dalles*

Settled 1854 **Pop** 4,632 **Elev** 155 ft **Area code** 541 **Zip** 97031 **Web** www.gorge.net/hrccc

Information Chamber of Commerce Visitor Center, 405 Portway Ave; 541/386-2000 or 800/366-3530

Hood River, located in the midst of a valley producing apples, pears, and cherries, boasts a scenic view of Oregon's highest peak, Mount Hood; its slopes are accessible in all seasons by road. OR 35, called the Loop Highway, leads around the mountain and up to the snowline. The Columbia River Gorge provides perfect conditions for windsurfing in the Hood River Port Marina Park.

What to See and Do

Bonneville Lock & Dam. The dam consists of 3 parts—1 spillway and 2 powerhouses. It has an overall length of 3,463 ft and extends across the Columbia River to Washington. It was a major hydroelectric project of the US Army Corps of Engineers. On the Oregon side is a 5-story visitor center with underwater windows into the fish ladders and new navigation lock with viewing facilities. Audiovisual presentations and tours of fish ladders, and the original powerhouse (June-Sep, daily or by appt; Oct-May, self-guided; closed Jan 1, Thanksgiving, Dec 25). Sternwheeler boat tours (June-Sep; fee). State salmon hatchery adj. Fishing (salmon and sturgeon ponds). Picnicking. Powerhouse II and Visitor Orientation Bldg on Washington side, WA 14; underwater fish viewing, audiovisual presentations, fish ladder and powerhouse tours (June-Sep, daily or by appt; Oct-May, self-guided; closed Jan 1, Thanksgiving, Dec 25); accessible via Bridge of the Gods from I-84. 23 mi W on I-84. Phone 541/374-8820. **FREE**

Columbia Gorge. Sternwheeler makes daytime excursions, sunset dinner and brunch cruises, harbor tours, and special holiday cruises. Res required exc for daily excursions (mid-June-Sep). Port of Cascade Locks. 10 mi W on I-84, Exit 44. Phone 541/223-3928 or 541/374-8427 for schedule and prices. ¢¢¢¢

Hood River County Museum. Items from early settlers to modern residents. An outdoor display that incl sternwheeler paddle wheel, beacon light used by air pilots in the Columbia Gorge, steam engine from the *Mary.* (Mid-Apr-Oct, daily) Port Marina Park. Phone 541/386-6772. **Donation**

Lost Lake. Swimming, fishing, boat rentals; hiking, picnicking, concession, day lodge. Camping. 28 mi SW off I-84 on Dee Secondary Hwy and paved Forest Service road in Mt Hood National Forest (see).

Mount Hood National Forest. (see) S & W of city.

Mount Hood Scenic Railroad. Historic railroad (1906); 44-mi round-trip excursions. (Apr-Dec, schedule varies) 110 Railroad Ave. Phone 541/386-3556. ¢¢¢¢¢

Panorama Point. Observation point for Hood River Valley and Mt Hood. ½ mi S on OR 35 to Eastside Rd.

Winery tours.

Flerchinger Vineyards. Tours; tasting rm. (Daily). 4200 Post Canyon Dr. Phone 541/386-2882. **FREE**

Hood River Vineyards. Tours; tasting rm. (Mar-Nov, daily) 4693 Westwood Dr. Phone 541/386-3772. **FREE**

Annual Events

Blossom Festival. Third wkend Apr.

Return of the Sternwheeler Days. Celebration of the sternwheeler *Columbia Gorge*'s return to home port for the summer. Wine and cheese tasting, crafts, food. Phone 541/374-8619. June.

Hood River County Fair. July.

Cross Channel Swim. Labor Day.

Hood River Valley Harvest Fest. Fresh local fruit, arts and crafts, wine tasting, contests. Third wkend Oct.

Motels/Motor Lodges

★ **LOVE'S RIVERVIEW LODGE.** *1505 Oak St (97031). 541/386-8719; fax 541/386-6671. Email wwwaana@ pacifier.* 20 rms, 2 story, 2 kit. units. June-mid-Sep: S $55-$62; D $69-$72; each addl $6; kit. units $79-$145; under 12 free; ski plans; lower rates rest of yr. Crib free. TV; cable (premium). Complimentary coffee in rms. Restaurant nearby. Ck-out 11 am. Business servs avail. Indoor pool; whirlpool. Refrigerators, microwaves. Some balconies. Cr cds: A, DS, MC, V.

D ⊠ ⊠ ⚒ SC

★★ **VAGABOND LODGE HOOD RIVER.** *4070 Westcliff Dr (97031). 541/386-2992; fax 541/386-3317; toll-free 877/386-2992. Email jcranmer@ gorge.net; www.vagabondlodge.com.* 42 rms, 7 suites. S $43-$53; D $52-$75; each addl $7; suites $63-$85; lower

rates winter. Crib $5. Pet accepted. TV; cable. Playground. Restaurant adj 7 am-midnight. Ck-out 11 am. Picnic tables. On 5 wooded acres; overlooks Columbia River Gorge. Cr cds: A, DS, MC, V.

D ⚒ ⚒ ⚒ ⚒ ⚒ ⚒

Hotel

★★ **BEST WESTERN HOOD RIVER INN.** *1108 E Marina Way (97031), I-84N Exit 64. 541/386-2200; fax 541/386-8905; res 800/528-1234; toll-free 800/828-7873. Email hrinn@gorge.net; www.hoodriverinn.com.* 142 rms, 3 story, 7 suites. May-Sep: S $84; D $119; each addl $12; suites $180; under 17 free; lower rates rest of yr. Crib avail. Pet accepted, some restrictions, fee. Parking lot. Pool, whirlpool. TV; cable (DSS). Complimentary coffee in rms, newspaper, toll-free calls. Restaurant 6 am-10 pm. Bar. Ck-out noon, ck-in 4 pm. Meeting rms. Business center. Bellhops. Dry cleaning, coin lndry. Gift shop. Golf. Tennis, 4 courts. Downhill skiing. Beach access. Bike rentals. Picnic facilities. Video games. Cr cds: A, C, D, DS, MC, V.

D ⚒ ⚒ ⚒ ⚒ ⚒ ⚒ ⚒ ⚒ ⚒ ⚒

Resort

★★★ **SKAMANIA LODGE.** *1131 SW Skamania Lodge Dr (98648), W on I-84, Exit 44, cross Bridge of the Gods to WA 14, then E to Stevenson. 509/427-7700; fax 509/427-2547; toll-free 800/376-9116. Email reservations@skamania.com; www. skamania.com.* 195 rms, 4 story, 5 suites. July-Sep: S, D $169; each addl $15; suites $279; under 11 free; lower rates rest of yr. Crib avail. Parking lot. Indoor pool, lap pool, whirlpool. TV; cable, VCR avail. Complimentary coffee in rms, newspaper, toll-free calls. Restaurant 7 am-9 pm. Bar. Ck-out 11 am, ck-in 4 pm. Meeting rms. Business center. Bellhops. Dry cleaning. Gift shop. Exercise rm, sauna. Golf, 18 holes. Tennis, 2 courts. Downhill skiing. Bike rentals. Hiking trail. Video games. Cr cds: A, D, DS, JCB, MC, V.

D ⚒ ⚒ ⚒ ⚒ ⚒ ⚒ ⚒ ⚒ ⚒ ⚒ ⚒

B&Bs/Small Inns

★★★ COLUMBIA GORGE HOTEL.
4000 Westcliff Dr (97031), I-84 Exit 62. 541/386-5566; fax 541/387-5414; toll-free 800/345-1921. Email cghotel@ gorge.net; www.columbiagorgehotel.com. 39 rms, 4 story. S, D $200. Pet accepted, fee. Parking lot. TV; cable, VCR avail. Complimentary full bkfst, coffee in rms, newspaper, toll-free calls. Restaurant. Bar. Ck-out noon, ck-in 4 pm. Meeting rms. Business center. Concierge. Gift shop. Golf. Downhill skiing. Beach access. Bike rentals. Hiking trail. Picnic facilities. Cr cds: A, C, D, DS, JCB, MC, V.

★★ INN OF THE WHITE SALMON.
172 W Jewett (98672), I-84 E to Exit 64, E on WA 14 for 1½ mi, 1.6 mi to Inn. 509/493-2335; toll-free 800/972-5226. Email innkeeper@gorge.net; www.innofthewhitesalmon.com. 11 rms, 2 story, 5 suites. S $87; D $112; each addl $25; suites $133; under 12 free. Crib avail. Pet accepted, fee. Street parking. TV; cable. Complimentary full bkfst. Restaurant nearby. Ck-out noon, ck-in 3 pm. Business center. Golf, 9 holes. Tennis, 2 courts. Downhill skiing. Hiking trail. Cr cds: A, C, D, DS, JCB, MC, V.

Restaurant

★★★ COLUMBIA RIVER COURT DINING ROOM. *4000 Westcliff Dr. 541/386-5566. Email cghotel@gorge. net; www.columbiagorge.com.* Specializes in wilted spinach salad with apple-smoked duck, fresh salmon, Hood River apple tarte. Own baking. Hrs: 8-11 am, noon-2 pm, 5-9 pm; Sun 8 am-1 pm, 3-8 pm. Res accepted; required hols. Bar. Wine list. Bkfst complete meals: $24.74; lunch prix fixe: 3-course $13.50; dinner a la carte entrees: $18-$30. Entertainment: pianist. View of river gorge. Cr cds: A, D, DS, MC, V.

Jacksonville

See also Ashland, Grants Pass, Medford

Founded 1852 **Pop** 1,896
Elev 1,569 ft **Area code** 541
Zip 97530
Web www.budget.net/~jville/ chamber

Information Historic Jacksonville Chamber of Commerce, PO Box 33; 541/899-8118

Gold was discovered here in 1851 and brought prospectors by the thousands. An active town until the gold strike played out in the 1920s, Jacksonville lost its county seat to the neighboring town of Medford (see) in 1927. Now a national historic landmark, the town is one of the best preserved pioneer communities in the Pacific Northwest. Approximately 80 original buildings can be seen and some visited. A Ranger District office of the Rogue River National Forest (see MEDFORD) is located about 20 miles southwest of town, in Applegate Valley.

What to See and Do

◪ Jacksonville Museum. In Old County Courthouse (1883), has exhibits of southern Oregon history, pioneer relics, early photographs, fashions, toys, Native American artifacts, quilts, natural history. (Memorial Day-Labor Day, daily; rest of yr, Tues-Sun; closed Jan 1, Thanksgiving, Dec 25) Children's Museum is in Old County Jail (1883). 206 N 5th St. Phone 541/773-6536. ¢ Also maintained by the Southern Oregon Historical Society is

Beekman House. (1875) Country Gothic house; former home of a prominent Jacksonville citizen. Living history exhibit. (Memorial Day-Labor Day, daily) 352 E California St. ¢

The Oregon Vortex Location of the House of Mystery. The Vortex is a spherical field of force half above the ground, half below. Natural, historical, educational, and scientific phenomena are found in former assay office and surrounding grounds. Guided lecture tours (Mar-Oct, daily). Approx 10 mi NW on county road, at 4303 Sardine Creek Rd, in Gold Hill. Phone 541/855-1543. ¢¢

Seasonal Event

Britt Musical Festivals. Hillside estate of pioneer photographer Peter Britt forms a natural amphitheatre. Festivals in classical, jazz, folk, country, dance, and musical theater. Phone 541/779-0847 or 800/882-7488. Mid-June-Sep 1.

Motel/Motor Lodge

★ **STAGE LODGE.** *830 N 5th St (97530). 541/899-3953; fax 541/899-7556; toll-free 800/253-8254. Email stgldg@cdsnet.net; www.stagelodge.com.* 25 rms, 2 story, 2 suites. May-Sep: S $69; D $79; each addl $6; suites $140; lower rates rest of yr. Crib avail, fee. Pet accepted, some restrictions, fee. Parking lot. TV; cable (premium), VCR avail. Complimentary continental bkfst, toll-free calls. Restaurant nearby. Ck-out 11 am, ck-in 2 pm. Business servs avail. Golf. Cr cds: A, D, DS, MC, V.

⬛ 🐾 🎿 🐾

B&Bs/Small Inns

★★ **JACKSONVILLE INN.** *175 E California St (97530). 541/899-1900; fax 541/899-1373; toll-free 800/321-9344. Email jvinn@mind.net; www. jacksonvilleinn.com.* 8 rms, 3 story, 3 suites. Mar-Sep: S $112; D $125; suites $224; lower rates rest of yr. Crib avail. Parking lot. TV; cable (DSS), VCR avail, CD avail. Complimentary full bkfst, coffee in rms, newspaper. Restaurant. Bar. Ck-out 11:30 am. Meeting rms. Business servs avail. Gift shop. Free airport transportation. Steam rm. Golf. Downhill skiing. Bike rentals. Picnic facilities. Cr cds: A, C, D, DS, V.

⬛ 🎿 🐾 🎿

★★ **TOUVELLE HOUSE BED & BREAKFAST.** *455 N Oregon St (97530). 541/899-8938; fax 541/899-3992; toll-free 800/846-8422. Email touvelle@wave.net; www.touvellehouse. com.* 4 rms, 3 story, 2 suites. May-Oct: S, D $140; each addl $25; suites $185; lower rates rest of yr. Parking lot. Pool. TV; cable, VCR avail. Complimentary full bkfst. Restaurant nearby. Bar. Ck-out 11 am, ck-in 3 pm. Meeting rm. Business center.

Concierge. Golf, 18 holes. Tennis, 2 courts. Downhill skiing. Bike rentals. Supervised children's activities. Hiking trail. Picnic facilities. Cr cds: A, DS, MC, V.

🐾 🎿 🎿 🐾

Restaurants

★★★ **JACKSONVILLE INN.** *175 E California St. 541/899-1900. Email jvinn@mind.net; www.jacksonvilleinn. com.* Specializes in prime rib, fresh salmon in season, veal scallopini. Hrs: 7:30 am-2 pm, 5-10 pm; Sun to 9 pm. Closed Thanksgiving, Dec 24, 25. Res accepted. Bar. Wine list. Bkfst $5.95-$9.95; lunch $6.95-$14.95; dinner $13.95-$41.95. Bldg dates to gold-rush era. Cr cds: A, C, D, DS, MC, V.

★★★ **MCCULLY HOUSE.** *240 E California (97530). 541/899-1942. Email mccully@ucive.net; www.mccully houseinn.com.* Specializes in international, New Orleans cuisine. Hrs: 10 am-2 pm; 5-9 pm; winter hrs vary. Res accepted. Bar. Lunch $8.95-$13.95; dinner $10.95-$24.95. Entertainment. One of the first houses built in town (1861). Rose garden. 3 guest rms avail. Cr cds: A, D, DS, MC, V.

⬛

John Day (C-6)

Pop 1,836 **Elev** 3,085 ft
Area code 541 **Zip** 97845
Information Grant County Chamber of Commerce, 281 W Main; 541/575-0547 or 800/769-5664

John Day, named for a heroic scout in the first Astor expedition, was once a Pony Express stop on trail to The Dalles. Logging and cattle raising are the major industries in the area. Headquarters for the Malheur National Forest is located here; two Ranger District offices of the forest are also located here.

What to See and Do

Grant County Historical Museum. Mementos of gold-mining days, Joaquin Miller cabin, Greenhorn jail (1910). (June-Sep, Mon-Sat, also Sun afternoons) 2 mi S on US 395 at 101 S Canyon City Blvd in Canyon City. Phone 541/575-0362 or 541/575-1993. ¢

John Day Fossil Beds National Monument. The monument consists of 3 separate units in Wheeler and Grant counties of north central Oregon; no collecting within monument. Wayside exhibits at points of interest in each unit. 40 mi W on US 26, then 2 mi N on OR 19. Phone 541/987-2333. **FREE** These units incl

Clarno Unit. Consists of hills, bluffs, towering rock palisades, and pinnacles. Self-guided Trail of the Fossils features abundant plant fossils visible in the 35-50 million-yr-old rock. Picnicking. 20 mi W of Fossil on OR 218.

Painted Hills Unit. Displays a colorful, scenic landscape of buff and red layers in the John Day Formation. Self-guided Painted Cove Trail and Leaf Hill Trail. Exhibits; picnicking. 9 mi NW of Mitchell, off US 26 on a county road.

John Day Fossil Beds National Monument

Sheep Rock Unit. Here are outstanding examples of the buff and green layers of the fossil-bearing John Day Formation, Mascall Formation, and Rattlesnake Formation. Visitor center offers picnicking and browsing among fossil displays. Self-guided Island in Time Trail and Story in Stone Trail incl exhibits. 7 mi W of Dayville on OR 19.

Kam Wah Chung & Company Museum. Originally constructed as a trading post on The Dalles Military Rd (1866-67). Now houses Chinese medicine herb collection, shrine, kitchen, picture gallery, Doc Hay's bedroom. (May-Oct, Sat-Thurs) 250 NW Canton, adj to city park. Phone 541/575-0028. ¢

Malheur National Forest. Nearly 1.5 million acres in southwestern part of Blue Mts incl Strawberry Mt and Monument Rock wilderness areas. Trout fishing in Magone, Yellowjacket, and Canyon Meadows Lakes, stream fishing; elk and deer hunting, hiking, winter sports, picnicking, camping. For further information contact Supervisor, PO Box 919. N & S on US 395; E & W on US 26. Phone 541/575-3000. **FREE**

Annual Events

"62" Day Celebration. Canyon City, 1 mi S. Celebrates the discovery of gold in 1862. Medicine wagon and fiddling shows, parade, booths, barbecue, dancing, selection of queen. Second wkend June.

Grant County Fair and Rodeo. Grant County Fairgrounds. Oregon's oldest continuous county fair. Early Aug.

Motels/Motor Lodges

★ **DREAMERS LODGE MOTEL.** *144 N Canyon Blvd (97845), N of jct US 26, 395.* 541/575-0526; fax 541/575-2733; toll-free 800/654-2849. 23 rms, 2 story, 2 suites. Oct-Mar: S $46; D $50; each addl $4; suites $60; under 17 free; lower rates rest of yr. Crib avail, fee. TV; cable (premium), VCR avail, CD avail. Ck-out 11 am, ck-in 2 pm. Golf, 9 holes. Tennis, 2 courts. Cr cds: A, D, DS, MC, V.
🏋️ 🐾 ✈️ 🔄 🐾 **SC**

★ **JOHN DAY SUNSET INN.** *390 W Main St (97845).* 541/575-1462; fax 541/575-1471; toll-free 800/452-4899. 43 rms, 1 suite. May-Sep: S $55; D

$65; each addl $4; children $4; under 8 free; lower rates rest of yr. Crib avail, fee. Pet accepted, some restrictions, fee. Parking lot. Indoor pool, whirlpool. TV; cable (DSS). Complimentary coffee in rms, toll-free calls. Restaurant, closed Mon. Ck-out 12 pm, ck-in 12 pm. Business servs avail. Coin lndry. Exercise privileges. Golf, 18 holes. Tennis, 4 courts. Hiking trail. Picnic facilities. Cr cds: A, C, D, DS, ER, JCB, MC, V.

Joseph (B-7)

Pop 1,073 **Elev** 4,190 ft
Area code 541 **Zip** 97846
Web www.eoni.com/~wallowa/
Information Wallowa County Chamber of Commerce, 107 SW 1st St, PO Box 427, Enterprise 97828; 541/426-4622 or 800/585-4121

Joseph is located in the isolated wilderness of northeast Oregon. Remote from industry, the town attracts vacationers with its beautiful surroundings. There are fishing lakes here and hunting in the surrounding area. At the north end of Wallowa Lake is Old Joseph Monument, a memorial to the Nez Perce chief who resisted the US government. A Ranger District office of the Wallowa-Whitman National Forest (see BAKER) is located in nearby Enterprise.

What to See and Do

Hells Canyon National Recreation Area. Created by the Snake River, at the Idaho/Oregon border, Hells Canyon is the deepest gorge in North America—1½ mi from Idaho's He Devil Mt (elevation 9,393 ft) to the Snake River at Granite Creek (elevation 1,408 ft). Overlooks at Hat Point, SE of Imnaha, and in Idaho (see GRANGEVILLE, ID); both are fire lookouts. The recreation area incl parts of the Wallowa-Whitman National Forest in Oregon, and the Nez Perce and Payette national forests in Idaho. Activities incl float trips, jet boat tours, boat trips into canyon from Lewiston, ID (see) or the Hells Canyon Dam (see WEISER, ID); auto tours; backpacking and horseback riding. Developed campgrounds in Oregon and Idaho; much of the area is undeveloped, some is designated wilderness. Be sure to inquire about road conditions before planning a trip; some are rough and open for a limited season. For a commercial outfitters guide list and further information contact Hells Canyon National Recreation Area Office, 88401 OR 82, Enterprise 97828. 30 mi NE on County Road 350 in Wallowa-Whitman National Forest (see BAKER). Phone 541/426-4978; for river information and float res contact PO Box 699, Clarkston, WA 99403, phone 509/758-1957.

Valley Bronze of Oregon. Company produces finished castings of bronze, fine and sterling silver, and stainless steel. Showrm displays finished pieces. Tours of foundry depart from showrm (by res). (May-Nov, daily; rest of yr, by appt) 018 S Main. Phone 541/432-7445. Showroom **FREE**; Foundry tours ¢¢

Wallowa Lake State Park. Park has 201 forested acres in an alpine setting formed by a glacier at the base of the rugged Wallowa Mts. Swimming, water sport equipment rentals, fishing, boating (dock, motor rentals), picnicking, concession, improved tent and trailer sites (dump station). Standard fees. Park at edge of Eagle Cap wilderness area; hiking and riding trails begin here. Horse stables nearby. 6 mi S on OR 82. Phone 541/432-4185.

Wallowa Lake Tramway. Gondola rises from valley to Mt Howard summit. Snack bar at summit. (June-Sep, daily; May, wkends, weather permitting) 6 mi S on OR 82. Phone 541/432-5331. ¢¢¢

Annual Event

Chief Joseph Days. PRCA rodeo, parades, Native American dances, cowboy breakfasts. Contact Chamber of Commerce. Last full wkend July.

Motels/Motor Lodges

★ **INDIAN LODGE MOTEL.** *201 S Main (97846). 541/432-2651; fax 541/432-4949; res 541/432-2651; toll-free 888/286-5484.* 16 rms. Apr: S $35; D $50; lower rates rest of yr. Crib avail, fee. Pet accepted, some restrictions. Parking lot. TV; cable.

Complimentary coffee in rms, toll-free calls. Restaurant 7 am-8 pm. Ck-out 11 am, ck-in 10 pm. Free airport transportation. Golf. Cr cds: DS, MC, V.

★★ **WALLOWA LAKE LODGE.** *60060 Wallowa Lake Hwy (97846), 6 mi S on OR 82. 541/432-9821; fax 503/432-4885. Email info@wallowa lake.com; www.wallowalake.com.* 22 units, 3 story, 2 suites, 8 kit. cottages. No A/C. No elvtr. No rm phones. No TVs. May-mid Oct: S, D $75-$165; family rates; lower rates rest of yr. Restaurant 7 am-1 pm, 5:30-9 pm. Ck-out 11 am. Meeting rms. Downhill ski 16 mi. On Wallowa Lake; swimming. Totally nonsmoking. Cr cds: DS, MC, V.

Resort

★ **FLYING ARROW RESORT.** *59782 Wallowa Lake Hwy (97846). 541/432-2951.* June-Sep: D $145; lower rates rest of yr. Street parking. Indoor/outdoor pools. TV; cable, VCR avail. Ck-out 11 am, ck-in 2 pm. Golf. Downhill skiing. Hiking trail. Cr cds: DS, MC, V.

B&B/Small Inn

★★ **CHANDLERS BED BREAD TRAIL INN.** *700 S Main St (97846). 541/432-9765; fax 541/432-4303; toll-free 800/452-3781. Email chanbbti@ eoni.com; www.eoni.com/~chanbbti.* 5 rms, 2 share bath, 2 story. No A/C. No rm phones. S $50-$70; D $60-$80; each addl $10. Children over 11 yrs only. Whirlpool. Complimentary full bkfst. Ck-out 11 am, ck-in 2 pm. Downhill/x-country ski 6 mi. Picnic tables. Cedar and log interiors with high vaulted ceilings. Outdoor gazebo. Totally nonsmoking. Cr cds: MC, V.

Klamath Falls (F-3)

Settled 1867 **Pop** 17,737 **Elev** 4,105 ft
Area code 541

Web www.klamathcountytourism. com

Information Klamath County Department of Tourism, 1451 Main St, 97601; 541/884-0666 or 800/445-6728

The closest sizable town to Crater Lake National Park (see) with more than 100 good fishing lakes nearby, Klamath Falls is host to sports-minded people. Upper Klamath Lake, the largest body of fresh water in Oregon, runs north of town for 30 miles. White pelicans, protected by law, nest here each summer, and a large concentration of bald eagles winter in the Klamath Basin. Headquarters and a Ranger District office of the Winema National Forest are located here.

What to See and Do

Collier Memorial State Park and Logging Museum. A 655-acre park located at the confluence of Spring Creek and Williamson River. Open-air historic logging museum with display of tools, machines, and engines; various types of furnished 1800s-era pioneer cabins; gift shop (daily; free). Fishing; hiking, picnicking, tent and trailer campsites (hookups, dump station). Standard fees. 30 mi N, on both sides of US 97. Phone 541/783-2471.

Favell Museum of Western Art and Native American Artifacts. Contemporary Western art; working miniature gun collection; extensive display of Native American artifacts. Also art and print sales galleries. Gift shop. (Mon-Sat; closed Jan 1, Thanksgiving, Dec 25) 125 W Main. Phone 541/882-9996. ¢¢

Fort Klamath Museum. Housed in a log replica of the original guardhouse built on the 8-acre Fort Klamath frontier post (established 1863 to promote peaceful relations between natives and early settlers). Contains displays of clothes, equipment, firearms, original artifacts from the fort, and other relics of the period. Picnic area. (June-Labor Day, Thurs-Mon; closed hols) 36 mi NW via US 97, OR 62 to Fort Klamath. Phone 541/883-4208. **Donation**

Jackson F. Kimball State Park. A 19-acre pine and fir timbered area at headwaters of Wood River, noted for its transparency and deep blue appearance. Fishing; picnicking, primitive campsites. Standard fees. 40 mi N on US 97, OR 62 to Fort Klamath, then 3 mi N on OR 232. Phone 541/783-2471.

Klamath County Baldwin Hotel Museum. Restored turn-of-the-century hotel contains many original furnishings. Guided tours (June-Sep, Tues-Sat; closed hols). 31 Main St. Phone 541/883-4207. ¢¢

Klamath County Museum. Local geology, history, wildlife, and Native American displays; research library has books on history, natural history, and anthropology of Pacific Northwest. (Mon-Sat; closed hols) 1451 Main St. Phone 541/883-4208. ¢

Migratory Bird Refuge. (in OR and CA) Major stopover on Pacific Flyway. There are 6 national wildlife refuges in the Klamath Basin. Upper Klamath and Klamath Marsh refuges lie to the N, and Lower Klamath, Bear Valley, Tule Lake, and Clear Lake lie to the S of the city. There is a visitor center with exhibits at refuge headquarters at Tule Lake (daily). Waterfowl (Mar-Apr, Oct-Nov); bald eagles (Dec-Mar); migratory birds (Mar-Apr); waterfowl and colonial bird nesting (summer). S on OR 39 and CA 139 to Tulelake, CA, then 5 mi W on East-West Rd. Phone 916/667-2231. **FREE**

Winema National Forest. This forest (more than 1 million acres) incl former reservation lands of the Klamath Tribe; high country of Sky Lakes; portions of Pacific Crest National Scenic Trail; recreation areas in Lake of the Woods, Recreation Creek, Mt Lakes Wilderness, and Mt Theilson Wilderness. Swimming, boating; picnicking, camping (some areas free). For information contact Supervisor, 2819 Dahlia St. N, E & W, reached by US 97, OR 62 or OR 140. Phone 541/883-6714. Camping ¢¢¢

Annual Events

Bald Eagle Conference. Mid-Feb.

Klamath Memorial Rodeo & Powwow. Late May.

Klamath County Fair. Early Aug.

Jefferson State Stampede. Early Aug.

Motels/Motor Lodges

★★ **BEST WESTERN KLAMATH INN.** *4061 S 6th St (97603), near Kingsley Field Airport. 541/882-1200; fax 541/882-2729; res 800/528-1234; toll-free 877/882-1200. www.best western.com/klamathinn.* 52 rms, 2 story. May-Sep: S $79; D $83; each addl $4; under 17 free; lower rates rest of yr. Crib avail, fee. Pet accepted, some restrictions. Parking lot. Indoor pool. TV; cable (premium). Complimentary continental bkfst, coffee in rms, toll-free calls. Restaurant. Ck-out 11 am, ck-in 2 pm. Meeting rm. Business servs avail. Dry cleaning. Free airport transportation. Golf, 18 holes. Tennis, 2 courts. Hiking trail. Picnic facilities. Cr cds: A, C, D, DS, MC, V.

D 🏊 👟 🛐 📠 🛏 🍴 🛝 🐾 SC

★ **CIMARRON MOTOR INN.** *3060 S 6th St (97603). 541/882-4601; fax 541/882-6690; toll-free 800/742-2648.* 163 rms, 2 story. S $45; D $50-$55; each addl $5; under 10 free. Crib avail. Pet accepted; $5. TV; cable (premium). Heated pool. Continental bkfst. Restaurant adj open 24 hrs. Ck-out noon. Meeting rm. Business servs avail. Cr cds: A, DS, MC, V.

D 🏊 🛝 🍴 🐾 SC

★★ **HOLIDAY INN EXPRESS.** *2500 S 6th St (97601). 541/884-9999; fax 541/882-4020; res 800/465-4329.* 57 rms, 2 story, 15 suites. S, D $62-$80; each addl $8; suites $95-$125; under 17 free; family rates. Crib free. TV; cable (premium), VCR avail. Indoor pool; whirlpool. Complimentary continental bkfst. Restaurant nearby. Ck-out noon. Coin lndry. Meeting rms. Business servs avail. Exercise equipt. Refrigerators, microwaves. Cr cds: A, C, D, DS, MC, V.

D 🛝 🛐 🍴 🍴 🐾

★★ **QUALITY INN & SUITES.** *100 Main St (97601). 541/882-4666; fax 541/883-8795; toll-free 800/732-2025. www.multi.com/molatore.* 80 rms, 2 story, 4 suites. S $63; D $63-$95.50; each addl $5; suites $93.50; under 18 free. Crib free. Pet accepted, some restrictions. TV; cable (premium). Heated pool. Complimentary continental bkfst. Coffee in rms. Restaurant adj. Ck-out noon. Coin lndry. Meeting rms. Business servs avail. In-rm modem link. Some in-rm whirlpools, microwaves. Cr cds: A, C, D, DS, JCB, MC, V.

[D] [icons] SC

★★ **SHILO INN SUITES HOTEL.** *2500 Almond St (97601), 2 mi NW on US 97 N (Business), Exit OIT.* 541/885-7980; fax 541/885-7959; toll-free 800/222-2244. 143 suites, 4 story. June-Sep: S, D $99-$119; each addl $10; kit. units $149; under 12 free; golf plans; lower rates rest of yr. Crib free. Pet accepted, some restrictions; $7. TV; cable (premium), VCR (movies). Complimentary continental bkfst, complimentary coffee in rms. Restaurant 6 am-11 pm. Bar 11-2 am. Ck-out noon. Meeting rms. Business center. In-rm modem link. Bellhops. Valet serv. Sundries. Coin lndry. Free airport, railroad station transportation. Exercise equipt; sauna. Health club privileges. Indoor pool; whirlpool. Bathrm phones, refrigerators, microwaves, wet bars. Cr cds: A, D, DS, MC, V.

[D] [icons] SC [icon]

★ **SUPER 8.** *3805 Hwy 97 (97601), near Oregon Tech.* 541/884-8880; fax 541/884-0235. www.super8.com. 61 rms, 3 story. No elvtr. June-mid-Sep: S $47.88-$51.88; D $51.88-$61.88; each addl $4; lower rates rest of yr. Crib free. TV; cable. Complimentary coffee in lobby. Restaurant nearby. Ck-out noon. Coin lndry. Whirlpool. Cr cds: A, D, DS, MC, V.

[D] [icons]

Hotel

★★ **BEST WESTERN OLYMPIC INN.** *2627 S 6th St (97603).* 541/882-9665; fax 541/884-3214; res 800/528-1234; toll-free 800/600-9665. www.bestwestern.com. 72 rms, 3 story. June-Sep: S, D $99; each addl $10; suites $129; under 12 free; lower rates rest of yr. Crib avail, fee. Parking lot. Pool, whirlpool. TV; cable (premium), VCR avail. Complimentary continental bkfst, coffee in rms, newspaper, toll-free calls. Restaurant nearby. Ck-out 11 am, ck-in 4 pm. Meeting rm. Business servs avail. Concierge. Dry cleaning. Exercise privileges. Golf. Hiking trail. Cr cds: A, D, DS, MC, V.

[D] [icons] SC

Restaurant

★★ **FIORELLA'S.** *6139 Simmer Ave (97603).* 541/882-1878. Specializes in pasticico, gnocchi, filet mignon. Hrs: 5-9 pm. Closed Sun, Mon; Dec 25. Res accepted. Bar. Extensive wine selection. Dinner $8.50-$19.95. Complete meals: $11.50-$22.50. Child's menu. Cr cds: A, DS, MC, V.

[D]

La Grande

(B-6) *See also Baker City, Pendleton*

Settled 1861 **Pop** 11,766 **Elev** 2,771 ft
Area code 541 **Zip** 97850
Web www.eoni.com/~visitlg

Information La Grande/Union County Visitors & Conventions Bureau, 1912 Fourth Ave, #200; 541/963-8588 or 800/848-9969

Located in the heart of Northeast Oregon amid the Blue and Wallowa mountains, La Grande offers visitors breathtaking scenery and numerous exhilarating activities. Rafting and fishing enthusiasts enjoy the Grande Ronde River; hikers and mountain bikers navigate the Eagle Cap Wilderness and the tracks of the Oregon Trail. A Ranger District office of the Wallowa-Whitman National Forest (see BAKER) is located here.

What to See and Do

Catherine Creek State Park. A 160-acre park in pine forest along creek. Fishing; biking, hiking, picnicking, camping. Standard fees. 8 mi SE on OR 203. Phone 541/963-0430 or 541/963-6444.

Eastern Oregon University. (1929) 1,900 students. Campus overlooks the town. Liberal arts college. Rock and mineral collection displayed in science bldg (Mon-Fri; closed hols; free). Nightingale Gallery, concerts, theatrical productions, in Loso Hall; changing exhibits. 1410 L Avenue. Phone 541/962-3672.

Hilgard Junction State Recreation Area. A 233-acre park on the old Oregon Trail. Fishing. Picnicking. Camping (daily). Exhibits at Oregon

Trail Interpretive Center (Memorial Day-Labor Day, daily). Standard fees. 8 mi W off I-84N. Phone 541/963-0430 or 541/963-6444.

Turns of the Brick. Self-guided walking tour of 30 turn-of-the-century bldgs and ghost signs. Approx 1-hr tour incl McGlasson's Stationery (1890), Masonic Lodge & JC Penney Co (ca 1900), Fire Station Bldg (1898), and Helm Bldg (1891). Unique brickwork and architecture explained in brochure avail from La Grande Downtown Development Assn. 105 Fir, Suite 321. Phone 503/963-0364. **FREE.**

Annual Events

Union County Fair. Union County Fairgrounds. Early Aug.

Oregon Trail Days. Celebration of pioneer heritage incl historical events, arts and crafts; oldtime fiddle contest. Mid-Aug.

Motels/Motor Lodges

★ **HOWARD JOHNSON INN.** *2612 Island Ave (97850), 1 mi E on OR 82, E of I-84N, Exit 261.* 541/963-7195; fax 541/963-4498; res 800/446-4656. Email 10239@hotel.cendant.com; www. hojo.com. 146 rms, 2 story. S, D $67-$77; each addl $8; under 18 free; lower rates rest of yr. Pet accepted. TV; cable (premium). Heated pool; whirlpool. Complimentary continental bkfst. Coffee in rms. Restaurant adj open 24 hrs. Ck-out noon. Free lndry. Meeting rms. Business servs avail. Exercise equipt; sauna. Refrigerators. Private patios, balconies. Cr cds: A, DS, MC, V.
D 🐾 🛠 ≈ 🏃 🦺

★ **ROYAL MOTOR INN.** *1510 Adams Ave (97850).* 541/963-4154; fax 541/963-3588; res 800/990-7575. 44 rms, 2 story. S, D $40-$52; each addl $5; under 17 free. Crib free. TV; cable (premium). Coffee in rms. Restaurant nearby. Ck-out 11 am. Cr cds: A, C, D, DS, MC, V.
≈ 🦺 SC

Guest Ranch

★★ **STANG MANOR BED & BREAKFAST.** *1612 Walnut St (97850).* 541/963-2400; toll-free 888/286-9463. Email innkeeper@stangmanor.com; www.stangmanor.com. 3 rms, 2 story, 1 suite. S $77; D $85;

each addl $15; suites $98; children $15. Parking lot. TV; cable (premium), VCR avail. Complimentary full bkfst. Restaurant nearby. Ck-out 11 am, ck-in 3 pm. Meeting rm. Bellhops. Exercise privileges. Golf. Downhill skiing. Cr cds: MC, V.
⊠ 🦺 🏃 ⛷ ≈ 🦺

Lakeview (F-4)

Founded 1876 **Pop** 2,526
Elev 4,798 ft **Area code** 541
Zip 97630
Web www.triax.com/lakecounty/lake co.htm
Information Lake County Chamber of Commerce, 126 North E Street; 541/947-6040

General John C. Fremont and Kit Carson passed through what is now Lake County in 1843. There are antelope and bighorn sheep in the area, many trout streams, and seven lakes nearby. A supervisor's office of the Fremont National Forest is located here; also here is a district office of the Bureau of Land Management and an office of the US Department of Fish and Wildlife.

What to See and Do

Drews Reservoir. Fishing, boating (launch); camping. 15 mi W on Dog Lake Rd.

Fremont National Forest. More than 2 million acres. Incl remnants of ice-age lava flows and the largest and most defined exposed geologic fault in North America, Abert Rim, on E side of Lake Abert. Abert Rim is most spectacular at the E side of Crooked Creek Valley. Many of the lakes are remnants of post-glacial Lake Lahontan. Gearhart Mt Wilderness is rough and forested with unusual rock formations, streams, and Blue Lake. Fishing; hunting, picnicking, camping. For information contact Supervisor, 524 N G St. E & W via OR 140, N & S via US 395 and OR 31. Phone 541/947-2151.

Geyser and Hot Springs. "Old perpetual," said to be largest continuous hot water geyser in the northwest. Spouts as high as 70 ft occur approximately every 90 seconds. Hot springs nearby. 1 mi N on US 395.

Paisley. Unspoiled old Western town. 45 mi N on OR 31.

Schminck Memorial Museum. Pressed-glass goblets, home furnishings, dolls, toys, books, clothing, quilts, guns, saddles, tools, and Native American artifacts. (Feb-Nov, Tues-Sat; also by appt; closed hols) 128 S E St. Phone 541/947-3134. ¢

Annual Events

Irish Days. Mid-Mar.

Junior Rodeo. Last wkend June.

World-Class Hang Gliding Festival. July 4 wkend.

Lake County Fair and Roundup. Labor Day wkend.

Motels/Motor Lodges

★★ **BEST WESTERN INN.** *414 N G St (97630). 541/947-2194; fax 541/947-3100; res 800/528-1234.* 38 rms, 2 story. S $48-$56; D $54-$60; each addl $6; suites $70-$110; higher rates special events. Crib $10. TV; cable (premium). Indoor pool; whirlpool. Complimentary continental bkfst, complimentary coffee in rms. Restaurant adj 6 am-8 pm. Ck-out 11 am. Business servs avail. In-rm modem link. Coin lndry. Downhill/x-country ski 10 mi. Refrigerators, microwaves avail. Cr cds: A, C, D, DS, MC, V.
🛏 🏊 ≈ 🐕 ≋ 🔥

★ **LAKEVIEW LODGE.** *301 N G St (97630), S of jct US 395, OR 140. 541/947-2181; fax 541/947-2572. Email bobkings@triax.com.* 30 rms, 2 story, 10 suites. May-Sep: S $50; D $54; each addl $5; suites $55; children $4; under 12 free; lower rates rest of yr. Crib avail, fee. Pet accepted, some restrictions. Parking lot. TV; cable (premium), VCR avail. Complimentary coffee in rms, newspaper, toll-free calls. Restaurant nearby. Ck-out 11 am, ck-in 3 pm. Business servs avail. Bellhops. Dry cleaning. Free airport transportation. Exercise equipt, whirlpool. Golf, 9 holes. Tennis, 4 courts. Downhill skiing. Hiking trail. Cr cds: A, C, D, DS, MC, V.
D 🐕 🏊 🛷 🎿 🚶 ⛷ ≈ 🔥 SC

Lincoln City

(B-1) *See also Depoe Bay, Newport, Tillamook*

Pop 5,892 **Elev** 11-115 ft
Area code 541 **Zip** 97367
Information Visitor & Convention Bureau, 801 SW Hwy 101, Suite #1; 541/994-8378 or 800/452-2151

Nicknamed the "kite capital of the world," Lincoln City is a popular recreation, art, and shopping area offering many accommodations with ocean view rooms.

What to See and Do

Alder House II. Set in a grove of alder trees, this is the oldest glass blowing studio in Oregon. Watch molten glass drawn from a furnace and shaped into pieces of traditional or modern design. (Mid-Mar-Nov; daily) 611 Immonen Rd, ½ mi E off US 101. **FREE**

Devil's Lake State Park. A 109-acre park with swimming, fishing, boating (ramp on E side of Devil's Lake), tent and trailer sites (on NW side of lake). Standard fees. S of town, off US 101. Phone 541/994-2002.

Theatre West. Community theater featuring comedy and drama. (Thurs-Sat) 3536 SE US 101. Phone 541/994-5663 for res.

Motels/Motor Lodges

★★ **BEST WESTERN LINCOLN SANDS.** *535 NW Inlet Ave (97367). 541/994-4227; fax 541/994-2232; res 800/528-1234; toll-free 800/445-3234.* 33 kit. suites, 3 story. Suites $99-$369. Crib $10. Pet accepted, some restrictions. TV; cable (premium), VCR. Heated pool; whirlpool. Complimentary continental bkfst, coffee in rms. Restaurant nearby. Ck-out 11 am. In-rm modem link. Exercise equipt; sauna. Microwaves. Balconies. On beach. Cr cds: A, DS, MC, V.
D 🐕 ≈ 🔥 SC

★ **COHO INN.** *1635 NW Harbor Ave (97367), W of US 101. 541/994-3684; fax 503/994-6244; toll-free 800/848-7006. www.thecohoinn.com.* 50 rms, 3 story, 31 kits. No A/C. No elvtr. June-Oct: S, D $100; each addl $6; suites $104-$128; lower rates rest of yr. Pet accepted, some restrictions; $6. TV; cable (premium). Complimentary coffee in lobby. Ck-out 11 am. Business servs avail. Sauna. Whirlpool. Some fireplaces. Some private patios, balconies. Oceanfront; beach nearby. Cr cds: A, DS, MC, V.

★ **COZY COVE BEACH FRONT RESORT.** *515 NW Inlet Ave (97367). 541/994-2950; fax 541/996-4332; toll-free 800/553-2683. Email cozybay@juno.com.* 70 rms, 2-3 story, 33 kits. S, D $55-$145; suites $145-$250; kit. units $79-$100. TV; cable, VCR avail (free movies). Heated pool; whirlpool. Complimentary coffee in lobby. Restaurant nearby. Ck-out 11 am. Business servs avail. Sauna. Some in-rm whirlpools, fireplaces. Some private patios, balconies. Picnic tables. On beach. Cr cds: A, DS, MC, V.

★★ **D SANDS MOTEL.** *171 SW US 101 (97367). 541/994-5244; fax 541/994-7484; toll-free 800/527-3925. www.o-t-b.com/dsands.htm.* 63 kit. units, 3 story. No elvtr. May-Oct: S, D $124-$149; each addl $10; under 8 free; lower rates mid-wk off-season. Crib free. TV; cable (premium), VCR (movies). Indoor pool; whirlpool. Complimentary coffee in lobby. Restaurant nearby. Ck-out 11 am. Business servs avail. Some fireplaces. Some private balconies. On ocean, beach. Cr cds: A, DS, MC, V.

★★★ **INN AT SPANISH HEAD.** *4009 S US 101 (97367). 541/996-2161; fax 541/996-4089; toll-free 800/452-8127. Email spanishhead@ newportnet.com.* 120 kit. units, 10 story. S, D $129-$169; each addl $15; suites $199-$289; under 16 free. Crib free. TV; cable, VCR avail (movies). Heated pool; whirlpool. Restaurant 8 am-2 pm, 5-9 pm; Sun-Thurs in winter to 8 pm. Bar 2 pm to close; winter from 5 pm. Ck-out noon. Meeting rms. Business servs avail. Bellhops. Valet parking. Exercise equipt; sauna. Game rm. Many private balconies. Built on side of cliff; ocean view. Cr cds: A, C, D, DS, MC, V.

★★ **NORDIC MOTEL.** *2133 NW Inlet Ave (97367). 541/994-8145; fax 541/994-2329; res 800/452-3558. Email nordicmotel@wcn.net; www. nordicmotel.com.* 52 rms, 3 story. July-Aug: S, D $79; each addl $10; suites $110; lower rates rest of yr. Crib avail. Parking lot. Indoor pool, whirlpool. TV; cable (premium), VCR avail, VCR avail. Complimentary continental bkfst, coffee in rms, toll-free calls. Restaurant nearby. Ck-out noon, ck-in 4 pm. Meeting rm. Business center. Sauna. Golf, 18 holes. Tennis, 2 courts. Beach access. Cr cds: A, C, D, DS, MC, V.

★ **PELICAN SHORES INN.** *2645 NW Inlet Ave (97367), W of US 101. 541/994-2134; fax 541/994-4963; toll-free 800/705-5505. Email stay@pelican shores.com; www.pelicanshores.com.* 35 rms, 3 story, 20 suites. June-Sep: S, D $79; each addl $5; suites $109; children $5; lower rates rest of yr. Crib avail, fee. Parking lot. Indoor pool. TV; cable (premium), VCR avail. Complimentary coffee in rms, newspaper, toll-free calls. Ck-out 11 am, ck-in 3 pm. Golf. Beach access. Cr cds: A, C, D, DS, MC, V.

★★ **SHILO INN OCEANFRONT RESORT.** *1501 NW 40th Pl (97367). 541/994-3655; fax 541/994-2199.* 247 rms, 3-4 story. Mid-June-mid-Sep: S $49-$102; D $84-$110; suites $169-$240; kit. unit $125-$160; under 12 free; lower rates rest of yr. Crib free. Pet accepted, some restrictions; $6/day. TV; cable (premium), VCR avail. Indoor pool; whirlpool. Restaurant adj 7-2 am. Bar 11-1 am. Ck-out noon. Coin lndry. Meeting rms. Business center. Free airport, bus depot transportation. Exercise equipt; sauna. Health club privileges. Refrigerators, microwaves; some bathrm phones. Picnic tables. On beach. Cr cds: A, C, D, DS, ER, JCB, MC, V.

Hotel

★★ **QUALITY INN.** *136 NE US 101 (97367). 541/994-8155; fax 541/ 994-5581; res 800/228-5151; toll-free 800/423-6240.* 28 rms, 3 story, 2 suites. June-Sep: S $149; D $159; each addl $10; suites $199; under 18 free; lower rates rest of yr. Parking lot. TV; cable (premium). Complimentary continental bkfst, coffee in rms, newspaper, toll-free calls. Restaurant. Ck-out 11 am, ck-in 4 pm. Business servs avail. Golf. Cr cds: A, C, D, DS, ER, MC, V.

Resort

★★★ **WESTIN SALISHAN LODGE.** *US 101 (97388), 1 blk E of US 101.* 541/764-2371; *fax* 541/764-3681; *toll-free* 800/452-2300. *Email sales@salishan.com; www.salishan.com.* 199 rms, 3 story, 3 suites. July-Oct: S, D $199; each addl $20; suites $375; lower rates rest of yr. Crib avail. Pet accepted, fee. Valet parking avail. Indoor pool, lap pool, whirlpool. TV; cable (premium), VCR avail. Complimentary coffee in rms, newspaper, toll-free calls. Restaurant 6 am-9:30 pm. 24-hr rm serv. Bar. Ck-out noon, ck-in 4:30 pm. Meeting rms. Business center. Bellhops. Concierge. Dry cleaning. Gift shop. Exercise equipt, sauna. Golf, 18 holes. Tennis, 4 courts. Beach access. Bike rentals. Supervised children's activities. Hiking trail. Picnic facilities. Video games. Cr cds: A, C, D, ER, JCB, MC, V.

Villa/Condo

★★ **DOCK OF THE BAY MOTEL.** *1116 SW 51st (97367).* 541/996-3549; *fax* 541/996-4759; *toll-free* 800/362-5229. *Email bhudson@wcn.net; www.dockofthebay-or.com.* 3 story, 24 suites. June-Sep: suites $225; each addl $10; under 13 free; lower rates rest of yr. Crib avail. Parking garage. TV; cable, VCR avail. Complimentary coffee in rms. Ck-out 11 am, ck-in 2 pm. Business servs avail. Golf. Beach access. Bike rentals. Hiking trail. Picnic facilities. Cr cds: DS, MC, V.

Restaurants

★★★ **BAY HOUSE.** *5911 SW US 101 (97367).* 541/996-3222. Specializes in fresh seafood, game, pasta. Hrs: 5:30-9 pm; Sat from 5 pm. Closed Dec 25; Mon, Tues Nov-Apr.

Res accepted. Dinner $18-$26. Overlooking Siletz Bay. Cr cds: A, DS, MC, V.

★★ **CHEZ JEANNETTE.** *7150 Old US 101 (97388).* 541/764-3434. Specializes in seafood, rack of lamb, game. Hrs: 5:30-10 pm. Res accepted. Dinner $20-$29. Child's menu. French cottage decor; built 1920. Cr cds: A, DS, MC, V.

★★ **THE DINING ROOM AT SALISHAN.** *7760 N US 101.* 541/764-2371. *www.salishan.com.* Specializes in Oregon lamb, fresh seafood, regional cuisine. Own baking. Hrs: 6-9 pm. Res accepted. Wine cellar. Dinner $10-$28. Child's menu. Entertainment. Valet parking. Cr cds: A, D, DS, MC, V.

★ **DORY COVE.** *5819 Logan Rd (97367), N on Logan Rd, adj to Roads End State Park.* 541/994-5180. Specializes in seafood. Hrs: 11:30 am-9 pm; Sun noon-8 pm; winter to 8 pm. Wine, beer. Lunch $4-$10; dinner $9-$20. Child's menu. Entertainment. Some tables have ocean view. Cr cds: A, DS, MC, V.

Madras

(C-4) *See also Prineville, Redmond*

Pop 3,443 **Elev** 2,242 ft
Area code 541 **Zip** 97741
Information Chamber of Commerce, 197 SE 5th St, PO Box 770; 541/475-2350 or 800/967-3564

Although the area was explored as early as 1825, settlement here was difficult because of Native American hostility. Settlement east of the Cascades, considered a wall of separation between the Native Americans and the settlers, was officially forbidden in 1856. In 1858 the order was revoked, and in 1862 the first road was built across the Cascades to provide a passage for traders. Shortly thereafter, settlement began in earnest.

What to See and Do

The Cove Palisades State Park. A 4,130-acre park on Lake Billy Chinook behind Round Butte Dam; scenic canyon of geological interest; spectacular views of the confluence of the Crooked, Deschutes, and Metolius rivers forming Lake Billy Chinook in a steep basaltic canyon. Swimming, fishing, boating (ramp, dock, rentals, marina with restaurant, groceries), houseboat rentals; hiking, picnicking, tent and trailer sites (dump station). Standard fees. 15 mi SW off US 97. Phone 541/546-3412.

Jefferson County Museum. Located in the old courthouse; old-time doctor's equipment; military memorabilia; homestead and farm equipment. (June-Sep, Tues-Fri afternoons) 34 Southeast D Street, 1 blk off Main St. Phone 541/475-3808. **Donation**

Rockhounding. Richardson's Recreational Ranch. All diggings accessible by road; highlight of ranch are famous agate beds, featuring Thunder Eggs and ledge agate material. Rockhound campground area (no hookups). Digging fee. 11 mi N on US 97, then right 3 mi to ranch office. Phone 541/475-2680.

Annual Events

Collage of Culture. Friendship Park. Music and balloon festival celebrating cultural diversity. Mid-May.

All Rockhounds Powwow Gem & Mineral Show. Jefferson County Fairgrounds. Field trips, entertainment, swapping. Late June or early July.

Motel/Motor Lodge

★★ **SONNY'S MOTEL.** *1539 SW Hwy 97 (97741). 541/475-7217; fax 541/475-6547; res 800/624-6137. www.sonnysmotel.com.* 44 rms, 2 story, 2 suites, 2 kits. S $47; D $55; each addl $8; suites $80-$105; kit. units $95; under 6 free. Crib $4. Pet accepted; $10. TV; cable (premium). Heated pool; whirlpool. Complimentary continental bkfst. Restaurant 3-10 pm. Bar to midnight. Ck-out 11 am. Coin lndry. Business servs avail. Lawn games. Some

microwaves; refrigerators avail. Cr cds: A, DS, MC, V.

Resort

★★★ **KAH-NEE-TA LODGE.** *100 Main St (97761), 14 mi NW on US 26 to Warm Springs, then 11 mi N. 541/553-1112; fax 541/553-1071; toll-free 800/554-4786. www.kah-nee-taresort. com.* 139 rms in 3-4 story lodge, 32 condos, 20 unfurnished teepees in village. Lodge: S, D $115-$140; suites $170-$275; condos: $109.95; village teepees for 5, $55; under 6 free in lodge; mid-wk packages (off-season). Pet accepted. TV; cable (premium). 2 heated pools; whirlpools; poolside serv, private hot mineral baths at village. Dining rm 7 am-10 pm. Snacks. Salmon Bake Sat (Memorial Day-Labor Day). Bars 11 am-2 pm. Ck-out 11:30 am, ck-in 4:30 pm. Lodge meeting rms. Gift shop. Tennis. 18-hole golf, greens fee $32, pro, putting green, driving range. Exercise rm; sauna. Massage. Kayak float trips. Trails. Bicycles. Rec dir; entertainment. Game rm. Authentic Native American dances Sun May-Sep. Varied accommodations. Owned by Confederated Tribes of Warm Springs Reservation. RV and trailer spaces avail. Casino. Cr cds: A, C, D, DS, MC, V.

McKenzie Bridge

Pop 200 (est) **Elev** 1,337 ft
Area code 541 **Zip** 97413
Web www.el.com/to/Mckenzieriver valley/
Information McKenzie River Chamber of Commerce and Information Center, MP 24 McKenzie Hwy East (OR 126), PO Box 1117, Leaburg 97489; 541/896-3330 or 541/896-9011

McKenzie Bridge and the neighboring town of Blue River are located on the beautiful McKenzie River, with covered bridges, lakes, waterfalls, and wilderness trails of the Cascades nearby. Fishing, float trips, skiing, and backpacking are some of the many activities available. Ranger District offices of the Willamette National Forest (see EUGENE) are located here and in Blue River.

What to See and Do

Blue River Dam & Lake. Saddle Dam Boating Site offers boat ramp. Mona Campground offers swimming, fishing; picnicking (fee). Dam is a US Army Corps of Engineers project. Recreation areas administered by the US Forest Service. Camping (mid-May-mid-Sep; fee). 7 mi W on OR 126, then N on Forest Road 15 in Willamette National Forest. Phone 541/822-3317 (Blue River Ranger Station).

Carmen-Smith Hydroelectric Development. Salmon spawning facility near Trail Bridge Dam; 3 stocked reservoirs—Trail Bridge, Smith, and Carmen (daily). Boat launching (free). Picnicking. Camping at Lake's End, N end of Smith Reservoir, at Ice Cap Creek on Carmen Reservoir and at Trail Bridge (10-day limit). 14 mi NE on OR 126, on Upper McKenzie River. Phone 541/484-2411 or the Ranger District stations. ¢¢¢

Cougar Dam and Lake. Six-mi-long reservoir. Echo Park is a day-use area with boat ramp (free). Slide Creek campground offers swimming, waterskiing; fishing, boat ramp; picnicking (free), camping (fee). Delta and French Pete campgrounds offer fishing; picnicking. Campgrounds maintained and operated by US Forest Service. Dam is a US Army Corps of Engineers project. (May-Sep; most areas closed rest of yr, inquire) For further info inquire at Blue River Ranger Station. 5 mi W on OR 126, then S on Forest Rd 19 (Aufderheide Forest Dr) in Willamette National Forest (see EUGENE). Phone 541/822-3317 or 541/896-3614.

Motel/Motor Lodge

★ **SLEEPY HOLLOW MOTEL.** *54791 McKenzie Hwy (97413), 3 mi W on OR 126.* 541/822-3805. 19 rms, 2 story. Apr-Oct: S $48; D $55; each addl $10; lower rates rest of yr. TV; cable, VCR avail. Restaurant nearby. Ck-out 11 am, ck-in 2 pm. Golf. Cr cds: MC, V.

Restaurant

★★ **LOG CABIN INN.** *56483 McKenzie Hwy (97413).* 541/822-3432. *Email lci@rio.com; www.logcabininn. com.* Specializes in mesquite-smoked barbecued fish, game. Hrs: noon-9 pm; Sun from 9 am. Res accepted. Bar. Lunch $5.95-$8.95; dinner $10.95-$17.95. Sun brunch $8.95. Child's menu. Built as stagecoach stop in 1906. Cr cds: A, MC, V.
D

McMinnville

(B-2) *See also Newberg, Oregon City, Salem*

Pop 17,894 **Elev** 160 ft **Area code** 503 **Zip** 97128
Web www.mcminnville.org
Information Chamber of Commerce, 417 N Adams; 503/472-6196

McMinnville is in the center of a wine-producing area. Many of the wineries offer tours.

What to See and Do

Community Theater. Musical, comedy, and drama productions by the Gallery Players of Oregon (Fri-Sun). Phone 503/472-2227.

Linfield College. (1849) 2,100 students. Liberal arts. On the 100-acre campus are Renshaw Art Gallery, Linfield Anthropology Museum, and the Linfield Theater. The music department offers concerts. Lectures and events throughout the yr. Phone 503/434-2000.

Annual Events

Wine & Food Classic. Mid-Mar.
Turkey Rama. Mid-July.
Yamhill County Fair. Late July-early Aug.

Motel/Motor Lodge

★★ **SAFARI MOTOR INN.** *345 NE Highway 99W (97128).* 503/472-5187; fax 503/474-6380; res 800/321-5543. 90 rms, 2 story. S $54; D $58; each addl $3; children $3. Crib avail. Parking lot. TV; cable. Complimentary coffee in rms, newspaper. Restaurant 6 am-9 pm. Bar. Ck-out noon, ck-in 3 pm. Meeting rms. Business center. Dry cleaning. Exercise privileges, whirlpool. Golf, 18 holes. Picnic facilities. Cr cds: A, C, D, DS, MC, V.

Resort

★★ **FLYING M RANCH.** *23029 NW Flying M Rd (97148), N on OR 47 to Yamhill, left on Oak Ridge Rd, left on Fairdale Rd, left on NW Flying M Rd.* 503/662-3222; fax 503/662-3202. Email flyingm@bigplanet.com; www. flying-m-ranch.com. 24 rms. S, D $60. Pet accepted, some restrictions. Parking lot. TV; cable. Restaurant. Bar. Ck-out 11 am, ck-in 3 pm. Meeting rms. Fax servs avail. Gift shop. Golf. Hiking trail. Picnic facilities. Cr cds: A, D, DS, MC, V.

B&B/Small Inn

★★ **STEIGER HAUS BED & BREAKFAST.** *360 SE Wilson St (97128).* 503/472-0821; fax 503/472-0100; toll-free 888/220-1142. Email steigerhaus@onlinemac.com; www. steigerhaus.com. 2 rms, 3 story, 3 suites. S $65; D $80; each addl $15; suites $130; under 12 free. Parking lot. TV; cable, VCR avail, CD avail. Complimentary full bkfst, toll-free calls. Restaurant nearby. Ck-out 11 am, ck-in 3 pm. Meeting rm. Business center. Concierge. Whirlpool. Golf, 18 holes. Tennis, 3 courts. Picnic facilities. Cr cds: DS, MC, V.

Medford

(F-2) *See also Ashland, Grants Pass, Jacksonville*

Founded 1885 **Pop** 46,951
Elev 1,380 ft **Area code** 541
Information Visitors and Convention Bureau, 101 E 8th St, 97501; 541/779-4847 or 800/469-6307

Medford is a name known throughout the United States for pears: Comice, Bartlett, Winter Nellis, Bosc, and d'Anjou. The city, on Bear Creek 10 miles from its confluence with the Rogue River, is surrounded by orchards. Trees make the city parklike; lumbering provides a large share of the industry. Mild winters and warm summers favor outdoor living and also encourage outdoor sports: boating and fishing on the Rogue River, fishing in 153 stocked streams and 17 lakes; camping and hunting in 56 forest camps within an 80-mile radius. The Rogue River National Forest headquarters is here.

What to See and Do

Butte Creek Mill. Water-powered grist mill (1872) grinds whole grain products with original millstones. Museum (summer, Sat). Mill (Mon-Sat; closed hols). 10 mi N on OR 62 in Eagle Point. Phone 541/826-3531. **FREE**

Crater Rock Museum. Gem and mineral collection; Native American artifacts; fossils, geodes, and crystals. Gift shop. (Tues, Thurs, and Sat; closed hols) N on I-5, Exit 35 then S on OR 99 in Central Point at 2002 Scenic Ave. Phone 541/664-6081. **Donation**

Joseph P. Stewart State Park. A 910-acre park located on lake formed by Lost Creek Dam. Swimming, fishing, boat dock and ramp to Rogue River; hiking and bike trails, picnicking, tent and improved campsites (daily; dump station). Some fees. 35 mi NE on OR 62. Phone 541/560-3334.

✪ **Rogue River National Forest.** Forest has 632,045 acres with extensive stands of Douglas fir, ponderosa, and sugar pine. Rogue-Umpqua National Forest Scenic Byway offers a day-long drive through southern Oregon's dramatic panorama of mountains, rivers, and forests; viewpoints. A part of the Pacific Crest National Scenic Trail and portions of 3 wilderness areas are incl in the forest. For anglers, the upper reaches of the Rogue River, other streams and lakes yield rainbow, cutthroat, and brook trout. Union Creek Historic District, on OR 62 near Crater Lake National Park. Forest is in 2 separate sections, located in the Siskiyou Mts (W of I-5) and

Cascade Range (E of I-5). Swimming; hiking, backpacking, downhill and cross-country skiing, picnic areas, camping. Some fees. For further info contact Info Receptionist, PO Box 520, 333 W 8th St. S off I-5 and NE on OR 62, 140. Phone 541/776-3600.

Southern Oregon History Center. More than 2,000 items from Southern Oregon Historical Society's cultural history collection. Exhibits, public programs, research library. Gift shop. (Mon-Fri) 106 N Central Ave. Phone 541/773-6536. **FREE**.

Tou Velle State Park. A 51-acre park. Fishing on Rogue River, boat ramp to Rogue River; picnicking. 3 mi NE on I-5, then 6 mi N on Table Rock Rd. Phone 541/582-1118. ¢

Annual Events

Pear Blossom Festival. Parade; 10-mi run; band festival. Second wkend Apr.

Jackson County Fair. Jackson County Fairgrounds. Entertainment, dance, music, 4-H fair. Third wkend July.

Motels/Motor Lodges

★★ **BEST INN & SUITES.** *1015 S Riverside Ave (97501). 541/773-8266; fax 541/734-5447; res 800/237-8466; toll-free 800/626-1900. www.bestinn. com.* 112 rms, 2 story, 14 suites. May-Oct: S $52-$60; D $58-$65; each addl $6; suites $89; under 12 free. Crib $6. TV; cable. Pool. Complimentary continental bkfst, coffee in rms. Restaurant nearby. Bar 10-2 am. Ck-out 11 am. Meeting rms. Business servs avail. Downhill/x-country ski 20 mi. Some microwaves. Cr cds: A, C, D, DS, MC, V.

⧉ 🐾 🎿 🏊 🛄 ✕ 🏔 🔥

★★ **BEST WESTERN HORIZON INN.** *1154 E Barnett Rd (97504), E of I-5 Exit 27. 541/779-5085; fax 541/772-6878; res 800/528-1234; toll-free 800/452-2255. Email horizon@vvi.net.* 129 rms, 2 story. S $50-$58; D $55-$61; each addl $5; suites $100-$150; under 17 free. Crib $5. Pet accepted; $10. TV; cable (premium). Heated pool; whirlpool. Complimentary coffee in lobby. Restaurant 6 am-midnight. Bar. Ck-out noon. Airport transportation. Downhill/x-country

ski 20 mi. Sauna. Some microwaves. Cr cds: A, DS, MC, V.

⧉ 🐾 🎿 🏊 🛄 🔥 SC

★★ **BEST WESTERN PONY SOLDIER INN.** *2340 Crater Lake Hwy (94504), E of I-5 Exit 30. 541/779-2011; fax 541/779-7304; res 800/528-1234; toll-free 800/634PONY. Email www.ponymp@aol.com.* 74 rms, 2 story. May-Sep: S $92; D $94; each addl $5; under 11 free; lower rates rest of yr. Crib avail. TV; cable (premium), VCR avail. Restaurant. Ck-out noon, ck-in 2 pm. Golf. Cr cds: A, C, D, DS, MC, V.

🛗 ✕ 🏔 🔥 SC

★ **CEDAR LODGE MOTOR INN.** *518 N Riverside (97501). 541/773-7361; fax 541/776-1033; res 800/282-3419. Email mencas@juno.com; www. ore.fishing.com.* 76 rms, 2 story, 3 suites. Apr-Oct: S $45; D $53; each addl $7; suites $65; children $7; under 12 free; lower rates rest of yr. Crib avail, fee. TV; cable (premium). Restaurant 11 am-2 pm. Ck-out 11 am, ck-in noon. Meeting rm. Golf, 18 holes. Tennis, 2 courts. Cr cds: A, C, D, DS, MC, V.

🛗 ⛷ 🏔 🔥 SC

★ **KNIGHTS INN.** *500 N Riverside Ave (97501). 541/773-3676; fax 541/857-0493; toll-free 800/531-2655.* 83 rms, 2 story. S $35; D $39-$46; each addl $4. Crib $4. Pet accepted, some restrictions. TV; cable. Pool. Restaurant adj 6 am-9 pm. Ck-out 11 am. Downhill/x-country ski 20 mi. Microwaves avail. Cr cds: A, C, D, DS, MC, V.

🐾 🎿 🏊 ✕ 🏔

Hotels

★ **RED LION HOTEL MEDFORD.** *200 N Riverside Ave (97501). 541/779-5811; fax 541/779-7961; res 800/733-5466. Email dougrlm@internetcds.com; www.redlionmedford.com.* 185 rms, 2 story, 2 suites. May-Sep: S $86; D $91; suites $250; lower rates rest of yr. Crib avail. Pet accepted. Parking garage. TV; cable (premium). Complimentary coffee in rms, newspaper, toll-free calls. Restaurant 6 am-10 pm. Bar. Ck-out noon, ck-in 3 pm. Meeting rms. Business center. Bellhops. Dry cleaning, coin lndry. Gift shop. Exercise privileges. Golf. Tennis, 8 courts. Hiking trail. Cr cds: A, C, D, DS, JCB, MC, V.

★★ **RESTON HOTEL.** *2300 Crater Lake Hwy (97504), E of I-5 Exit 30, near Medford-Jackson County Airport. 541/779-3141; fax 541/779-2623; toll-free 800/779-7829. Email sales@restonhotel.com; www.reston hotel.com.* 162 rms, 2 story, 3 suites. May-Aug: S, D $72; each addl $10; suites $120; under 17 free; lower rates rest of yr. Crib avail. Pet accepted, some restrictions, fee. Parking lot. Indoor pool, children's pool. TV; cable. Complimentary continental bkfst, newspaper, toll-free calls. Restaurant 11 am-9 pm. Bar. Ck-out noon, ck-in 3 pm. Meeting rms. Dry cleaning, coin lndry. Free airport transportation. Exercise privileges. Golf. Downhill skiing. Cr cds: A, D, DS, MC, V.

★★★ **ROGUE REGENCY INN.** *2345 Crater Lake Hwy (97504), at jct I-5, near Medford-Jackson County Airport. 541/770-1234; fax 541/770-2466; res 800/535-5805. Email regency@rogueregency.com; www. rogueregency.com.* 195 rms, 4 story, 8 suites. June-Sep: S $90; D $100; each addl $10; suites $200; lower rates rest of yr. Crib avail. Parking lot. Pool, whirlpool. TV; cable (premium). Complimentary coffee in rms, newspaper, toll-free calls. Restaurant 6 am-10 pm. Bar. Ck-out 11 am, ck-in 3 pm. Meeting rms. Business servs avail. Bellhops. Dry cleaning. Free airport transportation. Exercise privileges. Golf. Supervised children's activities. Video games. Cr cds: A, D, DS, JCB, MC, V.

★★ **WINDMILL INN.** *1950 Biddle Rd (97504), I-5 Exit 30, near Medford-Jackson County Airport. 541/779-0050; fax 541/779-0050; toll-free 800/547-4747. Email donda@jeld-wen.com; www.windmillinns.com.* 123 rms, 2 story, 2 suites. May-Sep: S, D $79; each addl $6; suites $79; under 17 free; lower rates rest of yr. Crib avail, fee.

Pet accepted. Parking lot. Pool, whirlpool. TV; cable (premium), VCR avail. Complimentary continental bkfst, newspaper, toll-free calls. Restaurant 6 am-11 pm. Ck-out 11 am, ck-in 3 pm. Meeting rm. Fax servs avail. Bellhops. Dry cleaning, coin lndry. Free airport transportation. Exercise privileges. sauna. Golf. Downhill skiing. Bike rentals. Hiking trail. Picnic facilities. Cr cds: A, D, DS, MC, V.

Restaurant

★★ **MON DESIR DINING INN.** *4615 Hanrick Rd (97502), I-5 Exit 33 E ¼ mi, then left on Hamrick Rd ¼ mi. 541/664-7558. www.so-menu.com.* Specializes in international cuisine. Hrs: 11 am-2 pm, 4-9 pm; Sat from 4 pm. Closed Sun, Mon. Res accepted. Bar. Lunch $4.95-$8.95; dinner $12.95-$24.95. Converted mansion. Fireplace, antiques, garden. Cr cds: D, MC, V.

Mount Hood National Forest

See also Hood River, The Dalles

(Crossed by US 26, approximately 50 mi E of Portland)

Web www.mthood.org

Mount Hood (11,235 ft) is the natural focal point of this 1,064,573-acre forest with headquarters in Sandy. Its white-crowned top, the

Mount Hood, the highest point in Oregon

highest point in Oregon, can be seen for miles on a clear day. It is also popular with skiers, who know it has some of the best slopes in the Northwest. There are five winter sports areas. Throughout the year, however, visitors can take advantage of the surrounding forest facilities for camping (1,600 camp and picnic sites), hunting, fishing, swimming, mountain climbing, golfing, horseback riding, hiking, and tobogganing. The Columbia Gorge, which cuts through the Cascades here, has many spectacular waterfalls, including Multnomah (620 ft). There are nine routes to the summit, which has fumed and smoked several times since the volcanic peak was discovered. Only experienced climbers should try the ascent and then only with a guide. For further info contact the Mount Hood Info Center, 65000 E US 26, Welches 97067; 503/622-7674, 503/622-4822, or 888/622-4822.

What to See and Do

River cruise. Two-hr narrated cruise of Columbia Gorge aboard the 599-passenger *Columbia Gorge,* an authentic sternwheeler. (Mid-June-Sep, 3 departures daily; res required for dinner cruise) Also here: museum; marina; travel information; picnicking; camping. 45 mi E of Portland via I-84 in Cascade Locks. Phone 503/223-3928. ¢¢¢¢

Skiing.

Mount Hood Meadows. Quad, triple, 7 double chairlifts, free rope tow; patrol, school, rentals; restaurant, cafeteria, concession, bar, 2 day lodges. Longest run 3 mi; vertical drop 2,777 ft. Also 550 acres of expert canyon skiing. (Nov-May, daily) Groomed, ungroomed cross-country trails; night skiing (Wed-Sun). 11 mi NE of Government Camp on OR 35. Phone 503/337-2222 or 503/227-7669 (snow conditions). ¢¢¢¢¢

Timberline Lodge. Quad, triple, 4 double chairlifts; patrol, school, rentals; restaurant, cafeteria, concession, bar, lodge. Longest run more than 2 mi; vertical drop 3,700 ft. (Mid-Nov-Apr, daily) Chairlift also operates May-Aug (daily, weather permitting; fee). 6

mi N of US 26. Phone 503/272-3311, 541/231-7979 (info), or 541/222-2211 (snow conditions). ¢¢¢¢¢

Motel/Motor Lodge

★ **MOUNT HOOD INN.** *87450 E Government Camp Loop (97028), on US 26.* 503/272-3205; fax 503/272-3307; toll-free 800/443-7777. 56 rms, 2 story, 4 suites. No A/C. S, D $125-$195; each addl $10; suites $145; under 12 free. Crib $5. Pet accepted; $5. TV; cable (premium), VCR avail. Complimentary continental bkfst. Restaurant nearby. Ck-out noon. Coin lndry. Meeting rms. Business servs avail. Downhill ski ¼ mi; x-country ski adj. Whirlpool. Some refrigerators, wet bars. Picnic tables. Cr cds: A, C, D, DS, MC, V.
🅳 🐾 ⚓ 👟 🏃 🇽 ⛷ 🔥

Resorts

★★★ **THE RESORT AT THE MOUNTAIN.** *68010 E Fairway Ave (97067), off US 26 at Welches Rd.* 503/622-3101; fax 503/622-2222; toll-free 800/669-7666. Email info@theresort.com; www.theresort.com. 151 rms, 2 story, 9 suites. May-Sep: S, D $149; each addl $20; suites $229; under 18 free; lower rates rest of yr. Crib avail. Parking lot. Pool, whirlpool. TV; cable, VCR avail. Complimentary coffee in rms, newspaper, toll-free calls. Restaurant. Bar. Ck-out noon, ck-in 4 pm. Meeting rms. Business center. Concierge. Dry cleaning, coin lndry. Gift shop. Salon/barber. Exercise equipt. Golf. Tennis, 4 courts. Downhill skiing. Bike rentals. Supervised children's activities. Hiking trail. Picnic facilities. Cr cds: A, DS, MC, V.
🅳 ⚓ 🏊 🏌 👟 🚣 🎾 🚴 🏃 🔥 🏂

★★ **TIMBERLINE LODGE.** *Timberline (97028), 6 mi NE of US 26.* 503/272-3311; fax 503/622-0710; toll-free 503/231-7979. www.timberlinelodge.com. 70 rms, 4 story. No A/C. S, D $65-$180; each addl $15; under 11 free; ski plans. Crib free. TV in most rms; cable, VCR avail (movies). Pool; whirlpool. Sauna. Supervised children's activities (Dec-Mar); ages 4-12. Dining rm 8-10 am, noon-2 pm, 6-8:30 pm. Snack bar. Bars 11 am-11 pm. Ck-out 11 am, ck-in 4 pm. Business servs avail. Downhill ski on site. Some fireplaces. Rustic rms; hand-carved furniture. Totally nonsmoking. Cr cds: A, D, DS, MC, V.

D ♿ 🛗 ⛷ ♒ 🏋 ⛺ 🔥

Restaurants

★★ **DON GUIDO'S ITALIAN CUISINE.** *73330 E US 26 (97049).* *503/622-5141.* Specializes in chicken marsala, halibut piccata, seafood fettucine. Hrs: 5-9:30 pm; hrs vary off-season. Closed hols. Res accepted. Bar. Dinner a la carte entrees: $9.95-$21.95. Child's menu. Entertainment. Parking. Built in 1928. Romantic atmosphere. Cr cds: A, DS, MC, V.

D

★★★ **HIGHLANDS DINING ROOM.** *68010 E Fairway Ave, off US 26 at Welches Rd. 503/622-2214.* *www.theresort.com.* Specializes in prime rib, salmon, Northwest cuisine. Hrs: 7 am-10 pm; Sun brunch 10 am-2 pm. Res accepted. Bar. Wine list. Bkfst $3.95-$7.95; lunch $5.50-$12; dinner $13.95-$17.95. Sun brunch $17.95. Child's menu. Entertainment: pianist Fri, Sat. Bright, cheerful atmosphere; view of pool, gardens. Cr cds: A, C, D, DS, ER, MC, V.

D

Newberg

(B-2) *See also Beaverton, Hillsboro, McMinnville, Oregon City, Portland, Salem*

Founded 1889 **Pop** 13,086 **Elev** 176 ft **Area code** 503 **Zip** 97132

Information Chamber of Commerce, 115 N Washington; 503/538-2014

Quakers made their first settlement west of the Rockies here and established Pacific Academy in 1885. Herbert Hoover was in its first graduating class (1888).

What to See and Do

Champoeg State Historic Area. A 615-acre park on site of early Willamette River settlement, site of settlers' vote in 1843 for a provisional territorial government, swept away by flood of 1861. Fishing, boat dock on Willamette River; hiking, picnicking, improved camping (dump station). Standard fees. Visitor information, interpretive center; monument. French Prairie Loop 40-mi auto or bike tour begins and ends here. (See SEASONAL EVENT) 5 mi W off I-5. Phone 503/678-1251. Per vehicle (Memorial Day wkend-Labor Day, wkends and hols) ¢¢ In the area are

Newell House Museum. Reconstructed home of Robert Newell, one-time mountain man and friend of the Native Americans. Contains period furnishings, quilts, coverlets, and examples of fine handiwork; collection of inaugural gowns worn by wives of Oregon governors; Native American artifacts. Old jail (1850) and typical pioneer 1-rm schoolhouse. (Feb-Nov, Wed-Sun; closed Thanksgiving) Just W of park entrance at 8089 Champoeg Rd NE. Phone 503/678-5537. ¢

Pioneer Mother's Memorial Log Cabin. A replica, much enlarged, of the type of log cabin built by early pioneers. Constructed of peeled hand-hewn logs, with a shake roof, it has a massive stone fireplace in the living room, a sleeping loft, and 2 small bedrms; many pioneer items incl an old Hudson's Bay heating stove, collection of guns and muskets dating from 1777-1853, a fife played at Lincoln's funeral, china and glassware, and original furnishings from pioneer homes. (Feb-Nov, Wed-Sun; closed Thanksgiving) Located in the park, on the banks of the Willamette River, at 8035 Champoeg Rd NE. Phone 503/633-2237. ¢

Visitor Center. Interpretive historical exhibits tell the story of "Champoeg: Birthplace of Oregon"; films; tours. (Memorial Day-Labor Day, daily; winter Mon-Fri) 8239 Champoeg Rd NE. Phone 503/678-1251. **Donation**

George Fox College. (1891) 1,700 students. Founded as Pacific Academy; renamed in 1949 for English founder of the Society of Friends. Herbert Hoover was a student here; Hoover Bldg has displays. Brougher Museum has Quaker and pioneer exhibits. Campus tours. 414 N Meridian. Phone 503/538-8383, ext 222.

Hoover-Minthorn House Museum.
Herbert Hoover lived here with his uncle, Dr. Henry Minthorn. Quaker house built in 1881 contains many original furnishings, photographs, and souvenirs of Hoover's boyhood. (Mar-Nov, Wed-Sun; Dec and Feb, Sat and Sun; closed Jan) 115 S River St. Phone 503/538-6629. ¢

Seasonal Event

Vintage Celebration. Classic automobiles and airplanes, arts and crafts, wine tasting. Phone 503/538-2014. Sat, Sun after Labor Day.

Motel/Motor Lodge

★★ **SHILO INN.** *501 Sitka Ave (97132). 503/537-0303; fax 503/537-0442; toll-free 800/222-2244.* 60 rms, 3 story. S, D $65-$79; each addl $10; suites $75; kit. units $79; under 12 free. Crib free. Pet accepted; $7/day. TV; cable (premium), VCR avail. Heated pool; whirlpool. Complimentary continental bkfst. Restaurant nearby. Ck-out noon. Coin lndry. Meeting rms. Business servs avail. Sundries. Exercise equipt; sauna. Bathrm phones, refrigerators, wet bars. Cr cds: A, C, D, DS, ER, JCB, MC, V.

Newport

(C-1) *See also Depoe Bay, Lincoln City, Yachats*

Settled 1882 **Pop** 8,437 **Elev** 160 ft
Area code 541 **Zip** 97365
Web www.newportchamber.org
Information Chamber of Commerce, 555 SW Coast Hwy; 541/265-8801 or 800/262-7844

This fishing port at the mouth of the Yaquina River has been a resort for more than 100 years. Crabbing is a popular activity here; Dungenness crabs can be caught in the bay year-round.

What to See and Do

Hatfield Marine Science Center of Oregon State University. Conducts research on oceanography, fisheries, water quality, marine science education, and marine biology; research vessel *Wecoma;* nature trail; aquarium-museum; films; special programs in summer. Winter and spring grey whale programs. Braille text and other aids for the hearing and visually impaired. (Daily; closed Dec 25) Marine Science Dr, S side of Yaquina Bay, just E of Newport Bridge, off US 101. Phone 541/867-0271. **Donation**

Lincoln County Historical Society Museums. Log Cabin Museum. Artifacts from Siletz Reservation; historical, pioneer, and maritime exhibits. (Tues-Sun; closed Jan 1, Thanksgiving, Dec 25) Also **Burrows House Museum.** Victorian-era household furnishings, clothing; history of Lincoln County. (Same days as log cabin museum) 545 SW 9th St. Phone 541/265-7509. **FREE**

Marine Discovery Tours. Whale-watching and river cruises. Hands-on activities. (Hrs vary seasonally; closed Dec 25) 345 SW Bay Blvd. Phone 541/265-6200 or 800/903-2628. ¢¢¢¢

Mineral collecting. Gemstones, marine fossils, other stones are found on beaches to N and S of Newport, particularly at creek mouths.

Oregon Coast Aquarium. Houses 190 species in unique habitats. (Daily; closed Dec 25) S side of Yaquina Bay. 2820 SE Ferry Slip Rd. Phone 541/867-3474. ¢¢¢

Ripley's—Believe It or Not. Exhibits incl replicas of a backwards fountain; King Tut's tomb; the *Titanic;* the Fiji mermaid. (Daily; closed Dec 25) 250 SW Bay Blvd. Phone 541/265-2206. ¢¢¢

State parks.

Beverly Beach. A 130-acre park with beach access, fishing; hiking, picnicking, tent and trailer sites (dump station, laundry tubs). Standard fees. 7 mi N on US 101. Phone 541/265-9278 or 800/452-5687.

Devil's Punch Bowl. An 8-acre park noted for its bowl-shaped rock formation that fills at high tide; ocean-carved caves, marine gardens, beach; trails, picnicking.

Observation point. 8 mi N off US 101. Phone 541/265-9278.

Ona Beach. A 237-acre day-use park with ocean beach, swimming, fishing, boat ramp on creek; picnicking. 8 mi S on US 101. Phone 541/867-7451.

South Beach. Over 400 acres. Botanically interesting area, sandy beach, dunes. Fishing; hiking, picnicking, improved campsites (dump station). Standard fees. 2 mi S on US 101. Phone 541/867-7451 (res).

Yaquina Bay. Over 30 acres. Ocean beach, fishing; picnicking. Agate beaches nearby. Old Yaquina Bay Lighthouse (1871) has been restored; exhibits. (Memorial Day-Labor Day, daily; rest of yr, wkends) N end of bridge on US 101. Phone 541/867-7451. **Donation**

Undersea Gardens. Visitors descend beneath the sea for underwater show. Watch native sea life through viewing windows; guides narrate as scuba divers perform; features Armstrong, the giant octopus. (Daily; closed Dec 25) 250 SW Bay Blvd, on Yaquina Bay just off US 101 in the Bay Front district. Phone 541/265-2206. ¢¢¢

Wax Works. Events of the past and future shown with animation and special effects. (Daily; closed Dec 25) 250 SW Bay Blvd. Phone 541/265-2206. ¢¢¢

Yaquina Head. Lighthouse here is a popular spot for whale watching and fully accessible tidal pool viewing. Also interpretive center. ½ mi N on US 101.

Annual Events

Seafood and Wine Festival. Last full wkend Feb.

Loyalty Days and Sea Fair Festival. Military ships, parade, sailboat races; entertainment. Phone 541/867-3798. First wkend May.

Motels/Motor Lodges

★★ **LITTLE CREEK COVE.** *3641 NW Oceanview Dr (97365), off US 101. 541/265-8587; fax 541/265-4576; toll-free 800/294-8025. Email lcc@newportnet.com; www.newportnet. com/lcc.* 29 kit. units, 2-3 story. No elvtr. S, D $99-$215; each addl $10. TV; cable (premium), VCR. Restaurant nearby. Ck-out noon. Business servs avail. Microwaves, fireplaces. Beach access. Cr cds: A, C, D, DS, MC, V.

Devil's Punch Bowl

★ **WHALER MOTEL.** *155 SW Elizabeth St (97365). 541/265-9261; fax 541/265-9515; toll-free 800/433-9444. Email information@whalernewport.com; www.whalernewport.com.* 61 rms, 3 story, 12 suites. June-Sep: S, D $95; suites $129; lower rates rest of yr. Crib avail, fee. Pet accepted, some restrictions. Parking lot. Indoor pool, whirlpool. TV; cable (premium). Complimentary continental bkfst, coffee in rms, newspaper, toll-free calls. Restaurant nearby. Ck-out noon, ck-in 3 pm. Coin lndry. Exercise equipt. Golf, 9 holes. Beach access. Cr cds: A, D, DS, MC, V.

Hotel

★★ **SHILO INN.** *536 SW Elizabeth St (97365), W of US 101. 541/265-7701; fax 541/265-5687; toll-free 800/222-2244. Email newport@shiloinns. com; www.shiloinns.com.* 179 rms. June-Aug: S, D $165; each addl $15;

suites $175; under 12 free; lower rates rest of yr. Pet accepted, some restrictions, fee. Parking lot. Indoor pool, lap pool, whirlpool. TV; cable (premium). Complimentary coffee in rms, newspaper, toll-free calls. Restaurant. Bar. Ck-out noon, ck-in 4 pm. Meeting rms. Business servs avail. Coin lndry. Sauna. Golf. Beach access. Supervised children's activities. Hiking trail. Picnic facilities. Video games. Cr cds: A, C, D, DS, ER, JCB, MC, V.

Resort

★★ **EMBARCADERO RESORT HOTEL.** *1000 SE Bay Blvd (97365). 541/265-8521; fax 541/265-7844; toll-free 800/547-4779. Email donna@ actionnet.net; www.embarcadero-resort. com.* 35 rms, 3 story, 45 suites. June-Sep: S, D $125; suites $155; lower rates rest of yr. Crib avail, fee. Parking lot. Indoor pool, whirlpool. TV; cable, VCR avail. Complimentary toll-free calls. Restaurant 7 am-9 pm. Bar. Ck-out noon, ck-in 4 pm. Meeting rms. Business servs avail. Coin lndry. Free airport transportation. Exercise equipt, sauna. Golf. Bike rentals. Cr cds: A, D, DS, MC, V.

Restaurant

★ **WHALE'S TALE.** *452 SW Bay Blvd (97365). 541/265-8660.* Specializes in seafood, natural foods. Own baking. Hrs: 8 am-9 pm; Fri to 10 pm; Sat 9 am-10 pm; Sun from 9 am. Closed Dec 24, 25; early Jan-mid-Feb; Wed in winter. Wine, beer. Bkfst $4-$8; lunch $4-$7; dinner $10.95-$18.95. Child's menu. Entertainment. Nautical decor. Local artwork. Cr cds: A, C, D, DS, MC, V.

North Bend

(D-1) *See also Bandon, Coos Bay, Reedsport*

Settled 1853 **Pop** 9,614 **Elev** 23 ft
Area code 541 **Zip** 97459
Web www.coos.or.us/~nbend

Information Bay Area Chamber of Commerce, PO Box 210, Coos Bay 97420; 541/269-0215 or 800/824-8486. North Bend Info Center is located at 1380 Sherman Ave in town; 541/756-4613

Commercial fisheries, lumbering, and manufacturing thrive in this city on a peninsula in Coos Bay.

What to See and Do

Coos County Historical Society Museum. Local history; permanent and changing exhibits. (Tues-Sat) In Simpson Park, on US 101, N edge of town. Phone 541/756-6320 or 541/756-4847. ¢

Oregon Dunes National Recreation Area. Area is 2 mi wide and 40 mi long. One of largest bodies of sand outside of the Sahara. (See REED-SPORT)

The Real Oregon Gift. Manufacturers of myrtlewood products. Tour of factory; gift shop. (Daily) 5 mi N on US 101. Phone 541/756-2220. **FREE**

Motel/Motor Lodge

★ **BAY BRIDGE MOTEL.** *66304 Hwy 101 (97459). 541/756-3151; fax 541/756-0749; toll-free 800/557-3156.* 16 rms, 3 kit. units. May-Oct: S $42-$52; D $52-$60; each addl $5; kit. units $59-$65; under 3 free; lower rates rest of yr. Crib $2. Pet accepted, some restrictions; $5/day. TV; cable. Complimentary coffee in lobby. Restaurant nearby. Ck-out 11 am. Some refrigerators. On Pacific Bay. Cr cds: A, DS, MC, V.

Restaurant

★★ **HILLTOP HOUSE.** *166 N Bay Dr (97459). 541/756-4160.* Specializes in steak, seafood, pasta. Hrs: 11:30 am-2:30 pm, 4:30-10 pm; winter to 9 pm. Res accepted. Lunch $4.25-$14.95; dinner $7.25-$29.95. View of bay harbor and sand dunes. Cr cds: A, D, MC, V.

Ontario

(C-7) *See also Caldwell, ID, Weiser, ID*

Founded 1883 **Pop** 9,392
Elev 2,154 ft **Area code** 541
Zip 97914
Information Visitors & Convention
Bureau, 88 SW 3rd Ave; 541/889-
8012 or 888/889-8012

Ontario, the largest town in Malheur
County, is a trading center at the
eastern border of Oregon. Irrigation
from the Snake River has made possible the cultivation of sugar beets,
potatoes, onions, corn, hay, and
alfalfa seed, but there is still a vast
wilderness of rangeland, lakes and
reservoirs, mountains, and canyons.
Quartz crystals, jaspers, thundereggs,
marine fossils, petrified wood, and
obsidian are abundant in the area.

What to See and Do

Fishing and hunting. Rainbow trout,
crappie, and bass are plentiful. Mal-
lard and Canada geese are found on
the Snake River; sage grouse,
chukars, antelope, mule deer in the
sagebrush areas; pheasant on irrigated land.

Owyhee Canyon. Fossils and utensils
of Native Americans; petroglyphs.
Boating, fishing; hunting.

State parks.

Farewell Bend. A 72-acre park
named by pioneers who left the
Snake River at this point in their
trek west. Swimming beach (bathhouse), fishing, boat ramp; picnicking, primitive and improved
camping (dump station). Standard
fees. 25 mi NW on I-84. Phone
541/869-2365.

Lake Owyhee. A 730-acre park
with 52-mi-long lake created by
Owyhee Dam. Fishing, boating
(ramp); picnicking, improved
camping (dump station). Standard
fees. 33 mi SW off OR 201. Phone
541/339-2444.

Ontario. A 35-acre day-use area.
Fishing, boat ramp; picnicking. On
I-84 at N end of town. Phone
541/869-2365.

Annual Events

American Musical Jubilee. Early June.

Obon Festival. Japanese dancing,
food; art show. Mid-July.

Malheur County Fair. First wk Aug.

Motels/Motor Lodges

★★ **BEST WESTERN & SUITES.**
*251 Goodfellow (97914), off I-84, Exit
376. 541/889-2600; fax 541/889-
2259; toll-free 800/828-0364.* 61 rms,
2 story, 14 suites. S $52-$57; D $75-
$80; each addl $4; suites $85-$95;
under 13 free. Pets accepted, some
restrictions; $25. TV; cable. Indoor
pool. Complimentary continental
bkfst. Restaurant nearby. Ck-out
noon. Coin lndry. Exercise equipt.
Regrigerators, microwaves; some
minibars. Crds: A, C, D, DS, ER, JCB,
MC, V.
🄳 🔧 ⚊ 🏋 ⊠ 🔥 SC

★★ **HOLIDAY INN.** *1249 Tapadera
Ave (97914). 541/889-8621; fax
541/889-8023; res 800/525/5333.*
100 rms, 2 story. S, D $55-$69;
under 18 free. Crib free. TV; cable.
Heated pool; whirlpool. Coffee in
lobby. Restaurant 6 am-11 pm. Ck-
out noon. Meeting rms. Local airport, railroad station, bus depot
transportation. Health club privileges. Some patios, balconies. Cr
cds: A, C, D, DS, MC, V.
🄳 ⚊ ⊠ 🔥 SC

★ **HOLIDAY MOTOR INN.** *615 E
Idaho Ave (97914). I-84, Exit 376.
541/889-9188; fax 541/889-4303.* 72
rms, 2 story. S $30-$35; D $40-$45;
each addl $5; under 12 free. Crib $5.
TV; cable (premium). Heated pool.
Coffee in lobby. Restaurant open 24
hrs, Sun, Mon 6 am-11 pm. Ck-out
11 am. Meeting rm. Business Servs
avail. Cr cds: A, C, D, DS, MC, V.
🄳 🔧 ⚊ ⊠ 🔥 SC

★ **MOTEL 6.** *275 NE 12th St
(97914), off I-84 Exit 376 and US 30
Payette exit. 541/889-6617; fax
541/889-8232; res 800/466-8356.* 126
rms, showers only, 2 story. S $25-
$30; D $30-$35; each addl $3; under
18 free. Crib free. TV; cable (premium). Restaurants nearby. Ck-out
noon. Coin lndry. Cr cds: A, C, D,
DS, MC, V.
🄳 🔧 ⚊ ⊠ 🔥

★ **SUPER 8 MOTEL.** *266 Goodfellow St (97914), off I-84 Exit 376. 541/889-8282; fax 541/881-1400; res: 800/800-8000.* 63 rms, 2 story. S $40-$45, D $50-$55; each addl $4; under 13 free. TV; cable (premium). Indoor pool; whirlpool. Complimentary continental bkfst. Restaurants nearby. Ck-out 11 am. Coin lndry. Exercise equipt. Cr cds: A, C, D, DS, ER, MC, V.

D ⊱ 🕇 ⊠ 🔥 SC

★ **YE OLDE COLONIAL MOTOR INN.** *1395 Tapadera Ave (97914). 541/889-9615; fax 541/889-9615; res 800/727-5014.* 84 rms, 2 story. S $27-$36, D $42-$45. Crib $2. TV; cable. Pets accepted, some restrictions. Indoor pool; whirlpool. Restaurant adj 6 am -noon. Ck-out 11 am. Business servs avail. In-rm modem link. Sundries. Cr cds: A, C, DS, MC, V.

D ⬟ ⊱ ⊠ 🔥 SC

Restaurant

★★ **NICHOLS STEAK HOUSE.** *411 SW 3rd St (83619). 208/452-3030.* Specializes in prime rib, 22-oz T-bone. Salad bar. Hrs: 11 am-9 pm; Fri to 10 pm; Sat 4-10 pm; Sun noon-8 pm. Closed Mon; hols. Wine, beer. Lunch $3-$10; dinner $9-$25. Child's menu. Western decor, antiques. Paintings by local artists. Cr cds: DS, MC, V.

D ⊰

Oregon Caves National Monument

See also Cave Junction, Grants Pass

(20 mi E of Cave Junction on OR 46)

This area was discovered in 1874, when hunter Elijah Davidson's dog followed a bear into the cave. After a visit in 1907, frontier poet Joaquin Miller called this "The Marble Halls of Oregon." In 1909 the cave and 480 acres of the Siskiyou Mountains were made a national monument.

The cave has many chambers—Paradise Lost, Joaquin Miller's Chapel,

Ghost Room, and others. Guide service is required. The average temperature is 42°F. Evening talks are given by National Park Service naturalists in summer.

On the surface, the area is covered with a beautiful old growth forest with abundant wildlife, birds, wildflowers, and an interesting variety of trees and shrubs. A maintained and marked system of trails provides access to these areas; stay on the trail. Dogs aren't allowed on trails.

Forest Service campgrounds (fee) are located 4 mi and 8 mi NW on OR 46 in Siskiyou National Forest (see GRANTS PASS). (Mid-May-Labor Day) Phone 541/592-3400.

Cave tours (daily; closed Thanksgiving, Dec 25). Children must be at least 3'-6" (42 inches) in height and complete a step test to be permitted into the cave. Cave tours are strenuous; recommended only for those in good physical condition. A jacket and walking shoes with nonslip soles should be worn. Lodge, dining room (May-mid-Oct). For further information contact Oregon Caves Co, 19000 Caves Hwy, Cave Junction 97523; 541/592-2100. Cave tours ¢¢¢

Oregon City

(B-2) *See also Beaverton, Forest Grove, Newberg, Portland, Salem*

Settled 1829 **Pop** 14,698 **Elev** 55 ft **Area code** 503 **Zip** 97045
Information Oregon City Chamber of Commerce and Visitors Center, PO Box 226; 503/656-1619 or 800/424-3002

Below Willamette Falls, where the river spills over a 42-foot drop, is historic Oregon City. Steamers were built here in the 1850s and locks around the falls opened the upriver to navigation in 1873. Salmon fishing in the Willamette and Clackamas rivers is from early March-mid-May. The city is built on terraces and there is an enclosed elevator to an observation platform.

What to See and Do

Holmes Family Home. (Rose Farm) Oldest standing American home in Oregon City, built in 1847. First Territorial governor gave his first address here in 1849; the upstairs ballroom was the scene of many social events. (Sun; closed hols and Jan-Feb) Holmes Lane & Rilance St. Phone 503/656-5146. ¢

John Inskeep Environmental Learning Center. Eight acres developed on former industrial site to demonstrate wildlife habitat in an urban setting. Incl extensive birds of prey exhibits, various plant and wildlife displays, and plant nursery. Haggart Astronomical Observatory (Wed, Fri, Sat; fee). 19600 S Molalla on N side of Clackamas Community College's campus. Phone 503/657-6958, ext 2351. ¢

McLoughlin House National Historic Site. Georgian frame bldg built in 1845-46 by Dr. John McLoughlin, chief factor of the Hudson's Bay Company, who ruled the Columbia River region from 1824-46. Period furnishings; many are original pieces, most having come around Cape Horn on sailing ships. (Tues-Sun; closed hols, also Jan) 713 Center St between 7th & 8th Sts. Phone 503/656-5146. ¢¢

Milo McIver State Park. On the Clackamas River, this 937-acre park offers a panoramic view of Mt Hood. Fishing, boating (ramp to river); hiking and horseback trails, picnicking, improved campsites (dump station). Standard fees. 4 mi N on OR 213, then 12 mi SE via OR 212, 211. Phone 503/630-7150.

The Old Aurora Colony Museum. Complex of bldgs forming historical museum of the Aurora Colony, a German religious communal society, founded by Dr. William Keil (1856-83). Incl Kraus House (1863), a colony house with original artifacts; Steinbach Cabin (1876); wash house used by colony women for washing, soap making, and canning; herb garden divided into various uses—teas, cooking, medicinal, fragrances. Exhibits of furniture, musical instruments, quilts, tools. Tours. (June-Aug, Tues-Sun; rest of yr, Wed-Sun; closed hols; also Jan) 15 mi SW via OR 99E at 15018 2nd St NE in Aurora. Phone 503/678-5754. ¢¢

Oregon Trail Interpretive Center. Exhibits on journey made by early settlers over the Oregon Trail. (Daily; closed hols) 1726 Washington St. Phone 503/657-9336. ¢

Stevens Crawford Museum. (Mertie Stevens Residence, 1907) Fifteen furnished period rms. Working kitchen, bedrms, living rm, dining rm; doll collection. (Feb-Dec, Tues-Sun) 603 6th St. Phone 503/655-2866. ¢¢

Willamette Falls Locks. National Historical site; oldest multi lift navagation lock, built 1873. Four locks, canal basin, and guard lock operated by US Army Corps of Engineers. Picnic areas. Information Center. (Daily) On Willamette River, in West Linn. Phone 503/656-3381. **FREE**

Hotel

★ **RIVERSHORE HOTEL.** *1900 Clackamette Dr (97045), off I-205. 503/655-7141; fax 503/655-1927; res 800/443-7777. www.rivershore.com.* 120 rms, 4 story. S $65; D $73; each addl $5; suites $122; under 12 free. Crib $5. Pet accepted, some restrictions; $5. TV; cable (premium). Heated pool; whirlpool. Restaurant 6 am-10 pm; Sun 7 am-9 pm. Bar noon-1 am. Ck-out noon. Most balconies overlook river. Cr cds: A, DS, MC, V.

Pendleton

(A-6) *See also Hermiston, La Grande, Umatilla*

Founded 1868 **Pop** 15,126
Elev 1,068 ft **Area code** 541
Zip 97801

Information Chamber of Commerce, 501 S Main; 541/276-7411 or 800/547-8911

Located on the old Oregon Trail, Pendleton is a trading center for the extensive cattle, wheat, and green pea production in the area. Seat of Umatilla County, it is famous for its annual Round-up.

What to See and Do

Emigrant Springs State Park. A 23-acre park near summit of Blue Mts (nearly 4,000 ft); ponderosa pine forest, winter sports, picnicking, lodge, tent and trailer sites. Oregon Trail display. Standard fees. 26 mi SE off I-84. Phone 541/983-2277.

Hamley's Western Store. Makers of fine Western saddles, custom leathercraft since 1883. Saddle making demonstrated. Tours (daily). 30 SE Court. Phone 541/276-2321. **FREE**

Pendleton Woolen Mills. Woolen manufacturing; carding, spinning, rewinding, and weaving processes. Guided tours (30 min; Mon-Fri). 1307 SE Court Place. Phone 541/276-6911. **FREE**

Ukiah-Dale Forest State Park. A 3,000-acre scenic forest canyon extending along Camas Creek and N Fork of John Day River. Fishing; camping. Standard fees. 50 mi S on US 395. Phone 541/983-2277.

✪ **Umatilla Indian Reservation.** Created by the Walla Walla Valley Treaty of 1855. Firsthand view and understanding of a Native American community in transition. Historic significance as well as a lifestyle different from modern-day, American-style development. One of the first Catholic missions in the US is here. Reservation always open for unguided touring. Indian Lake has good fishing, camping, and beautiful scenery. The foothills and lowlands of the Blue Mts provide excellent upland game and waterfowl hunting. In addition, the Umatilla Tribes have reestablished runs of chinook salmon and steelhead within the Umatilla River. Some fees. 5 mi E via Mission Hwy (US 30). Phone 541/276-3873.

Umatilla National Forest. More than 1 million acres, partly in Washington. Lewis and Clark passed through this region on the Columbia River in 1805. Incl spectacular views of the Tucannon, Umatilla, Grande Ronde, N Fork John Day, and Wenaha River canyons. Remnants of historic gold mining can be found in the Granite, OR, area in sight of the Greenhorn Mt Range. N Fork John Day, N Fork Umatilla, and the Wenaha-Tucannon wilderness areas may be reached on horseback or on foot. Stream fishing (steelhead, rainbow trout), boating, river rafting; big-game hunting (elk, deer), hiking, skiing, snowmobiling, picnicking, camping (fee at some campgrounds). NE & S of Pendleton. Reached by I-84, US 395, OR 11, 204, 82, 244, 207 & WA 12. Phone 541/276-3811 for further info. In forest are

    Ski areas. Spout Springs. Ski Bluewood. 45 mi NE to Walla Walla, WA, 29 mi NE on WA 12 to Dayton, then 23 mi SE on country road. 21 mi NE on OR 11 to Weston, then 20 mi E on OR 204 to Tollgate (see LA GRANDE).

Annual Event

Pendleton Round-up. Stadium. Rodeo and pageantry of Old West, annually since 1910. Gathering of Native Americans, PRCA working cowboys and thousands of visitors. Phone 800/457-6336. Mid-Sep.

Motels/Motor Lodges

★ **CHAPARRAL MOTEL.** *620 SW Tutuilla Rd (97801), S of I-84 Exit 209.* 541/276-8654; fax 541/276-5808. 51 rms, 3 story, 3 suites. June-Sep: S $37; D $47; each addl $5; suites $50; children $5; under 12 free; lower rates rest of yr. Crib avail, fee. Pet accepted, some restrictions, fee. Parking lot. TV; cable (premium). Complimentary coffee in rms, toll-free calls. Restaurant. Ck-out 11 am, ck-in 11 pm. Fax servs avail. Bellhops. Exercise privileges. Golf. Cr cds: A, D, DS, JCB, MC, V.

[D] [symbols] [SC]

★ ★ ★ **DOUBLETREE HOTEL.** *304 SE Nye Ave (97801), at I-84N Exit 210.* 541/276-6111; fax 541/278-2413; res 800/222-8733; toll-free 800/547-8010. www.doubletreehotels.com. 168 rms, 3 story. S, D $63-$73; each addl $10; under 18 free; wkend rates. Crib free. Pet accepted. TV. Heated pool. Coffee in rms. Restaurant 6 am-10:30 pm. Bar; entertainment. Ck-out noon. Meeting rms. Business servs avail. Free airport, railroad station, bus depot transportation. Health club privileges. Private patios, balconies. Cr cds: A, C, D, DS, ER, JCB, MC, V.

 D 🔄 ≈ 🖳 🐾 SC

★ **ECONOMY INN.** *201 SW Court Ave (97801). 541/276-5252; fax 541/278-1213.* 51 rms, 2 story. June-Sep: S $32-$36; D $40-$46; each addl $6; under 16 free; lower rates rest of yr. Closed during Pendleton Roundup. Crib free. Pet accepted; $5. TV; cable, VCR avail. Pool. Complimentary continental bkfst. Restaurant nearby. Ck-out noon. Refrigerators avail. Cr cds: A, D, DS, JCB, MC, V.

🔄 ≈ 🏋 ✈ 🖳 🐾

★ **TAPADERA MOTEL.** *105 SE Court Ave (97128). 541/276-3231; fax 541/276-0754; toll-free 800/722-8277.* 47 rms, 2 story. Mid-May-mid-Sep: S $35-$45; D $49-$55; each addl $5; under 12 free; lower rates rest of yr. Crib $5. Pet accepted; $5. TV; cable (premium). Restaurant 7 am-9 pm. Bar 11-2 am. Ck-out noon. Meeting rms. Business servs avail. Health club privileges. Cr cds: A, C, D, DS, MC, V.

🔄 🛎 🏋 🖳 🐾

Restaurant

★★ **CIMMIYOTTI'S.** *137 S Main St (97801). 541/276-4314.* Specializes in beef, chicken, fish. Hrs: 4-10 pm; Fri, Sat to 11 pm. Closed Sun. Res accepted. Bar. Dinner $8-$20. Child's menu. Western motif. Cr cds: A, D, MC, V.

D

Portland (B-2)

Founded 1851 **Pop** 437,319 **Elev** 77 ft
Area code 503 **Web** www.pova.com
Information Portland Oregon Visitors Association, 26 SW Salmon St, 97204; 503/222-2223 or 1-87PORT-LAND

Suburbs Beaverton, Forest Grove, Hillsboro, Newburg, Oregon City; also Vancouver, WA. (See individual alphabetical listings.)

Oregon's largest city sprawls across both banks of the Willamette River, just south of its confluence with the Columbia. The lush and fertile Willamette Valley brings it beauty and riches. Portland's freshwater harbor is visited by more than 1,400 vessels annually from throughout the world. The city enjoys plentiful electric power, captured from river waters, which drives scores of industries with minimal amounts of smoke or smog.

Portland is surrounded by spectacular scenery. The Columbia River Gorge, Mount Hood, waterfalls, forests, ski slopes, fishing streams, and hunting and camping areas are within easy access. It attracts many conventions, for which it is well-equipped with four large auditoriums, the Memorial Coliseum Complex, the Metropolitan Exposition Center, and the Oregon Convention Center. Portland's reputation as "The City of Roses" is justified by its leadership in rose culture, as seen in its International Rose Test Garden and celebrated during the annual Portland Rose Festival, which attracts visitors worldwide. Mount St. Helens (see WASHINGTON), in Washington's Gifford Pinchot National Forest, 50 miles to the northeast, can be seen from numerous vantage points in Portland.

Portland is also an educational center with Portland State University, the University of Portland (1901), Lewis & Clark College (1867), and Reed College (1911).

Transportation

Car Rental Agencies. See IMPORTANT TOLL-FREE NUMBERS.

Public Transportation. Buses, MAX light rail trains (Tri-County Metropolitan Transportation District), phone503/238-RIDE.

Rail Passenger Service. Amtrak 800/872-7245.

Airport Information

Portland International Airport. Information 503/460-4234; lost and found 503/460-4277; weather 503/275-9792; cash machines, Main Terminal, N & S ends of Oregon Market Place.

What to See and Do

American Advertising Museum. Museum devoted to the history and evolution of advertising and its impact on culture. Permanent and changing exhibits on print and broadcast advertising; reference library. (Mon-Fri by appt; Sat) 5035 SE 24th Ave. Phone 503/226-0000. ¢¢

Benson State Recreation Area. A 272-acre park with lake. Swimming, fishing, boating (no motors); picnicking. E on I-84, exit 30. Phone 503/695-2261. Per vehicle ¢¢

Children's Museum. Hands-on play spaces incl grocery store, baby rm, and clay shop. (Tues-Sun; closed hols) 3037 SW 2nd Ave. Phone 503/823-2227. ¢¢

Council Crest Park. Highest point in Portland (1,073 ft) for views of Tualatin Valley, Willamette River, Mt Hood, and Mt St. Helens. S on SW Greenway Ave (follow blue and white scenic tour signs). Phone 503/823-2223. **FREE**

Crystal Springs Rhododendron Garden. Approx 2,500 rhododendrons of 1,000 varieties and other woodland plants in woodland setting (more than 6 acres) and formal gardens with lake. (Daily) SE 28th Ave, N of SE Woodstock Blvd. Phone 503/823-2223. ¢

Forest Park. Park has 4,800 acres of wilderness with 50 mi of hiking

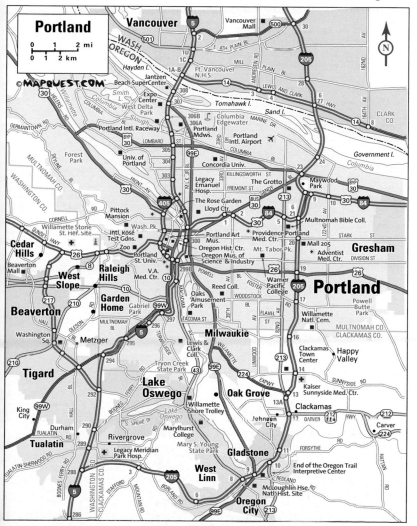

trails. Wildwood Trail begins at the Vietnam Veterans Living Memorial in Hoyt Arboretum and extends 28 mi, ending deep in the park beyond Germantown Rd. Bird-watching; small wild animals. Picnicking. (Daily) A map is avail from Hoyt Arboretum visitor center or phone 503/823-2223. Off US 30, NW of Fremont Bridge. Phone 503/228-8733. FREE]

Gray Line bus tours. Contact 4320 N Suttle Rd, PO Box 17306, 97217. Phone 503/285-9845 or 800/422-7042.

Grotto—The National Sanctuary of Our Sorrowful Mother. Religious sanctuary and botanical garden on 62 acres and 2 levels, created in 1924. Grotto carved in 110-ft cliff is surrounded by gardens. Elevator to the Natural Gallery in the woods featuring more than 100 statues. Landscaped top level with meditation chapel overlooking the Columbia River and Mt St. Helens (fee). (Daily; closed Thanksgiving, Dec 25) NE 85th Ave at Sandy Blvd, on OR 30. Phone 503/254-7371. ¢

Howell Territorial Park and The Bybee House. (1858) Restored house of early settlers; period furnishings. Pioneer orchard, agricultural museum on grounds. (June-Labor Day, wkend afternoons) 12 mi N via US 30, cross bridge to Sauvie Island, 1 mi W to Howell Territorial Park Rd. Phone 503/621-3344 or 503/222-1741. **Donation**

Hoyt Arboretum. More than 214 acres, with displays of more than 700 kinds of woody plants and one of the nation's largest collections of needle-bearing trees; self-guided trails with Vietnam Veterans Living Memorial. Also guided nature walk (Apr-Oct, Sat and Sun afternoons). Park and visitor center (daily). Picnicking. 4000 SW Fairview Blvd. Phone 503/228-8733. **FREE**

Lewis & Clark College. (1867) 3,400 students. Memorial Rose Garden with 1,500 plants; Tudor mansion (Mon-Fri), formal gardens. Tours of campus. SW Palatine Hill Rd, 3 mi E of I-5 Terwilliger Exit. Phone 503/768-7000.

Mount Hood-Columbia Gorge Loop Scenic Drive. This 163-mi scenic drive along the Columbia River and through Mt Hood National Forest (see) offers splendid views of the river basin, visits to waterfalls, many state parks, and spectacular mountain scenery. Drive E 17 mi on US 30, I-84 to Troutdale. At this point, for approx 24 mi, there are 2 routes: you may either turn right and take the mountainous upper-level scenic route, or continue on the main river-level freeway. The 2 roads rejoin about 10 mi W of Bonneville Dam (see HOOD RIVER). Continue E on US 30, I-84 for 23 mi to Hood River, turning S on OR 35 for 47 mi through Mount Hood National Forest to US 26. Drive NW on US 26, 56 mi back to Portland. A description of this tour may be found in a free visitors guide from the Portland Visitors Assn, or in "The Oregon Travel Guide" free from the Tourism Division, Oregon Economic Development Dept, 775 Summer St NE, Salem 97310. Phone 87-PORTLAND.

Mount Tabor Park. Extinct volcano; view of city and mountains. Picnicking. Summer concerts. (Daily) SE 60th Ave & Salmon St. Phone 503/823-2223. **FREE**

Multnomah Falls. Chief among the 11 waterfalls along 11 mi of this highway; 620-ft drop in 2 falls, 4th-highest in US. Hiking. Restaurant. Visitor center. 32 mi E on I-84. (See MOUNT HOOD NATIONAL FOREST)

Oaks Amusement Park. (1905) Thrill rides, children's area, roller rink (Tues-Sun; rentals), miniature golf; waterfront picnicking. Separate fees for activities. Park (two wks end of Mar, Apr-May, wkends; Mid-June-Sep, Tues-Sun). SE Oaks Park Way, E end of Sellwood Bridge. Phone 503/233-5777.

Oregon History Center. Regional repository of Northwest history; permanent and special exhibits; museum store; publishing house; regional research library (Wed-Sat). (Tues-Sun; closed hols) 1200 SW Park Ave. Phone 503/222-1741. ¢¢

Oregon Museum of Science and Industry. Six exhibit halls incl interactive exhibits on space, biological, life, Earth, physical, and computer science. Omnimax Theather (daily; fee); planetarium shows; laser light shows (fee). (Labor Day-Memorial Day, Tues-Sun; rest of yr, daily; closed Dec 25) 1945 SE Water Ave.

Phone 503/797-OMSI or 800/955-OMSI. ¢¢¢

Oregon Zoo. Specializes in breeding rare and endangered species. Features Asian elephants, Humboldt penguins, chimpanzees, Oregon native plants and animals; bears; musk oxen; wolves; animals of the African plains and rain forests. Train travels through zoo to Washington Park, stopping near the Intl Rose Test Garden and Japanese gardens (fee). (Daily; closed Dec 25) 4001 SW Canyon Rd. Phone 503/220-2789 or 503/226-1561. ¢¢¢

Peninsula Park and Community Center. Sunken rose gardens with 15,000 rose bushes; reflecting pond. Swimming (fee), wading pools; tennis, picnic grove, playground. Community Center (Mon-Fri). (Daily) N Portland Blvd & Albina Ave. Phone 503/823-2223. **FREE**

Pittock Mansion. (1914) Restored and furnished French Chateau-esque mansion surrounded by 46 forested and landscaped acres. Spectacular views of rivers, the city, and snow-capped mountains, incl Mt St. Helens and Mt Hood. (Daily; closed hols, also 1st 3 wks Jan) 3229 NW Pittock Dr. Phone 503/823-3624. ¢¢

Police Historical Museum. Collection of early police uniforms, badges, photos, and other police memorabilia. (Mon-Thurs; closed hols) 1111 SW 2nd Ave, 16th floor. Phone 503/823-0019. **FREE**

★ **Portland Art Museum.** Features 35 centuries of world art: European painting and sculpture from the Renaissance-present; 19th- and 20th-century American art; noted collections of NW Coast Native American art, Asian, pre-Columbian, West African, and classical Greek and Roman art; British silver; major print and drawings collection. Changing exhibits. Lectures, films, concerts, special events. Gift shop; rental sales gallery. (Daily; closed hols) 1219 SW Park Ave at Jefferson St. Phone 503/226-2811. ¢¢¢

Portland Saturday Market. One of largest, oldest open-air community markets in the US, with arts, crafts, food booths, produce, and street entertainers. (Sat-Sun, Mar-Dec 24) W Burnside St, under the Burnside Bridge. Phone 503/222-6072.

Portland State University. (1946) 14,700 students. Art and photography exhibits in Smith Memorial Center and Neuberger Hall. Campus tours. Visitor information center at SW Broadway & College Sts. Phone 503/725-3000.

Professional sports. NBA (Portland Trail Blazers). Rose Garden. 1 Center Court. Phone 503/224-4400.

State parks.

Crown Point. A 307-acre park with 725-ft-high point affords view of Columbia River Gorge with its 2,000-ft-high rock walls. Historic Vista House (1918), pioneer memorial of stone and marble. Visitor information service (summer). E on I-84, Exit 22; on US 30 Scenic Rte. Phone 503/695-2230. **FREE**

Dabney. A 135-acre park with fishing in Sandy River. Hiking, picnicking. 19 mi E off I-84 Exit 18, at Stark St Bridge on US 30 Scenic Rte. Phone 503/695-2261. Per vehicle ¢¢

Guy W. Talbot. A 371-acre park. Latourell Falls, 2nd-highest falls in the Columbia Gorge, drops 250 ft. Hiking, picnicking. Observation point. E on I-84, Exit 27; on US 30 Scenic Rte. Phone 503/695-2261. **FREE**

Lewis and Clark. A 56-acre park with fishing, boating (ramp); hiking, picnicking. 16 mi E on I-84, Exit 18. Phone 503/695-2261. **FREE**

Rooster Rock. A 1½-mi beach on Columbia River in 927-acre park. Swimming, fishing, boating (ramp, docks); hiking, picnicking, clothing optional beach area. E on I-84, milepost 25. Phone 503/695-2261. Per vehicle ¢

Willamette Stone. This 2-acre historic site marks the initial point of all government land surveys of Oregon and Washington; trail to stone monument. No water, rest rms. 4 mi W at Skyline Blvd & W Burnside. **FREE**

Sternwheeler Columbia Gorge. Riverboat scenic and dinner cruises on the Willamette River (Fri-Sun, Oct-mid-June), incl dinner dance cruises, champagne brunch cruises, narrated excursion trps, and special-event cruises. Leaves from Water-

© MAPQUEST.COM

The glory of Portland is its parks. Settled by idealistic New Englanders, Portland had an extensive park system in the 1850s, decades before other West Coast cities were even founded. Begin at Portland State University in the North Park Blocks, a swath of twenty blocks of parkland that cuts right through the heart of the city. The park was established in the 1850s and for generations was the best address for civic structures. Numerous historic churches, plus the Portland Art Museum, the Oregon History Center, the Portland Center for the Performing Arts, and the Schnitzer Concert Hall (home to Oregon Symphony) flank the park. The park is also home to the largest remaining stand of American elm (killed elsewhere by Dutch elm disease), numerous heroic statues, and a farmers market (on Wednesdays and Saturdays). Drop down to Pioneer Courthouse Square at 6th and Morrison, often referred to as Portland's living room. This is where many outdoor festivals, concerts, and demonstrations take place. (Dan Quayle got such a raucous reception here that he thenceforward refused to visit Portland, referring to the city as America's Beirut.) The Square is a great place for people-watching and sunbathing, and there are many food carts and cafes here. In the blocks around Pioneer Courthouse Square are many of Portland's major shopping venues. Adjacent is the Pioneer Courthouse itself, built in 1875. Follow 5th Avenue south, noting the abundance of public art along the pedestrian friendly bus mall. At 5th Avenue and Main Street is the Portland Building, a noted postmodern structure designed by Michael Graves. The front is surmounted by a massive statue called Portlandia. This is the second-largest hammered copper statue in the world, the largest being the Statue of Liberty. Drop down onto the Willamette River waterfront. The park that runs the length of downtown along the river is recent. In the 1970s, the city ripped out a freeway that ran along the river and replaced it with this park, which in summer is loaded with joggers, sun worshipers, and any number of summer festivals. Also along the river are boat tour operators, a large marina with some shops and cafes, and, at the north end, a memorial to Japanese American internment during WWII. Under the Burnside Bridge, adjacent to Waterfront Park, is the Portland Saturday Market (open both Saturday and Sunday), which is reputed to be the largest open-air crafts market in the nation. Turn north along 3rd Avenue, and walk through Portland's Old Town (most buildings dating from the 1880s) to Chinatown. Here, between 2nd and 3rd avenues and Everett and Flanders streets is the Portland Chinese Garden, a brand-new traditional Chinese garden that is a joint project of Portland and the city of Suzhou. It is the largest Chinese-style garden outside of China itself.

front Park, Portland. Phone 503/223-3928 for schedule and prices. Adults ¢¢¢¢-¢¢¢¢¢; Children ¢¢¢-¢¢¢¢¢

★ **Washington Park.** A 129-acre park on hill above city. Incl the Intl Rose Test Garden, with 8,000 bushes of more than 400 varieties (free); the Shakespeare Garden; Lewis and Clark monument; Sacajawea Memorial Statue. Two reservoirs. Archery, tennis. Picnic area. Sunken rose garden amphitheater has music productions, usually Aug-Sep (fee). Accessible via W Burnside St, SW Park Place, or Canyon Rd. Phone 503/823-2223 (wkdays). Also here is

> **Japanese Garden.** Five-and-a-half acres; acclaimed one of the most authentic Japanese gardens outside of Japan. Traditional gardens incl the Flat Garden (Hiraniwa), Strolling Pond Garden (Chisen-Kaiyu-Shiki), Tea Garden (Rojiniwa), Natural Garden (Shukeiyen), and the Sand and Stone Garden (Seki-tei); also an authentic Japanese pavilion. Special events include ikebana and bonsai exhibits. Gift shop. (Daily; closed Jan 1, Thanksgiving, Dec 25) Phone 503/223-1321 or 503/223-9233 (tours). ¢¢

Water Tower in Johns Landing. Former 3-story furniture factory (1903) with cobblestone courtyard; houses specialty shops and restaurants. (Daily; closed hols) 5331 SW Macadam Ave. Phone 503/274-2786.

World Forestry Center. Educational exhibits on regional and intl forests; 70-ft talking tree. Special exhibits, shows. (Daily; closed Dec 25) 4033 SW Canyon Rd. Phone 503/228-1367. ¢¢

Annual Events

St. Patrick's Irish Festival. One of the largest Irish festivals in the Pacific NW. Phone 503/227-4057. Five days Mar.

Portland Rose Festival. Held for more than 80 yrs, this festival incl the Grand Floral Parade (res required for indoor parade seats) and 2 other parades; band competition; rose show; championship auto racing; hot-air balloons; air show; carnival; Navy ships. Phone 503/227-2681. Late May-June.

Portland Scottish Highland Games. 15 mi E at Mt Hood Community College in Gresham. Phone 503/293-8501. Mid-July.

Multnomah County Fair. Agricultural and horticultural exhibits; entertainment. Phone 503/289-6623. Late July.

Mount Hood Jazz Festival. 15 mi E on I-84, in Gresham. Intl, national, and local jazz acts presented in outdoor festival. Phone 503/231-0161. First wkend Aug.

Portland Marathon. World-class running event featuring intl competition. Phone 503/226-1111. Early Oct.

Holiday Parade of Christmas Ships. Along Willamette and Columbia rivers. More than 50 boats cruise the 2 rivers in a holiday display. Phone 503/225-5555, code 2065. Early-mid Dec.

Seasonal Events

Greyhound Racing. Multnomah Greyhound Park, NE 223rd Ave between NE Halsey and Glisan Sts, 12 mi E off I-84, Exit 13 or 16A. Parimutuel betting. Matinee and evening races. Under 12 yrs not permitted at evening races. For schedule phone 503/667-7700. May-Oct.

Chamber Music Northwest. Catlin Gabel School and Reed College. Nationally acclaimed summer chamber music festival offers 25 concerts featuring 40-50 artists, Mon, Tues, Thurs-Sat. Catered picnic preceeding each concert. Children under 7 permitted only at Family Concert. Phone 503/223-3202. Mid-June-late July.

Horse racing. Portland Meadows, 1001 N Schmeer Rd, 6 mi N on I-5. Pari-mutuel betting. Thoroughbred and quarter horse racing. (Fri evenings, Sat and Sun matinee) Under 12 yrs not permitted at evening races. Phone 503/285-9144. Late Oct-Apr.

Portland Center Stage. Portland Center for the Performing Arts. Series of 5 contemporary and classical plays. Tues-Sun. For fees, performance, and title schedules phone 503/248-4335. Sep-Apr.

Additional Visitor Information

For further information contact the Portland Oregon Visitors Assn, 26 SW Salmon, 97204, phone 503/222-2223. For a recorded message describing major theater, sports, and music events in Portland for the current month, phone 503/225-5555, code 3608.

City Neighborhoods

Many of the restaurants, unrated dining establishments and some lodgings listed under Portland incl neighborhoods as well as exact street addresses. Geographic descriptions of these areas are given.

Downtown. S of I-405, W of the Willamette River, N of SW Lincoln, and East of I-30. **E of Downtown:** E of Willamette River. **W of Downtown:** W of I-30.

Nob Hill. W of Downtown; S of Vaughn St, W of I-405, N of Burnside St, and E of NW 23rd St.

Old Town. Area of Downtown S of Glisan St, W of Front St and the river, N of Burnside St, and E of NW 3rd St.

Motels/Motor Lodges

★★ **ALDERWOOD INN.** 7025 NE Alderwood Rd (97218), E of Downtown. 503/255-2700; fax 503/255-4700; res 888/987-2700. 150 rms, 4 story. June-Sep: S $75-$95; D $82-$102; each addl $7; suites $102-$122; under 12 free; lower rates rest of yr. Crib free. TV; cable. Complimentary full bkfst. Restaurant 6:30-9:30 am, 11:30 am-2 pm, 5-10 pm; Sun brunch 7 am-1 pm. Bar. Ck-out 11 am. Meeting rm. Business servs avail. In-rm modem link. Valet serv. Sundries. Coin lndry. Free airport transportation. Exercise equipt. Indoor pool; whirlpool. Refrigerators, microwaves. Cr cds: A, C, D, DS, MC, V.

D ⌖ ⟁ 🛪 ⟶ 🔥 **SC**

★★ **BEST WESTERN INN AT THE MEADOWS.** 1215 N Hayden Mdws Dr (97217), E of Downtown. 503/286-9600; fax 503/286-8020; toll-free 800/528-1234. 146 rms, 3 story. Feb-Oct: S, D $89-$99; suites $150; under 18 free; family rates; higher rates Indy Car races. Crib free. Pet accepted, some restrictions; $21.80. TV; cable (premium). Complimentary

continental bkfst, coffee in rms. Restaurant adj 6 am-11 pm. Ck-out noon. Meeting rms. Business servs avail. Valet serv. Sundries. Coin lndry. Free railroad station transportation. Some refrigerators, microwaves, wet bars. Cr cds: A, C, D, DS, JCB, MC, V.

D ⟶ ⟁ 🔥 **SC**

★ **CARAVAN MOTOR HOTEL & RESTAURANT.** 2401 SW 4th Ave (97201), S of Downtown. 503/226-1121; fax 503/274-2681. May, Nov: S $65; D $75; each addl $7; under 16 free; lower rates rest of yr. Crib avail, fee. TV; cable (premium), VCR avail. Restaurant 7 am-10:30 pm. Bar. Ck-out 1 pm, ck-in noon. Golf. Tennis. Cr cds: A, C, D, DS, ER, JCB, MC, V.

🛝 🎿 🛪 ⟶ 🔥

★ **CHESTNUT TREE INN.** 9699 SE Stark St (97216), E of Downtown. 503/255-4444; fax 503/255-4444; res 888/236-5660; toll-free 888/236-5600. 58 rms, 2 story. S $42; D $50; each addl $3. Crib free. TV; cable (premium). Complimentary coffee. Restaurant adj 6 am-11 pm. Ck-out noon. Business servs avail. Refrigerators. Cr cds: A, C, D, MC, V.

D ⟶ 🔥

★ **DAYS INN.** 9930 N Whitaker Rd (97217), I-5 Exit 306B, N of Downtown. 503/289-1800; fax 503/289-3778; toll-free 800/329-7466. 212 rms, 4 story. S, D $60-$70; each addl $5; under 12 free; wkly rates. Crib free. Pet accepted; $10/day. TV; cable (premium). Complimentary continental bkfst. Restaurant adj 6 am-11 pm. Ck-out noon. Coin lndry. Meeting rm. Business servs avail. In-rm modem link. Sundries. Free airport, railroad station, bus depot transportation. Park adj. Cr cds: A, C, D, DS, MC, V.

D ⌖ ⟶ 🔥

★ **DAYS INN PORTLAND SOUTH.** 9717 SE Sunnyside Rd (97015), I-205 Sunnyside Exit. 503/654-1699; fax 503/659-2702; res 800/DAYSINN; toll-free 800/241-1699. 110 rms, 3 story. S $55-$95; D $62-$102; each addl $7; studio rms $65-$130; under 12 free. Crib free. TV; cable (premium). Heated pool; whirlpool. Sauna. Complimentary continental bkfst. Ck-out noon. Business servs avail. Some refrigerators. Cr cds: A, DS, MC, V.

[D] [icons]

★★ **FAIRFIELD INN BY MAR-RIOTT.** *11929 NE Airport Way (97220), E of Downtown. 503/253-1400; fax 503/253-3889; res 800/228-2800. Email pdxfi@aol.com.* 106 rms, 3 story. Apr-Sep: S, D $75-$85; each addl $10; under 18 free; lower rates rest of yr. Crib free. TV; cable (premium). Pool; whirlpool. Complimentary continental bkfst. Restaurant nearby. Ck-out noon. Business servs avail. Sundries. Free airport transportation. Exercise equipt. Cr cds: A, DS, MC, V.

[D] [icons]

★★ **PHOENIX INN.** *14905 SW Bangy Rd (97035), S on I-5, Exit 292, at OR 217. 503/624-7400; fax 503/624-7405; toll-free 800/824-9992.* 62 rms, 4 story. June-Sep: S, D $94; each addl $5; suites $119-$129; under 18 free; lower rates rest of yr. Crib free. TV; cable (premium). Indoor pool; whirlpool. Complimentary continental bkfst. Coffee in rms. Restaurant adj 11 am-10 pm. Bar 11 am-10 pm. Ck-out noon. Coin lndry. Meeting rms. Business servs avail. In-rm modem link. Valet serv. Sundries. Airport transportation avail. Exercise equipt. Refrigerators; some minibars. Cr cds: A, C, D, DS, MC, V.

[D] [icons]

★★ **RESIDENCE INN BY MAR-RIOTT.** *1710 NE Multnomah St (97232), E of Downtown. 503/288-1400; fax 503/288-0241; res 800/331-3131. Email port2a@aol.com.* 168 suites, 3 story. June-Sep: suites $111-$159; package plans. Crib free. Pet accepted, some restrictions; $50, $10/day. TV; cable (premium). Complimentary continental bkfst, coffee in rms. Restaurant nearby. Ck-out noon. Meeting rms. Business servs avail. In-rm modem link. Valet serv. Sundries. Coin lndry. Free airport, railroad station transportation. Lighted tennis. Heated pool; whirlpools. Refrigerators, microwaves. Many fireplaces. Picnic tables. Cr cds: A, DS, MC, V.

[D] [icons]

★★ **RESIDENCE INN BY MAR-RIOTT.** *15200 SW Bangy Rd (97025), S on I-5, Exit 292. 503/684-2603; fax 503/620-6712; res 800/331-3131. Email ribmpdxlq@yahoo.com.* 112 kit. units, 2 story. 1 & 2-bedrm suites $130-$175. Crib $5. Pet accepted; $10/day. TV; cable (premium), VCR avail (free movies). Heated pool; whirlpool. Complimentary continental bkfst. Restaurant adj. Ck-out noon. Coin lndry. Business servs avail. Valet serv. Health club privileges. Fireplace in suites. Private patios, balconies. Picnic tables, grills. Cr cds: A, DS, MC, V.

[D] [icons]

★★ **SHILO INN.** *9900 SW Canyon Rd (97225), W of Downtown. 503/297-2551; fax 503/297-7708; toll-free 800/222-2244.* 142 rms, 2-3 story. S, D $79-$99; each addl $10; suites $99-$189; under 12 free. Crib free. Pet accepted; $7. TV; cable (premium), VCR avail (movies). Heated pool. Complimentary bkfst buffet. Restaurant 6 am-10 pm. Bar 11-2 am; entertainment Mon-Sat. Ck-out noon. Meeting rms. Business servs avail. Valet serv. Sundries. Free airport transportation. Exercise equipt. Refrigerators. Private patios, balconies. Cr cds: A, C, D, DS, ER, JCB, MC, V.

[D] [icons]

★★ **SHILO INN.** *10830 SW Greenburg Rd (97223), S on OR 217, Greenburg Rd Exit. 503/620-4320; fax 503/620-8277; res 800/222-2244. Email wahingtonsquare@shiloinns.com; www.shiloinns.com.* 78 rms, 4 story, 7 suites. S $59; D $69; each addl $10; suites $79; under 12 free. Crib avail. Pet accepted, fee. Parking lot. TV; cable (premium). Complimentary continental bkfst, coffee in rms, newspaper, toll-free calls. Restaurant. Ck-out noon, ck-in 2 pm. Meeting rm. Business servs avail. Dry cleaning, coin lndry. Gift shop. Exercise equipt, sauna, steam rm, whirlpool. Golf, 18 holes. Tennis, 3 courts. Video games. Cr cds: A, C, D, DS, ER, JCB, MC, V.

[D] [icons]

★ **SUPER 8 WILSONVILLE.** *25438 SW Parkway Ave (97070), I-5 Exit 286. 503/682-2088; fax 503/682-0453; res 800/800-8000.* 72 rms, 4 story. S $49.88; D $60.88-$67.88; each addl $4. Crib free. Pet accepted; $25 refundable. TV; cable (premium).

Complimentary coffee in lobby. Restaurant opp open 24 hrs. Ck-out noon. Coin lndry. Meeting rm. Business servs avail. Cr cds: A, DS, MC, V.

Hotels

★★★ 5TH AVENUE SUITES HOTEL.
506 SW Washington St (97204), Downtown. 503/222-0001; fax 503/222-0004; res 888/207-2201. www.5thavenuesuites.com. 86 rms, 10 story, 135 suites. June-Sep: S, D $185; suites $300; under 18 free; lower rates rest of yr. Crib avail. Pet accepted. Valet parking avail. TV; cable (premium), VCR avail, CD avail. Complimentary coffee in rms, newspaper. Restaurant 6 am-11 pm. 24-hr rm serv. Bar. Ck-out noon, ck-in 3 pm. Meeting rms. Business center. Bellhops. Concierge. Dry cleaning. Exercise privileges. Golf. Video games. Cr cds: A, C, D, DS, ER, JCB, MC, V.

★★★ BENSON HOTEL.
309 SW Broadway (97205), at Oak St, Downtown. 503/228-2000; fax 503/471-3920; res 800/426-0607; toll-free 888/523-6766. Email reservations@benson hotel.com; www.bensonhotel.com. 278 rms, 14 story, 9 suites. June-Aug: S, D $220; each addl $25; suites $500; under 18 free; lower rates rest of yr. Crib avail, fee. Pet accepted, some restrictions, fee. Valet parking avail. TV; cable (premium). Complimentary coffee in rms, newspaper, toll-free calls. Restaurant. 24-hr rm serv. Bar. Ck-out 1 pm, ck-in 3 pm. Conference center, meeting rms. Business center. Bellhops. Concierge. Dry cleaning. Gift shop. Exercise privileges. Golf. Tennis. Cr cds: A, C, D, DS, ER, JCB, MC, V.

★★ BEST WESTERN IMPERIAL HOTEL.
400 SW Broadway at Stark (97205), at Stark St, Downtown. 503/228-7221; fax 503/223-4551; res 800/528-1234; toll-free 800/452-2323. Email reservations@hotel-imperial.com; www.hotel-imperial.com. 128 rms, 9 story. S $100; D $125; each addl $10; under 12 free. Crib avail. Pet accepted, some restrictions, fee. Valet parking avail. TV; cable (premium). Complimentary continental bkfst, newspaper. Restaurant. Bar.

Ck-out 2 pm, ck-in 3 pm. Meeting rms. Business center. Bellhops. Dry cleaning. Exercise privileges, sauna, steam rm. Golf. Video games. Cr cds: A, C, D, DS, ER, JCB, MC, V.

★★ BEST WESTERN PONY SOLDIER INN AIRPORT.
9901 NE Sandy Blvd (97220), near Intl Airport, E of Downtown. 503/256-1504; fax 503/256-5928; res 800/528-1234; toll-free 800/634-7669. Email ponypdx@aol. com. 104 rms, 2 story, 15 suites. S $85; D $95; each addl $5; suites, kit. units $120; under 12 free. Crib $3. TV; cable (premium). Heated pool; whirlpool. Complimentary continental bkfst. Restaurant adj 6 am-10 pm. Ck-out noon. Free lndry facilities. Meeting rms. Business center avail. Valet serv. Sundries. Free airport transportation. Exercise equipt; sauna. Refrigerators, microwaves. Balconies. Cr cds: A, C, D, DS, ER, MC, V.

★★ BEST WESTERN ROSE GARDEN HOTEL.
10 N Weidler St (97227), E of Downtown. 503/287-9900; fax 503/287-3500; res 800/528-1234. Email jason@ipinc.net; www. bestwestern.com. 181 rms, 5 story. June-Oct: S $79; D $89; each addl $5; under 12 free; lower rates rest of yr. Crib avail. Parking garage. TV; cable (premium). Complimentary coffee in rms, toll-free calls. Restaurant 7 am-10 pm. Bar. Ck-out noon, ck-in 3 pm. Meeting rms. Business center. Golf. Cr cds: A, D, DS, MC, V.

★★ COURTYARD BY MARRIOTT.
11550 NE Airport Way (97220), near Intl Airport, E of Downtown. 503/252-3200; fax 503/252-8921; toll-free 800/321-2211. 140 rms, 6 story, 10 suites. S, D $102; suites $125; under 17 free. Crib avail. Parking lot. Pool, whirlpool. TV; cable (premium), VCR avail. Complimentary coffee in rms, newspaper, toll-free calls. Restaurant, closed Sun. Bar. Ck-out noon, ck-in 4 pm. Meeting rms. Business center. Bellhops. Dry cleaning, coin lndry. Free airport transportation. Exercise equipt. Golf. Downhill skiing. Video games. Cr cds: A, C, D, DS, JCB, MC, V.

★★★ **CROWNE PLAZA.** *14811 Kruse Oaks Blvd (97035), S on I-5 on OR 217.* 503/624-8400; fax 503/684-8324; res 800/227-6963; toll-free 800/465-4329. www.crowneplaza.com/hotels/pdxcp. 161 rms, 6 story. June-Aug: S, D $149; suites $161-$275; under 18 free; lower rates rest of yr. Crib free. Pet accepted. Valet parking $5. TV; cable (premium). Indoor/outdoor pool; whirlpool. Complimentary coffee in rms. Restaurant 6 am-2 pm, 5-10 pm. Rm serv to midnight. Bar 2 pm-midnight. Ck-out noon. Meeting rms. Business servs avail. Sundries. Gift shop. Valet serv. Exercise equipt; sauna. Cr cds: A, DS, MC, V.

D ◆ ⌷ ⟟ ⟟ ⟟ SC

★ **DAYS INN.** *1414 SW 6th Ave (97201), at Columbia, Downtown.* 503/221-1611; fax 503/226-0447; res 800/329-7466; toll-free 800/899-0248. Email daysinn@transport.com; www.daysinn.com. 173 rms, 5 story, 1 suite. June-Aug: S $109; D $129; each addl $10; suites $175; under 17 free; lower rates rest of yr. Crib avail. Parking garage. Pool. TV; cable. Complimentary newspaper. Restaurant 6:30 am-10 pm. Bar. Ck-out noon, ck-in 3 pm. Meeting rms. Business center. Dry cleaning. Exercise privileges. Golf. Tennis. Downhill skiing. Cr cds: A, C, D, DS, ER, JCB, MC, V.

D ⟟ ⟟ ⟟ ⟟ ⟟ ⟟ ⟟ SC ⟟

★★★ **DOUBLETREE HOTEL COLUMBIA RIVER.** *1401 N Hayden Island Dr (97217), W of I-5, Jantzen Beach Exit, N of Downtown.* 503/283-2111; fax 503/283-4718; toll-free 800/222-8733. www.doubletreehotels.com. 344 rms, 3 story, 8 suites. Apr-Sep: S, D $109; each addl $15; under 18 free; lower rates rest of yr. Crib avail. Pet accepted, some restrictions, fee. Parking lot. Pool, whirlpool. TV; cable (premium). Complimentary coffee in rms, newspaper, toll-free calls. Restaurant 11 am-10 pm. Bar. Ck-out noon, ck-in 4 pm. Conference center, meeting rms. Business servs avail. Bellhops. Dry cleaning, coin lndry. Gift shop. Salon/barber. Free airport transportation. Exercise privileges. Golf. Tennis, 2 courts. Downhill skiing. Cr cds: A, C, D, DS, ER, JCB, MC, V.

D ⟟ ◆ ⟟ ⟟ ⟟ ⟟ ⟟ ⟟ ⟟ SC

★★★ **DOUBLETREE HOTEL JANTZEN BEACH.** *909 N Hayden Island Dr (97217), E of I-5 Exit Jantzen Beach, N of Downtown.* 503/283-4466; fax 503/283-4743. www.doubletreehotels.com. 296 rms, 4 story, 24 suites. May-Aug: S $139; D $154; each addl $15; under 18 free; lower rates rest of yr. Crib avail. Pet accepted, some restrictions, fee. Parking lot. Pool, whirlpool. TV; cable (premium). Complimentary coffee in rms, newspaper. Restaurant 6 am-10 pm. Bar. Ck-out noon, ck-in 3 pm. Conference center, meeting rms. Business center. Bellhops. Dry cleaning, coin lndry. Gift shop. Free airport transportation. Exercise privileges. Golf. Tennis, 2 courts. Downhill skiing. Cr cds: A, C, D, DS, MC, V.

D ⟟ ◆ ⟟ ⟟ ⟟ ⟟ ⟟ ⟟ ⟟ ⟟ ⟟

★★★ **DOUBLETREE PORTLAND - LLOYD CENTER.** *1000 NE Multnomah St (97232), I-84 Exit 1 (Lloyd Blvd), E of Downtown.* 503/281-6111; fax 503/284-8553; toll-free 800/222-8733. Email sabo@jps.net; doubletreehotels.com. 459 rms, 15 story, 17 suites. May-Oct: S $159; D $169; each addl $10; suites $465; under 18 free; lower rates rest of yr. Crib avail. Pet accepted, some restrictions. Valet parking avail. Pool. TV; cable (premium). Complimentary coffee in rms, newspaper, toll-free calls. Restaurant 6 am-midnight. Bar. Ck-out noon, ck-in 3 pm. Conference center, meeting rms. Business center. Bellhops. Concierge. Dry cleaning. Gift shop. Free airport transportation. Exercise privileges. Golf. Tennis. Downhill skiing. Cr cds: A, C, D, DS, MC, V.

D ⟟ ◆ ⟟ ⟟ ⟟ ⟟ ⟟ ⟟ ⟟ ⟟ SC ⟟

★★★ **GOVERNOR HOTEL.** *611 SW 10th Ave (97205), at SW Alder Ave, Downtown.* 503/224-3400; fax 503/241-2122; toll-free 800/554-3456. Email hotelgov@aol.com; www.govhotel.com. 76 rms, 6 story, 24 suites. S $165; D $185; each addl $20; suites $240. Crib avail. Valet parking avail. Indoor pool, lap pool, whirlpool. TV; cable (premium), VCR avail. Complimentary coffee in rms, newspaper. Restaurant 6 am-11 pm. 24-hr rm serv. Bar. Ck-out noon, ck-in 4 pm. Meeting rms. Business center. Bellhops. Concierge. Dry cleaning. Exercise rm, sauna, steam rm. Golf. Video games. Cr cds: A, C, D, DS, ER, JCB, MC, V.

⊡ 🏋 ➰ 🏊 🎿 🈺 🚶

★★ **HAMPTON INN.** *8633 NE Airport Way (97220), E of Downtown. 503/288-2423; fax 503/288-2620; toll-free 800/426-7866. Email hampton@ spiritone.com; www.hamptoninn.com.* 130 rms, 4 story. S $89; D $94. Crib avail. Parking lot. Pool. TV; cable (premium). Complimentary continental bkfst, coffee in rms, newspaper, toll-free calls. Restaurant nearby. Ck-out noon, ck-in 3 pm. Meeting rm. Business servs avail. Dry cleaning. Gift shop. Free airport transportation. Exercise privileges. Golf. Downhill skiing. Video games. Cr cds: A, C, D, DS, JCB, MC, V.

⊡ ➤ 🏋 ➰ 🏊 🏋 🈺

★★ **HAWTHORN INN & SUITES.** *2323 NE 181st Ave (97230), I-84 Exit 13. 503/492-4000; fax 503/492-3271; res 800/527-1133. Email hiegresh@portland.quik.com; www. hotels-west.com.* 64 rms, 3 story, 6 suites. May-Aug: S $75; D $85; each addl $7; suites $130; under 18 free; lower rates rest of yr. Crib avail. Pet accepted. Parking lot. Indoor pool, whirlpool. TV; cable (DSS), VCR avail. Complimentary continental bkfst, coffee in rms, newspaper, toll-free calls. Restaurant nearby. Ck-out 1 pm, ck-in 3 pm. Business servs avail. Dry cleaning, coin lndry. Gift shop. Free airport transportation. Exercise privileges, sauna. Golf, 18 holes. Tennis. Downhill skiing. Cr cds: A, C, D, DS, ER, JCB, MC, V.

⊡ ➤ 🦮 ➤ 🏋 🎿 ➰ 🏋 🈺 SC

★★★ **THE HEATHMAN HOTEL.** *1001 SW Broadway (97205), Downtown. 503/241-4100; fax 503/790-7110; toll-free 800/551-0011. Email info@heathmanhotel.com; www. heathmanhotel.com.* 118 rms, 10 story, 32 suites. S, D $170; each addl $20; suites $215; under 17 free. Crib avail. Pet accepted, some restrictions, fee. Valet parking avail. TV; cable, VCR avail. Complimentary newspaper. Restaurant 5:30 am-11 pm. 24-hr rm serv. Bar. Ck-out noon, ck-in 3:30 pm. Meeting rms. Business center. Bellhops. Concierge. Dry cleaning. Exercise

equipt. Golf. Tennis. Downhill skiing. Cr cds: A, C, D, DS, JCB, MC, V.

⊡ ➤ ➤ 🏋 🎿 🏋 🈺 🈺

★★★ **HILTON PORTLAND.** *921 SW Sixth Ave (97204), Downtown. 503/226-1611; fax 503/220-2595; res 800/HILTONS. www.portland.hilton. com.* 449 rms, 23 story, 6 suites. June-Sep: S, D $195; each addl $3; suites $600; under 18 free; lower rates rest of yr. Crib avail. Valet parking avail. Indoor pool, whirlpool. TV; cable (premium), VCR avail. Complimentary coffee in rms, newspaper. Restaurant 6:30 am-11 pm. Bar. Ck-out 11 am, ck-in 4 pm. Conference center, meeting rms. Business center. Bellhops. Concierge. Dry cleaning. Gift shop. Exercise rm, sauna, steam rm. Golf, 18 holes. Cr cds: A, D, DS, JCB, MC, V.

⊡ 🏋 🏋 ➰ 🈺 🈺 🏋

★★ **HOLIDAY INN PORTLAND AIRPORT.** *8439 NE Columbia Blvd (97220), 2½ mi N of I-84, on I-205, Exit 23B/Columbia Blvd, near Intl Airport, E of Downtown. 503/256-5000; fax 503/256-5000; res 800/HOLIDAY.* 286 rms, 8 story, 17 suites. Oct: S $89; D $99; each addl $10; suites $150; under 12 free; lower rates rest of yr. Crib avail. Pet accepted, some restrictions, fee. Parking lot. Indoor pool, whirlpool. TV; cable (premium). Complimentary coffee in rms, newspaper, toll-free calls. Restaurant 6 am-10 pm. Bar. Ck-out noon, ck-in 3 pm. Conference center, meeting rms. Business center. Bellhops. Dry cleaning, coin lndry. Gift shop. Free airport transportation. Exercise equipt, sauna. Golf, 18 holes. Video games. Cr cds: A, D, DS, MC, V.

➤ 🏋 🏋 🎿 🈺 🈺 SC 🏋

★ **MALLORY HOTEL.** *729 SW 15th Ave (97205), W of I-405, Downtown. 503/223-6311; fax 503/223-0522; toll-free 800/228-8657. Email malloryhot@ aol.com; malloryhotel.com.* 117 rms, 8 story, 13 suites. S $85; D $90; each addl $5; suites $140; under 12 free. Crib avail. Pet accepted, fee. Valet parking avail. TV; cable (premium). Complimentary newspaper, toll-free calls. Restaurant. Bar. Meeting rms. Business servs avail. Bellhops. Dry cleaning. Exercise privileges. Golf. Tennis. Cr cds: A, D, DS, JCB, MC, V.

⊡ ➤ 🏋 🎿 🏋 🈺 🈺

★ **MARK SPENCER HOTEL PORT-LAND.** *409 SW 11th Ave (97205), Downtown. 503/224-3293; fax 503/223-7848; toll-free 800/548-3934. Email samiam@itinc.net; www.mark spencer.com.* 101 kit. units, 6 story. S, D $76-$119; each addl $10; suites $104-$119; studio rms $76; under 12 free; monthly rates. Crib free. Pet accepted; $200 refundable. TV; cable, VCR avail (free movies). Complimentary continental bkfst, coffee in lobby. Restaurant nearby. Ck-out noon. Coin lndry. Business servs avail. Health club privileges. Refrigerators; microwaves avail. Rooftop garden. Cr cds: A, C, D, DS, JCB, MC, V.
🏨 🏃 🏌 🛝 ⛵ 🔥

★★★ **MARRIOTT HOTEL.** *1401 SW Naito Pkwy (97201), Downtown. 503/226-7600; fax 503/221-1789; toll-free 800/228-9290.* 503 rms, 15 story. S $160-$190; D $170-$200; suites $400-$600; under 18 free. Crib free. Pet accepted. Valet parking in/out $14/day. TV; cable (premium), VCR avail. Indoor pool; whirlpool, poolside serv. Restaurant 6 am-11 pm; Fri, Sat to midnight. Bar 11:30-1 am; entertainment. Ck-out noon. Coin lndry. Convention facilities. Business center. Concierge. Gift shop. Exercise equipt; sauna. Massage. Some bathrm phones, wet bar in suites. Some private patios, balconies. Japanese garden at entrance. Luxury level. Cr cds: A, C, D, DS, ER, JCB, MC, V.
🅳 🐾 🏊 🏌 🛝 🔥 SC 🏃

★★★ **RADISSON HOTEL.** *1441 NE 2nd Ave (97232), E of Downtown. 503/233-2401; fax 503/233-0498; res 800/333-3333; toll-free 877/777-2704. Email radis1@ix.netcom.com.* 238 rms, 10 story, 1 suite. May-Oct: S, D $149; each addl $10; suites $250; under 12 free; lower rates rest of yr. Crib avail, fee. Parking lot. Pool. TV; cable (premium). Complimentary coffee in rms, newspaper, toll-free calls. Restaurant. Bar. Ck-in 3 pm. Meeting rms. Business center. Bellhops. Concierge. Dry cleaning. Exercise equipt. Golf. Tennis. Downhill skiing. Video games. Cr cds: A, D, DS, JCB, MC, V.
🅳 🏊 🎿 🏌 🛝 🔥 SC ⛷ 🏃

★★ **RAMADA INN.** *6221 NE 82nd Ave (97220), E of Downtown. 503/255-*

6511; fax 503/255-8417; res 800/ 2RAMADA. Email 1642@cendant.com; www.citysearch.com/pdx/ramadainn. 200 rms, 2 story, 2 suites. June-Aug: S, D $69; each addl $10; suites $150; under 17 free; lower rates rest of yr. Crib avail. Parking lot. Pool. TV; cable (premium). Complimentary coffee in rms, toll-free calls. Restaurant 6:30 am-10:30 pm. Bar. Ck-out noon, ck-in 3 pm. Business servs avail. Dry cleaning, coin lndry. Free airport transportation. Exercise equipt, sauna. Golf. Cr cds: A, C, D, DS, ER, JCB, MC, V.
🅳 🏃 🏊 🏌 ⛷ ✈ 🛝 🔥

★★★ **RIVER PLACE HOTEL.** *1510 SW Harbor Way (97201), Downtown. 503/228-3233; fax 503/295-6161; res 800/426-0670; toll-free 800/227-1333. Email sales@riverplacehotel.com; www. riverplacehotel.com.* 39 rms, 4 story, 45 suites. S $219; D $239; each addl $20; suites $229; under 18 free. Crib avail. Pet accepted, fee. Valet parking avail. Indoor pool, lap pool, lifeguard, whirlpool. TV; cable (premium), VCR avail, CD avail. Complimentary continental bkfst, newspaper. Restaurant. 24-hr rm serv. Bar. Ck-out 1 pm, ck-in 4 pm. Meeting rms. Business servs avail. Bellhops. Concierge. Dry cleaning. Exercise rm, sauna, steam rm. Golf. Tennis. Downhill skiing. Video games. Cr cds: A, C, D, DS, ER, JCB, MC, V.
🅳 🐾 🏊 🏌 ⛷ 🏊 🏌 ⛷ 🛝 🔥

★★ **SILVER CLOUD INN PORT-LAND.** *2426 NW Vaughn St (97210), W of Downtown. 503/242-2400; fax 503/242-1770; toll-free 800/205-6939. www.scinns.com.* 81 rms, 4 story. S $89; D $99; each addl $10; suites $109; under 18 free. Crib free. Pet accepted, some restrictions; $100. TV; cable (premium). Complimentary continental bkfst. Restaurant nearby. Ck-out noon. Business servs avail. In-rm modem link. Free lndry. Exercise equipt. Whirlpool. Refrigerators. Cr cds: A, DS, MC, V.
🅳 🐾 🏌 🛝 🔥 SC

★★★ **VINTAGE PLAZA.** *422 SW Broadway (97205), Downtown. 503/228-1212; fax 503/228-3598; res 800/243-0555. Email sales@vintage-plaza.com; www.vintageplaza.com.* 87 rms, 10 story, 20 suites. May-Aug,

Oct: S, D $180; suites $400; lower rates rest of yr. Crib avail. Pet accepted. Valet parking avail. TV; cable (DSS), VCR avail, CD avail. Complimentary newspaper, toll-free calls. Restaurant 24-hr rm serv. Bar. Ck-out 3 pm, ck-in noon. Meeting rms. Business servs avail. Bellhops. Concierge. Dry cleaning, coin lndry. Exercise rm, whirlpool. Golf, 18 holes. Tennis, 4 courts. Downhill skiing. Video games. Cr cds: A, C, D, DS, ER, JCB, MC, V.

⊡ ⬛ ⬛ ⬛ ⬛ ⬛ ⬛ ⬛ ⬛

★ ★ ★ ★ **THE WESTIN PORT-LAND.** *750 SW Alder St (97205). 503/294-9000; fax 503/241-9565; res 800/937-8461. Email aaron.babbie@westin.com; www.westinportland.com.* Located in the center of downtown Portland, this hotel is within walking distance to such area attractions as the Portland Convention Center. This facility offers guest internet access, coffee makers, in-room safes, and dual-line direct-dial telephones with fax and data ports. 187 rms, 18 story, 18 suites. June-Nov: S $220; D $245; each addl $25; suites $270; under 17 free; lower rates rest of yr. Crib avail. Pet accepted, fee. Valet parking avail. TV; cable (premium), VCR avail, CD avail. Complimentary coffee in rms, newspaper, toll-free calls. Restaurant 6:30 am-11 pm. 24-hr rm serv. Bar. Ck-out noon, ck-in 3 pm. Meeting rms. Business center. Bellhops. Concierge. Dry cleaning. Exercise equipt. Golf. Downhill skiing. Supervised children's activities. Video games. Cr cds: A, C, D, DS, ER, JCB, MC, V.

⊡ ⬛ ⬛ ⬛ ⬛ ⬛ ⬛ ⬛ ⬛ ⬛

Resorts

★ ★ ★ **FOUR POINTS SHERATON PORTLAND DOWNTWON.** *50 SW Morrison; Front Ave (97204), Downtown. 503/221-0711; fax 503/274-0312; res 800/325-3535; toll-free 800/899-0247. Email sales@fourpointsportland.com; www.fourpointsportland.com.* 140 rms, 5 story, 1 suite. June-Aug: S $129; D $144; suites $250; lower rates rest of yr. Crib avail. Pet accepted. Parking garage. TV; cable (premium). Complimentary coffee in rms, newspaper. Restaurant 6:30 am-10:30 pm. Bar. Ck-out noon, ck-in 3 pm. Meeting rms. Business servs avail. Dry cleaning. Exercise privileges. Golf. Downhill skiing. Bike rentals. Hiking trail. Video games. Cr cds: A, C, D, DS, ER, JCB, MC, V.

⊡ ⬛ ⬛ ⬛ ⬛ ⬛ ⬛ ⬛ SC

Dusk falls on the city of Portland

★ ★ **MCMENAMINS EDGEFIELD.** *2126 SW Halsey (97060), E on I-84, Wood Village Exit 16A. 503/669-8610; fax 503/665-4209; res 503/669-8610; toll-free 800/669-8610. Email edgefield@mcmenamins.com; www.mcmenamins.com/edge.* 114 rms, 3 story, 13 suites. S $50; D $105; each addl $15; suites $125. Parking lot. TV; cable (premium). Complimentary full bkfst, newspaper. Restaurant. Bar. Ck-out 11 am, ck-in 3 pm. Meeting rms. Business center. Concierge. Gift shop. Golf. Downhill skiing. Hiking trail. Cr cds: A, DS, MC, V.

⊡ ⬛ ⬛ ⬛ ⬛ ⬛ ⬛

B&Bs/Small Inns

★★ GENERAL HOOKER'S B&B.
125 SW Hooker St (97201). 503/222-4435; fax 503/295-6410; toll-free 800/745-4135. Email lori@general hokkers.com; www.generalhookers.com. 4 rms, 3 story. June-Sep: S $110; D $120; lower rates rest of yr. Street parking. TV; cable (premium), VCR avail, CD avail. Complimentary continental bkfst, newspaper, toll-free calls. Restaurant 7:30 am-7:30 pm. Ck-out 3 pm, ck-in 11 pm. Fax servs avail. Exercise privileges. Downhill skiing. Cr cds: A, MC, V.

🏊 🏋 ⛵ ♿

★★ HERON HAUS. *2545 NW Westover Rd (97210), in Nob Hill. 503/274-1846; fax 503/248-4055. www.heronhaus.com.* 3 rms, 3 story, 3 suites. Apr-Oct: S $95; D $135; each addl $65; suites $185; under 10 free; lower rates rest of yr. Parking lot. TV; cable (premium), VCR avail. Complimentary continental bkfst, newspaper, toll-free calls. Business servs avail. Exercise privileges. Cr cds: MC, V.

🏋 ♿ ⛵ ♿

★★★ PORTLAND'S WHITE HOUSE BED AND BREAKFAST.
1914 NE 22nd Ave (97212), E of Downtown. 503/287-7131; fax 503/249-1641; toll-free 800/272-7131. Email pdxwhi@aol.com; www.portlands whitehouse.com. 9 rms, 2 story. June-Sep: S $116; D $125; each addl $20; children $20; lower rates rest of yr. Crib avail. Street parking. TV; cable (premium), VCR avail. Complimentary full bkfst, newspaper. Restaurant nearby. Ck-out 11 am, ck-in 2 pm. Meeting rms. Business center. Concierge. Free airport transportation. Exercise privileges. Tennis. Cr cds: A, DS, MC, V.

🏊 🏋 ⛵ ♿ 🏊

★★ THE SWEET BRIAR INN. *7125 SW Nyberg Rd (97062), approx 10 mi S on I-5, Exit 289. 503/692-5800; fax 503/691-2894; toll-free 800/551-9167. www.sweetbrier.com.* 100 rms, 32 suites. S $65-$85; D $75-$95; suites $90-$165; under 18 free; wkend rates. Crib free. Pet accepted; $35 refundable. TV; cable (premium). Heated pool. Playground. Complimentary coffee in rms. Restaurant 6:30 am-10 pm. Bar; entertainment Tues-Sat. Ck-out noon. Meeting rms. Business servs avail. In-rm modem link. Sundries. Valet serv. Exercise equipt. Health club privileges. Refrigerator in suites. Some balconies, patios. Picnic tables. Cr cds: A, C, D, DS, JCB, MC, V.

🄳 🐾 ⛵ 🏋 🏊 ⛵ ♿

All Suites

★★★ EMBASSY SUITES DOWNTOWN. *319 SW Pine St (97204), Downtown. 503/279-9000; fax 503/220-0206; res 800/362-2779. Email msack@embassyportland.com; www.embassyportland.com.* 9 story, 276 suites. June-Aug: S $169; D $199; each addl $30; suites $169; under 18 free; lower rates rest of yr. Crib avail. Valet parking avail. Indoor pool, whirlpool. TV; cable (premium), VCR avail. Complimentary full bkfst, coffee in rms, newspaper, toll-free calls. Restaurant 11 am-11 pm. Bar. Ck-out 10 am, ck-in 4 pm. Meeting rms. Business center. Bellhops. Concierge. Dry cleaning, coin lndry. Gift shop. Salon/barber. Exercise equipt, sauna, steam rm. Golf, 18 holes. Video games. Cr cds: A, C, D, DS, JCB, MC, V.

🄳 🏋 🏊 ⛵ ♿ SC 🏊

★★ PHOENIX INN. *477 NW Phoenix Dr (97060), E on I-84. 503/669-6500; fax 503/669-3500; toll-free 800/824-6824. Email phoen901@ipinc.net; www.phoenixinn.com.* 69 rms, 3 story, 4 suites. June-Sep: S $65; D $70; each addl $7; suites $120; under 17 free; lower rates rest of yr. Crib avail. Pet accepted, fee. Parking lot. Indoor pool, whirlpool. TV; cable (DSS). Complimentary continental bkfst, coffee in rms, newspaper, toll-free calls. Restaurant. Ck-out noon, ck-in 4 pm. Meeting rms. Business servs avail. Concierge. Dry cleaning, coin lndry. Exercise privileges. Golf, 18 holes. Tennis, 2 courts. Hiking trail. Cr cds: A, C, D, DS, MC, V.

🄳 🐾 🦮 🏋 🎣 ⛵ 🏋 ⛵ ♿ SC

★★ SHILO INN PORTLAND AIRPORT. *11707 NE Airport Way (97220), near Intl Airport, E of Downtown. 503/252-7500; fax 503/254-0993; res 800/222-2244.* 200 rms, 4 story. S $95; D $105; each addl $15;

under 12 free. Crib avail. Parking lot. Indoor pool. TV; cable (DSS), VCR avail. Complimentary continental bkfst, coffee in rms, newspaper, toll-free calls. Restaurant 5:30 am-10 pm. Bar. Ck-out noon, ck-in 2 pm. Meeting rms. Business center. Bellhops. Concierge. Dry cleaning, coin lndry. Free airport transportation. Exercise equipt, sauna, steam rm. Golf, 18 holes. Video games. Cr cds: A, C, D, DS, MC, V.

⬛🛏🏂✈🏊🔥🏃

Conference Center

★★★ **SHERATON PORTLAND AIRPORT HOTEL.** *8235 NE Airport Way (97220), near Intl Airport, E of Downtown. 503/281-2500; fax 503/249-7602; res 800/325-3535. www. sheratonpdx.com.* 211 rms, 5 story, 9 suites. S $139; D $149; each addl $10; suites $275; under 12 free. Crib avail, fee. Parking lot. Indoor pool, whirlpool. TV; cable (premium). Complimentary coffee in rms, newspaper, toll-free calls. Restaurant 5:30 am-8:30 pm. Bar. Ck-out noon, ck-in 2 pm. Meeting rms. Business center. Bellhops. Concierge. Dry cleaning. Gift shop. Free airport transportation. Exercise equipt, sauna. Golf. Downhill skiing. Video games. Cr cds: A, C, D, DS, ER, JCB, MC, V.

⬛📲🛏🏊🏂✈🏊🔥SC🏃

Restaurants

★★ **AL-AMIR LEBANESE RESTAURANT.** *223 SW Stark St (97204), Downtown. 503/274-0010. www.savy diner.com.* Specializes in maza al-amir, kebab. Hrs: 11 am-2:30 pm, 4:30-10 pm; Fri, Sat 4:30 pm-1 am; Sun 4:30-9 pm. Closed Jan 1, Thanksgiving, Dec 25. Res required Fri, Sat. Bar. Lunch $5-$8; dinner $8.50-$16.50. Child's menu. Entertainment: Fri, Sat. Lebanese decor. Cr cds: A, DS, MC, V.

🍴

★★ **ALESSANDRO'S.** *301 SW Morrison (97204), Downtown. 503/222-3900. Email alessan@transport.com; www.citysearch.com.* Specializes in Roman-style Italian seafood, poultry, veal. Hrs: 11:30 am-2 pm, 5-10 pm; Fri, Sat 5-11 pm. Closed Sun; hols. Res accepted. Bar. Lunch complete meals: $5.75-$11; dinner

$10.50-$19.95. Complete meals: $32. Entertainment. Parking. Cr cds: A, D, MC, V.

⬛

★★ **ALEXIS.** *215 W Burnside (97209), in Old Town. 503/224-8577.* Specializes in deep-fried squid, eggplant casserole, grape leaves stuffed with ground lamb. Hrs: 11:30 am-2 pm, 5-10 pm; Fri to 11 pm; Sat 5-11 pm. Closed Sun; hols. Bar. Lunch $5.95-$8.95; dinner $8.95-$13.95. Entertainment: belly dancer Fri, Sat. Greek decor. Cr cds: A, D, DS, MC, V.

⬛🍴

★★★ **ATWATER'S.** *111 SW 5th Ave (97204), Downtown. 503/275-3600. www.atwaters.com.* Specializes in salmon, game, fowl. Hrs: 5-10 pm. Closed hols. Res accepted. Bar. Wine list. Dinner $18-$33. Child's menu. Entertainment: jazz Tues-Sat. Cr cds: A, D, DS, MC, V.

⬛

★★ **BLACK RABBIT.** *2126 SW Halsey. 503/492-3086. Email edge@ mcmenamins.com; www.mcmenamins. com.* Specializes in fresh Northwestern cuisine. Hrs: 7-11 am, 11:30 am-2:30 pm, 5-9 pm. Res accepted. Bar. Bkfst $5.25-$9.25; lunch $6.25-$12.50; dinner $13.50-$21. Child's menu. Entertainment. Parking. Cr cds: A, D, DS, MC, V.

⬛

★★ **BREWHOUSE TAP ROOM & GRILL.** *2730 NW 31st Ave (97210), W of Downtown. 503/228-5269. www.portlandbrew.com/portland.* Specializes in MacTarnahan's fish and chips, haystack-black baby ribs. Hrs: 11 am-10 pm; Mon to 9 pm; Fri to 11 pm; Sat noon-11 pm; Sun noon-9 pm. Closed hols. Bar. Lunch $4.75-$9.95; dinner $5.50-$12.95. Child's menu. Copper beer-making equipment at entrance. Cr cds: A, MC, V.

⬛

★★ **BUGATTI'S.** *18740 Williamette Dr (97068), Front St S to OR 43 (MacAdam). 503/636-9555.* Specializes in granchio, pollo capperi, prawns. Hrs: 5-9 pm; Fri, Sat to 10 pm. Closed hols. Res accepted. Beer, wine. Dinner a la carte entrees: $8.95-$16.95. Child's menu. Parking. Cr cds: MC, V.

⬛

★★ **BUSH GARDEN.** *900 SW Morrison (97205), Downtown. 503/226-7181.* Specializes in sashimi, sukiyaki. Sushi bar. Hrs: 11:30 am-9:30 pm. Closed hols. Res accepted. Bar. Lunch $5.75-$11.95; dinner $11.50-$24.95. Entertainment: karaoke. Parking. Dining in tatami rms. Cr cds: A, D, DS, MC, V.
D ⊡

★★ **CAFE AZUL.** *112 NW 9th Ave (97209), W of Downtown. 503/525-4422.* Specializes in codornices y empanada, mole oaxaqueño. Hrs: 5-10 pm. Closed Sun, Mon; hols. Res accepted. Bar. Dinner $15-$30. Entertainment. Street parking. Cr cds: D, DS, MC, V.
D

★★★ **CAFE DES AMIS.** *1987 NW Kearney (97209), W of Downtown. 503/295-6487. www.citysearch.com.* Specializes in filet of beef with port garlic. Own baking. Hrs: 5:30-10 pm. Closed Sun; hols. Res accepted. Dinner $13-$25. Parking. Country French decor. Cr cds: A, MC, V.
D

★★ **CAPRIAL'S BISTRO.** *7015 SE Milwaukee Ave (97202), E of Downtown. 503/236-6457.* Specializes in pasta, seafood. Hrs: 11 am-9 pm; Fri to 9:30 pm; Sat 11:30 am-9:30 pm. Closed Sun, Mon; hols. Res required. Wine, beer. Lunch $4.50-$10; dinner $17-$22. Casual decor. Cr cds: MC, V.
D

★★ **CHART HOUSE.** *5700 SW Terwilliger Blvd (97201), W of Downtown. 503/246-6963. Email portland@chart-house.com; www.chart-house.com.* Specializes in prime rib, steak, fresh seafood. Hrs: 11:30 am-10 pm; Sat, Sun from 5 pm. Res accepted. Bar. Lunch $6-$13; dinner $15-$25. Child's menu. Valet parking. 1,000 ft above Willamette River; panoramic view of Portland, Mt Hood, and Mt. St Helens. Fireplace. Cr cds: A, D, DS, MC, V.
D

★★★ **COUCH STREET FISH HOUSE.** *105 NW 3rd Ave (97213), N of OR 30, in Old Town. 503/223-6173. www.citysearch.com.* Specializes in Chinook salmon, live Maine lobster, Dungeness crab. Hrs: 5-10 pm; early-bird dinner 5-6 pm. Closed hols. Res accepted. Bar. Wine list. Dinner $16.95-$28.95. Entertainment. Valet parking. Old San Francisco decor. Cr cds: A, D, DS, MC, V.
D

★★★★ **COUVRON.** *1126 SW 18th Ave (97205), W of Downtown. 503/225-1844. Email couvron@aol.com; www.couvron.com.* Husband and wife team Anthony Demes and Maura Jarach preside over this tiny, French-inspired dining room where the dishes are near perfect and the pace is luxuriously relaxed; a rare quality in this day of multiple, nightly seatings. Chef Demes' passionate commitment to quality ingredients comes to light in three menus offered each evening: one based on the freshest of local ingredients, a vegetarian dinner, and the Grand Options—truly a culinary symphony. Specializes in foie gras, cherrywood-smoked Oregon quail, halibut. Hrs: 5:30-9 pm. Closed Sun, Mon; hols. Res accepted. Wine list. Dinner $30-$36. Prix fixe: 7-course $75. Cr cds: A, MC, V.
D

★ **DAN & LOUIS OYSTER BAR.** *208 SW Ankeny St (97204), in Old Town. 503/227-5906. Email danandlouis@integrity.com; www.danandlouiscitysearch.com.* Specializes in stewed, broiled, fried, pan-fried and raw oysters. Hrs: 11 am-10 pm; Fri, Sat to 11 pm. Closed hols. Beer, wine. Lunch $2.75-$7.25; dinner $5.95-$18.95. Child's menu. Antique seafaring decor; ship models. 19th-century bldg (1907). Family-owned. Cr cds: A, C, D, DS, MC, V.
D SC

★ **ESPARZA'S TEX MEX CAFE.** *2725 SE Ankeny St (97214), E of Downtown. 503/234-7909.* Specializes in stuffed pork loin with buffalo spicy cactus, carne asada rib-eye steak. Hrs: 11:30 am-10 pm. Closed Sun, Mon; hols. Bar. Lunch $5.50-$10.50; dinner $7.25-$12.50. Child's menu. Western decor. Cr cds: A, D, DS, MC, V.

★★ **ESPLANADE AT RIVERPLACE.** *1510 SW Harbor Way. 503/228-3233.* Specializes in Northwestern regional cuisine. Own desserts. Hrs: 6:30 am-2

pm, 5-10 pm; Sat 6:30-11:30 am, 5-10 pm; Sun 5-9 pm; Sun brunch 11 am-2 pm. Res accepted. Bar. Wine cellar. Bkfst $3.50-$10.50; lunch $6.95-$15; dinner $13.50-$28. Sun brunch $9-$13. Child's menu. Split-level dining; view of Willamette River and marina. Cr cds: A, C, D, DS, MC, V.
D

★★ **FERNANDO'S HIDEAWAY.** *824 SW First Ave (97204), Downtown. 503/248-4709. Email march2000@ aol.com.* Specializes in picanton catalan, churrasco, zarzuela de mariscos. Hrs: 4:30-10 pm; Sun to 9 pm. Closed Mon; Memorial Day, July 4. Res accepted. Bar. Dinner $15.50-$19.50. Street parking. Cr cds: A, C, D, DS, MC, V.
D

★★★★ **GENOA.** *2832 SE Belmont St (97214), E of Downtown. 503/238-1464. Email genoarestaurant@earth link.net; www.genoarestaurant.com.* It's worth more than 2 hours out of anyone's busy schedule to experience this northern-Italian restaurant's seven-course, prix-fixe extravaganza and warm, cozy atmosphere. This establishment, founded nearly 30 years ago by restaurateur Michael Vidor, is now co-owned by Cathy Whims and Kerry DeBuse and still carries on the tradition of highlighting a different region of Italy every two to three weeks. Italian menu. Specializes in authentic regional Italian dishes. Own baking. Hrs: 5:30-9:30 pm. Closed Sun; hols. Res accepted. Dinner prix fixe: 7-course $60, 4-course (Mon-Thurs) $50. Cr cds: A, D, DS, MC, V.
D

★★★ **HEATHMAN.** *1001 SW Broadway. 503/241-4100.* Specializes in Chinook salmon, halibut confit, Oregon lamb. Own baking. Hrs: 6:30 am-10 pm; Fri, Sat to 11 pm. Res accepted. Bar. Wine cellar. Bkfst $4-$11; lunch $8-$18; dinner $13-$29. Valet parking. Cr cds: A, D, DS, MC, V.
D

★★★ **HIGGINS.** *1239 SW Broadway (97205), Downtown. 503/222-9070. Email higgins@europa.com; www.city search.com.* Specializes in seafood, hamburger. Hrs: 11:30 am-10:30 pm; Sat, Sun from 5 pm. Closed hols. Res

accepted. Bar. Lunch a la carte entrees: $7-$13.50; dinner a la carte entrees: $14.50-$20.50. Child's menu. Contemporary decor. Cr cds: A, D, DS, MC, V.
D

★ **HUBER'S CAFE.** *411 SW 3rd Ave (97204), Downtown. 503/228-5686. www.hubers.com.* Specializes in roast turkey, flaming Spanish coffees. Hrs: 11:30 am-11 pm; Sat from noon. Closed Sun; hols. Res accepted. Bar. Lunch $4.95-$9; dinner $6.50-$18.95. Originally a saloon established in 1879 that became a restaurant during Prohibition. Arched stained-glass skylight, mahogany paneling, and terrazzo floor. Cr cds: A, D, DS, MC, V.
D 🖼

★★ **IL FORNAIO.** *115 NW 22nd Ave (97210), in Nob Hill. 503/248-9400. www.ilfornaio.com.* Italian menu. Specializes in pizza con la luganega, pollo toscano, ravioli pomodoro. Hrs: 11:30 am-10 pm; Fri to 11 pm. Closed Thanksgiving, Dec 25. Res accepted. Bar. Lunch $5-$15; dinner $6-$19. Child's menu. Free valet parking. Show kitchen; wood-burning pizza oven and rotisserie. Cr cds: A, MC, V.
D

★★★ **JAKE'S FAMOUS CRAW-FISH.** *401 SW 12th Ave (97205), Downtown. 503/226-1419. www. mccormickandschmicks.com.* Specializes in fresh regional seafood. Own baking. Hrs: 11:30 am-11 pm; Sat from 4 pm; Sun 4-10 pm. Closed July 4, Thanksgiving, Dec 25. Res accepted. Bar. Wine list. Lunch a la carte entrees: $4.95-$10; dinner a la carte entrees: $8.95-$28.95. Turn-of-the-century decor. Cr cds: A, D, DS, MC, V.
D

★★★ **JAKE'S GRILL.** *611 SW 10th St. 503/220-1850.* Specializes in steak, salmon. Hrs: 6:30 am-11 pm; Fri to midnight; Sat 7:30 am-midnight; Sun 7:30 am-10 pm. Res accepted. Bar. Bkfst $2.50-$11.95; lunch $4.95-$11.95; dinner $4.95-$18.50. Child's menu. Casual decor. Cr cds: A, D, DS, MC, V.
D 🖼

★★ **L'AUBERGE.** *2601 NW Vaughn (97210), W of Downtown. 503/223-*

3302. *www.laubergepdx.com*. Specializes in seafood, steak, lamb. Own baking. Hrs: 5:30-11:30 pm. Closed hols. Res accepted. Bar. Wine list. Dinner complete meals: $9.75-$36. Prix fixe: $42, $60. Parking. Tri-level dining; wall hangings, 2 fireplaces. Family-owned. Cr cds: A, D, DS, MC, V.

★★★ **LONDON GRILL.** *309 SW Broadway.* 503/295-4110. *www.benson hotel.com*. Specializes in Northwest salmon, rack of lamb, ostrich. Hrs: 6:30 am-9 pm; Fri, Sat to 10 pm; Sun brunch 9:30 am-2 pm. Res accepted. Bar. Wine cellar. Bkfst $4.95-$9.95; lunch $9-$13; dinner $19.95-$25. Sun brunch $19.50. Child's menu. Entertainment: harpist Wed-Sat. Valet parking. Jacket (dinner). Elegant dining in historic hotel. Cr cds: A, DS, MC, V.
D

★★ **MANDARIN COVE.** *111 SW Columbia (97201), Downtown.* 503/222-0006. Specializes in Hunan and Szechwan meats and seafood. Hrs: 11 am-10 pm; Fri to 11 pm; Sat noon-11 pm; Sun from 4 pm. Res accepted. Bar. Lunch $5.25-$7.50; dinner $6.50-$25.50. Cr cds: A, D, DS, MC, V.
D

★ **MAZZI'S ITALIAN-SICILIAN FOOD.** *5833 SW MacAdam Ave (97201), W of Downtown.* 503/227-3382. Specializes in fresh seafood, homemade pasta. Salad bar (lunch). Hrs: 11 am-10 pm; Fri to 11 pm; Sat 4-11 pm; Sun from noon. Closed Thanksgiving, Dec 24, 25. Bar. Lunch $3.25-$7.95; dinner $6.95-$16.95. Parking. Mediterranean decor; fireplaces. Cr cds: A, MC, V.
D

★★★ **MORTONS OF CHICAGO.** *213 SW Clay St (97201).* 503/248-2100. *www.mortons.com*. Specializes in double-cut filet migmon, porterhouse steak, lobster. Hrs: 5-11 pm. Closed hols. Res accepted. Wine list. Dinner $26.95-$32.95. Entertainment. Cr cds: A, D, JCB, MC, V.
D

★★ **MURATA.** *200 SW Market St (97201), W of Downtown.* 503/227-0080. Specializes in sushi ban, kaiseki. Hrs: 11:30 am-10 pm; Sat

from 5:30 pm. Closed Sun; hols. Res accepted. Wine, beer. Lunch $5.95-$14.75; dinner $15.50-$26.50. Complete meals: $45. Parking. Japanese atmosphere. Cr cds: A, D, MC, V.
D ⌐

★ **OLD SPAGHETTI FACTORY.** *0715 SW Bancroft (97201), W of Downtown.* 503/222-5375. *www.osf. com*. Specializes in pasta. Own sauces. Hrs: 11:30 am-10 pm; Fri, Sat to 11 pm. Closed Thanksgiving, Dec 24, 25. Bar. Lunch $3.50-$5.75; dinner $4.75-$8.50. Child's menu. Parking. 1890s decor; dining in trolley car. Family-owned. Cr cds: A, D, DS, MC, V.
D

★★★ **ORITALIA.** *750 SW Alder St.* 503/295-0680. *Email d.vacheresse@ worldnet.att.net; www.oritalia.net*. Specializes in seared eastern sea scallops, ginger steamed halibut. Hrs: 6:30 am-10 pm. Res accepted. Wine, beer. Lunch $3-$6.75; dinner $16-$26. Brunch $5.75-$14. Entertainment. Cr cds: A, D, DS, MC, V.
D

★★★ **PALEY'S PLACE.** *1204 NW 21st Ave (97209), W of Downtown.* 503/243-2403. *Email paleys@teleport. com; www.paleysplace.citysearch.com*. Specializes in local foods. Hrs: 5:30-11 pm; Fri, Sat to midnight; Sun from 5 pm. Closed hols. Res accepted. Wine list. Dinner $18-$25. Cr cds: A, MC, V.
D

★★★ **PAZZO RISTORANTE.** *627 SW Washington.* 503/228-1515. *www. pazzo.com*. Specializes in hardwood oven-baked seafood, meat, fowl. Own bread, pasta. Hrs: 7 am-10 pm; Fri to 11 pm; Sat 8 am-11 pm; Sun from 8 am. Closed hols. Res accepted. Bar. Bkfst a la carte entrees: $4-$8; lunch a la carte entrees: $8-$15; dinner a la carte entrees: $8-$18. Italian marble floors, mahogany bar; also dining in wine cellar. Cr cds: A, D, DS, MC, V.
D

★★★ **PLAINFIELD'S MAYUR.** *852 SW 21st Ave (97205), W of Downtown.* 503/223-2995. *Email rich@plainfields. com; www.plainfields.com*. Specializes in spiced lamb, rack of lamb, duck in almond sauce. Own baking. Hrs: 5:30-10 pm. Closed Thanksgiving, Dec 25. Res accepted. Wine cellar. Dinner a la carte entrees: $7.95-$15.95. Parking. Shingle-style mansion (1901). Centerpiece of dining room is functioning Indian clay oven (tandoor). Cr cds: A, D, DS, MC, V.

D

★ **POOR RICHARDS.** *3907 NE Broadway (97232), at Sandy Blvd, E of Downtown.* 503/288-5285. Specializes in steak, seafood. Hrs: 11:30 am-11 pm; Sat from 4 pm; Sun noon-9 pm. Closed hols. Res accepted. Bar. Lunch $5.50-$8; dinner $6.50-$16. Child's menu. Parking. Colonial decor; fireplace. Family-owned. Cr cds: A, DS, MC, V.

D

★★★ **PORTLAND STEAK & CHOPHOUSE.** *121 SW 3rd Ave, Downtown.* 503/223-6200. *www. portlandchophouse.com.* Specializes in cedar-plank salmon, filet mignon, double-cut pork chop. Hrs: 11 am-11 pm; Fri to midnight; Sat 8 am-midnight; Sun from 8 am. Res accepted. Bar. Lunch $8.95-$15; dinner $10-$30. Child's menu. Valet parking (dinner). Cr cds: A, D, DS, MC, V.

D

★★★ **RED STAR TAVERN & ROAST HOUSE.** *503 SW Alder (97204), Downtown.* 503/222-0005. *www.opentable.com.* Specializes in sage-roasted chicken with buttermilk mashed potatoes, rotisserie pork loin with sweet potato hash and roasted pear-onion jam. Hrs: 6:30 am-10 pm. Closed hols. Res accepted. Bar. Bkfst $5.50-$8.25; lunch $8.95-$12.95; dinner $13-$20. Child's menu. Wood-burning oven. Contemporary decor. Cr cds: A, DS, MC, V.

D

★★ **RHEINLANDER.** *5035 NE Sandy Blvd (97213), E of Downtown.* 503/288-5503. Specializes in hasenpfeffer, homemade sausage, rotisserie chicken. Hrs: 5-9 pm; Fri to 10 pm; Sat 4-10 pm; Sun from 3:30 pm. Closed Labor Day, Dec 24, 25. Res accepted. Bar. Dinner $3.95-$16.95. Child's menu. Entertainment: strolling accordionist, group singing. Parking. Family-owned. Cr cds: A, MC, V.

D

★★ **RINGSIDE.** *2165 W Burnside St (97210), W of Downtown.* 503/223-1513. *www.ringsidesteakhouse.com.* Specializes in steak, prime rib, seafood. Hrs: 5 pm-midnight; Sun 4-11:30 pm. Closed July 4, Thanksgiving, Dec 24, 25. Res accepted. Bar. Dinner $13.20-$39.95. Valet parking. Fireplace. Prizefight pictures; sports decor. Family-owned. Cr cds: A, D, DS, MC, V.

D ⌐

★★ **RINGSIDE EAST.** *14021 NE Glisan (97230), E of Downtown.* 503/255-0750. Specializes in prime rib, steak, seafood. Hrs: 11:30 am-11 pm; Fri to midnight; Sat 5 pm-midnight; Sun 4-10 pm. Closed hols. Res accepted. Bar. Lunch $4.50-$10.95; dinner $10.50-$36.75. Parking. Cr cds: A, DS, MC, V.

D

★★ **SALTY'S ON THE COLUMBIA.** *3839 NE Marnie Dr (97211), E of Downtown.* 503/288-4444. *www.saltys. com.* Specializes in halibut supreme, blackened salmon. Hrs: 11:15 am-10 pm. Closed Dec 25. Res accepted. Bar. Lunch $7.25-$18.95; dinner $14-$37. Sun brunch buffet $8.95-$17.95. Child's menu. Free valet parking. Overlooks Columbia River. Cr cds: A, D, DS, MC, V.

D ⌐

★★ **SAUCEBOX.** *214 SW Broadway (97205), Downtown.* 503/241-3393. *www.citysearch.com.* Specializes in roast Japanese salmon, steamed shrimp dumplings, hamachi and avocado. Hrs: 11:30 am-10 pm. Closed Sun, Mon; hols. Res accepted (dinner). Bar. Lunch $7-$11; dinner $9-$13. Street parking. Contemporary decor. Cr cds: A, MC, V.

D ⌐

★ **SAYLER'S OLD COUNTRY KITCHEN.** *10519 SE Stark (97216), E of I-205 Washington Exit, E of Downtown.* 503/252-4171. Specializes in steak, seafood, chicken. Hrs: 4-10 pm; Sat from 3 pm; Sun from noon. Closed hols. Bar. Lunch, dinner complete meals: $8.95-$35. Child's menu. Parking. Family-owned. Cr cds: A, DS, MC, V.

D SC

★ **SWAGAT INDIAN CUISINE.** *2074 NW Lovejoy (97209), W of Downtown.* 503/227-4300. Specializes in chicken tandoori, dosa. Hrs: 11:30 am-10 pm. Closed Thanksgiving, Dec 25. Bar. Lunch buffet: $5.95; dinner $9.95-$12.95. Parking. Indian atmosphere and decor. Cr cds: A, DS, MC, V.

D

★ **SYLVIA'S.** *5115 NE Sandy Blvd (97213), E of Downtown. 503/288-6828. www.sylvias.net.* Specializes in lasagne, fettucine Alfredo, veal parmigiana. Hrs: 4-10 pm; Fri, Sat to 11 pm; Sun 3-9 pm. Closed Thanksgiving, Dec 24, 25. Res accepted; required for theater. Bar. Dinner $7.75-$15.50. Child's menu. Parking. Dinner theater adj. Family-owned. Cr cds: A, DS, MC, V.

D

★★ **TYPHOON!.** *2310 NW Everett St (97201), W of Downtown. 503/243-7557.* Specializes in miang kum, drunken noodles. Hrs: 11:30 am-9 pm; Fri to 10 pm; Sat 5-10 pm; Sun from 4:30 pm. Closed hols. Res accepted. Wine, beer. Lunch $5.95-$8.95; dinner $6.95-$17.95. Thai decor. Cr cds: A, D, DS, MC, V.

D

★★ **WIDMER GASTHAUS.** *955 N Russell St (97227), Downtown. 503/281-3333. www.widmer.com.* Specializes in schnitzel, sauerbraten. Hrs: 11 am-10 pm; Sun noon-9 pm. Closed Jan 1, Thanksgiving, Dec 25. Res accepted. Bar. Lunch $6.25-$8.50; dinner $6.25-$13.95. Entertainment. Cr cds: A, DS, MC, V.

D

★★★ **WILDWOOD.** *1221 NW 21st Ave (97209), in Nob Hill. 503/248-9663. www.citysearch.com/pdx/wildwood.* Specializes in mussels, breast of duck, salmon. Hrs: 11:30 am-10 pm; Sun 10 am-8:30 pm. Closed Jan 1, Dec 25. Res accepted. Bar. Wine cellar. Lunch $8-$13; dinner $16-$27. Sun brunch $5.50-$13. Cr cds: A, MC, V.

D

★★ **WINTERBORNE.** *3520 NE 42nd (97213), E of Downtown. 503/249-8486.* Specializes in seafood. Hrs: 5:30-9:30 pm. Closed Sun-Tues; Dec 25. Res accepted. Dinner $13.50-

$19. Child's menu. Contemporary decor. Cr cds: A, DS, MC, V.

D

Unrated Dining Spots

IVY HOUSE. *1605 SE Bybee (97202), E of Downtown. 503/231-9528.* Eclectic menu. Specializes in European pastries, creamed soups, sandwiches. Hrs: 11 am-9 pm; Sat, Sun from 10 am. Closed Thanksgiving, Dec 25. Res accepted. Wine, beer. Lunch a la carte entrees: $3.65-$6.50; dinner a la carte entrees: $7.95-$18.95. Sun brunch Sat, $3.25-$9.95. Parking. Cr cds: MC, V.

ORIGINAL PANCAKE HOUSE. *8601 SW 24th Ave (97219), W of Downtown. 503/246-9007. Email oph@teleport.com; www.originalpancakehouse.com.* Specializes in omelettes, apple pancakes, cherry crepes. Hrs: 7 am-3 pm. Closed Mon, Tues. Bkfst $5-$10; lunch $5-$10. Parking. Colonial decor. No cr cds accepted.

PAPA HAYDN. *5829 SE Milwaukie (97202), E of Downtown. 503/232-9440.* Specializes in European pastries, desserts. Hrs: 11:30 am-10 pm; Fri, Sat to midnight; Sun 10 am-3 pm. Closed hols. Wine, beer. Lunch $4.95-$6.95; dinner $6.95-$13.95. Entertainment. Cr cds: A, MC, V.

PERRY'S ON FREMONT. *2401 NE Fremont (97212), E of Downtown. 503/287-3655.* Specializes in desserts, fish and chips, steak. Hrs: 4-10 pm; Sat from noon. Closed Sun, Mon; hols. Bar. Lunch, dinner $7.50-$16.50. Child's menu. Murals. Cr cds: DS, MC, V.

D

Port Orford

(E-1) *See also Bandon, Gold Beach*

Founded 1851 **Pop** 1,025 **Elev** 56 ft
Area code 541 **Zip** 97465
Web www.portorfordoregon.com
Information Chamber of Commerce, 502 Battle Rock City Pk, PO Box 637; 541/332-8055

Westernmost incorporated city in the contiguous United States, Port

Orford overlooks the Pacific Ocean with spectacular views. This was the first settlement in Coos and Curry counties. Captain George Vancouver sighted this area in 1792 and named it for the Earl of Orford. The cedar trees that grow in the area (sometimes called Lawson cypress and later named for the Earl) are highly favored for boat construction.

What to See and Do

Battle Rock Wayside. Site of one of the fiercest Native American battles on the Oregon Coast (1851); explanation of battle is inscribed on a marker in the park. Battle Rock offers one of the best seascapes in the state and has an ocean beach, surfing; hiking trail. S edge of town on US 101.

Cape Blanco State Park. A 1,880-acre park with unusual black sand ocean beach, observation point; historic lighthouse (1870). Fishing, boat ramp; hiking, picnicking, improved campsites. Standard fees. 9 mi N off US 101. Phone 541/332-6774. In the park is the

> **Historic Hughes House.** (1898) Restored Victorian Gothic-style house. (May-Sep, Thurs-Mon and hols) **Donation**

Fishing. Ocean fishing provides salmon, ling cod, perch, snapper, and crabs. Fall fishing in the Elk and Sixes rivers provides catches of chinook salmon and trout. **Garrison Lake**, at the NW edge of town, is open all yr for trout and bass fishing. Also swimming, waterskiing, boat ramp.

Humbug Mountain State Park. A 1,842-acre park with winding trail leading to summit (1,750 ft); peak looks out on virgin forest, trout streams, sand beach. Fishing; hiking, picnicking, tent and trailer sites (dump station). Standard fees. 6 mi S on US 101. Phone 541/332-6774.

Prineville

(C-4) *See also Bend, Madras, Redmond*

Founded 1868 **Pop** 5,355
Elev 2,864 ft **Area code** 541
Zip 97754

Information Prineville-Crook County Chamber of Commerce, 390 N Fairview; 541/447-6304

Two-thirds of the population of Crook County lives in or near Prineville. Livestock, alfalfa, wheat, mint, sugar beets, and lumbering are important in this county. Hunting, fishing, and rockhounding are popular. The City of Prineville Railroad, 19 miles of main line connecting the Union Pacific and Oregon Trunk Railway, is one of the few municipally-owned railroads in the US. Two Ranger District offices and headquarters of the Ochoco National Forest are located here.

What to See and Do

Mineral collecting. Agates of various types, obsidian, petrified wood, geodes, and other stones. More than 1,000 acres of digging space in Eagle Rock, Maury Mt, White Rock Springs, and other areas. Obtain map from Chamber of Commerce.

Ochoco Lake Park. A 10-acre juniper-covered promontory on the N shore of Ochoco Reservoir. Fishing; boating (ramp), hiking, picnicking, improved tent and trailer sites. Standard fees. 7 mi E on US 26. Phone 541/447-4363.

Ochoco National Forest. An approx 848,000-acre forest plus 111,000-acre Crooked River National Grassland; central Oregon high desert; thunderegg deposits; stands of ponderosa pine. Fishing in streams, Walton and Delintment lakes, Haystack and Antelope reservoirs; hunting, hiking trails, winter sports, picnicking, camping (fee). E on US 26. Phone 541/447-6247.

Redmond

(C-4) *See also Bend, Madras, Prineville*

Pop 7,163 **Elev** 2,997 ft
Area code 541 **Zip** 97756
Web www.nt.empnet.com/rchamber/
Information Chamber of Commerce, 446 SW 7th St; 541/923-5191 or 800/574-1325

Popular with sports enthusiasts and tourists, this is also the agricultural, lumbering, and industrial center of central Oregon. A Ranger District office of the Deschutes National Forest (see BEND) is located here. The US Forest Service Redmond Regional Air Center is located at Roberts Field.

What to See and Do

Firemen's Pond. Children's fishing pond. 3-acre lake stocked with bass, bluegill. Children under 14 and disabled persons only. (Mid-Apr-mid-Oct, daily) Lake Rd & Sisters Ave. Phone 541/548-6068. **FREE**

Petersen Rock Gardens. Model castles and bridges built with rock specimens; lagoons and flower beds; picnicking, fireplaces; museum. (Daily) 7930 SW 77th St, 7 mi S on US 97, then 2½ mi W. Phone 541/382-5574. ¢

State parks.

Cline Falls. A 9-acre park on the banks of the Deschutes River. Fishing; picnicking. 4 mi W on OR 126. Phone 541/388-6055.

Peter Skene Ogden Wayside. A 98-acre park wth canyon 400 ft wide, 304 ft deep. Picnicking. Observation point. 9 mi N on US 97. Phone 541/548-7501.

Smith Rock. A 623-acre park with view of unusual multicolored volcanic and sedimentary rock formations and the Crooked River Canyon. Crooked River Gorge (403 ft deep) is 3 mi N. Fishing; hiking, rock climbing, picnicking. 9 mi NE off US 97. Phone 541/548-7501.

Annual Event

Deschutes County Fair and Rodeo. First wk Aug.

Motels/Motor Lodges

★★ **BEST WESTERN RAMA INN.** *2630 SW 17th Pl (97756), off US 97 S. 541/548-8080; fax 541/548-3705; res 800/528-1234; toll-free 888/ramainn.* 49 rms, 2 story. S $57-$110; D $62-$130; under 12 free. Crib $4. TV; cable (premium), VCR avail. Indoor pool; whirlpool. Complimentary continental bkfst. Restaurant nearby. Ck-out 11 am. Coin lndry. Business servs avail. In-rm modem link. Free

airport transportation. Exercise equipt. Refrigerators. Cr cds: A, DS, MC, V.

★ **FRENCH-WELLS.** *1545 Hwy 97 S (97756). 541/548-1091; fax 541/548-0415; toll-free 800/833-3259.* 45 rms, 3 story. May-Sep: S $53; D $63; each addl $5; suites $80; under 12 free; lower rates rest of yr. Crib avail, fee. Pet accepted, fee. Parking lot. Pool. TV; cable (premium), VCR avail. Complimentary continental bkfst, coffee in rms, newspaper, toll-free calls. Restaurant 7 am-10 pm. Ck-out 11 am, ck-in 1 pm. Fax servs avail. Free airport transportation. Golf. Downhill skiing. Cr cds: A, C, D, DS, MC, V.

★ **VILLAGE SQUIRE MOTEL.** *629 SW 5th St (97756). 541/548-2105; toll-free 800/548-2102. Email info@ villagesquiremotel.com; www.village squiremotel.com.* 24 rms, 2 story. Apr-Sep: S $45; D $50; each addl $5; lower rates rest of yr. Pet accepted, some restrictions, fee. TV; cable, VCR avail. Restaurant nearby. Ck-out 11 am, ck-in 2 pm. Golf. Cr cds: A, DS, MC, V.

Hotel

★ **TRAVELODGE NEW REDMOND HOTEL.** *521 S 6th St (97756). 541/923-7378; fax 541/923-3949; res 800/578-7878; toll-free 800/726-2466.* 48 rms, 3 story. S, D $48-$70; each addl $5; suites $65-$80; under 12 free. TV; cable. Complimentary continental bkfst. Restaurant 11 am-10 pm. Bar to midnight. Ck-out 11 am. Meeting rms. Shopping arcade. Free airport transportation. Exercise equipt. Built 1927. Grand lobby; fireplace, wood beam ceiling, grandfather clock. Cr cds: A, C, D, DS, MC, V.

Resort

★★ **EAGLE CREST RESORT.** *1522 Cline Falls Rd (97756), 5 mi W on OR 126. 541/923-2453; fax 541/923-1720; toll-free 800/682-4786. www. eagle-crest.com.* 100 rms, 2 story, 43 kit. suites. Mid-Mar-Oct: S $69-$96; D $76-$101; kit. suites $93-$128; ski, golf plans; higher rates national hols; lower rates rest of yr. Crib free. TV; cable (premium), VCR avail. Heated pool; whirlpool. Playground. Super- vised children's activities (mid-June- early Sep); ages 6-12. Dining rm 7 am-9 pm. Bar from 4 pm. Ck-out noon, ck-in 4 pm. Coin lndry. Busi- ness servs avail. Grocery. Meeting rms. Gift shop. Beauty shop. Free air- port transportation. Lighted tennis, pro. Two 18-hole golf, greens fee $42, pro, putting green, driving range. Hiking, bicycle trails. Exercise rm. Lawn games. Microwave in suites. Balconies. Picnic tables, grills. On Deschutes River. Cr cds: A, D, DS, MC, V.

Restaurant

★★ **BEASLEY'S.** *1555 S Hwy 97 (97756). 541/548-4023.* Specializes in seafood, prime rib. Salad bar. Own baking. Hrs: 7 am-10 pm; Fri, Sat to 11 pm. Closed Dec 25. Bar. Bkfst $3- $6; lunch $4-$7; dinner $5-$24. Child's menu. Cr cds: A, D, DS, MC, V.

Reedsport

(D-1) *See also Coos Bay, Florence, North Bend*

Pop 4,796 **Elev** 10 ft **Area code** 541
Zip 97467
Web www.coos.or.us/~reewbycc
Information Chamber of Commerce, PO Box 11; 541/271-3495 or 800/247-2155

Surrounded by rivers, lakes, and the ocean, the area has an abundance and variety of fish, particularly striped bass, steelhead, and salmon. Two of the best bass fishing lakes in Oregon are nearby. Reedsport was originally marshland subject to flooding at high tides, so the earliest buildings and sidewalks were built three to eight feet above ground. A dike was built after the destructive

Christmastime flood of 1964 to shield the lower part of town.

What to See and Do

Dean Creek Elk Viewing Area. Area has 440 acres of pasture and bottom- land where Roosevelt elk (Oregon's largest land mammal) and other wildlife can be viewed. Interpretive center. No hunting. (Daily) Contact Bureau of Land Management, 1300 Airport Lane, North Bend 97459. 3 mi E on OR 38. Phone 541/756-0100. **FREE**

Oregon Dunes National Recreation Area. Large coastal sand dunes, forests, and wetlands comprise this 32,000-acre area in Siuslaw National Forest (see CORVALLIS). Beachcomb- ing, fishing; boating; hiking, horse- back riding, off-road vehicle areas, picnicking, camping (fee; some campgrounds closed Oct-May). Visi- tors center and headquarters in Reed- sport at US 101 and OR 38. (Daily; closed hols) W off US 101. Phone 541/271-3611.

Salmon Harbor. Excellent boat basin for charter boats, pleasure and fish- ing craft. Fishing for silver and chi- nook salmon in ocean, a short run from mouth of the Umpqua River (May-Sep, daily; rest of yr, Mon-Fri). Phone 541/271-3407.

Umpqua Discovery Center. Interpre- tive displays centering on cultural and natural history of area. (Daily; closed Jan 1, Thanksgiving, Dec 25) 409 Riverfront Way. Phone 541/271-4816. ¢¢

Umpqua Lighthouse State Park. This 450-acre park touches the mouth of the Umpqua River, borders the Umpqua Lighthouse Reservation, and skirts the ocean shore for more than 2 mi, with sand dunes rising 500 ft (highest in US). Noted for its marvelous, seasonal display of rhododendrons. Swimming, fishing; hiking, trail to beach and around Lake Marie, picnicking, tent and trailer sites, whale watching area. Standard fees. 6 mi S off US 101. Phone 541/271-4118.

William M. Tugman State Park. A 560- acre park in scenic coastal lake region. Swimming, bathhouse, fishing, boat- ing (ramp to Eel Lake); picnicking, improved tent and trailer sites (dump station). Standard fees. 8 mi S on US 101. Phone 541/759-3604.

Motels/Motor Lodges

★ **ANCHOR BAY INN.** *1821 Hwy 101 (97467). 541/271-2149; fax 541/271-1802; toll-free 800/767-1821.* June-Sep: S $48; D $59; each addl $5; suites $125; under 12 free; lower rates rest of yr. Pet accepted, fee. Pool. TV; cable (premium), VCR avail. Complimentary continental bkfst, newspaper, toll-free calls. Restaurant nearby. Ck-out 10 am, ck-in 1:30 pm. Coin lndry. Golf, 9 holes. Cr cds: A, C, D, DS, MC, V.

★★ **BEST WESTERN.** *1400 Hwy 101 (97467). 541/271-4831; fax 541/271-4832; res 800/528-1234.* 56 rms, 2 story, 9 suites, 2 kit. units. Late May-mid-Sep: S $64-$79; D $78-$98; each addl $5; suites $95-$130; kit. units $95-$120; lower rates rest of yr. Crib free. Pet accepted; $5. TV; cable (premium), VCR avail. Indoor pool; whirlpool. Complimentary continental bkfst. Restaurant nearby. Ck-out 11 am. Coin lndry. Meeting rms. Business servs avail. Exercise equipt. Minibars; refrigerators. Near Scholfield River. Cr cds: A, C, D, DS, MC, V.

★ **SALBASGEON INN OF REED-SPORT.** *1400 Hwy 101 (97467). 541/271-4831; fax 541/271-4831.* 12 rms, 2 story, 1 suite, 4 kit. units. Late May-mid-Sep: S $52-$68; D $65-$78; each addl $5; suite $71-$94; kit. units $73-$99; lower rates rest of yr. Pet accepted, some restrictions; $5/day. TV; cable (premium). Ck-out 11 am. Picnic tables. On Umpqua River. All rms have river views. Cr cds: A, C, D, DS, MC, V.

Rockaway

(A-1) *See also Cannon Beach, Seaside, Tillamook*

Pop 970 **Elev** 16 ft **Area code** 503 **Zip** 97136

Information Rockaway Beach Chamber of Commerce 103 S First St, PO Box 198; 503/355-8108 or 800/331-5928

Rockaway is an attractive resort area with a fine, wide beach.

Motels/Motor Lodges

★★ **SILVER SANDS MOTEL.** *215 S Pacific (97136), 1 blk W of US 101. 503/355-2206; fax 503/355-9690; res 800/457-8972.* 64 rms, 2 story, 40 kits. (no ovens). No A/C. May-Sep: S, D $94-$99; kit. units $104-$131; lower rates rest of yr. Crib free. TV; cable (premium). Indoor pool; whirlpool, sauna. Coffee in rms. Restaurant nearby. Ck-out 11:30 am. Refrigerators; some fireplaces. On ocean. Cr cds: A, DS, MC, V.

★ **SURFSIDE MOTEL.** *101 NW 11th Ave (97136). 503/355-2312; toll-free 800/243-7786.* 79 units, 1-2 story. No A/C. Mid-May-mid-Sep: S $48.50-$98.50; D $110.50-$149.50; kit. units $79.50-$149.50; lower rates rest of yr. Crib $5. Pet accepted; $10. TV; cable. Indoor pool. Restaurant nearby. Ck-out noon. Many fireplaces. On ocean; beach access. Cr cds: A, DS, MC, V.

Roseburg (E-2)

Settled 1853 **Pop** 17,032 **Elev** 459 ft **Area code** 541 **Zip** 97470
Web www.oregonnews.com/visitroseburg.html

Information Visitors and Convention Bureau, 410 Spruce St, PO Box 1262; 541/672-9731 or 800/444-9584

Roseburg is in one of Oregon's big stands of virgin timber that supports lumbermills and plywood plants. Although roses were the local pride, the town's name came not from the flower but from Aaron Rose, an early settler. This is the seat of Douglas County and headquarters for Umpqua National Forest.

What to See and Do

Douglas County Museum of History & Natural History. Exhibits incl early history and natural history displays of the region; photographic collection; research library. Also Regional Tourist Information. (Daily) 1 mi S via I-5, Exit 123 at fairgrounds. Phone 541/440-4507. ¢¢

Umpqua National Forest. Paved scenic byway takes 1 through magnificent scenery to Diamond Lake, which offers fishing (rainbow, steelhead trout) and forest camps. Mt Thielsen (9,182 ft) and Mt Bailey (8,363 ft) tower above the lake. The Colliding Rivers Visitor Information Center (daily) is located along OR 138 in Glide; Diamond Lake Visitor Center (summer) is located opp entrance to Diamond Lake Campground. The forest (nearly 1 million acres), named for Native Americans who once fished in the rivers, incl 3 wilderness areas: Boulder Creek, 19,100 acres, Mt Thielsen, 22,700 acres, and Roque-Umpqua Divide, 29,000 acres. Also the Oregon Cascades Recreation Area, 35,500 acres. Picnicking, lodging, hiking, camping (fee). For further info contact Forest Supervisor, 2900 NW Stewart Pkwy, PO Box 1008. Direct access from OR 138, along N Umpqua River. Phone 541/672-6601.

Wildlife Safari. A 600-acre drive-through animal park; 600 exotic specimens of African, Asian, and North American wildlife in natural habitats; petting zoo; elephant and train rides (seasonal); guided and walk-through tours by res; restaurant. (Daily) 6 mi S on I-5, exit 119 to OR 42 for 4 mi, in Winston. Phone 541/679-6761 or 800/355-4848. ¢¢¢

Wineries.

Callahan Ridge Winery. Tasting rm. (Apr-Oct, daily; other times call for appt) W of I-5; Garden Valley Exit 125, 2 mi W to Melrose then 1 mi S to Busenbark Lane, then right. Phone 541/673-7901 or 888/946-3487. **FREE**

Henry Estate Winery. Tours, tasting rm; picnic area. (Daily; closed hols) 13 mi NW via I-5, 1 mi W of Umpqua on County 6. Phone 541/459-5120, 541/459-3614, or 800/782-2686. **FREE**

Hillcrest Vineyard. Wine tastings; tours. (Daily; closed hols) Approx 10 mi W; I-5 exit 125, W on Garden Valley Rd, Melrose Rd, Doerner Rd then N on Elgarose and follow signs. Phone 541/673-3709 or 800/736-3709. **FREE**

Annual Events

Greatest of the Grape. Mid-Feb.

Spring Craft Fair. Late Mar.

Umpqua Valley Roundup. Wkend mid-June.

Roseburg Graffiti Week. First wk July.

Douglas County Fair. Early Aug.

Wildlife Safari Wildlights. Dec.

Motels/Motor Lodges

★ **BEST INN & SUITES.** *427 NW Garden Valley Blvd (97470), E of I-5 Veterans Hospital Exit 125. 541/673-5561; fax 541/957-0318.* 72 rms, 1-2 story. S $39-$55; D $49-$65; each addl $5; under 12 free. Crib $5. Pet accepted. TV; cable. Pool. Complimentary continental bkfst. Ck-out 11 am. Meeting rm. Business servs avail. Some microwaves. Cr cds: A, D, DS, MC, V.

🅳 ➜ 🅻 ⚌ 🕭 🖎 🔥

★★ **BEST WESTERN DOUGLAS INN.** *511 SE Stephens St (97470). 541/673-6625; fax 541/677-9610; res 800/528-1234; toll-free 877/368-4466.* 52 rms, 2 story. June-Sep: S $49-$68; D $60-$76; each addl $5; lower rates rest of yr. Crib $5. TV; cable (premium). Complimentary coffee. Restaurant opp 6 am-10 pm. Ck-out noon. Business servs avail. In-rm modem link. Exercise equipt; sauna. Whirlpool. Cr cds: A, DS, MC, V.

🅳 🕇 ⚌ 🖎 SC

★★ **BEST WESTERN GARDEN VILLA MOTEL.** *760 NW Garden Valley Blvd (97470). 541/672-1601; fax 541/672-1316; res 800/528-1234; toll-free 800/547-3446. Email bwgvmotel@mcsi.net.* 114 rms, 2 story, 6 suites. June-Aug: S $69; D $76; each addl $5; suites $82; under 12 free; lower rates rest of yr. Crib avail. Pet accepted, some restrictions. Parking lot. Pool. TV; cable (DSS), VCR avail. Complimentary continental bkfst, coffee in rms, newspaper, toll-free calls. Restaurant nearby. Ck-out noon. Meeting rms. Business center. Dry cleaning, coin lndry. Gift shop. Free airport transportation. Exercise equipt. Golf, 9 holes. Tennis, 2 courts. Downhill skiing. Hiking trail. Picnic facilities. Cr cds: A, C, D, DS, ER, JCB, MC, V.

🅳 ➜ 🕭 🕇 ➤ 🕇 🖛 ⚌ 🕇 🕭 🖎 🖎
🕇

★ **TRAVELODGE.** *315 W Harvard Ave (97470). 541/672-4836; fax 514/672-4836; toll-free 800/578-7878.* 2 story. July-Aug: S $65; D $80; each addl $5; under 17 free; lower rates rest of yr. Crib avail. Parking lot. Pool. TV; cable (DSS), VCR avail, VCR avail. Complimentary coffee in rms, newspaper, toll-free calls. Restaurant nearby. Ck-out 11 am, ck-in 1 pm. Fax servs avail. Dry cleaning. Golf. Picnic facilities. Video games. Cr cds: A, D, DS, MC, V.

⊡ 🕸 ⊠ ✕ ⊠ 🔥 **SC**

★★ **WINDMILL INN OF ROSE-BURG.** *1450 NW Mulholland Dr (97470). 541/673-0901; fax 541/673-0901; toll-free 800/547-4747. Email info@windmillinns.com; www.windmillinns.com.* 128 rms, 2 story. June-Aug: S, D $72; under 18 free; lower rates rest of yr. Crib avail, fee. Pet accepted. Parking lot. Pool, whirlpool. TV; cable (premium). Complimentary continental bkfst, coffee in rms, newspaper, toll-free calls. Restaurant. Ck-out 11 am, ck-in 3 pm. Meeting rms. Fax servs avail. Dry cleaning, coin lndry. Free airport transportation. Exercise privileges, sauna. Bike rentals. Cr cds: A, C, D, DS, MC, V.

⊡ 🔌 🕯 ⊠ 🕴 ✕ ⊠ 🔥 **SC**

Salem

(B-2) *See also Albany, McMinnville, Newberg, Oregon City, Portland, Silverton*

Settled 1840 **Pop** 107,786 **Elev** 154 ft **Area code** 503

Information Convention & Visitors Association, 1313 Mill St SE, 97301; 503/581-4325 or 800/874-7012

Capital and third-largest city in Oregon, Salem's economy is based on the state government, food processing, light manufacturing, agriculture, and wood products. Salem shares Oregon's sports attractions with other cities of the Willamette Valley.

What to See and Do

A.C. Gilbert's Discovery Village. Hands-on exhibits related to art, drama, music, science, and nature. (Tues-Sat, also Sun afternoons) 116 Marion St. Phone 503/371-3631. ¢¢

Bush House. Victorian mansion (1878) with authentic furnishings. (Tues-Sun; closed hols) Bush's Pasture Park. 600 Mission St SE, 6 blks S of capitol. Phone 503/363-4714. ¢¢ Also here is

> **Bush Barn Art Center.** Remodeled barn houses 2 exhibit galleries with monthly shows and a sales gallery featuring Northwest artists. (Tues-Sun; closed hols) Phone 503/581-2228. **FREE**

Enchanted Forest. Features storybook theme. Other exhibits incl reproduction of early mining town, haunted house (fee), log flume ride (fee), ice mountain bobsled ride (fee), old-world village, theater featuring live comedy and children's shows, water and light show. Picnic area; refreshments; gift stores. (Mid-Mar-Sep, daily) 7 mi S, off I-5 Sunnyside-Turner Exit 248, at 8462 Enchanted Way SE. Phone 503/363-3060. ¢¢¢

Historic Deepwood Estate. (1894) Queen Anne-style house and carriage house designed by W.C. Knighton. Povey Brothers stained-glass windows, golden oak woodwork; solarium; Lord & Schryver gardens with wrought-iron gazebo from 1905, boxwood gardens, perennial garden with English teahouse; nature trail. House (May-Sep, Sun-Fri; rest of yr, Mon, Wed, Fri, Sun; closed hols). 1116 Mission St SE. Phone 503/363-1825. ¢¢

Honeywood Winery. Oregon's oldest producing winery. Tours, tasting rm, gift shop. (Daily; closed Thanksgiving, Dec 25) 1350 Hines St SE. Phone 503/362-4111. **FREE**

Mission Mill Village. Thomas Kay Woolen Mill Museum (1889) shows process of processing fleece into fabric. Jason Lee House (1841), John D. Boon House (1847), Methodist Parsonage (1841), and Pleasant Grove-Presbyterian Church (1858) help interpret missionary family life. Shops, park, picnicking. Tours of woolen mill, historic houses (Tues-Sat, daily; closed Jan 1, Thanksgiving, Dec 25). 1313 Mill St SE. Phone 503/585-7012. Tours ¢¢

State Capitol. (1938) Marble, of modern Greek design. Atop the capitol is a fluted tower topped by a bronze, gold-leafed statue symbolic of the pioneers who carved Oregon out of the wilderness. Tours of capitol (June-Aug, daily; rest of yr by appt). Capitol bldg (daily; closed hols). Video; gift shop. 900 Court. Phone 503/986-1388. **FREE** N of here is the

Capitol Mall. Flanked by 4 state bldgs in modern Greek style, incl the Public Service, Transportation, Labor and Industries, and State Library bldgs. The grounds are an arboretum with historical statuary and monuments.

Willamette University. (1842) 2,500 students. Oldest institution of higher learning west of Missouri River, with several historic bldgs on campus incl Waller Hall (1867) and the Art Bldg (1905) with the Hallie Brown Ford Art Gallery. The Mark O. Hatfield Library has special area for research and viewing of Senator Hatfield's public papers. Campus tours; picnic area. 900 State St, between 12th & Winter Sts. Phone 503/370-6300.

Annual Events

Salem Art Fair & Festival. Bush's Pasture Park. Arts and crafts booths and demonstrations, children's art activities and parade, ethnic folk arts, performing arts, street painting, 5K run, food; tours of historic Bush House. Phone Salem Art Assn 503/581-2228. July.

West Salem Waterfront Parade. Mid-Aug.

Oregon State Fair. Fairgrounds, 2330 17th St NE. Horse racing, wine competition and tasting, agricultural exhibits, horse show, livestock, food, carnival, entertainment. Phone 800/833-0011. End of Aug through 1st week of Sep.

Motels/Motor Lodges

★★ **BEST WESTERN NEW KINGS INN.** *1600 Motor Ct NE (97301), off I-5 Exit 256. 503/581-1559; fax 503/364-4272; toll-free 877/594-1110. Email nkibw@aol.com.* 101 rms, 2 story. May-Oct: S $63; D $68; each addl $5; lower rates rest of yr. Crib avail, fee. Parking lot. Indoor pool, children's pool, whirlpool. TV; cable (premium). Complimentary continental bkfst, coffee in rms, newspaper, toll-free calls. Restaurant. Meeting rms. Business servs avail. Dry cleaning, coin lndry. Exercise

equipt, sauna. Golf. Tennis, 2 courts. Cr cds: A, C, D, DS, MC, V.

★ **PHOENIX INN.** *4370 Commercial St SE (97302), I-5 Exits 249 and 252. 503/588-9220; fax 503/585-3616; toll-free 800/445-4498. www.phoenixinn. com.* 89 rms, 4 story. S $62-$90; D $67-$90; each addl $5; suites $115-$125; under 17 free. Crib free. Pet accepted, some restrictions; $10. TV; cable (premium). Indoor pool; whirlpool. Complimentary continental bkfst. Ck-out noon. Coin lndry. Meeting rms. Business servs avail. Exercise equipt. Refrigerators. Some suites with whirlpool. Cr cds: A, C, D, DS, MC, V.

★ **TIKI LODGE.** *3705 Market St NE (97305), I-5 Market St Exit. 503/581-4441; fax 503/581-4445; toll-free 800/438-8458.* 50 rms, 20 with shower only, 2 story. Mid-May-Sep: S $49-$52; D $52-$58; each addl $4; under 12 free; wkly rates; lower rates rest of yr. Crib $2. Pet accepted. TV; cable (premium). Heated pool. Sauna. Complimentary coffee in lobby. Restaurant adj open 24 hrs. Ck-out noon. Meeting rms. Business servs avail. Cr cds: A, D, DS, MC, V.

Hotels

★ **RED LION HOTEL SALEM.** *3301 Market St (97301), I-5 Exit 256. 503/370-7888; fax 503/370-6305; res 800/REDLION; toll-free 800/248-6273. www.redlion.com.* 144 rms, 5 story, 6 suites. June-Sep: S, D $80; each addl $10; suites $130; under 18 free; lower rates rest of yr. Crib avail. Pet accepted, some restrictions, fee. Parking lot. Indoor pool, whirlpool. TV; cable. Complimentary coffee in rms, newspaper, toll-free calls. Restaurant. Bar. Ck-out noon, ck-in 4 pm. Meeting rms. Business servs avail. Dry cleaning, coin lndry. Exercise equipt. Downhill skiing. Cr cds: A, C, D, DS, ER, JCB, MC, V.

★★ **SHILO INN.** *3304 Market St NE (97301), I-5 Exit 256. 503/581-4001; fax 503/399-9385; toll-free 800/222-2244. Email salem@shiloinns.com; www.shiloinns.com.* 89 rms, 3 story. June-Aug: S $99; D $109; each addl $10; under 12 free; lower rates rest of yr. Parking lot. Indoor pool, whirl-pool. TV; cable (premium). Complimentary coffee in rms, newspaper, toll-free calls. Restaurant nearby. Ck-out noon, ck-in 2 pm. Meeting rm. Fax servs avail. Coin lndry. Free airport transportation. Exercise equipt, sauna, steam rm. Picnic facilities. Video games. Cr cds: A, C, D, DS, ER, JCB, MC, V.

D ≈ 🛪 ⊠ 🔥 SC

B&B/Small Inn

★★ **A CREEKSIDE INN THE MAR-QUEE HOUSE.** *33 Wyatt Ct NE (97301). 503/391-0837; fax 503/391-1713; toll-free 800/949-0837. Email rickiemh@open.org; www.marqueehouse. com.* 5 rms, 2 story. Aug-Oct: S $70; D $75; each addl $15; suites $90; lower rates rest of yr. Parking lot. TV; cable, VCR avail. Complimentary full bkfst, newspaper. Restaurant nearby. Ck-out 11 am, ck-in 4 pm. Business center. Golf. Cr cds: D, DS, MC, V.

🛪 ⊠ 🔥 🛪

Restaurant

★★★ **ALESSANDRO'S.** *120 NE Commercial St. (97301). 503/370-9951. Email alessandros@mailaty.com; www.alessandros@mailaty.com.* Specializes in seafood, poultry, veal. Hrs: 11:30 am-midnight; Sat, Sun from 5:30 pm. Closed hols. Res accepted. Bar. Wine cellar. Lunch $6.25-$10.50; dinner $9.50-$18.50. Prix fixe: $32. Child's menu. Overlooks park, waterfall. Cr cds: A, DS, MC, V.

D

★★ **KWAN ORIGINAL CUISINE.** *835 Commerical St SE (97302). 503/362-7711.* Specializes in emu, mango chicken with plum sauce, barbecue duck. Hrs: 11:30 am-10 pm; Fri, Sat to 11 pm; Sun to 9:30 pm. Closed hols. Res accepted. Bar. Lunch $5-$8; dinner $7-$12. Child's menu. Parking. Chinese decor; wooden Buddha. Cr cds: A, D, DS, MC, V.

D

Seaside

(A-1) See also Astoria, Cannon Beach

Pop 5,359 **Elev** 13 ft **Area code** 503
Zip 97138
Web www.clatsop.com/seaside
Information Chamber of Commerce, 7 N Roosevelt, PO Box 7; 503/738-6391 or 800/444-6740

Seaside is the largest and oldest seashore town in Oregon. It has a concrete promenade two miles long; ocean beaches provide clam digging, surfing, surf fishing, and beachcombing.

What to See and Do

Saddle Mountain State Park. A 2,922-acre park with trail to 3,283-ft summit, one of the highest in the Coastal Range. Hiking, picnicking, primitive campsites. Standard fees. 13 mi SE on US 26, then 9 mi N. For info. Phone 503/861-1671 or 503/436-2844.

Seaside Aquarium. Deep-sea life and trained seals; seal feeding (fee); (Mar-Nov, daily; rest of yr, Wed-Sun; closed Thanksgiving, Dec 24, 25) 200 N Prom, on beach. Phone 503/738-6211. ¢¢

Motels/Motor Lodges

★★ **EBB TIDE MOTEL.** *300 N Prom (97138), at 3rd Ave. 503/738-8371; fax 503/738-0938; toll-free 800/468-6232. Email ebbtide@seasurf.net; www. ebbtide.citysearch.com.* 99 rms, 3-4 story, 48 kits. No A/C. May-Sep: S, D $80-$120; kit. units $70-$120; lower rates rest of yr. Crib $5. TV; cable (premium), VCR avail. Indoor pool; whirlpool. Restaurant nearby. Ck-out noon. Coin lndry. Business servs avail. In-rm modem link. Exercise equipt; sauna. Refrigerators. On beach. Cr cds: A, D, DS, MC, V.

D ✦ 🔥 ≈ 🛪 🛪 ⊠ 🔥

★★ **GEARHART BY THE SEA RESORT.** *1157 N Marion Ave (97138), N on US 101, jct N Marion Ave and 10th St. 503/738-8331; fax 503/738-0881; toll-free 800/547-0115.* 80 condominiums, 1-5 story. No A/C. Condominiums $119-$184; each addl

$10. Crib $5. TV; cable, VCR avail (movies). Indoor pool. Restaurant 7 am-9 pm; off-season hrs vary. Bar to 2:30 am. Ck-out 11 am. Coin lndry. Meeting rm. 18-hole golf, greens fee $27, pro, putting green. Balconies. Ocean view. Cr cds: A, DS, MC, V.

★★ **HI-TIDE MOTEL.** *30 Ave G (97138). 503/738-8414; fax 503/738-0875; toll-free 800/621-9876. www. oregoncoastonlinehighway.com.* 64 rms, 3 story, 64 kits. (no ovens). No A/C. No elvtr. May-Sep: S, D, kit. units $85-$120; lower rates rest of yr. Crib $5. TV; cable (premium), VCR avail. Indoor pool; whirlpool. Restaurant nearby. Ck-out noon. Business servs avail. On ocean. Cr cds: A, C, D, DS, MC, V.

★★ **SHILO INN.** *900 S Holladay Dr (97138). 503/738-0549; fax 503/738-0532; res 800/222-2244. www.shilo inns.com.* 58 rms, 3 story. Mid-Apr-early Sep: S, D $59-$124; under 18 free; higher rates hols; lower rates rest of yr. Crib free. TV; cable (premium), VCR avail. Indoor pool; whirlpool. Steam rm, sauna. Complimentary continental bkfst. Restaurant nearby. Ck-out noon. Coin lndry. Business servs avail. Airport transportation. Health club privileges. Bathrm phones. Cr cds: A, C, D, DS, MC, V.

Hotel

★★ **BEST WESTERN OCEAN VIEW RESORT.** *414 N Prom (97138). 503/738-3334; fax 503/738-3264; res 800/528-1234; toll-free 800/234-8439. Email sales@oceanviewresort.com; www.oceanviewresort.com.* 84 rms, 5 story, 20 suites. May-Oct: S, D $250; suites $300; lower rates rest of yr. Crib avail. Pet accepted, some restrictions, fee. Parking lot. Indoor pool, whirlpool. TV; cable, VCR avail. Complimentary coffee in rms. Restaurant. Bar. Ck-out 11 am, ck-in 4 pm. Meeting rms. Fax servs avail. Coin lndry. Golf. Tennis. Beach access. Bike rentals. Supervised children's activities. Hiking trail. Picnic facilities. Cr cds: A, C, D, DS, MC, V.

Resort

★★ **SHILO INN.** *30 N Prom (97138). 503/738-9571; fax 503/738-0674; res 800/222-2244. Email sea sideoceanfront@shiloinns.com; www. shiloinns.com/oregon/seaside.html.* 112 rms, 5 story. June-Aug: D $239; each addl $15; under 12 free; lower rates rest of yr. Crib avail. Parking garage. Indoor pool, whirlpool. TV; cable (premium). Complimentary coffee in rms, newspaper, toll-free calls. Restaurant 7 am-11 pm. Bar. Meeting rms. Business center. Coin lndry. Free airport transportation. Exercise equipt, sauna, steam rm. Golf, 18 holes. Tennis. Beach access. Bike rentals. Hiking trail. Video games. Cr cds: A, C, D, DS, ER, JCB, MC, V.

B&Bs/Small Inns

★★ **CUSTER HOUSE BED & BREAKFAST.** *811 1st Ave (97138). 503/738-7825; fax 503/738-4324; toll-free 800/738-7852. Email custerbb@ seasurf.com; www.clatsop.com/custer.* 6 rms, 2 story. June-Sep: S, D $75; lower rates rest of yr. Parking lot. TV; cable, VCR avail. Complimentary full bkfst. Restaurant. Ck-out 11 am, ck-in 4 pm. Meeting rm. Business servs avail. Golf, 18 holes. Tennis, 6 courts. Beach access. Bike rentals. Supervised children's activities. Hiking trail. Picnic facilities. Cr cds: A, C, D, DS, JCB, MC, V.

★★★ **GILBERT INN BED & BREAKFAST.** *341 Beach Dr (97138). 503/738-9770; fax 503/717-1070; toll-free 800/410-9770. Email gilbertinn@theoregonshore.com; www. gilbertinn.com.* 9 rms, 2 story, 1 suite. May-Sep: S $120; D $125; each addl $10; suites $125; lower rates rest of yr. Parking lot. TV; cable, VCR avail. Complimentary full bkfst, newspaper. Restaurant nearby. Meeting rm. Fax servs avail. Exercise privileges. Golf. Tennis, 2 courts. Beach access. Bike rentals. Supervised children's activities. Hiking trail. Picnic facilities. Cr cds: A, DS, MC, V.

Restaurants

★ **CAMP 18.** *42362 Hwy 26 (97138), 25 mi E on US 26, at mile post 18.*

503/755-1818. Specializes in omelettes, family-style dinners. Hrs: 7 am-9 pm; Fri, Sat to 10 pm; hrs vary off-season. Closed Dec 25. Bar. Bkfst $3.25-$8.95; lunch $3.95-$8.95; dinner $10.95-$18.95. Sun brunch $11.95. Child's menu. Entertainment. In log bldg. Cr cds: A, DS, MC, V.

[D]

★★ **DOOGER'S SEAFOOD & GRILL.** *505 Broadway (97138). 503/738-3773.* Specializes in seafood, steak. Own clam chowder. Hrs: 11 am-10 pm; winter to 9 pm. Wine, beer. Lunch $4-$10.95; dinner $7.95-$22.95. Child's menu. Cr cds: A, DS, MC, V.

[D]

Silverton

(B-2) *See also Newberg, Oregon City, Salem*

Pop 5,635 **Elev** 249 ft **Area code** 503 **Zip** 97381
Information Chamber of Commerce, City Hall, 421 S Water St, PO Box 257; 503/873-5615

What to See and Do

Cooley's Gardens. Largest producer of bearded iris in the world. Display gardens feature many varieties; over 1 million blossom in fields (mid-May-early June). 11553 Silverton Rd NE. Phone 503/873-5463. **FREE.**

Country Museum/Restored Train Station. Ames-Warnock House (1908) contains local historical items dating from 1846. Southern Pacific Station (1906) contains larger items. (Mar-Dec, Thurs and Sun) Contact Chamber of Commerce. 428 S Water St. **Donation**

Silver Falls State Park. Oregon's largest state park, 8,706 acres, has 10 waterfalls, of which 5 are more than 100 ft high; 4 may be viewed from road, the others from forested canyon hiking trail. Swimming; bridle and bicycle trails, picnicking, tent and improved sites (dump station). Conference center. Standard fees. 15 mi SE on OR 214. Phone 503/873-8681.

Sweet Home

(C-2) *See also Albany*

Pop 6,850 **Elev** 525 ft **Area code** 541 **Zip** 97386
Web www.sweethome.or.us
Information Chamber of Commerce, 1575 Main St; 541/367-6186

Gateway to Santiam Pass and the rugged Oregon Cascades, the area around Sweet Home is popular for fishing, boating, skiing, hiking, and rockhounding. A Ranger District office of Willamette National Forest (see EUGENE) is located here.

What to See and Do

East Linn Museum. Nearly 5,000 artifacts of pioneer life in the area (1847). Period rms; rock collection and mining equipment; logging tools; maps, photos, portraits; guns, dolls, bottles; saddlery and blacksmith shop. (May-Sep, Tues-Sun; rest of yr, Thurs-Sun; also by appt; closed hols) 746 Long St, at jct OR 228, US 20. Phone 541/367-4580. **Donation**

Foster Lake. Swimming, water sports, fishing, boating. 2 mi E on US 20 at Foster.

Annual Events

Foster Mud Flat Races. First wkend Jan.

The Sweet Home Rodeo. Bull riding, barrel racing, bronc riding, mutton bustin'. Phone 541/367-6186. Second wkend July.

The Oregon Jamboree. Three-day country music and camping festival. Phone 541/367-8800. Second wkend Aug.

The Dalles

(B-4) *See also Biggs, Hood River*

Founded 1851 **Pop** 10,200 (est)
Elev 98 ft **Area code** 541 **Zip** 97058
Information Chamber of Commerce, 404 W 2nd St; 541/296-2231 or 800/255-3385

Multnonah Falls, Columbia River Gorge

Once The Dalles was the end of the wagon haul on the Oregon Trail. Here the pioneers loaded their goods on boats and made the rest of their journey westward on the Columbia River. The falls and rapids that once made the river above The Dalles unnavigable are now submerged under water backed up by the Columbia River dams. The Dalles Dam is part of a system of dams extending barge traffic inland as far as Lewiston, Idaho, and Pasco, Washington. The port has berthing space for all types of shallow draft vessels. The chief source of income in the area is agriculture. The Dalles is noted for its cherry orchards and wheat fields located in the many canyons along the river.

What to See and Do

Celilo Converter Station. N terminal for transmission of direct current between Pacific Northwest and Pacific Southwest (south terminal at Sylmar, CA). Interpretive display with educational and historical exhibits; visitors may also view control rm, equipment. (Daily) 1 mi SE on US 197. Phone 541/296-4694 or 541/296-3615. **FREE**

⭐ **Columbia Gorge Discovery Center.** Over 26,000-sq-ft bldg is official interpretive center for the Columbia River Gorge National Scenic Area. Hands-on and electronic exhibits detail the volcanic upheavals and raging floods that created the Gorge, describe the history and importance of the river, and look to the Gorge's future. Also Early Explorers, Steamboats and Trains, Industry and Stewardship exhibits. Guided tours, seminars, classes, and workshops (some fees). Library and collections (by appt). Cafe. (Daily; closed Jan 1, Thanksgiving, Dec 25) 3 mi NW at Crate's Point, 5000 Discovery Dr. Phone 541/296-8600. ¢¢¢ Admission incl

Wasco County Historical Museum. Reveals colorful history of over 10,000 yrs of county's occupation and importance of Columbia River on area history. Artifacts and exhibits feature Native Americans, missionaries, and early pioneers and explorers; history of area railroad industry, farming, and shipping. Interactive displays incl a late 19th-century town, railroad depot, and barn. (Schedule and phone same as Center) Also explore the

Oregon Trail Living History Park. Incl 80,000 sq ft of outdoor exhibits and gardens. Costumed interpreters demonstrate life of Oregon Trail emigrants, members of Lewis and Clark expedition, and Native Americans. Footpaths wind through park; offers stunning views of river from high bluff. (Schedule and phone same as Center)

Fort Dalles Museum. Only remaining bldg of the 1856 outpost is the Surgeon's Quarters. Rare collection of pioneer equipment; stagecoaches, covered wagons. (Mar-Oct, daily; rest of yr, Wed-Sun; closed hols, also 1st 2 wks Jan) 15th & Garrison Sts. Phone 541/296-4547. ¢¢

Mayer State Park. A 613-acre park comprised of an undeveloped area with overlook on Rowena Heights; and a developed area, on the shores of the Columbia River, with swimming beach, windsurfing, dressing rms, fishing, boat ramp; picnicking. 10 mi W, off I-84 Exit 77. Phone 541/695-2261.

Mount Hood National Forest. (see) W of city.

Sorosis Park. This 15-acre park overlooks the city from the highest point on Scenic Dr, with view of the Columbia River, Mt Adams, and Mt Hood. Located on part of the bottom of ancient Lake Condon. The bones of 3 types of camels, the ancient horse, and mastodons were found near here. Jogging trail, tennis courts, picnic area. Rose Garden.

Riverfront Park. Swimming beach, windsurfing, fishing, boating (launch), jet boat excursions; picnicking. Off I-84, exit 85.

The Dalles Dam and Reservoir. Two-mi train tour with views of historic navigation canal, visitor center, petroglyphs, and fish ladder facilities (Memorial Day-Labor Day, daily; Apr-May and Oct-Mar, Wed-Sun). 3 mi E of town off I-84 and 1 mi E of The Dalles Hwy Bridge, which crosses the Columbia just below the dam (use I-84 exit 87 in summer, Exit 88 off-season). Phone 541/296-1181. **FREE** On S shore, 8½ mi E of dam is

Celilo Park. Swimming, sailboarding, fishing, boating (ramp); picnicking, playground, comfort station. Recreational areas with similar facilities also are on N and S shores. Adj to ancient fishing grounds, now submerged under waters backed up by The Dalles Dam.

Annual Events

Cherry Festival. Fourth wkend Apr.

Fort Dalles Rodeo & Chili Cook-off. CASI sanctioned. Thurs-Sun, 3rd wk July.

Motels/Motor Lodges

★★ **BEST WESTERN UMATILLA HOUSE.** *112 W 2nd St (97058), at Liberty St. 541/296-9107; fax 541/296-*

3002; toll-free 800/528-1234. 65 rms, 2-4 story. S $51-$56; D $59-$63; each addl $7; under 12 free. Crib free. Pet accepted; $5. TV; cable (premium). Heated pool. Restaurant 6:30 am-9 pm. Bar 11 am-11 pm. Ck-out 11 am. Meeting rms. Business servs avail. In-rm modem link. Health club privileges. Some refrigerators. Cr cds: A, C, D, DS, ER, JCB, MC, V.

D ⊷ ≋ ⊠ 🖾 SC

★ **INN AT THE DALLES.** *3550 SE Frontage Rd (97058), S of I-84 Exit 87. 541/296-1167; fax 541/296-3920.* 45 rms, 4 kits. S, D $34-$57; each addl $5; suites, kit. units $45-$75. Crib $5. Pet accepted. TV; cable. Indoor pool. Coffee in lobby. Restaurant nearby. Ck-out 11 am. Business servs avail. Free airport transportation. View of Columbia River, Mt Hood, The Dalles Dam. Cr cds: A, C, D, DS, MC, V.

⊷ ⬧ ≋ ✈ ⊠ 🔥

★★★ **LONE PINE VILLAGE.** *351 Lone Pine Dr (97058), I-84, Exit 87, at US 197. 541/298-2800; fax 541/298-8282; toll-free 800/955-9626.* 56 rms, 2 story. June-Sep: S $56-$60; D $69-$74; each addl $6; suites $109; under 12 free; lower rates rest of yr. Pet accepted, some restrictions; $6. TV; cable (premium). Indoor pool; whirlpool. Complimentary full bkfst. Restaurant adj 6 am-10 pm. Bar 4 pm-2 am. Ck-out noon. Coin lndry. Meeting rms. Business servs avail. Sundries. Gift shop. Free airport transportation. Golf privileges, pro, driving range. Exercise equipt. Lawn games. Refrigerators, microwaves. Cr cds: A, D, DS, MC, V.

D ⊷ ⬧ ⧖ ≋ ⊼ 🔥 ⊠ 🖾

Hotel

★★ **QUALITY INN.** *2114 W 6th St (97058). 541/298-5161; fax 541/298-6411; toll-free 800/848-9378. Email info@qualityinn-thedalles.com; www. qualityinn thedalles.com.* 85 rms, 2 story, 4 suites. S $95. Crib avail. Pet accepted, fee. Parking lot. Pool, children's pool, whirlpool. TV; cable (premium), VCR avail. Complimentary coffee in rms, newspaper, toll-free calls. Restaurant 6 am-11 pm. Bar. Ck-out noon, ck-in 3 pm. Meeting rms. Business servs avail. Coin lndry.

Gift shop. Exercise privileges. Golf. Tennis, 4 courts. Downhill skiing. Hiking trail. Picnic facilities. Video games. Cr cds: A, C, D, DS, MC, V.

🅳 ⬛⬛⬛⬛⬛⬛⬛⬛⬛⬛⬛

Restaurant

★ **COUSIN'S.** *2115 W 6th St (97058). 541/298-2771. www.qualityinn.com.* Specializes in pot roast, turkey and dressing. Hrs: 6 am-10 pm; Fri, Sat to 11 pm. Closed Dec 25. Bar. Bkfst $1.95-$7.95; lunch $4.25-$6.25; dinner $6.50-$11.50. Child's menu. Frontier motif. Cr cds: A, C, D, DS, MC, V.

🅳 ⬛

Tillamook

(B-1) *See also Lincoln City, Rockaway*

Founded 1851 **Pop** 4,001 **Elev** 16 ft
Area code 503 **Zip** 97141
Information Tillamook Chamber of Commerce, 3705 US 101N; 503/842-7525

Located at the southern end of Tillamook Bay, this is the county seat. Dairying, cheese and butter making, timber, and fishing are the main industries. There are many beaches for swimming, crabbing, clamming, and beachcombing; boat landings and camping, picnicking, and fishing sites are also in the area.

What to See and Do

Cape Lookout State Park. A 1,974-acre park with virgin spruce forest, observation point; one of most primitive ocean shore areas in state. Hiking trail to end of cape, picnicking, tent and trailer sites (dump station). Standard fees. 12 mi SW off US 101 on Whiskey Creek Rd. Phone 503/842-4981.

⬛**Capes Scenic Loop Drive to Cape Meares and Oceanside.** (Approx 10 mi) W on 3rd St, NW on Bay Ocean Rd to Cape Meares; go S on Loop Rd to Cape Meares State Park. See Tillamook Bay County Boat Landing, Cape Meares Lake, beach with beachcombing; also Cape Meares Lighthouse; Native American burial Sitka spruce tree known as "Octopus Tree."

Continue S to Oceanside, site of Three Arch Rocks Federal Sea Lion and Migratory Bird Refuge, and beach area with beachcombing and agates. Continue S to Netarts; see Netarts Bay Boat Landing and Whiskey Creek Fish Hatchery. Go S on Cape Lookout Rd to Pacific City and Cape Kiwanda, then back to US 101S. (Or take Whiskey Creek Rd from Netarts boat launching site, continue over Cape Lookout Mt through Sandlake, Tierra Del Mar to Pacific City. Exceptionally scenic, it also avoids traffic on US 101.)

Tillamook County Pioneer Museum. Possessions of early settlers, replica of pioneer home and barn; blacksmith shop; logging displays, war relics; relics from Tillamook Naval Air Station and Blimp Base; minerals, guns, books, vehicles, natural history and wildlife exhibits incl 9 dioramas; "great grandma's kitchen." (Mar-Sep, daily; rest of yr, Tues-Sun; closed Thanksgiving, Dec 25) 2106 2nd St at Pacific Ave. Phone 503/842-4553. ¢

Annual Events

Tilamook Dairy Parade & Rodeo. Fairgrounds, 4603 3rd St. Fourth wkend June.

Tillamook County Fair. Fairgrounds, 4603 3rd St. First full wk Aug.

Motel/Motor Lodge

★★ **MARCLAIR INN.** *11 Main Ave (97141). 503/842-7571; fax 503/842-1071; toll-free 800/331-6857.* 47 rms, 1-2 story, 6 kits. No A/C. Mid-May-mid-Oct: S $60-$72; D $69-$80; suites, kit. units $85-$105; under 12 free; lower rates rest of yr. Crib $6. TV; cable. Heated pool; whirlpool. Sauna. Restaurant 7 am-9 pm. Ck-out 11 am. Sun deck. Cr cds: A, D, DS, MC, V.

⬛⬛⬛⬛⬛

Hotel

★★ **SHILO INN.** *2515 N Main St (97141). 503/842-7971; fax 503/842-7960; toll-free 800/222-2244. Email tillamook@shiloinns.com.* 101 rms, 2 story. July-Aug: S, D $69-$115; each addl $10; kit. units $120; under 12 free; higher rates County Fair; lower rates rest of yr. Crib avail, fee. Pet accepted, some restrictions, fee. Parking lot. Indoor pool, whirlpool. TV; cable

(DSS). Complimentary full bkfst, coffee in rms, newspaper, toll-free calls. Restaurant 6 am-10 pm. Ck-out noon, ck-in 4 pm. Meeting rms. Business servs avail. Coin lndry. Gift shop. Free airport transportation. Exercise equipt, sauna, steam rm. Golf. Video games. Cr cds: A, C, D, DS, ER, JCB, MC, V.

B&B/Small Inn

★★ **SANDLAKE COUNTRY INN.** *8505 Galloway Rd (97112), 11 mi S on US 101, right at Sandlake Exit, 5½ mi to Sandlake Grocery, right on Galloway Rd. 503/965-6745; fax 503/965-7425.* 4 rms, 2 story, 1 suite, 1 kit. unit. No A/C. Some rm phones. S, D $90-$135. TV; cable, VCR. Complimentary full bkfst. Ck-out 11 am, ck-in 3 pm. Concierge. In-rm whirlpools, fireplaces. Balconies. Farmhouse built of timbers washed ashore from a ship wreck in 1890. Antiques. Totally nonsmoking. Cr cds: A, DS, MC, V.

Umatilla

(A-5) *See also Hermiston, Pendleton*

Founded 1863 **Pop** 3,046 **Elev** 296 ft **Area code** 541 **Zip** 97882

Information Chamber of Commerce, PO Box 67; 541/922-4825 or 800/542-4944

What to See and Do

Columbia Crest Winery. Located amidst 2,000 acres of European-style vinifera grapes. Tours, incl wine production, cellar, and tastings. Picnicking; gardens. (Self-guided tours, Mon-Fri; guided tours, Sat-Sun; closed hols) 18 mi NW via WA 14, in Paterson, WA. Phone 509/875-2061. **FREE**

Hat Rock State Park. A 735-acre park on lake formed by McNary Dam. Swimming beach, fishing, boat ramp to the Columbia River; hiking, picnicking. Hat Rock is a large monolith that looks like a man's top hat; a landmark often referred to in diaries of early-day explorers and travelers. 9 mi E off US 730 near jct OR 207. Phone 541/567-5032.

McNary Lock and Dam. Single lift navigation lock. Dam is 7,365 ft long, 92 ft high. The Columbia River forms Lake Wallula, a 61-mi waterway partly in Washington. Swimming, waterskiing, fishing, boating (marinas); hunting, picnicking, primitive camping (2 areas; free). Tours of power, navigation, and fish passage facilities (June-Sep, daily). (Daily) 2 mi E on US 730. Phone 541/922-4388. **FREE**

Umatilla Marina Park. Swimming beach, boating (launch, storage, gas, oil); picnicking, RV trailer camping (fee). (Daily) NE edge of town on Columbia River. Phone 541/922-3939.

Annual Events

Sage Riders Rodeo. NRA sanctioned, Second wkend June.

Landing Days & Govenor's Cup Walleye Tournament. Labor Day wkend.

Yachats

(C-1) *See also Florence, Newport*

Pop 533 **Elev** 15 ft **Area code** 541 **Zip** 97498

Web www.pioneer.net/~yachat

Information Yachats Area Chamber of Commerce, US 101; PO Box 728; 541/547-3530

Yachats (YA-hots) is a resort area on the central Oregon coast, west of Siuslaw National Forest. Derived from a Native American phrase meaning "waters at the foot of the mountain," Yachats is along a rocky shore with a fine sandy beach.

What to See and Do

Cape Perpetua Campground. Beachcombing, fishing; hiking, camping. Summer campfire programs (Sat, Sun). 3 mi S on US 101. Camping ¢¢¢ Nearby is

Cape Perpetua Visitor Center. Interpretive displays of oceanography, natural history of coastal area, movies. Nature trails, auto tour. (May, Thurs-Sun; June-Labor Day, daily; rest of yr, Sat-Sun; closed Dec 25) In Suislaw National Forest. Phone 541/547-3289. **FREE**

Neptune State Park. This 302-acre park features Cook's Chasm (near N end), a long, narrow, deep fissure where the sea falls in with a spectacular fury; wind-depressed forest trees (near N end); slopes covered with huckleberry shrubs. A community of harbor seals makes its home on the rocks below Strawberry Hill. Surf fishing; hiking, picnicking. Observation point. 3 mi S on US 101. Phone 541/997-3641.

Tillicum Beach Campground. Ocean view, beachcombing; camping. Summer evening campfire programs Sat and Sun. 3½ mi N on US 101. Camping ¢¢¢

Yachats State Recreation Area. A 93-acre day-use park bordering the Yachats River, in the shadow of Cape Perpetua. Small picnic area. Observation point. On US 101. Phone 541/867-7451.

Motels/Motor Lodges

★★ **ADOBE RESORT MOTEL.** *1555 Hwy 101 (97498). 541/547-3141; fax 541/547-4234; toll-free 800/522-3623.* 93 rms, 2-3 story, 5 kits. S, D $58-$100; each addl $8; suites $150; kit. units $110-$135. Crib $8. Pet accepted, some restrictions. TV; cable (premium), VCR. Complimentary coffee in rms. Restaurant 8 am-2:30 pm, 5-9 pm. Bar. Ck-out 11 am. Meeting rm. Business servs avail. Gift shop. Exercise equipt; sauna. Whirlpool. Refrigerators; some fireplaces. Whirlpool in suites. Some balconies. On ocean. Cr cds: A, C, D, DS, MC, V.
D 🔁 🏊 🕊 🔄 🐾 SC

★ **FIRESIDE MOTEL.** *1881 Hwy 101 N (97498). 541/547-3636; fax 541/547-3152; toll-free 800/336-3573. Email reservations@overleaflodge.com; www.overleaflodge.com/fireside.* 44 rms, 2 story, 1 suite. June-Sep: S, D $99; each addl $7; suites $130; under 7 free; lower rates rest of yr. Crib avail. Pet accepted, fee. Parking lot. TV; cable (DSS), VCR avail. Complimentary coffee in rms, toll-free calls. Ck-out 11 am, ck-in 3 pm. Fax servs avail. Gift shop. Exercise privileges. Beach access. Supervised children's activities. Hiking trail. Picnic facilities. Cr cds: A, DS, MC, V.
D 🔁 🏊 🕊 🔄 🐾 SC

★★ **SHAMROCK LODGETTES.** *105 Hwy 101 S (97498), ¼ mi S. 541/547-3312; fax 541/547-3843; toll-*

free 800/845-5028. www.o-t-b.com. 19 rms, 11 kit. cottages. S, D, kit. units $71-$100; each addl $8; kit. cottages $91-$112; wkly rates. Crib $7. Pet accepted, some restrictions; $3/day. TV; cable (premium). Complimentary coffee in rms. Restaurant nearby. Ck-out 11 am. Massage. Refrigerators; some in-rm whirlpools; microwaves avail. Some private patios, balconies. Beach adj. Cr cds: A, D, DS, MC, V.
🔁 🐾

B&B/Small Inn

★★ **SEA QUEST BED & BREAKFAST.** *95354 Hwy 101 S (97498). 541/547-3782; fax 541/547-3719; toll-free 800/341-4878. Email seaquest@ newportnet.com; www.seaq.com.* 5 rms, 1 with shower only, 2 story. No rm phones. S, D $150-$160; each addl $20; wkends, hols (2-3-day min). Children over 14 yrs only. Complimentary full bkfst. Ck-out 11 am, ck-in 3 pm. Gift shop. Many in-rm whirlpools. On beach. Ocean view. Totally nonsmoking. Cr cds: MC, V.
D 🐾 🕊 🔄 🐾

WASHINGTON

The Stillaguamish, Steilacoom, and Hoh, Puyallup, Tulalip, and La Push, the Duckabush, the Dosewallips, and the Queets, the Skookumchuck, the Sol Duc, and the Pysht—all these are Washington towns and rivers. There are many more like them, named by Native Americans.

Ruggedly handsome Washington is like a bank in which nature has deposited some of her greatest resources. In addition to dramatic mountain ranges, expansive forests, and inviting harbors, it is also a cornerstone of American hydroelectric technology. Here are the majestic spectacles of mighty Mount Rainier—revered as a god by the Native Americans—and the Olympic Peninsula, where one of the wettest and one of the driest parts of the country are only a mountain away from each other; also here is Puget Sound, a giant inland sea where 2,000 miles of shoreline bend into jewellike bays.

Population: 4,866,692
Area: 68,192 square miles
Elevation: 0-14,410 feet
Peak: Mount Rainier (Pierce County)
Entered Union: November 11, 1889 (42nd state)
Capital: Olympia
Motto: *Al-ki* (By and by)
Nickname: Evergreen State
Flower: Rhododendron
Bird: Willow Goldfinch
Tree: Western Hemlock
Time Zone: Pacific
Website: www.tourism.wa.gov

Although British and Spanish navigators were the first Europeans to explore Washington's serrated shoreline, the first major discoveries were made in 1792, when an American, Captain Robert Gray, gave his name to Grays Harbor and the name of his ship, *Columbia,* to the great river. An Englishman, Captain George Vancouver, explored and named Puget Sound and christened Mount Baker and Mount Rainier, which he could see far inland. Fort Vancouver was the keystone of the British fur industry, dominating a Northwest empire. After conflicting US and British claims were resolved, Americans surged into this area by ship and wagon train.

Puget Sound

Part of the Oregon Territory until separated in 1853, the state's eastern boundary was established in 1863, when Idaho became a territory. Entering the last decade of the 19th century as a state of the Union, Washington found itself no longer America's last territorial frontier.

Civilization has not dissipated Washington's natural wealth. On the contrary, after more than a century of logging operations, Washington retains 24 million acres of superb forests, and miracles of modern engineering have almost completely erased the wastelands through which the wagon trains of the pioneers passed on their way to the sea.

The mighty but capricious Columbia River meanders through the heart of northeast and central Washington, then runs for 300 miles along the Oregon-Washington border. Through a series of dams and the Grand Coulee Reclamation Project, the energies of the Columbia have been harnessed and converted into what is presently one of the world's great sources of water power. Irrigation and a vast supply of inexpensive power gave a tremendous push to Washington's economy, sparking new industries and making possible the state's production of huge crops of grains, vegetables, and fruit.

Central Washington is the apple barrel of the country; dairying is a big industry in the western valleys. Forestry and wood products as well as the production of paper and allied products are of major importance in the western and northern sections of the state; one-third of the state is covered by commercial forests. In recent years Washington wines have enjoyed great popularity around the nation.

Since 1965, more than 25 percent of Washington's total manufacturing effort has been devoted to the production of transportation equipment, of which a large portion is involved in commercial jet aircraft. Along Puget Sound, industry means canning plants, lumber mills and pulp and paper plants; but even here there is a new economic dimension: petroleum refineries of four major companies have a daily capacity of 366,500 barrels of crude oil and gasoline; biotechnology and software development are growing industries. Tourism is the state's fourth largest industry, amounting to more than $8.8 billion a year.

When to Go/Climate

Moist air off the Pacific Ocean and Puget Sound creates the rainy conditions in western Washington and heavy snowfall in the Cascades. While the western slopes of the Cascades and Olympic Mountains are soaked with moisture, the eastern slopes and, indeed, the entire eastern part of the state is almost desert dry. Temperatures are seasonally mild, except for high in the mountains.

AVERAGE HIGH/LOW TEMPERATURES (°F)

SEATTLE

Jan 46/36	**May** 64/48	**Sep** 69/53
Feb 51/38	**June** 70/53	**Oct** 60/47
Mar 54/40	**July** 74/56	**Nov** 52/41
Apr 58/43	**Aug** 74/57	**Dec** 46/37

SPOKANE

Jan 33/21	**May** 66/42	**Sep** 72/46
Feb 41/26	**June** 75/49	**Oct** 59/36
Mar 48/30	**July** 83/54	**Nov** 41/29
Apr 57/35	**Aug** 83/54	**Dec** 34/22

Parks and Recreation Finder

Directions to and information about the parks and recreation areas below are given under their respective town/city sections. Please refer to those sections for details.

NATIONAL PARK AND RECREATION AREAS

Key to abbreviations. I.H.S. = International Historic Site; I.P.M. = International Peace Memorial; N.B. = National Battlefield; N.B.P. = National Battlefield Park; N.B.C. = National Battlefield and Cemetery; N.C.A. = National Conservation Area; N.E.M. = National Expansion Memorial; N.F. = National Forest; N.G. = National Grassland; N.H.P. = National Historical Park; N.H.C. = National Heritage Corridor; N.H.S. = National Historic Site; N.L. = National Lakeshore; N.M. = National Monument; N.M.P. = National Military Park; N.Mem. = National Memorial; N.P. = National Park; N.Pres. = National Preserve; N.R.A. = National Recreational Area; N.R.R. = National Recreational River; N.Riv. = National River; N.S. = National Seashore; N.S.R. = National Scenic Riverway; N.S.T. = National Scenic Trail; N.Sc. = National Scientific Reserve; N.V.M. = National Volcanic Monument.

Place Name	Listed Under
Colville N.F.	COLVILLE
Coulee Dam	same
Fort Vancouver N.H.S.	VANCOUVER
Gifford Pinchot N.F.	VANCOUVER
Klondike Gold Rush N.H.P.	SEATTLE
Mount Baker-Snoqualmie N.F.	BELLINGHAM, SEATTLE
Mount Rainier N.P.	same
Mount St. Helens N.V.M.	same
North Cascades N.P.	SEDRO WOOLLEY
Okanogan N.F.	OMAK
Olympic N.F.	OLYMPIA
Olympic N.P.	same
San Juan Island N.H.P.	SAN JUAN ISLANDS
Umatilla N.F.	CLARKSTON
Wenatchee N.F.	WENATCHEE
Whitman Mission N.H.S.	WALLA WALLA

STATE PARK AND RECREATION AREAS

Key to abbreviations. I.P. = Interstate Park; S.A.P. = State Archaeological Park; S.B. = State Beach; S.C.A. = State Conservation Area; S.C.P. = State Conservation Park; S.Cp. = State Campground; S.F. = State Forest; S.G. = State Garden; S.H.A. = State Historic Area; S.H.P. = State Historic Park; S.H.S. = State Historic Site; S.M.P. = State Marine Park; S.N.A. = State Natural Area; S.P. = State Park; S.P.C. = State Public Campground; S.R. = State Reserve; S.R.A. = State Recreation Area; S.Res. = State Reservoir; S.Res.P. = State Resort Park; S.R.P. = State Rustic Park.

Place Name	Listed Under
Alta Lake S.P.	CHELAN
Bay View S.P.	MOUNT VERNON
Belfair S.P.	BREMERTON
Birch Bay S.P.	BLAINE
Blake Island S.P.	BREMERTON
Bogachiel S.P.	FORKS
Brooks Memorial S.P.	GOLDENDALE
Conconully S.P.	OMAK
Deception Pass S.P.	ANACORTES
Federation Forest S.P.	ENUMCLAW
Fields Spring S.P.	CLARKSTON
Flaming Geyser S.P.	ENUMCLAW
Fort Canby S.H.P.	LONG BEACH

Fort Casey S.P.	COUPEVILLE
Fort Columbia S.H.P.	LONG BEACH
Fort Flagler S.P.	PORT TOWNSEND
Fort Simcoe S.H.P.	TOPPENISH
Fort Worden S.P.	PORT TOWNSEND
Ginkgo/Wanapum S.P.	ELLENSBURG
Illahee S.P.	BREMERTON
Kitsap Memorial S.P.	PORT GAMBLE
Lake Chelan S.P.	CHELAN
Lake Cushman S.P.	UNION
Lake Sammamish S.P.	ISSAQUAH
Lake Sylvia S.P.	ABERDEEN
Larrabee S.P.	BELLINGHAM
Lewis and Clark Trail S.P.	DAYTON
Millersylvania S.P.	OLYMPIA
Moran S.P.	SAN JUAN ISLANDS
Moses Lake S.P.	MOSES LAKE
Mount Spokane S.P.	SPOKANE
Old Fort Townsend S.P.	PORT TOWNSEND
Olmstead Place S.P.	ELLENSBURG
Potholes S.P.	MOSES LAKE
Rainbow Falls S.P.	CHEHALIS
Riverside S.P.	SPOKANE
Sacajawea S.P.	PASCO
Scenic Beach S.P.	BREMERTON
Schafer S.P.	ABERDEEN
Seaquest S.P.	KELSO
Sequim Bay S.P.	SEQUIM
Squilchuck S.P.	WENATCHEE
Steamboat Rock S.P.	COULEE DAM
Twanoh S.P.	UNION
Twenty-Five Mile Creek S.P.	CHELAN
Twin Harbors S.P.	WESTPORT
Wenberg S.P.	MARYSVILLE
Yakima Sportsman S.P.	YAKIMA

Water-related activities, hiking, riding, various other sports, picnicking, and visitor centers, as well as camping, are available in many of these areas. The 248,882 acres owned or managed by the Washington State Parks & Recreation Commission provide unusually good camping and trailer facilities at most locations, with a camping fee of $10/site; hookups $15; 10-day limit in summer; 15 days rest of yr. Most parks are open daily: Apr-mid-Oct, 6:30am-dusk; some are closed rest of yr. Pets on leash only. Further information may be obtained from the Washington State Parks & Recreation Commission, 7150 Cleanwater Lane, PO Box 42650, Olympia 98504-2650. Phone 360/902-8500, 800/233-0321, or 800/452-5687.

SKI AREAS

Place Name	Listed Under
Alpental Ski Area	NORTH BEND
Crystal Mountain Resort	MOUNT RAINIER NATIONAL PARK
Hurricane Ridge Winter Use Ski Area	OLYMPIC NATIONAL PARK
Hyak Ski Area	NORTH BEND
Mission Ridge Ski Area	WENATCHEE

CALENDAR HIGHLIGHTS

MARCH

Chocolate Fantasy (Yakima). Chocolate manufacturers from across the nation showcase candy, cookies, and pies; sampling, "chocolate bingo." Phone 509/966-6309.

APRIL

Daffodil Festival (Tacoma). In Tacoma and Puyallup Valley. Flower show, coronation, 4-city floral parade of floats, marine regatta, bowling tournament. Phone 253/627-6176.

MAY

Wooden Boat Festival (Olympia). Percival Landing in Harbor. Wooden boats on display, some open for public viewing. Wooden crafts fair. Phone 360/943-5404.

Ski to Sea Festival (Bellingham). Parades, carnival, art show, special events. Ski to Sea race; starts on Mount Baker, ends in Bellingham Bay, and involves skiers, runners, canoeists, bicyclists, and kayakers. Memorial Day weekend. Phone 360/734-1330.

JULY

San Juan Island Jazz Festival (San Juan Islands). Indoor/outdoor jazz festival featuring Dixieland, swing, zydeco, and blues/jazz. Friday Harbor. Phone 360/378-5509.

AUGUST

Seafair (Seattle). Citywide marine festival. Regattas, speedboat races, shows at Aqua Theater, parades, sports events, exhibits. Phone 206/728-0123.

Stampede and Suicide Race (Omak). Rodeo events; horses and riders race down a cliff and across the Okanogan River. Western art show. Native American dance contests. Encampment with more than 100 teepees. Phone 509/826-1002.

Southwest Washington Fair (Centralia). First held in 1909, this is the state's 2nd oldest fair and one of the largest. Phone 360/736-6072.

SEPTEMBER

Northeast Washington Fair (Colville). Stevens County Fairgrounds. Parade, livestock and horse shows, arts and crafts exhibits, carnival. Phone 509/684-2585.

Western Washington Fair (Puyallup). Pacific Northwest's largest fair; incl 3 statewide youth fairs, livestock shows, agricultural and commercial exhibits, free entertainment, midway, rodeo, top-name grandstand acts. Phone 253/841-5045.

Central Washington State Fair and Rodeo (Yakima). Fairgrounds. Thoroughbred racing. Pari-mutuel wagering. Phone 509/248-7160.

Mount Baker Ski Area	BELLINGHAM
Mount Spokane Ski Area	SPOKANE
Ski Acres Ski Area	NORTH BEND
Ski Bluewood Ski Area	DAYTON
Snoqualmie Ski Area	NORTH BEND
White Pass Village Ski Area	MOUNT RAINIER NATIONAL PARK

FISHING AND HUNTING

With 10,000 miles of bay and Pacific shoreline, 8,000 lakes, and rivers that stretch from Oregon to Canada, Washington provides something for every angler's whim. Fish hatcheries dot the state, stocking nature's waterways and those artificially created by irrigation and navigation dams. If you like salmon and steelhead, Washington is the state to try your luck.

Nonresident freshwater fishing license $40; 2-day license. A food fish license is required for salmon and saltwater bottomfish; nonresident food fish license, $20; nonresident saltwater fish license, $36; nonresident combination fresh water/saltwater fish license, $72. A shellfish/seaweed license is required for shellfish; nonresident license, $20. Razor clam season varies; contact the Dept of Fish & Wildlife for season dates, phone 360/902-2200. Nonresident small-game hunting license $150; 3-day $50; big game, $200-$660. Get hunting and freshwater fishing regulations and a complete list of license fees from Dept of Fish & Wildlife, 500 Capitol Way N, Olympia 98504. Fishing and Hunting regulation pamphlets are available in local sporting goods stores.

Driving Information

Safety belts are mandatory for all persons anywhere in vehicle. Children under 40 pounds in weight must be in an approved safety seat anywhere in vehicle. For further information phone 360/753-6197.

INTERSTATE HIGHWAY SYSTEM

The following alphabetical listing of Washington towns in *Mobil Travel Guide* shows that these cities are within 10 miles of the indicated Interstate highways. A highway map, however, should be checked for the nearest exit.

Highway Number	Cities/Towns within 10 miles
Interstate 5	Bellingham, Blaine, Centralia, Chehalis, Everett, Kelso, Longview, Marysville, Mount Vernon, Olympia, Puyallup, Seattle, Sedro Woolley, Snohomish, Tacoma, Vancouver.
Interstate 82	Ellensburg, Kennewick, Pasco, Richland, Sunnyside, Toppenish, Yakima.
Interstate 90	Bellevue, Ellensburg, Issaquah, Moses Lake, North Bend, Ritzville, Seattle, Spokane.
Interstate 182	Pasco, Richland.

Additional Visitor Information

Washington travel information and brochures on the state are available from the Washington State Tourism Department of Community, Trade, and Economic Development, 101 General Administration Bldg, PO Box 42500, Olympia 98504-2500. Phone 800/544-1800 for a copy of *Washington State Lodging and Travel Guide;* phone 800/638-8474 or 360/586-2088 for tourism information. *This is Washington* (Superior Publishing Co, Seattle) and *Sunset Travel Guide to Washington* (Sunset Publishing, Menlo Park, CA) are also helpful.

There are 180 visitor information centers in Washington; most are open May-Sep. Visitors who stop by will find information and brochures most helpful in planning stops to points of interest. The locations for the official state visitor centers at points of entry are as follows: 7 mi S of Blaine, near the Canadian border; E of Spokane at the Idaho/Washington border, I-90 Exit 299 westbound; 404 E 15th St, Vancouver; in Oroville on US 97, near the Canadian border; at the Oregon border on US 97, near Maryhill State Park and Sam Hill Bridge; and on WA 401 near the Astoria Bridge.

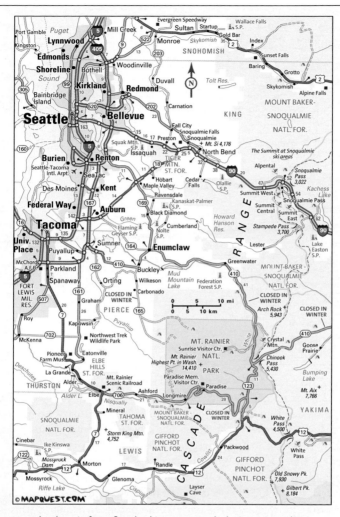

A very popular day trip from Seattle, this route rounds the imposing volcanic cone of Mount Rainier, the centerpiece of Mount Rainier National Park. Take Highway 410 east and climb along the White River with the towering white cone of 14,412-foot Mount Rainier rising above the forest. The park itself has a number of different viewpoints for taking in the peak, and each has its own personalities. Sunrise—the highest point reached by road in the park—is on the drier, east side of the peak; there are hikes to wildflower meadows and glacial overlooks, and mountain goats are often seen in the area. The aptly named Paradise area—on the southern side of the mountain atop a broad timberline shoulder—shares postcard views of the peak with the Paradise Inn, a vast historic stone-and-log lodge built in classic Arts-and-Crafts style. An extensive trail system explores flower-filled meadows and tumbling water falls. Other highlights of this route are Ohanapecosh, a riparian wetland with a stand of massive old-growth cedar trees, and Longmire, the original park headquarters with several turn-of-the 20th-century structures and another heritage hotel. A highlight of the return trip near Eatonville (on Highway 161) is the Northwest Trek Wildlife Park, a private refuge that rehabilitates wolves, cougars, and other Northwest native wildlife that have been injured or must be removed from the wild for other reasons. **(Approx 142 mi)**

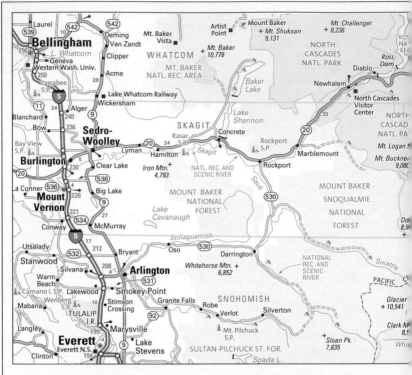

This route passes through spectacular mountain scenery in one of the West's most rugged national parks. Starting on the moist Pacific side of the Cascade range at Sedro-Wooley, Highway 20 follows the increasingly narrow Skagit River valley inland through dripping fir and cedar forests. Near Rockport, the landscape becomes wilder and steeper; this is a major wintering area for bald eagles, who come here to dine on migrating salmon. As the route enters the park near Marblemount, the Skagit is dammed in quick succession in a precipitous canyon by three early 20th-century hydrodams (this is where Seattle gets its power). Tours of the largest dam are the most popular activity in the park; getting up to the dam itself involves riding an incline railroad up a sheer cliff face. Around the dams are hikes to waterfalls and mist gardens. After climbing Rainy Pass, which has

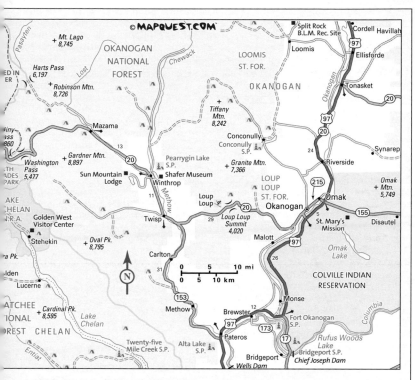

incredible views of tooth-edged mountain ranges and volcanoes in good weather, Highway 20 drops onto the dry side of the Cascades, where the forests are suddenly dominated by ponderosa pines and juniper. The highway follows the Methow River, a very lovely, semiarid valley, that was once the province of cattle ranches but is now lined with resort homes and golf courses. The town of Winthrop, which just 15 years ago was filled with feed stores and tractor dealerships, now epitomizes the wealthy New West culture with its art galleries, fine restaurants, and home-decor boutiques. From the delightfully named town of Twisp, follow Highway 153 through ranch land, which slowly gives way to apple orchards as the route joins Highway 97 and the Columbia River at Pateros. **(Approx 168 mi)**

Aberdeen

(D-2) *See also Hoquiam, Ocean Shores, Westport*

Settled 1878 **Pop** 16,565 **Elev** 19 ft
Area code 360 **Zip** 98520
Web www.chamber.grays-harbor.wa.us

Information Grays Harbor Chamber of Commerce, 506 Duffy St; 360/532-1924 or 800/321-1924

Aberdeen and Hoquiam are twin cities on the eastern tip of Grays Harbor. Born as a cannery named for the city in Scotland, Aberdeen later blossomed as a lumber town, with one of the greatest stands of Douglas fir ever found in the Pacific Northwest at its back. Many Harbor residents are descendants of Midwestern Scandinavians who came here to fell the forests. Today, the town's commerce consists of wood-processing, fishing, and ship building. The Port of Grays Harbor is located along the waterfront of the two towns.

What to See and Do

Aberdeen Museum of History. Special exhibits with 1880s-1940s furnishings and implements incl kitchen and bedroom, general mercantile store, 1-rm school; farm and logging equipment and displays; blacksmith shop, pioneer church, fire trucks. Slide show, photographs. (June-Labor Day, Wed-Sun; rest of yr, wkends) 111 E 3rd St. Phone 360/533-1976. **FREE**

Grays Harbor Historical Seaport. Historical interpretive center; classes in long boat building. Incl a museum with informational and active exhibits on the history of sailing in the Pacific Northwest. Also replica of Robert Gray's ship *Lady Washington* (seasonal; fee). (Daily; closed hols) 813 E Heron St. Phone 360/532-8611. **FREE**

Lake Sylvia State Park. Approx 235 acres of protected timber. Swimming, fishing; hiking, picnicking, concession, camping. Standard fees. 10 mi E on US 12, then 1 mi N on unnumbered road. Phone 360/249-3621.

Samuel Benn Park. Named for pioneer settler. Rose and rhododendron gardens, picnic facilities, playground, tennis. (Daily) East 9th & North I Sts. Phone 360/533-4100, ext 230. **FREE**

Schafer State Park. Approx 120 acres on Satsop River. Swimming, fishing; hiking, picnicking, camping (hookups; dump station). (Apr-mid-Dec, daily; rest of yr, wkends and hols) Standard fees. 13 mi E on US 12, then 10 mi N on unnumbered road. Phone 360/482-3852.

Motels/Motor Lodges

★ **OLYMPIC INN.** *616 W Heron St (98520). 360/533-4200; fax 360/533-6223; toll-free 800/562-8618.* 55 rms, 2 story, 3 kits. No A/C. S $43-$70; D $53-$73; each addl $7; suites, kit. units $65-$97. Crib $7. TV; cable (premium). Restaurant nearby. Ck-out noon. Coin lndry. Meeting rm. Business servs avail. Many refrigerators. Cr cds: A, C, D, DS, MC, V.
D ⬚ 🔥

★ **RED LION INN.** *521 W Wishkah St (98520). 360/532-5210; fax 360/533-8483; res 800/REDLION. www.redlion.com.* 67 rms, 2 story. June-Sep: S $68-$78; D $78-$98; each addl $10; under 18 free; lower rates rest of yr. Crib free. Pet accepted. TV; cable. Complimentary continental bkfst. Restaurant nearby. Ck-out noon. Sundries. Cr cds: A, C, D, DS, ER, JCB, MC, V.
D ⬚ 🐾 ⬚ ⬚ ⬚ ⬚ ⬚ 🔥 ⬚

B&B/Small Inn

★★ **ABERDEEN MANSION BED AND BREAKFAST.** *807 N M St (98520). 360/533-7079; toll-free 888/533-7079. Email jaonw@techline.com.* 5 rms, 2 story. No A/C. No rm phones. May-Oct: S, D $95-$125; lower rates rest of yr. Children over 12 yrs only. TV; cable. Complimentary full bkfst. Restaurant nearby. Ck-out 11 am, ck-in 4-6 pm. Victorian house built in 1905; antiques. Totally nonsmoking. Cr cds: A, DS, MC, V.
⬚ 🔥 SC

Restaurants

★★ **BILLY'S RESTAURANT.** *322 E Heron (98520). 360/533-7144.* Specializes in burgers, salad. Hrs: 7 am-11 pm. Closed Easter, Thanksgiving, Dec 25. Bar. Bkfst $2.50-$4.50; lunch, dinner $4.50-$12.95. Child's menu. In 1904 bldg with antique furnishings. Cr cds: A, D, MC, V.

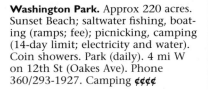

★★ **BRIDGES RESTAURANT.** *112 N G St (98520). 360/532-6563.* Specializes in prime rib, seafood, steak. Hrs: 11 am-11 pm; Fri, Sat to midnight; Sun 4-9 pm. Bar. Lunch $4.50-$10.95; dinner $6.50-$25.95. Child's menu. Entertainment. Solarium. Family-owned. Cr cds: A, D, DS, MC, V.

Anacortes

(B-3) *See also Coupeville, La Conner, Mount Vernon, Oak Harbor, San Juan Islands, Sedro Woolley*

Settled 1860 **Pop** 11,451 **Elev** 24 ft
Area code 360 **Zip** 98221
Web www.anacortes-chamber.com
Information Visitor Info Center at the Chamber of Commerce, 819 Commercial Ave, Suite G; 360/293-3832

Anacortes, at the northwest tip of Fidalgo Island, houses the San Juan Islands ferries. The town's name honors Anna Curtis, wife of one of the founders.

What to See and Do

Deception Pass State Park. More than 3,000 acres of sheltered bays and deep forests with fjord-like shoreline. Swimming (lifeguards in summer), scuba diving, fishing, clamming, boating (ramp, dock); hiking trails, picnicking, camping. Standard fees. 9 mi S on WA 20. Phone 360/675-2417.

San Juan Islands Trip. Ferryboats leave several times daily for major islands of the group. Either leave car at dock in Anacortes or disembark at any point and explore from paved roads. For schedules, fares contact the Visitor Information Center.

Washington Park. Approx 220 acres. Sunset Beach; saltwater fishing, boating (ramps; fee); picnicking, camping (14-day limit; electricity and water). Coin showers. Park (daily). 4 mi W on 12th St (Oakes Ave). Phone 360/293-1927. Camping ¢¢¢

Annual Events

Skagit Valley Tulip Festival. First 3 wkends Apr.
Waterfront Festival. Mid-May.
Shipwreck Day. Mid-July.
Barbershop Concert and Salmon Barbecue. Last wkend July.

Tulip Farm, Skagit Valley

Motels/Motor Lodges

★★ **ANACORTES INN.** *3006 Commercial Ave (98221). 360/293-3153; fax 360/293-0209; toll-free 800/327-7976.* 44 rms, 2 story, 5 kits. May-mid-Oct: S $65; D $70-$85; each addl $5; kit. units $10 addl; under 12 free. Pet accepted. TV; cable (premium). Heated pool. Coffee in rms. Restaurant nearby. Ck-out 11 am. Business servs avail. Refrigerators, microwaves. Cr cds: A, D, DS, MC, V.

★ **SHIP HARBOR INN.** *5316 Ferry Terminal Rd (98221). 360/293-5177; fax 360/299-2412; toll-free 800/852-8568. Email shi@shipharborinn.com;*

www.shipharborinn.com. 16 rms, 2 story, 4 suites. May-Sep: S $75; D $100; suites $125; lower rates rest of yr. Crib avail. Pet accepted, some restrictions, fee. Street parking. TV; cable (premium). Complimentary continental bkfst, toll-free calls. Restaurant nearby. Ck-out 11 am, ck-in 3 pm. Meeting rm. Business servs avail. Coin lndry. Gift shop. Golf, 18 holes. Tennis, 4 courts. Bike rentals. Hiking trail. Picnic facilities. Cr cds: A, C, D, DS, MC, V.

B&B/Small Inn

★★ **CHANNEL HOUSE BED & BREAKFAST.** *2902 Oakes Ave (98221). 360/293-9382; fax 360/299-9208; toll-free 800/238-4353. Email beds@sos.net; www.channel-house.com.* 6 rms, 3 story. June-Oct: S $79; D $95; each addl $20; lower rates rest of yr. Parking lot. TV; cable (premium). Complimentary full bkfst, coffee in rms. Restaurant nearby. Ck-out 1 pm, ck-in 3 pm. Concierge. Golf, 18 holes. Cr cds: A, DS, MC, V.

Bellevue

(C-3) *See also Issaquah, Seattle*

Pop 86,874 **Elev** 125 ft **Area code** 425 **Web** www.eastkingcounty.org
Information East King County Convention and Visitors Bureau, 520 112th Ave NE, Suite 101, 98004; 425/455-1926

Incorporated in 1953, Bellevue has rapidly become the state's fourth largest city. It is linked across Lake Washington to Seattle by the Evergreen Floating Bridge.

What to See and Do

Bellevue Art Museum. Contemporary NW art and craft exhibits and programs. (Daily) 301 Bellevue Square. Phone 425/452-2749. ¢¢

Bellevue Botanical Garden. Thirty-six acres feature woodlands, meadows, and display gardens including Waterwise Garden, Japanese Gardens, and Fuchsia Display. Garden shop. Visitor Center. (Daily) 12001 Main St. Phone 425/452-2749. **FREE**

Chateau Ste. Michelle. Located on an 87-acre estate; tours, wine tasting; summer concert series. Picnic area, gardens, gift shop with wine and picnic supplies. (Daily; closed hols) N on I-405 to exit 23B, at 14111 NE 145th St in Woodinville. Phone 425/488-1133. **FREE**

Rosalie Whyel Museum of Doll Art. Features curated collection of dolls, teddy bears, toys, and miniatures. Museum shop. (Daily; closed hols) 1116 108th Ave NE. Phone 425/455-1116. ¢¢

Motels/Motor Lodges

★★ **BEST WESTERN.** *11211 Main St (98004), W of I-405 Exit 12. 425/455-5240; fax 425/455-0654; res 800/528-1234.* 180 rms, 2 story. S $120; D $130; under 18 free; wkend rates. Crib free. Pet accepted; $30. TV; cable (premium), VCR avail. Heated pool; poolside serv. Coffee in rms. Restaurant 6:30 am-2 pm, 5-10 pm. Bar; entertainment Thurs-Sat. Ck-out noon. Meeting rms. Business servs avail. In-rm modem link. Bellhops. Valet serv. Sundries. Exercise equipt. Refrigerators; microwaves avail. Balconies. Cr cds: A, D, DS, JCB, MC, V.

★★ **RESIDENCE INN BY MARRIOTT.** *14455 NE 29th Pl (98007), off WA 520 148th Ave N Exit. 425/882-1222; fax 425/885-9260; res 800/331-3131.* 120 suites, 2 story. S, D $160-$240. Crib $5. Pet accepted; $10/day. TV; cable (premium), VCR avail (free movies). Heated pool. Complimentary continental bkfst, coffee in rms. Ck-out noon. Coin lndry. Meeting rms. Business servs avail. In-rm modem link. Valet serv. Lawn games. Refrigerators, microwaves. Private patios, balconies. Picnic tables, grills. Cr cds: A, D, DS, JCB, MC, V.

★★ **SILVER CLOUD INN.** *12202 NE 124th St (98034), N on I-405, Exit 20-B, E on NE 124 St. 425/821-8300; fax 425/823-1168; toll-free 800/205-6933. www.scinns.com.* 99 rms, 3 story. June-Sep: S $69-$97; D $77-$105; suites $98-$145; under 12 free; lower rates rest of yr. Crib free. TV;

cable (premium). Complimentary continental bkfst. Restaurant adj open 24 hrs. Ck-out noon. Meeting rms. Business servs avail. In-rm modem link. Concierge. Sundries. Guest lndry. Exercise equipt. Heated pool; whirlpool. Refrigerators. Microwaves avail. Cr cds: A, C, D, DS, MC, V.

[D] [icons]

★★ **WESTCOAST BELLEVUE HOTEL.** *625 116th Ave (98004), E of I-405, NE 8th St Exit. 425/455-9444; fax 425/455-2154; res 604/642-4129; toll-free 800/426-0670. Email wcbelle vue@aol.com.* 176 rms, 6 story. S $75-$85; D $85-$95; each addl $10; suites $100-$110; under 18 free. Crib free. TV; cable (premium). Heated pool; poolside serv. Complimentary coffee in rms. Restaurant 6 am-10 pm; Sat, Sun from 7 am. Rm serv. Bar 4-11 pm; closed Sun. Ck-out noon. Meeting rms. Business servs avail. In-rm modem link. Sundries. Exercise equipt. Cr cds: A, DS, MC, V.

[D] [icons] [SC]

Hotels

★★★★ **BELLEVUE CLUB HOTEL.** *11200 SE 6th St (98004), S of Downtown. 425/455-1616; fax 425/688-3101; toll-free 800/579-1110. www.bellevueclub.com.* On Seattle's east side, this beatifully appointed hotel and private club (open to registered guests) has a clean, award winning West Coast design with subtle Asian influences. The interiors are decorated in light eath tones, blond wood finishes, and exotic artwork. Each of the 67 guest rooms has an exquisite bathroom, rich in limestone, marble, and granite and featuring a deep soaking-tub and separate glass-enclosed shower, and a view of Mount Rainier, the plaza fountain, or the tennis courts. 67 rms, 2 with shower only, 4 story. S, D $190-$230; suites $370-$945; under 18 free; wkend rates. Crib free. Valet parking $5. TV; cable (premium), VCR avail. Indoor pool; whirlpool, poolside serv, lifeguard. Supervised children's activities; ages 1-12. Complimentary coffee in lobby. Restaurant (see also POLARIS). Rm serv 24 hrs. Bar 11 am-midnight;

entertainment Thurs-Sat. Ck-out 1 pm. Guest lndry. Meeting rms. Business center. In-rm modem link. Concierge. Gift shop. Indoor tennis, pro. Extensive exercise rm; sauna, steam rm. Massage. Minibars. Cr cds: A, C, D, MC, V.

[D] [icons]

★★★ **DOUBLETREE HOTEL.** *300 112th Ave (98094), W of I-405 Exit 12. 425/455-1300; fax 425/455-0466; res 800/222-8733.* 353 rms, 10 story. S, D $180-$225; each addl $15; suites $250-$495; under 18 free; wkend rates. Crib free. TV; cable (premium), VCR avail. Heated pool; whirlpool, poolside serv. Complimentary coffee in rms. Restaurant 6 am-11 pm. Bar 11-2 am; closed Sun, Mon. Ck-out noon. Convention facilities. Business servs avail. In-rm modem link. Concierge. Gift shop. Barber, beauty shop. Exercise equipt. Some bathrm phones. Balconies. Glass-enclosed elvtrs in lobby; multi-story glass canopy at entrance. Luxury level. Cr cds: A, DS, MC, V.

[D] [icons] [SC]

★★★ **HILTON HOTEL BELLEVUE.** *100 112th Ave NE (98004), off I-405 NE 4th St Exit. 425/455-3330; fax 425/451-2473; res 800/HILTONS; toll-free 800/235-4458. Email salesbell hilton@uswest.net; www.hilton.com.* 179 rms, 7 story, 2 suites. Crib avail. Parking lot. Indoor pool, whirlpool. TV; cable, VCR avail. Complimentary coffee in rms, newspaper, toll-free calls. Restaurant 6 am-11 pm. Bar. Ck-out noon, ck-in 3 pm. Meeting rms. Business center. Bellhops. Concierge. Dry cleaning. Exercise privileges, sauna. Golf. Tennis. Cr cds: A, D, DS, ER, MC, V.

[D] [icons]

★★★ **HYATT REGENCY BELLE-VUE.** *900 Bellevue Way NE (98004), at Bellevue Pl. 425/462-1234; fax 425/646-7567; res 800/233-1234. Email sales@bellepo.hyatt.com; www. bellevue.hyatt.com* 262 rms, 24 story, 20 suites. May-Aug: S $250; D $275; each addl $25; suites $375; under 18 free; lower rates rest of yr. Crib avail. Valet parking avail. Indoor pool, lap pool, whirlpool. TV; cable (premium). Complimentary coffee in rms, newspaper. Restaurant 5:45 am-10:30 pm. Bar. Ck-out noon, ck-in 3 pm. Conference center, meeting rms. Business center. Bellhops. Concierge. Dry cleaning. Salon/barber. Exercise privileges, sauna, steam rm. Golf. Downhill skiing. Cr cds: A, C, D, DS, ER, JCB, MC, V.

★★ **SILVER CLOUD INN-BELLVUE.** *10621 NE 12th St (98004). 425/637-7000; fax 425/455-0531; res 800/551-7207; toll-free 800/205-6937. Email managment@bellvue.scinns.com; www.scinns.com.* 86 rms, 4 story, 11 suites. May-Aug: S $114; D $124; each addl $10; suites $164; under 17 free; lower rates rest of yr. Crib avail. Parking lot. Pool, whirlpool. TV; cable (premium). Complimentary continental bkfst, coffee in rms. Restaurant nearby. Ck-out noon, ck-in 3 pm. Business servs avail. Dry cleaning. Exercise equipt. Golf. Video games. Cr cds: A, C, D, DS, MC, V.

★★★★ **WOODMARK HOTEL ON LAKE WASHINGTON.** *1200 Carillon Point (98033), N on Bellevue Way, continue onto Lake Washington Blvd NE. 425/822-3700; fax 425/822-3699; res 800/323-7500; toll-free 800/822-3700. www.thewoodmark.com.* Located on the shores of Lake Washington, seven miles east of Seattle, this low lying hotel is part of a 32-acre community that offers specialty shops, restaurants, a fitness center and spa, a scenic marina, and much more for visitors to enjoy. 72 rms, 4 story, 28 suites. S, D $190; each addl $25; suites $300; under 18 free. Crib avail. Valet parking avail. TV; cable (premium), VCR avail, CD avail. Complimentary coffee in rms, newspaper, toll-free calls. Restaurant 6:30 am-9 pm, closed Sat. 24-hr rm serv. Bar. Ck-out noon, ck-in 3 pm. Meeting rms. Business center. Bellhops. Concierge. Dry cleaning. Gift shop. Salon/barber. Exercise equipt. Golf. Beach access. Bike rentals. Video games. Cr cds: A, C, D, DS, JCB, MC, V.

B&B/Small Inn

★★★ **SHUMWAY MANSION.** *11410 99th Pl NE (98033), I-405 N Exit 20A, then 1½ mi W. 425/823-2303; fax 425/822-0421. Email info@ shumwaymansion.com; www.shumway mansion.com.* 8 rms, 2 story. No A/C.

Rm phone avail. S, D $70-$95; each addl $12; suite $105. Children over 12 yrs only. TV avail. Complimentary full bkfst; evening refreshments. Restaurant nearby. Ck-out 11 am, ck-in 3 pm. Business servs avail. In-rm modem link. Health club privileges. 24-rm historic mansion (1909), restored and moved to present site in 1985. Overlooks Juanita Bay. Totally nonsmoking. Cr cds: A, MC, V.

Restaurants

★★★ **BISTRO PROVENCAL.** *212 Central Way (98033), I-405 Kirkland Exit 18. 425/827-3300.* Specializes in seafood, rack of lamb. Own baking. Hrs: 5:30-10:30 pm. Closed hols. Res accepted. Dinner $13-$21. Complete meals: $23-$45. French country inn decor. Casual elegance. Fireplace. Cr cds: A, C, D, ER, MC, V.

★★★ **CAFE JUANITA.** *9702 120th Pl NE (98034), I-405 N Exit 20A, then approx 1½ mi W. 425/823-6533. Email holly@cafejuanita.com; www.cafe juanita.com.* Specializes in pollo pistacchi, venison shank, coniglio con funghi. Own baking, pasta, ice cream. Hrs: 5-10 pm. Closed Mon; hols. Res accepted. Dinner a la carte entrees: $14-$22.50. Child's menu. Casual dining in converted private home; wine bottle accents, open kitchen. Family-owned. Cr cds: A, D, MC, V.

★★ **JAKE O'SHAUGHNESSEY'S.** *401 Bellevue Sq (98004), in Bellevue Sq Mall. 425/455-5559.* Specializes in fresh salmon, prime rib, Caesar salad. Hrs: 9:30 am-9:30 pm. Closed Easter, Thanksgiving, Dec 25. Res accepted. Bar. Lunch $3.95-$9.95; dinner $9.95-$19.95. Child's menu. Club atmosphere with aquatic decor; several dining areas; open kitchen. Cr cds: A, D, DS, MC, V.

★★ **POLARIS.** *11200 SE 6th. 425/455-1616. www.bellevue.com.* Specializes in pasta, seafood, lamb. Hrs: 6:30-9 pm; Fri, Sat to 10 pm. Res accepted. Bar. Dinner $11.50-$24.95. Child's menu. Cr cds: A, MC, V.

★★ **SPAZZO MEDITERRANEAN GRILL.** *10655 NE 4th St (98004), on 9th Floor of Key Bank Bldg. 425/454-8255.* Specializes in Italian, Greek and Spanish dishes. Hrs: 11:30 am-10 pm; Fri to 11 pm; Sat 4-11 pm; Sun from 4:30 pm. Closed Dec 25. Res accepted. Bar. Lunch $6.95-$15.95; dinner $8.95-$23.95. Child's menu. View of Lake Washington and downtown. Cr cds: A, D, DS, MC, V. D

★★★ **THIRD FLOOR FISH CAFE.** *205 Lake St S (98033), I-405 N to Kirkland. 425/822-3553. www.fishcafe. com.* Specializes in spice-crusted Pacific halibut, pan-seared sturgeon, lamb shank. Own pastries. Hrs: 5-9:30 pm; Fri, Sat to 10 pm. Closed Jan 1, Thanksgiving, Dec 25. Res accepted. Bar. Wine list. Dinner a la carte entrees: $17-$35. Entertainment: jazz Wed, Sat. Three window-walls overlook Lake Washington and marina; dark woods create intimate atmosphere. Cr cds: A, D, DS, MC, V. D

Bellingham

(A-3) *See also Blaine, Sedro Woolley; also see Vancouver, BC Canada*

Founded 1853 **Pop** 52,179 **Elev** 68 ft
Area code 360
Web www.bellingham.org

Information Bellingham/Whatcom County Convention & Visitors Bureau, 904 Potter St, 98226; 360/671-3990 or 800/487-2032 (order information). The Bureau operates a Visitor Information Center off I-5 Exit 253; daily; closed hols.

This city, located on Bellingham Bay, has the impressive Mount Baker as its backdrop and is the last major city before the Washington coastline meets the Canadian border. The broad curve of the bay was charted in 1792 by Captain George Vancouver, who named it in honor of Sir William Bellingham. When the first settlers arrived here, forests stretched to the edge of the high bluffs along the shoreline. Timber and coal played major roles in the town's early economy.

Today, Bellingham has an active waterfront port, which supports fishing, cold storage, boat building, shipping, paper processing, and marina operations. Squalicum Harbor's commercial and pleasure boat marina accommodates more than 1,800 vessels, making it the second largest marina on Puget Sound. The marina is a pleasant area to dine, picnic, and watch the fishermen at work. The downtown area contains a mix of restaurants, art galleries, specialty shops, and other stores. Bellingham is also home to Western Washington University, located on Sehome Hill, which affords a scenic view of the city and bay.

What to See and Do

Chuckanut Drive. A 10-mi drive, mostly along highway cut into mountain sides; beautiful vistas of Puget Sound and San Juan Islands. S from Fairhaven Park on WA 11 along Chuckanut Bay to Larrabee State Park.

City recreation areas. More than 2,000 acres of parkland offer a wide variety of activities. (Daily) Fee for some activities. Phone 360/676-6985. Areas include

    Arroyo Park. Approx 40 acres of dense, second-growth forest in a canyon setting. Creek fishing; hiking, nature, and bridle trails. Off Chuckanut Dr on Old Samish Rd.

    Bloedel Donovan Park. Swimming beach, fishing, boat launch (fee); picnicking, playground, concession (summer). Community center with gym. Parking fee (summer). 2214 Electric Ave, NW area of Lake Whatcom.

    Boulevard Park. Fishing, boat dock; bicycle paths, picnicking, playground, craft studio. S State St & Bayview Dr.

    Civic Field Athletic Complex. Contains multiple athletic fields and indoor community pool. Lakeway Dr & Orleans St.

    Cornwall Park. Approx 65 acres. Wading pool, steelhead fishing in Squalicum Creek; fitness trail, tennis, other game courts and fields, picnicking, playground. Extensive rose garden in park. 2800 Cornwall Ave.

Fairhaven Park. Wading pool; hiking trails, tennis, picnicking, playground. Rose garden is test site for the American Rose Society. 107 Chuckanut Dr.

Lake Padden Park. Approx 1,000 acres with 152-acre lake. Swimming beach, fishing, boat launch (no motors); hiking and bridle trails, 18-hole golf course (fee), tennis, athletic fields, picnicking, playground. 4882 Samish Way.

Sehome Hill Arboretum. The 165-acre native plant preserve contains hiking and interpretive trails; scenic views of city, Puget Sound, San Juan Islands, and mountains from observation tower atop hill. 25th St & McDonald Pkwy.

Whatcom Falls Park. Approx 240 acres. Children's fishing pond; state fish hatchery. Hiking trails, tennis, athletic fields, picnicking, playground. 1401 Electric Ave, near Lake Whatcom.

🔟 **Fairhaven District.** In the late 1800s, this area was a separate city that had hopes of becoming the next Chicago. The 1890s bldgs are now restaurants and shops. Brass plaques detail history of the area. Walking tour brochures at the info gazebo. Centered at jct 12th St & Harris Ave.

Ferndale. Community founded in mid-1800s, with several preserved areas. **Hovander Homestead,** on Neilson Rd, is a county park with working farm and museum; interpretive center with nature trails and observation tower. Approx 9 mi NW off I-5, Exit 262. Phone 360/384-3444. ¢¢

Larrabee State Park. Approx 2,000 acres. Scuba diving, fishing, clamming, crabbing, tide pools, boating (ramp); hiking, picnicking, camping (hookups). Mountain viewpoints. Standard fees. 7 mi S on WA 11. Phone 360/676-2093.

Lynden Pioneer Museum. Exhibits on history of this Dutch community; antique car and buggy, farm equipment. (Mon-Sat) Approx 12 mi N via WA 539, at 217 Front St, Lynden. Phone 360/354-3675. ¢

Maritime Heritage Center. Salmon life-cycle facility and learning center. Outdoor rearing tanks; indoor displays detail development from egg to adult. Park (daily). Learning Center (Mon-Fri; closed hols). 1600 C Street. Phone 360/676-6806. **FREE**

Mount Baker-Snoqualmie National Forest. Mt Baker and Snoqualmie national forests were combined under a single forest supervisor in July, 1974. Divided into 5 ranger districts, the combined forest encompasses nearly 2 million acres. The Snoqualmie section lies E and SE of Seattle (see); the Mt Baker section lies E on WA 542 and includes the Mt Baker Ski Area. The forest extends from the Canadian border S to Mt Rainier National Park and incl rugged mountains and woodlands on the western slopes of the Cascades, the western portions of the Glacier Peak and Alpine Lakes, Henry M. Jackson, Noisy-Diobsud, Boulder River, Jackson, Clearwater, and Norse Peak wildernesses; 7 commercial ski areas; 1,440 mi of hiking trails; picnic areas and campsites. Mt Baker rises 10,778 ft in the N, forming a center for recreation all yr, famous for deep-powder snow skiing and snowboarding. Snoqualmie Pass (via I-90) and Stevens Pass (via US 2) provide all-yr access to popular, scenic destinations; Baker Lake provides excellent boating and fishing. Contact Forest Service/National Park Service Information. Phone 360/599-2714. E of forest is

North Cascades National Park. (See SEDRO WOOLLEY)

Mount Baker Ski Area. Two quad, 6 double chairlifts, rope tow; patrol, school, rentals; restaurant, cafeteria, bar, lodge. Longest run 1½ mi; vertical drop 1,500 ft. (Nov-Mar, daily; Apr, Fri-Sun; closed Dec 25) Also cross-country trails. Half-day rates (wkends, hols). 55 mi E on WA 542. Phone 360/734-6771 or 360/671-0211 (snow conditions). ¢¢¢¢

Western Washington Univ. (1893) 11,500 students. A 189-acre campus; internationally acclaimed outdoor sculpture collection; contemporary art at Western Gallery (360/650-3963). Theater (360/650-3876), music (360/650-3130), summer stock (360/650-3876). High St. Phone 360/650-3424.

Whatcom Museum of History & Art. Regional and historic displays; also changing art exhibits; in former city hall (1892) and 3 adj bldgs. Fee for special exhibitions. (Tues-Sun; closed hols) 121 Prospect St. Phone 360/676-6981. **FREE**

Annual Events

Ski to Sea Festival. Parades, carnival, art show, special events. Ski to Sea race starts on Mt Baker, ends in Bellingham Bay, and involves skiers, runners, canoeists, bicyclists, and kayakers. Memorial Day wkend.

Deming Logging Show. Log show grounds, in Deming. Log chopping, tree climbing, logger rodeo, salmon barbecue. Second wkend June.

Lummi Stommish. Lummi Reservation, 15 mi NW via I-5, exit 260 to WA 540. Water carnival with war canoe races, arts and crafts; salmon bake, Native American dancing. Wkend June.

Motels/Motor Lodges

★★ **BEST WESTERN INN.** *151 E McLeod Rd (98226). 360/647-1912; fax 360/671-3878; toll-free 800/528-1234. Email bheritage@aol.com.* 90 rms, 3 story. No elvtr. S $67-$80; D $77-$86; each addl $5; suites $135-$155; studio rms $67-$89; under 12 free. Crib free. TV; cable (premium), VCR avail. Heated pool; whirlpool. Complimentary continental bkfst. Restaurant 6 am-11 pm. Ck-out noon. Meeting rms. Business servs avail. Valet serv. Free airport transportation. Health club privileges. Some refrigerators, wet bars; microwaves avail. Cr cds: A, C, D, DS, MC, V.
D ⇔ ⊠ ⬚ SC

★ **DAYS INN.** *125 E Kellogg Rd (98226), I-5 Exit 256, near airport. 360/671-6200; fax 360/671-9491; res 800/329-7466; toll-free 800/831-0187.* 70 rms, 3 story. July-Sep: S $49.95; D $54.95; each addl $5; suites $79-$99; under 12 free, lower rates rest of yr. Crib free. Pet accepted; $5. TV; cable (premium). Heated pool; whirlpool. Complimentary continental bkfst. Restaurant nearby. Ck-out 11 am. Coin lndry. Meeting rms. Health club privileges. Some refrigerators; microwaves avail. Cr cds: A, C, D, DS, MC, V.
D ⬚ ⇔ ⬚ ⬚ ⬚

★★ **HAMPTON INN.** *3985 Bennett Dr (98225), I-5 Exit 258, near airport. 360/676-7700; fax 360/671-7557; res 800/426-7866. Email bllwa01@ hi-hotel.com.* 132 rms, 4 story. June-Sep: S $69-$74; D $79-$89 (up to 4); under 18 free; lower rates rest of yr. Crib free. TV; cable (premium). Pool. Complimentary continental bkfst, coffee in rms. Ck-out noon. Meeting rms. Business center. In-rm modem link. Free airport, railroad station transportation. Exercise equipt. Cr cds: A, C, D, DS, MC, V.
D ⇔ ⬚ ⬚ ⬚ ⬚

★★ **QUALITY INN.** *100 E Kellogg Rd (98226), I-5 Exit 256, near airport. 360/647-8000; fax 360/647-8094; toll-free 800/900-4661. www.hotelchoice. com/hotel/wao54.* 86 suites, 3 story. June-mid-Sep: S $64.95-$84.95; D $74.95-$94.95; each addl $10; under 18 free; lower rates rest of yr. Crib free. TV; cable (premium), VCR avail. Heated pool; whirlpool. Complimentary continental bkfst. Coffee in rms. Ck-out noon. Coin lndry. Meeting rms. Business center. In-rm modem link. Free airport, bus depot transportation. Exercise equipt. Refrigerators; microwaves avail. Balconies. Cr cds: A, D, DS, JCB, MC, V.
D ⇔ ⬚ ⬚ ⬚ ⬚

★★ **RAMADA INN.** *215 N Samish Way (81008). 360/734-8830; fax 360/ 647-8956; res 800/2RAMADA.* 66 rms, 3 story. June-Sep: S, D $90-$120; each addl $6; under 18 free; higher rates sporting events; lower rates rest of yr. Crib free. TV; cable (premium), VCR avail. Heated pool. Complimentary continental bkfst, coffee in rms. Restaurant nearby. Ck-out noon. Business servs avail. Valet serv. Refrigerators. Balconies. Cr cds: A, C, D, DS, MC, V.
D ⇔ ⬚ ⬚ ⬚

★★ **TRAVELERS INN.** *3750 Meridian St (98225). 360/671-4600; fax 360/671-6487; toll-free 800/633-8300.* 124 rms, 3 story. June-Sep: S $51.95; D $58.95; each addl $7; suites $64.95-$79.95; under 19 free; lower rates rest of yr. Crib free. Pet accepted, some restrictions. TV; cable (premium). Heated pool; whirlpool. Complimentary coffee in lobby. Restaurant nearby. Ck-out 11 am. Coin lndry. Meeting rms. Business servs avail. Some refrigerators. Cr cds: A, C, D, DS, MC, V.

★ **VAL-U INN MOTEL.** *805 Lakeway Dr (98226), I-5 Exit 253. 360/671-9600; toll-free 360/443-7777.* 80 rms, 2 story, 2 suites. May-Sep: S $54; D $62; each addl $5; suites $78; under 12 free; lower rates rest of yr. Crib avail. Pet accepted, some restrictions, fee. Parking lot. TV; cable, VCR avail. Complimentary continental bkfst, newspaper, toll-free calls. Restaurant nearby. Ck-out noon, ck-in 3 pm. Meeting rm. Fax servs avail. Coin lndry. Free airport transportation. Whirlpool. Cr cds: A, C, D, DS, MC, V.

Conference Center

★★ **BEST WESTERN LAKEWAY INN.** *714 Lakeway Dr (98226), off I-5 Exit 253. 360/671-1011; fax 360/676-8519; toll-free 888/671-1011. Email info@bellingham-hotel.com; www.bellingham-hotel.com.* 132 rms, 4 story, 8 suites. June-Aug: S $89; D $99; each addl $10; suites $120; under 12 free; lower rates rest of yr. Crib avail. Pet accepted, some restrictions, fee. Parking lot. Indoor pool, children's pool, whirlpool. TV; cable (premium), VCR avail. Complimentary coffee in rms, newspaper, toll-free calls. Ck-out noon, ck-in 3 pm. Meeting rms. Business center. Bellhops. Concierge. Dry cleaning, coin lndry. Salon/barber. Free airport transportation. Exercise equipt, sauna. Golf, 18 holes. Downhill skiing. Supervised children's activities. Video games. Cr cds: A, C, D, DS, ER, JCB, MC, V.

Restaurants

★★ **CHUCKANUT MANOR.** *3056 Chuckanut Dr (98232), 18 mi S on I-5 to Exit 250, then 2 mi W. 360/766-6191.* Specializes in seafood, steak. Hrs: 11:30 am-10 pm; Sun from 10:30 am; Sun brunch to 2:30 pm. Closed Mon; hols. Res accepted. Bar. Lunch $6-$12; dinner $14-$23. Sun brunch $13.50. Child's menu. Overlooks Samish bay, San Juan Islands. Cr cds: A, C, MC, V.

★★ **MARINA.** *985 Bell Wetherway (98225), on waterfront. 360/733-8292. www.bellwetheronthebay.com.* Specializes in seafood, steak. Hrs: 11:30 am-9:30 pm; Fri, Sat to 10 pm; Sun to 9 pm. Closed Dec 25. Res accepted Fri, Sat. Bar. Lunch a la carte entrees: $5.95-$12.95; dinner a la carte entrees: $10.95-$29.95. Child's menu. Cr cds: A, MC, V.

Blaine

(A-3) *See also Bellingham; also see Vancouver, BC Canada*

Pop 2,489 **Elev** 41 ft **Area code** 360 **Zip** 98231

Information Visitor Information Center, 215 Marine Dr, PO Box 4680; 360/332-4544 or 800/487-2032

What to See and Do

Birch Bay State Park. Approx 190 acres. Swimming, scuba diving, fishing, crabbing, clamming; picnicking, camping (daily, res advised Memorial Day-Labor Day; hookups, dump station). Standard fees. 10 mi SW via I-5, Exit 266, then 7 mi W via Grandview Rd, N via Jackson Rd to Helwig Rd. Phone 360/371-2800.

International Peace Arch. (1921) The 67-ft-high arch is on the boundary line between the US and Canada and marks more than a century of peace and friendship between the 2 countries. The surrounding park is maintained by the state of Washington and Province of British Columbia; gardens, picnicking, playground. N at point where I-5 reaches Canadian border.

Semiahmoo Park. A cannery once located on this 1½-mi-long spit was the last port of call for Alaskan fishing boats on Puget Sound. Restored bldgs now house museum, gallery, and gift shop (June-mid-Sep, Sat and Sun afternoons). Park (daily) offers clam digging. Picnicking, bird-watching. Off I-5, Exit 274, on Semiahmoo Sandspit, Drayton Harbor. Phone 360/371-2000. ¢¢

Annual Event

Peace Arch Celebration. Intl Peace Arch. Ceremony celebrates the relationship between the US and Canada; scouts and veterans from both nations. Second Sun June.

Resort

★ ★ ★ **RESORT SEMIAHMOO.** *9565 Semiahmoo Pkwy (98230), 3 mi S of Downtown, across Drayton Harbor; follow signs. 360/371-2000; fax 360/371-5490; res 800/323-7500; toll-free 800/770-7992. Email info@semiahmoo.com; www.semiahmoo.com.* 186 rms, 4 story, 12 suites. June-Sep: S, D $189; suites $229; lower rates rest of yr. Crib avail. Pet accepted, fee. Parking lot. Indoor/outdoor pools, whirlpool. TV; cable (premium), VCR avail. Complimentary coffee in rms, newspaper. Restaurant. Bar. Meeting rms. Business servs avail. Bellhops. Concierge. Dry cleaning. Gift shop. Salon/barber. Exercise rm, sauna, steam rm. Golf. Tennis, 5 courts. Downhill skiing. Beach access. Bike rentals. Supervised children's activities. Hiking trail. Picnic facilities. Video games. Cr cds: A, D, DS, MC, V.

Bremerton

(C-3) *See also Seattle*

Founded 1891 **Pop** 38,142 **Elev** 60 ft
Area code 360
Web www.visitkitsap.com
Information Kitsap Peninsula Visitor & Convention Bureau, 2 Rainier Ave, PO Box 270, Port Gamble, 98364; 360/297-8200 or 800/416-5615

The tempo of the Puget Sound Naval Shipyard is the heartbeat of Bremerton, a community surrounded on three sides by water. The six dry docks of the Naval Shipyard make Bremerton a home port for the Pacific fleet.

What to See and Do

⊠ **Bremerton Naval Museum.** Ship models, pictures, display of navy and

shipyard history. Naval artifacts. (Tues-Sun; closed hols) 130 Washington Ave. Phone 360/479-SHIP. **FREE**

Kitsap County Historical Society Museum. Re-creation of 1800s pioneer settlements. Photos and documents of history to WWII era. (Tues-Sat; closed hols) 280 4th St. Phone 360/692-1949. ¢

State parks.

Belfair. Approx 80 acres. Swimming; picnicking, camping (hookups; res Memorial Day-Labor Day, by mail only). Standard fees. 15 mi SW via WA 3 in Belfair. Phone 360/275-0668.

Illahee. Approx 75 acres. Swimming, scuba diving, fishing, clamming, boating (ramp, dock); hiking, picnicking, primitive camping. Standard fees. 3 mi NE off WA 306. Phone 360/478-6460.

Scenic Beach. Approx 90 acres. Swimming, scuba diving, limited fishing, oysters in season; nature trail, picnicking, primitive camping. Standard fees. 12 mi NW on WA 3. Phone 360/830-5079.

Blake Island. More than 475 acres. Saltwater swimming beach, scuba diving, fishing, boating (dock); hiking, picnicking, primitive camping. Standard fees. 6 mi SE, accessible only by boat. Phone 360/731-8330.

USS *Turner Joy.* Tours of Vietnam War era US Navy destroyer. (May-Sep, daily; rest of yr, Thurs-Mon; closed Dec 25) 300 Washington Beach Ave. Phone 360/792-2457. ¢¢

Annual Events

Armed Forces Day Parade. Mid-May.

Blackberry Festival. Late Aug.

Kitsap County Fair and Rodeo. Fairgrounds in Tracyton. Late Aug.

Seasonal Event

Mountaineers' Forest Theater. 8 mi W via WA 3, Kitsap Way, Seabeck Hwy, watch for signs. Oldest outdoor theater in the Pacific Northwest. Natural amphitheater surrounded by hundreds of rhododendrons beneath old-growth Douglas fir and hemlock. Log terraced seats. Family-oriented play. The ⅓-mile walk to theater is difficult for the physically disabled or elderly (assistance avail). Picnicking; concession. Contact 300 Third Ave W, Seattle 98119; 206/284-6310. Late May-early June.

Motels/Motor Lodges

★★ **BEST WESTERN BREMERTON INN.** *4303 Kitsap Way (98312). 360/405-1111; fax 360/377-0597; res 800/528-1234; toll-free 800/776-2291.* 90 rms, 3 story, 13 suites. S $71; D $79; each addl $8; under 15 free. Crib avail. Parking lot. Pool, whirlpool. TV; cable. Complimentary continental bkfst, newspaper, toll-free calls. Restaurant nearby. Ck-out 11 am, ck-in 2 pm. Meeting rm. Fax servs avail. Coin lndry. Exercise equipt. Golf. Cr cds: A, C, D, DS, ER, JCB, MC, V.

★★ **FLAGSHIP INN.** *4320 Kitsap Way (98312). 360/479-6566; fax 360/479-6745; toll-free 800/447-9396. Email desk@clerk.com, bremerton@ flagship-inn.com; www.flagship-inn. com.* 29 rms, 3 story. S $59.75; D $65.75-$71.75; each addl $6. Crib $6. TV; cable (premium), VCR (movies $2). Heated pool. Complimentary continental bkfst. Restaurant nearby. Ck-out noon. Business servs avail. In-rm modem link. Refrigerators. Balconies. On Oyster Bay. Cr cds: A, D, DS, MC, V.

★★ **MIDWAY INN.** *2909 Wheaton Way (98310). 360/479-2909; fax 360/479-1576; toll-free 800/231-0575.* 60 rms, 3 story, 12 kit. units. S $59; D $63; each addl $7; kit. units $65; under 10 free; wkly rates. Crib $5. Pet accepted, some restrictions; $10. TV; cable (premium), VCR (free movies). Complimentary continental bkfst, coffee in rms. Restaurant adj 4 pm-midnight. Ck-out 11 am. Coin lndry. Business servs avail. Refrigerators; microwaves avail. Cr cds: A, C, D, DS, MC, V.

★★ **WESTCOAST SILVERDALE HOTEL.** *3073 NW Bucklin Hill Rd (98383), approx 10 mi N on WA 3, Newberry Hill Rd Exit to Bucklin Hill Rd. 360/698-1000; fax 360/692-0972; toll-free 800/544-9799. Email sdhotel @silverlink.net.* 150 units, 2-3 story. S $70-$100; D $80-$110; each addl $10; suites $135-$325; under 18 free. Crib free. TV; cable. Indoor pool; whirlpool, poolside serv. Coffee in rms. Restaurant 6 am-11 pm. Rm serv. Bar 11-2 am; entertainment Fri-Sat. Ck-out noon. Meeting rms. Business servs avail. Bellhops. Valet serv. Lighted tennis. Exercise equipt; sauna. Game rm. Rec rm. Lawn games. Microwaves avail; refrigerator in suites. Private patios, balconies. Cr cds: A, DS, MC, V.

Restaurants

★★ **BOAT SHED.** *101 Shore Dr (98310). 360/377-2600.* Specializes in seafood, steak, pasta. Hrs: 11 am-11 pm. Closed Jan 1, Thanksgiving, Dec 25. Lunch $5.95-$9.95; dinner $5.95-$26.95. On waterfront. Cr cds: A, MC, V.

★★ **YACHT CLUB BROILER.** *9226 Bay Shore Dr (98383), 10 mi N on WA 3, Exit Newberry Hill, to Bucklin Hill Rd, turn right. 360/698-1601.* Specializes in prime steak, fresh salmon and halibut. Hrs: 11 am-10 pm; Fri, Sat to 11 pm; Sun brunch to 3 pm. Closed hols. Res accepted. Bar. Lunch $6-$12; dinner $10-$26. Sun brunch $4.95-$12. Child's menu. Overlooks Silverdale Bay. Cr cds: A, MC, V.

Cashmere

(C-5) *See also Leavenworth, Wenatchee*

Founded 1881 **Pop** 2,544 **Elev** 853 ft **Area code** 509 **Zip** 98815

Information Chamber of Commerce, PO Box 834; 509/782-7404

Cashmere's history dates back to the 1860s when a Catholic missionary came to the area to set up a school for Native Americans. Cashmere is located in the Wenatchee Valley in the center of the state on the North Cascade Loop. It has strong timber and fruit industries.

What to See and Do

Chelan County Historical Museum.
Pioneer relics, Native Americans artifacts; Columbia River archaeology exhibit; water wheel (1891); mineral exhibit; "pioneer village" with 21 cabins, mining displays. Great Northern railroad depot, passenger car, and caboose. (See ANNUAL EVENTS) (Apr-Oct, daily; rest of yr, by appt) 600 Cottage Ave, E edge of town. Phone 509/782-3230. ¢¢

Liberty Orchards Company, Inc.
Makes fruit-nut confections known as "aplets," "cotlets," "grapelets," and "fruit festives." Tour, samples. (May-Dec, daily; rest of yr, Mon-Fri; closed hols) Children with adult only. 117 Mission St, off US 2. Phone 509/782-2191. **FREE**

Annual Events

Founders' Day. Chelan County Historical Museum. Last wkend June.

Chelan County Fair. First wkend after Labor Day.

Apple Days. Chelan County Historical Museum. Apple pie contest, old-time crafts, Pioneer Village in operation, cider making. First wkend Oct.

Motels/Motor Lodges

★ **VILLAGE INN MOTEL.** *229 Cottage Ave (98815).* 509/782-3522; fax 509/782-2619; toll-free 800/793-3522. 21 rms, 2 story. S $45-$51; D $50-$60; each addl $5; higher rates festivals. Pet accepted, some restrictions; $5. TV; cable. Complimentary coffee in lobby. Restaurant nearby. Ck-out 11 am. Business servs avail. X-country ski 11 mi. Cr cds: MC, V.

★★ **WEDGE MOUNTAIN INN.** *7335 WA 2 (98815).* 509/548-6694; fax 509/664-3291; toll-free 800/666-9664. Email info@wedgemountain inn.com. 28 rms, 2 story. May-Dec: S $70; D $74; each addl $10; under 18 free; lower rates rest of yr. Crib $5. TV; cable. Heated pool. Complimentary coffee in lobby. Restaurant adj 6 am-9 pm. Ck-out 11 am. Coin lndry. Balconies. Cr cds: A, DS, MC, V.

Centralia

(D-2) *See also Chehalis*

Founded 1875 **Pop** 12,101 **Elev** 189 ft
Area code 360 **Zip** 98531
Web www.chamberway.com

Information The Centralia, Chehalis, and Greater Lewis County Chamber of Commerce, 500 NW Chamber of Commerce Way, Chehalis 98532; 360/748-8885 or 800/525-3323

Centralia was founded by a former slave named George Washington. George Washington Park is named for the founder, not for the country's first president.

What to See and Do

Borst Blockhouse (1852) and **Joseph Borst Family Farmstead** (1860). Fort built at confluence of Skookumchuck and Chehalis rivers as a strong point against Native American attacks; later moved to park entrance. Hewn log walls support upper fortification with loopholes for rifles, holes in 2nd floor to shoot through. Early steam locomotive; rhododendron gardens, arboretum. Homestead is refurbished and restored to its original state of the 1860s. (May-Sep, Sat and Sun; rest of yr, by appt) W of town in Fort Borst Park, off I-5, S of Harrison Ave. Phone 360/736-7687. **FREE**

Schaefer County Park. Swimming in the Skookumchuck River, fishing; hiking trails, picnicking (shelter), playground, horseshoe pits, volleyball. ½ mi N on WA 507. Phone 360/748-9121, ext 135. **FREE**

Annual Event

Southwest Washington Fair. One mi S on I-5. First held in 1909, this is the state's 2nd oldest fair and one of the largest. Third wk Aug.

Motels/Motor Lodges

★★ **INN AT CENTRALIA.** *702 W Harrison Ave (98531), I-5 Exit 82.* 360/736-2875; fax 360/736-2651. 89 rms, 2 story. June-Sep: S $55-$65; D

$65-$75; each addl $4; suites $80; under 12 free; lower rates rest of yr. Crib $4. TV; cable. Heated pool. Complimentary continental bkfst. Restaurant opp open 24 hrs. Ck-out 11 am. Business servs avail. Cr cds: A, C, D, DS, MC, V.

Chehalis

(D-2) *See also Centralia*

Settled 1873 **Pop** 6,527 **Elev** 226 ft
Area code 360 **Zip** 98532
Web www.chamberway.com

Information The Centralia, Chehalis, and Greater Lewis County Chamber of Commerce, 500 NW Chamber of Commerce Way; 360/748-8885 or 800/525-3323

First called Saundersville, this city takes its present name, Native American for "shifting sands," from its position at the point where the Newaukum and Chehalis rivers meet. Farms and an industrial park give economic sustenance to Chehalis and neighboring Centralia.

What to See and Do

Historic Claquato Church. (1858) Oldest church in state, original bldg on original site; handmade pews, pulpit. (Schedule varies) 3 mi W on WA 6, on Claquato Hill. Phone 360/748-4551 or 360/748-7755.

Lewis County Historical Museum. Restored railroad depot (1912). Pioneer displays; Native American exhibits. Cemetery, genealogical history; artifacts, newspapers, books, photographs, written family histories, oral histories of pioneers. (Tues-Sun; closed hols) 599 NW Front Way. Phone 360/748-0831. ¢

Rainbow Falls State Park. Approx 125 acres of woodland. Fishing, hiking trails, picnicking, camping (dump station). Standard fees. 18 mi W on WA 6. Phone 360/291-3767.

Annual Event

Music and Art Festival. Arts and craft vendors, food. Late July.

Restaurant

★ **MARY MCCRANK'S DINNER HOUSE.** *2923 Jackson Hwy (98532). 360/748-3662. Email marymccranks@ localaccess.com.* Own jams, jellies, breads, pies. Hrs: 11:30 am-8:30 pm; Sun noon-8 pm. Closed Mon; Dec 24, 25. Res accepted. Beer, wine. Lunch $5.50-$8.95; dinner $10.95-$18.50. Child's menu. Old-fashioned home cooking, farmhouse atmosphere. Fireplace, antiques. Established 1935. Cr cds: DS, MC, V.

Chelan

(C-5) *See also Wenatchee*

Settled 1885 **Pop** 2,969 **Elev** 1,208 ft
Area code 509 **Zip** 98816
Web www.lakechelan.com

Information Lake Chelan Chamber of Commerce, Box 216; (509)682-3503 or 800/4-CHELAN

Located in an apple-growing region, Chelan is a gateway to Lake Chelan and the spectacular northern Cascade mountains. A Ranger District office of the Wenatchee National Forest (see WENATCHEE) is located here.

What to See and Do

Lake Chelan. This fjordlike lake, the largest and deepest lake in the state, stretches NW for approx 55 mi through the Cascade Mts to the community of Stehekin in the North Cascades National Park (see SEDRO WOOLLEY); lake is nearly 1,500 ft deep in some areas. There are 2 state parks and several recreation areas along the lake.

Lake cruises. The passenger boats *Lady of the Lake II* and *Lady Express* make daily cruises on Lake Chelan to Stehekin. For details contact Lake Chelan Boat Co, 1418 W Woodin Ave, Box 186. Phone 509/682-4584 (recording). ¢¢¢¢

State parks.

Alta Lake. More than 180 acres. Swimming, fishing, boating (ramps); hiking, snowmobiling, ice-skating, camping (hookups). Standard fees. 20 mi N on US 97, then 2 mi W on WA 153. Phone 509/923-2473.

Lake Chelan. Approx 130 lakefront acres. Swimming, fishing, boating (ramps, dock); picnicking, camping (hookups; res required late May-Aug). (Apr-Oct, daily; rest of yr, wkends and hols) Standard fees. 9½ mi W via US 97 & South Shore Dr or Navarre Coulee Rd. Phone (800)452-5687.

Twenty-Five Mile Creek. Approx 65 acres. Fishing, boating (launch, mooring, gas); hiking, concession, camping (hookups). Standard fees. 18 mi NW on South Shore Dr. Phone (800)452-5687.

Annual Events

Apple Blossom Festival. 8 mi W via WA 150 in Manson. Second wkend May.

Taste of Chelan Street Fair. Late June.

WPRA Rodeo. Last wkend July.

Motel/Motor Lodge

★★ **CARVEL RESORT MOTEL.** *322 W Woodin Ave (98816). 509/682-2582; fax 509/682-3551; toll-free 800/962-8723. Email Carvel@nwi.net.* 92 rms, 1-4 story, 40 kits. Mid-June-mid-Sep: S, D $107-$165; suites $193-$500; wkly rate for kit. units; lower rates rest of yr. Crib $5. TV; cable. Heated pool. Restaurant nearby. Ck-out 11 am. Some refrigerators, fireplaces. Boat moorage. Cr cds: A, MC, V.

⬛ 🖼️ 🏕️ 😾 🔥

Resort

★★★ **CAMPBELL'S RESORT CONFERENCE CENTER.** *104 W Woodin (98816), on US 97, on Lake Chelan. 509/682-2561; fax 509/682-2177; toll-free 800/553-8225. Email res@ campbellsresort.com; www.campbells resort.com.* 175 rms, 3 suites. June-Aug: S, D $90; each addl $10; suites $172; under 18 free; lower rates rest of yr. Crib avail. Parking lot. Pool, whirlpool. TV; cable (premium), VCR avail. Complimentary coffee in rms, newspaper. Restaurant. Bar. Meeting rms. Business center. Concierge. Gift shop. Free airport transportation.

Exercise privileges. Golf. Tennis, 10 courts. Downhill skiing. Beach access. Supervised children's activities. Hiking trail. Picnic facilities. Video games. Cr cds: A, D, ER, JCB, MC, V.

⬛ 🐾 🖼️ 🍴 🎿 🏊 🛶 🎿 😾 🔥 SC 🚶

Cheney

(C-8) *See also Spokane*

Pop 7,723 **Elev** 2,350 ft
Area code 509 **Zip** 99004
Information Chamber of Commerce, 201 First St, PO Box 65; 509/235-8480

Cheney, on a rise of land that gives it one of the highest elevations of any municipality in the state, has been a university town since 1882. It is also a farm distribution and servicing center.

What to See and Do

Cheney Historical Museum. Features pioneer artifacts. (Mar-Nov, Tue and Sat afternoons) 614 3rd St. Phone 509/235-4343 or 509/235-4466. **FREE**

Eastern Washington University. (1882) 8,000 students. Tours of campus. Phone 509/359-2397. On campus are a theater, recital hall, and

Gallery of Art. Changing exhibits. (Academic yr, Mon-Fri; closed hols) Phone 509/359-2493. **FREE**

Museum of Anthropology. Teaching-research facility concerning Native Americans of North America. Phone 509/359-2433. **FREE**

Turnbull National Wildlife Refuge. Located on the Pacific Flyway; more than 200 species of birds have been observed in the area; also a habitat for deer, elk, coyotes, beaver, mink, chipmunks, red squirrels, and Columbia ground squirrels. Refuge named after Cyrus Turnbull, an early settler. A 2,200-acre public use area (daily). 4 mi S on Cheney-Plaza Rd, then 2 mi E. Phone 509/235-4723. Per vehicle (Mar-Oct) ¢

Annual Event

Rodeo Days. Rodeo, parade. Second wkend July.

Motel/Motor Lodge

★ **WILLOW SPRINGS MOTEL.** *5 B St (99004), I-90 Exit 270.* 509/235-5138; fax 509/235-4528. Email willow mngr@aol.com; www.nebsnow.com/ manager. 42 rms, 3 story. Apr-Sep: S $45; D $50; each addl $5; lower rates rest of yr. Crib avail. Pet accepted, fee. Parking lot. TV; cable (premium). Complimentary continental bkfst. Restaurant. Ck-out 11 am, ck-in 1 pm. Business center. Coin lndry. Cr cds: A, D, DS, MC, V.

Clarkston

(E-8) *See also Pullman*

Founded 1896 **Pop** 6,753 **Elev** 736 ft
Area code 509 **Zip** 99403
Information Chamber of Commerce, 502 Bridge St; 509/758-7712 or 800/933-2128

Clarkston is located on the Washington-Idaho boundary at the confluence of the Clearwater and Snake rivers. The town became a shipping center when the construction of four dams on the lower Snake River brought barge transportation here. Many recreation areas are located near Clarkston, especially along the Snake River and in the Umatilla National Forest. River trips are available into Hells Canyon.

What to See and Do

Asotin County Museum. Main museum contains sculptures, pioneer equipment, pictures, and clothing. On grounds are furnished pioneer house, shepherd's cabin, 1-rm schoolhouse, 1882 log cabin, blacksmith shop, a windmill, and Salmon River barge. (Tues-Sat; closed hols) Approx 6 mi S on WA 129, at 215 Filmore St, Asotin. Phone 509/243-4659. **FREE**

Fields Spring State Park. Approx 800 forested acres in the Blue Mts. A 1-mi uphill hike from parking lot to Puffer Butte gives view of 3 states. Wide variety of wildflowers and birdlife. Picnicking. Primitive camping. Stan-

dard fees. 30 mi S on WA 129. Phone 509/256-3332.

Petroglyphs. Ancient writings inscribed in cliffs of Snake River near Buffalo Eddy. Near town of Asotin.

Umatilla National Forest. Approx 319,000 acres of heavily forested mountain area extending into Oregon. Many recreation areas offer fishing; hunting, hiking, camping, downhill skiing (see DAYTON). For further info contact Supervisor, 2517 SW Hailey Ave, Pendleton, OR 97801. S of US 12, access near Pomeroy. Phone 541/276-3811.

Valley Art Center. Various types of art and crafts; changing monthly exhibits with featured artists and special showings. (Mon-Fri, closed hols) Northwest Heritage Show is held for 2 months in summer. 842 6th St. Phone 509/758-8331. **FREE**

Annual Events

Asotin County Fair. Incl cowboy breakfast, barbecue, parade. Last Thurs-Sun Apr.

Sunflower Days. Second Fri-Sat Aug.

Motels/Motor Lodges

★★ **BEST WESTERN RIVERTREE INN.** *1257 Bridge St (99403).* 509/758-9551; fax 509/758-9551; res 800/597-3621. 61 units, 2 story, 20 kits. (no equipt). S $59; D $69; each addl $5; suites $89-$130; kit. units $85 addl; higher rates university football games. Crib $5. TV; cable (premium). Heated pool; whirlpool. Restaurant opp 6-3 am. Ck-out noon. Business servs avail. Exercise equipt; sauna. Refrigerators. Balconies. Picnic tables, grills. Many rms with spiral staircase to loft. Cr cds: A, C, D, DS, ER, MC, V.

★★ **QUALITY INN.** *700 Port Dr (99403).* 509/758-9500; fax 509/758-5580; res 800/228-5151. Email quality inn@valint.net. 75 rms, 3 story. No elvtr. S $60-$89; D $65-$89; each addl $5; under 18 free. Crib free. TV; cable (premium). Pool. Coffee in rms. Restaurant 6 am-2 pm, 5-10 pm. Bar from 4 pm. Ck-out noon. Coin lndry. Meeting rms. Business servs avail. Valet serv. Balconies. On river. Convention center adj. Cr cds: A, D, DS, JCB, MC, V.

Restaurant

★ **ROOSTER'S LANDING.** *1550 Port Dr (99403). 509/751-0155.* Specializes in steak calypso, deer valley tenderloin, fish and chips. Hrs: 11 am-10 pm. Closed Thanksgiving, Dec 24. Res accepted. Bar. Lunch, dinner $5.95-$16.95. Child's menu. Parking. On river; view of countryside. Cr cds: A, DS, MC, V.
D SC

Colville

(B-7) *See also Spokane*

Pop 4,360 **Elev** 1,635 ft
Area code 509 **Zip** 99114
Information Chamber of Commerce, 121 E Astor, PO Box 267; 509/684-5973

Once a brawling frontier town, Colville, the seat of Stevens County, has quieted down and now reflects the peacefulness of the surrounding hills and mountains. Many towns flourished and died in this area—orchards, mills, and mines all had their day. The portage at Kettle Falls, a fort, and the crossing of several trails made Colville a thriving center.

What to See and Do

Colville National Forest. This million-acre forest is located in the NE corner of Washington bordering Canada. The forest extends along its western boundary from the Canadian border S to the Colville Reservation and E across the Columbia River to Idaho. Comprising conifer forest types, small lakes, and winding valleys bounded by slopes leading to higher mountainous areas, the forest offers good hunting and fishing and full-service camping. Also here is Sullivan Lake, offering recreation opportunities incl boating, fishing, swimming, developed and dispersed campground settings, hiking trails, and sightseeing. The bighorn sheep that inhabit adj Hall Mt can be viewed at a feeding station near the lake, which is cooperatively managed by the forest and the Washington Dept of Wildlife. For more info, contact the Forest Supervisor, Federal Bldg, 765 S Main St. Phone 509/684-7000. Also located here are a Ranger District office and

> **Lake Gillette Recreation Area.** Boating, swimming, fishing; picnicking, amphitheater with programs, camping (fee). (Mid-May-Sep) E via Tiger Hwy, WA 20. Phone 509/684-5657. **FREE**

Keller Heritage Center. Site of 3-story Keller home (1910), carriage house, blacksmith shop, farmstead cabin, gardens, museum, schoolhouse, machinery bldg, lookout tower. Local records, Native American artifacts. (Daily, May-Sep) 700 N Wynne St. Phone 509/684-5968. **Donation**

St. Paul's Mission. A chapel was built by Native Americans near here in 1845, followed by the hand-hewn log church in 1847. It fell into disuse in the 1870s and in 1939 was restored to its original state. Self-guided tour. Located at Kettle Falls in Coulee Dam National Recreation Area (see COULEE DAM). (All yr) 12 mi NW, near intersection of Columbia River & US 395. Phone 509/738-6266. **FREE**

Annual Events

Colville Professional Rodeo. Father's Day wkend.

Rendezvous. Arts and crafts, entertainment. First wkend Aug.

Northeast Washington Fair. Stevens County Fairgrounds. Parade, livestock and horse shows; arts and crafts exhibits; carnival. Wkend after Labor Day.

B&B/Small Inn

★★★ **MY PARENTS ESTATE BED & BREAKFAST.** *719 Hwy 395N (99141), 7 mi N. 509/738-6220.* 1 story, 1 suite. May-Sep: S, D $100; suites $100; lower rates rest of yr. Parking lot. TV; cable (premium). Complimentary full bkfst. Restaurant noon-9 pm. Ck-out 11 am, ck-in 4 pm. Golf, 9 holes. Tennis. Downhill skiing. Hiking trail. Picnic facilities. Cr cds: MC, V.

⊠ ⚐ 🏂 🎿 🐾 SC

Coulee Dam (B-6)

Founded 1934 **Pop** 1,087
Elev 1,145 ft **Area code** 509
Zip 99116
Web www.televar.com/~coulee

Information Grand Coulee Dam Area Chamber of Commerce, 306 Midway Ave, PO Box 760, Grand Coulee, 99133-0760; 509/633-3074 or 800/COULEE2

Established as a construction community for workers on the Grand Coulee Dam project, this town now is the home of service and maintenance employees of the dam and headquarters for the Lake Roosevelt National Recreation Area.

What to See and Do

Colville Tribal Museum. More than 8,000 years of history on 11 tribes. (Late May-Sep, daily; rest of yr, schedule varies) Mead Way. Phone 509/633-0751. **FREE**

✪ **Grand Coulee Dam.** Major structure of multipurpose Columbia Basin Project, built by Bureau of Reclamation. Water is diverted from the Columbia River to what in prehistoric days was its temporary course down the Grand Coulee (a deep water-carved ravine). The project will reclaim more than a million acres through irrigation and already provides a vast reservoir of electric power. One of the largest concrete structures in the world, the dam towers 550 ft high, has a 500-ft-wide base, and a 5,223-ft-long crest. Power plants contain some of world's largest hydro-generators. Self-guided tours begin at Visitor Arrival Center (daily, closed Jan 1, Thanksgiving, Dec 25). Major exhibits along tour route. Laser show (Memorial Day-Sep, nightly). Glass-enclosed elevator rides down face of 3rd power plant forebay dam; water recreation; camping. Near jct WA 155, 174. Phone 509/633-3074 or 509/633-3838. **FREE**

Lake Roosevelt National Recreation Area. Totals 100,059 acres incl Franklin D. Roosevelt Lake. Lake formed by Grand Coulee Dam serves as storage reservoir with 630-mi shoreline, extends 151 mi NE, reaching the Canadian border. Southern part is semi-arid; northern part mountainous, forested with ponderosa pine, fir, tamarack. Excellent for all sizes of motorboats with 151-mi waterway along reservoir and 200 mi of cruising water in Canada provided by Arrow Lakes, reached from Lake Roosevelt by the Columbia River. Thirty-eight areas have been specially developed; most provide camping (fee), picnicking, swimming, boating, and launching sites (fee). Fishing all yr in Roosevelt Lake. Contact Superintendent, 1008 Crest, 99116. Phone 509/633-9441. Within is

Fort Spokane. One of the last frontier military outposts of the 1800s. Four of 45 bldgs remain; brick guardhouse is now visitor center and small museum. Built to maintain peace between the settlers and Native Americans, no shot was ever fired. Self-guided trail around old parade grounds; interpretive displays. (Mid-June-Labor Day; daily) Living history programs performed on wkends in summer. Nearby are beach and camping (fee). Phone 509/725-2715. **FREE**

Steamboat Rock State Park. Approx 900 acres. Swimming, fishing, boating (launch); hiking, picnicking, camping (hookups; res recommended Memorial Day-Labor Day wkends) Standard fees. 11 mi S of Electric City on WA 155. Phone 509/633-1304 or 800/452-5687 (res).

Annual Events

Colorama Festival & PWRA Rodeo. Second wkend May.

Laser Light Festival. Memorial Day wkend.

Motel/Motor Lodge

★ **COLUMBIA RIVER INN.** *10 Lincoln Ave (99116). 509/633-2100; fax 509/633-2633; toll-free 800/633-6421. Email info@columbiariverinn.com; www.columbiariverinn.com.* 34 rms, 2 story. S, D $49-$95; under 12 free. Crib $5. TV; cable (premium). Pool;

whirlpool. Complimentary coffee in rms. Restaurant nearby. Ck-out 11 am. Coin lndry. Business servs avail. In-rm modem link. Gift shop. Some refrigerators, microwaves. Private patios, balconies. View of dam. Cr cds: A, DS, MC, V.

🛗 🖼 🏃

Hotel

★ **COULEE HOUSE MOTEL.** *110 Roosevelt Way (99116). 509/633-1101; fax 509/633-1416; res 800/715-7767. Email greit@televar.com; www.coulee house.com.* 61 rms, 2 story, 17 suites. May-Sep: S $64; D $74; each addl $4; suites $112; lower rates rest of yr. Crib avail, fee. Pet accepted, fee. Parking lot. Pool, whirlpool. TV; cable. Restaurant 6 am-10 pm. Ck-out 11 am, ck-in 3 pm. Business servs avail. Gift shop. Exercise privileges. Golf, 9 holes. Tennis, 5 courts. Hiking trail. Picnic facilities. Cr cds: A, C, D, DS, MC, V.

D 🏊 🛗 🍴 🏃 🖼 🎿 🏃 🛷 🔥

Coupeville

(B-3) *See also Oak Harbor, Port Townsend*

Pop 1,377 **Elev** 80 ft **Area code** 360 **Zip** 98239

Information Central Whidbey Chamber of Commerce, PO Box 152; 360/678-5434

One of the oldest towns in the state, Coupeville was named for Thomas Coupe, a sea captain and early settler, the only man to ever sail a full-rigged ship through Deception Pass. Fortified to protect the settlers and for the defense of Puget Sound, Coupeville was once the home of the only seat of higher education north of Seattle, the Puget Sound Academy. Today it is near Whidbey Island Naval Air Station, home of Naval Aviation for the Pacific Northwest.

What to See and Do

Alexander Blockhouse. (1855) One of 4 such bldgs built on Whidbey Island to protect settlers' homes from Native Americans during the White River Massacre. Near Front St, on waterfront.

Fort Casey State Park. Approx 140 acres. Scuba diving, saltwater fishing, boating (launch); picnicking, camping. Museum (May-mid-Sep). Standard fees. 3 mi S. Phone 360/678-4519.

Motel/Motor Lodge

★ **HARBOUR INN.** *1606 Main St, PO Box 1350 (98249), 20 mi S of Coupeville; 1 blk N off WA 525. 360/ 331-6900; fax 360/331-6900. Email harbrinn@whidbey.com.* 20 rms, 2 story. S $73; D $82; each addl $6; children $3; under 8 free. Crib avail. Pet accepted, some restrictions, fee. Parking lot. TV; cable, VCR avail. Complimentary continental bkfst. Restaurant. Ck-out 11 am, ck-in 3 pm. Fax servs avail. Golf. Beach access. Picnic facilities. Cr cds: A, MC, V.

D 🏊 🛗 🍴 🏃 🖼 🛷

B&Bs/Small Inns

★★ **CAPTAIN WHIDBEY INN.** *2072 W Captain Whidbey Rd (98239). 360/678-4097; fax 360/678-4110; toll-free 800/366-4097. Email info@captain whidbey.com; www.captainwhidbey. com.* 24 rms, 2 story, 3 suites. May-Oct: S $85; D $135; each addl $15; suites $155; lower rates rest of yr. Crib avail. Parking lot. TV; cable, VCR avail, VCR avail. Complimentary full bkfst, coffee in rms, newspaper, toll-free calls. Restaurant 5:30-10 pm. Bar. Ck-out noon, ck-in 4 pm. Meeting rm. Business servs avail. Gift shop. Golf. Tennis. Beach access. Bike rentals. Hiking trail. Picnic facilities. Cr cds: A, C, D, DS, MC, V.

D 🛗 🎿 🍴 🏃 🏃 🛷 🔥

★★★ **GUEST HOUSE BED & BREAKFAST COTTAGES.** *24371 WA 525 (98253), 10 mi S, on Whidbey Island. 360/678-3115. Email guesthse@ whidbey.net; www.whidbey.net/ logcottages.* 1 story, 6 suites. May-Sep: S, D $310; suites $310; lower rates rest of yr. Street parking. Indoor/outdoor pools, whirlpool. TV; cable (premium), VCR avail, CD avail. Complimentary full bkfst, coffee in rms. Restaurant nearby. Ck-out 11 am, ck-in 4 pm. Business servs avail. Exercise privileges. Golf. Downhill skiing. Hiking trail. Picnic facilities. Cr cds: A, DS, MC, V.

⛵ 🍴 ≈ 🛅 ⛷ 🔥

★★★ **INN AT LANGLEY.** *400 1st St (98260), S on WA 525 to Langley Rd then E. 360/221-3033; fax 360/221-3033. www.innatlangley.com.* 22 rms, 4 story, 2 suites. May-Sep: S, D $199; each addl $35; suites $325; lower rates rest of yr. Parking lot. TV; cable (premium), VCR avail. Complimentary continental bkfst, coffee in rms, newspaper. Restaurant. Ck-out noon, ck-in 3 pm. Meeting rm. Business servs avail. Concierge. Steam rm, whirlpool. Golf, 18 holes. Tennis, 6 courts. Beach access. Cr cds: A, MC, V.

🅳 ⛷ 🍴 ⛷ 🔥 ≈ 🔥

Restaurant

★★ **CAFE LANGLEY.** *113 1st St (98260), S on WA 525 to Maxwelton Rd, then E to Langley Rd to First St. 360/221-3090. www.langley-wa.com/cl.* Specializes in fresh seafood, locally grown products, Washington lamb. Hrs: 11:30 am-9 pm; Fri, Sat to 9:30 pm; Sun 11 am-8:30 pm. Closed hols; Tues Jan-Mar. Res accepted. Wine, beer. Lunch $5-$9; dinner $13.50-$17. Cr cds: A, MC, V.

🅳

Crystal Mountain

(see Mount Rainier National Park)

Dayton (Columbia County)

(E-7) *See also Walla Walla*

Settled 1859 **Pop** 2,468 **Elev** 1,613 ft
Area code 509 **Zip** 99328
Web www.HistoricDayton.com

Information Chamber of Commerce, 166 E Main St; 509/382-4825 or 800/882-6299

Once an important stagecoach depot and stopping-off place for miners, Dayton is now the center of a farm area in which sheep, cattle, wheat, apples, peas, asparagus, and hay are raised. Little Goose Lock and Dam, a multipurpose federal project and one of four such developments on the Snake River, is about 35 miles north of town. Vegetable canning and lumbering are local industries.

Dayton has many historic homes and buildings, including the Columbia County Courthouse (1886), oldest courthouse in the state still used for county government, and the Dayton Historic Depot (oldest in state).

What to See and Do

Kendall Skyline Drive. Scenic route through Blue Mts and Umatilla National Forest (see CLARKSTON). Usually open by July. Contact Chamber of Commerce for details. S of town.

Lewis and Clark Trail State Park. Approx 40 acres. Swimming; fishing; hiking, picnicking, camping. Standard fees. 5 mi SW on US 12. Phone 509/337-6457.

Palouse River Canyon. Deeply eroded gorge pierces wheatlands of region; cliffs rise hundreds of feet above river. At Palouse Falls, river roars over 198-ft cliff into deep ravine of basaltic rock, continues S to join Snake River. Nearby are Lyons Ferry and Palouse Falls state parks. 18 mi N on US 12, then 22 mi NW on unnumbered roads.

Ski Bluewood. Two triple chairlifts, platter pull, half pipe; patrol, school, rentals; cafeteria, bar. Longest run 2½ mi; vertical drop 1,125 ft. (Jan-Feb, daily; mid-Nov-Dec and Feb-Mar, Tues-Sun) Snowboarding. Half-day rates. 22 mi S via 4th St (North Touchet Rd), in Umatilla National Forest. Phone 509/382-4725. ¢¢¢¢

Annual Events

Dayton Depot Festival. Mid-July.
Columbia County Fair. Dayton Fairgrounds. Early Sep.

Palouse Falls

Ellensburg

(D-5) *See also Yakima*

Settled 1867 **Pop** 12,361 **Elev** 1,508 ft
Area code 509 **Zip** 98926
Web www.ellensburg-wa.com
Information Chamber of Commerce,
436 N Sprague; 509/925-3137 or
888/925-2204

Although this community has long
abandoned its first romantic name,
Robber's Roost, it cherishes the tradition and style of the West, both as a
center for dude ranches and as the
scene of one of the country's best
annual rodeos. At the geographic
center of the state, Ellensburg
processes beef and dairy products.
The county ranges from lakes and
crags in the west through irrigated
farmlands to sagebrush prairie along
the Columbia River to the east.

A Ranger District office of the
Wenatchee National Forest (see
WENATCHEE) is located here.

What to See and Do

Central Washington University.
(1890) 7,000 students. Liberal arts
and sciences, business, technology,
education. 8th Ave & Walnut St.
Phone 509/963-1111.

CWU Library. Regional depository
for federal docu-
ments; collection of
microforms, maps,
general materials.
(Daily) 14th Ave & D
St. Phone 509/963-
1777. **FREE**

**Sarah Spurgeon Art
Gallery.** Features
national, regional,
and advanced stu-
dents' art exhibits in
all media. (Sep-June,
Mon-Fri; closed
school hols) In Ran-
dall Hall. Phone
509/963-2665. **FREE**

**Clymer Museum of
Art.** Changing
gallery exhibits; local artists. (Sat and
Sun afternoons) 416 N Pearl. Phone
509/962-6416. ¢¢

Gallery I. Seven exhibit and sales
rooms surround a central atrium.
(Mon-Sat afternoons) 408 ½ N Pearl
St, on 2nd floor of the Stewart Bldg
(1889). Phone 509/925-2670. **FREE**

Ginkgo/Wanapum State Park. One
of world's largest petrified forests
(7,600 acres), with more than 200
species of petrified wood, incl prehistoric ginkgo tree. Waterskiing,
fishing, boating; hiking, picnicking,
camping (hookups). Standard fees.
28 mi E on I-90 Exit 136, in Vantage. Phone 509/856-2700. **FREE**

**★ Olmstead Place State Park-Her-
itage Site.** Turn-of-the-century Kittitas Valley farm, being converted to a
living historical farm. Originally
homesteaded in 1875. Eight bldgs;
wildlife, flowers, and trees; ½-mi
interpretive trail. Farm machinery
Tours. (June-Sep, wkends; rest of yr,
by appt) (See ANNUAL EVENTS). 4
mi E via Kittitas Hwy on Squaw
Creek Trail Rd. Phone 509/925-1943
or 509/856-2700. **FREE**

Wanapum Dam Heritage Center.
Self guided tour of center; fish-
viewing room, powerhouse, petroglyph rubbings, exhibits detail life of
the Wanapum, fur traders, ranchers,
miners. (Daily) 29 mi E on I-90, then
3 mi S on WA 243. Phone 509/754-
3541, ext 2571. **FREE**

Annual Events

National Western Art Show and Auction. Phone 509/962-2934. Third wkend May.

Ellensburg Rodeo. Kittitas County Fairgrounds. Calf roping, steer wrestling, bull riding, wild cow milking, Native American dances. Four days Labor Day wkend.

Kittitas County Fair. Carnival, exhibits, livestock, crafts, contests, entertainment. Four days Labor Day wkend.

Threshing Bee and Antique Equipment Show. Olmstead Place State Park. Steam and gas threshing, blacksmithing demonstrations, horse-drawn equipment, old-time plowing. Third wkend Sep.

Motel/Motor Lodge

★★ **ELLENSBURG INN.** *1700 Canyon Rd (98926). 509/925-9801; fax 509/925-2093; toll-free 800/321-8791. Email ellensburginn@yahoo.com.* 105 rms, 2 story. Aug: S $65; D $70; each addl $5; under 12 free; lower rates rest of yr. Crib avail. TV; cable (premium), VCR avail. Restaurant 6 am-10 pm. Bar. Ck-out noon, ck-in 2 pm. Meeting rms. Golf, 18 holes. Cr cds: A, C, D, DS, ER, JCB, MC, V.
🐾 🖼 🐾 SC

Restaurant

★★ **CASA DE BLANCA.** *1318 S Canyon Rd (98926). 509/925-1693.* Specializes in prime rib, steak. Hrs: 10:30 am-10:30 pm. Closed Thanksgiving, Dec 25. Res accepted. Bar. Lunch $3.99-$9; dinner $6.50-$15. Child's menu. Cr cds: A, D, DS, MC, V.
D 🖼

Enumclaw

(D-3) *See also Puyallup, Tacoma*

Pop 7,227 **Elev** 750 ft **Area code** 360
Zip 98022
Web www.chamber.enumclaw.wa.us

Information Chamber of Commerce/Visitor Information, 1421 Cole St; 360/825-7666

A Ranger District office of the Mount Baker-Snoqualmie National Forest (see BELLINGHAM, SEATTLE) is located here.

What to See and Do

Federation Forest State Park. Approx 620 acres of old growth timber. Catherine Montgomery Interpretive Center has displays on the state's 7 life zones. Three interpretive trails, hiking trails, and part of the Naches Trail, one of the first pioneer trails between eastern Washington and Puget Sound. Fishing; hiking, picnicking. 18 mi SE on WA 410. Phone 360/663-2207. **FREE**

Green River Gorge Conservation Area. Protects a unique 12-mi corridor of the Green River, which cuts through unusual rock areas, many with fossils. Views of present-day forces of stream erosion through caves, smooth canyon walls. 12 mi N on WA 169. **FREE** One of the many areas in the gorge is

> **Flaming Geyser State Park.** Two geysers (actually old test holes for coal), one burning about 6 inches high and the other bubbling methane gas through a spring. Fishing, boating, rafting; hiking, picnicking, playground. Abundant wildlife, wildflowers. No camping. Standard fees. (Daily) Phone 253/931-3930.

Mud Mountain Dam. One of the world's highest earth core and rock-fill dams. Vista-point structures; picnicking (shelters), playground, wading pool, nature trail. Day use only. (May-mid-Oct, daily; rest of yr, Mon-Fri) 7 mi SE via WA 410. Phone 360/825-3211. **FREE**

Annual Events

King County Fair. Fairgrounds. Phone 360/825-7777. Third wk July.

Pacific NW Scottish Highland Games. Fairgrounds. Phone 360/522-2541. Fourth wkend July.

Street Fair. Downtown. Phone 360/825-7666. Fourth wkend July.

Motel/Motor Lodge

★★ **BEST WESTERN PARK CEN-TER.** *1000 Griffin Ave (98022).* *360/825-4490; fax 360/825-3686; res 800/528-1234.* 40 rms, 2 story. June-Oct: S, D $63; each addl $5; under 12 free; lower rates rest of yr. Crib $10. Pet accepted; $10. TV; cable. Complimentary coffee in lobby. Restaurant 7 am-9 pm. Bar from 4 pm. Ck-out 11 am. Meeting rms. Business servs avail. In-rm modem link. Whirlpool. Some refrigerators, microwaves. Picnic tables. Cr cds: A, D, DS, MC, V.

Ephrata

(C-6) *See also Moses Lake, Quincy, Soap Lake*

Settled 1882 **Pop** 5,349 **Elev** 1,275 ft **Area code** 509 **Zip** 98823
Information Chamber of Commerce, 90 Alder NW, PO Box 275; 509/754-4656

Growth of this area is the result of the development of surrounding farmland, originally irrigated by wells, now supplied by the Columbia Basin irrigation project. Ephrata is the center of an area containing a series of lakes that offer fishing and water sports. There is excellent upland game bird hunting.

What to See and Do

Grant County Pioneer Village & Museum. Displays trace natural history and early pioneer development of area. Native American artifacts. Pioneer homestead and country village with 20 bldgs (some original, restored), incl church, schoolhouse, saloon, barbershop, Krupp-Marlin Jail, photography studio, bank, firehouse, livery stable, blacksmith shop; farm machinery exhibit. Guided tour. (Early May-Oct, Thurs-Tues; rest of yr, guided tour by appt) 742 Basin St N. Phone 509/754-3334. ¢

Oasis Park. Picnicking, 9-hole and par 3 golf (fee), children's fishing pond, playground, miniature golf

(fee). Camping (fee); swimming pool (free to campers). (Daily) 1½ mi SW on WA 28. Phone 509/754-5102.

Annual Event

Sage and Sun Festival. Parade, sports events, arts and crafts shows. Second wkend June.

Motel/Motor Lodge

★ **SHARLYN MOTEL.** *848 Basin St SW (98823).* 509/754-3575; *toll-free 800/292-2965.* 8 rms, showers only, 2 story. S, D $70-$90; each addl $10. TV; cable. Coffee in rms. Restaurant nearby. Ck-out 11 am. Refrigerators. Cr cds: A, C, D, DS, ER, MC, V.

B&B/Small Inn

★★ **IVY CHAPEL INN BED & BREAKFAST.** *164 D St SW (98823).* *509/754-0629; fax 509/754-0791. Email ivychapel@hotmail.com; www. ivychapelinn.com.* 6 rms, 1 with shower only, 3 story, 1 suite. No elvtr. No rm phones. S, D $75; suites $100. Children over 10 yrs only. Cable TV in many rms; VCR avail (movies). Complimentary full bkfst. Restaurant nearby. Ck-out 11 am, ck-in 3 pm. Street parking. Free airport, railroad station, bus depot transportation. Game rm. Microwaves avail. Picnic tables, grills. Built in 1948; was first Presbyterian church in Ephrata. Totally nonsmoking. Cr cds: A, D, DS, MC, V.

Everett

(B-3) *See also Marysville, Seattle*

Founded 1890 **Pop** 69,961 **Elev** 157 ft **Area code** 425
Information Everett/Snohomish County Convention and Visitor Bureau, 1710 W Marine View Dr, 98201; 425/252-5181

This lumber, aircraft, electronics, and shipping city is on a sheltered harbor where the Snohomish River empties into Port Gardner Bay. To the east is the snowcapped Cascade Mountain Range; to the west are the Olympic Mountains. Developed by Eastern industrial and railroad money, Everett serves as a major commercial fishing port and receives and dispatches a steady stream of cargo vessels. The Boeing 747 and 767 are assembled here.

Along the waterfront is an 1890s-style seaside marketplace, the Everett Marina Village.

What to See and Do

Boat tours. For information on companies offering sightseeing, dinner, and whale watching cruises, contact the Convention and Visitors Bureau. Phone 425/252-5181.

◪ **Boeing Everett Facility.** Audiovisual presentation; bus tour of assembly facility. Gift shop. (Mon-Fri; closed hols) No children under 10 yrs. I-5 Exit 189, approx 3 mi W on WA 526. Phone 206/655-1131. **FREE**

Mukilteo. This town, just W of Everett, is the major ferry point from the mainland to the S tip of Whidbey Island. Its name means "good camping ground." A lighthouse built in 1905 is open for tours (Sat). Phone 425/347-1456.

Recreation areas. There are many recreation areas in and near the city that offer swimming (fee), fishing, boat launch; hiking, picnicking, camping, nature centers, tennis, and golf (fee). Phone 425/257-8300. **FREE**

Totem Pole. 80 ft high, carved by Tulalip Chief William Shelton. Rucker Ave & 44th St.

Annual Event

Salty Sea Days. Festival, parade, displays, food, and carnival. Early June.

Seasonal Event

Auto racing. Evergreen Speedway, 15 mi SE via US 2, Exit 194 off I-5. NASCAR super and mini stocks, SVRA modifieds, hobby stocks, figure 8s; demolition events. Phone 360/805-6100. Apr-Sep.

Motels/Motor Lodges

★★ **BEST WESTERN CASCADIA INN.** *2800 Pacific Ave (98201).*

425/258-4141; fax 425/258-4755; res 800/528-1234; toll-free 800/822-5876. www.bestwesterncascadia.com. 134 rms, 3 story. S $69; D $99; each addl $4; suites $99-$149; under 18 free. Crib free. TV; cable (premium). Heated pool; whirlpool. Complimentary continental bkfst. Coffee in rms. Restaurant nearby. Bar 11-1 am. Ck-out noon. Coin lndry. Meeting rms. Business servs avail. Health club privileges. Some refrigerators; microwaves avail. Cr cds: A, D, DS, MC, V.

🄳 🐾 🛏 🕴 🕴 🖎 🔥

★ **WELCOME MOTOR INN.** *1205 Broadway (98201). 425/252-8828; fax 425/252-8880; toll-free 800/252-5512.* 42 rms, 2 story. July-Aug: S $38-$43; D $48-$52; each addl $5-$10; lower rates rest of yr. Crib $7. TV; cable (premium). Restaurant adj 5:30-10:30 pm. Ck-out 11 am. Microwaves avail. Cr cds: A, C, D, DS, MC, V.

🄳 🖎 🖎

Hotel

★★★ **MARINA VILLAGE INN.** *1728 W Marina View Dr (98201). 425/259-4040; fax 425/252-8419; toll-free 800/281-7037. Email mvi172@aol.com; www.gtesupersite.com/marinavilin.* 26 rms, 2 story, 20 suites. May-Sep: S, D $95; each addl $20; suites $145; children $10; lower rates rest of yr. Crib avail. TV; cable (DSS), VCR avail, CD avail. Restaurant. Meeting rms. Golf, 18 holes. Cr cds: A, C, D, DS, MC, V.

🕴 🖎 🖎

Conference Center

★ **HOWARD JOHNSON PLAZA HOTEL.** *3105 Pine St (98201), I-5 Exit 193N, 194S. 425/339-3333; fax 425/259-1547; res 800/446-4656; toll-free 800/556-7829.* 242 rms, 7 story, 5 suites. June-Aug: S $139; D $149; each addl $10; suites $199; under 16 free; lower rates rest of yr. Crib avail. Pet accepted, fee. Parking garage. Indoor pool, whirlpool. TV; cable (premium). Complimentary coffee in rms, newspaper, toll-free calls. Restaurant 6:30 am-10 pm. Bar. Ck-out noon, ck-in 3 pm. Meeting rms. Business center. Bellhops. Concierge. Dry cleaning. Exercise equipt, sauna. Golf. Downhill skiing. Supervised children's activities. Cr cds: A, C, D, DS, JCB, MC, V.

Forks (B-1)

Pop 2,862 **Elev** 375 ft **Area code** 360 **Zip** 98331

Information Chamber of Commerce, PO Box 1249; 360/374-2531 or 800/44-FORKS

The major town in the northwest section of the Olympic Peninsula, Forks takes its name from the nearby junction of the Soleduck, Bogachiel, and Dickey rivers. Timber processing is a major industry. A Ranger District office of the Olympic National Forest (see OLYMPIA) is located here.

What to See and Do

Bogachiel State Park. Approx 120 acres, on the shores of the Bogachiel River with swimming, fishing; hiking, camping (hookups, dump station). Standard fees. (Daily) 6 mi S on US 101. Phone 360/374-6356.

Olympic National Park. (see) 3 mi E on unnumbered road.

Motels/Motor Lodges

★★ **FORKS MOTEL.** *351 S Forks Ave (98331), 3 blks S on US 101. 360/374-6243; fax 360/374-6760; toll-free 800/544-3416. Email forksmotel@centurytel. net.* 73 rms, 1-2 story, 9 kits. Some A/C. June-Sep: S, D $50-$80; each addl $5; kit. from $85; lower rates rest of yr. Crib $5. TV; cable. Heated pool; wading pool. Restaurant nearby. Ck-out 11 am. Coin lndry. Business servs avail. Cr cds: A, DS, MC, V.

★ **PACIFIC INN MOTEL.** *352 S Forks Ave (98331). 360/374-9400; fax 360/374-9402; toll-free 800/235-7344. Email info@pacificinnmotel; www. pacificinnmotel.com.* 34 rms, 2 story. Mid-May-Sep: S $48; D $53-$57; each addl $5; under 13 free; lower rates rest of yr. Crib $5. TV; cable. Compli-

mentary coffee in lobby. Restaurant nearby. Ck-out 11 am. Coin lndry. Business servs avail. Cr cds: A, DS, MC, V.

Resort

★★ **KALALOCH LODGE.** *157151 US 101 (98331), 35 mi S. 360/962-2271; fax 360/962-3391. Email reservations@centurytel.net; www. visitkalaloch.com.* 18 rms, 2 story, 2 suites. June-Sep: S $120; D $135; each addl $10; suites $225; children $10; under 5 free; lower rates rest of yr. Crib avail. Pet accepted, fee. Parking lot. TV; cable (DSS). Complimentary coffee in rms. Restaurant 7 am-8:30 pm. Bar. Ck-out 11 am, ck-in 4 pm. Business servs avail. Gift shop. Beach access. Hiking trail. Picnic facilities. Cr cds: A, MC, V.

B&B/Small Inn

★ **MANITOU LODGE BED & BREAKFAST.** *813 Kilmer Rd (98331), 8 mi W on La Push Rd to Mora Rd, follow signs. 360/374-6295; fax 360/374-7495. Email manitou@olypen.com; www.manitoulodge.com.* 8 rms, 2 story. May-Oct: S, D $100; each addl $20; lower rates rest of yr. Pet accepted, some restrictions, fee. Street parking. TV; cable (DSS). Complimentary full bkfst, coffee in rms, toll-free calls. Ck-out 11 am, ck-in 4 pm. Meeting rm. Internet dock/port avail. Gift shop. Salon/barber. Beach access. Hiking trail. Cr cds: A, D, MC, V.

Goldendale

Settled 1863 **Pop** 3,319 **Elev** 1,633 ft **Area code** 509 **Zip** 98620

Information Greater Goldendale Area Chamber of Commerce, Box 524; 509/773-3411

Agriculture, aluminum smelting, and an assortment of small industries comprise the major business of Goldendale, named for John J. Golden, a pioneer settler.

What to See and Do

Brooks Memorial State Park. More than 700 acres. Fishing; hiking, picnicking, camping (hookups). Standard fees. 12 mi N on US 97. Phone 509/773-4611.

Goldendale Observatory. Nation's largest amateur-built Cassegrain telescope for public use; tours, demonstrations, displays, audiovisual programs. (Apr-Sep, Wed-Sun; rest of yr, schedule varies) 1602 Observatory Dr. Phone 509/773-3141. **FREE**

Klickitat County Historical Museum. Furniture and exhibits from early days of Klickitat County, in 20-rm restored mansion. Gift shop. (Apr-Oct, daily; rest of yr, by appt) 127 W Broadway. Phone 509/773-4303. ¢¢

Maryhill Museum of Art. Constructed by Samuel Hill. Permanent exhibits incl Rodin sculpture, European and American paintings, Russian icons, chess collection, French fashion mannequins, Native American baskets, and artifacts. (Mid-Mar-mid-Nov, daily) 11 mi S on US 97, then 2 mi W on WA 14; 35 Maryhill Museum Dr. Phone 509/773-3733. ¢¢

Mount Adams Recreation Area. Lakes, streams, forests; excellent fishing, bird hunting. NW of town.

Annual Event

Klickitat County Fair and Rodeo. Fourth wkend Aug.

Motels/Motor Lodges

★★ **FARVUE MOTEL.** *808 E Simcoe Dr (98620). 509/773-5881; fax 509/773-5881; toll-free 800/358-5881.* 48 rms, 2 story. S, D $49-$121; each addl $8. Crib free. TV; cable. Heated pool. Restaurant 6 am-11 pm. Bar from 5 pm. Ck-out 11 am. Business servs avail. Free airport transportation. Health club privileges. Refrigerators. View of Mt Adams and Mt Hood. Cr cds: A, C, D, DS, MC, V.
D ⇌ 🏋 🖂 🐾

★ **PONDEROSA MOTEL.** *775 E Broadway St (98620). 509/773-5842; fax 509/773-4049.* 28 rms, 2 story, 4 kits. S $38; D $45-$49; each addl $6; kit. units $5 addl. Pet accepted. TV;

cable. Ck-out 11 am. Business servs avail. Many refrigerators. Cr cds: A, D, DS, MC, V.
🐾 🐾 🏋 🖂 🐾

Hoquiam

(D-2) *See also Aberdeen, Ocean Shores, Westport*

Settled 1859 **Pop** 8,972 **Elev** 10 ft
Area code 360 **Zip** 98550
Web www.chamber.grays-harbor.wa.us

Information Grays Harbor Chamber of Commerce, 506 Duffy St, Aberdeen 98520; 360/532-1924 or 800/321-1924

Twin city to Aberdeen, Hoquiam is the senior community of the two and the pioneer town of the Grays Harbor region. A deepwater port 12 miles from the Pacific, it docks cargo and fishing vessels, manufactures wood products and machine tools, and cans the harvest of the sea.

What to See and Do

Hoquiam's "Castle." A 20-rm mansion built in 1897 by lumber tycoon Robert Lytle; antique furnishings; oak-columned entry hall; authentic Victorian atmosphere. (Summer, daily; rest of yr, wkends; closed Dec) 515 Chenault Ave. Phone 360/533-2005. ¢¢

Polson Park and Museum. (1924) Restored 26-rm mansion; antiques; rose garden. (June-Aug, Wed-Sun; rest of yr, wkends) 1611 Riverside Ave. Phone 360/533-5862. ¢¢

B&B/Small Inn

★★ **LYTLE HOUSE BED & BREAKFAST.** *509 Chenault Ave (98550). 360/533-2320; fax 360/533-4025; toll-free 800/677-2320. Email stay@lytle house.com; www.lytlehouse.com.* 6 rms, 3 story, 2 suites. May-Oct: S $100; D $115; each addl $15; suites $135; children $15; lower rates rest of yr. Parking lot. TV; cable (premium), VCR avail, CD avail. Complimentary full bkfst, coffee in rms, newspaper, toll-free calls. Restaurant nearby. Ck-out 11 am, ck-in 4 pm. Meeting rms. Business center. Coin lndry. Gift shop. Golf, 18 holes. Tennis, 6 courts. Hiking trail. Picnic facilities. Cr cds: A, MC, V.

Restaurant

★ **DUFFY'S.** *825 Simpson Ave (98550). 360/532-1519.* Specializes in seafood, veal, wild blackberry pie. Hrs: 6 am-9 pm. Bar. Bkfst $2.95-$8.50; lunch $3.25-$8.95; dinner $7.95-$13.95. Child's menu. Family-style dining. Cr cds: A, D, DS, MC, V.

Issaquah

See also Bellevue, North Bend, Seattle

Pop 7,786 **Elev** 100 ft **Area code** 425 **Zip** 98027
Information Chamber of Commerce, 155 NW Gilman Blvd; 425/392-7024

Historic buildings and homes of Issaquah have been renovated and moved to a seven-acre farm site, called Gilman Village, where they now serve as specialty shops.

What to See and Do

Boehm's Chocolate Factory. The home of Boehm's Candies was built here in 1956 by Julius Boehm. The candy-making process and the Edelweiss Chalet, filled with artifacts, paintings, and statues, can be toured. The Luis Trenker Kirch'l, a replica of a 12th-century Swiss chapel, was also built by Boehm. Tours by appt (May-Sep). 255 NE Gilman Blvd. Phone 425/392-6652. **FREE**

Lake Sammamish State Park. Approx 430 acres. Swimming, fishing, boating (launch); hiking, picnicking. Standard fees. 2 mi W off I-90. Phone 425/455-7010.

Annual Event

Salmon Days Festival. Welcomes return of Northwest salmon to original home. Phone 425/392-0661. First full wkend Oct.

Motel/Motor Lodge

★★ **HOLIDAY INN SEATTLE, ISSAQUAH.** *1801 12th Ave NW (98027), at I-90 Exit 15. 425/392-6421; fax 425/391-4650; res 800/465-4329. Email hiissaquah@aol.com.* 100 rms, 2 story. S $82; D $89; each addl $7; under 19 free. Crib free. TV; cable (premium). Heated pool; wading pool, poolside serv. Complimentary coffee in rms. Restaurant 6 am-2 pm, 5-10 pm. Bar. Ck-out noon. Coin lndry. Meeting rms. Business servs avail. In-rm modem link. Cr cds: A, DS, MC, V.

Kelso

(E-2) See also Longview

Founded 1847 **Pop** 11,820 **Elev** 40 ft
Area code 360 **Zip** 98626
Web www.tdn.com/kelso
Information Chamber of Commerce, 105 Minor Rd; 360/577-8058

Kelso straddles the Cowlitz River and is an artery for the lumber industry. The river also yields a variety of fish from giant salmon to tiny smelt.

What to See and Do

Cowlitz County Historical Museum. Exhibits depict history of the area. (Tues-Sun; closed hols) 405 Allen St. Phone 360/577-3119. **FREE**

Seaquest State Park. Approx 300 acres. Hiking, picnicking, camping (hookups). Nearby is Silver Lake with fishing (about 10,000 fish are caught here every summer). Standard fees. 10 mi N on I-5 Exit 49, then 5 mi E on WA 504. Phone 360/274-8633.

Volcano Information Center. Pictorial and scientific exhibits on the eruption of Mount St. Helens; three-dimensional narrated topographical display of the devastation. Also visitor information on surrounding area. (May-Oct, daily; rest of yr, Wed-Sun; closed hols) 105 Minor Rd, off I-5 Exit 39. Phone 360/577-8058. **FREE**

Motels/Motor Lodges

★★ **COMFORT INN.** *440 Three Rivers Dr (98626), I-5 Exit 39. 360/425-4600; fax 360/423-0762; res 800/228-5150. Email kelsogm@aol.com.* 57 rms, 2 story. S $60-$85; D $65-$90; each addl $5; under 18 free. Crib free. TV; cable (premium). Indoor pool; whirlpool. Complimentary continental bkfst. Restaurant nearby. Ck-out noon. Business servs avail. In-rm modem link. Valet serv. Cr cds: A, D, DS, JCB, MC, V.

D ⩳ ⏰ ⛶ ⬚ ⬚

★ **MOUNT ST. HELENS MOTEL.** *1340 Mount St. Helens Way (98611), 10 mi N on I-5, Exit 49. 360/274-7721; fax 360/274-7725. Email mtsthelensmotel@cetnet.net; www.mtsthelensmotel.com.* 32 rms, 2 story. Apr-Sep: S $55; D $72; lower rates rest of yr. Crib avail. Parking lot. TV; cable. Complimentary toll-free calls. Restaurant. Business servs avail. Coin lndry. Tennis, 4 courts. Cr cds: A, C, D, DS, MC, V.

D ⬚ ⬚ ⬚ ⬚ SC

Hotel

★ **RED LION HOTEL.** *510 Kelso Dr (98626), I-5 Exit 39. 360/636-4400; fax 360/425-3296; res 800/733-5466. www.redlion.com.* 159 rms, 2 story, 3 suites. June-Oct: S, D $81; each addl $10; suites $195; under 12 free; lower rates rest of yr. Crib avail. Pet accepted, some restrictions, fee. Parking lot. Pool, children's pool, whirlpool. TV; cable (premium). Complimentary coffee in rms, newspaper, toll-free calls. Restaurant 6 am-10 pm. Bar. Ck-out noon, ck-in 3 pm. Meeting rms. Business center. Dry cleaning. Exercise equipt. Golf. Cr cds: A, C, D, DS, MC, V.

D ⬚ ⬚ ⬚ ⏰ ⬚ ⬚ SC ⬚

Kennewick

(E-6) *See also Pasco, Richland*

Founded 1892 **Pop** 42,155 **Elev** 380 ft
Area code 509

Information Chamber of Commerce, 1600 N 20th St, PO Box 550, Pasco 99301; 509/547-9755

Huge hydroelectric dams harnessing the lower stem of the Columbia River have brought economic vitality to the "Tri-Cities" of Kennewick, Pasco, and Richland. On the south bank of Lake Wallula and near the confluence of the Columbia, Snake, and Yakima rivers, Kennewick has chemical and agricultural processing plants. Irrigation of the 20,500-acre Kennewick Highland project has converted sagebrush into thousands of farms, producing three cuttings of alfalfa annually, corn, and beans. Appropriately enough, this city with the Native American name "winter paradise" enjoys a brief winter and is the center of the state's grape industry.

What to See and Do

Columbia Park. Approx 300 acres. Waterskiing, fishing, boating (ramps); 18-hole golf, driving range (fee), tennis, picnicking, camping (hookups; fee). Park open all yr (daily). 2½ mi W on US 12 on Lake Wallula, formed by McNary Dam. Phone 509/783-3711. **FREE**

Two Rivers Park. Picnicking; boating (ramp), swimming, fishing. Park open all yr (daily). 5 mi E, off Finley Rd. Phone 509/783-3118. **FREE**

Motels/Motor Lodges

★ **NENDELS INN.** *2811 W 2nd Ave (99336). 509/735-9511; fax 509/735-1944; toll-free 800/547-0106.* 104 rms, 3 story, 3 kits. S $45; D $50-$53; each addl $5; kit. units $50; under 12 free; higher rates boat race wkends. Pet accepted; $5. TV; cable. Heated pool. Complimentary continental bkfst. Restaurant nearby. Ck-out 11 am. Business servs avail. Some refrigerators. Cr cds: A, C, D, DS, ER, MC, V.

D ⬚ ⬚ ⬚ ⬚ SC

★ **TAPADERA INN.** *300-A N Ely St (99336), on WA 395. 509/783-6191; fax 509/735-3854; toll-free 800/737-9804.* 61 rms, 2 story. S $40; D $47-$50; each addl $7; under 13 free; higher rates hydro races. Crib free. Pet accepted; $5. TV; cable (premium). Heated pool. Complimentary coffee in lobby. Restaurant adj 6 am-

11 pm. Ck-out noon. Coin lndry. Some refrigerators, microwaves. Cr cds: A, DS, MC, V.

D 🔾 ≋ 🏋 🏊 🔥

★★ **WESTCOAST TRI CITIES.** *1101 N Columbia Center Blvd (99336). 509/783-0611; fax 509/735-3087; res 800/325-4000.* 162 rms, 2 story. S $77, D $87; each addl $5; suites $90-$280; studio rms $75-$85; golf plans. Crib $5. Pet accepted. TV; cable (premium). Pool; whirlpool. Coffee in rms. Restaurant 6:30 am-9 pm. Bar 11-2 am; entertainment Fri, Sat. Ck-out noon. Meeting rms. Business servs avail. In-rm modem link. Sundries. Gift shop. Airport, railroad station, bus depot transportation. Health club privileges. Private patios, balconies. Cr cds: A, D, DS, MC, V.

D 🔾 ♨ ≋ 🏋 🏊 🔥 🛥

Hotel

★★ **SILVER CLOUD INN - KEN-NEWICK.** *7901 W Quinault Ave (99336). 509/735-6100; fax 509/735-3084; toll-free 800/205-6938. Email management@kennewick.scinns.com; www.scinns.com.* 100 rms, 4 story, 25 suites. May-Sep: S $84; D $94; each addl $10; suites $120; under 17 free; lower rates rest of yr. Crib avail. Indoor/outdoor pools. TV; cable (premium). Complimentary continental bkfst, coffee in rms, newspaper, toll-free calls. Ck-out noon, ck-in 3 pm. Meeting rm. Fax servs avail. Dry cleaning. Exercise privileges. Golf. Video games. Cr cds: A, C, D, DS, ER, MC, V.

D 🏋 ≋ 🏋 🏊 🔥 **SC**

Extended Stay

★ **KENNEWICK TRAVELODGE INN & SUITES.** *321 N Johnson St (99336). 509/735-6385; fax 509/736-6631.* 45 rms, 3 story. May-Sep: S $69; D $76; each addl $6; under 15 free; lower rates rest of yr. Crib avail, fee. Pet accepted, some restrictions, fee. Parking lot. Pool. TV; cable (premium). Complimentary continental bkfst, coffee in rms. Restaurant nearby. Ck-out 11 am, ck-in 3 pm. Business servs avail. Coin lndry. Golf. Cr cds: A, DS, MC, V.

D 🔾 🏋 ≋ 🏊 🔥

La Conner

See also Anacortes, Mount Vernon

Pop 656 **Area code** 360 **Zip** 98257
Information Chamber of Commerce, PO Box 1610; 360/466-4778

A picturesque town along the Swinomish Channel, La Conner is a popular destination for weekend travelers. Many of the town's homes and businesses are housed in the clapboarded structures built by its founders around the turn of the century. Numerous boutiques, galleries, and antique shops, some containing the works of local artists and craftspeople, line its streets.

What to See and Do

Museum of Northwest Art. Exhibits artist of the "Northwest School." (Tues-Sun; closed Jan 1, Thanksgiving, Dec 25) 121 S 1st St. Phone 360/466-4446. ¢¢

Skagit County Historical Museum. Exhibits depicting history of Skagit County. (Tues-Sun afternoons; closed Jan 1, Thanksgiving, Dec 25) 501 4th St. Phone 360/466-3365. ¢

Hotel

★★★ **LACONNER COUNTRY INN.** *107 S Second St (98257). 360/466-3101; fax 360/466-5902; toll-free 888/466-4113. www.laconnerlodging. com.* 26 rms, 2 story, 2 suites. Apr, June-Sep: S, D $95; each addl $20; suites $155; lower rates rest of yr. Crib avail. Pet accepted, some restrictions, fee. Parking lot. TV; cable (premium). Complimentary continental bkfst, coffee in rms, newspaper, toll-free calls. Restaurant 11 am-10 pm. Ck-out noon, ck-in 3 pm. Meeting rms. Business servs avail. Golf. Cr cds: A, D, DS, MC, V.

D 🔾 🏋 🔥 🛥

B&Bs/Small Inns

★★ **THE HERON.** *117 Maple Ave (98257). 360/466-4626; fax 360/466-3254; toll-free 877/883-8899. Email heroninn@ncia.com; www.theheron. com.* 9 rms, 3 story, 3 suites. Apr-Oct: D $100; each addl $20; suites $150;

lower rates rest of yr. Pet accepted, some restrictions, fee. Parking lot. TV; cable. Complimentary full bkfst, newspaper. Restaurant nearby. Ck-out 11 am, ck-in 3 pm. Meeting rms. Concierge. Golf. Downhill skiing. Bike rentals. Hiking trail. Picnic facilities. Cr cds: A, MC, V.

🄳 🐾 🕯️ 🛁 🖊️ 🍴 🏹 🛶 🖼️ SC

★★ **RAINBOW INN.** *12757 Chilberg Rd (98273). 360/466-4578; fax 360/466-3844; toll-free 888/266-8879. Email rainbow@rainbowinnbandb.com; www.rainbowinnbandb.com.* 8 rms, 3 story. Mar-Sep: S $85; D $95; each addl $20; children $10; under 3 free; lower rates rest of yr. Crib avail. Parking lot. TV; cable. Complimentary full bkfst, toll-free calls. Restaurant. Ck-out 11 am, ck-in 3 pm. Meeting rms. Business center. Gift shop. Whirlpool. Golf. Tennis, 2 courts. Beach access. Bike rentals. Hiking trail. Picnic facilities. Cr cds: DS, MC, V.

🛁 🖊️ 🍴 🏹 🛶 🖼️ SC 🎿

Leavenworth

(C-5) See also Cashmere, Wenatchee

Founded 1892 **Pop** 1,692
Elev 1,165 ft **Area code** 509
Zip 98826
Web www.leavenworth.org
Information Chamber of Commerce, PO Box 327; 509/548-5807

Surrounded by the Cascade Mountains, Leavenworth has an old world charm enhanced by authentic Bavarian architecture. Less than three hours from Seattle, the village is a favorite stop for people who enjoy river rafting, hiking, bicycling, fishing, golf, or skiing. Two Ranger District offices of the Wenatchee National Forest (see WENATCHEE) are located here.

What to See and Do

Icicle Junction. Family fun park offers 18-hole Bavarian-theme miniature golf, excursion train, bumper boats, ice-skating, interactive arcade. Party facilities. Fee for each activity. (Summer, daily; winter hrs may vary) Jct US 2 & Icicle Rd. Phone 509/548-2400.

National Fish Hatchery. Raises chinook salmon and steelhead. Educational exhibits. Hiking, interpretive trails. Fishing; boat ramp; picnicking, cross-country skiing. (Daily; closed Dec 25) 3½ mi S on Icicle Creek Rd. Phone 509/548-7641. **FREE**

Nutcracker Museum. Displays more than 3,000 nutcrackers. (May-Oct, daily; rest of yr, wkends; also by appt) 735 Front St. Phone 509/548-4708. ¢¢

Stevens Pass Ski Area. Quad, 4 triple, 6 double chairlifts; patrol, school, rentals; restaurant, cafeteria, bar, nursery. (Late Nov-mid-Apr, daily) 36 mi NW on US 2. Phone 206/973-2441. ¢¢¢¢

Annual Events

Bavarian Ice Fest. Snowshoe races, dogsled rides. Fireworks. Mid-Jan.

Maifest. Bandstand music, grand march, Maypole dance, art, chuck wagon breakfast. Early May.

Chamber Music in the Cascades. Icicle Creek Music Center. Professional chamber music festival featuring classical, jazz, new blue grass. Phone 509/548-6347. July.

Autumn Leaf Festival. Late Sep and Early Oct.

Lopez Island, Puget Sound

Bon Apetit. Mid-Nov.

Christmas Lighting. Sleigh rides, sledding. Early and mid-Dec.

Motels/Motor Lodges

★★ **DER RITTERHOF MOTOR INN.**
*190 US 2 (98826). 509/548-5845; fax
509/548-4098; toll-free 800/255-5845.
Email moreinfo@crcwnet.com; www.
derritterhof.com.* 48 rms, 2 story, 4
suites. June-Dec: S $74; D $82; each
addl $8; suites $150; children $8;
under 5 free; lower rates rest of yr.
Crib avail. Pet accepted, fee. Parking
lot. Pool, whirlpool. TV; cable (premium), VCR avail. Complimentary
continental bkfst. Restaurant. Meeting rms. Fax servs avail. Golf. Tennis.
Downhill skiing. Hiking trail. Picnic
facilities. Cr cds: A, MC, V.

★★ **ENZIAN MOTOR INN.** *590 US
2 (98826). 509/548-5269; fax
509/548-9215; toll-free 800/223-8511.*
104 rms, 2-4 story. S $80-$90; D $95-
$110; each addl $10; suites $140-
$170; under 6 free. Crib free. Pet
accepted; $10. TV; cable. 2 pools, 1
indoor; whirlpools. Complimentary
full bkfst. Restaurant nearby. Ck-out
11 am. Meeting rms. Putting green.
Exercise equipt. Some balconies. Cr
cds: A, C, D, DS, ER, MC, V.

Hotel

★ **RODEWAY INN.** *185 US 2
(98826). 509/548-7992; fax 509/548-
7143; res 800/228-2000; toll-free 800/
693-1225. Email rodeway@leavenworth
wa.com; www.leavenworthwa.com.* 64
rms, 3 story, 14 suites. June-Oct, Dec:
S $74; D $109; each addl $12; suites
$169; under 18 free; lower rates rest
of yr. Crib avail. Pet accepted, some
restrictions, fee. Parking lot. Indoor
pool, whirlpool. TV; cable (DSS), VCR
avail. Complimentary continental
bkfst, coffee in rms, newspaper, toll-
free calls. Restaurant nearby. 24-hr
rm serv. Ck-out 11 am, ck-in 3 pm.
Meeting rms. Business center. Coin
lndry. Exercise equipt. Golf. Tennis, 4
courts. Downhill skiing. Supervised
children's activities. Picnic facilities.
Cr cds: A, D, DS, MC, V.

Resort

★★ **BEST WESTERN ICICLE INN.**
*505 US 2 (98826). 509/548-7000; fax
509/548-7050; toll-free 800/558-2438.
Email info@icicleinn.com; www.icicle
inn.com.* 87 rms, 3 story, 6 suites.
July-Sep, Dec: S $99; D $109; each
addl $10; suites $189; under 18 free;
lower rates rest of yr. Crib avail. Parking lot. Pool, whirlpool. TV; cable
(premium), VCR avail. Complimentary continental bkfst, coffee in rms,
toll-free calls. Restaurant 4:30-9:30
pm. Ck-out noon, ck-in 3 pm. Meeting rms. Business servs avail. Coin
lndry. Gift shop. Exercise equipt.
Golf, 18 holes. Tennis, 2 courts.
Downhill skiing. Supervised children's activities. Hiking trail. Picnic
facilities. Cr cds: A, C, D, DS, ER,
JCB, MC, V.

B&Bs/Small Inns

★★ **ALL SEASONS RIVER INN.**
*8751 Icicle Rd (98826). 509/548-1425;
toll-free 800/254-0555. Email info@
allseasonsriverinn.com; www.allseasons
riverinn.com.* 4 rms, 3 story, 2 suites.
June-Oct, Dec: S, D $135; each addl
$20; suites $165; lower rates rest of
yr. Parking lot. TV; cable (premium),
VCR avail, VCR avail. Complimentary full bkfst. Restaurant nearby. Ck-
out 11 am, ck-in 3 pm. Concierge.
Gift shop. Golf, 18 holes. Tennis.
Downhill skiing. Beach access. Bike
rentals. Hiking trail. Picnic facilities.
Cr cds: DS, MC, V.

★ **HAUS ROHRBACH PENSION.**
*12882 Ranger Rd (98826). 509/548-
7024; fax 509/548-6455; toll-free 800/
548-4477. Email info@hausrohrbach.
com; www.hausrohrbach.com.* 10 units,
2 share bath, 1-3 story, 5 suites. No
elvtr. No rm phones. S, D $75-$95;
each addl $20; suites $125-$160;
wkly rates. Crib free. Heated pool;
whirlpool. Complimentary bkfst.
Restaurant nearby. Ck-out 11 am, ck-
in 2 pm. Free bus depot transportation. X-country ski 1 mi. Lawn
games. Balconies. Picnic tables. Austrian chalet-style inn. At base of
mountain. Totally nonsmoking. Cr
cds: A, DS, MC, V.

★★★ **MOUNTAIN HOME LODGE.**
*8201 Mountain Home Rd PO Box 687
(98826). 509/548-7077; fax 509/548-
5008; toll-free 800/414-2378. Email
info@mthome.com; www.mthome.com.*
9 rms, 3 story, 1 suite. Nov-Mar: S
$242; D $260; suites $180; lower
rates rest of yr. Valet parking avail.
Pool, whirlpool. TV; cable (premium), VCR avail, CD avail. Complimentary full bkfst, coffee in rms.
Restaurant. Bar. Ck-out noon, ck-in 3
pm. Meeting rms. Business center.
Concierge. Gift shop. Exercise rm.
Golf. Tennis. Downhill skiing. Hiking
trail. Cr cds: DS, MC, V.

★★★ **RUN OF THE RIVER BED &
BREAKFAST.** *9308 E Leavenworth Rd
(98826). 509/548-7171; fax 509/548-
7547; toll-free 800/288-6491. Email
rofther@runoftheriver.com; www.runof
theriver.com.* 6 air-cooled rms. No rm
phones. S, D $100-$155. Adults only.
TV; cable. Complimentary full bkfst.
Ck-out 11 am, ck-in 3 pm. Business
servs avail. Gift shop. X-country ski 2
mi. Mountain bicycles, snowshoes.
Whirlpool. Refrigerators. Balconies.
Picnic tables. Hand-hewn log furnishings and construction. Decks
with views of forest and mountains;
on bank of Icicle River. Totally nonsmoking. Cr cds: DS, MC, V.

Conference Center

★★ **SLEEPING LADY CONFER-
ENCE RETREAT.** *7375 Icicle Rd
(98826). 509/548-6344; fax 509/548-
6312; toll-free 800/574-2123. Email
info@sleepinglady.com; www.sleeping
lady.com.* 57 rms, 1 story, 1 suite. Jan-
Oct: S $185; D $250; each addl $35;
suites $295; under 4 free; lower rates
rest of yr. Crib avail. Parking lot.
Pool. TV; cable (premium), VCR
avail, CD avail, VCR avail. Complimentary full bkfst, coffee in rms,
newspaper. Restaurant. Bar. Ck-out
11 am, ck-in 3 pm. Meeting rms.
Business center. Coin lndry. Gift
shop. Exercise equipt, sauna. Golf, 18
holes. Downhill skiing. Beach access.
Hiking trail. Picnic facilities. Cr cds:
A, DS, MC, V.

Restaurant

★★ **LORRAINE'S EDEL HAUS.** *320
Ninth St (98826). 509/548-4412.* Specializes in peppercorn steak, Washington grown half chicken,
puttanesca. Hrs: 5-10 pm. Res
accepted. Wine, beer. Dinner a la
carte entrees: $9.25-$18.50. Child's
menu. Parking. Cottage-style atmosphere. Cr cds: DS, MC, V.
D

Long Beach (E-1)

Pop 1,236 **Elev** 10 ft **Area code** 360
Zip 98631
Information Peninsula Visitors
Bureau, PO Box 562; 360/642-2400
or 800/451-2542

This seashore resort is on one of the
longest hard sand beaches in the
world, stretching 28 miles along a
narrow peninsula, just north of
where the Columbia River empties
into the Pacific Ocean.

What to See and Do

Oysterville. Community founded in
1854; original settlers were lured by
oysters found on tidal flats of Willapa
Bay. Many original homes remain, as
well as church and schoolhouse. 15
mi N via Sandridge Rd. Phone
360/642-2400 or 800/451-2542.

Seascape scenic drive. 14 mi N from
Seaview on WA 103, through Long
Beach to Ocean Park.

State historic parks.

Fort Canby. (1864) More than
1,880 acres overlooking mouth of
Columbia River. Strategic base from
pioneer days through WWII. The
Lewis and Clark Interpretive Center,
built near an artillery bunker on a
hillside, has exhibits depicting the
historic expedition and the contri-
butions made by Native American
tribes; also multimedia presentations (daily). Fishing; hiking, picnicking, camping (hookups).
Standard fees. (Daily) 2 mi S on WA
100, in Ilwaco. Phone 360/642-
3078 or 800/452-5687 (res).

Fort Columbia. More than 580
acres. Site of former coastal
artillery corps post with Endicott-

period fortifications that protected mouth of Columbia River. Interpretive center in former barracks (Apr-Sep, daily) Also here is Columbia House, a former commander's residence. Hiking, picnicking. Grounds (Apr-Sep, Wed-Sun). 11 mi SE on US 101. Phone 360/777-8755. **FREE**

Motels/Motor Lodges

★★ **THE BREAKERS MOTEL & CONDO.** *26th and WA 103 (98631), 1 mi N, 360/642-4414; fax 360/642-8772; toll-free 800/219-9833. Email rooms@breakerslongbeach.com; www. breakerslongbeach.com.* 118 rms, 3 story, 53 kits. No A/C. June-Labor Day: S, D $74; suites $141-$186; kit. units $86; lower rates rest of yr. Crib free. Pet accepted; $10. TV; cable, VCR avail. Heated pool; whirlpool. Restaurant nearby. Ck-out 11 am. Meeting rm. Business servs avail. Some refrigerators. Private patios, balconies. Public golf adj. Cr cds: A, D, DS, MC, V.

★ **CHAUTAUQUA LODGE.** *304 14th St NW (98631). 360/642-4401; fax 360/642-2340; toll-free 800/869-8401.* 180 units, 3 story, 60 kits. No A/C. June-Sep: S, D $55-$100; each addl $5; suites $115-$160; kit. units $85-$115; lower rates rest of yr. Crib $2. Pet accepted, some restrictions; $8. TV, cable. Indoor pool; whirlpool, sauna. Complimentary coffee in rms. Restaurant adj 8 am-10 pm; winter from 11 am. Bar 4 pm-1 am. Ck-out 11 am. Coin lndry. Meeting rms. Business servs avail. Sundries. Rec rm. Refrigerators. Private patios, balconies. On beach. Cr cds: A, D, DS, MC, V.

★ **EDGEWATER INN.** *409 10th St (98631). 360/642-2311; fax 360/642-8018; res 800/561-2456.* 76 rms, 3 story, 8 suites. May, Sep: S $94; D $99; suites $104; lower rates rest of yr. Crib avail, fee. Pet accepted, some restrictions, fee. Parking lot. TV; cable (premium). Complimentary coffee in rms. Restaurant 11 am-9:30 pm. Bar. Ck-out 11 am. Meeting rms. Fax servs avail. Golf. Beach access. Hiking trail. Cr cds: A, D, DS, MC, V.

★ **OUR PLACE AT THE BEACH.** *1309 S Blvd (98631). 360/642-3793; fax 360/642-3896; toll-free 800/538-5107. Email tomson@aone.com.* 25 rms, 1-2 story, 4 kits. May-Oct: S, D $45-$59; each addl $5; kit. units $64-$75; some lower rates rest of yr. Crib $1. Pet accepted; $5. TV. Coffee in rms. Restaurant nearby. Ck-out 11 am. Meeting rms. Business servs avail. Exercise equipt; sauna, whirlpool. Refrigerators, microwaves. Picnic tables. Pathway to beach. Cr cds: A, C, DS, MC, V.

★★ **SHAMAN MOTEL.** *115 3rd St SW, PO Box 235 (98631), 1 blk W off WA 103. 360/642-3714; fax 360/642-8599; toll-free 800/753-3750. www. shamanmotel.com.* 42 rms, 2 story. July-Aug: S $84; D $94; under 5 free; lower rates rest of yr. Pet accepted, some restrictions, fee. Parking lot. Pool. TV; cable. Restaurant nearby. Business servs avail. Coin lndry. Exercise privileges. Golf. Tennis. Beach access. Cr cds: A, C, D, DS, JCB, MC, V.

Hotel

★ **SUPER 8.** *500 Ocean Beach Blvd (98631). 360/642-8988; fax 360/642-8986; res 800/800-8000; toll-free 888/478-3297. www.super8.com.* 46 rms, 2 story, 4 suites. Crib avail. Parking lot. TV; cable, VCR avail. Complimentary continental bkfst, coffee in rms, newspaper, toll-free calls. Restaurant nearby. Ck-out 11 am, ck-in 3 pm. Meeting rm. Fax servs avail. Coin lndry. Golf, 9 holes. Tennis. Beach access. Bike rentals. Supervised children's activities. Picnic facilities. Cr cds: A, C, D, DS, JCB, MC, V.

B&Bs/Small Inns

★★★ **BOREAS BED & BREAKFAST** *607 N Ocean Beach Blvd (98631). 360/642-8069; fax 360/642-5353; toll-free 888/642-8069. Email boreas@boreasinn.com; www.boreas inn.com.* 2 story, 5 suites. June-Oct: S, D $128; each addl $25; suites $128; lower rates rest of yr. Parking lot. TV; cable, VCR avail, VCR avail, CD avail. Complimentary full bkfst,

toll-free calls. Restaurant nearby.
Ck-out 11 am, ck-in 4 pm. Business
center. Concierge. Exercise privileges, whirlpool. Golf, 9 holes. Tennis, 4 courts. Beach access. Bike
rentals. Hiking trail. Picnic facilities.
Cr cds: A, D, DS, MC, V.

★ ★ ★ **THE INN AT ILWACO.** *120
Williams Ave NE (98642), S on WA 103.
360/642-8686; fax 360/642-8642; toll-
free 888/244-2523. Email bussone@
lonbeachlodging.com.* 9 rms, 2 story, 3
suites. No A/C. No rm phones. Apr-
Nov: S, D $99; each addl $15; suites
$180; lower rates rest of yr. Compli-
mentary full bkfst; afternoon refreshments. Restaurant nearby. Ck-out
noon, ck-in 2 pm. Business servs
avail. Free airport transportation.
Health club privileges. Located in
renovated church bldg. Totally nonsmoking. Cr cds: MC, V.

★ ★ **SCANDINAVIAN GARDENS
INN BED & BREAKFAST.** *1610 California Ave SW (98631). 360/642-8877;
fax 360/642-8764; toll-free 800/988-
9277. Email sginn@longbeachwa.com;
www.longbeachwa.com.* 4 rms, 2 story,
1 suite. July-Oct: S $105; D $115;
each addl $20; suites $145; lower
rates rest of yr. Crib avail. Parking
lot. TV; cable, VCR avail, CD avail.
Complimentary full bkfst. Restaurant. Ck-out 11 am, ck-in 3 pm. Business servs avail. Sauna, whirlpool.
Golf, 9 holes. Beach access. Bike
rentals. Hiking trail. Picnic facilities.
Cr cds: DS, MC, V.

Restaurants

★ ★ **SANCTUARY.** *794 US 101
(98631), 7 mi SE. 360/777-8380.
www.seattleintheround/sanctuary.com.*
Specializes in fresh local seafood,
pasta, chicken. Hrs: 5-9 pm; winter
hrs vary. Closed Mon, Tues. Res
accepted. Dinner $10.50-$17.95.
Child's menu. Entertainment. High
ceiling, stained glass, soft lighting.
Former church, built 1906. Cr cds: A,
DS, MC, V.
D

★ ★ **SHOALWATER.** *4503 Pacific
Hwy (98644), 1 mi S on WA 103, at
45th St. 360/642-4142. Email wine
dine@willapabay.org; www.shoalwater.*

com. Specializes in oysters, salmon,
regional meats. Own breads. Hrs:
11:30 am-9 pm; Fri, Sat to 10 pm.
Closed Dec 25. Res accepted. Bar.
Lunch $4.25-$13.50; dinner $13.50-
$24. Child's menu. Ingredients range
from the freshest local fish to mushrooms and salad greens gathered
from the peninsula's woods and gardens. Cr cds: A, D, DS, MC, V.
D

Longview

(E-2) *See also Chehalis, Kelso*

Settled 1923 **Pop** 31,499 **Elev** 21 ft
Area code 360 **Zip** 98632
Information Longview Area Chamber
of Commerce, 1563 Olympia Way;
360/423-8400

Longview is the home of one of the
largest forest products mill in the
world. Factories produce pulp, fine
and kraft papers, paper boxes, plywood, glassine, pig aluminum, concrete paint, caustic soda, and
chlorine. The first planned city in
the West, Longview is a deepwater
port fed by six railroad systems and
several highways. Fishing for steelhead, smelt, and salmon is excellent.
Longview is situated between Seattle,
WA and Portland, OR.

What to See and Do

Lake Sacajawea Park. A 120-acre
park with 60-acre lake; picnic areas,
playgrounds, gardens. Jogging, bike,
and fitness trails. Fishing, wildlife
refuge. (Daily) Between Kessler &
Nichols Blvds, US 30 & WA 432.

Monticello Convention Site. Here residents of Washington met to petition
the federal government to separate
Washington Territory from Oregon.
Olympia Way & Maple St.

Mount St. Helens Visitor Center. (See
MOUNT ST. HELENS NATIONAL
VOLCANIC MONUMENT) 10 mi N
on I-5 to Castle Rock, then 5 mi E on
WA 504.

Annual Events

International Festival. Lower Columbia College. Early May.

Cowlitz County Fair. Cowlitz County Expo Center. Exhibits, entertainment, carnival, pro rodeo. Last wk July.

Rain Fest. Cowlitz County Expo Center. Wine tasting, exhibit booths, music. Early Oct.

Marysville

(B-3) *See also Everett*

Settled 1872 **Pop** 10,328 **Elev** 15 ft
Area code 360 **Web** www.marysville-tulalip.com

Information The Greater Marysville Tulalip Chamber of Commerce, 4411 76th St NE, 98270; 360/659-7700

Natural surroundings, including lakes, rivers, and wooded countryside, make Marysville a popular spot for outdoor recreation.

What to See and Do

Tulalip Reservation. Within the community are St. Anne's Church (1904) with old mission bell, the Native American Shaker Church, and tribal community center. 6 mi NW via WA 506. Phone 360/651-4000.

Wenberg State Park. A 46-acre park. Swimming, fishing, boating (launch); picnicking, concession (summer), camping (some hookups). Standard fees. N via I-5 Exit 206, 2 mi W to Lakewood Rd, then 3 mi N to E Lake Goodwin Rd, then S. Phone 360/652-7417.

Annual Events

Strawberry Festival. Parade, art show, races. Phone 360/659-7664. Third wk June.

Home-Grown Festival. Third & State Sts. Open-air market, arts and crafts booths, street fair. Early Aug.

Merrysville for the Holidays. Watertower lighting, lighted holiday parade. Phone 360/659-3005. Early Dec.

Motel/Motor Lodge

★ **VILLAGE MOTOR INN.** *235 Beach St (98270). 360/659-0005; fax 360/658-0866; toll-free 877/659-0005.* 45 rms, 3 story, 6 suites. S $50-$57; D $55-$62; each addl $5; suites $75-$130; under 12 free; monthly rates. Pet accepted, some restrictions. TV; cable (premium). Complimentary continental bkfst, coffee in rms. Restaurant adj. Ck-out 11 am. Meeting rms. Business servs avail. In-rm modem link. Valet serv. Refrigerators, microwaves avail. Cr cds: A, C, D, DS, MC, V.

Restaurant

★ **VILLAGE.** *220 Ash Ave (98270), SE of I-5 Exit 199. 360/659-2305.* Specializes in steak, seafood. Own pies. Hrs: 5 am-10 pm; Sat, Sun from 6 am. Closed Dec 25. Bar. Bkfst $3.25-$7.50; lunch $4-$7; dinner $5-$12.95. Child's menu. Cr cds: A, D, DS, MC, V.

Moclips

Pop 700 (est) **Elev** 10 ft
Area code 360 **Zip** 98562

Information Washington Coast Chamber, 2602 WA 109, Ocean City 98569; 360/289-4552 or 800/286-4552

Motel/Motor Lodge

★ **HI-TIDE CONDOMINIUM RESORT.** *4890 Railroad Ave (98162), 3 mi N of Pacific Beach, off WA 109, on Pacific Ocean. 360/276-4142; fax 360/276-0156; res 360/276-4142; toll-free 800/662-5477. Email hitide@techline.com.* 25 kit. suites, 2 story. No A/C. Mid-June-mid-Oct: kit. suites $89-$159; each addl $10; under 11 free; wkly rates; lower rates rest of yr. Crib free. Pet accepted; $10/day. TV; cable, VCR avail. Restaurant nearby. Ck-out 11 am. Business servs avail. Lawn games. Fireplaces. Private patios, balconies. Cr cds: A, DS, MC, V.

Resort

★★ **OCEAN CREST RESORT.** *4651 WA 109 (98562), 1 mi S; 1 mi N of Pacific Beach. 360/276-4465; fax 360/276-4149; res 800/684-8439. Email ocncrest@techline.com.* 45 rms, 3 story. June-Aug: ; each addl $12; children $6; under 15 free; lower rates rest of yr. Crib avail. Pet accepted, some restrictions, fee. Parking lot. Indoor pool, whirlpool. TV; cable, VCR avail. Complimentary coffee in rms, newspaper, toll-free calls. Restaurant 8 am-9:30 pm. Bar. Ckout 11 am, ck-in 3 pm. Meeting rms. Business servs avail. Coin lndry. Gift shop. Exercise equipt, sauna. Beach access. Picnic facilities. Cr cds: A, DS, MC, V.

Moses Lake

(D-6) *See also Ephrata*

Settled 1910 **Pop** 11,235 **Elev** 1,060 ft
Area code 509 **Zip** 98837
Web www.moses-lake.com
Information Chamber of Commerce, 324 S Pioneer Way; 509/765-7888

Because of the water impounded by Grand Coulee Dam, the recreational and agricultural resources of this area have blossomed. Swimming, fishing, and hunting abound within a 25-mile radius. The city is also an important shipping and processing point for agricultural products.

What to See and Do

Adam East Museum. Native American artifacts, regional artwork, local history. (Tues-Sat afternoons; closed hols) 3rd & Ash Sts. Phone 509/766-9395. **FREE**

Moses Lake Recreation Area. S and W of city. **FREE** Incl

Moses Lake. Eighteen mi long. NW off I-90, WA 17.

Potholes Reservoir. Formed by O'Sullivan Dam (10 mi S). Swimming, boating, waterskiing, fishing. 14 mi SW off WA 17, I-90 on WA 170.

Potholes State Park. Approx 2,500 acres. Water sports, fishing, boat launch; hiking, picnicking, camping (hookups). Standard fees. 14 mi SW on WA 17 to WA 170.

Moses Lake State Park. A 78-acre park with swimming, fishing, boating (launch); picnicking. (Daily) 2 mi W on I-90. Phone 509/765-5852.

Cascade Park. Swimming, boating (launch), fishing, waterskiing; camping (fee). Park (mid-Apr-mid-Oct, daily). Valley Rd & Cascade Valley. Phone 509/766-9240.

Annual Events

Spring Festival. Memorial Day wkend.

Grant County Fair. Fairgrounds. Rodeo. Five days mid-Aug.

Motels/Motor Lodges

★ **BEST VALUE EL RANCHO MOTEL.** *1214 S Pioneer Way (98837), I-90 Exit 179, then 1½ mi N. 509/765-9173; fax 509/765-1137; res 888/315-BEST. Email elrancho@qwksilvr.com; www.bestvalueinn.com.* 20 rms, 1 story. May-Sep: S $50; D $60; each addl $5; under 11 free; lower rates rest of yr. Crib avail. Pet accepted, some restrictions. Parking lot. Pool. TV; cable (premium). Complimentary coffee in rms, toll-free calls. Restaurant nearby. Ck-out 11 am. Fax servs avail. Free airport transportation. Golf. Tennis. Picnic facilities. Cr cds: A, D, DS, MC, V.

★ **INTERSTATE INN.** *2801 W Broadway (98837), at I-90 Business Exit 176. 509/765-1777; fax 509/766-9452.* 30 rms, 2 story. S $39; D $49-$54; each addl $6; family, wkly rates. Crib $3.50. Pet accepted. TV; cable (premium), VCR avail. Indoor pool; whirlpool, sauna. Restaurant adj open 24 hrs. Ck-out 11 am. Business servs avail. Some refrigerators. Cr cds: A, D, DS, MC, V.

★ **MOSES LAKE MOTEL 6.** *2822 Wapato Dr (98837). 509/766-0250; fax 509/766-7762; res 800/466-8356.* 89 rms, 2 story. May-Sep: S $45; D $51; each addl $6; under 17 free; lower rates rest of yr. Crib avail. Pet accepted. Parking lot. Pool. TV; cable (premium). Complimentary toll-free calls. Restaurant nearby 1 pm-midnight. Ck-out noon, ck-in 3 pm. Business servs avail. Coin lndry. Cr cds: A, D, DS, MC, V.

★★ **SHILO INN.** *1819 E Kittleson (98837). 509/765-9317; fax 509/765-5058; res 800/222-2244.* 100 rms, 2 story. 6 kits. Late May-mid-Sep: S, D $69-$85; each addl $6; kits. $89-$105; under 12 free; wkly rates; lower rates rest of yr. Crib free. Pet accepted; $7. TV; cable (premium). Indoor pool; whirlpool. Coffee in rms. Restaurant open 24 hrs. Serv bar (beer) 11-2 am. Ck-out noon. Coin lndry. Meeting rms. Business servs avail. Valet serv. Sundries. Gift shop. Free airport, bus depot transportation. Exercise equipt; sauna. Bathrm phones, refrigerators, microwaves, wet bars. Cr cds: A, D, DS, MC, V.

Hotel

★★ **BEST WESTERN HALLMARK INN AND CONFERENCE CENTER.** *3000 Marina Dr (98837), I-90 Exit 176. 509/765-9211; fax 509/766-0493; res 888/448-4449; toll-free 800/235-4255. Email hisales@televar.com; www.hallmarkinns.com.* 151 rms, 3 story, 9 suites. May-Sep: S $69; D $79; each addl $5; suites $100; under 12 free; lower rates rest of yr. Pet accepted, some restrictions. Parking lot. Pool. TV; cable (premium). Complimentary coffee in rms, newspaper, toll-free calls. Restaurant. Bar. Meeting rms. Business servs avail. Dry cleaning, coin lndry. Free airport transportation. Exercise equipt; sauna. Golf, 18 holes. Tennis, 2 courts. Bike rentals. Hiking trail. Video games. Cr cds: A, C, D, DS, ER, JCB, MC, V.

Mount Rainier National Park

See also Packwood

Web www.nps.gov/mora/

Majestic Mount Rainier, towering 14,411 feet above sea level and 8,000 feet above the Cascade Range of western Washington, is one of America's outstanding tourist attractions. More than two million people visit this 378-square-mile park each year to picnic, hike, camp, climb mountains, or simply admire the spectacular scenery along the many miles of roadways.

The park's various "life zones," which change at different elevations, support a wide array of plant and animal life. Douglas fir, red cedar, and western hemlock, some rising 200 feet into the air, thrive in the old-growth forests. In the summer, the subalpine meadows come alive with brilliant, multi-colored wildflowers. These areas are home to more than 130 species of birds and 50 species of mammals. Mountain goats, chipmunks, and marmots are favorites among visitors, but deer, elk, bears, mountain lions, and other animals can also be seen here.

Mount Rainier

Mount Rainier is the largest volcano in the Cascade Range, which extends from Mount Garibaldi in southwestern British Columbia to Lassen Peak in northern California. The eruption of Mount St. Helens in 1980 gives a clue to the violent history of these volcanoes. Eruptions occurred at Mount Rainier as recently as the mid-1800s. Even today, steam emissions often form caves in the summit ice cap and usu-

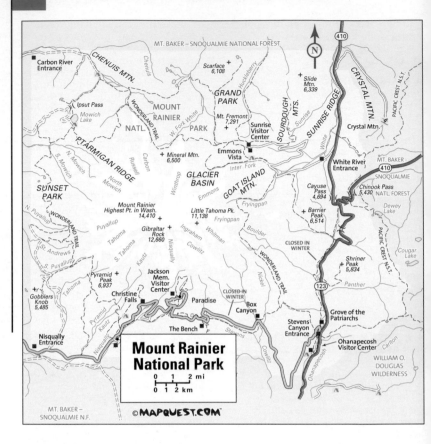

Mount Rainier
National Park

0   1   2 mi

0   1 2 km

©MAPQUEST.COM

ally melt the snow along the rims of the twin craters.

A young volcano by geologic standards, Mount Rainier was once a fairly symmetrical mountain rising about 16,000 feet above sea level. But glaciers and further volcanic activity shaped the mountain into an irregular mass of rock. The sculpting action of the ice gave each face of the mountain its own distinctive profile. The glaciation continues today, as Mount Rainier supports the largest glacier system in the contiguous United States, with 35 square miles of ice and 26 named glaciers.

Much of the park's beauty can be attributed to the glaciers, which at one time extended far beyond the park boundaries. The moving masses of ice carved deep valleys separated by high, sharp ridges or broad plateaus. From certain vantages, the valleys accentuate the mountain's height. The glaciers are the source of the many streams in the park, as well as several rivers in the Pacific North-

west. The meltwaters also nourish the various plants and animals throughout the region.

Winters at Mount Rainier are legendary. Moist air masses moving eastward across the Pacific Ocean are intercepted by the mountain. As a result, some areas on the mountain commonly receive 50 or more feet of snow each winter. Paradise, at 5,400 feet in elevation, made history in 1971-72, when it received 93 feet of snow, the heaviest snowfall ever recorded in this country; the three-story Paradise Inn is often buried up to its roof by snow. Because the mountain's summit is usually above the storm clouds, the snowfall there is not as great.

The park's transformation from winter wonderland to summer playground is almost magical. Beginning in June or July, the weather becomes warm and clear, although the mountain is occasionally shrouded in clouds. The snow at the lower elevations then disappears; meltwaters fill stream valleys and cascade over cliffs; wildflowers blanket the meadows, and visitors descend on the park for its many recreational activities.

There are several entrances to the park. The roads from the Nisqually entrance to Paradise and from the southeast boundary to Ohanapecosh are usually open year-round but may be closed temporarily during the winter. Following the first heavy snow, around November 1, all other roads are closed until May or June. The entrance fee is $10 per vehicle. For further info contact Mount Rainier National Park, Tahoma Woods, Star Rte, Ashford 98304; 360/569-2211.

What to See and Do

Camping. Major campgrounds are located at Cougar Rock, Ohanapecosh, and White River, and have fireplaces, tables, water, and sanitary facilities. Smaller campgrounds are at Sunshine Point and Ipsut Creek. No hookups; dump stations at Cougar Rock and Ohanapecosh only. All areas closed during winter exc Sunshine Point. Phone 800/365-2267 (res). Per site ¢¢¢¢

Fishing. No license required. Fishing season is open in lakes and ponds late Apr-Oct, in rivers and streams late May-Nov. Heavy snowfall restricts access to all water Nov-May. Most lakes are usually not ice-free until early July; ice-fishing not permitted. Specific regulations and details on special closure areas are available at ranger stations.

Hiking. More than 250 mi of trails wind throughout the park, offering unspoiled views of Mt Rainier, glaciers, meadows, lakes, waterfalls, and deep valleys; many trails converge at Paradise and Sunrise; trails vary in degree of difficulty. The **Wonderland Trail**, a 93-mi trail that circles the mountain, is linked with several other trails in the park. A *Pictorial Map* (1986) of the park's topography and *50 Hikes in Mount Rainier National Park,* an illustrated book with maps and hiking details, are available for purchase. Hiking information centers (summer, daily) are located at Longmire and White River. Permit is required yr-round for overnight backpacking; available at ranger stations and visitor centers (fee).

Interpretive programs and walks. Programs, incl nature walks and evening slide shows, are offered at several locations. Schedules are posted in visitor centers and at other locations. (Late June-Labor Day)

Longmire. Longmire is often the first stop for visitors in this area of the park. Visitor center, lodging, cafe, limited groceries. Facilities usually open yr-round. Near the Nisqually entrance, in SW corner of park.

Mountain climbing. The park has many opportunities for climbers; one of the most popular climbs is the 2-day trek to the summit of Mt Rainier. The guide service at Paradise conducts various programs for new and experienced climbers. Climbs should be attempted only by persons who are in good physical condition and have the proper equipment; deep crevasses and unstable ridges of lava are dangerous. All climbers must register with a park ranger (fee). Phone 360/569-2227.

Ohanapecosh. A preserve of rushing waters and dense old growth forest. Some of the largest trees in the park—many over 1,000 years old—are here. The Grove of the Patriarchs, a cluster of massive conifers on an island in the Ohanapecosh River, is reached by bridge along a popular trail that starts near the Steven's Canyon Entrance Station. At the Ohanapecosh Visitor Center, exhibits tell the story of the lowland forest ecosystem, where Douglas fir, western hemlock, and red cedar trees reign supreme. In SE corner of park.

Paradise. This is the most visited area of the park, featuring subalpine meadows covered with wildflowers, and hiking trails that provide views of Nisqually, Paradise, and Stevens glaciers. Visitor center with slide programs and films (May-mid-Oct, daily; rest of yr, wkends only); lodging (see MOTELS); cafe (summer, daily); snack bar (summer, daily; winter, wkends and hols only). The nearby Narada Falls drop 168 ft to Paradise River Canyon; viewpoints along stairway. Accessible from Nisqually entrance at SW corner of park, and from Stevens Canyon entrance at SE corner of park (summer only).

Skiing.

Paradise area. Cross-country skiing is popular here; equipment rentals and lessons are available at Longmire. For further info contact park HQ.

Crystal Mountain Resort. Three triple, 2 quad, 5 double chairlifts; patrol, school, rentals; restaurants, bars, day-care center, accommodations. Longest run 3½ mi; vertical drop 3,102 ft. (Nov-Apr, daily) Midweek, half-day, and twilight rates. Also summer season (late June-Labor Day): swimming, fishing; hiking, mountain biking, tennis, volleyball; chairlift rides to summit (fee); poolside cafe; accommodations. E via WA 410, then 6 mi E on Crystal Mt Rd, on NE boundary of Mt Rainier National Park, in Mt Baker-Snoqualmie National Forest. Phone 360/663-2265. Winter ¢¢¢¢

White Pass Village. Four double chairlifts, Pomalift, rope tow; patrol, school, rentals; accommodations, restaurant, bar, general store, service station. Longest run 2½ mi; vertical drop 1,500 ft. (Mid-Nov-mid-Apr, daily) Cross-country trails. On US 12, 12 mi E of Stevens Canyon (SE) entrance to the park. Phone 509/672-3100. ¢¢¢¢

Sunrise. On NE side of mountain; accessible only July-mid-Sep. This is the highest point reached by paved road within Washington (6,400 ft). The drive to Sunrise is worth the time; the crowds are smaller, and this area offers spectacular views of the mountain and Emmons Glacier, the largest in the US outside Alaska. Visitor center, snack bar, picnic area.

🌟 **Visitor centers.** Located at Longmire; at Paradise; at Sunrise (summer only); and at Ohanapecosh (summer only), near the Stevens Canyon entrance, in SE corner of park. All offer exhibits and publications.

Carbon River. Located on the Pacific side of Mt Rainier, the Carbon River area receives the most rainfall and contains the most luxurious forests. In fact, much of the woodland here is considered temperate rainforest. The main road into Carbon River and the NW corner of the park leads from Carbonado into Ipsut Creek, a seasonal ranger station and campground.

Motel/Motor Lodge

★★ **THE NISQUALLY LODGE.** *31609 WA 706 (98304). 360/569-8804; fax 360/569-2435; toll-free 888/674-3554. www.escapetothemountains. com.* 24 rms, 2 story. May-Sep: S, D $69-$79; each addl $10; lower rates rest of yr. Crib $5. TV; cable, VCR avail. Playground. Complimentary continental bkfst. Restaurant adj 7 am-9 pm. Ck-out 11 am. Whirlpool. Picnic tables. Totally nonsmoking. Cr cds: A, DS, MC, V.

D 🏊

Hotel

★★ **PARADISE INN.** *PO Box 108 (98304), in park, 20 mi E of Nisqually SW Entrance. 360/569-2275; fax 360/569-2770; res 360/569-2275.* 115 rms, 4 story, 2 suites. S, D $112; each addl $10; suites $151. Crib avail, fee. Parking lot. TV; cable (premium). Restaurant 7 am-8 pm. Bar. Ck-out 11 am, ck-in 4 pm. Fax servs avail. Bellhops. Gift shop. Hiking trail. Cr cds: A, D, DS, MC, V.

D 🐾 🏊 📠 🔥

B&B/Small Inn

★★ **ALEXANDER'S COUNTRY INN.** *37515 WA 706E (98304). 360/569-2300; fax 360/569-2323; res 800/654-7615. Email info@alexanders countryinn.com; www.alexanders countryinn.com.* 12 rms. May-Oct: S, D $110; each addl $15; suites $140; lower rates rest of yr. Crib avail. Parking lot. TV; cable (DSS), VCR avail, CD avail. Complimentary full bkfst. Restaurant 8 am. Ck-out 11 am, ck-in 3 pm. Gift shop. Whirlpool. Beach access. Hiking trail. Cr cds: MC, V.

🐾 🏊 🔥 📠 🔥

Restaurant

★★ **ALEXANDER'S COUNTRY INN.** *37515 WA 706E. 360/569-2300. Email info@alexanderscountryinn.com; www.alexanderscountryinn.com.* Specializes in seafood, steak, pie. Hrs: 8:30 am-8:30 pm; Sat, Sun from 8 am. Closed wkdays mid-Oct-mid-May. Res accepted. Bkfst $5.50-$8.50; lunch $5.95-$9.95; dinner $12.95-$19.95. Child's menu. Country decor. Cr cds: MC, V.

D

Mount St. Helens National Volcanic Monument

(From I-5 Exit 68: 48 mi E on US 12 to Randle, then S on Forest Service Rd 25; from I-5 exit 21: approx 35 mi NE on WA 503, Forest Service Rds 90, 25)

Web www.fs.fed.us/gpnf

In 1978, two geologists who had been studying Mount St. Helens warned that this youngest volcano in the Cascade Range could erupt again by the end of the century. On March 27, 1980, the volcano did just that, ending 123 years of inactivity. Less than two months later, on May 18, a massive eruption transformed this beautiful, snow-capped mountain and the surrounding forest into an eerie, desolate landscape with few signs of life.

The eruption sent a lateral blast of hot ash and gases out across the land at speeds up to 670 miles per hour, flattening 150 square miles of forest north of the volcano. An ash plume rising 13 miles into the atmosphere was spread eastward by the wind, coating many cities in Washington, Idaho, and Montana with a fine grit. Rivers were choked with logs and mud, huge logging trucks were toppled like small toys, and the mountain, having lost 1,300 feet of its summit, was left with a gaping crater 2,000 feet deep, ½ mile wide and a mile long.

Among the 57 people missing or killed by the eruption was 83-year-old Harry Truman, who for many years owned a lodge on Spirit Lake, just north of the mountain. Truman refused to heed evacuation warnings, believing his "beloved mountain" would not harm him; he and his lodge are now beneath hundreds of feet of mud and water.

The Monument, established in 1982, covers 110,000 acres within the Gifford Pinchot National Forest and provides a rare, natural laboratory in which scientists and visitors can view the effects of a volcanic eruption. Despite the destruction, the return of vegetation and wildlife to the blast zone has been relatively rapid. Within just weeks of the eruption, small plants and insects had begun to make their way through the ash. Today, herds of elk and other animals, as well as fir trees and wildflowers, have taken a strong foothold here.

Mount St. Helens

Forest Service Road 25, which runs north-south near the eastern boundary, provides access to views of the volcano. The roads are usually closed from approximately November-May because of snow; some roads are narrow and winding

Visitors are advised to phone ahead for current road conditions. Although volcanic activity at Mount St. Helens has decreased greatly in the last few years, some roads into the Monument could be closed if weather conditions dictate.

Admission to individual visitor areas incl Mount St. Helens Visitor Center, Coldwater Ridge Visitor Center (incl Coldwater Lake Recreation Area), Johnston Ridge Observatory, and Ape Cave ¢¢; One-day admission to all sites ¢¢¢. For further information, including a map with the locations of various facilities and attractions, contact the Monument Headquarters, 42218 NE Yale Bridge Rd, Amboy 98601; 360/247-3900.

What to See and Do

Ape Cave. At 12,810 ft in length, cave is said to be one of the longest intact lava tubes in continental US. Downslope portion of cave, extending approx 4,000 ft, is the most easily traveled. Upslope portion, extending nearly 7,000 ft, is recommended only for visitors carrying the proper equipment. All visitors are advised to carry three sources of light and wear sturdy shoes or boots and warm clothing; cave is a constant 42°F. An information station is also here; lantern rentals avail seasonally. On Forest Service Rd 8303, in southern part of monument.

Camping. Iron Creek Campground (fee) is located N of Mount St. Helens on Forest Service Rd 25. Other campgrounds ring Yale Lake and Swift Creek Reservoir S of the monument.

Coldwater Ridge Visitor Center. Major interpretive center at 5,000 feet offers views directly into mouth of crater. Lodge-like bldg overlooks Coldwater Lake created by eruption landslide. Films and viewing area; displays focus on rebirth of nature. Bookstore, cafeteria, interpretive hikes. (Daily) 45 mi E of Castle Rock. Phone 360/274-2131.

Hiking. An extensive system of trails offers hikers impressive views of the volcano and surrounding devastated areas. Trails vary in degree of difficulty. Some trails are accessible to wheelchairs. Temperatures can be very warm along the trails due to a lack of shade; hikers are advised to carry water.

Johnson Ridge Observatory. At 8,000 feet. State-of-the-art interpretive displays focus on sequence of geological events that drastically altered the landscape and opened up a new era in the science of monitoring an active volcano and forecasting erup-

tions. Wide-screen theater presentation, interpretive exhibits, staffed information desk, bookstore. Views of the lava dome, crater, pumice plain, and landslide deposit. Visitors can take ½-mi walk on Eruption Trail. Interpretive talks and hikes in summer. (Daily) 52 mi E of Castle Rock. Phone 360/274-2131.

✪ **Mount St. Helens Visitor Center.** (Center cannot be reached directly from the NE side Monument.) The center houses exhibits incl a walk-through model of the volcano, displays on the history of the mountain and the 1980 eruption, and volcano monitoring equipment. A 10-min slide program and a 22-min movie are shown several times daily, and special programs are held throughout the yr. Also here are volcano viewpoints and a nature trail along Silver Lake. (Daily; closed hols) Outside the Monument, off I-5 Exit 49, 5 mi east of Castle Rock on WA 504. Contact 3029 Spirit Lake Hwy, Castle Rock 98611. Phone 360/274-2100 or 360/274-2131.

Summit climb. Climbers are allowed to hike to the summit; free climbing permits are issued on a limited basis. Climb should be attempted only by persons in good physical condition. For climbing info contact the HQ. Phone 360/247-3961 or 360/247-3900.

Visitor information stations. Located at Pine Creek, on Forest Service Rd 90 near the SE side of the Monument; at Woods Creek, at the junction of Forest Service roads 25 and 76 near the NE side of the Monument; and at Ape Cave. (Summer, daily; may remain open until Labor Day)

Windy Ridge Viewpoint. Offers views directly into crater across log-strewn Spirit Lake. Snack bar, toilets. Interpretive hikes and talks. Off Forest Service Rd 99.

Mount Vernon

(B-3) *See also Anacortes, La Conner, Sedro Woolley*

Settled 1870 **Pop** 17,647 **Elev** 31 ft
Area code 360 **Zip** 98273
Web www.mvcofc.org

Information Chamber of Commerce, 117 N 1st St, #4, PO Box 1007; 360/428-8547

Developed by farmers and loggers, Mount Vernon is a major commercial center. Centrally located between Puget Sound and the North Cascades, the Skagit Delta's deep alluvial soil grows 125 varieties of produce including flowers and bulbs, fruit, and vegetables. Spring brings fields of daffodils, tulips, and irises to the country; a map of the fields is available at the Chamber of Commerce. The city is named for George Washington's plantation.

What to See and Do

Bay View State Park. Approx 25 acres. Sand beach (no swimming). Picnicking, camping (hookups). Standard fees. Interpretive center nearby. 7 mi W via WA 20, then right on Bay View-Edison Rd. Phone 360/757-0227.

Hillcrest Park. Approx 30 acres with playgrounds, tennis and basketball courts, hiking trails, covered and open picnic facilities, barbecue pits. 13th St & Blackburn Rd, ½ mi E of I-5 to Cedardale Rd, ½ mi N to Blackburn Rd, then E ¼ mi. Phone 360/336-6213. **FREE**

Little Mountain. Observation area atop 934-ft mountain, providing view of Skagit Valley, Olympic Mts, Mt Rainier, and San Juan Islands; surrounded by 480-acre forested park. Hiking, picnicking. (Daily) SE of city on Blackburn Rd W. Phone 360/336-6213.

Annual Events

Tulip Festival. Festival planned around tulip fields as they bloom. Tulip field tours, arts and crafts, exhibits. Apr.

Skagit County Fair. Second wk Aug.

Seasonal Event

Awesome Autumn Festival. Six wks of events including a 4-acre corn maze, arts and crafts fair, pumpkin festival. Phone 360/428-8547. Sep-Oct.

Motel/Motor Lodge

★★ **BEST WESTERN COLLEGE WAY INN.** *300 W College Way (98273), I-5 Exit 227, then 1 blk W. 360/424-4287; fax 360/424-6036; res 800/528-1234; toll-free 800/793-4024.* 66 rms, 56 A/C, 2 story, 10 kits. Mid-June-Sep: S $55; D $60-$65; each addl $5; kit. units $10 addl; under 12 free; lower rates rest of yr. Crib free. Pet accepted. TV; cable (premium). Heated pool; whirlpool. Complimentary continental bkfst. Coffee in rms. Restaurant adj 7 am-11 pm. Ck-out noon. Meeting rm. Business servs avail. In-rm modem link. Health club privileges. Some refrigerators; microwaves avail. Private patios, balconies. Cr cds: A, DS, MC, V.

D 🐾 ⌘ 🖼 🔥 SC

B&Bs/Small Inns

★★★ **RIDGEWAY "FARM" BED & BREAKFAST.** *14914 McLean Rd (98273). 360/428-8068; fax 360/428-8880; toll-free 800/428-8068. Email ridgeway@winstarmail.com; pts.places tostay.com/gen_prop.asp?hotel_id=1632.* 6 rms, 3 story. S $110; D $115; each addl $25; suites $175; children $25. Valet parking avail. TV; cable (premium), VCR avail, CD avail. Complimentary full bkfst, toll-free calls. Ck-out 11 am, ck-in 3 pm. Free airport transportation. Golf, 18 holes. Cr cds: A, DS, MC, V.

🏂 🖼 🔥

★★ **THE WHITE SWAN GUEST HOUSE.** *15872 Moore Rd (98273), I-5 Exit 221, 5¼ mi W on Fir Island Rd. 360/445-6805. www.thewhiteswan. com.* 3 rms, 2 story. Apr, July-Aug: S $70; D $85; each addl $10; lower rates rest of yr. TV; cable (premium), VCR avail, CD avail. Complimentary continental bkfst. Ck-out 11 am, ck-in 3 pm. Concierge. Golf. Cr cds: MC, V.

🏂 🖼 🔥

Conference Center

★★ **BEST WESTERN.** *2300 Market St (98273), I-5 Exit 229. 360/428-5678; fax 360/428-1844; res 800/528-1234; toll-free 800/662-6886. Email kristenw@cottontree.net; www. mountvernon@cottontree.net.* 120 rms, 3 story. Mar-Oct: S $89; D $99; each addl $10; under 18 free; lower rates rest of yr. Crib avail. Pet accepted, some restrictions, fee. Parking lot. Lap pool, children's pool, lifeguard, whirlpool. TV; cable (DSS). Complimentary continental bkfst, coffee in rms, newspaper, toll-free calls. Restaurant 11 am-9 pm. Bar. Ck-out noon, ck-in 3 pm. Meeting rms. Business servs avail. Dry cleaning, coin lndry. Gift shop. Exercise privileges. Golf. Tennis, 4 courts. Video games. Cr cds: A, C, D, DS, JCB, MC, V.

Neah Bay

(B-1) *See also Port Angeles*

Pop 916 **Elev** 0 ft **Area code** 360 **Zip** 98357

What to See and Do

Makah Cultural & Research Center. Exhibits on Makah and Northwest Coast Native Americans; 500-yr-old artifacts uncovered at the Ozette archaeological site, a Makah village dating back 2,000 yrs. Craft shop; dioramas; canoes; complete longhouse. (Memorial Day-mid-Sep, daily; rest of yr, Wed-Sun; closed Jan 1, Thanksgiving, Dec 25) WA 112, 1 mi E. Phone 360/645-2711. ¢¢

Newport

(B-8) *See also Spokane; also see Priest Lake Area, ID*

Settled 1890 **Pop** 1,691 **Elev** 2,131 ft **Area code** 509 **Zip** 99156
Web www.povn.com/~chamber
Information Chamber of Commerce, 325 W 4th St; 509/447-5812

A shopping, distribution, and lumbering center, Newport was born in Idaho. For a while there was a Newport on both sides of the state line, but the US Post Office interceded on behalf of the Washington community, which was the county seat of Pend Oreille County. Newport is known as "the city of flags"; flags from around the world are displayed on the main streets. A Ranger District office of the Colville National Forest (see COLVILLE) is located here.

What to See and Do

Historical Society Museum. In old railroad depot; houses historical artifacts of Pend Oreille County; 2 reconstructed log cabins. (Mid-May-Sep, daily) Washington & 4th Sts, in Centennial Plaza. Phone 509/447-5388. **Donation** Also here is

Big Wheel. Giant Corliss steam engine that for years powered the town's foremost sawmill. Flag display. A visitor info center is located here. Centennial Plaza.

North Bend

(C-4) *See also Seattle*

Founded 1889 **Pop** 2,578 **Elev** 442 ft **Area code** 425 **Zip** 98045
Information City of North Bend, 211 Main Ave N, PO Box 896; 425/888-1211 or 425/340-0928

A gateway to Mount Baker-Snoqualmie National Forest—Snoqualmie section (see SEATTLE)—and a popular winter sports area, North Bend also serves as a shipping town for a logging, farming, and dairy region. A Ranger District office of the Mount Baker-Snoqualmie National Forest(see BELLINGHAM) is located here.

What to See and Do

Skiing.

Snoqualmie Ski Area. Six double, 2 triple, quad chairlifts; 2 rope tows; 15 slopes and trails; patrol, school, rentals; bar, restaurant, cafeteria, day care center. Vertical drop 900 ft. (Mid-Nov-Apr, Tues-Sun) Intermediate chairs; half-day and eve rates. Shuttle bus to Ski Acres, Hyak, and Alpental (Fri nights, wkends, and hols); tickets interchangeable. 17 mi SE on I-90. Phone 425/434-6161 or 425/236-1600 (snow conditions). ¢¢¢¢

Ski Acres. Two triple, 6 double chairlifts, 5 rope tows; patrol, school, rentals; cross-country center; cafeteria, bar, day care center. Vertical drop 1,040 ft. (Wed-Mon) Shuttle bus to Snoqualmie, Hyak, and Alpental (Fri nights, wkends, and hols); tickets interchangeable.

18 mi SE on I-90 at Snoqualmie Pass. Phone 425/434-6671 or 425/236-1600 (snow conditions). ¢¢¢¢

Alpental. Four double chairlifts, 3 rope tows, platter pull; patrol, school, rentals; cafeteria, bar. Longest run 1½ mi; vertical drop 2,200 ft. (Hrs, fees same as for Snoqualmie) Shuttle bus to Snoqualmie, Hyak, and Ski Acres (Fri nights, wkends, and hols); tickets interchangeable. 17 mi SE on I-90, then 1 mi N on Alpental Rd. Phone 425/434-6112 or 425/236-1600 (snow conditions). ¢¢¢¢

Hyak. Two double chairlifts; patrol, school, rentals; cafeteria, bar. Vertical drop 960 ft. Shuttle bus to Ski Acres, Snoqualmie, and Alpental. (Late Dec-mid-Mar; Fri, Sat, Sun) Tickets interchangcable. 19 mi SE on I-90, at Snoqualmie Pass. Phone 425/434-7600 or 425/236-1600 (snow conditions). ¢¢¢¢

Snoqualmie Falls. Perpetual snow in the Cascade Mts feeds the 268-ft falls. Power plant; park area; trail to bottom of falls. Salish Lodge (see LODGE) overlooks falls. 4 mi NW via WA 202.

Snoqualmie Valley Historical Museum. Displays, rm settings of early pioneer life from 1890s; photos, Native American artifacts, logging exhibits; farm shed; reference material. Slide shows; changing exhibits. (Apr-mid-Dec, Thurs-Sun; tours by appt) 320 S North Bend Blvd. Phone 425/888-3200. **Donation**

Resort

★★★ SALISH LODGE AND SPA. 6501 Railroad Ave (98065), NW via WA 202. 425/888-2556; fax 425/888-2420; toll-free 800/826-6124. Email reservations@salishlodge.com; www.salishlodge.com. 87 rms, 4 story, 4 suites. July-Sep: S, D $369; suites $999; lower rates rest of yr. Crib avail. Pet accepted, some restrictions, fee. Valet parking avail. TV; cable (premium), VCR avail, CD avail. Complimentary coffee in rms, newspaper. Restaurant. Bar. Meeting rms. Business servs avail. Bellhops. Concierge. Dry cleaning. Gift shop. Exercise equipt, sauna, steam rm, whirlpool. Golf. Downhill skiing.

Bike rentals. Hiking trail. Picnic facilities. Video games. Cr cds: A, D, DS, JCB, MC, V.

[D] [icons]

Restaurant

★★★ SALISH LODGE AND SPA DINING ROOM. 6501 Railroad Ave. 425/831-6517. www.salish.com. Specializes in multicourse country bkfst, potlatch-style salmon, Northwest game. Hrs: 7 am-10 pm. Res accepted. Bar. Wine cellar. Bkfst $12.95-$24.95; lunch $10.95-$15.95; dinner $17.50-$31.95. Sun brunch $21.95-$24.95. Child's menu. Entertainment: Fri, Sat. Valet parking. Overlooks Snoqualmie Falls. Cr cds: A, DS, MC, V.

[D] [icon]

Oak Harbor

(B-3) *See also Anacortes, Coupeville, Everett, Port Townsend*

Settled 1849 **Pop** 17,176 **Elev** 115 ft
Area code 360 **Zip** 98277
Web www.whidbey.net/islandco

Information Chamber of Commerce Visitor Information Center, PO Box 883; 360/675-3535

This trading center on Whidbey Island was first settled by sea captains and adventurers and then in the 1890s by immigrants from the Netherlands who developed the rich countryside. The town's name was inspired by the oak trees that cloaked the area when the first settlers arrived and which have been preserved. Side roads lead to secluded beaches and some excellent boating and fishing with marinas nearby.

What to See and Do

Holland Gardens. Gardens of flowers and shrubs surround blue and white windmill; Dutch provincial flags, tulips, and daffodils decorate gardens during Holland Happening (see ANNUAL EVENTS). (Daily) SE 6th Ave W & Ireland St. **FREE**

Oak Harbor Beach Park. Authentic Dutch windmill; picnicking, barbecue pit; 1,800-ft sand beach, lagoon swimming, bathhouse, wading pools; tennis, baseball diamonds, playground, illuminated trails, camping (hookups, dump station; fee). (Daily) Phone 360/679-5551. **FREE**

Whidbey Island Naval Air Station. Only active naval air station in the Northwest. Guided group tours (min 10 persons); res required several months in advance. Approx 5 mi N on WA 20. Phone 360/257-2286. **FREE**

Annual Events

Holland Happening. Tulip show, arts and crafts, Dutch buffet, carnival, culture foodfest, square dance exhibition, parade. Late Apr.

Whidbey Island Jazz Festival. Mid-Aug.

Motels/Motor Lodges

★★★ **AULD HOLLAND INN.** *33575 WA 20 (98277). 360/675-2288; fax 360/675-2817; toll-free 800/228-0148. Email dutchvillage@oakharbor. net; www.auldhollandinn.com.* 36 rms, 2 story, 1 suite. May, Sep: S, D $55; each addl $5; suites $145; children $5; under 15 free; lower rates rest of yr. Crib avail, fee. Parking lot. Pool. TV; cable (premium), VCR avail. Complimentary continental bkfst, toll-free calls. Restaurant 5-11 pm. Bar. Ck-out 11 am, ck-in 2 pm. Meeting rm. Fax servs avail. Coin lndry. Gift shop. Exercise equipt, sauna. Golf. Tennis. Cr cds: A, C, D, DS, MC, V.

🦌 🖟 ⊶ 🕇 🔌 🔥

★★ **COACHMAN INN.** *32959 WA 20 (98277), at Goldie Rd. 360/675-0727; fax 360/675-1419; toll-free 800/ 635-0043. Email genmgr@thecoachman inn.com; www.thecoachmaninn.com.* 102 rms, 2-3 story, 47 kits. S $60; D $70; each addl (after 4th person) $5; suites $125-$175; kit. units $80-$95; under 12 free. Crib $5. TV; VCR avail. Heated pool; whirlpool. Playground. Complimentary continental bkfst, coffee in rms. Restaurant opp open 24 hrs. Ck-out noon. Coin lndry. Business servs avail. Exercise equipt. Refrigerators; microwaves avail. Picnic table, grill. Cr cds: A, DS, MC, V.

🄳 ⊶ 🕇 🔌 🔥 SC

Resort

★★ **BEST WESTERN HARBOR PLAZA.** *33175 WA 20 (98277). 360/679-4567; fax 360/675-2543; res 800/528-1234; toll-free 800/927-5478. www.bestwestern.com/harborplaza.* 64 rms, 3 story, 16 suites. May-Sep: S, D $99; each addl $10; suites $119; under 17 free; lower rates rest of yr. Crib avail. Pet accepted, some restrictions, fee. Parking lot. Pool, whirlpool. TV; cable (premium), VCR avail. Complimentary continental bkfst, coffee in rms, newspaper, toll-free calls. Restaurant. Bar. Meeting rms. Business servs avail. Dry cleaning. Exercise equipt. Golf, 18 holes. Tennis, 4 courts. Picnic facilities. Cr cds: A, D, DS, MC, V.

🄳 🦌 🕦 🖟 ⊶ 🕇 🔌 🔥 SC

Ocean Shores

(D-1) *See also Aberdeen, Hoquiam, Westport*

Pop 2,301 **Elev** 21 ft **Area code** 360 **Zip** 98569
Web www.oceanshores.com
Information Chamber of Commerce, Box 382; 360/289-2451 or 800/762-3224

This 6,000-acre area at the southern end of the Olympic Peninsula is a seaside resort community with six miles of ocean beaches, 23 miles of lakes and canals, and 12 miles of bay front. Clamming, crabbing, and trout and bass fishing are popular.

What to See and Do

Pacific Paradise Family Fun Center. Thirty-six-hole miniature golf (fee); entertainment center; Paradise Lake (fee). 767 Minard Ave. Phone 360/289-9537.

Motels/Motor Lodges

★★ **CANTERBURY INN.** *643 Ocean Shores Blvd (98569). 360/289-3317; fax 360/289-3420; toll-free 800/562-6678. Email condo@coastaccess.com; www.canterburyinn.com.* 12 rms, 3 story, 33 suites. Apr-Sep: S, D $106; each addl $10; suites $144; under 13 free; lower rates rest of yr. Crib avail.

Parking lot. Indoor pool. TV; cable (premium), VCR avail. Complimentary coffee in rms, newspaper, toll-free calls. Restaurant nearby. Ck-out noon, ck-in 4 pm. Meeting rm. Business servs avail. Coin lndry. Gift shop. Free airport transportation. Exercise equipt. Golf, 18 holes. Tennis. Beach access. Cr cds: A, D, DS, MC, V.

★★ SHILO BEACHFRONT RESORT. *707 Ocean Shores Blvd NW (98569). 360/289-4600; fax 360/289-0355; res 800/222-2244.* 113 rms, 4 story. S, D $119-$199; each addl $15; under 12 free. Crib free. TV; cable (premium), VCR (movies). Indoor pool; whirlpool. Coffee in rms. Restaurant 7 am-9 pm. Bar to midnight. Ck-out noon. Meeting rms. Business servs avail. Sundries. Coin lndry. Exercise equipt; sauna. Refrigerators, microwaves, wet bars. Cr cds: A, C, D, DS, JCB, MC, V.

Resort

★★ THE GREY GULL RESORT. *647 Ocean Shores Blvd NW (98569). 360/289-3381; fax 360/289-3673; toll-free 800/562-9712. Email greygull@the greygull.com; www.thegreygull.com.* 6 rms, 3 story, 32 suites. July-Aug: suites $139; lower rates rest of yr. Crib avail. Pet accepted, some restrictions, fee. Parking lot. Pool, whirlpool. TV; cable, VCR avail. Complimentary coffee in rms, newspaper. Restaurant nearby. Ck-out noon, ck-in 4 pm. Meeting rm. Business servs avail. Coin lndry. Exercise privileges, sauna. Golf, 18 holes. Tennis, 4 courts. Beach access. Bike rentals. Supervised children's activities. Hiking trail. Picnic facilities. Cr cds: A, DS, MC, V.

Olympia

(D-2) *See also Centralia, Tacoma*

Founded 1850 **Pop** 33,840 **Elev** 100 ft
Area code 360
Web www.olympiachamber.com
Information Olympia/Thurston County Chamber of Commerce, 521 Legion Way SE, PO Box 1427, 98507-1427; 360/357-3362 or 800/753-8474

As though inspired by the natural beauties that surround it—Mount Rainier and the Olympic Mountains on the skyline and Puget Sound at its doorstep—Washington's capital city is a carefully groomed, parklike community. Although concentrating on the business of government, Olympia also serves tourists and the needs of nearby military installations. It is a deep-sea port and a manufacturer of wood products, plastics, and mobile homes. The tiny village of Smithfield was chosen in 1851 as the site for a customhouse. The US Collector of Customs prevailed on the citizens to rename the community for the Olympic Mountians. Shortly afterwards, agitation to separate the land north of the Columbia from Oregon began. In 1853 the new territory was proclaimed, with Olympia as territorial capital. The first legislature convened here in 1854, despite Native American unrest that forced construction of a stockade ringing the town. (The 15-foot wall was later dismantled and used to plank the capital's streets.) The Olympia metropolitan area also includes the communities of Lacey and Tumwater, the oldest settlement in the state (1845) north of the Columbia River. The city today has a compact 20-square-block business section and a variety of stores, which attract shoppers from a wide area.

What to See and Do

Capitol Lake. Formed by dam at point where fresh water of Deschutes River empties into salt water of Budd Inlet. From top of dam thousands of salmon may be seen making their way upstream during spawning season starting in mid-Aug. Deschutes Pkwy skirts shore of Capitol Lake, providing scenic drive with dome of state capitol rising to the east. Boating, bicycle, and running trails, playground, picnic tables, concession. (Daily) **FREE**

Millersylvania State Park. More than 800 acres along Deep Lake. Swimming, fishing, boating; hiking, picnicking, camping (hookups). Standard fees. 10 mi S off I-5. Phone 360/753-1519.

Mima Mounds Natural Area. Mounds 8 to 10 feet high and 20 to 30 feet in diameter spread across miles of meadows west of Olympia. Once thought to be ancient burial chambers, they are now believed to be the result of Ice Age freeze-thaw patterns. Trails wind through 500-acre site. Information kiosk, picnic area. Contact Washington Dept of Natural Resources. I-5 S to exit 95 toward Littlerock (Hwy 121), then 128th Ave SW 1 mi to t-junction with Waddell Creek Rd. Turn N 1 mi to preserve. Phone 360/748-2383. **FREE**

Olympic National Forest. More than 630,000 acres. Picturesque streams and rivers, winding ridges, rugged peaks, deep canyons, tree-covered slopes; rain forest, world's largest stand of Douglas fir, public-owned oyster beds; populous herd of Roosevelt elk. Swimming, fishing; hiking, hunting, picnicking, camping (May-Sep). NW of city, reached via US 101, Exit 104. Contact Supervisor, Federal Bldg, 1835 Black Lake Blvd SW, 98502-5623. Phone 360/956-2400.

Percival Landing Park. Pleasant ½-mi walk along marina filled with pleasure crafts and seals. Observation tower; at S end is statue of *The Kiss*. Also Heritage Fountain, popular with children on summer days. On waterfront between Thurston St and 4th Ave. **FREE**

Priest Point Park. Playgrounds, hiking trails, picnic facilities in heavily wooded area with view of Olympic Mts. (Daily) E Bay Dr, overlooks Budd Inlet. **FREE**

State Capital Museum. A 1920 Spanish-style stucco mansion houses art gallery; Native American art and culture exhibits; pioneer exhibits. (Tues-Sun; closed hols) 211 W 21st Ave. Phone 360/753-2580. **Donation**

⭐ **State Capitol Campus.** On Capitol Way between 11th & 14th Aves. Phone 360/586-8687 or 360/586-3460 (tours). In 35-acre park overlooking Capitol Lake and Budd Inlet of Puget Sound are

> **Legislative Building.** A 287-ft dome with 47-ft lantern, neoclassical architecture, lavishly detailed interior. Guide service (daily). Phone 360/586-8687. **FREE**

> **Temple of Justice.** Houses State Supreme Court. (Mon-Fri; closed hols) **FREE**

> **Library Building.** Houses rare books, murals, mosaics. (Mon-Fri; closed hols) **FREE**

> **Capitol grounds.** Grounds lined with Japanese cherry trees attract hundreds of visitors in the spring; plantings are changed seasonally. Also here is a replica of Tivoli Gardens Fountain in Copenhagen, Denmark; sunken gardens, state conservatory (Memorial Day-Labor Day, daily); WWI and Vietnam memorials. Grounds (daily).

Tumwater Falls Park. Gentle walk (1 mi) follows spectacular falls of the Deschutes River. Landscaped grounds, picnicking, playground. Also here are Henderson House Museum, Crosby House, other bldgs from 1850s pioneer settlement. Good view of fall salmon run on man-made fish ladder. (Daily) S of city off I-5, 15 acres. Phone 360/943-2550. **FREE** Adj is

> **Tumwater Valley Athletic Club.** 18-hole golf course. (All yr) Phone 360/943-9500. Indoor swimming pools. Tennis and racquetball courts. Fee for activities. Phone 360/352-3400.

Wolf Haven America. Wolf rehabilitation center on 75 acres; also home to 40 wolves no longer able to live in the wild. Interpretive center, tours, and ecology center. (May-Sep, daily; rest of yr, Wed-Sun; closed Jan and Feb) 3111 Offut Lake Rd. Phone 360/264-4695 or 800/448-9653. ¢¢

Yahiro Gardens. Cooperative project between Olympia and sister city, Yashiro, Japan. Incl pagoda, bamboo grove, pond, and waterfall. (Daily, daylight hrs) At Plum St and Union Ave. **FREE**

Annual Events

Wooden Boat Festival. Percival Landing in Harbor. Wooden boats on display, some open for public viewing. Wooden crafts fair. Second wkend May.

Capital City Marathon and Relay. Eight-km run, children's run, 5-10-km walk, wheelchair division. Phone 360/786-1786. Wkend before Memorial Day wkend.

Super Saturday. Evergreen State College. Arts, crafts, food fair. Early June.

Lakefair. Capitol Lake. Parade, carnival midway, boating and swimming competition, naval vessel tours, flower shows. Mid-July.

Thurston County Fair. Fairgrounds in Lacey. Late July-early Aug.

Harbor Day Festival and Tug Boat Races. Labor Day wkend.

Seasonal Event

Olympia Farmers Market. 700 Capitol Way N. Incl fresh produce, baked goods, food booths, seafood, crafts. Phone 360/352-9096. First wkend in Apr through Dec; wkends only in Apr, Nov, and Dec.

Motels/Motor Lodges

★★ **BEST WESTERN TUMWATER INN.** 5188 Capitol Blvd (98501), S on I-5, Exit 102. 360/956-1235; fax 360/956-1235; res 800/528-1234; toll-free 800/848-4992. Email zmunns@aol.com; www.bestwestern.com. 90 rms, 2 story. June-Aug: S $70; D $83; suites $76; under 13 free; lower rates rest of yr. Crib avail. Pet accepted, some restrictions, fee. Parking lot. TV; cable (premium). Complimentary continental bkfst, coffee in rms, toll-free calls. Restaurant. Ck-out 11 am, ck-in 3 pm. Meeting rm. Business servs avail. Dry cleaning, coin lndry. Exercise equipt, sauna, steam rm. Golf. Hiking trail. Cr cds: A, C, D, DS, ER, JCB, MC, V.

★★ **TYEE HOTEL.** 500 Tyee Dr SW (98512), I-5 Exit 102. 360/352-0511; fax 360/943-6448; toll-free 800/386-8933. 145 rms, 2 story. S $76-$84 D $84; each addl $8; cabana suites $90-$150; studio rms $100; under 17 free; monthly rates. Crib free. TV; cable

(premium). Heated pool. Restaurant 6:30 am-9 pm. Bar 11-1:30 am; entertainment Fri, Sat. Ck-out noon. Meeting rms. Business servs avail. In-rm modem link. Valet serv. Sundries. Beauty salon. Tennis. Picnic tables. Cr cds: A, D, DS, MC, V.

★★★ **WEST COAST OLYMPIA HOTEL.** 2300 Evergreen Park Dr (98502), I-5 Exit 104. 360/943-4000; fax 360/753-9651; res 800/325-4000. www.westcoastolympiahotel.com. 177 rms, 3 story. S $105; D $115; each addl $10; suites $150-$200; under 18 free; some wkend rates. Crib free. Pet accepted. TV; Cable (premium). Heated pool; whirlpool. Complimentary coffee in rms. Restaurant 6 am-11 pm; Sun 7 am-2 pm. Bar 11:30-1 am. Ck-out noon. Coin lndry. Meeting rms. In-rm modem link. Valet serv. Exercise equipt. Lawn games. Wet bar in some suites. Some private patios, balconies. Cr cds: A, DS, MC, V.

Hotel

★★ **RAMADA INN GOVERNOR HOUSE.** 621 S Capitol Way (98501). 360/352-7700; fax 360/943-9349; res 800/272-6232. Email 198@hotel.cendant.com. 93 rms, 8 story, 32 suites. Jan-Mar, July-Sep: S $150; D $160; each addl $10; suites $225; under 19 free; lower rates rest of yr. Crib avail. Pet accepted, fee. Parking garage. Pool, whirlpool. TV; cable (premium), VCR avail, CD avail. Complimentary coffee in rms, newspaper, toll-free calls. Restaurant 7 am-9 pm. Bar. Ck-out noon, ck-in 3 pm. Meeting rms. Internet access avail. Dry cleaning, coin lndry. Exercise equipt, sauna. Golf, 18 holes. Tennis, 4 courts. Hiking trail. Picnic facilities. Cr cds: A, C, D, DS, ER, JCB, MC, V.

Restaurant

★★ **BUDD BAY CAFE.** 525 N Columbia St (98501). 360/357-6963. Email bbaycafe@olywa.net; www.olywa.net/bbaycafe. Specializes in fresh seafood, pasta, prime rib. Hrs: 11 am-10 pm; Sun brunch 9 am-1 pm.

Closed Dec 25. Res accepted. Bar. Lunch $4.25-$12.95; dinner $5.95-$24.95. Sun brunch $15.95. Child's menu. View of Budd Inlet and marina. Cr cds: A, DS, MC, V.

D

Olympic National Park

See also Forks, Port Angeles, Sequim

(119 mi NW of Olympia on US 101)

Web www.nps.gov/olym/

Information Park Headquarters, 600 E Park Ave, Port Angeles 98362; 360/452-0330

In these 1,442 square miles of rugged wilderness are such contrasts as the wettest climate in the contiguous United States (averaging 140-167 inches of precipitation a year) and one of the driest; seascapes and snow-cloaked peaks; glaciers and rain forests; elk and seals. With Olympic National Forest, State Sustained Yield Forest No 1, much private land, and several American Indian reservations, the national park occupies the Olympic Peninsula, due west of Seattle and Puget Sound.

The Spanish explorer Juan Perez was the first European explorer who spotted the Olympic Mountains in 1774. However, the first major western land exploration did not take place until more than a century later. Since then, generations of adventurous tourists have rediscovered Mount Olympus, the highest peak (7,965 feet), several other 7,000-foot peaks, and hundreds of ridges and crests between 5,000 and 6,000 feet high. The architects of these ruggedly contoured mountains are glaciers, which have etched these heights for thousands of years. About 60 glaciers are still actively eroding these mountains—the largest three are on Mount Olympus.

From approximately November through March, the west side of the park is soaked with rain and mist, while the northeast side is the driest area on the West Coast except southern California. The yearly deluge creates a rain forest in the western valleys of the park. Here Sitka spruce,

western hemlock, Douglas fir, and western red cedar grow to heights of 250 feet with eight-foot diameters. Mosses carpet the forest floor and climb tree trunks. Club moss drips from the branches.

Some 50 species of mammals inhabit this wilderness, including several thousand elk, Olympic marmot, black-tailed deer, and black bear. On the park's 60-mile strip of Pacific coastline wilderness, deer, bear, raccoon, and skunk can be seen; seals sun on the offshore rocks or plow through the water beyond the breakers. Mountain and lowland lakes sparkle everywhere. Lake Crescent is among the largest. Some roads are closed in winter.

What to See and Do

Camping. Limited to 14 days. Small camp trailers accommodated at most campgrounds. Campfire programs at some areas (July-Labor Day). ¢¢-¢¢¢

Fishing. Streams and lakes have game fish incl salmon, rainbow, Dolly Varden, eastern brook trout, steelhead, and cutthroat. No license required in the park; permit or punch card is necessary for steelhead and salmon. Contact Park HQ for restrictions. Phone 360/452-0330.

Hiking. Over 600 mi of trails. Obtain maps and trail guides in the park. Guided walks conducted July and Aug.

Mountain climbing. Something for everyone, from the novice to the experienced climber. Climbing parties must register at a ranger station.

Rain forests. Along Hoh, Queets, and Quinault river roads. Hall of Mosses and Spruce Nature Trails and trail to Mt Olympus start at end of Hoh River Rd.

⭐ **Visitor Center.** Has information, natural history exhibits, displays of American Indian culture, orientation slideshow. (Daily) From here, one can enter the park on Heart O' the Hills Pkwy to Hurricane Ridge (there is limited access Nov-Apr). 600 E Park Ave in Port Angeles. 3002 Mt Angeles Rd. Per vehicle ¢¢¢; per person ¢¢ Here is

   Skiing. Hurricane Ridge Winter Use Area. Pomalift, intermediate, and beginner's runs; school, rentals; snack bar. (Late Dec-late

Hall of Mosses in Hoh Rain Forest, Olympic National Park

Mar, Sat and Sun) Also snowshoeing and cross-country ski trails.

Resort

★ **SOL DUC HOT SPRINGS.** *Sol Duc Rd and US 101 (98362), 30 mi W of Port Angeles on US 101, then S 12 mi. 360/327-3583; fax 360/327-3593; res 360/327-3583. Email pamsdr@aol. com; www.northolympic.com/solduc.* Apr-Oct: S, D $98; each addl $15; lower rates rest of yr. Crib avail. Parking lot. Pool, children's pool, lifeguard. TV; cable (premium), VCR avail, CD avail. Restaurant 7:30 am-9 pm. Ck-out 11 am, ck-in 4 pm. Fax servs avail. Gift shop. Downhill skiing. Supervised children's activities. Hiking trail. Picnic facilities. Cr cds: A, DS, MC, V.

Omak

(B-6) *See also Winthrop*

Settled 1900 **Pop** 4,117 **Elev** 837 ft
Area code 509 **Zip** 98841

Information Tourist Information Center, 401 Omak Ave; 509/826-4218 or 800/225-6625

This lumber town is the largest in the north central part of Washington and is also known for its production of apples and its many orchards. The name of the town and nearby lake and mountain is derived from a Native American word meaning "good medicine." Omak is the "baby's breath capital of the world," a flower much used commercially by florists.

What to See and Do

Conconully State Park. Approx 80 acres along Conconully Reservoir; swimming, fishing, boating; picnicking, snowmobiling, camping. Standard fees. (Daily) 5 mi N on US 97, then 10 mi NW on Conconully Hwy (unnumbered road). Phone 509/826-7408.

Okanogan National Forest. Nearly 1.75 million acres. In the northern part of the forest is 530,031-acre Pasayten Wilderness. In the southwestern part of the forest is 95,976-acre Lake Chelan-Sawtooth Wilderness. Hunting and fishing are plentiful; picnicking and camping at 41 sites, most of which have trailer spaces; 8 boating sites.

Thirty-eight mi W of town at Methow Valley Airport, between Winthrop and Twisp, is the North Cascades Smokejumper Base; visitors welcome. One-mi paved wheelchair trail to Rainy Lake at Rainy Pass. NE and NW of town, reached via US 97, WA 20. Contact Supervisor, 1240 S Second Ave, Okanogan 98840. Phone 509/826-3275. **FREE**

Annual Event

Stampede and Suicide Race. Rodeo events; horses and riders race down a cliff and across the Okanogan River. Western art show. Native American dance contests. Encampment with more than 100 teepees. Phone 509/826-1002. Second wkend Aug.

Motels/Motor Lodges

★ **CEDARS INN.** *1 Apple Way (98840), S on WA 215 to jct WA 20 and US 97.* 509/422-6431; fax 509/422-4214. 78 rms, 3 story, 6 kits. No elvtr. S $46-$52; D, kit. units $52-$57; each addl $5; under 12 free; higher rates Stampede. Crib free. Pet accepted; $5. TV; cable, VCR avail (movies $1.50). Pool. Restaurant 6:30 am-10 pm. Bar 11 am-11:30 pm. Ck-out noon. Coin lndry. Meeting rms. Business servs avail. Cr cds: A, C, D, DS, ER, MC, V.

★ **MOTEL NICHOLAS.** *527 E Grape Ave (98841), ½ mi N on WA 215.* 509/826-4611; toll-free 800/404-4611. 21 rms, 1 story. May-Oct: S $34; D $42; each addl $4; lower rates rest of yr. Crib avail. Pet accepted, fee. TV; cable (premium). Complimentary coffee in rms, toll-free calls. Restaurant nearby. Ck-out 11 am, ck-in 10 pm. Fax servs avail. Picnic facilities. Cr cds: A, C, D, DS, MC, V.

Orcas Island

(see San Juan Islands)

Othello

(D-6) *See also Moses Lake*

Pop 4,638 **Elev** 1,038 ft
Area code 509 **Zip** 99344
Web www.ncw.net:80/chambers/othello

Information Chamber of Commerce, 33 E Larch; 509/488-2683 or 800/684-2556

Another beneficiary of the Grand Coulee project, Othello had a population of only 526 in 1950. The Potholes Canal runs by the town, linking the Potholes Reservoir and the smaller Scooteney Reservoir.

Annual Events

Sandhill Crane Festival. Wildlife Refuge. View migrating birds. Guided tours, wildlife workshops. Late Mar-early Apr.

Adams County Fair. Carnival, entertainment, tractor pull, exhibits. Mid-Sep.

Motels/Motor Lodges

★★ **BEST WESTERN LINCOLN INN.** *1020 E Cedar (99344).* 509/488-5671; fax 509/488-5084; res 800/528-1234; toll-free 800/240-7865. 50 rms, 2 story. S, D $58-$68; each addl $5; kit units $61-$71; higher rates hunting season, concerts at Gorge. Pet accepted; $10. TV; cable (premium), VCR. Pool. Coffee in rms. Restaurant opp 7 am-10 pm. Ck-out 11 am. Coin lndry. Business servs avail. Exercise equipt; sauna. Some refrigerators, microwaves. Cr cds: A, DS, MC, V.

★ **CABANA MOTEL.** *665 E Windsor St (99344).* 509/488-2605; fax 509/488-0885; toll-free 800/442-4581. 55 rms., 3 kit. units. S $30-$45; D $46-$55; each addl $5; kit. units $45-$70. Crib free. TV; cable (premium). Heated pool; whirlpool. Restaurant nearby. Ck-out 11 am. Some refrigerators, microwaves. Cr cds: A, DS, MC, V.

Packwood (E-4)

Pop 950 (est) **Elev** 1,051 ft
Area code 360 **Zip** 98361

Named for William Packwood, a colorful explorer who helped open this region, the town is a provisioning point for modern-day explorers of Mount Rainier National Park (see) and Snoqualmie and Gifford Pinchot national forests. A Ranger District office of the Gifford Pinchot National Forest (see VANCOUVER) is located here. The area abounds in edible wild berries and mushrooms; no permit is needed for picking. Winter and spring are popular with game watchers; elk, deer, bear, and goats can be spotted in the local cemetery as well as in the nearby parks.

What to See and Do

Goat Rocks Wilderness. Over 105,000 acres of alpine beauty with elevations from 3,000-8,200 ft. Jagged pinnacles rising above snowfields, cascading streams, mountain meadows with wildflowers; this is the home of the pika and mountain goat. E and S of town, in Gifford Pinchot National Forest.

Motels/Motor Lodges

★★ **COWLITZ RIVER LODGE.** 13069 US 12 PO Box 488 (98361). 360/494-4444; fax 360/494-2075; toll-free 888/305-2185. www. escapetothemountains.com. 32 rms, 2 story. June-Sep: S $57; D $62; each addl $5; under 6 free; lower rates rest of yr. Parking lot. TV; cable (premium), VCR avail. Complimentary continental bkfst. Restaurant 6 am-10 pm. Ck-out 11 am, ck-in 2 pm. Meeting rm. Fax servs avail. Bellhops. Coin lndry. Golf, 9 holes. Downhill skiing. Bike rentals. Hiking trail. Picnic facilities. Cr cds: A, D, MC, V.

D ⚹ 🐾 ≋ 👤 ≋ 🔥

★ **CREST TRAIL LODGE.** 12729 US 12 (98361). 360/494-4944; fax 360/494-6629; toll-free 800/477-5339. Email cresttrail@lewiscounty.com; www. mountsthelens.com. 27 rms, 2 story. June-Sep: S $58; D $66; each addl $5;

children $5; under 7 free; lower rates rest of yr. Crib avail, fee. Parking lot. TV; cable, VCR avail. Complimentary continental bkfst, coffee in rms, toll-free calls. Restaurant nearby 5 am-10 pm. Ck-out 11 am, ck-in 1 pm. Business servs avail. Bellhops. Whirlpool. Downhill skiing. Bike rentals. Hiking trail. Picnic facilities. Cr cds: A, DS, MC, V.

D ⚹ 🐾 ≋ 👤 ≋ 🔥 SC

★★ **TIMBERLINE VILLAGE RESORT.** 13807 US 12 (98004). 360/494-9224. 21 rms, 3 story. Some A/C. July-mid-Sep: S, D $45-$63; each addl $5; suites $73; under 10 free; lower rates rest of yr. Crib free. Pet accepted; $5. TV; cable. Complimentary continental bkfst, coffee in rms. Ck-out 11 am. Downhill ski 18 mi. Cr cds: A, MC, V.

D 🐾 ≋ 🐾 🔥

Pasco

(E-6) *See also Kennewick, Richland*

Founded 1880 **Pop** 20,337 **Elev** 381 ft
Area code 509 **Zip** 99301
Web www.cbvcp.com/pascochamber/

Information Greater Pasco Area Chamber of Commerce, 1600 N 20th, Suite A, PO Box 550; 509/547-9755

One of the "tri-cities" (see KENNEWICK and RICHLAND), Pasco has been nurtured by transportation throughout its history. Still a rail, air, highway, and waterway crossroads, Pasco is enjoying increased farm and industrial commerce thanks to the Columbia Basin project.

What to See and Do

Ice Harbor Lock and Dam. The first of four dams on Lower Snake River between Pasco and Lewiston, ID. One of the world's highest (103 ft) single-lift navigation locks. There is a powerhouse on the S shore and a fish ladder on each side of the river. (Daily) Visitor Center (Apr-Oct, daily), fish viewing rm, self-guided tours. Lake Sacajawea, with 4 developed parks, has swimming, waterskiing, fishing, boat ramps; picnicking, camping (May-Sep; hookups; fee). For info contact Resource Mgr, Rte 6, Box 693, 99301. 9 mi E, off WA 124. Phone 509/547-7781. **FREE**

Kahlotus. Town redone in Old West atmosphere. Many of the businesses and bldgs are museums in themselves. Near Palouse Falls (see DAYTON) and Lower Monumental Dam. 42 mi NE via US 395 and WA 260.

McNary Lock and Dam. Single-lift navigation lock. Dam is 7,365 ft long, 92 ft high, and is the easternmost of 4 multipurpose dams on the lower Columbia River between Portland, OR and Pasco. The Columbia River forms Lake Wallula here. The 61-mi long lake reaches beyond the Tri-Cities up to Ice Harbor Dam on Snake River. Developed parks with boating, marinas, water skiing, swimming, fishing; picnicking and camping nearby. Self-guided tours of hydropower, navigation, and salmon passage facilities. (Daily; guided tours in summer) For information contact Park Ranger, PO Box 1441, Umatilla, OR 97882. 3 mi S of WA 14 in Umatilla, OR. Phone 541/922-4388. **FREE**

Preston Estate Vineyards. Self-guided tour of tasting rm, oak aging casks, storage tanks, and bottling line; park with picnic and play area, amphitheater, gazebo, pond. (Daily; closed hols) 5 mi N via US 395, watch for road sign. Phone 509/545-1990. **FREE**

Sacajawea State Park. Site where Lewis and Clark camped in 1805. Approx 280 acres. Swimming, fishing, boating (launch, dock); picnicking. (Daily) 2 mi SE off US 12. Phone 509/545-2361.

Annual Events

Jazz Unlimited. Columbia Basin Community College. Phone 509/547-0511. Usually 2nd and 3rd wkend Apr.

Tri-Cities Water Follies. Events scheduled throughout month leading to hydroplane races on Columbia River on last wkend of month. Phone 509/547-5531. July.

Fiery Food Festival. Phone 509/545-0738. Wkend after Labor Day.

Motel/Motor Lodge

★ **VINEYARD INN.** *1800 W Lewis St (99301), near Tri-Cities Airport. 509/547-0791; fax 509/547-8632; toll-free 800/824-5457.* 165 rms, 2 story, 44 kits. S $40.50-$48; D $50-$60; each addl $5; kit. units, studio rms $50-$60; under 12 free; higher rates hydro races. Crib $6. Pet accepted; $5/day. TV; cable (premium), VCR avail. Indoor pool; whirlpool. Complimentary continental bkfst. Ck-out noon. Coin lndry. Business servs avail. Airport, railroad station, bus depot transportation. Cr cds: A, C, D, DS, MC, V.

🄳 ➡️ 🐾 ⌁ 🛬 ⬛ 🐾

Hotel

★★★ **DOUBLETREE HOTEL.** *2525 N 20th St (99301), N of downtown. 509/547-0701; fax 509/547-4278; res 800/222-8733. Email salesdt@double treepasco.com; www.hiltonhotels.com.* 269 rms, 3 story, 10 suites. Apr-Oct: S, D $114; suites $225; under 12 free; lower rates rest of yr. Crib avail. Pet accepted, some restrictions. Parking lot. Pool, whirlpool. TV; cable (premium), VCR avail. Complimentary coffee in rms, newspaper, toll-free calls. Restaurant. Bar. Ck-out noon, ck-in 3 pm. Conference center, meeting rms. Business center. Bellhops. Dry cleaning. Gift shop. Free airport transportation. Exercise equipt. Golf, 18 holes. Tennis, 8 courts. Video games. Cr cds: A, C, D, DS, MC, V.

🄳 ➡️ 🎿 ⛷️ ⌁ 🏃 ⬛ ✈️ 🐾 🎣

Port Angeles

(B-2) *See also Neah Bay, Sequim*

Pop 17,710 **Elev** 32 ft **Area code** 360 **Zip** 98362
Information Chamber of Commerce, 121 E Railroad; 360/452-2363

Sitting atop the Olympic Peninsula, Port Angeles has the Olympic Mountains at its back and Juan de Fuca Strait at its shoreline; just 17 miles across the Strait is Victoria, BC (see). Ediz Hook, a sandspit, protects the harbor and helps make it the first American port of entry for ships coming to Puget Sound from all parts of the Pacific; there is a US Coast Guard Air Rescue Station here. A Spanish captain who entered the harbor in 1791 named the village he found here Port of Our Lady of the Angels, a name that has survived in abbreviated form. The fishing fleet, pulp, paper and lumber mills, as well as tourism are its economic mainstays today.

Port Angeles is the headquarters for Olympic National Park (see). It is an excellent starting point for expeditions to explore the many faces of the peninsula.

What to See and Do

Ferry service to Victoria, BC Canada. (see) A 90-min trip; departs from Coho ferry terminal to Victoria's Inner Harbour. (Daily; summer, 4 trips; spring and fall, 2 trips; rest of yr, 1 trip) Contact Black Ball Transport Inc, 10777 Main St, Suite 106, Bellevue 98004. (For Border Crossing Regulations see MAKING THE MOST OF YOUR TRIP.) Phone 206/622-2222; or 604/386-2202 (Victoria). In Port Angeles phone 360/457-4491. Individuals ¢¢¢; Car and driver ¢¢¢¢¢

Olympic National Park. (see) HQ, 600 Park Ave.

Olympic Raft & Guide Service. River rafting in Olympic National Park. Phone 360/452-1443.

Olympic Van Tours, Inc. Depart from Coho ferry terminal. Unique, interpretive sightseeing tours into Olympic National Park (3 and 8 hrs). Tours coincide with ferry schedule. Res advised. Also shuttle service to and from Seattle. For schedule and fees contact PO Box 2201. Phone 360/452-3858.

Annual Event

Clallam County Fair. Mid-Aug.

Motels/Motor Lodges

★ **PORT ANGELES INN.** *111 E 2nd St (98362). 360/452-9285; fax 360/452-7935; res 800/421-0706. Email waterview@portangelesinn.com; www.portangelesinn.com.* 24 rms, 3 story, 3 suites. May-Oct: Crib avail. Parking lot. TV; cable (premium). Complimentary continental bkfst, coffee in rms, toll-free calls. Restau-

rant nearby. Ck-out 11 am, ck-in 3 pm. Business servs avail. Exercise privileges. Golf. Tennis. Downhill skiing. Beach access. Bike rentals. Hiking trail. Cr cds: A, C, D, DS, MC, V.

★★ **UPTOWN INN.** *101 E 2nd St (98362). 360/457-9434; fax 360/457-5915; toll-free 800/858-3812.* 35 rms, 1-3 story, 4 kits. No A/C. June-Oct: S, D $89-$130; each addl $5; kit. units $125; under 12 free; wkly, monthly rates; lower rates rest of yr. Crib free. Pet accepted, some restrictions. TV; cable (premium). Complimentary continental bkfst, coffee in rms. Restaurant nearby. Ck-out 11 am. Refrigerators, microwaves. Scenic view. Cr cds: A, DS, MC, V.

Resort

★ **RED LION HOTEL-PORT ANGELES.** *221 N Lincoln (98362). 360/452-9215; fax 360/452-4734; res 800/redlion. Email jbeckham@olypen.com; www.portangeleshotel.com.* 187 rms, 2 story. No A/C. May-Sep: S $100-$140; D $115-$155; suites $150-$175; each addl $10; under 18 free; some lower rates rest of yr. Crib free. Pet accepted. TV; cable. Heated pool; whirlpool. Complimentary coffee in rms. Restaurant 5:30 am-midnight. Ck-out noon. Sundries. Health club privileges. Private balconies. Overlooks harbor. Cr cds: A, DS, MC, V.

B&Bs/Small Inns

★★★ **DOMAINE MADELEINE.** *146 Wildflower Ln (98362), on Finn Hall Rd. 360/457-4174; fax 360/457-3037; toll-free 888/811-8376. Email romance@domainemadeleine.com; www. domainemadeleine.com.* 5 rms, 2 story, 2 suites. Mar-Oct: S $175; D $185; each addl $30; suites $195; children $25; under 17 free; lower rates rest of yr. Parking lot. TV; cable, VCR avail, CD avail. Complimentary full bkfst, coffee in rms, toll-free calls. Restaurant 5-10 pm, closed Mon. Ck-out 11 am, ck-in 4 pm. Meeting rm. Business servs avail. Golf. Downhill skiing. Picnic facilities. Cr cds: A, DS, MC, V.

⊠ ⚒ ▦ ▨ ♨

★★ **FIVE SEASUNS BED & BREAK-FAST.** *1006 S Lincoln St (98362), near airport. 360/452-8248; fax 360/417-0465; toll-free 800/708-0777. Email info@seasuns.com; www.seasuns.com.* 4 rms, 2 story. May-Oct: S $85; D $145; lower rates rest of yr. Parking lot. TV; cable, VCR avail. Complimentary full bkfst, coffee in rms. Restaurant nearby. Ck-out 11 am. Business servs avail. Gift shop. Free airport transportation. Golf, 18 holes. Tennis, 2 courts. Cr cds: A, DS, MC, V.

⊠ ⚒ ⛳ ▦ ♨

★★★ **TUDOR INN BED & BREAK-FAST.** *1108 S Oak St (98362). 360/452-3138; fax 360/452-3138; res 360/452-3138. Email info@tudorinn. com; www.tudorinn.com.* 5 rms, 2 story. No A/C. No rm phones. Mid-May-mid-Oct: S $80-$115; D $85-$125; lower rates rest of yr. Children over 12 yrs only. TV in sitting rm; VCR avail (free movies). Complimentary full bkfst; afternoon refreshments. Ck-out 11 am, ck-in 4-7 pm. Downhill/x-country ski 16 mi. View of Olympic Mts. Antiques, grand piano. English gardens. Totally non-smoking. Cr cds: A, DS, MC, V.

⊠ ✕ ▦ ♨

Restaurants

★★ **BELLA ITALIA.** *117 E 1st St #B (98362). 360/457-5442. Email bella@ olypen.com; www.northolympic.com/ bella.* Specializes in crab cakes, fresh seafood, organic produce. Own pastries. Hrs: 4-11 pm; winter hrs vary. Closed Thanksgiving, Dec 25. Res accepted. Bar. Dinner a la carte entrees: $6-$18. Child's menu. Two dining rms divided by espresso and wine bar; windows overlook courtyard. Cr cds: A, D, DS, MC, V.

D

★★ **BUSHWHACKER.** *1527 E 1st St (98362). 360/457-4113.* Specializes in prime rib, salmon, halibut. Salad bar. Hrs: 4:30-10 pm; Fri, Sat to 11 pm; Sun 5-9 pm. Closed Thanksgiving, Dec 24, 25. Bar. Dinner $6.95-$19.95. Child's menu. Parking. Northwest decor. Cr cds: A, DS, MC, V.

D

★★★ **C'EST SI BON.** *23 Cedar Park Dr (98362). 360/452-8888.* Specializes in French cuisine. Hrs: 5-11 pm. Closed Mon. Res accepted. Bar. Wine list. Dinner a la carte entrees: $19.25-$22.50. Child's menu. Parking. Romantic atmosphere. Cr cds: A, DS, MC, V.

D

★ **LANDINGS.** *115 E Railroad Ave Suite 101 (98362), adj Victoria Ferry Dock. 360/457-6768.* Specializes in seafood, hamburgers. Hrs: 6:30 am-9:30 pm. Closed Jan 1, Dec 25. Bar. Bkfst $3-$8; lunch, dinner $3-$12. Parking. Cr cds: A, D, DS, MC, V.

D

★★★ **TOGA'S INTERNATIONAL CUISINE.** *122 W Lauridsen Blvd (98362). 360/452-1952.* Specializes in beef fillets, prawns, lamb chops. Own baking. Hrs: 5-10 pm. Closed Sun, Mon; hols; Sep. Res required. Dinner $13.95-$24.95. Child's menu. Intimate dining in private residence; windows offer mountain view. Cr cds: MC, V.

D

Port Gamble

(B-3) *See also Port Ludlow, Seattle*

Settled 1853 **Pop** 300 (est)
Area code 360 **Zip** 98364
Information Pope and Talbot, Public Relations Dept, PO Box 217; 360/297-3341

Captain William Talbot, a native of Maine, discovered the vast Puget Sound timberlands and located what has become the oldest continuously operating sawmill in North America here. Spars for the ships of the world were a specialty. The community, built by the company and still owned by it, gradually developed a distinctive appearance because of its unusual (to this part of the country) New England architectural style.

The company, realizing an opportunity to preserve a bit of the past, has rebuilt and restored more than 30 homes, commercial buildings, and St. Paul's Episcopal Church. Replicas of gas lamps and underground wiring have replaced street lighting. The entire town has been declared a historic district.

What to See and Do

Hood Canal Nursery. Self-guided tour covers storage and maintenance building, soil mixing, pump house and chemical storage, water reservoir, greenhouses with a capacity of 3½ million seedlings. (Mon-Fri) W edge of town. Phone 360/297-7555. **FREE**

Kitsap Memorial State Park. Over 50 acres. Saltwater swimming, scuba diving, fishing, boating (mooring); hiking, picnicking, shelters, camping (dump station). Standard fees. 4 mi S on WA 3. Phone 360/779-3205.

Of Sea and Shore Museum. One of the largest shell collections in the country. Gift, book shop. (Mid-May-mid-Sep, Tues-Sun; rest of yr, wkends; closed Jan 1, Dec 25) Country Store Bldg, Rainier St. Phone 360/297-2426. **FREE**

Port Gamble Historic Museum. Exhibits trace the history of the area and the timber company. Displays arranged in order of time: replica of old saw filing rm; San Francisco office, captain's cabin from ship, individual rms from hotels and houses; Forest of the Future exhibit. (Memorial Day-Labor Day, daily) Downhill side of the General Store. Phone 360/297-8074. ¢

Port Ludlow

See also Port Gamble, Sequim

Settled 1878 **Pop** 500 (est) **Elev** 0-30 ft **Area code** 360 **Zip** 98365

Resort

★★ **PORT LUDLOW RESORT & CONFERENCE CENTER.** *200 Olympic Pl (98365). 360/437-2222; fax 360/437-2182; toll free 800/732-1239. Email resort@portludlowresort. com; www.portludlowresort.com.* 125 rms, 52 suites. May-Oct: S, D $120; each addl $20; suites $165; under 12 free; lower rates rest of yr. Crib avail. Parking lot. Indoor/outdoor pools, lifeguard, whirlpool. TV; cable, VCR avail. Restaurant. Bar. Meeting rms. Business servs avail. Coin lndry. Gift

shop. Exercise equipt, sauna. Golf. Tennis, 4 courts. Beach access. Bike rentals. Hiking trail. Picnic facilities. Cr cds: A, MC, V.

B&B/Small Inn

★★★ **HERON BEACH INN.** *1 Heron Rd (98365). 360/437-0411; fax 360/437-0310. www.portludlowconnect ions.com.* 37 rms, 3 story, 3 suites. No A/C. June-Oct: S, D $155-$215; each addl $35; suites $300-$450; under 18 free; golf plan; hol rates; summer wkends (2-day min); lower rates rest of yr. Crib avail. Pet accepted, some restrictions; $50 deposit. TV; VCR (free movies). Complimentary continental bkfst, coffee in rms. Restaurant (see HERON BEACH INN DINING ROOM). Ck-out 11 am, ck-in after 3 pm. Meeting rms. Business servs avail. In-rm modem link. Golf privileges; greens fee $50-$55, putting green, driving range. Lawn games. Refrigerators. Balconies. Built in 1994 to resemble estate in Maine. Views of Olympic and Cascade Mts. On shore, beach. Totally nonsmoking. Cr cds: A, D, DS, MC, V.

Restaurant

★★★ **HERON BEACH INN DINING ROOM.** *1 Heron Rd. 360/437-0411. www.heronbeachinn.com.* Specializes in fresh game and seafood. Own herbs. Hrs: noon-9:30 pm; Mon, Tues from 5:30 pm; winter hrs vary. Res accepted. Bar. Wine cellar. Lunch, dinner $12-$24. Child's menu. Views of bay, marina and Olympic Mts. Cr cds: A, D, DS, MC, V.

Port Townsend

See also Coupeville, Everett, Oak Harbor

Settled 1851 **Pop** 7,001 **Elev** 100 ft **Area code** 360 **Zip** 98368
Web www.olympus.net/ptchamber
Information Tourist Information Center, 2437 E Sims Way; 360/385-2722

Located on the Quimper Peninsula, at the northeast corner of the Olympic Peninsula, this was once a busy port city served by sailing vessels and sternwheelers. Captain George Vancouver came ashore in 1792 and named this spot Port Townshend, after an English nobleman. Port Townsend is a papermill town with boat building and farming.

What to See and Do

Rothschild House. (1868) Furnished in original style; flower and herb gardens. (May-Oct, daily; rest of yr, Sat, Sun, and hols only) Franklin & Taylor Sts. Phone 360/385-2722. ¢

State parks.

Old Fort Townsend (Historical). Approx 380 acres. Posted site of fort established in 1856, abandoned in 1895. Swimming, scuba diving, bank fishing; hiking, picnicking, camping. (Mid-Apr-mid-Sep) Standard fees. 3 mi S on WA 20. Phone 360/385-4730.

Fort Worden. Approx 340 acres. Home of Centrum Foundation, with poetry and visual arts symposiums. fiction writer's workshop; fiddle-tune, jazz, and folk dance festivals (phone 360/385-3102). Park has many historic bldgs, incl several Victorian houses (overnight stays avail by res). Swimming, underwater park with scuba diving, fishing, boating (launch, moorage); hiking, nature trails, tennis, picnicking, camping. Marine Science Center (Apr-Oct, Sat and Sun; summer hrs vary; fee). Coast Artillery Museum (summer months, Sat and Sun; fee). Youth hostel (phone 360/385-0655). Standard fees. 1 mi N. Phone 360/385-4730 or 800/233-0321.

Fort Flagler. More than 780 acres. Saltwater swimming, scuba diving, fishing, boating (launch, mooring); hiking, picnicking, camping (res required Memorial Day-Labor Day). Nature study; forested areas, some military areas. Standard fees. 20 mi SE on Marrowstone Island. Phone 360/385-1259.

Annual Events

Jefferson County Fair. Agricultural and 4-H displays, livestock shows. Wkend mid-Aug.

Wooden Boat Festival. Displays, classes, and lectures. First wkend after Labor Day.

House Tours. Phone 360/385-2722. Third wkend Sep.

Hotels

★★ **THE OLD ALCOHOL PLANT.** *310 Alcohol Loop Rd (98339), 9 mi S. 360/385-7030; fax 360/385-6955; toll-free 800/785-7030. www.alcoholplant. com.* 28 rms, 3 story. Mid-May-mid-Oct: S $49-$99; D $79-$99; each addl $10; suites $90-$250; under 14 free; wkly, monthly rates; lower rates rest of yr. Crib free. Pet accepted; $10. TV; cable (premium), VCR (movies $6). Restaurant 7 am-10 pm; Fri, Sat to 11 pm. Bar. Ck-out 11 am. Meeting rms. Exercise equipt. Game rm. Picnic tables. Former alcohol plant built 1910. Marina. Cr cds: A, DS, MC, V.

D 🔄 🛁 🎿 🏋 🎿 🏊 🔥

★★ **PALACE.** *1004 Water St (98368). 360/385-0773; fax 360/385-0780; toll-free 800/962-0741. Email palace@olympus.net; www.olympus.net/ palace.* 15 rms, 2 story. No A/C. No rm phones. May-mid-Sep: S, D $69-$139; each addl $10; suites $109-$129; under 13 free; lower rates rest of yr. Crib free. Pet accepted. TV; cable. Complimentary continental bkfst. Restaurant 6:30 am-10 pm. Ck-out noon. Meeting rms. Coin lndry. Some refrigerators. Cr cds: A, DS, MC, V.

🛁 🎿 🏋 🎿 🔥

B&Bs/Small Inns

★★★ **ANN STARRETT MANSION VICTORIAN BED & BREAKFAST.** *744 Clay St (98368). 360/385-3205; fax 360/385-2976; res 800/321-0644. Email edel@starrettmansion.com; www. starrettmansion.com.* 7 rms, 4 story, 2 suites. June-Sep: S, D $185; each addl $35; suites $225; children $35; lower rates rest of yr. Street parking. TV; cable, VCR avail. Complimentary full bkfst, coffee in rms, toll-free calls. Restaurant nearby. Meeting rms. Fax servs avail. Concierge. Exercise equipt. Golf, 18 holes. Tennis, 4 courts. Beach access. Bike rentals. Hiking trail. Cr cds: A, DS, MC, V.

🛁 🎿 🏋 🎿 🔥

★★ **BISHOP VICTORIAN GUEST SUITES.** *714 Washington St (98368). 360/385-6122; fax 360/379-1840; res 800/824-4738. Email bishop@waypt; www.bishopvictorian.com.* 3 story, 15 suites. May-Oct: S, D $119; each addl $15; suites $119; lower rates rest of yr. Crib avail. Pet accepted, some restrictions, fee. Parking lot. TV; cable, VCR avail. Complimentary continental bkfst, coffee in rms, toll-free calls. Restaurant nearby. 24-hr rm serv. Meeting rms. Business center. Exercise privileges. Golf. Tennis, 5 courts. Cr cds: A, DS, MC, V.

★★★ **CHANTICLEER INN.** *1208 Franklin St (98368). 360/385-6239; fax 360/385-3377; toll-free 800/858-9421. Email chanticleer@waypt.com; www.northolympic.com/chanticleer.* 5 rms, 3 with shower only, 2 story. S $90-$140; D $95-$145; each addl $10. Children over 12 yrs only. Complimentary full bkfst; afternoon refreshments. Restaurant nearby. Ck-out 10:30 am, ck-in 3-6 pm. Victorian house built in 1876; antiques. Totally nonsmoking. Cr cds: A, DS, MC, V.

★★ **THE ENGLISH INN.** *718 F St (98368). 360/385-5302; fax 360/385-5302; toll-free 800/254-5302. Email deborah@english-inn.com; www.english-inn.com.* 4 rms, 2 story. June-Sep: S $85; D $105; each addl $15; under 12 free; lower rates rest of yr. Street parking. TV; cable, VCR avail, CD avail. Complimentary full bkfst, coffee in rms. Restaurant nearby. Ck-out 11 am, ck-in 3 pm. Meeting rm. Golf, 18 holes. Hiking trail. Cr cds: MC, V.

★★★ **FW HASTINGS HOUSE OLD CONSULATE.** *313 Walker St (98368). 360/385-6753; fax 360/385-2097; toll-free 800/300-6753. Email info@oldconsulateinn.com; www.oldconsulateinn.com.* 8 rms, 5 with shower only, 3 story, 3 suites. No rm phones. June-Sep: S, D $96-$140; each addl $45; suites $140-$195; wkends (2-day min); lower rates rest of yr. Children over 12 yrs only. TVs; cable, VCR avail. Whirlpool. Complimentary full bkfst; afternoon refreshments. Ck-out 11 am, ck-in 3-6 pm.

Business servs avail. Free airport transportation. Queen Anne Victorian house built in 1889; many antiques. Totally nonsmoking. Cr cds: MC, V.

★★★ **HOLLY HILL HOUSE B&B.** *611 Polk St (98368). 360/385-5619; fax 360/385-3041; res 800/435-1454. Email hollyhill@olympus.net; www.hollyhillhouse.com.* 5 rms, 2 story, 1 suite. May-Oct: D $110; suites $155; under 12 free; lower rates rest of yr. Street parking. TV; cable. Complimentary full bkfst, newspaper. Restaurant nearby. Ck-out 10:30 am, ck-in 3 pm. Meeting rm. Beach access. Bike rentals. Hiking trail. Picnic facilities. Cr cds: MC, V.

★★★ **JAMES HOUSE.** *1238 Washington St (98368). 360/385-1238; fax 360/379-5551; toll-free 800/385-1238. Email innkeeper@jameshouse.com; www.jameshouse.com.* 12 rms, 3 story, 3 suites. May-Oct: S $100; D $135; each addl $30; suites $150; lower rates rest of yr. Street parking. TV; cable (premium), VCR avail. Complimentary full bkfst, newspaper, toll-free calls. Restaurant, closed Tue. Ck-out 11 am, ck-in 3 pm. Meeting rm. Internet dock/port avail. Concierge. Exercise privileges. Golf, 18 holes. Tennis, 6 courts. Beach access. Bike rentals. Hiking trail. Cr cds: A, DS, MC, V.

★★★ **LIZZIE'S BED & BREAKFAST.** *731 Pierce St (98368). 360/385-4168; fax 360/385-9467; toll-free 800/700-4168. Email wickline@olympus.net; www.lizziesvictorian.com.* 7 rms, 2 story. May-Oct: S, D $90; each addl $20; suites $135; lower rates rest of yr. Parking lot. TV; cable (premium), VCR avail. Complimentary full bkfst, newspaper. Restaurant. Ck-out 11 am, ck-in 4 pm. Meeting rm. Business servs avail. Concierge. Golf. Cr cds: DS, MC, V.

★★ **MANRESA CASTLE.** *7th and Sheridan (98368). 360/385-5750; fax 360/385-5883; toll-free 800/732-1281.* 40 rms, 3 story. No A/C. May-mid-Oct: S $65-$165; D $75-$175; each addl $10; lower rates rest of yr. TV;

cable (premium). Complimentary continental bkfst. Restaurant (see also MANRESA CASTLE). Bar 4-11 pm. Ck-out 11 am. Business servs avail. Castle built 1892; period furniture. View of bay from many rms. Cr cds: DS, MC, V.

★★★ **RAVENSCROFT.** *533 Quincy St (98368). 360/385-2784; fax 360/385-6724; toll-free 800/782-2691. Email ravenscroft@olympus.net; www. ravenscroftinn.com.* 8 rms, 4 story, 2 suites. May-Sep: S, D $190; suites $190; lower rates rest of yr. Parking lot. TV; cable (premium), VCR avail, VCR avail, CD avail. Complimentary full bkfst, newspaper. Restaurant nearby. Ck-out 11 am, ck-in 3 pm. Meeting rms. Business servs avail. Concierge. Gift shop. Exercise privileges. Golf, 18 holes. Downhill skiing. Beach access. Hiking trail. Picnic facilities. Cr cds: A, DS, MC, V.

★★ **THE SWAN HOTEL.** *222 Monroe St (98368). 360/385-1718; fax 360/379-1840; res 800/824-4738; toll-free 800/776-1718. Email bishop@ waypt.com; www.swanhotel.com.* 9 rms, 3 story, 5 kit. suites, 4 kit. cottages. May-Sep: kit. suites $105-$400; kit. cottages $85-$105; under 12 free; wkly rates; higher rates special events; lower rates rest of yr. Crib free. Pet accepted, some restrictions; $15 and daily fees. TV; cable, VCR avail (movies). Complimentary coffee in rms. Restaurant nearby. Ck-out 11 am, ck-in 3 pm. Meeting rms. Business servs avail. In-rm modem link. Refrigerators; microwaves avail. Some balconies. Cr cds: A, DS, MC, V.

Restaurants

★★ **KHU LARB THAI.** *225 Adams St (98368). 360/385-5023.* Hrs: 11 am-9 pm; Fri, Sat to 10 pm. Res accepted. Lunch, dinner a la carte entrees: $6.95-$10.95. Entertainment. Thai objets d'art. Cr cds: MC, V.

★★★ **LONNY'S.** *2330 Washington St (98368). 360/385-0700. www. lonnys.com.* Specializes in fresh seafood, local produce. Own baking, pasta. Hrs: 5-9 pm; winter hrs vary. Closed hols. Res accepted. Bar. Wine

cellar. Dinner $10.95-$18.95. Child's menu. Elegant dining in rustic Italian atmosphere. Cr cds: A, DS, MC, V.

★★★ **MANRESA CASTLE.** *Seventh and Sheridan Sts. 360/385-5750. www.manresacastle.com.* Specializes in curry chicken, fresh Northwest salmon. Own desserts. Hrs: 6-9 pm; Sun brunch 9 am-1 pm; winter hrs vary. Closed Jan 1, Dec 25. Res accepted. Bar. Dinner $9-$22. Sun brunch $3.25-$8.50. Child's menu. In 1892 castle; antique oak furnishings, ornate fireplace. Cr cds: DS, MC, V.

★★ **ORIGINAL OYSTER HOUSE.** *280417 US 101 (98368), 10 mi S. 360/385-1785.* Specializes in Northwest cuisine. Hrs: 4-8 pm; Fri, Sat to 9 pm. Res accepted. Bar. Dinner $9.95-$18. Child's menu. Parking. Overlooking Discovery Bay, beach. Cr cds: A, D, DS, MC, V.

★★ **SILVERWATER CAFE.** *237 Taylor St (98368). 360/385-6448.* Specializes in fresh local seafood, vegetarian dishes. Own desserts. Hrs: 11:30 am-9 pm; Fri-Sun to 10 pm. Closed Thanksgiving, Dec 25. Bar. Wine, beer. Lunch $4.50-$7.50; dinner $7.50-$15. Child's menu. Cr cds: MC, V.

Pullman

(D-8) *See also Clarkston*

Settled 1881 **Pop** 23,478 **Elev** 2,351 ft
Area code 509 **Zip** 99163
Web pullman-wa.com

Information Chamber of Commerce, 415 N Grand Ave; 509/334-3565 or 800/365-6948

A university town and an agricultural storage and shipping center in the fertile Palouse Hills, this community is named for George M. Pullman, the inventor-tycoon who gave his name to the railroad sleeping car.

What to See and Do

Parks. Kamiak Butte County Park. Timbered area with rocky butte rising 3,641 ft high, trails leading to summit. Approx 300 acres. Picnicking, hiking, interpretive programs (summer), camping (Apr-Oct; fee). Park (all yr). **Wawawai County Park.** 17 mi SW. Boating, fishing; picnicking, hiking. Earth-sheltered home (afternoon tours, call for dates). Camping (Apr-Oct; fee). Park (all yr). 10 mi N on WA 27. Phone 509/397-6238. **FREE**

Washington State University. (1890) 17,000 students. Guided tours at Office of Univ Affairs, Lighty Bldg. Rm 360. (Daily, afternoons) E of town center. Phone 509/335-4527. On campus are

> **Museum of Art.** Exhibitions, lectures, films. (Sep-May, daily, hrs vary) Fine Arts Center. Phone 509/335-1910 or 509/335-6607. **FREE**

> **Pullman Summer Palace Theater.** Daggy Hall. (Late June-early Aug) Phone 509/335-7236.

Annual Event

National Lentil Festival. Food booths, arts and crafts, musical entertainment, parade. Late Aug.

Motel/Motor Lodge

★ **AMERICAN TRAVEL INN.** *515 S Grand Ave (99163). 509/334-3500; fax 509/334-0549. Email greenbeard@ turbonet.com; www.palouse.net/all american/ATI-1.htm.* 35 rms, 2 story. Mid-May-Sep: S, D $40-$50; each addl $5; suites $59-$78; under 12 free; higher rates: graduation, football wkends, Mother's and Father's Day wkends. TV; cable. Pool. Restaurant adj 6 am-3 pm. Ck-out 11 am. Business servs avail. Cr cds: A, D, DS, MC, V.

D 🖼 🛠 ⛵ ♿

Hotel

★★ **QUALITY INN.** *1400 SE Bishop Blvd (99163). 509/332-0500; fax 509/334-4271; res 800/228-5151; toll-free 800/669-3212.* 53 rms, 2 story, 13 suites. Apr-May, Aug-Nov: S, D $99; each addl $10; suites $115; children $10; lower rates rest of yr. Crib avail. Pet accepted. Parking lot. Pool. TV; cable (premium), VCR avail. Complimentary continental bkfst, coffee in rms, newspaper, toll-free calls. Restaurant 11 am-2 pm. Ck-out

noon, ck-in 3 pm. Meeting rms. Business servs avail. Bellhops. Coin lndry. Gift shop. Free airport transportation. Exercise privileges, sauna. Golf. Hiking trail. Picnic facilities. Cr cds: A, D, DS, MC, V.

D ♻ 🛠 ⛵ ♿ 🛠 ⛵ 🛠 SC

Puyallup

See also Enumclaw, Tacoma

Founded 1877 **Pop** 23,875 **Elev** 40 ft
Area code 253
Web www.puyallupchamber.com
Information Chamber of Eastern Pierce County, 322 2nd St SW, PO Box 1298, 98371; 253/845-6755

Puyallup freezes the farm produce from the fertile soil and mild climate of the valley between Mount Rainier and Tacoma. A $2 million bulb industry (iris, daffodils, tulips) was born in 1923 when it was discovered the valley was ideal for growing. Ezra Meeker crossed the plains by covered wagon and named this city Puyallup (meaning "generous people") after a tribe that lived in the valley; Puyallups still live in the area.

What to See and Do

Ezra Meeker Mansion. (1890) The 17-rm Victorian house of Ezra Meeker, pioneer, farmer, 1st town mayor, author, and preserver of the Oregon Trail. Six fireplaces, period furnishings, stained-glass windows, and hand-carved woodwork. (Mar-mid-Dec, Wed-Sun; closed Easter, Thanksgiving) 312 Spring St. Phone 253/848-1770. ¢

Pioneer Park. Life-size statue of Ezra Meeker. Playground, wading pool (summer). S Meridian St at Elm Pl. Phone 253/841-5457. **FREE**

Annual Events

Ezra Meeker Community Festival. Fine arts show, crafts, entertainment; ice cream social at Meeker Mansion. Late June.

Sumner Summer Festival. Early Aug.

Pierce County Fair. 6 mi S in Graham. Early Aug.

Western Washington Fair. Pacific Northwest's largest fair; incl 3 statewide youth fairs, livestock shows, agricultural and commercial exhibits, free entertainment, midway, rodeo, top-name grandstand acts. Phone 253/841-5045. Seventeen days Sep.

Quinault

Pop 350 (est) **Elev** 221 ft
Area code 360 **Zip** 98575
Web www.chamber.grays-harbor.wa.us

Information Grays Harbor Chamber of Commerce, 506 Duffy St, Aberdeen 98520; 360/532-1924 or 800/321-1924

Quinault, on the shore of Lake Quinault, is the south entrance to Olympic National Park (see). In the heart of Olympic National Forest, it is the gateway to any of three valleys, the Hoh, Queets, and Quinault, which make up the rain forest, a lush green ecological phenomenon. It also provides an entrance to the Enchanted Valley area of the park. The Quinault Reservation is two miles west.

A Ranger District office of the Olympic National Forest (see OLYMPIA) is located here.

Motel/Motor Lodge

★★ **LAKE QUINAULT LODGE.**
345 S Shore Rd (98525), 2 mi NE of US 101. 360/288-2900; fax 360/288-2901; toll-free 800/562-6672. www. visitlakequinault.com. 92 rms, 1-3 story. No A/C. No rm phones. June-Sep: S, D $100-$150; each addl $10; under 5 free; lower rates rest of yr. Indoor pool; sauna. Restaurant 7 am-9:30 pm. Bar noon-11:30 pm. Ck-out 11 am. Meeting rms. Business servs avail. Gift shop. Boat rental. Lawn games. Game rm. Some fireplaces. Some balconies. On lake, beach. Cr cds: A, DS, MC, V.

Quincy

(D-5) *See also Ellensburg, Ephrata, Wenatchee*

Settled 1892 **Pop** 3,738 **Elev** 1,301 ft
Area code 509 **Zip** 98848

Information Quincy Valley Chamber of Commerce, 119 F Street SE, PO Box 668; 509/787-2140

Although there are only about eight inches of rain a year in this area, irrigation has turned the surrounding countryside green. Quincy processes and markets farm produce; more than 80 crops are grown in the area. Deposits of diatomaceous earth (soft chalky material used for fertilizers, mineral aids, and filters) are mined in the area and refined in Quincy. Fishing and game-bird hunting are good in the surrounding area.

What to See and Do

Crescent Bar Park. On Wanapum Reservoir in the Columbia River. Swimming, bathhouse, beaches, waterskiing, boating, fishing, marina; playground, picnicking, camping (Apr-Oct; hookups; fee), putting green, shops, pro shop, 9-hole golf (fee), four tennis courts (fee); restaurants, grocery. Park (all yr). 8 mi W off WA 28.

Annual Event

Farmer Consumer Awareness Day. Quincy High School, 16 Sixth Ave SE. Free tours to dairies, processing plants, packing houses, farms, harvesting operations. Exhibits, food booths, arts and crafts, petting zoo, antique autos, farm equipment, games, parade, 2K and 5K run, entertainment. Second Sat Sep.

Motel/Motor Lodge

★ **TRADITIONAL INNS.** *500 F St SW (98848). 509/787-3525; fax 509/ 787-3528. www.traditionalinns.com.* 24 rms, 2 story, 1 suite. May-Oct: S $58; D $66; each addl $8; suites $75; under 12 free; lower rates rest of yr. Crib avail. Pet accepted, some restrictions, fee. Parking lot. TV; cable.

Restaurant nearby. Ck-out 11 am, ck-in 3 pm. Business servs avail. Coin lndry. Golf, 18 holes. Tennis. Cr cds: A, C, D, DS, MC, V.

Richland

(E-6) *See also Kennewick, Pasco*

Pop 32,315 **Elev** 360 ft **Area code** 509 **Zip** 99352

Information Chamber of Commerce, 515 Lee Blvd, PO Box 637; 509/946-1651

Although one of the "tri-cities" (see KENNEWICK and PASCO), Richland has an entirely different personality, due to the 560-square-mile Hanford Works of the Department of Energy (DOE)—formerly the US Atomic Energy Commission. In 1943, Richland was a village of 250, dedicated to fruit cultivation. A year later Hanford was established by the government as one of four main development points for the atomic bomb—the others, Oak Ridge, TN; Los Alamos, NM; and the Argonne Laboratory, near Chicago. Hanford no longer is involved in the production of plutonium, and the more than 16,000 employees are now dedicated to environmental cleanup and safe disposal of nuclear and hazardous wastes. Important companies in Richland include Siemen's Nuclear Fuels Inc, Battelle Northwest, Boeing Computer Services, Washington Public Power Supply Service (WPPSS), Kaiser Engineers, and Fluor Daniel Hanford.

Once largely desert area, Richland today is surrounded by vineyards and orchards, thanks to irrigation from Grand Coulee Dam and the Yakima River Irrigation Projects. The city is at the hub of an area of spectacular scenery and outdoor activities within a short drive in any direction.

What to See and Do

CRESHT Museum. Displays, models, computer exhibits relating to US energy, science, and environmental topics. (Daily; closed hols) 95 Lee Blvd. Phone 509/943-9000. ¢¢

Annual Events

Cool Desert Nights Car Show. June.

Columbia Cup. Hydroplane races. July.

Benton-Franklin Fair and Rodeo. Franklin County Fairgrounds. Fair, parade, carnival. Aug.

Seasonal Event

NASCAR Auto Racing. June-Sep.

Motels/Motor Lodges

★ **BALI HAI MOTEL.** *1201 George Washington Way (99352).* 509/943-3101; fax 509/943-6363. 44 rms, 2 story. S $37-$40; D $37-$50; each addl $5; studio rms $37-$45; under 12 free; higher rates hydroplane races. Crib free. Pet accepted; $5. TV; cable (premium). Heated pool; whirlpool. Complimentary coffee in rms. Restaurant adj 7 am-11 pm. Ck-out noon. Coin lndry. Business servs avail. Refrigerators, microwaves. Cr cds: A, C, D, DS, ER, MC, V.

★ **DAYS INN.** *615 Jadwin Ave (99352), 1 blk S of George Washington Way.* 509/943-4611; fax 509/946-2271. 98 rms, 2 story. July-Aug: S $69; D $79; lower rates rest of yr. Crib avail. Parking lot. Pool. TV; cable (DSS), VCR avail. Complimentary continental bkfst, coffee in rms, newspaper, toll-free calls. Restaurant nearby. Ck-out noon, ck-in 3 pm. Meeting rm. Internet access avail. Coin lndry. Free airport transportation. Exercise privileges. Golf. Tennis. Beach access. Bike rentals. Hiking trail. Picnic facilities. Cr cds: A, D, DS, MC, V.

★★ **SHILO INN.** *50 Comstock St (99352), at George Washington Way.* 509/946-4661; fax 509/943-6741; res 800/222-2244. 150 rms, 2 story, 13 kits. Mid-May-mid-Sep: S, D $79-$99; each addl $10; kit. units $139-$155; under 13 free; golf packages; higher rates hydroplane races; lower rates rest of yr. Crib free. Pet accepted; $7/day. TV; cable (premium), VCR (movies $3). Heated pool; wading pool, whirlpool. Complimentary bkfst buffet. Coffee in rms. Restaurant 6 am-10 pm. Bar. Ck-out noon. Coin lndry. Meeting rms. Business servs avail. In-rm modem link. Valet serv. Airport, railroad station, bus depot transportation. Exercise equipt. Refrigerators, microwaves; some wetbars. On 12 acres. Cr cds: A, D, DS, JCB, MC, V.

Hotels

★★ **BEST WESTERN.** *1515 George Washington Way (99352). 509/946-4121; fax 509/946-2222; res 800/528-1234; toll-free 800/635-3980. Email towersales@nwinfo.net;www.towerinn. net.* 190 rms, 6 story, 5 suites. June-July: S $89; D $99; each addl $10; suites $159; under 18 free; lower rates rest of yr. Crib avail. Pet accepted, some restrictions, fee. Parking lot. Indoor pool, children's pool, whirlpool. TV; cable (premium). Complimentary continental bkfst, coffee in rms, newspaper, toll-free calls. Restaurant nearby. Ck-out noon, ck-in 4 pm. Meeting rms. Fax servs avail. Dry cleaning, coin lndry. Free airport transportation. Exercise privileges, sauna. Golf. Hiking trail. Picnic facilities. Video games. Cr cds: A, C, D, DS, ER, JCB, MC, V.

★ **RED LION HOTEL.** *802 George Washington Way (99352). 509/946-7611; fax 509/943-8564; toll-free 800/733-5466. Email jgibson@3-cities.com; www.redlion.com.* 143 rms, 2 story, 6 suites. Mar-Oct: S, D $88; suites $125; under 18 free; lower rates rest of yr. Crib avail. Pet accepted, some restrictions. Parking lot. Pool, whirlpool. TV; cable (premium), VCR avail. Complimentary coffee in rms, newspaper, toll-free calls. Restaurant. Bar. Meeting rms. Business center. Bellhops. Dry cleaning. Golf. Tennis, 4 courts. Beach access. Hiking trail. Picnic facilities. Cr cds: A, C, D, DS, ER, JCB, MC, V.

Restaurant

★ **R.F. MCDOUGALL'S.** *1705 Columbia Park Tr (99352). 509/735-6418.* Specializes in hamburgers, pasta. Hrs: 11 am-11 pm. Closed Thanksgiving, Dec 25. Bar. Lunch, dinner $3.50-$9.50. Antique advertising signs in Western-style restaurant. Cr cds: A, MC, V.

Ritzville

(D-7) *See also Moses Lake*

Settled 1878 **Pop** 1,725 **Elev** 1,815 ft **Area code** 509 **Zip** 99169
Information Chamber of Commerce, PO Box 122; 509/659-1936

Annual Events

BluesFest. Second Sat July.
Wheat Land Communities Fair. Parade, rodeo. Labor Day wkend.

Motel/Motor Lodge

★★ **BEST INN & SUITES.** *1513 S Smittys Blvd (99169). 509/659-1007; fax 509/659-1025; res 800/237-8466. Email bestinns@ritzcom.net; www. hotels-west.com.* 54 rms, 2 story, 2 suites. May-Sep: S $59; D $69; each addl $10; suites $159; under 18 free; lower rates rest of yr. Crib avail. Pet accepted. Parking lot. Pool. TV; cable (premium). Complimentary continental bkfst, coffee in rms, newspaper. Restaurant. Ck-out 1 pm, ck-in 3 pm. Meeting rm. Business servs avail. Coin lndry. Gift shop. Golf, 9 holes. Tennis, 4 courts. Cr cds: A, D, DS, ER, JCB, MC, V.

Restaurant

★ **CIRCLE T INN.** *214 W Main St (99169). 509/659-0922.* Specializes in steak, seafood. Own desserts. Hrs: 6 am-10 pm; Mon to 3 pm. Closed Jan 1, Thanksgiving, Dec 25. Bar. Bkfst $3.75-$6.50; lunch, dinner $4-$15.95. Cr cds: MC, V.

San Juan Islands

See also Anacortes; also see Victoria, BC Canada

Area code 360
Web www.sanjuanisland.org
Information Chamber of Commerce, PO Box 98, Friday Harbor 98250; 360/378-5240

These 172 islands nestled between the northwest corner of Washington and Vancouver Island, British Columbia, Canada, comprise a beautiful and historic area. Secluded coves, giant trees, freshwater lakes, fishing camps, modest motels, numerous bed & breakfasts, and plush resorts characterize the four major islands. Over 500 miles of paved or gravel roads swing through virgin woodlands and along lovely shorelines. The islands are accessible by ferry from Anacortes (see).

San Juan Island gave birth in 1845 to the expansionist slogan "Fifty-four forty or fight" and was the setting for the "pig war" of 1859, in which a British pig uprooted an American potato patch. The subsequent hostilities between the islands' 7 British and 14 American inhabitants reached such proportions that eventually Kaiser Wilhelm I of Germany was called in to act as arbiter and settle the boundaries. During the 13 years of controversy, the pig was the only casualty. This island was the last place the British flag flew within the territorial United States. Friday Harbor, most westerly stop in the United States on San Juan Islands ferry tour, is county seat of San Juan.

What to See and Do

Orcas Island. Largest in the chain; incl **Moran State Park** 15 mi NE. Has a 5,100-acre forest with swimming, fishing, boating (launch); hiking, picnicking, primitive camping (res suggested in summer). Mt Constitution (2,409 ft) with view site and tower. Standard fees. Phone 360/376-2326.

⭐ **San Juan Island.** Friday Harbor on E shore serves as base for salmon fleet; major commercial center of islands. Fishing lakes, camping facilities, golf, Intl Seaplane Base, and 2 airstrips are here. Also on San Juan is

San Juan Island National Historical Park. Commemorates settlement of boundary issue between the US and Great Britain. British Camp, 10 mi NW of Friday Harbor on Garrison Bay, has restored blockhouse, commissary, hospital, formal garden, and barracks built during the British occupation. American Camp, 6 mi SE of Friday Harbor, has remains of redoubt, the American defensive earthwork; laundresses' and officers' quarters. Picnicking; information specialist at both camps (June-Sep, daily; rest of yr, Thurs-Sun). Office and information center in Friday Harbor, 1st and Spring Sts (June-Aug, daily; May and Sep, Mon-Fri; closed rest of yr; closed hols) For further info contact Superintendent, Box 429, Friday Harbor 98250. Phone 360/378-2240. **FREE**

The Whale Museum. Art and science exhibits document the lives of whales and porpoises in this area. (Daily; closed hols) 62 1st St N in Friday Harbor. Phone 360/378-4710. ¢

Annual Event

Dixieland Jazz Festival. Friday Harbor and Roche Harbor. Phone 360/378-5509. Last wkend July.

Washington State Ferry, Orcas Island

Resorts

★★ ROCHE HARBOR RESORT AND HOTEL. *4950 Tarte Memorial Dr (98250), 10 mi NW on Roche Harbor Rd, on San Juan Island. 360/378-2155; fax 360/378-6809; toll-free 800/451-8910. www.rocheharbor.com.* 20 hotel rms, 4 with bath, 3 story, 9 kit. cottages (2-bedrm), 25 condos (1-3-bedrm). No A/C. No elvtr. May-Oct: S, D $79-$135; cottages $130-$195; condos $155-$265; under 6 free; lower rates rest of yr. Crib free. TV in condo. Pool. Restaurant opp 5-10 pm. Bar 11-1 am; entertainment (June-Aug). Ck-out 11 am, ck-in 3 pm. Business servs avail. Grocery. Coin lndry. Meeting rms. Business center. Gift shop. Tennis. Swimming beach; boats. Hiking. Microwaves avail. Some balconies. Picnic area; grills. On harbor. Totally nonsmoking. Cr cds: A, MC, V.

★★★ ROSARIO. *1 Rosario Way (98245), on Orcas Island, 5 mi SE of Eastsound, on Puget Sound. 360/376-2222; fax 360/376-3680; toll-free 800/562-8820.* 86 rms, 33 suites, 2 with kit., 1-2 story. No A/C. June-mid-Oct: S, D $180-$200; each addl $20; suites $200-$400; kit. units $140-$280; under 12 free; lower rates rest of yr. Crib $5. TV; VCR avail (movies $3). 3 pools, 1 indoor; whirlpool, poolside serv. Restaurant (by res) 7 am-2 pm, 6-10 pm. Box lunches, snacks. Bar 11-1 am. Ck-out 11 am, ck-in 4 pm. Grocery. Coin lndry. Package store 5 mi. Meeting rms. Airport transportation. Tennis. Golf privileges. Boating (marina). Lawn games. Music rm; piano, organ concerts. Entertainment. Exercise rm; sauna. Some wet bars, fireplaces. Private patios, balconies. On 30-acre estate. Totally nonsmoking. Cr cds: A, DS, MC, V.

B&Bs/Small Inns

★★ ARGYLE HOUSE BED & BREAKFAST. *685 Argyle Ave (98250). 360/378-4084; toll-free 800/624-3459. Email cmcarli@hotmail.com; www. argylehouse.net.* 5 rms, 2 story. May-Oct: D $120; suites $190; lower rates rest of yr. Street parking. TV; cable (premium), VCR avail. Complimentary full bkfst. Restaurant nearby. Ck-out 11 am, ck-in 3 pm. Free airport transportation. Whirlpool. Golf. Tennis. Cr cds: MC, V.

★★★ FRIDAY'S HISTORICAL INN. *35 1st St (98250), San Juan Island, near ferry terminal. 360/378-5848; fax 360/378-2881; toll-free 800/352-2632. Email fridays@interisland.net; www. friday-harbor.com.* 11 rms, 6 share bath, 3 story. No A/C. Some rm phones. June-Oct: S, D $90-$175; each addl $20; lower rates rest of yr. TV in some rms; cable (premium). Complimentary continental bkfst; afternoon refreshments. Restaurant nearby. Ck-out 11 am, ck-in 2 pm. Free airport transportation. Refrigerators; microwaves avail. Balconies. Built 1891. Antiques. Totally nonsmoking. Cr cds: MC, V.

★★ HARRISON HOUSE SUITES. *235 C St (98250). 360/378-3587; fax 360/378-2270; toll-free 800/407-7933. Email hhsuites@rockisland.com; www. san-juan-lodging.com.* 5 rms. No A/C. May-Sep: S, D $85-$225; under 2 free; wkends (2-day min); lower rates rest of yr. Crib free. TV; cable (premium), VCR (movies). Complimentary continental bkfst, coffee in rms. Restaurant nearby. Rm serv 24 hrs. Ck-out 3 pm, ck-in 11 am. Business servs avail. In-rm modem link. Free guest lndry. Free airport transportation. Massage. Heated pool; whirlpool. Refrigerators, microwaves; many in-rm whirlpools; some fireplaces. Many balconies. Built in 1904; eclectic furnishings. Totally nonsmoking. Cr cds: A, DS, MC, V.

★★★ HILLSIDE HOUSE BED & BREAKFAST. *365 Carter Ave (98250), near airport. 360/378-4730; fax 360/378-4715; toll-free 800/232-4730. Email info@hillsidehouse.com; www. hillsidehouse.com/.* 7 rms, 3 story. May-Sep: S $95; D $125; each addl $45; children $25; under 18 free; lower rates rest of yr. Parking garage. TV; cable (premium). Complimentary full bkfst, toll-free calls. Restaurant. Ck-out 11 am, ck-in 3 pm. Meeting rm. Fax servs avail. Gift shop. Golf, 9 holes. Tennis, 3 courts. Cr cds: A, DS, MC, V.

★★★ **INN AT SWIFTS BAY.** *856 Port Stanley Rd (98261), 1 mi past park entrance. 360/468-3636; fax 360/468-3637; toll-free 888/794-3846. Email vacation@swiftsbay.com; www.swifts bay.com.* 5 air-cooled rms, 2 with shower only, 2 story. No rm phones. S, D $95-$175. Adults only. TV in den; VCR. Complimentary full bkfst; afternoon refreshments. Ck-out 11 am, ck-in 3-7 pm. Business servs avail. Exercise equipt; sauna. Whirl-pool. Some refrigerators, fireplaces. Tudor-style inn in cedar grove; quiet atmosphere. Totally nonsmoking. Cr cds: A, DS, MC, V.

★★★ **LOPEZ FARM COTTAGES.** *555 Fisherman Bay Rd (98261). 360/468-3555; fax 360/468-3966; res 800/440-3556. www.lopezfarmcottages. com.* 4 kit. units, shower only. May-Oct: S, D $125; each addl $25; lower rates rest of yr. Complimentary con-tinental bkfst. Ck-out 11 am, ck-in 3-7 pm. Grocery, coin lndry, package store 1½ mi. Free airport transporta-tion. Hiking. Spa. Whirlpool. Refrig-erators, microwaves, wet bars, fireplaces. On historic family farm. Totally nonsmoking. Cr cds: MC, V.

★★ **ORCAS HOTEL.** *PO Box 155 (98280), at ferry landing, Orcas Island. 360/376-4300; fax 360/376-4399; toll-free 888/672 2792. Email orcas@orcashotel.com; www.orcashotel. com.* 12 rms. May-Oct: D $140; lower rates rest of yr. Crib avail. Parking lot. TV; cable (premium). Compli-mentary continental bkfst. Restau-rant 7:30 am-10 pm. Bar. Ck-out 11 am, ck-in 1:30 pm. Meeting rms. Business servs avail. Whirlpool. Golf. Beach access. Bike rentals. Hiking trail. Cr cds: A, MC, V.

★★ **PANACEA BED AND BREAK-FAST.** *595 Park St (98250). 360/378-3757; fax 360/378-8543; res 800/639-2762. Email panacea@pacificrim, www. friday-harbor.com/panacea.* 4 rms, 2 with shower only. No A/C. No rm phones. May-Oct: S, D $135-$165; lower rates rest of yr. Children over 17 yrs only. TV; cable. Complimen-tary full bkfst. Ck-out 10 am, ck-in 2 pm. Some in-rm whirlpools. Picnic tables, grills. Craftsman-style home

built in 1907. Totally nonsmoking. Cr cds: MC, V.

★★ **SAN JUAN.** *50 Spring St W (98250), ½ blk from ferry dock. 360/ 378-2070; fax 360/378-2027; toll-free 800/742-8210. Email sanjuaninn@ rockisland.com; www.san-juan.net/sjinn.* 8 rms, 2 story, 2 suites. May-Oct: S $75; D $105; each addl $25; suites $225; children $25; lower rates rest of yr. Street parking. TV; cable, VCR avail. Complimentary continental bkfst. Restaurant nearby. Ck-out 11 am, ck-in 2 pm. Meeting rm. Concierge. Exercise privileges, whirl-pool. Golf, 9 holes. Tennis, 4 courts. Picnic facilities. Cr cds: A, DS, MC, V.

★★ **TUCKER HOUSE BED & BREAKFAST.** *260 B St (98250). 360/378-2783; fax 360/378-6437; toll-free 800/965-0123. Email info@tucker house.com; www.tuckerhouse.com.* 6 rms, 3 share bath, 2 story, 2 kit. units. No A/C. No rm phones. May-mid-Oct: S, D $95-$145; each addl $25; wkly rates; lower rates rest of yr. Crib free. Pet accepted, some restric-tions; $15. TV; cable, VCR avail (movies). Complimentary full bkfst, coffee in rms. Ck-out 11 am, ck-in 2 pm. Refrigerators, microwaves. Picnic tables. Victorian home built in 1898. Totally nonsmoking. Cr cds: MC, V.

★★★ **TURTLEBACK FARM INN.** *1981 Crow Valley Rd (98245), on Orcas Island. 360/376-4914; fax 360/376-5329; toll-free 800/376-4914. Email turtleback@interisland.net; www.turtlebackinn.com.* 11 rms, 2 story. June-Oct: S $150; D $160; each addl $25; lower rates rest of yr. Park-ing lot. TV; cable, VCR avail. Com-plimentary full bkfst. 8-10. Ck-out 11 am, ck-in 1 pm. Meeting rm. Fax servs avail. Golf, 9 holes. Tennis, 4 courts. Beach access. Bike rentals. Hiking trail. Picnic facilities. Cr cds: DS, MC, V.

★★★ **WINDSONG BED & BREAK-FAST.** *213 Deer Harbor Rd (98280). 360/376-2500; fax 360/376-4453; toll-free 800/669-3948. Email windsong@ pacificrim.net; www.windsonginn.com.* 4 rms, 2 story. May-Oct: S $125; D

$135; each addl $25; lower rates rest of yr. Parking lot. TV; cable, VCR avail, VCR avail, CD avail. Complimentary full bkfst. Restaurant. Ck-out 11 am, ck-in 2 pm. Whirlpool. Golf, 18 holes. Beach access. Bike rentals. Hiking trail. Cr cds: MC, V.

Restaurants

★ ★ ★ **CHRISTINA'S.** *Horseshoe Hwy (98245), on Orcas Island. 360/376-4904. www.christinas.net.* Specializes in fresh Northwest seafood. Hrs: 5:30-10 pm. Closed Tues, Wed; Dec 25; 1st 3 wks in Nov, Jan. Res accepted. Bar. Wine list. Dinner a la carte entrees: $14.50-$26.50. Child's menu. Street parking. Extensive woodwork in several dining areas; large deck overlooks water. Cr cds: A, D, DS, MC, V.

★ ★ **DOWNRIGGERS.** *10 Front St (98250), San Juan Island (98250), adj ferry dock. 360/378-2700. Email debbier@rockisland.com.* Specializes in fresh local seafood, steak, pasta. Hrs: 11 am-10 pm; Sat, Sun from 9 am. Res accepted. Bar. Bkfst $4.95-$12.95; lunch $4.95-$12.95; dinner $8.95-$22.95. Several dining levels with views of harbor. Cr cds: A, MC, V.

[D]

★ ★ **LA FAMIGLIA RISTORANTE.** *Prune Alley at A St (98245), on Orcas Island, center of town. 360/376-2335.* Specializes in scallopine alla limone, seafood primavera. Hrs: 4:30-10 pm. Res required. Dinner $9.95-$17.95. Child's menu. Rustic decor; oak furnishings. Cr cds: A, DS, MC, V.

[D]

Seattle (C-3)

Founded 1852 **Pop** 516,259
Elev 125 ft **Area code** 206
Web www.seeseattle.org
Information Seattle-King County Convention & Visitors Bureau, 520 Pike St, Suite 1300, 98101; 206/461-5840

Suburbs Bellevue, Bremerton, Everett, Issaquah, Marysville, Port Gamble, Tacoma. (See individual alphabetical listings.)

Seattle has prospered from the products of its surrounding forests, farms, and waterways, serving as provisioner to Alaska and the Orient. Since the 1950s it has acquired a new dimension from the manufacture of jet airplanes, missiles, and space vehicles—which, along with tourism, comprise the city's most important industries.

The Space Needle, which dominated Seattle's boldly futuristic 1962 World's Fair, still stands, symbolic of the city's present-day, forward-looking character. The site of the fair is now the Seattle Center. Many features of the fair have been made permanent.

Seattle is on Elliott Bay, nestled between Puget Sound, an inland-probing arm of the Pacific Ocean, and Lake Washington, a 24-mile stretch of fresh water. The city sprawls across hills and ridges, some of them 500 feet high, but all are dwarfed by the Olympic Mountains to the west and the Cascades to the east. Elliott Bay, Seattle's natural harbor, welcomes about 2,000 commercial deep-sea cargo vessels a year. From Seattle's piers, ships wind their way 125 nautical miles through Puget Sound and the Strait of Juan de Fuca, two-thirds of them Orient-bound, the others destined for European, Alaskan, and Eastern ports.

On the same latitude as New-foundland, Seattle is warmed by the Japan Current, shielded by the Olympics from excessive winter rains, and protected by the Cascades from midcontinent winter blasts. Only twice has the temperature been recorded at 100°F; there isn't a zero on record.

Five families pioneered here and named the town for a friendly Native American chief. The great harbor, and the timber surrounding it, made an inviting combination; shortly thereafter a sawmill and a salmon-canning plant were in operation. Soon wagon trains were rolling to Seattle through Snoqualmie Pass, a tempting 3,022 feet, lower than any other in the Northwest.

Isolated at the fringe of the continent by the vast expanse of America, Seattle enjoyed great expectations

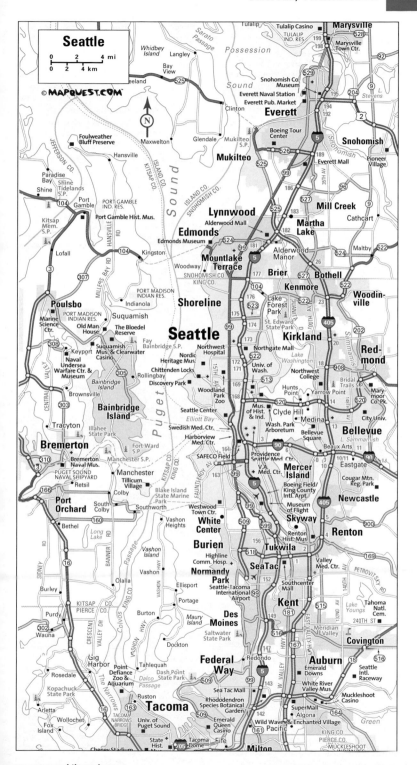

but few women, an obvious threat to the growth and serenity of the community. Asa Mercer, a civic leader and first president of the Territorial University, went East and persuaded 11 proper young women from New England to sail with him around the Horn to Seattle to take husbands among the pioneers. This venture in long distance matchmaking proved so successful that Mercer returned East and recruited 100 Civil War widows. Today many of Seattle's families proudly trace their lineage to these women.

When a ship arrived from Alaska with a "ton of gold" in 1897, the great Klondike Gold Rush was on, converting Seattle into a boomtown—the beginning of the trail to fortune. Since then Seattle has been the natural gateway to Alaska because of the protected Inside Passage; the commercial interests of the two remain tightly knit. Another major event for Seattle was the opening of the Panama Canal in 1914, a tremendous stimulant for the city's commerce.

Transportation

Airport. See SEATTLE-TACOMA INTL AIRPORT AREA.

Car Rental Agencies. See IMPORTANT TOLL-FREE NUMBERS.

Public Transportation. Metro Transit System, phone 206/553-3000.

Rail Passenger Service. Amtrak 800/872-7245.

What to See and Do

Alki Beach. Site where Seattle's first settlers built cabins; monument, scenic views, lighthouse at Alki Point (adj), boat ramp on Harbor Ave SW, concessions. Alki Ave SW & 59th Ave SW, Southwest Side. **FREE**

Carkeek Park. Approx 190 acres on Puget Sound. Beach, picnic area, model airplane meadow, hiking trail (1 mi). (Daily) NW 110th St, Northwest Side. **FREE**

Charles and Emma Frye Art Museum. Collection of American and European paintings from late 19th century; art competitions; traveling and changing exhibits. (Tues-Sun; closed Thanksgiving, Dec 25) 704 Terry Ave, at Cherry St, downtown. Phone 206/622-9250. **FREE**

Discovery Park. More than 500 acres of urban wilderness on the Magnolia bluff. Former US Army post. Nature trails, meadows, forests, cliffs, and beaches (no swimming). Picnicking, playground, tennis. Visitor center (daily; closed hols). Indian Cultural Center (Mon-Fri). Park (daily). Guided nature walks (Sat). 3801 W Government Way, NW Side. Phone 206/386-4236. **FREE**

Evergreen Floating Bridge. Almost 1½ mi long; connects downtown Seattle with Bellevue (see). On WA 520, near Montlake Pl, Southeast Side.

Experience Music Project. Interactive music museum that combines hands-on experiences with interpretive exhibits to tell the story of American rock 'n' roll. Features state-of-the-art sound technology; a world-class collection of artifacts, incl world's largest assortment of Hendrix memorabilia; a ridelike attraction; and exciting multimedia presentations. (Daily) Seattle Center, 5th & Harrison. Phone 206/770-2700. ¢¢¢¢

Ferry trips and cruises.

Argosy Harbor Cruise. One-hr narrated harbor tour. (Daily) From Pier 55, foot of Seneca St. Phone 206/623-1445. ¢¢¢-¢¢¢¢

Ferry trips. Access to Olympic Peninsula, a number of interesting ferry trips. Contact Washington State Ferries, Colman Dock, 98104. Seattle Ferry Terminal, Colman Dock, foot of Madison St. Phone 206/464-6400 or 800/843-3779 (WA). Per vehicle ¢¢-¢¢¢

Gallant Lady Cruises. Six-day inclusive summer cruises to San Juan Islands; also extended cruises along British Columbia. Contact PO Box 1250, Vashon 98070. Depart from Lake Union. Phone 206/463-2073.

Tillicum Village. Narrated harbor cruise to Blake Island incl baked-salmon dinner, stage show. Also on island is Northwest Coast Indian Cultural Center with museum and gift shop. (May-mid-Oct, daily; rest of yr, Sat; hrs vary) Res advised. Blake Island State Park. Excursion from Pier 55/56, ft of Seneca St. Phone 206/443-1244 or 800/426-1205. ¢¢¢¢

Freeway Park. Five-acre park features dramatic water displays. Free concerts (summer, Mon). (Daily) 6th and Seneca, downtown.

Gas Works Park. Views of downtown and Lake Union in 20-acre park. Towers of an old gas plant and imaginative reuse of industrial machinery. More than 26,000 boats/yr pass here to the ship canal. Your shadow marks the time on 28-ft sundial at top of Kite Hill. Kite-flying mound, picnic shelter, play barn, promenade. (Daily) N Northlake Way at Meridian N, Northwest Side. **FREE**

Golden Gardens. Saltwater swimming beach (no lifeguards; water temperature 54°F in summer), boat ramp (adj to Shilshole Bay Marina); picnic areas with views of Sound and mountains, volleyball courts, teen activity center. (Daily) N end of Seaview Ave NW, Northwest Side. **FREE**

Green Lake Park. Two swimming beaches (mid-June-early Sep, daily); indoor pool (Mon-Sat; fee); wading pool (May-Sep, daily); tennis; 3-mi pedestrian and bicycle path around lake; fishing pier, boat rentals; picnic and playfield aread, playground, pitch 'n' putt golf, concessions. On Aurora Ave (WA 99), between N 65th & 72nd Sts, Northwest Side. **FREE**

Industrial tour.

    Rainier Brewing Company. Guided tour of brewery; sample beer and root beer in Mountain Rm. (Mon-Sat; closed hols) Children must be able to walk and be accompanied by adult. (Mon-Fri) 3100 Airport Way S. Phone 206/622-2600. **FREE**

International District. Asian community with shops, restaurants, and the Nippon Kan Theatre, a national historic site at Kobe Park, where a giant lantern overlooks the terraced community gardens. SE of downtown, 4th Ave to I-5 and Yesler to S Dearborn Sts, downtown. Here is the

    Wing Luke Museum. Commemorates Asian and Pacific Asian culture and history in the Pacific Northwest. Notable exhibits focus on the culture clash between Chinese and white settlers in the 1880s and Japanese internment during WWII. (Tues-Sun) 407 7th Ave S. Phone 206/623-5124. ¢¢

Klondike Gold Rush National Historical Park-Seattle Unit. Visitor center in historic Pioneer Square District. Details gold rush stampede of 1897-98; displays, photomurals, artifacts, slide and film programs, gold-panning demonstrations. (Daily; closed Jan 1, Thanksgiving, Dec 25) 117 S Main St, Southwest Side. Phone 206/553-7220. **FREE**

Lake Union. Boatyards, seaplane moorages, houseboat colonies on lake. Seen from George Washington Memorial Bridge, Northwest Side.

Lake Washington Canal. Chittenden Locks raise and lower boats to link salt and fresh water anchorages. More than 400,000 passengers and 6 million tons of freight pass through annually. Commodore Park and a salmon ladder with viewing windows are on the S side. Can be seen from Seaview Ave NW or NW 54th St, Northwest Side.

Lake Washington Floating Bridge. Can be seen from Lake Washington Blvd and Lakeside Ave. Connects downtown Seattle with Mercer Island via I-90.

Lincoln Park. Trails, picnic areas, tennis; beach, bathhouse, saltwater pool (mid-June-early Sep, daily; fee), wading pool (June-Sep, daily). (Daily) Fauntleroy Ave SW & SW Rose St, Southwest Side. **FREE**

Mount Baker-Snoqualmie National Forest. Snoqualmie Section. Incl several ski areas (see MOUNT RAINIER NATIONAL PARK and NORTH BEND); 8 wilderness areas; picnic and campsites, fishing, hunting. More than 1 million acres. E and S of city, reached via I-90. Contact Outdoor Recreation Information Center, 915 2nd Ave, Suite 442, 98174. Phone 425/775-9702. **FREE**

Museum of Flight. Exhibits on aviation pioneers, industry. Spectacular Great Gallery focuses on modern flight, including space age; more than 40 aircraft on display, incl A-12 Blackbird. Adj is Red Barn (1909), original Boeing Aircraft Mfg Bldg, featuring exhibits emphasizing aviation from its beginnings through the 1930s. (Daily; closed Thanksgiving, Dec 25) Phone 206/764-5720. ¢¢

Museum of History and Industry. History of Seattle and Pacific Northwest, exhibits change frequently. (Daily;

closed Jan 1, Thanksgiving, Dec 25) Tues free. 2700 24th Ave E, on N side of WA 520, just S of Husky Stadium, Southeast Side. Phone 206/324-1125. ¢¢¢

Myrtle Edwards Park. One mi of shoreline, paved bike trail, views of Puget Sound, the Olympic Peninsula, and oceangoing vessels; Seamen's Memorial and a granite and concrete sculpture. N of Pier 70, NW Side. **FREE**

Nordic Heritage Museum. Center for Scandinavian community in Pacific Northwest. Represents all 5 Scandinavian countries. Historical exhibits, art gallery, performing arts. (Tues-Sat, also Sun afternoon) 3014 NW 67th St, Northwest Side. Phone 206/789-5707. ¢¢

☒ **Pike Place Market.** Oldest continuously operating farmer's market in the country. Buy anything from artichokes to antiques. More than 225 permanent shops, restaurants; handcrafts. (Daily; closed hols) First Ave and Pike St, in 9-acre historical district, downtown. Phone 206/682-7453. **FREE**

Pioneer Square. Restored bldgs of early Seattle now house galleries, shops, and restaurants. Bounded by 1st Ave, James St, and Yesler Way, downtown.

Professional sports.

American League baseball (Seattle Mariners). Safeco Field. Phone 206/628-3555.

NBA (Seattle SuperSonics). Key Arena. Seattle Center, 1st and Republic. Phone 206/281-5800.

NFL (Seattle Seahawks). Playing at Husky Stadium, Univ of Washington (see), until 2002. Phone 425/827-9777.

Schmitz Park. Section of forest as it was when first settlers arrived. Admiral Way SW & SW Stevens St, E of Alki Ave, SW Side. **FREE**

Seattle Art Museum. Museum houses modern art; ethnic art, incl the Katherine White Collection of African Art; Northwest Coast Native American collection; European painting, sculpture, and decorative arts. Changing exhibits. (Tues-Sun; closed Jan 1, Thanksgiving, Dec 25) 100 University St, downtown. Phone 206/654-3100. ¢¢¢ Ticket stub accepted as admission to

Seattle Asian Art Museum. This branch of the Seattle Art Museum features collection of Asian art incl Japanese, Chinese, and Korean collections. Japanese collection is one of top 5 in US. (Tues-Sun; closed Jan 1, Thanksgiving, Dec 25) 1400 E Prospect St, Volunteer Park. Phone 206/654-3100. **FREE** with ticket stub from Seattle Art Museum; otherwise ¢¢.

☒ **Seattle Center.** Site of 1962 World's Fair. 305 Harrison St, downtown. Phone 206/684-7200 or 206/684-8582 (recording). Its 74 acres incl

Monorail. Provides a scenic 90-second ride between Center House and Westlake Center in downtown. Legacy of 1962 World's Fair, the Swedish-built train makes frequent runs throughout the day. (Daily, closed Jan 1, Thanksgiving, Dec 25) ¢

Space Needle. A 605-ft tower. At 520-ft level, visitors can take in spectacular view from observation deck. Shops, lounge, and displays on observation deck; glass elevators. Two revolving restaurants at 500 ft; no elevator charge when dining. (Daily) Phone 800/937-9582. ¢¢¢

Fun Forest Amusement Park. Rides (fees), games in parklike setting. (June-Labor Day, daily; Mar-June and early Sep-Nov, wkends) Phone 206/728-1585. **FREE**

Center House. Three floors of specialty shops, restaurants, conference facilities, administrative offices. (Daily) Phone 206/684-7200 or 206/684-8582 (recording).

Seattle Center Opera House, Playhouse, Arena, Key Arena. The Opera House is home of the Seattle Opera Assoc and Pacific Northwest Ballet. Bagley Wright Theatre is home of Seattle Repertory Theatre (Phone 206/443-2222). The Arena seats up to 6,000 for hockey, boxing, concerts. Key Arena is home to the NBA SuperSonics and seats up to 15,000 for sports, concerts, conventions, and trade shows. Phone 206/684-7200.

International Fountain. Music and light show. (Daily)

Pacific Science Center. More than 200 hands-on exhibits plus IMAX Theater, live science demonstra-

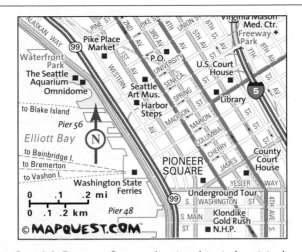

Begin in Seattle's Pioneer Square district, the city's original
downtown, which was built in the 1890s (after a disastrous fire) as
the money from the Yukon Gold Rush started pouring in. The
architecture is amazingly harmonious (one architect was
responsible for nearly 60 major buildings in a ten-block radius) and
graciously restored. The area also features the Underground tour
(see SIGHTSEEING TOURS) and many galleries, cafes, and antique
shops. A collection of totem poles can be found in tree-lined
Occidental Park and in Pioneer Square itself. Continue across
Alaskan Way (or take Waterfront Trolley, a vintage street car that
runs from Pioneer Square to the waterfront to Pike Place Market)
to the waterfront. Walk along the harbor, watching ferries dart to
and fro, or take a boat tour (see FERRY TRIPS AND CRUISES).
Stop at the Seattle Aquarium, located in Waterfront Park at Pier
59, then stop for clam chowder at Ivar's, located at Pier 54.
Continue north, recrossing Alaskan Way, and climb to Pike Place
Market, eight stories above the harbor on a bluff. There are two
ways to do this: there's an elevator hidden at the base of the
market, or you can take the Harbor Stairs, a new cascade of steps
flanked by shops and gardens. The Pike Place Market is Seattle's
most interesting destination, an old-fashioned public market (built
around 1910) in a warrenlike building with three floors of food,
baked goods, ethnic shops, fresh fish, and crafts. You could spend
hours here. Also in the Market are some of Seattle's best-loved
restaurants; many of them have great views over the harbor to the
islands and Olympic Mountains to the west. Just down the street is
the new Seattle Art Museum, with its excellent collection of
Northwest Native Art.

tions, planetarium shows, laser light shows, and special events. Science playground. (Daily; closed Thanksgiving, Dec 25) 200 2nd Ave N. Phone 206/443-2001. ¢¢¢

Seattle University. (1891) 4,800 students. Landscaped urban campus with more than 1,000 varieties of exotic flowers, trees, and shrubs; water fountain sculpture by George Tsutakawa. Tours of campus. 900 Broadway. Phone 206/296-6000.

Seward Park. Swimming beach (mid-June-early Sep, daily), bathhouse; picnic and play areas, tennis, amphitheater; Japanese lantern and *torii* (Japanese arch); fish hatchery. (Daily) Occupies peninsula off Lake Washington Blvd S & S Orcas St, Southeast Side. **FREE**

Space Needle, Seattle skyline

Shilshole Bay Marina. Moorage for 1,500 boats, fuel, repairs, launching ramp, marine supplies, restaurants. 7001 Seaview Ave NW, Northwest Side. Phone 206/728-3385.

Sightseeing tours.

Underground Tour. Informative, humorous lecture and guided walking tour of 5-block area where street level was raised 8-35 ft after the Seattle fire of 1889, leaving many storefronts and some interiors intact underground; 90-min tour goes both above and below ground. (Daily; closed hols; advance res recommended) 610 1st Ave. Phone 206/682-4646 or 888/608-6337. ¢¢¢

Gray Line bus tours. 4500 W Marginal Way SW, 98106. Phone 206/624-5077 or 800/426-7505.

Smith Cove. Navy ships at anchor; Seattle Annex, Naval Supply Center along N side of W Garfield St. Can be seen from Elliott Ave and W Garfield St, NW Side.

The Seattle Aquarium. Features 400,000-gallon underwater viewing dome; re-created Puget Sound habitats with tide that ebbs and flows, tropical Pacific exhibit, marine mammal exhibits of seals and sea otters. (Daily) Pier 59, Waterfront Park, downtown. Phone 206/386-4300. ¢¢

University of Washington. (1861) 34,400 students. Visitor Information Center, 4014 University Way NE. A 694-acre campus with 128 major bldgs, stadium. Special exhibits in Henry Art Gallery (Tues-Sun; closed hols; fee). Thomas Burke Memorial-Washington State Museum (Tues-Sun; closed hols; free); Henry Suzzallo Library. Meany Hall for the Performing Arts, 3 theaters; health sciences research center and teaching hospital; Waterfront Activities Center; Washington Park Arboretum. Parking fee. Main entrance, 17th Ave NE & NE 45th St, NE Side. Phone 206/543-9198.

Volunteer Park. Tennis, play area, wading pool (June-Sep, daily), picnic area, conservatory (daily), formal gardens, observation deck in water tower (520 ft) with view of mountains, city, Puget Sound (daily). 15th Ave E & E Prospect St, NE Side. **FREE**

Warren G. Magnuson Park. Approx 200 acres; 1-mi shoreline. Swimming beach (mid-July-early Sep, daily), boat ramp; picnicking, playfield, concessions. Fee for some activities. (Daily) NE 65th & Sand Point Way NE, NE Side.

Washington Park Arboretum. Arboretum Dr E winds over 200 acres containing more than 5,000 species of trees and shrubs from all parts of world. Rhododendrons, cherries, azaleas (Apr-June). Arboretum open daily all yr. Tours (Jan-Nov, Sun). On both sides of Lake Washington Blvd, between E Madison & Montlake, Southeast Side. Phone 206/543-8800. **FREE** Within is

Japanese Garden. Ornamental plants, glassy pools, 12-tier pagoda, and teahouse. Tea ceremony. 1502

Lake Washington Blvd E. Phone 206/684-4725. ¢¢

Woodland Park Zoological Gardens. Displays more than 1,000 specimens, many in natural habitats, incl nocturnal house, African savanna, and Asian primates exhibits. Children's Zoo. (Daily) Intl Test Rose Gardens (free). Phinney Ave N between N 50th & N 59th Sts, on WA 99, I-5 N 50th St Exit, SW of Green Lake, NW Side. Phone 206/684-4800 (recording). ¢¢¢

Annual Events

Pacific Northwest Arts and Crafts Fair. 4 mi E in Bellevue. Art exhibits, handicrafts. Late July.

Seafair. Citywide marine festival. Regattas, speedboat races, shows at Aqua Theater, parades, sports events, exhibits. Phone 206/728-0123. Late July-early Aug.

Seasonal Event

A Contemporary Theater (ACT). One of the major resident theaters in the country, ACT is a professional (Equity) theater. Tues-Sun. "A Christmas Carol," in Dec. 700 Union St. Phone 206/878-3285. May-Nov.

Seattle-Tacoma Internationl Airport Area

For additional accommodations, see SEATTLE-TACOMA INTERNATIONAL AIRPORT AREA, which follows SEATTLE.

City Neighborhoods

Many of the restaurants, unrated dining establishments, and some lodgings listed under Seattle incl neighborhoods as well as exact street addresses. Geographic descriptions of these areas are given.

Downtown. S of Denny Way, W of I-5, N of S King St, and E of Alaskan Way and Elliot Bay. **N of Downtown:** N of E Denny Way. **S of Downtown:** S of Dearborn St. **E of Downtown:** E of I-5.

International District. SE of Downtown; S of Yesler St, W of I-5, N of S Dearborn St, and E of 4th Ave S.

Pioneer Square. Downtown area on and around Pioneer Square; bounded by 1st and James Sts, Yesler Way, and 1st Ave S.

Queen Anne. S of W Nickerson St and Washington Ship Canal, W of Westlake Ave, N of Denny Way, and E of Elliot Ave W and 15th St W.

Seattle Center. S of Mercer St, W of 5th Ave N, N of Denny Way, and E of 1st Ave N.

Motels/Motor Lodges

★★ **BEST WESTERN LOYAL INN.** *2301 8th Ave (98121), at Denny Way, Downtown.* 206/682-0200; fax 206/467-8984. 91 rms, 4 story. July-Sep: S $98; D $102; each addl $6; suites $185; under 12 free; lower rates rest of yr. Crib $3. TV; cable. Complimentary continental bkfst. Ck-out noon. Coin lndry. Business servs avail. In-rm modem link. Sauna. Whirlpool. Some refrigerators, wet bars; microwaves avail. Cr cds: A, D, DS, MC, V.

D ⊠ 🔥

★★ **HOTEL EDGEWATER.** *2411 Alaskan Way; Pier 67 (98121), W of Downtown.* 206/728-7000; fax 206/441-4119; toll-free 800/624-0670. 237 rms, 4 story. S $129-$170; D $129-$240; each addl $15; suites $350-$1,000; under 18 free. Crib free. Valet parking (fee). TV; cable (premium). Coffee in rms. Restaurant 6 am-11 pm. Bar 11-1:30 am; entertainment Tues-Sat. Ck-out noon. Meeting rms. Business center. In-rm modem link. Bellhops. Valet serv. Gift shop. Exercise equipt. Guest bicycles. Minibars. Some balconies. Built entirely over water; adj to ferry terminal. Cr cds: A, C, D, DS, ER, MC, V.

D 🏋 ⊠ 🐾 SC 🏃

★★ **PIONEER SQUARE HOTEL.** *77 Yesler Way (98104), Pioneer Square.* 206/340-1234; fax 206/467-0707; toll-free 800/800-5514. May-Aug: S $169; D $179; each addl $15; suites $299; under 12 free; lower rates rest of yr. Crib avail. Parking garage. TV; cable, VCR avail. Complimentary continental bkfst, newspaper, toll-free calls. Restaurant nearby. Ck-out 11 am, ck-in 3 pm. Business servs avail. Bellhops. Concierge. Dry cleaning. Exercise privileges. Golf, 18 holes.

Tennis, 4 courts. Cr cds: A, C, D, DS, ER, JCB, MC, V.

D 🏋🔥🏃🤸✈🏊🔥 SC

★★★ **RADISSON HOTEL.** *17001 Pacific Hwy S (98188). 206/246-7000; fax 206/246-6835; toll-free 800/333-3333.* 138 rms, 3 story. June-Aug: S $79-$115; D $89-$125; each addl $10; suites $145; under 18 free; lower rates rest of yr. Crib free. TV; cable (premium). Heated pool. Complimentary continental bkfst. Coffee in rms. Restaurant adj 6 am-11 pm. Ck-out noon. Meeting rms. Business servs avail. In-rm modem link. Bellhops. Beauty shop. Free airport transportation. Exercise equipt. Cr cds: A, C, D, DS, ER, JCB, MC, V.

D 🏊🏃✈🏊🔥 SC

★★ **SIXTH AVENUE INN.** *2000 6th Ave (98121), Downtown. 206/441-8300; fax 206/441-9903; toll-free 800/648-6440.* 166 rms, 5 story, no ground floor rms. Mid-May-mid-Oct: S $81-$109; D $93-$121; each addl $12; suites $150; under 17 free. Crib free. TV; cable (premium). Restaurant 6:30 am-10 pm. Rm serv 7 am-9 pm. Bar 11 am-midnight. Ck-out noon. Meeting rms. Business servs avail. In-rm modem link. Bellhops. Valet serv. Sundries. Cr cds: A, C, D, MC, V.

🏊🔥 SC

★ **TRAVELERS INN.** *4710 Lake Washington Blvd (98056), S on I-405 Exit 7. 425/228-2858; fax 425/228-3055; toll-free 888/596-4777.* 116 rms, 2-3 story. No elvtr. S $42.99; D $49.99; each addl $4; suites $63.99-$79.99; under 18 free. Crib free. TV; cable (premium). Heated pool. Complimentary coffee in lobby. Restaurant adj open 24 hrs. Bar 11-2 am. Ck-out 11 am. Coin lndry. Business servs avail. Cr cds: A, D, DS, MC, V.

D 🏋🏊🏃🤸🏊🔥

Hotels

★★★ **ALEXIS.** *1007 1st Ave (98104), Downtown. 206/624-4844; fax 206/621-9009; toll-free 888/850-1155. www.alexishotel.com.* 109 rms, 6 story. S, D $210-$235; suites $245-$550; under 12 free; some wkend rates. Crib free. Pet accepted. Covered valet parking $18/day. TV; cable (premium), VCR avail. Restaurant 6:30 am-3 pm. Rm serv 24 hrs. Bar 11 am-midnight. Ck-out 1 pm. Meet-

ing rms. Business servs avail. In-rm modem link. Concierge. Shopping arcade. Exercise equipt; steam rm. Massage. Refrigerators; some bathrm phones; microwaves avail. Wet bar, minibar, beverages, whirlpool in suites. Eight wood-burning fireplaces. Some balconies. Cr cds: A, C, D, DS, JCB, MC, V.

D 🍴🏋🏃🤸🏊🔥

★★ **BEST WESTERN EXECUTIVE INN.** *200 Taylor Ave N (98109), Seattle Center. 206/448-9444; fax 206/441-7929; res 800/528-1234; toll-free 800/351-9444. Email info@exec-inn.com; www.exec-inn.com.* 123 rms, 5 story, 1 suite. Apr-Oct: S $119; D $134; each addl $15; under 17 free; lower rates rest of yr. Crib avail. Parking garage. TV; cable. Complimentary coffee in rms, newspaper, toll-free calls. Restaurant. Bar. Meeting rms. Business servs avail. Concierge. Dry cleaning. Exercise privileges, whirlpool. Golf, 18 holes. Downhill skiing. Picnic facilities. Cr cds: A, C, D, DS, ER, JCB, MC, V.

D 🏋🏋🏃🤸🏊🔥

★ **CAMLIN HOTEL.** *1619 9th Ave and Pine St (98101), Downtown. 206/682-0100; fax 206/682-7415; res 800/426-0670.* 136 rms, 36 A/C, 4-10 story. S, D $83-$114; each addl $10; suites $175; under 18 free. Crib free. TV; cable (premium). Pool. Restaurant 6-10:30 am, 11:30 am-2 pm, 6-10 pm; Sat 6:30-11 am, 5:30-10:30 pm; Sun 6:30-11 am, 5-9 pm. Bar; entertainment Tues-Sat. Ck-out noon. Business servs avail. Some balconies. Motor entrance on 8th Ave. Cr cds: A, D, DS, JCB, MC, V.

D 🏊🏃🤸🏊🔥

★★ **CROWNE PLAZA.** *1113 6th Ave and Seneca St (98101), at Seneca St, Downtown. 206/464-1980; fax 206/340-1617; res 800/227-6963; toll-free 800/521-2762. Email crowneplaza@crowneplazaseattle.com.* 415 rms, 34 story. June-Oct S, D $240; each addl $20; suites $260-$525; under 18 free; wkend rates; lower rates rest of yr. Crib free. Covered valet parking $18. TV; cable (premium), VCR avail. Coffee in rms. Restaurant 6 am-10 pm. Bar 11-2 am. Ck-out noon. Meeting rms. Business servs avail. In-rm modem link. Concierge. Exercise equipt; sauna. Whirlpool. Refrigerators avail. Luxury level. Cr cds: A, D, DS, JCB, MC, V.

★★★ **DOUBLETREE GUEST SUITES.** *16500 Southcenter Pkwy (98188), I-5 Southcenter Exit, S of Downtown. 206/575-8220; fax 206/575-4743; toll-free 800/222-8733. Email laurau@dtseattle.com; www. doubletreehotels.com.* 221 suites, 8 story. S, D $119-$238; each addl $15; under 18 free; wkend, seasonal rates. Crib free. TV; cable (premium), VCR avail. Indoor pool; outdoor pool privileges in summer; whirlpool. Coffee in rms. Restaurant 6 am-10 pm; wkends 7 am-11 pm. Bar 11-2 am; entertainment. Ck-out noon. Meeting rms. Business servs avail. Gift shop. Free airport transportation. Exercise equipt; sauna. Racquetball. Refrigerators; microwaves avail. Atrium lobby. Cr cds: A, DS, MC, V.

★★ **THE EDMOND MEANY HOTEL.** *4507 Brooklyn Ave NE (98105), E of I-5 Exit 45th St, N of Downtown. 206/634-2000; fax 206/547-6029; toll-free 800/899-0251. Email info@meany.com; www.meany.com.* 155 rms, 15 story. May-Oct: S $119; D $129; each addl $15; lower rates rest of yr. Crib avail, fee. Parking lot. TV; cable, VCR avail. Restaurant 6 am-10 pm. Bar. Ck-out noon, ck-in 3 pm. Meeting rms. Bellhops. Dry cleaning. Exercise equipt. Golf. Tennis. Video games. Cr cds: A, D, DS, MC, V.

★★★★ **FOUR SEASONS HOTEL SEATTLE.** *411 University St (98101), Downtown. 206/621-1700; fax 206/623-2271; res 800/332-3442; toll-free 800/223-8772.* Listed on the National Registry of Historic Places, this property was built in 1924 as the Olympic Hotel and has been meticulously restored to original Italian-Renaissance splendor. The 240-room, 210-suite destination has three restaurants, including the stunning Georgian dining room, Shucker's Oyster Bar, and Garden Court (great for Sunday brunch), and its own retail annex with 14 boutiques. 450 rms, 13 story. S $225-$255; D $265-$295; each addl $30; suites $330-$1,250; under 18 free; wkend rates. Crib free. Valet parking $21. TV; cable (premium), VCR avail (movies). Indoor pool; whirlpool, poolside serv. Restaurant (see also GEORGIAN ROOM). Rm serv 24 hrs. Bar 11-1 am. Ck-out 1 pm. Convention facilities. Business center. In-rm modem link. Concierge. Shopping arcade. Barber, beauty shop. Airport transportation. Exercise equipt; sauna. Health club privileges. Massage. Bathrm phones, minibars; some refrigerators. Cr cds: A, DS, MC, V.

★★ **HAMPTON INN & SUITES SEATTLE.** *700 Fifth Ave N (98109). 206/282-7700; fax 206/282-0899; res 800/HAMPTON. Email hamseadt@aol. com; www.hamptoninnandsuites.com.* 124 rms, 6 story, 74 suites. June-Sep: S $139; D $149; each addl $10; suites $159; under 18 free; lower rates rest of yr. Crib avail. Parking garage. TV; cable, VCR avail. Complimentary continental bkfst, coffee in rms, newspaper, toll-free calls. Restaurant nearby. Ck-out noon, ck-in 3 pm. Meeting rm. Business center. Dry cleaning, coin lndry. Exercise privileges. Golf. Tennis. Video games. Cr cds: A, C, D, DS, ER, JCB, MC, V.

★★ **HAWTHORN INN & SUITES.** *2224 8th Ave (98121), Downtown. 206/624-6820; fax 206/467-6926; toll-free 800/437-4867. Email hawthorn seattle@uswest.net; www.hotels-west. com.* 60 rms, 7 story, 12 suites. May-Sep: S $119; D $129; each addl $10; suites $169; under 17 free; lower rates rest of yr. Crib avail. Pet accepted, some restrictions, fee. Parking garage. TV; cable (premium). Complimentary full bkfst, coffee in rms, newspaper. Restaurant nearby. Ck-out noon, ck-in 3 pm. Business center. Concierge. Dry cleaning, coin lndry. Gift shop. Exercise equipt, sauna, whirlpool. Golf. Cr cds: A, C, D, DS, JCB, MC, V.

★★★ **HOTEL VINTAGE PARK.** *1100 Fifth Ave (98101), at Spring St, Downtown. 206/624-8000; fax 206/623-0568; res 800/624-4433. www.hotelvintagepark.com.* 126 rms, 11 story. S $185-$205; D $200-$220; suites $215-$375; under 12 free; wkend rates; package plans. Crib free. Valet parking $18. TV; cable,

VCR avail. Complimentary coffee in lobby. Restaurant (see also TULIO). Rm serv 24 hrs. Ck-out noon. Meeting rm. Business servs avail. In-rm modem link, fax. Concierge. Exercise equipt delivered to rms. Health club privileges. Bathrm phones, minibars. Wine tasting (Washington wines) in lobby Mon-Sat. Cr cds: A, D, DS, JCB, MC, V.

★★★ **INN AT THE MARKET.** *86 Pine St (98101), at Pikes Place Market, Downtown. 206/443-3600; fax 206/448-0631; toll-free 800/446-4484. Email info@innatthemarket.com; www.innatthemarket.com.* 63 rms, 6 story, 7 suites. May-Oct: S, D $170; each addl $10; suites $360; under 16 free; lower rates rest of yr. Crib avail. Valet parking avail. TV; cable, VCR avail. Complimentary coffee in rms, newspaper, toll-free calls. Restaurant 8 am-1 pm. Bar. Ck-out noon, ck-in 4 pm. Meeting rm. Business servs avail. Bellhops. Concierge. Dry cleaning. Salon/barber. Exercise privileges. Golf. Tennis. Video games. Cr cds: A, C, D, DS, ER, JCB, MC, V.

★★ **INN AT VIRGINIA MASON.** *1006 Spring St (98104), E of Downtown. 206/583-6453; fax 206/223-7545; toll-free 800/283-6453.* 79 air-cooled rms, 9 story. S, D $100-$120; suites $198-$220. TV; cable (premium), VCR (movies). Restaurant 7-10 am, 11:30 am-3 pm, 5-9 pm. Ck-out noon. Business servs avail. English country-style apartment house (1928); Queen Anne-style furnishings. Totally nonsmoking. Cr cds: A, D, DS, JCB, MC, V.

★★★ **MAYFLOWER PARK.** *405 Olive Way (98101), Downtown. 206/623-8700; fax 206/382-6996; toll-free 800/426-5100. Email mayflowerpark@mayflowerpark.com; www.mayflowerpark.com.* 153 rms, 12 story, 18 suites. Apr-Oct: S $175; D $190; each addl $15; suites $235; under 18 free; lower rates rest of yr. Crib avail. Valet parking avail. TV; cable (premium), VCR avail. Complimentary newspaper. Restaurant 6:30 am-10 pm. 24-hr rm serv. Bar. Ck-out noon. Meeting rms. Business center. Bellhops. Concierge. Dry cleaning. Exercise equipt. Golf. Supervised children's activities. Video

games. Cr cds: A, C, D, DS, JCB, MC, V.

★★★ **MONACO HOTEL.** *1101 4th Ave (81427). 206/621-1770; fax 206/624-0060; res 800/945-2240; toll-free 888/454-8397. Email sales@monaco-seattle.com; www.monaco-seattle.com.* 144 rms, 11 story, 45 suites. S $240; D $255; each addl $15; suites $305; under 16 free. Crib avail. Pet accepted. Valet parking avail. TV; cable (premium), VCR avail, CD avail. Complimentary coffee in rms, newspaper. Restaurant 6 am-10 pm. 24-hr rm serv. Bar. Ck-out noon, ck-in 3 pm. Meeting rms. Business servs avail. Bellhops. Concierge. Dry cleaning. Gift shop. Exercise privileges. Golf. Video games. Cr cds: A, C, D, DS, ER, MC, V.

★★ **PACIFIC PLAZA.** *400 Spring St (98104), Downtown. 206/623-3900; fax 206/623-2059; toll-free 800/426-1165. www.pacificplazahotel.com.* 159 rms, 8 story, 1 suite. May-July, Sep-Oct: S, D $106; suites $195; lower rates rest of yr. Crib avail. Parking garage. TV; cable (premium). Complimentary continental bkfst, coffee in rms, newspaper. Restaurant 11 am-midnight. Bar. Ck-out 11 am, ck-in 4 pm. Business servs avail. Bellhops. Concierge. Dry cleaning. Exercise privileges. Golf, 18 holes. Tennis. Video games. Cr cds: A, C, D, DS, JCB, MC, V.

★★★ **THE PARAMOUNT.** *724 Pine St (98101), Downtown. 206/292-9500; fax 206/292-8610; res 800/426-0670. Email troyt@paramounthotelseattle.com; www.westcoasthotels.com/paramount.* 144 rms, 11 story, 2 suites. Apr-Sep: S, D $220; each addl $10; suites $425; under 18 free; lower rates rest of yr. Crib avail. Valet parking avail. TV; cable (premium). Complimentary coffee in rms. Restaurant. Bar. Ck-out noon, ck-in 3 pm. Meeting rms. Bellhops. Concierge. Dry cleaning. Exercise equipt. Golf. Tennis. Video games. Cr cds: A, C, D, DS, MC, V.

★★★ **THE RENAISSANCE MADISON HOTEL.** *515 Madison St (98104), I-5 S Madison St Exit, Downtown. 206/583-0300; fax 206/622-*

8635; res 800/-HOTELS-1; toll-free 800/468-3571. www.renaissancehotels. com/madison. 75 rms, 28 story, 78 suites. May-Oct: S, D $179; suites $199; lower rates rest of yr. Crib avail. Valet parking avail. Indoor pool, whirlpool. TV; cable (premium), VCR avail. Complimentary coffee in rms, newspaper. Restaurant 6 am-10 pm. 24-hr rm serv. Bar. Ck-out noon, ck-in 3 pm. Business center. Bellhops. Concierge. Dry cleaning. Gift shop. Salon/barber. Exercise privileges. Golf. Downhill skiing. Cr cds: A, C, D, DS, ER, JCB, MC, V.

★★★ **SEATTLE HILTON.** *1301 6th Ave (98101), W of I-5 Seneca-Union Exit, Downtown. 206/624-0500; fax 206/624-9029; toll-free 800/445-8667.* 237 rms, 28 story. S $165-$210; D $185-$230; each addl $15; suites $310-$475; under 18 free; some wkend rates. Crib free. Garage $13. TV; cable (premium). Complimentary coffee in rms. Restaurants 6 am-10 pm. Rm serv 24 hrs. Bar 11-2 am; pianist. Ck-out 1 pm. Meeting rms. Business servs avail. Concierge. Gift shop. Exercise equipt. Refrigerators, minibars. View of Puget Sound. Cr cds: A, C, D, DS, ER, JCB, MC, V.

★★★ **SHERATON SEATTLE HOTEL & TOWERS.** *1400 Sixth Ave (98101), Downtown. 206/621-9000; fax 206/447-5534; res 800/544-5064.* www.sheraton.com. 789 rms, 35 story, 51 suites. Apr-Nov: S $209; D $229; each addl $20; suites $325; under 18 free; lower rates rest of yr. Crib avail. Valet parking avail. Indoor pool, lap pool, whirlpool. TV; cable (DSS). Complimentary coffee in rms, newspaper. Restaurant 6.30 am-10 pm. 24-hr rm serv. Bar. Ck-out noon, ck-in 3 pm. Conference center, meeting rms. Business center. Bellhops. Concierge. Dry cleaning. Gift shop. Salon/barber. Exercise equipt, sauna. Golf. Downhill skiing. Video games. Cr cds: A, C, D, DS, ER, JCB, MC, V.

★★ **SILVER CLOUD INN.** *5036 25th Ave NE (98105), N of Downtown. 206/526-5200; fax 206/522-1450; toll-free 800/205-6940. Email management@university.scinns.com; www.scinns.com.* 163 rms, 4 story, 17

suites. June-Oct: S $115; D $125; each addl $10; suites $154; under 17 free; lower rates rest of yr. Crib avail. Parking lot. Indoor pool, whirlpool. TV; cable (premium). Complimentary continental bkfst, coffee in rms, newspaper, toll-free calls. Restaurant nearby. Ck-out noon, ck-in 3 pm. Meeting rms. Business center. Concierge. Dry cleaning, coin lndry. Exercise equipt. Golf. Bike rentals. Video games. Cr cds: A, C, D, DS, MC, V.

★★★ **SORRENTO.** *900 Madison St (98104), I-5 N James, S Madison Exits, Downtown. 206/622-6400; fax 206/343-6155; res 800/323-7500; toll-free 800/426-1265. Email mail@hotel sorrento.com; www.hotelsorrento.com.* 34 rms, 7 story, 42 suites. May-Oct: S $205; D $230; each addl $20; suites $270; lower rates rest of yr. Crib avail. Valet parking avail. TV; cable, VCR avail, CD avail. Complimentary coffee in rms, newspaper, toll-free calls. Restaurant 7 am-11 pm. Bar. Ck-out noon, ck-in 4 pm. Meeting rms. Business center. Bellhops. Concierge. Dry cleaning. Gift shop. Salon/barber. Exercise privileges. Golf, 18 holes. Tennis. Bike rentals. Hiking trail. Picnic facilities. Cr cds: A, C, D, DS, ER, MC, V.

★★★ **SUMMERFIELD SUITES BY WYNDHAM.** *1011 Pike St (98101), Downtown. 206/682-8282; fax 206/682-5315; res 800/-wyndham; toll-free 800/833-4353. Email jgehrman@ summerfieldsuites.com; www.wyndham. com.* 22 rms, 8 story, 171 suites. May-Oct: S, D $199; each addl $20; suites $209; under 18 free; lower rates rest of yr. Crib avail. Valet parking avail. Pool, whirlpool. TV; cable (premium). Complimentary continental bkfst, coffee in rms, newspaper, toll-free calls. Restaurant nearby. Ck-out noon, ck-in 8 pm. Meeting rms. Bellhops. Concierge. Dry cleaning, coin lndry. Gift shop. Free airport transportation. Exercise privileges, sauna. Golf. Tennis. Video games. Cr cds: A, C, D, DS, JCB, MC, V.

★★★ **WARWICK HOTEL.** *401 Lenora St (98121), at 4th Ave, Downtown. 206/443-4300; fax 206/448-*

1662; toll-free 800/426-9280. 229 units, 19 story. May-Oct; S $190; D $210; each addl $10; suites $275-$500; under 18 free; lower rates rest of yr. Crib free. Covered valet parking $12. TV; cable, VCR avail. Indoor pool; whirlpool. Restaurant 6:30 am-2 pm, 5:30-10 pm. Rm serv 24 hrs. Bar 11-2 am; pianist Wed-Sat. Ck-out noon. Meeting rms. Business servs avail. In-rm modem link. Exercise equipt; sauna. Bathrm phones; many refrigerators, wet bars. In-rm whirlpool in suites. Balconies. Fireplace in lobby. Cr cds: A, C, D, DS, ER, JCB, MC, V.

D ⇌ 🏋 ⬛ 🔥 SC

★★ **WEST COAST GRAND HOTEL ON FIFTH AVENUE.** *1415 Fifth Ave (98101). 206/971-8000; fax 206/971-8100; toll-free 800/325-4000. www.westcoasthotels.com.* 297 rms, 20 story, 9 suites. May-Oct: S, D $179; each addl $15; suites $225; under 16 free; lower rates rest of yr. Crib avail. Pet accepted. Valet parking avail. TV; cable. Complimentary coffee in rms, newspaper, toll-free calls. Restaurant 6:30 am-10 pm. Bar. Ck-out noon, ck-in 3 pm. Conference center, meeting rms. Business center. Bellhops. Concierge. Dry cleaning. Gift shop. Exercise equipt. Golf, 18 holes. Video games. Cr cds: A, D, DS, ER, JCB, MC, V.

D ➟ 🏌 🛏 🏋 ⬛ ⬛ 🔥

★★ **THE WESTIN SEATTLE.** *1900 Fifth Ave (98101), at Westlake, Downtown. 206/728-1000; fax 206/728-2259; res 800/-WESTIN1; toll-free 800/228-3000. www.westin.com.* 891 rms, 47 story, 34 suites. Apr-Oct: S $250; D $275; each addl $30; suites $1200; under 18 free; lower rates rest of yr. Crib avail. Pet accepted, some restrictions. Valet parking avail. Indoor pool, lap pool, whirlpool. TV; cable (DSS), VCR avail. Complimentary coffee in rms, newspaper, toll-free calls. Restaurant 6 am-9 pm. 24-hr rm serv. Bar. Ck-out noon, ck-in 4 pm. Conference center, meeting rms. Business center. Bellhops. Concierge. Dry cleaning. Gift shop. Exercise equipt. Golf. Tennis. Downhill skiing. Supervised children's activities. Cr cds: A, C, D, DS, ER, JCB, MC, V.

D ➟ 🎿 🏌 🎣 ⇌ 🏋 🔥 ⬛ 🏃

★★★★ **W SEATTLE.** *1112 Fourth Ave (98101). 206/264-6000; fax 206/264-6100; res 877/WHOTELS. Email wseattle.sales@whotels.com; www.whotels.com.* All with a modern decor of earth tones and plush fabrics. Since this new hotel is designed for style-conscious, tech-savvy business travelers, rooms offer CD players, high-speed, Ethernet access, and cordless phones at a well equipped work station. Dream up desires to test the "whatever you want, whenever you want it" service motto. The lobby, adjcent bar and dining room are new contenders in the 'now' scene of Seattle. 417 rms, 26 story, 9 suites. May-Oct: S $395; D $415; each addl $20; suites $1000; under 17 free; lower rates rest of yr. Crib avail. Pet accepted. Valet parking avail. TV; cable (premium), VCR avail, CD avail. Complimentary coffee in rms, newspaper, toll-free calls. Restaurant. 24-hr rm serv. Bar. Ck-out noon, ck-in 3 pm. Conference center, meeting rms. Business center. Bellhops. Concierge. Dry cleaning. Exercise privileges. Tennis. Video games. Cr cds: A, C, D, DS, ER, JCB, MC, V.

D ➟ 🎣 🏌 ⬛ 🏋 SC 🏃

B&Bs/Small Inns

★★ **BEECH TREE MANOR.** *1405 Queen Anne Ave N (98109), Queen Anne. 206/281-7037; fax 206/284-2350.* 7 rms, 2 share bath, 2 story. No A/C. No rm phones. Mid-May-mid-Oct: S $64-$94; D $74-$94; suite $110; each addl $10; wkly rates; lower rates rest of yr. Pet accepted. TV in sitting rm; cable (premium), VCR. Complimentary full bkfst. Restaurant nearby. Ck-out 11 am, ck-in 4-7 pm. Business servs avail. Street parking. Turn-of-the-century mansion (1903) furnished with many antiques. Totally nonsmoking. Cr cds: MC, V.

➟ ⬛ 🏋

★★ **CHAMBERED NAUTILUS BED & BREAKFAST.** *5005 22nd Ave NE (98105), N of Downtown. 206/522-2536; fax 206/528-0898; toll-free 800/545-8459. Email chamberednautilus@msn.com; www.chamberednautilus.com.* 10 rms, 3 story. May-Oct: S $110; D $115; each addl $15; lower rates rest of yr. Street parking. TV; cable, VCR avail, CD avail. Complimentary full bkfst. Restaurant nearby. Ck-out 11 am, ck-in 4 pm. Business servs avail. Concierge. Golf. Bike rentals. Hiking trail. Cr cds: A, MC, V.

★★ **CHELSEA STATION BED & BREAKFAST.** *4915 Linden Ave N (98103), N of Downtown. 206/547-6077; fax 206/632-5107; toll-free 800/400-6077.* 2 rms, 2 story, 7 suites. D $95; suites $125. Parking lot. TV; cable, VCR avail, CD avail. Complimentary full bkfst, newspaper. Ck-out noon, ck-in 3 pm. Business servs avail. Concierge. Golf. Tennis, 4 courts. Cr cds: A, C, D, DS, ER, JCB, MC.

★★ **GASLIGHT INN.** *1727 15th Ave (98122), E of Downtown. 206/325-3654; fax 206/328-4803. Email inn keepr@gaslight-inn.com; www.gaslight-inn.com.* 9 rms, 3 story, 7 suites. S $98; D $108; suites $158; under 18 free. Parking lot. Pool. TV; cable. Complimentary continental bkfst, coffee in rms, newspaper. Restaurant. Business center. Concierge. Dry cleaning, coin lndry. Cr cds: A, MC, V.

★★ **HILL HOUSE BED & BREAKFAST.** *1113 E John St (98102), E of Downtown. 206/720-7161; fax 206/323-0772; toll-free 800/720-7161. Email visitus@seattlebnb.com; www.seattlebnb.com.* 5 rms, 3 story, 2 suites. Apr-Nov: S $95; D $120; suites $160; lower rates rest of yr. Parking lot. TV; cable, VCR avail. Complimentary full bkfst, newspaper, toll-free calls. Restaurant nearby. Ck-out 11 am. Meeting rm. Business servs avail. Concierge. Exercise privileges. Golf. Tennis. Picnic facilities. Cr cds: A, D, DS, MC, V.

★★★ **INN AT HARBOR STEPS.** *1221 1st Ave (98101), Downtown. 206/748-0973; fax 206/748-0533; toll-free 888/728-8910. www.foursisters.com.* 20 rms, 2 story. S, D $150-$200; each addl $15; hol rates. Crib $15. TV; cable, VCR avail. Complimentary full bkfst, afternoon refreshments, complimentary coffee in rms. Restaurant 8 am-10 pm. Ck-out noon, ck-in 2 pm. Business servs avail. In-rm

modem link. Exercise equipt. Indoor pool; whirlpool. In-rm whirlpools, refrigerators, fireplaces. Balconies. Ocean and garden views. Cr cds: A, C, D, ER, JCB, MC, V.

★★ **ROBERTA'S BED AND BREAKFAST.** *1147 16th Ave E (98112), E of Downtown. 206/329-3326; fax 206/324-2149. Email robertsbb@aol.com; www.robertasbb.com.* 5 rms, 3 story. S $82-$105; D $90-$125; each addl $20. Complimentary full bkfst, coffee in rms. Ck-out 11 am. Business servs avail. Built 1903; many antiques. Extensive library. Totally nonsmoking. Cr cds: MC, V.

★★★ **SALISBURY HOUSE BED & BREAKFAST.** *750 16th Ave E (98112), E of Downtown. 206/328-8682; fax 206/720-1019. Email sleep@salisburyhouse.com; www.salisburyhouse.com.* 4 rms, 1 suite. Apr-Oct: Street parking. TV; cable. Complimentary full bkfst, coffee in rms, newspaper, toll-free calls. Ck-out 11 am, ck-in 4 pm. Cr cds: A, MC, V.

★★ **UNIVERSITY INN.** *4140 Roosevelt Way NE (98105), N of Downtown. 206/632-5055; fax 206/547-4937; toll-free 800/733-3855. Email univinn@aol.com; www.university innseattle.com.* 90 rms, 4 story, 12 suites. June-Sep: S $114; D $124; each addl $1000; suites $134; under 18 free; lower rates rest of yr. Crib avail. Parking lot. Pool, whirlpool. TV; cable, VCR avail. Complimentary continental bkfst, coffee in rms, newspaper, toll-free calls. Restaurant. Ck-out noon, ck-in 3 pm. Meeting rms. Business center. Dry cleaning, coin lndry. Exercise privileges. Golf, 18 holes. Tennis, 8 courts. Downhill skiing. Picnic facilities. Cr cds: A, D, DS, MC, V.

Restaurants

★★★ **ADRIATICA.** *1107 Dexter N (98109), Queen Anne. 206/285-5000.* Specializes in lamb, pasta, seafood. Own pastries. Hrs: 5-10 pm; Fri, Sat to 11 pm. Closed hols. Res accepted. Bar. Wine list. Dinner $10.50-$26. Parking. Built 1922. European villa decor.

Overlooks garden, Lake Union. Cr cds: A, D, MC, V.

★★★ **AL BOCCALINO.** *1 Yesler Way (98104), Pioneer Square. 206/ 622-7688. www.alboccalino.com.* Specializes in fresh seafood, rissotto, veal chop. Hrs: 11:30 am-10 pm. Closed hols. Res accepted. Lunch $8-$12.50; dinner $11-$21. Bistro atmosphere. Cr cds: A, D, MC, V.

D

★★ **ANDALUCA.** *407 Olive Way (98101), Downtown. 206/382-6999. www.mayflowerpark.com.* Specializes in Northwestern cuisine with Mediterranean influence. Hrs: 6:30 am-10 pm; Fri, Sat to 11 pm; Sun from 7 am. Res required. Bkfst $4.50-$8.25; lunch $7.50-$12.50; dinner $14.50-$23. Cr cds: A, D, DS, MC, V.

D

★★ **ASSAGGIO RISTORANTE.** *2010 Fourth Ave (98121), Downtown. 206/441-1399. Email assaggiori@aol. com.* Specializes in seafood, risotto. Hrs: 11:30 am-10 pm; Sat from 5 pm. Closed Sun; hols. Res accepted. Lunch $8.95-$14.95; dinner $9.95-$20.95. Italian decor. Cr cds: A, D, DS, MC, V.

D

★★ **ATLAS FOODS.** *2820 NE University Village (98105). 206/522-6025. www.chowfoods.com.* Specializes in pastries, desserts. Hrs: 9 am-10 pm. Res accepted. Wine list. Lunch $4.25-$9.75; dinner $5.50-$15.25. Child's menu. Entertainment. Cr cds: MC, V.

D ⊒

★★ **BANDOLEONE.** *2241 Eastlake Ave E (98102), N of Downtown. 206/329-7559. www.bandoleone.net.* Specializes in ancho chile-marinated chicken, Jamaican jerk rack of lamb, pistachio-crusted Chilean sea bass. Own pastries. Hrs: 5:30-10:30 pm; Fri, Sat to 11 pm; Sat, Sun brunch 9 am-2:30 pm. Closed Thanksgiving, Dec 24, 25. Res accepted. Bar. Dinner $8.50-$15.95. Sun brunch, $4.50-$6.95. Child's menu. Entertainment: Latin music Sun. Casual, eclectic decor with original artwork. Cr cds: A, DS, MC, V.

D

★★★★ **BRASA.** *2107 3rd Ave (98121). 206/728-4220. Email seattle@brasa.com; www.brasa.com.*

Rich fabrics, terrazzo walkways, and iron create the ambiance for a Mediterranean-inspired meal at this hip restaurant. The daily-changing menu offers rustic, earthy flavors from the wood-fired oven such as roast suckling pig and braised lamb with Moroccan chutney. Wildly creative desserts complete the evening. Hrs: 5-10:30 pm; Fri, Sat to midnight. Closed hols. Res accepted. Wine, beer. Dinner $16-$27. Entertainment. Cr cds: A, C, D, MC, V.

D

★★ **BROOKLYN SEAFOOD, STEAK & OYSTER HOUSE.** *1212 Second Ave (98101), Downtown. 206/224-7000.* Specializes in seafood, steak. Oyster bar. Hrs: 11 am-10:30 pm; Sat from 4:30 pm; Sun 4-10 pm. Closed Dec 25. Res accepted. Bar. Lunch a la carte entrees: $7-$14; dinner a la carte entrees: $12-$33. Child's menu. Valet parking (dinner). In 1890s bldg; artwork. Cr cds: A, D, DS, MC, V.

D

★ **BUCA DI BEPPO.** *701 N 9th Ave (98109), Downtown. 206/244-2288. www.bucadibeppo.com.* Specializes in chicken cacciatore, tiramisu. Hrs: 5-10 pm; Fri to 11 pm; Sat, Sun from 4 pm. Closed Thanksgiving, Dec 24, 25. Res accepted Sun-Thurs. Bar. Dinner a la carte entrees: $7.95-$19.95. Eclectic decor; mural on dome ceiling; some seating in kitchen. Cr cds: A, D, DS, MC, V.

D ⊒

★ **BURRITO LOCO.** *9211 Holman Rd NW (98117), N of Downtown. 206/783-0719.* Specializes in chile relleno, chicken en mole, tacos de carnitas. Hrs: 11 am-10 pm. Closed hols. Wine, beer. Lunch $3.25-$4.75; dinner $7.50-$8.95. Child's menu. Colorful Mexican decor. Cr cds: A, DS, MC, V.

D

★★ **CACTUS.** *4220 E Madison (98112), E of Downtown. 206/324-4140.* Spanish menu. Specializes in flan, tapas, fresh fish. Hrs: 11:30 am-10 pm; Fri, Sat to 10:30 pm; Sun from 5 pm. Closed hols. Lunch $5.95-$9.95; dinner $7.95-$13.95. Child's menu. Southwestern atmosphere. Cr cds: A, C, D, DS, ER, MC, V.

D

★★★ **CAFE CAMPAGNE.** *1600 Post Alley (98101), Downtown. 206/728-2233.* Specializes in traditional cassoulet, homemade sausages, rotisserie meats. Hrs: 8 am-10 pm; Fri, Sat to 11 pm; Sun brunch 8 am-3 pm. Closed hols. Res accepted. Bar. Bkfst $6.95-$12.95; lunch $5.95-$15.95; dinner $8.95-$14.95. Sun brunch $6.95-$12.95. Entertainment. French bistro decor. Cr cds: A, D, MC, V.
D

★★ **CAFE FLORA.** *2901 E Madison (98112), E of Downtown. 206/325-9100. Email cafeflora@mindspring.com; www.cafeflora.com.* Specializes in Oaxca tacos, portabello Wellington, wheatberry burgers. Hrs: 11:30 am-10 pm; Sat from 9 am; Sun 9 am-9 pm; Sat, Sun brunch 9 am-2 pm. Closed Mon; hols. Wine, beer. Lunch $6.95-$9.95; dinner $9.95-$14.95. Sun brunch sat, $5.95-$9.95. Child's menu. Two large rms, one with stone fountain, decorated with original works of art. Cr cds: MC, V.
D

★★★ **CAFE LAGO.** *2305 24th Ave E (98112), N of Downtown. 206/329-8005.* Specializes in pasta, wood-fired pizza, grilled fish. Hrs: 5-9:30 pm; Fri, Sat to 10 pm. Closed hols; also 4th wk in Aug. Wine. Dinner a la carte entrees: $10-$20. Trattoria atmosphere. Cr cds: A, DS, MC, V.
D

★★ **CAMPAGNE.** *86 Pine St (98101), Downtown. 206/728-2800.* Specializes in rack of lamb, daily fish entrees, foie gras terrine. Hrs: 5:30-10 pm. Closed hols. Res accepted. Bar. Dinner a la carte entrees: $24-$30. Valet parking wkends only. Cr cds: A, D, MC, V.
D

★★★ **CANLIS.** *2576 Aurora Ave N (98109), Queen Anne. 206/283-3313. Email canlis@canlis.com; www.canlis.com.* Specializes in seafood, steak. Own sauces. Hrs: 5:30-10:30 pm. Closed Sun; hols. Res accepted. Bar. Extensive wine list. Dinner $20-$34. Entertainment: piano bar. Valet parking. Jacket. Fireplace. Open-hearth grill. Panoramic view of Lake Union, Cascade Mountains. Formal dining. Family-owned. Cr cds: A, D, DS, MC, V.
D

★★ **CARMELITA.** *7314 Greenwood Ave N (98103), Phinney Ridge, N of Downtown. 206/706-7703. www.carmelita.net.* Specializes in vegetarian and vegan fare with Mediterranean influences. Own baking, pasta. Hrs: 5-10 pm; Fri, Sat to 10:45 pm. Closed Mon; Jan 1, Dec 24, 25. Bar. Dinner $8.50-$13.95. Child's menu. Eclectic furnishings decorate this large dining area with high ceilings. Cr cds: MC, V.
D

★★★ **CHEZ SHEA.** *94 Pike St (98101), in Pike Place Market, Downtown. 206/467-9990. Email shea101@aol.com; www.chezshea.com.* Specializes in seafood. Hrs: 5:30-10:30 pm. Closed Mon; hols. Res accepted. Bar. Dinner a la carte entrees: $6-$12. Complete meals: 4-course $39. Child's menu. Contemporary decor. Cr cds: A, MC, V.

★★ **CHINOOK'S.** *1900 W Nickerson (98119), in Fisherman's Terminal, N of Downtown. 206/283-4665. Email chinooks@anthonys.com.* Specializes in Northwest seafood, salmon, halibut. Hrs: 11 am-10 pm; Sat, Sun from 7:30 am. Closed Thanksgiving, Dec 25. Bar. Bkfst complete meals: $4.95-$9.95; lunch complete meals: $4.95-$11.95; dinner complete meals: $5.95-$16.95. Child's menu. Parking. On Fisherman's Wharf. Nautical decor. Cr cds: A, MC, V.
D

★★ **CHUTNEY'S.** *519 1st Ave N (98109), Queen Anne. 206/284-6799.* Specializes in tandoori items, tikka masala, curried mussels. Own baking. Hrs: 11:30 am-10 pm; Fri, Sat to 10:30 pm; Sun from 5 pm. Closed Dec 25. Res accepted. Bar. Lunch, dinner $8.95-$13.95. Indian prints and carved deities decorate walls. Cr cds: A, D, DS, MC, V.
D

★★ **CUCINA! CUCINA!** *901 Fairview Ave N (98109), N of Downtown. 206/447-2782.* Specializes in pizza, pasta, salads. Hrs: 11:30 am-10 pm; Fri, Sat to 11 pm. Closed Thanksgiving, Dec 25. Res accepted (lunch). Bar. Lunch a la carte entrees:

$4.95-$10.95; dinner a la carte entrees: $4.95-$14.95. Child's menu. Valet parking. Bicycles hang from ceiling in lounge. Cr cds: A, D, DS, MC, V.

D

★★★ **DAHLIA LOUNGE.** *2001 Fourth Ave (98121), Downtown. 206/682-4142. www.dahlialounge.com.* Specializes in crab cakes, salmon, duck. Hrs: 11:30 am-10 pm; Fri to 11 pm; Sat 5:30-11 pm; Sun 5:30-10 pm. Closed hols. Res accepted. Lunch $6.50-$12; dinner $9.95-$22. Child's menu. Eclectic decor. Cr cds: A, DS, MC, V.

D

★ **DOONG KONG LAU.** *9710 Aurora Ave N (98103), N of Downtown. 206/526-8828.* Specializes in northern Hakka cuisine. Hrs: 9 am-11 pm. Res accepted. Lunch $3.95-$5.95; dinner $5.95-$10.95. Parking. Chinese prints, fish tanks. Cr cds: A, D, DS, MC, V.

⬛

★ **DRAGON FISH ASIAN CAFE.** *722 Pine St. 206/467-7777. Email eat@dragonfishcafe.com; www.dragon fishcafe.com.* Specializes in chicken lettuce cup, five spice salmon. Hrs: 7-2 am. Closed Thanksgiving, Dec 25. Res accepted. Wine, beer. Lunch $6.95-$11.95; dinner $8.95-$16.90. Entertainment. Cr cds: A, C, D, DS, JCB, MC, V.

D ⬛

★★ **DULCES LATIN BISTRO.** *1430 34th Ave (98122), E of Downtown. 206/322-5453. www.dulceslatinbistro. com.* Specializes in chiles rellenos, roasted red pepper ravioli, paella Valenciana. Own pasta, pastries. Hrs: 5-10 pm. Closed Mon; hols. Res accepted. Bar. Dinner $14.25-$18.50. Complete meal: $25. Entertainment: classical guitarist Wed, Thurs, Sun. Bistro decor with deep gold and bronze accents; completely separate cigar rm. Cr cds: A, DS, MC, V.

D ⬛

★★★ **EARTH AND OCEAN.** *1112 Fourth Ave (98101). 206/264-6060. www.hotels.com.* Hrs: 6:30 am-10:30 pm; Fri to 11:30 pm; Sat, Sun from 7:30 am. Res accepted. Wine, beer. Lunch $9-$14; dinner $13-$24.

Child's menu. Entertainment. Cr cds: A, C, D, DS, JCB, MC, V.

D ⬛

★★★ **EL GAUCHO.** *2505 1st Ave (98121), Downtown. 206/728-1337.* Scandanavian menu. Specializes in flaming shish kabob, chateaubriand, Angus steak. Own pastries. Hrs: 5 pm-1 am; Sun to 11 pm. Closed hols. Res accepted. Bar. Wine cellar. Dinner a la carte entrees: $13-$30. Entertainment: pianist. Valet parking. Former union hall for merchant seamen; formal, elegant dining. Cr cds: A, MC, V.

D

★★ **ELLIOTT'S OYSTER HOUSE.** *1201 Alaskan Way (98101), Pier 56, Downtown. 206/623-4340. www. elliottsoysterhouse.com.* Specializes in Pacific salmon, fresh Dungeness crab, fresh oysters. Hrs: 11 am-10 pm; Fri, Sat to 11 pm. Res accepted. Bar. Lunch $5.95-$15.95; dinner $10.95-$29.95. Child's menu. View of bay. Cr cds: A, D, DS, MC, V.

D SC

★★★ **ETTA'S SEAFOOD.** *2020 Western Ave (98121), Downtown. 206/443-6000. Email maureen@tomdouglas. com; www.tomdouglas.com.* Specializes in Northwestern seafood. Hrs: 11:30 am-10 pm; Fri to 11 pm; Sat 9 am-11 pm; Sun from 9 am. Closed hols. Res accepted. Bar. Lunch $5-$28; dinner $8-$30. Child's menu. Two dining rms. Cr cds: A, D, DS, MC, V.

D

★★ **F.X. MCRORY'S STEAK, CHOP & OYSTER HOUSE.** *419 Occidental Ave S (98104), Pioneer Square. 206/623-4800. www.mickmchughs. com.* Scandanavian menu. Specializes in steak, oysters, prime rib. Oyster bar. Hrs: 11:30 am-10 pm; Fri-Sun to 11 pm. Closed hols. Res accepted. Bar. Lunch $6-$12; dinner $10-$25. Child's menu. 1920s atmosphere. Cr cds: A, D, DS, MC, V.

D ⬛

★★★ **FLYING FISH.** *2234 1st Ave (98121), Downtown. 206/728-8595. www.flyingfishseattle.com.* Specializes in Thai crab cakes, whole fried snapper in lemon grass marinade. Hrs: 5 pm-1 am. Closed hols. Res accepted.

Bar. Dinner $9-$16.95. Eclectic decor. Cr cds: A, D, MC, V.

D

★ **FOUR SEAS.** *714 S King St (98104), International District. 206/ 682-4900. Email fourseasrestaurant@ msn.com; www.fourseas.com.* Chinese menu. Specializes in Hong Kong-style dim sum, garlic spareribs, moo goo gai pan. Hrs: 10:30 am-midnight. Res accepted. Bar. Lunch $5.75-$8.35; dinner $5.25-$15.95. Entertainment. Parking. Hand-carved Oriental screens. Cr cds: A, D, DS, MC, V.

D

★★★ **FULLERS.** *1400 6th Ave. 206/447-5544. www.sheraton.com.* Specializes in Northwest seafood, fowl, Ellensberg lamb. Own baking, pastas. Hrs: 5:30-10 pm. Closed Sun, Mon; hols. Res accepted. Bar. Wine list. Dinner a la carte entrees: $18-$30. Child's menu. Entertainment. Original works by Northwest artists. Marble pool and fountain in dining room. Cr cds: A, DS, MC, V.

D

★★★ **GENEVA.** *1106 Eighth Ave (98101), Downtown. 206/624-2222.* Specializes in rack of lamb, crab cakes, calf's liver. Hrs: 5-10 pm. Closed Sun, Mon; hols. Res accepted. Wine list. Dinner a la carte entrees: $14.50-$24. Intimate dining in European atmosphere. Cr cds: MC, V.

★★★★ **GEORGIAN ROOM.** *411 University St. 206/621-7889.* Located in the Four Seasons Olympic Hotel, this Italian Renaissance-style dining room has romantic appeal with its exquisite chandeliers, vaulted ceilings and lovely piano music. Showy, intricately prepared cuisine highlights the Pacific Northwest's seasonal ingredients and is complemented by an extensive, over-the-top wine list and attentive srevice. Come for breakfast (served until 1:00 pm on Sundays), lunch or dinner. Specializes in Pacific Northwest seafood, rack of lamb. Own baking. Menu changes seasonally. Hrs: 5:30-10 pm; Fri, Sat to 10:30 pm; Sun 7 am-1 pm. Res accepted. Bar. Wine cellar. Bkfst a la carte entrees: $4.50-$22; dinner a la carte entrees: $19-$36. Sun brunch $14.50-$32. Entertainment: pianist. Valet parking. Jacket (dinner). Cr cds: A, D, DS, MC, V.

D

★★ **HIDDEN HARBOR.** *1500 Westlake Ave N (98109), N of Downtown. 206/282-0501.* Mediterranean menu. Specializes in prime rib, fresh seafood. Hrs: 11 am-10 pm; Sun from 4 pm. Closed Dec 25. Res accepted. Bar. Lunch $6-$11; dinner $9.95-$29.95. Child's menu. Valet parking. Waterfront dining overlooking yacht harbor. Cr cds: A, D, DS, MC, V.

D

★ **HIRAM'S AT THE LOCKS.** *5300 34th St NW (98107). 206/784-1733. www.savvydiner.com.* Specializes in steak, seafood. Hrs: 4-10 pm; Sat, Sun 11 am-10 pm. Closed Thanskgiving, Dec 25. Res accepted. Wine, beer. Lunch $7.95-$14.95; dinner $16.95-$48.95. Child's menu. Entertainment. Cr cds: A, D, DS, JCB, MC, V.

D SC

★★★ **HUNT CLUB.** *900 Madison St. 206/343-6156. Email sorrento@ earthlink.net; www.hotelsorrento.com.* Specializes in local seafood. Hrs: 7 am-10 pm. Res accepted. Bar. Bkfst a la carte entrees: $6-$10; lunch a la carte entrees: $9-$18; dinner a la carte entrees: $18-$30. Free valet parking. Cr cds: A, DS, MC, V.

D

★★★ **IL BISTRO.** *93A Pike St (98101), Downtown. 206/682-3049. www.savvydiner.com.* Specializes in fresh seafood, pasta, rack of lamb. Hrs: 5:30 pm-2 am. Closed hols. Res accepted. Bar. Dinner a la carte entrees: $11.95-$29.95. Valet parking Thurs-Sat. Original art. Cr cds: A, MC, V.

D

★★★ **IL TERRAZZO CARMINE.** *411 1st Ave S (98104), Pioneer Square. 206/467-7797.* Specializes in osso buco, venison ravioli. Hrs: 11:30 am-10 pm; Sat from 5:30 pm. Closed Sun; hols. Res accepted. Bar. Lunch $8-$13; dinner $9.50-$28. Elegant decor. Cr cds: A, D, DS, MC, V.

D

★★ **IVAR'S ACRES OF CLAMS.** *Pier 54 (98104), Downtown. 206/624-6852. www.ivars.net.* Specializes in

Northwestern king salmon, oven-roasted seafood brochettes, dungeness crab-topped prawns. Hrs: 11 am-10 pm; Fri, Sat to 11 pm. Closed Thanksgiving, Dec 25. Res accepted. Bar. Lunch $6.95-$13.95; dinner $10.95-$19.95. Child's menu. On pier with windows overlooking waterfront; collection of old photos of the area. Cr cds: A, MC, V.

D

★★ **IVAR'S INDIAN SALMON HOUSE.** *401 NE Northlake Way (98105), on N Shore of Lake Union, N of Downtown.* 206/632-0767. Specializes in smoked salmon. Hrs: 11 am-10 pm; Sat to 11 pm; Sun from 10 am. Closed Thanksgiving, Dec 25. Res accepted. Bar. Lunch $7-$15; dinner $13-$25. Sun brunch $14.95. Child's menu. Parking. Indian long house decor. View of lake. Family-owned. Cr cds: A, MC, V.

D

★ **JITTERBUG.** *2114 N 45th St (98103), N of Downtown.* 206/547-6313. *Email jitterbug2114@aol.com.* Specializes in Italian farmhouse egg rumble, charmoula chicken sandwich, transcontinental tango. Own pasta, pastries. Hrs: 8 am-10 pm; Fri, Sat to 11 pm. Closed hols. Bar. Bkfst $2-$8.25; lunch $4-$8.25; dinner $8.25-$15.75. Child's menu. Lively atmosphere; counter service. Cr cds: MC, V.

D

★★★ **KASPAR'S.** *19 W Harrison St (98119), Queen Anne.* 206/298-0123. *Email kaspars@aol.com; www.uspan.com.* Eclectic menu. Specializes in Northwestern cuisine, vegetarian dishes, smoked salmon. Own ice cream and sorbets. Hrs: 5-10 pm; Fri, Sat to 11 pm. Closed Sun, Mon; Jan 1, July 4. Res accepted. Bar. Dinner a la carte entrees: $13-$21. Child's menu. Valet parking. 2 floors of dining. Cr cds: MC, V.

D

★★★ **LE GOURMAND.** *425 NW Market St (98107), at 6th Ave, N of Downtown.* 206/784-3463. Specializes in poached salmon with gooseberry and dill sauce, roast duckling with black currant sauce. Hrs: 5:30-10 pm. Closed Sun-Tues; Easter, Thanksgiving, Dec 24, 25. Res accepted. Wine, beer. Dinner complete meals: $18-$30. Original artwork. Cr cds: A, MC, V.

★★ **MADISON PARK CAFE.** *1807 42nd Ave E (98112), E of Downtown.* 206/324-2626. Specializes in fresh seasonal pastas and seafoods, homemade bkfst pastries. Own pasta, pastries. Hrs: 5-9 pm; Fri to 10 pm; Sat 8 am-10 pm; Sun 8 am-2 pm. Closed Mon; hols. Res accepted. Wine, beer. Bkfst $2.50-$7.25; lunch $2.50-$8.50; dinner $12.95-$16.95. Child's menu. French bistro atmosphere in converted house; brick courtyard. Cr cds: A, MC, V.

★★ **MALAY SATAY HUT.** *212 12th Ave S (98144).* 206/324-4091. *Email 6864yps@yahoo.com; www.sidewalk.com.* Specializes in Indian bread, satay, curry meats. Hrs: 11 am-11 pm. Res required. Wine, beer. Lunch $5-$9; dinner $7-$25. Entertainment. Cr cds: MC, V.

D

★★ **MARCO'S.** *2510 First Ave (98121), Downtown.* 206/441-7801. Eclectic menu. Specializes in jerk chicken, fried sage leaves. Hrs: 5:30-11 pm; Fri, Sat to midnight. Closed hols. Res accepted. Bar. Dinner $10.95-$15.95. Child's menu. Eclectic decor. Cr cds: A, MC, V.

D

★★ **MAXIMILIEN-IN-THE-MARKET.** *81A Pike Pl (98101), Pike Place Market, Downtown.* 206/682-7270. *Email maximilien@earthlink.net.* Specializes in French-style Northwest seafood. Hrs: 11:30 am-10 pm; Sun 9:30 am-3:30 pm. Closed Jan 1, Thanksgiving, Dec 25. Res accepted. Bar. Bkfst $3-$7.25; lunch $5.50-$13; dinner $8.25-$24. Sun brunch $1.75-$8.50. French marketplace decor; antiques. View of bay, mountains. Cr cds: A, D, DS, MC, V.

D

★★ **MCCORMICK & SCHMICK'S.** *1103 1st Ave (98101), Downtown.* 206/623-5500. *www.mccormickandschmicks.com.* Specializes in fresh seafood. Hrs: 11:30 am-11 pm; Sat from 4:30 pm; Sun 5-10 pm; summer hrs vary. Closed Thanksgiving, Dec 25. Res accepted. Bar. Lunch $4.95-$12.75; dinner $9.95-$20. Beamed ceilings. Irish bar. Original art. Cr cds: A, DS, MC, V.

D

Public Market, Seattle

★★ **MCCORMICK'S FISH HOUSE.** *722 4th Ave (98104), Downtown. 206/682-3900.* Specializes in fresh seafood. Oyster bar. Hrs: 11:30 am-11 pm; Fri to midnight; Sat 4 pm-midnight; Sun from 4:30 pm. Closed Memorial Day, Thanksgiving, Dec 25. Res accepted. Bar. Lunch $5.95-$11.95; dinner $5.95-$19.95. Vintage 1920s and 30s atmosphere; tin ceilings. Cr cds: A, D, DS, MC, V.
D ⊒

★★★ **METROPOLITAN GRILL.** *820 Second Ave (98104), at Marion St, Downtown. 206/624-3287. Email coleary@conrests.com.* Specializes in 28-day aged prime steak, Northwest seafood dishes. Hrs: 11 am-11 pm; Sat from 4 pm; Sun from 4:30 pm. Closed Thanksgiving. Res accepted. Bar. Wine list. Lunch $6.95-$15.95; dinner $10.95-$27.95. Child's menu. Cr cds: A, D, DS, MC, V.
D

★★ **NIKKO RESTAURANT.** *1900 5th Ave. 206/322-4641. www.nikko restaurant.com.* Specializes in sushi, sukiyaki, shabu shabu. Hrs: 11:15 am-2 pm, 5:30-10 pm. Closed Sun; hols. Res accepted. Wine, beer. Lunch $6.75-$19; dinner $16.95-$50.

Entertainment. Cr cds: A, D, JCB, MC, V.
⊒

★★★ **NISHINO.** *3130 E Madison (98112), E of Downtown. 206/322-5800.* Specializes in omakase, sushi. Hrs: 5:30-10:30 pm; Sun to 9:30 pm. Closed hols. Res accepted. Dinner $4-$16. Complete meal: $45-$60. Rooftop dining. Cr cds: A, MC, V.
D

★★★ **PALACE KITCHEN.** *2030 5th Ave (98121), Downtown. 206/448-2001. Email maureen@www.tom douglas.com; www.tomdouglas.com.* Specializes in applewood-grilled rotisserie dishes. Own baking, pasta. Hrs: 11:30-1 am; Sat, Sun 5 pm-1 am. Closed hols. Res accepted. Bar. Wine list. Lunch $8-$14; dinner $14-$19. Child's menu. Central kitchen and bar dominate dining rm. Cr cds: A, DS, MC, V.
D

★★ **PALISADE.** *2601 W Marina Pl (98199). 206/285-1000. www.savvy diner.com.* Specializes in cedar-plank roasted salmon, dungeness crab stuffed wood-oven roasted halibut. Hrs: 11:30 am-9:30 pm; Sat noon-10 pm; Sun 10 am-9 pm. Res accepted. Wine list. Lunch $7.99-$17.99; dinner $15.99-$44.99. Brunch $14.99-$19.99. Child's menu. Entertainment. Fish pond runs through part of restaurant. Cr cds: A, D, MC, V.
D ⚑ ⊒

★★ **PALOMINO.** *1420 Fifth Ave (98101), on 3rd Floor of Pacific First Center, Downtown. 206/623-1300. www.citysearch.com.* Specializes in grilled salmon, spit-roasted chicken, wood oven-roasted prawns. Hrs: 11:15 am-9:30 pm; Fri, Sat to 10:30 pm; Sun noon-9:30 pm. Closed hols. Res accepted. Lunch $6.95-$15.95; dinner $7.95-$19.95. Parking. Original art, exotic African wood. Overlooking atrium. Cr cds: A, D, DS, MC, V.
D

★★ **PARAGON.** *2125 Queen Anne Ave N (98109), Queen Anne. 206/283-4548. Email paragonbar@earth link.net.* Specializes in risotto, seafood. Hrs: 5-11 pm. Closed Dec

25. Res accepted. Bar. Dinner $9-$18. Bistro decor. Cr cds: A, D, MC, V.

D ⌐

★★ **PIATTI.** *2800 NE University Village (98105), N of Downtown.* 206/524-9088. Specializes in regional Italian cuisine. Hrs: 11 am-10 pm; Fri, Sat to 11 pm. Closed Dec 25. Res accepted. Bar. Lunch, dinner $6.95-$19.95. Child's menu. Casual decor. Cr cds: A, D, MC, V.

D

★★ **PINK DOOR.** *1919 Post Alley (98101), Pike Place Market, Downtown.* 206/443-3241. Specializes in rustic Italian dishes. Own baking, pasta. Hrs: 11:30 am-10 pm. Closed Sun, Mon; hols. Res accepted. Bar. Lunch $6.95-$11.50; dinner $6.95-$17.95. Child's menu. Eclectic decor with cherubs, mirrors and a swing; patio offers water view. Cr cds: A, MC, V.

★★★ **PLACE PIGALLE.** *81 Pike St (98101), in Pike Place Market, Downtown.* 206/624-1756. Specializes in rabbit reminiscence, seafood in tamarind broth, duck bijoux. Hrs: 11:30 am-10 pm; Fri to 11 pm; Sat to 10:30 pm. Closed Sun; hols. Res accepted. Bar. Lunch $8-$14; dinner $15-$23. Overlooks Elliott Bay. Casual decor. Cr cds: A, D, MC, V.

★★ **PONTI SEAFOOD GRILL.** *3014 3rd Ave N (98109), Queen Anne.* 206/284-3000. Specializes in Pacific rim seafood. Hrs: 11:30 am-10 pm; Fri, Sat to 11 pm. Closed Jan 1, July 4, Dec 25. Res accepted. Lunch a la carte entrees: $8.95-$12.95; dinner a la carte entrees: $11.95-$19.95. Child's menu. Entertainment. Valet parking. Formal dining in attractive surroundings. View of Lake Washington Canal. Cr cds: A, D, MC, V.

D

★ **PORTAGE BAY CAFE.** *4130 Roosevelt Way NE.* 206/547-8230. Specializes in cafe linguine, blackened salmon. Hrs: 7 am-9:30 pm; Fri, Sat to 10 pm; Sun from 7:30 am. Closed Jan 1, Dec 25. Res accepted. Bkfst $2-$7.95; lunch, dinner $4-$8.25. Child's menu. Bright, contemporary decor with floor-to-ceiling windows. Cr cds: A, MC, V.

D

★★★ **PREGO.** *515 Madison St, Downtown.* 206/583-0300. Specializes

in seafood, pasta. Hrs: 11:30 am-10 pm. Closed Dec 25. Res accepted. Bar. Lunch $6-$13; dinner $11-$25. Original Matisse art. Views of skyline, Puget Sound. Cr cds: A, D, DS, MC, V.

D

★★★ **QUEEN CITY GRILL.** *2201 1st Ave (98121), Downtown.* 206/443-0975. Email queencitygrill@seanet.com; www.queencitygrill.com. Specializes in pan-seared Chilean sea bass with chili-lime butter, grilled ahi tuna, aged Colorado Angus steak. Own pasta, desserts. Hrs: 11:30 am-11 pm; Fri to midnight; Sat 5 pm-midnight; Sun 5-11 pm. Closed hols. Res accepted. Bar. Wine cellar. Lunch a la carte entrees: $7.95-$13.95; dinner a la carte entrees: $8.95-$19.50. Child's menu. Exposed brick walls, original artwork, and mahogany woodwork accent this dining rm. Cr cds: A, D, DS, MC, V.

D ⌐

★★★ **RAY'S BOATHOUSE.** *6049 Seaview Ave NW (98107), N of Downtown.* 206/789-3770. Email rays@rays.com; www.rays.com. Specializes in Northwest seafood. Hrs: 11:30 am-9 pm; Fri, Sat to 10 pm. Closed Jan 1, Dec 25. Res accepted. Bar. Wine cellar. Lunch $5.95-$9.95; dinner $10.95-$25. Child's menu. Valet parking. View of Olympic Mts. Cr cds: A, D, DS, MC, V.

D

★★★★ **ROVER'S.** *2808 E Madison St (98112), E of Downtown.* 206/325-7442. www.rovers-seattle.com. Recognized as one of the Pacific-Northwest's best chefs, owner Thierry Rautureau serves regionally inspired, contemporary cuisine with French accents at this relaxed, homey restaurant. The wine list's 300 selections constantly change, as do the seasonal offerings presented in both regular and vegetarian 5-course and 8-course degustation menus. The country-house setting is awash in yellow, an appropriate color given the staff's sunny disposition and their friendly service. Specializes in seafood, Northwest game, vegetarian dishes. Hrs: 5:30-11 pm. Closed Sun, Mon; hols. Res required. Extensive wine list. Dinner complete meals: $59.50, $69.50,

$97.50. Entertainment. Cr cds: A, D, MC, V.

D

★ **ROY'S.** *1900 5th Ave. 206/256-7697. www.roysrestaurant.com.* Specializes in fresh seafood with Pacific Rim influence. Own desserts. Hrs: 6 am-10 pm; Fri, Sat to 10:30 pm. Res accepted. Bar. Wine cellar. Bkfst complete meals: $4.25-$14; lunch complete meals: $8.75-$15.75; dinner complete meals: $14.95-$23.95. Child's menu. Multi-leveled, semicircular dining rm with nautical theme. Cr cds: A, D, DS, MC, V.

D

★★★ **RUTH'S CHRIS STEAK HOUSE.** *800 5th Ave (98104), Downtown. 206/624-8524.* Specializes in steak, seafood. Hrs: 5-10 pm; Sun, Mon 4-9 pm. Closed hols. Res accepted. Bar. Dinner a la carte entrees: $16-$29.95. Valet parking. Cr cds: A, D, DS, MC, V.

D

★★★ **SAZERAC.** *1101 4th Ave. 206/624-7755. www.monaco-seattle. com.* Specializes in honey-glazed cedar plank salmon on collard greens. Own baking, pasta. Hrs: 7 am-11 pm. Res accepted. Bar. Wine list. Bkfst $5.95-$14; lunch $8.95-$15.95; dinner $14.95-$24. Child's menu. Valet parking. Cr cds: A, D, DS, MC, V.

D

★★ **SERAFINA.** *2043 Eastlake Ave E (98102), N of Downtown. 206/323-0807. Email serafina@wolfenet.com; www.serafinaseattle.com.* Specializes in rustic Italian dishes. Hrs: 11:30 am-10 pm; Fri to 11 pm; Sat 5:30-11 pm; Sun from 5:30 pm. Closed hols. Res accepted. Bar. Lunch a la carte entrees: $2.95-$8.95; dinner a la carte entrees: $7.95-$17.95. Entertainment. Murals. Cr cds: MC, V.

D

★★ **SHIRO'S.** *2401 2nd Ave (98121), Downtown. 206/443-9844.* Specializes in sushi, full Japanese dinners. Hrs: 5:30-9:45 pm. Closed hols. Res accepted. Wine, beer. Dinner $16-$19.50. Casual decor with large windows. Cr cds: A, MC, V.

D ⌐

★★ **SPACE NEEDLE.** *219 4th Ave N (98109), Seattle Center. 206/443-2100. www.spaceneedle.com.* Specializes in regional dishes. Hrs: 11 am-9:30 pm; Fri, Sat to 10:30 pm; Sun from 8 am. Res accepted. Bar. Bkfst $9.95-$14.95; lunch $14.95-$19.95; dinner $20.95-$31.95. Sun brunch $17.95-$21.95. Child's menu. Valet parking. Revolving dining rm. Family-owned. Cr cds: A, D, DS, MC, V.

D

★★★ **STARS BAR AND DINING.** *600 Pine St (98101). 206/264-1112.* Hrs: 11:30 am-midnight. Res accepted. Wine list. Lunch $8.50-$12.50; dinner $14.50-$22.50. Child's menu. Entertainment: jazz Thurs-Sat. Cr cds: A, C, D, ER, MC, V.

D ⌐

★ **STELLA'S TRATTORIA.** *4500 9th Ave NE (98105), N of Downtown. 206/633-1100.* Hrs: Open 24 hrs; Sun brunch 4 am-3 pm. Closed Thanksgiving, Dec 25. Bkfst $2.95-$6; lunch $6-$8.50; dinner $7-$13. Sun brunch $2.95-$8. Child's menu. Lively atmosphere. Cr cds: A, DS, MC, V.

D SC

★★★ **SZMANIA'S.** *3321 W McGraw (98199), N of Downtown. 206/284-7305. Email ludger@szmania.com; www.szmanias.com.* Specializes in German dishes, seasonal Pacific Northwest dishes. Hrs: 5-10 pm. Closed Mon; hols. Res accepted. Bar. Wine list. Dinner $9-$20. Child's menu. Parking. Fireplace; open kitchen. Cr cds: A, D, MC, V.

D

★ **TRATTORIA MITCHELLI.** *84 Yesler Way (98104), Pioneer Square. 206/623-3883.* Specializes in pizza, pasta, chicken. Hrs: 7-4 am; Mon to 11 pm; Sat from 8 am; Sun 8 am-11 pm. Closed Dec 25. Res accepted Sun-Thurs. Bar. Bkfst $2.75-$8.75; lunch $4.95-$9.95. Complete meals: (Mon-Fri) $4.95; dinner $6.75-$14.50. Child's menu. Antique furnishings. Cr cds: A, DS, MC, V.

D ⌐

★★★ **TULIO RISTORANTE.** *1100 5th Ave. 206/624-5500. Email marjorietulio@juno.com; www.seattle.sidewalk. com/tulio.* Specializes in regional Italian cuisine. Hrs: 7 am-10 pm; Sat,

Sun from 8 am. Closed hols. Res accepted. Bar. Wine cellar. Bkfst a la carte entrees: $5-$10; lunch a la carte entrees: $9-$15; dinner a la carte entrees: $9-$21. Child's menu. Valet parking. Open view of wood-burning pizza oven. Cr cds: A, D, DS, MC, V.

★★★ **UNION BAY CAFE.** *3515 NE 45th St (98105), N of Downtown. 206/527-8364.* Specializes in fresh seafood, organic produce, free-range chicken. Own pastries. Hrs: 5-10 pm; Sun 4:30-9 pm. Closed Mon; hols. Res accepted. Dinner a la carte entrees: $11.50-$18.75. Child's menu. Intimate dining in two dining rms with original artwork, wine and flower displays. Cr cds: A, D, DS, MC, V.

D

★★★ **UNION SQUARE GRILL.** *621 Union St (98101), Downtown. 206/224-4321.* Specializes in steaks, chops, Northwestern seafood. Hrs: 11 am-10 pm; Fri to 11 pm; Sat 5-11 pm; Sun from 5 pm. Closed hols. Res accepted. Bar. Wine list. Lunch $6.95-$15.95; dinner $15.95-$29.95. Valet parking. Several dining areas; mahogany furnishings, dividers. Cr cds: A, D, DS, MC, V.

D

★★★ **WILD GINGER.** *1400 Western Ave (98101), Downtown. 206/623-4450.* Specializes in fresh seafood, curry dishes. Satay bar. Hrs: 11:30 am-midnight; Sun from 4:30 pm. Closed Thanksgiving, Dec 25. Res accepted. Bar. Lunch $6.95-$12.95; dinner $9.95-$19.95. Located near Pike Place Market. Cr cds: A, D, DS, MC, V.

D

Unrated Dining Spots

CASCADIA. *2328 1st Ave (98121). 206/448-8884. www.cascadiarestaurant. com.* Specializes in wild salmon, mint cured rack of lamb, sweet corn and squash ravioli. Hrs: 5-10 pm; Fri, Sat to 10:30 pm. Closed Sun; hols. Res accepted. Wine, beer. Dinner $20-$34. Child's menu. Entertainment: pianist Thurs-Sat. Cr cds: A, D, MC, V.

D

PAINTED TABLE. *92 Madison St, Downtown. 206/624-3646. www.alexis hotel.com.* Eclectic menu. Specializes in French cuisine. Hrs: 6:30 am-10

pm; Sat, Sun from 7:30 am. Res required (dinner). Bar. Wine list. Bkfst $3.95-$9.95; lunch $6.95-$14.95; dinner $15.95-$29.95. Entertainment. Valet parking. Cr cds: A, D, DS, MC, V.

D

Seattle-Tacoma International Airport Area

(See also Seattle, Tacoma)

Services and Information

Information. 206/433-5312.

Lost and Found. 206/433-5312.

Airlines. Aeroflot, Air Canada, Alaska Airlines, America West, American, Asiana, British Airways, Canadian Airlines Intl, China Eastern, Continental, Delta, Eva Airways, Frontier Airlines, Hawaiian Airlines, Martinair Holland, Northwest, Reno Air, SAS, Southwest, Swissair, TWA, United, USAir, Western Pacific Airlines.

Motels/Motor Lodges

★★ **BEST WESTERN EXECUTIVE INN.** *31611 20th Ave S (98003), I-5 Exit 143S. 253/941-6000; fax 253/ 941-9500; res 800/528-1234; toll-free 800/648-3311. Email bwfedway@ ricochet.net.* 112 rms, 3 story. Mid-June-mid-Sep: S, D $99-$129; each addl $10; under 18 free; lower rates rest of yr. Crib free. Pet accepted; $20. TV; cable (premium). Heated pool; whirlpool. Restaurant 6 am-11 pm. Bar. Ck-out noon. Meeting rms. Business center. In-rm modem link. Bellhops. Valet serv. Free airport transportation. Health club privileges. Cr cds: A, C, D, DS, ER, JCB, MC, V.

D

★★ **CLARION HOTEL SEATAC.** *3000 S 176th St (98188). 206/242-0200; fax 206/242-1998; res 800/252-7466. Email clarionwa2@aol.com.* 211 rms, 3 story. June-Oct: S $60-$89; D $70-$99; each addl $10; under 19 free; higher rates Sea Fair; lower rates rest of yr. Crib free. TV; cable (premium), VCR avail. Complimentary coffee in rms. Restaurant 6 am-2 pm, 5-10 pm. Bar from 4 pm. Ck-out noon. Meeting rms. Business center. In-rm modem link. Coin lndry. Free airport transportation. Exercise equipt; sauna. Massage. Indoor pool; whirlpool. Game rm. Some refrigerators, microwaves. Cr cds: A, DS, MC, V.

★★ **COMFORT INN & SUITES SEA-TAC-SEATTLE.** *19333 Pacific Hwy S (98188), 1 mi S on WA 99, at S 193rd St.* 206/878-1100; fax 206/878-8678; res 800/228-5051; toll-free 800/826-7875. 119 rms, 4 story. S, D $75-$150; each addl $10; suites $135-$175; under 18 free. Crib free. TV; cable (premium), VCR avail. Complimentary continental bkfst. Restaurant adj open 24 hrs. Ck-out noon. Meeting rms. In-rm modem link. Bellhops. Sundries. Free covered parking. Free airport transportation. Exercise equipt. Whirlpool. Refrigerator in suites. Cr cds: A, C, D, DS, ER, JCB, MC, V.

★★★ **DOUBLETREE INN.** *205 Strander Blvd (98188), I-5, I-405 Southcenter Exit, S of Downtown.* 206/246-8220; fax 206/575-4743; res 800/222tree. Email reservations@dtseattle. com. 198 rms, 2 story. S, D $99-$178; each addl $10; suites $136-$142; under 18 free; wkend, seasonal rates. Crib free. TV; cable (premium), VCR avail. Heated pool; poolside serv. Playground. Restaurant 6 am-10 pm. Bar 11-2 am. Ck-out noon. Meeting rms. Business servs avail. Bellhops. Valet serv. Health club privileges. Microwaves avail. Some private patios. Cr cds: A, DS, MC, V.

★★★ **HILTON.** *17620 Pacific Hwy S (98188), at S 176th St.* 206/244-1800; fax 206/248-4499; res 800/HILTONS. 178 rms, 2-3 story. S, D $109-$159; suites $275-$350; under 18 free; wkend rates. Crib free. Pet accepted. TV; cable (premium), VCR avail. Heated pool; whirlpool, poolside serv. Complimentary coffee in rms. Restaurant 6 am-11 pm. Rm serv 24 hrs. Bar 11 am-midnight. Ck-out 1 pm. Meeting rms. Business center. In-rm modem link. Bellhops. Valet serv. Sundries. Free airport transportation. Exercise equipt. Private patios. Gar-

den setting. Cr cds: A, C, D, DS, ER, JCB, MC, V.

★ **LA QUINTA INN.** *2824 S 188th St (98188), 1 mi S on WA 99.* 206/241-5211; fax 206/246-5596; res 807/NUROOMS; toll-free 800/NUROOMS. 142 rms, 6 story. Late May-Sep: S $74; D $82; each addl $8; lower rates rest of yr; under 18 free. Crib free. Pet accepted, some restrictions. TV; cable (premium). Pool; whirlpool. Complimentary continental bkfst. Restaurant opp. Ck-out noon. Coin lndry. Meeting rm. Business servs avail. In-rm modem link. Sundries. Free airport transportation. Exercise equipt. Luxury level. Cr cds: A, DS, MC, V.

★★★ **MARRIOTT HOTEL.** *3201 S 176th St (98188), at International Blvd (WA 99).* 206/241-2000; fax 206/248-0789; toll-free 800/228-9290. 459 rms. S, D $111-$132; suites $200-$450; under 18 free; wkly, wkend rates. Crib free. Pet accepted. TV; cable (premium), VCR avail. Indoor pool; whirlpool, poolside serv. Restaurant 6 am-11 pm. Bar 11-2 am. Ck-out 1 pm. Convention facilities. Business center. In-rm modem link. Bellhops. Valet serv. Shopping arcade. Free airport transportation. Exercise equipt; sauna. Game rm. Microwaves avail. Luxury level. Cr cds: A, C, D, DS, ER, JCB, MC, V.

★★★ **RADISSON HOTEL.** *17001 Pacific Hwy S (98188), N on International Blvd (WA 99) at 170th St.* 206/244-6000; fax 206/206-6835. 170 rms, 2 story. S $119-$159; D $129-$169, each addl $10; under 18 free; wkend rates. Crib free. TV; cable. Heated pool; poolside serv. Coffee in rms. Restaurant 6 am-10 pm. Bar 4 pm-1 am. Ck-out noon. Convention facilities. Business servs avail. In-rm modem link. Bellhops. Sundries. Gift shop. Free airport transportation. Exercise equipt; sauna. Luxury level. Cr cds: A, C, D, DS, ER, JCB, MC, V.

★ **RED ROOF INN.** *16838 Pacific Hwy-International Blvd (98188), ¼ mi S on WA 99, at S 168th St.* 206/248-0901; fax 206/242-3170; res 800/843-

7663. 150 rms, 3 story. June-Sep: S, D $78-$87; each addl $10; suites $80; under 12 free; lower rates rest of yr. Crib free. Pet accepted. TV; cable (premium). Restaurant 7 am-10 pm. Ck-out noon. Meeting rm. Business servs avail. In-rm modem link. Sundries. Free airport transportation. Exercise equipt. Balconies. Cr cds: A, D, DS, ER, JCB, MC, V.

★ **TRAVELODGE.** 2900 S 192nd St (98188). 206/241-9292; fax 206/242-0681; res 800/578-7878; toll-free 800/393-1856. 106 rms, 3 story. July-Sep: S, D $65-$90; each addl $6; under 18 free; lower rates rest of yr. Crib free. TV; cable (premium). Complimentary coffee in rms. Restaurant adj open 24 hrs. Ck-out noon. Coin lndry. Business servs avail. In-rm modem link. Free airport transportation. Sauna. Cr cds: A, C, D, DS, ER, MC, V.

★★ **WESTCOAST-SEA-TAC HOTEL.** 18220 International Blvd (98188), at 182nd St. 206/246-5535; fax 206/246-9733; toll-free 800/426-0670. 146 rms, 5 story. S $95-$105; D $105-$115; each addl $10; suites $150; under 18 free; some wkend rates. Crib free. TV; cable (premium), VCR avail. Heated pool; whirlpool, poolside serv. Restaurant 6 am-10 pm. Bar 11:30-2 am. Ck-out noon. Meeting rms. Business servs avail. Bellhops. Valet serv. Free valet parking. Free airport transportation. Exercise equipt; sauna. Cr cds: A, C, D, DS, ER, JCB, MC, V.

Hotels

★★ **BEST WESTERN AIRPORT EXECUTEL.** 20717 International Blvd (98198), 1 mi S on WA 99, at S 207th St. 206/878-3300; fax 206/824-9000; res 800/528-1234; toll-free 800/648-3311. www.bestwestern.com/airport executel. 130 rms, 3 story, 8 suites. June-Sep: S $99; D $109; each addl $10; suites $149; under 18 free; lower rates rest of yr. Crib avail. Parking lot. Indoor pool. TV; cable. Complimentary continental bkfst, coffee in rms, newspaper. Restaurant 6 am-10 pm. Bar. Ck-out noon, ck-in 2 pm. Meeting rms. Fax servs avail. Bellhops. Dry cleaning. Free airport transportation. Exercise equipt, sauna. Golf. Downhill skiing. Beach access. Video games. Cr cds: A, C, D, DS, ER, JCB, MC, V.

★ **DOUBLETREE HOTEL.** 18740 Pacific Hwy S (98188). 206/246-8600; fax 206/901-5902; toll-free 800/222-8733. Email madelyna@doubletree-sea.com; www.doubletreehotels.com. 850 rms, 12 story, 12 suites. June-Aug: S, D $149; each addl $15; suites $750; under 18 free; lower rates rest of yr. Crib avail, fee. Pet accepted, some restrictions, fee. Valet parking avail. Pool, whirlpool. TV; cable (DSS). Complimentary coffee in rms, newspaper, toll-free calls. Restaurant. 24-hr rm serv. Bar. Conference center, meeting rms. Business center. Bellhops. Concierge. Dry cleaning. Gift shop. Salon/barber. Free airport transportation. Exercise equipt. Golf, 18 holes. Cr cds: A, C, D, DS, JCB, MC, V.

★★ **HOLIDAY INN SEATAC AIRPORT.** 17338 International Blvd (98188), at S 173rd St. 206/248-1000; fax 206/242-7084; res 800/HOLIDAY; toll-free 877/573-2822. Email hiseatac@seanet.com; www.basshotels.com. 260 rms, 12 story. June-Sep: S $139; D $149; each addl $10; under 17 free; lower rates rest of yr. Crib avail, fee. Pet accepted, some restrictions, fee. Parking lot. Indoor pool, whirlpool. TV; cable (DSS). Complimentary coffee in rms, toll-free calls. Restaurant 6 am-10 pm. Bar. Ck-out noon, ck-in 3 pm. Conference center, meeting rms. Fax servs avail. Bellhops. Concierge. Dry cleaning, coin lndry. Gift shop. Free airport transportation. Exercise equipt. Golf. Video games. Cr cds: A, C, D, DS, JCB, MC, V.

Restaurant

★ **SEAPORTS.** 18740 Pacific Hwy S. 206/246-8600. Specializes in tableside Caesar salad, tableside steak Diane. Hrs: 11:30 am-10 pm; Sun, Mon from 5 pm. Closed Dec 25. Res accepted. Bar. Lunch $10.95-$17.95; dinner $17.95-$39.95. Sun brunch $17.95. Child's menu. Valet parking. Elegant dining. Multi-level dining areas offer

views of mountains or airport. Family-owned. Cr cds: A, D, DS, MC, V.
☐

Unrated Dining Spot

THE CRUMPET SHOP. *1503 First Ave (98101). 206/682-1598.* Specializes in green eggs and ham, maple butter cream cheese and walnut. Hrs: 8 am-5 pm. Closed Sun. Child's menu. Entertainment. Cr cds: A, MC, V.
☐ ⌘

Sedro Woolley

(A-3) *See also Anacortes, Bellingham, Mount Vernon*

Founded 1889 **Pop** 6,031 **Elev** 509 ft
Area code 360 **Zip** 98284
Information Chamber of Commerce, 714-B Metcalf St; 360/855-1841 or 888/225-8365

A thick growth of cedar once cloaked the Skagit River Valley, but it has been replaced with fertile farms, for which Sedro Woolley is the commercial center. Lumbering is still one of the main industries. The town represents the merger of the town of Sedro (Spanish for "cedar") and its onetime rival, Woolley, named for its founder.

A Ranger District station of the Mount Baker-Snoqualmie National Forest (see BELLINGHAM, SEATTLE) is located here.

What to See and Do

Lake Whatcom Railway. A 7-mi, round-trip steam train ride in antique Northern Pacific passenger cars through countryside. (July-Aug, Sat and Tues; Dec, Sat only; rest of yr, charter trips) 11 mi N on WA 9, in Wickersham. Phone 360/595-2218. ¢¢¢

North Cascades National Park. Authorized in 1968, this 504,781-acre area has beautiful alpine scenery, deep glaciated canyons, more than 300 active glaciers, hundreds of jagged peaks, and mountain lakes. It is adj to the 576,865-acre Glacier Peak Wilderness dominated

by 10,541-ft-high Glacier Peak and to Ross Lake and Lake Chelan national recreation areas. Camping along WA 20 in Ross Lake area (June-Sep, fee), climbing, hiking, backpacking (by permit); fishing. Contact 2105 Hwy 20. 50 mi E on WA 20 (portions of this road are closed in winter). Phone 360/856-5700. **FREE**

Seattle City Light Skagit Hydroelectric Project. A 4½-hour tour incl 560-ft ride up mountain on incline lift, 4½-mi boat ride to Ross Dam and Powerhouse (tour), and return by boat to Diablo; family-style dinner. (Late June-Labor Day, Thurs-Mon) Res and advance payment required. Single 90-min tour also avail. (July-Labor Day, Thurs-Mon) Contact Skagit Tours, Seattle City Light, 1015 3rd Ave, Seattle 98104. 62 mi E of I-5/Mt Vernon on WA 20 (North Cascades Hwy) in Diablo, in Ross Lake National Recreation Area. Phone 206/684-3030. Museum in tour center. ¢¢¢¢ Self-guided mini-tours at Ross Lake National Recreation Area incl

> **Newhalem Visitor Information Center.** Information on Skagit Project and National Park/Recreation Area. (Mid-June-Labor day, daily) **FREE**

> **Trail of the Cedars.** (45 min) Informative nature walk on S bank of Skagit River. Begins at end of Main St, Newhalem. **FREE**

> **Gorge Powerhouse/Ladder Creek Falls & Rock Gardens.** Begins at Gorge Powerhouse, Newhalem; self-guided tour of powerhouse, walk through Gorge Rock Gardens to Ladder Creek Falls. Gardens lighted at night. (Late June-Labor Day, daily) **FREE**

Swimming, hiking, camping, boating, fishing, windsurfing. Also fishing in Skagit River. Clear Lake. 3 mi S on WA 9. RV sites in town.

Annual Events

Woodfest. Woodcarvers displaying their craft. Second wkend May.

Loggerodeo. Logging contests, rodeos, parades. One wk late June-early July.

Santa's City of Lights. Parade, tree lighting. First wkend Dec.

Sequim

(B-2) *See also Neah Bay, Port Angeles, Port Townsend*

Pop 3,616 **Elev** 183 ft **Area code** 360
Zip 98382
Web www.cityofsequim.com
Information Sequim-Dungeness Valley Chamber of Commerce, 1192 E Washington St, PO Box 907; 360/683-6197 or 800/737-8462

Sequim (pronounced SKWIM) is a Native American name meaning "quiet water."

What to See and Do

Dungeness Recreation Area. Approx 200 acres. Camping (Feb-Oct; fee). Access to Dungeness National Wildlife Refuge. (Daily) Clallam County Park, 6 mi NW. Phone 360/683-5847.

Olympic Game Farm. Wild animals; guided walking tour (summer; drive-through rest of yr). Endangered species breeding program. (Daily) 6 mi NW. Phone 360/683-4295. ¢¢- ¢¢¢

Sequim Bay State Park. Swimming, scuba diving, fishing, clamming, boating (dock); hiking, tennis, ballpark, picnicking, camping (hookups). Standard fees. 4 mi SE on US 101. Phone 360/683-4235.

Annual Event

Irrigation Festival. Oldest community festival in the state; celebrates the bringing of water to the Sequim Prairie. Picnics, parades, flower shows, contests. First full wk May.

Motels/Motor Lodges

★★ **BEST WESTERN.** *268522 US 101 (59730). 360/683-0691; fax 360/683-3748; toll-free 800/528-1234.* 54 rms, 1 with shower only, 36 with A/C, 3 story, 14 suites. No elvtr. May-Sep: S $75-$100; D $85-$110; each addl $8; suites $95-$145; under 12 free; lower rates rest of yr. Crib free. Pet accepted; $25 refundable. TV; cable. Heated pool. Complimentary continental bkfst Mid-Oct-mid Mar. Complimentary coffee in rms.

Restaurant adj 7 am-9 pm. Ck-out noon. Meeting rms. Business servs avail. 9-hole putting course. Lawn games. Refrigerator in suites. Balconies. Picnic tables. Cr cds: A, C, D, DS, MC, V.

★ **ECONO LODGE.** *801 E Washington St (98382). 360/683-7113; fax 360/683-7343; res 800/553-2666; toll-free 800/488-7113. Email econoldg@ olypen.com; www.sequimeconolodge. com.* 42 rms, 2 story, 2 suites. June-Sep: S $79; D $89; each addl $10; suites $125; under 18 free; lower rates rest of yr. Crib avail, fee. Pet accepted, fee. Parking lot. TV; cable, VCR avail. Complimentary continental bkfst. Restaurant nearby. Ck-out 11 am, ck-in 3 pm. Fax servs avail. Concierge. Coin lndry. Golf, 18 holes. Tennis, 2 courts. Downhill skiing. Supervised children's activities. Picnic facilities. Cr cds: A, C, D, DS, MC, V.

B&Bs/Small Inns

★★ **DIAMOND POINT INN.** *241 Sunshine Dr (98382), E on US 101, left on Diamond Point Rd, right on Eagle Creek Rd, right on Sunshine Rd. 360/797-7720; fax 360/797-7723; res 888/797-0393. Email dpinn@olypen. com.* 6 rms, 2 share bath, 2 story. No A/C. No rm phones. Apr-Sep: S, D $75-$125; each addl $20; lower rates Oct-Nov, Feb-Mar. Closed rest of yr. Children over 5 yrs only. Complimentary full bkfst. Ck-out 11 am, ck-in 3 pm. Business servs avail. Whirlpool. Lawn games. Some refrigerators. Picnic tables, grills. Surrounded by 10 acres of evergreens. Totally nonsmoking. Cr cds: MC, V.

★★★ **GREYWOLF INN.** *395 Keeler Rd (98382). 360/683-5889; fax 360/683-1487; toll-free 800/914-9653. Email info@greywolfinn.com; www. greywolfinn.com.* 5 rms, 2 story, 1 suite. June-Sep: D $100; each addl $25; suites $130; lower rates rest of yr. Parking lot. TV; cable, VCR avail, VCR avail. Complimentary full bkfst, coffee in rms, toll-free calls. Restaurant nearby. Ck-out 11 am, ck-in 4 pm. Business servs avail. Concierge. Exercise privileges, whirlpool. Golf. Tennis, 2 courts. Downhill skiing.

Hiking trail. Picnic facilities. Cr cds: A, DS, MC, V.

★★ **GROVELAND COTTAGE BED & BREAKFAST.** *4861 Sequim Dungeness Way (98382), 5 mi N. 360/683-3565; fax 360/683-5181; toll-free 800/879-8859. Email simone@olypen.com; www.northolympic.com/groveland.* 4 rms, 2 story. No A/C. June-Oct: S $70-$100; D $80-$110; each addl $15; wkly rates; lower rates rest of yr. Children over 12 yrs only. TV; cable, VCR (free movies). Complimentary full bkfst, coffee in rms. Restaurant nearby. Ck-out noon, ck-in 3 pm. Meeting rm. Business servs avail. Picnic tables. Former merchant's residence (1886); many antiques, Oriental rugs. Library/sitting rm. Totally nonsmoking. Cr cds: A, DS, MC, V.

★★ **MARGIES INN ON THE BAY BED AND BREAKFAST.** *120 Forrest Rd (98382). 360/683-7011; fax 360/683-7011; toll-free 800/730-7011. Email margies@olypen.com; www.northolympic.com/margie.* 5 rms, 2 story. No rm phones. May-mid-Oct: S, D $75-$142; each addl $20; lower rates rest of yr. Children over 12 yrs only. TV; VCR avail (movies). Whirlpool. Complimentary full bkfst. Restaurant nearby. Ck-out 11 am, ck-in 4 pm. Located on bay. Totally nonsmoking. Cr cds: A, DS, MC, V.

Restaurants

★★ **DUNGENESS INN.** *1965 Woodcock (98382). 360/683-3331. www.dungenessgcc.com.* Specializes in seafood, steak. Hrs: 7 am-8 pm; Fri, Sat to 9 pm. Closed Dec 25. Res accepted. Bar. Bkfst $3.50-$7.95; lunch $3.75-$12.95; dinner $6.95-$17.95. Sun brunch Sat, $5.95. Child's menu. Two-level dining with windows offering panoramic view of golf course. Family-owned. Cr cds: MC, V.

★ **MOON PALACE.** *323 E Washington (98382). 360/683-6898.* Specializes in Cantonese, mandarin dishes. Hrs: 11:30 am-8 pm; Sat 3-9 pm. Closed Mon; hols. Res accepted. Bar. Lunch $3.95-$5.50. Buffet: (Sun)

$5.95; dinner $5.25-$9.95. Parking. Oriental decor. Cr cds: A, DS, MC, V.

★★ **PARADISE.** *703 N Sequim Ave (98382). 360/683-1977.* Specializes in steak, seafood, pasta. Hrs: 11 am-9 pm. Closed Mon; July 4, Thanksgiving, Dec 25. Res accepted. Bar. Lunch $3.95-$12.95; dinner $6.95-$24.75. Parking. Many plants. Etched-glass booth dividers. Cr cds: A, DS, MC, V.

Snohomish

(B-3) *See also Everett, Marysville*

Settled 1853 **Pop** 6,499 **Elev** 64 ft
Area code 360 **Zip** 98290
Web www.historicsnohomish.org
Information Chamber of Commerce, 127 Ave A, Waltz Bldg, PO Box 135, 98291; 360/568-2526

Snohomish is sustained by dairy farms, tourism, and retail trade. The Boeing plant that manufactures 747s and 767s (see EVERETT) is nearby. Snohomish claims to be the antique capital of the Pacific Northwest, boasting 450 dealers and many specialty shops.

What to See and Do

Blackman Museum. Restored 1878 Victorian house; vintage furnishings. (June-Sep, daily; Mar-May and Oct-Dec, Wed-Sun afternoons; closed rest of yr) 118 Ave B. Phone 360/568-5235. ¢ Nearby is

Old Snohomish Village. Six authentic pioneer bldgs moved here incl general store (ca 1910) and weaver's shop, which displays antique looms. (June-Sep, daily; rest of yr, by appt) 2nd St & Pine St. Phone 360/568-5235. ¢

Star Center Antique Mall. More than 165 antique shops housed in a former armory. Restaurant, children's play area. (Daily) 829 2nd St. Phone 360/568-2131.

Stevens Pass Ski Area. Road goes past Eagle Falls. (See LEAVENWORTH) 53 mi E on US 2.

Walking tour of historical houses.
Contact Chamber of Commerce, 116
Ave B, Waltz Bldg, for brochure.
Phone 360/568-2526. **FREE**

Soap Lake

(C-6) See also Coulee Dam, Ephrata

Pop 1,149 **Elev** 1,075 ft
Area code 509 **Zip** 98851

The minerals and salts in Soap Lake
(Native American name *Smokiam,* or
"healing waters") give the community status as a health resort. They
also whip into a soaplike foam that
lines the shoreline on windy days.
This is the south entrance to the
Grand Coulee, the 50-mile channel
of the prehistoric Columbia River.

Motel/Motor Lodge

★★ **NOTARAS LODGE.** *13 Canna
N (98851). 509/246-0462; fax 509/
246-1054. Email notaras@televar.com;
www.notaraslodge.com.* 21 kit. units,
2 story. May-Sep: S $58; D $65; each
addl $7; suites $91-$110; under 6
free; lower rates rest of yr. Pet
accepted; $40 refundable and
$10/day. TV; cable. Restaurant 11
am-10 pm. Ck-out 11 am. Refrigerators, microwaves; some in-rm

whirlpools. Balconies. Picnic tables.
Some rms with skylights. Cr cds: DS,
MC, V.

Restaurant

★★ **DON'S.** *14 Canna St (98851).
509/246-1217.* Specializes in steak,
seafood, Greek dishes. Own baking.
Hrs: 11 am-9:30 pm; Fri to 10:30 pm;
Sat 4-10:30 pm; Sun from noon.
Closed Dec 25. Bar. Lunch $4-$10.95;
dinner $5.95-$18.95. Collection of
Louie Leininger photos. Cr cds:
MC, V.

Spokane

(C-8) See also Cheney

Settled 1871 **Pop** 177,196
Elev 1,898 ft **Area code** 509
Web www.spokane-areacvb.org

Information Spokane Area Visitor
Information Center, 201 W Main,
99204; 509/747-3230 or
888/SPOKANE

Spokane (Spo-KAN) is the booming
center of the vast, rich "Inland

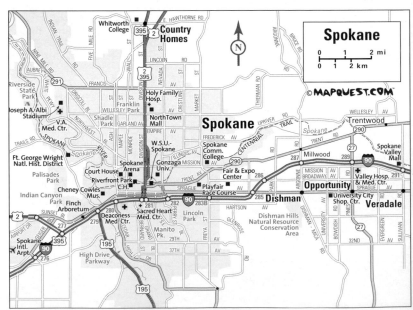

Northwest," an area including eastern Washington, northern Idaho, northeastern Oregon, western Montana, and southern British Columbia. A large rail center, the Spokane area also produces wheat, apples, hops, silver, gold, zinc, and lead. Spokane boasts more than 6,500 commercial and industrial firms. Thanks to the surrounding mountain ranges, Spokane enjoys what it likes to term New Mexico's climate in the winter and Maine's in the summer. The city itself is in a saucer-like setting amid pine-green hills with the Spokane River running through its 52 square miles.

Long a favorite Native American hunting and fishing ground, Spokane began as a sawmill, powered by Spokane Falls. This village, the name meaning "children of the sun," was the only point in a 400-mile-long north-south range of mountains where railroads could cross the Rockies and reach the Columbia Basin. Railroading sparked the city's early growth. The Coeur d'Alene gold fields in Idaho helped finance Spokane's continuing development and helped it to survive an 1889 fire that nearly leveled the city. Farming, lumbering, mining, and railroading aided Spokane's growth during the first decade of the century.

In 1974, the Havermale and Cannon islands in the Spokane River were the site of EXPO 74. The area has since been developed as Riverfront Park.

What to See and Do

Auto tour.

✪ **Loop drive.** A 33-mi city drive to major points of interest; route, marked with "city drive" signs, begins at Sprague Ave & Stevens St. Among points incl are

Cathedral of St. John the Evangelist. (Episcopal) Magnificent sandstone Gothic structure; stained-glass windows by Boston's Connick Studios; wood and stone carvings. Tours (Sat-Tues, Thurs; Sun after services). Recitals on 49-bell carillon (Thurs, Sun); also recitals on Aeolian-Skinner organ (schedule varies). 127 East 12th Ave. Phone 509/838-4277. **FREE**

Children's Museum. Children are permitted to touch, and encouraged to make noise and create. Weather exhibit; hydroelectric power station; music, art; regional and cultural history. (Daily) 110 N Post. Phone 509/624-5437. ¢¢

Comstock Park. Picnicking, tennis courts. Pool (mid-June-Aug, daily; fee for adults). Park (Daily). 29th Ave & Howard St. **FREE**

Manito Park. Duncan Formal Gardens (May-Sep, daily); conservatory (daily; closed Jan 1, Dec 25). Davenport Memorial Fountain with changing formations in 10-min cycle (May-Sep, daily); Japanese, lilac, and rose gardens (Apr-Oct, daily). Duck pond, picnicking. Grand Blvd at 18th Ave. Phone 509/625-6622. **FREE**

Cliff Park. Built around old volcanic island; Review Rock, ½ acre at base, offers highest point in city for viewing. (Daily) 13th Ave & Grove St. **FREE**

Cheney Cowles Museum. Museum closed for expansion until summer 2001. Houses collections of regional history and Native American culture. Fine Arts Gallery has changing art exhibits. Adj is **Campbell House** (1898), a restored mansion of Spokane's "age of elegance." W 2316 1st Ave. Phone 509/456-3931. ¢¢

Spokane Falls. Viewed from Bridge Ave at Monroe St or foot of Lincoln St. Spokane River roars over rocks in series of cascades; illuminated at night. Adj is

Riverfront Park. A 100-acre recreational park features outdoor amphitheater, IMAX theater, opera house, game rm. Spokane River runs through park; suspension bridges over Spokane River; foot bridges; skyride over falls. Miniature golf, roller coaster, carousel, children's petting zoo. Ponds; ice rink. Restaurant, vending carts, picnicking. Some fees. Spokane Falls Blvd from Division St to Post St. Phone 509/625-6600. **FREE**

Flour Mill. (1890) When it was built it was the most modern mill west of the Mississippi River. Today it is the home of boutiques, designer shops, galleries, restaurants. Overlooks Spokane River.

(Daily) 621 W Mallon, adj to Riverfront Park N entrance. **FREE**

Finch Arboretum. Approx 70 acres; incl Corey Glen Rhododendron Gardens, creek, 2,000 specimen plantings of ornamental trees and shrubs. (Daily) 3404 W Woodland Blvd, off Sunset Blvd. Phone 509/624-4832. **FREE**

Gonzaga University. (1887) 4,700 students. Rodin sculptures on display. In center of campus is Bing Crosby's gift to his *alma mater,* Crosby Student Center; Academy Award Oscar, gold records, certificates, trophies on display in Crosbyana Room (daily). Tours of campus (includes Crosby Center and St. Aloyisius Church; by appt). Boone Ave & Addison St. Phone 509/328-4220, ext 6531.

Mount Spokane State Park. More than 13,000 acres; incl Mt Spokane (5,881 ft), with excellent view from summit, and Mt Kit Carson (5,306 ft). Hiking, bridle trails, downhill skiing, cross-country skiing, snowmobiling (special parking permit required), picnicking, camping. Standard fees. 25 mi NE on WA 206. Phone 509/456-4169.

Riverside State Park. Approx 7,300 acres along Spokane River. Fishing, boating (launch); hiking, equestrian area, snowmobiling, picnicking, camping. Also 600-acre off-road vehicle area; outdoor stoves; interpretive center. Standard fees. 6 mi NW via Downriver Dr. Phone 509/456-3964.

Skiing. Mount Spokane. Five double chairlifts; patrol, school, rentals; cafeteria, bar, lodge. Longest run 1½ mi; vertical drop 2,000 ft. (Dec-mid-Apr, Wed-Sun) 30 mi NE on WA 206, in Mt Spokane State Park. Phone 509/238-2220. ¢¢¢¢

Worden's Winery. Tour and tasting of Gold Medal wines. Picnicking. (Daily; closed Jan 1, Dec 25) 7217 W 45th. Phone 509/455-7835. **FREE**

Annual Events

Ag Expo. Convention Center. Agricultural fair. Mid-Jan.

Spokane Interstate Fair. Interstate Fairgrounds. Broadway & Havana Sts. Phone 509/477-1766. Nine days mid-Sep.

Seasonal Events

Horse racing. Playfair Race Course. N Altamont & E Main Sts. Wed, Fri-Sun, hols. Phone 509/534-0505. July-mid-Nov.

Spokane Civic Theatre. 1020 N Howard. Live productions. Phone 509/325-2507. Thurs-Sun, Oct-mid-June.

Spokane Falls

Motels/Motor Lodges

★ **BUDGET INN.** *110 E 4th Ave (99202), I-90 Exit 281. 509/838-6101; fax 509/624-0733; res 800/325-4000.* 153 rms, 6 story. S $49; D $54; each addl $5; suites $59; under 18 free. Crib avail. Pet accepted. Parking lot. Pool. TV; cable. Complimentary continental bkfst, coffee in rms. Ck-out noon, ck-in 3 pm. Meeting rms. Business servs avail. Dry cleaning, coin lndry. Free airport transportation. Golf. Video games. Cr cds: A, D, DS, MC, V.

⌨ 🐾 🎿 ≈ ⛷ 🔥

★★ **COMFORT INN VALLEY.** *905 N Sullivan Rd (99037), 15 mi E on I-90, Exit 291. 509/924-3838; fax 509/921-6976; res 800/228-5150.* 76 rms, 2 story, 13 suites. May-Sep: S $59-$69; D $64-$74; each addl $5; suites $80-$135; under 18 free; lower rates rest of yr. Crib free. Pet accepted, some restrictions; $5/day. TV; cable, VCR avail. Pool; whirlpool. Complimentary continental bkfst. Restaurant nearby. Ck-out 11 am. Coin lndry. Meeting rms. Business servs avail. Refrigerator in suites. Cr cds: A, C, D, DS, MC, V.

⬜🔷🛏🏊🛒🔥

★ **DAYS INN AIRPORT.** *4212 W Sunset Blvd (99224). 509/747-2021; fax 509/747-5950; res 800/329-7466; toll-free 888/318-2611. Email 10000@ hotel.cendent.com.* 132 rms, 2 story. May-Aug: S, D $65; each addl $5; under 18 free; golf plans; lower rates rest of yr. Crib free. Pet accepted, some restrictions; $6. TV; cable (premium), VCR avail. Restaurant 7 am-10 pm. Bar 5 pm-midnight. Ck-out noon. Meeting rms. Business servs avail. In-rm modem link. Coin lndry. Free airport, railroad station, bus depot transportation. Heated pool. Picnic tables, grills. Cr cds: A, C, D, DS, MC, V.

⬜🔷♿⛷🏊🛒🏃🚴🛒🔥

★ **MOTEL 6.** *1919 N Hutchinson Rd (99212). 509/926-5399; fax 509/928-5974; res 800/466-8356.* 92 rms, 2 story. June-Sep: S $55; D $61; each addl $3; under 18 free; lower rates rest of yr. Crib free. TV; cable (premium). Complimentary coffee in lobby. Ck-out noon. Meeting rms. Business servs avail. Microwaves avail. Cr cds: A, D, DS, MC, V.

⬜🔷🛒🔥

★ **SHANGRI-LA.** *2922 W Government Way (99224), I-90 Business, Garden Springs Rd Exit. 509/747-2066; fax 509/456-8696; toll-free 800/234-4941.* 20 (1-3 rm) units, 2 story, 8 kits. S $42-$45; D $47-$50; each addl $5; kit units $50-$75. Crib free. Pet accepted. TV; cable, VCR avail. Heated pool. Playground. Coffee in rms. Restaurant nearby. Ck-out 11 am. Business servs avail. Free airport transportation. Health club privileges. Some refrigerators. Picnic tables. Cr cds: A, C, D, DS, MC, V.

🔷♿⛷🏊🛒🛒🔥🏃

★★ **SHILO HOTEL.** *923 E 3rd Ave (99202). 509/535-9000; fax 509/535-5740; res 800/222-2244.* 105 rms, 5 story. S, D $69-$99; each addl $8; under 12 free. Crib free. Pet accepted;

$7/day. TV; cable (premium), VCR (movies). Indoor pool. Complimentary full bkfst. Coffee in rms. Restaurant 6:30 am-10 pm. Bar 11:30 am-11 pm. Ck-out noon. Meeting rms. Business servs avail. In-rm modem link. Free airport transportation. Exercise equipt; sauna. Guest lndry. Refrigerators. Cr cds: A, C, D, DS, JCB, MC, V.

⬜🔷🛏🏃🛒🔥

★ **SUPER 8 MOTEL.** *N 2020 Argonne Rd (99212). 509/928-4888; fax 509/928-4888; res 800/800-8000. www.super8.com.* 187 rms, 3 story. May-Sep: S $50-$55; D $55-$65; each addl $5; under 13 free; higher rates special events; lower rates rest of yr. Crib free. Pet accepted. TV; cable (premium). Complimentary continental bkfst. Restaurant adj open 24 hrs. Ck-out 11 am. Meeting rms. Business servs avail. In-rm modem link. Coin lndry. Microwaves avail. Picnic tables. Cr cds: A, DS, MC, V.

🔷🛒🔥

★ **TRADE WINDS NORTH MOTEL.** *3033 N Division St (99207). 509/326-5500; fax 509/328-1357; res 800/528-1234; toll-free 800/621-8593.* 62 rms, 3 story, 1 suite. May-Sep: S, D $74; suites $104; under 17 free; lower rates rest of yr. Parking lot. Indoor pool, whirlpool. TV; cable (premium). Complimentary continental bkfst, coffee in rms, newspaper, toll-free calls. Restaurant. Ck-out noon, ck-in 3 pm. Dry cleaning, coin lndry. Sauna, steam rm. Golf. Cr cds: A, C, D, DS, MC, V.

🏃🛏🛒🔥 **SC**

★★★ **WEST COAST RIVER INN.** *N 700 Division St (99202). 509/326-5577; fax 509/326-1120; res 800/325-4000.* 245 rms, 2 story. S $80-$95; D $90-$105; each addl $10; suites $180; under 17 free. Crib free. Pet accepted, some restrictions. TV; cable. 2 heated pools; wading pool, whirlpool, poolside serv. Coffee in rms. Restaurant 6 am-10 pm. Bar 11-2 am; entertainment Wed-Sat. Ck-out noon. Meeting rms. Business servs avail. Bellhops. Sundries. Gift shop. Airport, railroad station, bus depot transportation. Tennis. Refrigerators avail. On river. Cr cds: A, C, D, DS, MC, V.

⬜🔷⛷🏊🛒🛏🏃🚴🛒🔥🏃

Hotels

★★ COURTYARD BY MARRIOTT.
N 401 Riverpoint Blvd (99202). 509/ 456-7600; fax 509/456-0969; toll-free 800/321-2211. 149 rms, 3 story. S, D $83; suites $119; under 12 free; wkly rates. Crib free. TV; cable. Indoor pool; whirlpool. Complimentary coffee in rms. Restaurant 6:30-10 am. Bar 5-10 pm. Ck-out noon. Coin lndry. Meeting rms. Business servs avail. Valet serv. Exercise equipt. Refrigerator in suites. Balconies. Cr cds: A, DS, MC, V.

★★★ DOUBLETREE HOTEL.
1100 N Sullivan Rd (99037), I-90 Exit 291. 509/924-9000; fax 509/922-4965; res 800/222TREE. Email reservations@ doubletreevalley.com; www.doubletree valley.com. 226 rms, 3 story, 10 suites. Apr-Sep: S $89; D $99; each addl $10; suites $119; under 18 free; lower rates rest of yr. Crib avail, fee. Pet accepted, some restrictions, fee. Parking lot. Pool, whirlpool. TV; cable (premium). Complimentary coffee in rms, newspaper, toll-free calls. Restaurant 6 am-11 pm. Bar. Ck-out noon, ck-in 3 pm. Meeting rms. Business center. Bellhops. Dry cleaning. Gift shop. Salon/barber. Free airport transportation. Exercise equipt. Golf, 18 holes. Downhill skiing. Hiking trail. Video games. Cr cds: A, C, D, DS, JCB, MC.

★★★ DOUBLETREE HOTEL SPOKANE CIT.
N 322 Spokane Falls Ct (99201), 3 blks W of US 2/395. 509/455-9600; fax 509/744-2343; res 800/222tree. Email sales@doubletree spokane.com. 369 rms, 15 story. June-Sep: S, D $119-$139; each addl $10; suites $125-$450; under 18 free; some wkend rates; higher rates: Bloomsday, AAUW dragster finals; lower rates rest of yr. Crib free. Valet parking. TV; cable (premium). Indoor/outdoor heated pool. Restaurant 6:30 am-10 pm. Bar 11-2 am; entertainment. Ck-out noon. Convention facilities. Business center. Concierge. Free airport, railroad station, bus depot transportation. Exercise equipt. Wet bar in some suites. On river in park. Cr cds: A, DS, MC, V.

★★ QUALITY INN VALLEY SUITES.
8923 E Mission Ave (99212). 509/928-5218; fax 509/928-5211; res 800/228-5151; toll-free 800/777-7355. Email qualitysales@spokanequalityinn. com; www.spokanequalityinn.com. 88 rms, 4 story, 40 suites. Apr-Sep: S, D $79; suites $190; lower rates rest of yr. Crib avail. Pet accepted, fee. Parking lot. Indoor pool, whirlpool. TV; cable (premium), VCR avail. Complimentary continental bkfst, coffee in rms, newspaper, toll-free calls. Restaurant. Meeting rms. Business center. Dry cleaning, coin lndry. Gift shop. Salon/barber. Exercise privileges, sauna. Golf, 18 holes. Tennis, 6 courts. Downhill skiing. Supervised children's activities. Hiking trail. Picnic facilities. Video games. Cr cds: A, D, DS, JCB, MC, V.

★★ RAMADA INN.
Spokane International Airport (99219). 509/838-5211; fax 509/838-1074; toll-free 800/272-6232. Email ramada705@aol.com; www.ramada.com. 165 rms, 2 story, 9 suites. May-Oct: S $85; D $95; each addl $10; suites $185; under 18 free; lower rates rest of yr. Crib avail. Pet accepted, some restrictions. Parking lot. Indoor/outdoor pools, whirlpool. TV; cable (DSS), VCR avail. Complimentary continental bkfst, coffee in rms, newspaper, toll-free calls. Restaurant. Bar. Meeting rms. Business servs avail. Bellhops. Dry cleaning, coin lndry. Gift shop. Free airport transportation. Exercise equipt. Golf. Downhill skiing. Supervised children's activities. Hiking trail. Video games. Cr cds: A, C, D, DS, ER, MC, V.

★ TRAVELODGE.
33 W Spokane Falls Blvd (99201). 509/623-9727; fax 509/623-9737; res 800/578-7878; toll-free 888/824-0292. Email mpaupst@ aol.com; www.spokanetravelodge.com. 80 rms, 4 story, 6 suites. Mar-Oct: S $90; D $100; each addl $10; suites $210; lower rates rest of yr. Crib avail. Pet accepted, some restrictions, fee. Parking garage. TV; cable (DSS), VCR avail. Complimentary continental bkfst, coffee in rms, newspaper, toll-free calls. Restaurant. Ck-out noon, ck-in noon. Meeting rm. Busi-

ness center. Dry cleaning, coin lndry. Exercise privileges. Golf. Tennis. Downhill skiing. Cr cds: A, C, D, DS, ER, JCB, MC, V.

★★ **WESTCOAST RIDPATH HOTEL.** *515 W Sprague Ave (99201), at Stevens St. 509/838-2711; fax 509/747-6970; res 800/325-4000. www.westcoasthotels.com.* 324 rms, 12 story, 18 suites. May-June: S, D $99; suites $199; lower rates rest of yr. Crib avail. Valet parking avail. Pool, lap pool. TV; cable (premium). Complimentary coffee in rms, newspaper, toll-free calls. Restaurant. Bar. Conference center, meeting rms. Business center. Bellhops. Dry cleaning, coin lndry. Gift shop. Salon/barber. Free airport transportation. Exercise privileges. Golf. Tennis. Downhill skiing. Bike rentals. Supervised children's activities. Hiking trail. Picnic facilities. Video games. Cr cds: A, D, DS, MC, V.

B&Bs/Small Inns

★★★ **ANGELICA'S BED & BREAKFAST.** *1321 W 9th Ave (99204). 509/624-5598; fax 509/624-5598; toll-free 800/987-0053. Email info@angelicas.com; www.angelicasbb.com.* 4 rms, 2 story. Apr-Dec: D $95; suites $110; lower rates rest of yr. Parking lot. TV; cable, VCR avail, CD avail. Complimentary full bkfst, coffee in rms, newspaper, toll-free calls. Restaurant nearby. Ck-out 10:30 am, ck-in 4 pm. Meeting rms. Business center. Exercise privileges. Golf. Downhill skiing. Bike rentals. Hiking trail. Picnic facilities. Cr cds: A, MC, V.

★★★ **FOTHERINGHAM HOUSE.** *2128 W 2nd Ave (99204). 509/838-1891; fax 509/838-1807. Email innkeeper@fotheringham.net; www.fotheringham.net.* 4 rms, 2 story. S, D $105. Street parking. TV; cable, VCR avail, CD avail. Complimentary full bkfst, coffee in rms, newspaper. Restaurant. Ck-out 11 am, ck-in 2 pm. Meeting rm. Business servs avail. Gift shop. Free airport transportation. Exercise privileges. Golf. Tennis. Cr cds: A, DS, MC, V.

★★★ **MARIANNA STOLTZ HOUSE BED & BREAKFAST.** *427 E Indiana Ave (99207). 509/483-4316; fax 509/483-6773; toll-free 800/978-6587. Email mstoltz@aimcomm.com; www.mariannastoltzhouse.com.* 3 rms, 2 story, 1 suite. May-Sep: S $79; D $89; each addl $10; suites $99; children $10; under 6 free; lower rates rest of yr. Parking lot. TV; cable, VCR avail. Complimentary full bkfst, coffee in rms, newspaper. Restaurant nearby. Business servs avail. Free airport transportation. Exercise privileges. Golf. Downhill skiing. Cr cds: A, DS, MC, V.

Restaurants

★ **CHAPTER XI.** *105 E Mission Ave (99202). 509/326-0466.* Specializes in prime rib, stuffed shrimp, mud pie. Salad bar. Hrs: 11:30 am-9 pm; Fri to 10 pm; Sat 4-10 pm; Sun from 4 pm. Closed Thanksgiving, Dec 25. Bar. Lunch $6-$10; dinner $6-$25. Cr cds: A, C, DS, MC, V.

★★ **CLINKERDAGGER.** *621 W Mallon (99201), I-90 Newport Exit. 509/328-5965.* Continental menu. Specializes in prime rib, fish. Hrs: 11:15 am-9 pm; Fri, Sat to 10 pm; Sun 4-9 pm. Closed July 4, Dec 25. Res accepted. Bar. Lunch a la carte entrees: $5.95-$12.95; dinner a la carte entrees: $12.95-$22. Child's menu. Parking. Converted flour mill; shops inside. Overlooks Spokane Falls. Cr cds: A, C, D, DS, ER, MC, V.

★ **OLD SPAGHETTI FACTORY.** *152 S Monroe St (99201), I-90 Lincoln St Exit. 509/624-8916.* Specializes in fettucine, tortellini, spaghetti dishes. Hrs: 4-9 pm; Fri, Sat to 11 pm. Closed Thanksgiving, Dec 24, 25. Bar. Dinner complete meal: $5-$9. Converted warehouse. Cr cds: A, D, DS, MC, V.

★★★ **PATSY CLARK'S.** *2208 W 2nd Ave (99204). 509/838-8300. Email senescall@aol.com; www.nwadv.com/patsy-clarks.* Specializes in seafood, steak, wild game. Own baking. Menu changes seasonally. Hrs: 11:30 am-9:30 pm. Res accepted. Bar. Lunch a la carte entrees: $10-$14; dinner a la carte entrees: $14-$27. Sun brunch $18. Entertainment: pianist. Valet parking. Mansion designed and built in 1898 by Kirkland K. Cutter for mining tycoon Patrick "Patsy" Clark. Antiques, handmade furniture, Tiffany stained glass. Cr cds: A, MC, V.

Sunnyside

(E-5) *See also Richland, Toppenish*

Founded 1893 **Pop** 11,238 **Elev** 743 ft **Area code** 509 **Zip** 98944
Information Chamber of Commerce, 520 S 7th St, PO Box 329; 509/837-5939 or 800/457-8089

This is the home of one of the first irrigation projects of more than 100,000 acres in the state. Its selection as a site for a large settlement of the Christian Cooperative movement brought growth and prosperity to this community. Irrigation continues to bring rich crops to the fields that circle the city.

The town is aptly named. Sunnyside averages over 300 days of sunshine every year with mild winters and dry summers.

What to See and Do

Darigold Dairy Fair. Tours of cheesemaking plant. (Daily; closed hols) 400 Alexander Rd. Phone 509/837-4321. **FREE**

Tucker Cellars Winery. Wine tasting. (Daily) Yakima Valley Hwy & Ray Rd. Phone 509/837-8701.

Washington Hills Cellar. Wine tasting. (Daily) 111 E Lincoln. Phone 509/839-WINE.

Tacoma (C-3)

Settled 1868 **Pop** 176,664 **Elev** 250 ft **Area code** 253
Web www.tpctourism.org
Information Tacoma-Pierce County Visitor & Convention Bureau, 1001 Pacific Ave, #400, PO Box 1754, 98402; 253/627-2836 or 800/272-2662

In its gemlike setting on Puget Sound, midway between Seattle and Olympia, Tacoma maintains its wood and paper products and its shipping traditions. Its harbor is a port of call for merchant vessels plying the oceans of the world. Backed by timber, shipping facilities, and low-cost water and power, more than 500 industries produce lumber, plywood, paper, millwork, furniture, foodstuffs, beverages, chemicals, and clothing. Major railroad and shipbuilding yards are also located here. Health care is a major employer, and high-tech industry continues to grow rapidly. The nearest metropolitan center to Mount Rainier National Park (see), Tacoma is a base for trips to Olympic National Park (see) and Puget Sound. Mild weather keeps parks and gardens green throughout the year.

In 1833 the Hudson's Bay Company built its second post (Fort Nisqually) on the North Pacific Coast in the forest, 18 miles south of the present site of Tacoma. In 1841 Charles Wilkes, commander of a US expedition, began a survey of Puget Sound from this point and named the bay around which Tacoma is built Commencement Bay. When the rails of the Northern Pacific reached tidewater here late in 1873, they sparked the industrial growth of the city.

What to See and Do

Emerald Downs. Thoroughbred horse racing. (Late June-early Nov, Thurs-Mon) 15 mi NE on I-5 to Auburn. Phone 253/288-7700 or 888/931-8400. ¢¢

Enchanted Village. Family entertainment park with rides for all ages; wax museum, antique toy and doll museum. Live entertainment. Concessions. (Mid-May-Labor Day, daily; early Apr-mid-May and Sep after Labor Day, wkends) 36201 Enchanted Pkwy S in Federal Way. Phone 253/661-8000 or 253/925-8000. ¢¢¢-¢¢¢¢ Also here is

Wild Waves Water Park. A 24,000-sq-ft wave pool with body and mat surfing in ocean-size waves; raging river ride, adult activity pool, 4 giant water slides with flashing lights and music, 2 speed slides, spas, children's pool. Game rm;

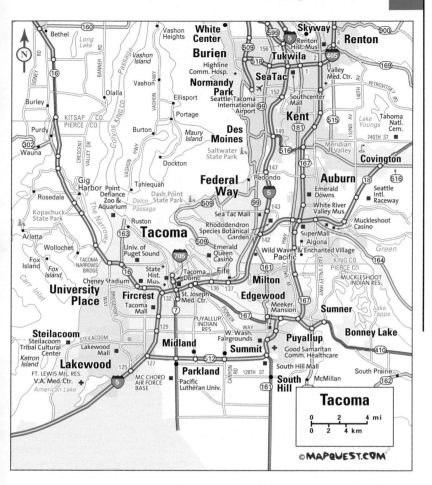

raft rentals. (Memorial Day wkend-Labor Day wkend, daily) Admission incl entry to Enchanted Village. Phone 253/661-8000 or 253/925-8000. ¢¢¢¢

Ferry. Point Defiance to Vashon Island. Contact Washington State Ferries, Seattle Ferry Terminal, Colman Dock, Seattle 98104. Phone 206/464-6400. Per vehicle ¢¢

Fort Lewis. Army center of the Northwest, home of I Corps, the 7th Infantry Division, and associated support units. Approx 86,000 acres with military bldgs and living quarters. Museum with exhibits on Northwest military history (Wed-Sun). 11 mi SW on I-5. Phone 253/967-7206.

McChord AFB. The 62nd Airlift Wing and 446th AW (Reserves) are based

here. Tours (Tues and Thurs; res required 1 month in advance). Museum (Tues-Sat, afternoons). 8 mi SW on I-5. Phone 253/984-2485.

Mount Rainier National Park. (see) Nisqually entrance, approx 56 mi SE on WA 7.

Narrows Bridge. Fifth-longest span for a suspension bridge in US (2,800 ft). Total length: 5,450 ft between anchorages. Successor to "Galloping Gertie," which collapsed in 1940, 4 months and 7 days after it had officially opened. W on Olympic Blvd; WA 16.

Tacoma Nature Center. Approx 50 acres of marshland, forest, thickets, and ponds providing a wildlife haven in heart of urbanized Tacoma. Nature trails, observation shelters; natural science library. Interpretive center; lectures and workshops. Park (daily). 1919 S Tyler St. Phone 253/591-6439. **FREE**

Northwest Trek. One-hr naturalist-guided and narrated tram tour takes visitors on 5½-mi ride through 600-acre wilderness and wildlife preserve, where native Northwest animals may be seen roaming free in their natural habitat; self-guided nature walks through wetlands and forest animal exhibits; nature trails including barrier-free trail; children's discovery center. Theater with 14-min film on history of facility. (Mar-Oct, daily; rest of yr, Fri-Sun and selected hols) 32 mi SE via I-5, WA 512, 161. Phone 360/832-6117. ¢¢¢

Pacific Lutheran University. (1890) 3,500 students. Swimming pool. Nine-hole golf course open to public. Self-guided tours. 11 mi SW on I-5. Off I-5, exit 127. Phone 253/535-7393 or 253/535-7430 (tours). On campus are

> **University Gallery.** Changing art exhibits (Mon-Fri). Rune stones sculpture on campus mall. Ingram Hall. Phone 253/535-7573 or 253/535-7430.

> **Robert Mortvedt Library.** African tribal art. (Mon-Sat) Phone 253/535-7500. **FREE**

Pioneer Farm. Replica of an 1887 homestead with animals; log cabin, barn, trading post, and other outbuildings; furnished with turn-of-the-century antiques. "Hands on" program, guided tours. (Mid-June-Labor Day, daily; Mar-mid-June and Labor Day-Thanksgiving, Sat and Sun only) 35 mi SE via WA 7, in the Ohop Valley. Phone 360/832-6300. ¢¢-¢¢¢

❚ **Point Defiance Park.** Approx 700 acres of dense forest, clay cliffs, driftwood-covered gravel beaches, and formal gardens. On bold promontory, nearly surrounded by water. Boating, fishing, swimming; hiking, picnicking. Park (daily). 6 mi N, entrance at N 54th & Pearl Sts. **FREE** Features of the park are

> **Boathouse Marina.** Bait and tackle shop. Boat and motor rentals. Moorage. Restaurant. Gift shop. (Daily; closed Thanksgiving, Dec 25) Phone 253/591-5325.

> **Point Defiance Zoo and Aquarium.** Zoo has polar bear complex, musk ox habitat, tundra waterfowl, ele-

phants, beluga whales, walrus, seals, and otters; World of Adaptions, Southeast Asia Complex, and "The Farm." Aquarium and 38 perimeter displays with hundreds of Pacific Northwest marine specimens. Reef Aquarium features sharks and other South Pacific sea life. (Daily; closed Thanksgiving, Dec 25) N 54th & Pearl Sts. Phone 253/591-5337. ¢¢¢

> **Never Never Land.** Sculptured storybook characters in 10-acre forest setting. Each wkend storybook characters visit and special events take place. (May-Aug, daily; Apr and Sep, wkends) Phone 253/591-5845. ¢

> **Fort Nisqually.** (1833) Restored fur-trading outpost of Hudson's Bay Co reflects period of English control when fur pelts were used as currency. Purchased by the US in 1869, moved to this site in 1937. Two remaining bldgs of original outpost are the Factor's House (1853) and the Granary (1843), oldest existing bldg in state; 8 other bldgs reconstructed according to original specifications using handmade hardware, lumber. Living history presentations. Fee for some special events. (Memorial Day-Labor Day, daily; rest of yr, Wed-Sun) Phone 253/591-5339. Summer wkends ¢; Rest of yr **FREE**

> **Camp Six Logging Exhibit (Western Forest Industries Museum).** Reconstructed steam logging camp set amid virgin timber. Dolbeer Donkey steam engine (1 of 2 in existence), 110-ft spar pole, restored water wagon, bunkhouses. (Jan-Oct, Wed-Sun) Logging train ride (Apr-Sep, Sat, Sun, and hols). A 90-ton shay steam locomotive operates in summer (wkends and hols). Santa train (3 wkends Dec). Phone 253/752-1164. Train rides ¢

> **Five-Mile Drive.** Around Point Defiance Park. Contains old growth forest with some 200-ft-high Douglas firs, variety of other evergreens, deciduous trees, shrubs. Scenic views of Puget Sound, Olympic Mts, Cascade Mts, Narrows Bridge. Drive closed to motor vehicles Sat mornings for cycling and walking.

> **Gardens.** Formal gardens in park incl an AARS rose garden, Japanese

Garden, Northwest Native garden, Pacific Northwest dahlia trial garden, rhododendron garden, and seasonal annual displays. **FREE**

St. Peter's Church. (Episcopal) Oldest church in city (1873); the organ came around Cape Horn in 1874; ½-ton bell, also shipped around the Horn, is mounted on tower beside church. (Sun; also by appt) 2910 Starr St, at N 29th St. Phone 253/272-4406.

Tacoma Art Museum. Permanent collection; changing exhibits; children's gallery with hands-on art activities. (Tues-Sun; closed Jan 1, Dec 25) 12th St & Pacific Ave. Phone 253/272-4258. ¢¢

Totem Pole. One of the tallest in US, carved from 105-foot cedar tree by Alaskan Native Americans; located in Firemen's Park with view of Commencement Bay and the Port of Tacoma. 9th & A Sts.

University of Puget Sound. (1888) 2,800 students. 37 Tudor Gothic bldgs on 72-acre campus. Many free cultural events, art gallery, theater, recital hall. Univ is older than state. 1500 N Warner St. Phone 253/879-3100. Also here is

> **James R. Slater Museum of Natural History.** Thompson Hall. Displays research specimens, particularly of Pacific Northwest flora and fauna; more than 11,000 birds, 4,600 egg sets; reptiles, amphibians, mammals, and pressed plants. (Mon-Fri; closed hols) **FREE**

Washington State History Museum. Exhibits incl collections of pioneer, Native American, and Alaskan artifacts and detail the history of the state and its people. Interactive, introductory, and changing exhibits. Indoor and outdoor theaters. Museum Cafe and Shop. (Memorial Day-Labor Day, daily; rest of yr, Tues-Sun; closed hols) 1911 Pacific Ave. Phone 888/238-4373. ¢¢ Adj is

> **Union Station.** Built in 1911 by Northern Pacific Railroad, the station, with its 98-ft-high dome, has been restored. Now home to the federal courthouse. The rotunda houses the largest single exhibit of sculptured glass by Tacoma-native Dale Chihuly. (Mon-Fri; closed hols) Phone 253/396-1768. **FREE**

Wright Park. More than 800 trees of 100 varieties in one of finest arboretums in Pacific Northwest. W.W. Seymour Botanical Conservatory, located in park at S 4th & G Sts, contains tropical plants, seasonal displays, and a botanical gift shop. Lawn bowling and horseshoe courts; playground, wading community center pool. (Daily) 6th Ave & I St. Phone 253/591-5330 (gift shop) or 253/305-1000 (pool). **FREE**

Annual Events

Daffodil Festival. In Tacoma and Puyallup Valley. Flower show, coronation, 4-city floral parade of floats, marine regatta, bowling tournament. Phone 253/627-6176. Two wks Apr.

Taste of Tacoma. Point Defiance Park. Entertainment, arts and crafts. Phone 206/232-2982. Early July.

Seasonal Events

Tacoma Little Theater. 210 N I Street. Six shows, incl comedies, dramas, and musicals. Phone 253/272-2281. Sep-June.

Tacoma Symphony Orchestra. Phone 253/272-7264. Late Sep-early Apr. 727 Commerce St.

Motels/Motor Lodges

★ **DAYS INN.** *6802 Tacoma Mall Blvd (98409), I-5 Exit 129.* 253/475-5900; fax 253/475-3540; toll-free 800/329-7466. 123 rms, 2 story. S, D $70-$89; each addl $10; suites $165; under 12 free. Crib free. Pet accepted. TV; cable (premium). Heated pool. Complimentary coffee in lobby. Restaurant 6:30 am-10 pm; Sat from 8 am; Sun 8 am-9 pm. Ck-out 11 am. Ck-in 3 pm. Meeting rms. Business center. In-rm modem link. Valet serv. Health club privileges. Refrigerator; microwaves avail. Cr cds: A, C, D, DS, ER, JCB, MC, V.
D 🐾 🏊 ☕ 🏋 SC 🚶

★ **LA QUINTA INN.** *1425 E 27th St (98421), I-5 Exits 134S, 135N.* 253/383-0146; fax 253/627-3280; toll-free 800/687-6667. 157 rms, 7 story. S $74-$110; D $82-$118; each addl $8; under 18 free. Crib free. Pet accepted. TV; cable (premium). Heated pool; whirlpool. Complimentary continental bkfst. Restaurant 6:30 am-10 pm.

Bar. Ck-out noon. Coin lndry. Meeting rms. Business center. In-rm modem link. Valet serv. Sundries. Exercise equipt. Microwaves avail. View of both Mt Rainier and Commencement Bay. Cr cds: A, C, D, DS, MC, V.

★★ **ROYAL COACHMAN INN, INC.** *5805 Pacific Hwy E (98424). 253/922-2500; fax 253/922-6443; toll-free 800/422-3051. Email service@royalcoachmaninn.com; www.royalcoachmaninn.com.* 93 rms, 2 story, 2 suites. Feb-Mar, June-Sep: S $65; D $71; each addl $8; suites $135; lower rates rest of yr. Crib avail. Pet accepted, some restrictions, fee. Parking lot. TV; cable (DSS), VCR avail. Complimentary continental bkfst, coffee in rms, newspaper, toll-free calls. Meeting rms. Business servs avail. Dry cleaning, coin lndry. Gift shop. Exercise equipt. Golf. Tennis. Downhill skiing. Cr cds: A, C, D, DS, ER, JCB, MC, V.

★★ **SHILO INN.** *7414 S Hosmer (98408), S on I-5, Exit 72nd St. 253/475-4020; fax 253/475-1236; res 800/222-2244. Email tacoma@shiloinns.com.* 132 rms, 4 story, 11 kits. S $79; D $85-$89; each addl $10; kit. units $99; under 12 free. Crib avail. Pet accepted; $7. TV; cable (premium), VCR (movies $3). Indoor pool; whirlpool. Complimentary continental bkfst. Restaurant opp 6 am-11 pm. Ck-out noon. Coin lndry. Meeting rms. Business servs avail. In-rm modem link. Valet serv. Exercise equipt; sauna, steam rm. Bathrm phones, refrigerators, microwaves. Cr cds: A, DS, MC, V.

Hotels

★★ **BEST WESTERN TACOMA INN.** *8726 S Hosmer St (98444), I-5 at 84th St Exit. 253/535-2880; fax 253/537-8379; res 800/528-1234; toll-free 800/305-2880. Email reservations@bwtacomainn.com; www.bwtacomainn.com.* 147 rms, 2 story, 2 suites. May-Sep: S, D $79; each addl $5; suites $130; under 12 free; lower rates rest of yr. Crib avail. Pet accepted, fee. Parking lot. Pool, whirlpool. TV; cable (premium). Complimentary coffee in rms, newspaper, toll-free calls. Restaurant 6 am-10 pm. Bar. Ck-out noon, ck-in 2 pm. Meeting rms. Business center. Dry cleaning, coin lndry. Exercise equipt. Golf, 18 holes. Downhill skiing. Picnic facilities. Cr cds: A, C, D, DS, ER, JCB, MC, V.

★★★ **SHERATON.** *1320 Broadway Plaza (98402), Downtown. 253/572-3200; fax 253/591-4105; res 800/325-3535; toll-free 800/845-9466. Email sales@sheratontacoma.com; www.sheratontacoma.com.* 298 rms, 26 story, 21 suites. Pet accepted, some restrictions. TV; cable. Complimentary coffee in rms, newspaper, toll-free calls. Restaurant 6 am-2 pm. Bar. Ck-out noon, ck-in 2 pm. Conference center, meeting rms. Business center. Bellhops. Dry cleaning. Gift shop. Salon/barber. Exercise privileges. Beach access. Video games. Cr cds: A, C, D, DS, ER, JCB, MC, V.

B&Bs/Small Inns

★ **BEST INN & SUITES.** *3100 Pacific Hwy E (98424). 253/922-9520; fax 253/922-2002; res 877/982-3781.* 105 rms, 2 story, 10 suites. June-Sep: S $58; D $65; each addl $7; suites $120; under 18 free; lower rates rest of yr. Crib avail. Pet accepted, fee. Parking garage. Pool, lap pool, whirlpool. TV; cable (DSS), VCR avail. Complimentary continental bkfst, coffee in rms, newspaper, toll-free calls. Restaurant 9 am-10 pm. Bar. Ck-out 11 am, ck-in 10 pm. Color printing avail. Dry cleaning, coin lndry. Tennis. Video games. Cr cds: A, DS, MC, V.

★★★ **CHINABERRY HILL.** *302 Tacoma Ave N (98403). 253/272-1282; fax 253/272-1335. Email chinaberry@wa.net; www.chinaberryhill.com.* 1 rms, 3 story, 4 suites. S $100; D $110; each addl $25; suites $175. Parking lot. TV; cable (premium), VCR avail. Complimentary full bkfst, coffee in rms, newspaper, toll-free calls. Restaurant nearby. Ck-out 11 am, ck-in 4 pm. Meeting rm. Business center. Whirlpool. Golf. Tennis. Downhill skiing. Picnic facilities. Cr cds: A, MC, V.

★★★ **COMMENCEMENT BAY BED & BREAKFAST.** *3312 N Union Ave (98407). 253/752-8175; fax 253/759-4025; toll-free 800/406-4088. Email greatviews@aol.com; www.great-views. com.* 3 rms, 3 story, 3 suites. Apr-Oct: S, D $110; suites $110; lower rates rest of yr. Street parking. TV; cable (premium), VCR avail, CD avail. Complimentary full bkfst, coffee in rms, newspaper, toll-free calls. Restaurant nearby. Ck-out 11 am, ck-in 4 pm. Meeting rms. Business center. Dry cleaning, coin lndry. Gift shop. Exercise privileges, whirlpool. Golf, 18 holes. Downhill skiing. Beach access. Bike rentals. Hiking trail. Picnic facilities. Cr cds: A, DS, MC, V.

★ **KEENAN HOUSE BED AND BREAKFAST.** *2610 N Warner St (98407). 253/752-0702; fax 253/756-0822. Email idvkeenan@aol.com.* 6 rms, 2 with bath, 2 story. No A/C. No rm phones. S $65-$70; D $70-$80; wkly rates. Crib free. TV in sitting rm. Complimentary full bkfst. Restaurant nearby. Ck-out 11 am, ck-in 2 pm. Street parking. Picnic tables. Two Victorian houses (ca 1890); antiques. Totally nonsmoking. Cr cds: MC, V.

★★★ **VILLA BED & BREAKFAST.** *705 N 5th St (98403). 253/572-1157; fax 253/572-1805; toll-free 888/572-1157. Email villabb@aol.com; www. tribnet.com/bb/villa.htp.* 4 rms, 1 with shower only, 2 story. No A/C. Guest phone avail. S, D $90-$145; each addl $15; wkly rates. Children over 12 yrs only. TV; cable (premium). Complimentary full bkfst. Ck-out noon, ck-in 3-9 pm. Business servs avail. In-rm modem link. Italianate villa built 1925; landscaped grounds; antiques. Totally nonsmoking. Cr cds: A, MC, V.

Restaurants

★★★ **ALTEZZO RISTORANTE.** *1320 Broadway Plaza. 253/591-4155.* Own baking. Hrs: 5-11 pm. Res accepted. Bar. Wine list. Dinner a la carte entrees: $8.95-$19.50. Valet parking. Penthouse dining; view of bay and mountains. Cr cds: A, D, DS, MC, V.
D

★★★ **CLIFF HOUSE.** *6300 Marine View Dr (98422). 253/927-0400. www.cliffhouserestaurant.com.* Specializes in Northwestern, continental cuisine. Hrs: 11 am-10 pm. Closed Dec 25. Res accepted. Bar. Lunch $6.95-$14; dinner $12.95-$25.95. Tableside cooking. Built on cliff; view of Commencement Bay and Mt Rainier. Cr cds: A, D, DS, MC, V.

★★ **COPPERFIELD'S.** *8726 S Hosmer St (98444). 253/531-1500.* Specializes in salmon, prime rib, pasta. Hrs: 6:30 am-10 pm; Fri, Sat to 11 pm; Sun from 7 am. Res accepted. Bar. Bkfst $2.50-$13.95; lunch $4.25-$7.25; dinner $6.50-$14.95. Sun brunch $13.95. Parking. Garden-like setting; wicker furniture. Cr cds: A, DS, MC, V.
D

★★ **HARBOR LIGHTS.** *2761 Ruston Way (98402). 253/752-8600.* Specializes in steak, seafood, veal. Hrs: 11 am-9:30 pm; Fri, Sat to 10:30 pm; Sun 2-9 pm. Closed hols. Res accepted. Bar. Lunch $5-$9.50; dinner $9.50-$32. Child's menu. Parking. Marine view. Family-owned. Cr cds: A, DS, MC, V.
D

★★ **JOHNNY'S DOCK.** *1900 East D St (98421). 253/627-3186.* Specializes in steak, seafood. Hrs: 10 am-8:30 pm; Fri to 9:30 pm; Sat to 10 pm; Sun, Mon to 8 pm. Res accepted. Bar. Bkfst $5.50-$7.95; lunch $5.95-$12.95; dinner $10.95-$24.95. Child's menu. Parking. Waterfront view; moorage. Family-owned. Cr cds: A, D, DS, MC, V.
D

★★★ **LOBSTER SHOP SOUTH.** *4013 Ruston Way (98402). 253/759-2165. www.lobstershop.com.* Specializes in steak, seafood, Australian lobster. Own pastries. Hrs: 11:30 am-10 pm; Sat from 4:30 pm; Sun brunch 9:30 am-1:30 pm. Closed Dec 25. Res accepted. Bar. Wine list. Lunch a la carte entrees: $6.95-$11.95; dinner a la carte entrees: $9.95-$25.95. Sun brunch $15.95.

Child's menu. Parking. Cr cds: A, D, DS, MC, V.

Toppenish

(E-5) *See also Sunnyside, Yakima*

Pop 7,419 **Elev** 755 ft **Area code** 509 **Zip** 98948
Web www.wolfenet.com/~cowboyup
Information Chamber of Commerce, PO Box 28; 509/865-3262 or 800/569-3982

Toppenish is a Native American word meaning "people from the foot of the hills." The Yakama Indian Agency is here, and the nearby million-acre Yakama Reservation is an important tourist attraction. The cultural differences offer good opportunities for sightseeing and dining. The Toppenish area produces hops, fruits, vegetables, and dairy products. Average rainfall is only about eight inches a year, but irrigation makes the countryside bloom.

What to See and Do

Fort Simcoe Historical State Park. Two hundred acres. Restoration of fort established 1856 to protect treaty lands from land-hungry settlers and to guard military roads. Five original bldgs restored; interpretive center with army and Native American relics. Picnicking, hiking. Park (Apr-Sep, daily; rest of yr, wkends and hols) 28 mi W on WA 220, Fort Rd. Phone 509/874-2372. **FREE**

Historical Murals. Painted on downtown buildings. For map or guided tour contact Mural Society, 5A Toppenish Ave. Phone 509/865-6516.

Yakama Nation Cultural Center. Located on ancestral grounds of the Yakamas. Incl museum depicting history of the Yakama Nation, library, theater, and restaurant. (Daily; closed Dec 25) S on US 97. Phone 509/865-2800. ¢¢

Annual Events

Native American Celebrations. Most at Yakama Reservation in White Swan, 23 mi W on WA 220. For details and locations phone 509/865-5121, ext 436. **Yakama Nation Treaty Day, Powwow and Rodeo.** (Phone 509/865-5313) Early June at Culture Heritage Center. **Bull-O-Rama.** Early July.

Old Fashioned Melodrama. Yakama Nation Cultural Center Theatre. Boo and hiss at the villain, cheer the hero. Late July-early Aug.

PRCA Rodeo. Early July. Old Fashioned Melodrama.

Western Art Show. Downtown. Three-day art show, cowboy poetry. Late Aug.

Union

See also Bremerton

Settled 1858 **Pop** 600 (est) **Elev** 10 ft
Area code 360 **Zip** 98592

This resort town at the curve of the Hood Canal almost became the saltwater terminus of the Union Pacific Railroad, but the failure of a British bank was a blow to Union's commercial future. There are public beaches, a marina, free launching sites, and a golf course in town.

What to See and Do

Lake Cushman State Park. Approx 600 acres. Swimming, fishing, boating (launch, fee); hiking trails, picnicking, camping (Apr-Nov; hookups). Standard fees. 5 mi SW via WA 106, 5 mi N via US 101 to Hoodsport, then 7 mi NW via Lake Cushman Rd. Phone 360/877-5491 or 800/233-0321 (info).

Tollie Shay Engine & Caboose #7. Refurbished 3-cylinder locomotive and Simpson logging caboose with coal-burning stove and unique sidedoor design. Caboose used by Shelton-Mason County Chamber of Commerce as office and tourist information center. (Daily; closed hols) 5 mi W on WA 106, 10 mi S on US 101 in Shelton. Phone 360/426-2021. **FREE**

Twanoh State Park. A 182-acre park along Hood Canal. Swimming, scuba diving, boating (launch, dock), fishing, clamming; hiking, picnicking, camping (hookups). Standard fees. 12 mi E on WA 106, off US 101. Phone 360/275-2222.

Vancouver

(F-3) *See also Portland, OR*

Founded 1824 **Pop** 46,380 **Elev** 89 ft **Area code** 360
Web www.vancouverusa.com
Information Greater Vancouver Chamber of Commerce, 404 E 15th St, Suite 11, 98663; 360/694-2588 or 800/377-7084

Vancouver treasures a national historic site, Fort Vancouver, now completely encircled by the city. The fort served as a commercial bastion for the Hudson's Bay Company, whose vast enterprises stretched far to the north and across the sea to Hawaii, bringing furs from Utah and California and dominating coastal trade well up the shoreline to Alaska. Around the stockaded fort, the company's cultivated fields and pastures extended for miles; drying sheds, mills, forges, and shops made it a pioneer metropolis. This community was a major stake in Britain's claim for all the territory north of the Columbia River, but by the treaty of 1846, Fort Vancouver became American. Settlers began to take over the Hudson's Bay Company lands, and an Army post was established here in 1849, continuing to the present day. In 1860, all of Fort Vancouver was turned over to the US Army.

The city is on the Columbia River, just north of Portland, Oregon. Vancouver has a diversified industrial climate, which includes electronics, paper products, fruit packing, malt production, and the manufacture of textiles, furniture, and machinery. The Port of Vancouver, one of the largest on the West Coast, is a deep-water seaport handling a wide range of commodities.

What to See and Do

Clark County Historical Museum. Exhibits incl 1890s store, doctor's office, printing press, doll collection, dioramas of area history, Native American artifacts; railroad exhibit; genealogical and historical research libraries. (Tues-Sat; closed hols) 1511 Main St. Phone 360/695-4681. **FREE**

⚡ Fort Vancouver National Historic Site. Over 150 acres. After extensive research and excavation, the fort has been partially reconstructed by the National Park Service. Now at the fort site: Chief Factor's house, kitchen, wash house, stockade wall, gates, the bastion, bake house, blacksmith shop, and trade shop-dispensary. Visitor center has museum exhibiting artifacts, information desk, video presentations. Tours, interpretive talks, and living history programs are offered. (Daily; closed hols) 1501 E Evergreen Blvd. Phone 360/696-7655. **¢¢**

Gifford Pinchot National Forest. Forest's 1,379,000 acres include 12,326-ft Mt Adams; 8,400-ft Mt St. Helens (see MOUNT ST. HELENS NATIONAL VOLCANIC MONUMENT); and 180,600 acres distributed among 7 wilderness areas. Fishing, swimming, boating; picnicking, camping, hunting. Some fees. Contact Public Affairs Assistant, PO Box 8944, 98668. NE of city, reached via WA 14, 25, 503. Phone 360/750-5001.

Officers' Row. Self-guided walking tour of 21 turn-of-the-century houses; 2 open to public.

Pearson Air Museum. At M.J. Murdock Aviation Center, one of the oldest operating airfields in the nation. Vintage aircraft and flying memorabilia. (Tues-Sun; closed hols) 1115 E 5th St. Phone 360/694-7026. **¢**

Motels/Motor Lodges

★ **BEST INN & SUITES CASCADE PARK.** *221 NE Chkalov Dr (98684), I-205 Exit 28. 360/256-7044; fax 360/256-1231; res 800/237-8466; toll-free 800/426-5110. Email bisvan@first world.net. 117 rms, 2 story. S $57; D $63; each addl $8; suites $95-$139; under 18 free. Crib free. Pet accepted; $15. TV; cable (premium). Indoor pool; whirlpool. Complimentary continental bkfst, coffee in rms.*

Restaurant 6 am-10 pm. Ck-out noon. Meeting rms. Business servs avail. Valet serv. Free airport transportation. Exercise equipt. Health club privileges. Cr cds: A, DS, MC, V.

★★ **COMFORT INN.** *13207 NE 20th (98686), I-5 Exit 7. 360/574-6000; fax 360/573-3746; res 800/228-5150.* 58 rms, 2 story. S $50-$55; D $60-$70; each addl $5; suites $115; under 18 free. Crib $3. TV; cable (premium). Indoor pool; whirlpool. Complimentary continental bkfst. Restaurant opp 6:30 am-9 pm. Ck-out 11 am. Coin lndry. Meeting rms. Business servs avail. In-rm modem link. Exercise equipt. Refrigerators. Cr cds: A, DS, MC, V.

★★★ **COMFORT SUITES.** *4714 NE 94th Ave (98662), I-205 Exit 30, near Vancouver Mall. 360/253-3100; fax 360/253-7998; res 800/228-5150. Email kimefox@aol.com.* 68 suites, 2 story. S $76-$86; D $81-$91; each addl $5; under 18 free. Crib free. TV; cable (premium). Indoor pool; whirlpool. Complimentary continental bkfst, coffee in rms. Restaurant nearby. Ck-out noon. Meeting rms. Business servs avail. Valet serv Mon-Fri. Airport transportation. Exercise equipt. Health club privileges. Refrigerators, microwaves; some in-rm whirlpools. Cr cds: A, D, DS, MC, V.

★ **FERRYMAN'S INN.** *7901 NE 6th Ave (98665), I-5 Exit 4. 360/574-2151; fax 360/574-9644.* 134 rms, 2 story, 9 kit. S $54-$65; D $63-$78; each addl $5; suites $65-$90.50; kit. units $65-$70; under 12 free. Crib free. Pet accepted; $3. TV; cable (premium). Heated pool. Complimentary continental bkfst. Restaurant adj open 24 hrs. Ck-out noon. Coin lndry. Meeting rms. Business servs avail. Cr cds: A, C, D, DS, JCB, MC, V.

★★ **HOLIDAY INN EXPRESS.** *9107 NE Vancouver Mall Dr (98662). 360/253-5000; fax 360/253-3137; toll-free 800/465-4329.* 56 rms, 2 story. S $65-$75; D $70-$80; each addl $5; under 18 free; special events (2-3 day min). Crib avail. TV; cable (premium). Complimentary continental bkfst. Ck-out noon. Sundries. Indoor pool; whirlpool. Health club privileges. Cr cds: A, C, D, DS, ER, JCB, MC, V.

★★ **SHILO INN.** *13206 NE Hwy 99 (98686), I-5 Exit 7. 360/573-0511; fax 360/573-0396; res 800/222-2244.* 66 rms, 2 story, 6 kits. S, D $75; each addl $10; kit. units $55-$79; under 13 free. Crib free. Pet accepted; $7. TV; cable (premium). Indoor pool; whirlpool. Complimentary continental bkfst. Restaurant adj 6:30 am-10:30 pm. Bar. Ck-out noon. Coin lndry. Meeting rms. Business servs avail. Valet serv. Free airport transportation. Sauna, steam rm. Health club privileges. Refrigerators. Cr cds: A, D, DS, MC, V.

Hotels

★ **BEST INN AND SUITES.** *7001 NE HWY 99 (98665), I-5 Exit 4. 360/696-0516; fax 360/693-8343; res 800/bestinn; toll-free 800/696-0516. Email gm@vanbestinn.com; www.vanbestinn.com.* 72 rms, 2 story. June-Aug: S $64; D $71; each addl $5; under 17 free; lower rates rest of yr. Crib avail. Pet accepted, some restrictions, fee. Parking lot. Pool, whirlpool. TV; cable (premium). Complimentary continental bkfst, coffee in rms, newspaper, toll-free calls. Restaurant nearby. Ck-out noon, ck-in 3 pm. Meeting rms. Business center. Coin lndry. Exercise privileges. Golf. Video games. Cr cds: A, D, DS, MC, V.

★★★ **THE HEATHMAN LODGE.** *7801 NE Greenwood Dr (98662). 360/254-3100; fax 360/254-6100; toll-free 888/475-3100. Email blwilkerson@heathmanlodge.com; www.heathmanlodge.com.* 121 rms, 4 story, 22 suites. S, D $119; each addl $15; suites $199; under 18 free. Crib avail. Parking lot. Indoor pool, whirlpool. TV; cable (premium), VCR avail, CD avail. Complimentary coffee in rms, newspaper, toll-free calls. Restaurant 6:30 am-10 pm. Bar. Ck-out noon, ck-in 4 pm. Meeting rms. Business center. Bellhops. Concierge. Dry cleaning, coin lndry. Gift shop. Exercise privileges, sauna. Golf. Tennis. Beach access. Hiking trail. Video games. Cr cds: A, C, D, DS, JCB, MC, V.

★ **RED LION HOTEL.** *100 Columbia St (98660). 360/694-8341; fax 360/694-2023; toll-free 800/222-8733. www.doubletreehotels.com.* 159 rms, 2 story, 1 suite. May-July: S $89; D $99; each addl $15; under 18 free; lower rates rest of yr. Crib avail. Pet accepted, some restrictions, fee. Parking lot. Pool. TV; cable (premium). Complimentary coffee in rms, newspaper, toll-free calls. Restaurant 60-10 pm. Bar. Ck-out noon, ck-in 2 pm. Meeting rms. Business center. Dry cleaning. Free airport transportation. Exercise privileges. Golf. Tennis. Downhill skiing. Video games. Cr cds: A, C, D, DS, ER, JCB, MC, V.

Walla Walla

(E-7) *See also Dayton*

Founded 1859 **Pop** 26,478 **Elev** 949 ft
Area code 509 **Zip** 99362
Web www.bmi.net/wwchamb/
Information Chamber of Commerce, 29 E Sumach, PO Box 644; 509/525-0850

Walla Walla Valley was first the site of a Native American trail and then an avenue for exploration and settlement of the West. Lewis and Clark passed through the area in 1805. Fur traders followed and Fort Walla Walla was established in 1818 as a trading post at the point where the Walla Walla and Columbia rivers meet. One of the key figures in the area's history was Dr. Marcus Whitman, a medical missionary, who in 1836 founded the first settler's home in the Northwest—a mission seven miles west of present-day Walla Walla. The Whitmans were killed by Native Americans in 1847. No successful settlement was made until after the Indian Wars of 1855-58.

In 1859 the city became the seat of Walla Walla County, which then included half of present-day Washington, all of Idaho, and one-quarter of Montana. It also had the first rail-

road in the Northwest, first bank in the state, first meat market and packing plant, and first institution of higher learning.

Walla Walla means "many waters," but local enthusiasts will tell you this is "the city they liked so much they named it twice." Agriculture is the major industry, with wheat the most important crop and green peas the second. Industries concentrate chiefly on food processing. And the Walla Walla Onion is known nationwide for its sweetness; a festival is held each July to honor the important crop. A Ranger District office of the Umatilla National Forest (see CLARKSTON, also see PENDLETON, OR) is located here.

What to See and Do

Fort Walla Walla Park. Camping (dump station; fee). (Apr-Sep, daily; limited facilities rest of yr) Dalles Military Rd. 1 mi W of WA 125, W edge of town. Phone 509/527-3770. Also in park is Audubon Society Nature Walk, outdoor amphitheater, and

Fort Walla Walla Museum Complex. Fourteen original and replica bldgs from mid-1800s. Schoolhouse, homestead cabin, railroad depot, blockhouse, doctor's office, blacksmith shop; largest horse-era agricultural museum in the West. Tours (Apr-Oct, by appt). Complex (Apr-Oct, Tues-Sun). Phone 509/525-7703. ¢¢

Pioneer Park. A 58-acre park with horticultural displays, exotic game bird display, playground, tennis courts, picnicking. Division & Alder Sts. Phone 509/527-4527. **FREE**

Whitman Mission National Historic Site. The memorial shaft, erected in 1897, overlooks the site of the mission established by Dr. Marcus and Narcissa Whitman in 1836. A self-guided trail with audio stations leads to mission grounds, Old Oregon Trail, memorial shaft, and grave. Visitor center, museum; cultural demonstrations (summer, wkends). (Daily; closed hols) 7 mi W on US 12, then ¾ mi S. Phone 509/522-6360. ¢

Motels/Motor Lodges

★★ **HAWTHORN INN AND SUITES.** *520 N 2nd Ave (99362).*

509/525-2522; fax 509/522-2565; res 800/527-1133. 61 rms, 3 story. May-Sep: S $60; D $60-$65; each addl $8; suites $110-$130; under 18 free; lower rates rest of yr. Crib free. Pet accepted, some restrictions. TV; cable (premium). Indoor pool. Complimentary continental bkfst. Coffee in rms. Restaurant adj 11 am-10 pm. Ck-out 1 pm. Meeting rm. Business servs avail. Gift shop. Exercise equipt; sauna. Some refrigerators. Cr cds: A, C, D, DS, MC, V.

★ **HOWARD JOHNSON EXPRESS INN.** *325 E Main (99362). 509/529-4360; fax 509/529-7463; res 800/igo-hojo. www.10236.cendant.com.* 85 rms, 2 story. S, D $72-$90; under 18 free. Crib free. Pet accepted. TV; cable (premium). Pool; whirlpool. Complimentary continental bkfst. Coffee in rms. Ck-out noon. Free lndry facilities. Meeting rms. Business servs avail. In-rm modem link. Exercise equipt; sauna. Some refrigerators. Some private patios, balconies. Cr cds: A, D, DS, MC, V.

★ **TRAVELODGE.** *421 E Main St (99362). 509/529-4940; fax 509/529-4943; res 800/578-7878.* 39 rms, 2 story. S $47; D $53-$58; each addl $5; under 17 free. Crib free. TV; cable (premium). Pool; whirlpool. Coffee in rms. Restaurant nearby. Ck-out noon. Business servs avail. Refrigerators. Cr cds: A, C, D, DS, ER, MC, V.

B&B/Small Inn

★★ **GREEN GABLES INN.** *922 Bonsella St (99362). 509/525-5501; toll-free 888/525-5501. Email greengables@ wwics.com; www.greengablesinn.com.* 4 rms, 2 story, 1 suite. D $110; each addl $25; suites $125. Crib avail. Parking lot. TV; cable (premium). VCR avail. Complimentary full bkfst, coffee in rms, newspaper, toll-free calls. Restaurant nearby. Ck-out 11 am, ck-in 3 pm. Fax servs avail. Golf, 18 holes. Tennis, 4 courts. Downhill skiing. Bike rentals. Picnic facilities. Cr cds: A, DS, MC, V.

Wenatchee

(C-5) *See also Cashmere, Leavenworth*

Founded 1888 **Pop** 21,756 **Elev** 727 ft **Area code** 509

Information Wenatchee Chamber of Commerce, PO Box 850, 98807; 509/662-2116 or 800/572-7753

The apple blossoms in the spring and the sturdy red of the grown fruit in the fall are the symbols of this community. Nestled among the towering mountains are fertile irrigated valleys where residents care for the orchards. Cherries, pears, peaches, and apricots are also grown here. With the establishment in 1952 of a huge aluminum smelter and casting plant, Wenatchee no longer has an economy based only on agriculture. The headquarters of the Wenatchee National Forest is located here.

What to See and Do

Mission Ridge Ski Area. Four double chairlifts, 2 rope tows; patrol, school, rentals, snowmaking; cafeteria, child care. Vertical drop 2,140 ft. (Mid-Nov-mid-Apr) Half-day rates. Limited cross-country trails. 12 mi SW on Squilchuck Rd. Phone 509/663-7631 or 800/374-1693 (snow conditions). ¢¢¢¢

North Central Washington Museum. Cultural Center; restored, operational 1919 Wurlitzer pipe organ; Great Northern Railway model; fine art gallery, apple industry exhibit, first trans-Pacific flight (Japan to Wenatchee) exhibit, archaeological and Native American exhibits. (Feb-Dec, daily; rest of yr, Mon-Fri; closed hols) 127 S Mission St. Phone 509/664-3340. ¢¢

Rocky Reach Dam. Visitors Center with underwater fish viewing gallery; theater. Powerhouse has Gallery of the Columbia and Gallery of Electricity; changing art exhibits. Landscaped grounds; picnic and play areas. (Daily; closed Dec 25; also Jan-mid-Feb) On Columbia River. 7 mi N on US 97A. Phone 509/663-7522 or 509/663-8121. **FREE**

Squilchuck State Park. This 287-acre park offers day use and group camping. (Mar-Nov) Standard fees. 9 mi SW on Squilchuck Rd. Phone 509/664-6373.

Wenatchee National Forest. Approx 2 million forested, mountainous acres lying W of Columbia River. Trail system leads to jagged peaks, mountain meadows, sparkling lakes. Hunting, fishing; picnicking, winter sports, many developed campsites (some fees). Forest map available (fee). Contact Supervisor, 215 Melody Ln, 98801-5933. N, S & W of town. Phone 509/662-4335.

Annual Event

Washington State Apple Blossom Festival. Parades, carnival, arts and crafts, musical productions; "Ridge to River Relay." Phone 509/662-3616. Last wkend Apr-1st wkend May.

Motels/Motor Lodges

★★ **HOLIDAY LODGE.** *610 N Wenatchee (98801). 509/663-8167; fax 509/663-8167; toll-free 800/772-0852.* 59 rms. May-Aug: S, D $60; each addl $5; under 12 free; lower rates rest of yr. Crib avail, fee. Pet accepted, some restrictions. Parking lot. Pool. TV; cable, VCR avail. Complimentary continental bkfst, newspaper, toll-free calls. Restaurant noon-midnight. Ck-out noon, ck-in noon. Fax servs avail. Coin lndry. Exercise equipt, sauna. Golf, 18 holes. Tennis, 2 courts. Downhill skiing. Hiking trail. Cr cds: A, C, D, DS, MC, V.

★★ **MICKEY O'REILLEY'S INN AT THE RIVER.** *580 Valley Mall Pkwy (98802), E Wenatchee. 509/884-1474; fax 509/884-9179; res 509/559-1474; toll-free 800/922-3199. Email info@ mickeyoreillys.com; www.mickeyoreillys. com.* 55 rms, 2 story. S $47-$57; D $62-$67; each addl $5; under 12 free. Crib free. TV; cable. Heated pool; whirlpool. Complimentary continental bkfst. Restaurant 11:30 am-10 pm. Bar 11:30-2 am. Ck-out 11 am. Business servs avail. Some refrigerators, microwaves. Some balconies. View of mountains. Cr cds: A, DS, MC, V.

★ **ORCHARD INN.** *1401 N Miller St (98801). 509/662-3443; fax 509/665-0715; res 800/368-4571.* 103 rms, 3 story. May-Aug: S $50-$55; D $55-$65; each addl $5; suites $70-$75; under 13 free; package plans; higher rates special events; lower rates rest of yr. Crib free. Pet accepted. TV; cable (premium). Complimentary coffee in lobby. Restaurant opp open 24 hrs. Ck-out 11 am. Meeting rms. Business servs avail. Sundries. Free airport, railroad station, bus depot transportation. Downhill ski 12 mi; x-country ski 10 mi. Pool; whirlpool. Some refrigerators, microwaves. Picnic tables. Cr cds: A, DS, MC, V.

★★ **RAMADA INN.** *1017 N Wenatchee Ave (98801). 509/663-8141; fax 509/665-8585; res 800/2RAMADA; toll-free 877/203-8585.* 105 rms, 1-2 story. S $45; D $65-$80; under 18 free. Crib free. Pet accepted. TV; cable (premium). Heated pool; whirlpool. Complimentary continental bkfst. Restaurant 11 am-10 pm. Bar; entertainment Fri, Sat. Ck-out noon. Meeting rms. Business servs avail. Lawn games. Private patios, balconies. Cr cds: A, C, D, DS, MC, V.

★ **TRAVELODGE.** *1004 N Wenatchee Ave (98801). 509/662-8165; fax 509/662-8165; res 800/578-7878; toll-free 800/235-8165. www. travelodge.com.* 48 rms, 2 story, 2 suites. May-Oct: S $59; D $79; suites $129; under 17 free; lower rates rest of yr. Crib avail. Pool, whirlpool. TV; cable, VCR avail. Complimentary continental bkfst, coffee in rms, newspaper, toll-free calls. Restaurant nearby. Ck-out 11 am, ck-in 2 pm. Coin lndry. Sauna. Golf. Downhill skiing. Cr cds: A, C, D, ER, JCB, MC, V.

Hotels

★ **RED LION HOTEL WENATCHEE.** *1225 N Wenatchee Ave (98801). 509/ 663-0711; fax 509/662-8175; toll-free 800/733-5466. Email knutson2@gte.net or scostelo@gte.net; www.redlionhotels. com.* 148 rms, 3 story, 1 suite. June-Aug: S $84; D $99; each addl $10; suites $150; under 17 free; lower rates rest of yr. Crib avail. Pet accepted. Parking lot. Pool, whirlpool. TV; cable (premium). Complimentary coffee in rms, newspaper, toll-free calls. Restaurant 6 am-10 pm. Bar. Ck-out noon, ck-in 4 pm. Meeting rms. Business center. Dry cleaning. Free airport transportation. Exercise equipt. Golf. Tennis. Downhill skiing. Cr cds: A, C, D, DS, ER, JCB, MC, V.

★★ **WESTCOAST WENATCHEE CENTER.** *201 N Wenatchee Ave (98801). 509/662-1234; fax 509/662-0782; res 800/426-0670.* 147 rms, 9 story. S $87-$99; D $95-$104; each addl $10; suites $135-$200; under 18 free; ski rates; higher rates Apple Blossom Festival. Crib free. Pet accepted; $50 deposit. TV. Indoor/outdoor pool; whirlpool, poolside serv. Coffee in rms. Restaurant 6:30 am-9 pm. Bar 11-2 am; entertainment Wed-Sat. Ck-out noon. Guest lndry. Meeting rms. Business servs avail. Free airport, railroad station, bus depot transportation. Downhill ski 12 mi. Exercise equipt. Some refrigerators. Cr cds: A, D, DS, MC, V.

Westport

(D-1) See also Aberdeen, Hoquiam, Ocean Shores

Settled 1858 **Pop** 1,892 **Elev** 12 ft **Area code** 360 **Zip** 98595
Information Westport-Grayland Chamber of Commerce, 2985 S Montesano St, PO Box 306, 98595-0306; 360/268-9422 or 800/345-6223

Near the tip of a sandy strip of land separating Grays Harbor from the Pacific, Westport is home to probably the largest sports fishing fleet in the Northwest. Pleasure and charter boats take novice and experienced anglers alike across Grays Harbor Bay into the Pacific for salmon fishing in the summer and deep-sea fishing nearly all year. In the winter, commercial fleets set their pots for crab and have their catch processed at one of Westport's large canneries.

Whale-watching excursions operate from March-May.

What to See and Do

Grays Harbor Lighthouse. (1900) Tallest lighthouse on W coast (107 ft). Ocean Ave.

Maritime Museum. Shipwreck and Coast Guard memorabilia; also on grounds are Coast Guard vessel *U/B 41332* and Whale Display House. (June-Sep, Wed-Sun afternoons, also hols) 2201 Westhaven Dr. Phone 360/268-0078. **Donation**

Twin Harbors State Park. More than 150 acres. Surf fishing, clamming, whale-watching; hiking, picnicking, camping (hookups; res advised Memorial Day-Labor Day). Ocean swimming permitted, but hazardous. Standard fees. 3 mi S on WA 105. Phone 360/268-9717.

Westport Aquarium. Large tank aquariums; performing seals. (Feb-Oct, daily; Nov, wkends; closed hols) 321 Harbor St. Phone 360/268-0471. ¢¢

Winthrop

(B-5) See also Omak

Pop 302 **Elev** 1,760 ft **Area code** 509 **Zip** 98862
Information Chamber of Commerce, Information Office, PO Box 39; 509/996-2125 or 888/463-8469

Redesigning the entire town on an old West theme has transformed it into the "old Western town of Winthrop," complete with annual events in the same vein.

Fifty-five miles west on the North Cascades Highway (WA 20) is North Cascades National Park (see SEDRO WOOLLEY). A Ranger District office of the Okanogan National Forest (see OMAK) is located here.

What to See and Do

Shafer Museum. Log house built by town founder, Guy Waring (1897). Incl early day farming and mining implements. (Memorial Day-Sep, daily) Castle Ave. Phone 509/996-2712. **FREE**

Motel/Motor Lodge

★ **THE WINTHROP INN.** *960 WA 20 (98862), 1 mi SE. 509/996-2217; fax 509/996-3923; toll-free 800/444-1972. Email wininn@methow.com.* 30 rms, 2 story. May-Oct: S $50-$75; D $55-$75; each addl $5; under 12 free; higher rates hols; lower rates rest of yr. Crib free. Pet accepted, some restrictions; $7. TV. Pool; whirlpool. Complimentary coffee in lobby. Restaurant nearby. Ck-out 11 am. Business servs avail. In-rm modem link. Downhill ski 15 mi; x-country ski on site. Picnic tables. Refrigerators, microwaves. Private patios, balconies. Cr cds: A, DS, MC, V.

Resort

★★★ **SUN MOUNTAIN LODGE.** *Patterson Lake Rd (98862), 9 mi SW. 509/996-2211; fax 509/996-3133; toll-free 800/572-0493. Email sunmtn@methow.com; www.sunmountainlodge.com.* 93 rms, 3 story, 6 suites. June-Oct: S, D $230; each addl $20; suites $315; under 12 free; lower rates rest of yr. Crib avail. Parking lot. Pool, whirlpool. TV; cable (premium). Complimentary coffee in rms, toll-free calls. Restaurant 7 am-9 pm. Bar. Ck-out noon, ck-in 4 pm. Meeting rms. Business servs avail. Bellhops. Concierge. Gift shop. Exercise equipt. Golf. Tennis. Downhill skiing. Beach access. Bike rentals. Supervised children's activities. Hiking trail. Picnic facilities. Cr cds: A, D, MC, V.

Restaurant

★★★ **THE DINING ROOM.** *Patterson Lake Rd. 509/996-2211. www.sunmountainlodge.com.* Specializes in wild mushroom strudel, tenderloin mignon. Hrs: 7 am-9 pm; Fri, Sat to 10 pm; winter hrs vary. Res accepted. Bar. Wine list. Bkfst $4-$10; lunch $6.50-$10; dinner $15-$25. Child's menu. Cr cds: A, MC, V.

Yakima

(D-5) *See also Ellensburg, Toppenish*

Settled 1861 **Pop** 54,827 **Elev** 1,068 ft
Area code 509
Information Yakima Valley Visitors & Convention Bureau, 10 N 8th St, 98901; 509/575-1300

Yakima (YAK-e-ma) County ranks first in the United States in production of apples, hops, sweet cherries, and winter pears. Irrigation was started as early as 1875, when early settlers dug crude canals. Orchards and farms replaced sagebrush and desert. The city takes its name from the Yakama Nation whose reservation lies to the south. There are about 300 days of sunshine annually, with an average yearly rainfall of eight inches.

What to See and Do

Ahtanum Mission. Founded in 1852, destroyed in Yakama Native American Wars, rebuilt in 1867; site of oldest irrigated apple orchards in valley (1872). 9 mi SW on unnumbered roads.

Historic North Front Street. Called "birthplace of Yakima," this 2-block section of downtown has restaurants and shopping.

Painted Rocks. Historic Yakima Nation pictographs. 7 mi NW on US 12.

Skiing. White Pass Village. 55 mi NW on US 12, in Mt Baker-Snoqualmie National Forest. (See MOUNT RAINIER NATIONAL PARK)

Yakima Interurban Trolley Lines. Trolley cars make trips around city and surrounding countryside. Boarding at car barns at 3rd Ave & W Pine St. (May-mid-Oct wkends; also evening rides July, Aug) 307 W Pine St. Phone 509/575-1700. ¢¢

Yakima Sportsman State Park. Approx 250 acres. Picnicking. Camping (hookups). Standard fees. 3 mi E on WA 24, Keyes Rd. Phone 509/575-2774.

Yakima Valley Museum. Exhibits relating to history of Yakima valley; Yakima Nation; fruit industry. Collection of horse-drawn vehicles. (Tues-Sun; closed hols) 2105 Tieton Dr, in Franklin Park. Phone 509/248-0747. ¢¢

Annual Events

Chocolate Fantasy. Chocolate manufacturers from across the nation showcase candy, cookies, and pies; sampling, "chocolate bingo." Phone 509/966-6309. Mid-Mar.

Spring Barrel Tasting. Area wineries participate. Last wkend Apr.

Yakima Air Fair. Phone 509/248-3425. First wkend June.

Central Washington State Fair and Rodeo. Fairgrounds. Phone 509/248-7160. Late Sep-early Oct.

Seasonal Event

Yakima Meadows Racetrack. Fairgrounds. Thoroughbred racing. Parimutuel wagering. Phone 509/248-3920 for schedule.

Motels/Motor Lodges

★★ **BEST WESTERN OXFORD INN.** *1603 Terrace Heights Dr (98901), 1 blk E of I-82 Exit 33. 509/457-4444; fax 509/453-7593; res 800/521-3050; toll-free 800/528-1234.* 96 rms, 4 story, 6 kits. S $59; D $65-$71; each addl $8; under 12 free; kit. units $69-$75. Crib free. TV; cable, VCR avail. Heated pool; whirlpool.

Fruit orchards of Yakima

Restaurant adj 6 am-10 pm. Bar 11-2 am. Ck-out noon. Coin lndry. Meeting rms. In-rm modem link. Sundries. Many refrigerators. Private patios, balconies. View of river. Cr cds: A, C, D, DS, ER, MC, V.

★ **NENDELS INN.** *1405 N 1st St (98901), I-82 Exit N 1st St. 509/453-8981; fax 509/452-3241; res 800/547-0106.* 53 rms, 2 story. S $39; D $45-$48; each addl $6; under 6 free. Crib free. Pet accepted. TV; cable (premium). Heated pool; whirlpools. Restaurant adj 24 hrs. Ck-out 11 am. Business servs avail. Cr cds: A, D, DS, MC, V.

★★ **QUALITY INN OF YAKIMA.** *12 E Valley Mall Blvd (98903), I-82 Union Gap Exit. 509/248-6924; fax 509/575-8470; toll-free 800/510-5670. www. qualityinn.com/hotel/wa718.* 85 rms, 2 story. Mar, May-Sep: S $64; D $74; each addl $10; under 12 free; lower rates rest of yr. Crib avail, fee. Pet accepted, some restrictions, fee. Parking lot. Pool. TV; cable (premium). Complimentary coffee in rms, newspaper, toll-free calls. Restaurant. Ck-out 11 am, ck-in 3 pm. Coin lndry. Golf. Cr cds: A, D, DS, MC, V.

★ **RED LION INN.** *818 N 1st St (98901), I-82 Exit N 1st St. 509/453-0391; fax 509/453-8384; res 800/REDLION.* 58 rms, 2 story. S $64-$79; D $74-$89; each addl $10; suites $120-$150; under 18 free. Crib free. Pet accepted, some restrictions. TV; cable (premium). Heated pool. Complimentary continental bkfst. Coffee in rms. Restaurant adj open 24 hrs. Ck-out noon. Business servs avail. Cr cds: A, D, DS, MC, V.

Hotels

★★★ **DOUBLE-TREE HOTEL YAKIMA.** *1507 N 1st Street (98901),*

I-82 Exit N 1st St. 509/248-7850; fax 509/575-1694; res 800/222TREE. Email ewalters@ixpnet.com; www.doubletreehotels.com. 204 rms, 2 story, 4 suites. May-Aug: S, D $94; each addl $10; suites $225; lower rates rest of yr. Crib avail, fee. Pet accepted, fee. Parking lot. Pool, whirlpool. TV; cable. Complimentary coffee in rms, newspaper. Restaurant. Bar. Ck-out noon, ck-in 3 pm. Meeting rms. Business servs avail. Dry cleaning. Gift shop. Free airport transportation. Exercise equipt. Golf. Downhill skiing. Video games. Cr cds: A, D, DS, MC, V.

D 🏌 ≈ 🏊 🏂 🚶 🎿 🍽 ♨ SC

★★ **WESTCOAST YAKIMA CENTER HOTEL.** 607 E Yakima Ave (98901). 509/248-5900; fax 509/575-8975; res 800/325-4000. Email margaret.murray@westcoasthotels.com; www.westcoasthotels.com. 148 rms, 2 story, 5 suites. Mar-Oct: S $97; D $107; each addl $10; suites $150; lower rates rest of yr. Crib avail. Pet accepted, fee. Parking lot. Pool, whirlpool. TV; cable (premium). Complimentary coffee in rms. Restaurant 6:30 am-10 pm. Bar. Ck-out noon, ck-in 3 pm. Meeting rms. Business center. Dry cleaning, coin lndry. Exercise privileges. Golf. Downhill skiing. Video games. Cr cds: A, D, DS, MC, V.

D 🏌 🏊 🏂 ≈ 🚶 🎿 🍽

★★ **WESTCOAST YAKIMA GATEWAY HOTEL.** 9 N 9th St (98901), I-82 City Center Exit 33. 509/452-6511; fax 509/457-4931; res 800/325-4000. Email margaret.murray@westcoast hotels.com; www.westcoasthotels.com. 169 rms, 3 story, 3 suites. May-Sep: S $75; D $85; each addl $10; suites $130; under 16 free; lower rates rest of yr. Crib avail. Pet accepted, some restrictions, fee. Parking lot. Pool, whirlpool. TV; cable (premium). Complimentary coffee in rms. Restaurant 6:30 am-10 pm. Bar. Ck-out noon, ck-in 3 pm. Meeting rms. Business servs avail. Bellhops. Dry cleaning, coin lndry. Free airport transportation. Exercise privileges. Golf. Downhill skiing. Video games. Cr cds: A, D, DS, MC, V.

D 🏌 🏊 🏂 ≈ 🚶 🎿 🍽

Restaurant

★★ **DELI DE PASTA.** 7 N Front St (98901). 509/453-0571. Specializes in seafood, steak, gourmet pasta dishes. Hrs: 5-10 pm. Closed Sun; hols. Res accepted. Wine, beer. Dinner $10.95-$21.95. Small, intimate dining area. Cr cds: A, MC, V.

D

WYOMING

From the high western plateaus of the Great Plains, the state of Wyoming stretches across the Continental Divide and into the Rocky Mountains. This is a land of scenic beauty and geographic diversity; mountain ranges, grasslands, and desert can all be found within Wyoming's borders.

The first Europeans to explore this region were French; brothers Louis and Francés François Verendrye trapped here in 1743. The first American to enter what is now Yellowstone National Park was John Colter, a member of the Lewis and Clark expedition, who was here during the winter of 1807-08. The 1820s saw a number of trappers and fur traders become established in the area. The territory became the site of important stops along the pioneer trails to the West Coast in the 1840s-60s.

The pioneer trails across Wyoming allowed pioneers to cross the rugged spine of the Rocky Mountains on an easy grade, following grass and water over the Continental Divide. Of the approximately 350,000 individuals who made their way along the various westward trails, some 21,000 died en route, claimed by disease, accidents, and mountain snow. After 1847 thousands of Mormons came along the Mormon Trail to join Brigham Young's settlement at Salt Lake. The situation improved dramatically for those bound for the West when the Union Pacific Railroad pushed across Wyoming during 1867-69. The "iron horse" made the journey considerably safer and easier, not to mention faster. Permanent settlement of the West then began in earnest.

The hard existence wrought from a sometimes inhospitable land bred a tough, practical people who recognized merit when they saw it. While still a territory, Wyoming in 1869 became the first area in the United States to grant women the right to vote. Subsequently, Wyomingites were the first in the nation to appoint a woman justice of the peace, the first to select women jurors, and the first to elect a woman, Nellie Tayloe Ross in 1924, governor. This reputation has earned Wyoming the nickname "the equality state."

Population: 453,588
Area: 96,988 square miles
Elevation: 3,100-13,804 feet
Peak: Gannett Peak (between Fremont and Sublette Counties)
Entered Union: July 10, 1890 (44th state)
Capital: Cheyenne
Motto: Equal rights
Nickname: Equality State, Cowboy State
Flower: Indian Paintbrush
Bird: Meadowlark
Tree: Cottonwood
Fair: Mid-August, in Douglas
Time Zone: Mountain
Website: www.state.wy.us

The pristine beauty of Yellowstone National Park

The civic-mindedness of its citizens spread beyond the political arena with equal vigor. Wyoming introduced the nation's first county library system and instituted a public education system that today ranks among the finest in the United States.

Cattle and sheep outnumber people by more than five

to one in Wyoming, which is the least populated state in the country. It is, therefore, easy to see how the cowboy has become such a prominent symbol here. The "bucking horse" insignia has appeared on Wyoming license plates since 1936. It also appears in various versions on road signs, storefronts, and newspapers.

Mineral extraction is the principal industry in Wyoming, which has the largest coal resources in the country. Tourism and recreation ranks second, with approximately four million visitors per year entering the state. Generally, they come to visit the numerous national parks, forests, and monuments. But Wyoming offers a wide range of attractions, from abundant camping to rustic guest ranching, all set among some of the finest natural beauty to be found in the nation.

The country's first national park (Yellowstone), first national monument (Devils Tower), and first national forest (Shoshone) are all located in Wyoming.

When to Go/Climate

Wyoming's climate is relatively cool and dry, though spring can be wet in the lower elevations and winter actually can be dangerous. Blizzards are frequent and have been known to arise from November through June. Temperatures can vary greatly on any given day in both spring and fall.

AVERAGE HIGH/LOW TEMPERATURES (°F)

CHEYENNE

Jan 38/15	May 65/39	Sep 71/44
Feb 41/18	June 74/48	Oct 60/34
Mar 45/22	July 82/55	Nov 47/24
Apr 55/30	Aug 80/53	Dec 39/17

LANDER

Jan 31/8	May 66/40	Sep 72/44
Feb 37/14	June 77/49	Oct 60/34
Mar 46/22	July 86/56	Nov 43/20
Apr 56/31	Aug 84/54	Dec 32/9

Parks and Recreation Finder

Directions to and information about the parks and recreation areas below are given under their respective town/city sections. Please refer to those sections for details.

NATIONAL PARK AND RECREATION AREAS

Key to abbreviations. I.H.S. = International Historic Site; I.P.M. = International Peace Memorial; N.B. = National Battlefield; N.B.P. = National Battlefield Park; N.B.C. = National Battlefield and Cemetery; N.C.A. = National Conservation Area; N.E.M. = National Expansion Memorial; N.F. = National Forest; N.G. = National Grassland; N.H.P. = National Historical Park; N.H.C. = National Heritage Corridor; N.H.S. = National Historic Site; N.L. = National Lakeshore; N.M. = National Monument; N.M.P. = National Military Park; N.Mem. = National Memorial; N.P. = National Park; N.Pres. = National Preserve; N.R.A. = National Recreational Area; N.R.R. = National Recreational River; N.Riv. = National River; N.S. = National Seashore; N.S.R. = National Scenic Riverway; N.S.T. = National Scenic Trail; N.Sc. = National Scientific Reserve; N.V.M. = National Volcanic Monument.

Place Name	Listed Under
Bighorn Canyon N.R.A.	LOVELL
Bighorn N.F.	SHERIDAN

CALENDAR HIGHLIGHTS

JUNE

Plains Indian PowWow (Cody). People from tribes throughout the western plains states and Canada gather to compete. Dancing and singing; ceremonial and traditional tribal dress.

JULY

Legend of Rawhide (Lusk). Live show performed since 1946. Concert, dances, trade show, golf tournament, gun show, parade, pancake breakfast.

1838 Mountain Man Rendezvous (Riverton). Council fire, primitive shoots, hawk and knife throw, games, food. Camping available. Phone 307/856-7306.

Central Wyoming Fair and Rodeo (Casper). Fairgrounds. Phone 307/235-5775.

Red Desert Round-Up (Rock Springs). One of the largest rodeos in the Rocky Mountains region.

Cheyenne Frontier Days (Cheyenne). Frontier Park arena. One of the country's most famous rodeos; originated in 1897. Parades, carnivals; USAF *Thunderbirds* flying team; pancake breakfast; entertainment, square dancing nightly.

AUGUST

Gift of the Waters Pageant (Thermopolis). Hot Springs State Park. Commemorates the deeding of the world's largest mineral hot springs from the Shoshone and Arapahoe to the people of Wyoming in 1896. Pageant features Native American dances, parade, buffalo barbecue.

SEPTEMBER

Jackson Hole Fall Arts Festival (Jackson). Three-wk celebration of the arts featuring special exhibits in more than 30 galleries, demonstrations, special activities. Also dance, theater, mountain film festival, Native American arts, and culinary arts. Phone 307/733-3316.

Bridger-Teton N.F.	JACKSON, PINEDALE
Devils Tower N.M.	same
Flaming Gorge N.R.A.	GREEN RIVER
Fort Laramie N.H.S.	same
Fossil Butte N.M.	KEMMERER
Grand Teton N.P.	same
Medicine Bow N.F.	LARAMIE
Shoshone N.F.	CODY
Thunder Basin N.G.	DOUGLAS
Yellowstone N.P.	same

STATE PARK AND RECREATION AREAS

Key to abbreviations. I.P. = Interstate Park; S.A.P. = State Archaeological Park; S.B. = State Beach; S.C.A. = State Conservation Area; S.C.P. = State Conservation Park; S.Cp. = State Campground; S.F. = State Forest; S.G. = State Garden; S.H.A. = State Historic Area; S.H.P. = State Historic Park; S.H.S. = State Historic Site; S.M.P. = State Marine Park; S.N.A. = State Natural Area; S.P. = State Park; S.P.C. = State Public Campground; S.R. = State Reserve; S.R.A. = State Recreation

Area; S.Res. = State Reservoir; S.Res.P. = State Resort Park; S.R.P. = State Rustic Park.

Place Name	Listed Under
Boysen S.P.	THERMOPOLIS
Buffalo Bill S.P.	CODY
Curt Gowdy S.P.	CHEYENNE
Edness K Wilkins S.P.	CASPER
Glendo S.P.	WHEATLAND
Guernsey S.P.	SAME
Hot Springs S.P.	THERMOPOLIS
Keyhole S.P.	GILLETTE
Seminoe S.P.	RAWLINS
Sinks Canyon S.P.	LANDER

Water-related activities, hiking, various other sports, picnicking, and visitor centers, as well as camping, are avail in many of these areas. State parks are open all yr, but some facilities may be closed Nov-Mar. Entrance fee per vehicle $5 nonresident, $2 resident; nonresident annual entrance pass $40, overnight camping $9. Entrance fee for state historical sites, $2. Camping is limited to 14 days per site unless otherwise posted (no res); $9/vehicle/night. Pets under control. Further information may be obtained from Wyoming State Parks & Historic Sites,122 W 25th, Herschler Bldg 1-E, Cheyenne 82002; 307/777-6323.

SKI AREAS

Place Name	Listed Under
Hogadon Ski Area	CASPER
Jackson Hole Ski Resort	JACKSON
Sleeping Giant Ski Area	CODY
Snow King Ski Resort	JACKSON
Snowy Range Ski Area	LARAMIE

FISHING AND HUNTING

For anglers there are 16,000 mi of fishing streams, 270,000 acres of fishing lakes, and 90 fish varieties, among which are 22 game fish. Throughout Wyoming pronghorn antelope, moose, elk, black bear, whitetail and mule deer, and bighorn sheep roam the mountain ranges and meadows, which are open to hunters.

Nonresident hunting and fishing license for one elk and one season of fishing: $410. Nonresident deer permit: $195; bighorn sheep permit (1 male): $1,510; moose permit (1 bull): $1,010; bird license: $50; turkey: $50; small game (cottontail) license: $50; (1-day, $10); nonresident fishing license: annual $65 (1-day, $6). Most hunting licenses must be applied for well in advance of the hunting season and are issued via computer drawing. Jan 31 is the deadline for elk applications, Feb 28 for bighorn sheep and moose, Mar 15 for deer and antelope. Persons missing date may apply for any leftover licenses. All license holders except for those purchasing a 1-day or 5-day fishing license must purchase a conservation stamp for $5 before hunting or fishing; one time fee/person/yr.

Visitors may take a self-guided tour of the visitor center in the headquarters office bldg, 5400 Bishop Blvd, Cheyenne.

Further information can be obtained from the State of Wyoming Game and Fish Department, 5400 Bishop Blvd, Cheyenne 82006; 307/777-4600.

Driving Information

Safety belts are mandatory for all persons in front seat of vehicle. Children under 3 yrs or under 40 pounds in weight must be in an approved safety seat. For further information phone 307/772-0824.

INTERSTATE HIGHWAY SYSTEM

The following alphabetical listing of Wyoming towns in *Mobil Travel Guide* shows that these cities are within 10 miles of the indicated Interstate highways. A highway map, however, should be checked for the nearest exit.

Highway Number	Cities/Towns within 10 miles
Interstate 25	Buffalo, Casper, Cheyenne, Douglas, Sheridan, Wheatland.
Interstate 80	Cheyenne, Evanston, Green River, Laramie, Rawlins, Rock Springs.
Interstate 90	Buffalo, Gillette, Sheridan.

Additional Visitor Information

Detailed visitor information is distributed by Wyoming Business Council Tourism Division, I-25 at College Dr, Cheyenne 82002; 307/777-7777 or 800/225-5996. There are several welcome centers in Wyoming; visitors will find the information provided at these stops most helpful in planning their stay in the state. Their locations are as follows: in the northern central part of Wyoming, N on I-90 in Sheridan; at the lower eastern corner, on I-25, S of I-80 in Cheyenne; on the western side, near Grand Teton National Park, on US 89 in Jackson; and in central Wyoming in Casper on Center St, S of I-25 (Mon-Fri); I-80 E at Exit 6 in Evanston; I-80, 10 mi E of Laramie (late May-mid-Oct); on I-90 in Sundance (late May-mid-Oct).

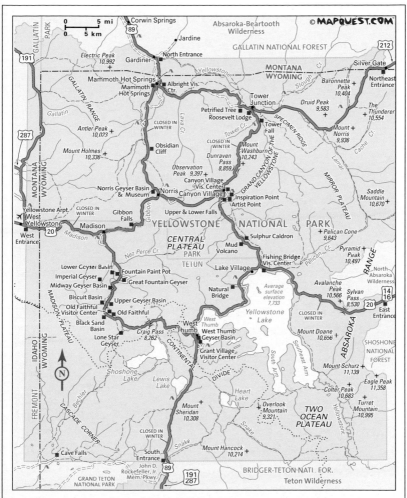

America's first national park, Yellowstone remains one of its most spectacular. It's best to allow two days to savor the sights along the park's figure-eight Grand Loop Road. Starting at the West Thumb/Grant Village area along Yellowstone Lake, head west to take in Old Faithful and the geyser basins. Continue north at Madison and Norris junctions toward Mammoth Hot Springs, a good place to stop overnight. From Mammoth, head east to Tower Junction, then south to the viewpoints of the Grand Canyon of the Yellowstone and its famous waterfalls. Drive south through the wildlife-rich Hayden Valley to Fishing Bridge; spend some time exploring the shores or surface of Lake Yellowstone. From Fishing Bridge, head south for Grand Teton National Park or east for Cody. **(Approx 121 mi, with many stops and slow-moving traffic)**

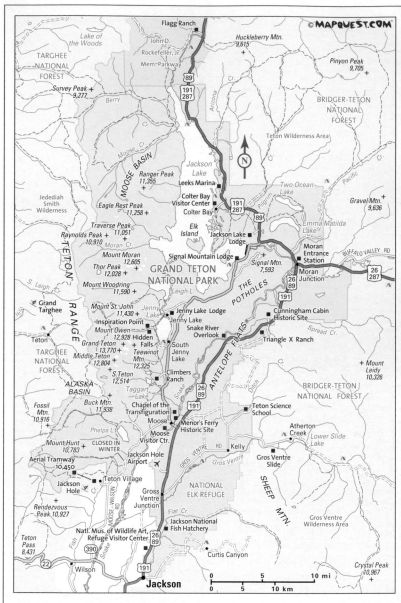

Much more compact than Yellowstone, Grand Teton National Park's highlights can easily be seen in a day. From Jackson, head north on US Highway 191 and enter the park at Moose. Teton Park Road accesses such sites as Menor's Ferry, the Chapel of the Transfiguration, Jenny Lake (with its boat cruises and hiking), and big Jackson Lake. Visit Colter Bay Village for a look at Plains Indian history; several good short trails leave from near here, too. Return to US 191 at Moran Junction and head south to return to Jackson or north to enter Yellowstone National Park. **(Approx 30 mi within park)**

Afton

(D-1) *See also Alpine*

Pop 1,394 **Elev** 6,239 ft
Area code 307 **Zip** 83110
Web www.starvalleychamber.com
Information Chamber of Commerce,
PO Box 1097; 307/883-2759 or
800/426-8833

An arch across Main Street composed
of 3,000 elk horns marks the entrance
to the town of Afton. For anglers and
big-game hunters there are outfitters
and experienced guides here who
rarely send their clients home empty-
handed. Afton is located in Star Valley, which is noted for its dairy
industry. A Ranger District office of
the Bridger-Teton National Forest (see
JACKSON) is located here.

What to See and Do

Bridger-Teton National Forest. (see
JACKSON)

Fishing. Excellent brown trout and
cutthroat trout fishing yr-round on
Salt River (within 2½ mi).

Intermittent spring. Spring flows out
of mountain for about 18 min, then
stops completely for the same period.
The theory behind this phenomenon
is that a natural siphon exists from
an underground lake. Canyon suitable for hiking or horseback riding.
Horses, guides avail. 7 mi E up Swift
Creek Canyon.

Outfitting and Big Game Hunting.
Inquire at the Chamber of Commerce.

Motels/Motor Lodges

★★ **BEST WESTERN HIGH COUN-
TRY INN.** *689 S Washington (83110),
¼ mi S on US 89. 307/886-3856; fax
307/885-9318.* 30 rms. No A/C. S
$45-$50; D $50-$55; each addl $5.
Crib free. Pet accepted, some restrictions. TV; cable. Heated pool; whirlpool. Complimentary coffee in
lobby. Restaurant adj 6 am-10 pm.
Ck-out 11 am. X-country ski 12 mi.
Cr cds: A, C, D, DS, MC, V.
⌨ ☒ ⌨ ☒ 🔥 SC

★ **CORRAL MOTEL.** *161 Washington (83110). 307/886-5424; fax
307/886-5464.* 15 rms, 2 kits. No

A/C. June-Oct: S $35; D $40-$45;
each addl $5; kits.; lower rates mid-
Apr-May. Closed Nov-mid-Apr. Crib
$2. Pet accepted, some restrictions.
TV; cable (premium). Restaurant
nearby. Ck-out 10 am. Some refrigerators. Picnic tables, grills. Totally
nonsmoking. Cr cds: A, C, D, DS,
MC, V.
⌨ ☒ 🔥 🖼

★ **MOUNTAIN INN MOTEL.** *83542
US Hwy 89 (83110), 1 mi S on US 89.
307/886-3156; fax 307/886-3156; toll-
free 800/682-5356.* 20 rms. No A/C.
Mid-May-mid-Oct: S $55; D $60;
each addl $5; lower rates rest of yr.
Crib $5. Pet accepted, some restric-
tions; $3/day. TV; cable (premium).
Heated pool; whirlpool. Sauna.
Restaurant nearby. Ck-out 11 am. Cr
cds: A, C, D, DS, MC, V.
⌨ ☒ ☒ 🔥

Alpine

(D-1) *See also Afton, Jackson*

Pop 200 **Elev** 5,600 ft **Area code** 307
Zip 83128

The Palisades Reservoir, just south of
town, offers fishing, boating, and
tent and trailer camping.

Motels/Motor Lodges

★★ **BEST WESTERN FLYING SAD-
DLE LODGE.** *118878 jct Hwy 89 &
26 (83128). 307/654-7561; fax
307/654-7563; toll-free 800/528-1234.*
20 rms, 6 cottages. June-Oct: S, D
$60-$150; each addl $5. Closed rest
of yr. Crib free. TV; cable (premium),
VCR avail (free movies). Heated pool;
whirlpools. Restaurant 7-11 am, 5-10
pm. Serv bar. Ck-out 11 am. Business
servs avail. Sundries. Tennis. Some
in-rm whirlpools, refrigerators. Western decor. On Snake River. Cr cds: A,
C, D, DS, MC, V.
🖼 ☒ ☒ 🖼

★ **ROYAL RESORT.** *Jct US 26 and 89
(83128). 307/654-7545; fax 307/654-
7546.* 45 rms, 3 story. S $58-$70; D
$65-$80; each addl $7; under 12 free.
Crib $10. Pet accepted. TV; cable
(premium); VCR avail (movies). Play-

ground. Restaurant 7 am-10 pm. Bar noon-1 am. Ck-out 11 am. Meeting rm. Gift shop. X-country ski on site. Whirlpool. Some refrigerators, minibars. Some balconies. Cr cds: A, D, DS, MC, V.

Buffalo

(B-5) *See also Sheridan*

Founded 1884 **Pop** 3,302
Elev 4,640 ft **Area code** 307
Zip 82834
Web www.buffalo.com/chamber/
Information Chamber of Commerce, 55 N Main; 307/684-5544 or 800/227-5122

Buffalo began as a trading center at the edge of Fort McKinney, one of the last of the old military posts. In 1892, trouble erupted here between big cattlemen and small ranchers with their allies, the nesters, in the Johnson County Cattle War. Several people were killed before Federal troops ended the conflict.

Located at the foot of the Big Horn Mountains, Buffalo attracts many tourists, hunters, and anglers; the economy is dependent on tourism, as well as lumber, minerals, and cattle. A Ranger District office of the Bighorn National Forest (see SHERIDAN) is located in Buffalo.

What to See and Do

Fort Phil Kearny Site. Cavalry post was the scene of a clash between Sioux, Arapahoe, Cheyenne, and US soldiers; site of Fetterman and Wagon Box battles; visitor center. (Mid-May-Sep, daily) 13 mi N on US 87. Phone 307/684-7629. ¢

Johnson County-Jim Gatchell Memorial Museum. Collection of Native American artifacts, local and regional history, pioneer equipment; natural history display. (Memorial Day-Labor Day, daily; May 2-Memorial Day and Labor Day-Nov 1, Mon-Fri; rest of yr, by appt; closed July 4) 100 Fort St, adj to courthouse. Phone 307/684-9331. ¢

Annual Event

Johnson County Fair and Rodeo. Features working cowhands; parade. Rodeo held last 3 days of fair. Phone 307/684-7357. Second wk Aug.

Motels/Motor Lodges

★ **CANYON MOTEL.** *997 Fort St (82834). 307/684-2957; toll-free 800/521-0723.* 18 rms, 3 kits. S $38, D $44-$48; each addl $3; kit. units $50-$55. Crib free. Pet accepted. TV; cable. Complimentary coffee in rms. Restaurant nearby. Ck-out 11 am. Airport transportation. Picnic tables. Cr cds: A, DS, MC, V.

★★ **COMFORT INN.** *65 US 16 E (82834). 307/684-9564; fax 307/684-9564; toll-free 800/638-7949.* 41 rms, 2 story. Late June-mid-Aug: S, D $79.95-$94.95; each addl $5; under 18 free; lower rates rest of yr. Crib $5. Pet accepted, some restrictions. TV; cable (premium). Complimentary continental bkfst. Restaurant nearby. Ck-out 11 am. Whirlpool. Cr cds: A, C, D, DS, JCB, MC, V.

★★★ **PARADISE.** *283 Hunter Creek Rd (82834), 12 mi W on US 16, then 4 mi NW on Hunter Creek Rd.* 307/684-7876; fax 307/684-5947. 18 kit. cabins. AP, July-Aug: S $1,400/wk; D $2,800/wk; each addl $1,400/wk; ages 6-12, $1,300/wk; under 6, $650/wk; lower rates June-Sep. Closed rest of yr. Crib free. Heated pool; whirlpool. Playground. Free supervised childrens activities. Complimentary coffee in cabins. Dining rm, sittings 7:30-8:30 am, 12:30 pm, 7 pm. Lunch rides. Cookouts. Bar 5-10 pm. Ck-out 10 am, ck-in 3 pm. Lndry facilities in most cabins. Package store 16 mi. Meeting rms. Free airport transportation. Lawn games. Entertainment. Fishing guides. Fireplaces. Private patios. Picnic tables. No cr cds accepted.

★★ **THE RANCH AT UCROSS.** *2373 US Hwy 14 (82835). 307/737-2281; fax 307/737-2211; toll-free 800/447-0194.* 31 rms, 2 story. S $115; D $130; each addl $20; under 18 free. Pet accepted. Heated pool. Complimentary full bkfst. Restaurant 6:30-9 am, 11:30 am-1 pm, 7-9 pm.

Bar 5-9 pm. Ck-out 1 pm. Meeting rm. Business servs avail. Bellhops. Sundries. Gift shop. Tennis. On creek. Cr cds: MC, V.

★ **WYOMING MOTEL.** *610 E Hart St (82834), ½ mi NE on US 16. 307/ 684-5505; fax 307/684-5442; toll-free 800/666-5505. Email wyomotel@vcn. com; www.buffalowyoming.com/wyo motel/.* 27 rms, 1 story. June-Sep: S $67; D $88; lower rates rest of yr. TV; cable (DSS). Restaurant nearby. Ck-out 11 am. Golf, 18 holes. Tennis. Cr cds: A, C, D, DS, MC, V.

Restaurant

★ **COLONEL BOZEMAN'S.** *675 E Hart St (82834). 307/684-5555.* Specializes in pasta, steaks, Mexican dishes. Hrs: 6 am-10 pm. Closed Dec 25. Bkfst $2.95-$6.95; lunch $3.95-$8.95; dinner $6.95-$16.95. Child's menu. Cr cds: A, D, MC, V.

Casper

(D-5) *See also Douglas*

Founded 1888 **Pop** 46,742
Elev 5,140 ft **Area code** 307
Web www.casperwyoming.org
Information Chamber of Commerce Visitor Center, 500 N Center St, PO Box 399, 82602; 307/234-5311 or 800/852-1889

Before oil was discovered, Casper was a railroad terminus in the cattle-rich Wyoming hinterlands, where Native Americans and emigrants on the Oregon Trail had passed before. Casper was known as an oil town after the first strike in 1890 in the Salt Creek Field, site of the Teapot Dome naval oil reserve that caused a top-level government scandal in the 1920s. World War I brought a real boom and exciting prosperity. A half-million dollars in oil stocks was traded in hotel lobbies every day; land prices skyrocketed and rents inflated while

oil flowed through some of the world's biggest refineries. The crash of 1929 ended the speculation, but oil continued to flow through feeder lines to Casper. Oil continues to contribute to the area's economy; also important are tourism, agriculture, light manufacturing, coal, bentonite, and uranium mining.

What to See and Do

Casper Mountain and Beartrap Meadow Parks. Nordic ski trails (fee). Snowmobile trails (registration required), mountain bike trails, picnicking, camping (fee), shelters (res required). (Daily) 10 mi S. Phone 307/235-9311. Located on the mountain is

Lee McCune Braille Trail. Flora, fauna, and geology are the focus of this trail (⅓ mi) geared for both the sighted and the visually impaired. The self-guided loop trail has signs in both Braille and English at 36 interpretive stations. Safety ropes are provided for guidance. **FREE**

Casper Planetarium. Three 1-hr shows every evening. (Early June-early Sep and Thanksgiving-Dec 24, daily) 904 N Poplar St. Phone 307/577-0310. ¢; Per family ¢¢

Devil's Gate. Pioneer landmark noted by emigrants moving W on the Oregon and Mormon Trails. Church of Jesus Christ of Latter-Day Saints interpretive center tells of the 1856 Martin's Cove disaster, in which as many as 145 people died when confronted by an early, severe winter. Hiking. (Daily; closed Dec 25) 63 mi S on WY 220. Phone 307/328-2953. **FREE**

Edness K. Wilkins State Park. Approx 300 acres on the Oregon Trail, bordered by the historic Platte River. Day-use park. Swimming pond, fishing; hiking paths, picnicking. 4 mi E via I-25, Hat Six Exit on US 87. Phone 307/577-5150. Per vehicle ¢¢

Fort Caspar Museum. On grounds of restored fort; exhibits of Platte Bridge Station/Fort Caspar, Oregon Trail, pony express, Mormon Trail, military artifacts, city of Casper, central Wyoming. (Mid-May-mid-Sep, daily; rest of yr, Sun-Fri) Fort bldgs closed in winter. 4001 Fort Caspar Rd. Phone 307/235-8462. **FREE**

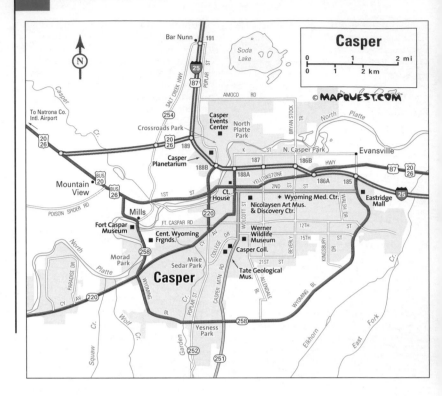

Hogadon Ski Area. Two chairlifts, Pomalift; patrol, school, rentals, snowmaking; cafeteria. Longest run ¾ mi; vertical drop 600 ft. (Late Nov-mid-Apr, Wed-Sun; closed Dec 25) 11 mi S via WY 251. Phone 307/235-8499 or 307/235-8369 (snow conditions). ¢¢¢¢

Independence Rock. "Register of the Desert," 193 ft high. Inscribed with more than 50,000 pioneer names, some dating back more than 100 yrs. Many names are obscured by lichen or worn away. 56 mi SW on WY 220.

Nicolaysen Art Museum and Discovery Center. Changing and permanent exhibits. (Tues-Sun; closed hols) 400 E Collins Dr. Phone 307/235-5247. ¢

Annual Event

Central Wyoming Fair and Rodeo. Fairgrounds, W of city. Mid-July.

Motels/Motor Lodges

★★ **COMFORT INN.** *480 Lathrop Rd (82636), on US 25 Exit 185. 307/235-3038; fax 307/235-3038; toll-free 800/228-5150.* 56 rms, 2 story.

June-Sep: S $70-$75; D $75-$80; each addl $5; suites $85-$95; under 18 free; lower rates rest of yr. Crib free. Pet accepted, some restrictions. TV; cable (premium). Complimentary continental bkfst. Restaurant nearby. Ck-out 11 pm. Business servs avail. Indoor pool; whirlpool. Refrigerator, microwave in suites. Cr cds: A, D, DS, MC, V.
🅳 🐾 ➰ 🏊 🔥 SC

★ **ECONO LODGE.** *821 N Poplar St (82601). 307/266-2400; fax 307/266-1146; toll-free 800/635-3559. Email eclodge@trib.com; www.ecolodge.com.* 103 rms, 2 story. June-Sep: S $64; D $70; each addl $6; lower rates rest of yr. Crib avail, fee. Pet accepted. Parking lot. TV; cable (premium), VCR avail. Complimentary continental bkfst, newspaper, toll-free calls. Restaurant. Ck-out 11 am, ck-in 6 pm. Meeting rm. Business center. Dry cleaning, coin lndry. Exercise privileges, sauna, whirlpool. Golf, 18 holes. Tennis, 4 courts. Downhill skiing. Hiking trail. Picnic facilities. Video games. Cr cds: A, C, D, DS, JCB, MC, V.
🅳 🐾 ⛷ 🏌 🎾 🏊 🏃 🏊 🔥 SC 🎿

★★ **HOLIDAY INN.** *300 West F St (82601). 307/235-2531; fax 307/473-3100.* 200 rms, 2 story. S, D $94-$99; each addl $10; suites $150-$175; under 18 free. Crib free. Pet accepted, some restrictions. TV; cable (premium). Indoor pool; whirlpool. Restaurant 6 am-2 pm, 5-10 pm. Bar. Ck-out noon. Coin lndry. Meeting rms. Business servs avail. Sundries. Free airport, bus depot transportation. Downhill/x-country ski 7 mi. Exercise equipt; sauna. Game rm. On river. Cr cds: A, C, D, DS, ER, JCB, MC, V.

⊡ 🔌 🦺 🏊 🛟 🍽 🎿 🏂 🔁 🔥

Hotels

★★ **HAMPTON INN.** *400 W F St (82601), I-25 Exit Poplar St. 307/235-6668; fax 307/235-2027; res 800/426-7966; toll-free 800/426-7866.* 122 rms, 2 story. May-Sep: S $69; D $79; under 18 free; lower rates rest of yr. Pet accepted, fee. Parking lot. Pool. TV; cable (premium). Complimentary continental bkfst, coffee in rms, newspaper, toll-free calls. Restaurant 11 am-10 pm. Ck-out 11 am, ck-in 1 pm. Meeting rms. Fax servs avail. Dry cleaning. Free airport transportation. Sauna. Golf. Downhill skiing. Picnic facilities. Cr cds: A, D, DS, MC, V.

⊡ 🔌 🦺 🏊 🛟 🍽 🎿 🔁 🔥 **SC**

★★★ **RADISSON HOTEL CASPER.** *800 N Poplar St (82601), 1 blk N of I-25, N Poplar Exit. 307/266-6000; fax 307/473-1010; res 800/333-3333. Email radcspr@trib.com.* 229 rms, 6 story. June-Sep: S, D $84; each addl $5; suites $99; under 18 free; lower rates rest of yr. Crib avail. Pet accepted, some restrictions, fee. Street parking. Indoor pool, whirlpool. TV; cable (premium), VCR avail. Complimentary coffee in rms, newspaper, toll-free calls. Restaurant 6 am-10 pm. Bar. Ck-out noon, ck-in 3 pm. Meeting rms. Business servs avail. Bellhops. Dry cleaning. Gift shop. Salon/barber. Free airport transportation. Exercise equipt. Golf. Tennis, 5 courts. Downhill skiing. Hiking trail. Cr cds: A, C, D, DS, JCB, MC, V.

⊡ 🔌 🦺 🏊 🛟 🍽 🎿 🏂 🔁 🔥

B&B/Small Inn

★★ **HOTEL HIGGINS.** *416 W Birch St (82637), 18 mi E on I-25, 1 mi N*

Exit 165. 307/436-9212; fax 307/436-9213; toll-free 800/458-0144. Email bdoll@trib.com. 6 rms, 2 story, 2 suites. S $56; D $70; suites $80. Crib avail. Street parking. TV; cable. Restaurant 11:30 am-9:30 pm. Bar. Ck-out noon, ck-in. Meeting rm. Fax servs avail. Dry cleaning, coin lndry. Exercise privileges. Golf, 9 holes. Tennis, 2 courts. Hiking trail. Cr cds: C, D, DS, MC, V.

⊡ 🦺 🏊 🛟 🎿 🔁 🔥

Restaurants

★★ **ARMOR'S SILVER FOX.** *3422 S Energy Ln (82604). 307/235-3000.* Specializes in veal, fettucine, prime rib. Hrs: 11 am-9:30 pm; Fri, Sat to 10:30 pm. Closed Sun; Dec 25. Res accepted. Bar. Lunch $5.95-$10.95; dinner $6.95-$21.95. Child's menu. Picture windows with mountain view. Cr cds: A, D, DS, MC, V.

⊡ 🍴

★★★ **PAISLEY SHAWL.** *416 W Birch St. 307/436-9212.* Specializes in prime rib, shrimp scampi. Own baking. Hrs: 11:30 am-1:30 pm, 6-9:30 pm; winter hrs vary. Closed hols. Res accepted. Bar. Lunch a la carte entrees: $5-$9; dinner a la carte entrees: $12-$25. Complete meals: $28. In 1916 bldg; turn-of-the-century decor. Cr cds: MC, V.

⊡ 🍴

Cheyenne

(F-7) *See also Laramie*

Founded 1867 **Pop** 50,008
Elev 6,098 ft **Area code** 307
Zip 82001 **Web** www.cheyenne.org
Information Cheyenne Convention & Visitors Bureau, 309 W Lincolnway; 307/778-3133 or 800/426-5009

Cheyenne was named for an Algonquian tribe that roamed this area. When the Union Pacific Railroad reached what is now the capital and largest city of Wyoming on November 13, 1867, there was already a town. Between July of that year and the day the tracks were actually laid, 4,000 people had set up living quarters and land values soared. Professional gunmen, soldiers, promoters, trainmen, gamblers, and confidence men enjoying quick money and cheap liquor gave the town the reputation of being "hell on wheels." Two railways and three transcontinental highways made it a wholesale and commodity jobbing point, the retail and banking center of a vast region. Cheyenne is the seat of state and county government. Agriculture, light manufacturing, retail trade, and tourism support the economy of the area.

What to See and Do

Cheyenne Botanic Gardens. Wildflower, rose gardens, lily pond, community garden. (Mon-Fri; wkends, hols, afternoons) 710 S Lions Park Dr. Phone 307/637-6458. **Donation**

Cheyenne Frontier Days Old West Museum. Incl collections of clothing, weapons, carriages, Western art. Gift shop. (Daily; closed hols) 4501 N Carey Ave. Phone 307/778-7290. ¢¢

⭐ **Cheyenne Street Trolley.** Two-hr historic tour of major attractions. (Mid-May-late Sep, daily) 309 W Lincolnway, Convention & Visitors Bureau. Phone 307/778-3133. ¢¢¢

Curt Gowdy State Park. The foothills of a mountain range separating Cheyenne and Laramie create the park formation. Two reservoirs provide trout fishing (no swimming), boating (ramps); hiking, picnicking, camping (standard fees). 26 mi W on Happy Jack *Rd* (WY 210). Phone 307/632-7946.

Historic Governors' Mansion. (1904) Residence of Wyoming's governors from 1905-76; first governors' mansion in the nation to be occupied by a woman, Nellie Tayloe Ross (1925-27). (Tues-Sat; closed hols) 300 E 21st St. Phone 307/777-7878. **FREE**

Holliday Park. One of world's largest steam locomotives, 4000-type UPRR, on grounds. Canoeing, tennis, picnicking, lighted horseshoe pit. (May-Oct) Morrie Ave & 19th St. Phone 307/637-6423. **FREE**

State Capitol. (1887) Beaux-arts bldg with murals in Senate and House chambers by Allen T. True. Ceiling of each chamber is of stained glass. Guided tours (Mon-Fri; closed hols). Head of Capitol Ave. Phone 307/777-7220. **FREE**

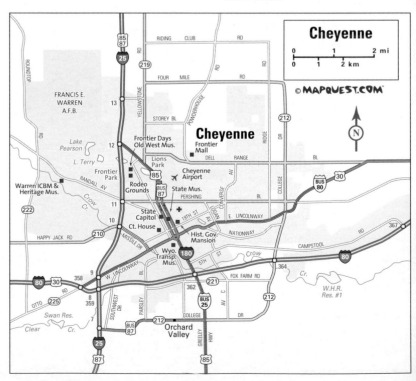

Plains Indian Dancer, Frontier Days

Warren AFB. Museum traces history of base from 1867-present (Daily; also by appt). (See ANNUAL EVENTS) Tours (by appt). W on Randall Ave. Phone 307/775-2980. **FREE**

Annual Events

Cheyenne Frontier Days. Frontier Park Arena, N on Carey Ave. One of country's most famous rodeos; originated in 1897. Parades, carnivals; USAF *Thunderbirds* flying team; pancake breakfast; entertainment, square dancing nightly. Phone 307/778-7290. Last full wk July.

Laramie County Fair. Frontier Park. Incl livestock and farm exhibits. Phone 307/633-4534. Early Aug.

Old-fashioned Melodrama. Atlas Theater. Phone 307/638-6543. July-mid-Aug.

Motels/Motor Lodges

★ **CHEYENNE SUPER 8.** *1900 W Lincolnway (82001), US 30, I-80 Business. 307/635-8741; fax 307/635-8741.* 61 rms, 3 story. No elvtr. May-Sep: S $47.88; D $52.98-$55.98; each addl $6; under 18 free; lower rates rest of yr. Crib free. TV; cable (premium), VCR avail (movies). Restaurant adj open 24 hrs. Ck-out 11 am. Cr cds: A, C, D, DS, ER, JCB, MC, V.

🄳 ⬥ ✈ ⬙ 🐾

★★ **COMFORT INN.** *2245 Etchepare Dr (82007). 307/638-7202; fax 307/635-8560; toll-free 800/777-7218.* 77 rms, 2 story. June-Aug: S, D $79.99; under 18 free. Crib free. Pet accepted. TV; cable (premium). Heated pool. Complimentary continental bkfst, coffee in lobby. Restaurant opp open 24 hrs. Ck-out noon. Coin lndry. Meeting rm. Business servs avail. Cr cds: A, C, D, DS, MC, V.

🄳 ⬥ ⬙ ⬙ 🐾 SC

★ **DAYS INN.** *2360 W Lincolnway (82001). 307/778-8877; fax 307/778-8697; res 800/329-7466. Email 6167@hotel.cendant.com.* 72 rms, 2 story. May-Sep: S, D $60-$75; each addl $5; suites $75-$80; lower rates rest of yr. Crib free. TV; cable (premium). Complimentary continental bkfst. Restaurant adj open 24 hrs. Ck-out noon. Meeting rm. Business servs avail. Whirlpool. Exercise equipt; sauna. Cr cds: A, DS, MC, V.

🄳 🛄 ⬙ 🐾 SC

★★ **FAIRFIELD INN.** *1415 Stillwater Ave (82001). 307/637-4070; fax 307/637-4070.* 62 rms, 3 story, 8 suites. May-Sep: S $63; D $74.95; each addl $6; suites $74.95-$89.95; under 18 free; higher rates Cheyenne Frontier Days; lower rates rest of yr. Crib free. TV; cable (premium). Indoor pool; whirlpool. Complimentary continental bkfst. Restaurant nearby. Ck-out 11 am. Business servs avail. Game rm. Refrigerator in some suites. Cr cds: A, D, DS, MC, V.

🄳 ⬥ ⬙ ⬙ ⬙ 🐾

★ **LA QUINTA INN.** *2410 W Lincolnway (82009). 307/632-7117; fax 307/638-7807; toll-free 800/687-6667.* 105 rms, 3 story. June-Aug: S $65; D $75; each addl $5; under 18 free; lower rates rest of yr. Crib free. Pet accepted. TV; cable (premium). Pool. Complimentary continental bkfst. Coffee in rms. Restaurant adj open 24 hrs. Ck-out noon. Sundries. Cr cds: A, C, D, DS, MC, V.

🄳 ⬥ ⬙ ⬙ 🐾 SC

★★★ **LITTLE AMERICA HOTEL.** *2800 W Lincolnway (82001), 1½ mi W at jct I-25, I-80. 307/775-8400; fax 307/775-8425; toll-free 800/445-6945.* 188 rms, 2 story. S $72; D $82-$89; each addl $10; suites $89-$149; under 12 free. Crib free. TV; cable (premium). Pool. Restaurants open 24 hrs. Bar 11-2 am; entertainment Thurs-Sat. Ck-out noon. Coin lndry. Meeting rms. Bellhops. Shopping arcade. Free airport, railroad station, bus depot transportation. 9-hole golf, putting green. Exercise equipt. Many bathrm phones, refrigerators. Private patios, balconies. Cr cds: A, C, D, DS, MC, V.

[D] [≈] [大] [⊿] [♨] [SC]

Conference Center

★★ **BEST WESTERN HITCHING POST INN RESORT & CONFERENCE CENTER.** *1700 W Lincolnway (82001), ½ mi E at I-25 and I-80. 307/638-3301; fax 307/778-7194; res 800/221-0125. Email www.sales@hitchingpostinn.com; www.hitchingpostinn.com.* 162 rms, 2 story, 4 suites. June-Aug: S $99; D $109; each addl $10; suites $150; under 17 free; lower rates rest of yr. Crib avail. Pet accepted, some restrictions. Parking lot. Indoor/outdoor pools, whirlpool. TV; cable (premium), VCR avail. Complimentary coffee in rms, toll-free calls. Restaurant 5 am-10 pm. Bar. Ck-out noon, ck-in 3 pm. Meeting rms. Business center. Bellhops. Concierge. Dry cleaning, coin lndry. Gift shop. Salon/barber. Free airport transportation. Exercise rm, sauna, steam rm. Golf. Tennis. Supervised children's activities. Picnic facilities. Video games. Cr cds: A, C, D, DS, ER, JCB, MC, V.

[D] [✦] [⊀] [⌿] [≈] [大] [⊀] [⊿] [♨] [SC] [大]

Restaurant

★ **POOR RICHARD'S.** *2233 E Lincolnway (82009). 307/635-5114.* Specializes in steak, fresh seafood. Salad bar. Hrs: 11 am-2:30 pm, 5-10 pm; Fri, Sat to 11 pm; Sat brunch 11 am-2:30 pm; Sun 5-10 pm. Closed Dec 25. Bar. Lunch $3.95-$6.95; dinner $6-$22.50. Brunch sat $4.75-$7.25. Child's menu. Cr cds: A, D, DS, MC, V.

[D]

Cody (B-3)

Founded 1896 **Pop** 7,897
Elev 5,002 ft **Area code** 307
Zip 82414
Web www.codychamber.org

Information Cody Country Chamber of Commerce, 836 Sheridan Ave; 307/587-2777

Buffalo Bill Cody founded this town, gave it his name, and devoted time and money to its development. He built a hotel and named it after his daughter Irma, arranged for a railroad spur from Montana and, with the help of his friend Theodore Roosevelt, had what was then the world's tallest dam constructed just west of town.

Cody is located 52 miles east of Yellowstone National Park (see); everyone entering Yellowstone from the east must pass through here, making tourism an important industry. A Ranger District office of the Shoshone National Forest is located here.

What to See and Do

★ **Buffalo Bill Historical Center.** Four-museum complex; gift shops. (Apr-Oct, daily; Nov-Mar, Thurs-Mon) 720 Sheridan Ave. Phone 307/587-4771. ¢¢ Admission incl

Buffalo Bill Museum. Personal and historical memorabilia of the great showman and scout incl guns, saddles, clothing, trophies, gifts, and posters.

Cody Firearms Museum. More than 5,000 projectile arms on display. Comprehensive collection begun in 1860 by Oliver Winchester.

Whitney Gallery of Western Art. Paintings, sculpture; major collection and comprehensive display of western art by artists from the early 1800s-present.

Plains Indian Museum. Extensive displays of memorabilia and artifacts representing the people of the Plains tribes and their artistic expressions; clothing, weapons, tools, and ceremonial items.

Buffalo Bill State Park. Wildlife is abundant in this area. Fishing, boating (ramps, docks); picnicking, primitive camping. 13 mi W on US 14, 16, 20, on Buffalo Bill Reservoir. Phone 307/587-9227. Camping ¢¢ Along the adj reservoir is

Buffalo Bill Dam and Visitor Center. (1910) A 350-ft dam, originally called the Shoshone Dam. The name was changed in 1946 to honor Buffalo Bill, who helped raise money for its construction. The Visitor Center has a natural history museum, dam overlook, gift shop. (May-Sep, daily) E end of reservoir. Phone 307/527-6076. **FREE**

Shoshone National Forest. This 2,466,586-acre area is one of the largest in the national forest system. Incl magnificent approach route (Buffalo Bill Cody's Scenic Byway) to the E gate of Yellowstone National Park (see) along N fork of the Shoshone River. The Fitzpatrick, Popo Agie, North Absaroka, Washakie, and a portion of the Absaroka-Beartooth wilderness areas all lie within its boundaries. Incl outstanding lakes, streams, big-game herds, mountains, and some of the largest glaciers in the continental US. Fishing; hunting, camping. Standard fees. W on US 14, 16, 20. Contact Forest Supervisor, PO Box 2140. Phone 307/527-6241.

Shoshone river trips.

Cody Boys River Trips. Two-hr to ½-day trips. (Mid-May-mid Sep, daily) PO Box 1446. Phone 307/587-4208. ¢¢¢¢

River Runners. Whitewater trips; 1½-hr and ½-day trips. (June-Labor Day, daily) 1491 Sheridan Ave. Phone 307/527-7238 or 800/535-RAFT. ¢¢¢¢

Wyoming River Trips. 1½-hr and ½-day trips. (Mid-May-late Sep, daily) 1701 Sheridan Ave, located at Holiday Inn Complex. Phone 307/587-6661 or 800/586-6661. ¢¢¢¢

Sleeping Giant Ski Area. Chairlift, T-bar; patrol, school, rentals; snack bar. Longest run ¾ mi; vertical drop 500 ft. (Dec-mid-Apr, Fri-Sun; closed Dec 25) Cross-country trails, snowmobiling. 46 mi W on US 14, 16, 20. Phone 307/587-4044 or 307/527-7669 (snow report). ¢¢¢¢

Trail Town and the Museum of the Old West. Twenty-four reconstructed bldgs dating from 1879-99 and cemetery on site of Old Cody City along the original wagon trails. Bldgs incl cabin used as rendezvous for Butch Cassidy and the Sundance Kid and cabin of Crow scout Curley, the only one of General Custer's troops that escaped from the Battle of Little Bighorn. Cemetery incl remains of Jeremiah "Liver Eating" Johnson.

(Mid-May-mid-Sep, daily) 2 mi W on Yellowstone Hwy. Phone 307/587-5302. ¢¢

Wyoming Vietnam Veteran's Memorial. Black granite memorial lists names of state residents who died or are missing in action in Vietnam. Off US 16/20 W of the airport.

⭐ **Yellowstone National Park.** (see) 52 mi W on US 14, 16, 20.

Annual Events

Cowboy Songs and Range Ballads. Buffalo Bill Historical Center. Early Apr.

Plains Indian PowWow. People from tribes throughout the western plains states and Canada gather to compete. Dancing and singing; ceremonial and traditional tribal dress. Late June.

Cody Stampede. Rodeo, parade. Phone 307/587-5155. Early July.

Frontier Festival. Buffalo Bill Historical Center. Demonstrations of pioneer skills, cooking crafts; musical entertainment. Mid-July.

Yellowstone Jazz Festival. Elks Club lawn. Mid-July.

Buffalo Bill Festival. City Park. Old West celebration; chili cook-off, kiddie festival. Mid-Aug.

Seasonal Event

Cody Nite Rodeo. Stampede Park. Phone 307/587-5155. Nightly, June-last Sat in Aug.

Motels/Motor Lodges

★★ **BUFFALO BILL VILLAGE.** *1701 Sheridan Ave (82414), (US 14, 16, 20, WY 120), in Buffalo Bill Village. 307/587-5544; fax 307/527-7757; toll-free 800/527-5544. Email blair@wavecom. net; www.blairhotels.com.* 82 rms, 1 story, 1 suite. May-Sep: S, D $89; suites $89; under 18 free; lower rates rest of yr. Crib avail. Parking lot. Pool. TV; cable. Complimentary coffee in rms, toll-free calls. Restaurant 6 am-7 pm. Bar. Ck-out 11 am, ck-in 3 pm. Meeting rms. Business servs avail. Bellhops. Dry cleaning. Gift shop. Exercise privileges. Golf, 18 holes. Tennis, 3 courts. Cr cds: A, C, D, DS, JCB, MC, V.

🄳 🛠 🍽 ⚓ 🍴 ✈ 🔲 ♨

★★ COMFORT INN BUFFALO BILL VILLAGE. *1601 Sheridan Ave (82414). 307/587-5556; fax 307/587-8727; toll-free 800/527-5544. Email blair@wavecom.net; www.blairhotels.com.* 75 rms, 2 story. Apr-Sep: S, D $129; each addl $6; under 18 free; lower rates rest of yr. Crib avail, fee. Parking lot. Pool. TV; cable (DSS). Complimentary continental bkfst, coffee in rms, toll-free calls. Restaurant 6 am-9 pm. Bar. Ck-out 11 am, ck-in 3 pm. Meeting rms. Business center. Bellhops. Dry cleaning. Gift shop. Free airport transportation. Exercise privileges. Golf, 18 holes. Tennis, 4 courts. Cr cds: A, C, D, DS, JCB, MC, V.

★ DAYS INN. *524 Yellowstone Ave (82414). 307/527-6604; fax 307/527-7341.* 52 rms, 2 story. Mid-May-Oct: S $115; D $125-$135; suites $150; each addl $10; under 12 free; lower rates rest of yr. Crib free. TV; cable (premium). Indoor pool; whirlpool. Complimentary continental bkfst. Restaurant nearby. Ck-out 11 am. Coin lndry. Cr cds: A, D, DS, MC, V.

★ KELLY INN. *2513 Greybull Hwy (82414), near regional airport. 307/527-5505; fax 307/527-5505.* 50 rms, 2 story. June-mid-Sep: S $75; D $92; each addl $5; lower rates rest of yr. Crib free. Pet accepted. TV; cable.

Buffalo Bill Historical Center, Cody

Complimentary coffee in lobby. Restaurant nearby. Ck-out 11 am. Coin lndry. Business servs avail. Free airport transportation. Whirlpool, sauna. Cr cds: A, D, DS, MC, V.

Guest Ranches

★ ABSAROKA MOUNTAIN LODGE. *1231 E Yellowstone Hwy (82414), 40 mi W on US 14, 16, 20, on Gunbarrel Creek in Shoshone National Forest; 12 mi E of Yellowstone National Park. 307/587-3963; fax 307/527-9628. Email bkudelsk@wyoming.com; www.absarokamtlodge.com.* 16 cabins. No A/C. AP, June-Sep: S, D $79-$96; lower rates May. Closed rest of yr. Crib $6. Playground. Dining rm 7:30-9:30 am, 6-8:30 pm. Bar 6-10:30 pm. Ck-out 11 am, ck-in 2 pm. Lawn games. Refrigerators avail. Picnic tables. Log cabins; western decor. Totally nonsmoking. Cr cds: DS, MC, V.

★ BILL CODY RANCH. *2604-MG Yellowstone Hwy (82414), 26 mi W on US 14, 16, 20. 307/587-2097; fax 307/587-6272; toll-free 800/615-2934. Email billcody@billcodyranch.com; www.billcodyranch.com.* 14 cabins. No A/C. Mid-June-late Aug: S, D $115; each addl $10; wkly rates, package plans; lower rates May-mid-June, late Aug-Sep. Closed rest of yr. Dining rm 7:30-9 am, 6-8 pm. Bar 4-10:30 pm. Entertainment Wed, Sat. Ck-out 10 am. Airport transportation. Whirlpool. River rafting. Chuck wagon cookout. Private porches. Picnic tables. On stream. Cr cds: DS, MC, V.

★★ ELEPHANT HEAD LODGE. *1170 Yellowstone Hwy (82450), 41 mi W on US 14, 16, 20; 11 mi E of Yellowstone National Park. 307/587-3980; fax 307/527-7922; res 307/587-3980. Email vacation@elephantheadlodge.com; www.elephantheadlodge.com.* 12 cabins. No A/C. Mid-May-mid-Oct: S $75; D $75-$100; AP avail. Closed rest of yr. Pet accepted. Playground. Dining rm 7:30-9:30 am, 11:30 am-1:30 pm, 6:30-8:30 pm. Bar 5:30-10 pm. Ck-out, ck-in noon. Hiking, nature trails. Picnic tables, grills. On river in Shoshone National Forest.

Trail rides avail. Totally nonsmoking. Cr cds: A, DS, MC, V.

★★ **SEVEN D RANCH.** *774 Sunlight Rd (82414), 17 mi N on WY 120, E on WY 296 to Sunlight Rd, 10 mi to Ranch.* 307/587-9885; fax 307/587-9885. *Email ranch7d@wyoming.com; www. 7dranch.com.* 11 cabins (1-4 bedrm). No A/C. No rm phones. AP, June-Aug, wkly: D $1,450/person; each addl $1,200/person; under 12, $1,125/person; lower rates Sep. Closed rest of yr. Supervised children's activities (June-Aug). Dining rm in lodge. Box lunches, cookouts. Ck-out 9:30 am, ck-in 3 pm. Guest lndry. Airport transportation. Horse corrals. Pack trips. Hiking. Trap shooting. Square dancing. Lawn games. Rec rm. Fishing/hunting guides. On creek in Shoshone National Forest. No cr cds accepted.

★ **SHOSHONE LODGE RESORT & GUEST RANCH.** *349 Yellowstone Hwy (82414), 46 mi W on US 14, 16, 20; 4 mi E of Yellowstone National Park.* 307/587-4044; fax 307/587-2681. *Email shoshone@shoshonelodge.com; www.shoshonelodge.com.* 16 cabins, 3 kits. (no equipt). No A/C. No rm phones. May-Oct: S $66; D $72; each addl $10; kit. units $20 addl. Closed rest of yr. Crib $2. Pet accepted. Dining rm 7-9 am, noon-1:30 pm, 6-8 pm. Ck-out 10 am. Coin lndry. Sundries. Lawn games. Downhill/X-country ski opp. Cookouts. Fireplace in lodge. Most cabins have porches. Cr cds: A, D, DS, MC, V.

Guest Ranches

★ **BLACKWATER CREEK RANCH.** *1516 Northfork Hwy (82414), 37 mi W on US 14, 16, 20; 15 mi E of Yellowstone National Park.* 307/587-5201; fax 307/587-5201. 15 cabins. No A/C. AP: S $1,150/wk; D $2,300/wk; under 10, $1,050/wk. Pool. Dining rm 7:30-8:30 am, 12:30-1:30 pm, 6:30-7:30 pm; closed mid-Sep-June. Cookouts. Bar. Ck-out 9:30 am, ck-in after 2 pm. Free airport transportation. Whitewater rafting. Horseback riding. Guided trips to Cody and Yellowstone. Hiking. Rodeos. Rec rm.

Whirlpool. Lawn games. Square dancing. Picnic tables. On Shoshone River and Blackwater Creek. Cr cds: MC, V.

★★★ **DOUBLE DIAMOND X.** *3453 Southfork Rd (82414), 35 mi SW.* 307/527-6276; fax 307/587-2708. *Email ddx@cody.wtp.net; www. ddxranch.com.* 12 units, 5 cabins, 7 rms in lodge. AP, Mid-June-mid-Sep, wkly: S, D $1,210-$1,460; children 6-14 $880-$1,020; under 6, $550; lower rates May-mid-June, mid-Sep-Oct. Closed rest of yr. Indoor pool; whirlpool. Supervised children's activities (June-Sep). Cookouts. Ck-out 11 am. Guest lndry. Meeting rms. Gift shop. Free airport transportation. Hiking. Entertainment nightly in summer. Square dancing. Fishing/hunting trips. Fly-fishing instruction. On South fork of Shoshone River. Cr cds: MC, V.

★★ **RIMROCK DUDE RANCH.** *2728 Northfork Hwy (82414), 27 mi W on US 14, 16, 20.* 307/587-3970; fax 307/527-5014; toll-free 800/208-7468. *Email fun@rimrockranch.com.* 9 cabins, 1-2 bedrms. No A/C. AP, June-Aug, wkly: S $1,100; D $2,000. Closed rest of yr. Crib free. Pool. Dining rm. Cookouts. Free airport transportation. Pack trips. Guided trip to Yellowstone Park. Float trip on Shoshone River. Clean and store. Rec rm. Refrigerators; some fireplaces, porches. Cr cds: MC, V.

★★ **UXU RANCH.** *1710 Northfork Hwy (82450), 35 mi W on US.* 307/587-2143; fax 307/587-8307; toll-free 800/373-9027. *www.uxuranch.com.* 11 cabins. No A/C. No rm phones. AP: wkly: S $1,320; D $2,375; each addl $1,050; ages 3-5 $525; under 3 free. Closed Oct-May. Playground. Supervised children's activities. Restaurant 8-9 am, 12:30-1:30 pm, 7:30-8:30 pm. Bar noon-11 pm; entertainment. Ck-out 11 am. Gift shop. Rec rm. Lawn games. Rustic former logging camp in forest setting. Cr cds: MC, V.

★ **VALLEY GOFF CREEK.** *995 Yellowstone Hwy (82414), 42 mi W on US 14, 16, 20; 10 mi E of Yellowstone*

National Park. 307/587-3753; fax 307/587-3753. 17 cabins. No A/C. Mid-May-mid-Oct: S $72; D $90; each addl $5; duplex cabins $100-$180; lower rates rest of yr. Crib $5. Pet accepted. TV in main lodge. Dining rm 7-9:30 am, 5-8 pm. Bar noon-11 pm. Ck-out 11 am. Sundries. Whitewater rafting. Lawn games. Private patios. Picnic tables. Trail rides. Cr cds: A, MC, V.

Restaurants

★★★ **FRANCA'S ITALIAN DINING.** *1421 Rumsey Ave (82414). 307/587-5354.* Italian menu. Specializes in homemade ravioli, focaccine bread, fresh seafood. Own desserts. Hrs: 6-11 pm. Closed Mon, Tues; mid-Jan-mid-May. Res accepted. Wine list. Dinner $12.50-$26. Elegant decor. No cr cds accepted.
D

★ **MAXWELL'S.** *937 E Sheridan St (82414). 307/527-7749.* Specializes in pasta, steaks, chicken. Hrs: 11 am-9 pm. Closed Sun; hols. Res accepted. Lunch $4.50-$6; dinner $10-$16. Child's menu. Cr cds: A, D, MC, V.
D

★★ **STEFAN'S.** *1367 Sheridan Ave (82414). 307/587-8511.* Specializes in stuffed filet mignon, homemade ravioli, fresh seafood pasta. Hrs: 11 am-10 pm. Closed Jan 1, Thanksgiving, Dec 25. Res accepted. Wine, beer. Lunch $2.95-$7.95; dinner $6.50-$22.50. Child's menu. Street parking. Garden decor; potted plants. Cr cds: A, D, MC, V.
D

Devils Tower National Monument

The nation's first national monument, Devils Tower was set aside for the American people by President Theodore Roosevelt in 1906. Located on 1,347 acres approximately five miles west of the Black Hills National Forest, this

Devils Tower

gigantic landmark rises from the prairie like a giant tree stump. Sixty million years ago volcanic activity pushed molten rock toward the earth's surface. As it cooled Devils Tower was formed. Towering 1,267 feet above the prairie floor and Ponderosa pine forest, the flat-topped formation appears to change hue with the hour of the day and glows during sunsets and in moonlight.

The visitor center at the base of the tower offers information about the area, a museum, and a bookstore. (Apr-Oct, daily). A self-guided trail winds around the tower for nature and scenery lovers. There are picnicking and camping facilities with tables, fireplaces, water, and restrooms (Apr-Oct). Contact Superintendent, PO Box 10, Devils Tower 82714; 307/467-5283. ¢¢-¢¢¢

Douglas

(D-6) *See also Casper*

Founded 1886 **Pop** 5,076
Elev 4,842 ft **Area code** 307
Zip 82633
Web www.chalkbuttes.com/jackalope

Information Douglas Area Chamber of Commerce, 121 Brownfield Rd; 307/358-2950

Cattlemen were attracted here by plentiful water and good grass. Homesteaders gradually took over, and agriculture became dominant. The town was named for Stephen Douglas, Lincoln's celebrated debating opponent. A Ranger District office for the Medicine Bow National Forest (see LARAMIE) is located in Douglas.

What to See and Do

Fort Fetterman State Museum. Located on a plateau above the valleys of LaPrele Creek and the North Platte River. Museum in restored officers' quarters; additional exhibits in ordnance warehouse. Picnic area. (Memorial Day-Labor Day, daily) 10 mi NW on WY 93 at Fort Fetterman State Historic Site. Phone 307/358-2864 or 307/777-7695. **FREE**

Medicine Bow National Forest. S of town on WY 91 or WY 94 (see LARAMIE).

Thunder Basin National Grassland. Approximately 572,000 acres; accessible grasslands, sagebrush, and some ponderosa pine areas. Bozeman and Texas trails cross parts of the grasslands. Large herds of antelope, mule deer, sage grouse. Hunting. N on WY 59. Phone 307/358-4690. **FREE**

Wyoming Pioneer Memorial Museum. Large collection of pioneer and Native American artifacts, guns, antiques. (June-Sep, daily; rest of yr, Mon-Fri; closed winter hols) State Fairgrounds, W end of Center St. Phone 307/358-9288. **FREE**

Annual Events

High Plains Old Time Country Music Show and Contest. Douglas High School Auditorium. 307/358-2950. Late Apr.

Jackalope Days. Carnival, entertainment, exhibitors. Usually 3rd wkend June.

Wyoming State Fair. Incl rodeo events, horse shows, exhibits. Phone 307/358-2398. Mid-Aug.

Conference Center

★★ **BEST WESTERN DOUGLAS INN.** *1450 Riverbend Dr (82633). 307/358-9790; fax 307/358-6251; res 800/528-1234; toll-free 800/344-2113.*

Email bwdouglas@netcommander.com; www.bwdouglas.com. 116 rms, 2 story, 1 suite. June-Sep: S $81; D $91; each addl $10; suites $150; under 18 free; lower rates rest of yr. Crib avail. Pet accepted, some restrictions. Parking lot. Indoor pool, whirlpool. TV; cable (premium), VCR avail. Complimentary coffee in rms. Restaurant 6 am-2 pm. Bar. Ck-out 11 am, ck-in 3 pm. Meeting rms. Business center. Bellhops. Dry cleaning, coin lndry. Gift shop. Exercise privileges, sauna. Golf, 18 holes. Hiking trail. Picnic facilities. Cr cds: A, C, D, DS, MC, V.

Dubois

(C-2) *See also Grand Teton National Park*

Founded 1886 **Pop** 895 **Elev** 6,940 ft
Area code 307 **Zip** 82513
Web www.dteworld.com/~duboiscc/

Information Chamber of Commerce, 616 W Ramshorn St, PO Box 632; 307/455-2556

On the Wind River, 56 miles from Grand Teton National Park (see), Dubois is surrounded on three sides by the Shoshone National Forest (see CODY). The Wind River Reservation (Shoshone and Arapahoe) is a few miles east of town. Dubois, in ranching and dude ranching country, is a good vacation headquarters. There are plentiful rockhounding resources, and a large herd of bighorn sheep roam within five miles of town. A Ranger District office of the Shoshone National Forest is located here.

What to See and Do

Big-game hunting. Elk, deer, moose, bear, and mountain sheep.

Fishing. There are 6 varieties of trout in nearby streams. 907 Ramshorn, off US 26, 287. Phone 307/455-3429. ¢

National Bighorn Sheep Interpretive Center. Major exhibit, "Sheep Mt," features full-size bighorns and the plants and animals that live around them. Other exhibits promote education, research, and conservation of the sheep and their habitats. (Memorial Day-Labor Day, daily; winter hrs vary) 907 Ramshorn, off US 26, 287. Phone 307/455-3429. ¢

Wind River Historical Center. Exhibits and displays depicting natural and social history of the Wind River Valley; incl Native American, wildlife, and archaeological displays; also Scandinavian tie-hack industries. (Mid-May-mid-Sep, daily; rest of yr, by appt) W on US 26, 287 at 909 W Ramshorn. Phone 307/455-2284. **FREE**

Annual Events

Pack Horse Races. Memorial Day wkend.

Wind River Rendezvous. Second wkend Aug.

Motel/Motor Lodge

★ **SUPER 8.** *1414 Warm Springs Dr (82513).* 307/455-3694; fax 307/455-3640. 32 rms, 2 story. July-Aug: S $45.88; D $48.88-$60.88; suite $85; each addl $5; under 12 free; lower rates rest of yr. Crib free. Pet accepted. TV; cable (premium). Whirlpool. Complimentary coffee. Ck-out 11 am. Cr cds: A, D, DS, MC, V.
🄳 🛪 ⬛ 🖼 🔥

Guest Ranch

★★ **ABSAROKA RANCH.** *PO Box 929 (82513), Dunoir Valley.* 307/455-2275. 4 cabins. AP (1-wk min), mid-June-mid-Sep: $1,150/person; family rates; lower rates early June-mid-June. Closed rest of yr. 10% serv charge. Crib free. Supervised children's activities (June-Sep). Dining rm. Cookouts. Box lunches. Ck-out 11 am, ck-in 2 pm. Horse stables. Guided hiking. Sauna. Lawn games. Game rm. On creek. Totally nonsmoking. Cr cds: A, DS, MC, V.
⬛ 🛪 🖼 🔥

★★★ **BROOKS LAKE LODGE.** *458 Brooks Lake Rd (82513), off US 26/287.* 307/455-2121; fax 307/455-2121. Email info@brookslake.com; www.brookslake.com. 6 rms in main bldg, 6 cabins (1- and 2-bedrm). Late June-late Sep, 3-day min: S, D $195-$450; each addl $195; family rates; wkly rates; lower rates late Sep, Jan-Mar. Closed rest of yr. Crib free. Whirlpool. Complimentary coffee in cab-

ins; full bkfst, lunch, dinner. Restaurant 7:30-9 am, 1 pm sitting, 7:30 pm sitting. Box lunches. Picnics, cookouts. Bar 6-10 pm; entertainment. Ck-out 11 am, ck-in 3 pm. Guest lndry. Gift shop. Meeting rms. Business servs avail. Boats. X-country ski on site. Horse stables. Snowmobiles, tobogganing, tubing. Hiking. Lawn games. Some refrigerators, minibars. Picnic tables. Cr cds: A, MC, V.
⬛ 🛪 ⬛ 🖼 🔥

★★ **LAZY L & B RANCH.** *1072 E Fork Rd (82513), 10 mi E on fork Rd, follow ranch sign 12 mi to ranch.* 307/455-2839; fax 307/455-2634; toll-free 800/453-9488. Email lazylb@aol.com; www.ranchweb.com/lazyl&b. 12 cabins. AP (1-wk min), Memorial Day-Sep: S $970 person; D $895/person; under 13 yrs $795. Closed rest of yr. Pet accepted. Heated pool. Supervised children's activities (May-Aug). Dining rm. Cookouts. Ck-out Sat 10 am, ck-in Sun 1 pm. Coin lndry. Gift shop. Airport transportation. River swimming. Hiking. Hayrides. Children's petting farm. Lawn games. Rec rm. 1,800 acres on mountain range bordering Shoshone National Forest. Totally nonsmoking. Cr cds: C.
⬛ 🛪 ⬛ 🛶 🎿 🖼 🔥

Evanston

(F-1) *See also Green River, Kemmerer*

Settled 1869 **Pop** 10,903 **Elev** 6,748 ft
Area code 307 **Zip** 82930
Web www.evanstonwy.com

Information Chamber of Commerce, 36 10th St, PO Box 365, 82931-0365; 307/783-0370 or 800/328-9708

Coal from the mines at Almy, six miles north of Evanston, supplied trains of the Union Pacific Railroad, which operated a roundhouse and machine shop in Evanston beginning in 1871. By 1872, the mines employed 600 men.

While cattle and sheep ranching remain important industries, the discovery of gas and oil has triggered a new "frontier" era for the town.

Evanston is also a trading center and tourist stopping point.

What to See and Do

Fort Bridger State Museum. Museum in barracks of partially restored fort named for Jim Bridger, scout and explorer. Pioneer history and craft demonstrations during summer; restored original bldgs. (May-Sep, daily; rest of yr, wkends; closed mid-Dec-Feb) Picnicking. 30 mi E on I-80, at Fort Bridger State Historic Site. Phone 307/782-3842. ¢

Annual Events

Chili Cook-off. Uinta County fairgrounds. Usually 3rd Sat June.

Uinta County Fair. Fairgrounds, US 30 E. 4-H, FFA exhibits; carnival, food. First full wk Aug.

Cowboy Days. PRCA rodeo with carnival, entertainment, parade, exhibits, booths, cookouts. Labor Day wkend.

Mountain Man Rendezvous. Fort Bridger State Museum (see). Black powder gun shoot, Native American dancing, exhibits, food. Labor Day wkend.

Seasonal Event

Horse Racing. Wyoming Downs. 12 mi N on WY 89. Thoroughbred and quarter horse racing. Pari-mutuel wagering. Phone 307/789-0511. Memorial Day-Labor Day, wkends and hols.

Motels/Motor Lodges

★★ **BEST WESTERN DUNMAR INN.** *1601 Harrison Dr (82930), W Entrance I-80 Exit #3, 1¼ mi W of I-80 Exit 3. 307/789-3770; fax 307/789-3758; res 800/528-1234; toll-free 800/654-6509.* 166 rms. May-Sep: S $79; D $85-$99; each addl $6; suites $85-$195; under 18 free; lower rates rest of yr. Crib $6. TV; cable. Heated pool. Restaurant 5:30 am-10 pm. Bar 11-2 am. Ck-out noon. Meeting rms. Gift shop. Exercise equipt. Bathrm phones; some refrigerators, wet bars. Cr cds: A, DS, MC, V.

★ **PRAIRIE INN MOTEL.** *264 Bear River Dr (82930). 307/789-2920.* 31

rms, 1 story. S $36; D $46. Crib avail. Pet accepted, some restrictions, fee. Parking lot. TV; cable. Complimentary continental bkfst, toll-free calls. Restaurant nearby. Ck-out 11 am, ck-in 1 pm. Golf, 9 holes. Tennis. Cr cds: A, C, D, DS, MC, V.

Fort Laramie National Historic Site

See also Torrington

Fort Laramie played an important role in much of the history of the old West. It was one of the principal fur-trading forts in the Rocky Mountain region from 1834-49 and one of the the most important army posts on the Northern plains from 1849-90. The first stockade built here, owned at one time by Jim Bridger and his fur-trapping partners, was Fort William, located on the strategic route to the mountains later to become the Oregon, California, and Mormon trails. In 1841, the decaying Fort William was replaced with an adobe-walled structure called Fort John on the Laramie River.

Gillette

(B-6) *See also Buffalo, Devils Tower National Monument*

Pop 17,635 **Elev** 4,608 ft
Area code 307
Web www.vcn.com/gillette_f/cvb

Information Convention & Visitors Bureau, 1810 S Douglas Hwy #A, 82718; 307/686-0040 or 800/544-6136

What to See and Do

Keyhole State Park. Within sight of Devils Tower (see). Surrounding mountains form the western boundary of the Black Hills. Antelope, deer, and wild turkeys are common to this area. Reservoir is excellent for water sports. Swimming, fishing, boating (ramps, marina); picnicking, lodging, camping; tent and trailer sites (standard fees). 45 mi E via I-90, then 8 mi N on Pine Ridge Rd. Phone 307/756-3596. Per vehicle ¢

Tours. Coal Mines. Res recommended. (Sep-May, Mon-Fri, daily; June-Aug, daily) 1810 S Douglas Hwy. Phone 307/686-0040 or 800/544-6136. **FREE**

Motels/Motor Lodges

★★ **BEST WESTERN TOWER WEST LODGE.** *109 N US (82716). 307/686-2210; fax 307/682-5105; res 800/528-1234; toll-free 800/762-7675.* 190 rms, 2 story. S $65; D $80; each addl $5; suites $125-$150; under 12 free. Crib free. TV; cable. Indoor pool; whirlpool. Complimentary coffee in rms. Restaurant 6 am-10 pm. Rm serv to 9 pm. Bar; entertainment. Ck-out noon. Coin lndry. Meeting rm. Business servs avail. Bellhops. Valet serv. Free airport transportation. Exercise equipt; sauna. Game rm. Refrigerators avail. Cr cds: A, C, D, DS, JCB, MC, V.

★★ **HOLIDAY INN.** *2009 S Douglas Hwy (82718). 307/686-3000; fax 307/686-4018; toll-free 800/465-4329.* 158 rms, 3 story. July-mid-Sep: S, D $90; suites $120-$150; under 18 free; lower rates rest of yr. Crib free. Pet accepted. TV; cable (premium). Indoor pool; whirlpool. Coffee in rms. Restaurant 6 am-2 pm; 5-10 pm. Bar 4:30 pm-2 am; entertainment Wed-Sat. Ck-out noon. Coin lndry. Meeting rms. Business center. Valet serv. Gift shop. Free airport transportation. Exercise equipt; sauna. Game rm. Rec room. Cr cds: A, C, D, DS, MC, V.

Restaurant

★ **HONG KONG.** *1612 W 2nd St (82716). 307/682-5829.* Specializes in Hunan beef, lemon chicken. Hrs: 11 am-9:30 pm. Closed Dec 25. Res accepted. Lunch $4-$5.50; dinner $5-$12.95. Cr cds: A, D, DS, MC, V.

Grand Teton National Park

See also Dubois, Jackson, Yellowstone National Park

These rugged, block-faulted mountains began to rise about nine million years ago, making them some of the youngest on the continent. Geologic and glacial forces combined to buckle and sculpt the landscape into a dramatic setting of canyons, cirques, and craggy peaks that cast their reflections across numerous clear alpine lakes. The Snake River winds gracefully through Jackson Hole ("hole" being the old fur trapper's term for a high-altitude valley surrounded by mountains).

John Colter passed through the area during 1807-08. French-Canadian trappers in the region thought the peaks resembled breasts and applied the French word *teton* to them.

Entering from the north, from Yellowstone National Park (see), US 89/191/287 skirts the eastern shore of Jackson Lake to Colter Bay, continuing to Jackson Lake Junction, where it turns eastward to the entrance at Moran Junction (at US 26). The Teton Park Road begins at Jackson Lake Junction and borders the mountains to Jenny Lake, then continues to park headquarters at Moose. US 89/191/26 parallels Teton Park Road on the east side of the Snake River to the south entrance from Moran Junction. All highways have a continuous view of the Teton Range, which runs from north to south. US 26/89/191 is open year-round from Jackson to Flagg Ranch, two miles south of Yellowstone National Park's South Gate, as is US 26/287 to Dubois. Secondary roads and Teton Park Road are open May-October.

The park is open year-round (limited in winter), with food and lodging available in the park from mid-May through September and in Jackson (see). There are three visitor centers with interpretive displays: Moose Visitor Center (daily; closed Dec 25); Colter Bay Visitor Center & Indian Arts Museum (mid-May-late Sep, daily); and Jenny Lake Visitor Center (June-Labor Day). Ranger-led hikes are available (mid-June-mid-

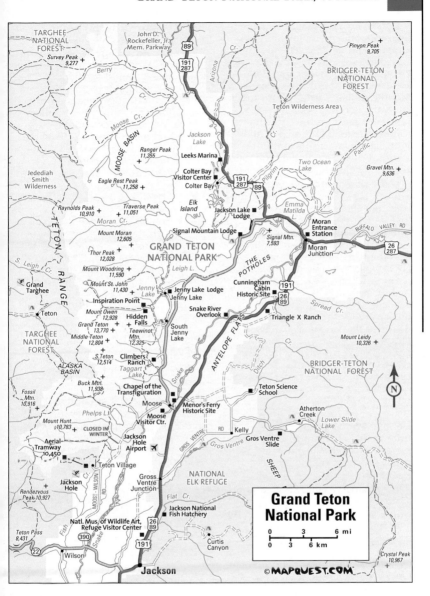

Grand Teton National Park

0 — 3 — 6 mi
0 — 3 — 6 km

© MAPQUEST.COM

Sep, daily; inquire for schedule), and self-guided trails are marked. A 24-hour recorded message gives information on weather; phone 307/739-3611.

The park can be explored by various means. There is hiking on more than 200 miles of trails. Corrals at Jackson Lake Lodge and Colter Bay have strings of horses accustomed to rocky trails; pack trips can be arranged. Boaters and anglers can enjoy placid lakes or wild streams;

the Colter Bay, Signal Mountain, and Leek's marinas have ramps, guides, facilities, and rentals. Climbers can tackle summits via routes of varying difficulty; the more ambitious may take advantage of Exum School of Mountaineering and Jackson Hole Mountain Guides classes that range from a beginner's course to an attempt at conquering the 13,770-foot Grand Teton, considered a major North American climbing peak.

Horses, boats, and other equipment can be rented. Bus tours, an airport, auto rentals, general stores, and guide services are available. Five National Park Service campgrounds are maintained: Colter Bay, Signal Mountain, Jenny Lake, Lizard Creek, and Gros Ventre (fee). Slide-illustrated talks on the park and its features are held each night (mid-June-Labor Day) at the amphitheaters at Colter Bay, Signal Mountain, and Gros Ventre.

Many river and lake trips are offered. Five-, ten-, and twenty-mile trips on rubber rafts float the Snake River. Visitors can choose an adventure to suit their individual tastes (see JACKSON). A self-guided trail tells the story of Menor's Ferry (1894) and the Maude Noble Cabin. Jenny Lake has boat trips and boat rentals. Jackson Lake cruises are available, some reaching island hideaways for breakfast cookouts. Boat rentals also are available at Jackson Lake. The Grand Teton Lodge Company offers a full-day, guided combination bus and boat trip covering major points of interest in the park (June-mid-Sep); phone 307/543-2855.

A tram with a vertical lift of 4,600 feet operates at Teton Village, rising from the valley floor to the top of Rendezvous Peak, just outside the park's southern boundary (see JACKSON).

The Chapel of the Transfiguration, located in Moose, is a log chapel with a large picture window over the altar framing the mountains. (Daily; services held late May-Sep)

The park is home to abundant wildlife, including pronghorn antelope, bighorn sheep, mule deer, elk, moose, grizzly and black bear, coyote, beavers, marmots, bald eagles, and trumpeter swans. Never approach or feed any wild animal. Do not pick wildflowers.

A park boat permit is required. A Wyoming fishing license is required for any fishing and may be obtained at several locations in the park. Camping permits are required for backcountry camping.

Grand Teton and Yellowstone national parks admission is $20/car. Contact Superintendent, PO Drawer 170, Moose 83012; 307/739-3399 or 307/739-3600 (recording).

CCInc Auto Tape Tours. This 90-minute cassette offers a mile-by-mile self-guided tour of the park. Written by informed guides, it provides information on history, points of interest, and flora and fauna of the park. Tapes may be purchased directly from CCInc, PO Box 227, 2 Elbrook Dr, Allendale, NJ 07401; 201/236-1666 or from the Grand Teton Lodge Co, 307/543-2855. ¢¢¢¢

Motel/Motor Lodge

★ **HATCHET RESORT.** *Hwy 287 (83013), 7½ mi E of Moran jct. 307/543-2413; fax 307/543-2034; toll-free 877/573-2413. Email hatchet@rmisp.com.* 22 cabins. No A/C. Memorial Day-Labor Day: S, D $80; each addl $5. Closed rest of yr. Pet accepted; $20. Restaurant 6:30 am-9:30 pm. Ck-out 10 am. Gift shop. Sundries. Picnic tables. Totally nonsmoking. Cr cds: A, DS, MC, V.
🔁 📧 🐾

Resort

★★ **DORNAN'S SPUR RANCH CABINS.** *10 Moose Ln (83012). 307/733-2522; fax 307/739-9098. Email spur@dornans.com; www.dornans.com.* 12 kit. cabins. No A/C. June-Oct: 1-bdrm $130-$160 (up to 4); 2-bdrm $190 (up to 6); lower rates rest of yr. Restaurant adj 7 am-9 pm. Ck-out 11 am. Totally nonsmoking. Cr cds: A, DS, MC, V.
🅳 🐾 ⚡ 🎿 📧 🔥

B&B/Small Inn

★★★ **INN AT BUFFALO FORK.** *18200 E Hwy 287 (83013), 6 mi E of Moran Entrance to Grand Teton National Park. 307/543-2010; fax 307/543-0935; toll-free 800/543-2010. Email innatbuff@blissnet.com.* 5 rms, 2 with shower only. No A/C. No rm phones. June-mid-Oct: S $139-$189; D $145-$195; each addl $20; under 5 free; lower rates rest of yr. TV in common rm; VCR avail (free movies). Complimentary full bkfst. Ck-out 11 am, ck-in 4 pm. X-country ski 11 mi. Whirlpool. Totally nonsmoking. Cr cds: A, MC, V.
🏊 📧 🐾

Guest Ranches

★ ★ ★ ★ **LOST CREEK RANCH.** *#1 Old Ranch Rd (83012), approx 8 mi N of Moose on US 26, 89, 187, 189, then 2 mi E on Gravel Rd. 307/733-3435; fax 307/733-1954. Email ranch@lostcreek.com; www.lostcreek.com.* Complimentary transfers from Jackson Hole Airport to this lodge and spa located between Grand Teton National Park and Bridger-Teton Forest. Rates for the 10 cabins and 20 rooms, available May through October, include meals. Consider visiting in the fall when the leaves are breathtaking and nearby fly-fishing is at its peak. 10 cabins, 7 with kit. No A/C. AP, June-mid-Oct, wkly rates: 1-4 persons $4,670-$10,450; each addl $860; under 6 free. Closed rest of yr. Crib free. Heated pool; whirlpool. Supervised children's activities (June-Aug). Coffee in cabins. Dining rm sittings: bkfst 7:30-8:30 am, lunch 12:30 pm, dinner 7 pm (children's dinner at 6 pm if desired). Ck-out 10 am, ck-in 3 pm. Free lndry serv. Meeting rms. Business servs avail. Airport transportation. Tennis. Hayrides. Exercise rm; sauna, steam rm. Spa. Massage. Lawn games. Entertainment. Game rm. Scenic float trips. Riding instruction avail. Refrigerators, fireplaces. Private porches. Picnic tables. Totally non-smoking. Cr cds: A.

The awe-inspiring mountains of Grand Teton N.P.

★ ★ ★ **MOOSE HEAD RANCH.** *Highway 89 (83012), 13 mi N of Moose, on US 26, 89, 187. 307/733-3141; fax 307/739-9097.* 14 cabins, 1-2 bedrm. No A/C. No rm phones. AP (incl riding), mid-June-Aug (5-day min): S $325; D $450; under 6, $100; 2-bedrm house (up to 6 people) $1,200-$1,650. Closed rest of yr. Crib free. Complimentary coffee in cabins. Dining rm 8-9 am, 12:30-1:30 pm, 7-8 pm. Cookouts. Meeting rm. Free airport transportation. Horseback riding instruction, trips; hiking trails. Fly-fishing, instruction. Rec rm. Lawn games. Refrigerators. Some fireplaces in cabins. Private porches. Library. On 120 acres; series of man-made trout ponds. No cr cds accepted.

Cottage Colonies

★ **COLTER BAY VILLAGE & CABINS.** *Grand Teton National Park (83013), 10 mi N of Moran jct. 307/543-3100; fax 307/543-3143; res 800/628-9988.* 166 cabins, 146 with shower only, 9 share bath. No A/C. No rm phones. S, D $35-$95; each addl $8.50; under 12 free. Closed Oct-mid-May. Crib free. Pet accepted, some restrictions. Restaurant 6:30 am-10 pm. Ck-out 11 am, ck-in 4 pm. Coin lndry. Gift shop. Grocery store. Airport transportation. Boat rentals, river and lake cruises. On Jackson Lake; marina. Cr cds: A, C, D, DS, MC, V.

★ ★ **FLAGG RANCH RESORT.** *Hwy 89 (83013), 5 mi N. 307/543-2861; fax 307/543-2356; res 800/443-2311. Email info@flaggranch.com; www.flaggranch.com.* 92 cabins. No A/C. Late June-

Aug: S, D $125; each addl $10; under 18 free; lower rates rest of yr. Crib free. Pet accepted; $5. Complimentary coffee in rms. Restaurant 7 am-10 pm. Bar 3-11 pm. Ck-out 11 am, ck-in 4 pm. Meeting rms. Business servs avail. Bellhops. Concierge. Gift shop. Grocery store. Cr cds: A, DS, MC, V.

⬛️🐾🍴🏊🛟🔥

Guest Ranches

★★★ GROS VENTRE RIVER RANCH.
18 Gros Ventre Rd (83011), 8 mi S to Gros Ventre jct, then 7 mi E on Gros Ventre Rd. 307/733-4138; fax 307/733-4292. 8 cabins, 4 kits. No A/C. No rm phones. AP, mid-June-Aug, wkly: S $1,190-$1,600; D $2,380-$3,200; each addl $1,000; lower rates rest of yr. Closed Nov, Apr. Crib free. TV in rec rm; VCR. Playground. Dining rm in lodge. Box lunches, cookouts. Ck-out 10 am, ck-in 3 pm. Meeting rms. Free airport transportation. Swimming in pond. Canoes. Hiking. Mountain bikes. Lawn games. Rec rm. Some fireplaces. On 160 acres. Cr cds: A, DS, MC, V.

🍴🛟🏊🔥

★★★★ JENNY LAKE LODGE.
Grand Teton National Park (83013), 14 mi SW of Moran, in park. 307/733-4647; fax 307/733-0324. Nestled at the base of the Tetons in Grand Teton National Park, this rustic, all-inclusive retreat is actually a cluster of 37 western-style cabins outfitted with down comforters and hand-made quilts. The pine-shaded property welcomes visitors from June through October for elegantly rustic accommodations and back-to-nature recreation including Jackson Hole Golf & Tennis Club, numerous hiking trails, and three lakes. 37 cabins. No A/C. No rm phones. MAP, late May-early Oct: S, D $305-$375; each addl $115; suite cabins $510-$535. Closed rest of yr. Crib free. Restaurant (see also JENNY LAKE LODGE DINING ROOM). Serv bar. Ck-out 11 am, ck-in 4 pm. Bellhops. Gift shop. Airport transportation. Bicycles; trail rides. Golf, tennis, and swimming privileges nearby. Some refrigerators. Wood stove in suites, lounge. Private patios. Totally nonsmoking. Cr cds: A, D, MC, V.

⬛️🍴🏌️🎾🔥🛟🔥

★★ COWBOY VILLAGE RESORT.
US 26/287 (83013), 17 mi E of Moran jct. 307/543-2847; fax 307/543-2391. 89 units, 3 story, 54 kit. cabins. No A/C. No elvtr. Mid-Nov-mid-Apr: S $241/person; D $211/person; suites $233/person; cabins $239/person; under 13, $40; lower rates June-mid-Oct. Closed rest of yr. TV; cable (premium). Dining rm 7 am-9:30 pm. Bar noon-midnight. Ck-out 11 am. Coin lndry. Sundries. Gift shop. Free airport transportation in winter. X-country ski on site. Snowmobiling. Whirlpools. Rec rm. Cabins have private porches, picnic tables, grills. Cr cds: A, DS, MC, V.

⬛️🛟🏂🎿🎿🔥🛟🔥

★★★ GRAND TETON NATIONAL PARK/JACKSON LAKE.
N Jackson Lake Lodge; N US 89 (83013), on US 89/287 in park. 307/543-3100; fax 307/543-3143; res 800/628-9988. 385 rms, 3 story. Mid-May-mid-Oct: S, D $102-$190; each addl $8.50; suites $350-$475; under 12 free. Closed rest of yr. Crib free. Heated pool; lifeguard. Dining rms 6 am-10:30 pm. Box lunches. Bar 11-1 am; entertainment Mon-Sat. Ck-out 11 am. Convention facilities. Business servs avail. Airport transportation. Bellhops. Concierge. Shopping arcade. Nightly programs July-Aug. Evening cookout rides. Float trips. Fly-fishing, instruction. Many private patios, balconies. Grand lobby has 2 fireplaces, 60-ft picture window. View of Mt Moran, Grand Tetons. Cr cds: A, C, D, DS, MC, V.

🛟🏂🔥🛟🔥

★★ SIGNAL MOUNTAIN LODGE.
Inner Park Rd (83013), 4½ mi W on Inner Park Rd, 3 mi SW of jct US 89/287 in Park. 307/543-2831; fax 307/543-2569; toll-free 800/672-6012. Email 102547.1642@compuserv.com; www.foreverresorts.com/signal.html. 79 cabins, 1-2 story, 30 kits. No A/C. Mid-May-mid-Oct: S, D $78-$160; kit. units $160. Closed rest of yr. Pet accepted, some restrictions. Crib free. Restaurant 7 am-10 pm in season. Bar noon-midnight. Ck-out 11 am. Meeting rms. Gift shop. Grocery store. Some refrigerators, fireplaces. Private patios, balconies. Marina; boat rentals; guided fishing trips. Scenic float trips on Snake River. On lake; campground adj. Cr cds: A, DS, MC, V.

🐾🛟🛟🔥

Restaurant

★ ★ ★ **JENNY LAKE LODGE DIN-ING ROOM.** *Inner Loop Rd. 307/733-4647. www.gtlc.com.* Specializes in range-fed buffalo, fresh Pacific salmon, Rocky Mt trout. Hrs: 7:30-9 am, noon-1:30 pm, 6-8:45 pm. Closed Oct-May. Res required dinner. Wine list. Bkfst complete meals: $13.50; lunch complete meals: $7-$9; dinner complete meals: $42.50. Child's menu. Entertainment: classical musicians. Dining in restored cabin. Cr cds: A, MC, V.

D

Unrated Dining Spot

MOOSE CHUCK WAGON. *10 Moose St (83012), Park Service Headquarters Visitor Center. 307/733-2415. Email dornans@dornans.com; www.dornans. com.* Specializes in beef and barbecue cooked over wood fires. Hrs: 7-11 am, noon-3 pm, 5-9 pm. Closed Sep-May. Bkfst a la carte entrees: $4.25-$6.25; lunch a la carte entrees: $3.35-$6.75; dinner buffet: $12. Open dutch oven. View of Tetons, Snake River. Family-owned. Cr cds: A, D, MC, V.

D **SC**

Green River

(F-2) *See also Evanston, Kemmerer, Rock Springs*

Settled 1862 **Pop** 12,711 **Elev** 6,109 ft
Area code 307 **Zip** 82935
Web www.grchamber.com
Information Chamber of Commerce, 1450 Uinta Dr; 307/875-5711

Green River, seat of Sweetwater County, is known as the trona (sodium sesquicarbonate) capital of the world. As early as 1852, Jim Bridger guided Captain Howard Stansbury on a Native American trail through the area. By 1862, a settlement here consisted mainly of the overland stage station, located on the east bank of the Green River. In 1868, Major John Wesley Powell started from here on his expedition of the Green and Colorado rivers.

This point of departure is now known as Expedition Island. The Green River, one of Wyoming's largest, is the northern gateway to the Flaming Gorge National Recreation Area.

What to See and Do

Flaming Gorge National Recreation Area. This area, administered by the US Forest Service, surrounds Flaming Gorge Reservoir in Wyoming (see ROCK SPRINGS) and Utah. Firehole campground and Upper Marsh Creek boat ramp are on the E shore of the reservoir; 2 other sites (Buckboard Crossing and Squaw Hollow) are on the W shore. Lucerne, Buckboard Crossing, Firehole, and Antelope Flats have camping and boat-launching ramps. Upper Marsh Creek and Squaw Hollow are boat ramp sites only. (Check road conditions locally before traveling during winter or wet periods.) There is usually ice fishing Jan-Mar. The Flaming Gorge Dam, administered by the US Bureau of Reclamation, the HQ, 3 visitor centers, and several other recreation sites are located along the S half of the loop in Utah. Campground fees; res required for group sites. For information contact District Ranger, Box 278, Manila, UT 84046. S on WY 530 or US 191. Phone 307/875-2871. Camping ¢¢¢

Sweetwater County Historical Museum. Historical exhibits on southwestern Wyoming; Native American, Chinese, and pioneer artifacts; photographic collection. (July-Aug, Mon-Sat; rest of yr, Mon-Fri; closed hols) Courthouse, 80 W Flaming Gorge Way. Phone 307/872-6435. **FREE**

Motel/Motor Lodge

★ ★ ★ **LITTLE AMERICA HOTEL.** *I-80 Exit 68 (82929). 307/875-2400; fax 307/872-2666; toll-free 800/634-2401 www.littleamerica.com.* 140 rms, 18 with shower only, 2 story. May-Sep: S $63; D $69; each addl $6; suites $85; under 12 free; lower rates rest of yr. Crib free. TV; cable (premium). Heated pool. Playground. Restaurant open 24 hrs. Bar 2:30 pm-1 am. Ck-out noon. Meeting rms. Business center. Sundries. Shopping arcade.

Coin lndry. Exercise equipt. Some refrigerators. Some balconies. Cr cds: A, C, D, DS, MC, V.

🏊 🏋 🏝 🔥 SC 🏃

Greybull

(B-4) *See Lovell*

Pop 1,789 **Elev** 3,788 ft
Area code 307 **Zip** 82426
Information Chamber of Commerce, 333 Greybull Ave; 307/765-2100

Just north of town are the rich geological sites Sheep Mountain and Devil's Kitchen. Sheep Mountain looks like a natural fortress surrounded by flatland when seen from the Big Horn Mountains. A Ranger District office of the Bighorn National Forest (see SHERIDAN) is located here.

What to See and Do

Greybull Museum. History and fossil displays; Native American artifacts. (June-Labor Day, Mon-Sat; Apr-May and Sep-Oct, Mon-Fri afternoons; rest of yr, Mon, Wed, and Fri afternoons; closed Jan 1, Thanksgiving, Dec 25) 325 Greybull Ave. Phone 307/765-2444. **FREE**

Annual Event

Days of '49 Celebration. Parades, rodeo, running races, demolition derby. Concert, dances. Second wkend June.

Jackson

(C-1) *See also Alpine, Grand Teton National Park, Pinedale*

Pop 4,472 **Elev** 6,234 ft
Area code 307 **Zip** 83001
Web www.jacksonholechamber.com
Information Jackson Hole Area Chamber of Commerce, 990 W Broadway, PO Box 550; 307/733-3316

Jackson, uninhibitedly western, is the key town for the mountain-rimmed, 600-square-mile valley of Jackson Hole, which is surrounded by mountain scenery, dude ranches, national parks, big game, and other vacation attractions. Jackson Hole is one of the most famous ski resort areas in the country, known for its spectacular views and its abundant ski slopes. It has three Alpine ski areas, five Nordic ski areas, and miles of groomed snowmobile trails. Annual snowfall usually exceeds 38 feet, and winter temperatures average around 21°F. The Jackson Hole area, which includes Grand Teton National Park, the town of Jackson, and much of the Bridger-Teton National Forest, has all the facilities and luxuries necessary to accommodate both the winter and summer visitor. Jackson Hole offers winter sports, boating, chuck-wagon dinner shows, live theater productions, symphony concerts, art galleries, rodeos, horseback riding, mountain climbing, fishing, and several white-water and scenic float trips. Two Ranger District offices of the Bridger-Teton National Forest are located in Jackson.

What to See and Do

Astoria Hot Springs. Swimming in a continuous flow of hot mineral water from 2-9 ft deep (mid-May-mid-Sep, daily), fishing; hiking, playground, basketball, camping (res advised). Float trips (by appt). 17 mi S of Jackson, 3½ mi from Hoback Junction. Swimming ¢¢; Camping ¢¢¢¢

Bridger-Teton National Forest. With more than 3.3 million acres, the forest literally surrounds the town of Jackson. Bridger-Teton was the site of one of the largest earth slides in US history, the Gros Ventre Slide (1925), which dammed the Gros Ventre River (to a height of 225 ft and a width of nearly ½ mi), forming Slide Lake, which is approximately 3 mi long. There are scenic drives along the Hoback River Canyon, the Snake River Canyon, and in Star Valley. Unspoiled backcountry incl parts of Gros Ventre, Teton, and Wind River ranges along the Continental Divide and the Wyoming Range. Teton Wilderness (557,311 acres) and Gros Wilderness (247,000 acres) are accessible on foot or horseback. Swimming, fishing, rafting; hiking, mountain biking, winter sports areas, camping (fee). Also in the forest is Bridger Wilderness (see PINEDALE).

Fishing, big-game hunting; boating. For further information contact Forest Supervisor, 340 N Cache, PO Box 1888. Phone 307/739-5500.

⭐ **Grand Teton National Park.** (see)

Gray Line bus tours. For information on tours in Jackson, Grand Teton, and Yellowstone national parks contact PO Box 411. Phone 307/733-4325 or 800/443-6133.

Jackson Hole Museum. Regional museum of early West, local history, and archeology. (Late May-Sep, daily) Walking tours offered. 105 N Glenwood. Phone 307/733-9605. ¢¢

National Elk Refuge. This 25,000-acre refuge is the winter home of thousands of elk and many waterfowl. Visitor center with slide show, exhibits, and horse-drawn sleigh rides (Mid-Dec-Mar, daily). 2 mi N of town. Phone 307/733-9212. Sleigh rides ¢¢

National Wildlife Art Museum. Art museum with large collection of North American wildlife paintings and sculpture; traveling exhibits, special programs. Children's play area. Overlooks National Elk Refuge. (Daily) Call ahead for admission fees. Rungus Rd, N of town. Phone 307/733-5771.

River excursions.

Barker-Ewing Float Trips. Ten-mi scenic trips on the Snake River, within Grand Teton National Park; meals avail. Res required. Phone 307/733-1800 or 800/365-1800. ¢¢¢¢

Lewis and Clark Expeditions. Scenic 3½- and 6-hr whitewater float trips through Grand Canyon of Snake River. (June-mid-Sep, daily) Also raft and canoe rentals. 145 W Gill St. Phone 307/733-4022 or 800/824-5375. ¢¢¢¢

Mad River Boat Trips, Inc. Three-hr whitewater Snake River Canyon trips (daily). Also combination scenic/whitewater trips, lunch/dinner trips. Res suggested. Phone 307/733-6203 or 800/458-RAFT. ¢¢¢¢

Triangle X Float Trips. Trips incl 5- and 10-mi floats; sunrise and evening wildlife floats; also cookout supper floats. Most trips originate at Triangle X Ranch. Booking offices are also located on the SW corner of Jackson Square. (June-Sep) On the Snake River in Grand Teton National Park. Phone 307/733-5500. ¢¢¢¢

Solitude Float Trips. Offers 5- and 10-mi scenic trips within Grand Teton National Park. Res suggested. Phone 307/733-2871.

Skiing.

Snow King Ski Resort. Three double chairlifts, surface tow; school, rental/repair shop; snack bar, resort facilities. Vertical drop 1,571 ft. (Dec-Apr, daily) 6 blks S of Town Square. Phone 307/733-5200. ¢¢¢¢

Jackson Hole Ski Resort. 2½-mi aerial tramway, 3 quad, triple, 3 double chairlifts, 2 surface tows; patrol, school, rentals; bar, restaurants, cafeterias, daycare, lodging. Longest run 4½ mi; vertical drop 4,139 ft. (Dec-mid-Apr, daily) Cross-country trails. Also summer swimming; tennis, horseback riding, hiking. 12 mi NW at Teton Village. Phone 307/733-2292 or 307/733-2291 (snow report). ¢¢¢¢ Also here is

Aerial Tramway. Makes 2½-mi ride to top of Rendezvous Mt for spectacular views. Free guided nature hike. (Late May-early Oct) Phone 307/733-2291. ¢¢¢¢

Teton Country Prairie Schooner Holiday. Four-day guided covered wagon trip between Yellowstone and Grand Teton national parks (see). Activities incl hiking, horseback riding; swimming and canoeing. Meals, tents, and sleeping bags incl. (Mid-June-late Aug) Phone 307/733-5386 or 800/772-5386. ¢¢¢¢ Also avail is

Covered Wagon Cookout and Wild West Show. Ride covered wagons to outdoor dining area; eating area covered in case of rain. Western entertainment. Departs from Bar-T-Five Corral (late May-mid-Sep, daily). Phone 307/733-5386. ¢¢¢¢

Teton County Historical Center. Fur trade exhibit. Research library (Daily) 105 Mercill Ave. Phone 307/733-9605. **FREE**

Teton Mountain Bike Tours. Guided mountain bike tours for all ability levels. Mountain bike, helmet, transportation, and local guides. Day, multiday, and customized group tours avail. Phone 800/733-0788. ¢¢¢¢

Wagons West. Covered wagon treks through the foothills of the Tetons. Gentle riding horses, chuck-wagon meals, campfire entertainment. Special guided horseback treks and hiking trips into surrounding mountains. Two-, four-, and six-day furnished trips. (June-Labor Day, Mon-Sat) Res necessary. Depart from motels in Jackson. Phone 307/886-9693 or 800/447-4711. ¢¢¢¢

Seasonal Events

Jackson Hole Rodeo. Snow King Ave. Phone 307/733-2805. Sat, Memorial Day-late Aug.

The Shootout. Town Square. Real-life Western melodrama. Mon-Sat nights, Memorial Day wkend-Labor Day.

Grand Teton Music Festival. 12 mi NW in Teton Village. Symphony and chamber music concerts. Virtuoso orchestra of top professional musicians from around the world. Many different programs of chamber music and orchestral concerts.

Box office, phone 307/733-1128. Early July-late Aug.

Jackson Hole Fall Arts Festival. Three-wk celebration of the arts featuring special exhibits in more than 30 galleries, demonstrations, special activities. Also dance, theater, mountain film festival, Native American arts, and culinary arts. Phone 307/733-3316. Mid-Sep-early Oct.

Motel/Motor Lodge

★ **4 WINDS.** *150 N Millward St (83001). 307/733-2474; fax 307/734-2796.* 21 rms, 1-2 story. June-Labor Day: S, D $82-$100; each addl $5; lower rates mid-late May-mid-June, after Labor Day-mid-Oct. Closed rest of yr. Crib $2. TV; cable (premium). Complimentary coffee in lobby. Restaurant adj 7 am-10 pm. Ck-out 11 am. Picnic tables, grill. City park, playground adj. Cr cds: A, DS, MC, V.

Begin at the Town Square, famous for its entrance arches of discarded elk antlers. Attractions here include a small log cabin dating from the early 1900s (but moved to the square in more recent years) and a nightly "shootout." Other landmarks include the Million Dollar Cowboy Bar, across from the west side of the square, and the Jackson Drug Company, across from its northeast corner. Continue north on Cache Street for a look at such notable buildings as the 1941 Teton Theater and the 1929 American Legion Hall. Go west on Gill Avenue then south on Glenwood, stopping to see St. John's Church and Rest House and the Jackson Hole Museum (with the covered wagon perched over its entrance).

★ **ANTLER INN.** *43 W Pearl St (83001).* 307/733-2535; *fax 307/733-4158; toll-free 800/522-2406. Email antlerjh@aol.com; www.townsquare inns.com.* 100 rms, 2 story, 12 suites. June-Sep: S $98; D $102; each addl $4; suites $130; children $4; under 12 free; lower rates rest of yr. Crib avail. Pet accepted, some restrictions. Parking lot. TV; cable (premium), VCR avail. Ck-out 11 am, ck-in 2 pm. Meeting rm. Business servs avail. Dry cleaning, coin lndry. Exercise equipt, whirlpool. Golf. Downhill skiing. Cr cds: A, C, D, DS, MC, V.

D ➡ ⛷ 🍴 🏊 🔏 ♨ SC

★★ **BEST WESTERN INN.** *80 Scott Ln (83001).* 307/739-9703; *fax 307/739-9168; res 800/528-1234; toll-free 800/458-3866. Email jacksonhole@ compuserve.com.* 154 rms, 3 story. Mid-June-mid-Sep: S, D $199; each addl $10; under 12 free; ski plan; lower rates rest of yr. Crib free. TV; cable, VCR (movies). Indoor/outdoor pool; whirlpools. Complimentary full bkfst; afternoon refreshments. Complimentary coffee in rms. Restaurant nearby. Ck-out 11 am. Coin lndry. Meeting rms. Business servs avail. In-rm modem link. Bellhops. Gift shop. Valet serv. Downhill/x-country ski 12 mi. Sauna. Health club privileges. Refrigerators, microwaves, minibars. Cr cds: A, C, D, DS, JCB, MC, V.

D ♨ 🏋 ⛷ 🏊 🎿 🔏 ♨

★★ **BEST WESTERN RESORT HOTEL AND CONFERENCE CENTER.** *3245 W McCollister Dr (83001), 12 mi W on Teton Village Rd.* 307/733-3657; *fax 307/733-9543; toll-free 800/445-4655. Email info@renaissanceutjh. com.* 101 rms, 5 story. Late June-Labor Day, late Dec-Feb: S $149-$169; D $179-$249; under 12 free; lower rates rest of yr. Crib free. TV; cable. Restaurant 7:30-10 am, 5-10 pm. Bar 11 am-midnight. Ck-out 11 am. Meeting rms. Business servs avail. In-rm modem link. Bellhops. Sundries. Gift shop. Coin lndry. Indoor/outdoor pool; whirlpool, poolside serv. Game rm. Cr cds: A, C, D, DS, MC, V.

D ♨ 🏋 ⛷ 🏊 🔏 ♨

★★ **BUCKRAIL LODGE INC.** *110 E Karns Ave (83001).* 307/733-2079. *www.buckraillodge.com.* 12 rms. No A/C. No rm phones. Mid-June-mid-Sep: S, D $70-$100; each addl $5; lower rates May-mid-June and mid-Sep-mid-Oct. Closed rest of yr. Crib $5. TV; cable (premium). Restaurant nearby. Ck-out 11 am. Whirlpool. Picnic table, grill. Totally nonsmoking. Cr cds: A, DS, MC, V.

⛷ 🔏 ♨

★ **DAYS INN.** *350 S US 89 (83001).* 307/739-9010; *fax 307/733-0044; res 800/329-7466.* 91 rms, 3 story. June-Labor Day: S, D $149-$209; each addl $10; suites $169-$209; under 12 free; lower rates rest of yr. Crib free. TV; cable (premium), VCR avail (movies). Complimentary continental bkfst. Coffee in rms. Restaurant adj. Ck-out 11 am. Sauna. Whirlpool. Some in-rm whirlpools, refrigerators, fireplaces; microwaves avail. Cr cds: A, D, DS, MC, V.

🍴 🎿 ⛷ ♨

★ **HITCHING POST LODGE.** *460 E Broadway (83001), 4 blks E of Town Square.* 307/733-2606; *fax 307/133-8221.* 33 rms in cabins, 16 kit. units. No A/C. Mid-June-mid-Sep: S $78 D $88-$92; kit. units $149-$179; each addl $5; lower rates rest of yr. Crib free. TV; cable (premium). Pool. Complimentary continental bkfst. Restaurant nearby. Ck-out 11 am. Coin lndry. Whirlpool. Refrigerators, microwaves. Picnic tables. Cr cds: DS, MC, V.

🍴 🎿 ⛷ 🏊 🎿 🔏 ♨

★★ **IMA TRAPPER INN.** *235 N Cache Dr (83001).* 307/733-2648; *fax 307/739-9351; toll-free 800/341-8000. Email info@trapperinn.com; www. trapperinn.com.* 52 rms, 2 story, 1 suite. June-Sep: S, D $115; each addl $7; suites $221; under 12 free; lower rates rest of yr. Crib avail. Parking lot. TV; cable (premium), VCR avail. Complimentary coffee in rms. Restaurant. Ck-out 11 am, ck-in 2 pm. Meeting rm. Fax servs avail. Concierge. Coin lndry. Whirlpool. Golf. Tennis, 4 courts. Downhill skiing. Hiking trail. Picnic facilities. Cr cds: A, C, D, JCB, MC, V.

D ⛷ 🍴 🎿 🔏 ♨ SC

Hotels

★★★ **ALPENHOF LODGE.** *3255 W McCollister Dr (83025), 12 mi NW on Teton Village Rd.* 307/733-3242; *fax*

307/739-1516; toll-free 800/732-3244. Email gm@alpenhoflodge.com; www. alpenhoflodge.com. 42 rms, 4 story, 1 suite. Dec-Mar, July-Aug: S, D $185; each addl $15; suites $375; under 10 free; lower rates rest of yr. Crib avail, fee. Valet parking avail. Pool, lap pool, whirlpool. TV; cable (premium), VCR avail. Complimentary newspaper, toll-free calls. Restaurant 7 am-10 pm. Bar. Ck-out 11 am, ck-in 3 pm. Meeting rm. Business center. Bellhops. Concierge. Dry cleaning, coin lndry. Gift shop. Sauna. Golf. Tennis, 8 courts. Downhill skiing. Hiking trail. Cr cds: A, C, D, DS, MC, V.

★★ **BEST WESTERN INN OF JACKSON HOLE.** 3345 W McCollister Dr (83025), 12 mi NW on Teton Village Rd. 307/733-2311; fax 307/733-0844; toll-free 800/842-7666. Email jacksonhole@compuserve.com; www.innatjh.com. 83 rms, 3 story. Jan-Mar, July-Aug: S, D $229; each addl $10; under 14 free; lower rates rest of yr. Crib avail. Parking lot. Pool, whirlpool. TV; cable. Complimentary coffee in rms, toll-free calls. Restaurant 7 am-10 pm. Bar. Meeting rm. Business center. Bellhops. Concierge. Coin lndry. Sauna. Golf. Downhill skiing. Hiking trail. Video games. Cr cds: A, D, DS, MC, V.

★★ **QUALITY 49'ER INN & SUITES.** 330 W Pearl St (83001). 307/733-7550; fax 307/733-2002; toll-free 800/451-2980. Email info@town squreinns.com; www.townsquareinns. com. 80 rms, 3 story, 62 suites. June-Sep: S $115; D $119; each addl $10; suites $189; under 12 free; lower rates rest of yr. Crib avail. Pet accepted, some restrictions, fee. Parking lot. Children's pool, whirlpool. TV; cable (premium), VCR avail. Complimentary continental bkfst, newspaper, toll-free calls. Restaurant 11 am-10 pm. Bar. Ck-out 11 am, ck-in 2 pm. Meeting rms. Business servs avail. Dry cleaning, coin lndry. Salon/barber. Exercise equipt, sauna. Golf. Downhill skiing. Hiking trail. Cr cds: A, C, D, DS, ER, JCB, MC, V.

★ **RED LION WYOMING INN.** 930 W Broadway (83002). 307/734-0035; fax 307/734-0037; toll-free 800/844-

0035. Email wyominginn@blissnet.com; www.wyoming-inn.com. 73 rms, 3 story, 1 suite. July-Aug: S, D $179-$249; each addl $10; kit. units $209; under 13 free; lower rates rest of yr. Crib avail. Pet accepted. Parking lot. TV; cable, VCR avail. Complimentary continental bkfst, coffee in rms, toll-free calls. Ck-out 11 am, ck-in 4 pm. Meeting rm. Business center. Bellhops. Concierge. Dry cleaning, coin lndry. Free airport transportation. Sauna. Downhill skiing. Bike rentals. Supervised children's activities. Hiking trail. Picnic facilities. Cr cds: A, DS, MC, V.

★★★★ **RUSTY PARROT LODGE.** 175 N Jackson St (83001), at Gill, opp mi Park. 307/733-2000; fax 307/733-5566; toll-free 800/458-2004. Email mail@rustyparrot.com; www.rusty parrot.com. Just minutes from Grand Teton and Yellowstone national parks and Jackson Hole, the lodge is just three blocks from Town Square. Rustic rooms are filled with mountain-style touches: antler chandeliers, hand-made furniture, and goose-down comforters. And, included in the rates, a hearty breakfast. To rejuvenate the body and the spirit after a day on the slopes, try one of the many treatments available at the The Body Sage, the on-site day spa. 30 rms, 3 story, 1 suite. Dec-Mar, June-Sep: S, D $250; each addl $30; suites $500; children $30; under 12 free; lower rates rest of yr. Crib avail, fee. Parking lot. TV; cable (premium), VCR avail. Complimentary full bkfst, newspaper, toll-free calls. Restaurant nearby. Ck-out 11 am, ck-in 4 pm. Fax servs avail. Bellhops. Concierge. Dry cleaning. Gift shop. Exercise privileges, whirlpool. Golf. Tennis. Downhill skiing. Bike rentals. Hiking trail. Cr cds: A, C, D, DS, MC, V.

★★★ **THE WORT HOTEL.** 50 N Glenwood St (83001). 307/733-2190; fax 307/733-2067; toll-free 800/ 322-2727. Email info@worthotel.com; www.worthotel.com. 57 rms, 2 story, 3 suites. Jan-Mar, June-Oct: S, D $220; each addl $25; suites $485; under 14 free; lower rates rest of yr. Crib avail. Pet accepted, some restrictions. Valet parking avail. TV; cable (premium), VCR avail. Complimentary newspaper, toll-free calls. Restaurant 7 am-

10 pm. Bar. Ck-out 11 am, ck-in 4 pm. Meeting rms. Business servs avail. Bellhops. Concierge. Dry cleaning. Gift shop. Exercise equipt, whirlpool. Golf. Downhill skiing. Hiking trail. Cr cds: A, D, DS, MC, V.

⬛🔌🛗🏊🏃🕴️🎿🛶🔥🆑

Resorts

★★ **JACKSON HOLE RESORT LODGING.** *3535 N Wilson Rd (83014), 9 mi W on Teton Village Rd.* 307/733-3990; fax 307/733-5551. 117 condo units. No A/C. June-Sep: 1-bedrm $99-$179; 2-bedrm $139-$225; 3-bedrm $169-$315; 4-bedrm $195-$349; house $175-$359; min stay required; higher rates Dec 25; lower rates rest of yr. Crib $10. TV; cable. Heated pool; whirlpool. Dining rm 6-10 pm. Bar 4 pm-2 am. Ck-out 11 am. Guest lndry. Meeting rms. Beauty shop. Downhill/x-country ski 4 mi. Exercise rm; sauna, steam rm. Massage. Refrigerators, microwaves, fireplaces. Private patios, balconies. Cr cds: A, DS, MC, V.

⬛🛗🏊🏊‍♂️🛶🏃🔥🛶🔥

★★★ **SNOW KING RESORT.** *400 E Snow King Ave (83001).* 307/733-5200; fax 307/733-4086; toll-free 800/ 522-5464. Email snowking@snowking. com; www.snowking.com. 193 rms, 7 story, 11 suites. Dec-Jan, May-Aug: S, D $205; each addl $10; suites $350; under 13 free; lower rates rest of yr. Crib avail, fee. Pet accepted, some restrictions, fee. Parking lot. Pool, whirlpool. TV; cable, VCR avail. Complimentary coffee in rms, newspaper, toll-free calls. Restaurant 6:30 am-9:30 pm. Bar. Ck-out noon, ck-in 4 pm. Meeting rms. Business center. Bellhops. Concierge. Dry cleaning, coin lndry. Gift shop. Salon/barber. Free airport transportation. Exercise equipt, sauna. Golf. Tennis, 2 courts. Downhill skiing. Hiking trail. Picnic facilities. Cr cds: A, C, D, DS, MC, V.

⬛🔌🛗🏊🏃🕴️🎿🛶🏊🔥🆑 🏃

★★★ **SPRING CREEK RANCH.** *1800 Spirit Dance Rd (83001), 3 mi NW on WY 22, then 3½ mi on Spring Gulch Rd.* 307/733-8833; fax 307/733-1524; toll-free 800/443-6139. Email reservations@springcreekresort.com; www.springcreekresort.com. 117 rms,

some kits. S, D $250; each addl $15; studio rms $275; condo units $450-$1,000; under 12 free; package plans. TV; cable (premium), VCR avail (movies). Heated pool; whirlpool. Complimentary coffee in rms. Restaurant 7:30 am-10 pm. Rm serv 7:30-10 am, noon-2 pm, 6-10 pm. Bar. Ck-out 11 am. Meeting rms. Business center. Bellhops. Valet serv. Concierge. Sundries. Gift shop. Airport transportation. Tennis. Downhill ski 12 mi; x-country ski. Lawn games. Refrigerators, fireplaces; microwaves avail. Private decks, balconies with view of Tetons. Picnic tables. Cr cds: A, DS, MC, V.

⬛🛗🏊🏊‍♂️🔥🛶🏃

★★★ **TETON PINES.** *3450 N Clubhouse Dr (83001), 7 mi W on Teton Village Rd.* 307/733-1005; fax 307/733-2860; toll-free 800/238-2223. Email info@tetonpines.com; www.teton pines.com. 16 rms, 2 story, 8 suites. June-Sep: S, D $395; suites $750; under 10 free; lower rates rest of yr. Crib avail. Parking lot. Pool, whirlpool. TV; cable, VCR avail. Complimentary full bkfst, coffee in rms, newspaper, toll-free calls. Restaurant, closed Sun. Bar. Ck-out 11 am, ck-in 4 pm. Meeting rms. Business center. Bellhops. Concierge. Dry cleaning. Gift shop. Salon/barber. Free airport transportation. Exercise privileges, sauna. Golf, 18 holes. Tennis, 8 courts. Downhill skiing. Hiking trail. Cr cds: A, D, V.

⬛🔌🏊🕴️🏊‍♂️🔥🛶🏃🛶🏃

B&Bs/Small Inns

★★ **DAVY JACKSON.** *85 Perry Ave (83001).* 307/739-2294; fax 307/733-9704; toll-free 800/584-0532. Email davyjackson@wyoming.com; www.davy jackson.com. 11 rms, 3 story. June-Sep: S, D $239; each addl $15; children $15; under 12 free; lower rates rest of yr. Crib avail. Parking lot. TV; cable (premium). Complimentary full bkfst, newspaper, toll-free calls. Ck-out noon, ck-in 3 pm. Business servs avail. Concierge. Dry cleaning. Gift shop. Whirlpool. Golf, 18 holes. Tennis. Downhill skiing. Bike rentals. Hiking trail. Cr cds: A, DS, MC, V.

⬛🛗🏊🏊🕴️🏊‍♂️🛶🔥🆑

★ **FLAT CREEK.** *1935 N US 89 (83002).* 307/733-5276; fax 307/733-0374; toll-free 800/438-9338. Email info@flatcreekmotel.com; www.flatcreek motel.com. 72 rms, 2 story, 3 suites. May-Sep: S $95; D $113; suites $250; under 18 free; lower rates rest of yr. Crib avail, fee. Pet accepted, some restrictions, fee. Parking lot. TV; cable (premium), VCR avail. Complimentary continental bkfst, coffee in rms. Restaurant. Ck-out 11 am, ck-in 3 pm. Business servs avail. Concierge. Dry cleaning, coin lndry. Gift shop. Free airport transportation. Whirlpool. Golf. Tennis, 4 courts. Downhill skiing. Cr cds: A, C, D, DS, MC, V.

★★★ **THE HUFF HOUSE INN BED & BREAKFAST.** *240 E Deloney (83001), 2 blks E of Town Square.* 307/733-4164; fax 307/739-9091. Email huffhousebnb@blissnet.com; www.jacksonwyomingbnb.com. 9 rms, 2 story. Feb-Mar, June-Sep, Dec: S, D $135; each addl $20; suites $205; children $20; lower rates rest of yr. Crib avail. Parking lot. TV; cable, VCR avail. Complimentary full bkfst, toll-free calls. Restaurant. Ck-out 11 am, ck-in 3 pm. Business center. Concierge. Exercise privileges, whirlpool. Golf, 18 holes. Downhill skiing. Bike rentals. Hiking trail. Picnic facilities. Cr cds: DS, MC, V.

★★★ **NOWLIN CREEK INN.** *660 E Broadway (83001).* 307/733-0882; fax 301/733-0106; toll-free 800/533-0882. Email nowlin@sisna.com. 5 rms, 2 story. June-Sep: S $150; D $160-$185; each addl $20; under 18 free; lower rates rest of yr. Complimentary full bkfst. Restaurant nearby. Ck-out 11 am, ck-in 4 pm. Whirlpool. Western ranch furnished with antiques. Totally nonsmoking. Cr cds: A, DS, MC, V.

★★★ **TETON TREE HOUSE BED & BREAKFAST.** *6175 Heck of a Hill Rd (83014), 7 mi W on WY 22, ½ mi S on Fall Creek Rd.* 307/733-3233; fax 307/733-0713. Email dbecker@rmisp.com; cruising-america.com/tetontreehouse. 6 rms, 3 story, 2 suites. July-Aug: D $160; each addl $25; under 10 free; lower rates rest of yr. Parking lot. TV; cable, VCR avail. Complimentary full

bkfst. Restaurant nearby. Ck-out 11 am. Fax servs avail. Whirlpool. Golf. Tennis. Downhill skiing. Cr cds: DS, MC, V.

★★★ **THE WILDFLOWER INN.** *3725 N Teton Village Rd (83001).* 307/733-4710; fax 307/739-0914. Email Wildflowerinn@compuserve.com. 5 rms, 1 suite, 2 story. No A/C. No rm phones. S, D $140-$180; suite $250; each addl $30; under 12 free. TV; cable (premium). Complimentary full bkfst. Restaurant nearby. Ck-out 11 am, ck-in 3-5 pm. Concierge serv. Downhill ski 4 mi. Whirlpool. Log house on 3 acres; pond; mountain views. Totally nonsmoking. Cr cds: A, DS, MC, V.

Restaurants

★★★★ **THE ALPENHOF DINING ROOM.** *3255 W McCollister, Hwy 390 to Teton Village.* 307/733-3462. Email alpenhof@sisna.com; www.jacksonhole.com/alpenhof. At the base of the Jackson Hole ski area, the restaurant at this Bavarian-style lodge is the most well-regarded dining room in the area. Here the emphasis is on hearty dishes of western-influenced continental cuisine. Variations on classic themes include the tableside preparation of Caribou Steak Diane or a great Bananas Foster. The property's upstairs bistro offers more casual fare. Own baking. Hrs: 7:30-10:30 am, 5:30-9 pm. Closed early Apr-mid-May and mid-Oct-early Dec. Res accepted. Bar. Wine list. Bkfst $3-$7.95; dinner $16-$30. Dinner for 2: $55-$61. Child's menu. Parking. Cr cds: A, D, DS, MC, V.

★★ **ANTHONY'S.** *62 S Glenwood (83001).* 307/733-3717. Specializes in lemon chicken, Cajun fettuccine, homemade bread. Hrs: 5:30-9:30 pm. Closed Thanksgiving, Dec 25. Bar. Dinner $10-$16. Art Deco Italian decor. Cr cds: A, D, MC, V.

★★★ **BLUE LION.** *160 N Millward St (83001).* 307/733-3912. Specializes in fresh seafood, lamb, fresh elk. Own baking. Hrs: 6-10 pm. Res accepted. Bar. Dinner $15-$25. In renovated old house. Herb garden. Cr cds: A, DS, MC, V.

★★★ **CADILLAC GRILLE.** *55 N Cache (83001). 307/733-3279. Email roncorp@brissiet.com.* Specializes in wild game, steak, fresh seafood, wood-oven pizza. Own baking. Hrs: 11:30 am-2:30 pm, 5:30-9:30 pm. Res accepted. Bar. Lunch a la carte entrees: $4.95-$8.95; dinner a la carte entrees: $14-$23.50. Child's menu. Contemporary art decor. Cr cds: A, MC, V.

D ⬛

★★ **CALICO.** *2650 Teton Village Rd (83025). 307/733-2460.* Specializes in pasta, pizza, seafood. Hrs: 5-10 pm; Sun brunch 10 am-2 pm. Bar. Dinner $7.95-$17.95. Sun brunch $6.95-$16.95. Child's menu. Old West decor. Cr cds: A, MC, V.

D

An elk snacks on lush Wyoming greenery

★ **JEDEDIAH'S.** *135 E Broadway (83001). 307/733-5671.* Specializes in sourdough pancakes, buffalo burgers, sourdough carrot cake. Hrs: 7 am-2 pm; 5:30-9 pm; winter hrs vary. Closed Thanksgiving, Dec 25. Res accepted. Bkfst $2.95-$8.95; lunch $4.50-$8.50; dinner $6-$15. Child's menu. Rustic decor in old house (1910); Western antiques. Cr cds: A, D, MC, V.

D SC

★★ **LAME DUCK.** *680 E Broadway (83001). 307/733-4311.* Specializes in seafood, sushi, sashimi. Hrs: 5-10 pm. Closed Thanksgiving, Dec 25. Dinner $3.95-$15.95. Child's menu. Parking. 3 tea rms. Cr cds: A, MC, V.

D

★★ **MILLION DOLLAR COWBOY STEAK HOUSE.** *25 N Cache St (83001), opp Town Square. 307/733-4790.* Steak menu. Specializes in steak, fresh seafood, wild game. Hrs: 5:30-10 pm; winter hrs vary. Closed Thanksgiving, Dec 25; Apr-early May, Nov. Bar. Dinner $14.95-$29.95. Knotty pine furnishings. Western decor. Cr cds: A, DS, MC, V.

D ⬛

★★ **OFF BROADWAY.** *30 S King St (83001). 307/733-9777. Email ob@onewest.net.* Continental menu. Specializes in fresh seafood, pasta, elk medallions. Hrs: 5:30-10 pm. Closed Dec 25. Res accepted. Dinner $11.95-$22.95. Child's menu. Cr cds: A, MC, V.

SC

★★★ **RANGE.** *225 N Cacat St (83001). 307/733-5481.* Specializes in medallions of elk, breast of turkey, Sonoma free-range cornish game hen. Hrs: 5:30-10 pm. Res accepted. Bar. Dinner $16-$31. Child's menu. Metropolitan high plains decor. Cr cds: A, MC, V.

D

★★★ **SNAKE RIVER GRILL.** *84 E Broadway (83001). 307/733-0557. srg@blissnet.com.* Specializes in fresh ahi tuna, roast elk loin, vegetarian lasagnette. Hrs: 6-10:30 pm. Closed Dec 25; Apr-mid-May, Nov-early Dec. Res accepted. Wine list. Dinner $16.95-$29.95. Child's menu. Upscale Western ranch decor and atmosphere; stone fireplace. Cr cds: A, DS, MC, V.

D

★★★ **STRUTTING GROUSE.** *Jackson Hole Golf and Tennis Club (83001), 7 mi N on US 89. 307/733-7788. www.gtlc.com.* Specializes in fresh salmon, bison medallions, venison sausage. Hrs: 11 am-9 pm. Closed Oct-mid-May. Res accepted. Bar. Lunch a la carte entrees: $5-$8.50; dinner a la carte entrees: $15.95-$22.95. Parking. Western decor; gardens. View of golf course, mountains. Cr cds: A, DS, MC, V.

★★ **SWEETWATER.** *King and Pearl Sts (83001).* 307/733-3553. Specializes in lamb, seafood, Greek phyllo pies. Hrs: 11:30 am-3 pm, 5:30-10 pm. Closed Thanksgiving, Dec 25. Res accepted. Bar. Lunch $5.95-$8.25; dinner $11.95-$24. Child's menu. Western decor. In log house built by pioneers. Cr cds: A, D, MC, V.

D

★★★ **TETON PINES.** *3450 N Clubhouse Dr.* 307/733-1005. *www.teton pines.com.* Specializes in wild game, fresh seafood, steak. Hrs: 11:30 am-2:30 pm, 6-9 pm. Closed Sun. Res accepted. Bar. Lunch $4.75-$11.75; dinner $16-$26.50. 15% serv charge. Parking. View of Tetons. Paintings of local scenes displayed. Cr cds: A, MC, V.

D

★★ **VISTA GRANDE.** *2550 Teton Village Rd (83001), 6 mi NW on WY 22, then 1½ mi N on Teton Village Rd.* 307/733-6964. Hrs: 5:30-10 pm. Bar. Dinner $7.50-$14.95. Child's menu. Parking. Mexican decor. View of mountains. Cr cds: A, MC, V.

D

Unrated Dining Spots

BAR J. *4200 Bar J Chuckwagon Rd (83001).* 307/733-3370. *www.barj chuckwagon.com.* Specializes in barbecue chuck-wagon dinner with beef, chicken, steak. Hrs: sittings: 7:30 pm (dinner), 8:30 pm (show). Closed Oct-May. Res accepted. Dinner complete meals: $14. Child's menu. Entertainment: western stage show. On working cattle ranch. Cr cds: DS, MC, V.

D

THE BUNNERY. *130 N Cache St (83001), in Hole in the Wall Mall.* 307/733-5474. Specializes in wholegrain waffles, broiled sandwiches. Own baking. Hrs: 7 am-9 pm. Closed Thanksgiving, Dec 25. Wine, beer. Bkfst $2.95-$5.95; lunch $3.95-$6.95; dinner $6.95-$9.95. Child's menu. Cr cds: MC, V.

D SC

Kemmerer

(E-1) *See also Evanston, Green River*

Pop 3,020 **Elev** 6,959 ft
Area code 307 **Zip** 83101

A Ranger District office of the Bridger-Teton National Forest (see JACKSON) is located here.

What to See and Do

Fossil Butte National Monument. On 8,198 acres is one of the most extensive concentrations of fossilized aquatic vertebrates, plants, and insects (some 50 million yrs old) in the US. (Daily) 11 mi W on US 30 N. Phone 307/877-4455. **FREE**

Lander

(D-3) *See also Riverton*

Settled 1875 **Pop** 7,023 **Elev** 5,360 ft
Area code 307 **Zip** 82520
Web www.landerchamber.org
Information Chamber of Commerce, 160 N 1st St; 307/332-3892 or 800/433-0662

Lander was once called the place where the rails end and the trails begin. Wind River Range, surrounding the town, offers hunting and fishing, mountain climbing, and rock hunting. The annual One-Shot Antelope Hunt opens the antelope season and draws celebrities and sports enthusiasts from all over the country. Sacajawea Cemetery (burial place of Lewis and Clark's Shoshone guide) is located in Fort Washakie, 15 mi NW on US 287. A Ranger District office of the Shoshone National Forest (see CODY) is located in Lander.

What to See and Do

Fremont County Pioneer Museum. Seven exhibit rms and outdoor exhibit area document the pioneer, ranching, Native American, and business history of the area. (Mon-Fri, also Sat afternoons) 630 Lincoln St. Phone 307/332-4137. ¢-¢¢

Sinks Canyon State Park. In a spectacular canyon, amid unspoiled Rocky Mt beauty, lies the middle fork of the Popo Agie River, which disappears into a cavern and rises again several hundred yards below in a crystal-clear, trout-filled spring pool. Abundant wildlife in certain seasons. Visitor center, observation points. Fishing (exc in the Rise of the Sinks); hiking, nature trails, groomed cross-country ski and snowmobile trails nearby. Limited tent and trailer sites (standard fees); other sites nearby. 7 mi SW on WY 131. Phone 307/332-6333.

South Pass City. An example of a once flourishing gold mining town. During the gold rush of 1868-72, 2,000 people lived here. Women were first given equal suffrage by a territorial act introduced from South Pass City and passed in Cheyenne on Dec 10, 1869. The town is currently being restored and has more than 20 historic bldgs on display (mid-May-Sep, daily). 33 mi S on WY 28, then 3 mi W. Phone 307/332-3684. ¢

Motels/Motor Lodges

★★ **BEST WESTERN, INN AT LANDER.** *260 Grand View Dr (82520). 307/332-2847; fax 307/332-2760; toll-free 800/528-1234.* 42 rms, 2 story, 4 suites. Crib avail. Parking lot. Pool. TV; cable. Complimentary continental bkfst. Ck-out 11 am, ck-in 2 pm. Meeting rms. Fax servs avail. Golf. Cr cds: A, D, DS, MC, V.

★★ **BUDGET HOST PRONGHORN.** *150 E Main St (82520). 307/332-3940; fax 307/332-2651; toll-free 800/283-4678. Email wgibson@wyoming.com; www.wyoming.com/~thepronghorn.* 50 rms, 2 story, 4 suites. May-Oct: S $54; D $74; each addl $5; suites $79; under 12 free; lower rates rest of yr. Crib avail, fee. Pet accepted, some restrictions, fee. Parking lot. TV; cable. Complimentary continental bkfst, toll-free calls. Restaurant. Meeting rms. Fax servs avail. Coin lndry. Golf, 18 holes. Tennis. Bike rentals. Hiking trail. Picnic facilities. Cr cds: A, C, D, DS, MC, V.

Laramie

(F-6) *See also Cheyenne*

Founded 1868 **Pop** 26,687
Elev 7,165 ft **Area code** 307
Zip 82070 **Web** www.laramietourism.org

Information Albany County Tourism Board, 800 S Third St; 307/745-4195 or 800/445-5303

Laramie had a rugged beginning as a lawless leftover of the westward-rushing Union Pacific. The early settlement was populated by hunters, saloonkeepers, and brawlers. When the tracks pushed on, Laramie stabilized somewhat, but for six months vigilantes were the only law enforcement available against desperate characters who operated from town. Reasonable folk finally prevailed; schools and businesses sprang up, and improved cattle breeds brought prosperity. A Ranger District office of the Medicine Bow National Forest is located here.

What to See and Do

Laramie Plains Museum. Victorian mansion (1892); each rm finished in a different wood; collections incl antique furniture, toys, china, ranching memorabilia, Western artifacts. Special seasonal displays. (Daily) 603 Ivinson Ave. Phone 307/742-4448. ¢¢

Lincoln Monument. World's largest bronze head (12½ ft high, 3½ tons), by Robert Russin of the Univ of Wyoming. 8 mi SE on I-80.

Medicine Bow National Forest. The more than 1 million acres incl the Snowy Range Scenic Byway; one 30-mi stretch on WY 130, W from Centennial, is particularly scenic with elevations as high as 10,800 ft at Snowy Range Pass. Winter sports areas, picnic grounds, camping (fee), commercial lodges. For further information contact the Forest Supervisor, 2468 Jackson St. W on WY 130, SW on WY 230, E on I-80, or N via US 30, WY 34, I-25, local roads. Phone 307/745-2300.

Snowy Range Ski Area. Triple, 3 double chairlifts, T-bar, 25 runs; school, rentals, snowmaking, guided snowmobile tours; cafeteria, bar. Vertical drop 1,000 ft; longest run 2 mi. Cross-country trails nearby. (Mid-Nov-mid-Apr, daily) 32 mi W on WY 130 (Snowy Range Rd). Phone 307/745-5750. ¢¢¢¢

University of Wyoming. (1886) 10,650 students. The state's only 4-yr univ. Its campus has the highest elevation of any in the US. The UW Visitor Information Center, 1408 Ivinson Ave, has displays, community and campus literature. Between 9th & 30th Sts, 1 blk N of US 30 (Grand Ave). Phone 307/766-4075 or 307/766-1121. On campus are

American Heritage Center and Art Museum. Nine galleries feature display of paintings, graphics, and sculpture from the 16th century-present. Manuscripts, rare books, artifacts relating to Wyoming and the West. Research facilities. (Tues-Sun; closed hols) 2111 Willet Dr. Phone 307/766-6622. **FREE**

Geological Museum. Houses rocks, minerals, vertebrate, invertebrate, mammal and plant fossils, incl 1 of 5 brontosaurus skeletons in the world. (Mon-Fri) S.K. Knight Geology Bldg. Phone 307/766-4218. **FREE**

Wyoming Territorial Prison and Old West Park. Western heritage park with living history programs. Frontier town, Territorial Prison, US Marshals' Museum (fee), dinner theater (fee), playground, gift shop. (May-Sep, daily) 975 Snowy Range Rd, just off I-80. Phone 800/845-2287, Ext 5. ¢

Vedauwoo. Sightseeing, camping, and climbing amid rock formations on the Medicine Bow National Forest. (Daily) Fee for camping. 21 mi SE of Laramie. Phone 800/280-2267. **FREE**

Motels/Motor Lodges

★★ **BEST WESTERN FOSTER'S COUNTRY INN.** *1561 Snowy Range Rd (82073), (WY 130, 230) at jct I-80 Snowy Range Exit 311. 307/742-8371; fax 307/742-0884.* 112 rms, 2 story. Mid-May-mid-Sep: S $58; D $64; each addl $6; under 12 free; higher rates special events; lower rates rest

of yr. Crib $6. Pet accepted. TV; cable. Indoor pool; whirlpool. Complimentary full bkfst. Restaurant open 24 hrs. Bar 8-2 am. Ck-out noon. Coin lndry. Meeting rms. Gift shop. Free airport, railroad station, bus depot transportation. Cr cds: A, C, D, DS, MC, V.

[D] [symbols]

★ **CAMELOT MOTEL.** *523 S Adams St (82070), I-80, Snowy Range Exit 311. 307/721-8860; toll-free 800/659-7915.* 33 rms, 2 story. S $45; D $55-$65; each addl $5. Crib $3. TV; cable. Restaurant opp open 24 hrs. Ck-out 11 am. Coin lndry. Cr cds: A, C, D, DS, MC, V.

[D] [symbols] [SC]

★ **ECONO LODGE.** *1370 McCue St (82072). 307/745-8900; fax 307/745-5806.* 51 rms, 2 story. June-Aug: S, D $64-$74; each addl $10; suites $94; under 13 free; lower rates rest of yr. Crib free. Pet accepted; $5. TV; cable. Indoor pool. Complimentary coffee in lobby. Restaurant nearby. Ck-out noon. Meeting rm. Some refrigerators. Cr cds: A, D, DS, MC, V.

[D] [symbols]

★★ **HOLIDAY INN.** *2313 Soldier Springs Rd (82070), at jct US 30, 287; I-80 Exit 313. 307/742-6611; fax 307/745-8371; toll-free 800/465-4329.* 100 rms, 2 story. Mid-May-mid-Sep: S $80; D $80-$120; each addl $8; under 18 free; lower rates rest of yr. Crib free. Pet accepted. TV; cable (premium). Indoor pool; whirlpool. Coffee in rms. Restaurant 6 am-10 pm. Bar. Ck-out noon. Coin lndry. Meeting rms. Gift shop. Free airport transportation. Cr cds: A, C, D, DS, MC, V.

[D] [symbols] [SC]

B&B/Small Inn

★★★ **A DRUMMOND'S RANCH BED & BREAKFAST.** *399 Happy Jack Rd (82007). 307/634-6042; fax 307/634-6042. Email adrummond@juno.com; www.adrummond.com.* 4 rms, 2 story. May-Aug: S, D $160; each addl $15; under 10 free; lower rates rest of yr. Crib avail. Pet accepted, some restrictions, fee. Street parking. TV; cable, VCR avail, CD avail. Complimentary full bkfst, coffee in rms. Ck-out 11 am, ck-in 4 pm. Business servs avail. Free airport transportation.

Sauna. Downhill skiing. Bike rentals. Hiking trail. Picnic facilities. Cr cds: DS, MC, V.

Lovell

(B-3) *See also Greybull*

Pop 2,131 **Elev** 3,837 ft
Area code 307 **Zip** 82431
Information Lovell Area Chamber of Commerce, 287 E Main, PO Box 295; 307/548-7552

A Ranger District office of the Bighorn National Forest (see SHERIDAN) is located here.

What to See and Do

Bighorn Canyon National Recreation Area. The focus of the area is 71-mi-long Bighorn Lake, created by the Yellowtail Dam in Fort Smith, MT. Boats may travel through Bighorn Canyon, which cuts across the northern end of the Bighorn Mts in north-central Wyoming and south-central Montana. The solar-powered Bighorn Canyon Visitor Center is just E of town on US 14A (daily). The Fort Smith Visitor Contact Station is in Fort Smith, MT (daily). Both centers are closed Jan 1, Thanksgiving, Dec 25. Yellowtail Visitor Center at the dam has tours (summer). Recreational and interpretive activities are avail at both ends of the area. Fishing, boating; picnicking, camping. For further information contact Bighorn Canyon Visitor Center, Hwy 14A E. S entrance 2 mi E on US 14A, then 8 mi N on WY 37. Phone 307/548-2251. Adj and accessible from town is

Pryor Mountain Wild Horse Range. This 32,000-acre refuge, established in 1968, provides a sanctuary for wild horses descended from Native American ponies and escaped farm and ranch horses. Administered jointly by the National Park Service and the Bureau of Land Management.

Annual Event

Mustang Days. Parade, rodeo, exhibits, entertainment, dancing, barbecue; 7-mi run. Late June.

Motel/Motor Lodge

★ **SUPER 8 MOTEL.** *595 E Main (82431). 307/548-2725; fax 307/548-2725; toll-free 800/800-8000.* 35 rms, 2 story. S $43.88; D $47.88-$51.88; each addl $3; under 12 free. Crib free. TV; cable (premium). Restaurant adj 6 am-9:30 pm. Ck-out 11 am. Cr cds: A, C, D, DS, MC, V.

Restaurant

★ **BIG HORN.** *605 E Main St (82431). 307/548-6811.* Specializes in seafood, steak. Salad bar. Hrs: 6 am-9 pm; Fri, Sat to 9:30 pm. Closed Jan 1, Dec 25. Bar. Bkfst $2.75-$7.50; lunch $2.50-$5.75; dinner $5-$14.50. Child's menu. Cr cds: A, C, D, DS, MC, V.

Lusk

(D-7) *See also Douglas*

Founded 1886 **Pop** 1,504
Elev 5,015 ft **Area code** 307
Zip 82225
Web www.wyoming.com/lusk
Information Chamber of Commerce, PO Box 457; 307/334-2950 or 800/223-LUSK

Raising livestock has always been important in Lusk; fine herds of Simmental, Angus, and sheep are the local pride. Hunting is excellent for deer and antelope.

What to See and Do

Stagecoach Museum. Relics of pioneer days, Native American artifacts, stagecoach. (May-June and Sep-Oct, Mon-Fri; July-Aug, Tues-Sun) 322 S Main. Phone 307/334-3444. ¢

Annual Events

Legend of Rawhide. Live show performed since 1946. Concert, dances, trade show, golf tournament, gun show, parade, pancake breakfast. Second wkend July.

Senior Pro Rodeo. Labor Day wkend.

Motels/Motor Lodges

★★ **BEST WESTERN.** *731 S Main (82225). 307/334-2640; fax 307/334-2642; toll-free 800/528-1234.* 30 rms. S $42; D $55-$66; each addl $4. Crib $4. TV; cable. Pool. Complimentary coffee in lobby. Restaurant nearby. Ck-out 11 am. Cr cds: A, C, D, DS, JCB, MC, V.

⌖ ⌖ ⌖

★ **IMA COVERED WAGON MOTEL.** *730 S Main St (82225), US 18, 20, 85. 307/334-2836; fax 307/334-2977. Email coveredwagon@wyoming.com.* 51 rms. Mid-June-mid-Oct: S $58; D $67-$71; each addl $5; suite $155; lower rates rest of yr. Crib $2. TV; cable. Indoor pool; whirlpool. Playground. Complimentary continental bkfst, coffee in lobby. Restaurant nearby. Ck-out 11 am. Coin lndry. Meeting rm. Sauna. Lawn games. Cr cds: A, C, D, DS, MC, V.

Ⓓ ⌖ ⌖ ⌖ SC

Newcastle (C-7)

Founded 1889 **Pop** 3,003
Elev 4,317 ft **Area code** 307
Zip 82701
Web www.trib.com/newcastle
Information Newcastle Area Chamber of Commerce, PO Box 68; 307/746-2739 or 800/835-0157

Originally a coal mining town, Newcastle is now an oil field center with its own refinery. It is also a tourist center, with fishing, hunting, and recreational facilities nearby. A Ranger District office of the Black Hills National Forest is located here.

What to See and Do

Anna Miller Museum. Museum of NE Wyoming, housed in stone cavalry barn. Log cabin from Jenney Stockade, oldest bldg in the Black Hills, and an early rural schoolhouse. More than 100 exhibits. (Mon-Fri, Sat by appt) Delaware and Washington Park. Phone 307/746-4188. **FREE**

Beaver Creek Loop Tour. Self-guided driving tour designed to provide the opportunity to explore a diverse and beautiful country; 45-mi tour covers 23 marked sites. Phone 307/746-2739. **FREE**

Pinedale

(D-2) *See also Jackson*

Settled 1878 **Pop** 1,181 **Elev** 7,175 ft
Area code 307 **Zip** 82941
Information Chamber of Commerce, 32 E Pine, PO Box 176; 307/367-2242

Pinedale is a place where genuine cowboys can still be found, and cattle drives still occur. Mountains, conifer and aspen forests, and lakes and rivers combine to make this a beautiful vacation area. There are fossil beds in the area, and rockhounding is popular. Cattle and sheep are raised on nearby ranches. A Ranger District office of the Bridger-Teton National Forest (see JACKSON) is located in Pinedale.

What to See and Do

Bridger-Teton National Forest. Lies along the Wind River Range, E, N, and W of town. Fishing; hunting, hiking, camping (fee). In forest is

Bridger Wilderness. Approx 400,000 acres of mountainous terrain entered only by foot or horseback. Trout fishing in snow-fed streams and more than 1,300 mountain lakes; hunting for big game. Backpacking. Permits required for some activities. Pack trips arranged by area outfitters.

Hunting. In-season hunting for elk, moose, deer, bear, antelope, mountain bighorn sheep, birds, and small game in surrounding mountains and mesas.

Museum of the Mountain Man. Houses exhibits on fur trade, western exploration, early history. (May-Oct, daily) Fremont Lake *Rd*. Phone 307/367-4101. ¢¢

⭐ **Scenic Drives. Skyline.** Up into the mountains 14 mi the fauna changes from sagebrush to an alpine setting. Lakes, conifers, beautiful mountain scenery; wildlife often seen. **Green River Lakes.** N via WY 352 to the lakes with Square Top Mt in the background; popular with photographers. Wooded campground, trails, backpacking.

Water sports. Fishing for grayling, rainbow, mackinaw, brown trout, golden and other trout in most lakes and rivers; ice-fishing, mostly located N of town. Swimming, waterskiing, boating, sailing regattas, float trips on New Fork and Green rivers.

Winter recreation. Cross-country skiing, groomed snowmobile trails, ice-fishing, skating.

Annual Event

Green River Rendezvous. Rodeo grounds, Sublette County. Noted historical pageant commemorating the meeting of fur trappers, mountain men, and Native Americans with the Trading Company's wagon trains at Fort Bonneville. Mid-July.

Motels/Motor Lodges

★★ **BEST WESTERN INN.** *850 W Pine St (82941). 307/367-6869; fax 307/367-6897.* 58 rms, 2 story. June-Labor Day: S, D $99; suites $125; under 12 free; lower rates rest of yr. Crib $5. Pet accepted. TV; cable. Indoor pool; whirlpool. Sauna. Complimentary continental bkfst. Restaurant nearby. Ck-out 11 am. Meeting rms. In-rm modem link. Exercise equipt. Some refrigerators. Cr cds: A, D, DS, MC, V.

⬛ ⬛ ⬛ ⬛ ⬛ **SC**

Restaurant

★★ **MCGREGOR'S PUB.** *21 N Franklin St (82941). 307/367-4443.* Specializes in prime rib, scallops, pasta. Own desserts, bread. Hrs: 11:30 am-2 pm, 5:30-11 pm; Sat, Sun from 5:30 pm. Closed hols. Res accepted. Bar. Lunch $4.95-$6.95; dinner $12.95-$29.95. Child's menu. Contemporary ranch decor. Cr cds: A, D, DS, MC, V.

D **SC**

Rawlins

(F-4) See also Lander, Thermopolis

Founded 1867 **Pop** 9,380
Elev 6,755 ft **Area code** 307
Zip 82301
Information Rawlins-Carbon County Chamber of Commerce, 519 W Cedar, PO Box 1331; 307/324-4111 or 800/228-3547

Rawlins, a division point of the Union Pacific Railroad, is located 20 miles east of the Continental Divide. In 1867, General John A. Rawlins, Chief of Staff of the US Army, wished for a drink of cool, clear water. Upon finding the spring near the base of the hills and tasting it, he said, "If anything is ever named after me, I hope it will be a spring of water." The little oasis was named Rawlins Springs, as was the community that grew up beside it. The city name was later shortened to Rawlins.

What to See and Do

Carbon County Museum. Houses artifacts of mining and ranching ventures. (Schedule varies) 9th & Walnut Sts. Phone 307/328-2740. **Donation**

Seminoe State Park. Seminoe Dam impounds a 27-mi-long reservoir surrounded by giant white sand dunes and sagebrush. Pronghorn antelope and sage grouse inhabit area. Swimming, fishing (trout, walleye), boating (ramps); hiking, picnicking, tent and trailer sites (standard fee). 6 mi E on I-80 to Sinclair, then 35 mi N on County Rd 351. Phone 307/328-0115 or 307/320-3013.

Wyoming Frontier Prison. Located on 49 acres, construction was begun in 1888. The prison operated from 1901-81. Tours (fee). (May-Sep, daily; rest of yr, by appt) 5th & Walnut. Phone 307/324-4422. Museum **FREE**; Tour ¢¢

Annual Event

Carbon County Fair and Rodeo. Fairgrounds, Rodeo Park off Spruce St.

Incl parades, exhibits, livestock, contests, demolition derby, old-timer rodeo. Second full wk Aug.

Motels/Motor Lodges

★ **DAYS INN.** *2222 E Cedar St (82301). 307/324-6615; fax 307/324-6615; toll-free 888/324-6615.* 118 rms, 2 story. June-mid-Sep: S $64; D $69; each addl $5; under 18 free; lower rates rest of yr. Crib free. Pet accepted. TV; cable (premium). Pool. Complimentary continental bkfst. Coffee in rms. Restaurant 11 am-2 pm, 5-9 pm. Bar 5 pm-2 am. Ck-out 11 am. Coin lndry. Meeting rms. Business servs avail. Cr cds: A, C, D, DS, MC, V.

[D] [🐾] [≈] [≍] [🖼] [SC]

★ **SLEEP INN.** *1400 Higley Blvd (82301), I-80 Exit 214. 307/328-1732; fax 307/328-0412; res 800/753-3746.* 81 rms, many with shower only, 2 story. June-Sep: S $53; D $58-$63; each addl $5; under 18 free; lower rates rest of yr. Crib free. TV; cable (premium), VCR avail (movies $3.50). Complimentary coffee in lobby. Restaurant adj open 24 hrs. Ck-out 11 am. Meeting rms. Business servs avail. Sauna. Cr cds: A, DS, MC, V.

[D]

Riverton

(D-3) *See also Lander, Thermopolis*

Founded 1906 **Pop** 9,202
Elev 4,964 ft **Area code** 307
Zip 82501
Information Chamber of Commerce, 1st & Main, Depot Bldg; 307/856-4801

Riverton is the largest city in Fremont County. Resources extracted from the region include natural gas, oil, iron ore, timber, and phosphate. Irrigation from the Wind River Range has placed 130,000 acres under cultivation, on which barley, alfalfa hay, beans, sunflowers, and grain are grown. The town is surrounded by the Wind River Reservation, where Arapaho and Shoshone live.

What to See and Do

Riverton Museum. Shoshone and Arapaho displays; mountain man display. General store, drugstore, post office, saloon, homesteader's cabin, church, bank, dentist's office, parlor, school, beauty shop. Clothing, quilts, cutters, buggies. 700 E Park St. Phone 307/856-2665. **FREE**

Annual Events

Wild West Winter Carnival. Depot Bldg. Early Feb.

State Championship Old-time Fiddle Contest. 21 mi NE via US 26, 789 in Shoshone. Divisional competition. Late May.

Powwows. Shoshone and Arapaho tribal powwows are held throughout the summer.

1838 Mountain Man Rendezvous. Council fire, primitive shoots, hawk and knife throw, games, food. Camping avail. Phone 307/856-7306. Early July.

Fremont County Fair and Rodeo. First full wk Aug.

Motels/Motor Lodges

★★ **HOLIDAY INN.** *900 E Sunset Dr (82501). 307/856-8100; fax 307/856-0266; toll-free 800/465-4329. Email jbartlow@wyoming.com.* 121 rms, 2 story. S, D $79; each addl $6; under 19 free. Pet accepted. TV; cable. Indoor pool; poolside serv. Restaurant 6 am-10 pm. Bar 4 pm-2 am. Ck-out noon. Coin lndry. Meeting rms. Sundries. Beauty shop. Airport transportation. Bathrm phones. Cr cds: A, C, D, DS, JCB, MC, V.

[D] [🐾] [♣] [✛] [≈] [🐾]

★★ **SUNDOWNER STATION.** *1616 N Federal Blvd (82501), US 26, WY 789. 307/856-6503; fax 307/856-6503; toll-free 800/874-1116.* 61 rms, 2 story. S $48; D $50-$54; each addl $4; under 12 free. Crib free. Pet accepted. TV; cable. Sauna. Restaurant 5:30 am-10 pm. Bar 4-11 pm. Ck-out 11 am. Meeting rms. Sundries. Free airport transportation. Balconies. Cr cds: A, DS, MC, V.

[🐾] [≍] [🖼] [SC]

Rock Springs

(F-3) *See also Green River*

Pop 19,050 **Elev** 6,271 ft
Area code 307 **Zip** 82901
Information Rock Springs Chamber of Commerce, 1897 Dewar Dr, PO Box 398, 82902; 307/362-3771 or 800/46-DUNES

Rock Springs traces its roots to a spring, which offered an ideal camping site along a Native American trail and, later, a welcome station on the Overland Stage route. Later still, Rock Springs became a supply station that provided millions of tons of coal to the Union Pacific Railroad. Noted for its multiethnic heritage, the town's first inhabitants were primarily Welsh and English immigrants brought in by the railroad and coal companies. West of town are large deposits of trona (sodium sesquicarbonate), used in the manufacture of glass, phosphates, silicates, soaps, and baking soda.

What to See and Do

Flaming Gorge Reservoir. This man-made lake, fed by the Green River, is 90 mi long with approx 375 mi of shoreline, which ranges from low flats to cliffs more than 1,500 ft high. Surrounded by a national recreation area (see GREEN RIVER), the reservoir offers excellent fishing. SW via I-80.

Annual Events

Desert Balloon Rally. Early July.
Red Desert Round-Up. One of the largest rodeos in the Rocky Mts region. Late July.
Sweetwater County fair. Late July-early Aug.

Motels/Motor Lodges

★★ **COMFORT INN.** *1670 Sunset Drive (82901), at I-80 Dewar Exit. 307/382-9490; fax 307/382-7333; res 800/228-5150.* 102 rms, 1 story, 41 suites. May-Aug: S $68; D $74; each addl $6; suites $83; under 18 free; lower rates rest of yr. Crib avail. Pet accepted, fee. Parking lot. Pool, chil-

dren's pool, whirlpool. TV; cable (premium). Complimentary continental bkfst, newspaper, toll-free calls. Restaurant nearby. Bar. Ck-out 11 am, ck-in 3 pm. Meeting rm. Business center. Dry cleaning, coin lndry. Free airport transportation. Exercise privileges. Golf. Picnic facilities. Cr cds: A, D, DS, MC, V.

🄳 🏊 🎿 🖥 🛁 🚶

★★ **RAMADA LIMITED.** *2717 Dewar Dr (82901). 307/362-1770; fax 307/362-2830; res 800/272-6232; toll-free 888/307-7890. Email marla@ sweetwater.net; www.ramada.com.* 130 rms, 2 story. May-early Sep: S $60-$70; D $70-$80; each addl $6; suites $78-$85; under 18 free; higher rates special events; lower rates rest of yr. Crib avail. Pet accepted. TV; cable (premium). Complimentary continental bkfst, coffee in rms. Restaurant adj open 24 hrs. Ck-out noon. Meeting rms. Business servs avail. Bellhops. Heated pool. Cr cds: A, DS, MC, V.

🄳 🏊 🖥 🛁

Hotel

★★ **HOLIDAY INN.** *1675 Sunset Dr (82901). 307/382-9200; fax 307/362-1064; res 800/465-4329. Email paanselm@wyoming.com; www.holiday-inn.com.* 113 rms, 4 story, 1 suite. Apr-Sep: S, D $83; suites $106; lower rates rest of yr. Crib avail. Pet accepted, some restrictions, fee. Parking lot. Indoor pool, children's pool. TV; cable. Complimentary coffee in rms, newspaper, toll-free calls. Restaurant 6 am-10 pm. Bar. Ck-out noon, ck-in 2 pm. Meeting rms. Fax servs avail. Bellhops. Dry cleaning, coin lndry. Free airport transportation. Exercise equipt. Golf, 18 holes. Cr cds: A, D, DS, JCB, MC, V.

🄳 🏊 🎿 🖥 🛁 🚶 🛁

Restaurant

★ **LOG INN.** *W Purple Sage Rd (82901), I-80 Flaming Gorge Exit 99. 307/362-7166. Email loginn@iopener. net.* Steak menu. Specializes in deep-fried lobster, barbecued ribs, blackened prime rib steaks. Hrs: 5:30-10 pm; Sun 5-9 pm. Closed hols. Res accepted. Bar. Dinner $11.50-$22.50.

Log bldg; rustic decor. Cr cds: A, D, DS, MC, V.

Sheridan

(B-4) *See also Buffalo*

Founded 1882 **Pop** 13,900
Elev 3,745 ft **Area code** 307
Zip 82801 **Web** visitsheridan.com
Information Convention and Visitors Bureau, PO Box 7155; 307/672-2485 or 800/453-3650

Sheridan, named for General Philip Sheridan, was not settled until the Cheyenne, Sioux, and Crow were subdued after a series of wars in the region. While the land, rich with grass, was ideal for grazing livestock, ranchers only moved in their herds after the tribes were driven onto reservations. For years the town had a reputation for trouble because of rustling and boundary disputes. Nevertheless, the first dude ranch in history was established near Sheridan in 1904.

Today, the town is a tourist center with dude ranches, hotels and motels, and sporting facilities. The nearby Big Horn Range, once a favored hunting ground of Native Americans, is rich in big game and fishing. A Ranger District office of the Bighorn National Forest is located in Sheridan.

What to See and Do

✪ **Bighorn National Forest.** The Big Horn Mts rise abruptly from the arid basins below to elevations of more than 13,000 ft. Fallen City, a jumble of huge rock blocks, is viewed from US 14, as are Sibley Lake and Shell Canyon and Falls. From Burgess Junction, US 14A passes by Medicine Mt, site of the "medicine wheel," an ancient circular structure. US 16 features Meadowlark Lake and panoramic views of Tensleep Canyon and the 189,000-acre Cloud Peak Wilderness. Forest has resorts, campgrounds (fee), backpacking and horseback trails, skiing at Antelope Butte Ski Area (60 mi W on US 14)

and High Park Ski Area (40 mi E of Worland). Fishing; hunting, cross-country skiing, snowmobiling. Contact the Forest Supervisor, 1969 S Sheridan Ave. More than 1,100,000 acres W and S of town, traversed by 3 scenic byways; US 14 (Bighorn Scenic Byway), US 14A (Medicine Wheel Passage); and US 16 (Cloud Peak Skyway). Phone 307/672-0751.

Bradford Brinton Memorial. Historic ranch house built in 1892; purchased in 1923 by Bradford Brinton and enlarged to its present 20 rms. Contains collections and furnishings that make this a memorial to the art and history of the West. More than 600 oils, watercolors, and sketches by American artists incl Russell and Remington. Also bronzes, prints, and rare books, ranch equipment, saddles, and Native American artifacts. (Mid-May-Labor Day, daily; also early Dec-Dec 24) 7 mi S on US 87, then 5 mi SW on WY 335. Phone 307/672-3173. ¢

King's Saddlery Museum. Collection of saddles; also Western memorabilia, Native American artifacts, old photographs, carriages. (Mon-Sat; closed hols) 184 N Main St, behind store. Phone 307/672-2702. **FREE**

Main Street Historic District. Take a walking tour of Sheridan, which boasts the largest collection of original late-1800s and early-1900s bldgs in the state. Phone 307/672-8881. **FREE**

Trail End Historic Center. Home of John B. Kendrick, Governor of Wyoming (1915-17), later US Senator (1917-33). Historical and family memorabilia. Mansion of Flemish-revival architecture; beautifully carved and burnished woodwork is outstanding. Botanical specimens on landscaped grounds. (Daily; closed hols) 400 Clarendon Ave adj to Kendrick Park. Phone 307/674-4589.

Annual Events

Sheridan-Wyo PRCA Rodeo. Carnival and parade. Mid-July.

Sheridan County Rodeo. Second wkend Aug.

Motels/Motor Lodges

★ ★ **BEST WESTERN SHERIDAN CENTER.** *612 N Main St (82801), (US 14, 87, I-90 Business). 307/674-7421;*

fax 307/672-3018; toll-free 800/528-1234. 138 rms, 2 story. June-Aug: S $69.95; D $79.95; each addl $6; under 12 free; lower rates rest of yr. Crib free. TV; cable. 2 pools, 1 indoor; whirlpool. Complimentary coffee in rms. Restaurant 6:30 am-9:30 pm. Bar noon-midnight. Ck-out 11 am. Meeting rms. Valet serv. Sundries. Free airport, bus depot transportation. Game rm. Some balconies. Cr cds: A, C, D, DS, MC, V.

⌖ ⌖ ⌖ SC

★ **DAYS INN.** *1104 Brundage Ln (82801).* 307/672-2888; fax 307/672-2888. 46 rms, 2 story. June-Aug: S, D $83-$88; each addl $5; suites $100-$150; under 12 free; lower rates rest of yr. Crib free. TV; cable (premium). Indoor pool; whirlpool. Sauna. Complimentary continental bkfst. Restaurant nearby. Ck-out 11 am. Coin lndry. Meeting rms. Near airport. Cr cds: A, D, DS, MC, V.

D ⌖ ⌖ ⌖ ⌖ ⌖ ⌖

B&B/Small Inn

★★★ **SPAHN'S BIG HORN MOUNTAIN BED & BREAKFAST.** *PO Box 579 (82833), I-90 Exit 25 or 33 to Big Horn, continue on WY 335 to end of pavement, then ½ mi on gravel road, follow sign.* 307/674-8150. Email spahn@bighorn-wyoming; www.bighorn-wyoming.com. 2 rms, 2 suites. June-Sep: D $140; each addl $25; children $25; lower rates rest of yr. Crib avail. Parking lot. TV; cable (DSS), VCR avail. Complimentary full bkfst, coffee in rms, toll-free calls. Restaurant. Ck-out 11 am, ck-in 4 pm. Golf. Supervised children's activities. Hiking trail. Cr cds: A, DS, MC, V.

⌖ ⌖ ⌖

Conference Center

★★ **HOLIDAY INN OF SHERIDAN.** *1809 Sugarland Dr (82801), I-90 Exit 25.* 307/672-8931; fax 307/672-6388; res 877/672-4011. Email holinn@cyberhighway.net; www.holiday-inn.com/sheridan. 209 rms, 5 story, 3 suites. May-Sep: S, D $99; suites $250; under 19 free; lower rates rest of yr. Crib avail. Pet accepted. Valet parking avail. Indoor pool, whirlpool. TV; cable (DSS), VCR avail. Complimentary coffee in rms, newspaper. Restaurant 6 am-10 pm. Bar. Ck-out noon, ck-in 3 pm. Meeting rms. Business servs avail. Bellhops. Dry cleaning, coin lndry. Gift shop. Free airport transportation. Exercise equipt, sauna, steam rm. Golf, 18 holes. Downhill skiing. Supervised children's activities. Picnic facilities. Cr cds: A, DS, MC, V.

D ⌖ ⌖ ⌖ ⌖ ⌖ ⌖ ⌖ ⌖ SC

Teton Village

(see Jackson)

Thermopolis

(C-3) *See also Riverton*

Founded 1897 **Pop** 3,247
Elev 4,326 ft **Area code** 307
Zip 82443
Web www.wyoming.com/~hotspot/
Information Chamber of Commerce, PO Box 768; 307/864-3192 or 800/786-6772

The world's largest mineral hot spring is at Thermopolis, which lies in a beautiful section of Big Horn Basin where canyons, tunnels, and buttes abound. The town is surrounded by rich irrigated farm and grazing land.

What to See and Do

Boysen State Park. Surrounded by the Wind River Reservation. Boysen Reservoir is 18 mi long and 3 mi wide. Beach on E shore, waterskiing, fishing for trout and walleye (all yr), boating (ramp, marina); picnicking, restaurant, lodging, tent and trailer sites (standard fees). 16 mi S on US 20. Phone 307/876-2772.

Hot Springs County Museum and Cultural Center. Home of "Hole-in-the-Wall" bar. Displays of arrowheads, minerals, gems; petroleum industry; country schoolhouse, agricultural bldg, railroad caboose, also period rms and costumes. (Mon-Sat; daily; closed hols) 7th & Broadway. Phone 307/864-5183. ¢¢

Hot Springs State Park. Beautiful terraces and mineral cones. Big Horn Spring, a hot mineral spring, pours out millions of gallons every 24 hrs at 135°F. The warm waters pour into the Big Horn River. Mineral swimming pools, indoor and outdoor, public bathhouse (massage avail); terrace walks, picnicking, playgrounds, campgrounds nearby. A state buffalo herd is also quartered here. Across the Big Horn River, 1 mi N on US 20. Phone 307/864-2176.

Wind River Canyon. Formations visible in canyon walls range from early to recent geologic ages. Whitewater rafting (fee). S on US 20.

Wyoming Dinosaur Center. Exhibits mounted dinosaurs and dioramas, fossils, guided tours of excavation sites. (Daily) Carter Ranch Rd. Phone 307/864-2997 or 307/864-3775. ¢¢¢-¢¢¢¢¢

Annual Events

Gift of the Waters Pageant. Hot Springs State Park. Commemorates the deeding of the world's largest mineral hot springs from the Shoshone and Arapahoe to the people of Wyoming in 1896. Pageant features Native American dances, parade, buffalo barbecue. First wkend Aug.

Currier & Ives Winter Festival. Downtown. Town is decorated in 19th-century holiday style. Christmas choir, sleigh rides. Beard contest; cookie contest. Nov-Dec.

Motels/Motor Lodges

★★ **COMFORT INN.** *100 N Rd 11 (82401), on US 16, 10 blks E of Town Center. 307/347-9898; fax 307/347-6734.* 50 rms, 2 story. Mid-June-mid-Aug: S $56-$80; D $64-$76; each addl $8; suites $100-$140; under 18 free; family rates; lower rates rest of yr. Crib avail. Pet accepted, some restrictions; $10. TV; cable (premium), VCR avail (movies). Complimentary continental bkfst. Restaurant nearby. Ck-out 11 am. Meeting rms. Business servs avail. Bellhops. Coin lndry. Airport transportation. Exercise equipt; sauna. Health club privileges. Indoor pool; whirlpool. Some in-rm whirlpools. Cr cds: A, C, D, DS, ER, JCB, MC, V.
Ⓓ 🔧 ♨ 🛗 ≈ 🏋 ♿ 🐾 🔥

★ **SUPER 8.** *Ln 5 Hwy 20 S (82443). 307/864-5515; fax 307/864-5447.* 52 rms, 2 story. June-Sep: S $76.88; D $80.88; each addl $5; suite $150; under 10 free; lower rates rest of yr. Crib $5. TV; cable (premium). Indoor pool; whirlpool. Complimentary coffee in lobby. Restaurant nearby. Ck-out 11 am. Meeting rms. Coin lndry. Cr cds: A, C, D, DS, ER, JCB, MC, V.
Ⓓ ♨ ≈ 🏋 🔥

Torrington (E-7)

Pop 5,651 **Elev** 4,098 ft
Area code 307 **Zip** 82240
Web www.prairieweb.com/goshen_cty_wy/

Information Goshen County Chamber of Commerce, 350 W 21st Ave; 307/532-3879

The town was a way station for the Oregon Trail, the Texas Trail, the Mormon Trail, and the pony express. It is now a livestock marketing center.

What to See and Do

Fort Laramie National Historic Site. (see) 20 mi NW on US 26, then W on WY 160; 3 mi SW of town of Fort Laramie. ¢

Homesteader's Museum. Historical items from the area's homesteading, ranching, and settlement period (1830-1940). Ranch collection, furnished homestead shack; artifacts, photographs, archaeological materials. Changing exhibits. (Summer, daily; winter, Mon-Fri; closed hols). 495 Main St. Phone 307/532-5612. **Donation**

Western History Center. Exhibits on prehistory, archeology, paleontology. Tours to dig sites (fee). (Tues-Sun, also by appt) 5 mi W of Hwy 26. Phone 307/837-3052. **Donation**

Annual Events

Goshen County Fair & Rodeo. Mid-Aug.

Septemberfest. Early Sep.

Motels/Motor Lodges

★ **SUPER 8.** *1548 Main St (82240). 307/532-7118; fax 307/532-7118.* 56

rms, 3 story. No elvtr. June-Sep: S $45; D $52-$58; each addl $5; lower rates rest of yr. Crib $5. TV; cable. Indoor pool; whirlpool. Complimentary coffee in lobby. Restaurant opp 5:30 am-10 pm. Ck-out 11 am. Meeting rm. Cr cds: A, D, DS, MC, V.

Wheatland

(E-6) *See also Cheyenne, Torrington*

Pop 3,271 **Elev** 4,748 ft
Area code 307 **Zip** 82201
Web www.wyoming.com/~platte/
Information Platte County Chamber of Commerce, 65 16th St, PO Box 427; 307/322-2322

The southern edge of Medicine Bow National Forest (see LARAMIE) is 20 miles west.

What to See and Do

Glendo State Park. Rising out of Glendo Resevoir's E side at Sandy Beach are a series of sand dunes, some reaching from the Great Divide Basin to the sand hills in Nebraska. Chips, scrapers, and arrowheads dating back 8,000 yrs are sometimes found. Abundant wildlife. Near historic crossings. Swimming, waterskiing, fishing, boating (marina, ramp, rentals); hunting, picnicking, restaurant, grocery, lodging, tent and trailer sites (standard fees). N on I-25. Phone 307/735-4433.

Guernsey State Park. On the shores of Guernsey Reservoir; high bluffs surround the park with Laramie Peak on the west. Surrounding area is rich in historical interest incl the Oregon Trail. Museum (mid-May-Labor Day, daily; free) has exhibits on early settlers, the Oregon Trail, geology. Park offers swimming, waterskiing; camping (standard fees). Some facilities may be closed Nov-Apr. 12 mi N on I-25, then 12 mi E on US 26, then N on WY 317. Phone 307/836-2334. Per vehicle ¢¢

Annual Events

Chugwater Chili Cookoff. Diamond Guest Ranch. Music, dancing, food. Family activities. Phone 307/322-2322. Second Sat June.

Guernsey Old Timer's & Street Dance. Parade, barbecue. July 3-4.

Summer Fun Fest and Antique Tractor Pull. Phone 307/322-2322. Second Sat July.

Platte County Fair and Rodeo. Incl parade, livestock sale, barbecue, pig wrestling. Phone 307/322-9504. Early Aug.

Motel/Motor Lodge

★★ **BEST WESTERN TORCHLITE INN.** *1809 N 16th St (82201).* 307/322-4070; fax 307/322-4072; res 900/528-1234; toll-free 800/662-3968. 50 rms, 2 story. S $40-$75; D $45-$75; each addl $5. Crib $8. Pet accepted. TV; cable (premium). Ck-out 11 am. Business servs avail. Airport transportation. Refrigerators. Cr cds: A, DS, MC, V.

Yellowstone National Park

See also Cody; also see West Yellowstone, MT

Pop 350 (est) **Area code** 307
Zip 82190

In 1872, the US Congress set aside more than 3,000 square miles of wilderness in the Wyoming Territory, establishing the world's first national park. More than a century later, Yellowstone boasts a marvelous list of sights, attractions, and facilities: A large freshwater lake, the highest in the nation (7,733 feet); a waterfall almost twice as high as Niagara, a dramatic, 1,200-foot-deep river canyon; and the world's most famous geyser—Old Faithful.

Most of the park has been left in its natural state, preserving the area's beauty and delicate ecological balance. The widespread fires at Yellowstone in 1988 were the greatest

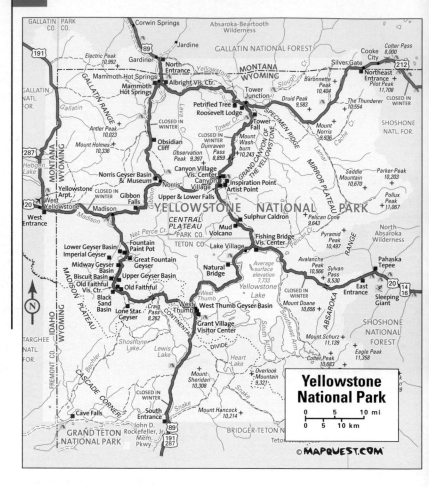

ecological event in the more than 100-year history of the park. Although large areas of forest land were affected, park facilities and attractions remained generally undamaged. Yellowstone is one of the world's most successful wildlife sanctuaries. Within its boundaries live a variety of species, including grizzly and black bears, elk, deer, pronghorn, and bison. Although it is not unusual to encounter animals along park roads, they are more commonly seen along backcountry trails and in more remote areas. Never approach, feed, or otherwise disturb any wild animal. Visitors should stay in their cars with the windows up if approached by wildlife. Animals may look friendly but are unpredictable.

The Grand Loop Road, a main accessway within the park, winds approximately 140 miles past many major points of interest. Five miles south of the North Entrance is Mammoth Hot Springs, the park headquarters and museum (year-round). The visitor center provides a general overview of the history of the park. High terraces with water spilling from natural springs are nearby. Naturalist-guided walks are conducted on boardwalks over the terraces (summer).

The Norris Geyser Basin is 21 miles directly south of Mammoth Hot Springs. The hottest thermal basin in the world provides a multitude of displays; springs, geysers, mud pots, and steam vents hiss, bubble, and erupt in a showcase of thermal forces at work. The visitor center has self-explanatory exhibits and dioramas (June-Labor Day, daily). A self-guided trail (2½ miles) offers views of the Porcelain and Back basins from boardwalks (mid-June-Labor Day). The Museum of the National Park Ranger is also nearby.

At Madison, 14 miles southwest of Norris, the West Entrance Road (US 20/91 outside the park) joins the Grand Loop Road. Heading south of Madison, it is a 16-mile trip to Old Faithful. Along the route are four thermal spring areas; numerous geysers, mud pots, and pools provide an appropriate prologue to the spectacle ahead. Old Faithful has not missed a performance in the more than 100 years since eruptions were first recorded. Eruptions occur on the average of every 75 minutes, although intervals have varied from 30 to 120 minutes. A nearby visitor center provides information, exhibits, and a film and slide program (May-Oct, mid-Dec-mid-Mar, daily).

From Old Faithful it is 17 miles east to West Thumb. Yellowstone Lake, the highest natural freshwater lake in the United States, is here. Early explorers thought that the shape of the lake resembled a hand-with the westernmost bay forming its thumb. A variety of rare species of waterfowl make their home along its 110 miles of shoreline. The 22-mile road from the South Entrance on the John D. Rockefeller Jr Memorial Parkway (US 29/287 outside the park) meets the Grand Loop Road here.

Northeast of West Thumb, about 19 miles up the western shore of Yellowstone Lake, the road leads to Lake Village and then to Fishing Bridge. Although fishing is not permitted at Fishing Bridge (extending one mile downstream, to the north and one-quarter mile upstream, to the south of Fishing Bridge), the numerous lakes and rivers in the park make Yellowstone an angler's paradise. At Fishing Bridge the road splits—27 miles east is the East Entrance from US 14/16/20, 16 miles north is Canyon Village. Canyon Village is near Upper Falls (109-ft drop) and the spectacular Lower Falls (308-ft drop). The colorful and awesome Grand Canyon of the Yellowstone River can be viewed from several points; there are self-guided trails along the rim and naturalist-led walks (summer). Groomed cross-country ski trails are open in winter. Museum (mid-May-late Sep, daily).

Sixteen miles north of Canyon Village is Tower. Just south of Tower Junction is the 132-ft Tower Fall, which can best be observed from a platform at the end of the path leading from the parking lot. The Northeast Entrance on US 212 is 29 miles east of Tower; Mammoth Hot Springs is 18 miles west.

The rest of the park is wilderness, with more than 1,100 miles of marked foot trails. Some areas may be closed for resource management purposes; inquire at one of the visitor centers in the area before hiking in backcountry. Guided tours of the wilderness can be made on horseback; horse rentals are available at Mammoth Hot Springs, Roosevelt, and Canyon Village.

Do not pick wildflowers or collect any natural objects. Read all regulations established by the National Park Service and comply with them—they are for the protection of all visitors as well as for the protection of park resources.

Recreational vehicle campsites are available by reservation at Fishing Bridge RV Park (contact TW Recreational Services, Inc, at 307/344-7901 for general information or 307/344-7311 for reservations). During July and August, demand often exceeds supply and many sites are occupied by mid-morning. Overnight vehicle camping or stopping outside designated campgrounds is not permitted. Reservations for Bridge Bay, Canyon, Madison, Grant Village, as well as Fishing Bridge RV Park. There are seven additional National Park Service campgrounds at Yellowstone; these are operated on a first-come, first-served basis, so it is advisable to arrive early to secure the site of your choice. Campfires are prohibited except in designated areas or by special permit obtained at ranger stations. Backcountry camping is available by permit only, no more than 48 hours in advance, in person, at ranger stations. Backcountry sites can be reserved for a $15 fee.

Fishing in Yellowstone National Park requires a permit. Anglers 16 years and older require a $10/10-day or $20/season permit. Rowboats, powerboats, and tackle may be rented at Bridge Bay Marina. Permits are also required for all vessels (seven-day permit: motorized, $10; nonmotorized, $5) and must be obtained in person at any of the following locations: South Entrance, Bridge Bay Marina, Mammoth Visitor Center, Grant Village Visitor Center, Lake Ranger Station, and Lewis Lake Campground. Information centers near Yellowstone Lake are located at Fishing Bridge and Grant Village (both Memorial Day-Labor Day, daily).

At several locations there are visitor centers, general stores for provisions, photo shops, service stations, tent and trailer sites, hotels, and lodges. There are bus tours through the park from mid-June to Labor Day (contact AmFac Parks and Resorts at 307/344-7311). Cars can be rented in some of the gateway communities.

CCInc Auto Tape Tours, two 90-minute cassettes, offer a mile-by-mile self-guided tour of the park. Written in cooperation with the National Park Service, it provides information on geology, history, points of interest, and flora and fauna. Tapes may be obtained at gift shops throughout the park. Tapes also may be purchased directly from CCInc, PO Box 227, 2 Elbrook Dr, Allendale, NJ 07401; 201/236-1666. ¢¢¢¢

TourGuide Self-Guided Car Audio Tours. Produced in cooperation with the National Park Service, this system uses the random-access capability of CD technology to instantly select narration on topics like wildlife, ecology, safety, history, and folklore. Visitors rent a self-contained player (about the size of a paperback book) that plugs into a car's cigarette lighter and broadcasts an FM signal to its radio. A screen on the unit displays menus of chapters and topics, which may be played in any order for an individualized, narrated auto tour (total running time approx 5 hrs). Players may be rented by contacting AmFac Parks and Resorts at 301/344-7311. For further information contact TIS, Inc, 1018 Burlington Ave, Suite 101, Missoula, MT 59801; 406/549-3800 or 800/247-1213. Per day ¢¢¢¢

The official park season is May 1-October 31. However, US 212 from Red Lodge, MT to Cooke City, MT (outside the Northeast Entrance) is not open to automobiles until about May 30 and closes about October 1. In winter, roads from Gardiner to Mammoth Hot Springs and to Cooke City, MT are kept open, but the road from Red Lodge is closed;

Morning Glory Pool, Yellowstone National Park

travelers must return to Gardiner to leave the park. The west, east, and south entrances are closed to automobiles from November 1 to about May 1, but are open to oversnow vehicles from mid-December-mid-March. Dates are subject to change. For current road conditions and other information, phone park headquarters at 307/344-7381. Entrance permit, $20/vehicle/visit, good for seven days to Yellowstone and Grand Teton.

Note: Weather conditions or conservation measures may dictate the closing of certain roads and recreational facilities. In winter, inquire before attempting to enter the park.

Motels/Motor Lodges

★ **CANYON LODGE CABINS.** *PO Box 165 (82190), 18 mi E of Old Faithful, then 2 mi S of Loop Rd on Yellowstone Lake. 307/344-7311; fax 307/ 344-7456. Email reserve@travelyellow stone.com; www.travelyellowstone.com.* 300 rms in 6 bldgs, 2 story. No A/C. Late May-Sep: S, D $85-$105; each addl $9; under 12 free. Closed rest of yr. Restaurant 6:30 am-10 pm. Bar 5 pm-midnight. Ck-out 11 am. Coin lndry. Meeting rms. Gift shop. On lake. Cr cds: A, D, MC, V.
[D] ⊠ 🅱

★ **CASCADE LODGE AT CANYON VILLAGE.** *Yellowstone National Park (82190), on Loop Rd at Canyon Village. 307/344-7311; fax 307/344-7456. Email reservations@ynp-lodges.com; www.ynp-lodges.com.* 35 rms, 3 story. No A/C. No elvtr. No rm phones. Early June-mid-Sep: S, D $106; each addl $9; under 9 free. Crib avail. Restaurant nearby. Ck-out 11 am. Sundries. Gift shop. Coin lndry. Cr cds: A, D, DS, JCB, MC, V.
[D] ⊠ 🅱

Hotel

★ **MAMMOTH HOT SPRINGS HOTEL AND CABINS.** *PO Box 165 (82190), 5 mi S of N Entrance on Loop Rd in Park. 307/344-7311; fax 307/344-7456. Email reserve@travel yellowstone.com; www.travelyellow stone.com.* 97 rms, 69 baths, 4 story, 126 cabins, 75 baths. No A/C. Late May-mid-Sep: S, D $45-$115; each

addl $9; suites $255; cabins $120; under 12 free; lower rates rest of yr. Closed Oct-Nov and Mar-Apr. Crib free. Restaurant opp 7 am-10 pm. No rm serv. Bar 11:30 am-midnight. Ck-out 11 am. Meeting rm. Gift shop. X-country ski on site. Cr cds: A, DS, MC, V.

Resorts

★★★ **LAKE YELLOWSTONE HOTEL.** *Yellowstone National Park (82190), ½ mi S of Lake jct on Loop Rd in Park. 307/344-7311; fax 307/344-7456. Email reserve@travelyellowstone. com; www.travelyellowstone.com.* 194 rms. No A/C. Late May-late Sep: S, D $100-$152; each addl $9; suite $390; under 12 free. Closed rest of yr. Crib free. Restaurant (see LAKE YELLOWSTONE DINING ROOM). No rm serv. Bar 11:30 am-midnight. Ck-out 11 am. Overlooks Yellowstone Lake. Cr cds: A, D, MC, V.
⊠ 🅱

★★ **OLD FAITHFUL INN.** *PO Box 165 (82190), adj to Old Faithful Geyser in Park. 307/344-7311; fax 307/344-7456. Email reserve@travelyellowstone .com; www.travelyellowstone.com.* 325 rms, 246 baths, 1-4 story. No A/C. Many rm phones. Early May-mid-Oct: S, D $55-$150; each addl $9; suites $330; under 12 free. Closed rest of yr. Crib free. Restaurant 6:30-10 am, 11:30 am-2:30 pm, 5-9:45 pm. No rm serv. Bar 11:30 am-midnight. Ck-out 11 am. Some refrigerators. Some rms have view of Old Faithful. Historic log structure (1904). Cr cds: A, D, MC, V.
⊠ 🅱

Restaurant

★★ **LAKE YELLOWSTONE DINING ROOM.** *307/344-7311. Email chef@imt.net; www.ynp-lodges.com.* Specializes in sauteed salmon, broiled duck, roasted tenderloin. Hrs: 6:30-10 am, 11:30 am-2:30 pm, 5-10 pm. Closed Oct-May. Res accepted. Bar. Bkfst $2.75-$5.95. Buffet: $6.75; lunch $3.75-$8.95; dinner $10.95-$18.95. Child's menu. Entertainment: string quartet; pianist. Overlooks lake. Cr cds: A, D, DS, MC, V.
[D]

CANADA

Just north of the United States, with which it shares the world's longest undefended border, lies Canada, the world's largest country in terms of land area. Extending from the North Pole to the northern border of the United States and including all the islands from Greenland to Alaska, Canada's area encompasses nearly four million square miles (10.4 million square kilometers). The northern reaches of the country consist mainly of the Yukon and Northwest territories, which make up the vast, sparsely populated Canadian frontier.

Jacques Cartier erected a cross at Gaspé in 1534 and declared the establishment of New France. Samuel de Champlain founded Port Royal in Nova Scotia in 1604. Until 1759 Canada was under French rule. In that year, British General Wolfe defeated French General Montcalm at Québec and British possession followed. In 1867 the British North America Act established the Confederation of Canada, with four provinces: New Brunswick, Nova Scotia, Ontario, and Québec. The other provinces joined later. Canada was proclaimed a self-governing Dominion within the British Empire in 1931. The passage in 1981 of the Constitution Act severed Canada's final legislative link with Great Britain, which had until that time reserved the right to amend the Canadian Constitution.

Population: 31,006,347
Area: 6,181,778 square miles (9,970,610 square kilometers)
Peak: Mount Logan, Yukon Territory, 19,850 feet (6,050 meters)
Capital: Ottawa
Speed Limit: 50 or 60 MPH (80 or 100 KPH), unless otherwise indicated

Today, Canada is a sovereign nation—neither a colony nor a possession of Great Britain. Since Canada is a member of the Commonwealth of Nations, Queen Elizabeth II, through her representative, the Governor-General, is the nominal head of state. However, the Queen's functions are mostly ceremonial with no political power or authority. Instead, the nation's chief executive is the prime minister; the legislative branch consists of the Senate and the House of Commons.

Visitor Information

Currency. The American dollar is accepted throughout Canada, but it is advisable to exchange your money into Canadian currency upon arrival. Banks and currency exchange firms typically give the best rate of exchange, but hotels and stores will also convert it for you with purchases. The Canadian monetary system is based on dollars and cents, and rates in *Mobil Travel Guide* are given in Canadian currency. Generally, the credit cards you use at home are also honored in Canada.

Goods and Services Tax (GST). Most goods and services in Canada are subject to a 7% tax. Visitors to Canada may claim a rebate of the GST paid on *short-term accommodations* (hotel, motel, or similar lodging) and on *most consumer goods* purchased to take home. Rebates may be claimed for cash at participating Canadian Duty Free shops or by mail. For further information and a brochure detailing rebate procedures and restrictions contact Visitors' Rebate Program, Revenue Canada, Summerside Tax Center, Summerside, PE C1N 6C6; phone 613/991-3346 or 800/66-VISIT (in Canada).

Driving in Canada. Your American driver's license is valid in Canada; no special permit is required. In Canada the liter is the unit of measure for gasoline. One US gallon equals 3.78 liters. Traffic signs are clearly understood and in many cities are bilingual. All road speed limits and mileage signs have been posted in kilometers. A flashing green traffic light gives vehicles turning left the right-of-way, like a green left-turn arrow. The use of safety belts is generally

Vermillion Lake, Banff National Park

mandatory in all provinces; consult the various provincial tourism bureaus for specific information.

Holidays. Canada observes the following holidays, and these are indicated in text: New Year's Day, Good Friday, Easter Monday, Victoria Day (usually 3rd Monday May), Canada Day (July 1), Labour Day, Thanksgiving (2nd Monday October), Remembrance Day (November 11), Christmas, and Boxing Day (December 26). See individual provinces for information on provincial holidays.

Liquor. The sale of liquor, wine, beer, and cider varies from province to province. Restaurants must be licensed to serve liquor, and in some cases liquor may not be sold unless it accompanies a meal. Generally there are no package sales on holidays. Minimum legal drinking age also varies by province. **Note:** It is illegal to take children into bars or cocktail lounges.

Daylight Saving Time. Canada observes Daylight Saving Time beginning the first Sunday in April through the last Sunday in October, except for most of the province of Saskatchewan, where Standard Time is observed year-round.

Tourist information is available from individual provincial and territorial tourism offices (see Border Crossing Regulations in MAKING THE MOST OF YOUR TRIP).

PROVINCE OF ALBERTA

With a history of ancient indigenous civilizations, missionary settlements, fur trading, "gold fever," and frontier development, Alberta thrives today as a vital industrial, agricultural, and recreational center. It possesses the widest variety of geographical features of any province in Canada, including a giant plateau "badlands" rich in dinosaur fossils, rolling prairie, and vast parkland. All along its western border are the magnificent Canadian Rockies.

Pop 2,513,100 **Land area** 246,423 sq mi (661,185 sq km) **Capital** Edmonton **Web** www.discoveralberta. com

Information Travel Alberta, Box 2500, Edmonton T5J 2Z4; 780/427-4321 or 800/661-8888

Easily accessible from Montana, visitors can enter Alberta from Waterton Lakes National Park and drive north to Calgary, where they intersect with the Trans-Canada Highway and can enjoy a variety of attractions. The view of the Rockies from the Calgary Tower and the excitement of the Calgary Stampede are not to be missed.

From Calgary drive northwest to Banff, Lake Louise, and Jasper National Park for some of the finest mountain scenery, outdoor activities, resorts, and restaurants on the continent.

Heading due north from Calgary visit Red Deer, a town famous for agriculture, oil, and its beautiful parkland setting. Farther north is the provincial capital, Edmonton. A confident, multicultural city, it is noted for its oil, its "gold rush" past, and its parks, cultural activities, magnificent sports facilities, and rodeos. Northwest of Edmonton, Alberta provides paved access to "Mile 0" of the Alaska Highway at Dawson Creek, BC. There is also paved access to the Northwest Territories—Canada's "frontier" land.

Drive southeast from Calgary and enter an entirely different scene: cowboy and Indian territory. Fort Macleod brings you back to the early pioneer days. Lethbridge is famous for its replica of the most notorious 19th-century whiskey fort—Fort Whoop-Up—and the Nikka Yuko Japanese Gardens. Farther east visit Medicine Hat, known for its parks, pottery, and rodeos. Alberta is truly a vacation destination for all seasons and tastes.

Alberta observes Mountain Standard Time and Daylight Saving Time in summer. Hunting is not permitted in national or provincial parks and a separate fishing license is required. For information on hunting and fishing in other areas of the province contact the Fish and Wildlife Division, Dept of Forestry, Lands, and Wildlife, 9920 108th St, Edmonton T5K 2C9.

In addition to national holidays, Alberta observes Heritage Day (1st Monday August and Family Day (3rd Monday Feburary).

Safety belts are mandatory for all persons anywhere in vehicle. Children under 6 years or under 40 pounds in weight must be in an approved child safety seat. For further information phone 780/427-8901.

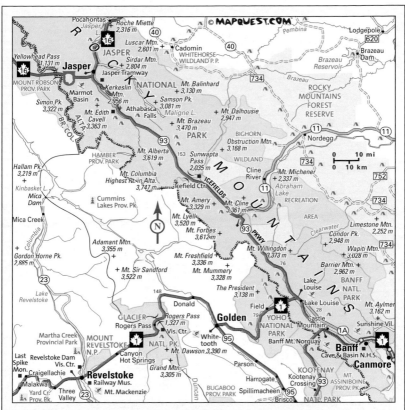

One of the most famous mountain highways in the world, the Icefield Parkway travels between Lake Louise and Jasper, along the crown of the Canadian Rockies. The scenery is absolutely dramatic: soaring peaks still under the bite of glaciers; turquoise green lakes surrounded by deep forests; roaring waterfalls; and, at the very crest of the drive, the Columbia Icefield, the largest nonpolar icecap in the world. Besides the scenery, there are activities and opportunities for recreation. A number of lakeside lodges offer canoe rentals, short horseback trail rides, whitewater rafting trips, and trips onto the Columbia Snowfield in specially designed snowcoaches. Wildlife is also abundant: mountain goats, mountain sheep, elk, moose, and bears are sighted frequently. **(Approx 142 mi; 229 km)**

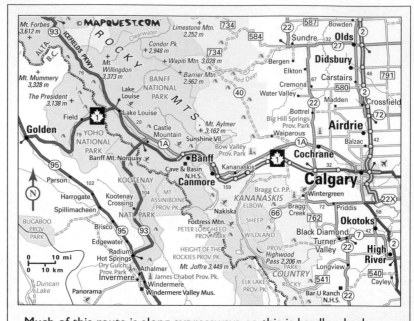

Much of this route is along expressways, so this is hardly a back road. Yet, on the edge of the Canadian prairies, the journey from Calgary up the Bow River valley and into the vastness of the Canadian Rockies is one of dramatically fast and beautiful geological transitions. From Calgary, Highway 1 heads west passing long-established ranches. Consider a stop at the Western Heritage Center at the historic Cochrane Ranch. The Rockies rise up fully grown from the prairies. One minute you're in ranch country, the next you're inside a narrow mountain valley surrounded by 10,000-foot-high peaks. At Canmore, Highway 1 enters Banff National Park, Canada's oldest national park. The town of Banff is a wonderfully scenic mountain town that's also one of the most cosmopolitan small communities in North America (Banff is apparently the single-most popular destination in Canada for foreign visitors). The setting is totally unlikely (how did they fit a town in between all these incredible mountain peaks?), and the amenities are superb. You'll find first-class hotels and dining, as well as the hiking, climbing, fishing, and rafting that you expect in the Rockies. Lake Louise and its smaller cousin, Morraine Lake, are both incredibly beautiful spots: eerily green lakes nestled in a glacial basin directly below the peaks of the Continental Divide. Again, the facilities are great. The Chateau Lake Louise, sitting at the lake's edge, is one of the most famous hotels in Canada. **(Approx 112 mi; 180 km)**

Banff

(F-3) *See also Calgary, Lake Louise*

Pop 6,800 (est) **Elev** 4,538 ft (1,383 m)
Area code 403
Information Banff-Lake Louise
Tourism Bureau, 224 Banff Ave, PO
Box 1298, T0L 0C0; 403/762-8421

Banff came to be because of the popularity of the hot springs in the area. The Banff Hot Springs Reservation was created in 1885 and by 1887 had become Rocky Mountains Park. Today we know this vast recreation area as Banff National Park, offering the visitor activity all year, plus the beauty of the Rocky Mountains.

Banff comes alive each summer with its music and drama festival at Banff Centre. In winter the Rockies provide some of the best skiing on the North American continent, including helicopter, downhill, and cross-country. The town of Banff itself has exciting nightlife, sleigh rides, Western barbecues, and indoor recreational activities. The area offers sightseeing gondola rides, boat and raft tours, concerts, art galleries, museums, hot springs, ice field tours, hiking, and trail rides.

What to See and Do

Cave & Basin Centennial Centre. The birthplace of Canada's national park system and a national historic site. Hot springs, cave, exhibits, trails, theater (daily; closed Jan 1, Dec 25). W on Cave Ave. Phone 403/762-1557. ¢¢

Jasper National Park. (see) 179 mi (287 km) N on Hwy 93.

Natural History Museum. More than 60 displays, slide and film shows depicting the national parks; prehistoric life, precious stones, trees, and flowers, origins of the earth, and formations of mountains and caves. (Daily; closed Dec 25) 112 Banff Ave, upstairs at Clock Tower Mall. Phone 403/762-4652. **FREE**

Sightseeing tours.

    Rocky Mountain Raft Tours. One-hr round-trip excursions (4 trips daily); also 3-hr round-trips (2 trips daily). Trip durations approx; incl transportation time to departure site. (June-mid-Sep) For schedule and fees contact Rocky Mt Raft Tours, PO Box 1771, T0L 0C0. Phone 403/762-3632.

    CCInc Auto Tape Tours. This 90-min cassette offers a mi-by-mi self-guided tour. Written by informed guides, it provides information on history, glaciers, points of interest, and flora and fauna of the area. Tapes are available at The Thunderbird on Banff Ave, opp the park Information Center. Rental incl player and tape: Banff tour or combination Banff/Jasper. Tapes also may be purchased directly from CCInc, PO Box 227, 2 Elbrook Dr, Allendale, NJ 07401. Phone 201/236-1666. ¢¢¢¢

Seasonal Event

Banff Festival of the Arts. St. Julien Rd. Mainstage productions and workshops in opera, ballet, music theater, drama, concerts, poetry reading, visual arts. Some events free. For information contact The Banff Centre Box Office, PO Box 1020, T0L 0C0; 403/762-6300. June-Aug.

Motels/Motor Lodges

★ **AKAI MOTEL.** *1717 Mountain Ave (T1W 2W1), E on Hwy 1. 403/678-4664; fax 403/678-4775; toll-free 877/900-2524.* 41 kit. units. July-Aug: S $75; D $80-$85; each addl $5; under 12 free; family rates; package plans; lower rates rest of yr. Crib free. Pet accepted, some restrictions. TV; cable. Complimentary coffee in lobby. Restaurant nearby. Ck-out 11 am. Bellhops. Downhill ski 15 mi; x-country ski 3 mi. Picnic tables. Cr cds: A, D, ER, MC, V.
🄳 🏊 🐾 ⛷ 🔥

★★ **BANFF VOYAGER INN.** *555 Banff Ave (T0L 0C0). 403/762-3301; fax 403/762-4131; toll-free 800/879-1991. Email res@banffvoyagerinn.com; www.banffvoyagerinn.com.* 87 rms, 2 story, 1 suite. June-Sep: S, D $130; each addl $15; suites $165; under 16 free; lower rates rest of yr. Crib avail. Parking lot. Pool, whirlpool. TV; cable (DSS). Restaurant 7 am-8 pm. Bar. Ck-out 11 am, ck-in 4 pm. Meeting rms. Fax servs avail. Golf. Downhill skiing.

Bike rentals. Hiking trail. Cr cds: A, JCB, MC, V.

[icons]

★★ **BREWSTER'S MOUNTAIN LODGE.** *208 Caribou St (T0L 0W0). 403/762-2900; fax 403/762-2970; res 888/762-2900; toll-free 800/762-2900. Email bml@brewsteradventures.com; www.brewsteradventures.com.* 73 air-cooled rms, 2 story, 15 suites. Mid-June-mid-Oct: S, D $189-$199; each addl $15; suites $275-$350; under 18 free; family rates; package plans; lower rates rest of yr. Crib avail. TV; cable (premium). Complimentary continental bkfst. Restaurant nearby. Bar 4-10 pm. Ck-out 11 am. Meeting rms. Business servs avail. Bellhops. Sundries. Shopping arcade. Downhill/x-country ski 5 mi. Sauna. In-rm whirlpool, refrigerator in suites. Some balconies. Cr cds: A, MC, V.

[icons] SC

★★ **CASTLE MOUNTAIN CHALETS.** *Jct Hwy 1-A, 93 S (T0L 0C0), 18 mi (29 km) E on Trans-Can Hwy 1, N of Castle Junction, in Banff National Park. 403/522-2783; fax 403/762-8629. Email info@castlemountain.com.* 19 kit. cottages, 2 with shower only, 12 suites. No A/C. No rm phones. S, D $175-$250. Crib $5. Pet accepted; $20. TV. Restaurant nearby. Ck-out 10:30 am. Coin lndry. Gift shop. Grocery store. Downhill ski 20 mi; x-country ski on site. Exercise equipt. Some in-rm whirlpools, fireplaces. Cr cds: A, MC, V.

[icons]

★ **CHARLTON'S CEDAR COURT.** *513 Banff Ave (T0L 0C0). 403/762-4485; fax 403/762-2744; res 800/661-1225. Email banff@charltonresorts.com.* 63 rms, 3 story, 16 kits. No A/C. June-Sep: S, D $170-$190; each addl $15; kit. units $190; under 16 free; lower rates rest of yr. Crib free. TV; cable. Indoor pool; whirlpool, steam rm. Complimentary coffee in rms. Restaurant nearby. Ck-out 11 am. Business servs avail. Free covered parking. Downhill ski 2 mi; x-country ski 1 mi. Cr cds: A, D, ER, JCB, MC, V.

[icons]

★★ **DYNASTY INN.** *501 Banff Ave (T0L 0C0). 403/762-8844; fax 403/762-4418; toll-free 800/667-1464.* 98 rms, 3 story. Mid-June-late Sep: S, D $155-$205; each addl $15; under 12 free; ski plan; lower rates rest of yr. Crib free. Garage parking. TV; cable. Restaurant nearby. Ck-out 11 am. Business servs avail. Bellhops. Downhill/x-country ski 3 mi. Sauna. Whirlpool. Balconies. Cr cds: MC, V.

[icons]

★★ **IRWIN'S MOUNTAIN INN.** *429 Banff Ave (T0L 0C0). 403/762-4566; fax 403/762-8220; toll-free 800/661-1721. Email irwins@banff.net; www.banff.net/irwins.* 65 rms, 3 story. No A/C. June-Sep: S $125; D $125-$195; each addl $10; suites $140-$215; under 16 free; lower rates rest of yr. Crib free. TV; cable (premium). Whirlpool. Complimentary coffee in rms. Restaurant 7-11 am, 5-11 pm. Ck-out 11 am. Meeting rms. Business servs avail. Gift shop. Valet serv. Coin lndry. Downhill ski 5 mi; x-country ski 1 mi. Exercise equipt; sauna. Some refrigerators. Cr cds: A, MC, V.

[icons]

★★★ **QUALITY RESORT - CHATEAU CANMORE.** *1720 Bow Valley Tr (T1W 2X3). 403/678-6699; fax 403/678-6954; res 800/424-6423; toll-free 800/261-8551. www.chateaucanmore.com.* 120 suites, 3 story. June-Oct: S, D $159-$189; kit. units $219-$249; under 18 free; lower rates rest of yr. Crib free. TV; VCR (movies). Indoor pool; whirlpool. Sauna. Playground. Supervised children's activities (July-Aug); ages 7-15. Complimentary coffee in rms. Restaurant 6 am-11 pm. Bar to 1 am. Ck-out 11 am. Meeting rms. Business servs avail. Lighted tennis. Downhill ski 18 mi; x-country ski 1 mi. Bicycles rental. Refrigerators, microwaves. Some balconies. Cr cds: A, DS, ER, JCB, MC, V.

[icons]

★ **RED CARPET INN.** *PO Box 1800 (T0L 0C0). 403/762-4184; fax 403/762-4894; toll-free 800/563-4609.* 52 rms, 3 story. No A/C. June-mid-Oct: S $100-$125; D $140-$150; lower rates rest of yr. Crib avail. Pet accepted. TV; VCR avail. Restaurant adj 7 am-11 pm. Business servs avail. Free garage parking. Whirlpool (winter only). Balconies. Cr cds: A, MC, V.

[icons]

★ **RUNDLE MOUNTAIN MOTEL.** *1723 Bow Valley Tr (T1W 1L7),*

15 mi E on Hwy 1, Canmore Exit, on Mountain Ave. 403/678-5322; fax 403/678-5813; res 800/661-1610. Email moreinfo@rundlemountain.com. 51 rms, 2 story, 14 suites, 18 kit. units. No A/C. Mid-June-mid-Sep: S, D $113; each addl $10; suites $235; kit. units $143; family, wkly rates; ski plans; lower rates rest of yr. TV; cable. Indoor pool; whirlpool. Playground. Complimentary coffee in rms. Restaurant 7 am-10 pm. Ck-out 11 am. Meeting rms. Refrigerators. Picnic tables. Cr cds: A, D, ER, MC, V.

Banff Avenue

Hotels

★★ **BANFF INTERNATIONAL.** *333 Banff Ave (T0L 0C0). 403/762-5666; fax 403/760-3281; toll-free 800/665-5666. Email banffih@banff.net; www. banffinternational.com.* 165 rms, 3 story. June-Sep: S, D $199; each addl $20; under 16 free; lower rates rest of yr. Crib avail. Pet accepted, fee. Parking garage. TV; cable (DSS). Complimentary coffee in rms. Restaurant 7 am-10 pm. Bar. Ck-out 11 am, ck-in 4 pm. Business servs avail. Bellhops. Concierge. Dry cleaning, coin lndry. Gift shop. Exercise equipt, sauna, steam rm, whirlpool. Golf. Tennis, 6 courts. Downhill skiing. Hiking trail. Video games. Cr cds: A, JCB, MC, V.

★★ **BANFF PARK LODGE.** *222 Lynx St (T0L 0C0). 403/762-4433; fax 403/762-3553; toll-free 800/661-9266.*

Email info@banffparklodge.com; www. banffparklodge.com. 198 rms, 3 story, 13 suites. June-Sep: S, D $239; each addl $15; suites $339; under 15 free; lower rates rest of yr. Crib avail. Valet parking avail. Indoor pool, whirlpool. TV; cable. Restaurant. Bar. Ck-out 11 am, ck-in 4 pm. Meeting rms. Business servs avail. Bellhops. Concierge. Dry cleaning. Gift shop. Salon/barber. Exercise privileges, steam rm. Golf. Tennis, 10 courts. Downhill skiing. Bike rentals. Hiking trail. Cr cds: A, D, ER, JCB, MC, V.

★★ **BANFF PTARMIGAN INN.** *337 Banff Ave (T0L 0C0). 403/762-2207; fax 403/762-3577; toll-free 800/661-8310. Email reservations@banff-caribou properties.com; www.banffcaribou properties.com.* 134 rms, 3 story. June-Oct: S, D $195; each addl $15; under 16 free; lower rates rest of yr. Crib avail. Parking garage. TV; cable. Complimentary coffee in rms. Restaurant. Bar. Ck-out 11 am, ck-in 4 pm. Meeting rm. Fax servs avail. Bellhops. Concierge. Dry cleaning. Gift shop. Exercise equipt, sauna, steam rm, whirlpool. Golf. Tennis. Downhill skiing. Bike rentals. Hiking trail. Cr cds: A, D, JCB, MC, V.

★★★ **BANFF SPRINGS.** *405 Spray Ave (T0L 0C0). 403/762-2211; fax 403/762-5755; res 800/866-5577. www.fairmont.com.* 770 rms, 9 story. No A/C. June-Aug: S, D $325-$390; each addl $21; suites $540-$975; under 18 free; lower rates rest of yr. Crib free. Pet accepted; $20. Garage $7/day, valet $11. TV; cable. 2 pools, 1 indoor; 2 whirlpools. Restaurant (see also BANFF SPRINGS). Bar noon-1 am. Ck-out noon. Convention facilities. Business center. Concierge. Shopping arcade. Barber, beauty shop. Tennis, pro. 27-hole golf, greens fee $65-$105, pro, putting green, driving range. Downhill ski 2 mi. Exercise equipt; sauna. Bowling. Rec rm. Mini-bars. Picnic tables. Cr cds: A, C, D, DS, ER, JCB, MC, V.

★★ BEST WESTERN GREEN GABLES INN. *1602 2nd Ave (T1W 1M8), 15 mi E on Hwy 1, at Canmore Exit. 403/678-5488; fax 403/678-2670; res 800/528-1234; toll-free 800/661-2133. Email g_gables@telusplanet.net; www.bestwestern.com/ca/greengables.* 60 rms, 2 story, 1 suite. June-Sep: S, D $149; each addl $10; suites $199; under 17 free; lower rates rest of yr. Parking lot. TV; cable. Complimentary continental bkfst, coffee in rms, newspaper, toll-free calls. Restaurant 7 am-10 pm. Bar. Ck-out 11 am, ck-in 4 pm. Meeting rms. Business servs avail. Dry cleaning. Exercise equipt, steam rm, whirlpool. Golf. Downhill skiing. Bike rentals. Hiking trail. Picnic facilities. Cr cds: A, C, D, ER, MC, V.

★★ BEST WESTERN SIDING 29 LODGE. *453 Marten St (T0L 0C0). 403/762-5575; fax 403/762-8866; res 800/528-1234. Email info@bestwestern banff.com; www.bestwesternbanff.com.* 45 rms, 3 story, 12 suites. June-Sep, Dec: S, D $195; each addl $10; suites $275; under 12 free; lower rates rest of yr. Crib avail. Pet accepted. Parking garage. Indoor pool, whirlpool. TV; cable. Complimentary coffee in rms. Restaurant nearby. Ck-out 11 am, ck-in 4 pm. Business center. Golf. Downhill skiing. Cr cds: A, D, DS, ER, JCB, MC, V.

★ HIDDEN RIDGE CHALETS. *901 Coyote Dr (T0L 0C0), at Tunnel Mt Rd. 403/762-3544; fax 403/762-2804; toll-free 800/661-1372.* 84 rms, 1 story. June-Sep, Dec: S, D $240; each addl $15; under 16 free; lower rates rest of yr. Crib avail. Parking garage. TV; cable. Restaurant nearby. Ck-out 11 am, ck-in 4 pm. Fax servs avail. Concierge. Dry cleaning. Whirlpool. Golf. Downhill skiing. Hiking trail. Picnic facilities. Cr cds: A, D, DS, ER, JCB, MC, V.

★★ HIGH COUNTRY INN. *419 Banff Ave (T0L 0C0). 403/762-2236;* fax 403/762-5084; toll-free 800/661-1244. Email highcinn@telusplanet.net; www.banffhighcountryinn.com.* 60 rms, 3 story, 10 suites. June-Sep: S, D $150; each addl $10; suites $220; under 12 free; lower rates rest of yr. Crib avail, fee. Parking garage. Indoor pool, whirlpool. TV; cable (DSS). Complimentary coffee in rms, toll-free calls. Restaurant 7:30 am-11 pm. Bar. Ck-out 11 am, ck-in 4 pm. Meeting rms. Business servs avail. Bellhops. Dry cleaning, coin lndry. Exercise privileges, sauna. Golf. Downhill skiing. Hiking trail. Cr cds: A, MC, V.

★★ INNS OF BANFF. *600 Banff Ave (T0L 0C0). 403/762-4581; fax 403/762-2434; toll-free 800/661-1272. Email resrv@innsofbanff.com; www.innsofbanff.com.* 180 rms, 5 story. Feb-Mar, June-Sep: S, D $235; each addl $20; under 16 free; lower rates rest of yr. Crib avail. Parking garage. Indoor/outdoor pools, whirlpool. TV; cable. Complimentary coffee in rms. Restaurant 7 am-10 pm. Bar. Ck-out 11 am, ck-in 4 pm. Meeting rms. Business servs avail. Bellhops. Concierge. Dry cleaning, coin lndry. Gift shop. Salon/barber. Sauna. Golf. Tennis. Downhill skiing. Bike rentals. Cr cds: A, D, ER, JCB, MC, V.

★★ MOUNT ROYAL. *138 Banff Ave (T0L 0C0). 403/762-3331; fax 403/762-8938; toll-free 800/267-3035. Email info@mountroyalhotel.com; www.mountroyalhotel.com.* 136 rms, 3 story, 10 suites. June-Oct: S, D $210; each addl $15; suites $335; under 16 free; lower rates rest of yr. Crib avail. Pet accepted, some restrictions, fee. Parking lot. TV; cable. Complimentary coffee in rms, newspaper. Restaurant 6:30 am-10 pm. Bar. Ck-out 11 am, ck-in 4 pm. Meeting rms. Business servs avail. Bellhops. Dry cleaning, coin lndry. Salon/barber. Exercise privileges, sauna, whirlpool. Golf. Tennis, 3 courts. Downhill skiing. Cr cds: A, D, JCB, MC, V.

★★★ RIMROCK RESORT. *301 Mountain Ave (T0L 0C0). 403/762-3356; fax 403/762-4132; toll-free 800/661-1587. Email info@rimrockresort. com.* 346 rms, 9 story, 45 suites. May-

Sep: S, D $225-$350; each addl $20; suites $450-$690; under 18 free; ski plan; lower rates rest of yr. Crib free. Garage parking $6; valet $10. TV; cable. Indoor pool; whirlpool, poolside serv. Restaurant (see THE PRIMROSE). Rm serv 24 hrs. Bar. Ck-out noon. Convention facilities. Business servs avail. Concierge. Shopping arcade. Downhill ski 3 mi; x-country ski on site. Exercise rm; sauna. Massage. Health club privileges. Minibars. Balconies Cr cds: A, D, DS, ER, JCB, MC, V.

★★ **RUNDLESTONE LODGE.** *537 Banff Ave (T0L 0C0). 403/762-2201; fax 403/762-4501; toll-free 800/661-8630. Email res@rundlestone.com; www.rundlestone.com.* 96 rms, 30 story, 2 suites. July-Aug: S $165; D $175; suites $280; lower rates rest of yr. Crib avail. Parking garage. Indoor pool, lap pool, whirlpool. TV; cable (premium). Complimentary coffee in rms, newspaper. Restaurant 7 am-10 pm. Bar. Ck-out 11 am, ck-in 3 pm. Meeting rm. Business servs avail. Concierge. Dry cleaning, coin lndry. Exercise equipt. Golf. Tennis. Downhill skiing. Bike rentals. Hiking trail. Cr cds: A, C, D, DS, ER, V.

Resorts

★★ **BANFF CARIBOU LODGE.** *521 Banff Ave (T0L 0C0). 403/762-5887; fax 403/762-5918; toll-free 800/563-8764. Email reservations@ banffcaribouproperties.com; www.banff caribouproperties.com.* 196 rms, 3 story, 4 suites. June-Oct: S, D $195; each addl $15; under 16 free; lower rates rest of yr. Crib avail. Parking garage. TV; cable (DSS). Complimentary coffee in rms. Restaurant 7 am-10 pm. Bar. Ck-out 11 am, ck-in 4 pm. Meeting rm. Bellhops. Concierge. Dry cleaning. Gift shop. Exercise equipt, sauna, steam rm, whirlpool. Golf. Tennis. Downhill skiing. Bike rentals. Hiking trail. Video games. Cr cds: A, D, DS, ER, JCB, MC, V.

★★ **BANFF ROCKY MOUNTAIN RESORT.** *1029 Banff Ave (T0L 0C0), Banff Ave at Tunnel Mt Rd, off Trans-Can Hwy 1. 403/762-5531; fax 403/762-5166; toll-free 800/661-9563.*

Email info@rockymountainresort.com; www.rockymountainresort.com. 36 rms, 2 story, 135 suites. June-Sep, Dec: S, D $240; each addl $15; suites $250; under 16 free; lower rates rest of yr. Crib avail. Pet accepted, some restrictions, fee. Parking lot. Indoor pool, whirlpool. TV; cable. Complimentary coffee in rms. Restaurant 6-9 pm. Bar. Ck-out 11 am, ck-in 5 pm. Meeting rms. Business servs avail. Bellhops. Concierge. Dry cleaning, coin lndry. Exercise equipt, sauna. Golf, 18 holes. Tennis, 2 courts. Downhill skiing. Bike rentals. Supervised children's activities. Hiking trail. Picnic facilities. Video games. Cr cds: A, D, DS, ER, JCB, MC, V.

★★★ **BUFFALO MOUNTAIN LODGE.** *700 Tunnel Mt Rd (T0L 0C0), 5 mi S off Trans-Can Hwy 1 via Moose St, Otter St to Tunnel Mt Rd. 403/762-2400; fax 403/762-4495; res 403/609-6199; toll-free 800/661-1367. Email bml@telusplanet.net; www. crmr.com.* 88 rms, 2 story, 20 suites. June-Sep: D $235; each addl $25; suites $310; lower rates rest of yr. Crib avail. Street parking. TV; cable, VCR avail. Complimentary coffee in rms, newspaper, toll-free calls. Restaurant 6:30 am-10 pm. Bar. Ck-out 11 am, ck-in 4 pm. Meeting rms. Business center. Bellhops. Concierge. Dry cleaning. Exercise equipt, sauna, steam rm, whirlpool. Golf. Downhill skiing. Cr cds: A, D, ER, MC, V.

B&Bs/Small Inns

★★ **BANFF AVENUE INN.** *433 Banff Ave (T0L 0C0). 403/762-4499; fax 403/760-3166; toll-free 888/762-4499. www.banffaveinn.com.* 14 rms, 3 story. No elvtr. Mid-June-Sep: S, D $159-$219; each addl $10; under 12 free; ski plans; lower rates rest of yr. TV; cable. Complimentary coffee in lobby. Restaurant 7-10:30 am, 5:30-10:30 pm. Ck-out 11 am, ck-in 4 pm. Downhill/x-country ski 10 mi. In-rm whirlpools, fireplaces. Many balconies. Contemporary decor. Totally nonsmoking. Cr cds: A, MC, V.

★★ **LADY MACDONALD COUNTRY INN.** *1201 Bow Valley Tr (P1W 1P5), 19 mi E on Hwy 1A. 403/678-3665; fax 403/678-9714; toll-free 800/*

567-3913. www.ladymacdonald.com.
11 rms, 2 story. No A/C. June-Sep
and Dec hols: D $125-$175; each
addl $10; under 12 free; lower rates
rest of yr. TV; cable (premium). Complimentary full bkfst. Restaurant adj
open 24 hrs. Ck-out 11 am. Downhill ski 10 mi; x-country ski 2 blks.
Victorian-style architecture; Shaker
pine furniture. Cr cds: A, MC, V.

★★ NORQUAY'S TIMBERLINE
INN. *PO Box 69 (T0L 0C0), off Trans-
Can Hwy 1 at base of Mt Norquay.
403/762-2281; fax 403/762-8331; toll-
free 877/762-2281. Email info@banff
timberline.com; www.banfftimberline.
com.* 48 rms, 2 story, 2 suites. June-
Sep: S, D $142; each addl $15; suites
$185; under 15 free; lower rates rest of
yr. Crib avail. Pet accepted, some
restrictions, fee. Parking lot. TV; cable
(DSS). Complimentary coffee in rms,
newspaper. Restaurant 7 am-10 pm.
Bar. Ck-out 11 am, ck-in 3 pm. Meeting rms. Business servs avail. Concierge. Dry cleaning. Whirlpool. Golf.
Tennis, 8 courts. Downhill skiing. Bike
rentals. Hiking trail. Picnic facilities.
Cr cds: A, MC, V.

Cottage Colony

★ KANANASKIS GUEST RANCH.
*(T0L 1X0), 60 mi W on Trans-Can
Hwy 1, Exit Hwy 1X. 403/673-3737;
fax 403/673-2100; res 800/691-5085.
www.brewsteradventures.com.* 33 cabins
(1-2-bedrm). No A/C. May-mid-Oct:
D $90-$110; each addl $15; under 12
free. Closed rest of yr. Crib free. TV
lounge. Dining rm 7:30-10:30 am, 6-
8:30 pm. Box lunches. Barbecues. Bar
4 pm-1 am. Ck-out 11 am, ck-in 4
pm. Grocery nearby. Meeting rms.
Business servs avail. Gift shop. Hiking. Trail rides. Whitewater rafting.
Lawn games. Whirlpool. Picnic
tables. On Bow River. Cr cds: A,
MC, V.

All Suite

★★ TUNNEL MOUNTAIN
CHALETS. *Tunnel Mt Rd and Tunnel
Mt Dr (T0L 0C0), 5 mi S of Trans-Can
Hwy 1 Via Moose St, Otter St to Tunnel
Mt Rd. 403/762-4515; fax 403/762-*

5183; toll-free 800/661-1859. Email
info@tunnelmountain.com; www.
tunnelmountain.com.* 24 suites. June-
Sep, Dec: suites $231; each addl $15;
under 15 free; lower rates rest of yr.
Crib avail. Parking garage. Indoor
pool, whirlpool. TV; cable (prmium).
Complimentary coffee in rms, toll-
free calls. Restaurant nearby. Ck-out
11 am, ck-in 4 pm. Meeting rm. Business servs avail. Dry cleaning. Exercise privileges, sauna, steam rm.
Golf. Tennis, 2 courts. Downhill skiing. Cr cds: A, DS, MC, V.

Conference Center

★★★ RADISSON HOTEL AND
CONFERENCE CENTER. *511 Bow
Valley Tr (T1W 1N7), approx 10 mi E
on Hwy 1. 403/678-3625; fax 403/
678-3765; res 800/333-3333.* 214 rms,
3 story, 10 suites. May-Oct: S, D
$189; each addl $10; suites $249;
under 17 free; lower rates rest of yr.
Crib avail. Pet accepted, fee. Parking
lot. Indoor pool, whirlpool. TV;
cable. Complimentary coffee in rms,
newspaper. Restaurant 6:30 am-10
pm. Bar. Ck-out noon, ck-in 4 pm.
Meeting rms. Business center. Bellhops. Dry cleaning, coin lndry. Gift
shop. Exercise equipt, steam rm.
Golf. Tennis, 3 courts. Downhill skiing. Picnic facilities. Cr cds: A, D, DS,
ER, JCB, MC, V.

Villa/Condo

★★★ DOUGLAS FIR RESORT.
*Tunnel Mt Rd (T0L 0C0), 5 mi S of
Trans-Can Hwy 1 via Lynx St, Wolf St
to Tunnel Mt Rd. 403/762-5591; fax
403/762-8774; toll-free 800/661-9267.
Email reservations@douglasfir.com;
www.douglasfir.com.* 121 rms, 4 story,
3 suites. S $108; each addl $15; suites
$218-$278; under 14 free. Parking
garage. Indoor pool, children's pool,
whirlpool. TV; cable. Complimentary
toll-free calls. Restaurant nearby. Ck-
out 11 am, ck-in 4 pm. Dry cleaning,
coin lndry. Exercise equipt, sauna,
steam rm. Golf. Tennis. Downhill skiing. Bike rentals. Hiking trail. Picnic
facilities. Cr cds: A, D, ER, MC, V.

Restaurants

★★ **BALKAN.** *120 Banff Ave (T0L 0C0). 403/762-3454.* Own desserts. Hrs: 11 am-11 pm. Closed Dec 25. Res accepted. Lunch $6.95-$12; dinner $10.99-$23. Child's menu. Greek wall hangings, statues. Cr cds: A, C, D, DS, ER, MC, V.

★★★ **BANFF SPRINGS.** *405 Spray Ave. 403/762-2211. www.cphotels.ca.* Specializes in fondues, schnitzel. Own baking. Hrs: 6 am-11 pm; Sun brunch 11 am-2 pm. Res accepted. Bar. Bkfst complete meals: $16; lunch a la carte entrees: $7-$15. Complete meals: $22-$45; dinner a la carte entrees: $16-$27. Complete meals: $22-$45. Sun brunch $23.95. Child's menu. Valet parking. Historical castle, built 1888. View of mountains. Cr cds: A, D, DS, MC, V.

★★ **THE BISTRO.** *229 Wolf St (T0L 0C0), in Wolf and Bear Mall. 403/762-8900. Email lebeaujolais@banff.net; www.info-pages.com/bistro.* Specializes in seafood, steak, European style cuisine. Hrs: 6 pm-midnight. Res accepted. Dinner $14-$20. Child's menu. Parking. Modern decor. Cr cds: C.

★★ **BUFFALO MOUNTAIN LODGE DINING ROOM.** *Tunnel Mt Rd. 403/760-4485. www.crmr.com.* Specializes in medallion of ranch elk with nectarine relish, port wine sauce, yukon potato hash, medallions of wild caribou. Hrs: 6:30 am-10 pm. Res required. Wine list. Lunch $6-$19; dinner $21-$33. Child's menu. Entertainment. Cozy, lodge style dinning with exposed beams and fieldstone fireplace. Cr cds: A, D, ER, MC, V.

★ **CABOOSE STEAK AND LOBSTER.** *Lynx and Elk Sts (T0L 0C0), in railroad station. 403/762-3622.* Steak menu. Specializes in prime rib, steak, seafood. Salad bar. Hrs: 5-10 pm. Closed Dec 25. Res accepted. Bar. Dinner a la carte entrees: $15-$30. Parking. Antiques and memorabilia from the railroad era. Cr cds: D, ER, MC, V.

★★ **CHEZ FRANCOIS.** *1604 2nd Ave. 403/678-6111.* Specializes in braised duck, poached fresh salmon, rack of lamb. Hrs: 6:30 am-11 pm. Res accepted. Bar. Bkfst $3.95-$8.50; lunch $5.50-$12.95; dinner $13.95-$22.95. Sun brunch $6.50-$12.95. Child's menu. Entertainment. Parking. Cr cds: A, D, DS, MC, V.

★★ **GIORGIO'S TRATTORIA.** *219 Banff Ave (T0L 0C0). 403/762-5114.* Specializes in veal, pasta, lamb. Hrs: 4:30-10 pm. Bar. Dinner a la carte entrees: $11.50-$24.25. Cr cds: MC, V.

★★★ **LE BEAUJOLAIS.** *212 Buffalo St (T0L 0C0). 403/762-2712. Email lebeaujolais@banff.net; www.info-pages.com/bistro.* Specializes in rack of lamb, Alberta beef. Own baking. Hrs: 6 pm-midnight. Res accepted. Wine cellar. Dinner a la carte entrees: $26-$33. Complete meals: $43-$50. Child's menu. Scenic view of mountains. Cr cds: MC, V.

★★ **PEPPERMILL.** *726 9th St (T1W 2V1). 403/678-2292.* Specializes in pepper steak, seafood. Hrs: 5-9:30 pm. Closed Tues; Dec 25; Nov. Res accepted. Dinner complete meals: $11.25-$20.75. Child's menu. Entertainment. Swiss atmosphere. Casual decor. Cr cds: A, MC, V.

★★★ **THE PRIMROSE.** *Mountain Ave. 403/762-3356. Email charlesstanford@rimrockresorthotel.com.* Specializes in pasta, veal, seafood. Hrs: Open 24 hrs. Res accepted. Bar. Wine list. Bkfst $7.75-$14.75. Buffet: $13; lunch $8-$23.75; dinner $15.50-$25. Child's menu. Valet parking. Large windows provide beautiful view. Cr cds: A, C, D, DS, ER, MC, V.

★★ **SINCLAIR'S.** *637 8th St (T1W 2B1). 403/678-5370.* Specializes in fresh glazed salmon, charbroiled lamb chops, seared halibut steak. Hrs: 11:30 am-2:30 pm, 5-9 pm; Fri to 10 pm; Sat 5-10 pm. Res accepted. Wine, beer. Lunch $8-$12; dinner $10-$20. Child's menu. Entertainment. Street parking. View of mountains. Original artwork, fireplace. Cr cds: A, D, DS, ER, MC, V.

★★★ **TICINO.** *415 Banff Ave. 403/762-3848. Email info@ticino restaurant.com; www.ticinorestaurant. com.* Specializes in veal dishes, beef and cheese fondue, pasta. Hrs: 5:30-10:30 pm. Res accepted. Bar. Wine list. Dinner a la carte entrees: $12-$26. Child's menu. European atmosphere. Family-owned. Cr cds: A, C, D, DS, ER, MC, V.

D SC ⊸

Unrated Dining Spot

RISTORANTE CLASSICO. *403/762-1840. Email therimrock@aol.com.* Specializes in leeks with prosciutto, grilled sea bass, bittersweet chocolate cake. Hrs: 11-2 am. Bar. Dinner $16-$25. Valet parking. Cr cds: A, MC, V.

D

Calgary

(F-4) *See also Banff*

Founded 1875 **Pop** 720,000 (est)
Elev 3,439 ft (1,049 m)
Area code 403
Web www.visitor.calgary.ab.ca

Information Convention & Visitors Bureau, 237 8th Ave SE, Rm 200, T2G 0K8; 403/263-8510 or 800/661-1678

Calgary, called "the gateway to the Canadian Rockies," was founded in 1875 by the North West Mounted Police at the confluence of the Bow and Elbow rivers. Surrounding the city are fertile farmlands and, to the west, the rolling foothills of the Rockies. It is partially due to this lush land that ranching and grain farming have played such a large part in the development of the city. In fact Calgary is a principal center for Canada's agribusinesses.

Calgary is also the major oil center in Canada. Since 1914 the petroleum industry has centered its activities here. Today more than 85 percent of Canada's oil and gas producers are headquartered in Calgary. As a result, Calgary has experienced a phenomenal growth rate. But the city has retained some of its earlier "small town" atmosphere, and Calgarians are still noted for their warmth and hospitality.

Site of the 1988 Olympic Winter Games, Calagary offers a broad array of pursuits for outdoors enthusiasts, ranging from its numerous golf courses to hiking and whitewater rafting in its foothills and alpine environs. Cultural activities abound as well and Calgary also provides its share of nightlife.

What to See and Do

Calaway Park. Amusement park with 24 rides, attractions, entertainment, games, shops, concessions. (July-Aug, daily; late May-June and Sep-Oct, wkends) 6 mi (10 km) W via Hwy 1, Springbank Exit. RR 2 Site 25. Phone 403/240-3822. All-inclusive fee ¢¢¢¢

Calgary Centre for Performing Arts. Three theaters noted for their excellent acoustics house the Calgary Philharmonic, Theatre Calgary, and other performing arts. Guided tours avail. 205-8 Ave SE. Phone 403/294-7455.

Calgary Science Centre. Discovery Dome, Pleiades Mystery Theatre, astronomy displays, exhibitions, observatory and self-guided tours; science and technology demonstrations. Souvenir shop, snack bar. Admission varies with program. (Tues-Sun; closed Dec 25) 701 11th St SW. Phone 403/221-3700. ¢¢

⊠ **Calgary Tower.** A 626-ft (191-m) tower with a spectacular view of Calgary and the Rocky Mts; revolving restaurant (see PANORAMA), observation terrace, lounge, souvenir shop. (Daily) 101 9th Ave SW. Phone 403/266-7171. ¢¢

The Calgary Zoo, Botanical Garden & Prehistoric Park. One of Canada's largest zoos, with more than 1,400 animals; botanical garden; Canadian Wilds (25 acres) features Canadian ecosystems populated by their native species. Prehistoric Park. (Daily) St. George's Island, 1300 Zoo Rd NE. Phone 403/232-9300 or 403/232-9372. ¢¢¢

Canada Olympic Park. Premiere site of XV Olympic Winter Games. Olympic Hall of Fame & Museum. Winter sports facilities incl double, 2 triple chairlifts, T-bar; ski school, rentals; snowmaking. Winter facilities (Nov-Mar, daily). Tours, special events (all yr). Trans-Canada Hwy & Bowfort Rd NW; 88 Canada Olympic Rd SW. Phone 403/247-5452. Lift ¢¢¢¢

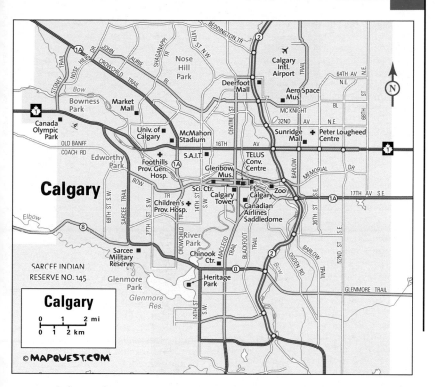

© MAPQUEST.COM

Devonian Gardens. Approx 2½ acres (1.25 hectares) of indoor vegetation in the heart of the city; waterfalls, fountains, ponds with rainbow trout, goldfish, and koi; seating for concerts; art displays; playground; reflecting pool. Below the gardens are stores and restaurants. (Daily) 7th Ave between 2nd & 3rd Sts SW. Phone 403/268-3830 (Calgary Parks & Recreation). **FREE**

Eau Claire Market & Prince's Island Park. Market is a 2-story warehouse, containing boutique shops, fish, meat, vegetable, and fruit stands, restaurants and bars, and 4-screen cinema. Also incl IMAX Theatre (phone 403/974-4629). Prince's Island Park is located on an island in the Bow River, lined with cottonwood trees and inhabited by Canada geese. Near 2nd Ave SW & 3rd St SW. Phone 403/264-6450.

Energeum. Public visitor center that involves guests in the story of Alberta's energy resources. Hands-on exhibits cover geology, exploration, conservation, and more; 1958 limited-edition Buick; theater with films, demonstrations, special events. (June-Aug, Sun-Fri; rest of yr, Mon-Fri) 640 5th Ave SW. Phone 403/297-4293. **FREE**

Fort Calgary Historic Park. (1875) Riverside park of 40 acres (16 hectares), site of original North West Mounted Police (NWMP) fort, at confluence of Bow and Elbow rivers. Abandoned in 1914, the site of the fort is now being rebuilt. Interpretive center focuses on NWMP, Calgary history. Exhibit hall, audiovisual presentation, Discovery Rm. Excellent views of rivers and St. George's Island. Adj is **Deane House** (1906), restored and open to public as restaurant; guided tours (by appt; phone 403/269-7747). (Daily) 750 9th Ave SE. Phone 403/290-1875. ¢¢

▲ **Glenbow Museum.** Museum, art gallery, library, and archives. Regional, national, and intl fine arts; displays of native cultures of North America and the development of the West; mineralogy, warriors, African and personal adornment. (Tues-Sun; closed hols) 130 9th Ave SE. Phone 403/268-4100 or 403/237-8988 (recording). ¢¢¢

Heritage Park Historical Village. Recreates life in western Canada before 1914. More than 100 exhibits; steam train, paddlewheeler, horse-drawn and electric streetcars, wagon rides, antique midway. (Mid-May-early Sep, daily; mid-Sep-early Oct, wkends and hols) 1900 Heritage Dr SW. Phone 403/259-1910 (recording) or 403/259-1900. ¢¢¢

Museum of the Regiments. One of Nort America's largest military museums, honors 4 Calgary Regiments. Films. Traveling art exhibits. (Thurs-Tues) 4520 Crowchild Trail SW. Phone 403/974-2850. ¢¢.

Professional sports.

NHL (Calgary Flames). Canadian Airlines Saddledome. 14th Ave & 5th St SE. Phone 403/777-2177.

⭐ **Royal Tyrrell Museum of Paleontology.** World's largest display of dinosaurs in state-of-the-art museum setting. More than 35 complete dinosaur skeletons; "Paleoconservatory" with more than 100 species of tropical and subtropical plants that once thrived in this region; hands-on exhibits, incl interactive terminals and games throughout. Souvenir shop, cafeteria. Inquire locally about summer bus service from Calgary. (Late May-Labour Day, daily; rest of yr, Tues-Sun; also Mon hols; closed Dec 25) 80 mi (128 km) NE via Hwy 9 in Drumheller. Phone 403/823-7707. ¢¢¢

Spruce Meadows. One of North America's finest equestrian facilities. Devoted to hosting the best show jumping tournaments on the continent, training young riders and young horses and breeding a super sport horse by crossing the North American Thoroughbred with the German Hanoverian. (Daily; closed Jan 1, Dec 25) (See ANNUAL EVENTS) Fee during tournaments. 3 mi (5 km) SW via Hwy 22X; RR 9. Phone 403/974-4200. ¢¢

Western Heritage Centre. Interpretive center with interactive displays about the past, present, and future of ranch, farm, and rodeo life. (Daily; summer hrs extended) Near jct of Hwy 22 and 1A, Conchrane, AB, T0L 0W0. Phone 403/932-3514. ¢¢¢

Annual Events

Calgary Winter Festival. 100 634 6th Ave SW. Music, entertainment, sports competitions, children's activities, carnival, dance. Eleven days mid-Feb. Phone 403/543-5480.

Calgary Stampede. Stampede Park. "The World's Greatest Outdoor Show." Parade, rodeo, chuck wagon races, stage shows, exhibition, square dances, marching bands, vaudeville shows. Ten days early July. Phone 403/261-0101, 800/661-1260, or 800/661-1767 (ticket info).

Spruce Meadows. Only internationally sanctioned outdoor horse jumping show held in North America; offers the world's richest show jumping purse. June-Sep. Phone 403/974-4200.

Motels/Motor Lodges

⭐⭐ **COMFORT INN.** *2363 Banff Tr NW (T2M 4L2). 403/289-2581; fax 403/284-3897; res 800/258-5051.* 70 rms, 2 story. Apr-Sep: S, D $100-$175; each addl $5; under 16 free; wkend rates; lower rates rest of yr. Crib $5. TV; cable. Sauna. Indoor pool; whirlpool. Complimentary continental bkfst. Coffee in rms. Restaurant adj 6 am-midnight. Ck-out 11 am. Business servs avail. Refrigerators. Some balconies. Cr cds: A, D, DS, ER, MC, V.
🅳 🏊 🛒 🔥

⭐ **DAYS INN - CALGARY WEST.** *1818 16th Ave NW (Trans-Can Hwy 1) (T2M 0L8). 403/289-1961; fax 403/289-3901; res 800/DAYSINN; toll-free 800/661-9564. Email info@daysinn calgarywest.com.* 130 rms, 4 story. Mid-June-Sep: S, D $65-$130; suites $130-$170; each addl $10; under 16 free; higher rates special events; lower rates rest of yr. Crib free. Pet accepted. TV; cable (premium), VCR avail. Heated pool; poolside serv. Coffee in rms. Restaurant 6:30 am-11:30 pm; pianist in dining rm Thurs-Sun. Bar 11-1:30 am. Ck-out 11 am. Meeting rms. Business servs avail. Bellhops. Gift shop. Airport transportation. Balconies. Cr cds: A, C, D, DS, ER, JCB, MC, V.
🅳 🐾 🏊 🛒 🧍 ✈ 🛥 🔥

⭐⭐ **HOLIDAY INN EXPRESS.** *2227 Banff Tr NW (T2M 4L2), 1 blk N of Trans-Can Hwy 1. 403/289-6600; fax 403/289-6767; res 800/HOLIDAY.* 64 rms, 3 story. S, D $60-$150; each addl $10; suites $100-$175; under 18 free. Crib free. TV; cable. Whirlpool.

Complimentary coffee in rms, continental bkfst. Restaurant adj. Ck-out noon. Meeting rms. Business servs avail. Valet serv Mon-Fri. Sauna. Cr cds: A, D, DS, ER, JCB, MC, V.

D ⬚ ⬚

★★ QUALITY HOTEL & CONFERENCE CENTRE.
3828 Macleod Tr S (T3J 3T5). 403/243-5531; fax 403/243-6962; res 800/361-3422. Email qualityhotel.calgary@home. 134 rms, 3 story. S, D $90-$150; suites $125-$175; each addl $10; under 18 free. Crib free. Pet accepted; $10. TV; cable. Heated pool; whirlpool. Coffee in rms. Restaurants 7 am-10 pm. Bar 11-2 am; closed Sun. Ck-out 11 am. Coin lndry. Meeting rms. Business servs avail. Bellhops in summer. Valet serv Mon-Fri. Gift shop. Cr cds: A, C, D, DS, ER, JCB, MC, V.

D ⬚ ⬚ ⬚

★ TRAVELODGE CALGARY SOUTH.
7012 Macleod Tr S (T2H 0L4). 403/253-1111; fax 403/253-2879; res 800/578-7878. 61 rms, 2 story, 1 suite. June-Sep: S, D $145; each addl $5; suites $175; under 17 free; lower rates rest of yr. Crib avail. Parking lot. Pool. TV; cable (premium), VCR avail. Complimentary coffee in rms, newspaper, toll-free calls. Restaurant nearby. Ck-out noon, ck-in 1 pm. Business servs avail. Dry cleaning. Golf. Tennis, 40 courts. Downhill skiing. Cr cds: A, D, ER, MC, V.

D ⬚ ⬚ ⬚ ⬚ ⬚ ⬚ SC

Hotels

★★ BEST WESTERN HOSPITALITY INN.
135 Southland Dr SE (T2J 5X5), at Macleod Tr (Hwy 2S). 403/278-5050; fax 403/278-5050; toll-free 877/278-5050. Email info@hospitalityinnsltd.com; www.bestwestern.com/ca/hospitalityinn. 249 rms, 8 story, 11 suites. May-Sep: S $149; D $154; each addl $5; suites $255; under 18 free; lower rates rest of yr. Crib avail. Pet accepted, some restrictions. Parking lot. Indoor pool, whirlpool. TV; cable (DSS). Complimentary coffee in rms, newspaper, toll-free calls. Restaurant 8 am-9 pm. Bar. Ck-out 11 am, ck-in 2 pm. Meeting rms. Business center. Bellhops. Dry cleaning. Gift shop. Salon/barber. Exercise privileges. Golf, 18 holes. Tennis. Downhill skiing. Supervised children's activities. Video games. Cr cds: A, C, D, DS, ER, MC, V.

D ⬚ ⬚ ⬚ ⬚ ⬚ ⬚ ⬚ ⬚ SC ⬚

★★ BEST WESTERN PORT O' CALL INN.
1935 McKnight Blvd NE (T2E 6V4). 403/291-4600; fax 403/250-6827; toll-free 800/661-1161. Email info@portocallinn.com; www.portocallinn.com. 198 rms, 7 story, 3 suites. S, D $139; each addl $5; suites $299; under 17 free. Crib avail. Parking garage. Indoor pool, whirlpool. TV; cable (DSS). Complimentary coffee in rms, newspaper, toll-free calls. Restaurant 7 am-10 pm. Bar. Ck-out noon, ck-in 4 pm. Meeting rms. Business center. Dry cleaning. Gift shop. Salon/barber. Free airport transportation. Exercise equipt, sauna, steam rm. Golf, 18 holes. Hiking trail. Video games. Cr cds: A, C, D, DS, ER, JCB, MC, V.

D ⬚ ⬚ ⬚ ⬚ ⬚ ⬚

★★ BLACKFOOT INN.
5940 Blackfoot Tr SE (T2H 2B5). 403/252-2253; fax 403/252-3574; toll-free 800/661-1151. Email info@blackfoot.com; www.blackfootinn.com. 196 rms, 7 story, 1 suite. May-July, Sep: S, D $169; each addl $10; suites $229; under 17 free; lower rates rest of yr. Crib avail. Pet accepted. Parking lot. Pool, whirlpool. TV; cable (premium), VCR avail, CD avail. Complimentary coffee in rms, newspaper. Restaurant 6:30 am-11 pm. Bar. Ck-out noon, ck-in 3 pm. Meeting rms. Business center. Bellhops. Concierge. Dry cleaning. Gift shop. Exercise privileges, sauna. Golf. Tennis. Downhill skiing. Supervised children's activities. Video games. Cr cds: A, D, ER, MC, V.

D ⬚ ⬚ ⬚ ⬚ ⬚ ⬚ ⬚ ⬚ SC ⬚

★★★ CALGARY MARRIOTT HOTEL.
110 9th Ave SE (T2G 0N6), in Calgary Center. 403/266-7331; fax 403/269-1961; res 800/228-9290, toll-free 800/896-6878. Email mhrs.yycdt.sales@marriott.com; www.marriott.com/yycdt. 372 rms, 23 story, 12 suites. May-Oct: S, D $188; each addl $20; suites $229; under 12 free; lower rates rest of yr. Crib avail. Pet accepted, some restrictions. Valet parking avail. Indoor pool, lap pool,

whirlpool. TV; cable (premium), VCR avail. Complimentary coffee in rms, newspaper, toll-free calls. Restaurant 6:30 am-11 pm. Bar. Ck-out noon, ck-in 3 pm. Conference center, meeting rms. Business center. Bellhops. Concierge. Dry cleaning. Gift shop. Exercise privileges. Golf. Tennis. Downhill skiing. Bike rentals. Supervised children's activities. Video games. Cr cds: A, D, DS, JCB, MC, V.

★★ **CARRIAGE HOUSE INN.** *9030 Macleod Tr S (T2H 0M4). 403/253-1101; fax 403/259-2414; toll-free 800/661-9566. Email sales@carriagehouse.net; www.carriagehouse.net.* 151 rms, 10 story, 6 suites. July-Aug: S, D $165; each addl $10; suites $195; under 17 free; lower rates rest of yr. Crib avail. Pet accepted, some restrictions, fee. Parking lot. Pool, whirlpool. TV; cable. Complimentary coffee in rms, newspaper, toll-free calls. Restaurant 6:30 am-11 pm. Bar. Ck-out noon, ck-in 3 pm. Meeting rms. Business center. Bellhops. Dry cleaning. Gift shop. Exercise privileges, sauna, steam rm. Golf, 18 holes. Tennis. Downhill skiing. Cr cds: A, D, DS, ER, JCB, MC, V.

★ **THE COAST PLAZA.** *1316 33rd St NE (T2A 6B6). 403/248-8888; fax 403/248-0749; toll-free 800/661-1464.* 248 rms, 7 and 12 story. S, D $135-$175; each addl $15; suites $295; under 18 free. Crib free. Pet accepted; $20. TV; cable, VCR avail. Heated pool; whirlpool. Complimentary coffee in rms. Restaurant 6:30 am-11 pm. Bar 11:30-2 am. Ck-out noon. Convention facilities. Business servs avail. Gift shop. Free airport transportation. Exercise equipt; sauna. Luxury level. Cr cds: A, D, DS, ER, MC, V.

★★ **DELTA BOW VALLEY.** *209 4th Ave SE (T2G 0C6). 403/266-1980; fax 403/266-0007; toll-free 800/268-1133.* 398 rms, 24 story, 41 suites. June-Sep: S, D $259; each addl $20; lower rates rest of yr. Crib avail. Pet accepted, fee. Valet parking avail. Indoor pool, lap pool, whirlpool. TV; cable (premium), VCR avail. Complimentary coffee in rms. Restaurant. 24-hr rm serv. Bar. Ck-out noon, ck-in 4 pm. Conference center, meeting rms. Business servs avail. Bellhops. Concierge. Dry cleaning. Gift shop. Exercise privileges, sauna. Golf. Tennis. Downhill skiing. Supervised children's activities. Video games. Cr cds: A, C, D, DS, ER, JCB, MC, V.

★★ **DELTA CALGARY AIRPORT.** *2001 Airport Rd NE (T2E 6Z8), at Intl Airport. 403/291-2600; fax 403/291-8722; res 800/268-1133. www.delta hotels.com.* 284 rms, 8 story, 12 suites. July: S, D $189; each addl $25; suites $289; under 18 free; lower rates rest of yr. Crib avail. Pet accepted. Parking garage. Indoor pool, whirlpool. TV; cable (premium). Complimentary coffee in rms, newspaper. Restaurant 6:30 am-10 pm. 24-hr rm serv. Bar. Ck-out noon, ck-in 4 pm. Conference center, meeting rms. Business center. Bellhops. Concierge. Dry cleaning. Gift shop. Salon/barber. Free airport transportation. Exercise equipt. Golf. Supervised children's activities. Hiking trail. Picnic facilities. Video games. Cr cds: A, C, D, DS, ER, JCB, MC, V.

★★★ **DELTA LODGE AT KANANASKIS.** *209 4th Ave SE (T0L 2H0), 60 mi SW on Trans-Can Hwy 1 and Kananaskis Tr (Hwy 40). 403/591-7711; fax 403/591-7770; res 800/268-1133. Email imiles@deltahotels.com.* 251 air-cooled rms, 3 story. S, D $299; each addl $20; suites $340-$550; under 18 free; ski plans. Crib free. Pet accepted; $100/stay. Covered parking $4. TV; cable. Indoor/outdoor pool; whirlpool. Restaurant (see PEAKS DINING ROOM). Bar; entertainment. Ck-out noon. Convention facilities. Business center. Concierge. Shopping arcade. Barber, beauty shop. Tennis. 36-hole golf course; greens fee, pro, putting green, driving range. Downhill ski 1 mi; x-country ski on site. Exercise equipt; sauna. Game rm. Rec rm. Minibars; some bathrm phones. Private patios, balconies. Cr cds: A, D, DS, ER, JCB, MC, V.

★★ **GLENMORE INN & CONVENTION CENTER.** *2720 Glenmore Tr SE (T2C 2E6), at Ogden Rd. 403/279-8611; toll-free 800/661-3163. Email sales@glenmoreinn.com; www.glenmore*

inn.com. 73 rms, 2 story. June-Aug: S, D $109-$119; each addl $10; suite $149; under 18 free; lower rates rest of yr. Crib free. TV; cable (premium), VCR avail. Whirlpool. Coffee in rms. Restaurant 6:30 am-11 pm. Bar 11-1 am. Ck-out noon. Meeting rms. Business servs avail. Valet serv. Exercise equipt; sauna. Cr cds: A, DS, MC, V.

D ⌧ 🖈 ⚑

★★ **HAMPTON INN & SUITES - CALGARY AIRPORT.** *2420 37th Ave NE (T2E 8S6). 403/250-4667; fax 403/ 250-5788; res 800/426-7566; toll-free 877/433-4667. Email yyacl01@hs-hotel.com; www.hamptoninn-suites. com.* 72 rms, 4 story, 32 suites. May-Sep: S $99; D $104; suites $124; under 17 free; lower rates rest of yr. Crib avail. Parking lot. Indoor pool. TV; cable (premium), VCR avail. Complimentary continental bkfst, coffee in rms, newspaper, toll-free calls. Restaurant. Meeting rms. Business servs avail. Dry cleaning, coin lndry. Free airport transportation. Exercise equipt. Golf, 18 holes. Downhill skiing. Supervised children's activities. Cr cds: A, D, DS, ER, MC, V.

D ⌧ 🖈 ⚑ 🚶 🏌 ⚑ ⚑ 🖈 SC

★★ **HOLIDAY INN.** *4206 Macleod Tr (T2G 2R7). 403/287-2700; fax 403/243-4721; toll-free 800/661-1889. Email mawood@cadvision.com; www. calgaryholidayinn.com.* 154 rms, 4 story, 3 suites. May-Sep: S, D $114; each addl $10; suites $135; under 19 free; lower rates rest of yr. Crib avail. Pet accepted, some restrictions, fee. Parking lot. Indoor pool, whirlpool. TV; cable (premium). Complimentary coffee in rms, newspaper, toll-free calls. Restaurant 7 am-10 pm. Bar. Ck-out noon, ck-in 2 pm. Meeting rms. Business servs avail. Bellhops. Dry cleaning, coin lndry. Exercise privileges. Golf. Supervised children's activities. Hiking trail. Video games. Cr cds: A, D, DS, ER, JCB, MC, V.

D 🚶 🏌 ⚑ 🖈 ⚑ ⚑ 🔥 🖈

★★ **HOLIDAY INN AIRPORT.** *1250 McKinnon Dr NE (T2E 7T7), Trans-Can Hwy 1 and 19th St NE. 403/230-1999; fax 403/277-2623; res 800/ 465-4329; toll-free 877/519-7113. Email reservations@holidayinn.cc; www. holiday-inn.com/calgary-upt.* 170 rms, 5 story. S, D $165; each addl $10;

suites $175; under 17 free. Crib avail. Pet accepted, some restrictions. Parking lot. Indoor pool. TV; cable (premium), VCR avail. Complimentary coffee in rms, newspaper, toll-free calls. Restaurant 6 am-11 pm. Bar. Ck-out 11 am, ck-in 3 pm. Meeting rms. Business center. Bellhops. Concierge. Dry cleaning. Free airport transportation. Exercise equipt, sauna. Golf. Downhill skiing. Video games. Cr cds: A, C, D, DS, ER, JCB, MC, V.

D 🚶 ⚑ ⌧ 🏌 ⚑ 🖈 ⚑ ⚑ 🔥 🖈

★★ **INTERNATIONAL HOTEL OF CALGARY.** *220 4th Ave SW (T2P 0H5). 403/265-9600; fax 403/265-6949; res 800/637-7200. Email book@ intlhotel.com; www.intlhotel.com.* 247 rms, 35 story. May-Sep: S $233; D $254; each addl $15; under 16 free; lower rates rest of yr. Valet parking avail. Indoor pool, whirlpool. TV; cable (premium). Complimentary newspaper. Restaurant 7 am-10:30 pm. Bar. Ck-out 1 pm, ck-in 3 pm. Meeting rms. Business servs avail. Bellhops. Concierge. Dry cleaning. Gift shop. Salon/barber. Exercise privileges, sauna. Golf. Video games. Cr cds: A, C, D, ER, MC, V.

D 🏌 ⚑ 🏌 ⚑ ⚑ 🔥

★★ **KANANASKIS INN AND CONFERENCE CENTER.** *PO Box 10 (T0L 2H0), 60 mi SW on Trans-Can Hwy 1 and Kananaskis Tr (Hwy 40). 403/ 591-7500; fax 403/591-7633; toll-free 888/591-7501. Email info@kananaskis inn.com.* 94 rms, 3 story. S, D $155-$175; each addl $15; suites $195-$295; under 18 free; ski, golf plans. Crib free. TV; cable (premium). Indoor pool; whirlpool, steam rm. Restaurant 7 am-10 pm. Bar. Ck-out 11 am. Meeting rms. Business servs avail. Gift shop. Free covered parking. Tennis. 36-hole golf; greens fee, putting green, driving range. Downhill ski 4 mi. Private patios, balconies. Cr cds: A, D, DS, ER, MC, V.

D ⚑ 🔥 🖈

★★★ **THE PALLISER.** *133 9th Ave SW (T2P 2M3). 403/262-1234; fax 403/260-1260; res 800/866-5577.* 405 rms, 12 story. S, D $240-$300; each addl $25; suites $400-$900; under 18 free. Crib free. TV; cable (premium), VCR avail. Coffee in rms. Restaurant (see THE RIMROCK ROOM). Rm serv

Calgary skyline

24 hrs. Bar 11-2 am. Ck-out noon. Convention facilities. Business center. In-rm modem link. Valet parking. Concierge. Gift shop. Barber, beauty shop. Airport transportation. Exercise equipt; steam rm. Massage. Minibars. Luxury level. Cr cds: A, C, D, DS, ER, JCB, MC, V.

★ **PRINCE ROYAL SUITES.** *618 5th Ave SW (T2P 0M7). 403/263-0520; fax 403/298-4888; toll-free 800/661-1592.* 301 air-cooled kit. suites, 28 story. S, D $145-$185; each addl $15; under 16 free. TV; cable. Coffee in rms. Restaurant 7 am-11 pm. Bar from noon. Ck-out noon. Coin lndry. Meeting rms. Airport transportation. Business servs avail. Exercise equipt; sauna, steam rm. Refrigerators. Cr cds: A, DS, MC, V.

★★ **QUALITY INN MOTEL VILLAGE.** *2359 Banff Tr NW (1A) (T2M 4L2), 1 blk N of Trans-Can Hwy 1. 403/289-1973; fax 403/282-1241; res 800/221-2222; toll-free 800/661-4667. Email info@qualityinnmotelvillage.com; www.qualityinnmotelvillage.com.* 100 rms, 2 story, 5 suites. May-Sep: S, D $169; each addl $5; suites $199; under 18 free; lower rates rest of yr. Crib avail. Pet accepted, some restrictions. Parking garage. Indoor pool, whirlpool. TV; cable. Complimentary continental bkfst, coffee in rms, newspaper. Restaurant. Bar. Meeting rms. Business servs avail. Bellhops. Concierge. Dry cleaning, coin lndry. Exercise equipt, sauna. Golf, 18

holes. Downhill skiing. Hiking trail. Cr cds: A, D, DS, ER, MC, V.

★★★ **RADISSON HOTEL CALGARY AIRPORT.** *2120 16th Ave NE (T2E 1L4), Trans-Can Hwy 1. 403/291-4666; fax 403/219-3069; res 800/333-3333. www.radisson.com/calgaryca_airport.* 177 rms, 10 story, 8 suites. June-Aug: S, D $159; each addl $10; suites $325; under 16 free; lower rates rest of yr. Crib avail. Pet accepted, some restrictions, fee. Parking lot. Indoor pool, whirlpool. TV; cable (premium), VCR avail. Complimentary coffee in rms, newspaper, toll-free calls. Restaurant 6 am-midnight. Bar. Ck-out 11 am, ck-in 3 pm. Meeting rms. Business center. Bellhops. Concierge. Dry cleaning. Gift shop. Free airport transportation. Exercise equipt. Golf. Tennis. Supervised children's activities. Picnic facilities. Video games. Cr cds: A, D, DS, ER, JCB, MC, V.

★★★ **SHERATON CAVALIER.** *2620 32nd Ave NE (T1Y 6B8). 403/291-0107; fax 403/291-2834; toll-free 800/325-3535. Email info@sheraton-calgary.com; www.sheraton-calgary.com.* 286 rms, 7 story, 20 suites. June-Sep: S, D $179; each addl $15; suites $339; under 18 free; lower rates rest of yr. Crib avail. Valet parking avail. Indoor pool, lap pool, children's pool, lifeguard, whirlpool. TV; cable. Complimentary coffee in rms, newspaper, toll-free calls. Restaurant. 24-hr rm serv. Bar. Ck-out noon, ck-in 3 pm.

Conference center, meeting rms. Business center. Bellhops. Concierge. Dry cleaning. Gift shop. Free airport transportation. Exercise privileges, sauna. Golf, 18 holes. Downhill skiing. Supervised children's activities. Video games. Cr cds: A, D, ER, MC, V.

★★★ **WESTIN CALGARY.** *320 4th Ave SW (T2P 2S6). 403/266-1611; fax 403/233-7471; toll-free 800/937-8461. Email kelga@westin.com; www.westin. com.* 504 rms, 20 story, 19 suites. July: S, D $275; each addl $20; suites $325; under 18 free; lower rates rest of yr. Crib avail. Pet accepted. Valet parking avail. Indoor pool, whirlpool. TV; cable, VCR avail. Complimentary coffee in rms, newspaper. Restaurant 6:30 am-10:30 pm. 24-hr rm serv. Bar. Ck-out 1 pm, ck-in 3 pm. Conference center, meeting rms. Business center. Bellhops. Concierge. Dry cleaning. Gift shop. Exercise equipt, sauna. Golf. Tennis. Video games. Cr cds: A, C, D, DS, ER, JCB, MC, V.

Resort

★★ **RAFTER SIX RANCH RESORT.** *(T0L 1X0). 403/673-3622; fax 403/673-3961; toll-free 888/267-2624. Email vacations@raftersix.com.* 18 rms in 3-story lodge, 8 cabins, 4 chalets. No A/C. AP: S, D $415-$740; 2-day min. TV in sitting rm. Heated pool; whirlpool. Playground. Dining rm 7:30 am-9 pm. Bar 4 pm-midnight. Ck-out noon. Coin lndry. Meeting rms. Business servs avail. Gift shop. Hiking. Hayrides. Entertainment. Horseback riding, chuck wagon bkfst, barbecues. Wilderness camping facilities. Lawn games. Some fireplaces. Balconies. Rustic; authentic Western Canadian ranch décor, furnishings; original Indian design door murals. Cr cds: A, MC, V.

Restaurants

★★ **ATRIUM STEAKHOUSE.** *2001 Airport Rd NE, in Airport. 403/291-2600.* Specializes in Alberta beef, fresh salmon, linguini Calabrese. Hrs: 6:30 am-10 pm. Res accepted. Bar. Bkfst $6.95-$9.95; lunch $9.95-$20.95; dinner $18-$26. Parking.

Bright atmosphere; fresh flowers. Cr cds: A, D, ER, MC, V.

★★★ **THE BELVEDERE.** *107 8th Ave SW (T2P 1B4). 403/265-9595. www.belevedercalgary.com.* Specializes in Arctic char with citrus honey and sake, sesame spinach and sticky coconut rice. Hrs: 11:30 am-midnight; Sat 5 pm-midnight. Closed Sun. Res accepted. Wine list. Lunch $14-$18; dinner $22-$36. View of the Calgary tower. Cr cds: A, D, ER, MC, V.

★ **CAESAR'S STEAK HOUSE.** *512 4th Ave SW (T2P 0J6). 403/264-1222.* Specializes in steak, seafood, ribs. Hrs: 11 am-1 pm, 4:30 pm-midnight; Sat from 4:30 pm. Closed Sun; hols. Res accepted. Bar. Wine list. Lunch $8-$18; dinner $18-$35. Valet parking. Greco-Roman motif; marble pillars, statues. Cr cds: A, D, MC, V.

★★ **HY'S CALGARY STEAK HOUSE.** *316 4th Ave SW (T2P 0H8). 403/263-2222. Email calgary@ hyssteakhouse.com..* Specializes in steak. Hrs: 11:30 am-11 pm; Sat from 5 pm; Sun 5-10 pm. Closed hols. Res accepted. Bar. Lunch $9.50-$17.95; dinner $17.95-$29.50. Parking. Rustic decor; antiques. Family-owned. Cr cds: Λ, D, MC, V.

★★ **INN ON LAKE BONAVISTA.** *747 Lake Bonavista Dr SE (T2J 0N2). 403/271-6711. www.calgarymenus. com/theinnonlakebonavista.* Specializes in Alberta beef, fresh seafood. Hrs: 11:30 am-2 pm, 5-11 pm; Sat from 4 pm. Res accepted. Bar. Wine list. Lunch á la carte entrées: $7.50-$14.50; dinner á la carte entrées: $17-$32. Sun brunch $18.95. Child's menu. Entertainment: Tues-Sat. On lake. Cr cds: A, C, D, DS, ER, MC, V.

★★ **THE KEG STEAKHOUSE AND BAR.** *7104 MacLeod Tr S (T2H 0L3). 403/253-2534. www.kegsteakhouse.com.* Steak menu. Specializes in prime rib, steak. Hrs: 4-10:30 pm; Fri to 11 pm; Sat noon-1 am; Sun 3-10 pm. Closed Dec 25. Res accepted Sun-Thurs. Bar. Lunch $6.99-$13.99; dinner $12.99-$26.99. Child's menu. 4-tier dining area; 2 fireplaces. Cr cds: A, C, D, DS, ER, MC, V.

[D] [=]

★★★ **MAMMA'S.** *320 16th Ave NW (T2M 0H6). 403/276-9744.* Specializes in pasta, veal, game birds. Own baking. Hrs: 11:30 am-2 pm, 5-11 pm; Sat from 5 pm. Closed Sun. Res required. Wine cellar. Lunch $7.95-$14.95; dinner $9.95-$24.95. Parking. Formal dining rm with chandeliers, Italian paintings. Cr cds: A, C, D, DS, ER, MC, V.

[D] [=]

★ **MESCALERO.** *1315 1st St SW (T2R 0V5). 403/266-3339.* Specializes in Tex-Mex, wild game, fresh seafood. Hrs: 11:30 am-2 pm; 5-10 pm; Sat to 11 pm; Sun to 9 pm. Closed Dec 25. Res accepted. Bar. Lunch a la carte entrees: $5-$13; dinner a la carte entrees: $5-$26. Sun brunch $8-$12. Parking. Rustic decor; imported Southwestern furnishings. Cr cds: A, D, ER, MC, V.

[D] [=]

★★★ **PANORAMA.** *101 9th Ave SW (T2P 1J9), in Tower Center. 403/266-7171. www.calgarytower.com.* Specializes in prime rib, tenderloin steak, fresh seafood. Hrs: 8 am-3 pm, 5-9 pm. Res accepted. Bar. Bkfst complete meals: $11; lunch complete meals: $10-$15; dinner complete meals: $17-$26. Child's menu. Revolving restaurant atop Calgary Tower; panoramic view of city, mountains. Cr cds: A, D, MC, V.

[D] [=]

★★ **PEAKS DINING ROOM.** *Hwy 40. 403/591-7711.* Specializes in cedar-planked salmon, roast rack of lamb, ribeye steak. Hrs: 6-11 am, 5-10 pm; Sun brunch 10:30 am-1:30 pm. Res accepted. Bar. Bkfst $6.50-$14.50. Buffet $13.95; dinner $14-$23. Sun brunch $21.95. Child's menu. Entertainment: pianist Fri-Sun. Parking. Contemporary decor. Cr cds: A, C, D, DS, ER, MC, V.

[D] [=]

★★ **QUINCY'S ON SEVENTH.** *609 7th Ave SW (T2P 0Y9). 403/264-1000. Email quincysonseventh@cadvision.com.* Specializes in steak, prime rib. Hrs: 11 am-midnight. Closed hols. Res accepted. Bar. Lunch a la carte entrees: $12.95-$18; dinner a la carte entrees: $19-$35. Child's menu.

Antique furnishings. Cr cds: A, C, D, DS, ER, MC, V.

[=]

★ **REGENCY PALACE.** *328 Centre St SE (T2G 2B8), Dragon City Plaza. 403/777-2288.* Specializes in duck, chicken, seafood. Salad bar. Hrs: 10 am-11 pm. Res accepted. Bar. Lunch $4.95-$14.95; dinner $7.95-$15.95. Oriental decor. Cr cds: A, C, D, DS, ER, MC, V.

[D] [=]

★★★ **THE RIMROCK ROOM.** *133 9th Ave SW. 403/262-1234. www. cphotels.ca.* Specializes in Alberta beef, Alberta lamb, wild game. Hrs: 11 am-2 pm, 6:30-10 pm; Fri, Sat to 11 pm. Res accepted. Bar. Bkfst $8-$12; lunch $12-$19; dinner $24-$30. Sun brunch $22.95. Child's menu. Valet parking. Formal atmosphere. Cr cds: A, C, D, DS, ER, MC, V.

[=]

★★ **RIVER CAFE.** *Prince's Island Park (T2G 0K7). 403/261-7670. Email rivercafe@cadvision.com; www.river cafe.com.* Specializes in cedar-planked Arctic char, Alberta caribou, seafood pasta. Hrs: 11 am-11 pm; Sun 10 am-10 pm; Sat, Sun brunch 10 am-3 pm. Closed Dec 25; also Jan. Res accepted. Bar. Lunch $8-$20; dinner $17-$35. Sat, Sun brunch, $5-$15. Canadian Northwoods decor. Cr cds: A, D, MC, V.

[D]

★★★ **SEASONS.** *1029 Banff Ave. 403/762-5531. www.rockymountain resort.com.* Specializes in marinated lamb kabobs, salmon florentine. Hrs: 7 am-10 pm. Res accepted. Wine, beer. Dinner $18-$22. Child's menu. Entertainment. View of the Rocky Mts. Cr cds: A, D, DS, ER, JCB, MC, V.

[D] [🔥]

★ **SILVER DRAGON.** *106 3rd Ave SE (T2G 0B6), in Chinatown. 403/264-5326.* Specializes in Cantonese, Peking-style cuisine. Hrs: 10 am-11:30 pm; Fri, Sat to 1:30 am. Closed Sun. Res accepted; required Sat, Sun. Wine. Lunch $6-$15; dinner $10-$30. Asian decor. Family-owned. Cr cds: A, D, MC, V.

[=]

★★ **SMUGGLER'S INN.** *6920 MacLeod Tr (T2H 0L3). 403/253-5355.* Specializes in Alberta beef, seafood, prime rib. Salad bar. Hrs: 11:30 am-midnight. Closed Jan 1, Dec 25. Res accepted. Bar. Lunch complete meals: $6-$10; dinner complete meals: $7-$25. Parking. Rustic atmosphere; antique furnishings. Family-owned. Cr cds: A, D, DS, MC, V.

[D] [⊸]

★★ **TEATRO.** *200 8th Ave SE (T2G 0K7), downtown, on Olympic Sq. 403/290-1012. Email teatro@teles planet.net; www.teatro-rest.com.* Specializes in lobster and scallop lasagna, rack of lamb, Italian market cuisine. Hrs: 11:30 am-midnight; Sat, Sun from 5 pm. Closed Jan 1, Dec 24, 25. Res accepted. Bar. Lunch a la carte entrees: $10-$16; dinner a la carte entrees: $18-$30. Parking. In old Dominion Bank bldg (1911). Cr cds: A, C, D, DS, ER, MC, V.

[D] [⊸]

Unrated Dining Spot

CONSERVATORY. *209 4th Ave SE (T2G 0C6). 403/266-1980.* Hrs: 11:30 am-2 pm, 5:30-10 pm; Sat from 5:30 pm. Lunch $11.50-$22.95; dinner $11.50-$22.95. Child's menu. Valet parking. Cr cds: A, D, MC, V.

[D] [SC]

Edmonton (D-5)

Settled 1795 **Pop** 854,200 (metro)
Elev 2,192 ft (671 m) **Area code** 780
Web www.tourism.ede.org

Information Edmonton Tourism, 9797 Jasper Ave NW, T5J 1N9; 708/426-4715 or 800/463-4667

As capital of a province whose economic mainstays are petroleum and agriculture, Edmonton has all the brash confidence of its position as a major supplier of one of the world's most sought-after resources, yet traces of the practical reticence nurtured by its past still linger.

The first Fort Edmonton, established in 1795, was named for Edmonton, England, now a suburb of London. The fort was relocated several times before its fifth site location near the present Alberta Legislature Building. With the close of the fur trade era, a settlement grew up around the fort and became the nucleus of the city. The sixth fort, a reconstruction from the fur-trading days, is now a major attraction in the city's river valley.

In the 1890s Edmonton became a major supply depot for the gold rush to the Yukon, since it was on the All-Canadian Route to the Klondike. Thousands of men stopped for days, weeks, or months before making the final 1,500-mile (2,400-kilometer) trip to Yukon gold. Many decided to stay in the town, turning a quiet village into a prosperous city. Each July the city returns to the colorful era of the gold rush for ten days of fun and frolic called Edmonton's Klondike Days (see ANNUAL EVENTS).

Edmonton prides itself in having more park area per capita than any other city in Canada. The park area winds along the banks of the North Saskatchewan River, Edmonton's most prominent physical characteristic. Capital City Recreation Park encompasses 3,000 acres (1,214 hectares) with 18 miles (29 kilometers) of biking and hiking trails along the river valley.

What to See and Do

Alberta Legislature Building. Tours of historic structure; Interpretive Centre incl displays of Alberta's history and legislature. Cafeteria. (Daily; closed hols) 10800 97th Ave. Phone 780/427-7362. **FREE**

Citadel Theatre. Five-theater complex located in downtown Edmonton is one of Canada's finest centers for the performing arts. Glass-enclosed atrium area; waterfall, plants. Three theater series (Sep-May). 9828 101 A Avenue. Phone 780/426-4811 (schedule and fees) or 780/425-1820 (tickets).

Commonwealth Stadium. Built for the XI Commonwealth Games; seating capacity is 61,336. Home of the Canadian Football League Edmonton Eskimos. The Stadium Recreation Centre houses gym, weights, and racquetball and squash courts. 11000 Stadium Rd. Phone 780/944-7400. ¢¢

Devonian Botanic Garden. Approx 200 acres (80 hectares) incl alpine and herb gardens, peony collection, and native plants; outstanding 5-acre

Japanese garden; nature trails; aspen and jackpine forests; lilac garden; butterfly pavilion; orchid greenhouse. Concession. (May-Sep, daily) 6 mi W via Yellowhead Hwy 16, then 9 mi S on Hwy 60. Phone 780/987-3054. ¢¢¢

Edmonton Queen Riverboat. Riverboat runs along the North Saskatchewan River, which travels through many local parks. Packages incl lunch, dinner, or cruise only. 9734 98th Ave. Phone 780/424-2628. Cruise only ¢¢¢-¢¢¢¢; Lunch or dinner cruise ¢¢¢¢-¢¢¢¢¢

✪ **Edmonton Space and Science Centre.** Multipurpose facility incl 220-seat planetarium theater; IMAX film theater (fee) with 4-story screen; extensive science exhibit hall dealing with latest discoveries in science, astronomy, and space exploration; artifacts (moon rock, telescopes). Challenger Learning Centre lets visitors cooperate in teams to complete a space flight simulation. Book, gift store. (Summer, daily; rest of yr, Tues-Sun) Varied fees for laser shows and IMAX films. 11211 142 St, in Coronation Park. Phone 780/451-3344. ¢¢¢-¢¢¢¢

Elk Island National Park. Forests, meadowlands, quiet lakes, and beaver ponds form an island in the area developed by man. A 75-sq-mi sanctuary for many species; moose, elk, deer, trumpeter swans, beaver, and coyote; large herd of plains bison and a small herd of rare wood bison; more than 200 species of birds. Camping (summer), hiking, golf, cross-country skiing. Visitor center and interpretive center (summer, wkends). Park (all yr). 28 mi (45 km) E on Yellowhead Hwy 16. Phone 780/922-2950 or 780/922-5790 (recording). Entrance fee/day ¢¢; Camping/night ¢¢¢¢

Fort Edmonton Park. Canada's largest historical park is a re-creation of sites of historic Edmonton incl Fort Edmonton, the Hudson's Bay Co Trading Post that gave the city its name, 1885 Street, 1905 Street, and 1920 Street. Demonstrations of artifacts and skills of earlier times by costumed interpreters. Steam train and streetcar rides. (Victoria Day-Labour Day, daily; rest of yr, days vary) Whitemud Dr & Fox Dr. Phone 780/496-8787. ¢¢¢ Adj is

John Janzen Nature Centre. Natural history events and programs; hands-on exhibits; active beehive, gopher colony, and nature trails; nature shop. (Daily; closed Dec 25) Phone 780/496-2939. ¢

Kinsmen Sports Centre. Built for the XI Commonwealth Games. Swim-

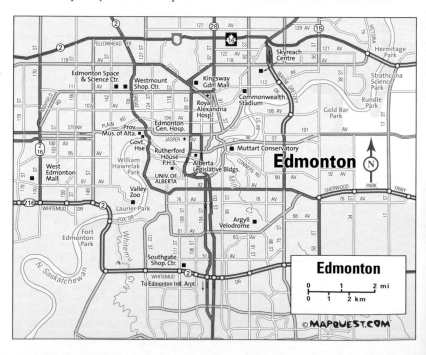

ming, diving, weight training; all types of racquet sports. Children under 8 must be accompanied by an adult. 9100 Walterdale Hill. Phone 780/496-7300. ¢¢

Muttart Conservatory. Glass pyramids house controlled growing environments: tropical, arid, and temperate. A 4th pyramid is a floral showcase, which is changed every few weeks. (Daily; closed Dec 25) 9626 96A St. Phone 780/496-8755. ¢¢

Parks. Capital City Recreation Park, winding through the city's river valley, is one of Canada's most extensive park systems. Bicycle, walking, and cross-country ski trails link the major parks, where barbecue, picnic facilities, public restrooms, and food concessions may be found. Contact River Valley Parks. Phone 780/496-7275.

Professional sports.

NHL (Edmonton Oilers). Edmonton Coliseum. 7424 118th Ave. Phone 780/474-8561.

Provincial Museum of Alberta. Contains excellent displays reflecting the many aspects of Alberta's heritage. Exhibits on natural and human history, incl aboriginal peoples, wildlife, geology, live insects, dinosaurs, and Ice Age mammals. (Daily; closed Dec 24-25) 12845 102 Ave. Phone 780/427-1786 (recording) or 780/453-9100. ¢¢¢

⭐ **Reynolds-Alberta Museum.** Interprets the mechanization of ground and air transportation, agriculture, and selected industries in Alberta from the turn of the 20th century. More than 100 major artifacts in museum bldg, hangar, and on 156-acre grounds. Displays incl vintage steam-powered farm equipment, automobiles, and aircraft; multimedia orientation show (17 min). (Daily; closed hols) Approx 40 mi (64 km) S via Hwy 2A in Wetaskiwin. Phone 780/361-1351. ¢¢¢ Also here is

Canada's Aviation Hall of Fame. More than 100 aviators have been inducted into the hall of fame; many artifacts. Vintage planes, free-standing exhibits; videos, large aviation library.

University of Alberta. 30,000 students. One of Canada's largest major research universities; 18 faculties and many research institutes. Tours (by appt). 114 St & 89 Ave. Phone 780/492-2325. On campus is

Rutherford House. (1911) Jacobean Revival home was residence of Alberta's first premier. Restored and refurnished to reflect lifestyle of post-Edwardian era. Costumed interpreters reenact life in 1915 with activities such as baking on wood stove, historical dramas, craft demonstrations, and musical performances. (Daily; closed Jan 1, Dec 25) Phone 780/427-3995. ¢

Valley Zoo. Features a wide variety of birds and mammals, fish, and reptiles. Train, merry-go-round, pony and camel rides; gift shop. (Daily) 133 St & Buena Vista Rd. Phone 780/496-6911. ¢¢

⭐ **West Edmonton Mall and Canada Fantasyland.** Mi-long (1.6-km) shopping and enterainment complex with more than 800 stores and services; 110 eating establishments, 19 movie theaters, aviary, aquaria, dolphin shows; 80-ft (24-m) replica of Spanish galleon, 4 submarines, water park with wave pool and water slides, bungee-jumping, ice skating rink, casino, Galaxyland amusement park with 14-story looping rollercoaster, 18-hole miniature golf course, IMAX Theatre. (Daily) 8770 170 St. Phone 780/444-5200.

Annual Events

Jazz City Festival. Jazz concerts, workshops, outdoor events. Late June-early July.

Edmonton's Klondike Days. Entertainment, exhibits, midway, parade; events incl Sourdough Raft Race, Sunday promenade, band extravaganza, chuckwagon races. Mid-late July. Northlands Park, 116 Ave & 73 St. Phone 780/471-7210.

Heritage Festival. William Hawrelak Park. More than 40 ethnic groups show Alberta's multicultural heritage in pageantry of color and music. Early Aug. 10715 124 St. Phone 780/488-3378.

Folk Music Festival. Three days of music at Alberta's largest outdoor music festival. Mid-Aug.

Fringe Theatre Event. Old Strathcona district. Dance, music, plays, mime, mask, street entertainers; more than 700 performances. Mid-late Aug.

Canadian Finals Rodeo. Edmonton Coliseum. Professional indoor rodeo to decide national championships. Mid-Nov. Northlands Park, 116 Ave & 73 St. Phone 780/471-7210.

Motels/Motor Lodges

★★ **BEST WESTERN CITY CEN-TRE INN.** *11310 109th St (T5G 2T7). 780/479-2042; fax 780/474-2204; res 800/528-1234; toll-free 800/666-5026.* 104 rms, 2 story, 5 suites. July-Aug, Nov: S $89; D $99; suites $145; lower rates rest of yr. Crib avail. Pet accepted. Parking lot. Indoor pool, whirlpool. TV; cable, VCR avail, VCR avail. Complimentary coffee in rms, toll-free calls. Restaurant. Bar. Ck-out noon, ck-in 1 pm. Meeting rms. Business center. Bellhops. Dry cleaning. Gift shop. Exercise privileges, sauna. Golf. Tennis. Cr cds: A, C, D, DS, ER, JCB, MC.

★★ **EXECUTIVE ROYAL INN WEST EDMONTON.** *10010 178th St (T5S 1T3). 780/484-6000; fax 780/489-2900; toll-free 800/661-4879. www. royalinn.com.* 194 rms, 4 story. S, D $82-$165; each addl $8. Crib free. TV; cable. Coffee in rms. Restaurants 6:30 am-10 pm. Bar noon-1 am. Ck-out 11 am. Meeting rms. Business servs avail. Bellhops. Valet serv. Sundries. Gift shop. Exercise equipt; steam rm. Whirlpool. Refrigerator in suites; some in-rm whirlpools. Cr cds: A, D, ER, MC, V.

★★ **WEST HARVEST INN.** *17803 Stony Plain Rd (T5S 1B4). 780/484-8000; fax 780/486-6060; toll-free 800/ 661-6993. Email inn@westharvest.ab.ca.* 161 rms, 3 story. S $65-$75; D $75-$85; each addl $10; under 16 free. Crib free. TV; cable. Coffee in rms. Restaurant 7 am-10:30 pm. Ck-out 11 am. Meeting rms. Business servs avail. Barber, beauty shop. Some refrigerators, in-rm whirlpools. Cr cds: A, D, ER, MC, V.

Hotels

★★ **BEST WESTERN CEDAR PARK INN.** *5116 Calgary Tr N (T6H 2H4). 780/434-7411; fax 780/437-4836; res 800/528-1234; toll-free 800/661-9461. Email res@cedarparkinn.com; www.*

albertahotels.ab.ca/cedarparkinn. 190 rms, 5 story. S, D $89-$109; each addl $5; suites $140-$160; family rates. Crib free. Pet accepted, some restrictions. TV; cable. Heated pool. Coffee in rms. Restaurant 7 am-11 pm; also 24-hr snack shop. Bar 11:30-1 am. Ck-out noon. Meeting rms. Business servs avail. Gift shop. Free airport transportation. Sauna. Cr cds: A, DS, MC, V.

★ **CHATEAU LOUIS HOTEL & CONFERENCE CENTRE.** *11727 Kingsway (T5G 3A1). 780/452-7770; fax 780/454-3436; toll-free 800/661-9843. Email info@chateaulouis.com; www.chateaulouis.com.* 140 rms, 3 story, 2 suites. S $79; D $89; each addl $10; suites $279; under 12 free. Crib avail, fee. Pet accepted, some restrictions, fee. Parking lot. TV; cable (premium), VCR avail, CD avail. Complimentary coffee in rms, newspaper, toll-free calls. Restaurant 6:30 am-midnight. 24-hr rm serv. Bar. Ck-out noon, ck-in 2 pm. Meeting rms. Business center. Dry cleaning. Exercise equipt. Golf. Cr cds: A, C, D, ER, MC, V.

★★★ **COAST TERRACE INN.** *4440 Calgary Tr N (T6H 5C2). 780/437-6010; fax 789/431-5801; toll-free 888/ 837-7223. www.coastterraceinn.com.* 240 rms, 4 story. S, D $150; suites $185-$250; under 18 free; wkend rates; package plans. Pet accepted, some restrictions. TV; cable. Heated pool; whirlpool. Coffee in rms. Restaurant 6:30 am-10 pm. Rm serv 24 hrs. Bar 11:30-1 am; entertainment. Ck-out noon. Meeting rms. Business servs avail. Bellhops. Gift shop. Underground parking. Exercise equipt; sauna, steam rm. Racquetball court. Minibars; some in-rm whirlpools. Balconies. Luxury level. Cr cds: A, D, MC, V.

★★★ **CROWNE PLAZA CHATEAU LACOMBE.** *10111 Bellamy Hill (T5J 1N7). 780/428-6611; fax 780/425-6564; toll-free 800/661-8801. Email cpcl@chateaulacombe.com; www. chateaulacombe.com.* 307 rms, 24 story, 25 suites. Apr-June, Sep-Nov: S, D $139; suites $175; under 17 free; lower rates rest of yr. Crib avail. Pet accepted, some restrictions. Valet parking avail. TV; cable (premium), VCR avail. Complimentary coffee in rms, newspaper, toll-free calls. Restaurant. Bar. Conference center, meeting rms. Business center. Bellhops. Concierge. Dry cleaning. Gift shop. Exercise privileges. Golf. Tennis, 10 courts. Bike rentals. Video games. Cr cds: D, DS, ER, JCB, MC, V.

★★★ DELTA CENTRE SUITES.

10222 102nd St (T5J 4C5), at Eaton Centre Shopping Mall. 780/429-3900; fax 780/428-1566; res 800/268-1133; toll-free 800/661-6655. Email deltaedm@compusmart.ab.ca; www. deltahotels.com. 40 rms, 4 story, 129 suites. S, D $129; each addl $10; suites $144; under 18 free. Crib avail. Pet accepted, some restrictions. Valet parking avail. TV; cable, VCR avail. Complimentary coffee in rms, newspaper. Restaurant 7 am-10 pm. Bar. Ck-out noon, ck-in 3 pm. Meeting rms. Business center. Bellhops. Concierge. Dry cleaning, coin lndry. Exercise privileges, steam rm, whirlpool. Golf. Downhill skiing. Supervised children's activities. Hiking trail. Video games. Cr cds: A, C, D, DS, ER, JCB, MC, V.

★★★ DELTA EDMONTON SOUTH.

4404 Calgary Tr (T6H 5C2). 780/434-6115; fax 780/434-5298; res 800/268-1133; toll-free 800/661-1122. Email deltasouth@compusmart.com. 237 rms, 11 story. S, D $159; each addl $10; suites $150-$325; under 18 free. Crib free. TV; cable. Heated pool; whirlpool. Coffee in rms. Restaurants 6 am-11 pm. Bar 11-2 am; entertainment. Ck-out noon. Meeting rms. Business center. Free indoor parking; valet. Exercise equipt. Many refrigerators. Cr cds: A, C, D, DS, ER, JCB, MC, V.

★★ FANTASYLAND HOTEL.

17700 87th Ave (P5T 4V4), in West Edmonton Mall. 780/444-3000; fax 780/444-3294; toll-free 800/737-3783. www.fantasylandhotel.com. 354 rms, 12 story. Mid-June-early Sep: S, D $165-$210; each addl $10; suites, theme rms $195-$225; under 18 free; lower rates rest of yr. Crib free. Some covered parking; valet $6.50. TV; cable. Restaurant 7 am-11 pm. Rm serv 24 hrs. Bar noon-1 am. Ck-out 11 am. Convention facilities. Business center. Concierge. Shopping arcade. Barber, beauty shop. Exercise equipt. Mall attractions incl indoor amusement park, water park, movie theaters. Cr cds: A, D, ER, JCB, MC, V.

★★ HOLIDAY INN PALACE.

4235 Calgary Tr N (T6J 5H2). 780/438-1222; fax 780/438-0906; res 800/465-4329; toll-free 800/565-1222. Email hipalace@telusplanet.net. 116 rms, 5 story, 20 suites. Mar-June, Sep-Nov: S $99; D $109; each addl $10; suites $135; lower rates rest of yr. Crib avail. Pet accepted, some restrictions, fee. Parking lot. TV; cable, VCR avail. Complimentary coffee in rms, newspaper, toll-free calls. Restaurant. Bar. Ck-out 11 am, ck-in 3 pm. Meeting rms. Business servs avail. Dry cleaning, coin lndry. Gift shop. Salon/barber. Free airport transportation. Exercise privileges, steam rm, whirlpool. Golf, 18 holes. Tennis, 4 courts. Downhill skiing. Supervised children's activities. Hiking trail. Picnic facilities. Video games. Cr cds: A, C, D, DS, ER, JCB, MC, V.

★★★★ HOTEL MACDONALD.

10065 100th St (T5J 0N6), downtown, across from River Valley on Jasper Ave, follow City Center signs. 780/424-5181; fax 780/424-8017; res 800/866-5577; toll-free 800/441-1414. www. fairmont.com. Originally built in 1915 during the era of grand hotels in Canada, the MacDonald has been fully restored to its original old-world elegance. High on the banks of the North Saskatchewan River and only minutes from the Shaw Convention Center and the city's main cultural attractions, this French-chateâu style hotel has a first-class fully equiped health club, squash courts, swimming pool, and whirlpools, and a fully equipped 24 hour business centre. 198 rms, 8 story. S, D $129-$229; each addl $20; suites $161-$349; under 18 free; wkend rates. Crib free. Pet accepted, some restrictions. Valet parking. TV; cable (premium). Indoor pool; wading pool, whirlpool, poolside serv. Restaurant (see HARVEST ROOM). Rm serv 24 hrs. Bar 11-1 am. Ck-out 1 pm. Meeting rms. Business center. In-rm modem link.

Concierge. Gift shop. Exercise rm; sauna, steam rm. Massage. Sun deck. Game rm. Minibars. Cr cds: A, DS, MC, V.

[icons]

★★ **INN ON 7TH.** *10001 107th St. 780/429-2861; fax 780/426-7225; toll-free 800/661-7327. Email reply@innon 7th.com; www.innon7th.com.* 163 rms, 16 story, 10 suites. S $85; D $95; each addl $10; suites $100; under 12 free. Pet accepted, some restrictions, fee. Parking lot. TV; cable (premium), VCR avail. Complimentary coffee in rms, toll-free calls. Restaurant 6 am-10 pm. Bar. Ck-out 11 am, ck-in 3 pm. Meeting rms. Business servs avail. Bellhops. Dry cleaning. Exercise privileges. Golf. Tennis. Downhill skiing. Hiking trail. Cr cds: A, C, D, DS, ER, MC, V.

[icons]

★★ **RAMADA INN.** *5359 Calgary Tr (T6H 4J9). 780/434-3431; fax 780/437-3714; res 800/272-6232; toll-free 800/661-9030. www.ramada.ca.* 121 rms, 7 story, 1 suite. Apr-Sep: S, D $89; each addl $5; suites $149; under 17 free; lower rates rest of yr. Crib avail. Parking lot. Indoor pool, children's pool, lifeguard, whirlpool. TV; cable. Complimentary coffee in rms, newspaper. Restaurant 6:30 am-9 pm. Ck-out 11 am, ck-in 2 pm. Meeting rms. Business center. Dry cleaning, coin lndry. Free airport transportation. Golf. Downhill skiing. Cr cds: A, D, ER, JCB, MC, V.

[icons]

★★★ **SHERATON GRANDE.** *10235 101st St (T5J 3E9), downtown. 780/428-7111; fax 780/441-3098; res 800/325-3535; toll-free 800/263-9030. Email sales@sheratonedmonton.com; www.sheratonedmonton.com.* 286 rms, 26 story, 27 suites. S, D $155; each addl $20; suites $195; under 17 free. Crib avail. Pet accepted, some restrictions. Valet parking avail. Indoor pool, whirlpool. TV; cable (DSS). Complimentary coffee in rms, newspaper, toll-free calls. Restaurant. Bar. Conference center, meeting rms. Business center. Bellhops. Concierge. Dry cleaning. Gift shop. Salon/barber. Exercise rm, sauna, steam rm. Golf, 18 holes. Tennis, 2 courts. Video games. Cr cds: A, C, D, ER, MC, V.

[icons]

★★★ **WESTIN EDMONTON.** *10135 100th St (T5J 0N7), downtown. 780/426-3636; fax 780/428-1454. Email sales@westin.ab.ca.* 413 rms, 12-20 story. S, D $175-$255; each addl $20; suites $400-$800; under 12 free; wkend rates. Crib free. Valet parking $17, garage $13. TV; cable. Heated pool. Coffee in rms. Restaurant 6:30 am-11 pm. Rm serv 24 hrs. Bar 11-1 am. Ck-out 1 pm. Meeting rms. Business center. Exercise equipt; sauna. Massage. Refrigerators, minibars; some bathrm phones and TVs. Luxury level. Cr cds: A, C, D, DS, ER, JCB, MC, V.

[icons]

All Suite

★ **TOWER ON THE PARK.** *9715 110th St (T5K 2M1). 780/488-1626; fax 780/488-0659; toll-free 800/720-2179. Email totp@telusplanet.net; www. toweronthepark.com.* 98 suites. Suites $79. Crib avail, fee. Pet accepted, some restrictions, fee. Parking garage. TV; cable, VCR avail. Complimentary continental bkfst, coffee in rms, newspaper, toll-free calls. Restaurant nearby. Ck-out noon, ck-in 4 pm. Meeting rms. Business center. Dry cleaning. Exercise privileges. Golf, 18 holes. Tennis. Hiking trail. Picnic facilities. Cr cds: A, D, ER, MC, V.

[icons]

Conference Centers

★★ **MAYFIELD INN AND SUITES.** *16615 109th Ave (T5P 5K8). 780/484-0821; fax 780/486-1634; toll-free 800/661-9804. www.mayfield-inn.com.* 210 rms, 10 story, 117 suites. S, D $109; each addl $15; suites $139. Pet accepted, some restrictions, fee. Parking lot. Indoor pool, whirlpool. TV; cable (premium). Complimentary full bkfst, coffee in rms, newspaper, toll-free calls. Restaurant 6:30 am-10 pm. Bar. Ck-out noon, ck-in 3 pm. Meeting rms. Bellhops. Dry cleaning. Gift shop. Salon/barber. Exercise rm, sauna, steam rm. Golf. Tennis. Video games. Cr cds: A, C, D, DS, ER, JCB, MC, V.

[icons]

★★ **NISKU INN AND CONFERENCE CENTER.** *Box 9801 Edmonton Intl Airport (T5J 2T2), off Hwy 2. 780/955-7744; fax 780/955-7743; toll-*

*free 800/661-6966. Email info@
niskuinn.ab.ca; www.niskuinn.ab.ca.*
152 rms, 2 story, 4 suites. S, D $99;
each addl $10; suites $149; under 18
free. Crib avail. Pet accepted, some
restrictions, fee. Parking lot. Indoor
pool, whirlpool. TV; cable (DSS), VCR
avail, CD avail. Complimentary continental bkfst, coffee in rms, newspaper. Restaurant 6 am-midnight. Bar.
Ck-out noon, ck-in 2 pm. Meeting
rms. Business center. Bellhops. Dry
cleaning. Gift shop. Salon/barber.
Free airport transportation. Exercise
privileges. Golf. Tennis, 6 courts.
Downhill skiing. Hiking trail. Cr cds:
A, D, ER, MC, V.

🔲 🏹 🛄 🎿 🎇 🏇 🏊 🏃 🔫 ✈ 🔲
🔲 🏃

Restaurants

★ **CHIANTI CAFE.** *10501 82nd Ave
(T6E 2A3), at Strathcona Square Market.* 780/439-9829. Specializes in
pasta, veal, chicken. Hrs: 11 am-11
pm; Fri, Sat to midnight. Closed Dec
25. Res accepted. Bar. Lunch, dinner
$4.50-$15.95. Renovated historic
post office bldg. Cr cds: A, D, DS,
MC, V.

🔲 🔲

★★ **COCOA'S.** *10222 102nd St.*
780/429-3900. *Email deltaedm@compus
mart.ab.ca; www.deltahotels.com.* Specializes in grilled Alberta bison, rack
of lamb, fresh maritime seafood
chowder. Hrs: 6:30 am-9 pm; Sat,
Sun from 7 am; Sun brunch 10 am-2
pm. Res accepted. Bar. Bkfst $6.95-
$12.95; lunch $7.25-$11.95; dinner
$11.95-$24.95. Sun brunch $14.95.
Child's menu. Valet parking. Art
Deco decor; atrium skylight. Cr cds:
A, DS, ER, MC, V.

🔲 🔲

★ **FIORE.** *8715 109th St (T6G 2L5).*
780/439-8466. Specializes in pasta,
seafood. Hrs: 11 am-10 pm; Fri to 11
pm; Sat 9 am-11 pm; Sun from 9 am.
Closed Dec 25. Res accepted. Bar.
Lunch $5-$8.50; dinner $8-$15.
Child's menu. Casual decor. Cr cds:
A, D, ER, MC, V.

🔲 🔲

★★★ **HARVEST ROOM.** *10065
100th St.* 780/424-5181. *www.cpho-
tels.ca.* Specializes in cream of wild

mushroom and artichoke soup, lamb
loin with rosemary, fresh British
Columbia salmon on cedar plank.
Hrs: 6:30 am-2 pm, 5:30-10 pm; Sat,
Sun from 7 am; Sun brunch 10:30
am-1:30 pm. Res accepted. Bar. Wine
cellar. Bkfst a la carte entrees: $7.75-
$11.95; lunch a la carte entrees: $9-
$15. Buffet: $12; dinner a la carte
entrees: $19-$28. Sun brunch $24.
Child's menu. Valet parking. Terrace
dining overlooking Saskatchewan
River and city. Elegant dining in historic hotel. Cr cds: A, C, D, DS, ER,
MC, V.

🔲 🆂🅲 🔲

★★ **HY'S STEAK LOFT.** *10013
101A Ave (T5J 0C3).* 780/424-4444.
Email edmonton@hyssteakhouse.com.
Specializes in Alberta beef. Hrs: 11:30
am-10 pm; Fri to 11 pm; Sat 5-11
pm; Sun 5-9 pm. Closed hols. Res
accepted. Bar. Wine cellar. Lunch a la
carte entrees: $10-$18; dinner a la
carte entrees: $19-$35. Elegant dining. Cr cds: A, D, MC, V.

🔲 🔲

★ **JAPANESE VILLAGE.** *10126
100th St (T5J 0N8).* 780/422-6083.
Specializes in sushi, tempura,
Teppanyaki cooking. Hrs: 11:30 am-
2 pm, 5-11 pm. Closed Victoria Day,
Nov 11, Dec 24, 25. Res accepted.
Lunch $7-$10; dinner $7-$17. Com-
plete meals: $18-$35. Child's menu.
Cr cds: A, C, D, DS, ER, MC, V.

🔲 🔲

★★★ **L'ANJOU.** *10643 123rd St
(T5N 1P3).* 780/482-7178. Specializes in stuffed chicken breast, roast
duck breast, grilled halibut with
mango salsa. Hrs: 6-8:30 pm. Closed
Sun-Tues; hols. Res required. Bar.
Dinner complete meals: $27-$35.
Parking. French country decor. Cr
cds: D, MC, V.

🔲

★★ **LA BOHEME.** *6427 112th Ave
(T5W 0N9).* 780/474-5693. *www.
labohedmonton.com.* Specializes in
seafood, lamb. Own pastries. Hrs: 11
am-midnight. Closed Dec 25. Res
required. Bar. Lunch a la carte
entrees: $15-$28; dinner a la carte
entrees: $15-$28. Complete meals:
$22-$32. Sun brunch $13.75. Park-
ing. Romantic European atmosphere.

Guest rms avail. Cr cds: A, D, DS, MC, V.

D ⬚ꜝ

★★★ **LA RONDE.** *10111 Bellamy Hill. 780/428-6611. Email cpcl@ chateaularonde.com.* Specializes in Alberta beef, fresh fish. Hrs: 5:30-10:30 pm; Sun brunch 10:30 am-2 pm. Res accepted. Bar. Dinner a la carte entrees: $18-$30. Sun brunch $21.95. Child's menu. Parking. Revolving restaurant with panoramic view of city. Cr cds: A, D, DS, MC, V.

D SC ⬚ꜝ

★★ **LA SPIGA.** *10133 125th St (T5N 1S7). 780/482-3100.* Specializes in rack of lamb, pasta. Own desserts. Hrs: 11:30 am-2 pm, 5-11 pm; Sat from 5 pm. Closed Sun; hols. Res accepted. Lunch, dinner a la carte entrees: $11.95-$22.95. Parking. Mansion built in 1915; beamed ceilings; fireplace. Cr cds: ER, MC, V.

D ⬚ꜝ

Unrated Dining Spot

CREPERIE. *10220 103rd St (T5J 0Y8). 780/420-6656. www.thecreperie. com.* French menu. Specializes in crepes, country French dishes. Hrs: 11:30 am-10 pm; Fri to 11 pm; Sat 5-11 pm; Sun 5-9 pm. Closed Dec 25. Res accepted; required Fri, Sat. Bar. Lunch a la carte entrees: $6-$10; dinner a la carte entrees: $6-$14. Child's menu. Cr cds: A, MC, V.

Fort Macleod

(H-5) *See also Lethbridge*

Settled 1874 **Pop** 3,139 **Elev** 3,105 ft (1,046 m) **Area code** 403
Web www.town.fortmacleod.ab.ca
Information Tourism Action Committee, PO Box 1959, T0L 0Z0; 403/553-2500 or 403/553-3204

Fort Macleod was the first North West Mounted Police post in Alberta, named in honor of Colonel James F. Macleod, who led the force on its march westward. The fort was successful in stamping out the illegal whiskey trade that had flourished previously in the area. Today the region has an abundance of mixed and grain farming.

What to See and Do

Fort Museum. Museum complex depicts history of North West Mounted Police, Plains tribes, and pioneer life in Fort Macleod, the first outpost in the Canadian west. A special feature is the Mounted Patrol Musical Ride (July-Aug, 4 times daily). (May-Oct, daily; rest of yr, Mon-Fri; closed hols) 25th St & 3rd Ave. Phone 403/553-4703. ¢¢

Head-Smashed-In Buffalo Jump Interpretive Centre. Buffalo jump site dating back approx 6,000 yrs. Interpretive tours, theater, cafeteria. (Daily; closed Easter, Dec 25) 2 mi (3 km) N on Hwy 2, then 10 mi (16 km) W on Spring Point Rd (S-785). Phone 403/553-2731. ¢¢¢

Remington-Alberta Carriage Centre. Displays one of the largest collections of horse-drawn vehicles in North America; over 200 carriages, wagons, and sleighs. Gallery has interactive displays, audiovisual productions, carriage factory. (Daily) 35 mi S on Hwy 2 at 623 Main St in Cardston. Phone 403/653-5139. ¢¢¢

Waterton Lakes National Park. (see) 30 mi SW on Hwy 3, then on Hwy 6.

Annual Events

Powwow & Tipi Village. Celebration features open tipi village, traditional native dances, games, food. Third wkend July. At Head-Smashed-In Buffalo Jump.

Santa Claus Parade & Festival. One of the oldest and largest Santa Claus parades west of Toronto. Last Sat in Nov.

Motel/Motor Lodge

★ **SUNSET MOTEL.** *104 Hwy 3W (T0L 0Z0), at W edge of town. 403/553-4448; fax 403/553-2784; toll-free 888/554-2784. Email sunsetmo@ teluselanet.net.* 22 rms, 3 kits. June-Sep: S $54; D $60; each addl $5; kit. units $76-$90; lower rates rest of yr. Crib free. Pet accepted. TV; cable. Restaurant nearby. Ck-out 11 am. Refrigerators. Cr cds: A, D, DS, ER, MC, V.

◀ ⬚ꜞ ⬚

Restaurant

★★★ **COBBLESTONE MANOR.** *173 7th Ave W, 26 mi E on Hwy 5.*

403/653-1519. Specializes in steaks, soups, home-style cooking. Own baking. Hrs: 4:30-9 pm. Closed Sun; early Jan-Mar. Res accepted. Dinner complete meals: $7.95-$17.95. Child's menu. Entertainment. Historic house (1889) built of rock with inlaid panels of fine wood from all over the world; antique furniture and woodwork. Cr cds: MC, V.

D

Jasper National Park

Area code 780
Information Jasper Tourism & Commerce, 632 Connaught Dr, PO Box 98, T0E 1E0; 780/852-3858

Established in 1907 and located in the Canadian Rockies, Jasper is one of Canada's largest and most scenic national parks. In its more than 4,200 square miles (10,878 square kilometers) are waterfalls, lakes, canyons, glaciers, and wilderness areas filled with varied forms of wildlife, in the midst of which is the resort town of Jasper.

Jasper has year-round interpretive programs, trips, and campfire talks. There are also guided wilderness trips, a sky tram, skating, skiing, ice climbing, and rafting and cycling trips. The park, the Rockies, and the resort atmosphere of Jasper make this trip enjoyable any time of the year.

What to See and Do

Marmot Basin. Quad, triple, 3 double chairlifts, 2 T-bars; patrol, school, rentals; repair shop; nursery, 3 cafeterias, bar. Vertical drop 2,300 ft (700 m). (Early Dec-late Apr) 13 mi (19 km) S of Jasper via Icefield Pkwy (93A). Phone 780/852-3816 or 780/488-5909 (snow conditions). Tows/lifts ¢¢¢¢

Miette Hot Springs. Pool uses natural hot mineral springs. (Mid-May-early Sep) Contact Canadian Parks Service, PO Box 10, Jasper, T0E 1E0; 780/852-6161. 38 mi (61 km) E of Jasper via Hwy 16, Pocahontas Junction. Phone 403/866-3750 (lodge). ¢¢

Sightseeing tours.

Boat cruise. Maligne Tours, Ltd. Narrated cruise (1½ hr) on Maligne Lake to world-famous Spirit Island. (June-Sep, daily) Fishing supplies and boat rentals, whitewater raft trips on Maligne River; hiking, horseback riding. 30 mi (48 km) S of Jasper via Hwy 16, Maligne Rd Exit. Phone 780/852-3370. Cruise ¢¢¢¢

Jasper Tramway. Two 30-passenger cars take 1¼ mi (2 km) trip up Whistlers Mt. Vast area of alpine tundra at summit; hiking trails, picnicking; restaurant, gift shop. (Apr-mid-Oct, daily) 4 mi (6 km) S of Jasper, Exit Jasper-Banff Hwy to Whistlers Mt Rd. Phone 780/852-3093. ¢¢¢

Other tours. Various tours are offered by bus, raft, gondola, and "snocoach" to Lake Louise, Jasper, Calgary, Banff, and the Athabasca Glacier. For further information contact Brewster Transportation & Tours, PO Box 1140, Banff, T0L 0C0. Phone 780/762-6700.

Motels/Motor Lodges

★ **AMETHYST LODGE.** *200 Connaught Dr (T0E 1E0).* 780/852-3394; *fax 780/852-5198; res 888/852-7737.* 97 rms, 3 story. June-Sep: S, D $165-$220; each addl $10; under 15 free; lower rates rest of yr. Pet accepted, some restrictions. TV; cable (premium). Complimentary coffee in rms. Restaurant 6:30 am-10 pm. Bar 5 pm-midnight. Ck-out 11 am. Meeting rms. Business center. Free railroad station, bus depot transportation. Downhill/x-country ski 15 mi. 2 whirlpools. Balconies. Cr cds: A, D, ER, JCB, MC, V.

★★ **MARMOT LODGE.** *86 Connaught Dr (T0E 1E0).* 780/852-4471; *fax 780/852-3280; toll-free 888/852-7737. www.mtn/park/lodges.com.* 107 rms, 47 A/C, 2 story, 32 kits. June-Sep: S, D $162-$182; each addl $10; suites $178-$325; under 16 free; ski plan; lower rates rest of yr. Pet accepted, some restrictions. TV; cable. Heated pool; whirlpool. Sauna. Restaurant 6:30-11 am, 5-10 pm. Bar 5 pm-1 am. Ck-out 11 am. Coin lndry. Meeting rm. Business servs avail. Valet serv. railroad station, bus depot transportation. Downhill/x-country ski 15 mi. Fireplace in some kit. units. Private patios, balconies. Grills. Ski waxing rm and lockers in winter. Cr cds: A, D, ER, JCB, MC, V.

★★ **SAW RIDGE HOTEL & CONFERENCE CENTER.** *82 Connaught Dr (T0E 1E0). 780/852-5111; fax 780/852-5942; toll-free 800/661-6427. Email shjres@telusplanet.net.* 154 rms, 3 story. June-Sep: S, D $209; each addl $20; suites $240-$280; under 18 free; lower rates rest of yr; MAP avail. Crib free. TV; cable (premium). Indoor pool; whirlpools. Restaurant 6:30 am-10:30 pm. Bar 4:30 pm-2 am. Ck-out 11 am. Meeting rms. Business servs avail. Valet serv. Free railroad station, bus depot transportation. Sauna. Downhill/x-country ski 5 mi. Some refrigerators; whirlpool in suites. Balconies. Ski lockers. Cr cds: A, DS, MC, V.

Hotels

★★★ **CHARLTON'S CHATEAU JASPER.** *96 Geikie St (T0E 1E0). 780/852-5644; fax 780/852-4860; res 800/661-9323. Email jasper@charlton resorts.com; www.charltonresorts.com.* 107 rms, 3 story, 12 suites. June-Sep: S, D $315; suites $390; lower rates rest of yr. Crib avail. Parking garage. Indoor pool, whirlpool. TV; cable (premium), VCR avail. Complimentary coffee in rms, newspaper. Restaurant 6:30 am-10 pm. Bar. Ck-out 11 am, ck-in 4 pm. Meeting rms. Business center. Bellhops. Dry cleaning. Exercise privileges. Golf, 18 holes. Tennis, 4 courts. Downhill skiing. Hiking trail. Video games. Cr cds: A, C, D, DS, ER, JCB, MC, V.

★★ **LOBSTICK LODGE.** *94 Geikie St (T0E 1E0), at Juniper. 780/852-4431; fax 780/852-4142; res 888/852-7737. www.mtn-park-lodges.com.* 139 rms, 3 story. June-Sep: S, D $202; each addl $10; suites $217; under 15 free; lower rates rest of yr. Crib avail. Pet accepted, some restrictions. Parking lot. Indoor pool, whirlpool. TV; cable, VCR avail. Complimentary coffee in rms, toll-free calls. Restaurant 7 am-9 pm. Bar. Ck-out 11 am, ck-in 4 pm. Meeting rm. Business

servs avail. Bellhops. Concierge. Dry cleaning, coin lndry. Gift shop. Sauna, steam rm. Golf, 18 holes. Downhill skiing. Hiking trail. Cr cds: A, D, ER, JCB, MC, V.

Resort

★★★ **JASPER PARK LODGE.** *(T0E 1E0), 2 mi E off Hwy 16. 780/852-3301; fax 780/852-5107; res 800/441-1414. Email reserve@jpl.cphotels.ca.* 450 units, 6 cabins. No A/C. Late May-mid-Oct: S, D $299-$419; each addl $25; under 18 free; MAP avail; lower rates rest of yr. Crib free. Pet accepted. TV; cable. Heated pool; whirlpool. Supervised children's activities; ages 2 and up. Dining rm (see EDITH CAVELL). Box lunches. Bar 11:30-1 am. Ck-out noon, ck-in 4 pm. Business servs avail. Shopping arcade. Airport, railroad station, bus depot transportation. Tennis. 18-hole golf, greens fee $45-$75, putting green. Swimming. Rowboats, canoes. Whitewater rafting. Downhill ski 15 mi; x-country ski on site. Bicycles. Lawn games. Soc dir; entertainment, movies. Barber, beauty shop. Rec rm. Game rm. Exercise rm; sauna, steam rm. Massage. Fishing guides. Minibars; fireplaces. Many private patios, balconies. Cr cds: A, D, DS, ER, JCB, MC, V.

B&B/Small Inn

★ **OVERLANDER MOUNTAIN LODGE.** *PO Box 6118 (T7V 1X5). 780/866-2330; fax 780/866-2332. Email overland@telusplanet.net; www. overlander-mtn-lodge.com.* 40 rms, 12 with shower only, 2 story. No A/C. No rm phone. May-Oct: S, D $100-$150; each addl $20; lower rates rest of yr. Crib free. Complimentary coffee in rms. Restaurant 7:30-10:30 am, 5:30-9:30 pm. Ck-out 11 am. Meeting rms. Business servs avail. X-country ski 15 mi. Some refrigerators, fireplaces. Some balconies. Cr cds: A, DS, MC, V.

Cottage Colony

★★ **ALPINE VILLAGE CABIN RESORT.** *Hwy 93A N; Box 610 (T0E 1E0), 1½ mi S on Hwy 93, then ¼ mi E*

on Hwy 93A. 780/852-3285; fax 780/
852-1955. www.alpinevillagejasper.com.
37 log cabins, 5 lodge suites, 29 kits.
No A/C. S, D $130; each addl $10;
suites, kit. units $140-$200. Closed
mid-Oct-Apr. TV; cable. Playground.
Coffee in rms. Ck-out 11 am. Many
fireplaces. Grills. Whirlpool. Cr cds:
MC, V.

D ☒ ☒ ☒

Restaurants

★★★ **EDITH CAVELL DINING
ROOM.** 82 Connaught Dr. 780/852-
6073. Email reserve@jpl.cphotels.ca;
www.cphotels.ca. Specializes in wild
mushroom chowder, beef tenderloin.
Hrs: 6-10 pm. Res accepted. Bar. Dinner $55-$65. Complete meals: $59.
Child's menu. Jacket. Cr cds: A, D,
MC, V.

D

★ **L & W.** Patricia St (T0E 1E0), at
Hazel St. 780/852-4114. Specializes in
pasta, pizza, Alberta prime rib. Salad
bar. Hrs: 10 am-midnight. Closed
Dec 25; Nov. Bar. Bkfst a la carte
entrees: $5-$7; lunch a la carte
entrees: $5-$7; dinner a la carte
entrees: $9-$16. Child's menu. Parking. Gardenlike setting. Family-
owned. Cr cds: MC, V.

D ☒

★★★ **LE BEAUVALLON.** 96 Geikie
St. 780/852-5644. www.charlton
resorts.com. Specializes in game, beef,
seafood. Own baking. Hrs: Open 24
hrs. Res accepted. Bar. Bkfst $8-$14;
lunch $9-$14; dinner $18-$38. Buffet: $21. Sun brunch $15. Child's
menu. Entertainment: harpist. Parking. Cr cds: A, DS, ER, MC, V.

D SC ☒

★ **SOMETHING ELSE.** 621 Patricia
(T0E 1E0). 780/852-3850. Own pizza.
Hrs: 11 am-11 pm. Lunch $6-$10;
dinner $10-$16. Child's menu. Open
kitchen. Cr cds: A, D, MC, V.

D ☒

★ **TOKYO TOM'S PLACE.** 410 Connaught Dr (T0E 1E0). 780/852-3780.
Specializes in sushi, deep fried tempura, sukiyaki. Hrs: noon-2:30 pm, 5-
10 pm. Closed Dec 25. Res accepted.
Bar. Lunch, dinner a la carte entrees:
$4.95-$18.95. Cr cds: A, D, MC, V.

★★ **TONQUIN PRIME RIB.** 94
Geikie St (T0E 1E0). 780/852-4966.
Specializes in prime rib, seafood. Hrs:
7-10:30 am, 4-11 pm. Res accepted;
required in season. Bar. Bkfst buffet:
$8.50-$9.50; dinner a la carte
entrees: $14-$24.95. Child's menu.
Parking. Views of mountains. Cr cds:
A, D, DS, ER, MC, V.

Lake Louise

(F-3) See also Banff

Pop 1,600 (est) **Elev** 5,018 ft (1,520
m) **Area code** 403
Information Banff-Lake Louise
Tourism Bureau, PO Box 1298, T0L
0C0; 403/762-8421; or Parks Canada
Lake Louise Info Centre; 403/522-
3833

In the heart of the Canadian Rockies,
Lake Louise is probably best known
as one of the finest year-round resort
towns in this area, along with Banff
(see) and Jasper. The Rockies provide
miles of summer hiking trails, natural beauty for the photographer,
and excellent skiing for a great part
of the year. Lake Louise also provides
the resort atmosphere of nightlife
and fun. During the summer, be sure
to view the town from the gondola.
The ride takes you to Mount White-
horn where there is a lodge, and you
can hike, picnic, explore, and relax.
Other popular activities incl canoeing, fishing, climbing, biking, riding,
tennis, and sightseeing tours.

Motels/Motor Lodges

★ **DEER LODGE.** 109 Lake Louise Dr
(T0L 1E0), 2¼ mi SE off Trans-Can
Hwy 1. 403/522-3991; fax 403/522-
4222; res 800/661-1595. Email
dlodge@telusplanet.net. 73 rms, 3
story. Some rm phones. June-Sep: S,
D $155-$220; each addl $25; under
12 free; lower rates rest of yr. Crib
free. Dining rm 7-11 am, 6-10 pm.
Bar 11 am-midnight. Ck-out 11 am.
Business servs avail. Downhill ski 3
mi; x-country ski adj. Sauna. Outdoor whirlpool. Some balconies. Former trading camp (1921); rustic
setting. Cr cds: A, D, ER, MC, V.

☒ ☒ ☒ ☒ ☒ ☒ ☒

★★ **EMERALD LAKE LODGE.** *1 Emerald Lake Rd; (V0A 1G0), 20 mi W on Trans-Can Hwy 1, in Yoho National Park. 250/343-6321; fax 250/343-6724; toll-free 800/663-6336. Email emlodge@rockies.net.* 85 suites in 24 cabin-style bldgs, 2 story. No A/C. June-Sep: suites $275-$455; under 12 free; ski plans; lower rates rest of yr. Crib free. Restaurant 6-11 pm. Bar. Ck-out 11 am. Meeting rms. Business servs avail. X-country ski on site; rentals. Sauna. Whirlpool. Boat rentals. Ice rink (winter). Game rm. Fireplaces. Private balconies. Picnic tables. On Emerald Lake in Canadian Rockies; canoeing. Cr cds: A, D, ER, MC, V.

🛁 🎿 ⛵ 🏞 🔥

★★ **MOUNTAINEER LODGE.** *101 Village Rd (T0L 1E0). 403/522-3844; fax 403/522-3902. Email mtnrldge@ telusplanet.net; www.mountaineerlodge. com.* 75 rms, 2 story, 3 suites. June-Sep: S $160; D $170; suites $260; lower rates rest of yr. Crib avail. Parking lot. TV; cable (DSS). Complimentary coffee in rms. Restaurant nearby. Ck-out 11 am, ck-in 4 pm. Business servs avail. Sauna, whirlpool. Tennis. Cr cds: A, MC, V.

D 🎿 🏞 🔥

Hotels

★★ **BAKER CREEK CHALETS.** *Hwy 1A, Bow Valley Pkwy (T0L 1E0). 403/522-3761; fax 403/522-2270.*

Lake Louise

Email bakercreek@expertcanmore.net; www.bakercreek.com. 33 rms, 1 story, 8 suites. June-Sep: S $165; D $240; each addl $15; suites $210; children $15; lower rates rest of yr. Crib avail, fee. TV; cable (DSS). Complimentary full bkfst, coffee in rms, newspaper. Restaurant. Bar. Ck-out 11 am, ck-in 3 pm. Fax servs avail. Gift shop. Free airport transportation. Exercise equipt, sauna, steam rm. Golf. Downhill skiing. Bike rentals. Hiking trail. Picnic facilities. Cr cds: MC, V.

🛁 🎿 🏞 🎿 🏃 🔥

★★★★ **POST HOTEL.** *200 Pipestone Rd (T0L 1E0). 403/522-3989; fax 403/522-3966; res 800/661-1586. Email info@posthotel.com; www.post hotel.com.* First known in 1942 as the Lake Louise Ski Lodge, this Alpine-style chalet enjoys a splendid, Canadian Rockies location in Banff National Park, just five minutes from the lake and ski area. Luxurious rooms are outfitted with goose-down comforters, slate floors, wood-burning fireplaces, and Jacuzzi tubs. The nationally recognized continental dining room is housed in the hotel's original log building. 68 rms, 3 story, 25 suites. Feb-Mar, July-Sep, Dec: Crib avail. Valet parking avail. Indoor pool, whirlpool. TV; cable (DSS). VCR avail, CD avail. Complimentary coffee in rms, newspaper, toll-free calls. Restaurant. Bar. Ck-out 11 am, ck-in 3 pm. Meeting rm. Business center. Bellhops. Concierge. Dry cleaning. Gift shop. Steam rm. Tennis, 2 courts. Downhill skiing. Bike rentals. Hiking trail. Picnic facilities. Cr cds: A, MC, V.

D 🛁 🎿 🏞 🎿 🔥 🏃 🔥 🏃

Lake Louise

Resorts

★★★ **CHATEAU LAKE LOUISE.** *111 Lake Louise Dr (T0L 1E0). 403/522-3511; fax 403/522-3834; res 403/522-3511; toll-free 800/441-1414. www.fairmont.com.* 488 rms, 8 story, 84 suites. June-Sep: S, D $545; each addl $25; suites $845; under 17 free; lower rates rest of yr. Crib avail. Pet accepted, some restrictions, fee. Valet parking avail. Indoor pool, lifeguard, whirlpool. TV; cable (DSS), VCR avail, CD avail. Complimentary coffee in rms, newspaper, toll-free calls. Restaurant noon-midnight. 24-hr rm serv. Bar. Ck-out noon, ck-in 4 pm.

Conference center, meeting rms. Bellhops. Concierge. Dry cleaning. Gift shop. Salon/barber. Exercise rm. Tennis. Downhill skiing. Bike rentals. Supervised children's activities. Hiking trail. Picnic facilities. Video games. Cr cds: A, D, DS, ER, JCB, MC, V.

★ **PARADISE LODGE AND BUNGALOWS.** *105 Lake Louise Dr. 403/522-3595; fax 403/522-3987. Email info@paradiselodge.com.* 24 rms in lodge, 21 cabins (shower only). No rm phones. June-Sep: suites $200-$250; cabins $145-$165; kit. cabins $165-$175; lower rates May and Oct. Closed rest of yr. Crib free. TV; cable. Playground. Restaurant nearby. Ck-out 11 am, ck-in 4 pm. Business servs avail. Refrigerators. Balconies. Picnic tables. Cr cds: MC, V.

Restaurants

★★★★ **POST HOTEL DINING ROOM.** *200 Pipestone Rd. 403/522-3989. www.posthotel.com.* Located five minutes from the lake and ski area, this continental dining room is housed in the hotel's original log building, is wrapped in Canadian pine and boasts a beautiful, field-stone fireplace. Creative, internationally influenced preparations of fish, Alberta beef and rack of lamb, caribou, venison, and veal are served in the Alpine-chalet ambiance, complimented by more than 900 wine selections. Specializes in veal, caribou strip loin, rack of lamb. Hrs: 7 am-9 pm. Closed Mid-Oct-early Dec. Res accepted. Wine list. Lunch $9.50-$23.50; dinner $27.50-$37.50. Child's menu. Entertainment: pianist. Cr cds: A, MC, V.

★★★ **VICTORIA DINING ROOM.** *3½ mi SE off Trans-Can Hwy 1. 403/522-3511.* Specializes in prime rib, salmon, rack of lamb. Own baking. Hrs: 6:30-9 am, 11 am-1 pm, 6-9 pm. Res accepted. Bar. Wine list. Bkfst buffet: $16; lunch buffet: $21; dinner complete meals: $28-$49. Child's menu. Valet parking. Cr cds: A, C, D, DS, ER, MC, V.

★★ **WALLISER STUBE.** *111 Lake Louise Dr. 403/522-3511.* Specializes in cheese and beef fondues, game. Hrs: 6-9:30 pm. Res accepted. Bar. Dinner complete meals: $25-$50. Child's menu. Swiss decor. Cr cds: A, D, DS, ER, MC, V.

Lethbridge

(H-5) *See also Fort Macleod*

Settled 1870 **Pop** 60,610 **Elev** 2,983 ft (909 m) **Area code** 403
Web www.albertasouth.com

Lethbridge, in Chinook Country, sits amid ranchland and irrigated farms. The chinook, an Alberta winter phenomenon, is a warm wind that reportedly can raise temperatures as much as 40 degrees within ten minutes.

Originally known to the Blackfoot as *Sik-okotoks* or "place of black rocks," Lethbridge was named after William Lethbridge, first president of the North-West Coal & Navigation Company. Among the many beautiful parks and gardens are the Brewery Gardens at the western edge of town; Indian Battle Park, site of the last battle between Native American nations in North America (1870), today a semiwilderness; and Henderson Lake Park.

In 1869 traders from the United States came north and built so-called "whiskey forts." One of the most notorious was Fort Whoop-Up near Lethbridge. The arrival of the North West Mounted Police in 1874 soon stamped out this illegal whiskey trade. The city has rebuilt this fort, and the flag that signaled the arrival of the latest load of whiskey is now the official flag of Lethbridge.

What to See and Do

Alberta Birds of Prey Centre. Living museum featuring hawks, owls, falcons, and other birds of prey from Alberta and around the world. Interpretive center has educational displays, wildlife art. Daily flying demonstrations; picnicking. (May-mid-Oct, daily, weather permitting) Approx 5 mi (8 km) E via Crowsnest

Hwy (Hwy 3), on 16 Ave in Coaldale. Phone 403/345-4262 or 800/661-1222, operator 20. ¢¢

Fort Whoop-Up. This is a replica of the original fort, a major whiskey trading post in southern Alberta in the 1870s. Interpretive gallery, theater; tours. (Mid-May-Sep, daily; rest of yr, Tues-Fri, Sun afternoons) In Indian Battle Park. Phone 403/329-0444. ¢¢

Nikka Yuko Japanese Garden. Built to commemorate Canada's Centennial in 1967, the authentic garden is a symbol of Japanese-Canadian friendship. Bldgs and bridges were built in Japan and reassembled in Lethbridge. The garden is an art form of peace and tranquility. (Mid-May-late Sep, daily) Henderson Lake Park. Phone 403/328-3511. ¢¢

Sir Alexander Galt Museum. Displays relate to early development of area. Featured exhibits incl indigenous culture, pioneer life, civic history, coal mining, farming history, irrigation, ethnic displays. Video presentations. (Daily; closed hols) W end 5th Ave S. Phone 403/320-3898. **FREE**

Annual Events

"Ag-Expo" Agricultural Exposition. Early Mar.

Whoop-Up Days. Fair, exhibitions, horse racing, rodeo, grandstand show. Early Aug.

International Air Show. Aug.

Hotels

★★ **BEST WESTERN HEIDELBERG INN.** 1303 Mayor Magrath Dr (T1K 2R1). 403/329-0555; fax 403/328-8846; toll-free 800/528-1234. June-Dec: S $92; D $97; each addl $5; under 17 free; lower rates rest of yr. Crib avail. Parking lot. TV; cable, VCR avail. Complimentary coffee in rms, newspaper, toll-free calls. Restaurant 6 am-11 pm. Bar. Ck-out noon, ck-in 2 pm. Business servs avail. Dry cleaning. Exercise equipt, sauna. Golf, 18 holes. Cr cds: A, C, D, DS, ER, JCB, MC, V.

⬛ 🏋 ⌘ 🛩 ✈ ⛷ 🏊

★★★ **LETHBRIDGE LODGE.** 320 Scenic Dr (T1J 4B4). 403/328-1123; fax 403/328-0002; toll-free 800/661-1232. Email kwatts@chipreit.com; www.lethbridgelodge.com. 155 rms, 4

story, 36 suites. July-Aug: S $129; D $139; each addl $10; suites $149; under 18 free; lower rates rest of yr. Crib avail. Pet accepted, some restrictions, fee. Parking lot. Indoor pool, whirlpool. TV; cable (premium). Complimentary coffee in rms, newspaper, toll-free calls. Restaurant 6:30 am-11 pm. Bar. Ck-out noon, ck-in 4 pm. Meeting rms. Business center. Bellhops. Dry cleaning. Gift shop. Exercise privileges. Golf. Hiking trail. Video games. Cr cds: A, C, D, DS, ER, JCB, MC, V.

⬛ 🏋 ⌘ 🛩 ✈ ⛷ 🔥 SC 🏊

Restaurants

★★ **BEEFEATER STEAK HOUSE.** 1917 Mayor Magrath Dr S (T1K 2R8). 403/320-6211. Specializes in Alberta prime rib, steak, seafood. Own desserts. Hrs: 11 am-2 pm, 4-11 pm; Sat from 4 pm; Sun to 9 pm; Sun brunch 10 am-2 pm. Res accepted. Bar. Lunch $5.95-$9.95; dinner $9.95-$24.95. Sun brunch $9.95. Child's menu. Entertainment. Atrium, garden setting. Cr cds: A, D, DS, MC, V.

⬛ 🍴

★★★ **COCO PAZZO.** 1264 3rd Ave S (T1J 0J9), Downtown. 403/329-8979. Specializes in wood-fired pizza, Alberta beef. Hrs: 11 am-11 pm; Thurs-Sat to midnight; Sun 5-9 pm. Closed hols. Res accepted. Bar. Lunch $4.95-$7.95; dinner $7.25-$16.50. Child's menu. Casual Italian cafe dining. Cr cds: A, MC, V.

⬛

★★ **NEW DYNASTY.** 103 7th St S. 403/328-1212. Specializes in shredded ginger beef, moo shu pork, shrimp and scallops with bacon wrap. Hrs: 11 am-midnight; Fri, Sat to 2 am. Closed Dec 25. Res accepted. Bar. Lunch $5-$7; dinner $8-$12. Child's menu. Modern Asian decor. Cr cds: A, D, DS, ER, MC, V.

⬛

★★★ **SVEN ERICKSEN'S.** 1715 Mayor Magrath Dr (T1K 2R7). 403/328-7756. Specializes in prime rib, seafood, roast beef. Own baking. Hrs: 11 am-9 pm. Closed Dec 25, 26. Res accepted. Bar. Lunch complete meals: $4.75-$7.95; dinner complete meals: $8.95-$31.95. Sun brunch $4.95-$6.75. Child's menu. Entertainment: Sat. Provincial decor; display of old photos, Lethbridge memorabilia; antique clock. Family-owned. Cr cds: A, ER, MC, V. D SC

Medicine Hat (G-7)

Settled 1883 **Pop** 42,929 **Elev** 2,365 ft (721 m) **Area code** 403 **Web** www.absouth.com

Information Medicine Hat & District Convention and Visitors Bureau, 8 Gehring Rd SE, PO Box 605, T1A 7G5; 403/527-6422 or 800/481-2822

The city of Medicine Hat is famous for its industries. Rich in clays and natural gas, the area was a natural site for brick, tile, and petrochemical plants. Its hot summer temperatures make it ideal for market gardens and greenhouses. There are many beautiful parks and excellent recreational facilities.

The name Medicine Hat is a translation of the Blackfoot name *Saamis* meaning "headdress of a medicine man." Supposedly a Cree medicine man lost his war bonnet in the river during a fight between the Cree and Blackfoot.

Natural gas was discovered here in 1883, and in 1909 the huge Bow Island gas field was founded. Because of these gas fields, the British poet Rudyard Kipling referred to the early settlement as "the town with all hell for a basement." Medicine Hat came into being with the arrival of the Canadian Pacific Railway.

What to See and Do

Cypress Hills Provincial Park. Oasis of mixed deciduous and coniferous forests in the middle of a predominantly grassland region. At a maximum elevation of 4,810 ft (1,466 m) above sea level, the hills are the highest point in Canada between the Rocky Mts and Labrador. The area offers a swimming beach, boating, canoeing, fishing; camping (fee), golf course, hiking trails, and nature interpretive programs. Fort Walsh National Historic Park is nearby. For further information contact PO Box 12, Elkwater T0J 1C0. E on Trans-Canada Highway 1, then S on Hwy 41. Phone 403/893-3777 or 403/893-3782 (camping, May-Sep). **FREE**

■ **Dinosaur Provincial Park.** A UNESCO World Heritage Site. Discoveries of extensive fossil concentrations in this area in the late 1800s led to the designation of this area as a provincial park. More than 300 complete skeletons have been recovered for display in museums worldwide. The 22,000-acre park consists mainly of badlands; large areas have restricted access and can be seen only on interpretive tours. Facilities incl canoeing, fishing; interpretive trails, dinosaur displays (at their actual site of discovery) along public loop drive, picnicking, primitive camping (firewood and water provided), guided tours and hikes, amphitheater events and talks (summer; fee; inquire in advance). A field station of the Royal Tyrell Museum of Paleontology in Drumheller is located here; also John Ware Cabin, with displays. Park (daily). Field station (mid-May-mid-Oct, daily; rest of yr, Mon-Fri). Some fees. Approx 25 mi (40 km) W on Hwy 1, then N on Hwy 884, W on Hwy 544. Phone 403/378-4342.

Medicine Hat Museum & Art Gallery. Displays depict the history of the Canadian West, featuring pioneer items, local fossils, relics, and Native artifacts. The archives contain a large collection of photographs and manu-

The natural wonders of Alberta

scripts. (Daily; closed Jan 1, Good Friday, Dec 25) 1302 Bomford Crescent SW. Phone 403/527-6266 or 403/526-0486. **FREE**

Annual Event

Exhibition and Stampede. Stampede Park. Cattle and horse shows, professional rodeo, midway rides. First wkend Aug.

Motels/Motor Lodges

★★ **BEST WESTERN INN.** *722 Redcliff Dr (T1A 5A3), 1½ mi W, 3 blks N of Hwy 3, near airport. 403/ 527-3700; fax 403/526-8689; toll-free 800/528-1234.* 110 rms, 2 story, 24 suites, 11 kits. S $69; D $75-$79; suites $119; kit. units $73-$83. Crib $3. Pet accepted. TV; cable (premium). 2 indoor pools; whirlpools. Complimentary continental bkfst. Restaurant adj 6 am-10:30 pm. Bar. Ck-out 11 am. Coin lndry. Meeting rms. Business servs avail. Sundries. Exercise equipt; sauna. Game rm. Refrigerators, microwaves. Cr cds: A, C, D, DS, ER, MC, V.

D ⊷ ≍ 🕇 ⊠ 🐾 SC

★ **SUPER 8.** *1280 Trans-Canada Way SE (T1B 1J5), opp Southview Mall. 403/528-8888; fax 403/526-4445; res 800/800-8000. Email medawat@telus planet.net.* 70 rms, 3 story, 8 kit. units. Late June-early Sep: S $59.88; D $63.88-$68.88; each addl $4; suite $114.88; kit. units $78.88; under 12 free; wkly rates; higher rates Exhibition and Stampede; lower rates rest of yr. Crib free. Pet accepted. TV; cable. Indoor pool; whirlpool. Complimentary continental bkfst. Restaurant opp open 24 hrs. Ck-out 11 am. Business servs avail. Cr cds: A, D, DS, ER, JCB, MC, V.

D ⊷ ≍ ⊠ 🐾

★ **TRAVELODGE.** *1100 Redcliff Dr SW (T1A 5E5), off Trans-Can Hwy 1. 403/527-2275; fax 403/526-7842; toll-free 800/442-8729.* 129 rms, 2 story. S $79; D $71-89. Crib free. TV; cable (premium). Heated pool; wading pool, whirlpool. Coffee in rms. Restaurant 6 am-11 pm; Sun 7 am-9 pm. Bar 11-2 am. Ck-out noon. Meeting rms. Business servs avail. Valet serv. Exercise equipt; sauna. Some refrigerators. Cr cds: A, D, DS, ER, MC, V.

D ≍ 🕇 ⊠ 🐾 SC

Hotel

★★★ **MEDICINE HAT LODGE.** *1051 Ross Glen Dr SE (T1B 3T8), jct Trans-Can Hwy 1 and Dunmore Rd. 403/529-2222; fax 403/529-1538; toll-free 800/661-8095. Email mhlodge@ memlane.com; www.medhatlodge.com.* 184 rms, 4 story, 6 suites. June-Aug: S $109; D $119; each addl $10; suites $149; lower rates rest of yr. Crib avail. Pet accepted, some restrictions. Valet parking avail. Indoor pool, children's pool, lifeguard. TV; cable (premium), VCR avail. Complimentary coffee in rms, newspaper, toll-free calls. Restaurant 6-11 pm. Bar. Ck-out noon, ck-in 4 pm. Meeting rms. Business center. Bellhops. Dry cleaning. Gift shop. Salon/barber. Free airport transportation. Exercise privileges, sauna, steam rm. Golf, 18 holes. Tennis, 4 courts. Downhill skiing. Bike rentals. Supervised children's activities. Hiking trail. Video games. Cr cds: A, C, D, DS, ER, JCB, MC, V.

D ⊷ ≍ 🕇 🕇 ⊫ ≍ 🕇 ⊠ 🐾 SC 🕇

Restaurant

★★ **BEEFEATER STEAK HOUSE.** *3286 13th Ave SE. 403/526-6925.* Specializes in beef, seafood. Salad bar. Hrs: 11 am-midnight; Sat from 4:30 pm; Sun 4:30-10 pm. Closed Dec 25, 26. Res accepted. Bar. Lunch $5.25-$12.50; dinner $8.50-$44. Child's menu. English motif. Cr cds: A, D, ER, MC, V.

⊟

Red Deer (E-5)

Settled 1885 **Pop** 58,252 **Elev** 2,816 ft (860 m) **Area code** 403
Web www.visitor.red-deer.ab.ca

Information Visitor & Convention Bureau, Greater Red Deer Visitor Centre at Heritage Ranch, PO Box 5008, T4N 3T4; 780/346-0180 or 800/215-8946

The city of Red Deer sits in the valley of the Red Deer River, which winds through the lush green parkland of central Alberta. Sylvan and Pine lakes are among the popular recreational lakes surrounding the city. Agriculture and the petroleum industry are the mainstays of the economy. To the west is the David Thompson Highway, leading through the foothills into Alberta's Canadian Rockies and Banff National Park (see BANFF).

In the early 1870s the Calgary-Edmonton Trail crossed the river at a point known as Red Deer Crossing. With the coming of the railway, traffic increased and a trading post and stopping place were established. When the Northwest Rebellion broke out in 1885, a small regiment was stationed at Fort Normandeau. A reconstruction of this fort stands near Red Deer.

The river was originally called *Waska-soo See-pi*, the Cree word for elk, because of the abundance of these animals. Early Scottish fur traders thought the elk were related to the red deer of their native land, hence the present name for the river and city.

What to See and Do

Canyon Ski Area. Triple, double chairlifts, 2 T-bars, handle tow; nordic jump; patrol, school, rentals; snowmaking; day lodge; bar, cafeteria. Longest run ½ mi (1 km); vertical drop 500 ft (164 m). (Nov-Mar, daily) X-country skiing. 6 mi (10 km) E on Ross St. Phone 403/346-5589, 780/346-5588 (snow conditions), or 780/346-7003 (off-season). ¢¢¢¢

Fort Normandeau. Rebuilt 1885 army fort and interpretive center with displays of cultural history. Slide program, living history interpreters. (May-Sep, daily) Picnic area, canoe launch. (See ANNUAL EVENTS) 2 mi (3 km) W off Hwy 2 on 32nd St. Phone 403/346-2010 or 403/347-7550. **Donation**

Red Deer and District Museum. Displays cover prehistory and early settlement of Red Deer; changing exhibits. Also here are Heritage Square and Red Deer and District Archives. (Daily; extended hrs July-early Sep; closed Jan 1, Dec 25) 4525 47 A Ave, adj to Recreation Centre. Phone 403/309-8405. **Donation**

Waskasoo Park. Large River Valley park extending throughout city. Incl fishing, canoeing, water park; 47 mi (75 km) of bicycle and hiking trails, equestrian area, 18-hole golf, picnicking (shelters). Campground (fee). Natural and cultural history interpretive centers; other attractions located within park. Fee for activities. (Daily) Phone 403/342-8159. **FREE**

Annual Events

Fort Normandeau Days. Fort Normandeau. Native American ceremonies and dances, parade, children's activities. Late May.

Highland Games. Westerner Park. Last Sat June.

International Folk Festival. Ethnic performers, displays, ethnic foods, fireworks. Early July.

Westerner Days. Fair and exhibition, midway, livestock shows, chuckwagon races. Mid-July.

Motels/Motor Lodges

★ **NORTH HILL INN.** *7150 50th Ave (T4N 6A5), (Hwy 2A).* 403/343-8800; fax 403/342-2334; toll-free 800/662-7152. 117 rms, 3 story. S $72; D $75-$85; under 18 free; wkend rates; golf plans. Crib free. Pet accepted, some restrictions. TV; cable (premium). Heated pool; whirlpool. Coffee in rms. Restaurant 6 am-10 pm. Bar. Ck-out 11 am. Meeting rms. Business center. Exercise equipt; sauna. Downhill ski 10 mi; x-country ski 3 mi. Cr cds: A, D, ER, MC, V.

⬛🔧🐾🏃🎿🏂🏃

★ **TRAVELODGE.** *2807 50th Ave (T4R 1H6).* 403/346-2011; res 800/578-7878; toll-free 888/383-2344. 136 rms, 3 story, 10 kits. S $69; D $75; suites $120. Crib avail. Pet accepted, some restrictions. TV; cable. Indoor pool; whirlpool. Restaurant 6:30 am-1 pm, 5-10 pm. Ck-out 11 am. Business servs avail. In-rm modem link. Coin lndry. Downhill ski 10 mi; x-country ski 3 mi. Cr cds: A, D, DS, ER, MC, V.

⬛🔧🐾🏃🏂

Hotels

★ ★ **BLACK KNIGHT INN.** *2929 50th Ave (T4R 1H1), (Hwy 2A).* 403/343-6666; fax 403/340-8970; toll-free 800/661-8793. www.blackknightinn.com. 91 rms, 8 story, 9 suites. S, D $88; each addl $10; suites $150; under 18 free. Crib avail. Parking lot. Indoor/outdoor pools, whirlpool. TV; cable. Complimentary coffee in rms, newspaper. Restaurant. Bar. Ck-out noon, ck-in noon. Meeting rms. Business servs avail. Bellhops. Concierge. Dry cleaning. Gift shop. Exercise privileges. Golf. Tennis. Downhill skiing. Hiking trail. Video games. Cr cds: A, D, ER, MC, V.

D ★ ⚑ ✗ ⚓ ⛄ ✗ ⚐ ⚒ ⚒

★★ HOLIDAY INN EXPRESS.

2803 50th Ave (T4R 1H1), (Hwy 2A). 403/343-2112; fax 403/340-8540; res 800/HOLIDAY; toll-free 800/223-1993. Email yrdab.hiexreddeerab@home.com; www.hiexpress.com/reddeer-exab. 88 rms, 2 story, 4 suites. Mar-Oct: S, D $104; each addl $10; suites $140; under 18 free; lower rates rest of yr. Crib avail, fee. Pet accepted, some restrictions, fee. Parking lot. Indoor pool, whirlpool. TV; cable (premium). Complimentary continental bkfst, coffee in rms, newspaper, toll-free calls. Restaurant nearby. Ck-out 11 am, ck-in 3 pm. Fax servs avail. Bellhops. Dry cleaning, coin lndry. Exercise privileges, steam rm. Golf, 18 holes. Tennis, 2 courts. Downhill skiing. Hiking trail. Video games. Cr cds: A, D, DS, ER, JCB, MC, V.

D ⚑ ✗ ⚓ ⛄ ✗ ⚐ ⚒ ⚒ SC

★★ HOLIDAY INN RED DEER.

6500 67th St (T3P 1A2). 403/342-6567; fax 403/343-3600; toll-free 800/661-4961. Email hotel@holidayinnred deer.com. 97 rms, 4 story. S, D $89; suites $99-$179; under 18 free; golf packages. Crib free. Pet accepted. TV; cable (premium). Complimentary coffee in rms. Restaurant 6 am-10 pm; Bar 10-2 am. Ck-out 11 am. Business center. Barber, beauty shop. Downhill ski 10 mi; x-country ski 2 mi. Exercise equipt; sauna. Massage. Whirlpool. Cr cds: A, DS, MC, V.

D ⚑ ✗ ⛄ ⚒ ⚒ SC ✗

Conference Center

★★ CAPRI HOTEL - CONVENTION & TRADE CENTRE.

3310 Gaetz 50th Ave (T4N 3X9), at top of S Hill. 403/346-2091; fax 403/346-4790; toll-free 800/662-7197. Email capcen@telus planet.net; www.capricentre.com. 208 rms, 14 story, 22 suites. Feb-Nov: S, D $110; each addl $20; suites $300; under 16 free; lower rates rest of yr. Crib avail. Parking lot. Pool, whirlpool. TV; cable (premium). Complimentary continental bkfst, coffee in rms, newspaper, toll-free calls. Restaurant 7 am-10 pm. Bar. Ck-out

noon, ck-in 3 pm. Meeting rms. Business center. Bellhops. Concierge. Dry cleaning. Gift shop. Salon/barber. Exercise equipt, sauna, steam rm. Golf. Tennis. Downhill skiing. Supervised children's activities. Hiking trail. Picnic facilities. Video games. Cr cds: A, C, D, DS, ER, MC, V.

D ⚑ ★ ⚑ ✗ ⚓ ✗ ⛄ ✗ ✗ ⚒ ⚒ ✗

Restaurant

★ **HOULIHAN'S.** *6791 Gaetz Ave #11 (T4N 4C9), in Pines Plaza. 403/342-0330.* Specializes in prime rib, beef Wellington, seafood. Hrs: 11 am-11 pm; Sat from 4:30 pm. Closed Sun; hols. Res accepted Mon-Thurs. Bar. Lunch $5-$7; dinner $10-$12. Child's menu. Various dining levels with fountain in center. Cr cds: A, D, DS, ER, MC, V.

D ⊟

Waterton Lakes National Park

Web www.worldweb.com/park scanada-waterton

Information Superintendent, Waterton Lakes National Park, T0K 2M0; 403/859-2224 (winter) or 403/859-5133 (summer).

Waterton Lakes National Park was established in 1895, taking its name from the lakes in the main valley which were named for the 19th-century English naturalist Squire Charles Waterton. In 1932 it was linked with Glacier National Park in Montana (see); the whole area is now known as Waterton-Glacier International Peace Park. This park contains 203 square miles (526 square kilometers) on the eastern slope of the Rocky Mountains, just north of the US-Canadian border.

Travelers from the US can reach the park via the Chief Mountain Highway along the east edge of Glacier National Park (mid-May-mid-Sep). The trails are well-maintained and afford an introduction to much of the scenery that is inaccessible by car. Whether by foot, car, or boat, exploring the park and its many wonders will make the trip most worthwhile.

Prince of Wales Hotel, Waterton Lakes National Park

The Red Rock Parkway goes from the town of Waterton Park to Red Rock Canyon after branching off Alberta Highway 5. A buffalo paddock is located on Highway 6, just inside the northeastern park boundary. Also from the town of Waterton Park, you can drive to Cameron Lake via the Akamina Parkway. Separate fees are charged at most parks.

Motels/Motor Lodges

★★ ASPEN VILLAGE INN. *111 Windflower Ave (T0K 2M0). 403/859-2255; fax 403/859-2033; res 888/859-8669. Email travel@watertoninsle.ab.ca.* 37 rms, 1-2 story, 2 suites, 12 kit. units. No A/C. No elvtr. Mid-May-Oct: S, D $122-$193; each addl $10; suites $159-$215; kit. units $126-$174; under 16 free; lower rates Easter-mid-June and Oct-Thanksgiving. Closed rest of yr. Crib $10. TV. Playground. Complimentary coffee in rms. Restaurant adj 7:30 am-10 pm. Ck-out 11 am. Gift shop. Sundries. Whirlpool. Grills. Cr cds: A, D, DS, ER, MC, V.

★ BEST WESTERN EMERALD ISLE MOTOR INN. *2306 Beacon Ave (V8L 1X2). 250/656 4141; fax 250/655-1351; res 800/528-1234; toll-free 800/315-3377. Email reservations@bwemerald isle.com; www.bwemeraldisle.com.* 54 rms, 2 story, 11 suites. May-Sep: S $129; D $159; each addl $20; suites $249; under 17 free; lower rates rest of yr. Crib avail. Pet accepted, some restrictions, fee. Parking lot. TV; cable. Complimentary coffee in rms. Restaurant 7 am-9 pm. Ck-out 11

am, ck-in 3 pm. Meeting rm. Business servs avail. Concierge. Dry cleaning, coin lndry. Gift shop. Sauna, whirlpool. Golf. Cr cds: A, C, D, DS, ER, JCB, MC, V.

★★★ KILMOREY. *117 Evergreen Ave (T0K 2M0). 403/859-2334; fax 403/859-2342; res 403/859-2252; toll-free 888/859-8669. Email travel@ watertoninfo.ab.ca.* 23 rms, 3 story, 3 suites. No A/C. No elvtr. No rm phones. S, D $86-$133; each addl $10; suites $117-$171; under 16 free. TV in lobby. Dining rm 7:30 am-10 pm. Ck-out 11 am, ck-in 3 pm. Country-style inn built in 1923. On Emerald Bay in Waterton Park. Cr cds: A, D, DS, ER, MC, V.

Hotel

★★ CRANDALL MOUNTAIN LODGE. *102 Mt View Rd (T0K 2M0). 403/859-2288; fax 403/859-2288. Email crandell@telusplanet.net; www.crandellmountainlodge.com.* 17 rms, 2 story, 8 kit. units. No A/C. No rm phones. June-Sep: S $88-$128; D $98-$158; each addl $10; kit. units $128-$188; hols (2-day min); lower rates rest of yr. Crib $7. Pet accepted, some restrictions. TV. Playground. Coffee in rms. Restaurant opp 7:30 am-10 pm. Ck-out 10 am. Meeting rms. Some fireplaces. Cr cds: A, DS, MC, V.

B&B/Small Inn

★ PRINCE OF WALES. *117 Evergreen Ave. 403/859-2231; fax 403/859-2630.* 87 rms, 7 story. No A/C. S $169-$221; D $175-$227; each addl $15; under 12 free. Closed late Sep-mid May. Crib free. Dining rm 6:30-9:30 am, 11:30 am-2 pm, 5-9 pm. Tearoom 2-5 pm. Bar 11:30 am-midnight. Ck-out 11 am. Bellhops. Gift shop. Large, gabled inn (built 1927) overlooking lake and mountains. Cr cds: A, MC, V.

PROVINCE OF BRITISH COLUMBIA

This huge territory, with its mixture of climate, geography, products, and people, began its modern history in 1843 while under British control. In 1871 British Columbia joined the Confederation and its steady progression can be traced through fur trading and gold rushes to urban development. Bordered on the south by Washington and on the north by the Yukon, the province has a wide range of weather conditions from the balmy warm breezes in Victoria to cold arctic winds in the far north. Thus many recreational possibilities, including skiing, sailing, swimming, spelunking, and river rafting, can be enjoyed.

Pop 3,100,000 (est) **Land area** 344,817 sq mi (893,073 sq km) **Capital** Victoria **Web** www.travel.bc.ca

Information Tourism British Columbia, Box 9830, Stn Prov Govt, Victoria V8W 9W5; 604/663-6000 or 800/663-6000

Vacation choices range from shopping for indigenous art, to gold panning, to flying over the magnificent wilderness of the Queen Charlotte Islands. No trip to British Columbia would be complete without a visit to Vancouver and Victoria. International in character, Vancouver boasts all the attractions of a modern city while preserving its vital past. Museums, galleries, parks, gardens, and fine dining blend well with beaches and marinas in this lovely peninsular city.

Victoria, the capital, is located on Vancouver Island and is noted for its many gardens and parks. Victoria offers sights that include the Parliament buildings, the Royal British Columbia Museum with its Natural History Gallery, and reconstructed areas that reflect the past.

Rogers Pass

Most of British Columbia is on Pacific Standard Time and observes Pacific Daylight Saving Time in summer. Tourists should note that there is strong anti-litter legislation in British Columbia which applies to boaters and hikers as well as drivers and pedestrians.

In addition to national holidays, British Columbia observes British Columbia Day (first Monday August).

Safety belts are mandatory for all persons anywhere in vehicle. Children under 40 pounds in weight must be in an approved passenger restraint anywhere in vehicle: 20-39 pounds may use an approved safety seat facing forward if in parents' or guardians' vehicle, or a regulation safety belt if in someone else's vehicle; under 20 pounds must be in an approved safety seat facing rear. For further information phone 250/387-3140.

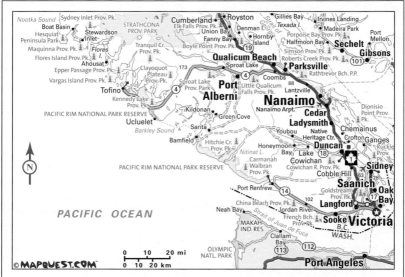

Only one paved road reaches the open ocean on Vancouver's western coast, which is an area of primordial beauty, tempestuous climate, abundant wildlife, and vast wilderness beaches. From Parksville on the island's east coast, Highway 4 passes a number of popular destinations, including a butterfly zoo and roaring Englishman Falls, before cresting Vancouver Island's central mountain range. Provincial parks protect Cathedral Grove, an old-growth forest preserve with millennium-old cedars and firs. Highway 4 reaches Port Alberni, where travelers can opt to take a day-long mail-boat trip out to far-flung communities scattered along Alberni Inlet. Highway 4 continues to Ucluelet, a fishing village and a popular departure point for whale-watching trips onto the Pacific and sea kayak trips to the Broken Group Islands (part of Pacific Rim National Park). The road to Tofino passes long beaches and rugged island-flecked shorelines, most of it preserved in Pacific Rim National Park. Tofino, at the end of the road, occupies a narrow peninsula between rocky, forested islands in churning seas. Once a backwoods village, Tofino is now one of the top resort destinations in British Columbia, with native art galleries and world-class hotels and restaurants. From Tofino, boat or float plane trips lead out to even more remote destinations, including shoreline hot springs on a remote island. **(Approx 107 mi; 173 km)**

This route parallels the western slopes of the Canadian Rockies along the Columbia River. Stirring mountain scenery mixes with great outdoor recreation, especially if you're a golfer. Highway 95 follows what's called the Rocky Mountain Trench, a broad U-shaped valley carved between the jagged peaks of the Rockies and the somewhat lower, but equally spectacular, peaks of the Selkirk, Columbia, and Purcell ranges. Besides miles and miles of mountain vistas, other highlights include Fairmont and Radium Hot Springs; a good railway museum at Cranbrook; Fort Steele, a reconstructed frontier town from the 1880s with summer interpretive programs and classic melodramas in the opera house; and the Columbia Wetlands, a 100-mile-long wildlife refuge that preserves the habitat of moose, coyote, mink, beaver, and hundreds of varieties of migrating birds. At Golden, travelers can enjoy a whitewater rafting trip in the Kicking Horse River, one of Canada's most thrilling rivers for rafters. (**Approx 154 mi; 248 km**)

Kamloops (E-6)

Pop 64,048 **Elev** 1,181 ft (360 m)
Area code 250
Web www.city.kamloops.bc.ca
Information Chamber of Commerce and Visitor Info Centre, 1290 W Trans-Canada Hwy, V2C 6R3; 250/374-3377 or 800/662-1994

Kamloops is located at the junction of the North and South Thompson rivers and is a trade center for a farming, mining, ranching, lumbering, and fruit-growing region. Kamloops trout are world famous; there are some 200 lakes within 60 miles (96 kilometers) of the city.

What to See and Do

Kamloops Museum & Archives. Natural history; Shuswap culture; fur trade; Gold Rush eras. (Daily; Tues-Sat in winter; summer hrs vary) 207 Seymour St. Phone 250/828-3576. **Donation**

Kamloops Wildlife Park. More than 300 animals, both native and intl. Nature trail. Miniature railroad (seasonal, fee). Park (daily). For further information contact PO Box 698, V2C 5L7. 11 mi (18 km) E, at 9055 E Trans-Canada Hwy 1. Phone 250/573-3242. ¢¢¢

Secwepemc Native Heritage Park. Located on the Kamloops Reserve, park interprets culture and heritage of the Secwepemc people. Incl archaeological site, full-scale winter village model, indoor museum exhibits, and native arts and crafts. Tours avail. (Summer, daily; rest of yr, Mon-Fri) N across Yellowhead Bridge, then 1st right. Phone 250/828-9801. ¢¢¢

Annual Event

International Air Show. Concession, beer garden. First Wed Aug. Fulton Field.

Motels/Motor Lodges

★★★ **THE COAST CANADIAN INN.** 339 St. Paul St (V2E 1J7). 250/372-5201; fax 250/372-9363; res 800/663-1144. Email i.striegan@coast hotels.com. 94 rms, 5 story. May-Sep:

S $110; D $120; each addl $10; under 18 free; ski plans; lower rates rest of yr. Crib free. Pet accepted. TV; cable (premium), VCR avail (movies). Pool. Restaurant 6:30 am-10 pm. Rm serv 24 hrs. Bar 1 pm-1 am; entertainment. Ck-out 1 pm. Meeting rms. Business center. In-rm modem link. Bellhops. Exercise equipt. Health club privileges. Minibars. Cr cds: A, DS, MC, V.

★ **DAYS INN.** 1285 W Trans-Can Hwy (V2E 2J7). 250/374-5911; fax 250/374-6922; res 800/329-7466; toll-free 800/561-5002. Email daysinn@ kamloops.net. 60 rms. June-Sep: S $99; D $109; each addl $10; suites $125-$250; kits. $150-$250; under 12 free; lower rates rest of yr. Crib free. Pet accepted, some restrictions. TV; cable (premium), VCR avail. Heated pool; whirlpool. Restaurant 7 am-9 pm. Ck-out noon. Meeting rms. Business servs avail. Refrigerators. Cr cds: A, D, ER, JCB, MC, V.

★★ **EXECUTIVE INN - KAMLOOPS.** 540 Victoria St (V2C 2B2). 250/372-2281; fax 250/372-1125; toll-free 800/663-2837. 150 rms, 5 story. May-Sep: S $105-$139; D $115-$149; each addl $10; suites $150-$250; under 14 free; lower rates rest of yr. Crib $10. TV; cable (premium). Coffee in rms. Restaurant 6 am-10 pm. Bar noon-1 am. Ck-out noon. Meeting rms. Business servs avail. Health club privileges. Casino. Cr cds: A, D, DS, ER, JCB, MC, V.

★★ **HOSPITALITY INN.** 500 W Columbia St (V2C 1K6). 250/374-4164; fax 250/374-6971; toll-free 800/663-5733. 77 rms, 2 story, 15 kits. June-Sep: S $92.50; D $96.50; each addl $6; kit. units $6 addl; under 12 free; lower rates rest of yr. Crib $6. TV; cable (premium). Sauna. Pool; whirlpool. Restaurant 7 am-10 pm. Ck-out 11 am. Meeting rms. Business servs avail. Refrigerators. Private patios. Cr cds: A, D, DS, ER, JCB, MC, V.

★★ **HOWARD JOHNSON PANORAMA INN.** 610 W Columbia St (V2C 1L1). 250/374-1515; fax 250/374-4116; toll-free 800/663-3813.

94 rms, 2-3 story, 11 suites, 40 kits. May-Sep: S $79-$85; D $85-$89; each addl $8; suites $95-$125; kits. $8 addl; under 12 free; lower rates rest of yr. Crib free. TV; cable. Sauna. Heated pool; whirlpool. Coffee in rms. Restaurant 7 am-11 pm. Ck-out 11 am. Business servs avail. In-rm modem link. Private balconies. View of city. Cr cds: A, D, DS, ER, MC, V.

🄳 ⌷ ⌷ 🄷 SC

★ **KAMLOOPS CITY CENTER TRAVELODGE.** *430 Columbia St (V2C 2T5).* 250/372-8202; fax 250/372-1459; toll-free 800/578-7878. Email sleepy@kam.com 68 rms, 2 story. May-Oct: S, D $84-$94; each addl $5; under 18 free; lower rates rest of yr. Crib free. TV; cable, VCR avail. Sauna. Heated pool; whirlpool. Restaurant 7 am-9 pm. Ck-out 11 am. Meeting rm. Business servs avail. Health club privileges. Cr cds: A, C, D, ER, MC, V.

🄳 ⌷ ⌷ 🄷 SC

★★ **RAMADA INN - KAMLOOPS.** *555 W Columbia St (V2C 1K7).* 250/374-0358; fax 250/374-0691; toll-free 800/663-2832. Email ramadakam@telus.net. 90 rms, 3 story, 12 kits. May-Sep: S $109; D $119; each addl $5; suites $100-$175; kit. units $10 addl; under 18 free; lower rates rest of yr. Crib free. TV; cable (premium), VCR avail. Sauna. Pool; whirlpool. Restaurant 7 am-10 pm. Bar; entertainment. Ck-out noon. Meeting rms. Business servs avail. Valet serv. Health club privileges. Refrigerators. Cr cds: A, D, DS, ER, JCB, MC, V.

🄳 ⌷ ⌷ ⌷ ⌷ ⌷ ⌷

★★ **SAGE BRUSH MOTEL.** *660 W Columbia St (V2C 1L1).* 250/372-3151; fax 250/372-2983; toll-free 888/218-6116. 60 rms, 2 story, 30 kits. May-mid-Sep: S $60; D $68-$78; each addl $5; kit. units $5 addl; higher rates hols; lower rates rest of yr. TV; cable (premium). Sauna. Heated pool; whirlpool. Restaurant 7 am-11 pm. Ck-out 11 am. Business servs avail. Health club privileges. Refrigerators. Cr cds: A, D, MC, V.

⌷ ⌷ 🄷 SC

★★ **STAY 'N SAVE.** *1325 Columbia St W (V2C 6P4).* 250/374-8877; fax 250/372-0507. 83 rms, 3 story, 25 kit. units. S $89; D $99; each addl $10; suites $120; kit. units $99-$130;

under 17 free; ski plans. Crib free. Pet accepted. TV; cable. Heated pool; whirlpool. Complimentary coffee in lobby. Restaurant adj open 24 hrs. Ck-out 11 am. Coin lndry. Meeting rms. Business servs avail. In-rm modem link. Valet serv. X-country ski 15 mi. Exercise equipt; sauna. Picnic tables. Cr cds: A, D, MC, V.

🄳 ⌷ ⌷ ⌷ ⌷ ⌷ ⌷ ⌷ ⌷ ⌷

Kelowna

(E-6) *See also Penticton*

Pop 78,000 (est) **Elev** 1,129 ft (344 m)
Area code 250
Web www.kelownachamber.org.
Information Visitors and Convention Bureau, 544 Harvey Ave, V1Y 6C9; 250/861-1515 or 800/663-4345

Kelowna is located on the shores of Okanagan Lake between Penticton (see) and Vernon, 80 miles (128 kilometers) north of the US border. The name Kelowna is a corruption of an indigenous word for grizzly bear. The history of Europeans in the area dates back to the fur brigades in the 19th century. Father Pandosy established a mission here in 1858. The apple trees that were planted by him were the beginning of one of the largest fruit-growing districts in Canada.

The Civic Centre complex, located in downtown Kelowna, includes government buildings, community theater, a curling rink, regional library, and centennial museum. The city also has 31 parks, seven on the lakeshore. Among the facilities in these parks are soccer fields, lawn bowling greens, and tennis courts.

Kelowna is a playground at almost any time of year. Water sports, golf, cricket, curling, baseball, and skiing are only a few of the sports played in the area. The winter highlight is the annual Snowfest.

Annual Events

Snowfest. "Smockey" game, Light Up Parade, polar bear dip, snowshoe relay, belly flop contest. Late Jan.
Okanagan Wine Festival. Races, ethnic events, baking contest, dance,

wine tasting (also see PENTICTON). May and Oct. Phone 250/861-1515.

Black Mountain Rodeo. Mid-May.

Kelowna Regatta. Mid-July.

Hydro Plane Races. Early Aug.

Motel/Motor Lodge

★ **SANDMAN HOTEL.** *2130 Harvey Ave (V1Y 6J8).* 250/860-6409; fax 250/860-7377; toll-free 888/526-1988. 120 rms, 3 story. S $77-$87; D $85-$89; each addl $5; kit. units $10 addl; under 12 free. Crib free. Pet accepted, some restrictions. TV; cable. Sauna. Pool; whirlpool. Restaurant open 24 hrs. Bar 11-1 am. Ck-out noon. Meeting rms. Business servs avail. Sundries. Refrigerators. Balconies. Cr cds: A, C, D, DS, ER, JCB, MC, V.

🐾 🏊 🐾 SC

Hotels

★★ **ACCENT INNS.** *1140 Harvey Ave (V1Y 6E7).* 250/862-8888; fax 250/862-8884; toll-free 800/663-0298. Email kelowna@staynsave.com; www. staynsave.com. 101 rms, 3 story, 12 suites. May-Sep: S $119; D $129; each addl $10; suites $139; under 16 free; lower rates rest of yr. Crib avail. Pet accepted, some restrictions. Parking lot. Pool, whirlpool. TV; cable (premium). Complimentary coffee in rms, newspaper, toll-free calls. Restaurant 7 am-9 pm. Ck-out 11 am, ck-in 3 pm. Meeting rm. Business servs avail. Dry cleaning, coin lndry. Exercise equipt, sauna. Golf, 18 holes. Downhill skiing. Video games. Cr cds: A, D, ER, MC, V.

D 🐾 🏊 🧍 🏊 🎿 🐾 SC

★★ **BEST WESTERN INN.** *2402 Hwy 97 N (V1X 4J1).* 250/860-1212; fax 250/860-0675; toll-free 888/860-1212. Email bestwest@silk.net; www. bestwestern.com/ca/innkelowna. 88 rms, 8 story, 59 suites. May-Sep: S $129; D $139; each addl $10; suites $229; under 17 free; lower rates rest of yr. Crib avail. Pet accepted, some restrictions, fee. Parking lot. Indoor pool, whirlpool. TV; cable (premium). Complimentary continental bkfst, coffee in rms, newspaper, toll-free calls. Restaurant 6:30 am-10 pm. Bar. Ck-out 11 am, ck-in 4 pm. Meeting rms. Concierge. Dry cleaning,

coin lndry. Gift shop. Exercise equipt, steam rm. Golf. Supervised children's activities. Video games. Cr cds: A, D, DS, MC, V.

D 🐾 🧍 🏊 🎿 🏊 SC

★★★ **COAST CAPRI HOTEL.** *1171 Harvey Ave (V1Y 6E8), Hwy 97.* 250/860-6060; fax 250/762-3430; toll-free 800/663-1144. www.coasthotels.com. 185 rms, 4-7 story. May-Sep: S $125-$135; D $135-$145; each addl $10; suites $175; under 18 free; ski, golf plans; lower rates rest of yr. Pet accepted. TV; cable, VCR avail. Sauna. Heated pool; whirlpool, poolside serv. Coffee in rms. Restaurant 6:30 am-10 pm. Rm serv 24 hrs. Bar. Ck-out noon. Meeting rms. Business center. In-rm modem link. Drugstore. Barber, beauty shop. Health club privileges. Balconies. Cr cds: A, C, D, ER, MC, V.

D 🐾 🏊 🐾 SC 🎿

★★ **HOLIDAY INN EXPRESS.** *2429 Hwy 97 N (V1X 4J2), at Banks Rd.* 250/763-0500; fax 250/763-7555; res 800/465-4329; toll-free 800/465-0200. Email express@cnx.net;www. hiexpress. com/kelownabc. 118 rms, 4 story, 2 suites. May-Oct: S, D $139; each addl $10; suites $199; under 19 free; lower rates rest of yr. Crib avail. Parking lot. Indoor pool, children's pool, whirlpool. TV; cable (premium), VCR avail. Complimentary continental bkfst, coffee in rms, newspaper, toll-free calls. Restaurant 6:30 am-8:30 pm. Ck-out noon, ck-in 4 pm. Meeting rm. Business center. Dry cleaning. Exercise privileges. Golf. Tennis, 2 courts. Downhill skiing. Video games. Cr cds: A, C, D, DS, ER, JCB, MC, V.

D 🏊 🧍 🎿 🏊 🎿 🏊 SC 🎿

★★★ **RAMADA LODGE.** *2170 Harvey Ave (V1Y 6G8).* 250/860-9711; fax 250/860-3173; toll-free 800/665-2518. Email lodge@cnx.net; www.rpbhotels. com. 105 rms, 3 story, 30 suites. May-Sep: S, D $119; each addl $10; suites $159; under 17 free; lower rates rest of yr. Crib avail. Pet accepted, some restrictions, fee. Parking lot. Indoor pool, whirlpool. TV; cable, VCR avail. Complimentary coffee in rms, newspaper, toll-free calls. Restaurant. 24-hr rm serv. Bar. Ck-out noon, ck-in 3 pm. Meeting rms. Fax servs avail. Bellhops. Dry cleaning. Gift shop.

Exercise equipt. Golf. Tennis. Downhill skiing. Picnic facilities. Video games. Cr cds: A, C, D, DS, ER, JCB, MC, V.

[icons]

★★ VILLAGE GREEN HOTEL & CASINO. *4801 27th St (V1T 4Z1), at 48th Ave. 250/542-3321; fax 250/549-4252; toll-free 800/663-4433. Email vilgreen@junction.net; www.village green.bc.ca.* 134 rms, 7 story, 3 suites. May-Sep: S $89; D $99; each addl $10; under 12 free; lower rates rest of yr. Crib avail. Parking lot. Indoor pool. TV; cable (premium), VCR avail. Complimentary coffee in rms. Restaurant 6:30 am-9 pm. Bar. Ckout noon, ck-in 3 pm. Meeting rms. Business center. Bellhops. Dry cleaning. Gift shop. Sauna. Golf. Downhill skiing. Cr cds: A, C, D, DS, ER, JCB, MC, V.

[icons]

Conference Center

★★ BEST WESTERN VERNON LODGE. *3914 32nd St (V1T 5P1), 30 mi N on Hwy 97. 250/545-3385; fax 250/545-7156; res 800/663-9400; toll-free 800/663-4422. Email vernonlodge@ rpbhotels.com; www.rpbhotels.com/vernon/verindex.html.* 127 rms, 3 story, 12 suites. June-Sep, Dec: S $99; D $109; each addl $10; suites $149; under 12 free; lower rates rest of yr. Crib avail. Pet accepted, some restrictions, fee. Parking lot. Indoor pool, whirlpool. TV; cable (premium), VCR avail. Complimentary coffee in rms. Restaurant 6:30 am-10 pm. Bar. Ckout noon, ck-in 2 pm. Meeting rms. Business servs avail. Dry cleaning. Salon/barber. Golf. Downhill skiing. Supervised children's activities. Hiking trail. Video games. Cr cds: A, C, D, DS, ER, JCB, MC, V.

[icons]

Nanaimo

(F-4) *See also Vancouver, Victoria*

Founded 1874 **Pop** 47,069 **Elev** 100 ft (30 m) **Area code** 250
Web www.tourism.nanaimo.bc.ca
Information Tourism Nanaimo, Beban House, 2290 Bowen Rd, V9T 3K7; 250/756-0106 or 800/663-7337

Nanaimo is located on Vancouver Island off the west coast of British Columbia, a main entry port for ferries from Vancouver and Horseshoe Bay. Because of its location it serves as a fine starting point to other attractions on the island as well as being a vacation highlight in itself. The name comes from the indigenous term "Sne-ny-mos" that referred to the gathering of the tribes. In 1849 coal was discovered and was mined here for 100 years.

What to See and Do

Bastion. Built in 1853 as a Hudson's Bay Co fort. Now a museum; cannon firing ceremony (summer months at noon). Restored to original appearance. (July-Aug) Front & Bastion Sts. Along harbor basin below is

Queen Elizabeth Promenade. Named to commemorate the vessel and landing of the first settlers in the area (1854); boardwalk offers pleasant view of waterfront and tidal lagoon.

Bowen Park. Swimming pool (fee); tennis courts, fitness circuit, game fields, picnic shelters, recreation complex, lawn bowling; totem poles, rose garden, rhododendron grove, petting farm, duck ponds, fish ladder. 500 Bowen Rd. ¢¢

Cyber City. Adventure park with laser tag, bumper cars, miniature golf, virtual reality arcade, spaceball. Restaurant. (Daily) 1815 Bowen Rd. Phone 250/755-1828. **FREE**

Ferry trips. BC Ferries. Service between Nanaimo and Horseshoe Bay, N of Vancouver (1½ hrs); or Duke Point and Tsawassen, S of Vancouver, near US border (2 hrs). For current schedule and fare information contact BC Ferry Corporation, 1112 Fort St, Victoria, V8V 4V2. Phone 250/669-1211 (Vancouver) or 250/386-3431 (Victoria).

Nanaimo Art Gallery & Exhibition Centre. Gallery with changing exhibits of art, science, and history. (Daily; closed hols) On Malaspina College campus. Phone 250/755-8790. **FREE**

Nanaimo District Museum. Walk-in replica of coal mine; turn-of-the-century shops, restored miner's cottage; dioramas; Chinatown display; changing exhibits. Tours avail. (May-Aug, daily; rest of yr, Tues-Sat; closed hols) 100 Cameron St. Phone 250/753-1821. ¢

Newcastle Island Provincial Marine Park. Boat docking (fee); camping (fee), hiking and bicycle trails, picnicking, pavilion with historical displays, concession (May-Sep). Dance and barbecue events in summer. No land vehicle access. Access by foot/passenger ferry from Maffeo Sutton Park (May-mid-Oct; fee); private boat rest of yr. **FREE**

Petroglyph Park. Established to preserve the many ancient indigenous rock carvings. 2 mi (3 km) S on Trans-Canada Hwy 1.

Totem pole

Annual Events

Polar Bear Swim. Prizes for all participants; free ice cream, bananas, and suntan lotion. Jan 1.

Nanaimo Marine Festival. Bathtub race (3rd or 4th Sun July) across the Straits of Georgia to Vancouver; many other events. Begins 1 wk prior to race day.

Vancouver Island Exhibition. Beban Park. Early or mid-Aug.

Motels/Motor Lodges

★★ **CASA GRANDE INN.** *3080 W Island Hwy (V9K 2C5). 250/752-4400; fax 250/752-4401; toll-free 888/720-2272. www.casagrandeinn.com.* 17 rms, 3 story. Feb, June-Sep: S $90; D $100; each addl $10; suites $150;

lower rates rest of yr. Crib avail. Pet accepted, some restrictions. Parking garage. TV; cable, VCR avail. Complimentary coffee in rms, toll-free calls. Restaurant nearby. Ck-out 11 am, ck-in 1 pm. Coin lndry. Golf, 18 holes. Tennis, 4 courts. Beach access. Picnic facilities. Cr cds: A, DS, ER, MC.

★ **DAYS INN HARBOURVIEW.** *809 Island Hwy S (V9R 5K1). 250/754-8171; fax 250/754-8557.* 79 rms, 2 story, 16 kits. June-Sep: S $83; D $93; each addl $10; suites $120; kit. units $85-$115; under 13 free; lower rates rest of yr. Crib $5. Pet accepted; $7/day. TV; cable (premium), VCR avail. Indoor pool; whirlpool. Restaurant 7 am-10 pm. Ck-out 11 am. Coin lndry. Meeting rms. Business servs avail. Sundries. Some refrigerators. Overlooking Nanaimo's inner harbour. Cr cds: A, D, DS, ER, JCB, MC, V.

★ **HOWARD JOHNSON HARBOUR SIDE HOTEL.** *1 Terminal Ave (V9R 5R4). 250/753-2241; fax 250/753-6522; toll-free 800/663-7322. Email tally-ho@nanaimo.ark.com.* 101 rms, 3 story. S, D $80-$110; each addl $10; suites $150; under 14 free; wknd rates. Crib free. TV; cable, VCR avail. Heated pool. Restaurant 6:30 am-9 pm. Bar 11:30-1:30 am. Ck-out noon. Meeting rms. Business servs avail. Valet serv. Sundries. Health club privileges. Cr cds: A, C, D, ER, MC, V.

Hotels

★★ **COAST BASTION INN.** *11 Bastion St (V9R 2Z9). 250/753-6601; fax 250/753-4155; res 800/663-1144. Email cbastion@nanaimo.ark.com; www.coasthotels.com.* 171 rms, 15 story, 4 suites. Apr-Nov: S $165; D $175; each addl $10; suites $250; under 18 free; lower rates rest of yr. Crib avail. Pet accepted, fee. Valet parking avail. TV; cable (premium), VCR avail. Complimentary coffee in rms, newspaper, toll-free calls. Restaurant. 24-hr rm serv. Bar. Meeting rms. Business center. Bellhops. Concierge. Dry cleaning. Salon/barber. Exercise equipt, sauna, whirlpool. Golf. Tennis, 20 courts. Beach access. Bike rentals. Hiking trail. Picnic facilities. Video games. Cr cds: A, D, DS, ER, JCB, MC, V.

⬛🔲🖐️🎿🏂🍴🏊🚶🏕️⛺🌲🎣

★★★ **FOUR POINTS SHERATON.** *4900 Rutherford Rd (V9T 5P1). 250/ 758-3000; fax 250/729-2808; toll-free 800/325-3535. Email fourpionts@ home.com; www.fourpoints.com.* 65 rms, 4 story, 7 suites. May-Sep: S, D $107; each addl $10; suites $236; under 12 free; lower rates rest of yr. Crib avail, fee. Valet parking avail. Indoor pool. TV; cable (premium), VCR avail. Complimentary coffee in rms, newspaper, toll-free calls. Restaurant. Bar. Ck-out noon, ck-in 3 pm. Meeting rms. Business center. Bellhops. Dry cleaning. Free airport transportation. Exercise equipt. Golf, 18 holes. Tennis, 4 courts. Cr cds: A, C, D, DS, ER, JCB, MC, V.

⬛🦽🖐️🎣🍴🏊🚶🏕️⛺🌲🎣

Resorts

CLAYOQUOT WILDERNESS RESORT. *(V0R 2Z0). 250/726-8235; fax 250/276-8558; toll-free 888/333-5405. www.wildretreat.com.* 21 rms, 2 story. June-Sep: S, D $369; each addl $269/369; lower rates rest of yr. Crib avail. TV; cable (premium), VCR avail, CD avail, VCR avail, CD avail. Complimentary full bkfst, coffee in rms, newspaper. Restaurant 6 am-11 pm. Bar. Ck-out 1 pm, ck-in 3:30 pm. Meeting rms. Business center. Bellhops. Gift shop. Free airport transportation. Exercise equipt. Golf, 18 holes. Beach access. Bike rentals. Supervised children's activities. Hiking trail. Picnic facilities. Cr cds: A, MC, V.

🦽🚶🏕️🍴🎣🌲🎣🎣

★★★ **FAIRWINDS SCHOONER COVE RESORT & MARINA.** *3521 Dolphin Dr (V9P 9J7), 15 mi (20 km) from BC Ferry Terminal. 250/468-7691; fax 250/468-5744; toll-free 800/ 663-7060. Email info@fairwinds.bc.ca; www.fairwinds.bc.ca.* 30 rms, 1 story. May-Sep: S, D $149; each addl $10; under 16 free; lower rates rest of yr. Crib avail. Pet accepted, some restrictions, fee. Parking lot. Pool, whirlpool. TV; cable, VCR avail. Complimentary coffee in rms, toll-free calls. Restaurant 7 am-10 pm. Bar. Ck-out 11 am, ck-in 3 pm. Meeting rms. Business servs avail. Bell-

hops. Coin lndry. Exercise equipt. Golf, 18 holes. Tennis, 2 courts. Downhill skiing. Beach access. Bike rentals. Hiking trail. Picnic facilities. Cr cds: A, D, DS, ER, MC, V.

⬛🔲🦽🖐️🎿🍴🎣🏊🚶🏕️⛺🌲🎣
SC

KINGFISHER OCEANSIDE RESORT AND SPA. Unrated for 2001. *4330 S Island Hwy (V9N 8H9). 250/338-1323; fax 250/338-0058; toll-free 800/663-7929. Email tor@kingfisher-resort-spa. com; www.kingfisher-resort-spa.com.* 27 rms, 2 story, 36 suites. S, D $100-$150. Crib avail. Pet accepted, fee. Parking garage. Pool, whirlpool. TV; cable (premium), VCR avail, CD avail. Complimentary coffee in rms, newspaper, toll-free calls. Restaurant 7 am-10 pm. Bar. Ck-out 11 am, ck-in 3 pm. Meeting rms. Business center. Concierge. Dry cleaning, coin lndry. Gift shop. Exercise equipt, sauna, steam rm. Golf, 18 holes. Tennis. Downhill skiing. Beach access. Hiking trail. Picnic facilities. Cr cds: A, D, DS, MC, V.

⬛🔲🦽🖐️🎿🍴🎣🏊🚶🏕️⛺🌲🎣
🎣

★★ **TIGH-NA-MARA RESORT HOTEL.** *1095 E Island Hwy (V9P 2E5). 250/248-2072; fax 250/248-4140; toll-free 800/663-7373. Email info@tigh-na-mara.com; www.tigh-na-mara.com.* 39 rms, 3 story, 55 suites. May-Oct: S, D $129; each addl $10; suites $189; children $5; under 16 free; lower rates rest of yr. Crib avail, fee. Pet accepted, fee. Parking lot. Indoor pool, whirlpool. TV; cable, VCR avail. Complimentary coffee in rms. Restaurant 7 am-9:30 pm. Bar. Ck-out 11 am, ck-in 3 pm. Meeting rms. Business center. Coin lndry. Gift shop. Exercise equipt, sauna, steam rm. Golf. Tennis. Beach access. Bike rentals. Supervised children's activities. Hiking trail. Picnic facilities. Cr cds: A, D, ER, MC, V.

⬛🔲🦽🖐️🍴🎣🏊🚶🏕️🌲🎣

Cottage Colony

★★ **YELLOW POINT LODGE.** *3700 Yellow Point Rd (V9G 1E8), 15 mi S via Trans-Can Hwy 1, follow signs. 250/ 245-7422; fax 250/245-7411.* 9 rms in main bldg, 4 story, 44 cottages, 19 with bath. No A/C. No elvtr. No rm phones. AP, May-Sep: S, cottages (1 or 2-bedrm) $112; D $177; each addl

$61; suites $177; higher rates Christmas hols; lower rates rest of yr. Children over 16 yrs only. Saltwater pool; whirlpool. Complimentary continental bkfst. Dining rm, 3 sittings: 8:30-9:30 am, 12:30 pm, 6:30 pm. Serv bar 11 am-11 pm. Ck-out noon, ck-in 3 pm. Coin lndry 8 mi. Meeting rms. Grocery 4 mi. Package store. Airport, railroad station, bus depot transportation. Tennis. Sauna. Beach; ocean swimming. Kayaks. Bicycles. Lawn games. Rec rm. Some refrigerators. Balconies. Picnic tables. Surrounded by 180 acres of preserved private forest; on Straits of Georgia. Cr cds: A, MC, V.

🏊 ⛱ 🔥

Restaurants

★ **THE CONSERVATORY RESTAURANT.** *399 Clubhouse. 250/703-5050. www.crowneisle.com.* Specializes in seafood and steaks. Hrs: 5-9 pm; Fri, Sat to 10 pm. Res accepted. Wine list. Dinner $15-$30. Child's menu. Entertainment. Glass dome over dining area. Cr cds: A, D, ER, MC, V.
D

★★ **THE MAHLE HOUSE RESTAURANT.** *2104 Hemer Rd (V9X 1L8). 250/722-3621. www.island.net/~mahle/.* Menu changes wkly. Hrs: 5-9 pm. Closed Mon, Tues. Res accepted. Wine, beer. Dinner $13.95-$26.95. Entertainment. Own vegetables. Old Victorian house. Cr cds: A, MC, V.
D

★★ **OLD HOUSE RESTAURANT.** *1760 Riverside Ln (V9N 8C7). 250/338-5406.* Specializes in steak, Paradise Meadows chicken breast, prime rib. Hrs: 11:30 am-9 pm; Fri, Sat to 9:30 pm. Closed Dec 25, Labour Day. Res accepted. Lunch $7.95-$11.95; dinner $10.95-$22.95. Child's menu. Entertainment. On the Courtney River, beautiful grounds. Cr cds: A, D, ER, MC, V.

★★ **THE RESTAURANT AT TIGH-NA-MARA RESORT.** *1095 E Island Hwy. 250/248-2333. Email info@tigh-na-mara.com; www.tigh-na-mara.com.* Specializes in rack of lamb, salmon. Hrs: 7 am-9:30 pm; Sun from 10 am. Res accepted. Wine list. Lunch $8.95-$12.95; dinner $15.95-$26.95. Brunch $9.95-$17.95. Child's menu.

Entertainment. Rustic atmosphere. Cr cds: A, D, ER, MC, V.
D

★★ **WESLEY STREET.** *1-321 Wesley St (V9R 2T5). 250/753-4004.* Specializes in free-range chicken breast, pan-seared sea scallops. Hrs: 11:30 am-11 pm. Res accepted. Wine list. Lunch $5.25-$12.50; dinner $16-$25. Child's menu. Entertainment: jazz Fri, Sat. In historic Nanaimo with views of ocean and mountains. Cr cds: A, MC, V.
D

Unrated Dining Spot

KINGFISHER RESTAURANT. *4330 S Island Hwy. 250/334-9600. Email dine@kingfisher-resort-spa.com; www.kingfisher-resort-spa.com.* Specializes in salmon, oysters, halibut. Hrs: 7:30 am-9 pm. Res accepted. Wine, beer. Lunch $5.95-$9.95; dinner $11.95-$21.95. Child's menu. Entertainment. Cr cds: A, D, DS, ER, JCB, MC, V.
D SC

Penticton

(F-6) *See also Kelowna*

Pop 23,181 **Elev** 1,150 ft (351 m)
Area code 250
Web www.penticton.org
Information Visitor InfoCentre, 888 Westminster Ave W, V2A 8R2; 250/493-4055 or 800/663-5052

Penticton is situated between the beautiful Okanagan and Skaha lakes on an alluvial plain. Beyond the lakes are fertile orchard lands and rolling hills. Penticton is famous for its peaches and other fruits. Because of its prime location, Penticton is sometimes called the land of peaches and beaches. Grape-growing and wine-making have become very important in the Okanagan Valley, producing some very fine wines.

What to See and Do

Agriculture Canada Research Station. Beautiful display of ornamental gardens; canyon view; picnicking.

Guided tours (July-Aug). 6 mi (10 km) N on Hwy 97. Phone 250/494-7711. ¢

Dominion Radio Astrophysical Observatory. Guided tours (July-Aug, Sun). Visitor Centre (daily). 9 mi (15 km) SW via Hwy 97, 5½ mi (9 km) S on White Lake Rd. Phone 250/493-2277. **FREE**

Okanagan Game Farm. Excellent selection of wild animals in natural setting. More than 900 animals on 600 acres (243 hectares). Gift, coffee shop; picnicking. (Daily) 5 mi (8 km) S on Hwy 97. Phone 250/497-5405. ¢¢¢

Penticton Museum. Collection of Salish artifacts; taxidermy, ghost town, and pioneer exhibits. Changing exhibits. At 1099 Lakeshore Dr W are 2 historic 1914 steamships: SS *Sicamous*, a 200-ft sternwheeler, and SS *Naramata*, a 90-ft steam tug (donation). (Mon-Sat; closed hols) 785 Main St. Phone 250/492-6025. **FREE**

Wonderful Water World. Waterpark has waterslides, miniature golf, slot car racing on 110-ft track. Concessions, picnic area. Campground on site. (Late May-Labour Day, daily) 225 Yorkton Ave. Phone 250/493-8121. ¢¢¢¢

Annual Events

Midwinter Breakout. Festival for the entire family. Second and 3rd wk Feb.

Okanagan Wine Festival. Wine tasting, grape stomping, seminars, and dinners (also see KELOWNA). Late Apr-early May; late Sep-mid-Oct.

British Columbia Square Dance Jamboree. Street dancing; dancing under the stars on perhaps North America's largest outdoor board floor. Early Aug. In King's Park.

Peach Festival. Parade, entertainment, family events. Mid-Aug.

Ironman Canada Championship Triathlon. Qualifier for Hawaiian Ironman. Late Aug.

Motels/Motor Lodges

★★ **BEL-AIR MOTEL.** *2670 Skaha Lake Rd (V2A 6G1). 250/492-6111; fax 250/492-8035; toll-free 800/766-5770. Email belairmotel@home.com; www.belairmotel.bc.ca.* 26 rms, 2 story, 16 suites. July-Aug: S $64; D $69; each addl $6; suites $86; lower rates rest of yr. Pet accepted, some restrictions, fee. Parking lot. Pool, whirlpool. TV; cable (premium). Complimentary coffee in rms. Restaurant nearby. Ck-out 11 am, ck-in 2 pm. Business servs avail. Coin lndry. Sauna. Golf. Downhill skiing. Picnic facilities. Cr cds: A, D, ER, MC, V.

★★ **BEST WESTERN INN AT PENTICTON.** *3180 Skaha Lake Rd (V2A 6G4), Hwy 97A. 250/493-0311; fax 250/493-5556; res 800/528-1234; toll-free 800/668-6746. Email bestwest@bestwestern.bc.ca.* 67 rms, 2 story, 24 kits. Mid-June-mid-Sep: S $109-$189; D $119-$189; each addl $10; kit. units $139-$189; suites $189-$275; under 18 free; lower rates rest of yr. Crib $10. TV; cable (premium). 2 pools, 1 indoor; whirlpool. Playground. Restaurant 7 am-10 pm. Ck-out 11 am. Coin lndry. Business servs avail. In-rm modem link. Valet serv. Refrigerators. Picnic tables. Cr cds: A, D, DS, ER, JCB, MC, V.

★★ **RAMADA COURTYARD INN.** *1050 Eckhardt Ave W (V2A 2C3). 250/492-8926; fax 250/492-2778; toll-free 800/665-4966.* 50 rms. Mid-May-mid-Sep: S, D $95; each addl $10; under 12 free; lower rates rest of yr. Pet accepted, some restrictions. TV; cable (premium). Heated pool. Restaurant nearby. Bar. Ck-out 11 am. Coin lndry. Meeting rms. Business servs avail. Valet serv. Lawn games. Some refrigerators, fireplaces. Private patios. Picnic tables, grill. Cr cds: A, D, DS, ER, MC, V.

★★ **SANDMAN HOTEL.** *939 Burnaby Ave W (V2A 1G7), off Hwy 97. 250/493-7151; fax 250/493-3767; toll-free 888/648-1118.* 141 rms, 3 story. Mid-May-Sep: S $71; D $81; each addl $5; under 16 free; lower rates rest of yr. Crib free. TV; cable (premium). Sauna. Indoor pool; whirlpool. Restaurant open 24 hrs. Bar noon-1 am. Ck-out noon. Meeting rms. Business servs avail. Valet serv. Sundries. Cr cds: A, C, D, DS, ER, JCB, MC, V.

★ **TRAVELODGE.** *950 Westminster Ave (B2A 1L2). 250/492-0225; fax 250/493-8340; toll-free 800/578-7878. Email travelodge@penticum.com.* 34 rms, 3 story. Mid-May-mid-Sep: S, D $85-$105; each addl $8; kit. units $8 addl; under 17 free; lower rates rest of yr. TV; cable (premium). Sauna. 2 pools, heated; whirlpool. Restaurant 7 am-1:30 pm. Ck-out noon. Meeting rms. Refrigerators. Private patios, balconies. Picnic tables. Cr cds: A, C, D, ER, MC, V.

[D] [symbols]

Hotel

★★★ LAKESIDE RESORT AND CONFERENCE CENTER. *21 Lakeshore Dr W (V2A 7M5). 250/493-8221; fax 250/493-0607; toll-free 800/663-9400. Email lakeside@rpbhotels. com.* 204 rms, 6 story. July-Aug: S, D $175-$195; each addl $15; under 16 free; golf plans; lower rates rest of yr. Crib free. Pet accepted, some restrictions. TV; cable (premium), VCR avail. Indoor pool; whirlpool. Supervised children's activities (late May-Labor Day); ages 3-14. Restaurant 7 am-11 pm. Bar noon-2 am; seasonal entertainment. Meeting rms. Business servs avail. In-rm modem link. Gift shop. Beauty shop. Tennis. Golf privileges. Downhill/x-country ski 20 mi. Exercise rm; sauna. Game rm. Balconies. On Okanagan Lake; swimming, boat rides. Cr cds: A, C, D, DS, ER, MC, V.

[D] [symbols]

Resort

★★ SPANISH VILLA. *890 Lakeshore Dr (V2A 1C1). 250/492-2922; fax 250/492-2922; res 800/552-9199. Email spanishvillaresort@home.com.* 14 rms, 2 story, 46 suites. July-Aug: S $108; D $118; each addl $10; suites $125; under 12 free; lower rates rest of yr. Crib avail, fee. Pet accepted, some restrictions. Parking lot. Indoor pool. TV; cable, VCR avail. Complimentary coffee in rms. Restaurant nearby. Ck-out 11 am, ck-in 3 pm. Fax servs avail. Dry cleaning, coin lndry. Exercise privileges. Golf, 18 holes. Tennis. Downhill skiing. Beach access. Picnic facilities. Cr cds: A, C, D, DS, ER, JCB, MC, V.

[D] [symbols] [SC]

Restaurant

★★ EDWARD'S. *2007 Main St (V2A 5H6). 250/492-0007.* Specializes in smorgasbord, Angus beef. Salad bar. Hrs: 11 am-10 pm. Wine, beer. Lunch, dinner $6-$20. Sun brunch $12.99. Child's menu. Early California decor; stained glass. Cr cds: A, MC, V.

[D] [SC]

Revelstoke (D-7)

Pop 5,544 **Elev** 1,499 ft (457 m)
Area code 250
Web www.revelstokecc.bc.ca/mountns

Information Chamber of Commerce, 204 Cambell Ave, PO Box 490, V0E 2S0; 250/837-5345 or 800/487-1493; or visit the Travel Info Centre, Trans-Canada Hwy 1 & BC 23N; 250/837-3522

Located in the towering Monashee and Selkirk ranges of the Columbia Mountains between the scenic Rogers and Eagle passes, Revelstoke is the gateway to Mount Revelstoke National Park, with Glacier National Park just to the east. Visitors may enjoy many activities all year. Especially popular is the skiing; with an annual average of 40 feet (13 m) of snow, Revelstoke offers multiple opportunities for downhill, cross-country, cat helicopter, ski touring adventures, and snowmobiling. Tennis, fishing, hiking, golf, caving, mountaineering, and swimming are also available throughout this exciting alpine city.

What to See and Do

Beardale Castle Miniatureland. Indoor attraction constructed in a European-style village setting. Handcrafted authentic miniature exhibits incl prairie town, Swiss mountain village, and medieval German village, each with a model railway running through it. Also animated toyland exhibits. (May-Sep, daily) 26 mi (42 km) W via Trans-Canada Hwy 1 at Craigellachie. Phone 250/836-2268. ¢¢

Provincial Building & Court House. (1912) Provincial bldg contains the original oak staircase connecting the 3 floors and basement; courtrm same as when built; marble walls in foyer; pillars; lighted dome. Tour (Mon-Fri, by appt; closed hols). 1123 W 2nd St. Phone 250/837-7636. **FREE**

Revelstoke Dam Visitor Centre. Displays, films, and photographs describe construction and operation of the hydroelectric powerhouse and relate the history of Revelstoke Dam. Self-guided tours. (Apr-Oct, daily) 3 mi (5 km) N via Hwy 23. Phone 250/837-6515. **FREE**

Three Valley Gap. Historic ghost town (guided tours; fee); lake. Lodging, restaurant. Cowboy show (nightly; fee). (Mid-Apr-mid-Oct, daily) 12 mi (19 km) W on Trans Canada Hwy 1. Phone 250/837-2109. ¢¢¢

Annual Events

Revelstoke Sno Fest. Outhouse races, parade, casino, dances, entertainment, cross-country skiing, downhill races, sno pitch, ice sculpture, snow golf tournaments. Jan. Phone 250/837-9351.

Revelstoke Mountain Arts Festival. Theatre, music, children's events. Third wkend Sep. Phone 250/837-5345.

Vancouver

(F-4) *See also Nanaimo, BC, Victoria, BC; also see Bellingham, WA*

Settled 1886 **Pop** 456,000 (est) **Elev** 38 ft (12 m) **Area code** 604 **Web** www.tourismvancouver.com

Information Tourism Vancouver Info-Centre, 200 Burrard St, V6C 3L6; 604/683-2000

Surrounded by the blue waters of the Strait of Georgia and backed by the mile-high peaks of the Coast Range, Vancouver enjoys a natural setting surpassed by few other cities on this continent. The waters that wash the city's shores protect it from heat and cold, making it a pleasant place to visit all year.

Captain George Vancouver, searching these waters for the Northwest Passage, sailed into Burrard Inlet and landed here in 1792. Fur traders, gold prospectors, and other settlers soon followed. In 1886 Vancouver

was incorporated as a city, only to be destroyed by fire several months later. The city was rebuilt by the end of that same year. In the next four years rail transportation from the east, along with the traffic of sailing vessels of the Canadian Pacific fleet, assured the future of its growth. Today Vancouver is one of Canada's largest cities—a major seaport, cultural center, tourist spot, and gateway to Asia.

Vancouver's population is primarily English, but its large number of ethnic groups—including Germans, French, Scandinavians, Dutch, Chinese, and Japanese—give the city an international flavor. Tourism, logging, mineral extraction equipment, marine supplies, chemical and petroleum products, and machine tools are among the city's major industries.

Vancouver is on the Canadian mainland, not on Vancouver Island as some people think. The downtown area, which includes many of the points of interest which follow, is a "peninsula on a peninsula." It juts out from the rest of Vancouver into Burrard Inlet, making it an especially attractive spot with beaches and marinas within easy walking distance of the city's busy heart. To the north across Burrard Inlet is North Vancouver; to the south is the mouth of the Fraser River and the island municipality of Richmond; to the east is Burnaby, and beyond that, the Canadian mainland.

For Border Crossing Regulations see MAKING THE MOST OF YOUR TRIP.

What to See and Do

Burnaby Art Gallery. Monthly exhibitions of local, national, and intl artists. Collection of contemporary Canadian works on paper. Housed in Ceperley Mansion, overlooking Deer Lake and the surrounding gardens. (Tues-Sat) 6344 Deer Lake Ave in Burnaby. Phone 604/291-2242. ¢

Burnaby Village Museum. Living museum of the period before 1925, with costumed attendants; more than 30 full-scale bldgs with displays and demonstrations. (Early Apr-late Dec, days vary) 6501 Deer Lake Ave in Burnaby, 9 mi (15 km) E. Phone 604/293-6501 (recording). ¢¢¢

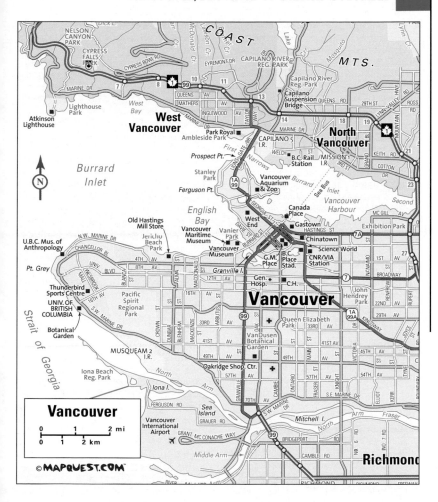

Capilano Suspension Bridge & Park.
Park flanks 1 mi (1.6 km) of the
canyon through which the Capilano
River flows. A 450-ft (137-m) gently
swaying footbridge spans the canyon
at a height of 230 ft (70 m). Park
contains gardens, totem poles, and
large Trading Post. Guided tours;
native wood carver on site; Story
Centre; restaurants. (Daily; closed
Dec 25) 3735 Capilano Rd. Phone
604/985-7474. ¢¢¢

Chinatown. This downtown area is
the nucleus of the 3rd-largest Chinese community in North America
(only San Francisco's and New York's
are larger.) At the heart lies the Chinese Market where 100-yr-old duck
eggs may be purchased; herbalists
promise cures with roots and pow-

dered bones. The Dr. Sun Yat-Sen
Classical Chinese Garden provides a
beautiful centerpiece. Chinese shops
display a variety of items ranging
from cricket cages to cloisonné vases.
Offices of 3 Chinese newspapers, and
one of the world's narrowest bldgs,
are located within the community's
borders. Resplendent Asian atmosphere offers fine examples of Chinese
architecture, restaurants, and nightclubs. East Pender St between Gore
& Carrall Sts.

Dr. Sun-Yat-Sen Classical Garden.
Unique to the Western hemisphere,
garden was originally built in China
ca AD 1492; transplanted to Vancouver for Expo '86. (Daily) 578 Carrall
St. Phone 604/689-7133. ¢¢

Exhibition Park. Approx 165 acres (70 hectares). Concert, convention, entertainment facilities. Thoroughbred racing (late spring-early fall) and Playland Amusement Park (Apr-June, wkends; July-Oct, daily; also evenings). Free tours of Challenger Relief Map. (See ANNUAL EVENTS) Hastings St between Renfrew & Cassiar Sts. Phone 604/253-2311.

Fort Langley National Historic Site. Restoration of Hudson's Bay Co post built in 1840 on the Fraser River; reconstructed palisade, bastion, and 4 bldgs plus one original bldg. Demonstrations of fur trade activities and period crafts of 1858. (Mar-Oct, daily; Nov-Feb, hrs vary; closed Jan 1, Dec 25, 26) 35 mi (48 km) E off Trans-Canada Hwy 1 or BC 7. Phone 604/513-4777. ¢¢

✪ Gastown. The original heart of Vancouver, named for "Gassy Jack" Deighton, who opened a saloon here in 1867. Restored late 19th- and early 20th-century bldgs now house antique shops, boutiques, art galleries, coffeehouses, restaurants, and nightclubs. Historic landmarks, cobblestone streets, and unique steam clock. Area bounded by Alexander, Columbia, Water, and Cordova Sts. Adj is

> **Harbour Centre-The Lookout.** Glass elevators to 360° viewing deck 553 ft (167 m) above street level; multimedia presentation, historical displays, tour guides. Revolving restaurant. (Daily; closed Dec 25) 555 W Hastings St. Phone 604/689-0421. Deck ¢¢¢

Gordon Southam Observatory. (Fri-Sun and hols, weather permitting) Phone 604/738-7827. **FREE**

Granville Island. Originally dredged for industrial purposes in 1913 from the False Creek Tidal Flats, now restored to retain flavor of boomtown industry. Public Market area houses many specialty shops. Electronic irrigation has helped Norway and red maples, which are cultivated here to adapt to the saline soil. Parks, supervised playground, craft studios, an art college, tennis, theaters. Harbor tours. (Daily; closed Mon in winter) 37-acre (15-hectare) area in heart of city, beneath S end of Granville Bridge. Phone 604/666-5784.

Industrial tours. The Tourism Vancouver Travel InfoCentre has information on avail tours.

Irving House Historic Centre. (1864) Fourteen rms of period furniture 1864-90. Adj is **New Westminster Museum,** on back of property, which has displays on local history, household goods, May Day memorabilia. (May-mid-Sep, Tues-Sun; rest of yr, Sat and Sun; closed Jan 1, Dec 25, 26) 302 Royal Ave, in New Westminster, 12 mi (19 km) S via Hwy 1A. Phone 604/527-4640. **Donation**

Maritime Museum. Changing maritime exhibits highlighting exploration, marine industries, model ships, and a harbor. Restored Arctic schooner *St. Roch,* first ship to navigate the Northwest Passage both ways; open to the public. (May-Sep daily; rest of yr, Tues-Sun; closed Dec 25) 1905 Ogden Ave. Phone 604/257-8300 (recording). ¢¢¢

Old Hastings Mill. (ca 1865) One of few bldgs remaining after fire of 1886; now houses indigenous artifacts, memorabilia of Vancouver's first settlers. (June-mid-Sep, daily; rest of yr, Sat and Sun afternoons) 1575 Alma Rd. Phone 604/734-1212. **FREE**

Pacific Space Centre. Visitors experience a journey through the night sky, backward or forward in time, or a search for other worlds. Shows are dramatic, informative, easy to understand. Shows (summer, daily; rest of yr, Tues-Sun). 1100 Chestnut St. Phone 604/738-7827 (recording) or 604/738-4431. ¢¢¢¢

Professional sports.

> **NBA (Vancouver Grizzlies).** General Motors Place. 800 Griffiths Way. Phone 604/899-4601.

> **NHL (Vancouver Canucks).** General Motors Place. 800 Griffiths Way. Phone 604/899-4600.

Queen Elizabeth Park. Observation point affords view of city, harbor, and mountains; Bloedel Conservatory has more than 100 free-flying birds; tropical, desert, and seasonal displays. (Daily; closed Dec 25) Off Cambie St & W 33rd Ave. Phone 604/257-8584 (conservatory) or 604/257-8570 (recording). ¢¢

Samson V **Maritime Museum.** Last steam-powered paddlewheeler to operate on the Fraser River now functions as a floating museum. Displays focus on the various paddlewheelers and paddlewheeler captains that have worked the river, and on river-related activities such as fishing and lumbering. (Sat and Sun afternoons; July and Aug, Wed-Sun; closed Jan 1, Dec 25, 26) Moored on the Fraser River at the Westminster Quay Market in New Westminster, 12 mi (19 km) S via Hwy 1A. Phone 604/527-4640. **Donation**

Sightseeing trips.

British Columbia Ferry Corp. Trips to the Nanaimo (2 hrs) or to Swartz Bay near Victoria (1½ hrs); both destinations are on Vancouver Island. Terminals at Horseshoe Bay, N of Vancouver via Trans-Canada Hwy 1 and Tsawwassen near US border, S of Vancouver via Hwy 99, 17. For current schedule and fare information contact BC Ferry Corporation, 1112 Fort St, Victoria V8V 4V2. Phone 604/669-1211 (Vancouver) or 250/386-34321 (Victoria). ¢¢-¢¢¢¢

Gray Line bus tours. Contact 255 E 1st Ave, V5T 1A7. Phone 604/879-9287.

Grouse Mountain tramway. Phone 604/984-0661.

Harbour Cruises Limited. Boat/train excursion (6½ hrs); also sunset dinner cruises; harbor tours, private charters. (May-Sep) Departures from northern foot of Denman St. Phone 604/688-7246 for schedule and fees. ¢¢¢¢¢

Royal Hudson Excursion. Six-hr round-trip steam train ride 80 mi (129 km) to Squamish; 2-hr stopover with optional tours. (May-Sep, Wed-Sun) Also train/boat combinations. Res requested; payment required 48 hrs in advance with res. 1311 W 1st St, N Vancouver. Phone 604/631-3500. ¢¢¢¢¢

SeaBus Harbour Ride. Makes 15-min crossing on twin-hulled catamaran design vessels every 15 min (30 min eve and Sun). Part of regional public transit system. Operates between Waterfront Station & Lonsdale Quay, across Burrard Inlet. Transit information 604/521-0400. ¢-¢¢

Simon Fraser University. (1965) 20,000 students. Located on Burnaby Mt; architecturally outstanding bldgs.

Original campus was completed in only 18 months. Hrly guided tours (July-Aug, daily; free) 10 mi (16 km) E off BC 7A (Hastings St) in Burnaby. Phone 604/291-3210 or 604/291-3111.

Skiing.

Cypress Bowl Ski Area. Four double chairlifts, rope tow; patrol, school, rentals; cafeteria. X-country trails; hiking trails. Snowshoe/winter hiking trail. (Dec-mid-Apr, daily) Provincial park offers spectacular views of Vancouver and the surrounding area and an accessible old-growth forest; scenic lookouts; picnic areas; hiking, self-guided interpretive trails. Park (all yr, daily). 7½ mi (12 km) NW via BC 99, in Cypress Provincial Park. Phone 604/926-5612. Ski area ¢¢¢¢

Grouse Mountain. All-yr recreational facility. Aerial tramway, 4 double chairlifts, 2 T-bars, 3 rope tows; 13 runs; patrol, school, rentals; lounge, restaurants. (Dec-mid-Apr, daily) Night skiing. Skyride (all yr; fee). Playground, hiking trails. "Our Spirit Soars" multimedia presentation; logging shows; helicopter tours, chairlift rides, horse-drawn wagon rides. 8 mi (13 km) N at 6400 Nancy Greene Way (top of Capilano Rd) in N Vancouver. Phone 604/984-0661. ¢¢¢¢

Seymour Ski Country. Three double chairlifts, rope tow; night skiing; patrol, school, rentals; cafeteria. (Mid-Nov-Apr, daily) Cross-country and snowshoe trails (Dec-Mar, daily). Chairlift also operates July-Aug (daily). Provincial park is a large semiwilderness with scenic roadside viewpoints overlooking Vancouver; picnic areas; hiking, self-guided interpretive trails. Park (all yr, daily). 1700 Mt Seymour Rd. Phone 604/986-2261. Ski area ¢¢¢¢

Stanley Park. Approx 1,000 acres (405 hectares) of beautifully land scaped gardens, lakes, totem poles, trails; swimming pool and sand beaches, golf, tennis. Children's farmyard (fee), miniature train (daily; fee). Horse-drawn tours avail from AAA Horse & Carriage Ltd (May-mid-Oct; phone 604/681-5115). NW of downtown. Phone 604/257-8400. Also here is

Vancouver Aquarium. One of the largest in North America; more than 8,000 marine and freshwater animals from around the world in 5 major viewing areas; killer whales, Beluga whales; Amazon Rain Forest gallery; North Pacific and Tropical galleries. (Daily) Phone 604/268-9900. ¢¢¢¢

University of British Columbia. (1915) 28,000 students. The 990-acre (401-hectare) campus features museums, galleries (some fees), many spectacular gardens; almost 400 bldgs complement the natural grandeur of the area. Free guided campus tours (May-Aug). Beautifully situated on scenic Point Grey. 8 mi (13 km) SW via Burrard St, 4th Ave. Phone 604/822-5355. Incl

Museum of Anthropology. World-renowned collection of artifacts from many cultures, with emphasis on art of first peoples of the Northwest Coast. **Great Hall** displays 30-ft totem poles and huge feast dishes; **Masterpiece Gallery** contains intricate works in gold, silver, wood, and stone; unique European ceramics collection; outdoor exhibit area has replicas of traditional Haida bldgs. "Visible storage" concept allows 90% of the museum's collection to be viewed at all times. Changing exhibits; public programs. Guided tours (free exc if by appt). (July-Aug, daily; rest of yr, Tues-Sun; closed Dec 25, 26) Free admission Tues in winter, Tues eve in summer. 6393 NW Marine Dr. Phone 604/822-3825 (recording). ¢¢¢

UBC Botanical Garden. Seven separate areas incl Asian, Physick, B.C. Native, Alpine, and Food gardens. (Daily; closed Jan 1, Dec 25) **Nitobe Garden,** authentic Japanese tea garden located behind Asian Centre (mid-Mar-early Oct, daily; rest of yr, Mon-Fri). 6804 SW Marine Dr. Phone 604/822-9666 (UBC Botanical Garden) or 604/822-6038 (Nitobe Garden). ¢¢

Frederic Wood Theatre. Summer stock and winter main stage productions. Phone 604/822-2678 for tickets and information.

Vancouver Art Gallery. Changing exhibits of contemporary and historical art, featuring masterworks of Emily Carr. Guided tours (by appt). Fine arts library. Restaurant, gift shop. (June-Sep, daily; rest of yr, Wed-Mon; closed Jan 1, Dec 25) 750 Hornby St. Phone 604/662-4719 (recording) or 604/682-4668. ¢¢¢

Vancouver Museum. One of Canada's largest civic museums. Decorative arts, Vancouver history, Northwest Coast indigenous culture, and touring exhibits. (Daily; closed Dec 25) 1100 Chestnut St, 1½ mi (2½ km) SW via Burrard, Cypress Sts. Phone 604/736-4431. ¢¢¢

VanDusen Botanical Garden. Approx 55 acres (22 hectares) of flowers and exotic plants. Seasonal displays, mountain views, restaurant. (Daily; closed Dec 25) 5251 Oak St. Phone 604/878-9274. ¢¢¢

Annual Events

Hyack Festival. 12 mi (19 km) S via Hwy 1A in New Westminster. Commemorates birthday of Queen Victoria, held yearly since 1871; 21-gun salute; band concerts, parade, carnival, sports events. Phone 604/522-6894. Ten days mid-May.

Symphony of Fire. English Bay Beach. Intl fireworks competition accompanied with music. July.

International Bathtub Race. Thirty-four-mi

Vancouver skyline

(55-km) race from Nanaimo to Vancouver. Phone 800/663-7337. Third or 4th Sun July.

Pacific National Exhibition Annual Fair. Exhibition Park. Second-largest fair in Canada. Hundreds of free exhibits, major theme event, concerts, thrill shows, world championship timber show; petting zoo, thoroughbred horse racing, commercial exhibits, roller coaster, agricultural shows, horse shows, livestock competitions, horticultural exhibits. Phone 604/253-2311. Usually mid-Aug-early Sep.

Christmas events. Christmas Carol Ship and lighted ship parade; New Year's Day Polar Bear swim.

Seasonal Event

A symphony orchestra, opera company, and many theater groups present productions around town, especially at the Queen Elizabeth Theatre & Playhouse and Orpheum Theatre. Consult local paper for details.

Additional Visitor Information

There are many more interesting things to see and do in Vancouver and the suburbs of Burnaby and New Westminster to the E, Richmond to the S, North Vancouver, and West Vancouver. The Tourism Vancouver InfoCentre has pamphlets, maps, ferry schedules, and additional information at Plaza Level, Waterfront Centre, 200 Burrard St, V6C 3L6; 604/683-2000.

City Neighborhoods

Many of the restaurants, unrated dining establishments, and some lodgings listed under Vancouver incl neighborhoods as well as exact street addresses. Geographic descriptions of these areas are given.

Chinatown. N of Pender St, E of Carrall St, S of Hastings St, and W of Gore St.

Downtown. N of Beatty St, E of Pacific Blvd, S of Burrard St, and W of Port Roadway. **S of Downtown:** S of Beatty St. **E of Downtown:** E of Port Roadway. **W of Downtown:** W of Burrard St.

Gastown. N of Cordova St, E of Cambie St, S of Water St, and W of Columbia St.

Granville Island. S of Downtown; bordered by Johnston St, Cartwright St, and Duranleau St.

West End. N of Burrard St, E of Pacific St, S of Park Lane, and W of Port Roadway.

Motels/Motor Lodges

★★ **BEST WESTERN KINGS INN.** *5411 Kingsway (V5H 2G1), (Hwy 1A/99A), 2 mi S.* 604/438-1383; fax 604/438-2954; res 800/528-1234; toll-free 800/211-1122. *Email bw_kings inn@telus.net.* 141 rms, 2 story. May-Sep: S $110; D $120; each addl $10; suites, kit. units $130-$135; under 12 free; lower rates rest of yr. Crib free. TV; cable. Pool. Complimentary coffee in rms. Restaurant 7 am-9 pm. Bar 11 am-midnight. Ck-out noon. Coin lndry. Meeting rms. Business servs avail. Sundries. Health club privileges. Game rm. Cr cds: A, C, D, DS, ER, JCB, MC, V.

★★ **BILTMORE HOTEL.** *395 Kingsway (V5T 3J7), S of Downtown.* 604/872-5252; fax 604/874-3003; res 800/663-5713. 100 rms, 7 story. Apr-Oct: S, D $79-$110; each addl $8; under 12 free; lower rates rest of yr. Crib free. TV; cable. Pool. Coffee in rms. Restaurant 6:30 am-8 pm; Sat from 7 am; Sun 8 am-2 pm. Bar noon-2 am. Ck-out noon. Meeting rms. Business servs avail. Cr cds: A, D, ER, MC, V.

Hotels

★★ **ACCENT INNS.** *10551 St. Edward Dr (V6X 3L8), Hwy 99 Exit 39, near Intl Airport.* 604/273-3311; fax 604/273-9522; toll-free 800/663-0298. *Email staynsave@staynsave.com; www.staynsave.com.* 206 rms, 3 story, 19 suites. May-June, Aug-Sep: S $124; D $134; each addl $10; suites $144; under 16 free; lower rates rest of yr. Crib avail. Pet accepted, some restrictions. Parking lot. TV; cable (premium). Complimentary coffee in rms, newspaper, toll-free calls. Restaurant 6 am-10 pm. Ck-out 11 am, ck-in 3 pm. Meeting rms. Fax servs avail.

Dry cleaning, coin lndry. Free airport transportation. Exercise equipt, whirlpool. Golf, 18 holes. Video games. Cr cds: A, D, ER, MC, V.

★★ BEST WESTERN ABERCORN INN. *9260 Bridgeport Rd (V6X 1S1), 9 mi S, near Intl Airport. 604/270-7576; fax 604/270-0001; toll-free 800 /663-0085. Email abercorn@ican.net; www.abercorn-inn.com.* 96 rms, 3 story. June-Sep: S $129; D $139; each addl $15; under 16 free; lower rates rest of yr. Crib avail. Parking lot. TV; cable (premium). Complimentary coffee in rms, newspaper, toll-free calls. Restaurant 6:30 am-10:30 pm. Bar. Ck-out noon, ck-in 4 pm. Meeting rms. Business center. Concierge. Dry cleaning. Free airport transportation. Exercise privileges. Golf. Downhill skiing. Hiking trail. Cr cds: A, D, DS, ER, JCB, MC, V.

★★ BEST WESTERN CHATEAU GRANVILLE. *1100 Granville St (V6Z 2B6), at Helmcken, Downtown. 604/669-7070; fax 604/669-4928; res 800/528-1234; toll-free 800/663-0575. Email sales@bwcg.com.* 148 rms, 15 story, 90 suites. May-Oct: S, D $133-$180; each addl $20; under 16 free; wknd rates; lower rates rest of yr. Crib free. Covered parking $5. TV; cable (premium). Restaurant 7 am-10 pm. Bar noon-1 am. Ck-out 11 am. Meeting rms. Business servs avail. Refrigerators, minibars. Private patios, balconies. Cr cds: A, C, D, DS, ER, JCB, MC, V.

★★ BEST WESTERN EXHIBITION PARK. *3475 E Hastings St (V5K 2A5), E of Downtown. 604/294-4751; fax 604/294-1269; res 800/528-1234; toll-free 800/296-4751.* 47 rms, 3 story, 11 suites. May-Sep: S, D $125; each addl $10; suites $199; under 12 free; lower rates rest of yr. Parking lot. TV; cable, VCR avail. Complimentary continental bkfst, coffee in rms, newspaper, toll-free calls. Restaurant nearby. Ck-out noon, ck-in noon. Business servs avail. Dry cleaning, coin lndry. Sauna, steam rm, whirlpool. Golf. Downhill skiing. Cr cds: A, C, D, DS, ER, MC, V.

★★ BEST WESTERN SANDS. *1755 Davie St (Z6G 1W5), 1 blk from English Bay, in the West End. 604/682-1831; fax 604/682-3546; res 800/528-1234; toll-free 800/663-9400. Email sands@rpbhotels.com; www.rpbhotels. com.* 115 rms, 6 story, 4 suites. May-Sep: S, D $199; each addl $15; suites $349; under 12 free; lower rates rest of yr. Crib avail. Pet accepted, some restrictions, fee. Valet parking avail. TV; cable (premium). Complimentary continental bkfst, coffee in rms, newspaper, toll-free calls. Restaurant 7 am-10 pm. Bar. Ck-out noon, ck-in 4 pm. Meeting rms. Business servs avail. Dry cleaning. Exercise equipt, sauna. Golf. Tennis, 6 courts. Video games. Cr cds: A, C, D, DS, ER, MC, V.

★★ BLUE HORIZON. *1225 Robson St (V6E 1C3), in the West End. 604/688-1411; fax 604/688-4461; toll-free 800/663-1333. Email info@blue horizonhotel.com; www.bluehorizon hotel.com.* 211 rms, 31 story, 3 suites. May-Sep: S $159; D $169; each addl $15; suites $275; under 16 free; lower rates rest of yr. Crib avail. Parking garage. Indoor pool, lap pool, whirlpool. TV; cable, VCR avail. Complimentary coffee in rms, newspaper, toll-free calls. Restaurant 6:30 am-8 pm. Bar. Ck-out 11 am, ck-in 3 pm. Meeting rms. Business servs avail. Bellhops. Concierge. Dry cleaning. Exercise equipt, sauna. Golf, 18 holes. Tennis, 5 courts. Downhill skiing. Cr cds: A, D, ER, MC, V.

★★★ COAST PLAZA SUITE HOTEL. *1763 Comox St (V6G 1P6), in the West End. 604/688-7711; fax 604/688-5934; toll-free 800/663-1144.* 267 rms, 35 story, 190 kits. No A/C. May-Oct: S $245-$315; D $285-$355; each addl $20; suites $295-$425; under 18 free; package plans. Crib free. TV; cable (premium), VCR avail. Indoor pool. Restaurants 6:30 am-10 pm. Rm serv 24 hrs. Bar 11:30-2 am. Ck-out noon. Coin lndry. Meeting rms. Business servs avail. In-rm modem link. Concierge. Shopping arcade. Valet parking. Free downtown transportation. Exercise rm; sauna. Refrigerators, minibars. Balconies. Luxury level. Cr cds: A, D, DS, ER, JCB, MC, V.

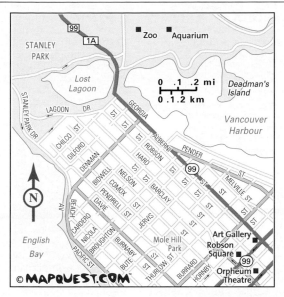

Vancouver is one of the most cosmopolitan cities in the world, and part of its considerable charm is the wonderful mix of people from all around the globe. Downtown Vancouver remains very dynamic, and a wander through the people-thronged streets is a great way to catch the energy of this city. Start at the Vancouver Art Gallery, which is the old City Hall. Walk up Robson Street, the city's primary boutique street, lined with all sorts of tiny shops, cafes, galleries, and food markets: this is a very busy place, and you'll hear dozens of languages in the bustle of the crowds. Grab a table at a coffee shop, and watch the world—literally—go by. Continue to Denman Street, and turn south (left). Denman is another busy commercial street, but less international. Here you'll find remnants of aging hippie Vancouver—bookstores, veggie restaurants, and little corner markets—rubbing shoulders with upscale, twenty-something cocktail bars and tattoo parlors for middle-class teenagers. Denman terminates at English Beach, where you can relax on the sand and enjoy the views of Vancouver's West Side across English Bay. Follow the seawall west (right) and, after a couple of blocks, enter Stanley Park, Vancouver's fantastic 1,000-acre park filled with old-growth forests, winding paths, and a number of tourist destinations. Of these, Vancouver Aquarium, reached by a forest path from the southern part of the park, is a must-see. One of the best in North America, it features performing orcas and porpoises, as well as ecosystem tanks from waters around the world. Nearby is Vancouver's small zoo, mostly of interest to children; stop and watch the sea otters play.

★★★ **CROWNE PLAZA HOTEL GEORGIA VANCOUVER.** *801 W Georgia St (V6C 1P7), Downtown. 604/682-5566; fax 604/642-5579; res 800/227-6963; toll-free 800/663-1111. Email hgsales@hotelgeorgia.bc.ca; www.hotelgeorgia.bc.ca.* 311 rms, 12 story, 2 suites. May-Sep: S, D $329; each addl $20; suites $400; under 16 free; lower rates rest of yr. Crib avail. Pet accepted, some restrictions. Valet parking avail. TV; cable (DSS). Complimentary coffee in rms, newspaper, toll-free calls. Restaurant 6:30 am-10 pm. 24-hr rm serv. Bar. Ck-out noon, ck-in 4 pm. Conference center, meeting rms. Business center. Bellhops. Concierge. Dry cleaning. Gift shop. Salon/barber. Exercise equipt. Golf, 18 holes. Tennis, 4 courts. Downhill skiing. Video games. Cr cds: A, D, DS, ER, JCB, MC, V.

⟦icons⟧

★★ **DELTA PACIFIC RESORT AND CONFERENCE CENTER.** *10251 St. Edwards Dr (V6X 2M9), 8 mi S via Hwy 99. 604/278-9611; fax 604/276-1121; res 800/268-1133. Email dpolowy@deltahotels.com; www.delta pacific.bc.ca.* 438 rms, 21 story, 44 suites. May-Sep: S, D $300; each addl $20; suites $450; under 18 free; lower rates rest of yr. Crib avail. Pet accepted, fee. Valet parking avail. Indoor/outdoor pools, children's pool, whirlpool. TV; cable (premium), CD avail. Complimentary coffee in rms, newspaper. Restaurant 6:30 am-11 pm. 24-hr rm serv. Bar. Ck-out noon, ck-in 3 pm. Conference center, meeting rms. Business center. Bellhops. Concierge. Dry cleaning. Gift shop. Salon/barber. Exercise rm, sauna. Golf. Tennis, 4 courts. Downhill skiing. Bike rentals. Supervised children's activities. Video games. Cr cds: A, C, D, ER, JCB, MC, V.

⟦icons⟧

DELTA PINNACLE. Unrated for 2001. *1128 W Hastings St (V6E 4R5). 604/684-1128; fax 604/298-1128; toll-free 800/268-1133. www.deltahotels. com.* 434 rms, 31 story, 10 suites. June-Oct: S, D $410; each addl $20; suites $560; under 18 free; lower rates rest of yr. Crib avail. Pet accepted. Indoor pool, whirlpool. TV; cable (premium), VCR avail, CD avail. Complimentary continental bkfst, coffee in rms, newspaper. Restaurant 6:30 am-midnight. Bar.

Ck-out noon, ck-in 3 pm. Conference center, meeting rms. Business center. Bellhops. Concierge. Dry cleaning. Gift shop. Salon/barber. Exercise equipt, sauna, steam rm. Golf. Downhill skiing. Beach access. Supervised children's activities. Hiking trail. Picnic facilities. Video games. Cr cds: A, C, D, DS, ER, JCB, MC, V.

⟦icons⟧

★★ **DELTA TOWN AND COUNTRY.** *6005 Hwy 17 (V4K 5B8), at Hwy 99. 604/946-4404; fax 604/946-5916; toll-free 888/777-1266. www.deltainn. com.* 50 rms, 2 story, 1 suite. June-Sep: S, D $99; each addl $10; suites $160; under 16 free; lower rates rest of yr. Crib avail, fee. Pet accepted, some restrictions, fee. Parking lot. Pool, lap pool. TV; cable (premium), VCR avail. Complimentary continental bkfst, coffee in rms. Restaurant 6 am-9 pm. Bar. Ck-out 11:30 am, ck-in 3 pm. Meeting rms. Business center. Dry cleaning, coin lndry. Gift shop. Exercise rm. Golf. Tennis, 5 courts. Downhill skiing. Supervised children's activities. Hiking trail. Picnic facilities. Video games. Cr cds: A, D, ER, MC, V.

⟦icons⟧

★★★ **DELTA VANCOUVER AIRPORT HOTEL AND MARINA.** *3500 Cessna Dr (V7B 1C7), 9 mi S, near Intl Airport. 604/278-1241; fax 604/276-1975; toll-free 800/268-1133.* 415 rms, 11 story. May-Sep: S, D $300; each addl $20; suites $395-$495; under 18 free; lower rates rest of yr. Crib free. TV; cable, VCR avail. Heated pool; poolside serv in season. Restaurant 6 am-10:30 pm. Bars 11-1 am. Ck-out 1 pm. Business center. In-rm modem link. Concierge. Gift shop. Airport transportation. Exercise equipt. Health club privileges. On Fraser River; marina. Cr cds: A, D, DS, ER, JCB, MC, V.

⟦icons⟧

★★ **EMPIRE LANDMARK HOTEL & CONFERENCE CENTRE.** *1400 Robson St (V6G 1B9), in the West End. 604/687-0511; fax 604/687-2801; toll-free 800/830-6144. Email ehlresa@ asiastandard.com; www.asiastandard. com.* 352 rms, 42 story, 5 suites. May-Oct: S $180; D $200; each addl $20; suites $395; lower rates rest of yr.

Crib avail. Parking garage. TV; cable (DSS). Complimentary coffee in rms. Restaurant 6:30 am-11 pm. Bar. Ck-out noon, ck-in 4 pm. Conference center, meeting rms. Business center. Bellhops. Concierge. Dry cleaning, coin lndry. Gift shop. Exercise equipt, sauna. Golf, 18 holes. Downhill skiing. Cr cds: A, D, DS, ER, JCB, MC, V.

★★★ **ENGLISH BAY INN.** *1968 Comox St (V6G 1R4). 604/683-8002. www.bbchannel.com/bbc/p216342.asp.* 7 rms. S, D: $117- $220. Complimentary full bkfst, pet accepted. 1 blk from beaches and parks. Cr cds: A, DS, MC, V.

★★ **EXECUTIVE AIRPORT PLAZA HOTEL.** *7311 Westminster Hwy (V6X 1A3), approx 10 mi S on Hwy 99, then 2½ mi W. 604/278-5555; fax 604/278-0255; res 888/388-3932; toll-free 800/663-2878. Email execcutivermd@acncanada.net; www.execcutiveinnhotels.com.* 231 rms, 18 story, 115 suites. May-Sep: S $129; D $149; each addl $20; suites $189; under 14 free; lower rates rest of yr. Crib avail. Parking garage. Indoor pool, whirlpool. TV; cable (premium). Complimentary coffee in rms, newspaper, toll-free calls. Restaurant 6:30 am 10 pm. Bar. Ck-out noon, ck-in 3 pm. Meeting rms. Business center. Bellhops. Concierge. Dry cleaning. Gift shop. Free airport transportation. Exercise privileges. Golf. Tennis, 10 courts. Cr cds: A, D, ER, MC, V.

★ **EXECUTIVE INN EXPRESS.** *9020 Bridgeport Rd (V6X 1S1). 604/270-6030; fax 604/270-6030; toll-free 800/663-2337. www.execcutiveinnhotels.com.* 85 rms, 3 story, 3 suites. June-Sep: S, D $99; each addl $10; suites $200; lower rates rest of yr. Crib avail. Parking lot. TV; cable (premium), VCR avail. Complimentary continental bkfst, coffee in rms, newspaper, toll-free calls. Restaurant 6 am-10 pm. Bar. Ck-out noon, ck-in 3 pm. Business center. Bellhops. Concierge. Dry cleaning, coin lndry. Free airport transportation. Exercise equipt, sauna. Golf, 18 holes. Beach

access. Video games. Cr cds: A, D, ER, MC, V.

★★ **EXECUTIVE INN HOTEL.** *1379 Howe St (V6Z 2R5). 604/688-7678; fax 604/688-7679; toll-free 800/570-3932. www.execcutiveinnhotels.com.* 98 rms, 8 and 18 story, 34 suites. May-Oct: S, D $179; each addl $20; suites $250; under 18 free; lower rates rest of yr. Valet parking avail. TV; cable, VCR avail. Complimentary coffee in rms. Restaurant 6:30 am-10 pm. Bar. Ck-out noon, ck-in 3 pm. Meeting rms. Business center. Bellhops. Concierge. Dry cleaning. Exercise equipt, whirlpool. Tennis, 10 courts. Downhill skiing. Beach access. Cr cds: A, C, D, ER, JCB, MC, V.

★★★★ **THE FAIRMONT VANCOUVER AIRPORT.** *3311 N Service Rd (V7B 1X9). 604/207-5200; fax 604/248-3219; toll-free 800/676-8922. Email fvares@fairmont.com; www.fairmont.com.* Not the stereotypical airport hotel, this elegant property has 392 technology friendly and very comfortable guestrooms for busy international travelers. Rooms include airline check-in, complimentary high-speed Internet access and portable phones. Great views of the mountains and Georgia Straits through the floor-to-ceiling soundproof widows. This elegant full-service hotel offers a fully equipped exercise room, spa, dining room and lounge, and full concierge service. 392 rms, 14 story, 2 suites. May-Oct: S, D $299; each addl $20; suites $600; under 17 free; lower rates rest of yr. Crib avail. Pet accepted, fee. Valet parking avail. Indoor pool, whirlpool. TV; cable (DSS), VCR avail, CD avail. Complimentary coffee in rms, newspaper, toll-free calls. Restaurant 6:30 am-11 pm. 24-hr rm serv. Bar. Ck-out noon, ck-in 3 pm. Conference center, meeting rms. Business center. Bellhops. Concierge. Dry cleaning. Gift shop. Salon/barber. Exercise rm, sauna. Beach access. Bike rentals. Video games. Cr cds: A, D, DS, ER, JCB, MC, V.

★★★★ **FOUR SEASONS HOTEL VANCOUVER.** *791 W Georgia St (V6C 2T4), Downtown. 604/689-9333;*

fax 604/689-3466. Located amidst the fine shops of the Pacific Centre, within walking distance of the convention centre, theatres, and other sports and entertainment facilities, this elegant hotel is noted for impeccable service and a renewed commitment to guest satisfaction. Relax with nightly entertainment in the Garden Terrace, lounge at the pool, or dine in the nationally recognized Chartwell. The 21,333 square feet of meeting space and complimentary downtown shuttle are great amenities for business guests. 385 rms, 28 story. May-Oct: S, D $315-$465; each addl $30; suites $450-$2,500; under 18 free; wkend rates; lower rates rest of yr. Crib free. Pet accepted. Garage $21/day. TV; cable (premium), VCR (movies). Heated pool; whirlpool. Restaurant 6:30 am-11 pm (see CHARTWELL). Rm serv 24 hrs. Bar 11:30-1 am. Ck-out noon. Meeting rms. Business center. In-rm modem link. Concierge. Shopping arcade. Tennis privileges. Downhill ski 10 mi. Exercise rm; sauna. Shuffleboard. Minibars. Cr cds: A, C, D, DS, ER, JCB, MC, V.

★★ **GEORGIAN COURT HOTEL.** *773 Beatty St (V6B 2M4), Downtown. 604/682-5555; fax 604/682-8830; toll-free 800/663-1155. Email info@ georgiancourt.com; www.georgiancourt. com.* 160 rms, 12 story, 20 suites. May-Sep: S $190; D $210; each addl $20; suites $215; under 17 free; lower rates rest of yr. Crib avail. Pet accepted, some restrictions. Parking garage. TV; cable. Complimentary coffee in rms, newspaper. Restaurant 7 am-11:30 pm. Bar. Ck-out noon, ck-in 3 pm. Meeting rms. Business center. Bellhops. Concierge. Dry cleaning. Gift shop. Exercise equipt, sauna, whirlpool. Golf. Tennis. Downhill skiing. Beach access. Bike rentals. Cr cds: A, D, ER, JCB, MC, V.

★★ **HAMPTON INN.** *8811 Bridgeport Rd (V6X 1R9). 604/232-5505; fax 604/232-5508; res 888/488-0101; toll-free 800/HAMPTON. Email yvrrh01@ hi-hotel.com; www.hamptoninnvancouver.com.* 111 rms, 5 story, 1 suite. May-Sep: S, D $115; each addl $10; suites $270; under 17 free; lower rates rest of yr. Crib avail. Parking lot. TV; cable (premium), VCR avail.

Complimentary continental bkfst, coffee in rms, newspaper, toll-free calls. Restaurant nearby. Ck-out noon, ck-in 3 pm. Meeting rm. Business center. Bellhops. Dry cleaning. Free airport transportation. Exercise equipt. Golf. Tennis, 6 courts. Beach access. Hiking trail. Video games. Cr cds: A, C, D, DS, ER, MC, V.

★★ **HOLIDAY INN.** *711 W Broadway (V5Z 3Y2), at Heather St, S of Downtown. 604/879-0511; fax 604/ 872-7520; res 800/HOLIDAY. Email info@holidayinnvancouver.com; www. holidayinnvancouver.com.* 194 rms, 16 story, 2 suites. May-Sep: S $189; D $209; each addl $10; suites $175; under 18 free; lower rates rest of yr. Crib avail. Pet accepted. Parking garage. Indoor pool. TV; cable (DSS) VCR avail. Complimentary coffee in rms. Restaurant. Bar. Meeting rms. Business servs avail. Bellhops. Dry cleaning. Gift shop. Exercise equipt, sauna. Golf. Downhill skiing. Cr cds: A, D, DS, ER, JCB, MC, V.

★★ **HOLIDAY INN HOTEL & SUITES DOWNTOWN.** *1110 Howe St (V6Z 1R2), Downtown. 604/684-2151; fax 604/684-2151; res 800/465-4329; toll-free 800/465-5329. Email hiotvan@intergate.bc.com; www.atlific. com.* 242 rms, 7 story. May-Oct: S $169; D $189; each addl $10; suites $199-$235; under 18 free; lower rates rest of yr. Crib free. Valet parking $8.95. TV; cable (premium), VCR avail. Indoor pool. Complimentary coffee. Restaurant 6:30 am-10 pm. Rm serv 24 hrs. Bars 11-2 am; entertainment on wkends. Ck-out noon. Meeting rms. Business center. Concierge. Gift shop. Game rm. Exercise equipt; sauna. Health club privileges. Some refrigerators. Balconies. Cr cds: A, C, D, DS, ER, JCB, MC, V.

★★ **HOLIDAY INN VANCOUVER AIRPORT.** *10720 Cambie Rd (V6X 1K8). 604/821-1818; fax 604/821-1819; res 800/465-4329; toll-free 888/ 831-3388. Email service@hi-airport.bc. ca; www.hi-airport.bc.ca.* 162 rms, 6 story, 1 suite. May-Sep: S, D $139; each addl $10; suite $279; under 18 free; lower rates rest of yr. Crib avail. Parking garage. TV; cable (DSS), VCR avail, CD avail. Complimentary coffee in rms, toll-free calls. Restaurant 6:30 am-midnight. Bar. Ck-out noon, ck-in 4 pm. Meeting rms. Business center. Bellhops. Concierge. Dry cleaning. Free airport transportation. Exercise equipt, whirlpool. Golf. Supervised children's activities. Video games. Cr cds: A, D, DS, ER, JCB, MC, V.

[D] [icons]

★★★ **HOTEL VANCOUVER.** *900 W Georgia St (V6C 2W6), Downtown. 604/684-3131; fax 604/662-1924; res 800/866-5577; toll-free 800/886-5577. Email reserve@hvc.cphotels.ca.* 550 rms, 14 story. Late Apr-early Oct: S $180-$340; D $205-$365; each addl $25; suites $305-$1,830; family, wkend rates; lower rates rest of yr. Pet accepted. TV; cable (premium), VCR avail. Indoor pool; wading pool, whirlpool. Restaurant 6 am-10 pm. Rm serv 24 hrs. Bars 11-1 am; entertainment. Ck-out noon. Meeting rms. Business center. In-rm modem link. Concierge. Shopping arcade. Beauty salon. Exercise rm; sauna. Refrigerator in suites. Luxury level. Cr cds: A, D, DS, ER, JCB, MC, V.

[D] [icons]

★★★ **HYATT REGENCY VANCOUVER.** *655 Burrard St (V6C 2R7), Downtown. 604/683-1234; fax 604/689-3707; res 800/233-1234. Email sales@yvrrvpo.hyatt.com; www. vancouver.hyatt.com.* 644 rms, 34 story, 13 suites. May-Oct: S, D $269; each addl $35; suites $1,295; under 18 free; lower rates rest of yr. Crib avail. Valet parking avail. Pool, lap pool. TV; cable (premium), VCR avail. Complimentary coffee in rms, newspaper, toll-free calls. Restaurant 6:30 am-11 pm. Bar. Ck-out noon, ck-in 4 pm. Conference center, meeting rms. Business center. Bellhops. Concierge. Dry cleaning. Gift shop. Salon/barber. Exercise privileges. Golf, 18 holes. Tennis, 10 courts. Downhill skiing. Cr cds: A, C, D, DS, ER, JCB, MC, V.

[D] [icons]

★★★★ **THE METROPOLITAN HOTEL.** *645 Howe St (V6C 2Y9), Downtown. 604/687-1122; fax 604/602-7846; toll-free 800/667-2300. www.metropolitan.com.* Located in the heart of Vancouver's financial, shop-

ping, and entertainment district this property surrounds guests with classic Asian art collectibles as the hotel was constructed according to the art of Feng Shui. The golden Chinese Temple Carving located in the lobby is a specially commissioned gilt Chinese temple screen placed there by the Feng Shui Master to bring prosperity to the hotel. 181 rms, 18 story, 16 suites. June-Oct: S $280; D $310; each addl $30; suites $365; under 18 free; lower rates rest of yr. Crib avail. Pet accepted. Valet parking avail. Indoor pool, lap pool, whirlpool. TV; cable, VCR avail, CD avail. Complimentary coffee in rms, newspaper. Restaurant. 24-hr rm serv. Bar. Ck-out 1 pm, ck-in 3 pm. Meeting rms. Business center. Bellhops. Concierge. Dry cleaning. Exercise equipt, sauna. Golf. Cr cds: A, D, ER, JCB, MC, V.

[D] [icons]

★★★ **PACIFIC PALISADES.** *1277 Robson St (V6E 1C4), in the West End. 604/688-0461; fax 604/688-4374.* 233 suites, 20-23 story. May-Oct: S, D $209-$249; each addl $30; suites to $800; under 16 free; lower rates rest of yr. Crib free. Parking $13. TV; cable, VCR avail. Indoor pool; whirlpool. Restaurant 6:30 am-10 pm. Rm serv 24 hrs. Bar 11:30-1 am; entertainment Thurs-Sat. Ck-out noon. Meeting rms. Business center. In-rm modem link. Concierge. Garage parking. Exercise rm; sauna. Some balconies. Cr cds: A, D, DS, JCB, MC, V.

[D] [icons]

★★★★ **THE PAN PACIFIC VANCOUVER.** *300-999 Canada Pl (V6C 3B5), adj Trade and Convention Center, Downtown. 604/662-8111; fax 604/685-8690; toll-free 800/937-1515. Email reservations@panpacific-hotel. com; www.panpacific-hotel.com.* This downtown waterfront property shares a complex with the World Trade Centre and Convention Centre. All 504 rooms and suites have a clean, Asian-influenced design and large windows with harbour, mountain or city views. Global Office Rooms are a great option for business travelers, providing a computer and high-speed Internet access. The soaring atrium lobby contains the lounge, the all-day restaurant, and, on the second level, the award-winning Five Sails dining room.

Stunning architecture and elegant Asian-influenced interiors make this a popular meeting spot for both locals and visitors alike. 465 rms, 15 story, 39 suites. May-Oct: S, D $515; suites $595; lower rates rest of yr. Crib avail. Pet accepted, some restrictions. Valet parking avail. Pool, lap pool, whirlpool. TV; cable, VCR avail, CD avail. Complimentary coffee in rms, newspaper, toll-free calls. Restaurant 6:30 am-3 pm. 24-hr rm serv. Bar. Ck-out noon, ck-in 3 pm. Conference center, meeting rms. Business center. Bellhops. Concierge. Dry cleaning. Gift shop. Salon/barber. Exercise rm, sauna, steam rm. Golf. Tennis. Video games. Cr cds: A, D, ER, JCB, MC, V.

★★ **QUALITY HOTEL - DOWN-TOWN.** *1335 Howe St (V6Z 1R7), Downtown. 604/682-0229; fax 604/662-7566; toll-free 800/663-8474. Email sales@qualityhotelvancouver.com; www.qualityhotelvancouver.com.* 132 rms, 7 story, 25 suites. June-Sep: S, D $139; each addl $20; suites $199; under 17 free; lower rates rest of yr. Crib avail. Pet accepted, some restrictions, fee. Parking garage. Pool. TV; cable (premium). Restaurant 7 am-9 pm. Bar. Ck-out 11 am, ck-in 3 pm. Meeting rms. Business servs avail. Bellhops. Concierge. Dry cleaning. Gift shop. Salon/barber. Exercise privileges. Golf. Tennis. Downhill skiing. Supervised children's activities. Cr cds: A, C, D, DS, ER, JCB, MC, V.

★★ **RADISSON HOTEL BURNABY.** *4331 Dominion St (V5G 1C7), 8 mi E via Trans-Can Hwy 1, Willingdon Ave S Exit. 604/430-2828; fax 604/430-9230; toll-free 800/667-6116. Email sales@villa.bc.ca; www.villa.bc.ca.* 275 rms, 21 story. S $131; D $141; each addl $10; suites $175-$1,000; under 18 free. Crib free. TV; cable. 2 pools, 1 indoor; poolside serv. Restaurant 6:30 am-10 pm. Bar 11-1 am. Ck-out noon. Meeting rms. Business center. In-rm modem link. Gift shop. Barber. Free covered parking. Exercise equipt. Refrigerators. Balconies. Cr cds: A, C, D, ER, MC, V.

★★★ **RADISSON PRESIDENT HOTEL AND SUITES.** *8181 Cambie Rd (V6X 3X9). 604/276-8181; fax 604/279-8381; toll-free 800/333-3333. Email sales@radissonvancouver.com.* 184 rms, 11 story. S, D $205; each addl $15; suites $225-$370; under 18 free. Crib free. TV; cable (premium), VCR avail. Indoor pool. Complimentary coffee in rms. Restaurant 6:30 am-2 pm, 5-10 pm. Rm serv 24 hrs. Ck-out 1 pm. Meeting rms. Business servs avail. In-rm modem link. Shopping arcade. Barber, beauty shop. Valet serv. Free airport transportation. Exercise equipt. Refrigerators. Cr cds: A, D, DS, JCB, MC, V.

★★★★ **RENAISSANCE VANCOUVER HOTEL HARBOURSIDE.** *1133 W Hastings (V6E 3T3), Downtown. 604/689-9211; fax 604/689-4358.* Found on the waterfront overlooking Vancouver Harbor, Burrard Inlet, and the North Shore Mountains is this 439 guestroom hotel. Located in the downtown area, it is only waling distance to the Tobson Street And the Pacific Center shopping area. 439 rms, 19 story. May-Oct: S, D $194-$244; each addl $25; suites $392-$1,400; under 19 free; lower rates rest of yr. Crib free. Pet accepted. Covered parking $15. TV; cable (premium). Indoor pool. Restaurant 6:30 am-11 pm. 2 bars; entertainment Mon-Sat. Ck-out noon. Convention facilities. Business servs avail. In-rm modem link. Exercise equipt; sauna. Minibars; refrigerators. Balconies. Cr cds: A, C, D, DS, ER, JCB, MC, V.

★★★★ **THE SUTTON PLACE HOTEL.** *845 Burrard St (V6Z 2K6), Downtown. 604/682-5511; fax 604/642-2926; res 800/810-6888. www.suttonplace.com.* Antiques and beautiful floral displays welcome guests in the elegant lobby of this downtown Vancouver hotel. This European-style hotel is located near businesses, art, and shopping. It offers 397 guestrooms and suites, a fitness center with indoor pool, and nearby tennis facilities, beaches, and winter skiing. 397 rms, 21 story, 47 suites. Mid-Apr-Oct: S $195-$395; D $215-$415; each addl $20; suites $445-$1,500; under 18 free; lower rates rest of yr. Crib free. Garage, valet parking $15. TV; cable (premium), VCR avail (movies). Indoor pool; whirlpool, poolside serv. Restaurant 6:30 am-11 pm. Rm serv

24 hrs. Bar 11:30-1:30 am; entertainment. Ck-out noon. Convention facilities. Business center. In-rm modem link. Concierge. Gift shop. Exercise rm; sauna, steam rm. Massage. Bathrm phones, refrigerators. Sun deck. Cr cds: A, C, D, DS, ER, JCB, MC, V.

★★★ **WATERFRONT CENTRE.**
900 Canada Place Way (V6C 3L5), at Burrard Inlet, in the West End. 604/691-1991; fax 604/691-1838; res 800/527-4727. www.fairmont. com. 489 units, 23 story. May-Oct: S, D $280-$395; each addl $25; suites $465-$1,700; under 18 free; lower rates rest of yr. Crib free. Pet accepted; $25. Garage parking $17. TV; cable, VCR avail. Heated pool; whirlpool, poolside serv. Restaurant 6:30 am-midnight. Rm serv 24 hrs. Bar from 11 am; entertainment Mon-Sat. Ck-out noon. Convention facilities. Business center. In-rm modem link. Concierge. Shopping arcade. Exercise equipt. Minibars. Luxury level. Cr cds: A, D, DS, JCB, MC, V.

★★★ **WEDGEWOOD.** *845 Hornby St (V6Z 1V1), Downtown. 604/689-7777; fax 604/608-5348; res 604/689-7777; toll-free 800/663-0666. Email info@wedgewoodhotel.com; www. wedgewoodhotel.com.* 51 rms, 13 story, 34 suites. May-Oct: S $200; D $220; suites $480; lower rates rest of yr. Crib avail. Valet parking avail. TV; cable (DSS), VCR avail, CD avail. Complimentary full bkfst, coffee in rms, newspaper, toll-free calls. Restaurant. 24-hr rm serv. Bar. Meeting rms. Business center. Bellhops. Concierge. Dry cleaning. Salon/barber. Exercise privileges, sauna. Golf, 18 holes. Tennis, 10 courts. Downhill skiing. Beach access. Bike rentals. Hiking trail. Picnic facilities. Video games. Cr cds: A, C, D, DS, ER, JCB, MC, V.

★★★★ **THE WESTIN GRAND VANCOUVER.** *433 Robson St (V6B 6L9). 604/602-1999; fax 604/647-2502; toll-free 888/625-5144. Email play@westingrandvancouver.com; www.westingrandvancouver.com.* This property resides in the entertainment district within walking distance of Yaletown's clubs and restaurants and Robson Street shopping. Rooms are decorated in black and beige tones

Pacific Rim National Park, Vancouver Island

with a contemporary style, and Grandview Floors (30 and 31) have wonderful city views. All of the rooms are suites, with a small live/work area, a kitchenette with microwave oven, 2 televisions (one with internet access), and a bathroom that has a separate bathtub and shower. 31 story, 207 suites. June-Oct: suites $329; each addl $25; under 18 free; lower rates rest of yr. Crib avail. Pet accepted, fee. Valet parking avail. Pool, lap pool, whirlpool. TV; cable (premium), VCR avail, CD avail. Complimentary coffee in rms, newspaper. Restaurant 6:30 am-10 pm. 24-hr rm serv. Bar. Ck-out noon, ck-in 3 pm. Meeting rms. Business center. Bellhops. Concierge. Dry cleaning. Gift shop. Exercise equipt, sauna, steam rm. Golf. Downhill skiing. Beach access. Bike rentals. Supervised children's activities. Hiking trail. Picnic facilities. Video games. Cr cds: A, D, ER, MC, V.

B&Bs/Small Inns

★★ **BEAUTIFUL BED AND BREAKFAST.** *428 W 40th Ave (V5Y 2R4), Downtown. 604/327-1102; fax 604/327-2299. Email sandbbb@portal.ca; www.beautifulbandb.bc.ca.* 4 rms, 3 story, 2 suites. Mar-Oct, Dec: D $85; suites $150; lower rates rest of yr. Street parking. TV; cable (premium), VCR avail, CD avail. Complimentary full bkfst, newspaper, toll-free calls. Restaurant. Ck-out 11 am. Golf, 18 holes. Tennis, 12 courts. Downhill skiing. Bike rentals. Hiking trail. Picnic facilities. No cr cds accepted.

★★★ **RIVER RUN COTTAGES.** *4551 River Rd W (V4K 1R9). 604/946-7778; fax 604/940-1970. Email river run@direct.ca.* 4 cottages, 1 story. June-Sep: S, D $130-$210; each addl $20; under 5 free; lower rates rest of yr. Pet accepted. Complimentary full bkfst. Restaurants nearby. Ck-out noon, ck-in 4 pm. Business servs avail. Bicycles, kayaks avail. On river. Totally nonsmoking. Cr cds: MC, V.

★★★ **WEST END GUEST HOUSE.** *1362 Haro St (V6E 1G2), in the West End. 604/681-2889; fax 604/688-8812; toll-free 888/546-3327. Email wegh@idmail.com; www.westendguesthouse.com.* 8 rms, 4 story. May-Oct: S $105; D $225; each addl $15; lower rates rest of yr. Valet parking avail. TV; cable (premium), VCR avail. Complimentary full bkfst, coffee in rms, newspaper, toll-free calls. Restaurant nearby. Business servs avail. Concierge. Golf, 18 holes. Tennis, 12 courts. Downhill skiing. Bike rentals. Cr cds: A, DS, MC, V.

★★★★ **THE WICKANINNISH INN.** *Osprey Ln at Chesterman Beach (V0R 2Z0), 5 mi from Tofino on Hwy 4, outside Pacific Rim Natl Park. 250/725-3100; fax 250/725-3110; toll-free 800/333-4604. Email info@wickinn.com; www.wickinn.com.* Along the rocky, wooded coastline of Vancouver Island's west shore sits this weathered cedar inn marking the gateway to Pacific Rim National Park. All 46 guestrooms have fireplaces, private balconies, and floor-to-ceiling windows with panoramic coast and ocean views. Visit Ancient Cedars Spa or have a private treatment on the sea-washed rocks. Take morning constitutionals, hiking the trails in the temperate rain forest, or take sunset walks on Chesterman Beach. End the day with a dinner at the resort's Pointe Restaurant perched high above the crashing waves of the Pacific Ocean. 46 rms, 3 story. June-Sep: S, D $360; each addl $20; under 18 free; lower rates rest of yr. Crib avail. Pet accepted, some restrictions, fee. Valet parking avail. TV; cable (premium), VCR avail, CD avail. Complimentary coffee in rms, newspaper, toll-free calls. Restaurant 8 am-9 pm. Bar. Ck-out noon, ck-in 3 pm. Meeting rm. Business center. Concierge. Gift shop. Steam rm. Golf, 9 holes. Beach access. Supervised children's activities. Hiking trail. Cr cds: A, C, D, ER, JCB, MC, V.

All Suites

★★ **EXECUTIVE INN HOTEL AND CONFERENCE CENTRE.** *4201 Lougheed Hwy (V5C 3Y6), between Gilmore and Willingdon Sts. 604/298-2010; fax 604/298-1123; res 888/388-3932; toll-free 800/590-3932. Email burnaby_resv@executiveinnhotels.com; www.executiveinnhotels.com.* 4 story, 125 suites. May-Sep: S, D $115-$160; each addl $10; under 12 free; wkend rates; lower rates rest of yr. Crib avail. Parking garage. Pool. TV; cable (premium), VCR avail. Complimentary coffee in rms, newspaper. Restaurant. Bar. Ck-out noon, ck-in 3 pm. Meeting rms. Business center. Bellhops. Dry cleaning. Gift shop. Free airport transportation. Exercise privileges. Golf. Tennis. Video games. Cr cds: A, D, MC, V.

★★★★ **SHERATON SUITES LE SOLEIL.** *567 Hornby St (V6C 2E8), Arthur Laing Bridge to Granville St, left on Davie St, right on Hornby St. 604/632-3000; fax 604/632-3001; res 800/325-3535; toll-free 877/632-3030. Email reservations@lesoleilhotel.com; www.lesoleilhotel.com.* In the heart of the city's financial and business districts sits this charming 122-suite boutique hotel. The stunning lobby boasts 30-foot, gilded ceilings, crystal chandeliers, and a Louis-XVI-style collection of imported, Italian furniture. Complimentary bottled water and fruit upon arrival are welcome surprises and the property's Oritalia restaurant — a cool hot spot — offers an eclectic Asian-Mediterranean cuisine. 10 rms, 16 story, 112 suites. May-Oct: S $400; D $420; each addl $20; suites $400; lower rates rest of yr. Crib avail, fee. Pet accepted, fee. Valet parking avail. Indoor pool, lap pool, lifeguard, whirlpool. TV; cable (DSS), VCR avail, CD avail. Complimentary coffee in rms, newspaper. Restaurant 6 am-11 pm. 24-hr rm serv. Bar. Ck-out noon, ck-in 3 pm. Meeting rms. Business center. Bellhops. Concierge. Dry cleaning. Exercise privileges. Golf, 18 holes. Tennis, 3 courts. Cr cds: A, D, ER, JCB, MC, V.

Villa/Condo

★ **HOWARD JOHNSON EXPRESS INN & SUITES.** *13245 King George Hwy (V3T 2T3), 15 mi SE on Hwy 99A.* 604/588-0181; fax 604/588-0180; res 800/446-4656. *www.hojo. com.* 42 rms, 2 story, 12 suites. May-Sep: S $70; D $75; each addl $10; suites $95; under 18 free; lower rates rest of yr. Crib avail. Parking lot. TV; cable (DSS), VCR avail. Complimentary continental bkfst, coffee in rms, newspaper, toll-free calls. Restaurant. Ck-out 11 am, ck-in noon. Business center. Coin lndry. Cr cds: A, C, D, DS, ER, MC, V.

Restaurants

★★ **A KETTLE OF FISH.** *900 Pacific (V6X 2E3), Downtown.* 604/682-6853. Email *theriley@axionet.com; www. andersonsrestaurants.com.* Seafood menu. Hrs: 11:30 am-2 pm, 5:30-9:30 pm; Sun from 5:30 pm. Closed Jan 1, Dec 24 eve, 25, 26. Res accepted. Lunch complete meals: $6.95 $12.95; dinner complete meals: $14.95-$32. English country garden atmosphere. Cr cds: A, D, MC, V.

★★ **ALLEGRO CAFI.** *888 Nelson St (V6J 2H1).* 604/683-8485. Specializes in rack of lamb, chicken, seafood. Hrs: 11:30 am-10 pm; Sat, Sun 5-9 pm. Closed Dec 25, Easter, Labor

Day. Res accepted. Wine list. Lunch $8-$10; dinner $12-$19. Entertainment. Cr cds: A, D, ER, MC, V.

★★ **AQUA RIVE.** *330200 Gramble St (V6C 1S4).* 604/683-5599. *www.aqua rive.com.* Specializes in wood-grilled Pacific salmon, wood-roasted rack of lamb, coriander crusted rack of prawns. Hrs: 11:30 am-10 pm; Fri, Sat to 10:30 pm; Sun 11 am-10 pm. Closed Dec 24, 25. Res accepted. Wine list. Lunch $9.95-$13.95; dinner $16.50-$27.95. Brunch $9.95-$13.95. Entertainment. Mountain view. Cr cds: A, D, ER, MC, V.

★★ **ARIA.** *433 Robson St (V6B 6L9).* 604/647-2521. Email *amaas@westin grandvacouver.com; www.westingrand vancouver.com.* Menu changes seasonally. Hrs: 6:30 am-11 pm; Thurs, Fri to midnight; Sat 7 am-midnight; Sun 7 am-11 pm. Res accepted. Wine, beer. Lunch $5-$18; dinner $18-$27. Brunch $5-$18. Child's menu. Entertainment. Cr cds: A, D, DS, ER, JCB, MC, V.

★★★ **BACCHUS.** *845 Hornby St, Downtown.* 604/689-7777. Email *info@wedgewoodhotel.com; www.travel. bc.ca/w/wedgewood.* Specializes in lamb, seafood. Hrs: 6:30 am-10:30 pm. Res accepted. Bar. Wine list. Bkfst $6.95-$12.25; lunch $12-$17; dinner $14-$30. Sun brunch $5-$14. Entertainment: pianist Mon-Sat. Valet parking. Jacket (dinner). European decor; many antiques, original artwork. Cr cds: A, D, DS, ER, MC, V.

★★★★ **BISHOP'S.** *2183 W 4th Ave (V6K 1N7), S of Downtown.* 604/738-2025. *www.bishops.net.* With chef Michael Allemeier in the kitchen and founder John Bishop the ever-genial host, this contemporary American restaurant is still highly regarded after ten years in business. Noted for fresh, simple preparations, dishes, highlighting local ingredients, are artfully presented, not overly contrived, and combine well with the predominantly West Coast wine list. The space is a stylish showroom for Bishop's Canadian art collection. Seafood menu. Specializes in con-

temporary Pacific Northwest cuisine. Hrs: 5:30-11 pm; Sun to 10 pm. Closed Dec 24-26. Res accepted. Wine list. Dinner $8-$34. Cr cds: A, D, ER, MC, V.
[D]

★★ **CAFE DE PARIS.** *761 Dennan St (V6G 2L6). 604/687-1418.* Specializes in bouillabaisse, cassoulet, rabbit. Hrs: 11:30 am-2 pm, 5:30-10 pm; Sun 11:30 am-3 pm, 5-9 pm. Closed Dec 25. Res accepted. Wine, beer. Lunch $10.50-$17.95; dinner $17.95-$25.95. Brunch $9.95-$17.95. Entertainment. Cr cds: A, MC, V.
[D]

★★★ **CAFFE DE MEDICI.** *1025 Robson St (V6E 1A9). 604/669-9322. www.medici.cc.* Specializes in scallops wrapped with prawn, crusted rack of lamb. Hrs: 11:30 am-10:30 pm; Sat noon-11 pm; Sun 5-11 pm. Closed Dec 25. Res accepted. Wine list. Lunch $14.95-$18.95; dinner $25.95-$32.95. Entertainment. Covered patio terrace. Cr cds: A, D, DS, ER, JCB, MC, V.
[D]

★★ **CANNERY.** *2205 Commissioner St (V5L 1A4), at foot of Victoria Dr, E of Downtown. 604/254-9606. www. canneryseafood.com.* Specializes in fresh seafood, mesquite-grilled dishes. Hrs: 11:30 am-2 pm, 5:30-10 pm; Sat, Sun from 5 pm. Closed Dec 24-26. Res accepted. Bar. Wine list. Lunch a la carte entrees: $8.95-$15.95; dinner a la carte entrees: $17.95-$31.95. Child's menu. Parking. Nautical motif; view of harbor. Cr cds: A, D, ER, MC, V.

★ **CAPILANO HEIGHTS.** *5020 Capilano Rd (V7R 4K7), 6 mi N, opp Cleveland Dam. 604/987-9511.* Specializes in prawns and broccoli with black bean sauce, Peking duck (24-hr notice). Hrs: noon-10 pm; Sat from 4:30 pm; Sun 4:30-9 pm. Closed Dec 25, 26. Res accepted. Bar. Lunch a la carte entrees: $7-$17; dinner a la carte entrees: $10-$20. Parking. Cr cds: A, MC, V.
[D]

★★ **CHARTHOUSE.** *3866 Bayview (V7E 4R7). 604/271-7000.* Specializes in seafood, beef. Hrs: 11 am-10 pm. Closed Dec 25. Res accepted. Lunch $5.95-$10.95; dinner $9.95-$21.95.

Sun brunch $8.95. Child's menu. Casual decor. Cr cds: MC, V.
[D]

★★★ **CHARTWELL.** *791 W Georgia St. 604/689-9333.* Specializes in Salt Spring Island lamb. Own baking. Hrs: 6:30 am-2:30 pm, 5:30-10 pm; Sat 6:30-11:30 am, 5:30-11 pm; Sun 6:30 am-10 pm. Res accepted. Bar. Wine cellar. Bkfst a la carte entrees: $9-$19; lunch a la carte entrees: $17-$23; dinner a la carte entrees: $18-$39. Parking. Cr cds: D, DS, ER, MC, V.
[D]

★★ **CHEZ MICHEL.** *1373 Marine Dr (V7T 1B6). 604/926-4913.* Specializes in prawns Nicoise, rack of lamb au jus, bouillabaisse. Hrs: 11:30 am-2:30 pm, 5:30-10:30 pm. Closed Sun; hols. Res required. Wine, beer. Lunch $8.95-$11.95; dinner $12.95-$19.95. Parking. French art on display. View of English Bay and Burrard Inlet. Cr cds: A, D, MC, V.

★★ **CINCIN ITALIAN WOOD GRILL.** *1154 Robson St (V6E 1V5). 604/688-7338. www.cincin.net.* Hrs: 11:30 am-midnight; Sat, Sun 5 pm-midnight. Res accepted. Wine list. Lunch $12.50-$16.50; dinner $14-$37. Entertainment. Cr cds: A, D, ER, MC, V.

★★ **CLOUD 9.** *1400 Robson St. 604/687-0511. Email resdept@empire landmark.com; www.empirelandmark. com.* Specializes in fresh seafood, baked salmon. Hrs: 6:30 am-midnight; Wed-Sat to 1 am. Res accepted. Bar. Bkfst a la carte entrees: $7.50-$15; lunch a la carte entrees: $8-$15; dinner a la carte entrees: $17-$40. Sun brunch $14-$25. Child's menu. Parking. Revolving dining rm on 42nd floor of hotel. Cr cds: A, C, D, ER, MC, V.
[D]

★ **THE CREEK RESTAURANT & BREWERY.** *1253 Johnston St. 604/685-7070.* Specializes in snapper, pork loin, salmon, ribeye. Hrs: 7-10:30 am, 11:30 am-2:30 pm, 5:30-10 pm; Thurs-Sat 5:30-11 pm; Sun 10:30 am-2:30 pm, 5:30-10 pm. Res accepted. Wine, beer. Lunch $8.95-$17.95; dinner $16.95-$25.95. Brunch $8.95-$12.95. Entertainment. Cr cds: A, DS, MC, V.
[D] [⊡]

★★★ **C RESTAURANT.** *1600 Howe St (V6O 2L9). 604/681-1164. www. crestaurant.com.* Specializes in smoked octopus, bacon wrapped scallops. Hrs: 11:30 am-11 pm; Sat 5:30-11 pm. Res accepted. Wine list. Lunch $12-$30; dinner $21-$39. Brunch $12-$30. Entertainment. Cr cds: A, D, ER, MC, V.
D

★★ **DELILAH'S.** *1789 Comox St (V6G 1P5), in the West End. 604/687-3424.* Specializes in rack of lamb, grilled salmon. Hrs: 5:30 pm-1 am. Closed Dec 24-26. Bar. Wine list. Dinner complete meals: 2-course $18.50, 5-course $29. Eclectic decor with Art Nouveau touches. Ceilings painted in oils by local artist. Cr cds: A, D, ER, MC, V.
D

★★★ **DIVA AT THE MET.** *645 Howe St (V6C 2Y9). 604/602-7788. Email reservations@divamet.com; www. divamet.com.* Specializes in Alaskan black cod, grilled Atlantic lobster tail with octopus bacon, paillard of veal with wild mushrooms. Hrs: 6:30-11 am, 11:30 am-2:30 pm, 5:30-10 pm; Sun brunch 11 am-2:30 pm. Res accepted. Bar. Extensive wine list. Bkfst $8-$17; lunch $13-$17; dinner $27-$40. Brunch $8-$17. Cr cds: A, D, DS, MC, V.
D

★★★ **DUNDRAVE PIER.** *150 25th St (V7B 4H8), on Dundrave Pier. 604/922-1414. Email beach@direct.ccl.* Specializes in rack of lamb, pasta, fresh seafood. Hrs: 11:30 am-10 pm; Fri, Sat to 11 pm; Sun from 11 am. Res accepted. Bar. Lunch a la carte entrees: $8.95-$13.95; dinner a la carte entrees: $9.95-$21. Sun brunch $8.95-$13. Child's menu. Valet parking. View of ocean, Vancouver Bay. Cr cds: A, MC, V.
D

★★ **FISH AND COMPANY.** *655 Burrard St. 604/639-4770. www.hyatt.com.* Specializes in kettle of "stoerte-becker," traditional Northern German fish soup, Pacific Rim plate, lamb, salmon, halibut. Hrs: 6:30-10 pm. Res accepted. Wine list. Dinner $10.50-$23. Child's menu. Entertain-

ment. Overlooking downtown Vancouver. Cr cds: A, D, ER, JCB, MC, V.
D

★★★ **FISH HOUSE IN STANLEY PARK.** *8901 Stanley Park Dr (V6G 3E2). 604/681-7275. Email drew@fish housestanleypark.com; www.fishhouse stanleypark.com.* Specializes in Northwest seafood bowl, grilled tuna steak Diane. Hrs: 11:30 am-10 pm; Sun 11 am-10 pm. Res accepted. Wine list. Lunch $10.95-$21.95; dinner $16.95-$59.95. Brunch $9.95-$21.95. Child's menu. Entertainment. Cr cds: A, D, ER, JCB, MC, V.
D

★★★ **FLEURI.** *845 Burrard St. 604/642-2900. Email info@vcr.sutton place.com.* Specializes in seared Dungeness crab cake, oolong tea-steamed sea bass, broiled Alberta beef tenderloin. Hrs: 6:30 am-11 pm; Sun brunch 11 am-2 pm. Bar. Extensive wine list. Bkfst a la carte entrees: $7.95-$15.50; lunch, dinner a la carte entrees: $15.50-$39. Brunch $27.95. Classic European decor. Cr cds: A, ER, MC, V.
D

★★ **GLOBE @ YVR.** *Vancouver International Airport. 604/248-3281. www. fairmont.com.* Specializes in seared halibut, asian vegetables, roasted duck confit. Hrs: 6-11 pm. Res accepted. Wine, beer. Lunch $9-$15.50; dinner $20-$29. Child's menu. Entertainment: pianist. Overlooks North Shore Mts, watch planes take off and land, panoramic view. Cr cds: A, C, D, ER, JCB, MC, V.
D SC

★★★ **GOTHAM STEAKHOUSE AND COCKTAIL BAR.** *615 Seymour St (V6B 3K3). 604/605-8282. www. gothamsteakhouse.com.* Specializes in filet mignon, porterhouse. Hrs: 11:30 am-3 pm, 5-10 pm. Closed Dec 25. Res accepted. Wine, beer. Lunch $13.95-$18.95; dinner $24.95-$49.95. Entertainment. Cr cds: A, D, ER, MC, V.
D

★ **GRANVILLE SUSHI.** *2526 Granville St (V6H 3G8). 604/738-0388.* Specializes in teriyaki, sushi, sashimi. Hrs: 11:30 am-2:30 pm, 5-10 pm; Fri, Sat 5-11 pm; Sun 11 am-2:30 pm, 5-

10 pm. Res accepted. Wine, beer. Lunch $5.25-$12.50; dinner $6.25-$20. Entertainment. Cr cds: V.
D

★★ **HY'S ENCORE.** *637 Hornby St (V6C 2G3), Downtown. 604/683-7671.* Specializes in steak. Hrs: 11:30 am-11:30 pm; Sat 5:30-11 pm; Sun 5:30-10 pm. Bar. Lunch a la carte entrees: $10-$22; dinner complete meals: $22-$40. Baronial decor. Cr cds: A, D, MC, V.
D

★★★ **IL GIARDINO DELI UMBERTO.** *1382 Hornby St, Downtown. 604/687-6316. www.umberto. com.* Specializes in rack of lamb, osso buco, filet of veal. Hrs: noon-11 pm; Sat from 5:30 pm. Closed Sun; Jan 1, Dec 25. Res accepted. Wine list. Lunch a la carte entrees: $9-$15; dinner a la carte entrees: $14-$30. Entertainment. Valet parking. In converted Victorian house (1896). Italian, Tuscan decor. Cr cds: A, D, MC, V.

★★ **IMPERIAL CHINESE SEAFOOD RESTAURANT.** *355 Burrard St (V6C 2G8). 604/688-8191. Email imperial@lynx.net; www.imperial rest.com.* Hrs: 11 am-11 pm; Sat, Sun from 10:30 am. Res accepted. Wine list. Lunch $3.30-$40; dinner $12.50-$52. Entertainment. Cr cds: D, ER, MC, V.
D

★★★★ **LA BELLE AUBERGE.** *4856 48th Ave (V4K 1V2). 604/946-7717. Email bruno@auberge.bc.ca; www.on/the.net/La_Belle_Auberge.* Since 1980, the aclaimed Chef Bruno Marti's restaurant has combined the old (circa 1900s farmhouse with Victorian decor) with the new (his marvelous contemporary interpretations of classic French cuisine). Menu changes seasonally. Hrs: 6 pm-midnight. Closed Mon. Res accepted. Wine, beer. Dinner $26-$33. Entertainment. Cr cds: A, C, D, ER, MC, V.

★★★ **LA TERRAZZA.** *1088 Canbie. 604/899-4449. Email laterrazza@ sprint.ca.* Specializes in rack of lamb, salmon. Hrs: 5 pm-midnight; Sun to 10:30 pm. Closed hols. Res accepted. Wine list. Dinner $27-$36. Setting is an impressive room with burnt sienna walls and murals; massive windows and vaulted ceilings. Cr cds: D, ER, MC, V.
D

★★★ **LE CROCODILE.** *Smythe St, at Burrard St, Downtown. 604/669-4298.* Specializes in veal, salmon. Own ice cream. Hrs: 11:30 am-2 pm, 5-10 pm; Fri to 10:30 pm; Sat 5-10:30 pm. Closed Sun; hols. Res accepted. Wine list. Lunch a la carte entrees: $9.50-$16.95; dinner a la carte entrees: $14.95-$22.95. Valet parking. Modern French decor; antiques. Cr cds: A, D, MC, V.
D

★ **LE GREC.** *2041 W 4th Ave (V6J 1N3). 604/733-7399.* Specializes in lamb shoulder, osso bucco, souvlakia. Hrs: 9:30 am-10 pm; Fri, Sat to 11 pm. Res accepted. Wine, beer. Lunch $6.25-$7.75; dinner $13.95-$15.95. Brunch $4.95-$8.95. Entertainment: vocalist Fri, Sat. Cr cds: A, D, DS, MC, V.
D

★★★★ **LUMIERE.** *2251 W Broadway (V6K 2E9), between Trafalgar and Larch. 604/739-8185.* Easily one of the most sophisticated dining experiences in Vancouver, this comfortable restaurant affords a terrific contemporary French meal. Chef/owner Robert Feenie has studied with the best of chiefs and his cooking shows it. The freshest, seasonal produce is perfectly prepared. The service is professional and very warm. A delightful experience. Specializes in vegetarian and seafood tasting menu. Hrs: 5:30-10:30 pm. Closed Mon; hols. Res accepted. Dinner $70-$150. Cr cds: A, C, D, DS, ER, MC, V.
D

★★ **MONK MCQUEENS.** *601 Stamps Landing (D5Z 3Z1). 604/877-1351. Email monks@monkmcqueens. com; www.monkmcqueens.com.* Specializes in smoked Alaskan black cod, ahi tuna steak. Hrs: 5:30-10 pm. Res accepted. Wine list. Dinner $19-$40. Child's menu. Entertainment: Thurs-Sat jazz, blues. Cr cds: A, MC, V.

★★ **MONTRI'S THAI.** *3629 W Broadway (3V6 R2B). 604/738-9888.* Hrs: 5-10:30 pm. Res accepted. Wine, beer. Dinner $9.95-$22.95. Entertainment. Cr cds: MC, V.
D

★★ **PAPI'S RISTORANTE ITAL-IANO.** *12251 Number 1 Rd (V7E 1T6). 604/275-8355.* Hrs: 11:30 am-9 pm; Fri, Sat 5-10 pm. Res accepted. Wine, beer. Lunch $8-$14; dinner $14-$27. Entertainment. Cr cds: A, MC, V.
D

★★★ **PICCOLO MONDO.** *850 Thurlow St (V6E 1W2), in the West End. 604/688-1633. www.piccolo mondoristorante.com.* Specializes in tortellini della Nonna, osso buco, bollito misto. Hrs: noon-2 pm, 6-10 pm; Sat from 6 pm. Closed Sun. Res accepted. Bar. Extensive wine selection. Lunch $10.75-$16; dinner $15-$30. Cr cds: A, D, MC, V.

★★ **PINK PEARL.** *1132 E Hastings St (V6A 1S2), E of Downtown. 604/253-4316. www.pinkpearl.com.* Specializes in Peking duck, spiced crab. Hrs: 9 am-10 pm. Res accepted. Bar. Bkfst a la carte entrees: $4.95-$8.95; lunch a la carte entrees: $6-$14; dinner a la carte entrees: $14-$28. Parking. Very large dining area. Cr cds: A, D, MC, V.
D

★★★ **THE POINTE.** *160 Gracie Rd. 250/725-2005.* Specializes in fish 'n' chips, homemade seafood chowder. Hrs: noon-7 pm. Closed Nov-Mar. Lunch $6.50-$9; dinner $8-$12.95. Entertainment. Located on Tofino Inlet. Waterfront dining. Cr cds: MC, V.
D

★★★ **PRESIDENT CHINESE SEAFOOD RESTAURANT.** *8181 Cambie Rd. 604/279-1997.* Specializes in Peking duck, crispy fried pigeon. Hrs: 8:30 am-3 pm, 5-10 pm. Res accepted. Wine, beer. Dinner $12-$50. Entertainment. Cr cds: A, D, MC, V.
D

★★★ **PROVENCE.** *4473 W 10th Ave (V6R 2H2). 604/222-1980. www. provencevancouver.com.* Specializes in Bouillabaisse, Tiger prawns. Hrs: 11:30 am-10 pm; Fri to 11 pm; Sat 10 am-11 pm; Sun 10 am-10 pm. Res accepted. Wine list. Lunch $8.75-$14.95; dinner $13.50-$25. Brunch $7.50-$14.95. Entertainment. Cr cds: A, D, ER, MC, V.
D

★★ **QUATTRO ON FOURTH.** *2611 W 4th (V6K 1P8). 604/734-4444.* Specializes in antipasta platters, pasta combination platter. Hrs: 5-9 pm. Closed Dec 24-27. Res accepted. Wine list. Dinner $15.95-$31.95. Entertainment. Cr cds: A, D, MC, V.
D

★ **RAINCITY GRILL.** *1193 Denman St (V6G 2N1). 604/685-7337. Email info@raincitygrill.com; www.raincity grill.com.* Specializes in grilled Caesar salad, albacore tuna sashimi. Hrs: 11:30 am-2:30 pm, 5-10 pm; Sat, Sun 10:30 am-2:30 pm, 5-9 pm. Closed Dec 24, 25. Res accepted. Wine list. Lunch $10-$18; dinner $15-$30. Brunch $10-$18. Entertainment. Cr cds: A, D, ER, MC, V.

★★ **SEASON'S RESTAURANT.** *33rd and Cambie (V6G 3E7). 604/874-8008. Email info@sequoiarestaurants. com; www.seasonsinthepark.com.* Hrs: 11:30 am-10 pm. Closed Dec 25. Res accepted. Wine list. Lunch $9-$22; dinner $12-$26. Brunch $9-$22. Child's menu. Entertainment. Cr cds: A, MC, V.
D

★★ **SHANGHAI CHINESE BISTRO.** *1124 Alberni St (V6E 1A5). 604/683-8222.* Specializes in general Tao chicken, Mongolian beef. Hrs: 11:30 am-midnight; Fri, Sat to 1 am. Closed Dec 25. Res accepted. Wine, beer. Lunch $7.50-$10; dinner $11-$17. Entertainment. Handmade noodle show. Cr cds: A, D, JCB, MC, V.
D

★★ **SHIJO JAPANESE RESTAU-RANT.** *1926 W 4th Ave, Suite 202 (V6J 1M5). 604/732-4676.* Specializes in sushi. Hrs: noon-2 pm, 5:30-10 pm; Sat, Sun 5:30-10 pm. Res accepted. Wine list. Lunch $8.50; dinner $25. Entertainment. Cr cds: A, D, JCB, MC, V.
D

★★★ **STAR ANISE.** *1485 W 12th St (V6H 1M6), S of Downtown. 604/737-1485.* Specializes in local seafood, game. Own desserts. Hrs: 5-10 pm. Closed Dec 24-26. Res accepted. Bar. Wine cellar. Dinner $18-$30. Parking. Elegant dining. Art by local artists. Cr cds: A, D, MC, V.
D

★★★ **SUN SUI WAH SEAFOOD RESTAURANT.** *388 Main St (V5V 3N9).* *604/872-8822. www.sunsuiwah. com.* Specializes in squab, seafood. Hrs: 10:30 am-10:30 pm; Fri, Sat from 10 am. Res accepted. Wine, beer. Lunch $2.75-$15; dinner $20-$30. Entertainment. Cr cds: A, MC, V.
[D] [⊟]

★★ **TAMA SUSHI.** *1595 W Broadway, Suite 200 (V6J 1W6).* *604/738-0119.* Specializes in spicy tuna sashimi, lobster sashimi, tama chili prones. Hrs: 11:30 am-2 pm, noon-2:30 pm, 5-10:15 pm; Fri, Sat to 10:45 pm. Res accepted. Wine list. Lunch $2.10-$19.25; dinner $2.10-$22.50. Entertainment. Tatami rms (Japanese Style rms). Cr cds: D, MC, V.
[D]

★★ **TEAHOUSE.** *7501 Stanley Park Dr (V6G 3E7), at Ferguson Point in Stanley Park, W of Downtown.* *604/669-3281.* Specializes in seafood, poultry, pasta. Own baking. Hrs: 11:30 am-5:30 pm; Sun 10:30 am-2:30 pm. Closed Dec 25. Res accepted. Wine cellar. Lunch a la carte entrees: $11.75-$17.95; dinner a la carte entrees: $9.95-$15.95. Sat, Sun brunch, $9.95-$15.50. Glass conservatory; view of harbor. Cr cds: A, MC, V.
[D]

★★★ **TOJO'S.** *777 W Broadway #202 (V5Z 4J7), W of Downtown.* *604/872-8050.* Specializes in traditional Japanese dishes. Sushi bar. Hrs: 5-11 pm. Closed Sun. Res accepted. Bar. Dinner $15-$28. Complete meals: $45-$100. Parking. Tatami rms avail. View of Japanese garden. Cr cds: A, DS, MC, V.

★★ **TOP OF VANCOUVER.** *555 W Hastings (V6B 4N4), Downtown.* *604/669-2220.* Specializes in local seafood, pasta. Hrs: 11:30 am-2:30 pm, 5-10 pm; Fri, Sat to 11 pm; Sun brunch 11 am-2:30 pm. Res accepted. Bar. Lunch, dinner a la carte entrees: $13-$42. Sun brunch $26.95. Child's menu. Entertainment. Revolving restaurant 550 ft above street level. Cr cds: A, D, DS, MC, V.
[D]

★★★ **VILLA DEL LUPO.** *689 Hamilton St (V6B 2R7).* *604/688-7436. www.villadellupo.com.* Specializes in lamb osso buco. Hrs: 5:30-10:30 pm. Res accepted. Extensive wine list.

Dinner $18.95-$29.95. Entertainment. Cr cds: A, D, ER, MC, V.

★★★ **WILLIAM TELL.** *765 Beatty St.* *604/688-3504. Email admin@ williamtell.bc.ca.* Specializes in veal, fresh seafood. Own baking, ice cream. Hrs: 7-10 am, 11:30 am-1 pm, 5:30-9 pm. Res accepted. Bar. Bkfst $6.50-$9.50; lunch $6-$13.25; dinner $18.75-$28. Valet parking. European decor. Cr cds: A, D, DS, MC, V.
[D]

★★★ **ZINFANDELLS.** *1355 Hornby St (V6Z 1W7).* *604/681-4444. Email zinfandells99@hotmail.com.* Hrs: 5-10:30 pm. Wine, beer. Dinner $15-$25. Prix-fixe: 3-courses $38. Entertainment. Cr cds: A, MC, V.
[D] [⊟]

Unrated Dining Spots

FIVE SAILS. *300-999 Canada Pl.* *604/662-8111. www.panpac.com.* Eclectic menu. Own baking. Hrs: 6:30-10 pm. Res accepted. Bar. Wine list. Dinner a la carte entrees: $38-$45. Valet parking. Pacific Rim cuisine. Cr cds: A, D, MC, V.
[D]

GREENS AND GOURMET. *2681 W Broadway (V6K 2G2), S of Downtown.* *604/737-7373.* Specializes in Greek moussaka, spinach pie, vegetarian dishes. Salad bar. Juice bar. Hrs: 11 am-9 pm. Closed Dec 25. Wine, beer. Lunch $4.95-$7.95; dinner $4.95-$10.95. Brunch $4.95-$7.95. Parking. California-style dining. Cr cds: MC, V.
[D] [SC] [⊠]

HART HOUSE ON DEER LAKE. *6664 Deer Lake Ave (V5E 4H3).* *604/298-4278. www.harthouse restaurant.com.* Specializes in beef, fish. Hrs: 11:30 am-2 pm, 5:30-10 pm. Closed Mon. Res accepted. Wine, beer. Lunch $12-$16; dinner $16-$28. Entertainment. Overlooking lake. Cr cds: A, D, MC, V.
[D]

TAPASTREE. *1829 Robson St (V6G 1E4).* *604/606-4680.* Specializes in seared ahi tuna, sauted wild mushrooms, lamb chops. Hrs: 5-10:30 pm; Fri, Sat 5 pm-midnight. Closed Jan 1, Dec 25. Res accepted. Wine list. Dinner $2.95-$10.95. Entertainment.

Black bear

Candelabras designed like arms. Cr cds: A, D, ER, MC, V.

D

TRUE CONFECTIONS. *866 Denman St (V6G 2L8), in the West End. 604/682-1292.* Specializes in devil's food cake with marshmallow icing, white chocolate raspberry cheesecake. Hrs: 4 pm-12:30 am; Sat, Sun from 1 pm. Wine, beer. Lunch, dinner a la carte entrees: $2.50-$7. 13-ft refrigerated display case filled daily with fresh cakes, pies and other desserts. Cr cds: A, DS, MC, V.

Vancouver Island

See also Nanaimo, BC, Vancouver, BC, Victoria, BC; also see Anacortes, WA, Bellingham, WA, Seattle, WA

The largest of the Canadian Pacific Coast Islands, Vancouver Island stretches almost 300 miles (480 kilometers) along the shores of western British Columbia. It is easily accessible by ferry from the city of Vancouver on the mainland as well as from other parts of British Columbia and the state of Washington. With most of its population located in the larger cities on the eastern coast, much of the island remains a wilderness and is very popular with outdoor enthusiasts.

The Vancouver Island Mountain Range cuts down the middle of the island, providing spectacular snow-capped scenery, fjords, and rocky coastal cliffs. Several provincial parks are dedicated to the preservation of wildlife: Columbia black-tailed deer and eagles are common to the southern tip; Roosevelt elk, black bears, and cougars inhabit the northern forests; and whales, sea lions, and seals are found along the shores. The surrounding ocean, as well as the inland lakes and rivers, offers anglers some of the world's best salmon and trout. Among the variety of activities to enjoy are sailing, canoeing, boating, scuba diving, camping, climbing, and caving.

The southern portion of the island contains more than half the island's total population and includes Victoria (see), British Columbia's capital city. Here, countryside resembles rural Britain with its rolling farmland, rows of hedges, and colorful flower gardens. Spain claimed the Sooke Inlet in the 18th century, giving the familiar Spanish names to much of the area. Later, British farmers arrived as well as thousands of prospectors looking for gold. A spectacular and demanding coastal trail—the West Coast Trail, which runs from Port Renfrew to Bamfield—and countless paths through Pacific rain forests traverse East Sooke Park on the southwest coast. On the southeast coast, Malahat Drive on the Island Highway provides a dramatic panorama of the Gulf Islands and the Saanich Peninsula. Inland is the Cowichan Valley, with many lakes and rivers teeming with fish. Whippletree Junction in Duncan is a reminder of the role played by Asian settlers in the island's mining and railway construction history. Just outside of Duncan are the British Columbia Forest Museum and Demonstration Forest and the Native Heritage Centre.

Island-hopping is pleasant in the Gulf Islands, located in the sheltered waters of the Strait of Georgia. These beautiful, isolated islands have become home to many artists. Salt Spring, the largest island, has a traditional market on Saturday in the town of Ganges where handmade crafts are featured.

Nanaimo (see) is the dominant town in the central region, an area known for excellent sandy beaches and beautiful parks. The spectacular waterfalls found on Englishman River and the natural caves in Horne Lake Provincial Park on the Qualicum River are worth a special trip. MacMillan Provincial Park contains the famous Cathedral Grove and features Douglas fir trees 800 years old with circumferences of 30 feet (9 meters). In the center of the island is the Alberni Valley, named for the Spanish sea captain who landed at the port in 1791 searching for gold and native treasures along the coast. Located in the valley are several parks with excellent swimming and fishing, the tallest falls found in North America—Della Falls—and a bird sanctuary and fish hatchery. From Port Alberni the mountain highway winds its way to the peaceful fishing village of Tofino, the northern boundary of the Long Beach section of the Pacific Rim National Park. The park encompasses 80 miles (129 kilometers) of rugged shoreline: Long Beach, only seven miles (11 kilometers) is the best-known and most easily accessible; south of Long Beach lies the Broken Island Group of Barkley Sound, 98 islands clustered in a huge bay surrounded by the Mackenzie Mountains; and south of Barkley Sound is the famous West Coast Lifesaving Trail of 45 miles (77 kilometers), originally a route to civilization for ship-wrecked sailors, now a test of strength and endurance for experienced hikers. Pacific Rim is especially popular among amateur naturalists who enjoy watching the whales and other sea life.

Settlements along the northern coast are primarily lumber towns or small villages. Cumberland, which once had the largest Chinese population in Canada, began as a coal mining town. Popular among sports enthusiasts are Forbidden Plateau and Mount Washington, excellent for skiing and hiking. The Campbell River is where the famous Tyee and Coho salmon are found in abundance. The Quinsam River fish hatchery keeps the area well-stocked. Inland from Campbell River is the

largest untouched wilderness area on the island—Strathcona Provincial Park. In the center of the park is the Golden Hinde, the island's highest peak (more than 7,000 feet/2,200 meters). Much of the rugged, mountainous wilderness is a wildlife sanctuary, but it also accommodates campers, hikers, climbers, and canoe and kayak enthusiasts. Nootka Sound, on the west coast, discovered by Captain Cook, remains pristine, with few towns and no roads along the coast. On the east coast, a major highway runs north of Kelsey Bay. Although this section of the north island is more heavily populated, it is still able to preserve its wilderness character. Visiting the tiny villages in this section is like stepping back in time to the days of the first settlers. Cape Scott, at the northernmost tip of the island, can be reached by a hiking trail which winds through Cape Scott Provincial Park, a stormy coastal wilderness with magnificent forests and various wildlife.

Adding to the beauty of Vancouver Island is its moderate climate, especially in the south where the land is protected from the open sea by mainland British Columbia on the southeast and Washington state on the southwest. On the west coast, however, winter storms can be bitter, and there is much rainfall throughout the year. All in all, Vancouver Island is an exciting place to visit with its fascinating terrain, sparkling waters, abundant wildlife, and delightful people.

Victoria

(F-4) *See also Nanaimo, BC, Vancouver, BC; also see San Juan Islands, WA*

Founded 1843 **Pop** 64,379 **Elev** 211 ft (64 m) **Area code** 250
Web www.tourismvictoria.com
Information Tourism Victoria, 812 Wharf St, V8W 1T3; 250/953-2233 or 800/663-3883

A major port with two harbors—the outer for ocean shipping and cruising, and the inner for coastal shipping, pleasure boats, ferries to the US mainland, amphibian aircraft, and fishing—Victoria has a distinctly

English flavor with many Tudor-style buildings and a relaxed way of life. It is a center of Pacific Northwest indigenous culture.

Victoria is a city of parks and gardens; even the five-globed Victorian lampposts are decorated with baskets of flowers in summer. One may take a horse-drawn carriage or double-decker bus tours through many historic and scenic landmarks; inquire locally for details. In winter, temperatures rarely go below 40°F (4°C). Victoria's climate is Canada's most moderate, making it a delightful place to visit any time of year.

What to See and Do

Art Gallery of Greater Victoria. Said to be the finest collection of Japanese art in Canada. Major holdings of Asian ceramics and paintings. Canadian and European art, with focus on prints and drawings. Decorative arts. Lectures, films, concerts. Only Shinto shrine outside Japan is located here. Japanese garden, bonsai. Gift shop. (Daily; closed hols) 1040 Moss St. Phone 250/598-9231. ¢¢

BC Forest Discovery Centre. Logging museum; old logging machines and tools, hands-on exhibits, logging camp, 1.5-mi (2.4 km) steam railway ride, sawmill, films, nature walk, picnic park, snack bar, gift shop. (May-Sep, daily) 40 mi (64 km) N on Hwy 1, near Duncan, 2892 Drinkwater Rd. Phone 250/715-1113. ¢¢¢

Beacon Hill Park. Approx 180 acres (75 hectares) with lakes, wildfowl sanctuary, children's petting farm, walks and floral gardens, cricket pitch; world's 2nd-tallest totem pole; beautiful view of the sea. For a list of additional recreational areas contact Tourism Victoria. From Douglas St to Cook St, between Superior St & waterfront. **FREE**

Butchart Gardens. Approx 50 acres (20 hectares). The "Sunken Garden" was created in the early 1900s by the Butcharts on the site of their depleted limestone quarry with topsoil brought in by horse-drawn cart. Already a tourist attraction by the 1920s, the gardens now incl the Rose, Japanese, and Italian gardens; also Star Pond, Concert Lawn, Fireworks Basin, Ross Fountain, and Show Greenhouse. Subtly illuminated at night (mid-June-mid-Sep). Fireworks (July-Aug, Sat eve). Musical stage

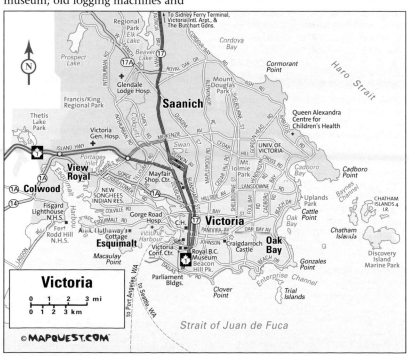

show (July-Aug, wkday eve). Restaurants; seed and gift store. 13 mi (21 km) N on Benvenuto Ave, near Brentwood Bay, 800 Benvenuto. Phone 250/652-5256 (recording) or 250/652-4422 for hrs and fees. ¢¢¢¢

Carr House. (1863) Italianate birthplace of famous Canadian painter/author Emily Carr. Ground floor restored to period. (Mid-May to Oct, daily; rest of yr, by appt) 207 Government St. Phone 250/383-5843. ¢¢

Centennial Square. Incl fountain plaza; Elizabethan knot garden of herbs and flowers. Occasional noontime concerts. Douglas & Pandora Sts.

Craigdarroch Castle. (1890) Historic house museum with beautifully crafted wood, stained glass; furnished with period furniture and artifacts. (Daily; closed Jan 1, Dec 25, 26) 1050 Joan Crescent. Phone 250/592-5323. ¢¢¢

Craigflower Farmhouse & Schoolhouse Historic Site. Farmhouse built in 1856 in simple Georgian style. 1854 schoolhouse is oldest in western Canada. Some original furnishings. (May-Oct) Craigflower Rd at Admirals Rd, 4 mi (6 km) NW. Phone 250/383-4627. ¢¢

Dominion Astrophysical Observatory. Public viewing through 72-in (185-cm) telescope; display galleries (Mon-Fri). Tours (Apr-Oct, Sat eve). 10 mi (16 km) NW at 5071 W Saanich Rd. Phone 250/363-0012 (recording). **FREE**

Empress Hotel. Historically famous bldg constructed by Canadian Pacific Railroad in 1908 and restored in 1989. Victorian in tradition, incl afternoon tea and crumpets served in the lobby. (See HOTELS) 721 Government St. Also here are

Crystal Garden. Glass bldg formerly housed the largest saltwater pool in the British Empire. Tropical gardens, waterfall, fountain, aviary, monkeys, free-flying butterflies, exotic fish pool; restaurant, shops. (Daily) 713 Douglas St, behind Empress Hotel. Phone 250/381-1213. ¢¢

Miniature World. More than 80 miniature, 3-dimensional scenes of fact, fiction, and history. Two large doll houses; very large rail diorama; villages; world's smallest operational sawmill. (Daily; closed Dec 25) 649 Humboldt St, at Empress Hotel. Phone 250/385-9731. ¢¢¢

Ferry trips. Black Ball Transport, Inc: between Victoria, BC and Port Angeles, WA (see), car ferry, phone 250/386-2202; Washington State Ferries: between Sidney, BC and Anacortes, WA, phone 250/381-1551; British Columbia Ferry Corp: between Victoria and British Columbia mainland or smaller island destinations, car ferry, phone 250/386-3431 or 604/669-1211 (Vancouver).

Fort Rodd Hill & Fisgard Lighthouse National Historic Site. A coastal artillery fort from 1895-1956; casemated barracks, gun, and searchlight positions, loopholed walls. Grounds (Daily; closed Dec 25). Historic lighthouse (1860) adj. For further information contact the Superintendent, 603 Fort Rodd Hill Rd, V9C 2W8. 8 mi (13 km) W, then ½ mi (1 km) S of BC 1A. Phone 250/478-5849. ¢¢

Hatley Castle. (Royal Roads University, 1908) Once the private estate of James Dunsmuir, former Lieutenant Governor of British Columbia. Bldgs are noted for their beauty, as are the grounds, with their Japanese, Italian, and rose gardens. Grounds (daily). 6 mi (10 km) W via Trans-Canada Hwy 1 and 1A, Colwood Exit, on Hwy 14 (Sooke Rd) in Colwood. 2005 Sooke Rd. Phone 250/391-2600. ¢¢

Helmcken House. (1852) Second-oldest house in British Columbia; most furnishings are original. Extensive 19th-century medical collection. (May-Oct, daily; rest of yr, by appt) 800 Johnson St. Phone 250/361-0021. ¢¢

Maritime Museum. Located in Old Provincial Courthouse. Depicts rich maritime heritage of the Pacific Northwest from early explorers through age of sail and steam; Canadian naval wartime history; large collection of models of ships used throughout the history of British Columbia. The *Tilikum,* a converted dugout that sailed from Victoria to England during the years 1901-04, is here. Captain James Cook display. On view, *Trekka* (1954), one of the smallest boats to circumnavigate the globe. (Daily; closed Jan 1, Dec 25) 28 Bastion Sq. Phone 250/385-4222. ¢¢

Pacific Undersea Gardens. Underwater windows for viewing of more than 5,000 marine specimens; scuba diver shows. (Daily; closed Dec 25) 490 Belleville St. Phone 250/382-5717. ¢¢¢

Parliament Buildings. Built in 1893-97 mostly of native materials, beautifully illuminated at night; houses British Columbia's Legislative Assembly. Guided tours (mid-June-Labour Day, daily; rest of yr, Mon-Fri; closed hols exc summer). Foreign language tours. Advance notice suggested for group tours. 501 Belleville St, at Inner Harbour. Phone 250/387-3046. **FREE**

Point Ellice House Museum. (1861) Original Victorian setting, furnishings. Afternoon tea served in restored garden. (Mid-June-Sep, Thurs-Mon; rest of yr, by appt) 2616 Pleasant St, off Bay St. Phone 250/380-6506. ¢¢

✪ **Royal British Columbia Museum.** Exhibits incl natural and human history, indigenous history and art; re-creation of a turn-of-the-century town. Natural history gallery, "Living Land-Living Sea" depicts natural history of British Columbia from Ice Age-present. (Daily; closed Dec 25) 675 Belleville St. Phone 250/387-3701. ¢¢¢-¢¢¢¢ Nearby are

> **Carillon.** Bells made in Holland; presented to the province by citizens of Dutch descent. Concerts; inquire locally for private tour.

> **Thunderbird Park.** Collection of authentic totem poles and indigenous carvings, representing the work of the main Pacific Coastal tribes. Indigenous carvers may be seen at work in the Carving Shed.

Royal London Wax Museum. More than 250 figures in theatrical settings. (Daily; closed Dec 25) 470 Belleville St, downtown on Inner Harbour. Phone 250/388-4461. ¢¢¢

Sightseeing tours.

> **Scenic Drives. North.** Malahat Dr (Trans-Canada Hwy 1), a continuation of Victoria's Douglas St, through Goldstream Park over Malahat Dr to Mill Bay, Cowichan Bay, Duncan, and the BC Forest Museum. **North.** On the continuation of Victoria's Blanshard St (Hwys 17 & 17A) through rural communities, pastoral valleys known as the Saanich Peninsula where on 50 acres (20 hectares) of manicured lawns, ponds, fountains, and formal gardens bloom the world-famous Butchart Gardens. **North.** Around the seashore along Dallas Rd through beautiful, traditionally English residential areas to Beach Dr, Oak Bay, and beyond to Cordova Bay. **West.** Leave the city behind on Trans-Canada Hwy 1 to Hwy 14, which winds through rural communities to the village of Sooke, where the population is still engaged in fishing, clamming, and logging. Unspoiled beaches, hiking trails, rocky seashores, are accessible from this West Coast road. Continuation on Hwy 14 will lead to Jordan River and to Port Renfrew, with its beautiful Botanical Beach.

Capital City Tally-Ho & Sightseeing Company. English horse-drawn carriage sightseeing tours: of city highlights, departing from Inner Harbour beside Parliament Bldgs; or past Victorian homes and through 200-acre (81-hectare) Beacon Hill Park and its extensive flower gardens (departs from Menzies & Belleville Sts). Fully narrated. (Apr-Sep, daily) 2044 Milton St. Phone 250/383-5067. ¢¢¢-¢¢¢¢

Gray Line bus tours. Several bus tours of Victoria and vicinity are offered (all yr). Contact 700 Douglas St, V8W 2B3. Phone 250/388-5248. ¢¢¢¢

Vancouver Island. (see) SW of mainland and accessible by ferry, aircraft, and jet catamaran.

Whale watching tours. Whale-watching boats line both the Wharf St waterfront and Inner Harbour. Half-day tours display marine life, incl orcas, sea lions, seals, and porpoises. Victoria Marine Adventures (phone 250/995-2211) and Prince of Whales (phone 250/383-4884) are 2 of the finer tour companies.

Annual Event

Victorian Days. Citizens dress in period costumes of 100 yrs ago; antique car display, parades, yacht race. Mid-May.

Motels/Motor Lodges

★★ **BEST WESTERN INNER HARBOR.** *412 Quebec St (V8V 1W5). 250/384-5122; fax 250/384-5113; res 800/528-1234; toll-free 888/383BEST. Email bestwest@victoriahotels.com.* 74 rms, 7 story. Mid-May-mid-Oct: S

$94-$140; D $110-$160; each addl $15; suites $190-$355; under 12 free; lower rates rest of yr. Crib free. TV; cable, VCR avail. Heated pool; whirlpool. Complimentary continental bkfst. Restaurant nearby. Ck-out 11 am. Coin lndry. Sauna. Refrigerators, microwaves. Cr cds: A, D, DS, MC, V.

⊡ ⬧ ⬧ ⬧ ⬧ ⬧ ⬧

★★ **CLARION HOTEL GRAND PACIFIC.** *455 Belleville St (V8V 1X3).* 250/386-2421; fax 250/383-7603. *Email grandpac@octonet.com; www. victoriabc.com/accom/quality.* 86 rms, 3 story, 11 kit. units. No A/C. June-Sep: S, D $145-$165; kit. units $160-$180; under 18 free; golf plans; lower rates rest of yr. Crib free. Pet accepted, some restrictions. TV; cable, VCR avail. Complimentary coffee in rms. Restaurant 7 am-10 pm. Bar 11-1 am. Ck-out 11 am. Meeting rms. Business servs avail. In-rm modem link. Bellhops. Valet serv. Sundries. Coin lndry. Free garage parking. Exercise equipt; sauna. Massage. Indoor pool; wading pool, whirlpool. Opp ocean. Cr cds: A, D, DS, ER, JCB, MC, V.

⊡ ⬧ ⬧ ⬧ ⬧ ⬧ SC

★ **PAUL'S MOTOR INN.** *1900 Douglas St (V8T 4K8).* 250/382-9231; fax 250/384-1435. *Email laurelpoint@ ampsc.com; www.islandnet.com/~ cvcprod/laurel.html.* 78 rms, 2 story. No A/C. May-Sep: S $83-$113; D $87-$117; each addl $5; under 11 free; lower rates rest of yr. Crib free. TV; cable. Restaurant open 24 hrs. Bar noon-2 am. Ck-out noon. Meeting rms. Business servs avail. Valet serv. Cr cds: A, ER, MC, V.

⬧ ⬧

★★ **ROYAL SCOT INN.** *425 Quebec St (V8V 1W7), ½ blk W of Parliament Bldgs.* 250/388-5463; fax 250/388-5452. 150 kit. suites, 4 story. No A/C. Mid-May-Sep: S, D $130-$305; each addl $15; under 16 free; wkly, monthly rates; lower rates rest of yr. TV; cable, VCR avail (movies $2.50). Indoor pool; whirlpool. Complimentary coffee in rms. Restaurant 7 am-9 pm. Ck-out 11 am. Coin lndry. Meeting rms. Business servs avail. Bellhops. Valet serv. Gift shop. Free covered parking. Exercise equipt; sauna. Rec rm. Some bathrm phones; microwaves. Balconies. Cr cds: A, DS, MC, V.

⬧ ⬧ ⬧ ⬧ ⬧ ⬧ ⬧

Hotels

★ **ACCENT INN.** *3233 Maple St (V8X 4Y9), at Mayfair Shopping Center.* 250/475-7500; fax 250/475-7599; res 800/663-0298. 111 rms, 3 story, 6 suites. May-Sep: S $124; D $134; each addl $10; suites $144; under 16 free; lower rates rest of yr. Crib avail. Pet accepted, some restrictions. Parking lot. TV; cable (premium). Complimentary coffee in rms, newspaper. Restaurant 6:30 am-9 pm. Ck-out 11 am, ck-in 3 pm. Meeting rms. Fax servs avail. Dry cleaning, coin lndry. Exercise privileges. Golf. Video games. Cr cds: A, D, ER, MC, V.

⊡ ⬧ ⬧ ⬧ ⬧ ⬧ ⬧ SC

★★★ **THE BEDFORD REGENCY.** *1140 Government St (V8W 1Y2).* 250/384-6835; fax 250/386-8930; toll-free 800/665-6500. *Email bedford@victoria bc.com; www.victoriabc.com/accom/ bedford.html.* 40 rms, 4 story. May-Oct: S, D $165-$215; each addl $20; under 16 free; lower rates rest of yr. Crib avail, fee. Parking garage. TV; cable. Restaurant. Bar. Ck-out 11 am, ck-in 3 pm. Meeting rms. Business servs avail. Bellhops. Dry cleaning. Exercise privileges. Golf. Cr cds: A, D, ER, MC, V.

⊡ ⬧ ⬧ ⬧ ⬧ ⬧ ⬧

★★ **BEST WESTERN CARLTON PLAZA.** *642 Johnson St (V8W 1M6).* 250/388-5513; fax 250/388-5343; toll-free 800/663-7241. *Email info@best westerncarlton.com; www.bestwestern carlton.com.* 103 rms, 6 story, 47 kit. suites. May-mid-Oct: S, D $129-$149; each addl $20; kit. suites $169-$189; under 18 free; wkly rates; lower rates rest of yr. Crib free. Garage parking; valet $8. TV; cable (premium). Complimentary coffee in rms. Restaurant 7 am-9 pm. Ck-out 11 am. Coin lndry. Business center. In-rm modem link. Shopping arcade. Barber, beauty shop. Health club privileges. Cr cds: A, DS, MC, V.

⊡ ⬧ ⬧ ⬧

★★ **CHATEAU VICTORIA.** *740 Burdett Ave (V8W 1B2).* 250/382-4221; fax 250/380-1950; toll-free 800/663-5891. *Email reservations@chateau victoria.com; www.chateauvictoria.com.* 59 rms, 18 story, 111 suites. May-Sep: S $117; D $147; each addl $15; suites $260; under 18 free; lower rates rest of yr. Crib avail. Parking lot. Indoor pool, whirlpool. TV; cable (premium), VCR avail. Complimentary coffee in rms, newspaper, toll-free calls. Restaurant 6:30 am-midnight. Bar. Ck-out 11 am, ck-in 3 pm. Meeting rms. Business center. Bellhops. Concierge. Dry cleaning. Exercise equipt. Golf. Tennis, 3 courts. Cr cds: A, C, D, DS, ER, JCB, MC, V.

⧉ 🏠 🏃 🍴 ➰ 🏊 🏄 🏋 🔥 🏃

★★ CLARION GRAND PACIFIC.

450 Quebec St (V8V 1W5). 250/386-0450; fax 250/380-4474; toll-free 800/663-7550. Email reserves@hotelgrandpacific.com. 145 rms, 8 story, 19 suites. June-Sep: S, D $289-$349; suites $369-$589; under 18 free; golf plans; lower rates rest of yr. Crib free. TV; cable, VCR avail. Complimentary coffee in rms. Restaurant 7 am-10 pm. Rm serv 24 hrs. Bar 11-1 am. Ck-out 11 am. Meeting rms. Business center. In-rm modem link. Concierge. Coin lndry. Free garage parking. 18-hole golf privileges. Exercise rm; sauna. Massage. Indoor pool; wading pool, whirlpool. Refrigerators, minibars. Opp ocean. Cr cds: A, C, D, DS, ER, JCB, MC, V.

⧉ 🏃 🏊 🍴 🏋 🏄 🔥

★★★ COAST HARBOURSIDE HOTEL & MARINA.

146 Kingston St (V9B 5X3). 250/360-1211; fax 250/ l360-1418; res 800/663-1144. 132 rms, 8 story. May-Oct: S $220; D $250; each addl $30; suites $270-$560; under 18 free; lower rates rest of yr. Crib free. Pet accepted. TV; cable, VCR avail. 2 pools, 1 indoor; whirlpool. Complimentary coffee in rms. Restaurant (see BLUE CRAB BAR AND GRILL). Rm serv 24 hrs. Bar. Ck-out noon. Meeting rms. Business servs avail. In-rm modem link. Concierge. Sundries. Valet serv. Exercise equipt; sauna. Refrigerators; microwaves avail. Balconies. Cr cds: A, D, DS, ER, JCB, MC, V.

⧉ 🐾 🏊 🏃 🏋 🏄 🔥

★ DAYS INN ON THE HARBOUR.

427 Belleville St (V8V 1X3). 250/386-3451; fax 250/386-6999; toll-free 800/665-3024. Email welcome2@daysinnvic.com; www.daysinnvictoria.com. 71 rms, 4 story. May-Sep: S, D $203; each addl $10; under 12 free; lower rates rest of yr. Crib avail. Parking lot. Pool, whirlpool. TV; cable, VCR avail. Complimentary coffee in rms. Restaurant 7 am-9 pm. Bar. Ck-out

noon, ck-in 3 pm. Meeting rm. Business center. Dry cleaning. Exercise privileges. Golf. Tennis. Cr cds: A, C, D, DS, ER, JCB, MC, V.

🏃 🍴 🏊 🏋 🏄 🔥 SC 🏋

★★ EMBASSY INN.

520 Menzies St (V8V 2H4), 1 blk S of Inner Harbour. 250/382-8161; fax 250/382-4224; toll-free 800/268-8161. Email embassy@pinc.com; www.travel.bc.ca/e/embassy. 88 rms, 4 story, 15 suites. June-Sep: S, D $135; each addl $15; suites $215; under 12 free; lower rates rest of yr. Crib avail. Parking garage. Pool. TV; cable. Complimentary coffee in rms. Restaurant 7 am-9:30 pm. Bar. Ck-out 11 am, ck-in 3 pm. Meeting rm. Business servs avail. Bellhops. Dry cleaning, coin lndry. Golf. Bike rentals. Cr cds: A, D, ER, MC, V.

⧉ 🏃 🏊 ✈ 🏄 🔥 SC

★★★ THE EMPRESS HOTEL.

721 Government St (V8W 1W5), Inner Harbour area. 250/384-8111; fax 250/381-4334; toll-free 800/441-1414. Email swilkins@emp.mhs.compuserve.com; www.vvv.com/empress/. 475 rms, 7 story. No A/C. Mid-May-Sep: S, D $255-$315; each addl $25; suites $405-$1,700; under 18 free; lower rates rest of yr. Crib free. Garage $14.50. TV; cable (premium), VCR avail. Indoor pool; whirlpool, wading pool. Restaurants 6 am-10 pm. Bar 11:30-1 am; entertainment Mon-Sat. Ck-out noon. Convention facilities. Business servs avail. In-rm modem link. Shopping arcade. Exercise equipt; sauna. Minibars; some refrigerators; microwaves avail. Opened in 1908. Cr cds: A, C, D, DS, ER, JCB, MC, V.

⧉ 🏊 🏃 🏄 🔥

★★ EXECUTIVE HOUSE.

777 Douglas St (V8W 2B5). 250/388-5111; fax 250/385-1323; res 800/663-7001. Email executivehouse@executivehouse.com; www.executivehouse.com. 179 rms, 17 story, 100 kits. No A/C. May-mid-Oct: S, D $99-$195; each addl $15; kit. units $15 addl; suites $195-$595; under 18 free; lower rates rest of yr. Pet accepted $15/day. Garage $2. TV; cable. Complimentary coffee. Restaurant 7 am-10 pm. Bars 11-1 am; entertainment. Ck-out noon. Meeting rm. Business servs avail. Exercise equipt; sauna, steam rm. Massage. Whirlpool. Many refrigerators; some bathrm phones. Private patios, balconies. Cr cds: A, DS, MC, V.

★★ **HARBOUR TOWERS.** *345 Quebec St (V8V 1W4), 1 blk S of Inner Harbour. 250/385-2405; fax 250/385-4453; toll-free 800/663-5896. Email harbour@pacificcoast.net; www.harbour towers.com.* 113 rms, 12 story, 80 suites. June-Oct: S, D $300; each addl $15; suites $500; lower rates rest of yr. Crib avail. Pet accepted. Parking garage. Indoor pool, whirlpool. TV; cable (premium), VCR avail, CD avail. Complimentary coffee in rms, newspaper. Restaurant. Bar. Ck-out noon, ck-in 4 pm. Meeting rms. Business center. Bellhops. Dry cleaning. Gift shop. Salon/barber. Exercise equipt, sauna. Golf. Tennis. Bike rentals. Supervised children's activities. Cr cds: A, D, ER, JCB, MC, V.

★★ **HOLIDAY INN.** *3020 Blanshard St (V5V 4E4). 250/382-4400; fax 250/382-4053; toll-free 800/465-4329. Email hivictoria@telus.net.* 123 rms, 3 story, 3 suites. June-July, Sep: S, D $159; each addl $10; suites $185; lower rates rest of yr. Crib avail, fee. Parking garage. TV; cable (premium). Complimentary coffee in rms. Restaurant 7 am-10 pm. Bar. Ck-out noon, ck-in 3 pm. Meeting rms. Business servs avail. Dry cleaning, coin lndry. Gift shop. Salon/barber. Exercise equipt, sauna, steam rm, whirlpool. Golf. Video games. Cr cds: A, D, DS, ER, JCB, MC, V.

★★★ **THE MAGNOLIA HOTEL & SUITES.** *623 Courtney St (V8W 1B8). 250/381-0999; fax 250/381-0988; toll-free 877/624-6654. Email sales@ magnoliahotel.com; www.magnolia hotel.com.* 64 rms, 7 story, 2 suites. May-Sep: S, D $279; each addl $20; suites $419; under 12 free; lower rates rest of yr. Crib avail. Valet parking avail. TV; cable (premium), VCR avail. Complimentary continental bkfst, coffee in rms, newspaper, toll-free calls. Restaurant 11:30 am-10 pm. Bar. Ck-out noon, ck-in 3 pm. Meeting rms. Business servs avail. Bellhops. Dry cleaning. Salon/barber. Free airport transportation. Exercise privileges. Golf, 18 holes. Tennis, 2 courts. Video games. Cr cds: A, C, D, DS, ER, JCB, MC, V.

★★★ **OAK BAY BEACH AND MARINE RESORT.** *1175 Beach Dr (V8S 2N2). 250/598-4556; fax 250/ 598-6180.* 50 rms, 3 story. No A/C. June-Sep, mid-Dec-early Jan: S, D $174-$214; each addl $25; suites $244-$399; lower rates rest of yr. Crib free. TV; cable, VCR avail. Restaurant 7-10:30 am, 2:30-9 pm. Bar from 11:30 am. Ck-out noon. Meeting rms. Business servs avail. In-rm modem link. Tennis, golf adj. Some refrigerators, bathrm phones. Some balconies. Tudor-style hotel (1927); some four-poster beds, many antiques. On beach. Cr cds: A, MC, V.

OLDE ENGLAND INN. Unrated for 2001. *429 Lampson St (V9A 5Y9), via Johnson St Bridge. 250/388-4353; fax 250/382-8311. www.oldengland.com.* 40 rms, 3 story, 10 suites. June-Sep, Dec: S $120; D $140; each addl $40; suites $200; lower rates rest of yr. Parking lot. TV; cable, VCR avail.

Parliament Building

Complimentary full bkfst, coffee in rms, toll-free calls. Restaurant 7 am-10 pm. Bar. Ck-out 11 am, ck-in 1 pm. Meeting rms. Business center. Bellhops. Concierge. Dry cleaning. Gift shop. Exercise privileges. Golf, 18 holes. Tennis, 6 courts. Bike rentals. Cr cds: A, MC, V.

★★ **QUEEN VICTORIA INN.** *655 Douglas St (V8V 2P9). 250/386-1312; fax 250/381-4312; toll-free 800/663-7007. Email info@queenvictoria.com;*

www.queenvictoria.com. 126 rms, 7 story, 20 suites. June-Sep: S, D $165; each addl $20; suites $205; under 15 free; lower rates rest of yr. Crib avail. Parking lot. Indoor pool, whirlpool. TV; cable, VCR avail. Complimentary coffee in rms. Restaurant 7 am-9 pm. Ck-out noon, ck-in 3 pm. Fax servs avail. Bellhops. Concierge. Dry cleaning, coin lndry. Exercise equipt, sauna. Golf. Cr cds: A, C, D, DS, ER, JCB, MC.

★★ **RAMADA HUNTINGDON MANOR.** 330 Quebec St (V8V 1W3), 1 blk S of Inner Harbour. 250/381-3456; fax 250/382-7666; res 800/2-RAMADA; toll-free 800/663-7557. Email huntingdon@bctravel.com; www.bctravel.com/huntingdon. 116 rms, 40 A/C, 3 story, 58 kits. Mid-June-mid-Sep: S, D $153-$233; each addl $15; suites $173-$233; kit. units $15 addl; under 18 free; wkly rates; lower rates rest of yr. Crib free. TV; cable. Coffee in rms. Restaurant 7 am-10 pm. Bar 3-10 pm. Ck-out 11 am. Coin lndry. Meeting rms. Business servs avail. Sauna. Massage. Whirlpool. Refrigerators, microwaves. Some private patios, balconies. Opp harbor. Cr cds: A, DS, MC, V.

★★★ **SWANS SUITE HOTEL.** 506 Pandora Ave (V8W 1N2). 250/361-3310; fax 250/361-3491; toll-free 800/668-7926. Email swans@swanshotel.com. 29 rms, 4 story. No A/C. July-Sep: S, D $165-$175; each addl $20; under 12 free; lower rates rest of yr. Crib $15. Garage $8. TV; cable, VCR avail (movies $3.50). Complimentary coffee in rms. Restaurant 7-1 am. Bar 11:30-2:30 am; entertainment Sun-Thurs. Ck-out noon. Coin lndry. Meeting rms. Business servs avail. Refrigerators, microwaves. Some balconies. Brewery, beer and wine shop on premises. Cr cds: A, D, MC, V.

★★★ **VICTORIA REGENT.** 1234 Wharf St (V8W 3H9), on Inner Harbour. 250/386-2211; fax 250/386-2622; toll-free 800/663-7472. Email reservations@victoria-regent-hotel.com; www.victoria-regent-hotel.com. 10 rms, 8 story, 34 suites. June-Oct: S, D $179; each addl $20; suites $239; under 16 free; lower rates rest of yr.

Crib avail, fee. Valet parking avail. TV; cable (premium), VCR avail. Complimentary continental bkfst, coffee in rms, newspaper, toll-free calls. Restaurant 7 am-11 pm. Ck-out noon, ck-in 3 pm. Meeting rm. Business center. Bellhops. Concierge. Dry cleaning, coin lndry. Exercise privileges. Golf. Cr cds: A, D, DS, ER, JCB, MC, V.

Resorts

★★★★ **THE AERIE RESORT.** 600 Ebedora Ln (V0R 2L0), 30 km (20 mi) N on Rte 1, Spectacle Lake turn. 250/743-7115; fax 250/743-4766; toll-free 800/518-1933. Email aerie@relais-chateaux.fr; www.aerie.bc.ca. This Mediterranean-style resort and spa is 30 minutes from Victoria in the mountains of Southern Vancouver Island. The 10-acre, parklike property of manicured grounds and breathtaking views is home to clusters of white, townhouselike bldgs nestled along the green mountainside holding 23 rms and suites. After a nature-filled day, relax in the Wellness and Beauty Centre or dine on Northwest-influenced French cuisine. 10 rms, 3 story, 13 suites. May-Sep: S, D $275; suites $495; lower rates rest of yr. Parking lot. Indoor pool, whirlpool. TV; cable, VCR avail, CD avail. Complimentary full bkfst, coffee in rms, newspaper. Restaurant. Bar. Meeting rms. Business servs avail. Bellhops. Concierge. Dry cleaning. Gift shop. Sauna. Golf. Tennis. Hiking trail. Picnic facilities. Cr cds: A, D, ER, MC, V.

★★ **LAUREL POINT INN.** 680 Montreal St (V8V 1Z8), 1 blk W of ferry dock. 250/386-8721; fax 250/386-9547; toll-free 800/663-7667. Email reservations@laurelpoint.com; www.laurelpoint.com. 135 rms, 65 suites. June-Sep: S, D $190; each addl $10; suites $250; under 12 free; lower rates rest of yr. Crib avail, fee. Pet accepted, fee. Valet parking avail. Indoor pool. TV; cable (DSS), VCR avail, CD avail. Complimentary coffee in rms, newspaper, toll-free calls. Restaurant. 24-hr rm serv. Bar. Meeting rms. Business center. Bellhops. Concierge. Dry cleaning. Gift shop. Exercise privileges, sauna. Golf. Tennis. Bike rentals. Cr cds: A, D, DS, ER, JCB, MC, V.

★★★ **OCEAN POINTE RESORT AND SPA.** *45 Songhees Rd (V9A 6T3), across Johnson St bridge. 250/360-2999; fax 250/360-1041; toll-free 800/667-4677. Email reservations@oprhotel.com; www.oprhotel.com.* 250 rms, 8 story, 5 suites. May-Oct: S, D $200; each addl $30; suites $600; lower rates rest of yr. Crib avail. Pet accepted, some restrictions. Valet parking avail. Indoor pool. TV; cable (premium), VCR avail, CD avail. Complimentary coffee in rms, newspaper, toll-free calls. Restaurant. 24-hr rm serv. Bar. Ck-out noon, ck-in 4 pm. Conference center, meeting rms. Business center. Bellhops. Concierge. Dry cleaning. Gift shop. Salon/barber. Exercise rm, sauna, steam rm. Golf. Tennis, 2 courts. Bike rentals. Supervised children's activities. Hiking trail. Picnic facilities. Cr cds: A, D, ER, JCB, MC, V.

B&Bs/Small Inns

★★★ **ABIGAIL'S HOTEL.** *906 McClure St (V8V 3E7). 250/388-5363; fax 250/388-7787; toll-free 800/561-6565. Email innkeeper@abigailshotel.com; www.abigailshotel.com.* 16 rms, 3 story, 6 suites. May-Sep: S $199; D $229; each addl $30; suites $329; lower rates rest of yr. Parking lot. TV; cable (premium), VCR avail, CD avail. Complimentary full bkfst, coffee in rms, newspaper. Restaurant nearby. Ck-out 11 am, ck-in 3 pm. Fax servs avail. Concierge. Dry cleaning. Gift shop. Exercise privileges. Golf. Tennis. Cr cds: A, MC, V.

★★ **ANDERSEN HOUSE.** *301 Kingston St (V8V 1V5). 250/388-4565; fax 250/388-4563. Email andersen@islandnet.com; www.islandnet.com/~andersen/.* 5 rms, 3 with shower only, 3 story, 2 suites, 1 kit. unit. No A/C. Mid-May-mid-Oct: S $145-$185; D $155-$195; each addl $35; suites $165-$205; lower rates rest of yr. Children over 12 yrs only. TV in some rms; cable. Complimentary full bkfst, coffee in rms. Restaurant nearby. Ck-out 11 am, ck-in 1 pm. Street parking. Some refrigerators. Some balconies. Picnic tables. Built in 1891; eclectic mix of antiques and modern art. A 1927 motor yacht is avail as guest rm. Totally nonsmoking. Cr cds: MC, V.

★★★ **BEACONSFIELD INN.** *998 Humboldt St (V8V 2Z8). 250/384-4044; fax 250/384-4052.* 9 rms, 4 story. No A/C. No elvtr. Rm phones avail. Mid-June-Sep: S, D $200-$350; each addl $65. Complimentary full bkfst; afternoon refreshments. Restaurant nearby. Ck-out 11 am, ck-in 3 pm. Business servs avail. Restored Edwardian mansion (1905); period antique furnishings, stained glass, mahogany floors. Library. Totally nonsmoking. Cr cds: MC, V.

★★★ **HATERLEIGH HERITAGE INN.** *243 Kingston St (V8V 1V5). 250/384-9995; fax 250/384-1935. Email paulk@haterleigh.com; www.haterleigh.com.* 6 rms, 1 suite. June-Oct: S, D $195; suites $215; lower rates rest of yr. Parking lot. TV; cable (premium), VCR avail, CD avail. Complimentary full bkfst, newspaper. Restaurant. Ck-out 11 am, ck-in 4 pm. Business servs avail. Concierge. Exercise privileges. Golf. Bike rentals. Hiking trail. Picnic facilities. Cr cds: MC, V.

★★ **HOLLAND HOUSE.** *595 Michigan St (V8V 1S7). 250/384-6644; fax 250/384-6117; toll-free 800/335-3466. Email hollandhouseinn@home.com; www.hollandhouse.victoria.bc.ca.* 17 rms. May-Sep: D $100; each addl $30; lower rates rest of yr. Parking lot. TV; cable, VCR avail. Complimentary full bkfst, coffee in rms, newspaper. Concierge. Dry cleaning. Cr cds: A, MC, V.

★★★ **PRIOR HOUSE B&B INN.** *620 St. Charles (V8S 3N7). 250/592-8847; fax 250/592-8223; res 877/924-3300. Email innkeeper@priorhouse.com; www.priorhouse.com.* 5 rms, 3 story, 3 suites. June-Sep: S, D $215; each addl $45; suites $243; lower rates rest of yr. Parking lot. TV; cable (premium), VCR avail. Complimentary full bkfst, coffee in rms, newspaper. Restaurant 8 am-9:30 pm. Ck-out 11 am, ck-in 3 pm. Business servs avail. Concierge. Coin lndry. Exercise privileges. Golf. Tennis, 3 courts. Video games. Cr cds: MC, V.

★★★ **SOOKE HARBOUR HOUSE.** *1528 Whiffen Split Rd (V0S 1N0), 23 mi NW via Hwy 1A and Hwy 14, thru*

Sooke, left on Whiffen Spit Rd.
250/642-3421; fax 250/642-6988; res
250/642-3421; toll-free 800/889-9688.
Email info@sookeharbourhouse.com. 28
rms, 1 with shower only, 4 story. No
A/C. Apr-Oct, MAP: S $175-$525;
each addl $35; under 12 free; lower
rates rest of yr. Closed 3 wks Jan.
Crib free. Pet accepted; $20. TV avail;
cable (premium), VCR avail (movies).
Whirlpool. Restaurant (see SOOKE
HARBOUR HOUSE). Ck-out noon,
ck-in 3 pm. Business servs avail. Free
airport transportation. Massage.
Refrigerators; Balconies. Picnic tables.
On ocean. Totally nonsmoking. Cr
cds: A, DS, MC, V.

Villa/Condo

★★★★ **HASTINGS HOUSE.** *160
Upper Ganges Rd (V8K 2S2), on Salt
Spring Island. 250/537-2362; fax
250/537-5333; toll-free 800/661-9255.
Email hasthouse@saltspring.com; www.
hastingshouse.com.* Nestled on Salt
Spring Island, one of British Columbia's beautiful Gulf Islands, this
retreat is both tranquil and romantic.
Five different bldgs, including a barn
with hayloft suite, make up the
accommodations, and all are decorated in warm, country-house style.
Dining is found in the main house
where guests can enjoy breakfast,
afternoon refreshments, and formal
dinner. The dining room provides
seasonal French cuisine featuring
local fresh ingredients and herbs and
vegetables from the gardens. Salt
Spring Island lamb is a special feature of the house and should not be
missed. 3 rms, 1 story, 15 suites.
June-Sep: S, D $410; each addl $80;
suites $520; lower rates rest of yr.
Parking lot. TV; cable (premium),
VCR avail, CD avail. Complimentary
full bkfst, coffee in rms. Restaurant 6-
8 pm. Bar. Ck-out 11 am, ck-in 3 pm.
Meeting rms. Business servs avail.
Bellhops. Concierge. Dry cleaning,
coin lndry. Gift shop. Free airport
transportation. Golf. Tennis, 3
courts. Beach access. Bike rentals.
Hiking trail. Picnic facilities. Cr cds:
A, MC, V.

Restaurants

★★★★ **AERIE DINING ROOM.**
*600 Ebedora Ln. 250/743-7115. Email
aerie@relaischateaux.fr; www.aerie.bc.
ca.* Located in the Mediterranean-
inspired resort and spa of the same
name, this renowned dining room
has absolutely stunning views of the
fjordlike Sound and the waters of the
Georgia Strait. Chef Christophe
Letard presents Northwest-inspired
French cuisie in each of the three
menus offered each day: seven-
course prix fixe, a market tasting
menu, plus a full a la carte option.
Specializes in fresh seafood, lamb,
game. Hrs: 6 pm-midnight. Res
accepted. Bar. Dinner a la carte
entrees: $27-$29.50. Complete meals:
$60. Child's menu. Parking. Cr cds:
A, D, MC, V.
D

★★★ **ANTOINE'S.** *2 Centennial Sq
(V8W 1P7), adj City Hall.* 250/384-
7055. Specializes in local seafood.
Hrs: 11 am-3 pm, 5-10 pm. Closed
Jan 1. Res required. Bar. Wine list.
Lunch a la carte entrees: $10-$12;
dinner a la carte entrees: $22-$30.
Complete meals: $22-$45. Parking.
Overlooks large fountain in Centen-
nial Sq. Cr cds: A, MC, V.

★★ **BLUE CRAB BAR AND GRILL.**
146 Kingston. 250/480-1999. Email
m.prins@costhotel.com. Specializes in
fresh local seafood. Hrs: 6:30 am-10
pm. Res accepted. Bar. Bkfst $5-$9.25;
lunch $8.50-$14.25; dinner $16-$27.
Sun brunch $10. Child's menu. Con-
temporary decor; view of harbor, skyline. Cr cds: A, D, DS, MC, V.
D

★★ **CAFE BRIO.** *944 Fort St (V8V
3K2).* 250/383-0009. www.cafe-brio.
com. Specializes in confit of duck.
Hrs: 11:45 am-10 pm; Sat-Mon 5:30-
10 pm. Closed Dec 25; 1st wk in Jan.
Res accepted. Wine list. Lunch $6-
$12; dinner $13-$28. Child's menu.
Entertainment. Italian Tuscan patio.
Cr cds: A, MC, V.
D

★★ **CAMILLE'S.** *45 Bastion Sq
(V8W 1J1).* 250/381-3433. Email
camilles@pacificcoast.net; www.
camillesrestaurant.com. Specializes in
seafood. Hrs: 5:30-9 pm. Closed Jan
1, Dec 24, 25. Res accepted. Bar. Din-

ner $14.95-$21.95. Romantic atmosphere. Cr cds: A, MC, V.

★★★ **DEEP COVE CHALET.** *11190 Chalet Rd (V8L 4R4), 18 mi N on 17 to 17A (Warn Rd). 250/656-3541. Email deep.cove.chalet@email.com; www.deep covechalet.com.* Hrs: noon-2:30 pm, 5:30-10 pm. Closed Mon. Res accepted. Bar. Wine cellar. Lunch $15-$35. Complete meals: $15-$22; dinner $20.50-$70. Complete meals: $20-$40. Entertainment: pianist Fri, Sat. Parking. Built in 1914; originally teahouse for a railroad station. View of Deep Cove Bay. Cr cds: A, MC, V.
D

★★★ **EMPRESS ROOM.** *721 Government St. 250/384-8111. www. fairmont.com.* Specializes in roasted rack of lamb, fresh seasonal fish. Hrs: 5:30-9 pm. Closed Mon, Tues in Nov & Feb. Res accepted. Wine list. Dinner $22-$56. Entertainment: harpist. Cr cds: A, D, DS, MC, V.
D

★★ **GATSBY MANSION.** *309 Belleville St (V8V 1X2), W of Parliament Bldg. 250/388-9191. Email huntingdon@bctravel.com; www. bctravel.com/huntingdon/gatsby.html.* Specializes in seafood, steak, poultry. Hrs: 7 am-10 pm. Res accepted. Bkfst $4.95-$8.95; lunch $4.95-$8.95; dinner $14.95-$23.95. Entertainment. Parking. Restored 3-story mansion (1897); antiques; garden. Cr cds: A, D, DS, MC, V.

★★★ **HERALD STREET CAFE.** *546 Herald St (V8W 1S6). 250/381-1441.* Specializes in seafood. Hrs: 11:30 am-3 pm, 5:30-10 pm; Fri, Sat to midnight. Closed Sun-Tues. Res accepted. Bar. Lunch $7-$11; dinner $11.95-$32.95. Eclectic decor. Cr cds: A, D, DS, ER, MC, V.
D

★★ **HUGO'S GRILL.** *625 Courtney St. 250/920-4844. www.hugoslounge. com.* Closed Dec 25. Res accepted. Wine, beer. Lunch $5.95-$12.95; dinner $9.95-$30.95. Entertainment. Cr cds: A, JCB, MC, V.
D ⚫

★★ **IL TERRAZZO.** *555 Johnson St (V8W 1M2), at Waddington Alley. 250/361-0028.* Specializes in wood-oven-baked meats and game, northern Italian dishes. Own baking,

pasta. Hrs: 11:30 am-3 pm, 5-10:30; Sun from 5 pm; winter hrs vary. Closed Jan 1, Dec 25. Two-level dining area features fireplaces, wood-fired pizza oven. Bar. Lunch a la carte entrees: $7.95-$11.95; dinner a la carte entrees: $13.95-$21.95. Child's menu. Cr cds: MC, V.
D

★ **INDIA TANDOORI HUT.** *1548 Fort St (V8S 5J2). 250/370-1880.* Specializes in tandoori chicken, lamb curry, chicken marsala. Own baking. Hrs: 11:30 am-2 pm, 5-9 pm; Sat, Sun from 5 pm. Closed Dec 25. Res accepted. Bar. Lunch a la carte entrees: $5-$18; dinner a la carte entrees: $11-$19. Colorful Indian decor. Cr cds: MC, V.
D SC

★★ **J&J WONTON NOODLE HOUSE.** *1012 Fort St (V8V 3K4). 250/383-0680.* Specializes in spicy beef or chicken noodle soup, sizzling hot pan prawns, spicy tofu hot pot. Own baking, noodles. Hrs: 11 am-2 pm, 4:30-8:45 pm. Closed Sun, Mon; hols. Bar. Lunch $3.95-$11; dinner $5.95-$16.95. Child's menu. Casual Chinese decor. Cr cds: MC, V.
D

★★ **JAPANESE VILLAGE STEAK AND SEAFOOD HOUSE.** *734 Broughton St (V8W 1E1). 250/382-5165. www.japanesevillage.bc.ca.* Specializes in teppan-style steak, salmon, lobster. Sushi bar. Hrs: 11:30 am-2 pm, 5-10 pm; Fri to 10:30 pm; Sat 5-11:30 pm; Sun 5-10 pm. Closed hols. Res accepted. Lunch complete meals: $6.50-$11.50; dinner complete meals: $16.50-$34.50. Child's menu. Entertainment: Sun. Tableside cooking. Japanese decor. Cr cds: A, C, D, DS, ER, MC, V.
D

★★ **THE MARINA.** *1327 Beach Dr (V8S 2N4). 250/598-8555.* Specializes in oysters Jim, seafood hot pot, chocolate fetish. Own baking. Hrs: 11:30 am-10 pm; Fri, Sat to 11 pm; Sun brunch 10 am-2:30 pm. Closed Dec 25. Res accepted. Bar. Wine list. Lunch $7.25-$13.95; dinner $9.95-$24.95. Sun brunch $21.95. Child's menu. Two-level dining area with large windows overlooking marina. Cr cds: A, D, DS, MC, V.
D

★★★★ **RESTAURANT MATISSE.**
512 Yates St (V8W 1K8). 250/480-0883. www.restayrabtnatusse.com.
Original artwork covers the exposed-red-brick walls and the scent of fresh flowers fills the air at this downtown, very traditional French restaurant steps from the Inner Harbour. The atmosphere is further enhanced by nostalgic French Chanteuse. Chef Philippe Renaudat offers specialties from his native France on the a la carte and prix fixe menus. The host/co-owner matches each course with wines from the wine menu if desired. Classic French menu. Specializes in lobster bisque, creme brulee, bouillabaisse. Hrs: 11:30 am-midnight; Sat, Sun 5 pm-midnight. Res accepted. Extensive wine list. Dinner $18.95-$27.95. Child's menu. Entertainment. Cr cds: A, MC, V.
D ⚓ SC

★★★ **SOOKE HARBOUR HOUSE.**
1528 Whiffen Spit Rd. 250/642-3421. Email info@sookeharbourhouse.com; www.sookeharbourhouse.com. Specializes in fresh seafood. Hrs: 5:30-9:15 pm. Res accepted. Bar. Dinner a la carte entrees: $20-$30. Entertainment. Cr cds: D, DS, MC, V.
D

★★ **SPINNAKER'S BREW PUB.**
308 Catherine St (V9A 3S8), across Johnson St bridge. 250/386-2739. Email spinnakers@spinnakers.com; www.spinnakers.com. Specializes in pasta, pot pies, fish and chips. Own baking, pasta. Hrs: 7 am-10 pm. Res accepted. Bar. Bkfst $1.99-$8.95; lunch $4.50-$11.95; dinner $4.50-$14.95. Child's menu. Entertainment: jazz, blues Fri, Sat. Views of harbor and city skyline; brewing vats can be seen from bar. Cr cds: A, D, MC, V.
D

★★★ **THE VICTORIAN.** *45 Songhees Rd. 250/360-5800. Email food.beverage@oprhotel.com; www. oprhotel.com.* Specializes in fresh seafood, rack of lamb. Hrs: 6-10:30 pm; winter hrs vary. Closed 1st 3 wks Jan. Res accepted. Bar. Dinner a la carte entrees: $21-$27. Complete meals: $39-$49. Child's menu. Valet parking. View of Inner and Outer Harbour. Cr cds: A, D, MC, V.
D

Unrated Dining Spots

BENTLEY'S ON THE BAY. *1175 Beach Dr (V8S 2N2). 250/598-4556. www.oakbaybeachhotel.com.* Hrs: 7 am-9 pm. Res accepted. Wine list. Lunch $7-$16; dinner $15-$28. Child's menu. Overlooking ocean, Mt. Baker. Cr cds: A, D, ER, JCB, MC, V.
D ⚓ SC

THE DINING ROOM RESTAURANT.
800 Benvenuto Ave (V8X 3X4). 250/ 652-8222. www.butchartgardens.com. Hrs: 11 am-9 pm. Closed Jan-Apr, Oct-Nov. Res accepted. Wine list. Lunch $10-15; dinner $15-$25. Entertainment. Cr cds: A, MC, V.
D

MURCHIE'S. *1110 Government St (V8W 1W5). 250/381-5451. Email order@murchies.com; www.murchies. com.* Specializes in cookies, shortbread, biscoti. Hrs: 9:30 am-6 pm; Thur, Fri to 9 pm; Sat to 5:30 pm; Sun 9 am-6 pm. Entertainment. Cr cds: MC, V.
D ⚓

THE TEA LOBBY - EMPRESS HOTEL. *721 Government St. 250/389-2727. www.cphotels.com.* Specializes in assorted tea sandwiches, homemade raisin scone with jersey cream, empress pastries. Sittings: 12:30 pm, 2 pm, 3:30 pm, 5 pm. Closed Dec 25. Res accepted. Wine list. Entertainment: pianist. Lobby with piano. Cr cds: A, C, D, DS, ER, JCB, MC, V.
D ⚓

VISTA 18. *740 Burdett Ave. 250/382-9258. www.vista18.com.* Specializes in lavender chicken, grilled ahi tuna, jumbo sea scallops. Hrs: 6:30 am-9:45 pm. Res accepted. Wine list. Lunch $6.95-$14.95; dinner $11.95-$23.95. Child's menu. Entertainment. Cr cds: A, D, DS, ER, JCB, MC, V.
D ⚓

WHITE HEATHER TEA ROOM.
1885 Oak Bay Ave (V8R 1C6). 250/595-8020. Specializes in grilled focaccia sandwiches, homemade soups, tarts, crepes, high tea. Hrs: 9:30 am-5 pm; Sun 10 am-5 pm. Closed Mon. Res accepted. Wine, beer. Lunch $6.95-$8.95. Entertainment. Cr cds: MC, V.
D

Whistler

(E-4) See also Vancouver

Pop 4,500 (est) **Elev** 2,200 ft
Area code 604 **Web** www.whistler
resort.com
Information Whistler Resort Assn,
4010 Whistler Way, V0N 1B4;
604/932-3928 or 800/944-7853; or
the Activity & Information Centre;
604/932-2394

The winning combination of Blackcomb and Whistler mountains makes
this an internationally famous ski
area. It is also a popular summer
vacation area. Five lakes dot the valley in Whistler, offering ample
opportunity to fish, swim, boardsail,
canoe, kayak, sail, or waterski; all of
the lakes are accessible by the Valley
Trail network that winds its way
through Whistler.

What to See and Do

Skiing. Patrol, school, sport shop;
snowmaking; cafeterias, restaurants,
bars; nursery, lodge. X-country skiing
(17.5 mi), heliskiing, snowboarding,
sleigh rides, snowshoeing. Multiday,
dual-mountain rates. (Mid-Nov-Apr,
daily) Gondola and some lifts also
operate in summer.

Blackcomb. Six high-speed quad
chairlifts (1 covered), 3 triple chairlifts, 3 handletows, 2 T-bars, platter
lift, magic carpet lift. More than
100 runs; longest run 8 mi, vertical
drop 5,280 ft. Glacier skiing (mid-
June-Aug, weather permitting).
High-speed gondola.

Whistler. Three high-speed quad,
double, 3 triple chairlifts, 2 handletows, 2 T-bars, platter pull.
More than 100 runs; longest run 7
mi, vertical drop 5,020 ft. Two
high-speed gondolas.

Hotels

★★ **BEST WESTERN LISTEL
WHISTLER HOTEL.** *4121 Village
Green (V0N 1B4). 604/932-1133; fax
604/932-8383; toll-free 800/663-5472.
Email info@listelhotel.com; www.listel
hotel.com.* 93 rms, 3 story, 5 suites.
Dec-Mar: S, D $299; each addl $30;
suites $429; under 18 free; lower
rates rest of yr. Crib avail. Pet
accepted, fee. Valet parking avail.

Indoor pool, whirlpool. TV; cable
(premium). Complimentary coffee in
rms. Restaurant 7 am-11 pm. Bar. Ck-
out 10 am, ck-in 4 pm. Meeting rms.
Business center. Concierge. Dry
cleaning, coin lndry. Exercise privileges, sauna. Golf, 18 holes. Tennis, 4
courts. Downhill skiing. Bike rentals.
Supervised children's activities. Hiking trail. Cr cds: A, D, DS, ER, JCB,
MC, V.

D 🐕 👤 🏌 🎿 🍴 🎰 ≈ 🚶 🏃 ⛷ ≈ 🔥
🏃

★★★ **CHATEAU WHISTLER
RESORT.** *4599 Chateau Blvd (V0N
1B4). 604/938-8000; fax 604/938-
2055; res 800/441-1414; toll-free 800/
606-8244. www.chateauwhistlerresort.
com.* 342 rms, 10-12 story. Mid-Dec-
mid-May: S, D $350-$375; each addl
$30; suites $475-$1,100; under 17
free; ski, golf plans; higher rates
Christmas hols; lower rates rest of yr.
Crib free. Pet accepted; $10. Valet
parking $15. TV; cable. Indoor/out-
door pool; whirlpool, poolside serv.
Supervised children's activities (June-
Sep). Restaurants 7 am-11 pm. Rm
serv 24 hrs. Bar 11 am-midnight;
entertainment. Ck-out 11 am. Meeting rms. Concierge. Shopping arcade.
Tennis, pro. 18-hole golf, greens fee
$109 (incl cart), pro, putting green.
Downhill/x-country ski adj. Exercise
equipt; sauna. Refrigerators avail.
Minibars; some bathrm phones. Cr
cds: A, D, DS, JCB, MC, V.

D 🐕 👤 🏌 🎿 🍴 ⛷ ≈ 🚶 🏃 ⛷ ≈ 🔥

★★ **CRYSTAL LODGE.** *4154 Village
Green (V0N 1B0). 604/932-2221; fax
604/932-2635; toll-free 800/667-3363.
Email info@crystal-lodge.bc.ca; www.
crystal-lodge.com.* 96 rms, 4 story, 41
suites. Feb-Mar, Dec: S, D $220; each
addl $25; suites $735; under 12 free;
lower rates rest of yr. Parking garage.
Pool, whirlpool. TV; cable. Complimentary coffee in rms, newspaper,
toll-free calls. Restaurant 6:30 am-10
pm. Bar. Ck-out 11 am, ck-in 4 pm.
Meeting rms. Business center. Bellhops. Dry cleaning, coin lndry. Gift
shop. Golf. Tennis, 5 courts. Downhill skiing. Bike rentals. Video games.
Cr cds: A, DS, ER, JCB, MC, V.

D 🎿 🍴 ⛷ ≈ 🔥 🏃

Resorts

★★ **DELTA WHISTLER RESORT.**
4050 Whistler Way (V0N 1B4). 604/

932-1982; fax 604/932-7332; toll-free 800/515-4050. www.delta-whistler.com. 268 rms, 24 suites. Nov-Apr: S, D $409; each addl $30; under 18 free; lower rates rest of yr. Crib avail. Pet accepted, fee. Valet parking avail. Pool, whirlpool. TV; cable (premium). Complimentary coffee in rms, newspaper. Restaurant 7 am-10 pm. Bar. Ck-out 11 am, ck-in 4 pm. Conference center, meeting rms. Business center. Bellhops. Concierge. Dry cleaning, coin lndry. Gift shop. Exercise equipt, sauna, steam rm. Golf. Tennis. Downhill skiing. Bike rentals. Supervised children's activities. Hiking trail. Video games. Cr cds: A, D, ER, JCB, MC, V.

★★ **LE CHAMOIS.** *4557 Blackcomb Way (V0N 1B4). 604/932-8700; fax 604/905-2576; toll-free 800/777-0185. Email reservations@powderresorts.com; www.powderresorts.com.* 45 rms, 6 story, 6 suites. Dec-Apr, July-Sep: S $336; D $440; suites $568; lower rates rest of yr. Crib avail. Valet parking avail. Pool, whirlpool. TV; cable (premium), VCR avail. Complimentary coffee in rms, newspaper. Restaurant. Bar. Ck-out 10 am, ck-in 4 pm. Meeting rm. Business servs avail. Bellhops. Concierge. Dry cleaning, coin lndry. Gift shop. Free airport transportation. Exercise equipt. Golf. Tennis, 16 courts. Downhill skiing. Bike rentals. Hiking trail. Picnic facilities. Cr cds: A, D, DS, ER, JCB, MC, V.

SUMMIT LODGE. Unrated for 2001. *4359 Main St (V0N 1B4). 604/932-2778; fax 604/932-2716; toll-free 888/913-8811. Email reservations@summitlodge.com; www.summitlodge.com.* 4 story, 81 suites. Dec-Mar, July-Sep: suites $425; each addl $20.50; under 18 free; lower rates rest of yr. Crib avail. Pet accepted, fee. Parking garage. Pool, whirlpool. TV; cable (premium), VCR avail. Complimentary continental bkfst, coffee in rms, newspaper. Restaurant 7 am-11 pm. Ck-out 11 am, ck-in 4 pm. Meeting rms. Business center. Bellhops. Concierge. Dry cleaning, coin lndry. Free airport transportation. Sauna. Golf. Tennis, 4 courts. Downhill ski-

ing. Supervised children's activities. Cr cds: A, D, DS, ER, MC, V.

★★★★ **THE WESTIN RESORT AND SPA.** *4090 Whistler Way (V0N 1B4). 604/905-5000; fax 604/905-5640; toll-free 888/634-5577. Email reservations@westinwhistler.net; www. westinwhistler.net.* This recently opened resort and spa is nestled at the foot of the famed Whistler Mountain, North America. This all suite hotel has fully equipped kitchenettes, extra large bathrooms with soaker tubs, a full range of in-room amenities, business-friendly work stations, and the usual electronics—including video checkout. Aubergine Grill with summer terrace, the Fire-Rock Lounge, 24-hour room service, and a state-of-the-art spa add to the enjoyment of this luxurious property. Combining business with pleasure? The Westin offers full conference facilities with on-site business services. 11 story, 419 suites. Dec-Apr, July-Sep: S, D $250-$300; each addl $30; suites $2500; under 18 free; lower rates rest of yr. Crib avail. Valet parking avail. Indoor/outdoor pools, lap pool, whirlpool. TV; cable (premium). Complimentary coffee in rms, newspaper. Restaurant 6 am. 24-hr rm serv. Bar. Ck-out noon, ck-in 4 pm. Meeting rms. Business servs avail. Bellhops. Concierge. Dry cleaning, coin lndry. Gift shop. Salon/barber. Exercise rm, sauna, steam rm. Golf, 18 holes. Tennis, 4 courts. Downhill skiing. Supervised children's activities. Hiking trail. Video games. Cr cds: A, DS, MC, V.

All Suite

★★★ **PAN PACIFIC LODGE.** *4320 Sundial Crescent (V0N 1S4). 604/905-2999; fax 604/905-2995; toll-free 888/905-9995. Email whistler@panpacific hotel.com; www.panpac.com.* 8 story, 121 suites. Dec-Mar: suites $309; lower rates rest of yr. Crib avail. Valet parking avail. TV; cable (premium), VCR avail. Complimentary coffee in rms, newspaper. Restaurant 7 am-2 pm. Bar. Ck-out 11 am, ck-in 3 pm. Meeting rm. Business center. Bellhops. Concierge. Dry cleaning, coin lndry. Gift shop. Exercise equipt. Golf. Tennis, 8 courts. Downhill skiing. Bike rentals. Supervised children's activities. Video games. Cr cds: A, C, D, DS, ER, JCB, MC, V.

[D] [symbols]

Restaurants

★★★★ **BEAR FOOT BISTRO.** *4121 Village Green.* 604/932-3433. Email info@bearfootbistro.com; www. bearfootbistro.com. Only a hard day of skiing can justify this four-hour, decadent feast-for-the-senses. Chef Eric Vernice (formerly of Troisgros in France) directs ten chefs in handcrafting each of eight courses from a huge range of rare, high-quality ingredients including caribou and pheasant. Add to this one of the most beautiful locations in North America and the result is a truly standout dining experience. Hrs: 5:30-11 pm. Res accepted. Wine list. Dinner $16-$50. Child's menu. Entertainment: jazz Mon-Sat. Cr cds: A, C, D, DS, ER, JCB, MC, V.
[D]

★★★ **LA RUA.** *4557 Blackcomb Way (V0N 1B0), in Le Chamois Hotel.* 604/932-5011. www.larua-restaurante. com. Specializes in Northwestern cuisine, seafood. Hrs: 6-9:30 pm. Res required. Bar. Wine cellar. Dinner $13.95-$29.95. Parking. Jacket. Formal dining in Mediterranean-style decor; many antiques. Cr cds: A, DS, MC, V.
[D]

★★ **RIMROCK CAFE.** *2117 Whistler Rd (V0N 1B0).* 604/932-5565. Email rimrock@direct.ca; www.rimrockwhistler. com. Specializes in fresh Northwest seafood, oysters. Hrs: 6-10 pm. Res accepted. Bar. Dinner $16-$25. Parking. Works of local artists. Built on and around a very large rock. Cr cds: A, D, ER, MC, V.

★★★ **RISTORANTE ARAXI.** *4222 Village Sq (V0N 1B4), Whistler Village Sq.* 604/932-4540. Email araxi@direct. ca; www.araxi.com. Specializes in fresh seafood, live lobster, local game. Own baking. Hrs: 10:30 am-10:30 pm; Sat, Sun to 11 pm. Res accepted. Bar. Wine list. Lunch a la carte entrees: $8-$14.95; dinner a la carte entrees: $10.50-$29.95. Mediterranean decor. Cr cds: A, D, MC, V.
[D]

★ **SUSHI VILLAGE.** *4272 Mountain Sq (V0N 1B4), Westbrook Hotel, 2nd fl.* 604/932-3330. Specializes in sushi, chicken teriyaki. Sushi bar. Hrs: 5:30-10 pm; off-season hrs vary. Closed Tues. Bar. Dinner complete meals: $7.95-$31.25. Entertainment. Tatami rms or traditional dining facilities. Cr cds: A, D, MC, V.
[D]

★★ **TRATTORIA DI UMBERTO.** *4417 Sundial Pl (V0N 1B0).* 604/932-5858. Specializes in rack of lamb, prawns sauteed in tomato and garlic sauce, Tuscan cuisine. Hrs: 11 am-2:30 pm, 5:30-10 pm. Res accepted. Bar. Lunch $5-$15; dinner $5-$26. Child's menu. Entertainment. Large mosaic tile imported from the Vatican. Cr cds: A, D, ER, MC, V.
[D]

★★★ **VAL D'ISERE.** *4314 Main St, #8 (V0N 1B0), St. Andrews House, 2nd fl.* 604/932-4666. Email valdisere@ direct.ca; www.valdisere-restaurant.com. Specializes in venison, Alsace-style onion pie. Hrs: 11 am-10 pm; winter hrs vary. Closed mid-Oct-mid-Nov. Res accepted. Wine list. Lunch $8.50-$15.50; dinner $14.50-$22.50. Overlooks large courtyard. Cr cds: A, D, ER, MC, V.
[D]

★★★ **WILDFLOWER RESTAURANT.** *4599 Chateau Blvd.* 604/938-2033. www.chateauwhistler.ca. Specializes in seafood. Hrs: 7 am-10 pm. Res accepted. Wine list. Lunch $13-$18; dinner $18-$42. Brunch $38. Child's menu. Entertainment. Cr cds: A, D, DS, ER, JCB, MC, V.
[D]

Unrated Dining Spot

SUSHI YA. *230-4370 Lorimer Rd (V0N 1B4).* 604/905-0155. Specializes in northern light sushi roll, blackcomb roll, whistler roll. Hrs: noon-10 pm; Sat, Sun 5-10 pm. Res accepted. Wine, beer. Lunch $7-$12; dinner $8-$13. Entertainment. Cr cds: A, DS, MC, V.
[D] [symbol]

PROVINCE OF MANITOBA

Manitoba is the most eastern of Canada's three prairie provinces. The capital city, Winnipeg, houses more than half of the province's population. Much of the remainder of the province is unspoiled recreational area. Entry into Manitoba can be made from Ontario on the east, Saskatchewan on the west, or from Minnesota and North Dakota on the south.

Many summer festivals are held that reflect the varied ethnic settlements in the province. Most representative of all ethnic backgrounds is Folklorama, a festival of the nations, which takes place in Winnipeg in August.

Pop 1,026,241 **Land area** 211,470 sq mi (547,705 sq km) **Capital** Winnipeg **Web** www.travelmanitoba.com

Information Travel Manitoba, Dept RK9, 155 Carlton St, 7th Floor, Winnipeg R3C 3H8; 204/945-3777 or 800/665-0040, ext RK9

Manitoba is also known for its 12 provincial parks and numerous recreation and heritage parks. Riding Mountain National Park is located near Dauphin. Fishing is good from May to September and water-related activities can be enjoyed in the many resorts and beaches on Lake Winnipeg, Lake Manitoba, and lakes in the provincial parks.

Outstanding attractions in Winnipeg include the zoo in Assiniboine Park, the Forks National Historic Site, the Manitoba Museum of Man and Nature, and the Winnipeg Art Gallery. The internationally acclaimed Royal Winnipeg Ballet, the Winnipeg Symphony Orchestra, the Manitoba Opera, and the Manitoba Theatre Centre have made Winnipeg a mecca for all who enjoy fine music and theater.

"Wheat City," Brandon

Manitoba observes Central Standard Time and Daylight Saving Time in summer.

In addition to national holidays, Manitoba observes Civic Holiday (first Monday August).

Seat belts are mandatory for all persons anywhere in vehicle. Children under 5 years or 50 pounds in weight must be in an approved safety seat anywhere in vehicle. For further information phone 204/945-4603.

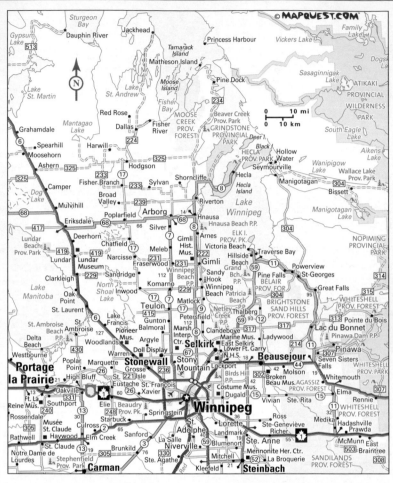

The La Verendrye Trail follows the path of the La Verendrye brothers, French explorers who traveled across central Canada and the United States in the 1780s on foot and canoe. The route begins along the east side of Lake Winnipeg, a portion of lake shore with an abundance of beaches. Grand Beach Provincial Park provides miles of sandy relaxation and swimming along the lake; the natural dunes tower nearly 30 feet. The route continues past more beach resorts and parks to the mouth of the Winnipeg River, part of the river "highway" system used by the early French voyagers. Turn to follow the river toward St. Georges, a French-speaking community along the river with a rebuilt fur-trading fort. At Seven Sisters Falls, turn and enter Whiteshell Provincial Park, which preserves thick spruce forests, rock-lined lakes, waterfalls, and the wildlife of the Great North Woods. In spring and summer, Alfred Hole Goose Sanctuary, near Rennie, is filled with young geese. Along park hiking trails, you may notice native petroforms, rock formations in the shape of snakes or turtles, constructed as sacred sites by early Native Americans. In the eastern portion of Whiteshell Park are more lakes, including Falcon Lake, with a number of excellent resorts and public beaches, and West Hawk Lake, which was formed by the impact of a meteorite. With a depth of 380 feet, the lake is popular with scuba divers.
(Approx 103 mi; 167 km.)

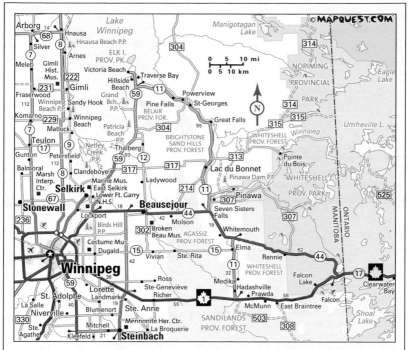

This route leaves Winnipeg to travel north along the western shores of Lake Winnipeg, the continent's seventh largest lake. The southern part of the lake is flanked by hardwood forests and is lined with beautiful white sand beaches. In the summer, provincial parks are popular with sunbathers, swimmers, and picnickers. Gimli, a small farming and fishing village, was settled almost exclusively by Icelandic settlers in the late 19th century; for many years it was capital of a semiautonomous region known as the Republic of New Iceland. The historic town still celebrates its Icelandic heritage in a series of summer festivals. An hour farther north is Hecla Island, also part of New Iceland, now preserved as Hecla/Grindstone Provincial Park. The island—which once was a fishing community—is linked to the mainland by a bridge and has a number of hiking trails through wildlife habitat. Nearby resorts rent canoes, cross-country skis, and other recreational gear. Island beaches are also popular for sunbathers and swimmers. **(Approx 73 miles; 117 km)**

Brandon (G-2)

Pop 42,000 (est) **Elev** 1,342 ft (409 m)
Area code 204
Web www.bedb.brandon.mb.ca

Information Brandon Economic Development Board, 1043 Rossler Ave, R7A 0L5; 204/728-3287 or 888/799-1111

Brandon has been named the "Wheat City" in honor of its rich agricultural heritage and reputation as a prosperous farming community. It is also the setting for the province's largest agricultural fairs.

What to See and Do

Commonwealth Air Training Plan Museum. Display of WWII aircraft, vehicles; photos, uniforms, flags, and other mementos of Air Force training conducted in Canada (1940-45) under the British Commonwealth Air Training Plan. (Daily) McGill Field, Hangar #1. Phone 204/727-2444. ¢¢

Annual Events

Royal Manitoba Winter Fair. Keystone Centre. Manitoba's largest winter fair. Equestrian events, heavy horses, entertainment. Late Mar.

Manitoba Summer Fair. Keystone Centre. Competition, children's entertainment, midway, dancing. June.

Manitoba Fall Fair. Keystone Centre. Manitoba's largest livestock show and sale; tractor pull, rodeo. Nov.

Motels/Motor Lodges

★★ **COLONIAL INN.** *1944 Queens Ave (R7B 0T1). 204/728-8532; fax 204/727-5969; toll-free 800/665-6373. Email colonial@westman.wave.ca; www.colonialinn.mb.ca.* 86 rms, 2 story, 1 suite. S $5195; D $62.95; suites $78.95. Crib avail. Pet accepted, some restrictions. Parking lot. Indoor pool, children's pool, whirlpool. TV; cable (premium), VCR avail. Complimentary coffee in rms, newspaper, toll-free calls. Restaurant 6 am-9 pm. Ck-out noon, ck-in 3 pm. Meeting rm. Business servs avail. Dry cleaning. Golf. Tennis. Downhill skiing. Hiking trail. Cr cds: A, D, DS, ER, MC, V.
🄳 🏊 🐕 🏊 🍴 🍽 🐾 🐕

★★ **COMFORT INN.** *925 Middleton Ave (R7C 1A8). 204/727-6232; fax 204/727-2246; res 800/228-5150. Email cn236@whgca.com; www.choicehotels.ca.* 81 rms, 2 story. Apr-Sep: S $85; D $95; each addl $10; under 18 free; lower rates rest of yr. Crib avail. Pet accepted, some restrictions. Parking lot. TV; cable (premium). Complimentary coffee in rms, newspaper, toll-free calls. Restaurant nearby. Ck-out 11 am, ck-in 2 pm. Business servs avail. Dry cleaning. Free airport transportation. Golf, 18 holes. Tennis, 4 courts. Downhill skiing. Picnic facilities. Cr cds: A, C, D, DS, ER, JCB, MC, V.
🄳 🏊 🐕 🍴 🏊 🍽 🐾 SC

★ **REDWOOD MOTOR INN.** *345 18th St N (R7A 6Z2). 204/728-2200; toll-free 877/728-2200.* 60 rms. S $51.95; D $61.95. Crib avail. TV; cable, VCR avail (movies). Indoor pool; whirlpool. Complimentary continental bkfst. Restaurant nearby. Ck-out noon. Business servs avail. In-rm modem link. Sundries. Cr cds: A, C, D, ER, MC, V.
🄳 🍽 🐾

★★ **ROYAL OAK INN.** *3130 Victoria Ave W (R7B 0N2). 204/728-5775; fax 204/726-5828; toll-free 800/852-2709.* 96 rms, 2 story. S $68.95-$78.95; D, suites $85.95-$95.95; each addl $10; package plans. Pet accepted. TV; cable, VCR avail (movies). Indoor pool; wading pool, whirlpool, poolside serv. Restaurant 7 am-10 pm; Sun 8 am-10 pm. Bar 11-2 am. Ck-out noon. Coin lndry. Meeting rms. Business servs avail. Valet serv. Sundries. Railroad station, bus depot transportation. Exercise equipt. Cr cds: A, C, D, ER, MC, V.
🄳 🏊 🍽 🏊 🍴 🐾 SC

Hotel

★★★ **VICTORIA INN.** *3550 Victoria Ave (R7B 2R4). 204/725-1532; fax 204/727-8282; res 204/725-1532. Email vicinn@mb.victoriainn.ca.* 121 rms, 2 story, 10 suites. Sep-Apr: S $82; D $89; suites $113; lower rates rest of yr. Crib avail. Pet accepted, some restrictions, fee. Parking lot. Indoor pool, whirlpool. TV; cable. Complimentary coffee in rms, newspaper, toll-free calls. Restaurant 7 am-11 pm. Bar. Ck-out noon, ck-in 2 pm. Meeting rms. Business servs avail. Dry cleaning. Exercise equipt, sauna. Golf, 18 holes. Video games. Cr cds: A, D, ER, MC, V.

🄳 🐾 🏗 ⛱ 🕴 🎿 ⤴ 🐾 SC

B&B/Small Inn

★ **THE CASTLE.** *149 2nd Ave SW (R0J 1E0). 204/867-2830; fax 204/ 867-5051. Email castlebb@escape.ca; www.minnedosa.com/castleeb&b.* 3 story, 4 suites. June-Aug: S $65; D $77; each addl $10; suites $99; lower rates rest of yr. Parking lot. TV; cable. Complimentary full bkfst, coffee in rms, newspaper. Restaurant nearby. Ck-out 11 am, ck-in 3 pm. Meeting rm. Gift shop. Golf, 9 holes. Tennis, 2 courts. Downhill skiing. Beach access. Supervised children's activities. Hiking trail. Picnic facilities. Cr cds: MC, V.

🛶 🎣 🏗 🎿 ⤴

Restaurant

★★★ **KOKONAS.** *1011 Rosser Ave (R7A 1A0), in Scotia Towers. 204/727-4395.* Specializes in steak, seafood. Salad bar. Own pastries. Hrs: 10:30 am-11:30 pm. Res accepted. Bar. Lunch $5.25-$10.95. Buffet: $7.95; dinner $8.95-$29.95. Nightly prime rib buffet. Cr cds: A, D, DS, MC, V.

🄳 SC ⤴

Turtle Mountain Provincial Park

See also Brandon, MB

(Adjacent to International Peace Garden on US-Canada border)

Turtle Mountain is one of Manitoba's smaller provincial parks, with 47,000 acres (19,020 hectares) of forested hills, ponds, and lakes. Its lakes provide a good environment for western painted turtle, beaver, muskrat, and mink. Arbor and Eagle islands have stands of elm, oak, and ash that have not been touched by fire, thereby remaining excellent examples of mature deciduous forests. Swimming, hiking trails, interpretive programs, fishing, and boating are available, as well as snowmobile and cross-country skiing trails and a winter day-use area at Lake Adam. Camping (primitive and improved) at Lake Adam, Lake William, and Lake Max campgrounds (hookups, dump stations).

Not far from the park is the town of Boissevain, where the annual Canadian Turtle Derby is held in mid-July. A large statue of Tommy Turtle welcomes the visitor at the south end of town. For further information phone 204/534-7204.

Winnipeg (G-4)

Pop 650,000 (est) **Elev** 915 ft (279 m)
Area code 204
Web www.tourism.winnipeg.mb.ca
Information Tourism Winnipeg, 279 Portage Rd, R3B 2B4; 204/943-1970 or 800/665-0204

Winnipeg, the provincial capital, is situated in the heart of the continent and combines the sophistication and friendliness of east and west. The city offers much for any visitor, including relaxing cruises on the Assiniboine and Red rivers, Rainbow Stage summer theater in Kildonan Park, the Manitoba Theatre Centre, the Winnipeg Symphony, the Manitoba Opera, and the renowned Royal Winnipeg Ballet. Sports fans will enjoy the Blue Bombers in football and the Manitoba Moose hockey team. Shopping, nightlife, gourmet restaurants—Winnipeg has it all.

What to See and Do

Assiniboine Park. A 376-acre (152-hectare) park features colorful English and formal gardens; the Leo Mol Sculpture Garden; conservatory with floral displays; duck pond; playgrounds; picnic sites; cricket and field hockey area; refreshment pavilion; miniature train; bicycle paths; fitness trail. **Assiniboine Park Zoo** has collection of rare and endangered species, tropical mammals, birds and reptiles; children's discovery area featuring variety of young

Winnipeg

© MAPQUEST.COM

animals (daily). Park (daily). 2355 Corydon Ave. Phone 204/986-3989. **FREE**

Birds Hill Provincial Park. A 8,275-acre (3,350-hectare) park situated on a glacial formation called an *eskar.* Large population of whitetail deer; many orchid species. Interpretive, hiking, bridle, and bicycle trails; snowshoe, snowmobile, and cross-country skiing trails (winter). Interpretive programs. Swimming; camping and picnicking at 81½ acre (33-hectare) lake (seasonal). Riding stables (phone 204/222-1137). (Daily) 8 mi N on Hwy 59. Phone 204/222-9151. Per vehicle (May-Sep) ¢¢

★ **Centennial Centre.** Complex incl concert hall, planetarium, Museum of Man and Nature, Manitoba Theatre Centre Bldg. 555 Main St. Phone 204/956-1360 for free tours of concert hall. Here are

Manitoba Museum of Man & Nature. Seven galleries interpret Manitoba's human and natural history: Orientation; Earth History (geological background); Grasslands (prairie); Arctic-Subarctic; Boreal Forest; *Nonsuch* (full-size replica of a 17th-century ship); and Urban. (Victoria Day-Labour Day, daily; rest of yr, Tues-Sun) 190 Rupert Ave. Phone 204/956-2830 or 204/943-3139 (program information). ¢¢ Also here is

Manitoba Planetarium. Circular, multipurpose audiovisual theater. Wide variety of shows; subjects incl UFOs, cosmic catastrophes, and the edge of the universe. In the **Touch the Universe Gallery,** visitors can learn about science through hands-on exhibits (separate admission fee). (Same days as museum) Phone 204/943-3142 (recording). ¢¢

"Dalnavert." Restored Victorian residence (1895) of Sir Hugh John Macdonald, premier of Manitoba, depicting lifestyle and furnishings of the period. Gift shop. Guided tours (Mar-Dec, Tues-Thurs, Sat and Sun;

rest of yr, Sat and Sun only) 61 Carlton St. Phone 204/943-2835. ¢¢

The Forks National Historic Site. Situated on 56 acres at the confluence of the Red and Assiniboine rivers. Riverside promenade; walkways throughout. Historical exhibits, heritage theater, children's programs, playground; evening performances. Special events. (May-Sep, daily) Grounds (all yr). Adj area open in winter for skating, x-country skiing. Pioneer Blvd, opp Water & Pioneer Aves at Provencher Bridge. Phone 204/983-2007 or 204/983-5988. **FREE**

Legislative Building. Example of neoclassical architecture. Grounds contain statues of Queen Victoria, Lord Selkirk, George Cartier. Tours (June-Aug, Mon-Fri; Sep-June, by appt) Broadway & Osborne. Phone 204/945-5813. **FREE**

Lower Fort Garry National Historic Site. Hudson's Bay Co fur trade post restored to the 1850s. Original bldgs; blacksmith shop, farmhouse, Ross cottage, furloft, Governor's house, sales shop; indigenous encampment. Visitor center with exhibits and artifacts of the fur trade society; costumed tour guides. Restaurant, gift shop. (Mid-May-Labour Day, daily) 20 mi (32 km) N on Hwy 9. Phone 204/785-6050. ¢¢

Oak Hammock Marsh Wildlife Management Area. More than 8,000 acres (3,238 hectares) of marshland and grassland wildlife habitat. Attracts up to 300,000 ducks and geese during spring (Apr-mid-May) and fall migration (Sep-Oct). nature trails; picnic sites, marsh boardwalk, viewing mounds, drinking water. Conservation center with displays, interpretive programs (daily; fee). 14 mi (23 km) N via Hwy 7 or 8, then 5 mi (8 km) to Hwy 67. Phone 204/945-6784. **FREE**

Ross House. (1854) Oldest bldg in the original city of Winnipeg; first post office in western Canada. Displays and period-furnished rms depict daily life in the Red River Settlement. (Mid-May-Labour Day, Wed-Sun) 140 Meade St N, between Euclid & Sutherland Aves. Phone 204/943-3958 or 204/947-0559. **FREE**

Royal Canadian Mint. (1976) One of the world's most modern mints; striking glass tower, landscaped interior courtyard. Tour allows viewing of coining process; coin museum. (Early May-late Aug, Mon-Fri; closed hols) 520 Lagimodière Blvd. Phone 204/257-3359. ¢

St.-Boniface Museum. (1846) Housed in oldest structure in the city, dating to the days of the Red River Colony; largest oak log construction in North America. 494 Ave Taché. Phone 204/237-4500.

Seven Oaks House Museum. Oldest habitable house in Manitoba (1851). Log construction, original furnishings, housewares. Adjoining bldgs incl general store, post office. (Mid-June-Sep, daily; mid-May-mid-June, Sat and Sun) Rupertsland Ave, in West Kildonan area. Phone 204/339-7429 or 204/986-3031. ¢

Sightseeing tours.

Paddlewheel/Gray Line/River Rouge boat & bus tours. Floating restaurant, moonlight dance and sightseeing cruises (May-Sep); also guided tours on double-decker buses. Bus/cruise combinations avail. Contact PO Box 3930, Postal Station B, R2W 5H9. Phone 204/942-4500. ¢¢-¢¢¢¢

Winnipeg Art Gallery. Canada's first civic gallery (1912). Eight galleries present changing exhibitions of contemporary, historical, and decorative art, plus North America's largest collection of Inuit art. (Summer, daily; rest of yr, Tues-Sun; closed hols) Programming incl tours, lectures, films, concerts. Cafeteria. 300 Memorial Blvd. Phone 204/786-6641. ¢¢

Annual Events

Festival du Voyageur. In St.-Boniface, Winnipeg's "French Quarter." Winter festival celebrating the French-Canadian voyageur and the fur trade era. Phone 204/237-7692. Ten days mid-Feb.

Red River Exhibition. Large event encompassing grandstand shows, band competitions, displays, agricultural exhibits, parade, entertainment, midway, petting zoo, shows, food. Late June-early July. Phone 204/888-6990.

Winnipeg Folk Festival. More than 100 regional, national, and intl

Legislative Building, Winnipeg

artists perform; 9 stages; children's village; evening concerts. Juried crafts exhibit and sale; intl food village. Birds Hill Provincial Park, 8 mi N on Hwy 59. Phone 204/780-3333. Early July.

Folklorama. Multicultural festival featuring up to 40 pavilions. Singing, dancing, food, cultural displays. Aug. Pavilions throughout city. Phone 204/982-6210 or 800/665-0234.

Seasonal Events

Winnipeg Symphony Orchestra. Classical, pops, and children's concerts. Sep-May. Centennial Concert Hall. Phone 204/949-3999 (box office).

Canada's Royal Winnipeg Ballet. Centennial Concert Hall. Performs mix of classical and contemporary ballets. Oct-May. Phone 204/956-2792.

Manitoba Opera Association. Nov-May. Portage Place. Phone 204/942-7479.

Motels/Motor Lodges

★★ **BEST WESTERN INTERNA-TIONAL INN.** *1808 Wellington Ave (R3H 0G3), near Intl Airport. 204/786-4801; fax 204/786-1329; res 800/528-1234; toll-free 800/928-4067. Email*

reservations@internationalinn.mb.ca. 288 rms, 5 story. S $78; D $83; each addl $5; suites $175; under 16 free; wkend rates. Crib $5. Pet accepted. TV; cable, VCR avail (movies free). 2 pools, 1 indoor; whirlpool, sauna, poolside serv. Restaurant 7 am-midnight. Bar 11:30-2 am. Ck-out 2 pm. Meeting rms. Business servs avail. In-rm modem link. Bellhops. Gift shop. Free airport transportation. Game rm. Some refrigerators. Cr cds: A, DS, MC, V.

⊛ ✈ ⊠ ⊠ 🔥 SC

★★ **COMFORT INN.** *1770 Sargent Ave (R3H 0C8), near Intl Airport. 204/783-5627; fax 204/783-5661; res 800/228-5150. www.hotelchoice.com.* 81 rms, 2 story. Mid-June-mid-Sep: S $57.99-$63.99; D $65.99-$71.99; each addl $4; under 18 free; wkend rates; lower rates rest of yr. Crib free. Pet accepted. TV; cable. Complimentary coffee in lobby. Continental bkfst avail. Restaurant nearby. Ck-out 11 am. Business servs avail. In-rm modem link. Valet serv. Cr cds: A, C, D, DS, MC, V.

D ⊛ ⊠ ⊠ ⊠ ⊠

★★ **COUNTRY INN AND SUITES.** *730 King Edward St (R3H 1B4), near Intl Airport. 204/783-6900; fax 204/*

775-7197; res 800/456-4000. 77 units, 3 story, 36 suites. S $65-$95; D $75-$105; each addl $10; under 18 free; wkend rates. Crib free. Pet accepted, some restrictions. TV; cable (premium), VCR (free movies). Complimentary coffee in rms, continental bkfst. Restaurant adj 7 am-11 pm. Ck-out noon. Coin lndry. Business servs avail. Sundries. Valet serv. Refrigerators. Cr cds: A, C, D, DS, MC, V.

[icons]

★ **HOWARD JOHNSON HOTEL.** *1740 Ellice Ave (R2K 0R2), near Intl Airport. 204/775-7131; fax 204/788-4685; res 800/446-4656; toll-free 800/665-8813. www.hojo.com.* 155 rms, 5 story. S, D $54-$72; each addl $5; under 16 free; wkend rates; package plans. Crib $5. TV; cable, VCR avail. Sauna. Indoor pool; whirlpool, poolside serv. Complimentary continental bkfst. Restaurant 7 am-11 pm. Bar 11-1 am; entertainment. Ck-out 1 pm. Coin lndry. Meeting rms. Business servs avail. Bellhops. Valet serv. Sundries. Gift shop. Free airport transportation. Cr cds: A, DS, MC.

[icons] **SC**

Hotels

★★ **CHARTER HOUSE.** *330 York Ave (R3C 0N9). 204/942-0101; fax 204/956-0665; toll-free 800/782-0175.* 90 rms, 5 story. S, D $75-$125; under 18 free; wkly, wkend rates. Crib avail. Pet accepted. TV; cable, VCR avail (movies). Heated pool; poolside serv. Restaurant 7 am-11 pm. Bar 11-1 am. Ck-out noon. Meeting rms. Business servs avail. In-rm modem link. Health club privileges. Balconies. Cr cds: A, C, D, DS, MC, V.

[icons]

★★ **DELTA WINNIPEG.** *350 St. Mary Ave (R3C 3J2). 204/942-0551; fax 204/942-6491. www.deltahotels. com.* 389 rms, 18 story. S $155; D $165; each addl $15; suites $195-$485; under 20 free. Crib avail. TV; cable (premium). 2 pools, 1 indoor; whirlpool; wading pool, lifeguard. Complimentary coffee in rm. Restaurants 6:30-1 am. 24-hr rm serv. Ck-out 1 pm. Coin lndry. Meeting rms. Business center. In-rm modem link. Airport transportation. Exercise rm;

sauna. Refrigerators. Balconies. Luxury level. Cr cds: A, DS, MC, V.

[icons]

★★ **HOLIDAY INN.** *1330 Pembina Hwy (R3T 2B4). 204/452-4747; fax 204/284-2751; res 800/465-4239; toll-free 800/423-1337. Email hiws@ gatewest.net; www.hi-winnipeg.mb.ca.* 169 rms, 11 story, 1 suite. S $159; D $169; each addl $10; suites $310; under 19 free. Crib avail. Pet accepted. Parking garage. Indoor pool, children's pool, whirlpool. TV; cable (premium), VCR avail, CD avail. Complimentary coffee in rms, newspaper, toll-free calls. Restaurant. Bar. Ck-out noon, ck-in 3 pm. Meeting rms. Business center. Bellhops. Dry cleaning, coin lndry. Free airport transportation. Golf, 18 holes. Tennis, 5 courts. Supervised children's activities. Cr cds: A, C, D, DS, ER, JCB, MC, V.

[icons]

★★ **HOLIDAY INN AIRPORT WEST.** *2520 Portage Ave (R3J 3T6). 204/885-4478; fax 204/831-5734; res 800/HOLIDAY. www.holidayinn.airport west.com.* 226 rms, 15 story, 8 kits. S $139; D $149; each addl $10; suites $145-$186; under 19 free; wkend rates. Crib free. TV; cable. Indoor pool; wading pool, whirlpool, poolside serv, lifeguard. Supervised children's activities, ages 3-11. Coffee in rms. Restaurant 6:30 am-11 pm. Bar 11:30-2 am; entertainment. Ck-out 1 pm. Coin lndry. Meeting rms. Business center. In-rm modem link. Free airport transportation. Game rm. Exercise equipt; sauna. Some minibars; refrigerators. Some balconies. Cr cds: A, D, DS, ER, JCB, MC, V.

[icons]

★★★ **RADISSON DOWNTOWN.** *288 Portage Ave (R3C 0B8). 204/956-0410; fax 204/947-1129; res 800/333-3333. www.radisson.com.* 272 rms, 29 story. S, D $129-$199; each addl $15; suites $229; under 18 free; wkend rates. Crib free. Pet accepted. Garage parking $3.75-$7; valet $3. TV; cable (premium), VCR avail (movies). Indoor pool; poolside serv. Supervised children's activities. Coffee in rms. Restaurant 6:30 am-10 pm; Sat, Sun from 7 am. Rm serv 24 hrs. Bars 11:30-1 am. Ck-out 1 pm. Meeting rms. Business center. In-rm modem link. Concierge. Gift shop. Exercise equipt; sauna. Minibars. Cr cds: A, D, DS, ER, JCB, MC, V.

[D] [symbols]

★★★ SHERATON WINNIPEG HOTEL. *161 Donald St (R3C 1M3). 204/942-5300; fax 204/943-7975; res 800/463-6400. Email reservations@ sheratonwinnipeg.mb.ca.* 266 rms, 21 story. S $130-$145; D $140-$155; each addl $15; under 18 free; wkend rates. Crib free. Pet accepted. Underground parking, valet $7.50/day. TV; cable (premium). Indoor pool; whirlpool, poolside serv. Coffee in rms. Restaurant 6:30 am-11 pm. Rm serv 24 hrs. Bar 11-1 am. Ck-out noon. Convention facilities. Business servs avail. In-rm modem link. Concierge. Gift shop. Airport transportation avail. Sauna. Health club privileges. Many refrigerators. Many balconies. Cr cds: A, D, DS, MC, V.

[D] [symbols]

All Suite

★★★ RADISSON SUITE HOTEL WINNIPEG AIRPORT. *1800 Wellington Ave (R3H 1B2), near Intl Airport. 204/783-1700; fax 204/786-6588; res 800/333-3333. Email radwinn@mb. sympatico.ca; www.radisson.com/ winnipegca_airport.* 6 story, 149 suites. Suites $195; under 17 free. Crib avail. Parking lot. Indoor/outdoor pools, whirlpool. TV; cable (premium), VCR avail. Complimentary full bkfst, coffee in rms, newspaper, toll-free calls. Restaurant 7 am-10 pm. 24-hr rm serv. Bar. Ck-out noon, ck-in 3 pm. Meeting rms. Business servs avail. Bellhops. Concierge. Dry cleaning. Gift shop. Free airport transportation. Exercise equipt, sauna. Golf. Tennis. Video games. Cr cds: A, D, DS, ER, MC, V.

[D] [symbols] [SC]

Restaurants

★★ AMICI. *326 Broadway (R3C 0S5). 204/943-4997.* Specializes in venison, veal, wild boar. Hrs: 11:30 am-2 pm, 5-10 pm; Sat from 5 pm. Closed Sun; hols. Res accepted. Bar. Lunch $6-$14.75; dinner $14.50-$36. Child's menu. Contemporary decor. Cr cds: A, D, DS, MC, V.

[D] [symbol]

★★ HY'S STEAK LOFT. *216 Kennedy (R3C 1T1). 204/942-1000.* Specializes in steak, seafood. Hrs: 4-11 pm; Fri, Sat 5 pm-midnight; Sun 5-9 pm. Closed hols. Res accepted. Bar. Wine list. Dinner $17-$31. Bi-level dining. Old English decor. Cr cds: A, D, ER, MC, V.

[symbol]

★★ ICHIBAN JAPANESE STEAKHOUSE AND SUSHI BAR. *189 Carlton St (R3C 3H8). 204/925-7400.* Specializes in Imperial dinner, Empress dinner, sushi. Hrs: 4:30-10 pm; Fri, Sat to 10:30 pm. Closed hols. Res accepted. Bar. Dinner $14.95-$28.95. Teppanyaki cooking. Japanese garden atmosphere. Cr cds: A, D, DS, MC, V.

[D] [SC] [symbol]

ATTRACTION LIST

Attraction names are listed in alphabetical order followed by a symbol identifying their classification and then city. The symbols for classification are: [A] for Annual Events, [S] for Seasonal Events, and [W] for What to See and Do.

1838 Mountain Man Rendezvous [A] *Riverton, WY*
"62" Day Celebration [A] *John Day, OR*
Aberdeen Museum of History [W] *Aberdeen, WA*
A.C. Gilbert's Discovery Village [W] *Salem, OR*
A Contemporary Theater (ACT) [S] *Seattle, WA*
Adam East Museum [W] *Moses Lake, WA*
Adams County Fair [A] *Othello, WA*
Aerial Fire Depot [W] *Missoula, MT*
Aerial Tramway [W] *Jackson, WY*
Ag Expo [A] *Spokane, WA*
"Ag-Expo" Agricultural Exposition [A] *Lethbridge, AB*
Agriculture Canada Research Station [W] *Penticton, BC*
Agriculture-Farm Show [A] *Kalispell, MT*
Ahtanum Mission [W] *Yakima, WA*
Alberta Birds of Prey Centre [W] *Lethbridge, AB*
Alberta Legislature Building [W] *Edmonton, AB*
Albertson College of Idaho [W] *Caldwell, ID*
Alder House II [W] *Lincoln City, OR*
Alexander Blockhouse [W] *Coupeville, WA*
Alki Beach [W] *Seattle, WA*
All Rockhounds Powwow Gem & Mineral Show [A] *Madras, OR*
Alpental [W] *North Bend, WA*
Alta Lake [W] *Chelan, WA*
Amazing May [A] *Grants Pass, OR*
American Advertising Museum [W] *Portland, OR*
American Falls Dam [W] *American Falls, ID*
American Heritage Center and Art Museum [W] *Laramie, WY*
American League baseball (Seattle Mariners) [W] *Seattle, WA*
American Musical Jubilee [A] *Ontario, OR*

Amfac Parks & Resorts, Inc [W] *West Yellowstone, MT*
Anaconda's Old Works [W] *Anaconda, MT*
Anna Miller Museum [W] *Newcastle, WY*
Annual Moon Tree Country Run [A] *Cave Junction, OR*
Anthony Lakes Ski Area [W] *Baker City, OR*
Ape Cave [W] *Mount St. Helens National Volcanic Monument, WA*
Appaloosa Museum & Heritage Center [W] *Moscow, ID*
Apple Blossom Festival [A] *Chelan, WA*
Apple Days [A] *Cashmere, WA*
Archie Bray Foundation, The [W] *Helena, MT*
Argosy Harbor Cruise [W] *Seattle, WA*
Armed Forces Day Parade [A] *Bremerton, WA*
Armitage County Park [W] *Eugene, OR*
Arroyo Park [W] *Bellingham, WA*
Art Gallery of Greater Victoria [W] *Victoria, BC*
Art on the Green [A] *Coeur d'Alene, ID*
Arts Chateau [W] *Butte, MT*
Arts in the Park [A] *Shoshone, ID*
Asotin County Fair [A] *Clarkston, WA*
Asotin County Museum [W] *Clarkston, WA*
Assiniboine Park [W] *Winnipeg, MB*
Astoria Column [W] *Astoria, OR*
Astoria Hot Springs [W] *Jackson, WY*
Astoria Regatta [A] *Astoria, OR*
Astoria-Warrenton Crab & Seafood Festival [A] *Astoria, OR*
Auto racing [S] *Everett, WA*
Auto tour [W] *Wallace, ID*
Auto tours [W] *Lewiston, ID*
Autumn Leaf Festival [A] *Leavenworth, WA*
Avalanche Creek [W] *Glacier National Park, MT*
Avery Park [W] *Corvallis, OR*

Awesome Autumn Festival [S] *Mount Vernon, WA*

Azalea Festival [A] *Brookings, OR*

Azalea Park [W] *Brookings, OR*

Bach Festival [A] *Eugene, OR*

Balanced Rock [W] *Buhl, ID*

Bald Eagle Conference [A] *Klamath Falls, OR*

Balloon Roundup [A] *Miles City, MT*

Bandon Museum [W] *Bandon, OR*

Banff Festival of the Arts [S] *Banff, AB*

Bannack Days [A] *Dillon, MT*

Bannack State Park [W] *Dillon, MT*

Bannock County Fair and Rodeo [A] *Pocatello, ID*

Bannock County Historical Museum [W] *Pocatello, ID*

Barbershop Ballad Contest [A] *Forest Grove, OR*

Barbershop Concert and Salmon Barbecue [A] *Anacortes, WA*

Barker-Ewing Float Trips [W] *Jackson, WY*

Basque Museum and Cultural Center [W] *Boise, ID*

Bastion [W] *Nanaimo, BC*

Battle Rock Wayside [W] *Port Orford, OR*

Bavarian Ice Fest [A] *Leavenworth, WA*

Bay Area Fun Festival [A] *Coos Bay, OR*

Bay View State Park [W] *Mount Vernon, WA*

BC Forest Discovery Centre [W] *Victoria, BC*

Beacon Hill Park [W] *Victoria, BC*

Beardale Castle Miniatureland [W] *Revelstoke, BC*

Bear Lake [W] *Montpelier, ID*

Bear Lake County Fair and Rodeo [A] *Montpelier, ID*

Bear Lake State Park [W] *Montpelier, ID*

Bear's Paw Battleground [W] *Chinook, MT*

Beartooth Highway (National Forest Scenic Byway) [W] *Red Lodge, MT*

Beaver Creek Loop Tour [W] *Newcastle, WY*

Beaver Creek Park [W] *Havre, MT*

Beaver Dick [W] *Rexburg, ID*

Beaverhead County Fair [A] *Dillon, MT*

Beaverhead County Museum [W] *Dillon, MT*

Beaverhead National Forest [W] *Dillon, MT*

Beekman House [W] *Jacksonville, OR*

Belfair [W] *Bremerton, WA*

Bellevue Art Museum [W] *Bellevue, WA*

Bellevue Botanical Garden [W] *Bellevue, WA*

Belly River Country [W] *Glacier National Park, MT*

Benewah, Round, and Chatcolet lakes [W] *St. Marie's, ID*

Benson State Recreation Area [W] *Portland, OR*

Benton County Fair and Rodeo [A] *Corvallis, OR*

Benton County Historical Museum [W] *Corvallis, OR*

Benton-Franklin Fair and Rodeo [A] *Richland, WA*

Berkeley Pit [W] *Butte, MT*

Beverly Beach [W] *Newport, OR*

Big Arm Unit [W] *Polson, MT*

Bigfork Art & Cultural Center [W] *Bigfork, MT*

Bigfork Summer Playhouse [S] *Bigfork, MT*

Big game hunting [W] *Dubois, WY*

Big Hole Basin [W] *Anaconda, MT*

Big Hole National Battlefield [W] *Anaconda, MT*

Big Hole National Battlefield [W] *Hamilton, MT*

Bighorn Canyon National Recreation Area [W] *Hardin, MT*

Bighorn Canyon National Recreation Area [W] *Lovell, WY*

Bighorn National Forest [W] *Sheridan, WY*

Big Mountain Ski and Summer Resort [W] *Whitefish, MT*

Big Sky Ski and Summer Resort [W] *Big Sky (Gallatin County), MT*

Big Sky Water Slide [W] *Columbia Falls, MT*

Big Spring Creek [W] *Lewistown, MT*

Big Springs [W] *Ashton, ID*

Big Wheel [W] *Newport, WA*

Bingham County Historical Museum [W] *Blackfoot, ID*

Birch Bay State Park [W] *Blaine, WA*

Birds Hill Provincial Park [W] *Winnipeg, MB*

Bitterroot National Forest [W] *Hamilton, MT*

Blackberry Arts Festival [A] *Coos Bay, OR*

Blackberry Festival [A] *Bremerton, WA*

Blackcomb [W] *Whistler, BC*

Blackfoot Pride Days [A] *Blackfoot, ID*

Blackman Museum [W] *Snohomish, WA*

Black Mountain Rodeo [A] *Kelowna, BC*

Blaine County Fair [A] *Chinook, MT*

Blaine County Museum [W] *Chinook, MT*

Blake Island [W] *Bremerton, WA*

Bloedel Donovan Park [W] *Bellingham, WA*
Bloomington Lake [W] *Montpelier, ID*
Blossom Festival [A] *Hood River, OR*
Blue River Dam & Lake [W] *McKenzie Bridge, OR*
Blue Rock Products Company-Pepsi Cola Bottling Plant [W] *Sidney, MT*
BluesFest [A] *Ritzville, WA*
Boat cruise. Maligne Tours, Ltd [W] *Jasper National Park, AB*
Boathouse Marina [W] *Tacoma, WA*
Boating [W] *Burley, ID*
Boatnik Festival [A] *Grants Pass, OR*
Boat tours [W] *Everett, WA*
Boehm's Chocolate Factory [W] *Issaquah, WA*
Boeing Everett Facility [W] *Everett, WA*
Bogachiel State Park [W] *Forks, WA*
Bogus Basin Ski Resort [W] *Boise, ID*
Bohemia Mining Days Celebration [A] *Cottage Grove, OR*
Boise Art Museum [W] *Boise, ID*
Boise Basin Museum [W] *Idaho City, ID*
Boise National Forest [W] *Boise, ID*
Boise National Forest [W] *Idaho City, ID*
Boise River Festival [A] *Boise, ID*
Boise Tour Train [W] *Boise, ID*
Bon Apetit [A] *Leavenworth, WA*
Bonner County Historical Society Museum [W] *Sandpoint, ID*
Bonneville Lock & Dam [W] *Hood River, OR*
Bonneville Museum [W] *Idaho Falls, ID*
Boot Hill [W] *Idaho City, ID*
Boot Hill [W] *Virginia City, MT*
Boothill Cemetery [W] *Billings, MT*
Border Days [A] *Grangeville, ID*
Borst Blockhouse [W] *Centralia, WA*
Boulevard Park [W] *Bellingham, WA*
Bowdoin National Wildlife Refuge [W] *Malta, MT*
Bowen Park [W] *Nanaimo, BC*
Boysen State Park [W] *Thermopolis, WY*
Bradford Brinton Memorial [W] *Sheridan, WY*
Bremerton Naval Museum [W] *Bremerton, WA*
Bridger Bowl Ski Area [W] *Bozeman, MT*
Bridger Raptor Festival [A] *Bozeman, MT*
Bridger-Teton National Forest [W] *Afton, WY*

Bridger-Teton National Forest [W] *Jackson, WY*
Bridger-Teton National Forest [W] *Pinedale, WY*
Bridger Wilderness [W] *Pinedale, WY*
British Columbia Ferry Corp [W] *Vancouver, BC*
British Columbia Square Dance Jamboree [A] *Penticton, BC*
Britt Musical Festivals [S] *Jacksonville, OR*
Brooks Memorial State Park [W] *Goldendale, WA*
Brownlee Dam [W] *Weiser, ID*
Brundage Mountain Ski Area [W] *McCall, ID*
Bruneau Canyon [W] *Mountain Home, ID*
Bucking Horse Sale [A] *Miles City, MT*
Buffalo Bill Dam and Visitor Center [W] *Cody, WY*
Buffalo Bill Festival [A] *Cody, WY*
Buffalo Bill Historical Center [W] *Cody, WY*
Buffalo Bill Museum [W] *Cody, WY*
Buffalo Bill State Park [W] *Cody, WY*
Buffalo Bus Lines [W] *West Yellowstone, MT*
Bullards Beach State Park [W] *Bandon, OR*
Burnaby Art Gallery [W] *Vancouver, BC*
Burnaby Village Museum [W] *Vancouver, BC*
Bush Barn Art Center [W] *Salem, OR*
Bush House [W] *Salem, OR*
Butchart Gardens [W] *Victoria, BC*
Butte Creek Mill [W] *Medford, OR*
Buzzard Day [A] *Glendive, MT*
C & M Stables [W] *Florence, OR*
Calaway Park [W] *Calgary, AB*
Caldwell Exchange Youth Rodeo [A] *Caldwell, ID*
Calgary Centre for Performing Arts [W] *Calgary, AB*
Calgary Science Centre [W] *Calgary, AB*
Calgary Stampede [A] *Calgary, AB*
Calgary Tower [W] *Calgary, AB*
Calgary Winter Festival [A] *Calgary, AB*
Calgary Zoo, Botanical Garden & Prehistoric Park, The [W] *Calgary, AB*
Callahan Ridge Winery [W] *Roseburg, OR*
Camping [W] *Mount Rainier National Park, WA*
Camping [W] *Mount St. Helens National Volcanic Monument, WA*

Camping [W] *Olympic National Park, WA*

Camping. Libby Ranger District; [W] *Libby, MT*

Camp Putt Adventure Golf Park [W] *Eugene, OR*

Camp Six Logging Exhibit (Western Forest Industries Museum) [W] *Tacoma, WA*

Canada Olympic Park [W] *Calgary, AB*

Canada's Aviation Hall of Fame [W] *Edmonton, AB*

Canada's Royal Winnipeg Ballet [S] *Winnipeg, MB*

Canadian Finals Rodeo [A] *Edmonton, AB*

Canyon County Fair [A] *Caldwell, ID*

Canyon County Historical Society Museum [W] *Nampa, ID*

Canyon Ferry State Park [W] *Helena, MT*

Canyon Ski Area [W] *Red Deer, AB*

Cape Arago [W] *Coos Bay, OR*

Cape Blanco State Park [W] *Port Orford, OR*

Cape Lookout State Park [W] *Tillamook, OR*

Cape Perpetua Campground [W] *Yachats, OR*

Cape Perpetua Visitor Center [W] *Yachats, OR*

Cape Sebastian State Park [W] *Gold Beach, OR*

Capes Scenic Loop Drive to Cape Meares and Oceanside [W] *Tillamook, OR*

Capilano Suspension Bridge & Park [W] *Vancouver, BC*

Capital City Marathon and Relay [A] *Olympia, WA*

Capital City Tally-Ho & Sightseeing Company [W] *Victoria, BC*

Capitol grounds [W] *Olympia, WA*

Capitol Lake [W] *Olympia, WA*

Capitol Mall [W] *Salem, OR*

Carbon County Fair and Rodeo [A] *Rawlins, WY*

Carbon County Museum [W] *Rawlins, WY*

Carbon River [W] *Mount Rainier National Park, WA*

Caribou National Forest [W] *Montpelier, ID*

Caribou National Forest [W] *Pocatello, ID*

Carillon [W] *Victoria, BC*

Carkeek Park [W] *Seattle, WA*

Carl G. Washburne Memorial [W] *Florence, OR*

Carmen-Smith Hydroelectric Development [W] *McKenzie Bridge, OR*

Carr House [W] *Victoria, BC*

Cascade Dam Reservoir [W] *McCall, ID*

Cascade Park [W] *Moses Lake, WA*

Casper Mountain and Beartrap Meadow Parks [W] *Casper, WY*

Casper Planetarium [W] *Casper, WY*

Cassia County Fair & Rodeo [A] *Burley, ID*

Cassia County Historical Museum [W] *Burley, ID*

Castle Museum [W] *Lewiston, ID*

Cathedral of St. Helena [W] *Helena, MT*

Cathedral of St. John the Evangelist [W] *Spokane, WA*

Catherine Creek State Park [W] *La Grande, OR*

Cave & Basin Centennial Centre [W] *Banff, AB*

CCInc Auto Tape Tours [W] *Banff, AB*

Celilo Converter Station [W] *The Dalles, OR*

Celilo Park [W] *The Dalles, OR*

Centennial Centre [W] *Winnipeg, MB*

Centennial Square [W] *Victoria, BC*

Center House [W] *Seattle, WA*

Central Montana Horse Show, Fair, Rodeo [A] *Lewistown, MT*

Central Washington State Fair and Rodeo [A] *Yakima, WA*

Central Washington Univ [W] *Ellensburg, WA*

Central Wyoming Fair and Rodeo [A] *Casper, WY*

Challis National Forest [W] *Challis, ID*

Chamber Music in the Cascades [A] *Leavenworth, WA*

Chamber Music Northwest [S] *Portland, OR*

Champoeg State Historic Area [W] *Newberg, OR*

Chariot Races [S] *Jerome, ID*

Charles and Emma Frye Art Museum [W] *Seattle, WA*

Charles M. Russell National Wildlife Refuge [W] *Lewistown, MT*

Charleston Marina Complex [W] *Coos Bay, OR*

Charlie Russell Chew-Choo [S] *Lewistown, MT*

Chateau Lorane Winery [W] *Cottage Grove, OR*

Chateau Ste. Michelle [W] *Bellevue, WA*

Chelan County Fair [A] *Cashmere, WA*

Chelan County Historical Museum [W] *Cashmere, WA*

Cheney Cowles Museum [W] *Spokane, WA*

Cheney Historical Museum [W] *Cheney, WA*

Cherry Festival [A] *The Dalles, OR*

Cheyenne Botanic Gardens [W] *Cheyenne, WY*

Cheyenne Frontier Days [A] *Cheyenne, WY*

Cheyenne Frontier Days Old West Museum [W] *Cheyenne, WY*

Cheyenne Street Trolley [W] *Cheyenne, WY*

Chief Black Otter Trail [W] *Billings, MT*

Chief Joseph Days [A] *Joseph, OR*

Chief Victor Days [A] *Hamilton, MT*

Children's Museum [W] *Portland, OR*

Children's Museum [W] *Spokane, WA*

Chili Cook-off [A] *Evanston, WY*

Chinatown [W] *Vancouver, BC*

Chocolate Fantasy [A] *Yakima, WA*

Chouteau County Fair [A] *Fort Benton, MT*

Christmas Dickens Festival [A] *Kellogg, ID*

Christmas events [A] *Vancouver, BC*

Christmas Lighting [A] *Leavenworth, WA*

Chuckanut Drive [W] *Bellingham, WA*

Chugwater Chili Cookoff [A] *Wheatland, WY*

Citadel Theatre [W] *Edmonton, AB*

City of Rocks National Reserve [W] *Burley, ID*

City recreation areas [W] *Bellingham, WA*

Civic Field Athletic Complex [W] *Bellingham, WA*

Clallam County Fair [A] *Port Angeles, WA*

Clam Chowder Festival [A] *Gold Beach, OR*

Clark County Historical Museum [W] *Vancouver, WA*

Clarno Unit [W] *John Day, OR*

Classic melodramas [S] *Virginia City, MT*

Classic Wooden Boat Show & Crab Feed [A] *Depoe Bay, OR*

Clearwater National Forest [W] *Lewiston, ID*

Cliff Park [W] *Spokane, WA*

Cline Falls [W] *Redmond, OR*

Clymer Museum of Art [W] *Ellensburg, WA*

C. M. Russell Museum Complex & Original Log Cabin Studio [W] *Great Falls, MT*

Cody Boys River Trips [W] *Cody, WY*

Cody Firearms Museum [W] *Cody, WY*

Cody Nite Rodeo [S] *Cody, WY*

Cody Stampede [A] *Cody, WY*

Coeur d'Alene Greyhound Park [W] *Coeur d'Alene, ID*

Coldwater Creek on the Cedar St Bridge [W] *Sandpoint, ID*

Coldwater Ridge Visitor Center [W] *Mount St. Helens National Volcanic Monument, WA*

Collage of Culture [A] *Madras, OR*

Collier Memorial State Park and Logging Museum [W] *Klamath Falls, OR*

Colorama Festival & PWRA Rodeo [A] *Coulee Dam, WA*

Columbia County Fair [A] *Dayton (Columbia County), WA*

Columbia Crest Winery [W] *Umatilla, OR*

Columbia Cup [A] *Richland, WA*

Columbia Gorge [W] *Hood River, OR*

Columbia Gorge Discovery Center [W] *The Dalles, OR*

Columbia Park [W] *Kennewick, WA*

Columbia River Maritime Museum [W] *Astoria, OR*

Colville National Forest [W] *Colville, WA*

Colville Professional Rodeo [A] *Colville, WA*

Colville Tribal Museum [W] *Coulee Dam, WA*

Commonwealth Air Training Plan Museum [W] *Brandon, MB*

Commonwealth Stadium [W] *Edmonton, AB*

Community Theater [W] *McMinnville, OR*

Comstock Park [W] *Spokane, WA*

Conconully State Park [W] *Omak, WA*

Concours d'Elegance [A] *Forest Grove, OR*

Conrad Mansion [W] *Kalispell, MT*

Cool Desert Nights Car Show [A] *Richland, WA*

Cooley's Gardens [W] *Silverton, OR*

Coos County Historical Society Museum [W] *North Bend, OR*

Copper King Mansion [W] *Butte, MT*

Copper Village Museum and Arts Center [W] *Anaconda, MT*

Cornwall Park [W] *Bellingham, WA*

Cottage Grove Lake [W] *Cottage Grove, OR*

Cottage Grove Museum [W] *Cottage Grove, OR*

Cougar Dam and Lake [W] *McKenzie Bridge, OR*

Council Crest Park [W] *Portland, OR*

Country Museum/Restored Train Station [W] *Silverton, OR*

Court's White Water Trips [W] *Gold Beach, OR*

Cove Palisades State Park, The [W] *Madras, OR*

Covered Bridge Celebration [A] *Cottage Grove, OR*

Covered Bridges [W] *Cottage Grove, OR*

Covered Wagon Cookout and Wild West Show [W] *Jackson, WY*

Cowboy Days [A] *Evanston, WY*

Cowboy Poet Festival [A] *St. Anthony, ID*

Cowboy Songs and Range Ballads [A] *Cody, WY*

Cowlitz County Fair [A] *Longview, WA*

Cowlitz County Historical Museum [W] *Kelso, WA*

Craigdarroch Castle [W] *Victoria, BC*

Craigflower Farmhouse & Schoolhouse Historic Site [W] *Victoria, BC*

Cranberry Festival [A] *Bandon, OR*

Crater Rock Museum [W] *Medford, OR*

Craters of the Moon National Monument [W] *Arco, ID*

Crescent Bar Park [W] *Quincy, WA*

CRESHT Museum [W] *Richland, WA*

Cross Channel Swim [A] *Hood River, OR*

Crow Fair [A] *Hardin, MT*

Crown Point [W] *Portland, OR*

Crystal Garden [W] *Victoria, BC*

Crystal Mountain Resort [W] *Mount Rainier National Park, WA*

Crystal Springs Rhododendron Garden [W] *Portland, OR*

Currier & Ives Winter Festival [A] *Thermopolis, WY*

Curry County Fair [A] *Gold Beach, OR*

Curry County Historical Museum [W] *Gold Beach, OR*

Curt Gowdy State Park [W] *Cheyenne, WY*

Custer County Art Center [W] *Miles City, MT*

Custer National Forest [W] *Hardin, MT*

Cut Bank [W] *Glacier National Park, MT*

CWU Library [W] *Ellensburg, WA*

Cyber City [W] *Nanaimo, BC*

Cypress Bowl Ski Area [W] *Vancouver, BC*

Cypress Hills Provincial Park [W] *Medicine Hat, AB*

Dabney [W] *Portland, OR*

Daffodil Festival [A] *Tacoma, WA*

Dalles Dam and Reservoir, The [W] *The Dalles, OR*

"Dalnavert" [W] *Winnipeg, MB*

Daly Mansion [W] *Hamilton, MT*

Darigold Dairy Fair [W] *Sunnyside, WA*

Darlingtonia [W] *Florence, OR*

Da Vinci Days [A] *Corvallis, OR*

Dawson County Fair & Rodeo [A] *Glendive, MT*

Days of '49 Celebration [A] *Greybull, WY*

Dayton Depot Festival [A] *Dayton (Columbia County), WA*

Deadman's Basin Fishing Access Site [W] *Harlowton, MT*

Dean Creek Elk Viewing Area [W] *Reedsport, OR*

Deception Pass State Park [W] *Anacortes, WA*

Deer Flat National Wildlife Refuge [W] *Nampa, ID*

Deerlodge National Forest [W] *Butte, MT*

Deerlodge National Forest [W] *Deer Lodge, MT*

Deming Logging Show [A] *Bellingham, WA*

Depoe Bay Park [W] *Depoe Bay, OR*

Depot Center [W] *Livingston, MT*

Deschutes County Fair and Rodeo [A] *Redmond, OR*

Desert Balloon Rally [A] *Rock Springs, WY*

Devil's Elbow [W] *Florence, OR*

Devil's Gate [W] *Casper, WY*

Devil's Lake State Park [W] *Lincoln City, OR*

Devil's Punch Bowl [W] *Newport, OR*

Devonian Botanic Garden [W] *Edmonton, AB*

Devonian Gardens [W] *Calgary, AB*

Dinosaur Provincial Park [W] *Medicine Hat, AB*

Discovery Center of Idaho [W] *Boise, ID*

Discovery Park [W] *Seattle, WA*

Dixieland Jazz Festival [A] *San Juan Islands, WA*

Dominion Astrophysical Observatory [W] *Victoria, BC*

Dominion Radio Astrophysical Observatory [W] *Penticton, BC*

Dorena Lake [W] *Cottage Grove, OR*

Douglas County Fair [A] *Roseburg, OR*

Douglas County Museum of History & Natural History [W] *Roseburg, OR*

Drag Races [S] *Lewistown, MT*
Drews Reservoir [W] *Lakeview, OR*
Driving Tour In Deschutes National
    Forest [W] *Bend, OR*
Dr. Sun-Yet-sen Classical Garden [W]
    Vancouver, BC
Dumas Brothel Museum [W] *Butte,
    MT*
Dungeness Recreation Area [W]
    Sequim, WA
Eagle Island State Park [W] *Boise, ID*
Eagle Watch [S] *Helena, MT*
Eastern Idaho State Fair [A] *Blackfoot,
    ID*
Eastern Montana Fair [A] *Miles City,
    MT*
Eastern Oregon Museum [W] *Baker
    City, OR*
Eastern Oregon University [W] *La
    Grande, OR*
Eastern Washington University [W]
    Cheney, WA
East Linn Museum [W] *Sweet Home,
    OR*
Eau Claire Market & Prince's Island
    Park [W] *Calgary, AB*
Ecola State Park [W] *Cannon Beach,
    OR*
Edmonton Queen Riverboat [W]
    Edmonton, AB
Edmonton's Klondike Days [A]
    Edmonton, AB
Edmonton Space and Science Centre
    [W] *Edmonton, AB*
Edness K. Wilkins State Park [W]
    Casper, WY
Elk Island National Park [W] *Edmonton, AB*
Ellensburg Rodeo [A] *Ellensburg, WA*
Elmore County Historical Foundation Museum [W] *Mountain
    Home, ID*
Elmo Unit [W] *Polson, MT*
Emerald Downs [W] *Tacoma, WA*
Emigrant Gulch [W] *Livingston, MT*
Emigrant Springs State Park [W]
    Pendleton, OR
Empress Hotel [W] *Victoria, BC*
Enchanted Forest [W] *Salem, OR*
Enchanted Village [W] *Tacoma, WA*
Energeum [W] *Calgary, AB*
Evergreen Floating Bridge [W] *Seattle,
    WA*
Exhibition and Stampede [A] *Medicine Hat, AB*
Exhibition Park [W] *Vancouver, BC*
Experience Music Project [W] *Seattle,
    WA*
Experimental Breeder Reactor Number 1 (EBR-1) [W] *Arco, ID*

Ezra Meeker Community Festival [A]
    Puyallup, WA
Ezra Meeker Mansion [W] *Puyallup,
    WA*
Face Rock State Park [W] *Bandon, OR*
Fairhaven District [W] *Bellingham,
    WA*
Fairhaven Park [W] *Bellingham, WA*
Fall Creek Dam and Lake [W] *Eugene,
    OR*
Fall Festival [A] *Corvallis, OR*
Fall Festival [A] *Florence, OR*
Farewell Bend [W] *Ontario, OR*
Farmer Consumer Awareness Day [A]
    Quincy, WA
Farmers Market [A] *Buhl, ID*
Farragut State Park [W] *Coeur d'Alene,
    ID*
Favell Museum of Western Art and
    Native American Artifacts [W]
    Klamath Falls, OR
Federation Forest State Park [W]
    Enumclaw, WA
Ferndale [W] *Bellingham, WA*
Ferry [W] *Tacoma, WA*
Ferry service to Victoria, BC, Canada
    [W] *Port Angeles, WA*
Ferry trips [W] *Seattle, WA*
Ferry trips [W] *Victoria, BC*
Ferry trips. BC Ferries [W] *Nanaimo,
    BC*
Festival du Voyageur [A] *Winnipeg,
    MB*
Festival of Nations [A] *Red Lodge, MT*
Festival of Quilts [A] *Gold Beach, OR*
Fiddlers' Hall of Fame [W] *Weiser, ID*
Fields Spring State Park [W] *Clarkston, WA*
Fiery Food Festival [A] *Pasco, WA*
Finch Arboretum [W] *Spokane, WA*
Finley Point Unit [W] *Polson, MT*
Firemen's Pond [W] *Redmond, OR*
Fishing [W] *Afton, WY*
Fishing [W] *Dubois, WY*
Fishing [W] *Glendive, MT*
Fishing [W] *Mount Rainier National
    Park, WA*
Fishing [W] *Olympic National Park,
    WA*
Fishing [W] *Port Orford, OR*
Fishing [W] *Twin Falls, ID*
Fishing and hunting [W] *Ontario, OR*
Fishing, camping. Martinsdale, Harris, and North Fork lakes [W]
    Harlowton, MT
Fishing, swimming, boating, camping [W] *Mountain Home, ID*
Five-Mile Drive [W] *Tacoma, WA*
Flaming Geyser State Park [W] *Enumclaw, WA*

Flaming Gorge National Recreation Area [W] *Green River, WY*

Flaming Gorge Reservoir [W] *Rock Springs, WY*

Flathead Lake [W] *Kalispell, MT*

Flathead Lake Biological Station, University of Montana [W] *Bigfork, MT*

Flathead Lake Cruise [W] *Polson, MT*

Flathead Lake State Park [W] *Bigfork, MT*

Flathead Lake State Park [W] *Polson, MT*

Flathead Music Festival [A] *Kalispell, MT*

Flathead National Forest [W] *Kalispell, MT*

Flattop Mountain [W] *Glacier National Park, MT*

Flavel House [W] *Astoria, OR*

Fleet of Flowers Ceremony [A] *Depoe Bay, OR*

Flerchinger Vineyards [W] *Hood River, OR*

Flinn's Heritage Tours [W] *Albany, OR*

Flour Mill [W] *Spokane, WA*

Fogarty Creek State Park [W] *Depoe Bay, OR*

Folklorama [A] *Winnipeg, MB*

Folk Music Festival [A] *Edmonton, AB*

Forest Park [W] *Portland, OR*

Forks National Historic Site, The [W] *Winnipeg, MB*

Fort Assinniboine [W] *Havre, MT*

Fort Bridger State Museum [W] *Evanston, WY*

Fort Calgary Historic Park [W] *Calgary, AB*

Fort Canby [W] *Long Beach, WA*

Fort Casey State Park [W] *Coupeville, WA*

Fort Caspar Museum [W] *Casper, WY*

Fort Clatsop National Memorial [W] *Astoria, OR*

Fort Clatsop National Memorial [W] *Cannon Beach, OR*

Fort Columbia [W] *Long Beach, WA*

Fort Dalles Museum [W] *The Dalles, OR*

Fort Dalles Rodeo & Chili Cook-off [A] *The Dalles, OR*

Fort Edmonton Park [W] *Edmonton, AB*

Fort Fetterman State Museum [W] *Douglas, WY*

Fort Flagler [W] *Port Townsend, WA*

Fort Henry Trading Post Site [W] *St. Anthony, ID*

Fort Klamath Museum [W] *Klamath Falls, OR*

Fort Langley National Historic Site [W] *Vancouver, BC*

Fort Laramie National Historic Site [W] *Torrington, WY*

Fort Lewis [W] *Tacoma, WA*

Fort Maginnis [W] *Lewistown, MT*

Fort Museum [W] *Fort Macleod, AB*

Fort Nisqually [W] *Tacoma, WA*

Fort Normandeau [W] *Red Deer, AB*

Fort Normandeau Days [A] *Red Deer, AB*

Fort Owen State Park [W] *Hamilton, MT*

Fort Peck Dam and Lake [W] *Glasgow, MT*

Fort Peck Summer Theater [S] *Glasgow, MT*

Fort Phil Kearny Site [W] *Buffalo, WY*

Fort Rodd Hill & Fisgard Lighthouse National Historic Site [W] *Victoria, BC*

Fort Sherman Museum [W] *Coeur d'Alene, ID*

Fort Simcoe Historical State Park [W] *Toppenish, WA*

Fort Spokane [W] *Coulee Dam, WA*

Fort Stevens State Park [W] *Astoria, OR*

Fort Union Trading Post National Historic Site [W] *Sidney, MT*

Fort Vancouver National Historic Site [W] *Vancouver, WA*

Fort Walla Walla Museum Complex [W] *Walla Walla, WA*

Fort Walla Walla Park [W] *Walla Walla, WA*

Fort Whoop-Up [W] *Lethbridge, AB*

Fort Worden [W] *Port Townsend, WA*

Fossil Butte National Monument [W] *Kemmerer, WY*

Foster Lake [W] *Sweet Home, OR*

Foster Mud Flat Races [A] *Sweet Home, OR*

Founders' Day [A] *Cashmere, WA*

Founders Day Corn Roast [A] *Forest Grove, OR*

Frederic Wood Theatre [W] *Vancouver, BC*

Freeway Park [W] *Seattle, WA*

Fremont County Fair [A] *St. Anthony, ID*

Fremont County Fair and Rodeo [A] *Riverton, WY*

Fremont County Pioneer Days [A] *St. Anthony, ID*

Fremont County Pioneer Museum [W] *Lander, WY*

Fremont National Forest [W] *Lakeview, OR*

Fringe Theatre Event [A] *Edmonton, AB*

Frontier Festival [A] *Cody, WY*

Frontier Gateway Museum [W] *Glendive, MT*

Frontier Montana [W] *Deer Lodge, MT*

Frontier Town [W] *Helena, MT*

Fun Forest Amusement Park [W] *Seattle, WA*

Gallant Lady Cruises [W] *Seattle, WA*

Gallatin County Fair [A] *Bozeman, MT*

Gallatin National Forest [W] *Bozeman, MT*

Gallery I [W] *Ellensburg, WA*

Gallery of Art [W] *Cheney, WA*

Gardens [W] *Tacoma, WA*

Gardiner Rodeo [A] *Gardiner, MT*

Gastown [W] *Vancouver, BC*

Gas Works Park [W] *Seattle, WA*

Gates of the Mountains [W] *Helena, MT*

Geological Museum [W] *Laramie, WY*

George Fox College [W] *Newberg, OR*

Georgetown Lake [W] *Anaconda, MT*

Geyser and Hot Springs [W] *Lakeview, OR*

Geyser Park [W] *Billings, MT*

Ghost towns & Sapphire mines [W] *Anaconda, MT*

Giant Springs State Park and State Trout Hatchery [W] *Great Falls, MT*

Gifford Pinchot National Forest [W] *Vancouver, WA*

Gift of the Waters Pageant [A] *Thermopolis, WY*

Gilbert's Brewery [W] *Virginia City, MT*

Ginkgo/Wanapum State Park [W] *Ellensburg, WA*

Glacier Jazz Stampede [A] *Kalispell, MT*

Glacier Maze [W] *Columbia Falls, MT*

Glacier National Park [W] *Kalispell, MT*

Glacier National Park [W] *Whitefish, MT*

Glacier Raft Company [W] *Glacier National Park, MT*

Glenbow Museum [W] *Calgary, AB*

Glendo State Park [W] *Wheatland, WY*

Goat Rocks Wilderness [W] *Packwood, WA*

Gold Collection [W] *Helena, MT*

Goldendale Observatory [W] *Goldendale, WA*

Golden Gardens [W] *Seattle, WA*

Gold Hill [W] *Idaho City, ID*

Gonzaga University [W] *Spokane, WA*

Good Nations Powwow [A] *Hamilton, MT*

Gordon Southam Observatory [W] *Vancouver, BC*

Gorge Powerhouse/Ladder Creek Falls & Rock Gardens [W] *Sedro Woolley, WA*

Goshen County Fair & Rodeo [A] *Torrington, WY*

Governor's Cup Marathon [A] *Helena, MT*

Grand Canyon in miniature [W] *Challis, ID*

Grand Coulee Dam [W] *Coulee Dam, WA*

Grand Targhee Ski and Summer Resort [W] *Driggs, ID*

Grand Teton Music Festival [S] *Jackson, WY*

Grand Teton National Park [W] *Jackson, WY*

Granite Park [W] *Glacier National Park, MT*

Grant County Fair [A] *Moses Lake, WA*

Grant County Fair and Rodeo [A] *John Day, OR*

Grant County Historical Museum [W] *John Day, OR*

Grant County Pioneer Village & Museum [W] *Ephrata, WA*

Grant-Kohrs Ranch National Historic Site [W] *Deer Lodge, MT*

Grants Pass Museum of Art [W] *Grants Pass, OR*

Granville Island [W] *Vancouver, BC*

Grasshopper Glacier [W] *Cooke City, MT*

Gray Line bus tours [W] *Jackson, WY*

Gray Line bus tours [W] *Portland, OR*

Gray Line bus tours [W] *Seattle, WA*

Gray Line bus tours [W] *Vancouver, BC*

Gray Line bus tours [W] *Victoria, BC*

Gray Line bus tours [W] *West Yellowstone, MT*

Grays Harbor Historical Seaport [W] *Aberdeen, WA*

Grays Harbor Lighthouse [W] *Westport, WA*

Great American Ski Chase [A] *West Yellowstone, MT*

Great Balloon Escape [A] *Albany, OR*

Great Columbia Crossing Bridge Run [A] *Astoria, OR*

Greatest of the Grape [A] *Roseburg, OR*

Great Northern Fair [A] *Havre, MT*

Great Northern Whitewater [W] *Glacier National Park, MT*

Great Salmon BalloonFest, The [A] *Salmon, ID*

Green Lake Park [W] *Seattle, WA*

Green River Gorge Conservation Area [W] *Enumclaw, WA*

Green River Rendezvous [A] *Pinedale, WY*

Greybull Museum [W] *Greybull, WY*

Greyhound Racing [S] *Portland, OR*

Grizzly Discovery Center [W] *West Yellowstone, MT*

Grotto—The National Sanctuary of Our Sorrowful Mother [W] *Portland, OR*

Grouse Mountain [W] *Vancouver, BC*

Grouse Mountain tramway [W] *Vancouver, BC*

Guernsey Old Timer's & Street Dance [A] *Wheatland, WY*

Guernsey State Park [W] *Wheatland, WY*

Guy W. Talbot [W] *Portland, OR*

Hamley's Western Store [W] *Pendleton, OR*

Harbor Day Festival and Tug Boat Races [A] *Olympia, WA*

Harbour Centre-The Lookout [W] *Vancouver, BC*

Harbour Cruises Limited [W] *Vancouver, BC*

Harney County Fair, Rodeo & Race Meet [A] *Burns, OR*

Harney County Historical Museum [W] *Burns, OR*

Harriman State Park [W] *Ashton, ID*

Harris Beach [W] *Brookings, OR*

Hatfield Marine Science Center of Oregon State University [W] *Newport, OR*

Hatley Castle [W] *Victoria, BC*

Hat Rock State Park [W] *Umatilla, OR*

Havre Beneath the Streets [W] *Havre, MT*

Havre Festival Days [A] *Havre, MT*

Hawaiian Luau [A] *Forest Grove, OR*

Headquarters Visitor Information Center [W] *Sun Valley Area, ID*

Head-Smashed-In Buffalo Jump Interpretive Centre [W] *Fort Macleod, AB*

H. Earl Clack Memorial Museum [W] *Havre, MT*

Heceta Head Lighthouse [W] *Florence, OR*

Heise Hot Springs [W] *Idaho Falls, ID*

Helena National Forest [W] *Helena, MT*

Hell Creek State Park [W] *Glasgow, MT*

Hellgate Jetboat Excursions [W] *Grants Pass, OR*

Hell's Canyon Adventures [W] *Weiser, ID*

Hells Canyon Dam [W] *Weiser, ID*

Hell's Canyon Excursions [W] *Lewiston, ID*

Hell's Canyon National Recreation Area [W] *Grangeville, ID*

Hells Canyon National Recreation Area [W] *Joseph, OR*

Hell's Canyon National Recreation Area [W] *Weiser, ID*

Hells Canyon Tours [W] *Baker City, OR*

Hell's Gate State Park [W] *Lewiston, ID*

Helmcken House [W] *Victoria, BC*

Hendricks Park Rhododendron Garden [W] *Eugene, OR*

Henry's Lake State Park [W] *Ashton, ID*

Henry Estate Winery [W] *Roseburg, OR*

Heritage Days [A] *Columbia Falls, MT*

Heritage Days [A] *Grants Pass, OR*

Heritage Festival [A] *Edmonton, AB*

Heritage Museum [W] *Libby, MT*

Heritage Park Historical Village [W] *Calgary, AB*

Herrett Center [W] *Twin Falls, ID*

Heyburn State Park [W] *St. Marie's, ID*

High Desert Museum, The [W] *Bend, OR*

Highland Games [A] *Red Deer, AB*

High Plains Old Time Country Music Show and Contest [A] *Douglas, WY*

High School Rodeo [A] *Salmon, ID*

Hiking [W] *Mount Rainier National Park, WA*

Hiking [W] *Mount St. Helens National Volcanic Monument, WA*

Hiking [W] *Olympic National Park, WA*

Hilgard Junction State Recreation Area [W] *La Grande, OR*

Hiline Festival games [S] *Glasgow, MT*

Hillcrest Park [W] *Mount Vernon, WA*

Hillcrest Vineyard [W] *Roseburg, OR*

Historical Murals [W] *Toppenish, WA*

Historical Museum at Fort Missoula [W] *Missoula, MT*

Historical points of 19th-century gold mining. Maiden. [W] *Lewistown, MT*

Historical Society Museum [W] *Newport, WA*

Historic Claquato Church [W] *Chehalis, WA*

Historic Deepwood Estate [W] *Salem, OR*

Historic Governors' Mansion [W] *Cheyenne, WY*

Historic Hughes House [W] *Port Orford, OR*

Historic Interior Homes Tours [A] *Albany, OR*

Historic North Front Street [W]
Yakima, WA

Hockaday Center for the Arts [W]
Kalispell, MT

Hogadon Ski Area [W] Casper, WY

Holiday Parade of Christmas Ships
[A] Portland, OR

Holland Gardens [W] Oak Harbor, WA

Holland Happening [A] Oak Harbor,
WA

Holliday Park [W] Cheyenne, WY

Holmes Family Home [W] Oregon
City, OR

Holter Museum of Art [W] Helena,
MT

Home-Grown Festival [A] Marysville,
WA

Homesteader's Museum [W] Torrington, WY

Honeywood Winery [W] Salem, OR

Hood Canal Nursery [W] Port Gamble, WA

Hood River County Fair [A] Hood
River, OR

Hood River County Museum [W]
Hood River, OR

Hood River Valley Harvest Fest [A]
Hood River, OR

Hood River Vineyards [W] Hood River,
OR

Hoover-Minthorn House Museum
[W] Newberg, OR

Hoquiam's "Castle" [W] Hoquiam,
WA

Horse-Drawn Trolley Tours [W] Baker
City, OR

Horse Racing [S] Evanston, WY

Horse Racing [A] Jerome, ID

Horse racing [S] Portland, OR

Horse racing [S] Spokane, WA

Hot Springs County Museum and
Cultural Center [W] Thermopolis, WY

Hot Springs State Park [W] Thermopolis, WY

House Tours [A] Port Townsend, WA

Howell Territorial Park and The
Bybee House [W] Portland, OR

Hoyt Arboretum [W] Portland, OR

Hughes River Expeditions [W] Weiser,
ID

Hult Center [W] Eugene, OR

Humbug Mountain State Park [W]
Port Orford, OR

Hungry Horse Dam and Power Plant
[W] Columbia Falls, MT

Hunting [W] Pinedale, WY

Hunt moss agates [W] Glendive, MT

Hyack Festival [A] Vancouver, BC

Hyak [W] North Bend, WA

Hydro Plane Races [A] Kelowna, BC

Ice Harbor Lock and Dam [W] Pasco,
WA

Icicle Junction [W] Leavenworth, WA

Idaho Botanical Gardens [W] Boise,
ID

Idaho Centennial Carousel [W]
Rexburg, ID

Idaho Falls [W] Idaho Falls, ID

Idaho Museum of Natural History
[W] Pocatello, ID

Idaho Panhandle National Forests—
Coeur d'Alene [W] Coeur d'A-
lene, ID

Idaho Panhandle National Forests—
Kaniksu [W] Priest Lake Area,
ID

Idaho Panhandle National Forests—
St. Joe [W] St. Marie's, ID

Idaho Powerboat Regatta [A] Burley,
ID

Idaho Repertory Theater [S] Moscow,
ID

Idaho Shakespeare Festival [S] Boise,
ID

Idaho State Historical Museum [W]
Boise, ID

Idaho State University [W] Pocatello,
ID

Illahee [W] Bremerton, WA

Independence Rock [W] Casper, WY

Indian Springs [W] American Falls, ID

Industrial tours [W] Vancouver, BC

Interagency Aerial Fire Control Center [W] West Yellowstone, MT

Intermittent spring [W] Afton, WY

International Air Show [A] Kamloops,
BC

International Air Show [A] Lethbridge,
AB

International Bathtub Race [A] Vancouver, BC

International District [W] Seattle, WA

International Festival [A] Longview,
WA

International Folk Festival [A] Red
Deer, AB

International Fountain [W] Seattle,
WA

International Peace Arch [W] Blaine,
WA

International Street Festival [A]
Rexburg, ID

International Wildlife Film Festival
[A] Missoula, MT

Interpretive programs and walks [W]
Mount Rainier National Park,
WA

Irish Days [A] Lakeview, OR

Ironman Canada Championship
Triathlon [A] Penticton, BC

Irrigation Festival [A] Sequim, WA

Irving House Historic Centre [W] *Vancouver, BC*

Jackalope Days [A] *Douglas, WY*

Jackson County Fair [A] *Medford, OR*

Jackson F. Kimball State Park [W] *Klamath Falls, OR*

Jackson Hole Fall Arts Festival [S] *Jackson, WY*

Jackson Hole Museum [W] *Jackson, WY*

Jackson Hole Rodeo [S] *Jackson, WY*

Jackson Hole Ski Resort [W] *Jackson, WY*

Jacksonville Museum [W] *Jacksonville, OR*

James R. Slater Museum of Natural History [W] *Tacoma, WA*

Japanese Garden [W] *Portland, OR*

Japanese Garden [W] *Seattle, WA*

Jasper National Park [W] *Banff, AB*

Jasper Tramway [W] *Jasper National Park, AB*

Jazz City Festival [A] *Edmonton, AB*

Jazz Festival [S] *Boise, ID*

Jazz Unlimited [A] *Pasco, WA*

Jedediah Smith Mountain Man Rendezvous & Buffalo Barbecue [A] *Grants Pass, OR*

Jefferson County Fair [A] *Port Townsend, WA*

Jefferson County Museum [W] *Madras, OR*

Jefferson State Stampede [A] *Klamath Falls, OR*

Jerome County Fair [A] *Jerome, ID*

Jerome County Historical Museum [W] *Jerome, ID*

Jerry's Rogue River Jet Boat Trips [W] *Gold Beach, OR*

Jessie M. Honeyman Memorial [W] *Florence, OR*

John Day Fossil Beds National Monument [W] *John Day, OR*

John Day Locks and Dam [W] *Biggs, OR*

John Inskeep Environmental Learning Center [W] *Oregon City, OR*

John Janzen Nature Centre [W] *Edmonton, AB*

John Scharff Migratory Bird Festival [A] *Burns, OR*

Johnson County Fair and Rodeo [A] *Buffalo, WY*

Johnson County-Jim Gatchell Memorial Museum [W] *Buffalo, WY*

Johnson Ridge Obervatory [W] *Mount St. Helens National Volcanic Monument, WA*

Josephine County Air Fair [A] *Grants Pass, OR*

Josephine County Fair [A] *Grants Pass, OR*

Joseph P. Stewart State Park [W] *Medford, OR*

Julia Davis Park [W] *Boise, ID*

Junior Rodeo [A] *Lakeview, OR*

Kahlotus [W] *Pasco, WA*

Kamloops Museum & Archives [W] *Kamloops, BC*

Kamloops Wildlife Park [W] *Kamloops, BC*

Kam Wah Chung & Company Museum [W] *John Day, OR*

Keller Heritage Center [W] *Colville, WA*

Kelowna Regatta [A] *Kelowna, BC*

Kendall Skyline Drive [W] *Dayton (Columbia County), WA*

Kerbyville Museum [W] *Cave Junction, OR*

Keyhole State Park [W] *Gillette, WY*

King County Fair [A] *Enumclaw, WA*

King's Saddlery Museum [W] *Sheridan, WY*

Kinsmen Sports Centre [W] *Edmonton, AB*

Kitsap County Fair and Rodeo [A] *Bremerton, WA*

Kitsap County Historical Society Museum [W] *Bremerton, WA*

Kitsap Memorial State Park [W] *Port Gamble, WA*

Kittitas County Fair [A] *Ellensburg, WA*

Klamath County Baldwin Hotel Museum [W] *Klamath Falls, OR*

Klamath County Fair [A] *Klamath Falls, OR*

Klamath County Museum [W] *Klamath Falls, OR*

Klamath Memorial Rodeo & Powwow [A] *Klamath Falls, OR*

Klickitat County Fair and Rodeo [A] *Goldendale, WA*

Klickitat County Historical Museum [W] *Goldendale, WA*

Klondike Gold Rush National Historical Park-Seattle Unit [W] *Seattle, WA*

Knight Library [W] *Eugene, OR*

Kootenai National Forest [W] *Libby, MT*

Kootenai National Wildlife Refuge [W] *Bonner's Ferry, ID*

Kootenai River Days [A] *Bonner's Ferry, ID*

Lake Chelan [W] *Chelan, WA*

Lake Coeur d'Alene [W] *Coeur d'Alene, ID*

Lake Coeur d'Alene Cruises, Inc [W] *Coeur d'Alene, ID*

Lake County Fair and Roundup [A] *Lakeview, OR*

Lake cruises [W] *Chelan, WA*

Lake Cushman State Park [W] *Union, WA*

Lakefair [A] *Olympia, WA*

Lake Gillette Recreation Area [W] *Colville, WA*

Lake Lowell [W] *Nampa, ID*

Lake McDonald [W] *Glacier National Park, MT*

Lake Owyhee [W] *Ontario, OR*

Lake Padden Park [W] *Bellingham, WA*

Lake Pend Oreille [W] *Sandpoint, ID*

Lake Roosevelt National Recreation Area [W] *Coulee Dam, WA*

Lake Sacajawea Park [W] *Longview, WA*

Lake Sammamish State Park [W] *Issaquah, WA*

Lake Sylvia State Park [W] *Aberdeen, WA*

Lake Umatilla [W] *Biggs, OR*

Lake Union [W] *Seattle, WA*

Lakeview Park [W] *Nampa, ID*

Lake Washington Canal [W] *Seattle, WA*

Lake Washington Floating Bridge [W] *Seattle, WA*

Lake Whatcom Railway [W] *Sedro Woolley, WA*

Landing Days & Govenor's Cup Walleye Tournament [A] *Umatilla, OR*

Lane County Fair [A] *Eugene, OR*

Lane County Historical Museum [W] *Eugene, OR*

LaPine [W] *Bend, OR*

Laramie County Fair [A] *Cheyenne, WY*

Laramie Plains Museum [W] *Laramie, WY*

Larrabee State Park [W] *Bellingham, WA*

Laser Light Festival [A] *Coulee Dam, WA*

Last Chance Stampede & Fair [A] *Helena, MT*

Last Chance Tour Train [W] *Helena, MT*

Latah County Fair [A] *Moscow, ID*

Latah County Historical Society [W] *Moscow, ID*

Lava Butte and Lava River Cave [W] *Bend, OR*

Lava Hot Springs [W] *Lava Hot Springs, ID*

Lavas, The [W] *Idaho Falls, ID*

Lawrence Park [W] *Kalispell, MT*

Lee McCune Braille Trail [W] *Casper, WY*

Legend of Rawhide [A] *Lusk, WY*

Legislative Building [W] *Olympia, WA*

Legislative Building [W] *Winnipeg, MB*

Lemhi County Fair & Rodeo [A] *Salmon, ID*

Lemhi Ghost Town [W] *Salmon, ID*

Lewis & Clark College [W] *Portland, OR*

Lewis and Clark [W] *Portland, OR*

Lewis and Clark Caverns State Park [W] *Three Forks, MT*

Lewis and Clark Expeditions [W] *Jackson, WY*

Lewis and Clark National Forest [W] *Great Falls, MT*

Lewis and Clark National Historical Trail Interpretive Center [W] *Great Falls, MT*

Lewis and Clark Trail State Park [W] *Dayton (Columbia County), WA*

Lewis County Historical Museum [W] *Chehalis, WA*

Lewiston Round-Up [A] *Lewiston, ID*

Libby Dam [W] *Libby, MT*

Liberty Orchards Company, Inc [W] *Cashmere, WA*

Library Building [W] *Olympia, WA*

Lincoln County Fair [A] *Shoshone, ID*

Lincoln County Historical Society Museums. Log Cabin Museum [W] *Newport, OR*

Lincoln Monument [W] *Laramie, WY*

Lincoln Park [W] *Seattle, WA*

Linfield College [W] *McMinnville, OR*

Lionel Hampton/Chevron Jazz Festival [A] *Moscow, ID*

Lion's Club Parade & Labor Day Festival [A] *Cave Junction, OR*

Lithia Park [W] *Ashland, OR*

Little Bighorn Battlefield National Monument [W] *Hardin, MT*

Little Big Horn Days [A] *Hardin, MT*

Little Mountain [W] *Mount Vernon, WA*

Loeb [W] *Brookings, OR*

Logger Days [A] *Libby, MT*

Loggerodeo [A] *Sedro Woolley, WA*

Lolo National Forest [W] *Missoula, MT*

Longest Dam Run [A] *Glasgow, MT*

Longmire [W] *Mount Rainier National Park, WA*

Lookout Pass Ski Area [W] *Wallace, ID*

Lookout Point and Dexter Dams and Lakes [W] *Eugene, OR*

Loop drive [W] *Spokane, WA*

Lost Creek State Park [W] *Anaconda, MT*

Lost Lake [W] *Hood River, OR*

Lower Fort Garry National Historic Site [W] *Winnipeg, MB*

Lower Mesa Falls [W] *Ashton, ID*

Loyalty Days and Sea Fair Festival [A] *Newport, OR*

Lucky Peak State Park [W] *Boise, ID*

Lummi Stommish [A] *Bellingham, WA*

Luna House Museum [W] *Lewiston, ID*

Lynden Pioneer Museum [W] *Bellingham, WA*

Madison Buffalo Jump State Monument [W] *Three Forks, MT*

Madison River Canyon Earthquake Area [W] *West Yellowstone, MT*

Mad River Boat Trips, Inc [W] *Jackson, WY*

Maifest [A] *Leavenworth, WA*

Mail Boat Whitewater Trips [W] *Gold Beach, OR*

Main Street Historic District [W] *Sheridan, WY*

Makah Cultural & Research Center [W] *Neah Bay, WA*

Makoshika [W] *Glendive, MT*

Malad Gorge State Park [W] *Jerome, ID*

Malheur County Fair [A] *Ontario, OR*

Malheur National Forest [W] *John Day, OR*

Malheur National Wildlife Refuge [W] *Burns, OR*

Malmstrom AFB [W] *Great Falls, MT*

Manitoba Fall Fair [A] *Brandon, MB*

Manitoba Museum of Man & Nature [W] *Winnipeg, MB*

Manitoba Opera Association [S] *Winnipeg, MB*

Manitoba Planetarium [W] *Winnipeg, MB*

Manitoba Summer Fair [A] *Brandon, MB*

Manito Park [W] *Spokane, WA*

Manty Shaw Fiddlers' Jamboree [A] *Shoshone, ID*

Many Glacier Area [W] *Glacier National Park, MT*

Marine Discovery Tours [W] *Newport, OR*

Maritime Heritage Center [W] *Bellingham, WA*

Maritime Museum [W] *Vancouver, BC*

Maritime Museum [W] *Victoria, BC*

Maritime Museum [W] *Westport, WA*

Maritime Week [A] *Astoria, OR*

Marmot Basin [W] *Jasper National Park, AB*

Marshall Mountain Ski Area [W] *Missoula, MT*

Maryhill Museum of Art [W] *Goldendale, WA*

Mary L. Gooding Memorial Park [W] *Shoshone, ID*

Marysville Ghost Town [W] *Helena, MT*

Massacre Rocks State Park [W] *American Falls, ID*

Maverick Mountain Ski Area [W] *Dillon, MT*

Mayer State Park [W] *The Dalles, OR*

McChord AFB [W] *Tacoma, WA*

McIntosh Apple Days [A] *Hamilton, MT*

McLoughlin House National Historic Site [W] *Oregon City, OR*

McNary Lock and Dam [W] *Pasco, WA*

McNary Lock and Dam [W] *Umatilla, OR*

Medicine Bow National Forest [W] *Douglas, WY*

Medicine Bow National Forest [W] *Laramie, WY*

Medicine Hat Museum & Art Gallery [W] *Medicine Hat, AB*

Merrysville for the Holidays [A] *Marysville, WA*

Middle Fork of the Salmon Wild and Scenic River [W] *Challis, ID*

Midwinter Breakout [A] *Penticton, BC*

Miette Hot Springs [W] *Jasper National Park, AB*

Migratory Bird Refuge [W] *Klamath Falls, OR*

Millersylvania State Park [W] *Olympia, WA*

Milo McIver State Park [W] *Oregon City, OR*

Mima Mounds Natural Area [W] *Olympia, WA*

Miner's Jubilee [A] *Baker City, OR*

Mineral collecting [W] *Newport, OR*

Mineral collecting [W] *Prineville, OR*

Mineral Museum [W] *Butte, MT*

Miniature World [W] *Victoria, BC*

Minnetonka Cave [W] *Montpelier, ID*

Mission Mill Village [W] *Salem, OR*

Mission Ridge Ski Area [W] *Wenatchee, WA*

Missoula Carousel [W] *Missoula, MT*

Missoula Museum of the Arts [W] *Missoula, MT*

Missoula Public Library [W] *Missoula, MT*

Missouri River Headwaters State Park [W] *Three Forks, MT*

M-K Nature Center [W] *Boise, ID*

MonDak Heritage Center [W] *Sidney, MT*

Monorail [W] *Seattle, WA*

Montana Cowboy Poetry Gathering [A] *Lewistown, MT*

Montana Fair [A] *Billings, MT*

Montana Governor's Cup Walleye Tournament [A] *Glasgow, MT*

Montana Historical Society Museum
[W] *Helena, MT*
Montana Pro Rodeo Circuit Finals [A]
Great Falls, MT
Montana Raft Company & Glacier
Wilderness Guides [W] *Glacier
National Park, MT*
Montana Snowbowl [W] *Missoula,
MT*
Montana State University [W] *Boze-
man, MT*
Montana Tech of the University of
Montana [W] *Butte, MT*
Montana Territorial Prison [W] *Deer
Lodge, MT*
Montana Traditional Jazz Festival [A]
Helena, MT
Montana Winter Fair [A] *Bozeman,
MT*
Monticello Convention Site [W]
Longview, WA
Moses Lake [W] *Moses Lake, WA*
Moses Lake Recreation Area [W]
Moses Lake, WA
Moses Lake State Park [W] *Moses
Lake, WA*
Moss Mansion [W] *Billings, MT*
Mount Adams Recreation Area [W]
Goldendale, WA
Mountain climbing [W] *Mount
Rainier National Park, WA*
Mountain climbing [W] *Olympic
National Park, WA*
Mountaineers' Forest Theater [S] *Bre-
merton, WA*
Mountain Man Rendezvous [A]
Evanston, WY
Mount Ashland Ski Area [W] *Ash-
land, OR*
Mount Bachelor Ski Area [W] *Bend,
OR*
Mount Baker Ski Area [W] *Belling-
ham, WA*
Mount Baker-Snoqualmie National
Forest [W] *Bellingham, WA*
Mount Baker-Snoqualmie National
Forest [W] *Seattle, WA*
Mount Hood-Columbia Gorge Loop
Scenic Drive [W] *Portland, OR*
Mount Hood Jazz Festival [A] *Port-
land, OR*
Mount Hood Meadows [W] *Mount
Hood National Forest, OR*
Mount Hood National Forest [W]
Hood River, OR
Mount Hood National Forest [W] *The
Dalles, OR*
Mount Hood Scenic Railroad [W]
Hood River, OR
Mount Rainier National Park [W]
Tacoma, WA

Mount Spokane State Park [W]
Spokane, WA
Mount St. Helens Visitor Center [W]
Longview, WA
Mount St. Helens Visitor Center [W]
*Mount St. Helens National Vol-
canic Monument, WA*
Mount Tabor Park [W] *Portland, OR*
Moyie Falls [W] *Bonner's Ferry, ID*
Mud Mountain Dam [W] *Enumclaw,
WA*
Mukilteo [W] *Everett, WA*
Multnomah County Fair [A] *Portland,
OR*
Multnomah Falls [W] *Portland, OR*
Museum of Anthropology [W]
Cheney, WA
Museum of Anthropology [W] *Van-
couver, BC*
Museum of Art [W] *Eugene, OR*
Museum of Art [W] *Pullman, WA*
Museum of Flight [W] *Seattle, WA*
Museum of History and Industry [W]
Seattle, WA
Museum of Montana Wildlife and
Hall of Bronze [W] *Browning,
MT*
Museum of North Idaho [W] *Coeur
d'Alene, ID*
Museum of Northwest Art [W] *La
Conner, WA*
Museum of the Mountain Man [W]
Pinedale, WY
Museum of the Northern Great
Plains [W] *Fort Benton, MT*
Museum of the Plains Indian [W]
Browning, MT
Museum of the Regiments [W] *Cal-
gary, AB*
Museum of the Rockies [W] *Bozeman,
MT*
Museum of the Upper Missouri River
[W] *Fort Benton, MT*
Music and Art Festival [A] *Chehalis,
WA*
Music Festival [A] *McCall, ID*
Music Festival [A] *Red Lodge, MT*
Mustang Days [A] *Lovell, WY*
Muttart Conservatory [W] *Edmonton,
AB*
Myrtle Edwards Park [W] *Seattle, WA*
Nanaimo Art Gallery & Exhibition
Centre [W] *Nanaimo, BC*
Nanaimo District Museum [W]
Nanaimo, BC
Nanaimo Marine Festival [A]
Nanaimo, BC
Narrows Bridge [W] *Tacoma, WA*
NASCAR Auto Racing [S] *Richland,
WA*

National Bighorn Sheep Interpretive Center [W] *Dubois, WY*
National Bison Range [W] *Polson, MT*
National Elk Refuge [W] *Jackson, WY*
National Fish Hatchery [W] *Ennis, MT*
National Fish Hatchery [W] *Leavenworth, WA*
National Geographic Theatre [W] *West Yellowstone, MT*
National Historic Oregon Trail Interpretive Center [W] *Baker City, OR*
National Lentil Festival [A] *Pullman, WA*
National Oldtime Fiddlers' Contest [A] *Weiser, ID*
National Western Art Show and Auction [A] *Ellensburg, WA*
National Wildlife Art Museum [W] *Jackson, WY*
Native American Celebrations [A] *Toppenish, WA*
Natural History Museum [W] *Banff, AB*
NBA (Portland Trail Blazers) [W] *Portland, OR*
NBA (Seattle SuperSonics) [W] *Seattle, WA*
NBA (Vancouver Grizzlies) [W] *Vancouver, BC*
Neptune State Park [W] *Yachats, OR*
Nevada City [W] *Virginia City, MT*
Nevada City Depot [W] *Virginia City, MT*
Never Never Land [W] *Tacoma, WA*
Newberry National Volcanic Monument [W] *Bend, OR*
Newcastle Island Provincial Marine Park [W] *Nanaimo, BC*
Newell House Museum [W] *Newberg, OR*
Newhalem Visitor Information Center [W] *Sedro Woolley, WA*
Nez Perce County Fair [A] *Lewiston, ID*
Nez Perce National Forest [W] *Grangeville, ID*
Nez Perce National Historical Park [W] *Lewiston, ID*
NFL (Seattle Seahawks) [W] *Seattle, WA*
NHL (Calgary Flames) [W] *Calgary, AB*
NHL (Edmonton Oilers) [W] *Edmonton, AB*
NHL (Vancouver Canucks) [W] *Vancouver, BC*
Nicolaysen Art Museum and Discovery Center [W] *Casper, WY*
Night Rodeo [A] *Caldwell, ID*

Nikka Yuko Japanese Garden [W] *Lethbridge, AB*
Ninepipe and Pablo National Wildlife Refuges [W] *Polson, MT*
Nordicfest [A] *Libby, MT*
Nordic Heritage Museum [W] *Seattle, WA*
North American Native American Days Powwow [A] *Browning, MT*
North Cascades National Park [W] *Bellingham, WA*
North Cascades National Park [W] *Sedro Woolley, WA*
North Central Washington Museum [W] *Wenatchee, WA*
Northeast Montana Fair & Rodeo [A] *Glasgow, MT*
Northeast Washington Fair [A] *Colville, WA*
Northern Forest Fire Laboratory [W] *Missoula, MT*
Northern Idaho Fair [A] *Coeur d'Alene, ID*
Northern International Livestock Exposition [A] *Billings, MT*
Northern Pacific Depot Railroad Museum [W] *Wallace, ID*
Northwest Microbrew Expo & Willamette Winter Wine Festival [A] *Eugene, OR*
Northwest Montana Fair & Rodeo [A] *Kalispell, MT*
Northwest Trek [W] *Tacoma, WA*
NRA/MRA Rodeo [A] *Big Timber, MT*
Nutcracker Museum [W] *Leavenworth, WA*
Oak Hammock Marsh Wildlife Management Area [W] *Winnipeg, MB*
Oak Harbor Beach Park [W] *Oak Harbor, WA*
Oaks Amusement Park [W] *Portland, OR*
Oasis Bordello Museum [W] *Wallace, ID*
Oasis Park [W] *Ephrata, WA*
Obon Festival [A] *Ontario, OR*
Ochoco Lake Park [W] *Prineville, OR*
Ochoco National Forest [W] *Prineville, OR*
Officers' Row [W] *Vancouver, WA*
Official Rogue River Mail Boat Hydro-Jet Trips [W] *Gold Beach, OR*
Of Sea and Shore Museum [W] *Port Gamble, WA*
Ohanapecosh [W] *Mount Rainier National Park, WA*
Okanagan Game Farm [W] *Penticton, BC*

Okanagan Wine Festival [A] *Kelowna, BC*

Okanagan Wine Festival [A] *Penticton, BC*

Okanogan National Forest [W] *Omak, WA*

Oktubberfest [A] *Grangeville, ID*

Old Aurora Colony Museum, The [W] *Oregon City, OR*

Old fashioned Melodrama [A] *Cheyenne, WY*

Old Fashioned Melodrama [A] *Toppenish, WA*

Old Fort Hall Replica [W] *Pocatello, ID*

Old Fort Townsend (Historical) [W] *Port Townsend, WA*

Old Governor's Mansion [W] *Helena, MT*

Old Hastings Mill [W] *Vancouver, BC*

Old Idaho Penitentiary [W] *Boise, ID*

Old Mission State Park [W] *Kellogg, ID*

Old No. 1 [W] *Butte, MT*

Old Snohomish Village [W] *Snohomish, WA*

Olmstead Place State Park-Heritage Site [W] *Ellensburg, WA*

Olympia Farmers Market [S] *Olympia, WA*

Olympic Game Farm [W] *Sequim, WA*

Olympic National Forest [W] *Olympia, WA*

Olympic National Park [W] *Forks, WA*

Olympic National Park [W] *Port Angeles, WA*

Olympic Raft & Guide Service [W] *Port Angeles, WA*

Olympic Van Tours, Inc [W] *Port Angeles, WA*

Ona Beach [W] *Newport, OR*

Ontario [W] *Ontario, OR*

Orcas Island [W] *San Juan Islands, WA*

Oregon Cabaret Theatre [S] *Ashland, OR*

Oregon Caves National Monument [W] *Cave Junction, OR*

Oregon Caves National Monument [W] *Grants Pass, OR*

Oregon Coast Aquarium [W] *Newport, OR*

Oregon Coast Music Festival [A] *Coos Bay, OR*

Oregon Connection/House of Myrtlewood, The [W] *Coos Bay, OR*

Oregon Dunes National Recreation Area [W] *North Bend, OR*

Oregon Dunes National Recreation Area [W] *Reedsport, OR*

Oregon Folklife Festival [A] *Corvallis, OR*

Oregon History Center [W] *Portland, OR*

Oregon Jamboree, The [A] *Sweet Home, OR*

Oregon Museum of Science and Industry [W] *Portland, OR*

Oregon Shakespeare Festival [S] *Ashland, OR*

Oregon State Fair [A] *Salem, OR*

Oregon State University [W] *Corvallis, OR*

Oregon Trail Days [A] *La Grande, OR*

Oregon Trail Interpretive Center [W] *Oregon City, OR*

Oregon Trail Living History Park [W] *The Dalles, OR*

Oregon Trail Regional Museum [W] *Baker City, OR*

Oregon Trail Rendezvous Pageant [A] *Montpelier, ID*

Oregon Vortex Location of the House of Mystery, The [W] *Jacksonville, OR*

Oregon Zoo [W] *Portland, OR*

Oswald West State Park [W] *Cannon Beach, OR*

Other tours [W] *Jasper National Park, AB*

Our Lady of the Rockies [W] *Butte, MT*

Outfitting and Big Game Hunting [W] *Afton, WY*

Owen Municipal Rose Garden [W] *Eugene, OR*

Owyhee Canyon [W] *Ontario, OR*

Oxbow Dam [W] *Weiser, ID*

Oysterville [W] *Long Beach, WA*

Pacific Lutheran University [W] *Tacoma, WA*

Pacific National Exhibition Annual Fair [A] *Vancouver, BC*

Pacific Northwest Arts and Crafts Fair [A] *Seattle, WA*

Pacific Northwest Sled Dog Championship Races [A] *Priest Lake Area, ID*

Pacific NW Scottish Highland Games [A] *Enumclaw, WA*

Pacific Paradise Family Fun Center [W] *Ocean Shores, WA*

Pacific Science Center [W] *Seattle, WA*

Pacific Space Centre [W] *Vancouver, BC*

Pacific Undersea Gardens [W] *Victoria, BC*

Pacific University [W] *Forest Grove, OR*

Pack Horse Races [A] *Dubois, WY*

Pack trips into Idaho primitive areas [W] *McCall, ID*

Paddlewheel/Gray Line/River Rouge boat & bus tours [W] *Winnipeg, MB*

Painted Hills Unit [W] *John Day, OR*

Painted Rocks [W] *Yakima, WA*

Painted Rocks State Park [W] *Hamilton, MT*

Paisley [W] *Lakeview, OR*

Palouse River Canyon [W] *Dayton (Columbia County), WA*

Panorama Point [W] *Hood River, OR*

Paradise [W] *Mount Rainier National Park, WA*

Paradise area [W] *Mount Rainier National Park, WA*

Pari-mutuel Horse Racing [A] *Grants Pass, OR*

Paris Gibson Square Museum of Art [W] *Great Falls, MT*

Park County Museum [W] *Livingston, MT*

Parks [W] *Edmonton, AB*

Parks. Airport, [W] *Blackfoot, ID*

Parks. Kamiak Butte County Park [W] *Pullman, WA*

Parliament Buildings [W] *Victoria, BC*

Paul Bunyan Days [A] *St. Marie's, ID*

Paxson Paintings [W] *Missoula, MT*

Payette National Forest [W] *McCall, ID*

Peace Arch Celebration [A] *Blaine, WA*

Peach Festival [A] *Penticton, BC*

Peaks to Prairies Triathlon [A] *Billings, MT*

Pear Blossom Festival [A] *Medford, OR*

Pearson Air Museum [W] *Vancouver, WA*

Pebble Creek Ski Area [W] *Pocatello, ID*

Pendleton Round-up [A] *Pendleton, OR*

Pendleton Woolen Mills [W] *Pendleton, OR*

Peninsula Park and Community Center [W] *Portland, OR*

Penticton Museum [W] *Penticton, BC*

Percival Landing Park [W] *Olympia, WA*

Perrine Memorial Bridge [W] *Twin Falls, ID*

Peter Paddlefish Day [A] *Sidney, MT*

Petersen Rock Gardens [W] *Redmond, OR*

Peter Skene Ogden Wayside [W] *Redmond, OR*

Peter Yegen, Jr—Yellowstone County Museum [W] *Billings, MT*

Petroglyph Park [W] *Nanaimo, BC*

Petroglyphs [W] *Clarkston, WA*

Phillips County Museum [W] *Malta, MT*

Pictograph Cave State Park [W] *Billings, MT*

Pierce County Fair [A] *Puyallup, WA*

Pike Place Market [W] *Seattle, WA*

Pilot Butte [W] *Bend, OR*

Pine Mountain Observatory [W] *Bend, OR*

Pioneer Cabin [W] *Helena, MT*

Pioneer Farm [W] *Tacoma, WA*

Pioneer Mother's Memorial Log Cabin [W] *Newberg, OR*

Pioneer Museum [W] *Glasgow, MT*

Pioneer Park [W] *Puyallup, WA*

Pioneer Park [W] *Walla Walla, WA*

Pioneer Square [W] *Seattle, WA*

Pittock Mansion [W] *Portland, OR*

Plains Indian Museum [W] *Cody, WY*

Plains Indian PowWow [A] *Cody, WY*

Platte County Fair and Rodeo [A] *Wheatland, WY*

Playmill Theater [S] *West Yellowstone, MT*

Point Defiance Park [W] *Tacoma, WA*

Point Defiance Zoo and Aquarium [W] *Tacoma, WA*

Point Ellice House Museum [W] *Victoria, BC*

Polar Bear Swim [A] *Nanaimo, BC*

Police Historical Museum [W] *Portland, OR*

Polson-Flathead Historical Museum [W] *Polson, MT*

Polson Park and Museum [W] *Hoquiam, WA*

Pomerelle Ski Area [W] *Burley, ID*

Ponderosa State Park [W] *McCall, ID*

Port Gamble Historic Museum [W] *Port Gamble, WA*

Portland Art Museum [W] *Portland, OR*

Portland Center Stage [S] *Portland, OR*

Portland Marathon [A] *Portland, OR*

Portland Rose Festival [A] *Portland, OR*

Portland Saturday Market [W] *Portland, OR*

Portland Scottish Highland Games [A] *Portland, OR*

Portland State University [W] *Portland, OR*

Portneuf Muzzleloader Blackpowder Rendezvous [A] *American Falls, ID*

Potholes Reservoir [W] *Moses Lake, WA*

Potholes State Park [W] *Moses Lake, WA*

Powell County Museum [W] *Deer Lodge, MT*

Powwow & Tipi Village [A] *Fort Macleod, AB*
Powwows [A] *Riverton, WY*
PRCA Rodeo [A] *Toppenish, WA*
Prehistoric Gardens [W] *Gold Beach, OR*
Preston Estate Vineyards [W] *Pasco, WA*
Priest Lake [W] *Priest Lake Area, ID*
Priest Lake State Park [W] *Priest Lake Area, ID*
Priest Point Park [W] *Olympia, WA*
Priest River [W] *Priest Lake Area, ID*
Professional sports [W] *Portland, OR*
Provincial Building & Court House [W] *Revelstoke, BC*
Provincial Museum of Alberta [W] *Edmonton, AB*
Pryor Mountain Wild Horse Range [W] *Lovell, WY*
Pullman Summer Palace Theater [W] *Pullman, WA*
Quarter Horse Show [A] *Kalispell, MT*
Queen Elizabeth Park [W] *Vancouver, BC*
Queen Elizabeth Promenade [W] *Nanaimo, BC*
"Race to the Sky" Dog Sled Races [A] *Helena, MT*
Rafting. Yellowstone Raft Company [W] *Gardiner, MT*
Rainbow Falls State Park [W] *Chehalis, WA*
Rain Fest [A] *Longview, WA*
Rain forests [W] *Olympic National Park, WA*
Rainier Brewing Company [W] *Seattle, WA*
Range Rider of the Yellowstone [W] *Billings, MT*
Range Riders Museum and Pioneer Memorial Hall [W] *Miles City, MT*
Ravalli County Fair, Rodeo, and Horse Races [A] *Hamilton, MT*
Real Oregon Gift, The [W] *North Bend, OR*
Recreation areas [W] *Everett, WA*
Red Deer and District Museum [W] *Red Deer, AB*
Red Desert Round-Up [A] *Rock Springs, WY*
Red Eagle Lake [W] *Glacier National Park, MT*
Redfish Lake Visitor Center [W] *Stanley, ID*
Red Lodge Mountain Ski Area [W] *Red Lodge, MT*
Red River Exhibition [A] *Winnipeg, MB*
Reeder's Alley [W] *Helena, MT*

Remington-Alberta Carriage Centre [W] *Fort Macleod, AB*
Rendezvous [A] *Colville, WA*
Rendezvous in the Park [A] *Moscow, ID*
Restored buildings [W] *Virginia City, MT*
Return of the Sternwheeler Days [A] *Hood River, OR*
Revelstoke Dam Visitor Centre [W] *Revelstoke, BC*
Revelstoke Mountain Arts Festival [A] *Revelstoke, BC*
Revelstoke Sno Fest [A] *Revelstoke, BC*
Reynolds-Alberta Museum [W] *Edmonton, AB*
Rhododendron Festival [A] *Florence, OR*
Richland County Fair and Rodeo [A] *Sidney, MT*
Ripley's—Believe It or Not [W] *Newport, OR*
River cruise [W] *Mount Hood National Forest, OR*
River Expeditions [W] *Stanley, ID*
Riverfront Park [W] *Spokane, WA*
Riverfront Park [W] *The Dalles, OR*
River Rafting [W] *Glacier National Park, MT*
River rafting, backpack, fishing, and pack trips [W] *Salmon, ID*
River Rafting. Flathead Raft Company [W] *Polson, MT*
River rafting. Salmon River Outfitters [W] *McCall, ID*
River Runners [W] *Cody, WY*
Riverside State Park [W] *Spokane, WA*
Riverton Museum [W] *Riverton, WY*
River trips. Yellowstone Raft Company [W] *Big Sky (Gallatin County), MT*
Robbers' Roost [W] *Virginia City, MT*
Robert Mortvedt Library [W] *Tacoma, WA*
Rockhounding. Richardson's Recreational Ranch [W] *Madras, OR*
Rocky Boy Powwow [A] *Havre, MT*
Rocky Mountain College [W] *Billings, MT*
Rocky Mountain Raft Tours [W] *Banff, AB*
Rocky Mountain River Tours [W] *Pocatello, ID*
Rocky Reach Dam [W] *Wenatchee, WA*
Rodeo [A] *Harlowton, MT*
Rodeo Days [A] *Cheney, WA*
Rogue River National Forest [W] *Medford, OR*
Rogue River Raft Trips [W] *Grants Pass, OR*

Rooster Rock [W] *Portland, OR*

Rosalie Whyel Museum of Doll Art [W] *Bellevue, WA*

Roseburg Graffiti Week [A] *Roseburg, OR*

Ross House [W] *Winnipeg, MB*

Ross Park [W] *Pocatello, ID*

Rothschild House [W] *Port Townsend, WA*

Round Lake State Park [W] *Sandpoint, ID*

Round-up Rodeo [A] *Livingston, MT*

Royal British Columbia Museum [W] *Victoria, BC*

Royal Canadian Mint [W] *Winnipeg, MB*

Royal Hudson Excursion [W] *Vancouver, BC*

Royal London Wax Museum [W] *Victoria, BC*

Royal Manitoba Winter Fair [A] *Brandon, MB*

Royal Tyrrell Museum of Paleontology [W] *Calgary, AB*

Ruins of Old Fort Benton [W] *Fort Benton, MT*

Rutherford House [W] *Edmonton, AB*

Sacajawea State Park [W] *Pasco, WA*

Saddle Mountain State Park [W] *Seaside, OR*

Sage and Sun Festival [A] *Ephrata, WA*

Sagebrush Days [A] *Buhl, ID*

Sage Riders Rodeo [A] *Umatilla, OR*

Salem Art Fair & Festival [A] *Salem, OR*

Salmon Bake [A] *Depoe Bay, OR*

Salmon Days Festival [A] *Issaquah, WA*

Salmon Harbor [W] *Reedsport, OR*

Salmon National Forest [W] *Salmon, ID*

Salmon River [W] *Stanley, ID*

Salmon River Days [A] *Salmon, ID*

Salty Sea Days [A] *Everett, WA*

Samson V Maritime Museum [W] *Vancouver, BC*

Samuel Benn Park [W] *Aberdeen, WA*

Samuel H. Boardman [W] *Brookings, OR*

Sandcastle Contest [A] *Cannon Beach, OR*

Sand Dunes Frontier [W] *Florence, OR*

Sandhill Crane Festival [A] *Othello, WA*

Sandpoint Public Beach [W] *Sandpoint, ID*

San Juan Island [W] *San Juan Islands, WA*

San Juan Island National Historical Park [W] *San Juan Islands, WA*

San Juan Islands Trip [W] *Anacortes, WA*

Santa Claus Parade & Festival [A] *Fort Macleod, AB*

Santa's City of Lights [A] *Sedro Woolley, WA*

Sarah Spurgeon Art Gallery [W] *Ellensburg, WA*

Sawtooth Mountain Mamas Arts & Crafts Fair [A] *Stanley, ID*

Sawtooth National Forest [W] *Bellevue, ID*

Sawtooth National Forest [W] *Burley, ID*

Sawtooth National Recreation Area [W] *Stanley, ID*

Sawtooth National Recreation Area [W] *Sun Valley Area, ID*

Sawtooth Quilt Festival [A] *Stanley, ID*

Sawtooth Twin Falls Ranger District [W] *Twin Falls, ID*

Sawtooth Valley & Stanley Basin [W] *Stanley, ID*

Sawtooth Wilderness [W] *Stanley, ID*

Scandinavian Midsummer Festival [A] *Astoria, OR*

Scenic Beach [W] *Bremerton, WA*

Scenic drives [W] *Coeur d'Alene, ID*

Scenic Drives. North [W] *Victoria, BC*

Scenic Drives. Skyline [W] *Pinedale, WY*

Schaefer County Park [W] *Centralia, WA*

Schafer State Park [W] *Aberdeen, WA*

Schminck Memorial Museum [W] *Lakeview, OR*

Schmitz Park [W] *Seattle, WA*

Scoggin Valley Park and Hagg Lake [W] *Forest Grove, OR*

SeaBus Harbour Ride [W] *Vancouver, BC*

Seafair [A] *Seattle, WA*

Seafood and Wine Festival [A] *Bandon, OR*

Seafood and Wine Festival [A] *Newport, OR*

Sea Lion Caves [W] *Florence, OR*

Seaquest State Park [W] *Kelso, WA*

Seascape scenic drive [W] *Long Beach, WA*

Seaside Aquarium [W] *Seaside, OR*

Seattle Aquarium, The [W] *Seattle, WA*

Seattle Art Museum [W] *Seattle, WA*

Seattle Asian Art Museum [W] *Seattle, WA*

Seattle Center [W] *Seattle, WA*

Seattle Center Opera House, Playhouse, Arena, Key Arena [W] *Seattle, WA*

Seattle City Light Skagit Hydroelectric Project [W] *Sedro Woolley, WA*

Seattle University [W] *Seattle, WA*

Secwepemc Native Heritage Park [W] *Kamloops, BC*

Sehome Hill Arboretum [W] *Bellingham, WA*

Semiahmoo Park [W] *Blaine, WA*

Seminoe State Park [W] *Rawlins, WY*

Senior Pro Rodeo [A] *Lusk, WY*

Septemberfest [A] *Torrington, WY*

Sequim Bay State Park [W] *Sequim, WA*

Seven Oaks House Museum [W] *Winnipeg, MB*

Seward Park [W] *Seattle, WA*

Seymour Ski Country [W] *Vancouver, BC*

Shafer Museum [W] *Winthrop, WA*

Sheep Rock Unit [W] *John Day, OR*

Sheridan County Rodeo [A] *Sheridan, WY*

Sheridan-Wyo PRCA Rodeo [A] *Sheridan, WY*

Shilshole Bay Marina [W] *Seattle, WA*

Shipwreck Day [A] *Anacortes, WA*

Shootout, The [S] *Jackson, WY*

Shore Acres [W] *Coos Bay, OR*

Shoshone-Bannock Indian Festival [A] *Blackfoot, ID*

Shoshone-Bannock Indian Festival [A] *Pocatello, ID*

Shoshone Falls [W] *Twin Falls, ID*

Shoshone Falls Park [W] *Twin Falls, ID*

Shoshone Indian Ice Caves [W] *Shoshone, ID*

Shoshone National Forest [W] *Cody, WY*

Showdown Ski Area [W] *White Sulphur Springs, MT*

Sierra Silver Mine Tour [W] *Wallace, ID*

Silver Falls State Park [W] *Silverton, OR*

Silver Mountain Ski Area [W] *Kellogg, ID*

Silverwood Theme Park [W] *Coeur d'Alene, ID*

Simon Fraser University [W] *Vancouver, BC*

Sinks Canyon State Park [W] *Lander, WY*

Sir Alexander Galt Museum [W] *Lethbridge, AB*

Siskiyou National Forest [W] *Grants Pass, OR*

Siuslaw National Forest [W] *Corvallis, OR*

Siuslaw Pioneer Museum [W] *Florence, OR*

Skagit County Fair [A] *Mount Vernon, WA*

Skagit County Historical Museum [W] *La Conner, WA*

Skagit Valley Tulip Festival [A] *Anacortes, WA*

Ski Acres [W] *North Bend, WA*

Ski areas. Spout Springs [W] *Pendleton, OR*

Ski Bluewood [W] *Dayton (Columbia County), WA*

Skiing [W] *Whistler, BC*

Skiing. Discovery Basin [W] *Anaconda, MT*

Skiing. Hurricane Ridge Winter Use Area [W] *Olympic National Park, WA*

Skiing. Lost Trail Powder Mountain [W] *Hamilton, MT*

Skiing. Mount Spokane [W] *Spokane, WA*

Skiing. Schweitzer Mountain Resort [W] *Sandpoint, ID*

Skiing. Snowhaven [W] *Grangeville, ID*

Skiing. White Pass Village [W] *Yakima, WA*

Ski to Sea Festival [A] *Bellingham, WA*

Sleeping Giant Ski Area [W] *Cody, WY*

smART Festival [A] *St. Marie's, ID*

Smith Cove [W] *Seattle, WA*

Smith Rock [W] *Redmond, OR*

Smokejumper Center [W] *Missoula, MT*

Snake River Heritage Center [W] *Weiser, ID*

Snake River Stampede [A] *Nampa, ID*

Snoqualmie Falls [W] *North Bend, WA*

Snoqualmie Ski Area [W] *North Bend, WA*

Snoqualmie Valley Historical Museum [W] *North Bend, WA*

Snowfest [A] *Kelowna, BC*

Snow King Ski Resort [W] *Jackson, WY*

Snowy Range Ski Area [W] *Laramie, WY*

Soldier Mountain Ski Area [W] *Mountain Home, ID*

Solitude Float Trips [W] *Jackson, WY*

Sorosis Park [W] *The Dalles, OR*

South Bannock County Historical Center [W] *Lava Hot Springs, ID*

South Beach [W] *Newport, OR*

Southern Oregon History Center [W] *Medford, OR*

South Hills Ridgeline Trail [W] *Eugene, OR*
South Pass City [W] *Lander, WY*
South Slough National Estuarine Research Reserve [W] *Coos Bay, OR*
Southwest Washington Fair [A] *Centralia, WA*
Space Needle [W] *Seattle, WA*
Spencer Butte Park [W] *Eugene, OR*
Sperry and Grinnell Glaciers [W] *Glacier National Park, MT*
Spokane Civic Theatre [S] *Spokane, WA*
Spokane Falls [W] *Spokane, WA*
Spokane Interstate Fair [A] *Spokane, WA*
Spring Barrel Tasting [A] *Yakima, WA*
Spring Craft Fair [A] *Roseburg, OR*
Spring Festival [A] *Moses Lake, WA*
Spring Festival [A] *Priest Lake Area, ID*
Spruce Meadows [W] *Calgary, AB*
Spruce Meadows [A] *Calgary, AB*
Squilchuck State Park [W] *Wenatchee, WA*
Stagecoach Museum [W] *Lusk, WY*
Stampede and Suicide Race [A] *Omak, WA*
Standrod House [W] *Pocatello, ID*
Stanley Park [W] *Vancouver, BC*
St. Anthony Sand Dunes [W] *St. Anthony, ID*
Star Center Antique Mall [W] *Snohomish, WA*
State Capital Museum [W] *Olympia, WA*
State Capitol [W] *Boise, ID*
State Capitol [W] *Cheyenne, WY*
State Capitol [W] *Helena, MT*
State Capitol [W] *Salem, OR*
State Capitol Campus [W] *Olympia, WA*
State Championship Old-time Fiddle Contest [A] *Riverton, WY*
State Fair [A] *Great Falls, MT*
St.-Boniface Museum [W] *Winnipeg, MB*
Steamboat Rock State Park [W] *Coulee Dam, WA*
Ste. Chapelle Winery & Vineyards [W] *Caldwell, ID*
Steens Mountain Rim Run [A] *Burns, OR*
Sternwheeler Columbia Gorge [W] *Portland, OR*
Stevens Crawford Museum [W] *Oregon City, OR*
Stevens Pass Ski Area [W] *Leavenworth, WA*
Stevens Pass Ski Area [W] *Snohomish, WA*

St. Francis Xavier Church [W] *Missoula, MT*
St. Joe Baldy Mountain [W] *St. Marie's, ID*
St. Joe River [W] *Coeur d'Alene, ID*
St. Joe River [W] *St. Marie's, ID*
St. Mary Lake [W] *Glacier National Park, MT*
St. Mary's Mission [W] *Hamilton, MT*
St. Michael's Episcopal Cathedral [W] *Boise, ID*
Stock Car Racing [S] *Hermiston, OR*
St. Patrick's Irish Festival [A] *Portland, OR*
St. Paul's Episcopal Church [W] *Virginia City, MT*
St. Paul's Mission [W] *Colville, WA*
St. Peter's Church [W] *Tacoma, WA*
Strawberry Festival [A] *Marysville, WA*
Street Fair [A] *Enumclaw, WA*
Succor Creek Canyon [W] *Caldwell, ID*
SUDS Festival [A] *Gold Beach, OR*
Summer [W] *Sun Valley Area, ID*
Summer Band Concert Series [S] *Pocatello, ID*
Summer Celebration [A] *Fort Benton, MT*
Summerfest [A] *St. Anthony, ID*
Summer Fun Fest and Antique Tractor Pull [A] *Wheatland, WY*
Summit climb [W] *Mount St. Helens National Volcanic Monument, WA*
Sumner Summer Festival [A] *Puyallup, WA*
Sumpter Valley Railroad [W] *Baker City, OR*
Sunflower Days [A] *Clarkston, WA*
Sunrise [W] *Mount Rainier National Park, WA*
Sunrise Festival of the Arts [A] *Sidney, MT*
Sunset Bay [W] *Coos Bay, OR*
Sunshine Mine Disaster Memorial [W] *Kellogg, ID*
Sun Valley Resort. Year-round activities [W] *Sun Valley Area, ID*
Super Saturday [A] *Olympia, WA*
Swan Lake [W] *Bigfork, MT*
Sweet Home Rodeo, The [A] *Sweet Home, OR*
Sweet Pea Festival [A] *Bozeman, MT*
Sweetwater County fair [A] *Rock Springs, WY*
Sweetwater County Historical Museum [W] *Green River, WY*
Swimming, hiking, camping, boating, fishing, windsurfing [W] *Sedro Woolley, WA*
Symphony of Fire [A] *Vancouver, BC*
Table Rock [W] *Boise, ID*

Tacoma Art Museum [W] *Tacoma, WA*

Tacoma Little Theater [S] *Tacoma, WA*

Tacoma Nature Center [W] *Tacoma, WA*

Tacoma Symphony Orchestra [S] *Tacoma, WA*

Targhee National Forest [W] *Ashton, ID*

Taste of Chelan Street Fair [A] *Chelan, WA*

Taste of Tacoma [A] *Tacoma, WA*

Tautphaus Park [W] *Idaho Falls, ID*

Temple of Justice [W] *Olympia, WA*

Territorial Days [A] *Deer Lodge, MT*

Teton Country Prairie Schooner Holiday [W] *Jackson, WY*

Teton County Historical Center [W] *Jackson, WY*

Teton Flood Museum [W] *Rexburg, ID*

Teton Mountain Bike Tours [W] *Jackson, WY*

Theatre West [W] *Lincoln City, OR*

Thompson-Hickman Memorial Museum [W] *Virginia City, MT*

Thoroughbred racing [S] *Boise, ID*

Three Valley Gap [W] *Revelstoke, BC*

Threshing Bee and Antique Equipment Show [A] *Ellensburg, WA*

Thunder Basin National Grassland [W] *Douglas, WY*

Thunderbird Park [W] *Victoria, BC*

Thundering Seas [W] *Depoe Bay, OR*

Thurston County Fair [A] *Olympia, WA*

Tillamook Dairy Parade & Rodeo [A] *Tillamook, OR*

Tillamook County Fair [A] *Tillamook, OR*

Tillamook County Pioneer Museum [W] *Tillamook, OR*

Tillicum Beach Campground [W] *Yachats, OR*

Tillicum Village [W] *Seattle, WA*

Timberline Lodge [W] *Mount Hood National Forest, OR*

Tollie Shay Engine & Caboose #7 [W] *Union, WA*

Totem Pole [W] *Everett, WA*

Totem Pole [W] *Tacoma, WA*

Tours. Coal Mines [W] *Gillette, WY*

Tou Velle State Park [W] *Medford, OR*

Towe Ford Museum [W] *Deer Lodge, MT*

Trail End Historic Center [W] *Sheridan, WY*

Trail of the Cedars [W] *Sedro Woolley, WA*

Trail Town and the Museum of the Old West [W] *Cody, WY*

Trenner Memorial Park [W] *American Falls, ID*

Triangle X Float Trips [W] *Jackson, WY*

Tri-Cities Water Follies [A] *Pasco, WA*

Tri-County Fair and Rodeo [A] *Deer Lodge, MT*

Trips into Hell's Canyon [W] *Weiser, ID*

Tucker Cellars Winery [W] *Sunnyside, WA*

Tulalip Reservation [W] *Marysville, WA*

Tulip Festival [A] *Mount Vernon, WA*

Tumalo [W] *Bend, OR*

Tumalo Falls [W] *Bend, OR*

Tumwater Falls Park [W] *Olympia, WA*

Tumwater Valley Athletic Club [W] *Olympia, WA*

Turkey Rama [A] *McMinnville, OR*

Turnbull National Wildlife Refuge [W] *Cheney, WA*

Turner Mountain Ski Area [W] *Libby, MT*

Turns of the Brick [W] *La Grande, OR*

Twanoh State Park [W] *Union, WA*

Twenty-Five Mile Creek [W] *Chelan, WA*

Twin Bridges [W] *Rexburg, ID*

Twin Falls [W] *Twin Falls, ID*

Twin Falls County Fair & Rodeo [A] *Twin Falls, ID*

Twin Falls County Fair and Rodeo [A] *Buhl, ID*

Twin Falls Park [W] *Twin Falls, ID*

Twin Harbors State Park [W] *Westport, WA*

Two Medicine Valley [W] *Glacier National Park, MT*

Two Rivers Park [W] *Kennewick, WA*

Tyee Wine Cellars [W] *Corvallis, OR*

UBC Botanical Garden [W] *Vancouver, BC*

Uinta County Fair [A] *Evanston, WY*

Ukiah-Dale Forest State Park [W] *Pendleton, OR*

Umatilla Indian Reservation [W] *Pendleton, OR*

Umatilla Marina Park [W] *Umatilla, OR*

Umatilla National Forest [W] *Clarkston, WA*

Umatilla National Forest [W] *Pendleton, OR*

Umpqua Discovery Center [W] *Reedsport, OR*

Umpqua Lighthouse State Park [W] *Reedsport, OR*

Umpqua National Forest [W] *Roseburg, OR*

Umpqua Valley Roundup [A] *Roseburg, OR*
Underground Tour [W] *Seattle, WA*
Undersea Gardens [W] *Newport, OR*
Union County Fair [A] *La Grande, OR*
Union Station [W] *Tacoma, WA*
Unity Lake State Park [W] *Baker City, OR*
University Gallery [W] *Tacoma, WA*
University of Alberta [W] *Edmonton, AB*
University of British Columbia [W] *Vancouver, BC*
University of Great Falls [W] *Great Falls, MT*
University of Idaho [W] *Moscow, ID*
University of Montana [W] *Missoula, MT*
University of Oregon [W] *Eugene, OR*
University of Puget Sound [W] *Tacoma, WA*
University of Washington [W] *Seattle, WA*
University of Wyoming [W] *Laramie, WY*
Upper Mesa Falls [W] *Ashton, ID*
USS *Turner Joy* [W] *Bremerton, WA*
Valley Art Center [W] *Clarkston, WA*
Valley Bronze of Oregon [W] *Joseph, OR*
Valley of the Rogue State Park [W] *Grants Pass, OR*
Valley Zoo [W] *Edmonton, AB*
Vancouver Aquarium [W] *Vancouver, BC*
Vancouver Art Gallery [W] *Vancouver, BC*
Vancouver Island [W] *Victoria, BC*
Vancouver Island Exhibition [A] *Nanaimo, BC*
Vancouver Museum [W] *Vancouver, BC*
VanDusen Botanical Garden [W] *Vancouver, BC*
Vedauwoo [W] *Laramie, WY*
Veteran's Day Parade [A] *Albany, OR*
Victorian Days [A] *Victoria, BC*
Vigilante Rodeo [A] *Butte, MT*
Vintage Celebration [S] *Newberg, OR*
Virginia City-Madison County Historical Museum [W] *Virginia City, MT*
Visitor Center [W] *Anaconda, MT*
Visitor Center [W] *Missoula, MT*
Visitor Center [W] *Newberg, OR*
Visitor Center [W] *Olympic National Park, WA*
Visitor centers [W] *Mount Rainier National Park, WA*
Visitor information stations [W] *Mount St. Helens National Volcanic Monument, WA*

Volcano Information Center [W] *Kelso, WA*
Volunteer Park [W] *Seattle, WA*
Wadopana Powwow [A] *Wolf Point, MT*
Wagon Days [A] *Sun Valley Area, ID*
Wagons West [W] *Jackson, WY*
Wahkpa Chu'gn [W] *Havre, MT*
Walking tour of historical houses [W] *Snohomish, WA*
Wallace District Mining Museum [W] *Wallace, ID*
Wallowa Lake State Park [W] *Joseph, OR*
Wallowa Lake Tramway [W] *Joseph, OR*
Wallowa-Whitman National Forest [W] *Baker City, OR*
Wanapum Dam Heritage Center [W] *Ellensburg, WA*
War Bonnet Roundup [A] *Idaho Falls, ID*
Warhawk Air Museum [W] *Caldwell, ID*
Warren AFB [W] *Cheyenne, WY*
Warren G. Magnuson Park [W] *Seattle, WA*
Wasco County Historical Museum [W] *The Dalles, OR*
Washington Hills Cellar [W] *Sunnyside, WA*
Washington Park [W] *Anacortes, WA*
Washington Park [W] *Portland, OR*
Washington Park Arboretum [W] *Seattle, WA*
Washington State Apple Blossom Festival [A] *Wenatchee, WA*
Washington State History Museum [W] *Tacoma, WA*
Washington State University [W] *Pullman, WA*
Waskasoo Park [W] *Red Deer, AB*
Waterfront Festival [A] *Anacortes, WA*
Water sports [W] *Pinedale, WY*
Waterton Lakes National Park [W] *Fort Macleod, AB*
Water Tower in Johns Landing [W] *Portland, OR*
Wax Works [W] *Newport, OR*
Wayfarers Unit [W] *Bigfork, MT*
Wayne Estes Memorial Tournament [A] *Anaconda, MT*
Wenatchee National Forest [W] *Wenatchee, WA*
Wenberg State Park [W] *Marysville, WA*
West Coast Game Park [W] *Bandon, OR*
West Edmonton Mall and Canada Fantasyland [W] *Edmonton, AB*
Western Art Show [A] *Toppenish, WA*
Western Days [A] *Twin Falls, ID*

Westerner Days [A] *Red Deer, AB*
Western Heritage Center [W] *Billings, MT*
Western Heritage Centre [W] *Calgary, AB*
Western History Center [W] *Torrington, WY*
Western Idaho Fair [A] *Boise, ID*
Western Montana Fair [A] *Missoula, MT*
Western Montana Quarter Horse Show [A] *Missoula, MT*
Western Rendezvous of Art [A] *Helena, MT*
Western Washington Fair [A] *Puyallup, WA*
Western Washington Univ [W] *Bellingham, WA*
Westport Aquarium [W] *Westport, WA*
West Salem Waterfront Parade [A] *Salem, OR*
Westward Ho! Sternwheeler [W] *Florence, OR*
Whale Museum, The [W] *San Juan Islands, WA*
Whale of a Wine Festival [A] *Gold Beach, OR*
Whale-watching tours [W] *Victoria, BC*
Whatcom Falls Park [W] *Bellingham, WA*
Whatcom Museum of History & Art [W] *Bellingham, WA*
Wheat Land Communities Fair [A] *Ritzville, WA*
Whidbey Island Jazz Festival [A] *Oak Harbor, WA*
Whidbey Island Naval Air Station [W] *Oak Harbor, WA*
Whistler [W] *Whistler, BC*
White Bird Hill [W] *Grangeville, ID*
Whitefish Lake [W] *Whitefish, MT*
Whitefish State Park [W] *Whitefish, MT*
White Pass Village [W] *Mount Rainier National Park, WA*
Whitewater rafting [W] *Eugene, OR*
Whitewater Rafting. Sun Country Tours [W] *Bend, OR*
Whitman Mission National Historic Site [W] *Walla Walla, WA*
Whitney Gallery of Western Art [W] *Cody, WY*
Whoop-Up Days [A] *Lethbridge, AB*
Wild Blackberry Festival [A] *Cave Junction, OR*
Wild Horse Stampede [A] *Wolf Point, MT*
Wildlife Safari [W] *Roseburg, OR*

Wildlife Safari Wildlights [A] *Roseburg, OR*
Wild River Adventures [W] *Glacier National Park, MT*
Wild Waves Water Park [W] *Tacoma, WA*
Wild West Day [A] *Bigfork, MT*
Wild West Winter Carnival [A] *Riverton, WY*
Willamette Falls Locks [W] *Oregon City, OR*
Willamette National Forest [W] *Eugene, OR*
Willamette Pass Ski Area [W] *Eugene, OR*
Willamette Science & Technology Center [W] *Eugene, OR*
Willamette Stone [W] *Portland, OR*
Willamette University [W] *Salem, OR*
William M. Tugman State Park [W] *Reedsport, OR*
Wind River Canyon [W] *Thermopolis, WY*
Wind River Historical Center [W] *Dubois, WY*
Wind River Rendezvous [A] *Dubois, WY*
Windy Ridge Viewpoint [W] *Mount St. Helens National Volcanic Monument, WA*
Wine & Food Classic [A] *McMinnville, OR*
Winema National Forest [W] *Klamath Falls, OR*
Wing Luke Museum [W] *Seattle, WA*
Winnipeg Art Gallery [W] *Winnipeg, MB*
Winnipeg Folk Festival [A] *Winnipeg, MB*
Winnipeg Symphony Orchestra [S] *Winnipeg, MB*
Winter [W] *Sun Valley Area, ID*
Winter Carnival [A] *McCall, ID*
Winter Carnival [A] *Red Lodge, MT*
Winter Carnival [A] *Sandpoint, ID*
Winter Carnival [A] *Whitefish, MT*
Winter recreation [W] *Pinedale, WY*
Wolf Haven America [W] *Olympia, WA*
Wonderful Water World [W] *Penticton, BC*
Wooden Boat Festival [A] *Olympia, WA*
Wooden Boat Festival [A] *Port Townsend, WA*
Woodfest [A] *Sedro Woolley, WA*
Woodland Park [W] *Kalispell, MT*
Woodland Park Zoological Gardens [W] *Seattle, WA*
Worden's Winery [W] *Spokane, WA*

World Center for Birds of Prey [W] *Boise, ID*

World Championship Timber Carnival [A] *Albany, OR*

World-Class Hang-Gliding Festival [A] *Lakeview, OR*

World Forestry Center [W] *Portland, OR*

World Museum of Mining and 1899 Mining Camp [W] *Butte, MT*

World Snowmobile Expo [A] *West Yellowstone, MT*

WPRA Rodeo [A] *Chelan, WA*

Wright Park [W] *Tacoma, WA*

Wyoming Dinosaur Center [W] *Thermopolis, WY*

Wyoming Frontier Prison [W] *Rawlins, WY*

Wyoming Pioneer Memorial Museum [W] *Douglas, WY*

Wyoming River Trips [W] *Cody, WY*

Wyoming State Fair [A] *Douglas, WY*

Wyoming Territorial Prison and Old West Park [W] *Laramie, WY*

Wyoming Vietnam Veteran's Memorial [W] *Cody, WY*

Yachats State Recreation Area [W] *Yachats, OR*

Yahiro Gardens [W] *Olympia, WA*

Yakama Nation Cultural Center [W] *Toppenish, WA*

Yakima Air Fair [A] *Yakima, WA*

Yakima Interurban Trolley Lines [W] *Yakima, WA*

Yakima Meadows Racetrack [S] *Yakima, WA*

Yakima Sportsman State Park [W] *Yakima, WA*

Yakima Valley Museum [W] *Yakima, WA*

Yamhill County Fair [A] *McMinnville, OR*

Yaquina Bay [W] *Newport, OR*

Yaquina Head [W] *Newport, OR*

Yellow Bay Unit [W] *Bigfork, MT*

Yellowstone Art Museum [W] *Billings, MT*

Yellowstone Jazz Festival [A] *Cody, WY*

Yellowstone National Park [W] *Cody, WY*

Yesterday's Playthings [W] *Deer Lodge, MT*

Youth Horse Show [A] *Kalispell, MT*

Zoo Boise [W] *Boise, ID*

ZooMontana [W] *Billings, MT*

LODGING LIST

Establishment names are listed in alphabetical order followed by a symbol identifying their classification and then city and state. The symbols for classification are: [AS] for All Suites, [BB] for B&Bs/Small Inns, [CAS] for Casinos, [CC] for Cottage Colonies, [CON] for Villas/Condos, [CONF] for Conference Centers, [EX] for Extended Stays, [HOT] for Hotels, [MOT] for Motels/Motor Lodges, [RAN] for Guest Ranches, and [RST] for Resorts.

4 WINDS [MOT] *Jackson, WY*
5TH AVENUE SUITES HOTEL [HOT] *Portland, OR*
ABERDEEN MANSION BED AND BREAKFAST [BB] *Aberdeen, WA*
ABIGAIL'S HOTEL [BB] *Victoria, BC*
ABSAROKA LODGE [MOT] *Gardiner, MT*
ABSAROKA MOUNTAIN LODGE [RAN] *Cody, WY*
ABSAROKA RANCH [RAN] *Dubois, WY*
ACCENT INN [HOT] *Victoria, BC*
ACCENT INNS [HOT] *Kelowna, BC*
ACCENT INNS [HOT] *Vancouver, BC*
A CREEKSIDE INN THE MARQUEE HOUSE [BB] *Salem, OR*
ADOBE RESORT MOTEL [MOT] *Yachats, OR*
A DRUMMOND'S RANCH BED & BREAKFAST [BB] *Laramie, WY*
AERIE RESORT, THE [RST] *Victoria, AB*
AIRPORT INN [MOT] *Sun Valley Area, ID*
AKAI MOTEL [MOT] *Banff, AB*
ALDERWOOD INN [MOT] *Portland, OR*
ALEXANDERS COUNTRY INN [BB] *Mount Rainier National Park, WA*
ALEXIS [HOT] *Seattle, WA*
ALL SEASONS RIVER INN [BB] *Leavenworth, WA*
ALPENHOF LODGE [HOT] *Jackson, WY*
ALPINE VILLAGE CABIN RESORT [CC] *Jasper National Park, AB*
AMERICAN INN [MOT] *Hardin, MT*
AMERICAN TRAVEL INN [MOT] *Pullman, WA*
AMERITEL INN [MOT] *Idaho Falls, ID*
AMERITEL INN [MOT] *Pocatello, ID*
AMERITEL INN-TWIN FALLS [MOT] *Twin Falls, ID*
AMETHYST LODGE [MOT] *Jasper National Park, AB*

ANACORTES INN [MOT] *Anacortes, WA*
ANCHOR BAY INN [MOT] *Reedsport, OR*
ANDERSEN HOUSE [BB] *Victoria, BC*
ANGELICA'S BED & BREAKFAST [BB] *Spokane, WA*
ANGEL POINT GUEST SUITES [BB] *Kalispell, MT*
ANN STARRETT MANSION VICTORIAN BED & BREAKFAST [BB] *Port Townsend, WA*
ANTLER INN [MOT] *Jackson, WY*
APPLETON INN BED & BREAKFAST [BB] *Helena, MT*
ARGYLE HOUSE BED & BREAKFAST [BB] *San Juan Islands, WA*
ASPEN VILLAGE INN [MOT] *Waterton Lakes National Park, AB*
ASTORIA DUNES MOTEL [MOT] *Astoria, OR*
AULD HOLLAND INN [MOT] *Oak Harbor, WA*
AVERILL'S FLATHEAD LAKE LODGE [RAN] *Bigfork, MT*
BAD ROCK COUNTRY BED & BREAKFAST [BB] *Columbia Falls, MT*
BAKER CREEK CHALETS [HOT] *Lake Louise, AB*
BALI HAI MOTEL [MOT] *Richland, WA*
BANFF AVE INN [BB] *Banff, AB*
BANFF CARIBOU LODGE [RST] *Banff, AB*
BANFF INTERNATIONAL [HOT] *Banff, AB*
BANFF PARK LODGE [HOT] *Banff, AB*
BANFF PTARMIGAN INN [HOT] *Banff, AB*
BANFF ROCKY MOUNTAIN RESORT [RST] *Banff, AB*
BANFF SPRINGS [HOT] *Banff, AB*
BANFF VOYAGER INN [MOT] *Banff, AB*
BARRISTER BED & BREAKFAST [BB] *Helena, MT*

BAY BRIDGE MOTEL [MOT] *North Bend, OR*
BAYSHORE MOTOR INN [MOT] *Astoria, OR*
BEACONSFIELD INN [BB] *Victoria, BC*
BEAR PAW COURT [MOT] *Chinook, MT*
BEAUTIFUL BED AND BREAKFAST [BB] *Vancouver, BC*
BEAVERTON FAIRFIELD INN [HOT] *Beaverton, OR*
BED & BREAKFAST ON THE GREEN [BB] *Corvallis, OR*
BEDFORD REGENCY, THE [HOT] *Victoria, BC*
BEECH TREE MANOR [BB] *Seattle, WA*
BEL-AIR MOTEL [MOT] *Penticton, BC*
BELLEVUE CLUB HOTEL [HOT] *Bellevue, WA*
BENSON HOTEL [HOT] *Portland, OR*
BEST INN & SUITES [HOT] *Coeur d'Alene, ID*
BEST INN & SUITES [MOT] *Medford, OR*
BEST INN & SUITES [MOT] *Ritzville, WA*
BEST INN & SUITES [MOT] *Roseburg, OR*
BEST INN & SUITES [BB] *Tacoma, WA*
BEST INN & SUITES CASCADE PARK [MOT] *Vancouver, WA*
BEST INN AND CONFERENCE CENTER [MOT] *Missoula, MT*
BEST INN AND SUITES [MOT] *Caldwell, ID*
BEST INN AND SUITES [MOT] *Eugene, OR*
BEST INN AND SUITES [HOT] *Vancouver, WA*
BEST INN NORTH [MOT] *Missoula, MT*
BEST INNS & SUITES [MOT] *Corvallis, OR*
BEST REST INN [MOT] *Boise, ID*
BEST VALUE EL RANCHO MOTEL [MOT] *Moses Lake, WA*
BEST WESTERN [MOT] *Ashland, OR*
BEST WESTERN [MOT] *Baker City, OR*
BEST WESTERN [MOT] *Bellevue, WA*
BEST WESTERN [MOT] *Lusk, WY*
BEST WESTERN [MOT] *Mount Vernon, WA*
BEST WESTERN [MOT] *Reedsport, OR*
BEST WESTERN [HOT] *Richland, WA*
BEST WESTERN [MOT] *Sequim, WA*
BEST WESTERN, INN AT LANDER [MOT] *Lander, WY*
BEST WESTERN/YELLOWSTONE MOTOR INN [MOT] *Livingston, MT*
BEST WESTERN ABERCORN INN [HOT] *Vancouver, BC*

BEST WESTERN AIRPORT EXECUTEL [HOT] *Seattle-Tacoma International Airport Area, WA*
BEST WESTERN AIRPORT MOTOR INN [MOT] *Boise, ID*
BEST WESTERN BILLINGS [MOT] *Billings, MT*
BEST WESTERN BREMERTON INN [MOT] *Bremerton, WA*
BEST WESTERN BUCKS T-4 LODGE [MOT] *Big Sky (Gallatin County), MT*
BEST WESTERN BURLEY INN & CONVENTION CENTER [MOT] *Burley, ID*
BEST WESTERN BY MAMMOTH HOT SPRINGS [RST] *Gardiner, MT*
BEST WESTERN CANYON SPRINGS PARK HOTEL [MOT] *Twin Falls, ID*
BEST WESTERN CARLTON PLAZA [HOT] *Victoria, BC*
BEST WESTERN CASCADIA INN [MOT] *Everett, WA*
BEST WESTERN CAVANAUGH'S TEMPLIN'S RESORT [MOT] *Coeur d'Alene, ID*
BEST WESTERN CEDAR PARK INN [HOT] *Edmonton, AB*
BEST WESTERN CHATEAU GRAN-VILLE [HOT] *Vancouver, BC*
BEST WESTERN CITY CENTRE INN [MOT] *Edmonton, AB*
BEST WESTERN CLOVER CREEK INN [MOT] *Montpelier, ID*
BEST WESTERN COLLEGE WAY INN [MOT] *Mount Vernon, WA*
BEST WESTERN COTTON TREE INN [MOT] *Idaho Falls, ID*
BEST WESTERN COTTON TREE INN [HOT] *Pocatello, ID*
BEST WESTERN COTTON TREE INN [MOT] *Rexburg, ID*
BEST WESTERN DOUGLAS INN [MOT] *Douglas, WY*
BEST WESTERN DOUGLAS INN [MOT] *Roseburg, OR*
BEST WESTERN DUNMAR INN [MOT] *Evanston, WY*
BEST WESTERN EMERALD ISLE MOTOR INN [MOT] *Waterton Lakes National Park, AB*
BEST WESTERN ENTRADA LODGE [MOT] *Bend, OR*
BEST WESTERN EXECUTIVE INN [HOT] *Seattle, WA*
BEST WESTERN EXECUTIVE INN [MOT] *Seattle-Tacoma International Airport Area, WA*
BEST WESTERN EXHIBITION PARK [HOT] *Vancouver, BC*

BEST WESTERN FLYING SADDLE LODGE [MOT] *Alpine, WY*

BEST WESTERN FOOTHILLS MOTOR INN [MOT] *Mountain Home, ID*

BEST WESTERN FOSTER'S COUNTRY INN [MOT] *Laramie, WY*

BEST WESTERN GARDEN VILLA MOTEL [MOT] *Roseburg, OR*

BEST WESTERN GRAND MANOR INN [MOT] *Corvallis, OR*

BEST WESTERN GRAND MANOR [MOT] *Eugene, OR*

BEST WESTERN GRANT CREEK INN [HOT] *Missoula, MT*

BEST WESTERN GRANTREE INN [HOT] *Bozeman, MT*

BEST WESTERN GRANTS PASS INN [MOT] *Grants Pass, OR*

BEST WESTERN GREEN GABLES INN [HOT] *Banff, AB*

BEST WESTERN HALLMARK INN AND CONFERENCE CENTER [HOT] *Moses Lake, WA*

BEST WESTERN HAMILTON INN [MOT] *Hamilton, MT*

BEST WESTERN HARBOR PLAZA [RST] *Oak Harbor, WA*

BEST WESTERN HEIDELBERG INN [HOT] *Lethbridge, AB*

BEST WESTERN HERITAGE INN [HOT] *Great Falls, MT*

BEST WESTERN HIGH COUNTRY INN [MOT] *Afton, WY*

BEST WESTERN HITCHING POST INN RESORT & CONFERENCE CENTER [MOT] *Cheyenne, WY*

BEST WESTERN HOLIDAY MOTEL [MOT] *Coos Bay, OR*

BEST WESTERN HOOD RIVER INN [HOT] *Hood River, OR*

BEST WESTERN HORIZON INN [MOT] *Medford, OR*

BEST WESTERN HOSPITALITY INN [HOT] *Calgary, AB*

BEST WESTERN ICICLE INN [RST] *Leavenworth, WA*

BEST WESTERN IMPERIAL HOTEL [HOT] *Portland, OR*

BEST WESTERN INN [MOT] *Bellingham, WA*

BEST WESTERN INN [MOT] *Jackson, WY*

BEST WESTERN INN [HOT] *Kelowna, BC*

BEST WESTERN INN [MOT] *Lakeview, OR*

BEST WESTERN INN [MOT] *Medicine Hat, AB*

BEST WESTERN INN [MOT] *Miles City, MT*

BEST WESTERN INN [MOT] *Pinedale, WY*

BEST WESTERN INN AT PENTICTON [MOT] *Penticton, BC*

BEST WESTERN INN AT THE MEADOWS [MOT] *Portland, OR*

BEST WESTERN INN AT THE ROGUE [HOT] *Grants Pass, OR*

BEST WESTERN INNER HARBOR [MOT] *Victoria, BC*

BEST WESTERN INN OF JACKSON HOLE [HOT] *Jackson, WY*

BEST WESTERN INTERNATIONAL INN [MOT] *Winnipeg, MB*

BEST WESTERN KENTWOOD LODGE [MOT] *Sun Valley Area, ID*

BEST WESTERN KINGS INN [MOT] *Vancouver, BC*

BEST WESTERN KLAMATH INN [MOT] *Klamath Falls, OR*

BEST WESTERN KWATAQNUK RESORT [RST] *Polson, MT*

BEST WESTERN LAKEWAY INN [RST] *Bellingham, WA*

BEST WESTERN LINCOLN INN [MOT] *Othello, WA*

BEST WESTERN LINCOLN SANDS [MOT] *Lincoln City, OR*

BEST WESTERN LISTEL WHISTLER HOTEL [HOT] *Whistler, BC*

BEST WESTERN LOYAL INN [MOT] *Seattle, WA*

BEST WESTERN LUPINE INN [MOT] *Red Lodge, MT*

BEST WESTERN MCCALL [MOT] *McCall, ID*

BEST WESTERN NEW KINGS INN [MOT] *Salem, OR*

BEST WESTERN NEW OREGON MOTEL [MOT] *Eugene, OR*

BEST WESTERN OCEAN VIEW RESORT [HOT] *Seaside, OR*

BEST WESTERN OLYMPIC INN [HOT] *Klamath Falls, OR*

BEST WESTERN OUTLAW HOTEL [MOT] *Kalispell, MT*

BEST WESTERN OXFORD INN [MOT] *Yakima, WA*

BEST WESTERN PARADISE INN [MOT] *Dillon, MT*

BEST WESTERN PARK CENTER [MOT] *Enumclaw, WA*

BEST WESTERN PIER POINT INN [MOT] *Florence, OR*

BEST WESTERN PONDEROSA INN [MOT] *Billings, MT*

BEST WESTERN PONY SOLDIER INN [HOT] *Albany, OR*

BEST WESTERN PONY SOLDIER INN [MOT] *Medford, OR*

BEST WESTERN PONY SOLDIER INN AIRPORT [HOT] *Portland, OR*

BEST WESTERN PORT O' CALL INN [HOT] *Calgary, AB*

BEST WESTERN RAMA INN [MOT] *Redmond, OR*

BEST WESTERN RESORT HOTEL AND CONFERENCE CENTER [MOT] *Jackson, WY*

BEST WESTERN RIVERTREE INN [MOT] *Clarkston, WA*

BEST WESTERN ROSE GARDEN HOTEL [HOT] *Portland, OR*

BEST WESTERN SAFARI INN [MOT] *Boise, ID*

BEST WESTERN SANDS [HOT] *Vancouver, BC*

BEST WESTERN SHERIDAN CENTER [MOT] *Sheridan, WY*

BEST WESTERN SIDING 29 LODGE [HOT] *Banff, AB*

BEST WESTERN TACOMA INN [HOT] *Tacoma, WA*

BEST WESTERN TETON WEST [HOT] *Driggs, ID*

BEST WESTERN TORCHLITE INN [MOT] *Wheatland, WY*

BEST WESTERN TOWER WEST LODGE [MOT] *Gillette, WY*

BEST WESTERN TUMWATER INN [MOT] *Olympia, WA*

BEST WESTERN TYROLEAN LODGE [MOT] *Sun Valley Area, ID*

BEST WESTERN UMATILLA HOUSE [MOT] *The Dalles, OR*

BEST WESTERN UNIVERSITY INN [HOT] *Moscow, ID*

BEST WESTERN VERNON LODGE [HOT] *Kelowna, BC*

BEST WESTERN VILLAGE GREEN [MOT] *Cottage Grove, OR*

BEST WESTERN VISTA INN [HOT] *Boise, ID*

BEST WESTERN WALLACA INN [HOT] *Wallace, ID*

BEST WESTERN WINDSOR INN [MOT] *Ashland, OR*

BIG SKY RESORT [RST] *Big Sky (Gallatin County), MT*

BILL CODY RANCH [RAN] *Cody, WY*

BILLINGS INN, THE [MOT] *Billings, MT*

BILTMORE HOTEL [MOT] *Vancouver, BC*

BISHOP VICTORIAN GUEST SUITES [BB] *Port Townsend, WA*

BLACK BUTTE RANCH [RST] *Bend, OR*

BLACKFOOT INN [HOT] *Calgary, AB*

BLACK KNIGHT INN [HOT] *Red Deer, AB*

BLACKWATER CREEK RANCH [HOT] *Cody, WY*

BLACKWELL HOUSE [BB] *Coeur d'Alene, ID*

BLUE HORIZON [HOT] *Vancouver, BC*

BOISE RIVER INN [MOT] *Boise, ID*

BOREAS BED & BREAKFAST [BB] *Long Beach, WA*

BOZEMAN'S WESTERN HERITAGE INN [HOT] *Bozeman, MT*

BREAKERS MOTEL & CONDO, THE [MOT] *Long Beach, WA*

BREWSTER'S MOUNTAIN LODGE [MOT] *Banff, AB*

BROOKS LAKE LODGE [MOT] *Dubois, WY*

BUCKRAIL LODGE INC [MOT] *Jackson, WY*

BUDGET HOST PRONGHORN [MOT] *Lander, WY*

BUDGET INN [MOT] *Great Falls, MT*

BUDGET INN [MOT] *Spokane, WA*

BUFFALO BILL VILLAGE [CABINS] [MOT] *Cody, WY*

BUFFALO MOUNTAIN LODGE [RST] *Banff, AB*

CABANA MOTEL [MOT] *Othello, WA*

CALGARY MARRIOTT HOTEL [HOT] *Calgary, AB*

CAMELOT MOTEL [MOT] *Laramie, WY*

CAMLIN HOTEL [HOT] *Seattle, WA*

CAMPBELL - A CITY INN, THE [BB] *Eugene, OR*

CAMPBELL'S RESORT CONFERENCE CENTER [RST] *Chelan, WA*

CAMPUS INN LLC [MOT] *Eugene, OR*

CANTERBURY INN [MOT] *Ocean Shores, WA*

CANYON LODGE CABINS [MOT] *Yellowstone National Park, WY*

CANYON MOTEL [MOT] *Buffalo, WY*

CAPRI HOTEL - CONVENTION & TRADE CENTRE [MOT] *Red Deer, AB*

CAPTAIN WHIDBEY INN [BB] *Coupeville, WA*

CARAVAN MOTOR HOTEL & RES-TAURANT [MOT] *Portland, OR*

CARRIAGE HOUSE INN [HOT] *Calgary, AB*

CARVEL RESORT MOTEL [MOT] *Chelan, WA*

CASA GRANDE INN [MOT] *Nanaimo, BC*

CASCADE LODGE AT CANYON VILLAGE [MOT] *Yellowstone National Park, WY*

CASTLE, THE [BB] *Brandon, MB*

CASTLE MOUNTAIN CHALETS [MOT] *Banff, AB*

CAVANAUGH'S COLONIAL HOTEL [MOT] *Helena, MT*
CAVANAUGH'S PARKCENTER SUITES [MOT] *Boise, ID*
CEDAR LODGE MOTOR INN [MOT] *Medford, OR*
CEDARS INN [MOT] *Omak, WA*
CEDARWOOD INN MOTEL ASHLAND [MOT] *Ashland, OR*
CENTENNIAL INN, THE [BB] *Dillon, MT*
CHAMBERED NAUTILUS BED & BREAKFAST [BB] *Seattle, WA*
CHANDLERS BED BREAD TRAIL INN [BB] *Joseph, OR*
CHANNEL HOUSE [BB] *Depoe Bay, OR*
CHANNEL HOUSE BED & BREAKFAST [BB] *Anacortes, WA*
CHANTICLEER INN [BB] *Ashland, OR*
CHANTICLEER INN [BB] *Port Townsend, WA*
CHAPARRAL MOTEL [MOT] *Pendleton, OR*
CHARLTON'S CEDAR COURT [MOT] *Banff, AB*
CHARLTON'S CHATEAU JASPER [HOT] *Jasper National Park, AB*
CHARTER HOUSE [HOT] *Winnipeg , MB*
CHATEAU LAKE LOUISE [RST] *Lake Louise, AB*
CHATEAU LOUIS HOTEL & CONFERENCE CENTRE [HOT] *Edmonton, AB*
CHATEAU VICTORIA [HOT] *Victoria, BC*
CHATEAU WHISTLER RESORT [HOT] *Whistler, BC*
CHAUTAUQUA LODGE [MOT] *Long Beach, WA*
CHELSEA STATION BED & BREAKFAST [BB] *Seattle, WA*
CHESTNUT TREE INN [MOT] *Portland, OR*
CHEYENNE SUPER 8 [MOT] *Cheyenne, WY*
CHICO HOT SPRINGS RESORT [RST] *Livingston, MT*
CHINABERRY HILL [BB] *Tacoma, WA*
CIMARRON MOTEL SOUTH [MOT] *Bend, OR*
CIMARRON MOTOR INN [MOT] *Klamath Falls, OR*
CLARION GRAND PACIFIC [HOT] *Victoria, BC*
CLARION HOTEL GRAND PACIFIC [MOT] *Victoria, BC*
CLARION HOTEL SEATAC [MOT] *Seattle-Tacoma International Airport Area, WA*

CLAYOQUOT WILDERNESS RESORT [RST] *Vancouver, BC*
C'MON INN [MOT] *Billings, MT*
COACHMAN INN [MOT] *Oak Harbor, WA*
COAST BASTION INN [HOT] *Nanaimo, BC*
COAST CANADIAN INN, THE [MOT] *Kamloops, BC*
COAST CAPRI HOTEL [HOT] *Kelowna, BC*
COAST HARBOURSIDE HOTEL & MARINA [HOT] *Victoria, BC*
COAST PLAZA, THE [HOT] *Calgary, AB*
COAST PLAZA HOTEL AT CALGARY [HOT] *Calgary, AB*
COAST PLAZA SUITE HOTEL [HOT] *Vancouver, BC*
COAST TERRACE INN [HOT] *Edmonton, AB*
COEUR D'ALENE - A RESORT ON THE LAKE, THE [RST] *Coeur d'Alene, ID*
COEUR D'ALENE INN & CONFERENCE CENTER [MOT] *Coeur d'Alene, ID*
COHO INN [MOT] *Lincoln City, OR*
COLONIAL INN [MOT] *Brandon, MB*
COLTER BAY VILLAGE & CABINS [CC] *Grand Teton National Park, WY*
COLUMBIA GORGE HOTEL [BB] *Hood River, OR*
COLUMBIA RIVER INN [BB] *Astoria, OR*
COLUMBIA RIVER INN [MOT] *Coulee Dam, WA*
COMFORT INN [MOT] *Big Sky (Gallatin County), MT*
COMFORT INN [MOT] *Billings, MT*
COMFORT INN [MOT] *Boise, ID*
COMFORT INN [MOT] *Bozeman, MT*
COMFORT INN [MOT] *Brandon, MB*
COMFORT INN [MOT] *Buffalo, WY*
COMFORT INN [MOT] *Calgary, AB*
COMFORT INN [MOT] *Casper, WY*
COMFORT INN [MOT] *Cheyenne, WY*
COMFORT INN [MOT] *Grants Pass, OR*
COMFORT INN [MOT] *Great Falls, MT*
COMFORT INN [MOT] *Helena, MT*
COMFORT INN [MOT] *Idaho Falls, ID*
COMFORT INN [MOT] *Kelso, WA*
COMFORT INN [MOT] *Livingston, MT*
COMFORT INN [MOT] *Miles City, MT*
COMFORT INN [MOT] *Pocatello, ID*
COMFORT INN [MOT] *Red Lodge, MT*
COMFORT INN [MOT] *Rexburg, ID*
COMFORT INN [MOT] *Rock Springs, WY*

COMFORT INN [MOT] *Thermopolis, WY*

COMFORT INN [MOT] *Vancouver, WA*

COMFORT INN [HOT] *West Yellowstone, MT*

COMFORT INN [MOT] *Winnipeg, MB*

COMFORT INN & SUITES SEA-TAC-SEATTLE [MOT] *Seattle-Tacoma International Airport Area, WA*

COMFORT INN BUFFALO BILL VILLAGE [MOT] *Cody, WY*

COMFORT INN OF BUTTE [HOT] *Butte, MT*

COMFORT INN OF DILLON [HOT] *Dillon, MT*

COMFORT INN OF HAMILTON [HOT] *Hamilton, MT*

COMFORT INN VALLEY [MOT] *Spokane, WA*

COMFORT SUITES [MOT] *Vancouver, WA*

COMMENCEMENT BAY BED & BREAKFAST [BB] *Tacoma, WA*

CONNIE'S HAWTHORN INN & SUITES [HOT] *Sandpoint, ID*

CORRAL MOTEL [MOT] *Afton, WY*

COTTONWOOD INN [MOT] *Glasgow, MT*

COULEE HOUSE MOTEL [HOT] *Coulee Dam, WA*

COUNTRY INN AND SUITES [MOT] *Winnipeg, MB*

COUNTRY WILLOWS BED & BREAKFAST INN [BB] *Ashland, OR*

COURTYARD BY MARRIOTT [HOT] *Beaverton, OR*

COURTYARD BY MARRIOTT [HOT] *Portland, OR*

COURTYARD BY MARRIOTT [HOT] *Spokane, WA*

COWBOY VILLAGE RESORT [HOT] *Grand Teton National Park, WY*

COWLITE RIVER LODGE [MOT] *Packwood, WA*

COYOTE ROADHOUSE INN [BB] *Bigfork, MT*

COZY COVE BEACH FRONT RESORT [MOT] *Lincoln City, OR*

CRANDALL MOUNTAIN LODGE [HOT] *Waterton Lakes National Park, AB*

CRATER LAKE LODGE [HOT] *Crater Lake National Park, OR*

CREST MOTEL [MOT] *Astoria, OR*

CREST TRAIL LODGE [MOT] *Packwood, WA*

CROWNE PLAZA [HOT] *Portland, OR*

CROWNE PLAZA [HOT] *Seattle, WA*

CROWNE PLAZA CHATEAU LACOMBE [HOT] *Edmonton, AB*

CROWNE PLAZA HOTEL GEORGIA VANCOUVER [HOT] *Vancouver, BC*

CROWN ISLE RESORT & GOLF COMMUNITY [HOT] *Nanaimo, BC*

CRYSTAL LODGE [HOT] *Whistler, BC*

CUSTER HOUSE BED & BREAKFAST [BB] *Seaside, OR*

DAVY JACKSON [BB] *Jackson, WY*

DAYS INN [MOT] *Bellingham, WA*

DAYS INN [MOT] *Billings, MT*

DAYS INN [HOT] *Bozeman, MT*

DAYS INN [HOT] *Butte, MT*

DAYS INN [MOT] *Cheyenne, WY*

DAYS INN [MOT] *Cody, WY*

DAYS INN [MOT] *Coeur d'Alene, ID*

DAYS INN [MOT] *Glendive, MT*

DAYS INN [MOT] *Jackson, WY*

DAYS INN [MOT] *Kalispell, MT*

DAYS INN [MOT] *Kamloops, BC*

DAYS INN [MOT] *Portland, OR*

DAYS INN [MOT] *Rawlins, WY*

DAYS INN [MOT] *Sheridan, WY*

DAYS INN [MOT] *Tacoma, WA*

DAYS INN [MOT] *West Yellowstone, MT*

DAYS INN AIRPORT [MOT] *Spokane, WA*

DAYS INN - CALGARY WEST [MOT] *Calgary, AB*

DAYS INN HARBOURVIEW [MOT] *Nanaimo, BC*

DAYS INN OF GREAT FALLS [MOT] *Great Falls, MT*

DAYS INN ON THE HARBOUR [HOT] *Victoria, BC*

DAYS INN PORTLAND SOUTH [MOT] *Portland, OR*

DEER CROSSING BED & BREAKFAST [BB] *Hamilton, MT*

DEER LODGE [BB] *Lake Louise, AB*

DELTA BOW VALLEY [HOT] *Calgary, AB*

DELTA CALGARY AIRPORT [HOT] *Calgary, AB*

DELTA CENTRE SUITES [HOT] *Edmonton, AB*

DELTA EDMONTON SOUTH [HOT] *Edmonton, AB*

DELTA LODGE AT KANANASKIS [HOT] *Calgary, AB*

DELTA PACIFIC RESORT AND CONFERENCE CENTER [HOT] *Vancouver, BC*

DELTA PINNACLE [HOT] *Vancouver, BC*

DELTA TOWN AND COUNTRY [HOT] *Vancouver, BC*

DELTA VANCOUVER AIRPORT HOTEL AND MARINA [HOT] *Vancouver, BC*

DELTA WHISTLER RESORT [RST]
    Whistler, BC
DELTA WINNIPEG [HOT] *Winnipeg,*
    MB
DER RITTERHOFF MOTOR INN
    [MOT] *Leavenworth, WA*
DESERT INN [MOT] *Nampa, ID*
DIAMOND POINT INN [BB] *Sequim,*
    WA
DOCK OF THE BAY MOTEL [BB]
    Lincoln City, OR
DOMAINE MADELEINE [BB] *Port*
    Angeles, WA
DORNAN'S SPUR RANCH CABINS
    [RST] *Grand Teton National*
    Park, WY
DOUBLE DIAMOND X [RST] *Cody,*
    WY
DOUBLETREE [HOT] *Boise, ID*
DOUBLETREE CLUB HOTEL - BOISE
    [HOT] *Boise, ID*
DOUBLETREE GUEST SUITES [HOT]
    Seattle, WA
DOUBLETREE HOTEL [HOT] *Bellevue,*
    WA
DOUBLETREE HOTEL [HOT] *Pasco,*
    WA
DOUBLETREE HOTEL [MOT]
    Pendleton, OR
DOUBLETREE HOTEL [HOT] *Seattle-*
    Tacoma International Airport
    Area, WA
DOUBLETREE HOTEL [HOT] *Spokane,*
    WA
DOUBLETREE HOTEL COLUMBIA
    RIVER [HOT] *Portland, OR*
DOUBLETREE HOTEL JANTZEN
    BEACH [HOT] *Portland, OR*
DOUBLETREE HOTEL RIVERSIDE
    [HOT] *Boise, ID*
DOUBLETREE HOTEL SPOKANE CIT
    [HOT] *Spokane, WA*
DOUBLETREE HOTEL YAKIMA [HOT]
    Yakima, WA
DOUBLETREE INN [MOT] *Seattle-*
    Tacoma International Airport
    Area, WA
DOUBLETREE PORTLAND - LLOYD
    CENTER [HOT] *Portland, OR*
DOUGLAS FIR RESORT [HOT] *Banff,*
    AB
DREAMERS LODGE MOTEL [MOT]
    John Day, OR
D SANDS MOTEL [MOT] *Lincoln City,*
    OR
DYNASTY INN [MOT] *Banff, AB*
EAGLE CREST RESORT [RST]
    Redmond, OR
EBB TIDE MOTEL [MOT] *Seaside, OR*
ECONO LODGE [MOT] *Boise, ID*
ECONO LODGE [MOT] *Casper, WY*

ECONO LODGE [MOT] *Laramie, WY*
ECONO LODGE [MOT] *Sequim, WA*
ECONOMY INN [MOT] *Hermiston,*
    OR
ECONOMY INN [MOT] *Pendleton, OR*
EDGEWATER INN [MOT] *Long Beach,*
    WA
EDGEWATER RESORT [MOT]
    Sandpoint, ID
EDMOND MEANY HOTEL, THE
    [HOT] *Seattle, WA*
ELDORADO INN [MOT] *Baker City,*
    OR
ELEPHANT HEAD LODGE [RAN]
    Cody, WY
ELKHORN RESORT [RST] *Sun Valley*
    Area, ID
ELKINS ON PRIEST LAKE [RST] *Priest*
    Lake Area, ID
ELLENSBURG INN [MOT] *Ellensburg,*
    WA
EL WESTERN RESORT [EX] *Ennis, MT*
EMBARCADERO RESORT HOTEL
    [RST] *Newport, OR*
EMBASSY INN [HOT] *Victoria, BC*
EMBASSY SUITES DOWNTOWN [AS]
    Portland, OR
EMERALD LAKE LODGE [MOT] *Lake*
    Louise, AB
EMILY A BED & BREAKFAST, THE
    [BB] *Missoula, MT*
EMPIRE LANDMARK HOTEL &
    CONFERENCE CENTRE [HOT]
    Vancouver, BC
EMPRESS HOTEL, THE [HOT]
    Victoria, BC
ENGLISH BAY INN [HOT] *Vancouver,*
    BC
ENGLISH INN, THE [BB] *Port*
    Townsend, WA
ENZIAN MOTOR INN [MOT]
    Leavenworth, WA
EXECUTIVE AIRPORT PLAZA HOTEL
    [HOT] *Vancouver, BC*
EXECUTIVE HOUSE [HOT] *Victoria,*
    BC
EXECUTIVE INN EXPRESS [HOT]
    Vancouver, BC
EXECUTIVE INN HOTEL [HOT]
    Vancouver, BC
EXECUTIVE INN HOTEL AND
    CONFERENCE CENTER [AS]
    Vancouver, BC
EXECUTIVE INN - KAMLOOPS
    [MOT] *Kamloops, BC*
EXECUTIVE ROYAL INN WEST
    EDMONTON [MOT] *Edmonton,*
    AB
FAIRFIELD INN [MOT] *Bozeman, MT*
FAIRFIELD INN [MOT] *Cheyenne, WY*

FAIRFIELD INN [MOT] *Great Falls, MT*

FAIRFIELD INN [MOT] *Helena, MT*

FAIRFIELD INN [MOT] *West Yellowstone, MT*

FAIRFIELD INN BY MARRIOTT [MOT] *Billings, MT*

FAIRFIELD INN BY MARRIOTT [MOT] *Portland, OR*

FAIRMONT HOT SPRINGS RESORT [RST] *Anaconda, MT*

FAIRMONT VANCOUVER AIRPORT, THE [HOT] *Vancouver, BC*

FAIRWINDS SCHOONER COVE RESORT & MARINA [RST] *Nanaimo, BC*

FAN MOUNTAIN INN [MOT] *Ennis, MT*

FANTASYLAND HOTEL [HOT] *Edmonton, AB*

FARVUE MOTEL [MOT] *Goldendale, WA*

FERRYMAN'S INN [MOT] *Vancouver, WA*

FIRESIDE MOTEL [MOT] *Yachats, OR*

FIVE SEASUNS BED & BREAKFAST [BB] *Port Angeles, WA*

FLAGG RANCH RESORT [CC] *Grand Teton National Park, WY*

FLAGSHIP INN [MOT] *Bremerton, WA*

FLAMINGO MOTEL [MOT] *Coeur d'Alene, ID*

FLAT CREEK [BB] *Jackson, WY*

FLERY MANOR [BB] *Grants Pass, OR*

FLYING ARROW RESORT [RST] *Joseph, OR*

FLYING M RANCH [RST] *McMinnville, OR*

FOREST GROVE INN [MOT] *Forest Grove, OR*

FORKS MOTEL [MOT] *Forks, WA*

FORT THREE FORKS [MOT] *Three Forks, MT*

FOTHERINGHAM HOUSE [BB] *Spokane, WA*

FOUR POINTS SHERATON [HOT] *Nanaimo, BC*

FOUR POINTS SHERATON PORTLAND DOWNTWON [RST] *Portland, OR*

FOUR SEASONS HOTEL SEATTLE [HOT] *Seattle, WA*

FOUR SEASONS HOTEL VANCOUVER [HOT] *Vancouver, BC*

FOX HOLLOW BED & BREAKFAST [BB] *Bozeman, MT*

FRANKLIN STREET STATION BED & BREAKFAST [BB] *Astoria, OR*

FRENCH-WELLS [MOT] *Redmond, OR*

FRIDAY'S HISTORICAL INN [BB] *San Juan Islands, WA*

FW HASTINGS HOUSE OLD CONSULATE [BB] *Port Townsend, WA*

GALLATIN GATEWAY [BB] *Bozeman, MT*

GASLIGHT INN [BB] *Seattle, WA*

GEARHART BY THE SEA RESORT [MOT] *Seaside, OR*

GENERAL HOOKER'S B&B [BB] *Portland, OR*

GEORGIAN COURT HOTEL [HOT] *Vancouver, BC*

GILBERT INN BED & BREAKFAST [BB] *Seaside, OR*

GLENMORE INN & CONVENTION CENTER [HOT] *Calgary, AB*

GOLDSMITH'S BED & BREAKFAST INN [BB] *Missoula, MT*

GOOD MEDICINE LODGE [BB] *Whitefish, MT*

GOVERNOR HOTEL [HOT] *Portland, OR*

GRAND TARGHEE [RST] *Driggs, ID*

GRANDVIEW RESORT [RST] *Priest Lake Area, ID*

GRAN TETON NATIONAL PARK/JACKSON LAKE [RST] *Grand Teton National Park, WY*

GRAY WOLF INN & SUITES [HOT] *West Yellowstone, MT*

GREEN GABLES INN [BB] *Walla Walla, WA*

GREENWOOD INN [MOT] *Beaverton, OR*

GREY GULL RESORT, THE [RST] *Ocean Shores, WA*

GREY WHALE INN [BB] *Cannon Beach, OR*

GREYWOLF INN [BB] *Sequim, WA*

GROS VENTRE RIVER RANCH [BB] *Grand Teton National Park, WY*

GROUSE MOUNTAIN LODGE [RST] *Whitefish, MT*

GROVELAND COTTAGE BED & BREAKFAST [BB] *Sequim, WA*

GUEST HOUSE BED & BREAKFAST COTTAGES [BB] *Coupeville, WA*

HALLMARK RESORT [MOT] *Cannon Beach, OR*

HAMPTON INN [MOT] *Bellingham, WA*

HAMPTON INN [HOT] *Bend, OR*

HAMPTON INN [MOT] *Bozeman, MT*

HAMPTON INN [HOT] *Casper, WY*

HAMPTON INN [MOT] *Idaho Falls, ID*

HAMPTON INN [MOT] *Kalispell, MT*

HAMPTON INN [MOT] *Missoula, MT*

HAMPTON INN [HOT] *Portland, OR*

HAMPTON INN [HOT] *Vancouver, BC*

HAMPTON INN & SUITES - CALGARY AIRPORT [HOT] *Calgary, AB*

HAMPTON INN & SUITES SEATTLE [HOT] *Seattle, WA*
HAMPTON INN SEATTLE AIRPORT [HOT] *Seattle, WA*
HARBOR VIEW MOTEL [MOT] *Bandon, OR*
HARBOUR INN [MOT] *Coupeville, WA*
HARBOUR TOWERS [HOT] *Victoria, BC*
HARRISON HOUSE BED & BREAKFAST [BB] *Corvallis, OR*
HARRISON HOUSE SUITES [BB] *San Juan Islands, WA*
HASTINGS HOUSE [BB] *Victoria, BC*
HATCHET RESORT [MOT] *Grand Teton National Park, WY*
HATERLEIGH HERITAGE INN [BB] *Victoria, BC*
HAUS ROHRBACH PENSION [BB] *Leavenworth, WA*
HAWTHORN INN & SUITES [HOT] *Portland, OR*
HAWTHORN INN & SUITES [HOT] *Seattle, WA*
HAWTHORN INN AND SUITES [MOT] *Albany, OR*
HAWTHORN INN AND SUITES [MOT] *Walla Walla, WA*
HEARTHSTONE INN [BB] *Cannon Beach, OR*
HEATHMAN HOTEL, THE [HOT] *Portland, OR*
HEATHMAN LODGE, THE [HOT] *Vancouver, WA*
HEIDELBERG INN [MOT] *Sun Valley Area, ID*
HERON, THE [BB] *La Conner, WA*
HERON BEACH INN [BB] *Port Ludlow, WA*
HERON HAUS [BB] *Portland, OR*
HI-TIDE MOTEL [MOT] *Seaside, OR*
HIDDEN RIDGE CHALETS [HOT] *Banff, AB*
HIGH COUNTRY INN [HOT] *Banff, AB*
HIGH COUNTRY MOTEL [MOT] *Cooke City, MT*
HILANDER MOTEL & STEAK HOUSE [MOT] *Mountain Home, ID*
HILLCREST MOTEL [MOT] *Moscow, ID*
HILL HOUSE BED & BREAKFAST [BB] *Seattle, WA*
HILLSIDE HOUSE BED & BREAKFAST [BB] *San Juan Islands, WA*
HILLS RESORT [RST] *Priest Lake Area, ID*
HILLTOP INN [MOT] *Billings, MT*
HILTON [HOT] *Eugene, OR*
HILTON [MOT] *Seattle-Tacoma International Airport Area, WA*

HILTON HOTEL BELLEVUE [HOT] *Bellevue, WA*
HILTON PORTLAND [HOT] *Portland, OR*
HITCHING POST LODGE [MOT] *Jackson, WY*
HI TIDE CONDOMINIUM RESORT [MOT] *Moclips, WA*
HOLIDAY INN [HOT] *Boise, ID*
HOLIDAY INN [HOT] *Bozeman, MT*
HOLIDAY INN [HOT] *Calgary, AB*
HOLIDAY INN [MOT] *Casper, WY*
HOLIDAY INN [MOT] *Gillette, WY*
HOLIDAY INN [HOT] *Great Falls, MT*
HOLIDAY INN [MOT] *Laramie, WY*
HOLIDAY INN [MOT] *Pocatello, ID*
HOLIDAY INN [MOT] *Riverton, WY*
HOLIDAY INN [HOT] *Rock Springs, WY*
HOLIDAY INN [HOT] *Vancouver, BC*
HOLIDAY INN [HOT] *Victoria, BC*
HOLIDAY INN [HOT] *Winnipeg, MB*
HOLIDAY INN AIRPORT [HOT] *Calgary, AB*
HOLIDAY INN AIRPORT WEST [HOT] *Winnipeg, MB*
HOLIDAY INN EXPRESS [MOT] *Bozeman, MT*
HOLIDAY INN EXPRESS [MOT] *Calgary, AB*
HOLIDAY INN EXPRESS [MOT] *Eugene, OR*
HOLIDAY INN EXPRESS [MOT] *Florence, OR*
HOLIDAY INN EXPRESS [MOT] *Helena, MT*
HOLIDAY INN EXPRESS [HOT] *Kelowna, BC*
HOLIDAY INN EXPRESS [MOT] *Klamath Falls, OR*
HOLIDAY INN EXPRESS [HOT] *Miles City, MT*
HOLIDAY INN EXPRESS [HOT] *Missoula, MT*
HOLIDAY INN EXPRESS [HOT] *Red Deer, AB*
HOLIDAY INN EXPRESS [MOT] *Vancouver, WA*
HOLIDAY INN EXPRESS GRANTS PASS [HOT] *Grants Pass, OR*
HOLIDAY INN EXPRESS-PARKSIDE [MOT] *Butte, MT*
HOLIDAY INN GRAND MONTANA [HOT] *Billings, MT*
HOLIDAY INN HOTEL & SUITES DOWNTOWN [HOT] *Vancouver, BC*
HOLIDAY INN OF SHERIDAN [HOT] *Sheridan, WY*
HOLIDAY INN PALACE [HOT] *Edmonton, AB*

HOLIDAY INN PARKSIDE [MOT] *Missoula, MT*

HOLIDAY INN PORTLAND AIRPORT [HOT] *Portland, OR*

HOLIDAY INN RED DEER [HOT] *Red Deer, AB*

HOLIDAY INN SEATAC AIRPORT [HOT] *Seattle-Tacoma International Airport Area, WA*

HOLIDAY INN SEATTLE, ISSAQUAH [MOT] *Issaquah, WA*

HOLIDAY INN SUNSPREE RESORT [MOT] *West Yellowstone, MT*

HOLIDAY INN VANCOUVER AIRPORT [HOT] *Vancouver, BC*

HOLIDAY LODGE [MOT] *Wenatchee, WA*

HOLLAND HOUSE [BB] *Victoria, BC*

HOLLY HILL HOUSE B&B [BB] *Port Townsend, WA*

HOME FARM BED AND BREAKFAST [BB] *Grants Pass, OR*

HOOSIER'S MOTEL & BAR [MOT] *Cooke City, MT*

HOSPITALITY INN [MOT] *Kamloops, BC*

HOTEL EDGEWATER [MOT] *Seattle, WA*

HOTEL HIGGINS [BB] *Casper, WY*

HOTEL MACDONALD [HOT] *Edmonton, AB*

HOTEL MCCALL [HOT] *McCall, ID*

HOTEL VANCOUVER [HOT] *Vancouver, BC*

HOTEL VINTAGE PARK [HOT] *Seattle, WA*

HOWARD JOHNSON [MOT] *Lewiston, ID*

HOWARD JOHNSON EXPRESS INN [MOT] *Billings, MT*

HOWARD JOHNSON EXPRESS INN [MOT] *Coeur d'Alene, ID*

HOWARD JOHNSON EXPRESS INN & SUITES [MOT] *Vancouver, BC*

HOWARD JOHNSON EXPRESS INN [MOT] *Walla Walla, WA*

HOWARD JOHNSON HARBOUR SIDE HOTEL [MOT] *Nanaimo, BC*

HOWARD JOHNSON HOTEL [MOT] *Winnipeg, MB*

HOWARD JOHNSON INN [MOT] *La Grande, OR*

HOWARD JOHNSON PANORAMA INN [MOT] *Kamloops, BC*

HOWARD JOHNSON PLAZA HOTEL [MOT] *Everett, WA*

HUFF HOUSE INN BED & BREAKFAST, THE [BB] *Jackson, WY*

HYATT REGENCY BELLEVUE [HOT] *Bellevue, WA*

HYATT REGENCY VANCOUVER [HOT] *Vancouver, BC*

IDAHO COUNTRY INN [BB] *Sun Valley Area, ID*

IDAHO HERITAGE INN [BB] *Boise, ID*

IDAHO ROCKY MOUNTAIN RANCH [RAN] *Stanley, ID*

IMA COVERED WAGON MOTEL [MOT] *Lusk, WY*

IMA RAINBOW VALLEY MOTEL [MOT] *Ennis, MT*

IMA TRAPPER INN [MOT] *Jackson, WY*

INDIAN LODGE MOTEL [MOT] *Joseph, OR*

INN AMERICA [MOT] *Boise, ID*

INN AMERICA [MOT] *Nampa, ID*

INN AMERICA - A BUDGET MOTEL [MOT] *Lewiston, ID*

INN AT BUFFALO FORK [BB] *Grand Teton National Park, WY*

INN AT CENTRALIA [MOT] *Centralia, WA*

INN AT HARBOR STEPS [BB] *Seattle, WA*

INN AT ILWACO, THE [BB] *Long Beach, WA*

INN AT LANGLEY [BB] *Coupeville, WA*

INN AT NESIKA BEACH [BB] *Gold Beach, OR*

INN AT OTTER CREST [MOT] *Depoe Bay, OR*

INN AT SPANISH HEAD [MOT] *Lincoln City, OR*

INN AT SWIFTS BAY [BB] *San Juan Islands, WA*

INN AT THE DALLES [MOT] *The Dalles, OR*

INN AT THE MARKET [HOT] *Seattle, WA*

INN AT VIGINIA MASON [HOT] *Seattle, WA*

INN OF THE SEVENTH MTN, THE [RST] *Bend, OR*

INN OF THE WHITE SALMON [BB] *Hood River, OR*

INN ON 7TH [HOT] *Edmonton, AB*

INNS OF BANFF [HOT] *Banff, AB*

INTERMOUNTAIN LODGE [MOT] *Driggs, ID*

INTERNATIONAL HOTEL OF CALGARY [HOT] *Calgary, AB*

INTERSTATE INN [MOT] *Moses Lake, WA*

IRWIN'S MOUNTAIN INN [MOT] *Banff, AB*

IVY CHAPEL INN BED & BREAKFAST [BB] *Ephrata, WA*

IZAAK WALTON INN [BB] *West Glacier Area, MT*

JACKSON HOLE RESORT LODGING [RST] *Jackson, WY*

JACKSONVILLE INN [BB] *Jacksonville, OR*

JACOBSON'S COTTAGES [CC] *East Glacier Area, MT*

JAMES HOUSE [BB] *Port Townsend, WA*

JASPER PARK LODGE [RST] *Jasper National Park, AB*

JENNY LAKE LODGE [RST] *Grand Teton National Park, WY*

JOHN DAY SUNSET INN [MOT] *John Day, OR*

JORGENSON'S INN AND SUITES [MOT] *Helena, MT*

KAH-NEE-TA LODGE [RST] *Madras, OR*

KALALOCH LODGE [RST] *Forks, WA*

KALISPELL GRAND HOTEL [HOT] *Kalispell, MT*

KAMLOOPS CITY CENTER TRAVELODGE [MOT] *Kamloops, BC*

KANANASKIS GUEST RANCH [CC] *Banff, AB*

KANANASKIS INN AND CONFERENCE CENTER [HOT] *Calgary, AB*

KANDAHAR LODGE [HOT] *Whitefish, MT*

KATYS INN [BB] *La Conner, WA*

KEENAN HOUSE BED AND BREAKFAST [BB] *Tacoma, WA*

KELLY INN [MOT] *Cody, WY*

KELLY INN [MOT] *West Yellowstone, MT*

KENNEWICK TRAVELODGE INN & SUITES [EX] *Kennewick, WA*

KILMOREY [EX] *Waterton Lakes National Park, AB*

KINGFISHER OCEANSIDE RESORT AND SPA [RST] *Nanaimo, BC*

KNIGHTS INN [MOT] *Ashland, OR*

KNIGHTS INN [MOT] *Medford, OR*

KOOTENAI VALLEY MOTEL [MOT] *Bonner's Ferry, ID*

LACONNER COUNTRY INN [HOT] *La Conner, WA*

LADY MACDONALD COUNTRY INN [BB] *Banff, AB*

LAKE MCDONALD LODGE [HOT] *West Glacier Area, MT*

LAKE QUINAULT LODGE [HOT] *Quinault, WA*

LAKESIDE INN [HOT] *Sandpoint, ID*

LAKESIDE RESORT AND CONFERENCE CENTER [HOT] *Penticton, BC*

LAKEVIEW LODGE [MOT] *Lakeview, OR*

LAKE YELLOWSTONE HOTEL [RST] *Yellowstone National Park, WY*

LA QUINTA INN [MOT] *Cheyenne, WY*

LA QUINTA INN [MOT] *Seattle-Tacoma International Airport Area, WA*

LA QUINTA INN [MOT] *Tacoma, WA*

LAUREL POINT INN [RST] *Victoria, BC*

LAZY L & B RANCH [RAN] *Dubois, WY*

LE CHAMOIS [RST] *Whistler, BC*

LETHBRIDGE LODGE [HOT] *Lethbridge, AB*

LEWISTOWN SUPER 8 MOTEL [MOT] *Lewistown, MT*

LITTLE AMERICA HOTEL [MOT] *Cheyenne, WY*

LITTLE AMERICA HOTEL [MOT] *Green River, WY*

LITTLE CREEK COVE [MOT] *Newport, OR*

LIVINGSTON SUPER 8 [MOT] *Livingston, MT*

LIZZIE'S BED & BREAKFAST [BB] *Port Townsend, WA*

LOBSTICK LODGE [HOT] *Jasper National Park, AB*

LONE MOUNTAIN [RAN] *Big Sky (Gallatin County), MT*

LONE PINE VILLAGE [MOT] *The Dalles, OR*

LOPEZ FARM COTTAGES [BB] *San Juan Islands, WA*

LOST CREEK RANCH [RAN] *Grand Teton National Park, WY*

LOVE'S RIVERVIEW LODGE [MOT] *Hood River, OR*

LYTLE HOUSE BED & BREAKFAST [BB] *Hoquiam, WA*

MAGNOLIA HOTEL & SUITES, THE [HOT] *Victoria, BC*

MALLORY HOTEL [HOT] *Portland, OR*

MALTANA [MOT] *Malta, MT*

MAMMOTH HOT SPRINGS HOTEL AND CABINS [HOT] *Yellowstone National Park, WY*

MANITOU LODGE BED & BREAKFAST [BB] *Forks, WA*

MANRESA CASTLE [BB] *Port Townsend, WA*

MAPLE ROSE INN [BB] *Port Angeles, WA*

MARCLAIR INN [MOT] *Tillamook, OR*

MARGIES INN ON BAY THE BED AND BREAKFAST [BB] *Sequim, WA*

MARIANNA STOLTZ HOUSE BED & BREAKFAST [BB] *Spokane, WA*

MARINA CAY RESORT & CONFERENCE CENTER [RST] *Bigfork, MT*

MARINA VILLAGE INN [HOT] *Everett, WA*

MARK IV MOTOR INN [MOT] *Moscow, ID*

MARK SPENCER HOTEL PORTLAND [HOT] *Portland, OR*

MARMOT LODGE [MOT] *Jasper National Park, AB*

MARRIOTT HOTEL [HOT] *Portland, OR*

MARRIOTT HOTEL [MOT] *Seattle-Tacoma International Airport Area, WA*

MAYFIELD INN AND SUITES [MOT] *Edmonton, AB*

MAYFLOWER PARK [HOT] *Seattle, WA*

MCCALL HOUSE [BB] *Ashland, OR*

MCMENAMINS EDGEFIELD [RST] *Portland, OR*

MEADOW LAKE [RST] *Columbia Falls, MT*

MEDICINE HAT LODGE [HOT] *Medicine Hat, AB*

METROPOLITAN HOTEL, THE [HOT] *Vancouver, BC*

MICKEY O'REILLEY'S INN AT THE RIVER [MOT] *Wenatchee, WA*

MIDWAY INN [MOT] *Bremerton, WA*

MONACO HOTEL [HOT] *Seattle, WA*

MONEY SAYER MOTEL [MOT] *Florence, OR*

MOOSE HEAD RANCH [RAN] *Grand Teton National Park, WY*

MORRISON'S ROGUE RIVER LODGE [BB] *Grants Pass, OR*

MOSES LAKE MOTEL 6 [MOT] *Moses Lake, WA*

MOTEL 6 [MOT] *Coeur d'Alene, ID*

MOTEL 6 [MOT] *Spokane, WA*

MOTEL 6 GARDINER [MOT] *Gardiner, MT*

MOTEL DEL ROGUE [MOT] *Grants Pass, OR*

MOTEL NICHOLAS [MOT] *Omak, WA*

MOTEL ORLEANS [MOT] *Albany, OR*

MOUNTAINEER LODGE [MOT] *Lake Louise, AB*

MOUNTAIN HOME LODGE [BB] *Leavenworth, WA*

MOUNTAIN INN MOTEL [MOT] *Afton, WY*

MOUNTAIN PINE [MOT] *East Glacier Area, MT*

MOUNTAIN SKY GUEST RANCH [MOT] *Livingston, MT*

MOUNTAIN TIMBERS LODGE [BB] *Columbia Falls, MT*

MOUNTAIN VILLAGE LODGE [RST] *Stanley, ID*

MOUNT ASHLAND INN [BB] *Ashland, OR*

MOUNT ST. HELENS MOTEL [MOT] *Kelso, WA*

MOUNT BACHELOR VILLAGE RESORT [MOT] *Bend, OR*

MOUNT HOOD INN [MOT] *Mount Hood National Forest, OR*

MOUNT ROYAL [HOT] *Banff, AB*

MY PARENTS ESTATE BED & BREAKFAST [BB] *Colville, WA*

NENDELS INN [MOT] *Kennewick, WA*

NENDELS INN [MOT] *Yakima, WA*

NINE QUARTER CIRCLE RANCH INC. [RAN] *Big Sky (Gallatin County), MT*

NISKU INN AND CONFERENCE CENTER [RAN] *Edmonton, AB*

NISQUALLY LODGE, THE [MOT] *Mount Rainier National Park, WA*

NORDIC MOTEL [MOT] *Lincoln City, OR*

NORQUAY'S TIMBERLINE INN [BB] *Banff, AB*

NORTHGATE INN [MOT] *Challis, ID*

NORTH HILL INN [MOT] *Red Deer, AB*

NOTARAS LODGE [MOT] *Soap Lake, WA*

NOWLIN CREEK INN [BB] *Jackson, WY*

OAK BAY BEACH AND MARINE RESORT [HOT] *Victoria, BC*

OAK HILL BED & BREAKFAST [BB] *Ashland, OR*

OCEAN CREST RESORT [RST] *Moclips, WA*

OCEAN POINTE RESORT AND SPA [RST] *Victoria, BC*

O'DUACHAIN COUNTRY INN [BB] *Bigfork, MT*

OLD ALCOHOL PLANT, THE [RST] *Port Townsend, WA*

OLDE ENGLAND INN [HOT] *Victoria, BC*

OLD FAITHFUL INN [RST] *Yellowstone National Park, WY*

OLYMPIC INN [MOT] *Aberdeen, WA*

ORANGE STREET BUDGE MOTOR INN MISSOULA [MOT] *Missoula, MT*

ORCAS HOTEL [BB] *San Juan Islands, WA*

ORCHARD INN [MOT] *Wenatchee, WA*

OREGON CAVES LODGE [MOT] *Cave Junction, OR*

OUR PLACE AT THE BEACH [MOT] *Long Beach, WA*

OVERLANDER MOUNTAIN LODGE [BB] *Jasper National Park, AB*

OWYHEE PLAZA HOTEL [HOT] *Boise, ID*

PACIFIC 9 MOTOR INN [MOT]
  Eugene, OR
PACIFIC INN MOTEL [MOT] *Forks,*
  WA
PACIFIC PALISADES [HOT] *Vancouver,*
  BC
PACIFIC PLAZA [HOT] *Seattle, WA*
PALACE [HOT] *Port Townsend, WA*
PALLISER, THE [HOT] *Calgary, AB*
PANACEA BED AND BREAKFAST [BB]
  San Juan Islands, WA
PAN PACIFIC LODGE [AS] *Whistler,*
  BC
PAN PACIFIC VANCOUVER, THE
  [HOT] *Vancouver, BC*
PARADISE [HOT] *Buffalo, WY*
PARADISE INN [MOT] *Livingston, MT*
PARADISE INN [MOT] *Mount Rainier*
  National Park, WA
PARADISE LODGE AND
  BUNGALOWS [RST] *Lake*
  Louise, AB
PARAMOUNT, THE [HOT] *Seattle, WA*
PAUL'S MOTOR INN [MOT] *Victoria,*
  BC
PEDIGRIFT HOUSE B&B [BB]
  Ashland, OR
PELICAN SHORES INN [MOT] *Lincoln*
  City, OR
PEPPERTREE INN [MOT] *Beaverton,*
  OR
PHOENIX INN [HOT] *Eugene, OR*
PHOENIX INN [MOT] *Portland, OR*
PHOENIX INN [AS] *Portland, OR*
PHOENIX INN [MOT] *Salem, OR*
PHOENIX INN TIGARD [MOT]
  Beaverton, OR
PINE LODGE [HOT] *Whitefish, MT*
PINE MEADOW INN [BB] *Grants Pass,*
  OR
PIONEER SQUARE HOTEL [MOT]
  Seattle, WA
PLAZA SUITE HOTEL [HOT] *Boise, ID*
PLUM CREEK HOUSE [BB] *Columbia*
  Falls, MT
POCATELLO SUPER 8 [MOT]
  Pocatello, ID
POLLARD HOTEL [HOT] *Red Lodge,*
  MT
PONDEROSA [MOT] *Burns, OR*
PONDEROSA MOTEL [MOT]
  Goldendale, WA
PORT ANGELES INN [MOT] *Port*
  Angeles, WA
PORTLAND'S WHITE HOUSE BED
  AND BREAKFAST [BB] *Portland,*
  OR
PORT LUDLOW RESORT &
  CONFERENCE CENTER [RST]
  Port Ludlow, WA
POST HOTEL [HOT] *Lake Louise, AB*

PRAIRIE INN MOTEL [MOT]
  Evanston, WY
PRINCE OF WALES [BB] *Waterton*
  Lakes National Park, AB
PRINCE ROYAL SUITES [HOT]
  Calgary, AB
PRIOR HOUSE B&B INN [BB] *Victoria,*
  BC
QUALITY 49'ER INN & SUITES [HOT]
  Jackson, WY
QUALITY HOTEL & CONFERENCE
  CENTRE [MOT] *Calgary, AB*
QUALITY HOTEL - DOWNTOWN
  [HOT] *Vancouver, BC*
QUALITY INN [MOT] *Baker City, OR*
QUALITY INN [MOT] *Bellingham, WA*
QUALITY INN [HOT] *Billings, MT*
QUALITY INN [MOT] *Clarkston, WA*
QUALITY INN [HOT] *Lincoln City, OR*
QUALITY INN [HOT] *Pullman, WA*
QUALITY INN [HOT] *The Dalles, OR*
QUALITY INN & SUITES [MOT]
  Klamath Falls, OR
QUALITY INN AIRPORT SUITES
  [MOT] *Boise, ID*
QUALITY INN MOTEL VILLAGE
  [HOT] *Calgary, AB*
QUALITY INN OF YAKIMA [MOT]
  Yakima, WA
QUALITY INN VALLEY SUITES [HOT]
  Spokane, WA
QUALITY RESORT - CHATEAU
  CANMORE [MOT] *Banff, AB*
QUEEN VICTORIA INN [HOT]
  Victoria, BC
RADISSON DOWNTOWN [HOT]
  Winnipeg, MB
RADISSON HOTEL [HOT] *Portland,*
  OR
RADISSON HOTEL [MOT] *Seattle, WA*
RADISSON HOTEL [MOT] *Seattle-*
  Tacoma International Airport
  Area, WA
RADISSON HOTEL AND
  CONFERENCE CENTER [MOT]
  Banff, AB
RADISSON HOTEL BURNABY [HOT]
  Vancouver, BC
RADISSON HOTEL CALGARY
  AIRPORT [HOT] *Calgary, AB*
RADISSON HOTEL CASPER [HOT]
  Casper, WY
RADISSON NORTHERN HOTEL
  [HOT] *Billings, MT*
RADISSON PRESIDENT HOTEL AND
  SUITES [HOT] *Vancouver, BC*
RADISSON SUITE HOTEL WINNIPEG
  AIRPORT [AS] *Winnipeg, MB*
RAFTER SIX RANCH RESORT [RST]
  Calgary, AB
RAINBOW INN [BB] *La Conner, WA*

RAINBOW RANCH [BB] *Big Sky (Gallatin County), MT*
RAMADA COURTYARD INN [MOT] *Penticton, BC*
RAMADA HUNTINGDON MANOR [HOT] *Victoria, BC*
RAMADA INN [MOT] *Beaverton, OR*
RAMADA INN [MOT] *Bellingham, WA*
RAMADA INN [MOT] *Billings, MT*
RAMADA INN [MOT] *Bozeman, MT*
RAMADA INN [MOT] *Butte, MT*
RAMADA INN [HOT] *Edmonton, AB*
RAMADA INN [HOT] *Portland, OR*
RAMADA INN [HOT] *Spokane, WA*
RAMADA INN [MOT] *Wenatchee, WA*
RAMADA INN GOVERNOR HOUSE [HOT] *Olympia, WA*
RAMADA INN- KAMLOOPS [MOT] *Kamloops, BC*
RAMADA LIMITED [MOT] *Rock Springs, WY*
RAMADA LODGE [HOT] *Kelowna, BC*
RANCH AT UCROSS, THE [HOT] *Buffalo, WY*
RAVENSCROFT [BB] *Port Townsend, WA*
RED CARPET INN [MOT] *Banff, AB*
RED LION HOTEL [HOT] *Coos Bay, OR*
RED LION HOTEL [HOT] *Kelso, WA*
RED LION HOTEL [MOT] *Lewiston, ID*
RED LION HOTEL [HOT] *Richland, WA*
RED LION HOTEL [HOT] *Vancouver, WA*
RED LION HOTEL EUGENE [HOT] *Eugene, OR*
RED LION HOTEL MEDFORD [HOT] *Medford, OR*
RED LION HOTEL-PORT ANGELES [RST] *Port Angeles, WA*
RED LION HOTEL SALEM [HOT] *Salem, OR*
RED LION HOTEL WENATCHEE [HOT] *Wenatchee, WA*
RED LION INN [MOT] *Aberdeen, WA*
RED LION INN [RST] *Astoria, OR*
RED LION INN [MOT] *Missoula, MT*
RED LION INN [MOT] *Yakima, WA*
RED LION INN NORTH [MOT] *Bend, OR*
RED LION WYOMING INN [HOT] *Jackson, WY*
RED ROOF INN [MOT] *Seattle-Tacoma International Airport Area, WA*
REDWOOD MOTEL [MOT] *Grants Pass, OR*
REDWOOD MOTOR INN [MOT] *Brandon, MB*

RENAISSANCE VANCOUVER HOTEL HARBOURSIDE [HOT] *Vancouver, BC*
RENAISSANCE MADISON HOTEL, THE [HOT] *Seattle, WA*
RESIDENCE INN BY MARRIOTT [MOT] *Bellevue, WA*
RESIDENCE INN BY MARRIOTT [AS] *Boise, ID*
RESIDENCE INN BY MARRIOTT [MOT] *Portland, OR*
RESIDENCE INN BY MARRIOTT [MOT] *Portland, OR*
RESORT AT GLACIER, THE [MOT] *East Glacier Area, MT*
RESORT AT THE MOUNTAIN, THE [RST] *Mount Hood National Forest, OR*
RESORT SEMIAHMOO [RST] *Blaine, WA*
RESTON HOTEL [HOT] *Medford, OR*
RICHLAND DAYS INN [MOT] *Richland, WA*
RIDGEWAY "FARM" BED & BREAKFAST [BB] *Mount Vernon, WA*
RIMROCK DUDE RANCH [BB] *Cody, WY*
RIMROCK RESORT [HOT] *Banff, AB*
RIVERBEND INN [MOT] *Coeur d'Alene, ID*
RIVER HOUSE MOTEL [MOT] *Florence, OR*
RIVERHOUSE RESORT [RST] *Bend, OR*
RIVER PLACE HOTEL [HOT] *Portland, OR*
RIVER ROCK LODGE [HOT] *Big Sky (Gallatin County), MT*
RIVER RUN COTTAGES [BB] *Vancouver, BC*
RIVERSHORE HOTEL [HOT] *Oregon City, OR*
RIVERSIDE INN [HOT] *Grants Pass, OR*
RIVER STREET INN, THE [BB] *Sun Valley Area, ID*
RIVERVIEW INN [MOT] *Lewiston, ID*
RIVIERA [MOT] *Biggs, OR*
ROBERTA'S BED AND BREAKFAST [BB] *Seattle, WA*
ROCHE HARBOR RESORT AND HOTEL [RST] *San Juan Islands, WA*
ROCK CREEK RESORT [RST] *Red Lodge, MT*
ROCK SPRINGS GUEST RANCH [RST] *Bend, OR*
ROCKY MOUNTAIN LODGE [HOT] *Whitefish, MT*
RODEWAY INN [MOT] *Ashland, OR*
RODEWAY INN [MOT] *Boise, ID*

RODEWAY INN [HOT] *Leavenworth, WA*
RODEWAY INN & SUITES [HOT] *Gardiner, MT*
ROGUE REGENCY INN [HOT] *Medford, OR*
ROGUE VALLEY MOTEL [MOT] *Grants Pass, OR*
ROMEO INN [BB] *Ashland, OR*
ROOSEVELT, THE [BB] *Coeur d'Alene, ID*
ROSARIO [RST] *San Juan Islands, WA*
ROSE BRIAR HOTEL [BB] *Astoria, OR*
ROYAL 7 [MOT] *Bozeman, MT*
ROYAL COACHMAN INN, INC. [MOT] *Tacoma, WA*
ROYAL MOTOR INN [MOT] *La Grande, OR*
ROYAL OAK INN [MOT] *Brandon, MB*
ROYAL RESORT [MOT] *Alpine, WY*
ROYAL SCOT INN [MOT] *Victoria, BC*
ROYAL VIEW MOTOR HOTEL [MOT] *Grants Pass, OR*
RUNDLE MOUNTAIN MOTEL [MOT] *Banff, AB*
RUNDLESTONE LODGE [HOT] *Banff, AB*
RUN OF THE RIVER BED & BREAKFAST [BB] *Leavenworth, WA*
RUSTY PARROT LODGE [HOT] *Jackson, WY*
SACAJAWEA SELECT INN [MOT] *Lewiston, ID*
SAFARI MOTOR INN, INC [MOT] *McMinnville, OR*
SAGE BRUSH MOTEL [MOT] *Kamloops, BC*
SALBASGEON INN OF REEDSPORT [MOT] *Reedsport, OR*
SALIBURY HOUSE BED & BREAKFAST [BB] *Seattle, WA*
SALISH LODGE AND SPA [RST] *North Bend, WA*
SANDERS - HELENA'S BED & BREAKFAST, THE [BB] *Helena, MT*
SANDLAKE COUNTRY INN [BB] *Tillamook, OR*
SANDMAN HOTEL [MOT] *Kelowna, BC*
SANDMAN HOTEL [MOT] *Penticton, BC*
SANDPOINT QUALITY INN [MOT] *Sandpoint, ID*
SAN JUAN [BB] *San Juan Islands, WA*
SAW RIDGE HOTEL & CONFERENCE CENTER [MOT] *Jasper National Park, AB*
SAWTOOTH INN BEST WESTERN [HOT] *Jerome, ID*

SCANDINAVIAN GARDENS INN BED & BREAKFAST [BB] *Long Beach, WA*
SCHOONERS COVE OCEAN FRONT MOTEL [RST] *Cannon Beach, OR*
SEA QUEST BED & BREAKFAST [BB] *Yachats, OR*
SEATTLE HILTON [HOT] *Seattle, WA*
SEVEN D RANCH [RAN] *Cody, WY*
SHAMAN MOTEL [MOT] *Long Beach, WA*
SHAMROCK LODGETTES [MOT] *Yachats, OR*
SHANGRI-LA [MOT] *Spokane, WA*
SHANICO INN [MOT] *Corvallis, OR*
SHARLYN MOTEL [MOT] *Ephrata, WA*
SHERATON [HOT] *Billings, MT*
SHERATON [HOT] *Tacoma, WA*
SHERATON CAVALIER [HOT] *Calgary, AB*
SHERATON GRANDE [HOT] *Edmonton, AB*
SHERATON PORTLAND AIRPORT HOTEL [HOT] *Portland, OR*
SHERATON SEATTLE HOTEL & TOWERS [HOT] *Seattle, WA*
SHERATON SUITES LE SOLEIL [AS] *Vancouver, BC*
SHERATON WINNIPEG HOTEL [HOT] *Winnipeg, MB*
SHILO BEACHFRONT RESORT [MOT] *Ocean Shores, WA*
SHILO HOTEL [MOT] *Spokane, WA*
SHILO INN [HOT] *Astoria, OR*
SHILO INN [HOT] *Bend, OR*
SHILO INN [HOT] *Coeur d'Alene, ID*
SHILO INN [MOT] *Eugene, OR*
SHILO INN [MOT] *Grants Pass, OR*
SHILO INN [MOT] *Helena, MT*
SHILO INN [HOT] *Idaho Falls, ID*
SHILO INN [MOT] *Moses Lake, WA*
SHILO INN [MOT] *Nampa, ID*
SHILO INN [MOT] *Nampa, ID*
SHILO INN [MOT] *Newberg, OR*
SHILO INN [HOT] *Newport, OR*
SHILO INN [MOT] *Portland, OR*
SHILO INN [MOT] *Portland, OR*
SHILO INN [MOT] *Richland, WA*
SHILO INN [HOT] *Salem, OR*
SHILO INN [MOT] *Seaside, OR*
SHILO INN [RST] *Seaside, OR*
SHILO INN [MOT] *Tacoma, WA*
SHILO INN [HOT] *Tillamook, OR*
SHILO INN [HOT] *Twin Falls, ID*
SHILO INN [MOT] *Vancouver, WA*
SHILO INN AIRPORT [MOT] *Boise, ID*
SHILO INN OCEANFRONT RESORT [MOT] *Lincoln City, OR*

SHILO INN PORTLAND AIRPORT [AS] *Portland, OR*
SHILO INN RIVERSIDE [HOT] *Boise, ID*
SHILO INN SUITES HOTEL [MOT] *Klamath Falls, OR*
SHIP HARBOR INN [MOT] *Anacortes, WA*
SHORE CLIFF INN [MOT] *Gold Beach, OR*
SHORE LODGE [RST] *McCall, ID*
SHOSHONE LODGE RESORT & CUEST RANCH [RAN] *Cody, WY*
SHUMWAY MANSION [BB] *Bellevue, WA*
SIGNAL MOUNTAIN LODGE [BB] *Grand Teton National Park, WY*
SILVER CLOUD INN [MOT] *Bellevue, WA*
SILVER CLOUD INN [HOT] *Seattle, WA*
SILVER CLOUD INN-BELLVUE [HOT] *Bellevue, WA*
SILVER CLOUD INN - KENNEWICK [HOT] *Kennewick, WA*
SILVER CLOUD INN PORTLAND [HOT] *Portland, OR*
SILVER FOREST [BB] *Bozeman, MT*
SILVERHORN MOTOR INN & RESTAURANT [MOT] *Kellogg, ID*
SILVER SANOS MOTEL [MOT] *Rockaway, OR*
SILVER SPUR MOTEL [HOT] *Burns, OR*
SIXTH AVENUE INN [MOT] *Seattle, WA*
SKAMANIA LODGE [RST] *Hood River, OR*
SLEEPING LADY CONFERENCE RETREAT [RST] *Leavenworth, WA*
SLEEP INN [MOT] *Billings, MT*
SLEEP INN [MOT] *Boise, ID*
SLEEP INN [MOT] *Bozeman, MT*
SLEEP INN [MOT] *Jerome, ID*
SLEEP INN [MOT] *Missoula, MT*
SLEEP INN [MOT] *Mountain Home, ID*
SLEEP INN [MOT] *Rawlins, WY*
SLEEPY HOLLOW MOTEL [MOT] *McKenzie Bridge, OR*
SNOW KING RESORT [RST] *Jackson, WY*
SOL DUC HOT SPRINGS [RST] *Olympic National Park, WA*
SONNY'S MOTEL [MOT] *Madras, OR*
SOOKE HARBOUR HOUSE [BB] *Waterton Lakes National Park, AB*
SORRENTO [HOT] *Seattle, WA*

SPAHN'S BIG HORN MOUNTAIN BED & BREAKFAST [BB] *Sheridan, WY*
SPANISH VILLA [RST] *Penticton, BC*
SPRINDRIFT MOTOR INN [MOT] *Brookings, OR*
SPRING CREEK RANCH [RST] *Jackson, WY*
STAGECOACH INN [MOT] *West Yellowstone, MT*
STAGECOACH INN MOTEL [MOT] *Salmon, ID*
STAGE LODGE [MOT] *Jacksonville, OR*
STANG MANOR BED & BREAKFAST [RAN] *La Grande, OR*
STARDUST MOTEL [MOT] *Wallace, ID*
STATEHOUSE INN [HOT] *Boise, ID*
STAY 'N SAVE [MOT] *Kamloops, BC*
STEIGER HAUS BED & BREAKFAST [BB] *McMinnville, OR*
STRATFORD INN [MOT] *Ashland, OR*
SUMMERFIELD SUITES BY WYNDHAM [HOT] *Seattle, WA*
SUMMIT LODGE [RST] *Whistler, BC*
SUNDOWNER MOTEL [MOT] *Caldwell, ID*
SUNDOWNER STATION [MOT] *Riverton, WY*
SUN MOUNTAIN LODGE [RST] *Winthrop, WA*
SUNRIVER RESORT [RST] *Bend, OR*
SUNSET MOTEL [MOT] *Bonner's Ferry, ID*
SUNSET MOTEL [MOT] *Fort Macleod, AB*
SUNSET OCEANFRONT ACCOMMODAT [MOT] *Bandon, OR*
SUN VALLEY RESORT [RST] *Sun Valley Area, ID*
SUPER 8 [MOT] *Boise, ID*
SUPER 8 [MOT] *Dubois, WY*
SUPER 8 [MOT] *Klamath Falls, OR*
SUPER 8 [HOT] *Long Beach, WA*
SUPER 8 [MOT] *Medicine Hat, AB*
SUPER 8 [MOT] *Missoula, MT*
SUPER 8 [MOT] *Missoula, MT*
SUPER 8 [MOT] *Montpelier, ID*
SUPER 8 [MOT] *Moscow, ID*
SUPER 8 [MOT] *Red Lodge, MT*
SUPER 8 [MOT] *Rexburg, ID*
SUPER 8 [MOT] *Thermopolis, WY*
SUPER 8 [MOT] *Torrington, WY*
SUPER 8 LIONSHEAD RESORT [MOT] *West Yellowstone, MT*
SUPER 8 MOTEL [MOT] *Baker City, OR*
SUPER 8 MOTEL [MOT] *Big Timber, MT*
SUPER 8 MOTEL [MOT] *Billings, MT*
SUPER 8 MOTEL [MOT] *Butte, MT*

SUPER 8 MOTEL [MOT] *Coeur d'Alene, ID*
SUPER 8 MOTEL [MOT] *Deer Lodge, MT*
SUPER 8 MOTEL [MOT] *Dillon, MT*
SUPER 8 MOTEL [MOT] *Hardin, MT*
SUPER 8 MOTEL [MOT] *Helena, MT*
SUPER 8 MOTEL [MOT] *Kellogg, ID*
SUPER 8 MOTEL [MOT] *Lewiston, ID*
SUPER 8 MOTEL [MOT] *Lovell, WY*
SUPER 8 MOTEL [MOT] *Sandpoint, ID*
SUPER 8 MOTEL [MOT] *Spokane, WA*
SUPER 8 MOTEL [MOT] *Whitefish, MT*
SUPER 8 TETON WEST [MOT] *Driggs, ID*
SUPER 8 WILSONVILLE [MOT] *Portland, OR*
SURFRIDER RESORT [MOT] *Depoe Bay, OR*
SURFSAND RESORT HOTEL [RST] *Cannon Beach, OR*
SURFSIDE MOTEL [MOT] *Rockaway, OR*
SUTTON PLACE HOTEL, THE [HOT] *Vancouver, BC*
SWAN HOTEL, THE [BB] *Port Townsend, WA*
SWANS SUITE HOTEL [HOT] *Victoria, BC*
SWAN VALLEY SUPER 8 LODGE [MOT] *Bigfork, MT*
SWEET BRIAR INN, THE [BB] *Portland, OR*
SWIFTCURRENT INN [MOT] *East Glacier Area, MT*
TAMARACK LODGE [MOT] *Sun Valley Area, ID*
TAPADERA INN [MOT] *Kennewick, WA*
TAPADERA MOTEL [MOT] *Pendleton, OR*
TETON MOUNTAIN VIEW LODGE [MOT] *Driggs, ID*
TETON PINES [RST] *Jackson, WY*
TETON RIDGE RANCH [RST] *Driggs, ID*
TETON TREE HOUSE BED & BREAKFAST [BB] *Jackson, WY*
TIGH-NA-MARA RESORT HOTEL [RST] *Nanaimo, BC*
TIKI LODGE [MOT] *Salem, OR*
TIMBERLINE LODGE [RST] *Mount Hood National Forest, OR*
TIMBERLINE VILLAGE RESORT [MOT] *Packwood, WA*
TIMBERS [MOT] *Bigfork, MT*
TLC INN [MOT] *Bozeman, MT*
TOLOVANA INN [RST] *Cannon Beach, OR*

TORCH & TOES BED & BREAKFAST [BB] *Bozeman, MT*
TOUVELLE HOUSE BED & BREAKFAST [BB] *Jacksonville, OR*
TOWER ON THE PARK [AS] *Edmonton, AB*
TOWN & COUNTRY MOTEL [MOT] *Bonner's Ferry, ID*
TOWNHOUSE INN [MOT] *Havre, MT*
TOWN HOUSE INN OF GREAT FALLS [HOT] *Great Falls, MT*
TRADE WINDS NORTH MOTEL [MOT] *Spokane, WA*
TRADITIONAL INNS [MOT] *Quincy, WA*
TRAVELERS INN [MOT] *Bellingham, WA*
TRAVELERS INN [MOT] *Seattle, WA*
TRAVEL LODGE [MOT] *Hillsboro, OR*
TRAVELODGE [MOT] *Boise, ID*
TRAVELODGE [MOT] *Eugene, OR*
TRAVELODGE [MOT] *Medicine Hat, AB*
TRAVELODGE [MOT] *Missoula, MT*
TRAVELODGE [MOT] *Penticton, BC*
TRAVELODGE [MOT] *Red Deer, AB*
TRAVELODGE [MOT] *Roseburg, OR*
TRAVELODGE [MOT] *Seattle-Tacoma International Airport Area, WA*
TRAVELODGE [HOT] *Spokane, WA*
TRAVELODGE [MOT] *Walla Walla, WA*
TRAVELODGE [MOT] *Wenatchee, WA*
TRAVELODGE CALGARY SOUTH [MOT] *Calgary, AB*
TRAVELODGE NEW REDMOND HOTEL [HOT] *Redmond, OR*
TRAVELODGE SUITES [MOT] *Forest Grove, OR*
TRIPLE CREEK RANCH [MOT] *Hamilton, MT*
TUCKER HOUSE BED & BREAKFAST [BB] *San Juan Islands, WA*
TUDOR INN BED & BREAKFAST [BB] *Port Angeles, WA*
TUNNEL MOUNTAIN CHALETS [AS] *Banff, AB*
TURTLEBACK FARM INN [BB] *San Juan Islands, WA*
TU TU' TUN LODGE [BB] *Gold Beach, OR*
TWIN FALLS COMFORT INN [MOT] *Twin Falls, ID*
TYEE HOTEL [MOT] *Olympia, WA*
UNIVERSITY INN [MOT] *Boise, ID*
UNIVERSITY INN [BB] *Seattle, WA*
UPTOWN INN [MOT] *Port Angeles, WA*
UXU RANCH [MOT] *Cody, WY*

VAGABOND LODGE HOOD RIVER [MOT] *Hood River, OR*

VALLEY GOFF CREEK [MOT] *Cody, WY*

VALLEY RIVER INN [HOT] *Eugene, OR*

VAL-U INN [MOT] *Missoula, MT*

VAL-U INN MOTEL [MOT] *Bellingham, WA*

VICTORIA INN [HOT] *Brandon, MB*

VICTORIA REGENT [HOT] *Victoria, BC*

VILLA BED & BREAKFAST [BB] *Tacoma, WA*

VILLAGE GREEN HOTEL & CASINO [HOT] *Kelowna, BC*

VILLAGE INN [MOT] *Challis, ID*

VILLAGE INN [MOT] *East Glacier Area, MT*

VILLAGE INN MOTEL [MOT] *Cashmere, WA*

VILLAGE MOTOR INN [MOT] *Marysville, WA*

VILLAGE SQUIRE MOTEL [MOT] *Redmond, OR*

VINEYARD INN [MOT] *Pasco, WA*

VINTAGE PLAZA [HOT] *Portland, OR*

VOSS INN [BB] *Bozeman, MT*

WALLOWA LAKE LODGE [MOT] *Joseph, OR*

WARWICK HOTEL [HOT] *Seattle, WA*

WATERFRONT CENTRE [HOT] *Vancouver, BC*

WEASKU INN [BB] *Grants Pass, OR*

WEDGE MOUNTAIN INN [MOT] *Cashmere, WA*

WEDGEWOOD [HOT] *Vancouver, BC*

WELOME MOTOR INN [MOT] *Everett, WA*

WESTCOAST-SEA-TAC HOTEL [MOT] *Seattle-Tacoma International Airport Area, WA*

WESTCOAST BELLEVUE HOTEL [MOT] *Bellevue, WA*

WEST COAST GRAND HOTEL ON FIFTH AVENUE [HOT] *Seattle, WA*

WEST COAST KALISPELL CENTER [MOT] *Kalispell, MT*

WEST COAST OLYMPIA HOTEL [MOT] *Olympia, WA*

WESTCOAST POCATELLO HOTEL [HOT] *Pocatello, ID*

WESTCOAST RIDPATH HOTEL [HOT] *Spokane, WA*

WEST COAST RIVER INN [MOT] *Spokane, WA*

WESTCOAST SILVERDALE HOTEL [MOT] *Bremerton, WA*

WESTCOAST TRI CITIES [MOT] *Kennewick, WA*

WESTCOAST WENATCHEE CENTER [HOT] *Wenatchee, WA*

WESTCOAST YAKIMA CENTER HOTEL [HOT] *Yakima, WA*

WESTCOAST YAKIMA GATEWAY HOTEL [HOT] *Yakima, WA*

WEST END GUEST HOUSE [BB] *Vancouver, BC*

WEST HARVEST INN [MOT] *Edmonton, AB*

WESTIN BAYSHORE RESORT AND MARINA [HOT] *Vancouver, BC*

WESTIN CALGARY [HOT] *Calgary, AB*

WESTIN EDMONTON [HOT] *Edmonton, AB*

WESTIN GRAND VANCOUVER, THE [HOT] *Vancouver, BC*

WESTIN PORTLAND, THE [HOT] *Portland, OR*

WESTIN RESORT AND SPA, THE [RST] *Whistler, BC*

WESTIN SALISHAN LODGE [RST] *Lincoln City, OR*

WESTIN SEATTLE, THE [HOT] *Seattle, WA*

WHALER MOTEL [MOT] *Newport, OR*

WHITE SWAN GUEST HOUSE, THE [BB] *Mount Vernon, WA*

WICKANINNISH INN, THE [BB] *Vancouver, BC*

WILDFLOWER INN, THE [BB] *Jackson, WY*

WILLOW SPRINGS MOTEL [MOT] *Cheney, WA*

WINCHESTER COUNTRY INN [BB] *Ashland, OR*

WINDMILL INN [HOT] *Ashland, OR*

WINDMILL INN [HOT] *Medford, OR*

WINDMILL INN OF ROSEBURG [MOT] *Roseburg, OR*

WINDSONG BED & BREAKFAST [BB] *San Juan Islands, WA*

WINTHROP INN, THE [MOT] *Winthrop, WA*

WOODMARK HOTEL ON LAKE WASHINGTON [HOT] *Bellevue, WA*

WOODS HOUSE BED & BREAKFAST [BB] *Ashland, OR*

WOODSMAN MOTEL AND CAFE [MOT] *McCall, ID*

WORT HOTEL, THE [HOT] *Jackson, WY*

W SEATTLE [HOT] *Seattle, WA*

WYNDHAM GARDEN HOTEL - SEATTLE [HOT] *Seattle, WA*

WYOMING MOTEL [MOT] *Buffalo, WY*

YELLOW POINT LODGE [CC] *Nanaimo, BC*

YELLOWSTONE SUPER 8 [MOT] *Gardiner, MT*

YELLOWSTONE VILLAGE INN [HOT] *Gardiner, MT*

RESTAURANT LIST

Establishment names are listed in alphabetical order followed by a symbol identifying their classification and then city and state. The symbols for classification are: [RES] for Restaurants and [URD] for Unrated Dining Spots.

ADRIATICA [RES] *Seattle, WA*
AEIRE DINING ROOM [RES]
     Victoria, AB
A KETTLE OF FISH [RES] *Vancouver, BC*
AL-AMIR LEBANESE RESTAURANT
     [RES] *Portland, OR*
AL BOCCALINO [RES] *Seattle, WA*
ALESSANDRO'S [RES] *Portland, OR*
ALESSANDRO'S [URD] *Salem, OR*
ALEXANDER'S COUNTRY INN [RES]
     Mount Rainier National Park, WA
ALEXIS [RES] *Portland, OR*
ALLEGRO CAFI [RES] *Vancouver, BC*
ALPENHOF DINING ROOM, THE
     [RES] *Jackson, WY*
ALTEZZO RISTORANTE [RES] *Tacoma, WA*
AMBROSIA [RES] *Eugene, OR*
AMICI [RES] *Winnipeg, MB*
ANDALUCA [RES] *Seattle, WA*
ANTHONY'S [RES] *Jackson, WY*
ANTOINE'S [RES] *Victoria, BC*
AQUA RIVE [RES] *Vancouver, BC*
ARIA [RES] *Vancouver, BC*
ARMOR'S SILVER FOX [RES] *Casper, WY*
ASHLAND BAKERY & CAFE [RES]
     Ashland, OR
ASSAGGIO RISTORANTE [RES]
     Seattle, WA
ATLAS FOODS [RES] *Seattle, WA*
ATRIUM STEAKHOUSE [RES] *Calgary, AB*
ATWATER'S [RES] *Portland, OR*
BACCHUS [RES] *Vancouver, BC*
BALKAN [RES] *Banff, AB*
BANDOLEONE [RES] *Seattle, WA*
BANDON BOATWORKS [RES]
     Bandon, OR
BANFF SPRINGS [RES] *Banff, AB*
BANGKOK CUISINE [RES] *Sandpoint, ID*
BARCLAY II [RES] *Anaconda, MT*
BAR J [URD] *Jackson, WY*
BAY HOUSE [RES] *Lincoln City, OR*
BEAR FOOT BISTRO [RES] *Whistler, BC*

BEASLEY'S [RES] *Redmond, OR*
BEEFEATER STEAK HOUSE [RES]
     Lethbridge, AB
BEEFEATER STEAK HOUSE [RES]
     Medicine Hat, AB
BELLA ITALIA [RES] *Port Angeles, WA*
BELVEDERE, THE [RES] *Calgary, AB*
BENTLEY'S ON THE BAY [URD]
     Victoria, BC
BEVERLY'S [RES] *Coeur d'Alene, ID*
BIGFORK INN [RES] *Bigfork, MT*
BIG HORN [RES] *Lovell, WY*
BILLY'S RESTAURANT [RES] *Aberdeen, WA*
BISHOP'S [RES] *Vancouver, BC*
BISTRO, THE [RES] *Banff, AB*
BISTRO PROVENCAL [RES] *Bellevue, WA*
BLACK RABBIT [RES] *Portland, OR*
BLUE CRAB BAR AND GRILL [RES]
     Victoria, BC
BLUE LION [RES] *Jackson, WY*
BOAT SHED [RES] *Bremerton, WA*
BOODLES [RES] *Bozeman, MT*
BRASA [RES] *Seattle, WA*
BREWHOUSE TAP ROOM & GRILL
     [RES] *Portland, OR*
BRIDGES RESTAURANT [RES]
     Aberdeen, WA
BROOKLYN SEAFOOD, STEAK &
     OYSTER HOUSE [RES] *Seattle, WA*
BRUNO'S ITALIAN SPECIALTIES [RES]
     Billings, MT
BUCA DI BEPPO [RES] *Seattle, WA*
BUDD BAY CAFE [RES] *Olympia, WA*
BUFFALO MOUNTAIN LODGE
     DINING ROOM [RES] *Banff, AB*
BUGATTI'S [RES] *Portland, OR*
BUNNERY, THE [URD] *Jackson, WY*
BURRITO LOCO [RES] *Seattle, WA*
BUSH GARDEN [RES] *Portland, OR*
BUSHWHACKER [RES] *Port Angeles, WA*
CABOOSE STEAK AND LOBSTER
     [RES] *Banff, AB*
CACTUS [RES] *Seattle, WA*
CADILLAC GRILLE [RES] *Jackson, WY*

CAESAR'S STEAK HOUSE [RES]
Calgary, AB
CAFE AZUL [RES] *Portland, OR*
CAFE BRIO [RES] *Victoria, BC*
CAFE CAMPAGNE [RES] *Seattle, WA*
CAFE DE PARIS [RES] *Vancouver, BC*
CAFE DES AMIS [RES] *Portland, OR*
CAFE EDELWEISS [RES] *Big Sky
(Gallatin County), MT*
CAFE FLORA [RES] *Seattle, WA*
CAFE JUANITA [RES] *Bellevue, WA*
CAFE LAGO [RES] *Seattle, WA*
CAFE LANGLEY [RES] *Coupeville, WA*
CAFE NAVARRO [RES] *Eugene, OR*
CAFFE DE MEDICI [RES] *Vancouver,
BC*
CALICO [RES] *Jackson, WY*
CAMILLE'S [RES] *Victoria, BC*
CAMP 18 [RES] *Seaside, OR*
CAMPAGNE [RES] *Seattle, WA*
CANLIS [RES] *Seattle, WA*
CANNERY [RES] *Vancouver, BC*
CAPILANO HEIGHTS [RES] *Vancouver,
BC*
CAPRIAL'S BISTRO [RES] *Portland, OR*
CARMELITA [RES] *Seattle, WA*
CASA DE BLANCA [RES] *Ellensburg,
WA*
CASCADIA [URD] *Seattle, WA*
C'EST SI BON [RES] *Port Angeles, WA*
CHANDLER'S RESTAURANT [RES]
Sun Valley Area, ID
CHANTERELLE [RES] *Eugene, OR*
CHAPTER XI [RES] *Spokane, WA*
CHART HOUSE [RES] *Portland, OR*
CHARTHOUSE [RES] *Vancouver, BC*
CHARTWELL [RES] *Vancouver, BC*
CHATEAULIN [RES] *Ashland, OR*
CHEZ FRANCOIS [RES] *Banff, AB*
CHEZ JEANNETTE [RES] *Lincoln City,
OR*
CHEZ MICHEL [RES] *Vancouver, BC*
CHEZ SHEA [RES] *Seattle, WA*
CHIANTI CAFE [RES] *Edmonton, AB*
CHINOOK'S [RES] *Seattle, WA*
CHOWDERHEAD [RES] *Gold Beach,
OR*
CHRISTINA'S [RES] *San Juan Islands,
WA*
CHUCKANUT MANOR [RES]
Bellingham, WA
CHUTNEY'S [RES] *Seattle, WA*
CIMMIYOTTI'S [RES] *Pendleton, OR*
CINCIN ITALIAN WOOD GRILL
[RES] *Vancouver, BC*
CIRCLE T INN [RES] *Ritzville, WA*
CLIFF HOUSE [RES] *Tacoma, WA*
CLINKERDAGGER [RES] *Spokane, WA*
CLOUD 9 [RES] *Vancouver, BC*
COBBLESTONE MANOR [RES] *Fort
Macleod, AB*
COCOA'S [RES] *Edmonton, AB*

COCO PAZZO [RES] *Lethbridge, AB*
COLONEL BOZEMAN'S [RES] *Buffalo,
WY*
COLUMBIA RIVER COURT DINING
ROOM [RES] *Hood River, OR*
CONSERVATORY [URD] *Calgary, AB*
CONSERVATORY RESTAURANT, THE
[RES] *Nanaimo, BC*
COPPERFIELD'S [RES] *Tacoma, WA*
COTTAGE [RES] *Cottage Grove, OR*
COUCH STREET FISH HOUSE [RES]
Portland, OR
COUSIN'S [RES] *The Dalles, OR*
COUVRON [RES] *Portland, OR*
COYOTE RIVERHOUSE [RES] *Bigfork,
MT*
CREEK RESTAURANT & BREWERY,
THE [RES] *Vancouver, BC*
CREPERIE [URD] *Edmonton, AB*
C RESTAURANT [RES] *Vancouver, BC*
CRUMPET SHOP, THE [URD] *Seattle-
Tacoma International Airport
Area, WA*
CUCINA! CUCINA! [RES] *Seattle, WA*
DAHLIA LOUNGE [RES] *Seattle, WA*
DAN & LOUIS OYSTER BAR [RES]
Portland, OR
DEEP COVE CHALET [RES] *Victoria,
BC*
DELI DE PASTA [RES] *Yakima, WA*
DELILAH'S [RES] *Vancouver, BC*
DEPOT [RES] *Missoula, MT*
DINING ROOM, THE [RES] *Winthrop,
WA*
DINING ROOM AT SALISHAN, THE
[RES] *Lincoln City, OR*
DINING ROOM RESTAURANT, THE
[URD] *Victoria, BC*
DIVA AT THE MET [RES] *Vancouver,
BC*
DON'S [RES] *Soap Lake, WA*
DON GUIDO'S ITALIAN CUISINE
[RES] *Mount Hood National
Forest, OR*
DOOGER'S [RES] *Cannon Beach, OR*
DOOGER'S SEAFOOD & GRILL [RES]
Seaside, OR
DOONG KONG LAU [RES] *Seattle,
WA*
DORY COVE [RES] *Lincoln City, OR*
DOWNRIGGERS [RES] *San Juan
Islands, WA*
DRAGON FISH ASIAN CAFE [RES]
Seattle, WA
DUFFY'S [RES] *Hoquiam, WA*
DULCES LATIN BISTRO [RES] *Seattle,
WA*
DUNDARAVE PIER [RES] *Vancouver,
BC*
DUNGENESS INN [RES] *Sequim, WA*
EARTH AND OCEAN [RES] *Seattle,
WA*

EDDIE'S SUPPER CLUB [RES] *Great Falls, MT*
EDITH CAVELL DINING ROOM [RES] *Jasper National Park, AB*
EDWARD'S [RES] *Penticton, BC*
EL GAUCHO [RES] *Seattle, WA*
ELLIOTT'S OYSTER HOUSE [RES] *Seattle, WA*
EMPRESS ROOM [RES] *Victoria, BC*
ERNESTO'S ITALIAN RESTAURANT [RES] *Bend, OR*
ESPARZA'S TEX MEX CAFE [RES] *Portland, OR*
ESPLANADE AT RIVERPLACE [RES] *Portland, OR*
ETTA'S SEAFOOD [RES] *Seattle, WA*
EVERGREEN BISTRO [RES] *Sun Valley Area, ID*
EXCELSIOR INN [RES] *Eugene, OR*
FENDERS [RES] *Whitefish, MT*
FERNANDO'S HIDEAWAY [RES] *Portland, OR*
FIORE [RES] *Edmonton, AB*
FIORELLA'S [RES] *Klamath Falls, OR*
FIRST AVENUE WEST [RES] *Kalispell, MT*
FIRST PLACE [RES] *Big Sky (Gallatin County), MT*
FISH AND COMPANY [RES] *Vancouver, BC*
FISH HOUSE IN STANLEY PARK [RES] *Vancouver, BC*
FIVE SAILS [URD] *Vancouver, BC*
FLEURI [RES] *Vancouver, BC*
FLOATING RESTAURANT [RES] *Sandpoint, ID*
FLYING FISH [RES] *Seattle, WA*
FOUR SEAS [RES] *Seattle, WA*
FRANCA'S ITALIAN DINING [RES] *Cody, WY*
FRONTIER PIES RESTAURANT [RES] *Rexburg, ID*
FULLERS [RES] *Seattle, WA*
F.X. MCRORY'S STEAK, CHOP & OYSTER HOUSE [RES] *Seattle, WA*
GABLES [RES] *Corvallis, OR*
GALLATIN GATEWAY INN [RES] *Bozeman, MT*
GATSBY MANSION [RES] *Victoria, BC*
GENEVA [RES] *Seattle, WA*
GENOA [RES] *Portland, OR*
GEORGE HENRY'S [RES] *Billings, MT*
GEORGIAN ROOM [RES] *Seattle, WA*
GIORGIO'S TRATTORIA [RES] *Banff, AB*
GLACIER VILLAGE [RES] *East Glacier Area, MT*
GLOBE @ YVR [RES] *Vancouver, BC*

GOTHAM STEAKHOUSE AND COCKTAIL BAR [RES] *Vancouver, BC*
GOVINDA'S VEGETARIAN BUFFET [URD] *Eugene, OR*
GRAND, THE [RES] *Big Timber, MT*
GRANVILLE SUSHI [RES] *Vancouver, BC*
GREAT WALL [RES] *Billings, MT*
GREENLEE'S [RES] *Red Lodge, MT*
GREENS AND GOURMET [URD] *Vancouver, BC*
GRETCHEN'S [RES] *Sun Valley Area, ID*
HARBOR LIGHTS [RES] *Tacoma, WA*
HART HOUSE ON DEER LAKE [URD] *Vancouver, BC*
HARVEST ROOM, THE [RES] *Edmonton, AB*
HEATHMAN [RES] *Portland, OR*
HERALD STREET CAFFE [RES] *Victoria, BC*
HERON BEACH INN DINING ROOM [RES] *Port Ludlow, WA*
HIDDEN HARBOR [RES] *Seattle, WA*
HIGGINS [RES] *Portland, OR*
HIGHLANDS DINING ROOM [RES] *Mount Hood National Forest, OR*
HILLTOP HOUSE [RES] *North Bend, OR*
HIRAM'S AT THE LOCKS [RES] *Seattle, WA*
HONG KONG [RES] *Gillette, WY*
HOULIHAN'S [RES] *Red Deer, AB*
HUBER'S CAFE [RES] *Portland, OR*
HUGO'S GRILL [RES] *Victoria, BC*
HUNT CLUB [RES] *Seattle, WA*
HYDRA [RES] *Sandpoint, ID*
HY'S CALGARY STEAK HOUSE [RES] *Calgary, AB*
HY'S ENCORE [RES] *Vancouver, BC*
HY'S STEAK LOFT [RES] *Edmonton, AB*
HY'S STEAK LOFT [RES] *Winnipeg, MB*
ICHIBAN JAPANESE STEAKHOUSE AND SUSHI BAR [RES] *Winnipeg, MB*
IL BISTRO [RES] *Seattle, WA*
IL FORNAIO [RES] *Portland, OR*
IL GIARDINO DELI UMBERTO [RES] *Vancouver, BC*
IL GIARDINO DI UMBERTO RISTORANTE [RES] *Vancouver, BC*
IL TERRAZZO [RES] *Victoria, BC*
IL TERRAZZO CARMINE [RES] *Seattle, WA*
IMPERIAL CHINESE SEAFOOD RESTAURANT [RES] *Vancouver, BC*
INDIA TANDOORI HUT [RES] *Victoria, BC*

INN ON LAKE BONAVISTA [RES] *Calgary, AB*
IRON HORSE [RES] *Coeur d'Alene, ID*
IVANO'S RISTORANTE [RES] *Sandpoint, ID*
IVAR'S ACRES OF CLAMS [RES] *Seattle, WA*
IVAR'S INDIAN SALMON HOUSE [RES] *Seattle, WA*
IVY HOUSE [URD] *Portland, OR*
J & J WONTON NOODLE HOUSE [RES] *Victoria, BC*
JACKSONVILLE INN [RES] *Jacksonville, OR*
JADE GARDEN [RES] *Helena, MT*
JAKE O'SHAUGHNESSEY'S [RES] *Bellevue, WA*
JAKER'S [RES] *Twin Falls, ID*
JAKER'S STEAK, RIBS & FISH HOUSE [RES] *Great Falls, MT*
JAKERS [RES] *Idaho Falls, ID*
JAKE'S FAMOUS CRAWFISH [RES] *Portland, OR*
JAKE'S GRILL [RES] *Portland, OR*
JALAPENO'S [RES] *Sandpoint, ID*
JAMESON [RES] *Wallace, ID*
JAPANESE VILLAGE [RES] *Edmonton, AB*
JAPANESE VILLAGE STEAK AND SEAFOOD HOUSE [RES] *Victoria, BC*
JEDEDIAH'S [RES] *Jackson, WY*
JENNY LAKE LODGE DINING ROOM [RES] *Grand Teton National Park, WY*
JIMMY D'S CAFE [RES] *Coeur d'Alene, ID*
JITTERBUG [RES] *Seattle, WA*
JOHN BOZEMAN BISTRO [RES] *Bozeman, MT*
JOHNNY'S DOCK [RES] *Tacoma, WA*
JULIANO'S [RES] *Billings, MT*
KASPAR'S [RES] *Seattle, WA*
KEG STEAKHOUSE AND BAR, THE [RES] *Calgary, AB*
KHU LARB THAI [RES] *Port Townsend, WA*
KINGFISHER RESTAURANT [URD] *Nanaimo, BC*
KOJI OSAKAYA [RES] *Beaverton, OR*
KOKONAS [RES] *Brandon, MB*
KWAN ORIGINAL CUISINE [RES] *Salem, OR*
L & W [RES] *Jasper National Park, AB*
L'ANJOU [RES] *Edmonton, AB*
L'AUBERGE [RES] *Portland, OR*
LA BELLE AUBERGE [RES] *Vancouver, BC*
LA BOHEME [RES] *Edmonton, AB*
LA FAMIGLIA RISTORANTE [RES] *San Juan Islands, WA*

LAKE YELLOWSTONE DINING ROOM [RES] *Yellowstone National Park, WY*
LAME DUCK [RES] *Jackson, WY*
LANDINGS [RES] *Port Angeles, WA*
LA RONDE [RES] *Edmonton, AB*
LA RUA [RES] *Whistler, BC*
LA SPIGA [RES] *Edmonton, AB*
LA TERRAZZA [RES] *Vancouver, BC*
LEAF & BEAN COFFEE HOUSE [URD] *Bozeman, MT*
LE BEAUJOLAIS [RES] *Banff, AB*
LE BEAUVALLON [RES] *Jasper National Park, AB*
LE CROCODILE [RES] *Vancouver, BC*
LE GOURMAND [RES] *Seattle, WA*
LE GREC [RES] *Vancouver, BC*
LIVINGSTON [RES] *Livingston, MT*
LOBSTER SHOP SOUTH [RES] *Tacoma, WA*
LOG CABIN CAFE [RES] *Cooke City, MT*
LOG CABIN INN [RES] *McKenzie Bridge, OR*
LOG INN [RES] *Rock Springs, WY*
LONDON GRILL [RES] *Portland, OR*
LONE MOUNTAIN RANCH DINING ROOM [RES] *Big Sky (Gallatin County), MT*
LONNY'S [RES] *Port Townsend, WA*
LORD BENNETT'S [RES] *Bandon, OR*
LORRAINE'S EDEL HAUS [RES] *Leavenworth, WA*
LUMIERE [RES] *Vancouver, BC*
LYDIA'S [RES] *Butte, MT*
MACARONI'S [RES] *Ashland, OR*
MACKENZIE RIVER PIZZA [URD] *Bozeman, MT*
MADISON PARK CAFE [RES] *Seattle, WA*
MAHLE HOUSE RESTAURANT, THE [RES] *Nanaimo, BC*
MALAY SATAY HUT [RES] *Seattle, WA*
MAMMA'S [RES] *Calgary, AB*
MANDARIN COVE [RES] *Portland, OR*
MANRESA CASTLE [RES] *Port Townsend, WA*
MARCO'S [RES] *Seattle, WA*
MARINA [RES] *Bellingham, WA*
MARINA, THE [RES] *Victoria, BC*
MARY MC CRANK'S DINNER HOUSE [RES] *Chehalis, WA*
MATTHEW'S TASTE OF ITALY [RES] *Billings, MT*
MAXIMILIEN-IN-THE-MARKET [RES] *Seattle, WA*
MAXWELL'S [RES] *Cody, WY*
MAZZI'S ITALIAN-SICILIAN FOOD [RES] *Portland, OR*
MCCORMICK & SCHMICK'S [RES] *Seattle, WA*

MCCORMICK'S FISH HOUSE [RES] Seattle, WA

MCCULLY HOUSE [RES] Jacksonville, OR

MCGREGOR'S PUB [RES] Pinedale, WY

MEADOWS [RES] Bend, OR

MESCALERO [RES] Calgary, AB

METROPOLITAN GRILL [RES] Seattle, WA

MICHAEL'S LANDING [RES] Corvallis, OR

MILFORD'S FISH HOUSE [RES] Boise, ID

MILLION DOLLAR COWBOY STEAK HOUSE [RES] Jackson, WY

MILL STEAKS & SPIRITS [RES] McCall, ID

MON DESIR DINING INN [RES] Medford, OR

MONK MCQUEENS [RES] Vancouver, BC

MONTRI 'S THAI [RES] Vancouver, BC

MOON PALACE [RES] Sequim, WA

MOOSE CHUCK WAGON [URD] Grand Teton National Park, WY

MORTONS OF CHICAGO [RES] Portland, OR

MURATA [RES] Portland, OR

MURCHIE'S [URD] Victoria, BC

NEW DYNASTY [RES] Lethbridge, AB

NICHOLS STEAK HOUSE [RES] Ontario, OR

NIKKO RESTAURANT [RES] Seattle, WA

NISHINO [RES] Seattle, WA

NORTH BANK [RES] Eugene, OR

NOR'WESTER SEAFOOD [RES] Gold Beach, OR

OFF BROADWAY [RES] Jackson, WY

OLD HOTEL, THE [RES] Dillon, MT

OLD HOUSE RESTAURANT [RES] Nanaimo, BC

OLD PINEY DELL [RES] Red Lodge, MT

OLD SPAGHETTI FACTORY [RES] Portland, OR

OLD SPAGHETTI FACTORY [RES] Spokane, WA

ONATI-THE BASQUE RESTAURANT [RES] Boise, ID

ON BROADWAY [RES] Helena, MT

OREGON ELECTRIC STATION [RES] Eugene, OR

ORIGINAL OYSTER HOUSE [RES] Port Townsend, WA

ORIGINAL PANCAKE HOUSE [URD] Portland, OR

ORITALIA [RES] Portland, OR

PAINTED TABLE [URD] Seattle, WA

PAISLEY SHAWL [RES] Casper, WY

PALACE KITCHEN [RES] Seattle, WA

PALEY'S PLACE [RES] Portland, OR

PALISADE [RES] Seattle, WA

PALOMINO [RES] Seattle, WA

PANHANDLE RESTAURANT [RES] Bonner's Ferry, ID

PANORAMA [RES] Calgary, AB

PAPA HAYDN [URD] Portland, OR

PAPI'S RISTORANTE ITALIANO [RES] Vancouver, BC

PARADISE [RES] Sequim, WA

PARAGON [RES] Seattle, WA

PATSY CLARK'S [RES] Spokane, WA

PAVILION [RES] Beaverton, OR

PAZZO RISTORANTE [RES] Portland, OR

PEAKS DINING ROOM [RES] Calgary, AB

PEPPERMILL [RES] Banff, AB

PERRY'S ON FREMONT [URD] Portland, OR

PIATTI [RES] Seattle, WA

PICCOLO MONDO [RES] Vancouver, BC

PIER 11 FEED STORE [RES] Astoria, OR

PINE ROOM CAFE [RES] Burns, OR

PINE TAVERN [RES] Bend, OR

PINK DOOR [RES] Seattle, WA

PINK PEARL [RES] Vancouver, BC

PLACE PIGALLE [RES] Seattle, WA

PLAINFIELD'S MAYUR [RES] Portland, OR

POINTE, THE [RES] Vancouver, BC

POLARIS [RES] Bellevue, WA

PONTI SEAFOOD GRILL [RES] Seattle, WA

POOR RICHARD'S [RES] Cheyenne, WY

POOR RICHARD'S [RES] Portland, OR

PORTAGE BAY CAFE [RES] Seattle, WA

PORTLAND STEAK & CHOPHOUSE [RES] Portland, OR

PORTSIDE [RES] Coos Bay, OR

POST HOTEL DINING ROOM[RES] Lake Louise, AB

PREGO [RES] Seattle, WA

PRESIDENT CHINESE SEAFOOD RESTAURANT [RES] Vancouver, BC

PRIMROSE, THE [RES] Banff, AB

PROVENCE [RES] Vancouver, BC

QUATTRO ON FOURTH [RES] Vancouver, BC

QUEEN CITY GRILL [RES] Seattle, WA

QUINCY'S ON SEVENTH [RES] Calgary, AB

RAINCITY GRILL [RES] Vancouver, BC

RANGE [RES] Jackson, WY

RAY'S BOATHOUSE [RES] Seattle, WA

RED APPLE [RES] Walla Walla, WA

RED STAR TAVERN & ROAST HOUSE
    [RES] *Portland, OR*
REGENCY PALACE [RES] *Calgary, AB*
RESTAURANT AT TIGH-NA-MARA
    RESORT, THE [RES] *Nanaimo,*
    BC
RESTAURANT MATISSE [RES] *Victoria,*
    BC
REX [RES] *Billings, MT*
R.F. MCDOUGALL'S [RES] *Richland,*
    WA
RHEINLANDER [RES] *Portland, OR*
RICK'S CAFE AMERICAN AT THE
    FLICKS [RES] *Boise, ID*
RIMROCK CAFE [RES] *Whistler, BC*
RIMROCK ROOM, THE [RES] *Calgary,*
    AB
RINGSIDE [RES] *Portland, OR*
RINGSIDE EAST [RES] *Portland, OR*
RISTORANTE ARAXI [RES] *Whistler,*
    BC
RISTORANTE CLASSICO [URD] *Banff,*
    AB
RIVER CAFE [RES] *Calgary, AB*
ROOSTER'S LANDING [RES]
    Clarkston, WA
ROSZAK'S FISH HOUSE [RES] *Bend,*
    OR
ROVER'S [RES] *Seattle, WA*
ROY'S [RES] *Seattle, WA*
RUTH'S CHRIS STEAK HOUSE [RES]
    Seattle, WA
SALISH LODGE AND SPA DINING
    ROOM [RES] *North Bend, WA*
SALMON RIVER COFFEE SHOP [RES]
    Salmon, ID
SALTY'S ON THE COLUMBIA [RES]
    Portland, OR
SAM'S SUPPER CLUB [RES] *Glasgow,*
    MT
SANCTUARY [RES] *Long Beach, WA*
SAUCEBOX [RES] *Portland, OR*
SAYLER'S OLD COUNTRY KITCHEN
    [RES] *Beaverton, OR*
SAYLER'S OLD COUNTRY KITCHEN
    [RES] *Portland, OR*
SAZERAC [RES] *Seattle, WA*
SEAPORTS [RES] *Seattle-Tacoma*
    International Airport Area, WA
SEASONS [RES] *Calgary, AB*
SEASON'S RESTAURANT [RES]
    Vancouver, BC
SERAFINA [RES] *Seattle, WA*
SHANGHAI CHINESE BISTRO [RES]
    Vancouver, BC
SHIJO JAPANESE RESTAURANT
    [RES] *Vancouver, BC*
SHIP INN [RES] *Astoria, OR*
SHIRO'S [RES] *Seattle, WA*
SHOALWATER [RES] *Long Beach, WA*
SHOWTHYME [RES] *Bigfork, MT*
SILVER DRAGON [RES] *Calgary, AB*

SILVERWATER CAFE [RES] *Port*
    Townsend, WA
SINCLAIR'S [RES] *Banff, AB*
SMUGGLER'S INN [RES] *Calgary, AB*
SNAKE RIVER GRILL [RES] *Jackson,*
    WY
SNOW GOOSE GRILLE [RES] *East*
    Glacier Area, MT
SOMETHING ELSE [RES] *Jasper*
    National Park, AB
SOOKE HARBOUR HOUSE [RES]
    Waterton Lakes National Park,
    AB
SPACE NEEDLE [RES] *Seattle, WA*
SPAGHETTINI'S [RES] *Butte, MT*
SPANISH PEAKS BREWERY [RES]
    Bozeman, MT
SPAZZO MEDITERRANEAN GRILL
    [RES] *Bellevue, WA*
SPINNAKER'S BREW PUB [RES]
    Victoria, BC
STAR ANISE [RES] *Vancouver, BC*
STARS BAR AND DINING [RES]
    Seattle, WA
STEFAN'S [RES] *Cody, WY*
STELLA'S TRATTORIA [RES] *Seattle,*
    WA
STONEHOUSE [RES] *Helena, MT*
STRUTTING GROUSE [RES] *Jackson,*
    WY
SUN SUI WAH SEAFOOD
    RESTAURANT [RES] *Vancouver,*
    BC
SUSHI VILLAGE [RES] *Whistler, BC*
SUSHI YA [URD] *Whistler, BC*
SVEN ERICKSEN'S [RES] *Lethbridge,*
    AB
SWAGAT INDIAN CUISINE [RES]
    Portland, OR
SWEETWATER [RES] *Jackson, WY*
SWEETWATERS [RES] *Eugene, OR*
SYLVIA'S [RES] *Portland, OR*
SZMANIA'S [RES] *Seattle, WA*
TAMA SUSHI [RES] *Vancouver, BC*
TAPASTREE [URD] *Vancouver, BC*
TEAHOUSE [RES] *Vancouver, BC*
TEA LOBBY - EMPRESS HOTEL, THE
    [URD] *Victoria, BC*
TEATRO [RES] *Calgary, AB*
TETON PINES [RES] *Jackson, WY*
THIRD FLOOR FISH CAFE [RES]
    Bellevue, WA
THREE BEAR [RES] *West Yellowstone,*
    MT
TICINO [RES] *Banff, AB*
TOGA'S INTERNATIONAL CUISINE
    [RES] *Port Angeles, WA*
TOJO'S [RES] *Vancouver, BC*
TOKYO TOM'S PLACE [RES] *Jasper*
    National Park, AB
TONQUIN PRIME RIB [RES] *Jasper*
    National Park, AB

TONY'S [RES] *Bend, OR*
TOP OF VANCOUVER [RES]
    Vancouver, BC
TRATTORIA DI UMBERTO [RES]
    Whistler, BC
TRATTORIA MITCHELLI [RES] *Seattle,*
    WA
TRUE CONFECTIONS [URD]
    Vancouver, BC
TULIO RISTORANTE [RES] *Seattle, WA*
TYPHOON! [RES] *Portland, OR*
UNCLE LOOIE'S [RES] *Livingston, MT*
UNION BAY CAFE [RES] *Seattle, WA*
UNION SQUARE GRILL [RES] *Seattle,*
    WA
UPTOWN CAFE [RES] *Butte, MT*
VAL D'ISERE [RES] *Whistler, BC*
VICTORIA DINING ROOM [RES] *Lake*
    Louise, AB
VICTORIAN, THE [RES] *Victoria, BC*
VILLA DEL LUPO [RES] *Vancouver, BC*
VILLAGE [RES] *Marysville, WA*
VISTA 18 [URD] *Victoria, BC*
VISTA GRANDE [RES] *Jackson, WY*
WALKER'S GRILL [RES] *Billings, MT*
WALLISER STUBE [RES] *Lake Louise,*
    AB
WARM SPRINGS RANCH
    RESTAURANT [RES] *Sun Valley*
    Area, ID
WESLEY STREET [RES] *Nanaimo, BC*
WESTSIDE BAKERY & CAFE [URD]
    Bend, OR
WHALE'S TALE [RES] *Newport, OR*
WHEELHOUSE [RES] *Bandon, OR*
WHITE HEATHER TEA ROOM [URD]
    Victoria, BC
WHOLE FAMDAMILY [RES]
    Lewistown, MT
WIDMER GASTHAUS [RES] *Portland,*
    OR
WILDFLOWER RESTAURANT [RES]
    Whistler, BC
WILD GINGER [RES] *Seattle, WA*
WILDWOOD [RES] *Portland, OR*
WILLIAM TELL [RES] *Vancouver, BC*
WINCHESTER COUNTRY INN [RES]
    Ashland, OR
WINDBAG SALOON [RES] *Helena, MT*
WINDWARD INN [RES] *Florence, OR*
WINTERBORNE [RES] *Portland, OR*
YACHT CLUB BROILER [RES]
    Bremerton, WA
YANKEE POT ROAST [RES] *Grants*
    Pass, OR
YELLOWSTONE MINE [RES] *Gardiner,*
    MT
ZENON CAFE [RES] *Eugene, OR*
ZIMORINO RED PIES OVER
    MONTANA [RES] *Missoula, MT*
ZINFANDELLS [RES] *Vancouver, BC*

CITY INDEX

Aberdeen, WA, 234
Afton, WY, 357
Albany, OR, 125
Alpine, WY, 357
American Falls, ID, 8
Anaconda, MT, 60
Anacortes, WA, 235
Arco, ID, 8
Ashland, OR, 126
Ashton, ID, 8
Astoria, OR, 129
Baker City, OR, 131
Bandon, OR, 133
Banff, AB, 407
Beaverton, OR, 134
Bellevue, ID, 9
Bellevue, WA, 236
Bellingham, WA, 239
Bend, OR, 135
Bigfork, MT, 61
Biggs, OR, 139
Big Hole National Battlefield, MT, 63
Big Sky (Gallatin County), MT, 63
Big Timber, MT, 65
Billings, MT, 65
Blackfoot, ID, 9
Blaine, WA, 242
Boise, ID, 10
Bonner's Ferry, ID, 17
Bozeman, MT, 70
Brandon, MB, 494
Bremerton, WA, 243
Brookings, OR, 140
Browning, MT, 74
Buffalo, WY, 358
Buhl, ID, 18
Burley, ID, 18
Burns, OR, 140
Butte, MT, 74
Caldwell, ID, 19
Calgary, AB, 414
Cannon Beach, OR, 141
Cashmere, WA, 244
Casper, WY, 359
Cave Junction, OR, 143
Centralia, WA, 245
Challis, ID, 20
Chehalis, WA, 246
Chelan, WA, 246
Cheney, WA, 247
Cheyenne, WY, 361
Chinook, MT, 76
Clarkston, WA, 248
Cody, WY, 364

Coeur d'Alene, ID, 20
Columbia Falls, MT, 77
Colville, WA, 249
Cooke City, MT, 78
Coos Bay, OR, 143
Corvallis, OR, 144
Cottage Grove, OR, 146
Coulee Dam, WA, 250
Coupeville, WA, 251
Crater Lake National Park, OR, 147
Craters of the Moon National Monument, ID, 24
Crystal Mountain, WA, 252
Dalles, OR, 148
Dayton (Columbia County), WA, 252
Deer Lodge, MT, 79
Depoe Bay, OR, 149
Devils Tower National Monument, WY, 368
Dillon, MT, 79
Douglas, WY, 369
Driggs, ID, 24
Dubois, WY, 369
East Glacier Area, MT, 85
Edmonton, AB, 423
Ellensburg, WA, 253
Ennis, MT, 81
Enterprise, OR, 150
Enumclaw, WA, 254
Ephrata, WA, 255
Eugene, OR, 150
Evanston, WY, 370
Everett, WA, 255
Florence, OR, 155
Forest Grove, OR, 156
Forks, WA, 257
Fort Benton, MT, 81
Fort Clatsop National Memorial, OR, 157
Fort Hall, ID, 25
Fort Laramie National Historic Site, WY, 371
Fort Macleod, AB, 430
Gardiner, MT, 82
Gillette, WY, 371
Glacier National Park, MT, 83
Glasgow, MT, 86
Glendive, MT, 88
Gleneden Beach, OR, 158
Gold Beach, OR, 158
Goldendale, WA, 257
Grand Teton National Park, WY, 372
Grangeville, ID, 25
Grants Pass, OR, 159

Great Falls, MT, 88
Green River, WY, 377
Greybull, WY, 378
Hamilton, MT, 90
Hardin, MT, 92
Harlowton, MT, 92
Havre, MT, 93
Helena, MT, 93
Hermiston, OR, 162
Hillsboro, OR, 163
Hood River, OR, 163
Hoquiam, WA, 258
Idaho City, ID, 26
Idaho Falls, ID, 27
Issaquah, WA, 259
Jackson, WY, 378
Jacksonville, OR, 165
Jasper National Park, AB, 431
Jerome, ID, 28
John Day, OR, 166
Joseph, OR, 168
Kalispell, MT, 97
Kamloops, BC, 445
Kellogg, ID, 29
Kelowna, BC, 446
Kelso, WA, 259
Kemmerer, WY, 386
Kennewick, WA, 260
Ketchum, ID, 29
Klamath Falls, OR, 169
La Conner, WA, 261
La Grande, OR, 171
Lake Louise, AB, 433
Lakeview, OR, 172
Lander, WY, 386
Laramie, WY, 387
Lava Hot Springs, ID, 30
Leavenworth, WA, 262
Lethbridge, AB, 435
Lewiston, ID, 30
Lewistown, MT, 99
Libby, MT, 99
Lincoln City, OR, 173
Little Bighorn Battlefield National
    Monument, MT, 100
Livingston, MT, 101
Long Beach, WA, 264
Longview, WA, 266
Lovell, WY, 389
Lusk, WY, 389
Madras, OR, 175
Malta, MT, 102
Marysville, WA, 267
McCall, ID, 32
McKenzie Bridge, OR, 176
McMinnville, OR, 177
Medford, OR, 178
Medicine Hat, AB, 437
Miles City, MT, 103
Missoula, MT, 103
Moclips, WA, 267

Montpelier, ID, 33
Moscow, ID, 34
Moses Lake, WA, 268
Mountain Home, ID, 35
Mount Hood National Forest, OR,
    180
Mount Rainier National Park, WA,
    269
Mount St. Helens National Volcanic
    Monument, WA, 273
Mount Vernon, WA, 274
Nampa, ID, 36
Nanaimo, BC, 448
Neah Bay, WA, 276
Newberg, OR, 182
Newcastle, WY, 390
Newport, OR, 183
Newport, WA, 276
North Bend, OR, 185
North Bend, WA, 276
Oak Harbor, WA, 277
Ocean Shores, WA, 278
Olympia, WA, 279
Olympic National Park, WA, 282
Omak, WA, 283
Ontario, OR, 186
Orcas Island, WA, 284
Oregon Caves National Monument,
    OR, 187
Oregon City, OR, 187
Othello, WA, 284
Packwood, WA, 285
Pasco, WA, 285
Pendleton, OR, 188
Penticton, BC, 451
Pinedale, WY, 390
Pocatello, ID, 37
Polson, MT, 108
Port Angeles, WA, 286
Port Gamble, WA, 288
Portland, OR, 190
Port Ludlow, WA, 289
Port Orford, OR, 209
Port Townsend, WA, 289
Priest Lake Area, ID, 39
Prineville, OR, 210
Province of Alberta, AB, 404
Province of British Columbia, BC,
    442
Province of Manitoba, MB, 491
Pullman, WA, 292
Puyallup, WA, 293
Quinault, WA, 294
Quincy, WA, 294
Rawlins, WY, 391
Red Deer, AB, 438
Red Lodge, MT, 109
Redmond, OR, 210
Reedsport, OR, 212
Revelstoke, BC, 453
Rexburg, ID, 40
Richland, WA, 295

Ritzville, WA, 296
Riverton, WY, 392
Rockaway, OR, 213
Rock Springs, WY, 393
Roseburg, OR, 213
Salem, OR, 215
Salmon, ID, 41
Sandpoint, ID, 42
San Juan Islands, WA, 297
Seaside, OR, 217
Seattle, WA, 300
Seattle-Tacoma International Airport
    Area, WA, 322
Sedro Woolley, WA, 325
Sequim, WA, 326
Sheridan, WY, 394
Shoshone, ID, 44
Sidney, MT, 110
Silverton, OR, 219
Snohomish, WA, 327
Soap Lake, WA, 328
Spokane, WA, 328
Stanley, ID, 46
St. Anthony, ID, 45
St. Marie's, ID, 45
Sunnyside, WA, 334
Sun Valley Area, ID, 46
Sweet Home, OR, 219
Tacoma, WA, 334
Teton Village, WY, 395
The Dalles, OR, 219
Thermopolis, WY, 395
Three Forks, MT, 111

Tillamook, OR, 222
Toppenish, WA, 340
Torrington, WY, 396
Turtle Mountain Provincial Park, MB,
    495
Twin Falls, ID, 49
Umatilla, OR, 223
Union, WA, 340
Vancouver, BC, 454
Vancouver, WA, 341
Vancouver Island, BC, 474
Victoria, BC, 476
Virginia City, MT, 111
Wallace, ID, 50
Walla Walla, WA, 343
Waterton Lakes National Park, AB,
    440
Weiser, ID, 51
Wenatchee, WA, 344
West Glacier Area, MT, 86
Westport, WA, 346
West Yellowstone, MT, 112
Wheatland, WY, 397
Whistler, BC, 487
Whitefish, MT, 114
White Sulphur Springs, MT, 116
Winnipeg, MB, 495
Winthrop, WA, 346
Wolf Point, MT, 116
Yachats, OR, 223
Yakima, WA, 347
Yellowstone National Park, WY, 397

Mobil Travel Guides

Please check the guides you would like to order:

☐ 0-7853-4629-5
California
$16.95

☐ 0-7803-4630-9
Florida
$16.95

☐ 0-7853-4635-X
Great Lakes
Illinois, Indiana, Michigan
Ohio, Wisconsin
$16.95

☐ 0-7853-4636-8
Great Plains
Iowa, Kansas, Minnesota,
Missouri, Nebraska, North
Dakota, Oklahoma, South
Dakota
$16.95

☐ 0-7853-4633-3
Mid-Atlantic
Delaware, Maryland,
Pennsylvania, Virginia,
Washington DC, West
Virginia
$16.95

☐ 0-7853-4631-7
**New England and Eastern
Canada**
Connecticut, Maine, Massachu-
setts, New Hampshire, Rhode
Island, Vermont, Canada
$16.95

☐ 0-7853-4632-5
New York/New Jersey
$16.95

☐ 0-7853-4638-4
Northwest
Idaho, Montana, Oregon, Wash-
ington, Wyoming, Canada
$16.95

☐ 0-7853-4634-1
Southeast
Alabama, Arkansas, Georgia, Ken-
tucky, Louisiana, Mississippi,
North Carolina, South Carolina,
Tennessee
$16.95

☐ 0-7853-4637-6
Southwest
Arizona, Colorado, Nevada, New
Mexico, Texas, Utah
$16.95

Please ship the books above to:

Name: _____

Address: _____

City: _____ State _____ Zip _____

Total Cost of Book(s)	$_____	☐ Please charge my credit card.
Shipping & Handling (Please add $2.00 for first book $1.00 for each additional book)	$_____	☐ Discover ☐ Visa ☐ MasterCard ☐ American Express
Add 8.75% sales tax	$_____	Card #_____
Total Amount	$_____	Expiration _____
☐ My Check is enclosed.		Signature _____

Please mail this form to: **Mobil Travel Guides
7373 N. Cicero Avenue
Lincolnwood, IL 60712**

Mobil
Travel Guide®

Northwest
Idaho
Montana
Oregon
Washington
Wyoming
Alberta
British Columbia
Manitoba

Great Plains
Iowa
Kansas
Minnesota
Missouri
Nebraska
North Dakota
Oklahoma
South Dakota

Great Lakes
Illinois
Indiana
Michigan
Ohio
Wisconsin

**New England
Eastern Canada**
Connecticut
Maine
Massachusetts
New Hampshire
Rhode Island
Vermont
New Brunswick
Nova Scotia
Ontario
Prince Edward
  Island
Quebec

California

**New York
New Jersey**

Southwest
Arizona
Colorado
Nevada
New Mexico
Texas
Utah

Southeast
Alabama
Arkansas
Georgia
Kentucky
Louisiana
Mississippi
North Carolina
South Carolina
Tennessee

Florida

Mid-Atlantic
Delaware
Maryland
Pennsylvania
Virginia
Washington, D.C.
West Virginia

Add your opinion!

Help make the Guide even more useful. Tell us about your experiences with the hotels and restaurants listed in the Guide (or ones that should be added).

Find us on the Internet at **www.exxonmobiltravel.com/feedback**

Or copy the form below and mail to Mobil Travel Guide, 7373 N. Cicero Ave, Lincolnwood, IL 60712 or fax to 847/329-5877. All information will be kept confidential.

Your name _____   Were children with you on trip? ☐ Yes ☐ No

Street _____   Number of people in your party _____

City/State/Zip _____   Your occupation _____

Establishment name _____
☐ Hotel ☐ Resort ☐ Restaurant
☐ Motel ☐ Inn ☐ Other

Street _____   City _____ State _____

Do you agree with our description? ☐ Yes ☐ No. If not, give reason _____

Please give us your opinion of the following::

Decor	Cleanliness	Service	Food
☐ Excellent	☐ Spotless	☐ Excellent	☐ Excellent
☐ Good	☐ Clean	☐ Good	☐ Good
☐ Fair	☐ Unclean	☐ Fair	☐ Fair
☐ Poor	☐ Dirty	☐ Poor	☐ Poor

2001 Guide rating _____ ★

Check your suggested rating
☐ ★good, satisfactory
☐ ★★very good
☐ ★★★excellent
☐ ★★★★outstanding
☐ ★★★★★ one of best in country

Date of visit _____   First visit? ☐ Yes ☐ No

☐ ✓unusually good value

Comments _____

Establishment name _____
☐ Hotel ☐ Resort ☐ Restaurant
☐ Motel ☐ Inn ☐ Other

Street _____   City _____ State _____

Do you agree with our description? ☐ Yes ☐ No. If not, give reason _____

Please give us your opinion of the following::

Decor	Cleanliness	Service	Food
☐ Excellent	☐ Spotless	☐ Excellent	☐ Excellent
☐ Good	☐ Clean	☐ Good	☐ Good
☐ Fair	☐ Unclean	☐ Fair	☐ Fair
☐ Poor	☐ Dirty	☐ Poor	☐ Poor

2001 Guide rating _____ ★

Check your suggested rating
☐ ★good, satisfactory
☐ ★★very good
☐ ★★★excellent
☐ ★★★★outstanding
☐ ★★★★★ one of best in country

Date of visit _____   First visit? ☐ Yes ☐ No

☐ ✓unusually good value

Comments _____

Notes